ACCLAIM FOR THE HOLLANDER TRANSLATIONS OF *INFERNO* AND *PURGATORIO*

"The Hollanders' [translation] is probably the most finely accomplished and may well prove the most enduring."

—R. W. B. Lewis, *Los Angeles Times*

"This is the translation for our time and probably beyond."

—*National Review*

"The virtues of prose raised to a quiet, sometimes stunning elegance. . . . Reading Dante with Hollander could become addictive."

—*The Providence Journal*

"There has seldom been such a useful [version]. . . . The Hollanders . . . act as latter-day Virgils, guiding us through the Italian text that is printed on the facing page."

—*The Economist*

"[The Hollander *Inferno*] makes the poem accessible to the lay reader and appealing to the specialist: the translation is both faithful to the original and highly readable; the introduction and notes are dense without being overly scholarly. . . . A highly worthy new *Inferno* that is the mature fruit of years of scholarly, pedagogical, and creative work."

—*Choice*

"A distinguished act of poetry and scholarship in one and the same breath, the Hollander Dante, among the strong translations of the poet, deserves to take its own honored place."

—Robert Fagles, translator of *The Illiad* and *The Odyssey*

"The new *Inferno* . . . is both majestic and magisterial and the product of a lifelong devotion to Dante's poetry and to the staggering body of Dante scholarship. . . . The Hollanders' adaptation is not only an intelligent reader's Dante, but it is meant to enlighten and move and ultimately to give us a Dante so versatile that he could at once soar to the hereafter and remain unflinchingly earthbound."

—André Aciman, author of *Out of Egypt*

"A brisk, vivid, readable—and scrupulously subtle—translation, coupled with excellent notes and commentary. Every lover of Dante in English should have this volume."

—Alicia Ostriker

"This new version of the *Inferno* wonderfully captures the concision, directness, and pungency of Dante's style. . . . A grand achievement."

—Richard Lansing, Professor of Comparative Literature, Brandeis University

"English-speaking lovers of Dante are doubly in the Hollanders' debt: first for this splendidly lucid and eminently readable version of Dante's Hell, and second, for the provocative, elegantly written commentary."

—John Ahern, Antolini Professor of Italian Literature, Vassar College

"This new Hollander translation deserves to sweep the field. . . . [The Hollanders] have produced an English text of remarkable poetic sensitivity while never traducing the original Italian or pretending to supplant Dante's poem with one of their own."

—John Fleming,
Professor of English and Comparative Literature,
Princeton University

"The Hollanders have rendered both the supple lyricism and the rich imagery of the *Purgatorio* with an admirably informed expertise. . . . A model for all translators."

—*Literary Review*

JEAN HOLLANDER
AND ROBERT HOLLANDER
PARADISO

JEAN HOLLANDER has taught literature and writing at Brooklyn College, Columbia University, Princeton University, and the College of New Jersey, where she was director of the Writers' Conference for twenty-three years. She recently published her third book of poems.

ROBERT HOLLANDER, her husband, taught Dante's *Divine Comedy* to Princeton students for forty-two years, and is the author of a dozen books and more than seventy articles on Dante, Boccaccio, and other Italian authors. He is Professor in European Literature Emeritus at Princeton and the founding director of both the Dartmouth Dante Project and the Princeton Dante Project. He has received many awards, including the gold medal of the city of Florence and the gold florin of the Dante Society of America, in recognition of his work on Dante.

ALSO TRANSLATED BY

JEAN HOLLANDER AND ROBERT HOLLANDER

Inferno
Purgatorio

ALSO BY JEAN HOLLANDER

Crushed into Honey: Poems
Hugo von Hoffmansthal, *The Woman Without a Shadow* (translator)
I Am My Own Woman: The Outlaw Life of Charlotte Von Mahlsdorf, Berlin's Most Distinguished Transvestite (translator)
Moondog: Poems
Organs and Blood: Poems

ALSO BY ROBERT HOLLANDER

Allegory in Dante's Commedia
Walking on Dante: Poems
Boccaccio's Two Venuses
Studies in Dante
Il Virgilio dantesco: Tragedia nella "Commedia"
André Malraux, *The Temptation of the West* (translator)
Giovanni Boccaccio, *Amorosa Visione* (translated with Timothy Hampton and Margherita Frankel)
Boccaccio's Last Fiction: Il Corbaccio
Dante and Paul's "five words with understanding"
Dante's Epistle to Cangrande
Boccaccio's Dante and the Shaping Force of Satire
Dante: A Life in Works

PARADISO

Dante Alighieri

PARADISO

A VERSE TRANSLATION BY ROBERT & JEAN HOLLANDER

INTRODUCTION & NOTES BY ROBERT HOLLANDER

ANCHOR BOOKS
A Division of Random House, Inc.
New York

FIRST ANCHOR BOOKS EDITION, SEPTEMBER 2008

The Library of Congress has cataloged the Doubleday edition as follows:
Dante Alighieri, 1265–1321.
[Paradiso. English]
Paradiso / Dante Alighieri ; a verse translation by Robert & Jean Hollander ; introduction & notes by Robert Hollander.
p. cm.
I. Hollander, Robert, 1933– II. Hollander, Jean, 1928–
III. Title.
PQ4315.4.H65 2007
851'.1—dc22
2007018070

Anchor ISBN: 978-1-4000-3115-3

Author photographs © Pryde Brown
Book design by Pei Loi Koay

www.anchorbooks.com

PRINTED IN THE UNITED STATES OF AMERICA
10 9 8 7 6 5 4 3 2 1

for

Cornelia (A.R.)

& Dr. Buzz

NOTE ON THE TRANSLATION

Since our goals in translating the third *cantica* of Dante's poem are not in substance different from those that animated our translation of the first and second, the reader is asked to consult the similar notices that precede our translations of *Inferno* (Doubleday 2000; Anchor 2002) and of *Purgatorio* (Doubleday 2003; Anchor 2004). *Paradiso*, however, presents some challenges different from those encountered in the first two *cantiche*. Needless to say, we have again attempted to give as accurate a sense of the poetry and meaning of the Italian text as the English language and our abilities allow. The language and style of this part of the poem are, in many respects, dramatically different from those to which the reader has become accustomed in the previous *cantiche*. As we suggested in the front matter for the second volume, "While surely we must acknowledge that *Inferno* and *Purgatorio* are very different poetic places, they nonetheless maintain some arrestingly similar elements. From the vantage point of *Paradiso* the second canticle looks much more like its predecessor than like its successor." Indeed, *Paradiso* is not only unique within Dante's oeuvre; it is simply unique. Theology set to music, as it were, it pushes its reader (not to mention its translators) to the limit.

A particular problem facing translators of the *Paradiso* involves one of its distinguishing features: neologisms, or words new to the Italian language and essentially invented by their creator. The current estimate of the number of neologisms in the poem runs to around ninety, with the great bulk of these appearing in *Paradiso* (see Ferrante [Ferr.1983.1], p. 131, n. 10). It seems appropriate that the requirements of expressing the higher realities of God's realm involve linguistic novelties of the most radical kind. Some of these we have attempted to bring over into English, when Dante's coinage seems so striking that *any* reader would have to pay astonished attention to the violence done "standard Italian"; for example, the verb *intrearsi* (*Par.* XIII.57), literally "to inthree itself," which Dante employs to speak of the Holy Spirit's involvement with the other two Persons of the Trinity, and which we have translated with an English neologism, "the Love that is *intrined* with them." Others we have not, especially when it seemed to us that his usage borders on the "ordinarily daring" language one associates with almost any poetic making, for example, the verb *ingigliarsi* (*Par.* XVIII.113), which literally means "to enlily itself," but is fairly obviously meant to indicate what our translation suggests it does, i.e., "to make itself into a lily." In other words, the first class of neologisms is the linguistic equivalent of self-consciously audacious metaphor, and, like it, is obviously intended to make a reader reel, while the second is closer to our normal expectations of heightened poetic language; it may surprise, but does not shock. It is, naturally, not exactly easy to make such distinctions. It is also true that the difficulty of bringing the effect of a neologism into a second language is another complicating factor. Sometimes Dante's daring thrusts simply do not "feel right" in English. In short, the reader should be aware that our practice in this regard is various.

We are once again grateful to two friends born in Italy and born to Dante for their willingness to sample our translations and my footnotes with a knowing eye. Margherita Frankel, formerly a professor of Italian at New York University, was her usual careful and exacting self as she examined our materials. The same must be said of Simone Marchesi, who studied with me when he was a graduate student at Princeton and has now returned to the university to teach students how to read Dante in his own courses. We are pleased to express our continuing gratitude to them both. This translation has brought us into contact with people whom we did not know before. It has been pleasing to hear from readers in this country, England, and Australia who have enjoyed our English-speaking Dante. And two of them were not only appreciative, but helpful. Professors of law Clayton Gillette (NYU) and Stephen Morse (Pennsylvania) paid for their enjoyment of *Inferno* by reading the penultimate drafts of *Purgatorio* and of *Paradiso* and sharing their questions and comments with us; we are deeply grateful to both of them, in part for demonstrating to me exactly why I have always used the adjective "lawyerly" (as in "a lawyerly argument") in a positive sense. Finally, I would like to acknowledge those graduate students who worked with me on this *cantica*, first in 1980 (Carolyn Calvert Phipps, Micaela Janan, Albert Rossi, Stephen Rupp, Alex Sheers) and then in 1986 (Sheila Colwell, Roberta Davidson, Martin Elzinga, Frank Ordiway, Lauren Scancarelli Seem). I hope that their memories of those seminars glow half as bright as mine.

Gerald Howard, in addition to his more significant titles and duties at Random House, has been our editor for some years now. It was his support that made publication of our work possible and his continuing clear-headed and keen-eyed editorial supervision that has helped keep the project on an even keel. And we are grateful as well to all at Random House and Anchor Books (including three former students of mine at Princeton: Rakesh Satyal, Alice Van Straalen, and Anne Merrow) who have taken such obvious pleasure in their association with this project.

27 November 2005 (Hopewell)

This first Anchor edition has some sixty changes in the translation, some thirty in the commentary, and six additions to the bibliography.

30 January 2008 (Hopewell)

TABLE OF ABBREVIATIONS & LIST OF COMMENTATORS

1. Dante's works:

Conv.	*Convivio*
Dve	*De vulgari eloquentia*
Egl.	*Egloghe*
Epist.	*Epistole*
Inf.	*Inferno*
Mon.	*Monarchia*
Par.	*Paradiso*
Purg.	*Purgatorio*
Quest.	*Questio de aqua et terra*
Rime	*Rime*
Rime dub.	*Rime dubbie*
VN	*Vita nuova*
Detto	*Il Detto d'Amore* ("attributable to Dante" [Contini])
Fiore	*Il Fiore* ("attributable to Dante" [Contini])

2. Commentators on the *Commedia*. These seventy-three texts are all currently available in the database known as the Dartmouth Dante Project (http://dante.dartmouth.edu). Dates, particularly of the early commentators, are often approximate. The order followed here is that found in the DDP, which at times seems to violate chronology, and sometimes does so, in order to keep various versions of the same commentator (e.g., Pietro Alighieri) or teacher and pupil (e.g., Trifon Gabriele and Bernardino Daniello) next to one another.

Jacopo Alighieri (1322) (*Inferno* only)
Graziolo de' Bambaglioli (1324) (Latin) (*Inferno* only)
Jacopo della Lana (1324)
Anonymus Lombardus (1325[?]) (Latin) (*Purgatorio* only)
Guido da Pisa (1327) (Latin) (*Inferno* only)
L'Ottimo (1333)
Anonimo Selmiano (1337) (*Inferno* only)
Pietro Alighieri (1) (1340–42) (Latin)
Pietro Alighieri (2) (1344–55[?])
Pietro Alighieri (3) (1359–64[?])
Codice cassinese (1350–75[?]) (Latin)
Chiose ambrosiane (1355[?])
Guglielmo Maramauro (1369–73)
Chiose cagliaritane (1370[?])
Giovanni Boccaccio (1373–75) (*Inferno* I–XVII only)
Benvenuto da Imola (1380) (Latin)
Francesco da Buti (1385)
"Falso Boccaccio" (1390[?])
Anonimo Fiorentino (1400)
Filippo Villani (1405) (*Inferno* I only)
Giovanni da Serravalle (1416) (Latin)
Guiniforto Barzizza (1440) (*Inferno* only)
Cristoforo Landino (1481)
Alessandro Vellutello (1544)
Pier Francesco Giambullari (1538–48)
Giovan Battista Gelli (1541–63)
Benedetto Varchi (1545) (*Paradiso* I & II only)
Trifon Gabriele (1525–41)
Bernardino Daniello (1547–68)
Torquato Tasso (1555–68)
Lodovico Castelvetro (1570)
Pompeo Venturi (1732)
Baldassare Lombardi (1791–92)
Luigi Portirelli (1804–5)
Paolo Costa (1819–21)
Gabriele Rossetti (1826–40) (*Inferno & Purgatorio* only)
Niccolò Tommaseo (1837)
Raffaello Andreoli (1856)
Luigi Bennassuti (1864)
Henry W. Longfellow (1867) (English)

Gregorio Di Siena (1867) (*Inferno* only)
Brunone Bianchi (1868)
G. A. Scartazzini (1874; but the 2nd ed. of 1900 is used)
Giuseppe Campi (1888)
Gioachino Berthier (1892)
Giacomo Poletto (1894)
Hermann Oelsner (1899) (English)
H. F. Tozer (1901) (English)
John Ruskin (1903) (English; not in fact a "commentary")
John S. Carroll (1904) (English)
Francesco Torraca (1905)
C. H. Grandgent (1909) (English)
Enrico Mestica (1921)
Casini/Barbi (1921)
Carlo Steiner (1921)
Isidoro Del Lungo (1926)
Carlo Grabher (1934)
Ernesto Trucchi (1936)
Luigi Pietrobono (1946)
Attilio Momigliano (1946)
Manfredi Porena (1946)
Natalino Sapegno (1955)
Daniele Mattalia (1960)
Siro A. Chimenz (1962)
Giovanni Fallani (1965)
Giorgio Padoan (1967) (*Inferno* I–VIII only)
Giuseppe Giacalone (1968)
Charles S. Singleton (1973) (English)
Bosco/Reggio (1979)
Pasquini/Quaglio (1982)
Robert Hollander (2000–7) (English)
Nicola Fosca (2003–6)

NB: The text of the *Paradiso* is that established by Petrocchi, *Dante Alighieri: La Commedia secondo l'antica vulgata*, ed. Giorgio Petrocchi (Florence: Le Lettere, 1994 [1966–67]), vol. IV. (This later edition has two minor changes to the text of this *cantica*, which is thus essentially identical with the earlier text.) All references to other works are keyed to the List of Works Cited found at the back of this volume (e.g., Adve.1995.1), with the exception of references to commentaries contained in the Dartmouth

Dante Project. Informational notes derived from Paget Toynbee's *Concise Dante Dictionary of Proper Names and Notable Matters in the Works of Dante* (Oxford: Clarendon, 1914) are followed by the siglum (T). References to the *Enciclopedia dantesca*, 6 vols. (Rome: Istituto della Enciclopedia Italiana, 1970–78) are indicated by the abbreviation *ED*. Commentaries by Robert Hollander are (at times) shorter versions of materials found in the Princeton Dante Project, a multimedia edition of the *Commedia*. Consultation (without charge to the user) is possible at www.princeton.edu/dante.

(1) Paradiso: *An Impossible Poem.*

It is difficult to imagine what life must have been like for Dante, having to manage the details of everyday existence in his exile while his mind was occupied with details of quite another sort. Indeed, the subjects treated in the last *cantica* represent both implausible and daring choices for a poet (an awareness reflected in the title of the three-part Canadian Broadcasting Corporation's series for radio in 2002, *Dante, Poet of the Impossible*). In fact, it seems almost beyond human capacity to have written the *Comedy*. The whole poem might be considered an experiment in pushing back the boundaries of human expression, at times surprising even its creator. What is most surprising (and, to some, offensive) is the incorporation of subjects previously reserved exclusively for prose in an Italian poem: for example, moral philosophy (*Inf.* XI and *Purg.* XVI) and biology (*Purg.* XXV). However, this tactic becomes most noteworthy in *Paradiso*. There we find astronomy (*Par.* II, where Dante takes on the task of a Ptolemy or an Alfraganus); free will (Canto V, where he rehearses this topic so dear to Augustine); the theology of history (VI, Orosius); municipal politics (XVI, Cicero and Brunetto Latini); and angelology and its relation to astronomy (XXVIII–XXIX, the Pseudo-Dionysius). If the entire project of the *Divine Comedy* must have caused its author understandable anxiety, the choice of a strategy for making the part of the poem that is called *Paradiso* must have caused its author considerable effort in wrestling with weighty concerns. If Giorgio Petrocchi's work to establish the dates of composition for the various parts of the poem is correct (and it must be considered a provisional, if still the most convincing, attempt), Dante spent the years 1313 to 1317 revising *Inferno* and *Purgatorio*, and planning *Paradiso* (see Petrocchi [Petr.1957.1 and Petr.1969.1]). Perhaps because of the time he took for revision, only occasionally in the first two *cantiche* does one sense Dante laboring under his load (as, one might suggest, is apparent in the opening fifty or so verses of *Inferno* I). There is a "finished" quality to the first two *cantiche* that *Paradiso* sometimes does not have. To take a single example, the text of Canto III clearly suggests that Dante originally planned to portray the souls of the saved as dwelling in the stars (indeed, any number of commentators forget themselves from time to time and display a similar misunderstanding), while Canto IV makes it plain that they are ordinarily to be found in the Empyrean [pronounced em-PEER-ian] and only on this very special occasion manifest themselves to a celestial visitor in each of the first eight heavens. Further, a passage in Canto IX seems to drop back into the same mistake overruled in Canto IV. It is possible that a later revision of the poem would have done a better job ironing out this rather alarming inconsistency. And the issue seems worth raising. Are we reading, in *Paradiso*, less finished work than we found in the first two *cantiche*? Given the near-total absence of any hard evidence (there is anecdotal reference, narrated by Boccaccio in his biography of Dante, to the discovery of the last thirteen cantos by the poet's sons only after his death), a resolution of this question is probably not possible.

Even a veteran reader is startled each time he or she begins rereading the third *cantica* of this "theological epic." For here the usual accoutrements of poetic narrative are downstaged by the language of Scholastic discourse and, finally, of mystical devotion. Dante's *Paradiso* is surely one of the most daring poetic initiatives we have—perhaps it is simply the most daring. Its extraordinary popular success (in December 2002, Roberto Benigni recited and discussed its final canto to an Italian television audience reported to be more than 12 million in number) is testament to Dante's stubbornness and to his genius. Its at times endless-seeming theological disquisitions, to be sure, have addled many a reader; one finds few who will claim (or admit) that it is their favorite *cantica*. At the same time, the poetic technique found in it reflects a supreme confidence and, in its greatest moments, attains a sublimity that sweeps all cynicism before it. It is perhaps worth the effort to report on one's own experience in this regard. The writer has twice offered graduate seminars on *Paradiso* at Princeton (in 1980 and 1986). In both of these, the same thing happened. His students found the going difficult (as did he). They did not look forward to breaking their heads each week over the niceties of Scholastic distinction and other arcana. Nonetheless, once each seminar began, it was as though all present became a single instrument working toward a common understanding (perhaps in unconscious imitation of the speaking eagle in the heaven of Jupiter). Rarely have seminars flown by so quickly for all involved (or so it was reported even by the students), and rarely have students taught their teacher quite so well. *Paradiso* is certainly the most challenging part of the poem, but may also be the most rewarding for those who give themselves to it and let it do its work on them.

(2) *A Poem of the Stars.*

This poem about a journey through the heavens has little to do with our own notions of astronomy. (For Dante's astronomy see, in English, at least Moore [Moor.1903.1], pp. 1–108; Orr [Orr.1914.1]; and Cornish [Corn. 2000.2]). Measured in the time that the protagonist is absent from the earth, the *Paradiso* seems to take a little more than twenty-four hours, although the temporal indications are less precise than they have been in the first two *cantiche*. He zooms up from the garden of Eden at noon on Wednesday, March 30 (or April 13, depending on the view of the matter accepted by the reader's favorite discussant of the problem—see the notes to *Inf.* I.1 and *Inf.* XXI.38) and returns to earth sometime during the evening of the next day. This return is the only temporally unmarked portion of his reported voyage to the three realms of the afterworld, but the rough indications found in crucial passages late in the *cantica* encourage us to believe that the completed adventure, which ostensibly ends with the undescribed reentry of the protagonist, has taken one week, Thursday evening to Thursday evening. Giovanni Agnelli (Agne.1891.1), Table XI, has tried to demonstrate that the time consumed by Dante's trip through Paradise takes exactly twenty-four hours (with some timeless time allowed for the visionary final four cantos). But even a rough calculation of the duration of time as presented in the text itself would seem to show that the time Dante spent in the heavens, as measured by earthly duration, is somewhat more than twenty-four hours (see the note to *Par.* XXVII.79–81). The first twenty-four hours were spent on earth and began Thursday evening (*Inf.* I and II); the next full day was consumed exploring Hell (*Inf.* III–XXXIV.69); and the next in the ascent to see again the stars (*Inf.* XXXIV.70–139), which brings us to 6 PM on Sunday evening Jerusalem time, or 6 AM Sunday morning at the Antipodes, where begins the three-and-one-half-day trip up the mountain (what we call Purgatory) that ended with our hero in the earthly paradise at the propitious time of noon.

The heavens, conceived by Dante and the astronomers of his time as a series of concentric circular spheres, nine in all, surrounding the center of the universe, this our paltry earth, are formed by transparent crystal bodies, the first seven of which each mounts a single gem. These for

Dante are the planets: Moon, Mercury, Venus, Sun, Mars, Jupiter, Saturn. (In Dante's eyes, they all shine with their own light alone.) The eighth sphere contains all the other stars (shining with reflected light, once again precisely reversing the understanding of our time). The ninth, the Primum Mobile or Crystalline Sphere, contains no other physical body besides itself, but, by loving God, propels the movement of the entire universe. Strictly speaking, Dante's physical universe contains only these nine spheres. Surmounting it, existing beyond time and space and yet containing all space and time, is the home of God, of the angels, and of the souls of the saved (with seats reserved for those few yet to come). This placeless place is known as the Empyrean. As we will learn in Cantos III and IV (and the learning is not come by easily), no soul whom we meet in the eight lower spheres actually has a home in them, but has only appeared in a particular sphere to give Dante instruction of a certain hierarchical bent, for while all the blessed are equally blessed (as all the damned are equally damned), there is nonetheless here, as there was in Hell, an order of rank among those present. All the blessed are equally blessed, only some are less blessed than others—or, perhaps better put, some have fewer apparent credentials for salvation than others (e.g., Piccarda the traduced nun, as compared with St. Benedict; or Folco the former lover and poet, with St. John).

We also learn that each of these heavens, which are "ruled" by one of the nine orders of angels (about which see notes found in Canto XXVIII), is associated with a particular virtue: faith, hope, and love, respectively, in the first three spheres (Moon, Mercury, Venus), but each of these theological virtues in an imperfect form (see Ordiway [Ordi.1982.1]). The next four planetary spheres (Sun, Mars, Jupiter, Saturn) present in turn the four cardinal virtues: prudence, fortitude, justice, and temperance. In the Starry Sphere we encounter the three theological virtues in their perfected form; in the Primum Mobile the nine ranks of angels, reflecting each of the nine virtues over which each of their orders presides.

As even this brief description indicates, Dante's celestial bodies are less important for their physical traits (which are, nonetheless, duly noted) as for their influence on the character of a given human soul. Dante's astronomy is thus, to us today, a curious blend of consideration of the physical characteristics of the heavens and of their influence on human life (see Kay [Kay.1983.1 and Kay.1994.2]). It is at once both astronomy and astrology, but an astrology "cleaned up," drained of its deterministic elements, an astrology that would pass muster with St. Augustine, who cried out so eloquently against it (e.g., *Confessions* VII.vi). The notion that our actions are determined by the stars is simply anathema to Christian theologians, for whom the resultant pleas (e.g., "I was born under Venus; how could I resist the call of sexual pleasure?") were the early version of the dog-ate-my-homework defense. Thus Dante's age combined Ptolemaic astronomy and what we would rightly call astrology in such ways as to maintain the doctrine of Free Will. The stars, we will learn from Charles Martel in *Paradiso* VIII.97–148, predispose us toward certain abilities (thus explaining why we become either warriors or poets, for example) but in no way control our moral choices. And it is these that prepare us for our eternal lives, whether in Heaven or in Hell.

(3) *The Drama of* Paradiso.

This drama is not nearly so much moral, as was that described in the first two *cantiche*, as it is intellectual. *Inferno* and *Purgatorio* are both centrally moral in the reactions that they summon in the reader. This pertains at least through *Purgatorio* XXVII; once we arrive in the earthly paradise, we can feel the ground moving beneath our feet, compelling us to take a more historical and religious direction. Turning the corner into the heavens, we are soon aware of a more theological (indeed Scholastic) dimension to the poem, one that is, if not altogether a surprise, dramatically different. Here is another way in which the third *cantica* differs from the first two. The motivation of much of the discourse in the canticle comes from Dante's puzzled questions, the result of his shaky understanding of God's justice. Beatrice, given the role that one waggish commentator has characterized as resulting from her having been forced to act the part of St. Thomas in drag, takes over the role of guide from Virgil. And while she fields most of Dante's questions, there are others who do so as well. It is quite a cast of teachers that he is privileged to have, including four eventual saints of the Church: Thomas, Bonaventure, Benedict, and Bernard.

And who is the protagonist of this bildungsroman? Pertile (Pert.1998.2), p. 19, describes him as follows: "A Florentine excluded from his city, aristocrat deprived of means, fervent Christian and unswerving anticlerical, politician constrained to stand on the sidelines, partisan without a party, layman swept up in his own religious mission, intellectual *déclassé*, Dante is a microcosm of all the tensions and contradictions of his time." And now, when he has reached the final portion of his journey, the traces of his worldly identities and cares are, if anything, even more pressing, even more visible.

While the first actual presence of Beatrice in the poem, in the earthly paradise, puts her in the role of moral preceptor rather than that of guide to revealed truth, once we enter *Paradiso*, that becomes precisely her role. It is no wonder that Romantic readers insist that they find her less attractive than Francesca. (And, in the wake of De Sanctis and Croce, there follow many others who try to turn the poem into something it simply refuses to be.) Dante's heavenly preceptor sounds like a Doctor of the Church, exactly as Dante wanted her to. Her role, some have argued, is to supervise the correction of Dante's intellect. In such a formulation, Virgil supervises the correction of Dante's will in *Inferno* and the perfection of his will in *Purgatorio*, while Beatrice has a similar role in the correction of Dante's intellect in the first nine heavenly spheres, and Bernard presides over the perfection of Dante's intellect in the Empyrean (see Hollander [Holl.1976.2]). That role makes the gamut of Scholastic distinctions that she forces Dante (and us) to run through seem only a reasonable course. It is probably true that no one has ever poeticized theology at such length and with better art than Dante has done in *Paradiso*.

There are many large theological and philosophical subjects addressed by Beatrice. (In *Convivio*, Dante might have referred to the passages containing them as *digressioni* [digressions]—and in *Paradiso* XXIX.127, he again uses that word.) This is not to consider those offered by Justinian, Charles Martel, Thomas Aquinas, Cacciaguida, or still others. Beatrice's topics include the following: the paradoxical nature of heavenly "gravity," drawing one up and not down (*Par.* I); the spiritual reason for the spots on the Moon (II—another refutation of arguments found in *Convivio* [II.xiii.9]); the information that saved souls do not return to their star but proceed directly (once they have finished their purgation, if they have had to pass through that realm; at least some saints and most or all martyrs apparently did not) to the Empyrean (IV); the relation between the absolute and the conditional will (IV); the repayment of broken vows and the freedom of the will (V); the *primo mobile* and the roots of time (XXVII); the ranks of the angels (XXVIII); the nature of and reason for God's creation of the universe (XXIX); the fallen angels (XXIX); those members of religious orders who teach false doctrines (XXIX); the numberless ranks of the angels (XXIX).

Given this array of subjects, we may be excused if we wonder what Dante expected in the reader of *Paradiso* by way of education. We are puzzled by the always interesting and surely difficult question of the writer's intended audience. To have garnered the respect and popularity he apparently did within a short period of time, his audience would have had to understand many at least recondite allusions and be able to follow some fairly sophisticated theological disquisition. How broad an audience could Dante have had that fully appreciated his achievement? (We should not forget that there also sprang up an enthusiastic illiterate audience for the work, memorizing the text from the recitals of others, a tradition that has continued into our own times (see Ahern [Aher.1982.3]). Obviously, it had to be literate, which we may safely assume means that he had a small audience to begin with (but for the growth of that potential audience from the tenth century on and the development of an "intellectual elite," see the classic study of Le Goff, *Les intellectuels au Moyen Âge* [English ed., Lego.1957.1]; and for laymen's interests in and knowledge of formal philosophy, see Imbach [Imba.1996.1], pp. 1–128). That audience is expected to be conversant with all the disciplines on which Dante relies to convey his thoughts, not only theology, not only the so-called liberal arts (divided into two parts, the *trivium* and *quadrivium* [see below]), but with developing issues in what we would refer to as philosophy and natural science. This was not the nineteenth century, when there were numerous readers of a professional preparation (doctors, lawyers, and others whose schooling included literature at a fairly advanced level in *liceo*) who entered into debate in the *Giornale dantesco* or other literary periodicals over some of the poem's finer points in a kind of "official amateur" role. There were, in the fourteenth century, perhaps no more than a happy few with such preparation. The educated readers to whom Dante addresses his poem had perhaps surprisingly similar educational backgrounds, having been subjected to the seven liberal arts: grammar, rhetoric, dialectic (roughly what is covered less cogently by preparation for what is measured by the "verbal" portion of the Standard Achievement Tests, familiar to American high school students); arithmetic, music, geometry, and astronomy (disciplines that were all associated with mathematics, and thus something like the preparation for the SATs in math). The most educated were mainly priests; they had also studied theology, the "highest science," the only field for the "PhD" in most medieval universities, on the model of Paris, where Thomas Aquinas taught. And so, while we may feel challenged by any or all of the "fields" that are represented in the poem, the educated elite probably could manage to understand a lot more of it than we, as is evidenced by the early commentaries, which produce a good deal of lore regarding what we would call astronomy, biology, geology, and physics.

(4) *Language and Style in* Paradiso.

Most of the diction of *Paradiso* is solemn, but some is surprisingly lighthearted (Canto V.139: "il seguente canto canta" [the next song sings]), exalted, but also giddily playful (Canto V.122–123: "Dì, dì . . . a dii"

[Speak, speak . . . in gods]); and, at times, colloquial and salty (Canto XVII.129: "e lascia pur grattar dov' è la rogna" [and let the one who itches scratch]). If the low comic speech we heard so much of in *Inferno* and a good smattering of in *Purgatorio* is less often present in *Paradiso*, the fact that it is there at all tells us something about Dante's determination to keep that low comic thread present in the fabric of the last canticle. It is probably correct to say that *Purgatorio* is the more "churchly" of the last two *cantiche*, while *Paradiso* is the more "Scholastic." Nonetheless, the very presence of a few low-vernacular moments determines our sense of the linguistic range that defines the enterprise. Jean Racine, who was grandly alert to such problems, once wrote that one cannot have a character say the word *mouchoir* (handkerchief) in a tragedy (because it violates the stylistic register of the genre). In even the most exalted parts of *Paradiso*, Dante keeps the low-mimetic present, as for instance in the last canto (*Par.* XXXIII.7) when he refers to Mary's womb, not in a Petrarchan and noble and politely metaphorical way (as one commentator thought he should have, by saying *virginal chiostro* [virginal cloister]), but by the unvarnished plainness of *ventre* ("womb" or "belly").

All the speakers overheard by us, eavesdropping at Dante's shoulder, are saved. This fact understandably colors the intonations that we hear. The more academic and abstract subjects normally addressed by Beatrice and by those Dante meets in the heavens would seem to call for different stylistic registers, and indeed we do hear a lot of Scholastic discourse, most notably from St. Thomas and from Dante's three apostolic examiners, Peter, James, and John, on the theological virtues. Nonetheless, we catch the inflection not only of that speech appropriate to such discourse, but also of Franciscan narrative (see Canto XI), with plenty of room left for a Christian version of Old Testament prophetic rage in the various denunciations of earthly behavior we hear in the first nine heavens. As Fredi Chiappelli (Chia.1967.3) suggested, in moving to *Paradiso* we encounter, at first (and as we might expect), a much greater degree of abstraction, both linguistic and conceptual, than we have become accustomed to in the earlier parts of the poem. However, and as Chiappelli points out, starting in Canto XXII the poet begins to move back to the concrete. This paradox is surely allied to the Incarnational basis of the Christian faith as well as of the poetics of the *Commedia*.

On the overall newness of the treatment of the subjects in the final canticle, see E. H. Wilkins (Wilk.1961.1), p. 3: "Certain differences between the *Inferno* and the *Purgatorio* on the one hand and the *Paradiso* on the other may be noted briefly. In each of the first two *cantiche* the number of lines that are spoken is a little less than half the total number of lines in the *cantica*: in the *Paradiso* considerably more than half of all the lines are spoken. In each of the first two *cantiche* the number of spoken passages is about three hundred and fifty; in the *Paradiso* it is about one hundred and fifty. In each of the first two *cantiche* the spoken passages average about six lines in length: in the *Paradiso* they average about twenty lines in length. In each of the first two *cantiche* the number of individual speakers is somewhat more than fifty: in the *Paradiso* it is less than twenty." Wilkins's census confirms what readers probably generally feel without extensive reflection: the third *cantica* is essentially different from the first two because of the sharp reduction in the amount of narrative it deploys. If, indeed, we examine the speeches of the twenty or so speakers in *Paradiso*, we quickly realize not only that *Paradiso* is characterized by having fewer speakers with more to say, but that very few of these speeches are devoted to narrative. In *Inferno* and *Purgatorio*, for Virgil to hold forth on the nature of sin (*Inf.* XI) or for Marco Lombardo to explain the nature of love (*Purg.* XVI) seemed unusual. We had become enthusiastically accustomed to the experience of sinners and penitents revealing their histories through riveting narratives. Even Beatrice's reproofs to Dante in *Purgatorio* XXX–XXXI generally took a narrative form, a retelling of the dark side of the protagonist's emergent new life. In the third *cantica*, on the other hand, embedded narratives are few and far between. To be sure, the poet will continue to tell how the protagonist moves from place to place in brief descriptions. What is comparatively absent, however, is narrative, narrative deployed in those self-revealing tales told by the souls whom the protagonist encounters in the first two canticles. (These are so prominent a feature of Dante's writing in the *Commedia* that they may seem to be its single most defining characteristic; witness their effect on Robert Browning.) Ugolino's self-narrative, for instance, runs 72 verses (*Inf.* XXXIII.4–75). The eleven speakers in *Paradiso* who tell their own stories, ranging from Piccarda in Canto III (through Justinian, Charles Martel, Cunizza, Folco, Thomas, Bonaventure, Cacciaguida [perhaps, as Dante's ancestor, unsurprisingly the longest-winded, at 19 verses], Peter Damian, Benedict) to Adam in Canto XXVI, tell all eleven of these in some 150 verses scattered over twenty-four cantos (there are none in the first two cantos, exactly as we might expect, nor in the last seven, a fact that may surprise us, until we reflect that the extinction of self-consciousness is one hallmark of the shared behavior of all the saints in Heaven). In short, the total number of verses devoted to self-narrative in the third *cantica* is barely more than double that allotted to a single speaker, albeit the most loquacious one, in *Inferno*.

The language of *Paradiso* is exceptional, in every sense of that word.

There are words here that literally were never before used in a poem (or sometimes anywhere else, as far as we know), some simply transferred from one linguistic field to a new one, others made up by our poet. For Dante's versification, his wide-ranging lexicon (e.g., Latinisms, dialectical speech, Gallicisms, neologisms), his rhymes, and his stylistic traits, see the admirably clear and complete summary produced by John A. Scott (pp. 261–80) in his helpful introduction to the study of Dante (Scot.2004.2).

(5) *Politics in* Paradiso.

In attempting to come to grips with *Purgatorio*, some readers experience difficulty because they take Dante's views as being more "human" than they in fact are (e.g., the episode involving Matelda in Canto XXVIII may seem to some to valorize sensual love, while in fact it shows the need to transcend it). Others, dealing with *Paradiso*, make the mistake of considering the interests found in this *cantica* to be only "divine" (one oft-repeated view is that after we leave *Purgatorio* behind, the poem reveals no further interest in the political affairs of the world below—which is simply untrue). There is small need to insist on the political nature of so much of Dante's interest in the first two canticles. (For a fairly recent bibliography, see Di Scipio [Disc.1983.1], p. 282, n. 1.) *Paradiso*, however, is frequently portrayed either as having left such worldly concerns behind or as, if they are seen as present, downplaying their importance. Such a view is countered by even casual attention to the text. The reader may want to consider Canto VI, in which Justinian narrates the history of the eagle of imperial Rome; Cantos XV–XVII, in the course of which Cacciaguida describes, in detail, the political life of Florence in the "good old days" and the city's decline, as well as the future, political and personal, of its most famous exile, Dante Alighieri (see Davis [Davi.1968.1]); Canto XXVII (vv. 136–148), in which the poet offers the final political prophecy in the poem; and Canto XXX (vv. 133–148), where Beatrice shows Dante the vacant throne of the emperor Henry VII and savages the sitting pope (much to the dismay of some commentators, who think the poem should be more pacific at a point so near its vision of God). This is not to exhaust the passages showing a pronounced political concern in the final *cantica*, but does give a rapid sense of the importance of politics in it. Dante's political views are less surprisingly found in *Paradiso* than one at first may think. From their very first presence in the poem (e.g., the prophecy of the *veltro* in *Inf.* I, Ciacco's discussion of better times in Florence's earlier history in *Inf.* VI), they are not mere political views, but reveal themselves as having a religious, even a providential, component.

Endword.

"This commentary, as demanding of our labor as it was of our publisher's support, represents, published in these times, an act of faith in our schools and even more in the values found in our culture and in our history that some, shamefully and foolishly, attempt to make matters of debate. In order to preserve our humanity, we believe that it is indispensable to continue to practice philology, criticism, and literary history, that is, to make every effort to understand as precisely as possible the messages passed along to us by our common culture, which we in turn bear the responsibility of passing along to those to come. To be witnesses to and actors in a civilizational moment that reaches toward the future does not in any way deny the value of the past, the very source of our nourishment." These words (here translated from the Italian), dated Easter 1978, were written by Umberto Bosco, coauthor (along with Giovanni Reggio) of, in the opinion of the author of these notes, one of the finest commentaries to *Paradiso* available. Bosco's remarks, found on p. x of his *Premessa*, reflect the distress felt by many in Italy during one of the most difficult times of the postwar era, when Italian universities were besieged (often literally) by enemies, both external and internal, as the undersigned, a member of a commission of foreign scholars preparing a report on that situation, had opportunity to observe less than a year after Bosco wrote these words. A quarter of a century later, one hardly senses that the forces of civilization are winning the "culture wars" that seem almost embedded in university life and in the culture that lies outside the gates. On the other hand, one may take some comfort in the fact that Homer, Dante, Shakespeare, and other geniuses in the human arts, in whatever form they are appreciated, are still vital presences if only they are read or seen or heard. Whenever they cease their posthumous vitality, their extinction, like that of the dead canary in its cage within the confines of the coal mine, will tell those still breathing among us that it is time to get back to the surface or else, perhaps, to abandon hope.

Robert Hollander
Tortola, 21 January 2005

Map of Dante's Paradise

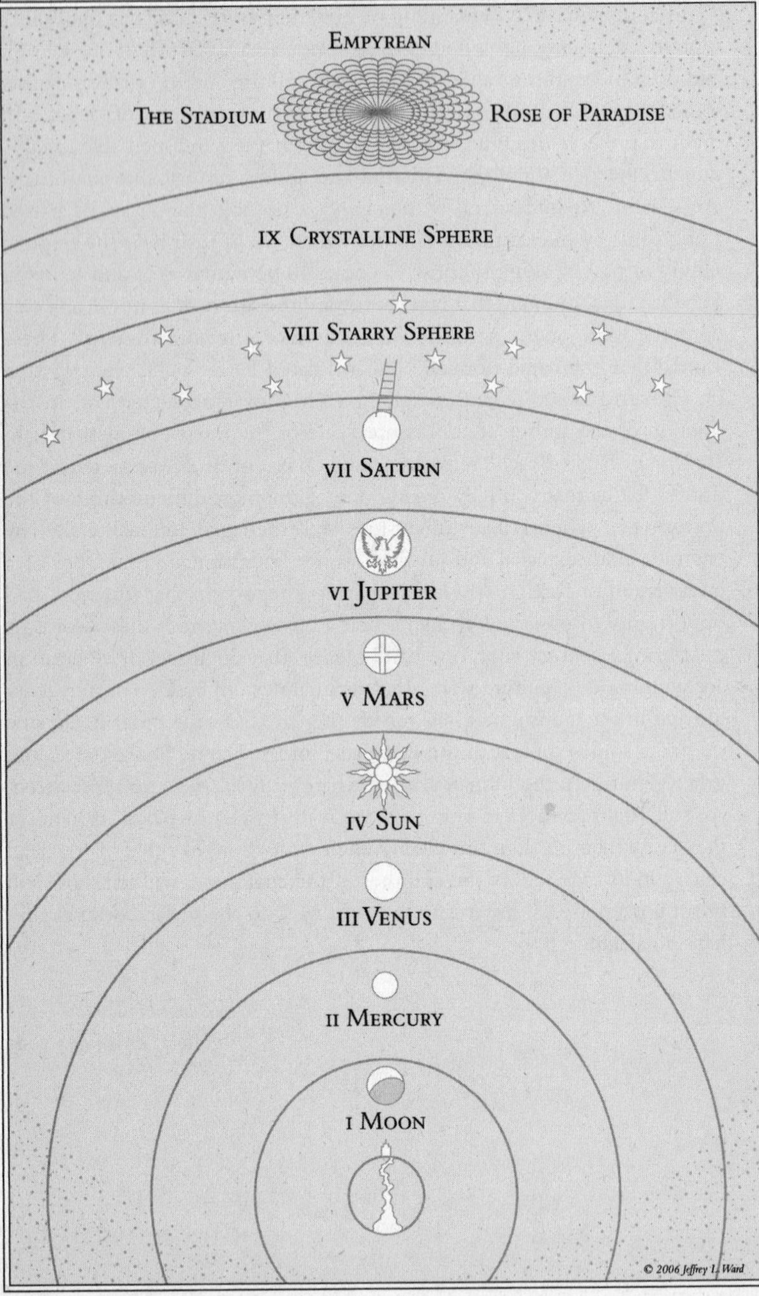

Empyrean

The Stadium

Rose of Paradise

IX Crystalline Sphere

VIII Starry Sphere

VII Saturn

VI Jupiter

V Mars

IV Sun

III Venus

II Mercury

I Moon

Empyrean	**XXX.16–XXXIII.145**
ascent	XXX.1–15

---

(9) Crystalline Sphere	**XXVII.100–XXIX.145**
ascent	XXVII.88–99
(8) Starry Sphere	**XXII.112–XXVII.87**
ascent	XXII.99–111
(7) Saturn	**XXI.16–XXII.98**
ascent	XXI.1–15
(6) Jupiter	**XVIII.70–XX.148**
ascent	XVIII.52–69
(5) Mars	**XIV.88–XVIII.51**
ascent	XIV.82–87
(4) Sun	**X.40–XIV.81**
ascent	X.28–39
(3) Venus	**VIII.16–X.27**
ascent	VIII.1–15
(2) Mercury	**V.100–VII.148**
ascent	V.86–99
(1) Moon	**II.31–V.85**
ascent	II.19–30

Proem: Eden	**I.1–II.18**

PARADISO I

OUTLINE

- 1–12 proem: looking back at the completed journey and the promise to narrate the rest of its course
- 13–36 invocation (fifth in the poem): the aid of **"Apollo"**
  - 13–21 invocation proper
  - 22–36 result of such inspiration; justification for it
- 37–60 the narrative begins: Dante still in earthly paradise
  - 37–42 the constellation Aries
  - 43–48 noon: Dante looking as Beatrice looks into the sun
  - 49–54 simile: the sun in her eyes and reflecting rays
  - 55–60 Dante can look directly at the sun
- 61–81 the ascent toward the Moon
  - 61–63 rising, Dante seems to see a second sun above him
  - 64–66 he looks back to see the stars reflected in her eyes
  - 67–72 simile: **Glaucus** and Dante's own "transhumanation"
  - 73–75 the poet cannot say whether he ascended in body
  - 76–81 reaching the sublunary ring of fire: *son et lumière*
- 82–141 Dante's questions and Beatrice's responses
  - 82–93 the first question: where is he? and the response
  - 94–99 the second: how can he pass through air and fire?
  - 100–126 response: the upward inclination of all things
  - 127–135 response: how things diverge from their true goal
  - 136–141 response: but not Dante, now freed from sin
- 142 coda: Beatrice looks back up.

PARADISO I

La gloria di colui che tutto move
per l'universo penetra, e risplende
in una parte più e meno altrove.

Nel ciel che più de la sua luce prende
fu' io, e vidi cose che ridire
né sa né può chi di là sù discende;

perché appressando sé al suo disire,
nostro intelletto si profonda tanto,
che dietro la memoria non può ire.

Veramente quant' io del regno santo
ne la mia mente potei far tesoro,
sarà ora materia del mio canto.

O buono Appollo, a l'ultimo lavoro
fammi del tuo valor sì fatto vaso,
come dimandi a dar l'amato alloro.

Infino a qui l'un giogo di Parnaso
assai mi fu; ma or con amendue
m'è uopo intrar ne l'aringo rimaso.

Entra nel petto mio, e spira tue
sì come quando Marsïa traesti
de la vagina de le membra sue.

O divina virtù, se mi ti presti
tanto che l'ombra del beato regno
segnata nel mio capo io manifesti,

vedra'mi al piè del tuo diletto legno
venire, e coronarmi de le foglie
che la materia e tu mi farai degno.

The glory of Him who moves all things
pervades the universe and shines
in one part more and in another less.

I was in that heaven which receives
more of His light. He who comes down from there
can neither know nor tell what he has seen,

for, drawing near to its desire,
so deeply is our intellect immersed
that memory cannot follow after it.

Nevertheless, as much of the holy kingdom
as I could store as treasure in my mind
shall now become the subject of my song.

O good Apollo, for this last labor
make me a vessel worthy
of the gift of your belovèd laurel.

Up to this point, one peak of Mount Parnassus
has been enough, but now I need them both
in order to confront the struggle that awaits.

Enter my breast and breathe in me
as when you drew out Marsyas,
out from the sheathing of his limbs.

O holy Power, if you but lend me of yourself
enough that I may show the merest shadow
of the blessèd kingdom stamped within my mind,

you shall find me at the foot of your belovèd tree,
crowning myself with the very leaves
of which my theme and you will make me worthy.

Sì rade volte, padre, se ne coglie
per trïunfare o cesare o poeta,
colpa e vergogna de l'umane voglie,

che parturir letizia in su la lieta
delfica deïtà dovria la fronda
peneia, quando alcun di sé asseta.

Poca favilla gran fiamma seconda:
forse di retro a me con miglior voci
si pregherà perché Cirra risponda.

Surge ai mortali per diverse foci
la lucerna del mondo; ma da quella
che quattro cerchi giugne con tre croci,

con miglior corso e con migliore stella
esce congiunta, e la mondana cera
più a suo modo tempera e suggella.

Fatto avea di là mane e di qua sera
tal foce, e quasi tutto era là bianco
quello emisperio, e l'altra parte nera,

quando Beatrice in sul sinistro fianco
vidi rivolta e riguardar nel sole:
aguglia sì non li s'affisse unquanco.

E sì come secondo raggio suole
uscir del primo e risalire in suso,
pur come pelegrin che tornar vuole,

così de l'atto suo, per li occhi infuso
ne l'imagine mia, il mio si fece,
e fissi li occhi al sole oltre nostr' uso.

Molto è licito là, che qui non lece
a le nostre virtù, mercé del loco
fatto per proprio de l'umana spece.

So rarely, father, are they gathered
to mark the triumph of a Caesar or a poet—
fault and shame of human wishes—

that anyone's even longing for them,
those leaves on the Peneian bough, should make
the joyous Delphic god give birth to joy.

Great fire leaps from the smallest spark.
Perhaps, in my wake, prayer will be shaped
with better words so Cyrrha may respond.

The lamp of the world rises on us mortals
at different points. But, by the one that joins
four circles with three crossings, it comes forth

on a better course and in conjunction
with a better sign. Then it tempers and imprints
the wax of the world more to its own fashion.

Its rising near that point had brought out morning there
and evening here, and that hemisphere
was arrayed in light, this one in darkness,

when I saw that Beatrice had turned toward her left
and now was staring at the sun—
never had eagle so fixed his gaze on it.

And, as a second ray will issue from the first
and rise again up to its source,
even as a pilgrim longs to go back home,

so her gaze, pouring through my eyes
on my imagination, made itself my own, and I,
against our practice, set my eyes upon the sun.

Much that our powers here cannot sustain is there
allowed by virtue of the nature of the place
created as the dwelling fit for man.

Io nol soffersi molto, né sì poco,
ch'io nol vedessi sfavillar dintorno,
com' ferro che bogliente esce del foco;

e di sùbito parve giorno a giorno
essere aggiunto, come quei che puote
avesse il ciel d'un altro sole addorno.

Beatrice tutta ne l'etterne rote
fissa con li occhi stava; e io in lei
le luci fissi, di là sù rimote.

Nel suo aspetto tal dentro mi fei,
qual si fé Glauco nel gustar de l'erba
che 'l fé consorto in mar de li altri dèi.

Trasumanar significar *per verba*
non si poria; però l'essemplo basti
a cui esperïenza grazia serba.

S'i' era sol di me quel che creasti
novellamente, amor che 'l ciel governi,
tu 'l sai, che col tuo lume mi levasti.

Quando la rota che tu sempiterni
desiderato, a sé mi fece atteso
con l'armonia che temperi e discerni,

parvemi tanto allor del cielo acceso
de la fiamma del sol, che pioggia o fiume
lago non fece alcun tanto disteso.

La novità del suono e 'l grande lume
di lor cagion m'accesero un disio
mai non sentito di cotanto acume.

Ond' ella, che vedea me sì com' io,
a quïetarmi l'animo commosso,
pria ch'io a dimandar, la bocca aprio

I could not bear it long, yet not so brief a time
as not to see it sparking everywhere,
like liquid iron flowing from the fire.

Suddenly it seemed a day was added to that day,
as if the One who has the power
had adorned the heavens with a second sun.

Beatrice had fixed her eyes
upon the eternal wheels and I now fixed
my sight on her, withdrawing it from above.

As I gazed on her, I was changed within,
as Glaucus was on tasting of the grass
that made him consort of the gods in the sea.

To soar beyond the human cannot be described
in words. Let the example be enough to one
for whom grace holds this experience in store.

Whether I was there in that part only which you
created last is known to you alone, O Love who rule
the heavens and drew me up there with your light.

When the heavens you made eternal,
wheeling in desire, caught my attention
with the harmony you temper and attune,

then so much of the sky seemed set on fire
by the flaming sun that neither rain nor river
ever fed a lake so vast.

The newness of the sound and the bright light
lit in me such keen desire to know their cause
as I had never with such sharpness felt before.

And she, who knew me as I knew myself,
to calm my agitated mind
before I even had begun to speak, parted her lips

e cominciò: "Tu stesso ti fai grosso
col falso imaginar, sì che non vedi
ciò che vedresti se l'avessi scosso.

Tu non se' in terra, sì come tu credi;
ma folgore, fuggendo il proprio sito,
non corse come tu ch'ad esso riedi."

S'io fui del primo dubbio disvestito
per le sorrise parolette brevi,
dentro ad un nuovo più fu' inretito

e dissi: "Già contento *requïevi*
di grande ammirazion; ma ora ammiro
com' io trascenda questi corpi levi."

Ond' ella, appresso d'un pïo sospiro,
li occhi drizzò ver' me con quel sembiante
che madre fa sovra figlio deliro,

e cominciò: "Le cose tutte quante
hanno ordine tra loro, e questo è forma
che l'universo a Dio fa simigliante.

Qui veggion l'alte creature l'orma
de l'etterno valore, il qual è fine
al quale è fatta la toccata norma.

Ne l'ordine ch'io dico sono accline
tutte nature, per diverse sorti,
più al principio loro e men vicine;

onde si muovono a diversi porti
per lo gran mar de l'essere, e ciascuna
con istinto a lei dato che la porti.

Questi ne porta il foco inver' la luna;
questi ne' cor mortali è permotore;
questi la terra in sé stringe e aduna;

and said: 'You make yourself dull-witted
with false notions, so that you cannot see
90 what you would understand, had you but cast them off.

'You are not still on earth, as you believe.
Indeed, lightning darting from its source
93 never sped as fast as you return to yours.'

If I was stripped of my earlier confusion
by her brief and smiling words,
96 I was the more entangled in new doubt

and said: 'I was content to be released
from my amazement, but now I am amazed
99 that I can glide through these light bodies.'

Then she, having sighed with pity,
bent her eyes on me with just that look
102 a mother casts on her delirious child,

and said: 'All things created have an order
in themselves, and this begets the form
105 that lets the universe resemble God.

'Here the higher creatures see the imprint
of the eternal Worth, the end
108 for which that pattern was itself set forth.

'In that order, all natures have their bent
according to their different destinies,
111 whether nearer to their source or farther from it.

'They move, therefore, toward different harbors
upon the vastness of the sea of being,
114 each imbued with an instinct that impels it on its course.

'This instinct carries fire toward the moon,
this is the moving force in mortal hearts,
117 this binds the earth to earth and makes it one.

né pur le creature che son fore
d'intelligenza quest' arco saetta,
120 ma quelle c'hanno intelletto e amore.

La provedenza, che cotanto assetta,
del suo lume fa 'l ciel sempre quïeto
123 nel qual si volge quel c'ha maggior fretta;

e ora lì, come a sito decreto,
cen porta la virtù di quella corda
126 che ciò che scocca drizza in segno lieto.

Vero è che, come forma non s'accorda
molte fïate a l'intenzion de l'arte,
129 perch' a risponder la materia è sorda,

così da questo corso si diparte
talor la creatura, c'ha podere
132 di piegar, così pinta, in altra parte;

e sì come veder si può cadere
foco di nube, sì l'impeto primo
135 l'atterra torto da falso piacere.

Non dei più ammirar, se bene stimo,
lo tuo salir, se non come d'un rivo
138 se d'alto monte scende giuso ad imo.

Maraviglia sarebbe in te se, privo
d'impedimento, giù ti fossi assiso,
com' a terra quïete in foco vivo."
142 Quinci rivolse inver' lo cielo il viso.

'This bow impels not just created things
that lack intelligence, but also those
that have both intellect and love.

'Providence, which regulates all this,
makes with its light forever calm the heaven
that contains the one that whirls with greatest speed,

'and there now, as to a place appointed,
the power of that bowstring bears us,
aimed, as is all it shoots, at a joyful target.

'It is true that as a work will often fail
to correspond to its intended form, its matter
deaf and unresponsive to the craftsman's plan,

'so sometimes a creature, having the capacity
to swerve, will, thus impelled, head off another way,
in deviation from the better course

'and, just as sometimes we see fire
falling from a cloud, just so the primal impulse,
diverted by false pleasure, turns toward earth.

'If I am correct, you should no more wonder
at your rising than at a stream's descent
from a mountain's peak down to its foot.

'It would be as astounding if you, set free
from every hindrance, had remained below,
as if on earth a living flame held still.'
Then she turned her face up to the heavens.

1–36. Dante clearly offers these verses as an introduction to the third and final *cantica* as a whole. So much is dealt with in them, and in precisely such a way as to set *Paradiso* off from the rest of the poem, that it is perhaps worth considering them as a unit before attempting to come to grips with particular lines. One burden of these remarks (and of the specific glosses that follow them) is that Dante is once again (see, e.g., *Purg.* XXIV.52–54) playing a dangerous game as he addresses his role as poet. He presents himself, if in hidden ways (in modern political parlance, he "preserves deniability"), as being inspired by God to write this part of the poem (a barely hidden claim in the first two canticles as well). At the same time he allows us to believe, if we are uncomfortable with that claim here, that he is only doing what all poets do, invoking deities for poetic inspiration as has been conventional since Homer's time. And so here we shall find him referring to Apollo (I.13), Mt. Parnassus (I.16), the satyr Marsyas (I.20), and Daphne (in the form of the laurel tree—I.25). Yet all those classicizing gestures do not quite obfuscate the clear postclassical network of the necessary Christian appurtenances of a poem that begins by remembering its culmination and conclusion, the vision of God in the Empyrean.

We are fortunate in the fact that the first dozen of these opening verses are the subject of a commentary written by no less an expert than Dante himself, in his *Epistle to Cangrande*, which now, after the evidence that it was known and extensively cited by Andrea Lancia circa 1345, as Luca Azzetta (Azze.2003.1) has demonstrated, cannot easily be denied its Dantean paternity (and especially not by those for whom a major piece of negative evidence against the authenticity of the document was the complete absence of direct reference to Dante's authorship in the fourteenth century). Dante himself marks off these thirty-six verses as introductory, referring to the rest of the *cantica* (*Par.* I.37–XXXIII.145) as its *pars executiva* (executive portion), i.e., the narrative (of which he says nothing, if he seems to promise to do so). In fact, his detailed treatment (the *pars executiva*, as it were, of his epistle) is reserved, interestingly enough, only for the first dozen of these three dozen lines, which receive some four pages of analysis (we might reflect that, had the commentator continued at this rate, he would have produced a document of some sixteen hundred pages for *Paradiso* alone). Then the commentator begins to treat his subject at breakneck speed: The last *terzina* of the group (vv. 10–12) receives only a single brief sentence of attention, while the following fifteen verses (13–27) are glossed even more hurriedly.

Except for Scartazzini, a happy and fairly early exception, few exegetes have made wide use of the *Epistle* in their responses to the opening of the *Paradiso* (if Charles Singleton, in his "Special Note" to the canto, and Umberto Bosco/Giovanni Reggio [comm. to vv. 1, 2, 3, 4, 6, 7–9, 12, 13] offer notable exceptions; see also Baldelli [Bald.1993.2]). To do so properly would overburden these pages; therefore, the interested reader is directed to a fuller treatment of this document in the commentary to the opening five tercets of the canto in the Princeton Dante Project (www.princeton.edu/dante).

Dante's practice as composer of prologues to each of his three *cantiche* is diverse, as may be readily observed in the following table:

	Introduction	Invocation	Narrative Begins
Inferno I	1–9	II.7 [delayed]	I.10
Purgatorio I	1–6	I.7–12	I.13
Paradiso I	1–12	I.13–36	I.37

Paradiso, it seems clear, required more painstaking justification than anything before it, and this, the fifth of the nine invocations in the poem (see the note to *Inf.* II.7–9) is by far the most elaborate, requiring eight tercets for its development. We shall return to the invocatory portion of the introduction to *Paradiso* shortly; here we may simply observe that the self-reflective poetic gestures made in those eight tercets occupy fully two-thirds of this introductory poetic space.

1. The phrasing "di colui che tutto move" (of Him who moves all things) is unmistakably derived from Aristotle's "unmoved mover" (see *Metaphysics* XII.7), familiar in Scholastic writings, as Scartazzini (1900, comm. to this verse) insists. "La gloria," on the other hand, initiates and controls the Scholastic definition in order to Christianize its terminology. ("Glory" is notably and understandably absent from Aristotle's or Thomas's discussion of the first mover.) The word has various possible meanings in the *Commedia* (see the article "gloria" by Sebastiano Aglianò [*ED* III (1975)], pp. 240–42): for example, it may represent earthly renown, a shining quality, the state of blessedness. Here it may retain some of its more earthly resonance, but in only the highest sense: God's shining forth from his beatitude, the most "famous" of all things that exist.

2–3. The *Letter to Cangrande* devotes well over a page to these verses, arguing that we are to find the glory of God's Being reflected in all that exists in His secondary creation; likewise, His essence, or His intellect, lies at the heart of all the substances found in the created universe. Thus it is not surprising that we find a gradation among even the things that God has made, some being more or less corruptible than others. Dante offers no examples in this difficult passage, but it is clear that he is thinking of the angels at the highest end of creation, and the less exalted forms of matter (e.g., rocks, mud) at the lowest. The words *penetra* (pervades, penetrates) and *risplende* (shines [with reflected light]) distinguish between God's unmediated glory and its reflection, its quality various as what it is reflected by.

4–12. For the interrelated phenomena in *Paradiso* (beginning with this passage) of "the seeing and understanding of the protagonist—with their related difficulties—and the ability to remember and to express his experience—with *their* related difficulties," see the densely supported observations of Giuseppe Ledda (Ledd.2002.1), pp. 243–98.

4–6. The reference to St. Paul's ascent to the heavens is unmistakable (II Corinthians 12:3–4) and has long been acknowledged (at least since the time [ca. 1385] of Francesco da Buti [comm. to vv. 1–12]). For a particularly incisive treatment, see Landino on this tercet. More recently, see the extended treatment by Giuseppe Ledda (Ledd.2002.1), pp. 243–59. And see Di Scipio (Disc.1995.1), p. 253, for the pertinence here of the concept of *excessus mentis* (but see the previous recognitions of Sapegno [in his comment to vv. 6–9] and a few other modern commentators). For the Pauline background of the concept, see Di Scipio (Disc.1995.1), pp. 153–55.

4. Some commentators, perhaps beginning with Pietrobono (comm. to this verse), put forward the notion that the reference is to all ten heavens, that is, to the totality of this superterrestrial world. A few have also argued that the reference is to the outermost of the physical heavenly spheres, either the Crystalline or the Primum Mobile. However, it seems utterly clear that Dante is referring to the Empyrean, God's "home" (insofar as He who is everywhere can be thought of as located in a particular anywhere as well). Scartazzini (comm. to this verse) was perhaps the first to refer to the *Epistle to Cangrande* as eventual justification of this reading: "And it is called the Empyrean, which is as much as to say, the heaven glowing with fire or heat; not that there is material fire or heat therein, but spiritual, which is holy love, or charity" (XIII.68—tr. P. Toynbee).

5. It is difficult *not* to think of the heavenly experience granted St. Paul.

7. For his several discussions of the language of desire in Dante, with special reference to *Paradiso*, see Lino Pertile (Pert.1990.1); (Pert.1993.2); (Pert.1998.2), pp. 87–133; (Pert.2001.1). And now see his global study of this subject (Pert.2005.2).

9. On this verse, "che dietro la memoria non può ire" (that memory cannot follow after it), see Bruno Nardi (Nard.1960.3), who examines the understanding of the nature of memory as it is reflected in the traditions that develop from Aristotle and Augustine and come down into Albertus Magnus and Thomas Aquinas in order to establish that "when our intellect comes near to the beatific vision of God . . . , it so immerses itself in it . . . that the memory and the image-receiving capacity of the mind are unable to contain it any longer" (p. 273). As Poletto and Tozer point out (comms. to vv. 7–9), Dante has explained this verse in the *Epistle to Cangrande* (XIII.77): "Et reddit causam dicens 'quod intellectus in tantum profundat se' in ipsum 'desiderium suum', quod est Deus, 'quod memoria sequi non potest' " (And he gives the reason, saying that "the intellect plunges itself to such depth" in its very longing, which is for God, "that the memory cannot follow" [tr. P. Toynbee]). There is (mainly unexpressed) disagreement among the commentators as to whether the memory is with the intellect in its first experience of the Godhead and only loses that perception afterward, or, as Dante seems to be saying, is left behind at the outset in the intellect's excitement. Whatever hypothesis one accepts, the result is the same, as the last verses of the poem will also announce: The vision of God cannot be contained in human memory; rather, we can only claim a memory of having had a memory, now lost.

10–12. As though in preparation for the invocation that is to come in the following tercet, Dante resorts to a series of phrases or words laden with literary overtone, whether intrinsically or by the context offered from their other appearances in the *Commedia*: *veramente* (discussed in the following note), *regno santo, mente, tesoro, materia, il mio canto*. For instance, the "holy kingdom" (*regno santo*) that is Paradise may remind us of medieval poets' assigning themselves geographic/political areas as subjects of their work (e.g., the "matter of Troy," the "matter of France," etc.); all the rest of these terms are also used by Dante in passages that refer to the writing of his poem. For *materia*, see *Paradiso* X.27, where Dante refers to the text of *Paradiso* as "that matter of which I have become the scribe."

10. While it is clear that, as commentators have pointed out, Dante's conjunction (*veramente*, here "nevertheless") mirrors the formality of the Latin conjunction *verumtamen*, it also necessarily exhibits the only partly hidden claim that this poem is a record of things that have truly (*veramente*) been observed. In 1791, Lombardi (comm. to this verse) was perhaps the first commentator to insist on the force of the Latin root, specifically denying the meaning of *con verità, certamente,* found in the earlier commentaries. It is, however, difficult to accept the notion that the obvious Italian meaning is utterly effaced in the Latinism. In accord with that view, Benvenuto (comm. to vv. 1–12) glosses *veramente* as "not in empty dreams." Poetry, as commentators should realize perhaps more often than we do, has the propensity to open into a plurality of meanings that cannot be fully rendered in prose. (Dante, however, in *Vita nuova* XXV.10 clearly himself sponsors the notion that the meaning of poems are known to those who make them: "For, if any one should dress his poem in images and rhetorical coloring and then, being asked to strip his poem of such dress in order to reveal its true meaning, would not be able to do so—this would be a veritable cause for shame. And my best friend [Guido Cavalcanti] and I are well acquainted with some who compose so clumsily" [tr. M. Musa].)

Since most of the seven of the preceding uses of the adverb fairly obviously offer only the more usual Italian sense of the word (i.e., "truly," "really"—as will most of the seven that follow), its undertone here is not easily muffled.

11. The word *tesoro* is focal in a number of contexts as we move through the poem. For these, see the note to *Paradiso* XVII.121–122. Here Dante claims to have laid up in his memory the "treasure of Heaven" (see Matthew 19:21).

12. For the concept behind Dante's word *materia*, see the note to vv. 10–12, above. As for the noun *canto*, when it signifies "song" (and not "side" or "edge," a meaning it has fully seven times, interspersed through all three *cantiche*), it is used twenty-four times in the poem, and includes reference to a gamut of "songs": (1) classical epic (*Inf.* IV.95); (2) a specific canto or passage in the *Commedia* (*Inf.* XX.2; XXXIII.90; *Purg.* I.10; *Par.* V.16; V.139); (3) Dante's *former* song, the second ode of the *Convivio* (*Purg.* II.107; II.131); (4) the Ulysses-seducing song of the Siren in Dante's second Purgatorial dream (*Purg.* XIX.23); (5) songs of biblical derivation sung as part of the rite of purgation, that is, the *Miserere* sung by the peni-

tents in ante-purgatory (*Purg.* V.27) and the *Gloria in excelsis* sung by the penitent avaricious at Statius's liberation from *his* penitence (*Purg.* XX.140); (6) Charity's directive song to which Faith and Hope measure the steps of their dance (*Purg.* XXIX.128); and finally (7) twelve songs in the *Paradiso* directed to or emanating from Heaven, first the holy songs of the Seraphim (*Par.* IX.77) and, last, the *Gloria* sung by the Church Triumphant (if not by Jesus and Mary, already returned to the Empyrean—*Par.* XXVII.3).

13–36. The author of the *Epistle to Cangrande* himself divides the introduction to *Paradiso* into two parts, vv. 1–12 and 13–36 (see *Epist.* XIII.48). While the invocation proper occupies only three verses, this entire passage supports and extends it. (For an intense consideration of Dante's use of invocation, see Ledda [Ledd.2002.1], pp. 55–63.)

13–15. The invocation of God, even if as the "good Apollo," is, once one considers the poetic moment, almost a necessity. (Paulinus of Nola apostrophizes Christ as follows: "Salve o Apollo vere" [Save us, O true Apollo—*Carmina* II.51], as noted by Kantorowicz [Kant.1951.1], p. 228, among a plethora of similar expressions found in Greek [and some Latin] syncretistic passages.) Who else but God Himself can serve as the ultimate "muse" for a poem about the ultimate mysteries of the Christian faith? If the first two of these three verses indirectly but clearly associate Apollo with God (the word *valore* in verse 14 is used at least thrice again undoubtedly to refer to the Power of God the Father [*Par.* I.107, X.3, and XXXIII.81]), while the second indirectly but clearly associates Dante with St. Paul (see *Inf.* II.28, "lo Vas d'elezïone" [the Chosen Vessel]), since Dante, likewise, will be made God's chosen vessel (*vaso*). And what of the gift that this poet seeks? The "belovèd laurel," in this exalted context, becomes more than poetic fame, but the true immortality of those who are blessed for eternity, another and better kind of immortality: the "laurel" granted by God to his immortal (i.e., saved) poet, rewarded, among other things, for having written, under His inspiration, of Him. In the *Epistle to Cangrande*, Dante offers the following explanation of the reason poets call on higher authority: "For they have need of invocation in a large measure, inasmuch as they have to petition the superior beings for something beyond the ordinary range of human powers, something almost in the nature of a divine gift" (tr. P. Toynbee—the last phrase reads *quasi divinum quoddam munus*, representing an only slightly veiled reference to the theologized nature of his "Apollo"). For Dante's single use of the

Latinism *muno*, based on *munus*, see *Paradiso* XIV.33. We should not forget, if we insist on the pagan valence of Apollo, that Dante has already twice "transvaluated" a pagan god into the Christian deity: See *Inferno* XXXI.92 and *Purgatorio* VI.118 for the expression *sommo Giove* (highest Jove). This is surely the same phenomenon that we witness here.

Do these "transvaluations" of the more usual understandings of poetic inspiration and success entirely erase the traces of their original reference among poets and their audiences? We are, after all, reading a poem. And we should have no doubt but that its human agent was as interested in earthly success as any other poet (and perhaps more than most). However, the context makes a pagan understanding of these grand poetic gestures at the same time both impossible and desirable. We are almost forced to recognize the divine claims made by this very human agent, but we are allowed to understand them in completely human terms as well. We find ourselves in a usual dilemma: If we take the truth claims made by the poet on behalf of his poem seriously, we feel greatly troubled (mortal agents are not allowed such claims unless they are *demonstrably* chosen, as, to Christian believers, was Paul); on the other hand, if we insist that these claims are in fact not true, we sense that we have failed to deal with something that, if it makes us uncomfortable, nonetheless must be dealt with; other poets do not make such stringent demands upon our belief. In another way of phrasing this, we can only say No after we have said Yes, that is, by understanding Dante's veiled claims, no matter what we eventually decide to think of them.

13. It seems clear that, whatever the eventual identity we are meant to assign to Ovid's amorous god, there is one that this personage cannot possibly have in its higher context, that of Apollo, pagan god of the Sun, music, and so on. Ovid's Apollo (*Metam.* I.452–567), pursuing Daphne with immediate disastrous consequence for the girl, is, we are probably meant to understand, the "bad" Apollo. The later poet's "sun God" is in antithetic relationship to him when Dante reconstructs the Ovidian tale into a sort of Christian riddle. Since the pagan Apollo was understood as the poet seeking immortality (Daphne is metamorphosed, of course, into the laurel tree), we are left to consider what the laurel becomes in this rarefied circumstance. The best understanding of it is perhaps that Dante is invoking the aid of the true God in his triune majesty (see the note to *Par.* II.7–9) to make his inspired poem so that he himself may achieve immortal glory, eternal life in the Empyrean. This understanding of the laurel should be set against that found earlier in the poem (see *Purg.* XI.91–93

and note), for unlike the green crown of mortal achievements, which adorns its winner's brow only until someone is eventually adjudged better by the crowd, this one is the reward of true immortality for the writing of the poem "to which both heaven and earth have set their hand" (*Par.* XXV.2). The passage sounds exactly like the usual petition for aid in making a poem, but has this subtle and absolutely crucial difference. Apollo is a familiar Christian analogue for Christ (for later manifestations of this medieval tradition in Calderón, see Curtius [Curt.1948.1], pp. 245, 568), and here it is perhaps the Second Person of the Trinity that first shines through to the reader as the dominant Person present in these lines (see Giacalone's comment on vv. 20–21: "Here Apollo is a figure of Christ"). As we shall see, the other two Persons are both referred to, clearly if obliquely.

16–18. This tercet explains its predecessor (i.e., why the poet feels he must turn to "the Delphic god" [verse 32] now), although it is fair to say that elements in it have remained a puzzle through the centuries. If previously he has seemingly not needed to appeal directly to a higher authority for inspiration, relying only on the Muses, Dante now turns to the god himself. Whatever the meanings and references of the details put before us here, almost every commentator agrees that this is their basic significance.

Dante, however, is apparently confused about the configuration of the actual Mt. Parnassus in Greece. See Tozer's explanation (1901) of this material (which Dante borrows, without perhaps recognizing the problem he inherits in doing so, from his Latin precursors): "That mountain rises to a single conspicuous summit; and when the Greek poets speak of its two summits (Soph., *Ant.* 1126; Eurip., *Bacch.* 307; cf. *Ion.* 86–8) they mean, not the real summit of the mountain, but the two peaks that rise above Delphi, which are several thousand feet lower. These expressions were misunderstood by the Roman poets, who regularly describe Parnassus as rising to two summits; for example, Ov., *Met.* I.316–317, 'Mons ibi verticibus petit arduus astra duobus, Nomine Parnassus' (There Mount Parnassus lifts its two peaks skyward, high and steep—tr. F. J. Miller); Lucan, *Phars.* V.72, 'Parnassus gemino petit aethera | colle' (the twin peaks of Parnassus soar to heaven—tr. J. D. Duff). Dante followed them, and naturally fell into the same mistake."

Nonetheless, if Dante knew what many of his commentators, from the earliest through those of the last century, report at verse 16 (e.g., the Ottimo, Pietro di Dante, the author of the *Chiose ambrosiane*, Benvenuto, the Anonimo Fiorentino, John of Serravalle, Lombardi, Portirelli,

Tommaseo, Scartazzini, Campi), namely, that Cyrrha was sacred to Apollo, Nissa to Bacchus, how could he have made the second "peak" of Parnassus sacred to the Muses? At *Purgatorio* XXIX.37–42, Dante's second invocation of that *cantica* makes reference to the Heliconian residence of the Muses. However, two other passages in *Purgatorio* (XXII.65 and XXXI.141) make oblique reference to the Castalian spring on Mt. Parnassus as also being home to these ladies. It does seem possible that Dante has deliberately conflated two homes of the Muses, the spring on Parnassus with that on Helicon (which Dante may not have known as a mountain but as itself a spring).

18. For the phrase "m'è uopo," here translated "I need," see Landino (comm. to vv. 16–18): "chome in latino diciamo 'mihi est opus' " (as in Latin we say, "I have this to do").

The word *aringo* (here translated loosely and, in reverse metonymy, as "struggle") actually descends from a Gothic word referring to the space in which troops were gathered (and subsequently a contest took place)—see Giacalone (comm. to vv. 16–18). The English "ring" (definition 13 in the *OED*) offers, if not perhaps a true cognate, a useful analogue, as in the phrase "I would not get into the ring with him, if I were you."

19. In this second piece of his invocation proper (in the first, at verse 14, he had asked to be made God's vessel), the poet asks to be, literally, inspired ("Enter my breast and breathe in me"). If the first petition seems to have been aimed in particular at the Second Person of the Trinity, Christ as Apollo, this one seems to be directed to the Holy Spirit, as has been the case in the *Comedy* when Dante has represented inspiration, reflecting the "spiration of the Holy Spirit" (e.g., see the notes to *Inf.* XXXIII.106–108; *Purg.* XXIV.52–54). And now see Picone (Pico.2005.1), pp. 10–11.

20–21. If the reader has accepted the possibility (even the likelihood) that Dante's guarded speech is to be unriddled as an invocation of Christian dimension and scope, these next two verses seem to undo such a formulation with a certain exigency, for the story of Marsyas does not seem to lend itself to such understandings (but see the similar treatment of Apollo discussed in the note to verse 13).

Dante probably did not have access to the fragmentary accounts knit together to make the story of Marsyas that modern readers can find in various compendia. The prehistory of Marsyas was, if known to him, interesting. Minerva, having invented the wind instrument that we know as the flute, or panpipes, saw herself, playing it, reflected in water and noticed how ugly the exercise made her face. She hurled it away, only to have it picked up by Marsyas, who found that he quickly learned the skill to make his tunes. He became so convinced of his ability that he challenged Apollo to a musical contest (cf. those similar Ovidian challengers of the gods' aesthetic abilities, the daughters of King Pierus [*Purg.* I.9–12] and Arachne [*Purg.* XII.43–45]). Naturally, Apollo and his lyre outdo Marsyas and his flute. Since each combatant was to have his will if victorious, Apollo flays Marsyas alive (presumptuous mortals are always taught their lesson by the Ovidian gods whom they offend, but never seem to learn it). Ovid's account (in the sixth book of the *Metamorphoses*) of the early stages of the myth are brief (vv. 383–386 [he spends the core of his account, vv. 387–391, on the flaying in graphic detail and then, in the quieter conclusion, vv. 392–400, on the sadness of Marsyas's fellow fauns and satyrs at his death and transformation into the clearest stream in Phrygia]). He is a satyr defeated in a contest by Apollo on Minerva's rejected reed and punished by the god; but do we not catch a glimpse in him of a potentially failed Dante, his vernacular low instrument contrasted with the lofty Apollonian lyre? In the account of Marsyas's punishment that Dante knew best (Ovid, *Metam.* VI.383–400), his musical instrument has evidently humble origins: It is a reed (*harundo* [verse 384]) such as a yokel might pluck to make a tuneful sound; it is also a flute (*tibia* [verse 386]). Thus, along with presenting in Marsyas a coded figure of the poet as *vas electionis*, Dante also would seem to encourage us to fashion a further understanding: As Marsyas, he is a proponent of the comic muse, of the low style, against the higher forms of artistry intrinsically represented by Apollo, the flute versus the lyre. We have learned to read Dante's controversial self-identifications with a certain perspicuity. At one remove, he goes out of his way (and we readily follow him with great relief) to show that he is *not* at all like Uzzah (see the note to *Purg.* X.56–57) or, for that matter, Arachne (see the note to *Purg.* XII.43–45). On the other hand, we never rid ourselves of the suspicion that the poet is also confessing that he, secretly, for all his protestation by the use of contrary exemplars, acknowledges precisely his resemblance to these outlaws, these challengers to divine authority, these chafers at divine constraint upon human knowledge and capacity. Ovid's Marsyas is the opposite of Dante's, who has been turned inside out, as it were. (See Levenstein's succinct remark [Leve.2003.1, p. 412]: "While Ovid portrays the god's removal of the skin from the satyr, Dante describes the god's removal of the satyr from the skin.")

22–24. Apollo now becomes God the Father, addressed by the first of his Trinitarian attributes, Power. His highest creation, the Empyrean, is referred to as the "kingdom," of which Dante hopes to be allowed to retain a weak but true copy in his mind; he will bring that back and write it down for us. The phrase "l'ombra del beato regno" (the shadow of the blessèd kingdom—verse 23) reflects the Latin technical term *umbra* found in discussions of figure and fulfillment in biblical exegesis. See Ledda (Ledd.2002.1), pp. 302–3; Hollander (Holl.1969.1), pp. 196–97; (Holl.1993.5), pp. 19–21; and Ledda (Ledd.1997.1), p. 137.

25–27. The language here admits of two referential fields; in the Ovidian one, the tree is Apollo's laurel, to which Dante comes to crown himself with its leaves, as his subject and the god himself shall make him worthy. However, poets are not usually portrayed as crowning themselves. Perhaps that is a clue to our necessary radical transformation of the pagan myth as it applies to Dante. In the Christian version of the myth, Apollo is Christ (see the note to vv. 13–15) whose "tree" (the cross) the Christian poet approaches to gather to himself the Christian version of the laurel wreath, the immortality won for humankind by Christ, which his poem and Christ's love will make him worthy to receive. In this vein see Goffis (Goff.1964.1): "E così il 'diletto legno,' a cui si rivolgerà Dante, è certo l'alloro, ma è anche il *lignum crucis*, e le foglie d'alloro non saranno segno di gloria terrena soltanto" (And thus the "beloved tree," to which Dante shall address himself, is, to be sure, the laurel, but it is also the wood of the Cross; and the laurel's leaves shall not be a sign of earthly glory alone). In Dante's world, however, as the next tercet will make clear, there are none or few who even long for such reward.

The word *legno* occurs in nineteen passages in the poem, nine times as metonymic for "ship," seven times to mean "tree," twice to mean "a piece of wood," and once to refer to the cross, the "tree" to which Jesus was nailed (*Par.* XIX.105).

28–33. Far from worrying about not having enough laurel leaves to accommodate all those worthy of them (intrinsically the condition in earlier times, i.e., classical ones), Dante's Apollo must take joy whenever, in this leaden age, *anyone*, no matter how undeserving, desires to be crowned with the leaves of "the Peneian bough," that is, those of the laurel (or bay tree), in Daphne's transformed state; Daphne's father, god of a Thessalian river, was named Peneus, and the river after him. See, as Scartazzini (comm. to vv. 31–33) suggests, Ovid (*Metam.* I.452): "Primus amor Phoebi Daphne Peneia" (Apollo's first love, Peneus's daughter, Daphne).

29. Dante abruptly broadens the subject area to include emperors alongside of poets. Since, up to now (vv. 9–27), the focus has been exclusively on poetry, it comes as something of a surprise to find the imperial crown beneath our gaze, no matter how usual the reference to both laureations may be in our minds. Dante's sense of himself as political poet may account for this expansion; nothing else in the immediate context would seem to do so.

34. Arianna Punzi (Punz.1999.1) sees this line as an example of "false modesty"; however, the line reads more ordinarily as modesty itself ("the smallest spark leaps from a great fire"), a reading that is ridiculous and thus never attempted (e.g., how could Dante say the *Commedia* was "a small spark"?). On the other hand, normal grammatical usage would point in that direction. This is not to suggest that Dante wanted us to read the verse that way, but that when we do (as he surely knew we would in our first reading of the verse, before we discard that reading as impossible), we excuse him from the potential sin of pride. Nonetheless, it is clear that his little spark is meant to kindle a vast flame in us. That, however, is not necessarily to be understood as a prideful thought, when we consider the matter in light of the given of this poem (namely, that it is derived directly from God in order to help us to pray better), rather the completion of a chosen poet's duty.

35–36. The translation is based on an interpretation that may strike those who know the commentary tradition as erroneous (but see Hollander [Holl.1993.7], pp. 20–21; [Holl.1993.2], p. 91). These verses are usually (nearly universally) interpreted to refer to other *better* poets who will be inspired to write by reading Dante (and who, because of his example, will have even more success in finding Apollo's favor). Michelangelo Picone has in fact suggested (Pico.2002.4, p. 212n.) that Cino da Pistoia may be one such. And even the generally skeptical Scartazzini (1900, comm. to verse 35) falls victim to a probably unwise spirit of unanimity, although he is plainly uncomfortable with the portrait of the poet that results from this interpretation. "Troppa umiltà" (overabundant humility) is his muttered response. Indeed, the very notion that Dante might envision the possibility that a single other poet (much less a whole crowd) might outdo him in poetic accomplishment seems nothing less than preposterous. In the later twentieth century, several commentators tried another solution, one first reflected in the commentary tradition by Daniele Mattalia (1960), who cites Giuseppe Toffanin's remarks (Toff.1947.1), pp. 80–82, even though he does not agree with them, that try to make the case for the saints in Heaven, including Beatrice, as being those whose prayers will be amended by Dante's poem. That also seems a strained interpretation, since self-interested prayer is a necessary instrument only for those who are on earth, not yet experiencing their salvation. Nonetheless, the view impressed Rocco Montano (Mont.1963.1), p. 321, enough to make its way to print yet again and, through him, in 1968, to the commentator Giuseppe Giacalone (comm. to vv. 34–36). This minority position, however, does not hold up very well to scrutiny, either, though it is a welcome, if belated, response to the standard, if unlikely, gloss. There is a "third way," fortunately, of solving the problem. (See Hollander [Holl.2005.2 and 2006.1].) Literally, the verses seem to express the (not immodest) hope that the *Comedy* will help those who will read it to pray more effectively (and thus put themselves in the way of salvation—that would seem to be the necessary conclusion). It is no wonder that for centuries most of Dante's readers avoided recognition of the barely hidden daring in such religious claims as this. But it seems to be the simplest explanation of these verses, one that is in harmony with the avowed aim of this poet, which is to move those living in the bondage of the sins of this life toward the liberty of eternal glory (see the *Epistle to Cangrande*, v. 21).

See the similar dispute that dogs a similar passage, *Paradiso* XXX.34.

37–45. This long and difficult beginning of the narrative portion of the final *cantica* may be paraphrased as follows: The Sun ("the lamp of the world") rises on us mortals from various points along the horizon, but from that point at which four circles intersect in such a way as to form three crosses (generally understood as the circles of the horizon, the equator, the zodiac, the colure of the equinoxes, the last three of which intersect the horizon in this way on the vernal equinox, March 21), it comes forth conjoined with a better constellation (Aries) and takes a better course, and it better tempers and imprints the material compound of the world with its informing power. And from that point on the horizon it had made morning there, where almost all was light (Purgatory), and evening here, where almost all was dark (i.e., in the Northern Hemisphere). As Bosco/Reggio (comm. to vv. 37–42) point out, Dante has marked the beginnings of all three *cantiche* with references to the time (*Inf.* II.1–5; *Purg.* I.13–30, 115–117). Singleton refines the point (comm. to vv. 44–45): Where *Inferno* begins at evening (around 6 PM) and *Purgatorio* at dawn (shortly before 6 AM), *Paradiso* begins, more propitiously, at noon, the most "noble" hour of the day (see *Purg.* XXXIII.104 and *Conv.* IV.xxiii.15). And see the note in Bosco/Reggio to the following tercet (vv. 43–45) for some of the elaborate exegesis attached to the astronomical problems here. For a detailed discussion in English, see Alison Cornish (Corn.2000.2), pp. 87–92.

46–48. The lengthy opening description of the heavens yields to the first presence and first naming of Beatrice in *Paradiso*. Her superhuman ability to gaze directly and fixedly at the Sun reflects a tradition insisting on eagles' ability to do so found in Aristotle among the ancients (*De animalibus* IX.xxxiv) and in Brunetto Latini among the moderns (*Tresor* I.v.8). And see *Paradiso* XX.31–32. As Carroll points out (comm. to vv. 49–64), we probably should not draw allegorical conclusions about Beatrice's turning leftward (a movement frequently symptomatic, in this poem, of moral deficiency); here her turning in this direction is necessitated by her being in the Southern Hemisphere where Beatrice was facing east; north, where the Sun shone, was thus to her left.

49–54. This, the first formally developed simile of *Paradiso*, is in fact double (and that its second element deploys the image of a completed pilgrimage should not surprise us). We may sense an increasing degree of abstraction in the similes of this *cantica* (but not always—see vv. 67–69, where Dante's "transhumanation" is cast in physical terms; he is changed as was Glaucus). For the increasingly abstract nature of the poetry of roughly the first two-thirds of *Paradiso*, see Chiappelli (Chia.1967.3). And for two bibliographies of studies devoted to the Dantean simile, see Sowell (Sowe.1983.1) and Varela-Portas (Vare.2002.1).

Beatrice's miraculous (to ordinary mortals) ability to look into the Sun is momentarily granted to Dante, who sees the reflection of the Sun in her eyes and somehow is able to look up into that planet with his returning gaze. When we reflect that, according to *Purgatorio* IV.62, the Sun itself is a mirror (*specchio*), Beatrice then becomes a mirror of the mirror of God.

55–57. Some of the early commentators make the understandable mistake (since "here" obviously refers to the earth) of thinking that "there" applies to the heavens and not the pinnacle of the Mount of Purgatory; however, both Benvenuto da Imola (comm. to vv. 49–57) and Francesco da Buti (comm. to vv. 49–63) comprehend that Dante and Beatrice are still in the earthly paradise, a fact that the title of this new *cantica* tends to make us forget.

58–60. Dante is able to make out the corona of the Sun. The reader must assume that his greater sight results from his greater closeness to the Sun at this highest point on the earth's surface as well as from his regaining the vision of innocence (see the note to vv. 55–57).

61–63. Venturi (comm. to vv. 62–63) believes that this additional brightness was caused by the sight of the Moon, now grown larger in its appearance because Dante is so much higher. However (and as Lombardi [comm. to this tercet] correctly objects), this cannot be the sphere of the Moon, which awaits Beatrice and Dante in the next canto, but is the sphere of fire, in the outermost situation of the four elements that constitute our earth (water and earth, then air, and finally fire), a solution at first proposed in 1333 or so by the Ottimo (comm. to vv. 58–63). And see verse 115 of this canto ("This instinct carries fire up toward the moon"), where the sphere of fire is apparently again alluded to.

64–66. The guide and her charge presumably have passed through the (unnamed) sphere of fire that girds the earth just below the sphere of the Moon; Dante's eyes are guided by Beatrice's beyond this home of earth's highest-dwelling element and to a first sight of the heavenly spheres.

67–72. Glaucus's transformation, described by Ovid (*Metam.* XIII. 904–968), is a dazzling rendition of how an ordinary fisherman, chancing upon a magic herb, is metamorphosed into a god of the sea. Dante can sharply reduce the poetic space he devotes to the Ovidian scene because it is so familiar to his readers (at least the ones he most cares about). For the classical history of Glaucus as it comes into Ovid, Dante's primary source, see Diskin Clay (Clay.1985.1).

For Dante's Glaucus (along with Marsyas) as figures of Dante's own divinization, see Rigo (Rigo.1994.1), pp. 109–33. For the theme of *deificatio* in St. Bernard's *De diligendo Deo* as clarifying Dante's notion of "transhumanation," see Migliorini-Fissi (Migl.1982.1), who indeed sees traces of Bernard's work throughout the poem, as does Mazzoni (Mazz.1997.1), especially pp. 178–80, 192–230.

68. For Glaucus's "tasting" of the grass that transforms him as "reversing" Adam's "tasting" of the forbidden tree (*Par.* XXVI.115), see Rigo (Rigo.1994.1), p. 113. (The notion of Glaucus as Adam in his refound innocence goes well with that of Dante in his: See Carroll's observation in his note to vv. 49–64.) We observe here a conflation of Ovid's *Heroides* XVIII.160, a verse (cited by Rigo.1994.1, p. 114) referring to Glaucus: "reddidit herba deum" (whom a plant once deified—tr. H. C. Cannon).

The two major classical myths evoked in this canto, Apollo and Glaucus, along with the associated references to arrows and the ingestion of food, indicate the two main ways to understanding that we will hear about all through the *cantica*, intellectual penetration and a more passive reception of the truth.

That Dante has turned to Ovid for three major myth/motifs in this canto (Apollo and Daphne/immortality; Apollo and Marsyas/being drawn out of one's bodily limits; Glaucus/transhumanation) would almost seem to indicate that, for Dante's purposes, Ovid's poem about the gods, transmogrified by Dante's Christian intellect into shadows of a higher truth, is a more adaptable source than Virgil's martial epic for this more exalted and final component of the *Comedy*. If, after our encounter with the first cantos of *Paradiso*, we are of that opinion, we are not altogether incorrect. However, if we believe that Virgil's text is no longer a valued source in the poem's most Christian precincts, we will eventually be disabused of this notion, particularly in Cantos XV and XXXIII.

70–72. For Dante "transhumanation" is the passing beyond normal human limits by entering into a state at least approaching that enjoyed by divinity.

Chiarenza (Chia.1972.1), p. 83, holds this passage up to Hugh of St. Cher's comparison of the difficulty of conveying one's "intellectual vision" to someone else to the difficulty of describing the flavor of wine to one who had never tasted it.

See Migliorini-Fissi (Migl.1982.1), pp. 41–44, for St. Bernard's relevant concept of *deificatio*.

70. Dante's claim is lodged in self-conscious language that, in a single verse, includes an Italian neologism (*trasumanar*), literally "to transhumanate," an intransitive verb signifying "to become more than human," and a Latin phrase, *per verba* (in words).

73–75. This tercet reflects the three Persons of the Trinity, one per verse (Power, Knowledge, Love); we also learn in a single line (75) how Dante and Beatrice move upward: drawn instantaneously by God Himself, not propelled gradually by themselves.

73. This citation of II Corinthians 12:3 has not escaped many commentators. There Paul is not certain as to whether he was in body or not in his ascent through the heavens. For his phrase "third heaven" as meaning, not

the heaven of Venus, to which the phrase would ordinarily refer in Dante, but the highest part of God's kingdom, see St. Thomas, *Summa Theologica* II–II, q. 175, a. 3, r. to obj. 4 (cited from the online edition of the *Catholic Encyclopedia* [www.newadvent.org/cathen/]): "In one way by the third heaven we may understand something corporeal, and thus the third heaven denotes the empyrean (I Tim. 2:7; Cf. I, 12, 11, ad 2), which is described as the 'third,' in relation to the aerial and starry heavens, or better still, in relation to the aqueous and crystalline heavens. Moreover, Paul is stated to be rapt to the 'third heaven,' not as though his rapture consisted in the vision of something corporeal, but because this place is appointed for the contemplation of the blessed. Hence the gloss on 2 Cor. 12 says that the 'third heaven is a spiritual heaven, where the angels and the holy souls enjoy the contemplation of God: and when Paul says that he was rapt to this heaven he means that God showed him the life wherein He is to be seen forevermore.' "

On the Pauline stance of the poet here and elsewhere, see Mazzeo, "Dante and the Pauline Modes of Vision" (Mazz.1960.1), pp. 84–110. (And see his earlier book *Structure and Thought in the "Paradiso"* [Mazz.1958.1] for a wider consideration of the poetics of this *cantica*.) See *Paradiso* XXVII.64–65, where St. Peter finally makes it plain that Dante is present, ascending through the heavens, in the flesh. Bosco/Reggio (comm. to vv. 73–75) make the point that, since Dante eventually allows us to believe that he went up in body (they cite *Par.* XXI.11 and 61, passages that are perhaps less decisive than that in *Par.* XXVII), all this coy uncertainty has a main purpose: to give himself Pauline credentials, since Paul himself either cannot or will not say in what state he was during his rapture. Gragnolati (Grag.2005.1), pp. 162–74, joins those who believe that Dante contrives to make us see that he wants to be understood as having made the final ascent in the flesh.

74. For Dante's phrasing describing God's love as manifest in His creation, commentators beginning with Scartazzini (comm. to this verse) have suggested the resonance of Boethius (*Cons. Phil.* II.m8.15), "coelo imperitans amor" (love governing the heavens).

75. God is portrayed as drawing Dante upward through His beam of light; whether the protagonist possesses physical weight or not, it is a spiritual force that lifts him, not a physical one.

76–81. If God loved the universe in creating it, it loves him back. These two tercets create a picture of the totality of God's spheres. Having created them in time, He also made eternal (sempiternal, as Dante rightly says, i.e., having a beginning but not an end) their desire to reunite themselves with Him.

78. The reference is pretty clearly to the "music of the spheres," that harmony created by the movement initiated by the love of the spheres themselves for God. As early as the Ottimo (1333; comm. to vv. 76–81), students of the poem attributed the notion of the harmony of the spheres (as do other early commentators) to Macrobius's commentary to the Ciceronian *Somnium Scipionis* (for a brief overview of the vexed topic, the extent of Dante's knowledge of this early-fifth-century neoplatonist, see Georg Rabuse, "Macrobio," *ED* III [1971], pp. 757–59 [Rabuse enthusiastically supports the view that Dante knows both the *Somnium Scipionis* and the *Saturnalia* well]). Among the moderns, since Lombardi (1791 [comm. to vv. 76–78]), commentators have suggested the dependence here upon that concept, and, closer to our own time, Bosco/Reggio (comm. to vv. 76–77) point out that it is clear that Dante refers to the so-called "music of the spheres." Such music is a pleasing notion, but all of Aristotle's three greatest commentators—Averroës, Albert the Great, and Thomas Aquinas—quash its possibility. Dante, as poet, seems to like the idea well enough that he is willing to be its sponsor despite such firm and authoritative opposition. Bosco/Reggio go on to point out that this reference to the music of the spheres is the only one found in *Paradiso*, where all later music will be in the form of the singing of the saved and of the angels—less suspect musical forms, we might conclude.

79–81. Perhaps because humans are accustomed to seeing no measurable space-consuming object more vast than a lake or a sea, the poet compares the extended fire he saw in the sky to a watery body. How we are to understand the exact nature of the phenomenon at which he gazed is not clear, although some believe (see the note to vv. 61–63) it is the fiery ring that surrounds the sphere of the Moon, a common fixture of medieval astronomy that would otherwise have remained unmentioned in the poem. But there is simply no certainty on this matter.

82–84. Both the beautiful sound (the music of the spheres? [see the note to verse 78]) and the brilliant and extended pool of light (the sphere of fire between the earth and Moon? [see the note to vv. 61–63]) increase Dante's intense desire to know their realities. It will at least seem that Beatrice's answer (vv. 88–93) does little to answer either of Dante's questions in ways that we, earthlings like him, would consider satisfying. However, it certainly does seem that the poet means us to be aware of our unslaked curiosity about the identity of these two heavenly phenomena. An attractive hypothesis is that he means us to draw exactly these conclusions without having left himself tainted by incredible claims (e.g., "I passed through the sphere of fire and listened to the music of the spheres").

85–87. We learn definitively that Beatrice truly reads the protagonist's mind, a capacity that Virgil at times claimed but was rarely, if ever, capable of demonstrating (see the notes to *Inf.* XVI.115–123; XXIII.25–30; *Purg.* XV.133–135). Her lips open in response before Dante's question has been voiced.

The reason for the agitation experienced by the protagonist is explained by verses 82–84.

88–90. Beatrice avers that, were only Dante thinking in an otherwordly way, he would not have asked his two questions. He thinks of what his senses are experiencing as though it were sensed on earth. Her point is that it is precisely his earthly home that he has left behind and is indeed racing from as quickly as lightning flies. This response apparently does not satisfy readers' inquisitiveness much better than it satisfies the protagonist's. On the other hand, Benvenuto da Imola suggests (in his comm. to *Par.* I.91–93) that the sounds of celestial harmony could not be heard from earth ("audit sonum coeli, non quia sit ibi factus de novo, sed quia dum staret in terra non poterat ipsum audire"). Thus Beatrice is intrinsically answering Dante's first question; his earthly ears confounded the reality (the music of the spheres) of what they heard. As for the second, commentators, beginning perhaps with Lombardi (1791 [to verse 92]), have understood that Dante's allusion is to the sphere of fire that circled the earth above the other elements, near the Moon; in other words, that Beatrice's words "lightning darting from its place" contain a specific reference to the sphere of fire, as is now recognized in most discussions of this tercet.

91–93. For a study devoted to the paradoxes that flow from Dante's combined corporeal heaviness and lightness, see Simon Gilson (Gils.2004.1), pp. 170–73: Beatrice's words gather up and redeploy Aristotle's statements concerning the rapid and violent movement of celestial bodies (*De caelo* II.2 and *Meteora* II.9), combining them with the views of St. Augustine (*Confessions* XIII.9) on the *pondus amoris*, the downward-tending direction of earthly affection and the liberating fire of love for God. (Both Sapegno [1955, comm. to vv. 124–126] and Singleton [1975, comm. to verse 116] cite this passage from the *Confessions* to make a similar point.) Dante's rational soul is returning to its "birthplace" in the heavens, where God breathed it into the being he was to become, his characteristics set by the Fixed Stars, as we learn, for instance at *Paradiso* VIII.94–114.

94. Dante has conflated his two previous questions as one, since they have both been answered in the same way.

95. Beatrice's smiling words (*sorrise parolette*) here contain the first reference to smiles and smiling that run through this canticle. There are roughly twice as many references (two dozen) to smiling in *Paradiso* as there were in *Purgatorio* (see the note to *Purg.* II.83).

96–99. Dante's new question probably does not refer to a concern that will arise later (if he is in the body, as he plainly seems to believe he is): How can he pass through the matter of the planetary spheres? See *Par.* II.37–45 and the accompanying note; rather, it more likely relates to his surprise that he in his bodied state can rise above not only land and water back on earth, but, far more puzzling to him, the lighter elements of air and fire. In the view of the author of the Codice Cassinese (comm. to verse 99), the reference is to two of the four elements: "scilicet. aerem et etherem, qui leves sunt respectu aliorum duorum corporum gravium ut est terra et aqua" (that is, air and fire, which are light in comparison to those other two bodies [elements] that are heavy, as are earth and water), a formulation that shows us a fourteenth-century commentator using the word *corpo* not to refer to the material heavenly spheres (as some modern commentators believe it must), but to the four elements. For the identity of *ether* and *ignis*, see Guido da Pisa (comm. to *Inf.* XIV.52–60).

97. While rhyme may have forced the Latin verb *requïevi* (I was content), Dante surely enjoyed Latinizing his own speech as a character in his own poem (for the first [and last] time since his first word in the poem [*Inf.* I.65, *Miserere*]). He is, as his bibliography attests, a writer in vernacular *and* in Latin.

100–102. We have been made aware of the wonder of those in beatitude at the obtuseness of mortals at least since we first observed the angel finding the plight of Dante at the gates of Dis of absolutely no interest (*Inf.* IX.100–103).

103–141. Beatrice's response fills the rest of the canto, with the exception of its final line of narrative. It is divided into three parts. In the first (vv.

100–126), she deals with Dante's puzzlement as to his upward inclination, given his mortal condition; in the second (vv. 127–135), she admits that fallen human nature is prone to being drawn downward, away from this true inclination; in the third (vv. 136–141), she avers that Dante is now proof against such wrong directionality because he has been freed of sin.

103–105. While hardly answering Dante's question directly (vv. 98–99: How can his heaviness pass through lighter zones in the atmosphere above the earth?), Beatrice begins her discourse on the nature of the universe, the formal disposition of which is ordered, in resemblance of its Creator.

106–108. In the structure of the created universe, where the divine form first became manifest, angels (and humans?) possess the capacity to understand that form. The Scholastic word "form" is akin to the Platonic term "idea," a spiritual essence inhering in its physical manifestations.

109–120. Beatrice now presents the components of the universe's order: All things in nature, whether nearer to God or farther, have a natural inclination toward the good. While their destinations differ, each responds to its own inborn impulse in finding its goal, whether fire (guided toward the lunar sphere), the sensitive soul in irrational creatures, the force of gravity in inanimate things—and not only irrational things (animals, inanimate nature), but angels and humans as well. Both these classes of being possess not only intellect, but love; the latter, as Bosco/Reggio point out (comm. to verse 120) in the sense of "capable of willing," as in *Purgatorio* XVII.92–93 ("amore . . . d'animo" [*love*, whether natural or *of the mind*]).

109–111. For a possible poetic precursor to Dante's formulation of the laws of gravity, see Ovid (*Metam.* I.29–30), as pointed out by Rossini (Ross.2000.1), p. 172. The passage was first noted by Daniello (comm. to this tercet): "Densior his tellus, elementaque grandia traxit et pressa est gravitate sua" (the earth was heavier than these [the elements of fire and air], and, drawing with it the grosser elements, sank to the bottom of its own weight [tr. F. J. Miller]). And see the note to vv. 91–93, above.

112–117. Reverting to nautical metaphor (see vv. 67–69) for the life-journeys of all created things, whether capable of willing or not, the poet equates the purposes of inanimate and one kind of animate life with voyages toward various ports, the ends for which God has ordained these of His creations. This impulse is exemplified in three kinds of being: a light element (fire) with its inherent "desire" to rise to its own sphere (see the note to vv. 61–63); creatures possessed of an animal (but not a rational) soul; and a heavy element (earth) with its obedience to the law of gravity, expressed as a "desire" to become compacted (the opposite impulse from that of fire).

118–120. We now realize, if we did not at first, that "mortal hearts" did not refer to those of humans, in whom hearts are bound with immortal souls, guided by intellect and by choice in their loving (their will), but to the hearts of animals and to the "instinct" in matter.

121–126. It is God's plan that the Empyrean, bathed in His light, is unmoving, peaceful, while the uppermost and neighboring heaven, the Primum Mobile, itself most agitated, imparts motion to the other spheres below. It is humans' eventual goal to be drawn toward God.

127–135. Dante, aware of our awareness that not all creatures possessed of immortal souls tend toward the good, explains why not all arrows hit their target. The fault is not in the archer (God), but in the material (Beatrice switches metaphoric equivalence in mid-metaphor, moving from archery to the production of artifacts): Some of the craftsman's work is faulty because of the innate shortcomings of his material. It is a paradox that God's more noble creatures may swerve in their movement while the lesser follow more predictable paths; that paradox results from the unique gift of the freedom of the will to humans and to angels (see *Par.* V.19–24).

136–141. Having offered the necessary philosophic background, Beatrice now more or less answers Dante's question: His natural inclination is to move upward. To be sure, his quandary (vv. 98–99) was how he, as an object possessing mass and weight, could penetrate matter, and this concern is not, strictly speaking, answered in her remarks so much as it is bypassed for a higher degree of abstraction.

Bosco/Reggio (comm. to verse 141) set into relief the paradox that underlies these two *terzine*. While Dante's voyage through the heavens is itself miraculous in any terms, his upward tendency, which seems paranormal to him, is utterly natural; that he was called to witness, as was Paul, is a mystery that only God can explain; that, once called, he rises through the spheres is explained by the merest science, the result of a spiritual force of gravity, as it were.

142. The final verse of the canto, returning to the narrative mode, describes Beatrice's renewed contemplation of Heaven, to which she is obviously pleased to return, having had to lower her intellectual powers in order to explain what to her is intuited and obvious to such an auditor as Dante, with his as yet necessarily lesser capacity to experience and to understand the highest truths.

PARADISO II

OUTLINE

MOON

- 1–9 apostrophe of readers (class one): turn back
  - 1–6 certain readers are warned not to read *Paradiso*
  - 7–9 the untraveled sea of the poem and Dante's guides
- 10–18 apostrophe of readers (class two): *you* may follow
  - 10–15 if early on you tasted the bread of angels
  - 16–18 implicit simile: readers/Dante = Jason's crew/**Jason**
- 19–30 ascent to the Moon
  - 19–26 flight upward toward the Moon
  - 27–30 Beatrice to Dante: thank God for bringing us here
- 31–45 arrival in the lunar landscape
  - 31–36 Dante's penetration of this space
  - 37–45 this possible penetration of matter by matter stirs further thought (relating to the Incarnation)
- 46–51 Dante's question: what accounts for these moonspots?
- 52–148 Beatrice's answer: not the quantity (density and rarity), but the quality of light
  - 52–58 incorrect sense-based reason surely won't help here; but tell me what *you* think of this problem
  - 59–60 Dante: I think it's about rare and dense matter
  - 61–63 Beatrice: you don't know what you are talking about
  - 64–148 Beatrice's exposition:
    - 64–72 (a) the fixed stars, too, seem diverse; if rarity and density were the only

distinguishing marks for them, no other power would mark them;

73–84 (b) further, if rarity caused the dark spots, then the Moon would (i) either have "holes" or (ii) be mixed in its composition. Eclipses show (i) is false. Therefore, I shall work on (ii) and destroy that argument as well.

85–111 the experiment involving three mirrors

112–148 the "formal principle" of distribution for the universe's matter is spiritual, not physical.

PARADISO II

O voi che siete in piccioletta barca,
desiderosi d'ascoltar, seguiti
dietro al mio legno che cantando varca,

tornate a riveder li vostri liti:
non vi mettete in pelago, ché forse,
perdendo me, rimarreste smarriti.

L'acqua ch'io prendo già mai non si corse;
Minerva spira, e conducemi Appollo,
e nove Muse mi dimostran l'Orse.

Voi altri pochi che drizzaste il collo
per tempo al pan de li angeli, del quale
vivesi qui ma non sen vien satollo,

metter potete ben per l'alto sale
vostro navigio, servando mio solco
dinanzi a l'acqua che ritorna equale.

Que' gloriosi che passaro al Colco
non s'ammiraron come voi farete,
quando Iasón vider fatto bifolco.

La concreata e perpetüa sete
del deïforme regno cen portava
veloci quasi come 'l ciel vedete.

Beatrice in suso, e io in lei guardava;
e forse in tanto in quanto un quadrel posa
e vola e da la noce si dischiava,

giunto mi vidi ove mirabil cosa
mi torse il viso a sé; e però quella
cui non potea mia cura essere ascosa,

O you, eager to hear more,
who have followed in your little bark
my ship that singing makes its way,

turn back if you would see your shores again.
Do not set forth upon the deep,
for, losing sight of me, you would be lost.

The seas I sail were never sailed before.
Minerva fills my sails, Apollo is my guide,
nine Muses point me toward the Bears.

You other few who craned your necks in time
to reach for angels' bread, which gives us life on earth,
yet never leaves us satisfied,

you may indeed set out, your ship afloat
upon the salty deep, keeping to the furrow
I have made, before the sea goes smooth again.

Those famous men who made their way to Colchis,
when they saw Jason had become a plowman,
were not as stunned as you shall be.

The innate and never-ending thirst for God
in His own kingdom drew us up,
almost as swiftly as you know the heavens turn.

Beatrice was gazing upward, my gaze fixed on her,
when, perhaps as quickly as a bolt strikes,
flies, and releases from its catch,

suddenly I found myself there
where my eyes were drawn to an astounding sight.
And she, from whom my thoughts could not be kept

volta ver' me, sì lieta come bella,
"Drizza la mente in Dio grata," mi disse,
"che n'ha congiunti con la prima stella."

Parev' a me che nube ne coprisse
lucida, spessa, solida e pulita,
quasi adamante che lo sol ferisse.

Per entro sé l'etterna margarita
ne ricevette, com' acqua recepe
raggio di luce permanendo unita.

S'io era corpo, e qui non si concepe
com' una dimensione altra patio,
ch'esser convien se corpo in corpo repe,

accender ne dovria più il disio
di veder quella essenza in che si vede
come nostra natura e Dio s'unio.

Lì si vedrà ciò che tenem per fede,
non dimostrato, ma fia per sé noto
a guisa del ver primo che l'uom crede.

Io rispuosi: "Madonna, sì devoto
com' esser posso più, ringrazio lui
lo qual dal mortal mondo m'ha remoto.

Ma ditemi: che son li segni bui
di questo corpo, che là giuso in terra
fan di Cain favoleggiare altrui?"

Ella sorrise alquanto, e poi "S'elli erra
l'oppinïon," mi disse, "d'i mortali
dove chiave di senso non diserra,

certo non ti dovrien punger li strali
d'ammirazione omai, poi dietro ai sensi
vedi che la ragione ha corte l'ali.

turned to me, as full of joy as she was fair,
to say: 'Direct your grateful mind to God,
who has conjoined us with the nearest star.'

It seemed to me that we were in a cloud,
shining, dense, solid, and unmarred,
like a diamond struck by sunlight.

The eternal pearl received us in itself,
as water does a ray of light
and yet remains unsundered and serene.

If I was there in flesh—on earth we can't conceive
how matter may admit another matter to it,
when body flows into, becomes another body—

that, all the more, should kindle our desire
to see the very One who lets us see
the way our nature was conjoined with God.

What now we take on faith will then be seen,
not demonstrated but made manifest,
like *a priori* truths, which we accept.

I replied: 'My Lady, with absolute devotion
I offer thanks to Him
who has removed me from the world of death.

'But tell me, what are the dark spots
on this body that make those down on earth
repeat their preposterous tales of Cain?'

She smiled a little, then: 'If the understanding
of mortals errs,' she said, 'there where the key
of the senses fails in its unlocking,

'surely the shafts of wonder should no longer
strike you, since you see that, dependent
on the senses, reason's wings fall short.

Ma dimmi quel che tu da te ne pensi."
E io: "Ciò che n'appar qua sù diverso
credo che fanno i corpi rari e densi."

Ed ella: "Certo assai vedrai sommerso
nel falso il creder tuo, se bene ascolti
l'argomentar ch'io li farò avverso.

La spera ottava vi dimostra molti
lumi, li quali e nel quale e nel quanto
notar si posson di diversi volti.

Se raro e denso ciò facesser tanto,
una sola virtù sarebbe in tutti,
più e men distributa e altrettanto.

Virtù diverse esser convegnon frutti
di principi formali, e quei, for ch'uno,
seguiterieno a tua ragion distrutti.

Ancor, se raro fosse di quel bruno
cagion che tu dimandi, o d'oltre in parte
fora di sua materia sì digiuno

esto pianeto, o, sì come comparte
lo grasso e 'l magro un corpo, così questo
nel suo volume cangerebbe carte.

Se 'l primo fosse, fora manifesto
ne l'eclissi del sol, per trasparere
lo lume come in altro raro ingesto.

Questo non è: però è da vedere
de l'altro; e s'elli avvien ch'io l'altro cassi,
falsificato fia lo tuo parere.

S'elli è che questo raro non trapassi,
esser conviene un termine da onde
lo suo contrario più passar non lassi;

'But tell me what you make of this yourself.'
And I: 'The different shadings here
60 are caused, I think, by bodies rare or dense.'

And she: 'No doubt but you shall see that this belief
lies deep in error—if you consider well
63 the arguments that I shall lodge against it.

'The eighth sphere shows you many lights,
which, both in magnitude and luminosity,
66 may be seen as having different aspects.

'If this were caused by *rare* and *dense* alone,
a single power would be in them all:
69 here more, there less—or equally.

'Different powers must be the fruit resulting from
formative principles, but these, except for one,
72 according to your reasoning, would be annulled.

'What is more, if that dark of which you ask
had rareness as its cause, this planet
75 would be lacking matter in some parts,

'or else, just as fat and lean
alternate in mass upon a body, this planet
78 would alternate the pages of its volume.

Were the first case true, this would be shown
in the sun's eclipse, when light showed through,
81 as when it shines through any rarer medium.

'But such is not the case: therefore, let us consider
your other argument and, if I show it to be false,
84 then your opinion will be proven wrong.

'If this rarer substance does not go all the way,
there must be a point at which its denser opposite
87 would not allow the light to pass on through

e indi l'altrui raggio si rifonde
così come color torna per vetro
lo qual di retro a sé piombo nasconde.

Or dirai tu ch'el si dimostra tetro
ivi lo raggio più che in altre parti,
per esser lì refratto più a retro.

Da questa instanza può deliberarti
esperïenza, se già mai la provi,
ch'esser suol fonte ai rivi di vostr' arti.

Tre specchi prenderai; e i due rimovi
da te d'un modo, e l'altro, più rimosso,
tr'ambo li primi li occhi tuoi ritrovi.

Rivolto ad essi, fa che dopo il dosso
ti stea un lume che i tre specchi accenda
e torni a te da tutti ripercosso.

Ben che nel quanto tanto non si stenda
la vista più lontana, lì vedrai
come convien ch'igualmente risplenda.

Or, come ai colpi de li caldi rai
de la neve riman nudo il suggetto
e dal colore e dal freddo primai,

così rimaso te ne l'intelletto
voglio informar di luce sì vivace,
che ti tremolerà nel suo aspetto.

Dentro dal ciel de la divina pace
si gira un corpo ne la cui virtute
l'esser di tutto suo contento giace.

Lo ciel seguente, c'ha tante vedute,
quell' esser parte per diverse essenze,
da lui distratte e da lui contenute.

'and thus a ray of light would be thrown back
just as color is reflected from the glass
by the hidden layer of lead that lies beneath.

'Now, you will object, the ray shows dark there
more than in the other parts
because it is reflected from a farther source.

'From this objection, an experiment—
should you ever try it—may set you free, experiment,
the source that feeds the streams of all your arts.

'Take three mirrors, placing two at equal distance
from you, letting the third, from farther off,
also meet your eyes, between the other two.

'Still turned to them, have someone set,
well back of you, a light that, shining out,
returns as bright reflection from all three.

'Although the light seen farthest off
seems smaller in its size, still you will observe
that it must shine with equal brightness.

'Now, as the substantial form of snow,
if struck by warming rays, is then deprived
both of its former color and its cold,

'I shall now reshape your intellect,
thus deprived, with a light so vibrant
that your mind will quiver at the sight.

'Beneath the heaven of divine repose
revolves a body in whose power resides
the being of all things contained in it.

'The next heaven, which holds so many sights,
distributes its being among various forms,
contained in it and yet distinct from it.

Li altri giron per varie differenze
le distinzion che dentro da sé hanno
dispongono a lor fini e lor semenze.

Questi organi del mondo così vanno,
come tu vedi omai, di grado in grado,
che di sù prendono e di sotto fanno.

Riguarda bene omai sì com' io vado
per questo loco al vero che disiri,
sì che poi sappi sol tener lo guado.

Lo moto e la virtù d'i santi giri,
come dal fabbro l'arte del martello,
da' beati motor convien che spiri;

e 'l ciel cui tanti lumi fanno bello,
de la mente profonda che lui volve
prende l'image e fassene suggello.

E come l'alma dentro a vostra polve
per differenti membra e conformate
a diverse potenze si risolve,

così l'intelligenza sua bontate
multiplicata per le stelle spiega,
girando sé sovra sua unitate.

Virtù diversa fa diversa lega
col prezïoso corpo ch'ella avviva,
nel qual, sì come vita in voi, si lega.

Per la natura lieta onde deriva,
la virtù mista per lo corpo luce
come letizia per pupilla viva.

Da essa vien ciò che da luce a luce
par differente, non da denso e raro;
essa è formal principio che produce,
conforme a sua bontà, lo turbo e 'l chiaro."

'All the other spheres, in varying ways,
direct their distinctive qualities
120 to their own purposes and influence.

'Thus do these organs of the universe proceed,
as now you see, step by step,
123 rendering below what they take from above.

'Observe well how I pass along this way
to the truth you seek, so that in time
126 you may know how to ford the stream alone.

'The motion and the power of the holy wheels
must be derived from the blessèd movers,
129 as the work of the hammer from the smith.

'And the heaven made fair by all these lights
takes its stamp from the intellect that makes it turn,
132 making of itself the very seal of that imprinting.

'And as the soul within your dust
is distributed through the different members,
135 conforming to their various faculties,

'so angelic intelligence unfolds its bounty,
multiplied down through the stars,
138 while revolving in its separate oneness.

'Each differentiated power makes a different alloy
with each precious body that it quickens,
141 with which, even as does life in you, it binds.

'From the joyous nature whence it springs,
the mingled potency shines through its star,
144 as joy shines in the living pupil of an eye.

'From this power is derived the difference seen
from light to light, and not from dense and rare.
This is the formative principle that creates,
148 according to its worth, the dark and bright.'

1–18. For the Ovidian resonances in this passage, so marked by classical motif (the poem as voyage across a sea, the poet as inspired by gods and/or muses) and allusion (Jason and the voyage of the Argonauts), see Picone (Pico.1994.1), pp. 191–200.

1–6. The canto begins apparently by discouraging the "average reader" from attempting to understand it. As we shall shortly discover, only some of us are welcomed to the attempt (vv. 10–18). We may be put in mind of the similar gesture near the beginning of *Convivio* (I.i.2–6). That passage continues (I.i.7): "Blessed are the few who sit at the table where the bread of the angels is eaten, and most unfortunate those who share the food of sheep" (tr. R. Lansing). See O'Brien (Obri.1979.1) for a strong differentiation of the references to the "bread of angels" in these two passages, the first accommodating secular knowing, this one based on faith and the Scriptures. For the differing audiences sought for *Convivio* and *Paradiso*, see Vincenzo Placella (Plac.1995.1).

1. Despite the distraction of an address to the reader, we realize that, beginning with the opening of this canto, we are in the sphere of the Moon. There is only one other occasion in the ten heavens when the entrance to a celestial realm coincides with the beginning of a canto: *Paradiso* XXI (Saturn). Those who are overwhelmed by the organized quality of Dante's mind might like to be aware of its "disorderly" side as well.

The "little bark" inevitably reminds readers of the "small bark" (*navicella*—*Purg.* I.2) that represents Dante's intellect at the beginning of *Purgatorio*. His capacities, we may infer, have increased in accord with his nearness to God; his ship, we understand by implication, is now a mighty craft; ours is the "little bark."

2. For only the second time in the poem (see *Inf.* XXII.118), Dante addresses his readers as listeners, as Aversano (Aver.2000.2), p. 10, points out.

3. The phrase "ship that singing makes its way" once again capitalizes on the equation ship = poem (see *Purg.* I.2). The word *legno* as metaphoric expression, the material of construction being referred to as the thing itself, has a classical heritage and a heavy Dantean presence. While in *Purgatorio* it appears four times without once having this meaning, in *Inferno* it

had appeared ten times, in fully seven of which it denotes "ship" or "boat." Now in the last *cantica* it is used six times, twice (here and in Canto XIII.136) with the meaning "ship."

The self-consciously "literary" language continues that strain from the first 36 verses of the opening canto in less lengthy but similar behavior in the first 18 of this one. And see Paola Allegretti (Alle.2004.1) for a consideration of the opening passage of this canto (II.1–15) as the centerpiece between two other important passages involving ships, *Purgatorio* II.10–51 and *Paradiso* XXXIII.94–96, with ample consideration of classical sources, in a revisitation of Curtius's often-cited essay, "The Ship of the Argonauts" (Curt.1950.1).

4–6. The warning sounds "elitist," even scornful (and see the note to vv. 13–15). But if we think about what is at stake, nothing less than our salvation, its exclusionary nature seems only necessary. Did Dante really mean that those of us who have no Christian upbringing either cannot be saved or at least cannot be saved by reading Dante's poem? The latter is what the passage apparently asserts, for if we lose track of him, we may lose track of God. It is perhaps necessary to remind ourselves that the voice we hear belongs to an unsuccessful, exiled Florentine, with one completed work longer than a single *canzone* (*Vita nuova*, some twenty years behind him), who has banked all that he is and has on this text that he will barely manage to finish before his death. The intervening centuries have allowed Dante an authority only doubtfully accorded him by his early commentators, who by and large manage to avoid paying sufficient attention to this amazing claim, with possibly the single exception of Benvenuto (comm. to vv. 5–6), perhaps the sole interpreter to put the potential failure of Dante's readership in specifically Christian terms: "quia cum vestro parvo ingenio non possetis intelligere meam profundam materiam, et possetis *errare a via rectae fidei*" (lest, with your limited understanding, you fail to understand the depth of my material, and *wander from the path of the true faith* [italics added]). Benvenuto goes on to cite Anicius Manlius Severinus Boethius, not the *Consolation of Philosophy*, but the specifically Christian treatise, *The Trinity Is One God Not Three Gods*.

7–9. For a discussion of the triune God, see Canto I, note 13. And for the "triune Apollo," see Di Scipio (Disc.1995.1), pp. 258–59, who offers a passage in Alain de Lille's *Anticlaudianus* as a potential source for Dante's Christianized Apollo. For the presence of a text of Alanus in another context, the river of light in *Paradiso* XXX, see the note to *Par.* XXX.61–69.

7. Familiar by now (e.g., *Inf.* I.22–24, *Purg.* I.1–3) is the watery expression for nonaqueous spaces. The assertion that the poet is the first to report his travel over such "seas" is essentially true; for an exhaustive discussion of the topos of novelty in the *Commedia*, see Ledda (Ledd.2002.1), pp. 57–86.

9. Benvenuto (comm. to vv. 7–9) thinks that Dante's "nove," not only indicating the number "nine," is more subtly construed as a form of the adjective *nuovo* (new), and believes that the poet felt the need for new muses since he was writing of the Christian God, not the pagan divinities. While that argument probably needs to be more accommodating (since the phrase "nine Muses" is bypassed only with considerable difficulty), it should have alerted readers to the unlikely presence of pagan goddesses at this height in the poem's development. Suffice it to say that such concerns were expressed from time to time in the commentary tradition, but have never won the day, so that there results a certain unsureness of exactly how to deal with this verse. Scartazzini (comm. to this verse) has a useful review of such puzzlement, but does not attempt to solve the riddle himself. However, possibly the most compelling gloss to this verse was written by Giovan Battista Gelli halfway into the sixteenth century, and not in response to this verse, but to *Inferno* II.7–9: "Ma perchè io mi persuado che il Poeta nostro, per trattar di quelle cose divine, le quali son veramente divine, e non fabulose come quelle delle quali trattano quasi tutti gli altri poeti, abbia in tutte le cose ancor concetti molto più alti e più profondi di loro, dico ancora io (ascendendo con lo intelletto più alto, . . .) che le Muse, propiamente e divinamente parlando, significano quelle intelligenze, o sieno anime o sieno motori, che muovono e guidano le nove sfere celesti, cioè quelle de' sette pianeti, quella del cielo stellato e quella del primo mobile" (However, since I am persuaded that our poet, in order to treat of things divine—indeed truly divine, not the stuff of fable, such as almost all other poets deal with—had in all things ideas both more lofty and more profound than they do; and I say further, ascending higher with my intellect, that the Muses, properly and divinely speaking, signify those intelligences, whether they be souls or movers, that move and direct the nine heavenly spheres, that is those of the seven planets, that of the Starry Sphere, and that of the Primum Mobile.) See Hollander (Holl.1993.3), p. 227, for a highly similar solution without, however, reference to Gelli. If the verse is read in this way, the discomfort of Benvenuto is addressed without twisting the literal sense of the line. It is the nine heavens that are referred to as "muses"; they are the sign of God's creating power and lead Dante's mind to port. (Several commentators, beginning with Vellutello,

refer to the Muses in this context as Dante's *bussola* [compass], but only one [Campi, comm. to vv. 7–9] sees that metaphor in a Christian conceptual frame, i.e., that these are not the classical Muses.)

10–12. The handful of Christian readers who will be able to navigate the third canticle are marked by long devotion to the study of religious truth (not necessarily demonstrating, as several commentators urge, a more general philosophical interest). For the distinction, see Attilio Mellone, "Pane degli angeli," *ED* (IV [1973]), p. 266, contrasting what is conveyed by the expression "bread of angels" when it is used in *Convivio* (I.i.7) to its meaning here; there it covers all kinds of knowing, but here only revealed truth.

The opening tercet looks to the Bible and to Dante's *Convivio*, as Singleton points out (comm. to Par.I.1–6 and 10–11). While the biblical phrase (Psalms 77 [78]:25, Wisdom 16:20) is clearly theological in meaning, the passage from *Convivio* (I.i.7) is not: "Blessed are the few who sit at the table where the bread of the angels is eaten, and most unfortunate those who share the food of sheep!" (tr. R. Lansing). It seems likely that the author of the *Comedy* would look back upon these words with a shudder, noting this hostility to the most Christian of images, the faithful as a flock to which Jesus is shepherd.

10. "Voi altri pochi" (you other few): This is the fifteenth address to the reader in the poem. See the note to *Inferno* VIII.94–96; and see Ledda (Ledd.2002.1), pp. 117–58, for a full discussion of Dante's addresses to the reader (nineteen in all, according to him [pp. 119–21]), as part of the poet's larger authorial strategies.

11. For the meaning of the Eucharist in the liturgy for the Wednesday after Easter as informing this scene (which just happens to take place on the Wednesday after Easter, the day that Beatrice ascends with the protagonist), see O'Brien (Obri.1979.1), pp. 99–100. The offertory verse from the mass for that day, O'Brien reports, quoting the Roman Missal, contains the phrase "the bread of angels" in the following exalted context: "The Lord God opened the gates of Heaven and rained down manna upon them (the disciples in company of the risen Jesus) so that they might eat; He gave them heavenly bread; and, hallelujah, man ate the bread of angels (*panem Angelorum manducavit homo*)."

12. Christians on earth will never be able to attain angelic understanding of the doctrine that nourishes them; for that they must await their afterlife in Paradise.

13–15. We are warned that even a Christian reader, losing track of the ship that is *Paradiso*, may get lost in these precincts. The daring of these lines, far beyond approaching what in Yiddish is referred to as *chutzpah*, is perhaps not imaginable in any other poet.

16. The "famous men" are the Argonauts who accompanied Jason on the first voyage made on a ship, in the thirteenth century B.C., to Colchis, a voyage already referred to (*Inf.* XVIII.86–87) and that will furnish the matter for the ultimate "historical" reference in the poem (*Par.* XXXIII.95–96), a final look at the voyage of the *Argo*.

Dante refers to Colchis by the singular form of the adjectival noun of place, "colco."

17–18. In order to gain the Golden Fleece, Jason, aided by Medea's herbal concoctions, performs wondrous deeds in Colchis (*Metam.* VII.100–158). In Ovid, however, it is not Jason's shipmates who stand amazed at what they witness of Jason's astounding feats (e.g., plowing a field by means of the iron-tipped horns of two bulls, turned upside down and serving as Jason's plow, and seeding it with serpents' teeth, with a resulting harvest of soldiers), but the onlooking Colchians ("mirantur Colchi" [*Metam.* VII.120]). Dante is here not nodding, but "rewriting" the classical text in order to make it more worthy of bearing a Christian message, as Picone is aware (Pico.2002.2), p. 47.

19–22. The narrative continues with Dante and Beatrice being drawn heavenward by their desire for God, she with her eyes fixed on Heaven, he with his fixed on hers, which serve as his mirrors. This is the first of the formulaic ascents that will precede the arrival and description of each new heaven. For a listing of them all, see the page facing the "map" of Paradise in the front matter.

21. While some complicate the meaning of the comparison, it is perhaps better to see it in simple terms: The poet, who knows that the stars are actually moving rather rapidly in their orbits, compares their movement to the rapid upward movement of Beatrice and himself.

23–26. One of the most frequently discussed examples of Dante's employment of the device *hysteron proteron*, a rhetorical figure that, to denote speed and the resultant difficulty of knowing which event in a sequence preceded which other(s), reverses the normal order. As a speeding arrow (actually a bolt shot from a crossbow) is suddenly released from the catch (or "nut" or "peg" [according to Tozer on vv. 23–24]) on the bow, flies, and strikes its target, that is how quickly Dante finds himself within the surface of the Moon, so quickly indeed that the constituent moments of the ascent seem to have been experienced in reverse order. Gabriele (comm. to vv. 23–24) informs us that this iron "arrow" (the bolt) was usually four-sided.

30. Beatrice makes plain what we have probably fathomed: Dante is in the sphere of the Moon, within the body of this "star" itself. Dante's terms for the heavenly bodies are, from a modern point of view, both inconsistent and, at times, different from ours, as the reader has already probably noted. (Later on in this canto, he will refer to the Moon as a planet [*pianeto*, verse 76] and not, as here, a "star." He uses the terms interchangeably; for us the Moon is neither of the above.)

31–36. Dante's first impression of the physicality of the Moon tells us that its matter is less "material" than Earth's: For all its rocklike qualities, it seems a cloud. As Singleton (comm. to verse 31) points out, Aristotle taught in *De caelo* that the Moon and all above is physically different from our material world. It is thus that Dante must describe it as "eternal," since, unlike Earth, it is imperishable. That Beatrice, pure form, penetrates the matter of the Moon, is not surprising; that Dante also does so raises the question in his mind that we find referred to in vv. 37–39.

32. The poet is of the opinion that the Moon shines with its own light as well as reflecting the light of the Sun (*Mon.* III.iv.17–18), as Singleton observes (comm. to verse 32). In this canto, Dante refers only to the second phenomenon (vv. 79–81).

37–45. The poet raises the question once more (see *Par.* I.4–6, *Par.* I.73, *Par.* I.98–99) of his presence in the heavens with his flesh in such a way as to make us feel that he wants us to believe he was there in body (otherwise the "bonus" referred to in the tercet that concludes this passage will not apply).

Singleton (comm. to *Par.* I.98–99) refers to St. Thomas's words that were clearly meant to calm fearful Christians, worried that at the general resurrection, saved souls would be kept from approaching Heaven by the substance of the spheres. Here is Thomas's answer (*Summa contra Gentiles* IV.87): "Neither does this divine promise meet an impossibility in the assertion that celestial bodies are unbreakable so that the glorious bodies may not be elevated above them. For the divine power will bring it about that the glorious bodies can be simultaneously where the other bodies are; an indication of this was given in the body of Christ when He came to the disciples, 'the doors being shut' (John 20:26)."

See Picone (Pico.2000.1), pp. 7–12, for discussion of Dante's bodily assumption; and again (Pico.2002.2), pp. 35–39, hammering home his essential observation, that Dante wants us to acknowledge his presence in paradise in the flesh, without, perhaps, paying sufficient attention to the deliberate coyness of his claim, only made indirectly (if clearly enough) some three-quarters of the way into the *cantica* (see the note to *Par.* I.73).

39. The double presence of the word *corpo* in a single verse is a sign of the poet's concern with materiality here; *corpo* (body) appears nine times in this canto, far more often than in any other (nearly one-sixth of its fifty-five appearances throughout the poem; *Inferno* XXXIII is the closest challenger, with five).

46–51. Having done what Beatrice exhorted him to do (vv. 29–30; thank God for raising him from the earth to the Moon), Dante now asks the question the resolution of which will occupy the rest of the canto—the cause of the dark spots on the Moon.

51. For the legend that Cain was confined to the Moon and bore a bundle of thorns, see the note to *Inferno* XX.124–126. For a study of the question of these "lunar spots," see at least Bruno Nardi (Nard.1985.1) and Giorgio Stabile (Stab.1989.1), pp. 47–55; according to the latter, p. 48, Dante puts forward "tre interpretazioni: del mago, del filosofo naturale e del teologo" (three interpretations, that of the magus, that of the "scientist," that of the theologian) only to destroy the first two in favor of the last.

52–57. Beatrice gently chides those rationalists (including Dante) who analyze ineffectively, since they lack the principle that informs the phenomena that they observe, evidence found through the senses.

58. Beatrice's simple (if loaded) question brings forth ninety verses of response.

59–60. Dante restates (as Beatrice knew he would) his previous argument, found in *Convivio* II.xiii.9, that the dark places in the Moon are the result of rarer matter (which does not reflect the Sun's rays as well as denser matter does) in the surface of the Moon. However, and as Bosco/Reggio point out (comm. to this passage), the protagonist has here gone deeper into error by making this phenomenon more inclusive and even, perhaps, general, using the plural in line 60, *corpi*, and thus indicating other celestial bodies in addition to the Moon.

Where most critics believe Dante's source for this view is Averroës, André Pézard, as is duly reported by Sapegno in his introductory note to his commentary on this canto, believes it lies in the *Roman de la Rose* (vv. 16803–16850 [ed. Lecoy], vv. 16833–16880 [tr. Dahlberg]). And Vasoli (Vaso.1972.1), p. 36, cites Pézard (Peza.1965.1), pp. 1377–78, for Jean de Meun's passage with its view of the moonspots. What is most fascinating about Jean's words to the student of the *Commedia* is how clearly reflected they seem to be in Dante's. (And the closeness is all the more arresting because *Il Fiore* contains no similar passage; there can be no question of the *Roman*'s direct influence on Dante here, no question that Dante is here citing a putative earlier self in *Il Fiore*.) In the *Roman*, Nature, confessing to Genius, resolves the question of the moonspots more or less precisely as Dante had in *Convivio*: "It seems to men that the moon (*la lune*) may indeed not be clean and pure (*necte et pure*), because in some places it shows up dark (*obscure*). But it is because of its double nature that it appears opaque and cloudy (*espesse et trouble*) in some places . . . because it is both clear and opaque (*clere et espesse*). . . ." Jean is arguing that the Moon has two kinds of matter, clear and opaque, and that the Sun's beams pass right through the clear but are reflected by the opaque; and then, beginning at verse 16825 (16855 in Dahlberg's translation), Nature, like Beatrice, turns to experimental means of demonstration: "But if one took lead, or something dense (*plom ou quelque chose espesse*) that does not allow rays to pass through, and placed oneself on the side opposite to that from which the Sun's rays come, the form would return immediately." It is difficult to believe that Dante did not have this passage in mind when he developed his own discussion, also involving "experimental science," if coming up with a very different solution, one that objects strenuously to the mere physicality of Nature's explanation, as we shall see. Thus, if Dante reveals his knowledge of the French text here, he does not reveal himself as an uncritical admirer.

This discussion touches on one of the great unresolved issues confronting readers of the *Commedia*: Dante's knowledge of the Old French masterpiece of Guillaume de Lorris and Jean de Meun. To deal with the state of the unresolved issue briefly, we should be aware of at least three possible answers to the spiny question: (1) *Il Fiore* is indeed by Dante, and thus he knew the *Roman* from his youth (since the latter work is a sort of free translation of passages from the Old French work, and Contini—as well as almost all who make the *Fiore* a part of Dante's bibliography—places it very early in Dante's career, in the 1280s or, at the latest, in the early 1290s [see Rossi (Ross.2003.1), p. 20]). (2) *Il Fiore* was indeed read by Dante, but someone else wrote it, which explains why he cites this Italian "translation" of the *Rose* (for some textual resonances of *Il Fiore* in the *Commedia*, see *ED* II [1970], pp. 898–900) but not the original; there is thus no direct relationship between the French work and Dante's. (3) Another view would hold that, beginning with this passage, Dante reveals his recent reading of the *Roman*, a text that he encountered only after he had finished composing *Purgatorio*. In recent years the dispute has intensified, even in Italy, where—while Contini, much of whose later life was devoted to demonstrating Dantean authorship, remained among the living—dissenting voices were not very often heard. See the balanced volume, edited by Baranski and Boyde (Bara.1997.3), devoted in part to the question of the work's authorship; Leonardi (Leon. 1996.1), who believes it is authentic; Malato (Mala.1999.1), pp. 138–48, considering arguments *pro et contra*, and tending toward a negative view; and Pasquini (Pasq.2001.1), p. 43, denying Dantean authorship. For what had earlier become the standard view and the basic bibliography, see Gianfranco Contini, *Fiore, Il* (*ED* II [1970]), pp. 895–901; and for a listing of some more agnostic views, see Hollander (Holl.2001.1), pp. 182–83. More recently, we have Luciano Rossi's attempt to start the investigation over again (Ross.2003.1), reminding us of his senior colleague's early attempt to accomplish a similar task: Picone's remarks on the problems of attribution (Pico.1974.1).

61–63. Beatrice begins with a sweeping denunciation of Dante's position in a thoroughly Scholastic manner, making clear the nature of the thesis that she will set about to destroy (Dante's hypothesis regarding alternating layers of rarity and density). For this tercet as reflecting the poet's disavowal of his earlier Averroist views of the issue, see Cassell (Cass.2004.1), pp. 54–55.

64–148. See Russo (Russ.1971.1), pp. 103–58, 161–208, for an impassioned defense of the poetic qualities of such lengthy and ostensibly "scientific" or "philosophical" passages as this one, which he links with the only slightly shorter lesson in embryology offered up by Statius (*Purgatorio* XXV.37–108). For a careful study of the central theological and scientific issues here and the history of their reception among Dante's critics, see Vasoli (Vaso.1972.1). And for an immensely helpful basic bibliography on Dante in relation to the various sciences that make their presence felt in the poem, see the extended note by Simon Gilson (Gils.2001.2), pp. 58–65. For a useful review of some current writing on Dante's knowledge and use of the sciences, with bibliography, see Ledda (Ledd.2001.1).

64–72. The first part of Beatrice's discourse attacks the notion (introduced by Dante in verse 60) that various stars in the Starry Sphere shine brighter or less bright and, indeed, have other distinguishing characteristics (e.g., color, size, shape), simply because they are more or less dense. This would make the differentiating power single, and would be at odds with what we know of the variety of God's formal principles. So much for the larger issue at stake here. For discussion of the passage, see Moore (Moor.1903.1), pp. 87–91.

73–105. Turning to the phenomenon itself, Beatrice adduces two arguments to destroy Dante's position, the first involving two points (vv. 73–82), the second, a single one (vv. 83–105), building on the second point in the first argument, an extended disproof by imagined experiment.

73–82. If the dark spots on the Moon were the result of rarer matter, then matter rare and dense would be distributed either randomly or in strips, as meat and fat in creatures or pages in a book (for this second image, vv. 77–78, see Hatcher [Hatc.1971.1]). Were the first case true (i.e., were there "holes" without density in the Moon), we would verify that fact during eclipses of the Sun; and, since we cannot, Beatrice says, we must look to the second possible cause put forward by Dante.

For studies of the problem presented by the dark spots on the Moon, see Paget Toynbee, "Dante's Theories as to the Spots on the Moon" (Toyn.1902.1), pp. 78–86 (for a discussion of possible sources and of some of the confusion caused by the passage). See also Manlio Pastore Stocchi (Past.1981.1). And see Nardi (Nard.1985.1), Stabile (Stab.1989.1), pp. 47–55 & nn., and Picone (Pico.2000.1), pp. 21–25.

83–90. If then, Beatrice reasons, there are no "holes" for the Sun's light to come through, we must hypothesize the presence of dense matter that will act as a mirror for whatever light has penetrated the rare matter beneath the Moon's surface.

91–93. Dante will object, Beatrice says, that the farther reflection, because of its greater distance, will seem dimmer, a proposition that she will spend four tercets tearing down.

94–105. In Aristotelian manner, Beatrice extols the virtue of experiment. In this "thought experiment" that she proposes for Dante to perform, the two equidistant mirrors (one of which is, strictly speaking, unnecessary) represent the surface of the Moon, while the one set farther back stands in for the indented portion, where the dense part begins. The three lights reflected in the mirror will show equal brightness, if not equal size. Thus, as Beatrice clearly means to instruct Dante, the quality of the light is not affected by distance; only the quantity is.

For a discussion of this passage and the significance of mirrors in *Paradiso*, see Miller (Mill.1977.1). See also Tate (Tate.1961.1), offering a first "Trinitarian" reading of the third experimentally unnecessary mirror. Boyde (Boyd.1995.1), pp. 14–16, actually performed a version of the experiment in order to test Dante's method (it passed his test). Gilson (Gils.1997.1), pp. 204–6, discusses various other similar "experiments" described by earlier writers (Pseudo-Thomas on the *Meteorologica*, Chalcidius on the *Timaeus*, Roger Bacon, Albert the Great on the *De causis*), concluding that, while Albert's is the closest to Dante's, in this (as in so much else) Dante simply cannot be pinned down. And now see Turelli (Ture.2004.1), in polemic with Kleiner (Klei.1994.1), p. 104 (who believes that "dopo il dosso" means "directly behind your back," thus making the experiment literally impossible). But see Landino's gloss to vv. 100–108; he simply (and understandably) assumes that the light is *above* the experimenter's head ("et sopra el capo tuo ti sia un lume"). In our own time, Turelli convincingly defends the experimental "correctness" of Beatrice's verbal demonstration; Moevs (Moev.2005.1), p. 115, however, accepts Kleiner's presupposition, arguing that in the thought experiment we must realize that Dante possesses—meaningfully, of course—a transparent body.

106–111. Beatrice turns to simile (one of the fairly infrequent occasions on which the poet puts the simile-forging power into the hands of a character [but cf. *Inf.* XXVII.94–97]): As the Sun's rays reduce snow to its underlying essence (water), stripping it of its accidental qualities (cold, whiteness), so Beatrice's mind will rid Dante's intellect of its improper qualities and return it to its original condition.

112–114. Going back, in thought, to the Beginning, the Empyrean, Beatrice turns her attention to the Primum Mobile, the ninth sphere, where nothing may be seen but where all the powers that course through the universe have their origins in space and time. See *Convivio* II.xiv.15: "For, as the Philosopher says in the fifth book of the Ethics, 'legal justice disposes the sciences for our learning, and commands that they be learned and taught in order that they not be forsaken'; so with its movement *the aforesaid heaven governs the daily revolution of all the others*, by which every day they all receive and transmit here below the virtue of all their parts" (tr. R. Lansing, italics added).

115–117. The Sphere of the Fixed Stars is where the angelic powers, undifferentiated in the Primum Mobile, are differentiated among the stars. It is from here that they exercise their influence on earth.

118–120. Perhaps it is best to follow Bosco/Reggio's interpretation of this difficult tercet, which they understand in light of lines from *Purgatorio* XXX.109–110: "Not only by the working of the wheels above / that urge each seed to a certain end. . . ." They argue that this tercet then means that the seven lower heavens (after the Primum Mobile and the Starry Sphere) dispose in diverse ways the various essences or powers that they receive from the Starry Sphere, adapting them to their own precise purposes.

121–123. These "organs" of the universe, resembling in their workings the effective parts of the human body, as Dante now understands, take their powers from the realms closest to God and disperse them below.

124–126. Beatrice's admonition prepares Dante to do his own reasoning (and do better than he has done so far). If he learns from this experience, he will not only understand the principle that explains the phenomenon of the moonspots, but other things as well.

127–129. Only now does Beatrice turn her attention to the angels ("the blessèd movers"), the artisans of all creation. Up to now we have heard exclusively of the incorruptible material universe; now we find out what animates it.

130–132. And the Starry Sphere, into the stars of which the powers are distributed, receives that imprinting from the Intelligences (angels) in the Primum Mobile. There is a possible ambiguity here, as Dante uses the singular (*mente profonda*) to indicate either the Cherubim (the angels of knowledge) or all nine angelic orders, as the context would seem to demand.

133–138. The "dust" that in Genesis (3:19 ["pulvis es, et in pulverem reverteris"]) is our flesh is seen here as activated in its various members by the angelic intelligences—unless we are once again to take the singular (*intelligenza*—verse 136) at face value (see the note to vv. 130–132), in which case Beatrice is speaking only of the Cherubim, which seems unlikely.

139–141. The undivided power of primal angelic intelligence (found in the ninth sphere), descending, makes a different union with each star that it animates, similar to the way in which it binds with human souls. For this notion, Pietrobono (comm. to this tercet) cites *Convivio* II.v.18: "These movers by their intellect alone produce the revolution in that proper subject which each one moves. The most noble form of heaven, which has in itself the principle of this passive nature, revolves at the touch of the motive power which understands it; and by touch I mean contact, though not in a bodily sense, with the virtue which is directed toward it" [tr. R. Lansing].

Fraccaroli (Frac.1906.1) offers these verses as an example of Dante's frequent divergence from the text of Plato's *Timaeus* when it counters the opinions of Aristotle (Fraccaroli is among those scholars who believe that Dante actually knew the text of that work in Chalcidius's translation rather than from some other intermediary—see the note to *Par.* IV.24). In Plato the stars are self-propelled.

142–144. The greater or lesser effulgence of a star results from the conjoined qualities that a particular star has in conjunction with the informing virtues, or powers, of its angelic informant. And this is the answer to Dante's quandary. He had attempted to analyze the moonspots in physical terms; Beatrice has just accounted for them in metaphysical ones (notably poetic though these are, comparing the relative brightness of/in a heavenly body to the relative brightness in a joyful eye, an ocular smile, as it were).

145–148. The difference between light and dark in heavenly bodies is not to be accounted for quantitatively, in terms of density/rarity, but qualitatively, by the amount of angelic potency found in a given body.

PARADISO III

OUTLINE

MOON (continues)

- 1–9 Dante's intellect corrected (about the moonspots)
  - 1–9 Dante would confess his error and newfound certitude, but he is distracted by a presence
- 10–24 souls in the Moon
  - 10–18 simile: image in Moon and reflection on mirror or water
  - 19–24 Dante as counter-**Narcissus,** looking away
- 25–33 Beatrice's smiling reproof and correction
  - 25–27 silly fellow, looking into vacancy,
  - 28–33 these are real beings; speak to them
- 34–41 Dante focuses on questioning **Piccarda:**
  - 34–41 (a) who are you? (b) what is your condition?
- 42–57 Piccarda's responses
  - 42–45 our charity conforms to such a wish as yours
  - 46–51 (a) I am the nun Piccarda
  - 52–57 (b) with cause are we low in celestial rank
- 58–66 Dante's reaction and follow-up question
  - 58–63 your words allow me to recognize you
  - 64–66 don't you long to be higher in the heavens?
- 67–87 Piccarda's response
  - 67–87 our will is His will
- 88–96 Dante returns to his first question
  - 88–90 Dante understands Piccarda's precision
  - 91–96 simile: Dante wants to order a second course
- 97–108 Piccarda's response
  - 97–108 Piccarda narrates her vocation and dereliction
- 109–120 Piccarda tells of **Costanza**
  - 109–120 she never gave up her will to be a nun
- 121–130 Piccarda withdraws

121–125 Dante follows the sight of her as long as he can,

126–130 then turns back to Beatrice, whose splendor quiets his questioning.

PARADISO III

Quel sol che pria d'amor mi scaldò 'l petto,
di bella verità m'avea scoverto,
provando e riprovando, il dolce aspetto;

e io, per confessar corretto e certo
me stesso, tanto quanto si convenne
leva' il capo a proferer più erto;

ma visïone apparve che ritenne
a sé me tanto stretto, per vedersi,
che di mia confession non mi sovvenne.

Quali per vetri trasparenti e tersi,
o ver per acque nitide e tranquille,
non sì profonde che i fondi sien persi,

tornan d'i nostri visi le postille
debili sì, che perla in bianca fronte
non vien men forte a le nostre pupille;

tali vid' io più facce a parlar pronte;
per ch'io dentro a l'error contrario corsi
a quel ch'accese amor tra l'omo e 'l fonte.

Sùbito sì com' io di lor m'accorsi,
quelle stimando specchiati sembianti,
per veder di cui fosser, li occhi torsi;

e nulla vidi, e ritorsili avanti
dritti nel lume de la dolce guida,
che, sorridendo, ardea ne li occhi santi.

"Non ti maravigliar perch' io sorrida,"
mi disse, "appresso il tuo püeril coto,
poi sopra 'l vero ancor lo piè non fida,

That sun which first made warm my breast with love
had now disclosed, by proof and refutation,
the sweet and lovely features of the truth.

To confess myself corrected and convinced
I raised my head no higher
than saying so required,

but then appeared a sight
which so drew my attention
that my confession quickly slipped from mind.

As through clear, transparent glass
or through still and limpid water,
not so deep that its bed is lost from view,

the outlines of our faces are returned
so faint a pearl on a pallid forehead
comes no less clearly to our eyes,

I saw many such faces eager to speak,
at which I fell into the error opposite to that
which inflamed a man to love a fountain.

As soon as I became aware of them,
believing them to be reflections,
I turned around to see from whom they came

and, seeing nothing, I returned my gaze
to the light of my sweet guide,
whose holy eyes were glowing as she smiled.

'Be not surprised,' she said, 'if I am smiling
at your childish thoughts, since they as yet trust not
their steps to truth but turn you back,

ma te rivolve, come suole, a vòto:
vere sustanze son ciò che tu vedi,
qui rilegate per manco di voto.

Però parla con esse e odi e credi;
ché la verace luce che le appaga
da sé non lascia lor torcer li piedi."

E io a l'ombra che parea più vaga
di ragionar, drizza'mi, e cominciai,
quasi com' uom cui troppa voglia smaga:

"O ben creato spirito, che a' rai
di vita etterna la dolcezza senti
che, non gustata, non s'intende mai,

grazïoso mi fia se mi contenti
del nome tuo e de la vostra sorte."
Ond' ella, pronta e con occhi ridenti:

"La nostra carità non serra porte
a giusta voglia, se non come quella
che vuol simile a sé tutta sua corte.

I' fui nel mondo vergine sorella;
e se la mente tua ben sé riguarda,
non mi ti celerà l'esser più bella,

ma riconoscerai ch'i' son Piccarda,
che, posta qui con questi altri beati,
beata sono in la spera più tarda.

Li nostri affetti, che solo infiammati
son nel piacer de lo Spirito Santo,
letizian del suo ordine formati.

E questa sorte che par giù cotanto,
però n'è data, perché fuor negletti
li nostri voti, e vòti in alcun canto."

'as is their custom, toward emptiness.
These are real beings that you see,
assigned this place for failing in their vows.

'Therefore speak with them, listen, and believe,
for the true light that brings them peace
does not allow their steps to stray.'

And, addressing myself to the shade
that seemed most keen to speak, I began,
like a man muddled by excessive zeal:

'O spirit made for bliss, who in the beams
of life eternal savor the sweetness
that, untasted, cannot be understood,

'I shall take it as a kindness if you share with me
your name and lot, and the lot of others here.'
Then she, eager and with smiling eyes:

'Our love shuts not its doors against just will,
any more than does the love of God, who wills
that all His court be like Himself.

'In the world I was a virgin sister.
If you search your memory,
my having grown more fair will not conceal my name

'and you will recognize me as Piccarda,
placed here among these other blessèd souls,
and blessèd am I in the slowest of these spheres.

'Our affections, which are inflamed
only when they please the Holy Spirit,
take joy in their adherence to His plan,

'and this our lot, which seems so very low,
is given us because of vows neglected
and, in part, no longer valid.'

Ond' io a lei: "Ne' mirabili aspetti
vostri risplende non so che divino
che vi trasmuta da' primi concetti:

però non fui a rimembrar festino;
ma or m'aiuta ciò che tu mi dici,
sì che raffigurar m'è più latino.

Ma dimmi: voi che siete qui felici,
disiderate voi più alto loco
per più vedere e per più farvi amici?"

Con quelle altr' ombre pria sorrise un poco;
da indi mi rispuose tanto lieta,
ch'arder parea d'amor nel primo foco:

"Frate, la nostra volontà quïeta
virtù di carità, che fa volerne
sol quel ch'avemo, e d'altro non ci asseta.

Se disïassimo esser più superne,
foran discordi li nostri disiri
dal voler di colui che qui ne cerne;

che vedrai non capere in questi giri,
s'essere in carità è qui *necesse*,
e se la sua natura ben rimiri.

Anzi è formale ad esto beato *esse*
tenersi dentro a la divina voglia,
per ch'una fansi nostre voglie stesse;

sì che, come noi sem di soglia in soglia
per questo regno, a tutto il regno piace
com' a lo re che 'n suo voler ne 'nvoglia.

E 'n la sua volontade è nostra pace:
ell' è quel mare al qual tutto si move
ciò ch'ella crïa o che natura face."

Then I said to her: 'From your transfigured faces
shines forth a divinity I do not know,
and it transforms the images I can recall.

'That is why my memory worked so slowly,
but now what you have said has helped me
and I more readily recall your features.

'But tell me, do you, who are here content,
desire to achieve a higher place, where you
might see still more and make yourselves more dear?'

Along with the other shades, she smiled,
then answered me with so much gladness
she seemed alight with love's first fire:

'Brother, the power of love subdues our will
so that we long for only what we have
and thirst for nothing else.

'If we desired to be more exalted,
our desires would be discordant
with His will, which assigns us to this place.

'That, as you will see, would not befit these circles
if to be ruled by love is here required
and if you consider well the nature of that love.

'No, it is the very essence of this blessèd state
that we remain within the will of God,
so that our wills combine in unity.

'Therefore our rank, from height to height,
throughout this kingdom pleases all the kingdom,
as it delights the King who wills us to His will.

'And in His will is our peace.
It is to that sea all things move,
both what His will creates and that which nature makes.'

Chiaro mi fu allor come ogne dove
in cielo è paradiso, *etsi* la grazia
del sommo ben d'un modo non vi piove.

Ma sì com' elli avvien, s'un cibo sazia
e d'un altro rimane ancor la gola,
che quel si chere e di quel si ringrazia,

così fec' io con atto e con parola,
per apprender da lei qual fu la tela
onde non trasse infino a co la spuola.

"Perfetta vita e alto merto inciela
donna più sù," mi disse, "a la cui norma
nel vostro mondo giù si veste e vela,

perché fino al morir si vegghi e dorma
con quello sposo ch'ogne voto accetta
che caritate a suo piacer conforma.

Dal mondo, per seguirla, giovinetta
fuggi'mi, e nel suo abito mi chiusi
e promisi la via de la sua setta.

Uomini poi, a mal più ch'a bene usi,
fuor mi rapiron de la dolce chiostra:
Iddio si sa qual poi mia vita fusi.

E quest' altro splendor che ti si mostra
da la mia destra parte e che s'accende
di tutto il lume de la spera nostra,

ciò ch'io dico di me, di sé intende;
sorella fu, e così le fu tolta
di capo l'ombra de le sacre bende.

Ma poi che pur al mondo fu rivolta
contra suo grado e contra buona usanza,
non fu dal vel del cor già mai disciolta.

Then it was clear to me that everywhere in heaven
is Paradise, even if the grace of the highest Good
does not rain down in equal measure.

But, as happens, when one food may satisfy
while still we crave another, we give thanks
for the one we have, while asking for the other,

so did I with both word and gesture,
to learn from her about the web through which
she had not drawn her shuttle to completion.

'Perfect life and high desert,' she said to me,
'set in a higher sphere a lady by whose rule
down in your world they take the robe and veil

'so that till death they wake and sleep
in union with that Bridegroom who accepts each vow
that love makes fitting for His pleasure.

'To follow her, still young, I fled the world
and, cloaking myself in her habit,
I promised to follow the rule of her order.

'Then men more used to evil than to good
carried me off, away from the sweet cloister.
God knows what after that my life became.

'And this other splendor who appears to you
upon my right, who blazes up
with all the brightness of this sphere:

'What I told of myself applies to her as well.
She was a sister and, like me, she had the shadow
of the holy veil torn from her head.

'But, even after she was cast into the world
against her will and against all proper custom,
the veil was never loosened from her heart.

Quest' è la luce de la gran Costanza
che del secondo vento di Soave
generò 'l terzo e l'ultima possanza."

Così parlommi, e poi cominciò *"Ave,*
Maria" cantando, e cantando vanio
come per acqua cupa cosa grave.

La vista mia, che tanto lei seguio
quanto possibil fu, poi che la perse,
volsesi al segno di maggior disio,

e a Beatrice tutta si converse;
ma quella folgorò nel mïo sguardo
sì che da prima il viso non sofferse;
e ciò mi fece a dimandar più tardo.

'This is the light of the great Constance,
who bore to the second blast of Swabia
the third and final emperor.'

Thus she spoke to me, and then began to sing
Ave Maria, and, still singing, vanished,
like something heavy through deep water.

My eyes, which watched her as long as they could,
turned, once she was lost to view,
to the goal of their greater desire

and were wholly bent on Beatrice.
But she so blazed upon my sight
at first my gaze could not sustain her light
and that delayed my plying her with questions.

1–3. If many readers have responded to the previous canto—for some the most labored and unwelcoming of the entire poem—with a certain impatience (e.g., if *Paradiso* is going to be like this, I'd prefer to spend my time in *Inferno* and/or *Purgatorio*), here they are placed on notice that, for Dante, Beatrice's instruction in spiritual astronomy is more aesthetically pleasing than any possible worldly attraction. It is notable that each of the verses of this tercet contains words or phrases that are often associated with sensual or aesthetic pleasure (*amor, scaldò il petto, bella, dolce*), yet here conjoined with the language of Scholastic argumentation (see the note to vv. 2–3, below).

1. It is not surprising, given its Christian valence, that Dante should have used the Sun as metaphoric equivalent for Beatrice (it is a nice touch that the professor in the matter pertaining to, in the phrasing of St. Francis's *Laudes creaturarum*, "Sister Moon" should be her "brother," the Sun).

This evident recollection of the first significant events recorded in the second chapter of the *Vita nuova*, Beatrice's appearance to the nearly nine-year-old Dante and his immediate *innamoramento*, sets the stage for the entrance of his newly reconstituted instructor and guide ("Bëatrice, dolce guida e cara!" [my sweet belovèd guide] of *Par.* XXIII.34) in the next twenty-eight cantos. She will illumine his intellect as she first stirred all his soul. (Or, as Benvenuto da Imola puts it, "idest que primo amoravit cor meum carnaliter, deinde mentaliter" [that is, who first set my heart in carnal affection, then in intellectual love]). It is not that she has changed in any way; what has changed is *his* ability to comprehend the deeper truths available from her. Such a transformation—from physical to intellectual love—has roots in Plato's *Phaedrus*, surely unknown to Dante by direct encounter, but perhaps having some influence on him and on others in his time (those who wrote of the ennobling potential of carnal love) at least from its diffusion through a lengthy and various tradition (see Joseph A. Mazzeo, "Dante and the Phaedrus Tradition of Poetic Inspiration," in Mazz.1958.1).

2–3. The development of the opening metaphor (Beatrice as Sun) has it that the light of his guide illumines the truth behind the conundrum of the causes of the Moon's dark spots as the light in a lover's eyes makes beautiful the face of his beloved. The poet is joining the two main aspects of his Beatricean versifying, that based on appreciations of her physical beauty and that dependent upon a spiritual understanding of a more lasting attraction. It is jarring, perhaps, but exhilarating to watch the "old poetry" being conjoined with the new, the rhymes of carnal love being forced into collaboration with the language of Scholastic discourse, "provando e riprovando" (by proof and refutation). The words clearly refer, in reverse order, to Beatrice's refutation of Dante's erroneous ideas (*Par.* II.61–105) and to her truthful assertions (*Par.* II.112–117).

4–9. Dante presents himself as both rebuked and corrected (the terms relate to *provando* and *riprovando* in verse 3) in this "confession." His previous confession (*Purg.* XXXI.1–42) involved recanting his past improper loves. That this scene marks the beginning, in *Paradiso*, of what has been described as "the correction of Dante's intellect" in a program that began with the correction and perfection of his will (*Inferno* and most of *Purgatorio*) seems likely. (See the note to *Purg.* XXVII.139–141.) This process will carry through until St. Bernard appears and the program of the perfection of Dante's intellect is begun.

Dante's confession is once again impeded (see *Purg.* XXXI.7–9). This time, however, not through any failing on his part, but because his attention has been drawn to higher things. (Further, Beatrice already knows his thoughts and so expression of them is not necessary.)

7. What is the precise character of the sight (*visïone*) appearing to him? Is it a dream? Is it an experience of the noumenal world in a Pauline face-to-face encounter? From the prose of the *Vita nuova* onward, these have been the two kinds of "visions" that weave their way through Dante's works. It would thus seem here that what he is seeing is actual, not dreamed; and it would further seem that, in seeing his first saved souls as they are for eternity (if not yet with their bodies [see *Par.* XXV.127–129]), he is experiencing a higher form of vision than he has previously known, gazing on the presence of two heavenly souls in the very Moon, a collocation that causes, as we shall see, considerable difficulty in a reader's attempt to comprehend the ground rules governing the appearances of the saved in the spheres of the heavens.

10–16. As though to reward us for having had to deal with his theologized poetry, Dante now engages us in a pleasing aesthetic moment (so often associated in the poem with similes, a mode offering Dante the very stuff of lyric expression). It is charged with the erotic energy of thirteenth-century Italian and Provençal lyric. What is perhaps surprising is the fact that this poet is able to bring that energy to bear *here*, in the highest realm. At the same time, we should note the way in which he twice in this canto invites us to carnal impressions of love only to warn us that these are valuable only if they are markers of a higher form of affection. These lines and the earlier verses that also seem erotically charged (vv. 1–3) look forward to the stories of two nuns who are delighted to renounce sexuality. They also glance back to Beatrice's explanation of the moonspots.

17–18. The "opposite error" into which Dante falls results from the fact that, where Narcissus looked into a mirroring surface of water and thought the beautiful visage he saw in it was that of someone else, Dante believes that the faces before him are reflections of those who are now suddenly present alongside him and Beatrice, not these actual new beings themselves. See Bernardino Daniello (comm. to these verses): "quelle faccie, ch'erano vere, gli paresser false, et a Narciso la falsa, vera pareva" (those faces, which were real, seemed to him to be false, while to Narcissus the false seemed real).

For the "Narcissus program" in the poem as a whole (*Inf.* XXX; *Purg.* XXX; *Par.* III, XXX, XXXIII), see the note to *Inferno* XXX.126–129 and articles by Brownlee (Brow.1978.1) and Shoaf (Shoa.1983.1), pp. 21–100.

19–24. Dante, bending his eye on vacancy, allows Beatrice the chance to get off a good schoolmarmish rebuke of her pupil, whose actions mirror those of untutored humankind, unable to read the very facts of human relations—for example, who is standing where; who is reflected, who is not.

25–28. For Dante's *puerizia* and subsequent "childish" behavior, see *Purgatorio* XXX.40–54. Francesco da Buti's comment to that passage (comm. to *Purg.* XXX.37–51) shares elements with his comment (to vv. 19–33) on this one, which has it that from the ages of one through seven a male is a child (*fanciullo*), while from eight through fourteen he is a boy (*garzone*). The commentator continues by saying that Beatrice means to associate her confused pupil with the latter stage of development. In the garden of Eden his failings were portrayed as being based on affectional disorder; here, as is always the case after his tasting of Lethe and Eunoe (and his moral coming of age—belated though it may have been), it is his intellect that is behaving in a juvenile manner.

29–30. Dante's misprision has set up Beatrice's explanation, central to our understanding of the epistemology of the heavenly spheres. All whom we meet here are the living souls of real people with real histories (i.e., they are not part of some "symbolic" or otherwise less "real" manifestation) and a place in Heaven, that is, the Empyrean, not one of the lower spheres, where they manifest themselves to Dante *only* on the occasion of his Pauline visit to the heavens. It is this last detail to which particular attention must be paid, since later discussion in this canto might lead one to believe that the souls whom we meet in the Moon are indeed its permanent residents. See vv. 49–50, 55–57, 64–66, 73–75, 88–90, 97, and 121–123 (and discussion in the accompanying notes). Virgil describes himself, in the only previous (and only other) use of the verb in the poem (*Purg.* XXI.18), as situated in the Limbus, which "mi rilega nell'etterno essilio" (confines me in eternal exile), hardly envisioned as a temporary state. (The form "rilegollo" has, by common consent, a different meaning; at *Inf.* XXV.7, his blasphemous act of freedom required that Vanni Fucci be bound again.) But what exactly does *rilegare* (or *relegare*, a form that shows up in some manuscripts) mean? Either "relegate" or "bind fast," according to Andrea Mariani ("rilegare," *ED* IV [1973], p. 929). And, as Simone Marchesi has suggested in conversation, whether the form that Dante used was "relegato" or "rilegato," the word may refer to the Roman punishment of "relegation," the lesser form (because it was not necessarily permanent) of exile. This description would surely fit the condition of Piccarda and Constance rather well.

Beatrice's words may easily be understood as verifying that the souls in the heaven of the Moon are indeed permanently here, as Francesco da Buti believed (comm. to vv. 19–33): "sono nell'ultimo grado di sotto (di Dio) in vita eterna" (they are on the last level farthest from God in the life eternal). As we move through the relevant passages, it will be clear that Dante is far from having shut the door on such an explanation—but that is precisely what he will do in the next canto (in *Par.* IV.28–39). In consequence, one would be excused for believing that Beatrice means that Piccarda, Constance, and other Moon-dwellers are *rilegate* (bound, or, as in our translation, "assigned") here on a permanent basis. See also the note to *Paradiso* IX.119–123.

31–33. Having potentially undermined the authority of the next speaker by pointing out that she was one who had broken her vows, Beatrice quickly restores it in these words that guarantee her ability to speak God's truth and nothing but that truth.

34. The use of the word *ombra* to identify a saved soul is puzzling. We expect it and find it, amply present, in *Inferno* (some two dozen occurrences) for the damned. It is surprising to find that its use to indicate the souls of the dead, now saved, increases in *Purgatorio*. While it appears there 49 times in all, it is present with this meaning 34 times. Here, in Paradise, to see the first saved soul whom we meet in this *cantica* referred to as a "shade" is disconcerting. The term that becomes normative in *Paradiso* is *vita*, generally translated "living soul" (IX.7; XII.127; XIV.6; XX.100; XXI.55; XXV.29). It is perhaps the association of those present in the first three heavens with flawed activities (broken vows, ambition, and lust) that moved Dante to begin his descriptions of the inhabitants of Paradise with the word that would surely seem to connect them with the damned; it is repeated at verse 67, in the plural, to refer to all the souls found in the Moon. The souls who appear in Mercury (*Par.* V.107) will be the next and the last heavenly presences to be referred to as *ombre*.

35–36. The soul whom we meet will shortly (at verse 49) be identified as Piccarda Donati. It seems clear from her eagerness to speak with Dante that we are meant to understand that she has recognized him from their days in Florence.

Piccarda joins a select few, those personages who appear at the opening of their respective canticles as the first representative of sin and then of redemption: Celestine V (if it is indeed he, as seems nearly certainly to be the case) in *Inferno* III, Manfred in the third canto of *Purgatorio*, and now Piccarda. Each of these figures is a surprise, and was surely meant to be one: a damned pope, a saved libertine and possible murderer, and a woman who, no matter how unwilling her subjection to the world, was certainly no St. Clare.

The protagonist's "muddled" condition results, in the opinion of Manfredi Porena (comm. to verse 36), from his excitement at being able, for the first time, to speak with a soul who lives in Heaven.

While it is impossible to tell from the text, it would seem that Piccarda, unlike Beatrice and heavenly souls we meet farther along, does not read Dante's mind, but needs to have a spoken question in order to respond (see vv. 91–96). Dante also voices questions to Justinian (*Par.* V.127–129), to Charles Martel (*Par.* VIII.44; 91–93), and to Cunizza (*Par.* IX.19–21). It is only when he encounters Folquet of Marseille (*Par.* IX.73–79) that he expects anyone other than Beatrice to read his thoughts. This is another detail setting those below the heaven of the Sun apart from the more exalted souls of Paradise, for Dante never has to verbalize another question, although Cacciaguida wants to savor his unnecessary voicing of one (see *Par.* XV.64–69).

37. Piccarda is a spirit who is "ben creato" (spirit made for bliss), in sharp opposition to those in Hell referred to as being "mal nati" ("ill-born souls" at *Inf.* XVIII.76; "born for sorrow" at *Inf.* XXX.48).

43–45. While there is much that is personal in the interaction between Dante and Piccarda, her first words show how "impersonal" the feelings of the saved are, both for one another and for this very special visitor. They are more than glad to welcome him, and his coming increases the love they feel in general (see *Par.* V.105) by adding one more soul for them to love. Nonetheless (with the major exception of Cacciaguida, whose familial ties to the protagonist are much [some might say shamelessly] exploited), almost all of the exchanges between Dante and the blessed show that they are at a postpersonal level of development. If we keep in mind some of the great scenes of personal remembrance found in the first two *cantiche* (e.g., those presenting Ciacco, Cavalcante, Brunetto, Casella, Belacqua, and Forese), the starkness of the contrast is evident.

46–49. "Piccarda, daughter of Simone Donati, of the celebrated Florentine family of that name, and sister of Corso and Forese Donati. Piccarda was a connection by marriage of Dante, he having married Gemma, daughter of Manetto Donati. . . . The commentators state that Piccarda was forced from her convent by her brother Corso, while he was Podestà of Bologna (i.e., in 1283 or 1288), in order to marry her to a Florentine, Rossellino della Tosa, and that she died soon after her marriage. . . ." (T).

47–48. It is a "post-Proustian" touch that here the recognition of things past is not tinged by the tragic sense of mortality, of age that strips the loveliness from the human form, but rather is complicated by the souls having become more beautiful, and almost unrecognizable for that reason. We may remember what her brother Forese said of Piccarda: "I cannot say whether my sister was more virtuous / than she was beautiful" (*Purg.* XXIV.13–14). In her new life she is more of both.

For the absence of the perfected forms of the three Theological Virtues in those who display themselves in the subsolar planets (i.e., Moon, Mercury, and Venus), see Ordiway (Ordi.1982.1). But see Carroll, introduction to *Paradiso* and *Proem* to Canto X, for a much earlier version of this thesis. And see Andreoli (comm. to verse 16): "The fact is that it is only in the fourth heaven that we shall begin to find souls that are completely without reproach." Bosco/Reggio rightly point out (comm. to *Par.* XIV.68) that, beginning in the Sun, the souls who appear take on definite shapes—circle, cross, eagle, ladder—thus further distinguishing themselves from these who appear in the first three subsolar heavens.

49–50. Naming herself (and thus answering the first of Dante's questions), Piccarda for a second time speaks of her placement in this heaven as though it might be permanent. See the other relevant passages indicated in the note to vv. 29–30.

51. The Moon is "the slowest of these spheres" because, in Dante's astronomy, each successive heaven, of the nine revolving around the earth, is moving at a faster rate of speed. See the apparently contradictory notice (*Par.* XXVIII.22–39) in which the nine ranks of angels, each associated with one of the planetary spheres, rotating around the point that represents the Godhead, rotate faster the *nearer* they are to that point.

52–54. A difficult tercet because it is hard to be certain whether the *piacere* associated with the Holy Spirit is directed by the souls toward the Spirit or by the Spirit toward the souls. We are in accord with that branch of the tradition, a majority, represented by Francesco da Buti's gloss (to vv. 46–57), in which the souls whom we see in the Moon "altro desiderio non ànno, se non di piacere allo Spirito Santo dal quale procede la carità" (have no other care except to be pleasing to the Holy Spirit, from whom holy love comes forth).

For the nature of love represented by the earthly (and now heavenly) Piccarda, see Battaglia Ricci (Batt.1989.1), pp. 51–65, 68–70, pointing out that Dante is probably relying on various expressions of mystical devotion, especially those found in the *Epistola ad Severinum de caritate* by one "frate Ivo."

55–57. The "lot" of these souls reflects their earthly failings (as will also be true of those we meet in each of the next two heavens), their failure to maintain the strict sense of their vows. While this is a particularly monastic concern, since vows were a part of the requirements for entrance, as it were, and while the only beings we hear about here were in fact nuns, the failing is probably not meant to be understood as being limited to the clergy.

On yet another occasion the phrasing at the very least admits the possibility that Piccarda's "lot" (*sorte*) is permanently to be present in the Moon. See discussions indicated in the note to vv. 29–30.

58–63. Once again the nature of heavenly transfiguration is alluded to (see vv. 47–48). Only after he knows her story can Dante begin to recognize the features of the earthly woman he once knew. That even this much "physicality" is possible is singular; Dante will not recognize anyone else whom he once knew and whom he meets in the various heavens, not Charles Martel (*Par.* VIII), not his ancestor Cacciaguida (*Par.* XV). From this, we may choose to believe that only here, in the Moon, is there even the slightest amount of physical resemblance of a soul to its earlier mortal self. Dante, however, does not choose to raise (or answer) this question for us. But see *Par.* XXXI.46–48, where St. Bernard tells Dante that the heavenly infants are recognizable as such.

64–66. It is clear that the protagonist believes that Piccarda and the other souls with her are bound in the Moon for eternity unless the desire he attributes to them to be closer to God should one day be consummated. This, of course, is the opinion of the protagonist and is not necessarily shared by the poet. See the note to vv. 29–30.

67. See the discussion of the use of the word *ombra* (shade) in *Paradiso* (in the note to verse 34).

69. The exact nature of the love displayed by Piccarda is a subject for disagreement among the commentators, some arguing that the phrase is to be understood as indicating the "first fire of love," that is, the first enamorment of a young woman; others understand that the phrase rather indicates the fire of divine love, that given expression through the Holy Spirit. Those who hold to this second view find confirming evidence in the phrase found both at *Inferno* III.6 and *Paradiso* VI.11, "primal Love" (*primo amor*), referring to the love expressed in the Holy Spirit, forcing the phrase to be understood (or translated) as "love in the First Fire," that is, the Holy Spirit. While this is surely a possible explanation, it does require a somewhat forced understanding of the verse. Would it be so strange for Piccarda, burning with reciprocal affection for God's love of her, to seem to Dante like a young woman just fallen in love? It is hard to see the harm in such a reading. See the similar views of Bosco/Reggio (comm. to vv. 67–69). One might also be reminded of the distance between this scene and the one containing Dante's recognition of the love felt for him by Matelda (*Purg.* XXVIII.43–51). In that passage Dante imagines that Matelda is amorously disposed toward him in the normal mortal way; there he is incorrect. Here he is fully aware of the kind of love that motivates Piccarda, but sees it in terms reminiscent of our mortal sort of loving.

70–84. The bulk of Piccarda's answer to Dante's question (vv. 64–66) begins with the word *frate* (brother), the word that was nearly absent from Hell (eleven uses, predominantly to indicate a member of a religious order [nomenclature that the Infernal context makes obviously suspect at once], and only once to express human fraternity [by Ulysses, addressing his shipmates, at *Inf.* XXVI.112—with, according to some readers, an unmistakable whiff of Julius Caesar's fulsome address to his soldiers, *captatio benevolentiae* on all fours, as it were]). It frequently appeared as a term of address in *Purgatorio* (thirteen times). Now, in the heavens, it appears less frequently as a term of address, first here, and then a total of four other times. In a sense it contains a central message of Piccarda's speech in that it insists on the relationship that binds all saved Christians in their fellowship in God, a sense that overcomes the inevitable hierarchical distinctions found among them in this life. The love that governs their will is nothing less than charity, with the result that it is impossible for them to want advantage over their brothers and sisters in grace. To wish things other than they are, to desire one's own "advancement," is nothing less than to oppose the will of God. And thus all members of this community observe the gradations among themselves, but find in them the expression of their general and personal happiness.

Verses 80–85 return to forms for the word *volontà* (will), which opened (at verse 70) Piccarda's concluding discourse as its main subject, five times (*voglia, voglie, voler, 'nvoglia, volontade*), underlining the importance of the will's direction of human love to divine ends. The celestial form of will in brotherhood is vastly different from the will that destroys fraternity here on earth. But it is as natural in the realms of Paradise as it is absent from Hell (and rarely enough found on earth).

73–75. At first reading, a certain indeterminacy seems possible. Does Piccarda mean "higher in the heavens" or "higher in the Rose"? Since the concluding words of the tercet, "that which assigns us to this place," seem to refer to the sphere of the Moon, it is difficult to conclude that she means other than in a higher heaven. See, again, the note to vv. 29–30.

79. Our translation reflects Weatherby's discussion (Weat.1975.1), p. 24, of the Scholastic nature of the term *forma*. Thus our choice of "essence" (in the sense of "formative principle").

85. Piccarda's last tercet makes her point with two differing linguistic gestures, this first a summarizing citation, the second a powerful

metaphor. Exactly which text she is citing is a matter for consideration, but a list of suggested candidates includes Luke 2:14 ("Et in terra pax hominibus bonae voluntatis" [And on earth peace to men of good will]); Ephesians 2:15 ("Ipse enim est pax noster" [For he (Christ Jesus) is our peace]); and Augustine's *Confessions* XIII.9 ("In bona voluntate pax nobis est" [Our peace lies in willing the good]). The greater closeness of the last ("E 'n la la sua voluntade è nostra pace" [And in His will we find our peace]) makes it the most likely to have been on Dante's mind as he created his Piccarda. (Grandgent [comm. to this verse], followed by Singleton, in his commentary to this line, cites the passage from Ephesians. John Sinclair [Sinc.1946.1], p. 59, cites the passage from Augustine.) Readers of these notes may remark upon the parallel then found between Francesca and Piccarda, each quoting a crucial text of St. Augustine as the climactic gesture of her speech; see *Inferno* V.138 and the note thereto.

86–87. Piccarda's metaphor for the totality of the peace found in God reverses our normal sense of the proclivity of bodies to descend or to ascend (a phenomenon that is almost the trademark of *Paradiso*, beginning with Beatrice's explanation that it here is as natural to be drawn up toward God as on earth to be drawn down by gravity; see *Par.* I.136–141). In *Paradiso* I.113, Beatrice has used the phrase "lo gran mar de l'essere" (the vastness of the sea of being) to refer to all of God's creation, both here and above. Now Piccarda redeploys this metaphor to apply it only to God Himself, seen as the ocean to which all creation, whether direct or indirect, flows up.

While many commentators, moved by Piccarda, think of Francesca da Rimini, only Singleton (comm. to these verses) adverts to Francesca's very words (*Inf.* V.98–99) as being remembered here. Both ladies use watery metaphors to express the peace that they either long for or enjoy.

88–90. Piccarda's words have finally made it plain to Dante how one can be nearer or closer to God in Heaven and yet feel equally blessed with all who share beatitude, disregarding the matter of relative rank. Once again the phrasing, now representing not so much the response of the protagonist (see vv. 64–66) as the understanding of the poet, raises the question that is necessarily so persistent for a reader of this canto: Do references to paradisal "placement" speak of the ranked order of the saved in the Rose in the Empyrean or of their presences in the celestial spheres? Once we arrive in the Rose (*Par.* XXXII), we will see that there is a ranking (by one's row in the Rose bowl); on the other hand, there does not seem to be much in the way of ranking going on within each sphere (there may be some in Jupiter), if the spheres themselves are ranked, progressing from lowest to most exalted. Again, see the note to vv. 29–30.

91–96. The second simile of the canto (see vv. 10–18 for the first) is an elaborate way of describing the protagonist's reminder to his colloquist that she had not fully answered his second question (verse 41), the one dealing with her and her companions' "lot" in the afterworld. As is frequent in the post-Convivial *Paradiso*, the material for the simile proper is drawn from alimentation. In a real sense, as Robin McCallister suggested in a paper in 1968, for Dante the *Paradiso* offered him the opportunity to complete the *Convivio*, now in better, more "orthodox," form.

95–96. The as yet unexpressed portion of Piccarda's self-explanation is, in metaphor, compared to the unfinished portion of a woven fabric, an image that undoubtedly reflects the Florence of Dante's day, in the heart of which the wool merchants plied their trade.

97–99. Piccarda is referring to the companion and fellow citizen of St. Francis of Assisi, founder (in collaboration with Francis) of her own order in 1212, the Clarisse, St. Clare (1194–1253). "[S]he was canonized by [Pope] Alexander IV in 1255. The rule of her order, which was confirmed in 1247, and again in 1253, two days before her death, by Pope Innocent IV, was characterized by extreme austerity" **(T)**.

As Lauren Scancarelli Seem suggested in conversation many years ago, Piccarda's reference to St. Clare, as being loftier than she, parallels, in opposition, Francesca's reference to her husband, Gianciotto, as being fated to a place lower in Hell than she (see *Inf.* V.107). And see the note to *Purgatorio* XXIV.13–15 for another set of "family resemblances."

The resemblances and differences among the first three women in the three *cantiche* (Francesca in *Inf.* V, Pia de' Tolomei in *Purg.* V, and Piccarda) have offered occasion for frequent comment. See Stefanini (Stef.1992.1), pp. 26–31, for a study of structural similarities in these three narratives.

97. Dante's coinage, *inciela* (inheavens, "set[s] in a higher sphere"), again raises the issue of whether he refers to the Empyrean (in which Clare [whom we do not see there] is seated higher in the Rose than Piccarda) or to yet another heavenly sphere (e.g., that of the Sun, where we learn of St. Francis in Canto XI). It is very difficult to be certain, despite Bosco/Reggio's assurances that all is under control (see their note to vv.

28–30). The second alternative, however, does seem more likely (i.e., St. Clare, in Piccarda's view [the poet's also?], is in the Sun [or perhaps in Saturn]). Once more, see the note to vv. 29–30.

100–102. Piccarda's language recollects various biblical passages equating the love of God with marriage to Christ. Compare the Song of Solomon, passim, as read by Christian interpreters; Matthew 9:15 and 25:1–12; Mark 2:19; and Luke 5:34, but in particular the parable of the wise and foolish virgins in Matthew 25.

106–108. This celebrated tercet condenses a moment of horror followed by a life of despondency into a single unit of verse. As for the events to which Piccarda refers, the most frequent understanding among the commentators is that her brother Corso wanted to marry her off to one Rossellino della Tosa in order to further his political/financial ambition and, for this reason, had her abducted from her convent.

109–120. Constance of Sicily is the only companion mentioned by Piccarda (and one wonders, here and elsewhere, why, if the souls appear in the spheres only for the instruction of visiting Dante, they always seem to be accompanied by crowds of anonymous others, who are thus temporarily deprived of the joys of the Empyrean).

Bosco/Reggio offer a succinct account of the significant facts about her as they were known to Dante (in their comment to verse 118): "Constance, daughter of Roger II, king of Sicily, born in 1154, last heir of the Norman kingdom of Naples and Sicily, in 1185 married Henry VI of Swabia, son of Frederick Barbarossa. By marrying her, the emperor was finally obtaining dominion over southern Italy, which he had in vain attempted to conquer by force of arms. In 1194 Frederick II was born of this marriage. Constance, widowed in 1197, until her death in 1198 knew how to govern the kingdom with a shrewd sort of wisdom. With sure political instinct, sensing that she was near death, she named Pope Innocent III guardian of her three-year-old son, Frederick. During the time that the latter was emperor, the Guelphs spread the story that Constance had been made a nun against her will and that, at the age of 52, taken from the convent by the archbishop of Palermo, she had been joined in matrimony to Henry VI. Frederick II, the 'Antichrist,' would then have been born to an ex-nun who was at the same time a woman of a certain age, and thus opposing the precepts of every law, whether human or divine. In this way did Guelph propaganda attempt to discredit the emperor. Constance, in fact, had never been a nun and had married Henry at the age of 31. Dante accepted the story that she had become a nun, but omitted any negative elements from it, thus being able to illumine the figure of the empress in a lofty poetic light, making her the innocent victim of political machinations and violent acts. The halo of light that surrounds her, the refulgence in her of all of the light of this heaven, the attributes accorded her, all these tell us of Dante's high esteem for the 'Great Norman,' with the negative elements of Guelph propaganda transformed into a luminous attestation of the poet's reverence."

Piccarda's remarks at vv. 112–117 will puzzle Dante in the next canto (*Par.* IV.19–21).

109. This is the first time the word "splendor" (*splendore*) is used to describe the appearance of a soul in *Paradiso* (but see also at least V.103; IX.13; XI.39; XIV.95; XXI.32; XXIII.82; XXV.106; XXIX.138). In the heaven of the Sun we learn that the souls are enclosed in their own light (e.g., *Par.* XIII.48), thus explaining why we would not be able to recognize them even had we previously known them—as well as why Dante *can* recognize the features of Piccarda; that is, she still possesses features, if they are but faint. Thus for Constance to be treated in this way, as though she were appearing in a higher heaven, tells us a good deal about Dante's admiration for her.

118. Her name, Constance, plays with and against her former weakness, inconstancy, in that, if she was inconstant in her vows when forced (as she was at least in Dante's sense of her life) back into the world, she was also constant in her heart (see verse 117). It is also interesting that there are reports that the name assumed by Piccarda, in the convent of the Clarisse, was Constance (see Lombardi's commentaries [1791] to *Purg* XXIV.10 and *Par.* III.49). In *Purgatorio* (III.113), Constance is remembered with great affection by her grandson, Manfred (like his grandmother in this, not mentioning the name of the magnificent but hated "last of the Roman emperors," Frederick II [*Conv.* IV.iii.6]). As was suggested in the note to *Purgatorio* III.143, that canto is also a "canto of two Constances."

120. Frederick is referred to as the third powerful figure in the line of Frederick Barbarossa and Henry VI, the three Swabian emperors. See Grandgent (comm. to verse 119): "The Swabian Emperors are called 'blasts' because of the violence and the brief duration of their activity. Frederick I (Barbarossa) was the first; the 'second wind' was Constance's husband, Henry VI; the third and last was her son, Frederick II."

121–123. Where do these two Constances go after they recede from view? Opinions are divided, some more recent commentators (beginning with Costa in 1819 [comm. to verse 122]) claiming that they head back to the Empyrean (as will, apparently, many souls encountered later in the *cantica*); others are of the opinion that they go deep into the mass of the Moon (e.g., Benvenuto [comm. to vv. 115–123]: "disparuit in corpore lunae frigido" [disappeared into the cold matter of the Moon]). This is also maintained by Francesco da Buti (comm. to vv. 121–130): "profondò nel corpo lunare" (sank deep into the matter of the Moon). Most, however, do not even raise the question of where Piccarda (not to mention Constance or, indeed, any of their companions) is headed.

This is the last passage in the canto that makes the reader confront the problem of the permanent residence of the souls we see in the Moon (see the note to vv. 29–30). Here, the sense of descent would seem to make the second hypothesis more likely. The fact that, among the early commentators, only Benvenuto and Francesco da Buti tried to assign a destination to their departure makes the problematic nature of the passage apparent. In the later nineteenth century, Scartazzini (comm. to verse 123) and Campi (comm. to this tercet) also draw the conclusion that Costa did, basing it on what the next canto (vv. 28–39) will make clear: The souls are all in the Empyrean and descend from there to manifest themselves in the planets (or so Dante called both Moon and Sun along with those to which we reserve that appellation). However, twentieth-century exegetes preferred to admire the aesthetic attractiveness of the passage rather than apply themselves to this little conundrum. The result is that there is no "official" view of the problem, which remains unsolved. Dante should have shown Piccarda and the others going up, returning to God; he did not, and we have either, like Scartazzini, tried to be more correct than our author or, like Benvenuto, followed our poetic sense to make Dante seem to violate his own rules—at least the rules that he would lay down in the next canto. There is, according to an Italian proverb, always a third way ("C'è sempre una terza via"). In this case, that has proven more popular than the first two, the way of avoidance, whether knowingly chosen or not.

121–122. For the program of song in the last *cantica*, see the note to *Paradiso* XXI.58–60.

124–130. In the wake of the disappearance of the two nuns, the poet prepares us for the answers to the questions to which they have given rise. These lines could, without disrupting the reader's sense of order, have been moved forward into the next canto. As we have seen (since at least

Inferno VIII, which opens with the often-noted self-consciousness of the words "Io dico, seguitando . . ." [To continue, let me say . . .]), the reader experiences a sense that there was a kind of willful and arbitrary process at work in the poet's decisions about how a given canto should begin (or end). That Dante was increasingly amused by this practical poetic problem is evidenced in the growing number of ungainly narrative restarts as we move into *Purgatorio*. Dante obviously enjoyed playfully challenging our sense of proper beginnings and endings.

Battaglia Ricci (Batt.1989.1), p. 29, cites with approval Marti's argument (Mart.1964.1), p. 1385, for the circular movement of the canto, from Beatrice as Sun to Beatrice as Sun. (Dante is in the first case rewarded with an understanding of the dark places in the Moon; in the second he is promised an answer [if in rather disquieting terms] to the two questions that his interview with Piccarda has given rise to in him. Marti characterizes the first Beatrice as the "sun of love" and the second as the "sun of knowledge.")

PARADISO IV

OUTLINE

MOON (continues)
[a canto devoted to three questions of Dante]

1–63 *(1) do our [saved] souls return to our birth star?*

- 1–9 triple simile: man between two foods; lamb between two wolves; hound between two does: all compared to Dante between his first two questions
- 10–18 Beatrice (**Daniel**) comforts Dante (**Nebuchadnezzar**)
- 19–27 treating first the question that has more venom:
- 28–48 "accommodative metaphor" is her answer to it
- 49–63 hedging **Plato**'s wrongness (did *he* use metaphor?)

64–117 *(2) distinction between absolute and conditional will?*

- 64–72 Beatrice: this question has less of harm in it
- 73–90 Beatrice: **Lawrence** and **Mucius Scaevola**: wills firm
- 91–114 Beatrice: Piccarda's view does not contradict mine
- 115–117 coda: Dante's two questions now are fully answered

118–142 *(3) can broken vows be made good?*

- 118–132 Dante's gratitude for Beatrice's responses
- 133–138 her willingness to be of help and his curiosity urge another query: can a broken vow be made good?
- 139–142 Beatrice is so pleased by this question that her splendor overpowers Dante.

PARADISO IV

Intra due cibi, distanti e moventi
d'un modo, prima si morria di fame,
che liber' omo l'un recasse ai denti;

sì si starebbe un agno intra due brame
di fieri lupi, igualmente temendo;
sì si starebbe un cane intra due dame:

per che, s'i' mi tacea, me non riprendo,
da li miei dubbi d'un modo sospinto,
poi ch'era necessario, né commendo.

Io mi tacea, ma 'l mio disir dipinto
m'era nel viso, e 'l dimandar con ello,
più caldo assai che per parlar distinto.

Fé sì Beatrice qual fé Danïello,
Nabuccodonosor levando d'ira,
che l'avea fatto ingiustamente fello;

e disse: "Io veggio ben come ti tira
uno e altro disio, sì che tua cura
sé stessa lega sì che fuor non spira.

Tu argomenti: 'Se 'l buon voler dura,
la vïolenza altrui per qual ragione
di meritar mi scema la misura?'

Ancor di dubitar ti dà cagione
parer tornarsi l'anime a le stelle,
secondo la sentenza di Platone.

Queste son le question che nel tuo *velle*
pontano igualmente; e però pria
tratterò quella che più ha di felle.

Between two foods, equally near at hand and tempting,
left free to choose, a man would die of hunger
before he could bring either to his teeth—

so would a lamb stand still, caught between the cravings
of two ferocious wolves, in equal fear of both,
so would a hound, stock-still between two does:

just so, if I kept silent, urged in equal measure
by my doubts, I merit neither praise nor blame,
since my silence was forced, not freely chosen.

I kept silent, but my longing
and my questions all were painted on my face
more ardently than words could have expressed.

Beatrice did what Daniel did
when he freed Nebuchadnezzar from his wrath,
which had made him cruel unjustly,

by her words: 'It is clear to me you feel the pull
of two desires, so that your divided craving
binds itself so tight it can't breathe out.

'You reason: "If the will does not even waver
in devotion to the good, how can the violence
of another reduce my measure of reward?"

'Still another cause for your perplexity
is that you think, in accord with Plato's teaching,
the souls return to their own stars.

'These are the questions that weigh equally
upon your will. First I shall deal
with the one that has more venom in it.

D'i Serafin colui che più s'india,
Moïsè, Samuel, e quel Giovanni
che prender vuoli, io dico, non Maria,

non hanno in altro cielo i loro scanni
che questi spirti che mo t'appariro,
né hanno a l'esser lor più o meno anni;

ma tutti fanno bello il primo giro,
e differentemente han dolce vita
per sentir più e men l'etterno spiro.

Qui si mostraro, non perché sortita
sia questa spera lor, ma per far segno
de la celestïal c'ha men salita.

Così parlar conviensi al vostro ingegno,
però che solo da sensato apprende
ciò che fa poscia d'intelletto degno.

Per questo la Scrittura condescende
a vostra facultate, e piedi e mano
attribuisce a Dio e altro intende;

e Santa Chiesa con aspetto umano
Gabrïel e Michel vi rappresenta,
e l'altro che Tobia rifece sano.

Quel che Timeo de l'anime argomenta
non è simile a ciò che qui si vede,
però che, come dice, par che senta.

Dice che l'alma a la sua stella riede,
credendo quella quindi esser decisa
quando natura per forma la diede;

e forse sua sentenza è d'altra guisa
che la voce non suona, ed esser puote
con intenzion da non esser derisa.

'Not the Seraph that most ingods himself,
not Moses, Samuel, or whichever John you please—
none of these, I say, not even Mary,

'have their seats in another heaven
than do these spirits you have just now seen,
nor does their bliss last fewer years or more.

'No, all adorn the highest circle—
but they enjoy sweet life in differing measure
as they feel less or more of God's eternal breath.

'Those souls put themselves on view here
not because they are allotted to this sphere
but as a sign of less exalted rank in Heaven.

'It is necessary thus to address your faculties,
since only in perceiving through the senses can they grasp
that which they then make fit for intellect.

'For this reason Scripture condescends
to your capacity when it attributes hands and feet
to God, but has another meaning,

'and for your sake Holy Church portrays
Gabriel and Michael with the faces of men
and that other angel who made Tobit well again.

'What Timaeus has to say about the souls
does not resemble what one here observes
because he seems to take his words for facts.

'He claims the soul returns to its own star,
from which he thinks that it was drawn
when nature gave it bodily form.

'But perhaps his meaning differs
from what his words seem to express
and may have an intention not lightly mocked.

S'elli intende tornare a queste ruote
l'onor de la influenza e 'l biasmo, forse
in alcun vero suo arco percuote.

Questo principio, male inteso, torse
già tutto il mondo quasi, sì che Giove,
Mercurio e Marte a nominar trascorse.

L'altra dubitazion che ti commove
ha men velen, però che sua malizia
non ti poria menar da me altrove.

Parere ingiusta la nostra giustizia
ne li occhi d'i mortali, è argomento
di fede e non d'eretica nequizia.

Ma perché puote vostro accorgimento
ben penetrare a questa veritate,
come disiri, ti farò contento.

Se vïolenza è quando quel che pate
nïente conferisce a quel che sforza,
non fuor quest' alme per essa scusate:

ché volontà, se non vuol, non s'ammorza,
ma fa come natura face in foco,
se mille volte vïolenza il torza.

Per che, s'ella si piega assai o poco,
segue la forza; e così queste fero
possendo rifuggir nel santo loco.

Se fosse stato lor volere intero,
come tenne Lorenzo in su la grada,
e fece Muzio a la sua man severo,

così l'avria ripinte per la strada
ond' eran tratte, come fuoro sciolte;
ma così salda voglia è troppo rada.

'If he intends to assign to these wheels
the honor of their influence and the blame,
then his shaft may strike a certain truth.

'This principle, wrongly understood, once misled
nearly all the world so that it went astray
and named stars Jupiter, Mercury, and Mars.

'The other doubt that troubles you
contains less venom because its harm
could not lead you away from me.

'For divine justice to appear unjust
in mortal eyes is evidence of faith,
not of heretical iniquity.

'Since your human understanding is quite able
to penetrate this truth,
I shall content you as you wish.

'Even if violence is done when the one who bears it
in no way consents to the one who deals it out,
these souls were not excused on that account.

'For the will, except by its own willing, is not spent,
but does as by its nature fire does in flame,
though violence may force it down one thousand times.

'Thus, if it stays bent, whether much or little,
it then accepts that force, as indeed did these,
since they could have retreated to their holy place.

'Had their will remained unbroken,
as did the will that fastened Lawrence to the grate
and which made Mucius harsh to his own hand,

'then, once freed, it would have drawn them back
along the path from which they had been dragged.
But will so firm is all too rare.

E per queste parole, se ricolte
l'hai come dei, è l'argomento casso
che t'avria fatto noia ancor più volte.

Ma or ti s'attraversa un altro passo
dinanzi a li occhi, tal che per te stesso
non usciresti: pria saresti lasso.

Io t'ho per certo ne la mente messo
ch'alma beata non poria mentire,
però ch'è sempre al primo vero appresso;

e poi potesti da Piccarda udire
che l'affezion del vel Costanza tenne;
sì ch'ella par qui meco contradire.

Molte fïate già, frate, addivenne
che, per fuggir periglio, contra grato
si fé di quel che far non si convenne;

come Almeone, che, di ciò pregato
dal padre suo, la propria madre spense,
per non perder pietà si fé spietato.

A questo punto voglio che tu pense
che la forza al voler si mischia, e fanno
sì che scusar non si posson l'offense.

Voglia assoluta non consente al danno;
ma consentevi in tanto in quanto teme,
se si ritrae, cadere in più affanno.

Però, quando Piccarda quello spreme,
de la voglia assoluta intende, e io
de l'altra; sì che ver diciamo insieme."

Cotal fu l'ondeggiar del santo rio
ch'uscì del fonte ond' ogne ver deriva;
tal puose in pace uno e altro disio.

'And these words, if you have correctly understood them,
have destroyed an argument
that would have often troubled you again.

'But now before your eyes you find
another obstacle, so vast that your attempt
to overcome it on your own would leave you spent.

'Assuredly I have set it firmly in your mind
that a soul in bliss could never tell a lie,
since it is always near the primal Truth.

'But then you may have heard Piccarda say
that Constance kept her true love for the veil,
so that in this she seems to contradict me.

'Many times, brother, has it occurred
that, if unwillingly, to escape from harm,
one does a thing that had better not been done,

'as Alcmaeon, exhorted by his father,
slew his own mother: so as not to fail
in piety, he steeled himself to pity.

'At this point, I would ask you to reflect,
the threat of violence so mingles with the will
that these offenses cannot be excused.

'An absolute will consents not to the wrong,
but the will *does* consent to the extent it fears,
if it draws back, to fall into still greater harm.

'Piccarda, thus, in that which she affirms,
speaks of the absolute will, while I refer
to the other, so that we both maintain a truth.'

Such was the rippling of the holy stream,
issuing from the source from which all truth derives,
that put each one of my desires at peace.

"O amanza del primo amante, o diva,"
diss' io appresso, "il cui parlar m'inonda
e scalda sì, che più e più m'avviva,

non è l'affezion mia tanto profonda,
che basti a render voi grazia per grazia;
ma quei che vede e puote a ciò risponda.

Io veggio ben che già mai non si sazia
nostro intelletto, se 'l ver non lo illustra
di fuor dal qual nessun vero si spazia.

Posasi in esso, come fera in lustra,
tosto che giunto l'ha; e giugner puollo:
se non, ciascun disio sarebbe *frustra*.

Nasce per quello, a guisa di rampollo,
a piè del vero il dubbio; ed è natura
ch'al sommo pinge noi di collo in collo.

Questo m'invita, questo m'assicura
con reverenza, donna, a dimandarvi
d'un'altra verità che m'è oscura.

Io vo' saper se l'uom può sodisfarvi
ai voti manchi sì con altri beni,
ch'a la vostra statera non sien parvi."

Beatrice mi guardò con li occhi pieni
di faville d'amor così divini,
che, vinta, mia virtute diè le reni,
e quasi mi perdei con li occhi chini.

'O belovèd of the first Lover,' I said then,
'divine creature whose speech so floods and scalds me
that I am more and more alive,

'not all the depth of my affection
is enough to requite You grace for grace.
But may He who sees, and has the power, reward You.

'I now see clearly that our intellect
cannot be satisfied until that truth enlighten it
beyond whose boundary no further truth extends.

'In that truth, like a wild beast in its den, it rests
once it has made its way there—and it can do that,
or else its every wish would be in vain.

'Like a shoot, doubt springs
from the root of truth, and its nature
urges us toward the summit, from ridge to ridge.

'It is this, lady, that invites and assures me
to ask You, with reverence, about another truth
that still remains obscure to me.

'I would like to know if one can satisfy your court
with such other works for vows left unfulfilled
that in your scale their weight would not be scant.'

Beatrice looked at me with eyes so full
of the radiance of love and so divine
that, overcome, my power of sight faded and fled,
and, eyes cast down, I almost lost my senses.

1–9. This three-part opening simile is not so much difficult as it is puzzling. The residue of the confusion resulting from what he has seen and heard in the previous canto, it prepares the ground for the protagonist's two-pronged question for Beatrice about human liability. (1) How can a person not be guilty of a sin who wills to live the good life but somehow comes up short of doing so? (2) Where will this kind of saved soul be located in the afterlife? While readers are probably eventually able to make sense of the relationship between the tenor and the vehicle(s) of the simile, not a few nonetheless wonder about Dante's practice here. To deal with the tenor first, the prose sense of what is at stake is simple. The protagonist is so eager to have answers to both of his questions (and so afraid of what the answers might be) that he simply cannot decide which one to ask first and, instead of speaking, he is silent (vv. 7–9). As for the vehicles, to some only the first seems necessary, while the second may initially seem otiose, and the third redundant, since it only seems to repeat the substance of the first.

1–3. Bruno Nardi (Nard.1944.1), pp. 301–3, has argued that the widespread notion that these lines are a recasting of Buridan's famed paradox (starving donkey between two equally distant piles of straw) should be rejected. As Nardi and others have shown, the more certain source lies in the *Summa theologica* (I–II, q. 13, a. 6): "If any two things are absolutely equal, a man is not moved to the one more than to the other; just as a starving man, if he has food equally appetizing in different directions and at an equal distance, is not moved to the one more than to the other" (English text as found in Carroll's commentary to *Par.* IV.1–9). Further, and as Fallani (in his comm. to these verses) points out, Buridan's ass was posterior to Dante's *Paradiso*. Beginning with Lombardi (comm. to this tercet), and continuing into the twentieth century, one finds insistence on Thomas as source, neglecting Aristotle, for example, Tommaseo (comm. to this tercet); Andreoli (comm. to this tercet); Scartazzini (comm. to vv. 1–2); Poletto (comm. to vv. 1–6); Carroll (comm. to vv. 1–9), etc. The first commentators to put the two together, as is in our day fairly commonplace, were apparently Tozer in 1901 and Torraca in 1905, both in response to this tercet. However, if one reads farther in Thomas's passage, it is striking, as Sapegno points out (comm. to vv. 1–9), citing Nardi (Nard.1944.1), pp. 297–303, that Thomas has proposed this paradox only to refute its relationship to practical reality—as might any sensible person. Zeno's arrow and Buridan's ass (and Thomas's starving man, as Thomas himself insists) are the sorts of logically developed paradoxes that "philosophers" enjoy creating and that poets generally enjoy mocking. Here Thomas, Dante's "philosopher," rejects philosophical nonsense while Dante, our poet, seems to sponsor it.

4–5. The second vehicle of the simile seems, from what one may find in the commentary tradition, not to have a discernible source anywhere. If that is true, what we have here is pure Dantean invention, a post-Scholastic paradox added to Thomas's. Whereas in the first tercet Dante the questioner is likened to a hungry man unable to decide between two equally tempting foods (so long a time that he will, undirected by external agency, die), in these two lines he becomes the potential victim of his lupine questions, unable to decide which one to run from, since each looks equally fierce. While this part of the extended comparison surely seems askew, given the fact that Dante must choose which question to ask rather than which to avoid, the passage does impart something that will later be brought back into play (at verse 27): These questions are potentially destructive, and thus like (or at least not unlike) ravening wolves. And so, after initial puzzlement, a reader must admit that the apparently otiose comparison does pay its passage in the greater scheme. Angiolillo (Angi.1986.1) complains about the "incongruity" of this comparison, since it portrays immobility, not indecision; passivity, not aggression. But this is to miss Dante's point: Solutions of his two doubts seem equally attractive and, potentially at least, the concerns that give rise to each of them are equally destructive. For a hypothesis relating to Dante's own broken vow, which may account for the poet's "overkill" in this simile, offering a sense of what makes the questions both attractive and dangerous, see the second paragraph of the note to vv. 139–142.

6. While in the actual world two deer are capable of accomplishing more damage to a single dog than Dante's text allows, it is clear that the third vehicle of the simile displays exactly the same relationship as the first: hungry Dante between two equally tempting viands. Here some commentators do suggest a source (see Bosco/Reggio on this verse: Ovid [*Metam.* V.164–167], first suggested by Pietro di Dante and then by Daniello, and/or possibly, if Mattalia is correct, Virgil [*Georg.* III.539–540], as was first suggested by the author of the Codice Cassinese). Angiolillo (Angi.1986.1) proposes the passage from Ovid, and then adds another

from Seneca's drama *Thyestes*, 707–711. Whatever the source, what seems puzzling is the fact that our usually orderly and rigorous poet (or so we like to conceive him) here seems to have allowed himself an unnecessary repetition. It seems fair to say that, while detractors of the poet's inclusion of the second piece of business (see the note to vv. 4–5) have failed to take the point behind it, the several expressions of discomfort with the third part of the simile have not had sufficient response. However, experience teaches that Dante knows his business far better than we; if we fail to fathom his purposes, that does not necessarily require that he was without them. A possible solution is to suggest that the three-part simile mirrors the process of the protagonist's actual inner thoughts, moving from philosophical eagerness to fearful worry and then back to the first eagerness.

13–15. The simile puts into parallel Beatrice (placating Dante's anxiety) and Daniel (stilling Nebuchadnezzar's wrath). It thus also necessarily puts into parallel Dante and Nebuchadnezzar, a relation that at first seems to make no sense at all. The poet has already visited this text in the Bible (the second book of the prophet Daniel), the king's dream and the prophet's interpretation of it (see *Inf.* XIV.94–111 for Dante's version of that dream, embodied in the representation of the *veglio di Creta*). Here he fastens on its perhaps strangest aspect: the new king's desire to kill all the wise men in his kingdom of Babylon who could neither bring his forgotten dream back to mind nor then interpret it—about as unseemly a royal prerogative as anyone has ever sought to enjoy. Thus it seems natural to wonder in what way(s) Dante may possibly be conceived of as resembling the wrathful king of Babylon. The entire commentary tradition observes only a single link: Nebuchadnezzar's displeasure and Dante's puzzlement are both finally relieved by (divinely inspired—see Trucchi on these verses) external intervention on the part of Daniel, in the first case, of Beatrice in the second. Why should Dante have cast himself as the tyrannical Babylonian ruler? That is a question that has stirred only the shorelines of the ponds of commentaries and has never had an answer. If one looks in the *Epistle to Cangrande* (77–82), however, one finds a gloss to *Paradiso* I.4–9 that is germane here. And apparently, in any discussion of this passage, only G. R. Sarolli, in his entry "Nabuccodonosor" (*ED* IV [1973]), has noted the striking similarity in the two texts, going on to argue that this similarity serves as a further proof of the authenticity of the epistle. In that passage Dante explains that his forgetting of his experience of the Empyrean (because he was lifted beyond normal human experience and could not retain his vision) has some egregious precursors: St. Paul, three of Jesus' disciples, Ezechiel (their visionary capacity certified by the testimony of Richard of St. Victor, St. Bernard, and St. Augustine); and then he turns to his own unworthiness to be included in such company (if not hesitating to insist that he had been the recipient of such exalted vision): "But if on account of the sinfulness of the speaker [Dante himself, we want to remember] they should cry out against his claim to have reached such a height of exaltation, let them read Daniel, where they will find that even Nebuchadnezzar by divine permission beheld certain things as a warning to sinners, and straightway forgot them" (81—tr. P. Toynbee). Dante, like the Babylonian king, has had a vision that was God-given, only to forget it. And now he is, Nebuchadnezzar-like, distraught; Beatrice, like the Hebrew prophet, restores his calm. Thus the typological equation here is not idle; Dante *is* the new Nebuchadnezzar in that both he and the wrathful king, far from being holy men (indeed both were sinners), had access to visionary experience of God, only to forget their vision. The king enters this perhaps unusual history, that of forgetting a divine revelation on the part of those who were less than morally worthy, as "the first forgettor"; Dante, as the second (see Hollander [Holl.2005.1]).

16–18. We are now reminded that all the fuss (vv. 1–12) over Dante's paralyzed will, rendering him unable to choose which question to ask, was eventually in vain, since Beatrice can read his thoughts in God anyway. The poem, of course, needs to hold our attention and thus make Dante's choices important, even when they are technically unnecessary. His development, as sinner gradually being made worthy of the visionary experience of God and thus of salvation itself, is the major strand of the narrative of the *cantica*. And thus the poet may at times allow himself a certain latitude with the rules of his own game, making his work the richer for it.

19–27. Beatrice addresses the nature of Dante's questions. The first concerns the apparent fact that even a person who never ceases willing the good, and who ceases doing good only by virtue of the force of others, is in some way responsible for that failure. The second, zeroing in on a problem that we frequently encountered throughout the previous canto (see the note to *Par.* III.29–30), concerns the ultimate abode of the blessed: whether or not they return to dwell forever in the stars that most shaped their personalities. This is the more pernicious of these two dangerous questions and will thus be addressed first, if at lesser length, vv. 28–63 (Beatrice's answer to the first question will be found at vv. 64–114).

19–21. Beatrice makes the need to deal with Dante's first question seem even more pressing by revealing that for him it has a personal interest: It is *he* who wonders if his own merit might be diminished through no fault of his own.

24. Beatrice refers to Plato's teaching as it is found in his *Timaeus*. See the note to vv. 49–54. Torraca, in his comment to this verse, the phrase "secondo la sententia di Platone," cites Thomas's *Summa contra gentiles* (II.83), "secundum Platonis sententiam." Bosco/Reggio posit the possibility that, if Dante did not know the text of the *Timaeus* directly, he might have been acquainted with key portions of it through St. Augustine, St. Thomas, Albertus Magnus, Cicero, or Macrobius. This is the position, assumed tentatively, by most students of the question; some, however, take it that Dante did have direct knowledge of at least this one Platonic text. For Dante's knowledge of Plato in general and the *Timaeus* in particular, see Edward Moore (Moor.1896.1), pp. 156–64. The great British Dantist makes a sound case for Dante's direct acquaintance with Chalcidius's text of the *Timaeus* (41 D and E, 42 B, p. 157) in the relevant passages of this canto and *Convivio* IV.xxi.2 and II.xiii.5, although on one occasion he admits to a reasonable doubt in that respect, offering a near disclaimer in the clause "in whatever form it found its way to Dante" (p. 160). Margherita de Bonfils Templer (Debo.1987.1), building on her previous investigations (see p. 90, n. 5 for these), makes her case for Dante's use of the glosses to the *Timaeus* of Guillaume de Conches. And see her study of Platonic gnoseology in *Convivio* (Debo.1987.2). More recently, see Giuliana Carugati's investigation (Caru.1994.1) of Dante's reliance on Proclus in *Convivio* II and III. For a view counseling caution in attributing direct knowledge of the *Timaeus* to Dante, who refers to the work by name only once in *Convivio* (III.v.6) and then here, see Marta Cristiani, "Timeo," *ED* V (1976), pp. 604–5. See also her entries "Platone," *ED* IV (1973), pp. 546–50, and "platonismo," *ED* IV (1973), pp. 550–55.

25–27. Both of the protagonist's questions reflect a dangerous uncertainty on his part about the nature of free will, which will be the subject of Beatrice's urgent lecture at the beginning of the next canto. If he believes that compromise in making vows is possible or that our souls' choices are controlled by the stars that govern our natures, he is in heresy. The second doubt, since it would destroy the notion of free will utterly (and not just partially), is the more dangerous, which is why Beatrice chooses to address it first. As Trucchi, discussing this tercet, points out, Plato's notion that souls return to their formative stars, embraced by some early Christians, was finally condemned at the Council of Constantinople in the year 540.

25. Dante's use of the Latin infinitive as a noun is not without precedent in the work: See *Purgatorio* V.24, *Miserere*; *Paradiso* III.79, *esse* (to be [as substantive, "being"]); *Paradiso* XIX.2, *frui*; and, more interestingly in this context, *Paradiso* XXXIII.143, where *velle* (to will [as substantive, "the will"]) itself reappears, once again rhyming with *stelle* (stars). That only other recurrence of this Latin word may be more programmatic than has been noticed. Plato's apparent doctrine, rejected here, receives a final disapproving glance in the last lines of the poem, in which Dante has his final vision of the universe as it truly is, and not as Plato's *Timaeus* (and Dante's *Convivio* [IV.xxi.2]: "Plato and others maintained that they issued from the stars and were more or less noble according to the nobility of their star"—tr. Lansing; and see also *Conv.* II.xiii.5) might have us believe.

There are some seventy-five Latin words or passages incorporated in this insistently vernacular work, more than half of them in its most "churchly" *cantica*, *Purgatorio*, as is not surprising.

28–39. Beatrice's refutation is in three main parts:

- (1) Scriptural justification for God's showing saved souls in the stars, vv. 28–39.
  - (1a) why such ways of presenting divine truth are necessary, vv. 40–48.
- (2) Plato's possible error in the *Timaeus*, vv. 49–54.
- (3) Plato's potential agreement with Christian doctrine, vv. 55–63.

The first part refutes not only what Dante has shown himself to believe in the previous canto, namely that the souls in the Moon are there permanently (see the note to *Par.* III.29–30), but resolves what Piccarda and even Beatrice (depending on how one reads verse 30 of *Par.* III) had left an open question. Now we are told by Beatrice, definitively, that no soul of Paradise is present in any star, except for the occasion of Dante's visit to the spheres. Thus if, while reading the ending of the last canto, we may (quite reasonably) have thought that Piccarda and Constance were heading back into the matter of the Moon, we now probably have to understand that they have returned to their home in the Empyrean.

28. Indicating only the highest rank of angels, the Seraphim, Beatrice reminds Dante that *all* the nine ranks of angels are in the Empyrean and

are the beings closest to God. Here the poet resolves a potential problem, similar to that caused by the appearance of the souls in the spheres, in that readers might eventually assume that the angelic order most associated with a certain heaven actually dwells in that heaven. This verse cancels that potential reading before it can be applied.

29–30. Moses, Samuel, John the Baptist, John the Evangelist, and Mary are all to be found in that same placeless place known as the Empyrean. When we read *Paradiso* XXXII, we will find all of these but Samuel represented as having been seen by the protagonist among the eighteen souls actually pointed out there by St. Bernard. Beatrice's little list is "ecumenical," involving two Hebrews (Moses and Samuel in the role of the first and last "great jurists" of Israel, as it were), one "Hebrew-Christian" (the Baptist), and two Christians (John and Mary). Since all four whom we do eventually see in the Rose are in its highest tier, we may assume that Samuel is at that level also. (Why Dante has chosen Samuel, rather than Abraham, Solomon, David, or still another, is not immediately clear; see the discussion in the note to verse 29.) It would also seem likely that Dante is paralleling elements in his angelic and human populations of the Rose, referring only to the highest rank of each, thus distinguished from all who are at lower levels.

29. The meaning of Beatrice's remark is not difficult to grasp. The angels (she refers to the highest order, the Seraphim, but from the context we know that she means all nine orders) and all the blessed are found, and found only, in the Empyrean. From *Par.* XXXII we know that four of the five saints referred to here are in the highest rank of the stadium-rose: Moses (vv. 131–132), John the Baptist (vv. 31–33), John the Evangelist (vv. 127–128), Mary (vv. 88–93). Samuel is not among the eighteen saints referred to in that canto, but since all four who have been, like their Seraphic counterparts, elevated to the topmost rank, we are probably meant to understand that Samuel has been also; that is, we are to understand that he is there, even if we do not see him.

But why Dante singles him out here (and why he passes him over in silence in *Par.* XXXII) are questions rarely formed and perhaps never answered. Tommaseo (comm. to vv. 28–30) was perhaps the first to refer to the fact that Moses and Samuel were referred to only once in the same passage of Scripture, Jeremiah 15:1: "Then said the Lord unto me, Though Moses and Samuel stood before me, yet my mind could not be toward this people: cast them out of my sight, and let them go forth." G. R. Sarolli, "Samuele," *ED* IV (1973), does improve upon the relatively sorry record of the commentators, who just do not seem to realize that this sudden appearance of Samuel in the poem calls for study. Why, for instance, if Dante wants to pick a pair of Old Testament "heroes," does he not couple Moses with his favorite Hebrew figure, David? Perhaps, since Samuel was the last of the Judges of Israel, in Dante's mind he balances the first Hebrew "law-giver," Moses (see *Inf.* IV.57). Sarolli points to Samuel's position among the exegetes as *typus Christi* as well as a figure of John the Baptist and to his role in transferring the kingly power from Saul to David as clues to Dante's reasons for his lofty placement in the *Commedia*. (But why, we wonder, was not that lofty placement confirmed, as it was for his four fellow nominees, in *Par.* XXXII?) Toynbee had already made the point that the rest of Dante's references to Samuel by name (*Mon.* II.vii.8; III.vi.1–6; *Epist.* VII.19) have to do with Samuel's intervention that resulted in the termination of Saul's kingship. (This last passage is a casuistic argument, in which Dante insists that Samuel had the power to depose Saul *not* because he was God's vicar, which the hierocrats insisted was indeed true [thus buttressing their case for papal intervention in imperial affairs], but because God selected him as an "angelic" messenger, His direct emissary.) Such is dramatically true of Dante's second epistle to Henry VII (*Epist.* VII.19), in which he compares Henry to Saul, about to be dethroned by Samuel (I Samuel 15), and in which his accusations put Dante unmistakably in Samuel's place. If the order of composition of these Samuel-Saul passages is *Epistle* VII (late 1311), *Paradiso* IV, *Monarchia* II and III, the last three likely written within only a few months of one another in circa 1314, we may begin to have an inkling of why Samuel, so long absent from Dante's pages, should suddenly have sprung to life in them. Henry's foundering kingship shows the need for a new Samuel to hector the struggling king, a role that Dante, no stranger to answering an elevated call to action, tries to take on. For Henry's increasing similarity to Saul, see the article referred to by Filippo Bognini (Bogn.2007.1), p. 93 (n. 54). By the time he is writing *Paradiso* XXXII, Henry is dead, and thus well beyond useful hectoring.

31–32. Piccarda and Constance, we are told, are in the same space as that occupied by these glorious figures. Thinking of it this way, we can understand why they are not in the least disturbed by their lower rank within the Rose (*Par.* III.70–87). Exactly where in the celestial rose they are seated is never revealed to us; we know only that they are fairly low in it (but at least halfway up, above the innocent babes [see *Par.* XXXII.37–48] and yet beneath the height attained by St. Clare [see *Par.* III.98–99], whatever that may be).

33. The souls in Plato's *Timaeus* are said to remain longer periods in their stars in accord with their greater goodness, a bit of doctrine slapped aside in this single verse. The slap also hits the cheek of Dante himself: See the text of *Convivio* IV.xxi.2, cited in the note to verse 25, above.

34. Rhyme apparently forces Dante into a self-contradiction. The Empyrean is not a *giro* (circle), like the revolving physical heavens, but a point, both infinitely large (*Par.* XXXIII.85–93) and infinitely small (*Par.* XXVIII.16–21). Nonetheless, here he says it is a *giro*.

35. The phrase *dolce vita* (sweet life), here used for the first time to indicate the life of the blessed in God's eternal presence (see also *Par.* XX.48, XXV.93), has a biting resonance in Federico Fellini's Dante-haunted film of 1960, *La dolce vita*.

36. The relative beatitude of the blessed is defined as the result of their greater or lesser ability to respond to the breath of the Holy Spirit. Normal human competitiveness makes it hard to imagine human beings, even fairly selfless and generous ones, taking joy in their lesser ability to respond to God's love. On the other hand, our experience of some artists, musicians, and athletes reveals that there are indeed professionals who gladly admire the greater ability of their betters and enjoy participation in the same activity in which these "stars" excel. Unfortunately, there is probably less such admirable conduct than one might hope.

37. This verse seals Beatrice's presentation of the temporary nature of the souls' presence in the Moon, as she uses a past definite (*si mostraro* [put themselves on view here]) to indicate that they no longer do so—their time in the Moon is over. See the similar use of the past definite in verse 32, *appariro* (appeared), which probably also indicates that they are no longer present.

39. Beatrice's words have given rise to a series of misreadings. What Dante says is that Piccarda and her companions in the Moon occupy a less exalted rank in Heaven; commentators (and translators) tend to say that they occupy *the least* (i.e., the very lowest) of the heavenly ranks. However, the comparative adverb *meno* (less) is never used in the *Commedia* as a superlative. The reason for this attempt to turn Dante's vague placement of them into something far more definite is perhaps found in an assumption that, if these women are here encountered in the lowest heaven, they must

then be in the lowest rank of Heaven. The poem does not permit any such certainty. See the note to vv. 31–32.

40–42. The need to speak to the human intellect in terms reflecting the experience of the senses will be more fully explored in the next two tercets, the corollary, as it were, to what has just been said here. And here Dante presents familiar Thomistic insistence on the priority (and usefulness) of sense data, an Aristotelian position and most certainly a counter-Platonic one.

40. For a study of the word *ingegno* in the *Commedia* (a word introduced at *Inf.* II.7 and then found some eighteen times, with a last appearance in *Par.* XXIV.81), taking this passage as his point of departure, see Dumol (Dumo.1998.1), pp. 1–13, 177–95. And for the source of Dante's concept in Aristotle (*Ethics* VI.1), as commented upon and developed by Aquinas, see pp. 95–124. This is the faculty called "racionativum," the *vis cogitativa*, that is, practical or scientific knowledge.

43–48. The phenomenon referred to by Beatrice, of ancient Christian lineage, is known as accommodative metaphor. Put simply (and Dante's text does this admirably), it is the metaphoric presentation of higher things and higher beings that ordinary mortals simply have not the experiential background to understand. (For the closeness of Dante's presentation of it here to the exposition made by St. Thomas, see Hollander [Holl.1969.1], p. 192, and Dumol [Dumo.1998.1], pp. 5–6.) For example, angels are pure being (or, as Dante would say, "pure act" [see *Par.* XXIX.33]) and have no visible aspect. So that we may better conceive them, we are allowed to think of them as having wings, faces, voices, and other attributes. Similarly, God Himself is beyond any anthropomorphic human imagining, but Scripture allows us to think of Him as having hands and feet and so on.

In an important sense, almost all of Dante's experience of the afterworld in the first thirty cantos of this canticle is metaphoric, that is, what he sees in the stars is there only temporarily, and for illustrative purposes. For similar understandings, see Freccero, "*Paradiso* X: The Dance of the Stars" (Frec.1986.1 [1968]), pp. 221–26; Hollander (Holl.1969.1), pp. 192–201; Chiarenza (Chia.1972.1); Mazzotta (Mazz.1979.1), pp. 246–47; Barolini (Baro.1992.1), pp. 143–65; and Moevs (Moev.1999.1). And see the appreciation of a Harvard freshman, Chris Hampson, in a seminar in the autumn of 2005: "The whole point is that this is *not* what it's really like."

46–48. As examples of ways in which we may have a graphic sense of exactly what the phrase "accommodative metaphor" signifies, church windows to this day represent angels with human features, while even seven hundred years ago Dante knew that angels were disembodied, were "pure act" (*Par.* XXIX.33). Humans are allowed to conceive of such higher realities in more concrete and familiar terms. Unnamed, Raphael joins periphrastically his two fellow Archangels, the ones most frequently referred to in literature and life. Indeed, only Gabriel and Michael enjoy a presence in the standard Bible, while Raphael's is limited to the Book of Tobit (see the note to verse 48).

48. Raphael is generally accounted one of the seven angels "who stand before the Lord" (Apocalypse 8:2). The apocryphal book of Enoch (chapter 21) furnishes the names of the four others, of whom only Uriel is much known today (and then mainly through his presence in Milton's *Paradise Lost*). The story of how this Archangel allowed Tobias to cure the blindness of his father, Tobit, is told in the now apocryphal Book of Tobias (11:2–15). That Dante elected to use this particular circumlocutory detail to identify Raphael may seem puzzling. However, it was one of the few concrete details associated with this Archangel known to him. And consult *Paradiso* XXVI.12 for another brief reference to a miraculous cure for blindness, that conferred by the laying on of hands by Ananias. For a substantial recounting, one nearly as controlled and entertaining as a *novella* by Boccaccio, of the startling biblical narrative concerning Tobias and Raphael, see the commentary of Jacopo della Lana to vv. 40–48.

49–54. The *Timaeus* argues that the souls of the dead return to the stars that gave them birth. This is heresy, *tout court*, if it is meant literally. Beatrice's correction of Dante's error, concocted in the previous canto as a recapitulation of the error he had in fact first made in the *Convivio*, should end our own confusion as to the presence of the souls in the spheres. They appear in a sort of cosmic accommodative metaphor, thus suggesting that all the last canticle up to its thirtieth canto (with a brief hiatus in the twenty-third—see the note to *Par.* XXIII.61–63) is a vast metaphoric preparation for the seeing face-to-face that will occur in the Empyrean. Further, such an understanding reminds us how "historical," how "real" everything described and seen in the first two canticles has seemed in comparison.

51. The verb *par[e]* (seems) begins to open the door to Dante's attempt to hedge his attack on certain of Plato's views in vv. 55–60.

54. The reference to "form" here indicates, in language reflective of Scholastic terminology, an individuated human soul that inhabits a specific body.

55–63. Dante opens the question of the potential truth to be found in Plato's literally untrue teachings. Here again (see the note to vv. 13–15) the reader will want to turn to the *Epistola a Cangrande*, again near its conclusion (84): "For we perceive many things by the intellect for which language has no terms—a fact which Plato indicates plainly enough in his books by his employment of metaphors; for he perceived many things by the light of the intellect which his everyday language was inadequate to express" (tr. P. Toynbee).

Dante's view of Plato would seem to indicate great respect (if not as much as for Aristotle, given greater praise than his teacher in *Inferno* IV), a sense that some of his teaching was potentially or actually heretical, and a further sense of admiration, perhaps based principally on what in Plato he found most poetlike, his use of metaphor to express truth slantwise. In both major moments in which Dante discusses Plato, here and in the *Epistle*, the salient subject is, indeed, Plato's use of metaphor. It is possible that Dante is fervently opposed to those who read Plato as a teller of literal truth (in which reading he is nothing short of a heretic *avant-la-lettre*, as are, on historical grounds, the neoplatonists, in Dante's view). It seems possible, however, that Dante is willing to allow the philosopher himself a potential escape route; he may have seemed to him, in the end, more like a poet than a philosopher. Dante's teacher, Thomas Aquinas, is cited by Oelsner (comm. to verse 51) as allowing for the possibility, just as we have seen Dante do here, of a possible metaphoric truth in some of Plato's *dicta* that are literally untrue.

55–57. Bosco/Reggio, in their comment on this passage, point out that its source may lie in Albertus Magnus, *De natura et origine animae* (II.7), since that is a sure source for the embryology of *Purgatorio* XXV, as was established by Bruno Nardi ("L'origine dell'anima umana secondo Dante" [1931–32], repr. in Nard.1960.2). Should that be true (and, as they argue, it seems likely that it is, since there is little to suggest Dante really knew any Plato directly, even in Latin translation), it would deeply undercut the notion that Dante's acquaintance with the *Timaeus* was firsthand. And this would also reveal that Dante had a noted precursor in trying at least to open the question of Plato's possible acceptability to Christian thinkers, as one tradition has even no less a rigorist than Thomas Aquinas doing (see the last sentence of the note to vv. 55–63).

55. For the view that the meaning of *sentenza* here must be "intention," see Sanguineti (Sang.1999.2). But Dante's usual practice and the likely significance of this tercet point rather in the direction of "meaning," as any number of commentators believe. And see, for a previous use of the word in this canto, verse 24, "secondo la sentenza di Platone" (in accord with Plato's teaching).

58–60. The nature of Dante's own "modified astrology" has already been made clear in Marco Lombardo's discussion of free will and its relationship to astral influence, particularly in *Purgatorio* XVI.67–84. While any astrology at all seems mere foolishness to most modern readers, Dante's position, which mirrors that of St. Augustine, is that whatever influence the stars have on us, it in no way reduces our ability to choose the good. Our birth stars may incline us in one direction or another (see *Par.* VIII.122–135), but we remain totally responsible for our choices, our actions.

61–63. The "unenlightened" theory of astral influence sponsored by the ancients (and possibly by Plato) resulted in the naming of the planets for the powers (and limitations) they conferred on human beings. Dante's version supersedes that theory and restores free will to human conduct.

62. The exceptions among the ancients were, naturally, the monotheistic Hebrews.

64–117. Dante's first question, dealt with second because it has less "venom" in it (verse 27), finally has its day in court. That it is less potentially dangerous to the health of the soul does not mean that it is not worrisome, as the amount of space it receives now (over fifty lines) attests. It, too, centrally involves freedom of the will.

64–66. Beatrice suggests that the protagonist's failure to understand the precise rules that govern the keeping of vows, unlike the larger issue of freedom of the will, is less likely to interfere with his love for her, his guide to the truth found in God. His potential problem with his second "doubt" is a total one, while this one is only partial.

67–69. Beatrice offers up another paradox (see her argument in *Purg.* XXXIII.94–99 that Dante's inability to remember his sins is the very proof that he committed them): For mortals *not* to understand divine justice is evidence (the probable meaning of *argomento* here, though there is debate on the point) that it exists.

70–72. Because the nature of this question concerning vows is not so lofty that a closer-to-divine intelligence is required for its solution, Beatrice will be able to explain it fully to mortal Dante.

73–81. Beatrice is brutally clear: Since the will by its very nature always seeks the good, any capitulation to external force is a violation of God's love. A modern reader may sense a certain outrage at this line of thought. It would seem to call for martyrdom as the only adequate response if another would divert us from our true path by use of force or the threat of force. As the following examples will make plain (vv. 82–87), that is exactly what is called for. If we fail to keep our absolute will intact (the term is employed at verse 109; see the note to that passage, vv. 109–114), allowing it to be swayed by fear, we are guilty of the sin that afflicted both Piccarda and Constance, who should have found some way to return to the cloister, no matter what harm they thought they might have faced in so doing. Dante's doctrine is as simple and as terrifying as that. For discussion of these questions, see Singleton's commentary to vv. 73–74; 76–78.

77–78. The image of the flame that, temporarily twisted by external force from its natural upright position, will always by its very nature raise itself back up underlines the natural propensity of the will to the good, despite the force that may be used against it.

82–87. As he did so often in *Purgatorio*, Dante combines a Christian and a pagan exemplary figure to make his point: "St. Lawrence, a deacon of the Church of Rome, said to have been a native of Huesca in Spain who suffered martyrdom under the Emperor Valerian, Aug. 10, 258. The tradition is that, being commanded by the prefect of Rome to deliver up the treasures of the Church which had been entrusted to his charge by Pope Sixtus II, he replied that in three days he would produce them. On the expiration of the appointed time he presented to the prefect all the sick and poor to whom he had given alms, with the words 'Behold the treasures of Christ's Church.' The prefect thereupon directed St. Lawrence to be tortured, in order to make him reveal where the treasures were hidden. But, torture proving ineffectual, he was stretched on an iron frame with bars, like a gridiron, beneath which a fire was kindled so that his body was gradually consumed. In the midst of his agony he is said to have remained steadfast, and to have mocked his executioners, bidding them to turn his body that it might be equally roasted on both sides (cf. Prudentius, *Peristephanon liber* 401–9)" (T). "Gaius Mucius Scaevola, Roman citizen who, when Lars Porsena of Clusium was besieging Rome, made his way into the enemy's camp with the intention of killing Porsena; by mistake, however, he stabbed the king's secretary instead of the king himself. Being seized, Mucius was ordered by the king to be burned alive, whereupon he thrust his right hand into a fire, which was already lighted for a sacrifice, and held it in the flames without flinching. Porsena, struck with admiration at his fortitude, ordered him to be set free; in return Mucius informed him that there were 300 noble youths in Rome who had sworn to take the king's life, that the lot had fallen upon him to make the first attempt, and that his example would be followed by the others, each as his turn came. Porsena, impressed with this account of the determination of the Romans, made proposals of peace and withdrew from the siege. From the circumstance of the loss of his right hand, Mucius was thenceforward known as Scaevola ('left-handed'). Dante [also] mentions Mucius in connexion with this incident [in] *Conv.* IV.v.13; and, with a reference to Livy (*Ab urbe* II.12) as his authority in *Mon.* II.v.14" (T). Will so firm as that, however, is rarely found. Nonetheless, willingness to accept even martyrdom remains the only eventual solution for this problem. And the example of Scaevola makes the message even more painful: One must be prepared to do violence even against oneself in the service of liberty.

89–90. For Beatrice's paraphrase of Dante's unthinking analysis of the problem addressed here, see vv. 19–21. It has now been "canceled" and should trouble him no more.

91–99. Beatrice now offers a sort of corollary to the message she has just delivered, anticipating Dante's further question: How can Piccarda be telling the truth when she says that neither she nor Constance ever ceased wanting to be back in their convents (*Par.* III.112–117), if what Beatrice has just said is true?

94–96. This passage makes crystal clear what has surely been evident earlier (most recently at *Par.* III.31–33, but as early as the second canto of *Inferno*, when we see Beatrice through Virgil's eyes, in his description of her and her "vere parole" [*Inf.* II.135]): The souls of those in bliss never tell less than the absolute truth.

100–108. Starting with a general remark, Beatrice attempts to clarify her position. Humans frequently do things they know they should not do, both against their own will and to escape from harm. The example she adduces, that of Alcmaeon, does not, however, seem to fulfill the second part of her precision. Further, Dante seems to have muddled his version of the story of Alcmaeon, nearly certainly derived from Statius (*Thebaid* II.265–305). (And see also Ovid, *Metamorphoses* IX.406–415.) In Statius, Alcmaeon is the son of Amphiaraus and Eriphyle; he avenged his father's death by killing his mother, who, bought off by the gift of a necklace, revealed Amphiaraus's hiding place to those who wanted to take him into battle with them and, because of her intervention, succeeded in doing so (see *Purg.* XII.49–51 [and note]).

Beatrice's description, in any case, does fit Piccarda's tale perfectly. She did something she did not want to do (leaving her convent) and did not return from fear of what might be done to her if she tried to—at least that is what Dante would seem to want us to believe.

109–114. Beatrice's distinction is between the absolute will (the Latin term, *absoluta voluntas*, reflects its root in the verb *absolvere*, to release from obligation) and another will, unnamed, that theologians refer to as the "conditioned" (or "conditional") will, that is, a will conditioned by circumstance. "*Assoluta* here means 'absolute' as contrasted with 'relative.' Independently of the circumstances (i.e., of the pressure of fear) the will does not consent to the wrong forced upon it; but when affected by fear of worse suffering in case of withdrawing itself from the pressure of that force, so far it does consent. So Piccarda, when she speaks of Constance's life, does not take into account her yielding to fear, while Beatrice does take it into account, and therefore regards her as defective in the observance of her vows. Thus both their statements are true" (Tozer to vv. 109–114). For example, one wants desperately to stop smoking but, like Svevo's Zeno, continually yields to the abysmal need to smoke one last cigarette. Piccarda's absolute will was always to desire the life of her convent; her conditioned will was to accept the marriage into which she was forced. And thus there is no contradiction between what she says of herself and what Beatrice describes as a blameworthy failure in her vows. They are speaking of two differing aspects of willing.

115–116. In a poem controlled by large metaphoric constructs (e.g., light, road, forest, mountain, sea, ship, wings, city, tree, plant, beast, etc.), the third *cantica* nonetheless stands out for its metaphoric exertions. The last developed metaphor in a canto that began by studying the justification for metaphor, this passage (and many another after it) shows Dante's determination to up the "poetic ante" for his reader, asked to follow a difficult mind, setting about its work giving expression to theological/philosophical concepts in emotionally charged lyric language. On the subject of metaphor in Dante (far less visited than the related topic of simile), see at least Raimondi (Raim.1986.1) and Pasquini (Pasq.1996.2 and Pasq.2001.1, pp. 179–217).

This particular metaphor has furnished the opening of *Purgatorio* XXI with its biblical material, the water of life that Jesus offers the Samaritan woman. And here it is Beatrice who is equated with Jesus, bringing the source of that water to humankind.

118–138. Dante's lengthy and flowery expression of his gratitude to Beatrice for her explanation and of his humility before God's mysteries serves as *captatio benevolentiae* in disposing Beatrice to answer still one more question—not that she requires any such suasion. Once again, the needs of the poem come first.

122. Dante addresses Beatrice with the respectful *voi*, as he will also do at verse 134; but see the note to vv. 136–138.

130–132. Tozer (comm. to this tercet) explains this difficult text as follows: " 'Owing to this desire of knowing the Divine Verity, doubt arises at the foot of truth as saplings rise from the foot of a tree.' *Appiè del vero*: This is another way of saying that it springs from the root of truth, that idea being suggested by the metaphor: the doubt is a germ of truth. *è natura*, &c.: 'it is a natural process, which impels us from height to height unto the summit.' By the questions which arise from learning a truth, we are led on to the apprehension of a higher truth, and so onwards till the highest is reached."

136–138. Dante's third question will be the subject of the first eighty-four verses of the following canto. Thus all of the present canto and over half of the next is devoted to three questions concerning the freedom of the will, the most important issue confronting a moralizing Christian writer. It is probably not accidental that Dante chose to put this discussion here, in the first sphere, that of the Moon, reflecting the fact that the first three realms of the heavens present saved souls whose virtues were unmistakably marred by significant defect (see the note to *Par.* III.47–49). Most of *Paradiso* is concerned with the correction and perfection of Dante's intellect. Its beginning offers a chance to reengage with the world of moral choice, so inviting to a writer who never gave up his engagement with the affairs of humankind in this life.

139–142. This passage offers a variant on the theme of blindness already present in this canto in the reference to Tobias in verse 48 (and see the note to that verse) and reworked in Canto XXVI.12, with its reference to Ananias's restoration of Saul's sight. There Beatrice's increasingly evident power completely (if only temporarily) destroys his power of sight; here Dante is weakened by Beatrice's overpowering glance, his eyes so overcome that they, in a trope developed from military behavior, are temporarily routed by the Beatricean ocular "army." Most unmilitary, Dante nearly faints, as he did, for very different reasons, at the conclusions of *Inferno* III and V.

A possible reason for the poet's desire to underline the protagonist's guilty feelings about Beatrice comes from the context we have just now entered, his first enunciation (at vv. 136–138) of his question (see Beatrice's rephrasing of it in the following canto, *Par.* V.13–15) about the possibility of redemption for broken vows. We do know that Dante had made at least one vow that he had spectacularly failed to fulfill. In *Vita nuova* XLII.2 he had made a solemn promise: "Sì che, se piacere sarà di colui a cui tutte le cose vivono, che la mia vita duri per alquanti anni, io spero di dicer di lei quello che mai non fue detto d'alcuna" (Accordingly, if it be the pleasure of Him through whom all things live that my life continue for a few more years, I hope to write of her that which has never been written of any other woman [tr. M. Musa]).

And so, while Bosco/Reggio (comm. to verse 138) are probably correct that Dante's question is meant to be understood as being addressed formally to all in bliss with Piccarda (and see Tommaseo comm. to vv. 136–138, citing verse 67, where Beatrice mentions "la nostra giustizia" [our justice] in much the same context), the earlier addresses to Beatrice (vv. 122, 134) stay in our ears and cause a certain ambiguity. Is Dante still addressing his *guida*, or is he pondering the opinion of the saints? This is perhaps a case of Dante trying to hide behind the mask of a more general appeal: "Do you all up here know if mortals are allowed to make broken vows good by substituting other things for them?". That is preferable to asking Beatrice if God can ever forgive his not making good the vow he made to honor her at the end of the *Vita nuova*, only to write *Convivio* instead, a work in which she is abandoned for the Lady Philosophy. Dante, hidden behind that impersonal formulation (delivered by that noun used as a pronoun, *l'uom* [one]), wonders whether or not he might still make amends for his broken promise with this poem in Beatrice's honor. Such a decision is not in the lap of these "gods," in fact, but belongs to the Father. He has obviously decided in favor of the claimant, otherwise the voyage would not have been granted him.

PARADISO V

OUTLINE

MOON and MERCURY

(1) *Dante's third question (from Canto IV)*

1–12 Beatrice: Dante's inability to look at her is only to be expected, given the divine love that she reflects

13–15 Beatrice rephrases Dante's question (see IV. 136–138)

16–18 the poet's interruption: the beginning of this canto

19–33 her answer: free will God's greatest gift to angels and humans; thus the importance of vows taken freely

34–42 she adds: but the Church does allow substitution (she apparently contradicts herself but will soon clarify)

43–45 two things are essential to this sacrifice: that which is promised and the form of the promise:

46–51 the second (the "form") can never be "canceled" short of fulfillment (see vv. 32–33);

52–54 as for what is offered, some change is possible—

55–60 but only with sacerdotal permission and if the thing substituted is of greater value;

61–63 if the original vow is "heavier," the substitution is not permitted.

64–72 Beatrice (indirectly) addresses mortals: do not take vows lightly, as did **Jephthah** and **Agamemnon**

73–84 she now addresses Christians directly: given their authorities (Bible and pope), they have no excuses

(2) *The ascent to Mercury*

85–87 Dante as "scribe" of Beatrice, who looks upward

88–90 her silence and new appearance quell several questions in Dante as they speed upward

91–93 simile: arrow striking target before bowstring stops vibrating: that's how quickly they arrive in Mercury;

94–96 Beatrice's increased joy makes the planet brighter,

97–99 and if the planet changed, think how Dante changed

(3) *The saved who appear in Mercury*

100–108 simile: fish in pond thinking they'll be fed compared to spirits approaching Dante, joyfully effulgent

109–114 address to reader: "if *you* would like to hear more, only think how much more *I* wanted to hear!"

115–120 Dante is welcomed by a heavenly soul who promises to satisfy him (this is **Justinian**, as we shall learn)

121–123 Dante is urged by Beatrice to speak and believe

124–129 Dante wants to know who this spirit is and why he possesses this degree of beatitude

130–132 the "light" grows brighter at this request

133–139 simile: as the sun hides itself in its own light once its "vapors" burn away, this soul hid himself in his.

PARADISO V

"S'io ti fiammeggio nel caldo d'amore
di là dal modo che 'n terra si vede,
sì che del viso tuo vinco il valore,

non ti maravigliar, ché ciò procede
da perfetto veder, che, come apprende,
così nel bene appreso move il piede.

Io veggio ben sì come già resplende
ne l'intelletto tuo l'etterna luce,
che, vista, sola e sempre amore accende;

e s'altra cosa vostro amor seduce,
non è se non di quella alcun vestigio,
mal conosciuto, che quivi traluce.

Tu vuo' saper se con altro servigio,
per manco voto, si può render tanto
che l'anima sicuri di letigio."

Sì cominciò Beatrice questo canto;
e sì com' uom che suo parlar non spezza,
continüò così 'l processo santo:

"Lo maggior don che Dio per sua larghezza
fesse creando, e a la sua bontate
più conformato, e quel ch'e' più apprezza,

fu de la volontà la libertate;
di che le creature intelligenti,
e tutte e sole, fuoro e son dotate.

Or ti parrà, se tu quinci argomenti,
l'alto valor del voto, s'è sì fatto
che Dio consenta quando tu consenti;

'If I flame at you with a heat of love
beyond all measure known on earth
so that I overcome your power of sight,

'do not wonder, for this is the result
of perfect vision, which, even as it apprehends,
moves its foot toward the apprehended good.

'I see clearly how, reflected in your mind,
the eternal light that, once beheld,
alone and always kindles love, is shining.

'And, if anything else beguiles your mortal love,
it is nothing but a remnant of that light, which,
incompletely understood, still shines in it.

'You want to know if a vow left unfulfilled
may be redeemed by some exchange
that then secures the soul from challenge.'

Thus did Beatrice begin this canto and,
like a man who does not interrupt his speech,
continued thus her holy discourse:

'The greatest gift that God in His largesse
gave to creation, the most attuned
to His goodness and that He accounts most dear,

'was the freedom of the will:
all creatures possessed of intellect,
all of them and they alone, were and are so endowed.

'Now will be clear to you, reasoning from this,
the lofty worth of vows, as long as they are such
that God consent when you consent.

ché, nel fermar tra Dio e l'omo il patto,
vittima fassi di questo tesoro,
tal quale io dico; e fassi col suo atto.

Dunque che render puossi per ristoro?
Se credi bene usar quel c'hai offerto,
di maltolletto vuo' far buon lavoro.

Tu se' omai del maggior punto certo;
ma perché Santa Chiesa in ciò dispensa,
che par contra lo ver ch'i' t'ho scoverto,

convienti ancor sedere un poco a mensa,
però che 'l cibo rigido c'hai preso,
richiede ancora aiuto a tua dispensa.

Apri la mente a quel ch'io ti paleso
e fermalvi entro; ché non fa scïenza
sanza lo ritenere, avere inteso.

Due cose si convegnono a l'essenza
di questo sacrificio: l'una è quella
di che si fa; l'altr' è la convenenza.

Quest' ultima già mai non si cancella
se non servata; e intorno di lei
sì preciso di sopra si favella:

però necessitato fu a li Ebrei
pur l'offerere, ancor ch'alcuna offerta
si permutasse, come saver dei.

L'altra, che per materia t'è aperta,
puote ben esser tal, che non si falla
se con altra materia si converta.

Ma non trasmuti carco a la sua spalla
per suo arbitrio alcun, sanza la volta
e de la chiave bianca e de la gialla;

'For when man makes a pact with God,
this treasure, as I have suggested, then becomes
the sacrificial pledge, an action freely chosen.

'What, then, may you render in its place?
If you think of doing good with what you've offered,
you would do good works with gains ill-gotten.

'Now you may be certain of the major point.
Since Holy Church gives dispensations in this matter—
which seems to contradict the truth I have declared—

'you'll have to linger longer over dinner,
for the tough food that you have swallowed
still requires some aid for your digesting.

'Open your mind to what I now explain
and fix it in your memory, for to hear
and not remember does not lead to knowledge.

'Two things compose the essence
of this sacrificial act,
first that which is promised, then the pact itself.

'This pact can never be annulled
until it is fulfilled. It was of this
I spoke just now with such precision.

'Thus it was incumbent on the Hebrews
still to offer sacrifice, even if some offerings
allowed for substitution, as surely you must know.

'The first part, as has been explained, is the object
of the vow. It may indeed be such there is no fault
in substituting other objects for it.

'But let no man shift the burden on his shoulders
at the call of his own will, for such change requires
that both the white and yellow keys be turned.

e ogne permutanza credi stolta,
se la cosa dimessa in la sorpresa
come 'l quattro nel sei non è raccolta.

Però qualunque cosa tanto pesa
per suo valor che tragga ogne bilancia,
sodisfar non si può con altra spesa.

Non prendan li mortali il voto a ciancia;
siate fedeli, e a ciò far non bieci,
come Ieptè a la sua prima mancia;

cui più si convenia dicer 'Mal feci,'
che, servando, far peggio; e così stolto
ritrovar puoi il gran duca de' Greci,

onde pianse Efigènia il suo bel volto,
e fé pianger di sé i folli e i savi
ch'udir parlar di così fatto cólto.

Siate, Cristiani, a muovervi più gravi:
non siate come penna ad ogne vento,
e non crediate ch'ogne acqua vi lavi.

Avete il novo e 'l vecchio Testamento,
e 'l pastor de la Chiesa che vi guida;
questo vi basti a vostro salvamento.

Se mala cupidigia altro vi grida,
uomini siate, e non pecore matte,
sì che 'l Giudeo di voi tra voi non rida!

Non fate com' agnel che lascia il latte
de la sua madre, e semplice e lascivo
seco medesmo a suo piacer combatte!"

Così Beatrice a me com'ïo scrivo;
poi si rivolse tutta disïante
a quella parte ove 'l mondo è più vivo.

'Let each exchange be reckoned vain
unless the burden laid aside is found,
as four is found in six, in the one assumed.

'Whatever, therefore, has such worth
as would unbalance any scale
shall not be replaced, no matter what the cost.

'Let not mortals take vows lightly.
Be faithful and, as well, not injudicious,
as was Jephthah, offering up what first he saw,

'who had done better had he said "I have done ill"
than keeping faith and doing worse. And you can find
this sort of folly in the leader of the Greeks,

'who made Iphigenia lament the beauty of her face
and who made all those, whether wise or foolish,
who heard reports of such a rite lament as well.

'Be more grave, Christians, in your endeavors.
Do not resemble feathers in the wind, nor think
that any sort of water has the power to wash you clean.

'You have the Testaments, both New and Old,
and the shepherd of the Church to guide you.
Let these suffice for your salvation.

'If wicked greed should call you elsewhere,
be men, not maddened sheep, lest the Jew
there in your midst make mock of you.

'Be not like the lamb that leaves
its mother's milk and, silly and wanton,
pretends to battle with itself in play.'

Just as I am writing, thus did Beatrice speak.
And then, still filled with longing, she turned
to where the universe shines brightest.

Lo suo tacere e 'l trasmutar sembiante
puoser silenzio al mio cupido ingegno,
90 che già nuove questioni avea davante;

e sì come saetta che nel segno
percuote pria che sia la corda queta,
93 così corremmo nel secondo regno.

Quivi la donna mia vid' io sì lieta,
come nel lume di quel ciel si mise,
96 che più lucente se ne fé 'l pianeta.

E se la stella si cambiò e rise,
qual mi fec' io che pur da mia natura
99 trasmutabile son per tutte guise!

Come 'n peschiera ch'è tranquilla e pura
traggonsi i pesci a ciò che vien di fori
102 per modo che lo stimin lor pastura,

sì vid' io ben più di mille splendori
trarsi ver' noi, e in ciascun s'udia:
105 "Ecco chi crescerà li nostri amori."

E sì come ciascuno a noi venìa,
vedeasi l'ombra piena di letizia
108 nel folgór chiaro che di lei uscia.

Pensa, lettor, se quel che qui s'inizia
non procedesse, come tu avresti
111 di più savere angosciosa carizia;

e per te vederai come da questi
m'era in disio d'udir lor condizioni,
114 sì come a li occhi mi fur manifesti.

"O bene nato a cui veder li troni
del trïunfo etternal concede grazia
117 prima che la milizia s'abbandoni,

Her falling silent and her transformed look
imposed a silence on my eager mind,
which was already teeming with new questions.

And next, like a shaft that strikes its target
before the cord is still,
we sped into the second realm.

There I saw my lady so radiant with joy
as she passed into that heaven's brightness
that the planet shone the brighter for it.

And if even that star then changed and smiled,
what did I become who by my very nature
am subject to each and every kind of change?

As to the surface of a fishpond, calm and clear,
the fish draw close to what they see above them,
believing it to be their food,

so I saw more than a thousand splendors
drawing toward us, and from each was heard:
'Oh, here is one who will increase our loves!'

And as these shades approached,
each one of them seemed filled with joy,
so brilliant was the light that shone from them.

Merely consider, reader, if what I here begin
went on no farther, how keen would be
your anguished craving to know more.

But you shall see for yourself what great desire
I felt to hear about their state from them
as soon as they appeared to me.

'O spirit born for bliss, whom grace allows
to see the thrones of the eternal triumph
before you leave the battlefield,

del lume che per tutto il ciel si spazia
noi semo accesi; e però, se disii
di noi chiarirti, a tuo piacer ti sazia."

Così da un di quelli spirti pii
detto mi fu; e da Beatrice: "Dì, dì
sicuramente, e credi come a dii."

"Io veggio ben sì come tu t'annidi
nel proprio lume, e che de li occhi il traggi,
perch' e' corusca sì come tu ridi;

ma non so chi tu se', né perché aggi,
anima degna, il grado de la spera
che si vela a' mortai con altrui raggi."

Questo diss' io diritto a la lumera
che pria m'avea parlato; ond' ella fessi
lucente più assai di quel ch'ell' era.

Sì come il sol che si cela elli stessi
per troppa luce, come 'l caldo ha róse
le temperanze d'i vapori spessi,

per più letizia sì mi si nascose
dentro al suo raggio la figura santa;
e così chiusa chiusa mi rispuose
nel modo che 'l seguente canto canta.

'we are on fire with the light that fills all Heaven.
And so, if you would like us to enlighten you,
content yourself as you desire.'

This came to me from one of those good spirits.
And Beatrice began: 'Speak, speak with confidence,
having faith in them as you would trust in gods.'

'I clearly see you nest in your own light,
and that you flash it from your eyes,
because it sparkles when you smile.

'But I know not who you are, nor why,
worthy soul, you take your rank here from the sphere
most veiled from mortals in another's rays,'

I said, addressing myself to the radiance
that had been first to speak,
which then became more brilliant than before.

As the sun, once its heat has gnawed away
the dense and tempering vapors,
hides itself in its own excess of light,

so, with increasing joy, the holy form
concealed itself from me within its rays
and, thus concealed, it made response
in the very manner that the next song sings.

1–12. Beatrice explains that she has flamed more brightly into Dante's eyes, temporarily blinding him at the end of the last canto (vv. 141–142), because she enjoys perfect vision in God. Further, she sees (vv. 7–9) that the process that leads to such sight has now begun in Dante as well. In him it is at its earliest stage, since he interprets what he knows of God in human terms, as is reflected in his recently expressed desire (*Par.* IV.136–138) to know the "economics" of divine forgiveness.

1–6. For a presentation of the *status questionis* of a problem that has bothered many readers of these verses, see Giuseppe Ledda (Ledd.2002.1), pp. 263–64. Whose sight (*veder*, verse 5) is perfect (*perfetto*), Beatrice's or Dante's? Plausible cases can be (and have been) made for each alternative. As is evident from our translation, we are inclined to side with those who think that the improved sight is Beatrice's, as her apprehension of the divine Essence draws her farther into God's sight, thus also causing her to shine with greater effulgence. But see the early gloss of Francesco da Buti to vv. 1–18; in our own time Leonella Coglievina (Cogl.1990.1), p. 50; Marina De Fazio (Defa.1995.1), p. 85; Anna Maria Chiavacci Leonardi (Chia.1997.1), comm. to vv. 4–6, all have worked on this passage; all of them believe that the more perfect vision mentioned by Beatrice belongs to Dante. Their case is made more difficult by the fact that currently the protagonist is having a very hard time seeing anything at all. And while majority vote is probably not a valid procedure for disentangling knotted skeins of Dante's text, we are in accord with the wider opinion, given summarizing voice by Alessandro Niccoli, "perfetto," *ED* IV [1973]. The most imposing criticism of Beatrice's candidacy is based on verse 6: How can her will be described as being in motion toward God? Is she not already there? And the answer to that is found in the several expressions of eagerness on her part to get her peripatetic instruction of Dante completed so that she can get back "home," first as she enters the poem (*Inf.* II.71); then in the earthly paradise when she makes clear that the temporary nature of a stay even in that most agreeable place is preferable to a permanent one (*Purg.* XXXII.100–102; XXXIII.10–12); finally, when she asks Dante to look back down the "ladder" he has climbed up through the heavens in order to reach the "ultima salute" (*Par.* XXII.124–132).

1–2. The "heat of love" with which Beatrice is aflame may remind the reader of the kind of affection found in a previous fifth canto, that presenting Francesca in *Inferno*; it is, however, better understood, as it was by John of Serravalle (comm. to vv. 1–6), specifically as the love breathed into Beatrice by the Holy Spirit.

1. This first occurrence of a character's speaking the opening verse of a canto in *Paradiso* may make a reader wonder how unusual it is to find the first verse(s) of a canto *spoken* by a person other than the narrator. In fact, this is not that unusual a phenomenon, occurring thirteen times in all. For a study of the nature of Dante's *exordia*, see Blasucci (Blas.2000.1).

6. For the image of the soul as having a foot, see (as Chiavacci Leonardi [Chia.1997.1], ad loc., points out) Augustine, *Enarr. in Ps.* IX.15: "pes animae recte intelligitur amor" (the foot of the soul is rightly construed as love).

7. Marina De Fazio (Defa.1995.1), p. 72, cites Cesare Garboli's notice (Garb. 1971.1, p. 7) of the highly probable dependence of Dante's verse "Io veggio ben sì come già resplende" (I see clearly how, reflected in your mind) on Guido Cavalcanti's line "Io veggio che negli occhi suoi risplende" (I see that, shining from her eyes . . .), verse 11 of his *Rime* XXV, "Posso degli occhi miei novella dire." She goes on to discuss the contrastive use to which the verse is put, since Guido's *amor* ("fundamentally unknowable and therefore conducive to error") has a quite different valence, and since the love that Beatrice teaches (and represents) "is knowledge and leads to salvation."

10–12. See Tozer's paraphrase of these verses and his comment on them: " 'And if aught else leads men's . . . desires astray, this is nothing but a faint trace of that eternal light, misunderstood, which makes itself seen in the object of desire.' The view here stated is the same which is found in *Purg.* XVII.103–5 and 127–9, viz., that both virtue and vice in man proceed from love, or the desire of what is good, only in the case of vice the desire is misled by a false appearance of good."

11. As for the word *vestigio*, Poletto was apparently the first commentator (comm. to vv. 7–12) to cite *Monarchia* I.viii.2: "cum totum universum nichil aliud sit quam *vestigium* quoddam divine bonitatis" (since the whole universe is simply an imprint of divine goodness [tr. P. Shaw]). The word is a "triple hapax," that is, a word that appears exactly once in each *cantica* (cf. also *Inf.* XXIV.50 and *Purg.* XXVI.106; and, for occurrences of this phenomenon in general, see Hollander [Holl.1988.3], Appendix).

13–15. Beatrice repeats the burden of Dante's third question (*Par.* IV.136–138). It is fair to say that it is urged by a single concern, but one that has both objective and personal focus for him (for the latter, see *Par.* IV.19–21 and note): If one has not fulfilled one's vow, is there anything that may be offered in its place in order to make it good? Obviously there is, we may think, since Piccarda and Constance are both found in Paradise. The problem is, nonetheless, worked out painstakingly in the following seventy verses.

On the concept of the vow (*voto*), see Aglianò (*ED* V [1976], pp. 1150a–1152b); for Dante's barely hidden polemic here against the Decretalist position on how broken vows may be amended (and thus finally become acceptable to God), see Pastore Stocchi (Past.1972.1), pp. 16–18; and see the study of the three canti devoted to the question (III, IV, V) in Mazzotta (Mazz.1993.1), pp. 34–55.

Beatrice's lengthy intervention (vv. 1–15 and 19–84) brings the second-longest visit to any planetary heaven in *Paradiso* to its conclusion (I.73–V.85); only the space devoted to the Sun is greater (as is of course the longest heavenly episode, that of the Fixed Stars, which extends nearly five cantos). Had the poet not interrupted her here, her eighty-one-verse speech would have been the longest uninterrupted speech in the poem until this point (see the note to *Purg.* XVII.91–139). Reading the poem a second time, we probably anticipate the fact that Justinian will have the honor of having the longest uninterrupted speaking part in the *Commedia*, 145 verses (all of the next canto and the first three of VII).

16–17. It is as though Dante were playing with the conventions of his art. This self-conscious introduction, naming the intermediate unit of division (between *cantica* and verse) of the poem (*canto*—see Baranski [Bara.1995.3] for an appropriately theoretical consideration of this term) for the first time since *Inferno* XX.2 and XXXIII.90, makes Beatrice, as it were, the "author" of this canto (see De Fazio [Defa.1995.1], pp. 74–75), and then, while interrupting her speech (and thus depriving her of her "record"), compares her to one who does *not* interrupt his or her speech. Such playfulness will be found again in the last verse of the canto, once more deploying the word *canto* in a self-conscious way.

19–24. Promised by Virgil (at *Purg.* XVIII.73–75), here begins Beatrice's disquisition on freedom of the will, the property of, among all things in God's creation, angels and humans alone.

It is this passage that a virtual unanimity of contemporary Dante scholars believes is referred to in the famous tag "sicut in *Paradiso Comoedie* iam dixi" (as I have already said in the *Paradiso* of the *Comedy* [*Mon.* I.xii.6, tr. p. Shaw]), referring to God's gift of free will to humankind. After the work of Ricci, Mazzoni, and Shaw (see Hollander [Holl.2001.1], pp. 150–51), not to mention Scott (Scot.1996.1, pp. 51–52) and Kay (Kay.1998.1, pp. xxiv–xxxi, giving probable cause for a date *after* 31 March 1317), there can be little doubt as to the genuineness of this passage, which probably dates the theologically minded political treatise as contemporary with the composition of the early cantos of *Paradiso*, and no earlier than 1314 (Mazzoni's estimate) and almost surely not as late as Padoan's choice of 1320. Mineo (Mine.1987.1), pp. 90–92nn., dates the composition of Canto VI to the second half of 1316. If he is correct, then a date of 1317 for *Monarchia* would be reasonable. This is a complex and vexed problem, one that cannot be said to be entirely resolved; however, whenever the treatise was written, it was almost certainly written between 1314 and 1321 (and nearly certainly—*pace* Padoan [Pado.1993.1, p. 116]—earlier between these poles rather than later), despite the recent claims of Palma di Cesnola (Palm.2003.1), pp. 43–46, for as early as 1313. In any case, neither set of previous arguments for an earlier composition, whether for a date preceding Henry VII's stay in Italy (1307 [Nardi]) or during it (1310–13 [Macarrone, Vinay]), seems viable any longer.

For the most recent discussion of the dates of composition of the *Commedia*, with a helpful summary of the modern debate (begun by Francesco Egidi in 1927), see Enrico Fenzi (Fenz.2005.1).

23–24. One wonders whether, without the account of the one-tenth of the angelic host who chose to rebel against their maker (for Dante's version of the event, see *Par.* XXIX.49–51), Dante would have felt the need even to discuss the attribution of free will to angelic intelligences.

25–33. Given the special status of the freedom of our will and given the nature of a vow to God, made freely (no other kind is acceptable), the free will itself becomes part of what is pledged, that is, one sacrifices the right to will any differently in the future without forfeiting the vow. In a real sense it is a pledge to will no further—at least with respect to the matter of a particular vow. The result is that one is not free to make substitution for what is originally promised, since that would be to replace the original sacrifice with something of less value, or simply to attempt to use again what had already been surrendered.

According to Bosco/Reggio (comm. to vv. 26–27), Dante's rigorism with respect to the conditions for the substitution of that which was vowed is in polemic with the laxity in this respect of practitioners of canon law.

34–39. The point of the argument, for which Beatrice prepares Dante with a certain urgency, is that there is no possible substitution for a vow, but that "Holy Church" (the sarcasm is stinging) does in fact allow such substitution.

43–63. These verses contain the core of Beatrice's position. Here is a portion of Carroll's discussion of them: "She draws a distinction between the matter of a vow, and the compact or agreement itself, the latter of which, as the previous discourse showed, could never be cancelled, save by being fulfilled. Even the Hebrews had still to offer, though sometimes the thing offered was allowed to be changed. Among Christians the surrender of the will in a vow must still be made, but in certain cases the 'matter' of the vow may be exchanged for something else. This commutation, however, is to take place under the strictest conditions. First of all, no man is at liberty to shift the burden at his own pleasure: since the vow is to God, only God's representative can alter it—'both the white key and the yellow' [verse 57] must turn in the lock, the knowledge and the authority of the Church. Even the Church, in the second place, ought not to commute the 'matter' of a vow save for something else of greater value. In the Mosaic law, the increase of value was assessed at one-fifth; Dante raises it to one-half—the proportion is to be as four to six. It follows from this, in the next place, that there are some things of such supreme value that this exchange of a half more is impossible; and in this case there can be no commutation, far less dispensation. It is commonly assumed that Dante is here referring to the vow of chastity, which 'draws down every scale,' and can have no equivalent. The question is carefully discussed by Aquinas, who holds that even the Papal authority has no power to cancel this vow."

43–45. Beatrice's discussion of the two elements of a vow now begins to modulate, and seems to mirror her earlier discussion of absolute and conditional will (see *Par.* IV.109–114 and note). Vows have two components, the vow itself (equivalent to the sacrifice of free will), like the absolute will, in that it may never acceptably be relinquished; and the thing vowed. We now realize that Beatrice has been hiding, in her urgent rebuttal of those clergy who want to keep their "customers" happy, the fact that there is a loophole in the laws regarding the second component of a vow, the beloved thing itself that is freely sacrificed.

46–48. The vow itself, the sacrifice of free will, may never be withdrawn except by being finally adhered to; this position is what results, Beatrice says, from her previous argument.

49–51. The last chapter of Leviticus repeatedly (27:13, 15, 19, 27, 31) sets the official rate of exchange: Whatever is put forth in substitution must be of 20 percent greater value.

Here we, for the first time, have an example of an acceptable substitution for something vowed, even if exactly what may be substituted is less than immediately clear, while its worth seems nitpickingly precise (120 percent). Reading these verses, Benvenuto da Imola (comm. to vv. 40–51) found himself reminded of Genesis 22:13, where Abraham substitutes a ram for Isaac as his sacrifice to his Lord: "sicut filius Abrae in arietem." It is difficult to understand how a ram might be worth 120 percent of one's beloved son, much less the 150 percent to which Beatrice will later raise the ante (verse 60). But such are the ways of God, not easily interpreted by us mere humans, whether we are by trade commentators or not.

51. Beatrice means that Dante should know these conditions from his knowledge of Leviticus.

52–63. And now Beatrice makes plain the rules governing allowable substitution in the "matter" of the vow: The new pledge's worth must be 150 percent (6 to 4) of what was first offered. This seems a nearly impossible condition to fulfill (and is even harsher than the condition imposed in Leviticus 27, as we have seen [see the note to vv. 49–51]) without trivializing the nature of the initial vow. It is probably fair to say that this is exactly Beatrice's (and Dante's!) point, for she wants essentially to ban all negotiations with God on the part of scheming prelates and, for that matter, of those selfish members of their flocks.

57. The two keys refer to mercy and justice (see the note to *Purg.* IX.117–126) as these are administered by the Church, through the power vested in its priests. One may not, in other words, take it upon oneself to decide exactly what is of greater value than the object first offered.

64–72. Beatrice now adds a sort of corollary to her previous instruction, warning us in indirect address ("Let not mortals take vows lightly") not to make foolish vows that are better broken than kept. This constitutes a special case; it is clear that we are meant to consider most vows as being both wise and well intentioned.

Jephthah's keeping of his vow is joined with Agamemnon's equally disastrous pledge with regard to Iphigenia. Dante pairs a scriptural and a pagan source (cf. the similar proceeding at *Par.* IV.82–83, linking St. Lawrence and Mucius Scaevola) to underline his point. See Judges 11:30–40 and Cicero, *De officiis* III.25 (according to Moore [Moor.1896.1], p. 263). But see also, as various commentators point out, Virgil (*Aen.* II.116–117) and Ovid (*Metam.* XII.27–38). Both Jephthah and Agamemnon make unexamined vows that result in the deaths of their daughters.

64. This is the seventh and final occurrence of the word *voto* (vow) in Cantos III through V. Underlining how heavily it dominates the discourse in these cantos, its presence is found in only two other places in the rest of the poem (*Inf.* XXVIII.90; *Par.* XXXI.44).

66–68. For the troublesome word *mancia*, which, in modern Italian, usually refers to the gratuity left for someone who performs a service, see its only other use in the poem at *Inferno* XXXI.6, where it also would seem to mean "offering" or "gift." Not all agree that this is what the word means in Dante. One alternative reading is based on the Old French word *manche*, with the meaning "assault," "(military) encounter," as Bosco/Reggio (comm. to verse 66) point out. They also remind us that St. Thomas, too, presents Jephthah as an exemplary maker of a foolish vow (*ST* II-II, q. 88, a. 2); Thomas cites St. Jerome: "He was only being foolish when he made such a vow, but he turned impious when he kept it."

70. Iphigenia had to mourn her beauty because Agamemnon, her father, had promised to sacrifice the most beautiful thing to be born in his realm that year if Diana would grant favoring winds so that the Greek fleet might set sail from Aulis for Troy. From Dante's point of view, the vow itself is tinctured with worse things than foolishness, since Troy was the sacred birthplace of what becomes, after its destruction at the hands of perfidious Greeks, Rome. For an earlier and less frontal encounter with this classical matter, see *Inferno* XX.110–111.

For Dante's transposition of the tears of Jephthah's daughter, weeping for her lost youth in the mountains of her sorrow (Judges 11:37–38), to Iphigenia's cheeks, see Torraca (comm. to vv. 70–72).

73–84. Beatrice joins a second (and now direct) address to her last one (vv. 64–72), now specifically referring to Christians, who are ipso facto more guilty than the rest of humankind if they make foolish vows.

74–75. There is a continuing debate (if not one of particular consequence) about the precise meaning of this "water." Some take it in the wider sense, that is, Christians are warned not to take vows lightly in the hopes that they will "cleanse" them of guilt; others stay closer to the literal, seeing in *acqua* the cleansing holy water of easy absolution granted by an all-too-human priestly intercessor for an ill-considered vow. The following tercet would seem to support this second line of interpretation, which informs our translation, by implicitly calling into question the authority of such inept priests.

In such a reading, the two verses thus would have a chronological relation: Christians should (1) be hesitant before reaching out for God's help by taking vows without due consideration of their ensuing indebtedness and then (2), once having made that initial mistake, not be so sure that all priestly intervention will work to release them from their lightly considered (but nonetheless binding) vows. This does seem to be the more likely meaning. If it seems that such a reading blurs the traditional Catholic view, one that protects the individual believer from the captious behavior of his or her priest, it should be remembered that a vow is a pact (see verse 28, above, and *Par.* XII.17) made directly by the individual with God Himself.

76–78. This tercet, if understood as a general statement, would badly undercut the role of the clergy in the human search for salvation, as a sort of Catholic version of each believer praying in his or her closet (albeit guided by the pope). The word "salvamento" occurs only here in the poem, and in final-rhyme position (where the poet's imagination is most forced, one admits, to find ingenious rhymes). Could it be used with a more limited sense? That is, does it mean "solution" to a particular problem involving vows? This would be a difficult argument to sustain. Among the earliest commentators (e.g., Jacopo della Lana to these verses, interpreting " 'l pastor de la Chiesa" as follows: "le predicazioni che vi fanno li pastori della Chiesa" [the preaching that the priests of the Church make for you]), the reading " 'l pastor" was plural (" 'i pastor"). However, Benvenuto's text was as ours, and he nevertheless interprets the singular as a plural (comm. to vv. 73–78): "praelatos praedicantes et dirigentes vos" (prelates offering you direction in their preaching). Francesco da Buti (comm. to vv. 73–84) is the first to understand the pope (and only the pope), but he seems totally comfortable with that meaning. In any case, and as Carroll suggests (comm. to vv. 64–84), what Dante, through Beatrice, is really saying is that vows are not necessary to salvation, that we should enter into them only with due consideration. Porena (comm. to this tercet) puts the matter with admirable concision: "Per salvare l'anima basta, invece, osservare i comandamenti di Dio, i precetti di Cristo nel Vangelo e i precetti della Chiesa guidata dal papa" (To save one's soul, on the other hand, it is sufficient to follow God's commandments, Christ's precepts, and those of His Church, guided by the pope).

79–81. See Carroll's gloss on this tercet (comm. to vv. 64–84): "Dante appeals to Christians to be on their guard against the wicked greed which will tell them that the Old and the New Testament and the Shepherd of the Church are not sufficient to salvation, and induces them to take vows under promise of an easy absolution for the breaking of them."

81. The Jew (introduced to this subject at verse 49) living among Christians knows the Law, and therefore the rules regarding the making and keeping of vows, as well as they do; he is thus uniquely, among non-Christians, capable of recognizing their hypocrisy.

85. Here the poet presents himself as the "scribe" of Beatrice. (Mestica [comm. on this verse] looks back to two moments in the earthly paradise in which his lady requires such duty of him, *Purg.* XXXII.104–5 and XXXIII.52–54.) What, however, is lacking in some such comments, those that tend to emphasize Dante's loyalty to his beloved guide, is the force of the gesture, which reinforces his pose, one that makes him not the inventor of a fiction but the reporter of a series of actual encounters. In *Paradiso* X.27, Dante will again refer to himself as a scribe (*scriba*), only setting down (and not inventing) what has been revealed to him. This verse anticipates that gesture, presenting him as *scriba Beatricis*, seventy lines ago herself presented as the "author" of this canto (see verse 16). For the influential and groundbreaking study of the poet's self-presentation as "scriba Dei," see Sarolli (Saro.1971.1), esp. pp. 215–16, 233–43, 335–36.

87. There is surprisingly much debate about the exact location of this brightness upon which Beatrice fastens her gaze. Suffice it to say that, since they are still beneath the Sun, that is a possible terminus; but where the universe is brightest is where God is, the Empyrean. Compare the similar view expressed by John of Serravalle (comm. to vv. 85–87).

88–99. The ascent to the second heaven, that of Mercury, is, like all of the ascents from sphere to sphere, instantaneous, God drawing Dante and Beatrice up another level toward Him.

90. The nature of Dante's unasked questions, which some have attempted to puzzle out, is never made known. It is probably best simply to understand that he, naturally enough, has many of them.

94–99. Beatrice's increased joy at being, with Dante, closer to God makes even the immutable planet glow more brightly. If this is so, we are asked to imagine how much changed was mortal and transmutable Dante himself.

100–104. This simile immediately reminds the reader of the similar formal comparison that preceded the exchange between Dante and the souls who appeared to him in the Moon (*Par.* III.10–18), in a position parallel, that is, to this one's. There Dante believes that the forms he sees as though they were under water or glass are reflections of himself and of Beatrice. He avoids such Narcissistic error here, where he understands at once that these are souls that welcome him with love. We can see that, having experienced a single heaven, he has learned much about heavenly love.

105. Their loves are for one another in God. How will Dante help increase these? This line has been variously interpreted. It seems first of all true that these saved souls, finding a mortal in the heavens, know that they will help him become more holy by answering his questions and preparing him for Paradise, thus increasing the objects of their affection by one and the heat of their affection for one another. It also seems at least possible that they refer to a second future increase in their affections, for one another and for him, when he joins them after his death, one more to love and be loved in God.

107. This marks the last (of three occurrences) in this final *cantica* of the word *ombra* (shade), perhaps surprisingly used to indicate a saved soul. See the note to *Paradiso* III.34.

109–114. The second address to the reader in *Paradiso* underlines the importance of the scene that will follow. Once we realize that we are about to encounter Justinian, we have some sense of heightened expectation; first-time readers are merely encouraged to pay close attention.

115. The speaker, as we shall learn in the next canto (verse 10), is the shade of the Roman emperor Justinian. His reference to Dante as "bene nato" (born for bliss) has Virgilian (and thus imperial?) resonance, in that in the *Aeneid* the hero is referred to as *natus* (meaning "son") some three

dozen times (see Hollander [Holl.1989.1], p. 90, n. 28). He greets Dante, then, as the new Aeneas.

116–117. Justinian's words for triumph and warfare reflect his imperial background and concerns; here they have a modified sense, the triumph over death found in Christ and the Christian sense of militancy reflected, for example, in Job 7:1, "Life is a warfare," cited by Aversano (Aver.2000.2), p. 24.

118. The light to which Justinian refers is the light of God's love for his creatures.

122–123. The poetic playfulness of the canto, so evident near its beginning and at its end (see the second part of the note to vv. 16–18), is present here as well, both in the *rima composta "Dì, dì"* (Say, say) and in the rapidly repeated sounds of *di* in these verses ("*Dì, dì* . . . cre*di* come a *dii* . . . t'an-ni*di*"). Beatrice excitedly urges Dante (whose name happens to begin with that sound) on in his increasing hunger for knowledge of heavenly things. (For an even more exhilarated passage, see *Paradiso* VII. 10–12.)

Why all these repetitions in the concluding verses of the canto? Here *dì dì* (pronounced, in order to rhyme with *annidi* and *ridi*, "dìdi"), and then in verse 138: *chiusa chiusa*, and in 139: *canto canta*? Does the device of anaphora (repetition) have a thematic purpose, mirroring things that can be represented only by themselves (as is the case with vows)?

124–126. Whereas Dante could eventually make out the facial features of Piccarda (*Par.* III.58–63), as his ascent continues he is able to make out less of such detail in the next subsolar heaven; then, in the last of them, in Venus, Charles Martel (whom he knew on earth as he did Piccarda [at least within the claims made in the poem]) is, unlike Piccarda, not recognizable, and makes it clear that he is simply not visible as himself to Dante's mortal sight (*Par.* VIII.52–54). Occupying a middle ground, as it were, Justinian's former facial features are all, with the exception of his eyes, elided by his joy. This may reflect a "program" for the gradual effacement of the signs of human personality in Dante's first three heavenly spheres.

127–128. Dante's two questions addressed to Justinian will be answered in the next canto at vv. 1–27 and 112–126. His second question reflects his similar one to Piccarda (*Par.* III.64–66): Why is this spirit in so relatively low a sphere? Dante may have forgotten Beatrice's instruction in the last canto (*Purg.* IV.28–36), which makes it plain that such heavenly gradation is only temporary. Or he may have grasped the point that temporary presence in a planet is part of God's universal plan for his instruction and wants to know more.

129. It was perhaps more than ten years earlier that Dante had compared the planet Mercury to the branch of knowledge known as dialectic (*Conv.* II.xiii.11): "The heaven of Mercury may be compared to Dialectics because of two properties: for Mercury is the smallest star of heaven, because the magnitude of its diameter is not more than 232 miles . . . ; the other property is that in its passage it is veiled by the rays of the sun more than any other star" (tr. R. Lansing).

130–137. When the Sun finally overwhelms the cool temperatures that yield a mist through which we at times can look at its disk through that mediating layer, it burns that away, with the consequence that we now cannot look at this unveiled star, which seems wrapped in its own effulgence. Just so, Dante tells us, Justinian, the love he feels increased by Dante's affection for him and by his own for Dante, was swathed increasingly in his own light so that he, too, becoming brighter, became less visible as a human semblance.

138–139. If anaphora has the result of intensifying the effect of what is said, here we confront two lines, each of which contains a repeated pair of words, *chiusa chiusa* and *canto canta*, a configuration that is perhaps unique in the poem. Justinian's dramatic appearance on the scene has been carefully prepared for (see the note to vv. 122–123).

PARADISO VI

OUTLINE

MERCURY

1–27 **Justinian** answers Dante's first question: his involvement in the Empire; his identity; his former heresy; **Belisarius**; his inspired reform of Roman law

28–33 Giustinian justifies what will follow (vv. 34–96), a history of Rome, by saying that it will explain the failures of both **Guelphs** and **Ghibellines**:

34–36 death of **Pallas**: the Eagle "takes flight"

37–39 from **Ascanius** to the **Horatii** and **Curiatii**

40–42 from **Romulus** to **Tarquin** (rapes of **Sabines** and **Lucrece**)

43–54 the republican period and its military triumphs

55–96	empire	[Benvenuto da Imola's list:
55–72	(1) **Julius Caesar**	Julius
73–81	(2) **Augustus**	Augustus
82–90	(3) **Tiberius** [!]	Trajan
91–93	(4) **Titus** [!]	Constantine
	(5) Justinian	Justinian
94–96	(6) **Charlemagne**	Theodosius
		Charlemagne]

97–111 Justinian returns to Guelphs and Ghibellines:

- 97–102 it is they who cause Italy's unhappiness
- 103–105 Ghibellines remove justice from the ensign
- 106–111 but let not **Charles II** oppose it with his Guelphs

112–126 Response to Dante's second question: the spirits here

- 112–117 seekers of honor and fame fell short in charity,
- 118–123 but they now may rejoice as though they had not

124–126 the heavenly polyphony made by their lesser merit

127–142 **Romeo** di Villanova:

127–132 his worthiness and Provençal envy

133–138 **Raimondo**'s four daughters queens; his gratitude?

139–142 Romeo's graceful, Dante-like exile.

PARADISO VI

"Poscia che Costantin l'aquila volse
contr' al corso del ciel, ch'ella seguio
dietro a l'antico che Lavina tolse,

cento e cent' anni e più l'uccel di Dio
ne lo stremo d'Europa si ritenne,
vicino a' monti de' quai prima uscìo;

e sotto l'ombra de le sacre penne
governò 'l mondo lì di mano in mano,
e, sì cangiando, in su la mia pervenne.

Cesare fui e son Iustinïano,
che, per voler del primo amor ch'i' sento,
d'entro le leggi trassi il troppo e 'l vano.

E prima ch'io a l'ovra fossi attento,
una natura in Cristo esser, non piùe,
credea, e di tal fede era contento;

ma 'l benedetto Agapito, che fue
sommo pastore, a la fede sincera
mi dirizzò con le parole sue.

Io li credetti; e ciò che 'n sua fede era,
vegg' io or chiaro sì, come tu vedi
ogne contradizione e falsa e vera.

Tosto che con la Chiesa mossi i piedi,
a Dio per grazia piacque di spirarmi
l'alto lavoro, e tutto 'n lui mi diedi;

e al mio Belisar commendai l'armi,
cui la destra del ciel fu sì congiunta,
che segno fu ch'i' dovessi posarmi.

'Once Constantine reversed the eagle's flight,
counter to the course of heaven it had followed
behind that ancient who took Lavinia to wife,

'for two hundred years and more the bird of God
remained at Europe's borders,
near the mountains from which it first came forth.

'There it ruled the world beneath the shadow
of its sacred wings, passing from hand to hand
and, changing in this way, at last came into mine.

'Caesar I was and am Justinian,
who, by will of the Primal Love I feel,
pruned from the laws what was superfluous and vain.

'Before I had set my mind to that hard task
I believed Christ had but a single nature,
and not a second, and was content in that belief.

'But the blessèd Agapetus,
the most exalted of our shepherds,
brought me to the true faith with his words.

'I believed him. What he held by faith
I now see just as clearly as you understand
that any contradiction is both false and true.

'As soon as my footsteps moved at the Church's side,
it pleased God, in His grace, to grant me inspiration
in the noble task to which I wholly gave myself,

'entrusting my weapons to Belisarius,
with whom Heaven's right hand was so conjoined
it was a sign for me to give them up.

Or qui a la question prima s'appunta
la mia risposta; ma sua condizione
mi stringe a seguitare alcuna giunta,

perché tu veggi con quanta ragione
si move contr' al sacrosanto segno
e chi 'l s'appropria e chi a lui s'oppone.

Vedi quanta virtù l'ha fatto degno
di reverenza; e cominciò da l'ora
che Pallante morì per darli regno.

Tu sai ch'el fece in Alba sua dimora
per trecento anni e oltre, infino al fine
che i tre a' tre pugnar per lui ancora.

E sai ch'el fé dal mal de le Sabine
al dolor di Lucrezia in sette regi,
vincendo intorno le genti vicine.

Sai quel ch'el fé portato da li egregi
Romani incontro a Brenno, incontro a Pirro,
incontro a li altri principi e collegi;

onde Torquato e Quinzio, che dal cirro
negletto fu nomato, i Deci e ' Fabi
ebber la fama che volontier mirro.

Esso atterrò l'orgoglio de li Aràbi
che di retro ad Anibale passaro
l'alpestre rocce, Po, di che tu labi.

Sott' esso giovanetti trïunfaro
Scipïone e Pompeo; e a quel colle
sotto 'l qual tu nascesti parve amaro.

Poi, presso al tempo che tutto 'l ciel volle
redur lo mondo a suo modo sereno,
Cesare per voler di Roma il tolle.

'Here, then, ends my reply to your first question,
but its nature still constrains me
to follow up with something further

'so you may consider if with reason some rebel
against that sacred standard, both those opposed
and those who take it as their own.

'Consider how much valor has made it worthy
of reverence, beginning with the hour
when Pallas gave his life to give it sway.

'You know it made its home in Alba
for three hundred years and more until, at last,
again for its sake, three made war on three.

'And you know what it accomplished under seven kings,
from the wrongs done Sabine women to Lucretia's woes,
conquering the nearby people all around.

'You know what it accomplished when it was held aloft
by the noble Romans against Brennus, against Pyrrhus,
against the other kingdoms and republics,

'so that Torquatus, Quintius—named
for his unkempt locks—the Decii, the Fabii:
all achieved the fame that I am glad to keep.

'It brought the pride of Arabs low
when they followed Hannibal along the Alpine crags
from which, O river Po, you fall.

'Under it triumphed youthful Scipio and Pompey,
and to that hill beneath which you were born
it seemed indeed a bitter sight.

'Then, as the time approached when Heaven willed
to bring the world to its own state of peace,
Caesar, by the will of Rome, laid hold on it.

E quel che fé da Varo infino a Reno,
Isara vide ed Era e vide Senna
e ogne valle onde Rodano è pieno.

Quel che fé poi ch'elli uscì di Ravenna
e saltò Rubicon, fu di tal volo,
che nol seguiteria lingua né penna.

Inver' la Spagna rivolse lo stuolo,
poi ver' Durazzo, e Farsalia percosse
sì ch'al Nil caldo si sentì del duolo.

Antandro e Simeonta, onde si mosse,
rivide e là dov' Ettore si cuba;
e mal per Tolomeo poscia si scosse.

Da indi scese folgorando a Iuba;
onde si volse nel vostro occidente,
ove sentia la pompeana tuba.

Di quel che fé col baiulo seguente,
Bruto con Cassio ne l'inferno latra,
e Modena e Perugia fu dolente.

Piangene ancor la trista Cleopatra,
che, fuggendoli innanzi, dal colubro
la morte prese subitana e atra.

Con costui corse infino al lito rubro;
con costui puose il mondo in tanta pace,
che fu serrato a Giano il suo delubro.

Ma ciò che 'l segno che parlar mi face
fatto avea prima e poi era fatturo
per lo regno mortal ch'a lui soggiace,

diventa in apparenza poco e scuro,
se in mano al terzo Cesare si mira
con occhio chiaro e con affetto puro;

'And what it accomplished, from the Var to the Rhine,
the Isère and the Loire and the Seine beheld,
as did all the valleys that supply the Rhone.

'What it accomplished when it issued from Ravenna
and leapt the Rubicon was such a flight
that neither tongue nor pen could follow it.

'Toward Spain it wheeled in arms,
then toward Durazzo, and smote Pharsalia,
thus bringing grief to the tepid waters of the Nile.

'Antandros and the Simois, where it had set out,
it saw again, and the place where Hector lies.
Then it roused itself—at Ptolemy's expense.

'From there, like lightning, it fell on Juba,
then turned toward the region to your west,
where it heard the sound of Pompey's trumpet.

'For what it wrought with the one who bore it next
Brutus and Cassius bark in Hell,
and both Modena and Perugia were aggrieved.

'Wretched Cleopatra still weeps because of it.
She, fleeing before its advancing front,
took from the asp her quick and baleful death.

'With him it raced to the shore of the Red Sea.
With him it brought the world such peace
that the doors of Janus's shrine were locked.

'But what the standard that promotes my speech
had done before and had yet to do
in the mortal realm where it holds sway

'comes to seem both small and dim
if we observe it, with clear eyes and pure affection,
held in the hand of the third Caesar.

ché la viva giustizia che mi spira,
li concedette, in mano a quel ch'i' dico,
gloria di far vendetta a la sua ira.

Or qui t'ammira in ciò ch'io ti replìco:
poscia con Tito a far vendetta corse
de la vendetta del peccato antico.

E quando il dente longobardo morse
la Santa Chiesa, sotto le sue ali
Carlo Magno, vincendo, la soccorse.

Omai puoi giudicar di quei cotali
ch'io accusai di sopra e di lor falli,
che son cagion di tutti vostri mali.

L'uno al pubblico segno i gigli gialli
oppone, e l'altro appropria quello a parte,
sì ch'è forte a veder chi più si falli.

Faccian li Ghibellin, faccian lor arte
sott' altro segno, ché mal segue quello
sempre chi la giustizia e lui diparte;

e non l'abbatta esto Carlo novello
coi Guelfi suoi, ma tema de li artigli
ch'a più alto leon trasser lo vello.

Molte fïate già pianser li figli
per la colpa del padre, e non si creda
che Dio trasmuti l'armi per suoi gigli!

Questa picciola stella si correda
d'i buoni spirti che son stati attivi
perché onore e fama li succeda:

e quando li disiri poggian quivi,
sì disvïando, pur convien che i raggi
del vero amore in sù poggin men vivi.

'For the living justice that inspires me
allowed it, in his hand of whom I speak,
the glory of the vengeance for His wrath.

'And now marvel at what I unfold for you:
Afterward it raced with Titus, doing vengeance
upon the vengeance for the ancient sin.

'Then, beneath its wings,
when Lombard tooth bit Holy Church,
Charlemagne, in victory, gave her comfort.

'Now you may judge such men as I accused before
and consider their offenses,
the very cause of all your ills.

'One sets against the universal standard
yellow lilies, while the other claims it for a party,
so that it's hard to see which one offends the more.

'Let the Ghibellines ply them, ply their tricks
beneath another standard, for he follows
this one poorly who severs it from justice.

'And let not this new Charles strive to fell it
with his Guelphs, but let him fear its claws,
which have ripped the hides from greater lions.

'Many a time have children wept
for the father's sin, and let him not think
that God will change His ensign for those lilies.

'This little star is ornamented
with righteous spirits, those whose deeds were done
for the honor and the glory that would follow.

'When such errant desires arise down there,
then the rays of the one true love
must rise with less intensity.

Ma nel commensurar d'i nostri gaggi
col merto è parte di nostra letizia,
perché non li vedem minor né maggi.

Quindi addolcisce la viva giustizia
in noi l'affetto sì, che non si puote
torcer già mai ad alcuna nequizia.

Diverse voci fanno dolci note;
così diversi scanni in nostra vita
rendon dolce armonia tra queste rote.

E dentro a la presente margarita
luce la luce di Romeo, di cui
fu l'ovra grande e bella mal gradita.

Ma i Provenzai che fecer contra lui
non hanno riso; e però mal cammina
qual si fa danno del ben fare altrui.

Quattro figlie ebbe, e ciascuna reina,
Ramondo Beringhiere, e ciò li fece
Romeo, persona umìle e peregrina.

E poi il mosser le parole biece
a dimandar ragione a questo giusto,
che li assegnò sette e cinque per diece,

indi partissi povero e vetusto;
e se 'l mondo sapesse il cor ch'elli ebbe
mendicando sua vita a frusto a frusto,
assai lo loda, e più lo loderebbe."

'But noting how our merit equals our reward
is part of our happiness,
120 because we see them being neither less nor more.

'So much does living justice sweeten our affection
we cannot ever then take on
123 the warp of wickedness.

'Differing voices make sweet music.
Just so our differing ranks in this our life
126 create sweet harmony among these wheels.

'Within this very pearl shines
the shining light of Romeo,
129 whose great and noble work was poorly paid.

'But those of Provence who schemed against him
have not had the last laugh—he takes an evil road
132 to whom another's good deed seems a wrong.

'Raymond Berenger had four daughters,
each of them a queen, and Romeo, a man
135 of little standing and a stranger, made that happen.

'And when malicious tongues moved Raymond
to go over accounts with this just man,
138 who had rendered him seven plus five for ten,

'Romeo left there, poor in his old age.
And, if the world knew the heart he had within
when, crust by crust, he begged his bread,
142 much as it praises him, it would praise him more.'

1–27. Justinian's response to Dante's first inquiry allows the poet to present his version of the biography of the emperor who codified Roman law. "Justinian I, surnamed the Great, emperor of Constantinople, A.D. 527–565. Justinian is best known for his legislation. He appointed a commission of jurists to draw up a complete body of law, which resulted in the compilation of two great works; one, called *Digesta* or *Pandectae* (533), in fifty books, contained all that was valuable in the works of preceding jurists; the other, called *codex constitutionum*, consisted of a collection of the imperial constitutions. To these two works was subsequently added an elementary treatise in four books, under the title of *Institutiones* (533); and at a later period Justinian published various new constitutions, to which he gave the name of *Novellae constitutiones* (534–65). These four works, under the general name of *Corpus iuris civilis*, form the Roman law as received in Europe" (T).

The sixth canto in each *cantica*, as has often been appreciated, is devoted to an increasingly wide political focus: first to Florentine politics, then to Italian politics, and now to Dante's theologically charged imperial politics. For a clear statement of what had become the standard view, see Brezzi (Brez.1968.1), p. 176. The three spokesmen for these three subjects are also of increasing distinction: Ciacco, Sordello, and Justinian; we get another clue as to Dante's high esteem for Ciacco despite his deforming gluttony and resulting damnation.

The canto is divided into four parts, the first and third as direct responses to Dante's preceding questions (*Par.* V.127–129). The second (vv. 28–111) is coyly characterized by Justinian himself, here serving as Dante's stand-in, as a "digression" (*alcuna giunta*—verse 30). It is not only the longest but also clearly the central element in Justinian's discourse. The final section (vv. 127–142) is devoted to a second spirit in Mercury, Romeo di Villanova. Mineo (Mine.1987.1), pp. 91–92, believes that the theme holding this canto together is earthly justice. And see Mazzoni (Mazz.1982.1), p. 159. We need look no farther than the first line of his *Institutiones* (I.i.1) to see how important that concept was to this man, who had the root of the word inscribed in his very name (*iustus* is Latin for "just"): "Iustitia est constans et perpetua voluntas ius suum cuique tribuens" (Justice is the constant and perpetual desire to render each his due).

1. It has been suggested (Holl.2001.1, p. 140) that this canto, the only one in the poem spoken by a single voice, is a sort of Dantean version of a miniaturized *Aeneid*, become, in this handling, a theologized history of

Rome. This first verse lends aid to such a view, as it rather dramatically opens this "mini-epic" in medias res, as indeed did the poem that contains it (see the note to *Inferno* I.1). The uniqueness of Justinian's canto, the only one in the poem dedicated to a single speaker and to the longest single speech in the poem, reflects the phenomenon addressed in great detail by Wilkins (see the section "Style in *Paradiso*" in the introduction): The third *cantica* has fewer speakers, but these speak at greater length than do most of those found in the first two canticles.

2–3. The Eagle, symbol of the Roman Empire, originally, with Aeneas, followed the course of the heavens, encircling the earth from east to west. Subsequently it moved from west (Italy) to east (Constantinople), where Constantine had transferred the seat of the empire in 330, and where Justinian governed from 527 until 565.

Aeneas's taking Lavinia to wife, not recounted in the *Aeneid*, is the only Virgilian detail that is reprocessed in Justinian's epic narrative.

4–6. Dante's chronology is different from that of most historians; he perhaps reflects one tradition found in some manuscripts of Brunetto Latini's *Tresor*, which has it that the initial transfer took place in 333 (and not in 330) and that Justinian assumed the eastern throne only in 539 (and not in 527), some 206 years later, thus accounting for Dante's error (in verse 4: "two hundred years and more"). For speculation regarding these dates in relation to Dante's sense of imperial prophecy in the *Aeneid*, see Hollander and Russo (Holl.2003.1).

The mountains of the Troad, in Asia Minor, are presented as the site of Troy.

4. For Dante's phrase "the bird of God" (*l'uccel di Dio*), see its earlier presence in slightly different form: "l'uccel di Giove" (*Purg*. XXXII.112).

7. Justinian's words allow a reader to glimpse the heavily theologized nature of this history lesson. The citation (first noted by Baldassare Lombardi, in his comm. to this verse) of Psalm 16:8 (17:8), "sub umbra alarum tuarum" (beneath the shadow of your wings), building on the phrase "l'uccel di Dio" (the bird of God) in verse 4, invests the passage with a sense of divinity that is surely and specifically Christian.

8–9. The succession of the emperors has, in Dante, much the same feeling as that of the popes. One feels in both the presence of divine selection. It is not even a paradox that in Dante a greater solemnity is associated with the emperors, seen as carrying out God's work even before there were Christian emperors.

10. This verse performs a perfectly balanced five-word chiasmus:

Cesare Giustiniano
fui son
e

Justinian *was* a ruler and *is* a citizen of Heaven.

This verse makes a reader mindful of that classical (and modern) poetic convention in which the dead open a colloquy with passersby through the agency of the words inscribed on their tombstones; see Stefano Carrai (Carr.2002.1), pp. 99–105.

11–12. One key element in Justinian's self-presentation as inspired lawgiver is perhaps surprisingly similar to a key element in Dante's self-description as inspired poet (see *Purgatorio* XXIV.52–54 and the note to that tercet). Hollander [Holl.1999.1], pp. 279–81, calls attention to the similarity in the presentations of Dante and Justinian as divinely inspired writers; see vv. 23–24, below: "it pleased God, in His grace, to grant me inspiration / in the noble task to which I wholly gave myself."

It may seem odd that Dante thought of the *Digesta*, Justinian's great winnowing of Roman law into fifty volumes, as having been inspired by the Holy Spirit—but not much more so than that he could have made the same claim for his own poetry. Moments like these make it difficult to deny the daring of the claims this poet makes for the veracity of his own fiction. He had to know how much discomfort this claim would cause, broadening, as it does, the range of those to whom the Spirit had chosen to speak beyond the wildest imagining. (See Mazzoni [Mazz.1982.1], pp. 139–40, for acknowledgment of this dimension of Dante's strategy [which may seem surprising to those who wish to keep theology and politics separate], pointing to Kantorowicz's previous and entirely similar understanding.)

The words "[il] primo amor ch'i' sento" are potentially problematic. We have followed tradition in translating the verb *sentire* as meaning "feel." However, it certainly could mean "hear." The verb is used some 92 other times in the poem; some 32 of these mean "hear," while some 60 indicate a more general sense of sense perception. See the clear examples of both meanings in a single verse: *Purgatorio* XXIV.38. Thus we have no reason to believe it could not mean "hear" here. And see the parallel with the phrase "ch'i'odo" at *Purgatorio* XXIV.57, pointed out by Hollander (Holl.1999.1), p. 279.

13–18. Justinian confesses that he had believed in the monophysite heresy, embraced by Eutyches, which allowed Jesus only a divine nature, that is, denied His humanity. Credit for bringing his view into conformity with orthodoxy is conferred upon Pope Agapetus I (533–536). As Carroll points out (comm. to vv. 1–27), however, Dante has, whether innocently or not, twisted several facts in order to manufacture his version of a Justinian cured of heresy before he did his inspired work on Roman law; for example, Agapetus came to Constantinople only *after* the books were finished, while Dante's account (vv. 22–24) is quite different. Our poet simply must have a Christian compiler of the laws that were to govern Christian Europe; and so he manages to find ("create" might be the better word) him.

19–21. Agapetus is given credit for arguing his case so convincingly that Justinian was persuaded, as would be a contemporary of Dante, by Aristotle's "law of contradictories." Tozer (comm. to this tercet) paraphrases as follows: " '[Agapetus's] article of faith (the two Natures in Christ) I now see clearly, in the same way as you see that of two contradictories one must be false, the other true'; i.e. not as a matter of opinion or inference, but with absolute certainty."

22–24. Justinian now makes still more specific the dependence of his legal writing on the Holy Spirit. See the note to vv. 11–12. Dante is insistent in establishing the emperor's conversion as preceding his formulation of the laws, no matter what the facts may have been.

25–27. Belisarius (ca. 500–565), Justinian's greatest general, is portrayed by Dante in unproblematic and glowing terms, either despite what the poet knew of his eventual difficulties with his emperor or in ignorance of them. If Dante did know the extravagant and unverified tale (but he may not have, we must remember) that Justinian finally had all his possessions stripped from Belisarius and also had him blinded, we would sense even more strongly how willing Dante was to let the ideality of the situation trump its actuality. For here is a realm that a Dante can love, its supreme leader completely dedicated to the practical intellectual concerns of governance, the law, while his "right hand," loyal and true, takes care of problems with the Vandals in Africa and the Goths in Italy. In any case, this pair of heroic figures offers Dante an emblem of the successful collaboration between representatives of the active and of the contemplative life (here in the form of the lower part of Boethius's familiar binome, practical [rather than theoretical] thought; see *Cons. Phil.* I.1[pr.]).

This is, according to the *Grande Dizionario*, one of the very few times in the history of the Italian language that the verb *commendare* is used to signify "affidare" (entrust)—the only other example put forward comes from Castiglione two centuries later. In Dante the word more usually signifies "praise, celebrate."

30. Narrowing the principal activity of his own life on behalf of Rome triggers in Justinian the need to "add" something more, a "digression" of sorts (vv. 34–111), which naturally enough has begun (vv. 31–33) by touching on the criminally irresponsible struggles between Guelphs and Ghibellines in Dante's Italy. It will, also naturally enough, conclude with the same concern (vv. 97–111). Thus ancient history has a most modern relevance and is framed by that topic.

31–33. The outcome of the struggle of the Eagle, a great Hegelian bird moving through history to make manifest the Spirit, is hardly a cause for optimism, at least not at the moment in which Dante is writing. The "covers" of Justinian's historical essay both depict the disastrous present day in Italy. The ensuing narrative of the Eagle's flight through time and space is put to the service of showing that it has become the corrupt emblem of a corrupt party (the Ghibellines of 1300), opposed by equally corrupt Guelphs.

Justinian speaks ironically (employing the trope *antiphrasis*, saying the opposite of what is meant).

34–96. The core of the canto, offering what is perhaps the poem's crucial political self-definition, presenting an absolutely unorthodox "history of the Caesars," that is, one principally shaped by a Christian point of view, is divided into sixteen segments:

(1) death of Pallas (35–36)
(2) Ascanius founds Alba Longa (37–38)
(3) Horatians' victory over the Curiatii (39)
(4) kings: rape of the Sabines (Romulus) (40)
(5) kings: rape of Lucretia (the Tarquins) (41–42)
(6) republic: vs. Gauls of Brennus (43–44)

(7) republic: vs. Tarentini of Pyrrhus (44–45)
(8) republic: Torquatus and Cincinnatus (46)
(9) republic: Decii and Fabii (47–48)
(10) republic: defeat of Hannibal (49–51)
(11) republic: Scipio and Pompey (vs. Catiline) (52–54)
(12) empire: Julius Caesar (55–72)
(13) empire: Augustus Caesar (73–84)
(14) empire: Tiberius Caesar (85–90)
(15) empire: Titus (91–93)
(16) empire: Charlemagne (94–96)

34. The Eagle is marked by *virtù* (usually "power" but, at times, as here, "virtue"), precisely what the opposing Italian political parties lack. The ensuing list of virtuous founding presences harps upon the moral virtues that separated Romans from their enemies. See *Convivio* IV.iv.11 for an earlier expression of Dante's firm belief in the moral superiority of the Romans: "Therefore, since this office [rulership] could not be attained without the greatest virtue, and since its exercise required the greatest and most humane kindness, this was the people best disposed to receive it" (tr. R. Lansing).

35–36. Roman imperial virtue begins with the death of Pallas, son of Evander. Despite the special protection of Aeneas, Pallas is killed in battle by Turnus (*Aen.* X.479–489). Thus the founding event of the empire is presented here as the death of Pallas, an event that seems to have the status of sacrifice. For a discussion in this vein, see Rachel Jacoff (Jaco.1985.1). The death of Cato has a similar resonance; he died for liberty, as Virgil tells Dante (*Purg.* I.71–72; and see the note to vv. 71–74). Pallas dies in order to give virtue a homeland in Italy where, for a time at least, it prospered. "His death led to that of Turnus, because Aeneas would have spared the latter's life, had he not seen the belt of Pallas, which [Turnus] was wearing (*Aen.* XII.940–950). By Turnus' death Aeneas became possessed of Lavinia, and of the Kingdom of Latinus. Thus the death of Pallas ultimately caused the eagle to obtain the sovereignty" (Tozer's commentary to vv. 35–36).

Of the death of Pallas, Dante (*Monarchia* II.ix.14) has this to say: "In this combat [with Turnus] the clemency of the victor Aeneas was so great that, had he not caught sight of the belt which Turnus had taken from Pallas when he killed him, the victor would have granted life as well as peace to the vanquished, as our poet's closing lines testify" (tr. P. Shaw).

37–39. Dante refers to Alba Longa, "the most ancient town in Latium, built according to tradition by Ascanius, son of Aeneas" (T). The Eagle would remain there some three hundred years until the defeat of the local Curiatii by the Roman Horatii.

40–42. Dante (*Conv.* IV.v.11) includes three Tarquins among the first seven kings of Rome: ". . . the seven kings who first governed her—namely Romulus, Numa, Tullus, Ancus, and the Tarquin kings who were the rulers and the tutors, so to speak, of her youth" (tr. R. Lansing). That means Dante counts the sixth king, Tullius Servius, related by marriage but not by birth, as one of the Tarquins, as Toynbee explains ("Tarquinii").

It is probably significant that the first period of Roman history is marked, at either end, by rape, that of the Sabine women in Romulus's rule and that of Lucrece by her husband's cousin, Sextus Tarquinius, son of Lucius Tarquinius Superbus, seventh king of Rome. That second act of sexual violence eventually had the result of ending Tarquin rule (510 B.C.).

43–45. Dante records two major military victories of the ensuing republican period. "Brennus, leader of the Senonian Gauls, who in 390 B.C. crossed the Apennines, defeated the Romans at the Allia, and took Rome; after besieging the capitol for six months he quitted the city upon receiving 1,000 pounds of gold as a ransom for the capitol and returned home safe with his booty. According to later tradition (followed by Livy), at the moment when the gold was being weighed and Brennus, declaring the Roman weights to be false, had thrown his sword into the scale, Camillus and a Roman army appeared, fell upon the Gauls, and slaughtered them" (T). "Pyrrhus, king of Epirus, born 318 B.C., died 272 B.C.; he claimed descent from Pyrrhus, the son of Achilles and great-grandson of Aeacus. In 280 Pyrrhus crossed over into Italy at the invitation of the Tarentines to help them in their war against the Romans" (T).

This tercet begins a passage dedicated to the Roman republic (vv. 43–54). For a clear understanding of Dante's allegiance to republican ideals and principles, see Davis, "Ptolemy of Lucca and the Roman Republic" (1974) and "Roman Patriotism and Republican Propaganda: Ptolemy of Lucca and Pope Nicholas III" (1975), both reprinted in Davi.1984.1, pp. 254–89 and 224–53, respectively; and see Hollander and Rossi (Holl.1986.1) and the note to *Paradiso* XXVII.61–63.

45. The words *principi e collegi* refer to other political organisms on the peninsula, whether kingdoms or republics; for *collegi* with this meaning,

Porena (comm. to this verse) cites *Monarchia* II.v.7: These bodies "seem in some sense to function as a bond between individuals and the community" (tr. P. Shaw).

46. "Titus Manlius, surnamed Torquatus, from the collar (*torques*) which he took from a fallen foe; and Quinctius, surnamed Cincinnatus, or the 'curly-haired' " (Longfellow, comm. on this verse).

47. The Decii and the Fabii: "Decii, famous Roman family, three members of which, father, son, and grandson, all bearing the same name, Publius Decius Mus, sacrificed their lives for their country" (T); "the Fabii, ancient patrician family at Rome, which claimed descent from Hercules and the Arcadian Evander. It is celebrated as having furnished a long line of distinguished men" (T).

48. Dante uses a rare (or coins his own new) verb, *mirrare*, meaning either "to embalm, to preserve with myrrh." See Scartazzini (comm. to this verse) for an acerbic discussion of the vagaries of the ancient debate over this word. Some early commentators think Dante was only deliberately (because of the exigencies of rhyme) misspelling *miro* (admire) with a double "rr"; others see that it means "preserve," as Scartazzini argues it indeed does, if he dislikes any sense of the odoriferous, favored by some but inappropriate, in his view, in Paradise.

49–51. To refer to the Cathaginians as Arabs is (as Bosco/Reggio [comm. on this tercet] explain) to commit an anachronism, since Arabs populated that part of North Africa only in Dante's day, not in Roman times. Hannibal (247–183 B.C.) was Rome's perhaps most glorious and successful antagonist, over a period of some fifteen years defeating them in several major battles, until, at the battle of Zama, in 202 B.C., he was utterly crushed by Scipio (who received his surname, "Africanus," as a result).

52–53. "Publius Cornelius Scipio Africanus Major, one of the greatest of the Romans, born 234 B.C., died ca. 183; while just a youth he fought against Hannibal at the Battle of the Ticinus (218); he was elected consul 205, and in the next year crossed over into Africa, and at last brought to an end the long struggle between Rome and Hannibal by his decisive victory over the latter at the Battle of Zama, Oct. 19, 202; he returned to Italy in 201, and entered Rome in triumph, receiving the surname of Africanus in commemoration of his brilliant services; he served in the war against Antiochus the Great in 190, and, being afterwards accused of taking bribes from Antiochus, was tried in Rome in 185, on the anniversary of the Battle of Zama; the prosecution was, however, dropped, and Scipio left Rome, to which he never returned; he died not long after, probably in 183" (T). "Pompey the Great, born 106 B.C., died 48 B.C.; in his youth he distinguished himself as a successful general and earned the surname of Magnus on account of his victories in the African campaign; he was consul with Crassus in 70 B.C., and in 59 B.C. joined Julius Caesar and Crassus in the first triumvirate. Caesar's increasing power made it inevitable that a struggle for supremacy should take place between them sooner or later, and in 49 B.C. the Civil War broke out; in the next year Pompey was completely defeated by Caesar at the Battle of Pharsalia, and fled to Egypt, where he was murdered by order of Ptolemy's ministers" (T).

Scipio is the Roman hero who is most often referred to by Dante; see Hollander and Rossi (Holl.1986.1), pp. 64–68.

54. The Roman standards seemed bitter to the inhabitants of the ancient hill town of Fiesole, beneath which lies Dante's Florence, when the army destroyed it in the war against Catiline. According to Giovanni Villani (*Cron.* I.36–37), Pompey was among the generals at the siege.

55–72. After seven tercets, each of which is devoted to one event (and sometimes more) in pre-imperial history, Dante will turn to his gallery of Roman emperors, one that will eventually resemble no other such listing ever found. But he deals with the first of them, Julius, here. (Post-Shakespearean readers may need to be reminded that, for Dante and historians in his time, Julius [and not Augustus] was the first emperor.)

Dante's "life of Caesar" is immediately put (forced?) into a Christian context. It was Julius's task to set the world in better order so that it would be prepared for the coming of Christ. Next Dante turns to Caesar's military triumphs in Gaul (vv. 58–60). The six rivers mentioned in these verses may derive from Lucan, *Pharsalia* I.399–434, as is suggested by Scartazzini (comm. to verse 58).

The next four tercets (vv. 61–72) essentially recount the main Caesarean events of Lucan's version of the civil wars between Julius and the republicans: (1) his crossing of the Rubicon and march on Rome (*Phars.* I–III); (2) his attack on the republican forces in Spain (*Phars.* IV; see *Purg.* XVIII.101–102); (3) his landing on the Dalmatian coast in pursuit of Pompey (V–VI); (4) the battle of Pharsalus, with the death of Cato and flight of Pompey to Egypt, where he was betrayed and killed by Ptolemy (VII–IX); (5) his tour of some sites of the Trojan War (IX); (6) his deposition of Ptolemy, placing Cleopatra in his stead (X); (7) his defeat of Juba, king of Numidia, one of Pompey's supporters (not included in the unfinished epic, but since Juba is referred to at some length in *Phars.* IV.670–824, he was probably scheduled for a final, sad appearance); (8) a return to Spain, where Caesar annihilated the remainder of Pompey's followers (Lucan looks forward to this last battle, at Munda, in *Phars.* I.40). While most of these events seem to have sources in Lucan's text, and follow the order in which they occur in that text, what is utterly lacking is Lucan's biting sarcasm about Julius so sharply felt in most of these scenes. Indeed, Dante's own hostility toward Julius seems largely absent from this passage (see Stull and Hollander [Stul.1991.1], pp. 33–43, for discussion of Julius's ups and [mainly] downs in Dante's eyes). In these lines, as in his presence as an *exemplum* of zeal in *Purgatorio* XVIII.101–102 (and see the note to the passage), only a positive view of Caesar is appropriate, since he is seen here as the first and theologically necessary emperor of Rome. The reference to Troy (vv. 67–68) also seems to have radically different purposes here and in Lucan; here it ties Julius to the Trojan founders of Rome, while there (*Pharsalia* IX.961–1003) it mocks his pretensions. See Mineo (Mine.1987.1), pp. 121–29, for the problematic nature of Dante's changing views of Julius.

55–57. For Dante's similar sense of "kairos," of the "fullness of time," under Augustus, see *Convivio* IV.v.4–8, a text that also includes the following details about the birth of Rome: "David was born when Rome was born—that is, when Aeneas came to Italy from Troy, which was the origin of the Roman city, according to written records" (IV.v.6 [tr. R. Lansing]). And see *Monarchia* I.xvi.2: "That mankind was then [in the reign of Augustus] happy in the calm of universal peace is attested by all historians and by famous poets; even the chronicler of Christ's gentleness deigned to bear witness to it; and finally Paul called that most happy state 'the fullness of time' [*plenitudinem temporis*]" (tr. P. Shaw).

61–63. Here, once more, Dante's apparent sentiments are far from Lucanian. This nefarious crime of Julius is treated in this passage as a great and necessary step forward. See, however, Dante's previous harsh treatment of Curio, who encouraged Julius to cross the Rubicon and march on Rome (*Inf.* XXVIII.97–99). There the context was the destruction of the republic; here it is the establishment of the empire.

65–66. Pompey, although he managed to avoid death at Caesar's hand in Greece, was betrayed by his host, the young king, Ptolemy, and killed in Egypt (*Phars.* VIII).

69. The young king suffers his own misfortune: Julius replaces him on the throne with Cleopatra.

73. The word *baiulo* here means "standard-bearer." It refers to Octavian, the second of Dante's "world-historical" emperors, eventually known as Augustus Caesar. The Ottimo (comm. to vv. 73–81) traces it to the first-conjugation verb *baiuolo* (carry).

74. See *Inferno* XXXIV.64–67 for Dante's initial portrayal of this pair. Now he adds a detail: They are barking. In the previous passage we are told that Brutus is silent, and Cassius is not described as uttering sounds. Their "next-door neighbor" in Cocytus, however, Bocca, does bark (*Inf.* XXXII.105 and 108). Has Dante conflated that noise here? If we decide that such a solution seems unlikely, we are faced with another loose end in *Paradiso* (see the note to *Par.* III.34).

75. Octavian's forces defeated Mark Antony at Modena and also sacked the city of Perugia. Tozer points to Lucan (*Phars.* I.40) for a source: "Though to these be added the famine of Perusia and the horrors of Mutina" (tr. J. D. Duff).

76–78. Antony, who survived defeat in the battles against the imperial army in Italy, did not choose to live much longer, after losing the naval battle near Actium (31 B.C.), and committed suicide. Cleopatra, fleeing before the imperial ensign, held aloft now by Octavian, did not choose to die with her lover; she put herself to death by means of the bite of an asp that she held to her breast (some commentators insist that she in fact employed two venomous snakes to do away with herself). Over the centuries many potential sources have been cited for the mode of her suicide, which occurred only once she perceived that, unlike Julius, Octavian was firm against her charms and intended to take her back to Rome as a captive.

79. For a possible source, see *Aeneid* VIII.685–688, where Antony is criticized for his deportment with Cleopatra (this scene is one of those portrayed on the shield that Venus presents to Aeneas, *Aen.* VIII.626–731). As

Fairclough points out in his note to this passage, the "ruddy sea" is the Indian Ocean, not the Red Sea. The first commentator to cite this phrase (*litore rubro*) in the *Aeneid* (VIII.686) was apparently Scartazzini (comm. to this verse). Most modern commentators also cite it, but, like Scartazzini, without noting that Virgil is not referring to the Red Sea. If he is in fact citing the *Aeneid*, Dante either makes the same mistake his modern commentators make or else forces the passage out of context, and has Augustus establishing his dominion over that most propitious part of the Mediterranean world, where Christ became flesh, as part of the *plenitudo temporis* (see the note to vv. 55–57). And see the note to *Paradiso* VII.6 for a possible resonance of another segment of this Virgilian text.

80–81. See the great prophecy of Augustus as bearer of world peace in *Aeneid* I.286–296, esp. verse 294, "claudentur Belli portae" (the gates of War shall be shut), as was first observed by Pietro di Dante (comm. to vv. 79–81, along with passages from Lucan, esp. *Phars.* I.62). For both these *loci*, see also Tommaseo (comm. to vv. 79–81).

81. The word *delubro* is a Latinism (from *delubrum*, "temple").

82–91. "Tiberius Claudius Nero, stepson and adopted son and successor of Augustus; Roman emperor, A.D. 14–37" (T). There is apparently a certain tongue-in-cheek quality to Dante's words in support of his selection of the third emperor in his most unusual pantheon. Julius is a bit problematic, given even Dante's own slurs on his character (see the notes to *Purg.* IX.133–138 and *Purg.* XXVI.77–78), but we understand that, for Dante and his time, he was the first emperor and thus is a necessary presiding presence. About Augustus no one ever could (and no one ever has wanted to) complain. But Tiberius (not to mention Titus!) has caused more than a little discomfort. And the protagonist does indeed marvel at these words (in *Paradiso* VII.19–24). But see *Monarchia* II.xi.5: "Thus if Christ had not suffered under an authorised judge, that penalty would not have been a punishment. And no judge could be authorised unless he had jurisdiction over the whole of mankind, since the whole of mankind was punished in that flesh of Christ 'who bore our sorrows', as the prophet says. And Tiberius Caesar, whose representative Pilate was, would not have had jurisdiction over the whole of mankind unless the Roman empire had existed by right" (tr. P. Shaw).

Benvenuto (comm. to vv. 79–81) made clear his amazement at Dante's having included Tiberius among the great emperors, referring to him as "the worst sort of successor" to Augustus. (And see Benvenuto's own list of seven emperors, dropping Tiberius and Titus in favor of Trajan and Constantine and adding Theodosius, in the outline of this canto.) It is possible that Dante's "final list" is indeed seven, since it eventually includes Henry VII or his successor (see the note to *Par.* XXX.133–138) as the seventh emperor in the line adumbrated here. See Hollander and Rossi (Holl.1986.1), pp. 62 and 78n.

88–90. Justinian is making the case for the justness of Christ's death at the hands of the Romans (Pontius Pilate, acting as agent of Tiberius). This "vendetta" pursued by the Roman Eagle (as Justinian, inspired by the justice of God even as he now speaks, insists) is what makes the accomplishments of even Julius and Augustus seem paltry, for Christ's death atoned for all previous human sin and made sinners to come redeemable as well. Thus the apparently specious hyperbole in the passage regarding Tiberius (vv. 82–91) must be seen as serious. His greatness is precipitated out of the event he presided over, the Crucifixion. See Carroll on vv. 82–90: "The wrath is the just anger of God against the human race for its sins; and the 'doing of vengeance' is the death of Christ, regarded as the bearing of the punishment inflicted by that anger. The extraordinary thing is that Dante regards the crucifixion as the supreme glory of Roman justice, inasmuch as it was the agent by which 'the Living Justice' 'did vengeance for His wrath.' "

88. See the quotation of the first line of Justinian's *Institutiones* in the note to vv. 1–27. Again Dante puts words reflecting the spiration of the Holy Spirit in Justinian's mouth; see verse 23 and the note to vv. 22–24. And see *Inferno* XXIX.55–57 and the note to vv. 54–57 for Dante's association of himself with similar inspiration, not to mention *Purgatorio* XXIV.52–54. Aversano (Aver.2000.2), p. 28, is one of the relatively few commentators to take clear notice of Justinian's insistence on divine inspiration for his work on Roman law.

92–93. "Titus, son and successor of Vespasian, Roman emperor, A.D. 79–81; he served under his father in the Jewish wars, and when Vespasian was proclaimed emperor and returned to Italy in 70 he remained in Palestine in order to carry on the siege of Jerusalem, which he captured, after a siege of several months, in September of that year; in the following year he returned to Rome and celebrated the conquest of the Jews in a triumph with his father" (T). For a clear explanation of this tercet, see Tozer (comm. to vv. 91–93): "The repetition is that of the word *vendetta* in two different applications, corresponding to the twofold mission of the eagle; first it avenged God's wrath against Adam's sin (*vendetta del peccato antico*) by putting Christ to death; then it took vengeance on the Jews for bringing about Christ's death by the destruction of Jerusalem by Titus."

Giorgio Padoan (Pado.1965.2), pp. 7–17, looks away from the canto of his *Lectura Dantis Romana* (*Par.* VII) to consider these verses and their problematic view of Jewish history.

94–96. Charlemagne gets short shrift as the sixth (Justinian does not, of course, refer to himself as a member of this elite group, but commentators have done so for him) and last of these "world-historical" emperors. See Tozer (comm. to these verses): "[W]hen Desiderius, king of the Lombards, persecuted the Church, Pope Adrian I called in Charles the Great to its defence. *[V]incendo:* by his victory over Desiderius. The date of this was 774, and Charles was not crowned emperor of the West until 800, so that at the time when it took place he was not under the protection of the Roman eagle (*sotto le sue ali*). Dante's error here is of a part with his more serious mistake in *Mon.* [III.xi.1] where he says that Charles was crowned emperor by Adrian I while the emperor Michael was on the throne of Constantinople—whereas in reality he was crowned by Leo III during the reign of Irene." The process of *translatio imperii* has now been insisted on, as the Eagle has flown out of Italy and into France. This tercet thus accomplishes a great deal, introducing and defending the concept of the Holy Roman Empire in the space of three lines.

97–111. Having finished with the "Roman" past of imperial power, from Julius to Charlemagne, a period of just over eight hundred years, Justinian now turns to the present political ills of Italy. This subject is not treated as formally as the history of Roman institutions, but it is at once clear that, for Dante, it is of extraordinary importance.

97–99. For Justinian's earlier references to Guelphs and Ghibellines and their battle over control of the *sacrosanto segno* (that most holy standard), see vv. 31–33 and the notes to those verses and to verse 30. In a real sense then, vv. 34–96 *are* a digression (they are referred to as a *giunta* [an addendum] at verse 30), only preparing for Dante's pressing business, to show how poorly ordered the political affairs of the peninsula were in his own time.

100–102. While the Guelphs oppose the imperial ensign with their (French) golden lilies, the Ghibellines try to make it only their own, desiring to deprive others of their rightful imperial homeland.

103–105. The Ghibellines, for ridding the sacred sign of empire of justice, are told to find another symbol to represent their conniving spirit.

106–108. Charles II, king of Naples (ruled 1289–1309), is referred to as "new" to distinguish him from his father, also king of Naples (and Sicily, in his case), who died in 1285. Justinian warns him not to let his Guelph troops attempt to wrest the ensign of imperial rulership from the Ghibellines (who have their own problems in meriting it), for the empire has defeated mightier enemies before.

108. The imperial Eagle's claws are portrayed as having "ripped the hides from larger lions" than Charles represents. The general sense is clear, but there have been any number of interpretations of what exactly is meant. The majority believes that there is no specific reference, only a generic prophecy of Charles's doomed experiment with increasing his dominions, should he try to accomplish that.

109–110. Strangely enough, not a single commentator (at least not among the seventy-two currently gathered in the DDP) makes reference to Ugolino's narrative here (see, e.g., *Inf.* XXXIII.38–39). In this poem there is hardly another more evident case of sons weeping for the sins of their father.

112–117. In these two tercets Justinian explains the nature of what was lacking in these souls (as Ordiway has pointed out [Ordi.1982.1], pp. 82–85, it is the theological virtue of hope in its perfected form). As the temporary Moon-dwellers displayed a marred version of faith, so Justinian and the others here, while they were alive, displayed hope in an immature form, rendering their love of God less vibrant than it should have been.

118–123. In the following pair of tercets (these twelve verses indeed form a group, the two equal parts of which are joined by a triumphant "But") Justinian, as has frequently been noted, sounds very much like Piccarda (*Par.* III.70–87). We can safely assume that neither he nor Romeo would be among the higher petals of the rose in *Paradiso* XXXII; but that only makes them love God the more, for accepting them in Heaven with a history of such galling imperfections.

121. This verse marks the third occurrence of the noun *giustizia* in the canto, a density shared by only two previous cantos (*Inf.* III and *Purg.* XIX;

however, see *Par.* VII, where that noun appears only once, but other forms of the word [*giusta* (3), *guistamente* (2), *giuste*] appear six times; see the note to *Par.* VII.20).

127–142. Romeo, seneschal (chief steward) of Raymond Berenger IV, count of Provence: "The only foundation, apparently, for the story, adopted by Dante and Villani (vi.90), of the 'pilgrim' who became the minister of the Provençal count, is the fact that the name of count Berenger's grand seneschal was Romieu (or Romée) of Villeneuve. Romeo, a friend of Sordello (*Purg.* VI.74) was born c. 1170. In Aug. 1229 he was in Genoa as ambassador to the *podestà* of that city, and in the same year was serving as Raymond Berenger's chief minister, and by him was granted certain possessions in Genoa and her territories, and the next year received other properties. Early in 1241, on another mission as ambassador, he became involved in a battle at sea, from which he escaped unscathed, even managing to capture a Pisan vessel laden with merchandise which he had taken to Nice. On Aug. 19, 1245 Raymond Berenger died, leaving his daughter Beatrice his heir, and Romeo as 'baiulus totius terrae suae et filiae suae' [guardian of all his lands and those of his daughter]. Beatrice then married Charles of Anjou while under Romeo's guardianship. Romeo died in 1250" (T).

130–132. Those courtiers, we suppose, who spoke ill of Romeo to Raymond succeeded in forcing his removal from a position of trust (see vv. 136–139), but in the end suffered the tyrannical rule of Raymond's successors.

134. When we read or hear Raymond's name, we may reflect on how many names or references to historical figures we have encountered in this canto (all but two of them in the first 106 verses). The total (Constantine, Aeneas, Lavinia, Justinian, Agapetus, Belisarius, Pallas, the Curiatii, the Horatii, the seven first kings of Rome, Sabine women, Lucrece, unnamed republicans, Brennus, Pyrrhus, Torquatus, Cincinnatus, the Decii, the Fabii, Hannibal, Scipio Africanus, Pompey, Julius Caesar, Hector, Ptolemy, Juba, Augustus, Brutus, Cassius, Mark Antony, Cleopatra, Tiberius, Titus, Desiderius, Charlemagne, Charles II of Anjou, Romeo, and Raymond), even if we count some plural presences as single units, as here, is an impressive thirty-eight, and that excludes the several-times-alluded-to Guelphs and Ghibellines. If we have bought into the discredited but still supported notion that in the last *cantica* Dante has given over

worldly concerns, it may come as something of a surprise to have a canto in *Paradiso* make so obvious a gesture toward history.

137. The phrase *dimandar ragione* is a term used for requesting a review of the financial situation between involved parties.

138. For example, Romeo's accounts always returned more than he had accepted into his care. The numbers seem merely casually chosen, but would indicate a healthy 20 percent gain in Raymond's holdings under Romeo's management.

139–142. Where the opening verses of the canto imply the presence of Virgil, as author of the *Aeneid*, the concluding ones summon the image of the exiled and "mendicant" Dante (cf. *Par.* XVI.58–60, Cacciaguida's admonition: "You shall learn how salt is the taste / of another man's bread and how hard it is / to go down and then up another man's stairs"). See Mazzoni (Mazz.1982.1), p. 157; and see Woodhouse (Wood.1997.1), for a treatment in English of Romeo's resemblance to Dante: It is he who, "by recalling, in his person and in his name, *Romeus*, pilgrim to Rome, the tragic figure of Dante himself" (p. 7). His name also binds the two seemingly disparate parts of the canto, ancient and modern. This is a "Roman canto," even when it turns its attention to recent events in Provence; its first part is a sort of vernacular version of a theologized *Aeneid*; its last, a comic (i.e., happily resolved) version of a lament for a courtier.

PARADISO VII

OUTLINE

MERCURY

1–3 **Justinian**'s double-tongued canto opening
4–6 his "double light"
7–9 the dancing disappearance of the "Mercurians"
10–12 Dante's question and eagerness to share it with Beatrice
13–18 he holds it back, yet she divines his thoughts
19–24 Beatrice reveals his question ("how can a just vendetta be justly punished?") and prepares to answer

(1) Beatrice's response to Dante's first question

25–27 **Adam**, not reining in his will, took us down with him
28–33 thus the human race was "infirm" until the Incarnation
34–39 the flesh of **Christ** was both pure (like new-made Adam's) and, because flesh after original sin is what it is, impure in itself;
40–45 if one pays attention to Christ's flesh as flesh, the pain of the Cross was justly felt,
46–48 thus a single act had diverse effects, pleasing God and the Jews (for different reasons), earthquake and the opening of heaven the differing signs
49–51 and thus let it no longer be difficult for you to acknowledge that a just vengeance (the killing of Jesus) was itself avenged justly (by Titus)

(2) Dante's second doubt and Beatrice's response

52–57 I see you are again confused; what you want to know is "Why did God decide to save humankind by agency of the death of Jesus and not in some other way?"
58–63 This is hidden, brother, from those who have not been brought up in the flame of divine love
64–78 man's privileged position in the universe
79–81 the Fall: man lost most of that privilege

82–93 only two ways to recover his position: (1) he himself had to repay or (2) God had to pardon him

94–105 since he had no means to accomplish the first of these, it remained to God to ransom him

106–120 the Incarnation and death of Jesus

(3) *Dante's third doubt; Beatrice's resolution of it*

121–123 Anticipating a problem Dante may derive from her previous words, Beatrice resolves yet another doubt:

124–129 you say, "I see the four elements, and they, created by God, in fact die; they should not do so";

130–138 angels and heavens fully formed by God

139–141 souls of beasts and plants drawn forth by the stars

142–144 but your life is breathed into you directly by God,

145–148 hence you are immortal (as are Adam and Eve).

PARADISO VII

"Osanna, sanctus Deus sabaòth,
superillustrans claritate tua
felices ignes horum malacòth!"

Così, volgendosi a la nota sua,
fu viso a me cantare essa sustanza,
sopra la qual doppio lume s'addua;

ed essa e l'altre mossero a sua danza,
e quasi velocissime faville
mi si velar di sùbita distanza.

Io dubitava e dicea "Dille, dille!"
fra me, "dille" dicea, "a la mia donna
che mi diseta con le dolci stille."

Ma quella reverenza che s'indonna
di tutto me, pur per *Be* e per *ice*,
mi richinava come l'uom ch'assonna.

Poco sofferse me cotal Beatrice
e cominciò, raggiandomi d'un riso
tal, che nel foco faria l'uom felice:

"Secondo mio infallibile avviso,
come giusta vendetta giustamente
punita fosse, t'ha in pensier miso;

ma io ti solverò tosto la mente;
e tu ascolta, ché le mie parole
di gran sentenza ti faran presente.

Per non soffrire a la virtù che vole
freno a suo prode, quell' uom che non nacque,
dannando sé, dannò tutta sua prole;

'Osanna, sanctus Deus sabaoth,
superillustrans claritate tua
felices ignes horum malacoth!'—

thus, wheeling to the notes of his own melody,
I saw that being, in whom a double light
is twinned, caught up in song,

he and the others moving in their dance
and, like the fastest-flying sparks,
veiled from me by their sudden distance.

I was in doubt, saying to myself, 'Tell her,
tell her,' saying to myself, 'tell this to my lady,
who slakes my thirst with her sweet drops.'

But the reverence that is mistress over me
at the mere sound of *Be* or *ice*
bowed down my head, as when a man nods off.

Not long did Beatrice leave me in this state
before she spoke, shining with the rays of such a smile
as would content a man if he were set on fire:

'In my infallible opinion this idea,
that just revenge itself perhaps deserves
just punishment, has set you thinking.

'But I will quickly free your mind of doubt.
Still, you must listen closely, for my words
shall set before you things of great importance.

'By not enduring, for his own good, a rein
upon his will, that man who was not born,
damning himself, damned all his offspring.

onde l'umana specie inferma giacque
giù per secoli molti in grande errore,
fin ch'al Verbo di Dio discender piacque

u' la natura, che dal suo fattore
s'era allungata, unì a sé in persona
con l'atto sol del suo etterno amore.

Or drizza il viso a quel ch'or si ragiona:
questa natura al suo fattore unita,
qual fu creata, fu sincera e buona;

ma per sé stessa pur fu ella sbandita
di paradiso, però che si torse
da via di verità e da sua vita.

La pena dunque che la croce porse
s'a la natura assunta si misura,
nulla già mai sì giustamente morse;

e così nulla fu di tanta ingiura,
guardando a la persona che sofferse,
in che era contratta tal natura.

Però d'un atto uscir cose diverse:
ch'a Dio e a' Giudei piacque una morte;
per lei tremò la terra e 'l ciel s'aperse.

Non ti dee oramai parer più forte,
quando si dice che giusta vendetta
poscia vengiata fu da giusta corte.

Ma io veggi' or la tua mente ristretta
di pensiero in pensier dentro ad un nodo,
del qual con gran disio solver s'aspetta.

Tu dici: 'Ben discerno ciò ch'i' odo;
ma perché Dio volesse, m'è occulto,
a nostra redenzion pur questo modo.'

'As a result, for centuries the human race
lay sick in an abyss of error
until the Word of God chose to descend,

'uniting human nature, estranged now
from its Maker, with Himself in His own person
by a single act of His eternal Love.

'Now direct your inner sight on what evolves from that.
This nature, united with its Maker,
was pure and good, even as it was when first created.

'But through the fault of its own doing
it was expelled from Eden
because it turned away from truth and life.

'If, then, the penalty exacted by the cross
is measured by the nature He assumed,
no other ever stung so justly.

'Yet it is also true that there was never done
so great an outrage with regard to Him who suffered,
having taken on that nature.

'From a single act, then, came diverse effects,
for the same death delighted God as well as Jews.
Because of it earth quaked and Heaven opened.

'No longer, from now on, should it seem puzzling
when you hear it said that a just vengeance
was afterward avenged in a just court.

'But now I see your mind entangled,
by one thought and another in a knot
from which, eager, it waits to be untied:

'You say, "I follow closely what I hear,
but why God wanted this to be the very way
for our redemption is obscure to me."

Questo decreto, frate, sta sepulto
a li occhi di ciascuno il cui ingegno
ne la fiamma d'amor non è adulto.

Veramente, però ch'a questo segno
molto si mira e poco si discerne,
dirò perché tal modo fu più degno.

La divina bontà, che da sé sperne
ogne livore, ardendo in sé, sfavilla
sì che dispiega le bellezze etterne.

Ciò che da lei sanza mezzo distilla
non ha poi fine, perché non si move
la sua imprenta quand' ella sigilla.

Ciò che da essa sanza mezzo piove
libero è tutto, perché non soggiace
a la virtute de le cose nove.

Più l'è conforme, e però più le piace;
ché l'ardor santo ch'ogne cosa raggia,
ne la più somigliante è più vivace.

Di tutte queste dote s'avvantaggia
l'umana creatura, e s'una manca,
di sua nobilità convien che caggia.

Solo il peccato è quel che la disfranca
e falla dissimìle al sommo bene,
per che del lume suo poco s'imbianca;

e in sua dignità mai non rivene,
se non rïempie, dove colpa vòta,
contra mal dilettar con giuste pene.

Vostra natura, quando peccò *tota*
nel seme suo, da queste dignitadi,
come di paradiso, fu remota;

'The reason for this decree, brother, lies buried,
hidden from the eyes of all
whose minds have not been ripened in the flame of love.

'Nonetheless, because so many strive to hit this mark,
while so few can even see it, I shall explain
why that was the most fitting choice.

'Spurning any kind of envy, Divine Goodness,
burning within, so sparkles
that it unfolds Eternal Beauty.

'That which, unmediated, derives from it
is thus without an end, because its imprint,
once stamped, can never wear away.

'That which, unmediated, rains down from it
is wholly free, because it is not subject
to the influence of things more recent,

'is more like that Goodness and thus more pleases Him.
The holy ardor that irradiates all things
shines brightest in what most resembles it.

'In all these gifts the human creature
is advantaged, but, if a single gift is lacking,
he must fall from his exalted state.

'Sin alone is what enslaves him,
making him unlike the highest good
so that he is illumined by its light but little,

'never returning to his privilege
unless he fills the void created by his fault
with penalties fit for his sinful pleasure.

'Your nature, when it sinned *in toto*
in its seed, was separated
from these privileges and from its Eden.

né ricovrar potiensi, se tu badi
ben sottilmente, per alcuna via,
sanza passar per un di questi guadi:

o che Dio solo per sua cortesia
dimesso avesse, o che l'uom per sé isso
avesse sodisfatto a sua follia.

Ficca mo l'occhio per entro l'abisso
de l'etterno consiglio, quanto puoi
al mio parlar distrettamente fisso.

Non potea l'uomo ne' termini suoi
mai sodisfar, per non potere ir giuso
con umiltate obedïendo poi,

quanto disobediendo intese ir suso;
e questa è la cagion per che l'uom fue
da poter sodisfar per sé dischiuso.

Dunque a Dio convenia con le vie sue
riparar l'omo a sua intera vita,
dico con l'una, o ver con amendue.

Ma perché l'ovra tanto è più gradita
da l'operante, quanto più appresenta
de la bontà del core ond' ell' è uscita,

la divina bontà che 'l mondo imprenta,
di proceder per tutte le sue vie,
a rilevarvi suso, fu contenta.

Né tra l'ultima notte e 'l primo die
sì alto o sì magnifico processo,
o per l'una o per l'altra, fu o fie:

ché più largo fu Dio a dar sé stesso
per far l'uom sufficiente a rilevarsi,
che s'elli avesse sol da sé dimesso;

'Nor could they be recovered—
if you consider closely—by any other recourse
except to ford one of these crossings:

'either that God, in His own clemency,
had pardoned, or that man, of himself,
had given satisfaction for his foolish pride.

'Now fix your eyes deep in the abyss
of the everlasting will of God
and give your strict attention to my words.

'With his limitations, man could never offer
satisfaction, for he could not descend as deep
into humility, by latter-day obedience,

'as, by disobeying, he had thought to rise.
And this is the reason for which he was denied
the power of giving satisfaction on his own.

'Thus it was necessary that God in His own ways
restore man to the fullness of his life—
by the one way, that is, or by both of them.

'But since the deed more gratifies the doer
the more it shows the goodness
of the heart from which it springs,

'divine goodness, which puts its imprint
on the world, was pleased to proceed
in both its ways to raise you up again.

'Nor between the last night and the first day
was, or will there be, a deed performed—in the first way
or the second—so sublime or generous.

'More bountiful was God when He gave Himself,
enabling man to rise again, than if,
in His sole clemency, he had simply pardoned.

e tutti li altri modi erano scarsi
a la giustizia, se 'l Figliuol di Dio
non fosse umilïato ad incarnarsi.

Or per empierti bene ogne disio,
ritorno a dichiararti in alcun loco,
perché tu veggi lì così com' io.

Tu dici: 'Io veggio l'acqua, io veggio il foco,
l'aere e la terra e tutte lor misture
venire a corruzione, e durar poco;

e queste cose pur furon creature;
per che, se ciò ch'è detto è stato vero,
esser dovrien da corruzion sicure.'

Li angeli, frate, e 'l paese sincero
nel qual tu se', dir si posson creati,
sì come sono, in loro essere intero;

ma li alimenti che tu hai nomati
e quelle cose che di lor si fanno
da creata virtù sono informati.

Creata fu la materia ch'elli hanno;
creata fu la virtù informante
in queste stelle che 'ntorno a lor vanno.

L'anima d'ogne bruto e de le piante
di complession potenzïata tira
lo raggio e 'l moto de le luci sante;

ma vostra vita sanza mezzo spira
la somma beninanza, e la innamora
di sé sì che poi sempre la disira.

E quinci puoi argomentare ancora
vostra resurrezion, se tu ripensi
come l'umana carne fessi allora
che li primi parenti intrambo fensi."

'All other means fell short of justice
save that the Son of God
120 should humble Himself by becoming flesh.

'Now, to satisfy each of your desires,
I go back to clarify one point,
123 that you may understand it just as I do.

'You say: "I see water, I see fire, air,
and earth—and all their combinations—
126 become corrupted, lasting only briefly.

' "And yet these things were created,
so that, if what was said is true,
129 they should be proof against corruption."

'The angels, brother, and this pure country
where you are may be said to have been created
132 just as they are and in their entire being,

'but those elements that have been named
and those other things made from them
135 take their form from a created power.

'Created was the matter that is in them,
created, the informing power
138 in these stars that wheel about them.

'The soul of every beast and every plant
is drawn from a complex of potentials
141 by the shining and the motion of the holy lights.

'But supreme goodness breathes life in you,
unmediated, and He so enamors your soul
144 of Himself that it desires Him forever after.

'From this you may, in consequence, deduce
your resurrection, if you but recall
how then your flesh was made
148 in the making of the first two parents.'

1–15. If one were to select a single passage from the entire *Commedia* that seems most self-consciously wrought and thoroughly marked by poetic exuberance, it might be difficult to find one more fitting that description than this, with its opening mixture of Hebrew and Latin, the mysterious "double light" glowing upon Justinian, the sudden departure of that soul and his dancing fellows, the protagonist's wild excitement in his bafflement over a theological question, and, finally, the linguistic playfulness of the poet's reference to Beatrice's name. It is as though Dante were apologizing in advance for the lack of poetic energy that typifies the rest of the canto, turned over to the theological needs of its protagonist as ministered to by his guide.

Canto VII almost seems to be offered as reassurance to readers with a religious and/or theological bent that we've closed the books on Roman history and Italian politics and now will stick to our good Christian knitting—for a while, at least.

1–3. See Tozer's translation and note (comm. to vv. 1–3): " 'Hosanna, holy God of hosts, who by Thy brightness dost illuminate from above the happy fires of these realms.' These verses appear to have been Dante's own, not a hymn of the Church; but they are in Latin, to correspond to other mediaeval hymns. *malacoth*: as Dante required a rhyme for *Sabaoth*—no easy thing to find—he availed himself of the word *malachoth*, which he met with in St. Jerome's Preface to the Vulgate, where it is translated by *regnorum* (realms). The proper form of this, which is read in modern editions of the Vulgate, is *mamlachot*, but in Dante's time *malachoth* was the accepted reading."

For *glossolalia* ("speaking in tongues") as a concern to Dante, see Hollander (Holl.1992.1). And see Di Scipio (Disc.1995.1), p. 281, for another assertion that *Inferno* VII.1 is a parodic version of *glossolalia*. Sarolli, who almost gets credit for being the first writer to connect, in an oppositional relation, the first lines of this canto with those of the seventh canto of *Inferno, "Pape Satàn, pape Satàn, aleppe!"* (Saro.1971.1, pp. 289–90), also unaccountably urges a reader to understand that the macaronic passage includes not only Hebrew and Latin, but Greek. (Tommaseo, in passing, does mention *Inf.* VII.1 in conjunction with the opening of *Par.* VII, thus depriving Sarolli of an honor he merits, since Tommaseo makes no effort to deal with the significance of the phenomenon he has observed.)

1. See the note to *Paradiso* V.1. This is the third consecutive canto that begins with a speaker's voice (rather than narration) and the second consecutive canto to begin with the same speaker's voice, both of these phenomena unique occurrences.

Justinian's first word of his last speech, *Osanna*, has a history in the poem: see *Purgatorio* XI.11 and XXIX.51. After this appearance, it also appears in *Paradiso* VIII.29; XXVIII.118; and XXXII.135. Its six appearances make it the most present "foreign" word in the poem. The Ottimo hears its resonance from the shouts for the entry of Jesus into Jerusalem (e.g., Matthew 21:9). Benvenuto, discussing (comm. to *Par.* VIII.22–30) the word's appearance in *Paradiso* VIII.29, has this to say: "Ista vox hebraica significat immensam affectionem mentis quae non potest bene exprimi graece vel latine" (This Hebrew word signifies immense mental affection which cannot be properly expressed either in Greek or in Latin). The second Hebrew word in this line, *sabaòth*, is genitive plural "of the armies" (or "hosts," as Tozer translates, an English version of Latin *hostis* [enemy], but without its sense of opposition).

For the program of song in the last *cantica*, see the note to *Paradiso* XXI.58–60.

3. God is depicted as shining down from above and illumining these saved souls who, along with Justinian, have appeared to Dante in Mercury in the moments before they withdraw from Dante's presence.

4–5. Justinian is now presented as a "substance," an irreducible human soul, singing this holy song. We perhaps now understand why Dante has gone to such lengths to associate the emperor, inspired keeper of the Roman laws, and himself, inspired poet of empire, in the preceding canto (see *Par.* VI.11; VI.23; VI.88); their tasks are not dissimilar.

6. The neologism *s'addua* is problematic. Readers are divided as to what exactly the double light represents, and there are widely various opinions. Mazzoni (Mazz.1982.1), p. 142, suggests that these lights are, the one, earthly, the other, heavenly, that is, the emperor's past and present identities. Bosco/Reggio (comm. to this verse) are of the opinion that the lights are of the warrior and of the legislator. However, as we have seen in the preceding canto, Justinian seems most eager to put the military life behind him (*Par.* VI.25–27); thus it would be strange for Dante to treat him in such wise. And see Jacoff (Jaco.1985.1), pp. 323–24, arguing for Virgil's phrase "geminas . . . flammas," the description of Augustus at the helm

during the Battle of Actium, his brows casting a double flame, as he is portrayed on the shield of Aeneas (*Aen.* VIII.680, part of the same passage visited in the last canto: See the note to *Par.* VI.79–81). That seems a promising lead to follow. However, it would probably be strange for Dante to have "borrowed" Augustus's identity for Justinian. There is also a possibility that Dante is thinking of the passage in Acts 2:3–4 in which the apostles are given the gift of *glossolalia.* There appeared to them cloven tongues of fire; these settled on each of them; they were then filled with the Holy Spirit and began to speak such languages as the Spirit gave them to utter. That is possibly reflected in what has been occurring in the opening lines of Canto VII; however, there may be a problem with the "dispertitae linguae tanquam ignis," which may not be all that well described by the phrase "doppio lume."

8–9. Whereas the souls in the Moon may have been portrayed as vanishing downward into the matter of that body (*Par.* III.122–123), these pretty clearly travel a great distance upward very rapidly. Dante has now got his logistics under control: The souls that appear in the planets return to the Empyrean once they have completed their mission, which is to instruct Dante.

10–12. This is the third and final time Dante uses repetitions of the word *dì* (see *Purg.* XXXI.5 and *Par.* V.122 for identical paired presences of the imperative form of *dire*) to give a greater sense of intensity to a speaker's urging. The first two times Beatrice is speaking to the protagonist; now Dante speaks to himself, in phrasing that is still more insistent.

The tercet, a dizzying display of alliteration (there are nine *d* sounds in three lines), also contains a possible pun. Beatrice's "sweet drops" in Italian (*dolci stille*) sound reasonably like Bonagiunta's new sweet style (*dolce stil[e] novo* [*Purg.* XXIV.57]), which he attributes to Dante's poetry in praise of Beatrice. The likelihood of intention behind such a play on words is increased by the presence of the same three rhymes later on in this canto, vv. 53–57 (*nodo, ch'i' odo,* and *modo*) as are found in *Purgatorio* XXIV.53–57. These are the only two occurrences of these constituents of *terza rima* in the poem; that they occur at the same numerical placemarks (vv. 53, 55, 57) is hardly conclusive evidence, but doesn't hurt the case, either.

12. For Dante's phrase "dolci stille" (sweet drops), see Chiamenti (Chia.1995.1), p. 178 (see also Sarteschi [Sart.1999.1], p. 186), indicating a possible source in Augustine, *Confessiones* XIII.30.45: "Et audivi, domine

deus meus, et elinxi *stillam dulcedinis* ex tua veritate" (And I heard, O Lord my God, and drank up a *drop of sweetness* out of Thy truth [tr. E. B. Pusey]).

13–15. In an exerted tercet, the poet says that he bowed his head, under the sway of his devotion to Beatrice, just as does a man who nods off to sleep. For the same phrase, "t'assonna," see *Paradiso* XXXII.139. There it precedes the vision of the Godhead, featuring the miracle of the Incarnation. It is perhaps not accidental that this is a central subject in Beatrice's long disquisition that begins at verse 19 and runs the rest of the canto.

14. Surely what is meant is "any part of her name," but we may want to reflect that the parts referred to just happen to be the first and the last, mirroring, perhaps, the alpha and omega that represent God. "Bice" was, of course, Beatrice's nickname (see *Vita nuova* XXIV.8, the ninth line of the sonnet "Io mi senti' svegliar dentro a lo core": "monna Vanna e monna Bice," where Dante observes Guido Cavalcanti's lady, Giovanna, preceding his lady, Beatrice.)

18. Some commentators try to associate the *foco* with the fires of Hell, but it seems more likely that Dante is saying that Beatrice's smile had the power to calm even one who had been set on fire. And see *Purgatorio* XXVII.10–54 for Dante's hesitant encounter with the purging flames of the terrace of Lust.

19–24. Had not Justinian just spoken at even greater length, this would have been the longest single speech in the poem, extending 130 lines from verse 19 to the end of the canto (148). The passage beginning here is described by Carroll (comm. to vv. 10–66) as "the chief theological discourse in the *Paradiso*." All the rest of the canto is, in fact, a Beatricean commentary on two passages in the preceding canto, first (vv. 19–51) Justinian's presentation of Titus's doing "vengeance for vengeance" in his destruction of Jerusalem (*Par.* VI.91–93), second (vv. 52–120) his previous claim that Tiberius, by having sovereignty when Christ was put to death (*Par.* VI.89–90), took "vengeance" for God's wrath by presiding over the Crucifixion. It is interesting that Dante makes his two unusual choices for a short list of the most significant Roman emperors the focus of Beatrice's commentary in verse.

This stylistic tour de force (having Beatrice, presented playfully in the fifth canto as the author of the poem [vv. 16–17], now reappear as the commentator on two passages from the sixth canto) is not calculated to set enthusiasts of lyric poetry aflutter. *Terza rima* is about the only thing poetic that we find in the rest of the canto, as Beatrice's language is Scholastic-sounding and severe, her interests only instructional, and correctively so.

19. The only other appearance of the word *infallibile* occurs in *Inferno* XXIX.56, where it modifies *giustizia*. Here Beatrice gives her infallible (because she speaks with the authority of her Maker) idea of the justness of God's vengeance, the "negative form" of his justice, punishment.

20–21. For a consideration of the way in which Christ's prediction of the fall of Jerusalem (Luke 19:36–46) and the city's conquest by the Romans in A.D. 70 are reflected in this and other passages (and also look forward to the coming punishment of Florence), see Martinez (Mart.2003.1).

20. The presence of two words directly related to "justice" in this verse begins by far the largest single deployment in any canto of such words: *giusta* and *giustamente* here; *giustamente* (42); *giusta* (50 and 51); *giuste* (84); *giustizia* (119). The neighboring canto (VI) is tied for second place with four, thus making these two cantos the center of this concern in a poem that is perhaps more concerned with justice than with any other single concept. See the note to *Inferno* III.4.

25–33. Adam's sin of transgression (and it is significant that Dante here is placing on *his* shoulders the sin of Eve) was what "brought sin into the world and all our woe" (Milton, *Paradise Lost* 1.3), to borrow the words of another major poet's reference to that transgression. It is this for which the Word of God chose, in his love for humankind, to offer Himself as flesh in sacrifical atonement for all sin since Adam. (It was precisely this humanity of Jesus in which Justinian did not at first believe [see *Par.* VI.13–15].)

26. Adam was not born; he was created directly by God, as was (almost) Eve.

28. Scartazzini/Vandelli (comm. on vv. 28–33) point to *Monarchia* III.iv.14 for the phrase *infirmitas peccati* (infirmity of sin) as corresponding to the sickness afflicting the human race after Adam's fall.

29. Later Dante will spell out the exact amount of time that passed between Adam's sin and his redemption—5,232 years. See *Paradiso* XXVI.118–123.

30. The "Word of God" is Jesus, as Second Person of the Trinity.

31–33. This tercet includes reference to the two other aspects of the triune God, the Sapience represented by the Son having been mentioned in verse 30 (where Beatrice refers to the Word becoming flesh); the Power represented by the Father, "Maker" of all things; the Love represented by the Holy Spirit.

34–45. Humankind, a combination of immortal soul and mortal body, as present in Adam and Eve, quickly (for exactly how quickly, see *Par.* XXVI.139–142) turned from God to sin, and was sent out of Eden. If we measure what was done to Christ upon the Cross by the enormous burden of sin He took on, His penalty was utterly just; if, on the other hand, we measure the worth of the one who was punished, no greater outrage was ever committed, especially when we consider what He had voluntarily consented to.

39. The verse repeats, as Benvenuto da Imola (comm. to vv. 34–39) was perhaps the first to realize, Christ's dictum (John 14:6) "Ego sum via, et veritas, et vita" (I am the way, and the truth, and the life). The text continues, "No one comes to the Father unless through me."

46–48. The paired results of Christ's sacrifice are expressed in a chiasmus: The death of Jesus pleased (a) God and (b) the Jews; it caused both (b) the earthquake at the Crucifixion and (a) the opening of Heaven to humankind. The Jews took perverse pleasure at the killing of Jesus for which reason God made the earth shake, expressing His displeasure; at the same time, and of far greater importance, God accepted Jesus' sacrifice and opened Heaven to redeemed humanity.

49–51. Beatrice's repetition of the adjective *giusta* (just) underlines her main concern for Dante, that he understand that God never acts unjustly. She has taken care of his first doubt, which arose from what Justinian said about the reign of Titus.

52–120. Next Beatrice turns to the problem that arose for the protagonist in Justinian's remarks about the reign of Tiberius. This is one of the most pernicious stumbling blocks for nonbelievers and even some Christians. It is the question posed (and answered) by Beatrice here (see Scartazzini's lengthy gloss to this passage, which deals with Dante's complex discussion clearly). The two main sources for Dante's thinking about the justification for the death of Jesus on the Cross are, according to Scartazzini, St. Thomas (*ST* III, q. 46, a. 1–3) and St. Anselm of Canterbury (*Cur Deus homo*). For insistence on the primacy, for Dante's thinking on this subject, of Anselm's tract, see Fallani (Fall.1989.1), pp. 233–34.

52–63. Now, reading Dante's mind, Beatrice sees what is troubling him; there must have been some other way for human sin to have been canceled short of having the incarnate Godhead be slain upon a cross. Beatrice warns that her proof will be difficult, because only those nourished over time by the warmth of God's affection ever understand this mystery, that is, only those inspired by the Holy Spirit are able to understand the love for humankind that impelled Jesus to give up his life for us.

57. From Lombardi (1791, comm. to vv. 56–57) to Grabher (1934, comm. to vv. 55–63), most commentators think the word *pur* here means "only." Starting with Trucchi (1936, comm. to vv. 52–57), the tide begins swinging to *proprio* (precisely, exactly); Chimenz (1962, comm. to vv. 56–57) prefers this meaning to "only," as do Bosco/Reggio (1979, comm. to vv. 56–57); as our translation indicates, we do, too.

64–120. Tozer's summary of these passages may be helpful: "Man, inasmuch as his soul proceeded direct from God, possessed the gifts of immortality, free will, and likeness to God, and on these depended his high position (vv. 64–78). By the Fall the freedom of his will and his likeness to God were impaired, and his position was lost (vv. 79–81). There were only two ways by which he could recover this, i.e., either (1) that he should make satisfaction himself for his sin, or (2) that God in His mercy should pardon him freely (vv. 82–93). The former of these it was impossible for man to do, because he could not render any adequate recompense; it remained therefore for God to guarantee his pardon (vv. 94–105). This God did in a manner at once most consonant with His own nature, as being perfect Goodness, and most advantageous to man, and most in accordance with the demands of justice. He followed both the way of mercy and the way of justice. By the Incarnation and death of Christ He enabled man to regain his lost position, and at the same time made the satisfaction for his sins which justice required" (vv. 106–20).

64–65. For an attempt to demonstrate the closeness of the thought here to that found in Plato's *Timaeus*, see Fraccaroli (Frac.1906.1), pp. 393–97, disputing the more usual nineteenth-century claim of a dependence upon Boethius. However, see Richard Green's note to the passage, in his translation of the *Consolatio* (Gree. 1962.1), p. 60, pointing out that the poem ("O qui perpetua mundum ratione gubernas" [O you who govern the world with eternal reason]) in Boethius (*Consolatio* III.m9) is recognized as being an epitome of the first section of the *Timaeus*. Among the early commentators, Pietro di Dante (comm. to vv. 64–78) cites Boethius ("Rather it was the form of the highest good, existing within You without envy, which caused You to fashion all things according to the external exemplar"), while Benvenuto da Imola (comm. to vv. 64–66) and Francesco da Buti (comm. to vv. 64–75) cite *Timaeus* 29e (the opening of Book I): "Optimus erat, et ab optimo omnis invidia relegata est" (He [the god who made universal disorder into order] was good: and in the good no jealousy in any matter can ever arise [tr. F. M. Cornford]—Plato is speaking of the divine mind, as is Boethius). For more support of Plato's candidacy and general consideration of the problem, see Galimberti (Gali.1968.1), pp. 227–35. Sapegno (comm. to vv. 64–66) was perhaps the first to cite both (Boethius, *Cons.* III.m9.1–6; Plato, *Tim.* I). Giacalone (comm. to vv. 64–66) offers helpful discussion and a bibliography.

67. Those things created directly, that is, without mediation, by God include the angels, the heavenly spheres, unformed matter (e.g., the earth's surface, awaiting the formal intervention of God to be given its definitive shape), and the rational part of the tripartite human soul. For the distinction between this unformed God-created matter, Augustine's *materia informis*, and "prime matter" (*materia prima*), see O'Keeffe (Okee.1924.1), pp. 51–57.

68–69. That which God creates unmediated is eternal and unvarying.

72. The "more recent" things were created not directly by God, but with some mediation (e.g., planetary influence), since all of these were part of a "secondary creation."

85–87. In Adam we all sinned, and have been denied the privileges that once were his, particularly three things: immortality, the earthly paradise, and our resemblance to God.

97–100. We were not capable of abasing ourselves in humility deep enough to make up for the amount we had risen up in pride.

103–111. Thus it remained for God to ransom us using either mercy or justice. He elected to employ both of these.

112–120. Dante employs *hysteron proteron* yet again to mark either end of human history, the last night of life on earth (see the Apocalypse) and the first day (see Genesis). In the period of time sectored in that arc no greater act ever was or shall be than Jesus' act of self-humiliation to save humankind.

124–138. This passage and the rest of the canto deal with the ontology of God's creation, specifically the distinctions between the nature of being in that which is created directly by God (things eternal or, more properly, since they have a beginning in time, sempiternal) and in that which, though created by God (for nothing that exists owes or can owe its existence to any other first cause), has other participation in its making (i.e., they are made by the intervention of other already existent things, as are almost all things that we encounter: butterflies, the cliffs of Dover, rain). On this question see Moore's late essay, "Dante's Theory of Creation" (Moor.1917.1), pp. 134–65, and the stern response by David O'Keeffe (Okee.1924.1); Moevs's discussion (Moev.2005.1), pp. 122–26, agrees with O'Keeffe's objections to Moore's formulations, which underlie many later (mis)understandings of the basic cosmic views put forward here by Beatrice, and which, as a result, are incorrect. As Moevs points out (pp. 123–24), Beatrice fears lest Dante, mistaking her words at vv. 67–69, fail to distinguish between primary creation (i.e., directly by God) and secondary creation (God acting in collaboration with other agents). As Moevs rightly insists, for Dante there is no such thing as creation independent of God; but there is (1) direct creation and (2) indirect creation; in the latter other agents besides the deity have a role. All such entities, Beatrice concludes, are "mortal," including the four elements. This passage is not made easier by its frequent use of the past participle of the verb *creare*. The word *creature* at verse 127 has the sense of "things created" (by God). But this, mirroring the protagonist's confusion, blurs the crucial distinction that Beatrice will make; all things are created by God, some few directly (and they are eternal or, to use the correct term, sempiternal) but most parts of the made universe, as the four elements, indirectly. At verse 131 *creati* also refers to divine creation, but this time (and for the only time in this passage) of direct creation by God, and hence of eternal things, both angels and the heavenly spheres. In verse 135 *creata* refers to the secondary creation of the informative power in the stars, as it does in both of its iterations in vv. 136 and 137. The next could not be clearer, but its use of the same term, *creare*, for both kinds of creation, primary and secondary (i.e., direct and indirect), makes a reader's task more difficult.

124–129. This is the second consecutive canto in which Dante has not spoken (he is in fact silent from *Par.* V.129 until *Par.* VIII.44 [for his considerably longer period of abstention from speech, see *Par.* IX.81–*Par.* XIV.96]). In this canto his suppressed speech is reported (but not uttered) at vv. 10–12 and Beatrice speaks his doubt for him in vv. 55–57 and then once more here in this passage.

139–144. For a paraphrase of the first tercet, see Tozer (comm. to vv. 139–141): "From speaking of things without life Beatrice passes to those which possess the sensitive or the vegetative life without the rational soul. These also are not incorruptible, because their life is produced mediately by the influence of the stars, acting on those elements of their nature (i.e., of the matter of which they are composed) which are capable of being affected by them. 'The brightness and the motion of the holy lights (the stars) draws forth the life of brutes and plants from the combination of elements (*complession*) in them, which is endued with power (*potenziata*) thereto,' i.e., to be so affected. *Complession* in its technical use means 'a combination of elements,' e.g., of humours of the body, or properties of matter." And see Moevs (Moev.2005.1), p. 125, on this passage: "The souls of all plants and animals are 'drawn from' varying compounds of the sublunar elements (*complession potenzïata*) by the influence of the stars, but human life (the human intelligence or rational soul) 'breathes directly' from the 'supreme beneficence,' from Intellect-Being itself. That is why the human mind or soul is always in love with, and never ceases to seek union with, the ground of its being, of all being."

145–148. Moevs (Moev.2005.1), pp. 130–132, points out an error underpinning some commentators' responses to the Dantean formulation of a central theological issue in this canto: the corruptibility of the first bodies given to humankind directly by God. Their usual position is that this body, created as home of the soul in both Adam and Eve, was incorruptible; thus its "true nature" is incorruptible, despite original sin; with resurrection we regain that incorruptible body. But what, we may ask, of the damned? Clearly their bodies are not of the incorruptible kind, since the damned all-too-painfully recollect the corruptions of the body and live repeating them eternally, as we have seen often enough in *Inferno*. That is a negative argument, if perhaps a useful one. Moreover, and as Moevs, following O'Keeffe (Okee.1924.1), pp. 61–62, points out, the argument is heretical on its own terms. No Christian authority ever said that the human body was eternal, even in its original Edenic condition (but exactly this opinion is found among some commentators; see, e.g., Fallani [Fall.1989.1], p. 236, holding that it is indeed immortal). And so the question arises: Will we be given what we originally had, a corruptible body washed clean of its sins (unlike the maculate body that is the property of anyone damned), as our soul has been? Or will we receive a truly incorruptible body? In one way of understanding, the body has always been, and always will be, corruptible (even if, resurrected, it will not decay anymore). To triumph in it is also to triumph over it. Moevs concludes his treatment of this problematic passage as follows (p. 132): "Beatrice has re-expressed the great Clementine dictum that God became man so that man may learn from man how to become God." But see Paul's discussion of the raising of the dead in I Corinthians 15:35–54, which certainly seems to promise incorruptible flesh to those who participate in the general resurrection.

PARADISO VIII

OUTLINE

VENUS

1–12 Venereal preamble: what the ancient pagans used to believe about this planet (**"veneral trinity"**); **Dido**

13–15 the ascent to Venus accomplished without awareness

16–21 double simile: as a spark within a flame and as one voice is distinguished from another because it varies its note, so the lights of souls stood out from the light of Venus

22–27 pseudo-simile: lightning or windstorm, to one who had seen these movements, would seem slow compared to them;

28–30 those in front sing "Osanna" (the first song of the canto)

31–32 one of the saved **[Charles Martel]** approaches to speak:

33–39 "We revolve here with the order of angels known as **'Principalities,'** to whom you once referred as **'Thrones'**

40–42 Dante looks reverently at Beatrice; with her permission

43–48 he turns his eyes back to Charles: "Who are you?"

49–84 Charles's story:

- 49–51 I died young (twenty-four years old in 1295), and this will cause the world more woe than had I not
- 52–54 the joy that swathes me makes me like a silkworm
- 55–57 you (Dante) loved me much; had I lived, you would have enjoyed the rewards of that love
- 58–75 the realms deprived of his guidance by his death: **Provence**, the kingdom of **Naples**, **Hungary**
- 76–84 Charles castigates his brother **Robert**'s future rule

85–90 Dante takes joy in seeing his joy seen by Charles in God

91–93 Dante continues by wondering, on the basis of vv. 82–83, how a good father can have a bad son

94–96 Charles agrees to deal with Dante's quandary:

97–111 "God's providence is present in the heavenly bodies"

112–114 Charles: "is that clear?" Dante: "Yes"

115–135 Charles continues: "humans have diverse dispositions, as **[Aristotle]** says (thus **Solon, Xerxes, Melchizedek, [Daedalus]**, **[Icarus]**); but Nature does not favor one family over another: **Esau, Jacob; Romulus**";

136–138 Charles now offers a corollary as a "cloak":

139–148 the world should not insist on forcing humans to take on roles that do not fit their natures.

PARADISO VIII

Solea creder lo mondo in suo periclo
che la bella Ciprigna il folle amore
raggiasse, volta nel terzo epiciclo;

per che non pur a lei faceano onore
di sacrificio e di votivo grido
le genti antiche ne l'antico errore;

ma Dïone onoravano e Cupido,
quella per madre sua, questo per figlio,
e dicean ch'el sedette in grembo a Dido;

e da costei ond' io principio piglio
pigliavano il vocabol de la stella
che 'l sol vagheggia or da coppa or da ciglio.

Io non m'accorsi del salire in ella;
ma d'esservi entro mi fé assai fede
la donna mia ch'i' vidi far più bella.

E come in fiamma favilla si vede,
e come in voce voce si discerne,
quand' una è ferma e altra va e riede,

vid' io in essa luce altre lucerne
muoversi in giro più e men correnti,
al modo, credo, di lor viste interne.

Di fredda nube non disceser venti,
o visibili o no, tanto festini,
che non paressero impediti e lenti

a chi avesse quei lumi divini
veduti a noi venir, lasciando il giro
pria cominciato in li alti Serafini;

To its own cost, there was a time the world believed
that the fair Cyprian beamed rays of maddened love,
revolving in the wheel of the third epicycle,

so that the ancient peoples in their ancient error
not only did her honor
with sacrifice and votive cry

but honored Dïone, and Cupid too,
one as her mother, the other as her son,
and told how once he sat in Dido's lap.

And from her with whom I here begin they took
the name of the star that is wooed by the sun,
now at her nape, now at her brow.

I had not been aware of rising to that star,
but was assured of being in it
when I observed my lady turn more beautiful.

And, as one sees a spark within a flame
or hears, within a song, a second voice,
holding its note while the other comes and goes,

so I saw within that light still other lights,
swifter and slower in their circling motions,
it seemed in measure to their inner sight.

Winds racing down from a cold cloud,
in their swift motion, whether visible or not,
would seem impeded, slow,

to one who had seen these heavenly lights
come toward us, pausing in the dance
begun among the lofty Seraphim.

e dentro a quei che più innanzi appariro
sonava "*Osanna*" sì, che unque poi
di rïudir non fui sanza disiro.

Indi si fece l'un più presso a noi
e solo incominciò: "Tutti sem presti
al tuo piacer, perché di noi ti gioi.

Noi ci volgiam coi principi celesti
d'un giro e d'un girare e d'una sete,
ai quali tu del mondo già dicesti:

'Voi che 'ntendendo il terzo ciel movete';
e sem sì pien d'amor, che, per piacerti,
non fia men dolce un poco di quïete."

Poscia che li occhi miei si fuoro offerti
a la mia donna reverenti, ed essa
fatti li avea di sé contenti e certi,

rivolsersi a la luce che promessa
tanto s'avea, e "Deh, chi siete?" fue
la voce mia di grande affetto impressa.

E quanta e quale vid' io lei far piùe
per allegrezza nova che s'accrebbe,
quando parlai, a l'allegrezze sue!

Così fatta, mi disse: "Il mondo m'ebbe
giù poco tempo; e se più fosse stato,
molto sarà di mal, che non sarebbe.

La mia letizia mi ti tien celato
che mi raggia dintorno e mi nasconde
quasi animal di sua seta fasciato.

Assai m'amasti, e avesti ben onde;
che s'io fossi giù stato, io ti mostrava
di mio amor più oltre che le fronde.

And from among the closest that appeared
rang out *Hosanna* so that ever since
I have not been without the wish to hear it.

Then one, alone, drew nearer and began:
'All of us desire to bring you pleasure
so that you may in turn delight in us.

'In one orbit we revolve with these celestial princes—
in one circle, with one circling, and with a single thirst—
to whom, from the world, you addressed these words:

' "You who, by understanding, move the third heaven."
We are filled with love but, to give you pleasure,
a little respite will be no less sweet to us.'

After I had raised my reverent eyes
to my lady and she had made them glad
and made them sure of her consent,

I turned them back to the light that had made
such a promise, and 'Oh, who are you?'
I asked, my voice expressing great affection.

I watched the light grow larger
and more luminescent as I spoke
with new joy added to its joys!

Thus changed, it said to me: 'The world kept me
but a little while below, and, had that time been longer,
much evil that shall be would not have been.

'It is my happiness that hides me from you,
as it enfolds and hides me in its shining rays,
like the creature that is wrapped in its own silk.

'You loved me well, and with good reason.
Had I remained below, to you I would have shown
much more than the mere fronds of my affection.

Quella sinistra riva che si lava
di Rodano poi ch'è misto con Sorga,
per suo segnore a tempo m'aspettava,

e quel corno d'Ausonia che s'imborga
di Bari e di Gaeta e di Catona,
da ove Tronto e Verde in mare sgorga.

Fulgeami già in fronte la corona
di quella terra che 'l Danubio riga
poi che le ripe tedesche abbandona.

E la bella Trinacria, che caliga
tra Pachino e Peloro, sopra 'l golfo
che riceve da Euro maggior briga,

non per Tifeo ma per nascente solfo,
attesi avrebbe li suoi regi ancora,
nati per me di Carlo e di Ridolfo,

se mala segnoria, che sempre accora
li popoli suggetti, non avesse
mosso Palermo a gridar: 'Mora, mora!'

E se mio frate questo antivedesse,
l'avara povertà di Catalogna
già fuggeria, perché non li offendesse;

ché veramente proveder bisogna
per lui, o per altrui, sì ch'a sua barca
carcata più d'incarco non si pogna.

La sua natura, che di larga parca
discese, avria mestier di tal milizia
che non curasse di mettere in arca."

"Però ch'i' credo che l'alta letizia
che 'l tuo parlar m'infonde, segnor mio,
là 've ogne ben si termina e s'inizia,

'The left bank that is moistened by the Rhone
once it mingles waters with the Sorgue
awaited me as sovereign at a time to come,

'as did Ausonia's horn, from where it borders Bari,
Gaeta, and Catona, to the place
where the Tronto and the Verde flow into the sea.

'On my brow already shone the crown
of the country furrowed by the Danube
once it leaves behind its German banks.

'And fair Trinacria, overcast and murky
between Pachynus and Pelorus,
above the bay most vexed by the Sirocco,

'darkened not by Typhon but by rising sulphur—
would still have waited for its kings,
born through me of Charles and Rudolph,

'had not bad governance, which ever grieves the hearts
of subject peoples, impelled Palermo
to cry out, "Kill them, kill!"

'And if my brother but foresaw this
he would shun the greedy poverty of Catalonia
so that it not afflict him.

'For truly there is need that he or someone else
should look to it, lest on his overloaded bark
be laid a load of even greater weight.

'His stingy nature, though he came from worthy stock,
would require officials who do not set their hearts
on filling up their coffers.'

'Since I sense that the deep joy
your words have filled me with, my lord,
is seen by you as clearly as it's seen by me

per te si veggia come la vegg' io,
grata m'è più; e anco quest' ho caro
perché 'l discerni rimirando in Dio.

Fatto m'hai lieto, e così mi fa chiaro,
poi che, parlando, a dubitar m'hai mosso
com' esser può, di dolce seme, amaro."

Questo io a lui; ed elli a me: "S'io posso
mostrarti un vero, a quel che tu dimandi
terrai lo viso come tien lo dosso.

Lo ben che tutto il regno che tu scandi
volge e contenta, fa esser virtute
sua provedenza in questi corpi grandi.

E non pur le nature provedute
sono in la mente ch'è da sé perfetta,
ma esse insieme con la lor salute:

per che quantunque quest' arco saetta
disposto cade a proveduto fine,
sì come cosa in suo segno diretta.

Se ciò non fosse, il ciel che tu cammine
producerebbe sì li suoi effetti,
che non sarebbero arti, ma ruine;

e ciò esser non può, se li 'ntelletti
che muovon queste stelle non son manchi,
e manco il primo, che non li ha perfetti.

Vuo' tu che questo ver più ti s'imbianchi?"
E io "Non già; ché impossibil veggio
che la natura, in quel ch'è uopo, stanchi."

Ond' elli ancora: "Or dì: sarebbe il peggio
per l'omo in terra, se non fosse cive?"
"Sì" rispuos' io; "e qui ragion non cheggio."

'there where every good begins and ends,
my joy is greater. And I also hold it dear
90 that you discern this as you gaze on God.

'You have made me glad, now bring me light,
for, listening to your words, I am confused:
93 How from sweet seed may come a bitter fruit?'

Thus I to him, and he: 'If I can prove a truth to you,
then you will have before your eyes
96 an answer to the question on which you turn your back.

'The Good, which revolves and gladdens
all the realm you now are climbing,
99 puts its plan to work through these great bodies.

'Not only are the natures of the souls foreseen
within the Mind that in Itself is perfect,
102 but, along with their natures, their well-being,

'and thus whatsoever this bow shoots
falls predisposed to a determined end,
105 as a shaft directed to its target.

'Were this not so, the heavens you traverse
would engender such effects
108 as would not seem crafted but chaotic,

'and such cannot be, unless the intellects that impel
the spheres here were defective and defective, too,
111 the primal Intellect, for failing to perfect them.

'Would you like to have this truth made clearer?'
And I: 'No, for I understand it cannot be
114 that nature should weary in her necessary chores.'

And he continued: 'Now tell me, would it be worse
for man on earth if he were not a social being?'
117 'Yes,' I agreed, 'and here I ask no proof.'

"E puot' elli esser, se giù non si vive
diversamente per diversi offici?
Non, se 'l maestro vostro ben vi scrive."

Sì venne deducendo infino a quici;
poscia conchiuse: "Dunque esser diverse
convien di vostri effetti le radici:

per ch'un nasce Solone e altro Serse,
altro Melchisedèch e altro quello
che, volando per l'aere, il figlio perse.

La circular natura, ch'è suggello
a la cera mortal, fa ben sua arte,
ma non distingue l'un da l'altro ostello.

Quinci addivien ch'Esaù si diparte
per seme da Iacòb; e vien Quirino
da sì vil padre, che si rende a Marte.

Natura generata il suo cammino
simil farebbe sempre a' generanti,
se non vincesse il proveder divino.

Or quel che t'era dietro t'è davanti:
ma perché sappi che di te mi giova,
un corollario voglio che t'ammanti.

Sempre natura, se fortuna trova
discorde a sé, com' ogne altra semente
fuor di sua regïon, fa mala prova.

E se 'l mondo là giù ponesse mente
al fondamento che natura pone,
seguendo lui, avria buona la gente.

Ma voi torcete a la religïone
tal che fia nato a cignersi la spada,
e fate re di tal ch'è da sermone;
onde la traccia vostra è fuor di strada."

'And can he be such if men down there on earth
live not in different ways for different tasks?
Not if your master is correct in this.'

Thus he brought his thesis to its point
and then concluded, 'The roots of your activities,
therefore, are necessarily diverse:

'Thus one is born Solon and another Xerxes,
one Melchizedek, another one the man
who flew up through the air and lost his son.

'Circling nature, which sets its seal
on mortal wax, plies its craft with skill,
but does not distinguish one house from another.

'Thus it happens that Esau differs even in the seed
from Jacob, and Quirinus is born
of so rude a father he is ascribed to Mars.

'Nature, once begotten, would always follow
a course like that of its begetters
if Divine Providence did not intervene.

'Now what was behind you is before you.
But that you may know how much it is you please me,
I want you to wear this corollary as your cloak.

'Always, if nature meets a fate
unsuited to it, like any kind of seed
out of its native soil, it comes to a bad end,

'and if the world below paid more attention
to the foundation nature lays
and built on that, it would be peopled well.

'But no, you force into religion one born
to wear the sword, and make a king
of one more fit for sermons,
so that your path departs from the true way.'

1–12. The elaborate and classicizing beginning of the canto is marked by fully six verbs in the imperfect tense (*solea, raggiasse, faceano, onoravano, dicean, pigliavano*). (For a characterization of their effect, see Ragni's response, cited in the note to vv. 13–15.) This is one of the longest "single-sentence" canto-openings up to this point in the poem, superseded only by *Inferno* XXIV.1–15.

2. Venus is "Cyprian" because she was born on the island of Cyprus.

3. Two words in this verse may benefit from closer attention. The verb *raggiare* is here used in the imperfect subjunctive, thus connoting a certain dubiety about the pagan opinion that the planet Venus was responsible for errors of erotic adventure. Compare *Convivio* II.vi.9: ". . . the rays of each heaven are the paths along which their virtue descends [directly from the planet itself] upon these things here below" (tr. R. Lansing). Dante is speaking of Venus there, as he is here. For awareness of this connection, see Poletto (comm. to vv. 1–12).

The concept epicycle (*epiciclo*), another example of *hapax legomenon*, was the invention of ancient astronomers because their calculations of planetary movement, based on the belief that the earth was the center of the universe, around which the planets revolved, needed regularizing. And thus all the planets except the Sun supposedly had epicyclical movement. Here is Tozer on the nature of that motion (comm. to vv. 1–3): "The term 'epicycle' means a circle, the centre of which is carried round upon another circle; cp. *Convivio* [II.iii.16–17]. To account for the apparent irregularities in the orbits of the heavenly bodies which resulted from the view that they revolved round the earth which was stationary, Ptolemy suggested that each planet moved in such a circle of its own in addition to the revolution of the sphere to which it belonged. In the case of Venus this is called the third epicycle, because the sphere of Venus is the third in order in the heavens."

And see Carroll (comm. to vv. 1–21): "Translating all this into its spiritual equivalent, the meaning appears to be: as Venus had one movement round the Earth and another round the Sun, so these souls had two movements of the heart, cyclic and epicyclic, one round some earthly centre, the other round God, of whom the Sun is the natural symbol."

4–6. The second iteration of the word "ancient" flavors the first, which looks innocent enough when first we notice it: "ancient peoples" is not ordinarily a slur. But it becomes one once it is conjoined with "ancient error," at once represented by the slaughter of innocent animals ("sacrifice") and nefarious vows ("votive cry").

7. Now to the amorous "pantheon," featuring the pagan goddess Venus, are conjoined her mother, Dione, and her son, Cupid. These three divinities constitute a sort of pagan trinity: Mother, Daughter, Holy Son.

9. See *Convivio* IV.xxvi.8 for Dido and the promise of eventual further reference to her in the seventh treatise, which, of course, was never completed. Is this Dante's fulfillment of that promise?

Pietro Alighieri (Pietro1, comm. to vv. 7–9) cites the Virgilian passage, including the line (*Aen.* I.718) in which Dido's name, accompanied by *gremio* (translated by Dante's *grembo,* "lap"), appears, a line that describes Venus's maternal ruse, placing Cupid in Dido's lap disguised as Ascanius.

Paratore (Para.1989.1), p. 250, points out that the presence of Dido in this canto is yet another connection to *Inferno* V, such as others find revealed in vv. 32–33, 38–39, 45.

10. Dante "takes his start" with Venus (*la bella Ciprigna*) at verse 2. However, Vellutello (comm. to vv. 10–12) expands her meaning into the familiar "two Venuses," the first earthly and carnal, the second heavenly and spiritual. He does not say so, but Dante is possibly loading his phrase with a double sense, talking both about the carnal Venus, with reference to whom he begins this canto, and also his spiritual awakening in his love for Beatrice.

12. The meaning is that the Sun courts Venus, now from behind her (at her neck), now approaching her from the front (his attention fixed on her brow). The celestial phenomenon referred to is the epicyclical movement of Venus around the Sun, in which she moves from west to east, describing a circle around the circumference of her sphere, which, like every planetary sphere, is itself moving in a westerly direction. Thus the countering motion of the planet itself, on its epicycle, takes her from a position in which she has the Sun behind her in the morning, when she is known as Lucifer, to one in which she has him before her in the evening, when she is known as Hesperus. As Bosco/Reggio (comm. to this verse) point out, Venus is not both morning star and evening star on the same day, a fact of which Dante is aware (*Conv.* II.ii.1).

13–15. Once again the poet allows us to wonder how the protagonist, especially if he is in fact in the body (see *Par.* I.99), manages to penetrate the physical matter of the planets.

Ragni (Ragn.1989.2), pp. 137–39, points out that the imperfect tense used in the long opening passage (vv. 1–12) is now replaced by the past definite as we move from the hazy distant pagan times and into the hard-edged recent experience of the reality of the Christian afterworld beheld by the protagonist.

It is notable that the rising into the next planet on its epicyclical sphere is accomplished in a single tercet. By comparison, the arrivals in the Moon (*Par.* II.19–30) and in Mercury (*Par.* V.86–99) both take considerably more poetic space.

16–30. The five tercets that serve as introduction to Venus are followed by another five tercets that serve to introduce the souls of the saved who descend from the Empyrean to greet Dante here (Charles Martel in this canto, Cunizza, Folco, and Rahab in the next; the last three clearly are associated with an inclination toward carnal love that impaired their moral function, a fact that calls into question the reasons for Charles's presence here [see the note to vv. 55–57]).

Dante employs first a double simile (vv. 16–21) and then an implicit simile (it is one in content, if not quite in form, vv. 22–27) to describe these souls, before reporting on what they do (vv. 28–30), which is to sing "Hosanna."

17–18. For the difficulties in ascertaining the actual polyphonic music Dante might have had in mind as he wrote this passage, see Heilbronn (Heil.1984.2), pp. 42–45.

19. We observe that the term *lucerne* ("lamps," or "lights") has now replaced *ombre* as the term for the souls of the saved. See the note to *Paradiso* III.34. And for the two following uses of *lucerna* with this meaning, see *Paradiso* XXI.73 and XXIII.28.

20–21. Once again the speed at which a spirit moves suggests how intensely it is capable of seeing/loving God.

23. The phrase "whether visible or not" refers to lightning (according to Aristotle, winds made visible by ignition [Carroll, comm. to vv. 22–26]), or windstorms (e.g., hurricanes).

26–27. Against the many commentators who believe that Dante here refers to the Empyrean, where the Seraphim (and the other eight angelic orders are located), Bosco/Reggio (comm. to these verses) point out that, yes, Dante could have been using synecdoche in order to signify *all* the angelic orders by naming only one, but that the angels are probably meant to be considered seated, as we see that the blessed are. And so they quite reasonably conclude that Dante is referring to the Primum Mobile, where the angelic dance has its beginning with the Seraphim and moves down through the spheres (where we catch a glimpse of it here).

29. For the other occurrences of *osanna* (a joyous and affectionate shout) in the poem, see the note to *Paradiso* VII.1. And for the program of song in the last *cantica*, see the note to *Paradiso* XXI.58–60.

31–33. One of the souls (we will eventually be able to recognize him as Charles Martel, although he is never named) comes forward to speak for all of them. Indeed, his opening remarks (which conclude at verse 39) are not in any way personal. He in fact is the mouthpiece for all those who have come down. That will no longer be true once Dante asks him who he is, when he has reason to personalize his response.

34–39. Charles informs Dante that here they are whirling with the Principalities, the order of angels that govern the heaven of Venus, which Dante had once (incorrectly) said was that of the Thrones (*Conv.* II.v.6). He now has firsthand experience of exactly how wrong he was.

Dante is obviously revising a previous opinion about angelology. (For the clarification that in *Convivio* he had followed the views of Gregory the Great as found in the *Moralia*, but here as found in his *Homilies*, see Muscetta [Musc.1968.1], p. 258.) However, something far worse than a scholarly slip by an amateur of angelic lore is probably at stake here. The first ode of *Convivio*, the opening verse of which is cited, specifically rejects Beatrice in favor of Lady Philosophy. And a good deal of energy in the *Commedia* is put to the task of retracting the views that reflect that wrongful love. Some scholars, rejecting this notion, point out that Dante *never* gives over his predilection for philosophical investigation (e.g., Scott [Scot.1995.1], Dronke [Dron.1997.1], and Scott again [Scot.2004.2], pp. 126–29). Such a view is surely correct yet may be said to miss the point: Dante needs to separate himself from his choice of Lady Philosophy over Beatrice, and this requires jettisoning certain of his philosophical baggage, especially that displayed in the first decade of the fourteenth century, that is, not Aristotle, but perhaps Plato (author of the *Timaeus*) and/or the neoplatonist Proclus (see the note to *Par.* IV.24); not Aristotle, but perhaps the "radical Aristotelians" (see Corti [Cort.1983.1]).

The modern notion of a palinodic aspect in Dante's more mature view of his earlier work, in particular *Convivio*, featuring a certain amount of stern remonstrance on the part of the author of the *Commedia* against his younger self, began perhaps with Freccero, "Casella's Song" (1973) (reprinted in Frec.1986.1, pp. 186–94). His position was shared by Hollander (Holl.1975.1), Jacoff (Jaco.1980.1 [to a lesser degree]), Barolini (Baro.1984.1 [also to a lesser degree]), pp. 31–40, 57–84; and see Hollander (Holl.1990.1). For a considerably earlier understanding of the conflict between the two Dantes, see Giovanni Federzoni's note (Fede.1920.1) to vv. 36–39: "The reason for the reference to the *canzone* here is that the amatory life, to which the spirits encountered in this planet offered themselves, the Epicurean existence condemned by the austerity of the Christian religion, is, on the contrary, justified by pagan philosophy, the philosophy that Dante himself celebrated in the second treatise of the *Convivio* and most of all in this very *canzone*." And now see Picone (Pico.2002.3).

34. The angelic spirits are now not seated in the Empyrean but whirling in "dance" with the rotation of Venus, its sphere governed by these Principalities.

38. The love that fills the speaker and his companions is obviously *caritas*, not the lust that they knew from their earthly lives. See the note to vv. 55–57.

39. While the literal sense of his remark is clearly that staying still and quiet to welcome Dante will be no less sweet to them than are their whirling dance and accompanying song, Charles's way of implicitly reprimanding Dante for his divagation from Beatrice is courtesy itself: "let our *not* singing your ode seem a favor to you." Compare Casella's singing of the ode from *Convivio* III in *Purgatorio* II and Cato's rebuke.

40–41. While Dante turns to Beatrice to gain permission to pose a question to these souls, it seems likely that he might have looked at her to see if she is reflecting upon his disloyalty when he turned away from her to the *donna gentile*. But he has been through Lethe, and himself cannot remember his fault. But if he cannot remember, we can. He did not behave so reverently to her memory in *Convivio*, when, as he tells it, after the death of Beatrice he read Boethius and Cicero looking for consolation (silver) and, in his reacquaintance with philosophy, found gold (*Conv.* II.xii.4): "I who sought to console myself found not only a remedy for my tears but also the words of authors, sciences, and books. Pondering these, I quickly determined that Philosophy, who was the lady of these authors, sciences, and books, was a great thing" (tr. R. Lansing).

44. Here we find the much-debated phrase "Deh, chi siete?" Perhaps the solution is simpler than the discussion surrounding it might indicate. In 1894, Poletto (comm. to vv. 40–45) made the only sensible suggestion that this is not only the correct reading (there is much textual evidence on its side, as Scartazzini demonstrated [comm. to vv. 43–44]), but (as even Scartazzini failed to see) more than acceptable phrasing on Dante's part and a perfectly sensible way for the protagonist to frame his question: "You (the one to whom I am speaking), say who all the rest of you are" (i.e., at least the three others whom we will meet in the next canto).

45. Dante's affection responds to the fondness the anonymous speaker has shown him (see vv. 32–33, 38–39).

46–48. Dante's presence in the heavens has already been presented as increasing the paradisiac joy of the blessèd (see, for example, *Par.* V.105).

49–51. Charles presents himself as the good ruler, whose early death deprived Europe of his many virtues, but also unleashed the evil of others who came to power in his absence from the scene. "Charles Martel, eldest son of Charles II of Naples and Anjou and Mary, daughter of Stephen IV (V) of Hungary; he was born in 1271; and in 1291 he married Clemence of Habsburg, daughter of the Emperor Rudolf I, by whom he had three children, Charles Robert (Carobert) (afterwards king of Hungary), Clemence (married Louis X of France), and Beatrice; he died at Naples in 1295 at the age of 24" (T). He died, narrowly predeceasing his wife, Clemenza, of the plague, although some were of the opinion that he had been poisoned. Dante's other great hope, for his own political ends as well as his idealistic sense of the imperial role of Italy, Henry VII, had died recently (24 August 1313). That event, dashing even Dante's unrealistic hopes for the triumph of the principle of restored imperial leadership, probably colored his reflections about the untimely death of Charles eighteen years earlier.

52–54. Carroll (comm. to these verses) has this to say about this tercet: "It is a mistake to say, as is sometimes done, that this is a mere temporary concealment due to the sudden increase of joy caused by this meeting with his friend. Doubtless there was this increase of joy, and therefore of light, for Dante expressly says so (*Par.* VIII.46–48); but from the very first he describes them as 'lamps' and 'sparks' within a flame [see the note to verse 19]. There is no indication that at any time he saw them in their own proper forms."

55–57. Whatever fantasy Dante may have had of a better (nonexilic) existence had Charles remained alive and a power on the peninsula, his use of the verb *amare* and the noun *amore* in this tercet, spoken by Charles in Venus, shows how the poet has reconceptualized the nature of love from Dido's kind to spiritual friendship (see the note to *Inf.* II.61). For an essay on the two Venuses, see Landino's proem to this canto. Pertile (Pert.2001.1), p. 60, is not alone in objecting that Charles does not seem to be present here in the role of lover, if Cunizza, Folchetto, and Rahab (found in the next canto) all do. Indeed, his lengthy self-presentation (vv. 49–84) is exclusively political in nature. For an attempt to link Charles and Venus, see Boyde (Boyd.1993.1), p. 285: "Perhaps we are meant to infer that the rays of Venus may dispose a 'gentle heart' to disinterested friendship, as well as to *luxuria*." That is a reasonable response to Dante's situation of Charles in this planet. Nonetheless, Benvenuto da Imola portrays Charles as a "son of Venus" (comm. to vv. 31–39): "fuit vere filius Veneris quia amorosus, gratiosus, vagus, habens in se quinque invitantia hominem ad amorem, scilicet, sanitatem, pulcritudinem, opulentiam, otium, et juventutem" (. . . he was indeed a son of Venus, amorous, graceful, eager, possessing five qualities that promote a man's disposition to love, i.e., good health, physical attractiveness, wealth, leisure, and youth).

Ragni (Ragn.1989.2), pp. 145–52, shows that Dante's presentation of Charles Martel accords with his presentation of the ideal ruler in *Monarchia* (I.xi.6–18).

See Arnaldi (Arna.1992.1), pp. 55–56 (cited by Picone [Pico.2002.3], p. 124) for the appealing notion that, when Charles visited Florence in 1294, he and Dante met in the environment of S. Maria Novella, where at this period visiting heads of state were customarily lodged and where Dante may have also been involved. See his own words: "I began to go where she [Philosophy] was truly revealed, namely to the schools of the religious orders [Dominicans at S. Maria Novella, Franciscans at S. Croce] and to the disputations held by the philosophers" (*Conv.* II.xii.7—tr. R. Lansing). Thus the context of Dante's new "love" (for the Lady Philosophy) is understandably referred to. It must have permeated his and Charles's discussions at the time, as may be evidenced by Charles's reference to the first ode of the *Convivio*, usually dated to around this time (ca. 1293–94).

58–63. The familiar technique of locating territories by their watery limits is employed here to identify Provence, part of the dowry (see *Purg.* XX.61) of Beatrice, daughter of Raymond Berenger, wife of Charles I of Anjou, and grandmother of Charles Martel. Upon the death of his father, Charles II (who in fact survived him by fourteen years, dying in 1309), he would have inherited the titles to lordship as Count of Provence.

The second tercet points to southern Italy, where Charles would have inherited kingship over the kingdom of Naples (as a result of the *Vespri Siciliani* [1282], no longer of Sicily as well): "The kingdom of Apulia in Ausonia, or Lower Italy, embracing Bari on the Adriatic, Gaeta in the Terra di Lavoro on the Mediterranean, and C[a]tona in Calabria; a region bounded on the north by the Tronto emptying into the Adriatic, and the Verde (or Garigliano) emptying into the Mediterranean" (Longfellow's comm. to verse 61).

64–66. Charles inherited the kingship of Hungary through his mother. Crowned *in absentia* (1292), in Aix, he never exercised his rights to rulership, a king in title only. Hungary is farther along the Danube, past Austrian lands ("its German banks"), to the east and south.

67–75. The fourth realm, which might have been Charles's to lose by his untimely death had not it already been lost because of the Sicilian Vespers (1282), was actually referred to in Dante's time by its classical name "Trinacria" (see Bosco/Reggio, comm. to vv. 67–70), possibly to avoid reminding people that the kingdom of Sicily (currently an independent entity, under the control of the House of Aragon) used to contain the territories of Naples.

Picone (Pico.2002.3), p. 127, following Arnaldi's suggestion (Arna. 1992.1, pp. 51, 57), thinks that Dante may here be imagining a second cultural "golden age" in Sicily if Charles and his heirs had only governed the island.

68–69. Pachynus and Pelorus are the ancient names for Capes Passero and Faro, which form "arms" that stretch out at either end of the eastern shore of Sicily (the present-day Gulf of Catania). For Pelorus, see the note to *Purgatorio* XIV.31–42.

70. *Tifeo* (Typhon [or Typhoeus]), also referred to by the variant *Tifo* (*Inf.* XXXI.124), was a hundred-headed monster who attempted to acquire power over all creatures. Jupiter struck him down with his thunderbolt and buried him in Tartarus under Mt. Aetna, the eruptions of which were

supposedly due to his exertions to escape (see Ovid, *Metamorphoses* V.346–358, where Typhon's two hands are said to be pilloried by Pelorus and Pachynus). Dante dispenses with "classical erudition" in the name of "modern science": The clouds of smoke hanging over the area are not the result of Typhon's struggles to escape, but of sulphur burning in the earth. For this explanation, Tozer (comm. to verse 72) suggests that Dante found a source in Isidore of Seville (*Etym.* XIV.8).

75. The so-called *Vespri siciliani* were begun at the hour of Vespers on Easter Monday of 1282 in Palermo. The uprising resulted in the French losing control, eventually of all Sicily, which ended up being ruled by Spain.

76–78. The debate over the most likely interpretation of these lines goes back to the fourteenth century, one school of interpretation insisting that the phrase "l'avara povertà di Catalogna" (the greedy poverty of Catalonia) refers to the Spanish courtiers who will accompany Charles's brother Robert to Italy once he is "put on" (in 1309), the other, that it is Robert's own avarice that is worthy of a Spaniard. The first interpretation currently is the most favored, but counterarguments are presented by Bosco/Reggio (comm. to this tercet) and Picone (Pico.2002.3), pp. 128–29. Picone (p. 128n.) argues that *antivedere* does not here have its usual meaning ("see in advance"), but refers to a past event (a necessary choice if one believes that the event referred to does not lie in Robert's future). However, see the note to vv. 79–84. And see Barolini (Baro.1984.1), p. 65n., documenting the three other appearances of the verb in the poem (*Inf.* XXVIII.78; *Purg.* XXIII.109; *Purg.* XXIV.46). In all four contexts the prediction of future occurrences is the subject.

Charles's brother was a great enemy to Henry VII. Less than a year after Henry's death, on 15 March 1314, Pope Clement V announced Robert's appointment as imperial vicar, a position that Henry had held. Robert reigned as king of Naples until 1343, long enough, that is, to place the laurel wreath on Petrarch's head on 6 April 1341. Dante was spared knowledge of that coronation. If Canto VI is about the triumphs of Rome, this canto is concerned with political defeats, those suffered by Charles and by Dante: Charles's death brought his brother to the throne and into collaboration with Clement.

79–84. Robert and his "ship of state" (the kingdom of Naples) are already so heavily burdened with difficulties that it is in greater danger of foundering if it is loaded with still more deadweight. Since Robert's avarice is already "on board," that comes close to ruling out the second interpretation of verse 77 (see the note to vv. 76–78), leaving the avarice of his Spanish followers as the better reading. For *barca* with this sense ("ship of state"), see *Paradiso* XVI.96.

82. This verse has long been the cause of dispute: To whom precisely does the phrase "worthy stock" refer? Since Charles's following discourse centers on the differing virtues of fathers and sons (with fathers generally getting the better of the comparisons), some suggest that the reference here is to the otherwise despised Charles II of Anjou, Charles Martel's father (see, e.g., Lombardi, comm. to vv. 82–84, for this view). Tozer (comm. to vv. 82–84) finds justification in such a reading in *Paradiso* XIX.128, where the elder Charles is granted a single virtue (and thus a certain native liberality). As uncomfortable as it may leave one feeling, that is perhaps the best available gloss.

83. This also is currently a disputed verse. What is the reference of the noun *milizia*? It was only in the twentieth century, with Torraca's complex and interesting gloss (comm. to vv. 82–84), that the possibility that the word might refer to soldiers is even broached. All who have a previous opinion are certain that the word refers to administrators, government officials, or the like. We have accepted their view for our translation. It allows, by the way, the understanding that the members of Robert's Spanish entourage may be included in the group, which perhaps accounts for Bosco/Reggio's insistence that the word refers to "mercenary soldiers" (comm. to this verse), a reading in which they are the first.

85–90. Dante tells Charles that he is glad on two counts, first that his royal friend knows of Dante's gladness without his needing to express it; second, that he knows of it in God, because he is saved.

91–93. Dante continues by wondering, on the basis of vv. 82–83, how a good father can have a bad son. See Picone (Pico.2002.3), pp. 129–31, for a clarifying discussion of this passage and the rest of the canto, which, he argues, relies for its basic point on a biblical text, the parable of the sower (Matthew 13:3–23).

94–96. For the insistent presence of this image in the canto, see the note to verse 136.

97–111. Tozer (comm. to these verses) summarizes Charles's thoughts: "The argument is as follows: God, in creating the universe, provided not only for the existence of things, but for their working in the most perfect manner; and the instrumentality which He appointed for that purpose was the stellar influences, which are directed by the angels or Intelligences who preside over them: Were it not for these, chaos and not order would prevail."

97–99. God sets the mark of his Providence upon his creatures, not through his direct creation (which is reserved for the individual human soul), but indirectly, through the stars and planets associated with the eight lowest celestial spheres. This arrangement maintains human freedom of the will and yet allows God the role of ordering his Creation, thus avoiding chaos (see verse 108).

100–102. God foresees not only the nature of the composite human soul (not only the part that he makes directly, the rational soul, but the animal and vegetative souls, that he helps shape indirectly, by agency of the celestial bodies), but its ultimate perfection as it prepares to leave its body. The word *salute*, as readers of the *Vita nuova* (where it also puns on *saluto* [salutation]) will recall, is utilized by Dante in such ways as to run the gamut from physical "health" to more generalized "well-being" to Christian "salvation," and it probably has polyvalent significance here.

103–105. The image of an arrow striking its mark once again meets the reader's eyes (see *Par.* I.119 and V.91). If one had to pick one passage in the poem that might lead a reader to believe that Dante's view of predestination verges on determinism, this tercet might be a popular selection. Yet, once we reflect on the way Dante has held back, avoiding dangerous formulations in the previous tercet, we can sense that he is both aware of the pitfall and determined to avoid it. For the wider meaning in Dante's use of the verb *disporre* (verse 104), see the note to *Paradiso* XXX.138.

106–108. As he concludes his "lecture" on predestination, Charles makes it clear why he has had to come so close to the shoals of determinism, where, after Augustine, many Christian thinkers have come close to sinking: If God does not order the universe, it would not have any order at all. Nature, left to its own, would produce only chaos, as King Lear discovered. Insistence on God's control of so much of the field of human action might seem to whittle away the uses of free will to a point approaching nullity. Yet Dante, through Beatrice (see *Par.* V.19–24), has already insisted on the efficacy of God's greatest gift to humankind.

109–111. Charles ends his exposition by an argument from impossibles. For God and his informed angels to produce chaos, they would have to be deficient, and that is impossible.

112–114. This brief exchange may remind readers of the similar sort of question-and-answer drill performed by Socrates and one of his "student" interlocutors (whose response is the deferential "yes, Socrates" that still strikes readers as comical) in Platonic dialogues. As Bosco/Reggio point out (comm. to verse 114), Dante is here citing an Aristotelian maxim, "Nature never fails to provide the things that are necessary," which he also cites in *Convivio* IV.xxiv.10, *Monarchia* I.x.1, and *Questio* 44.

115–117. Aristotle again sets Charles's agenda; see the opening of the *Politics*: "Man is by nature a political animal" (the Latin Aristotle in fact said that he is a *civile* [civic] one, thus accounting for Dante's *cive*, which we have translated as "social").

118–120. To the next proposition (that diversity among humankind is desirable [see Aristotle, *Politics* I.i.2]), Charles himself supplies Dante's agreement (the poet having in fact already done so in *Conv.* IV.iv.5, when he speaks not only of the social needs of human life, but of the need for diversity of occupation among the members of the community).

121. The poet now characterizes Charles's method of argumentation as "deductive," reminding the reader of the Scholastic style of his conversation.

122–126. And so, Charles concludes, your natural dispositions to take up one thing or something else must differ one from another. It results that, in order to have leading practitioners of various necessary human tasks, one of you becomes Solon (a legislator), another Xerxes (a general), still another Melchizedech (a priest), and finally Daedalus (an artisan). These four "orders" of society include the most necessary activities.

Why Dante chose to identify Daedalus by the tragic flight of his son, Icarus, is not clear, unless we are to understand the reference as blending with the next topic (as some commentators do), the differences between members of the same family.

127–129. See Tozer's paraphrase and interpretation of these lines: " '[T]he nature of the revolving spheres, which, like a seal on wax, imprints itself on mankind, exercises its art well, but does not distinguish one house from another.' In other words: The stellar influences produce individuality of character in men, but do not favour one family more than another by perpetuating excellence in it. Dante is returning to the question, How can a bad son proceed from a good father?"

127. The word *natura* is focal to this discussion. Aversano (Aver.2000.2), p. 37, points out that its seven appearances in this canto represent the heaviest concentration of the word in the poem. That is about one-eleventh of its roughly seventy-seven occurrences.

130–132. Quirinus was the name given to Romulus, Rome's first king, posthumously, when he was celebrated as a god. His mother, Rhea Silvia, a Vestal Virgin (in some versions of the story), gave birth to twins and claimed that Mars had lain with her. Daniello (comm. to this tercet) may have been the first to refer, in this context, to Virgil (*Aen.* I.292–293). But see Tommaseo (comm. to this tercet), who "adjusts" the Virgilian passage to the more appropriate verse 274, where, according to Virgil, Ilia (another name for Rhea Silvia?), a priestess, bears to Mars her twin offspring, Romulus and Remus. (It is striking that neither here nor anywhere in this or in his other works does Dante mention Remus, Romulus's twin, especially here, given the facts that he has just considered Jacob and Esau and that their story has obvious similarities to that of this pair of emulous fraternal twins, one of whom [Romulus] eventually killed the other.) And thus Dante's view (and the standard view in the commentaries) is at some variance from Virgil's presentation of the immortal bloodlines of the founder of Rome. See, for example, Umberto Cosmo (Cosm.1936.1), p. 78, referring to the fact that: ". . . il figlio di un ignoto plebeo può accogliere in sé la virtù di fondare una città come Roma, e salire tanto alto nella riputazione universale da esser ritenuto per disceso da un Dio" (. . . the son of an unknown commoner may harbor the potency exhibited in founding a city like Rome, in making his way to the pinnacle of general approbation so as to be considered descended from a god [Mars]). In the instance of Jacob and Esau, Dante would seem to be interested only in making the point that twins may differ from one another, while in that of Romulus and his unnamed plebeian father, the difference involves father and son. But the reader, as Dante must have known, will also consider Remus as a Roman Esau.

133–135. Charles finishes with a flourish: The lives of fathers would always map in advance the lives of their offspring (we must remind ourselves of the sexually skewed biology sponsored by the poet in *Purg.* XXV.43–48, which has it that only the paternal seed shapes the human characteristics of the infant [the rational soul is inbreathed directly by God]). Thus, were it not for the mediating "interference" of Providence rayed down by the stars, we would all be precisely like our fathers.

136. As Heilbronn points out (Heil.1984.2), pp. 45–46, this phrasing joins with that found in vv. 11–12 and 95–96 to connect with a passage in *Convivio* (II.xiii.14): "and [rhetoric] appears in the morning when the rhetorician speaks before the face of his hearer, and it appears in the evening (that is, behind) when the rhetorician speaks through writing, from a distance." Whether or not Dante's associations of the planets with the seven liberal arts in *Convivio* is binding in *Paradiso* is a question that remains to be settled, but, at the very least, a certain skepticism seems called for. It is probably just to reflect that, had he wanted to insist on these identities, he easily could have. That he did not would seem to make their application here dubious.

138. For the only other occurrence of the word *corollario* in the poem, see *Purgatorio* XXVIII.136.

139–141. In the guise of sound practical advice, Dante levels his guns at Robert, as we shall see in the concluding lines of the canto. Paratore (Para.1989.1), pp. 260–62, gives evidence that reveals Dante's accord in this view of Nature with that expressed by St. Thomas in his *Summa contra Gentiles* (III.80–81).

Raoul Manselli, "Carlo Martello" *ED* I (1970), p. 843a, thinks of Hugh Capet, of whom Charles Martel turns out to be the only "good fruit" (*Purg.* XX.45).

142–144. If we feel that we are hearing the voice of Rousseau in these lines, we should remember that *natura naturata* is the result of a process very much under the control of God through his instruments, the stars. As we have just learned, God intervenes not only directly, when He creates our rational souls, but indirectly, in controlling our innate propensities through the stellar influences. Thus today it might seem an expression of a Dantean point of view whenever we hear an athlete or a singer referring to his or her "God-given talent."

145–147. A part of John S. Carroll's gloss to vv. 137–148 is worth having: "There is little doubt that Charles is referring to two of his own brothers. Louis, the next to himself in age, almost immediately after his release from captivity in Aragon, renounced his hereditary rights, joined the Franciscan Order, and was made Bishop of Toulouse [Louis died in 1297 and was canonized in 1311]. This renunciation of the sword, for which Dante evidently thought him better fitted, gave the throne to his younger brother Robert, who had in him more of the preacher than the king. Villani says of him: 'This King Robert was the wisest king that had been among Christians for five hundred years, both in natural ability and in knowledge, being a very great master in theology and a consummate philosopher' [*Chronicle*, xii.10]. Robert was surnamed 'the Wise.' Petrarch, who regarded him as the king of philosophers and poets, submitted to be examined by him for the space of two days and a half, in the presence of the entire Court, on every known branch of learning. Gregorovius sweeps aside Robert's claims to wisdom with contempt: 'The King enjoyed an undeserved reputation as a lover of learning, and was himself the author of tedious lucubrations on religious and profane questions.' His character reminds us of James, 'the British Solomon,' who held that 'a sovereign ought to be the most learned clerk in his dominions,' and took himself seriously as a great theologian."

PARADISO IX

OUTLINE

VENUS

1 “Fair **Clemenza**”: Charles’s wife or daughter?

2–3 his son, **Caroberto**, deprived of Naples by Uncle Robert

4–6 Charles’s prophecy, perhaps indicating the battle of **Montecatini** (1315)

7–9 the “life” of Charles turns its attention back to God

10–12 denunciation of vain mortals, who turn away from God

13–15 another “splendor” comes toward Dante

16–18 Beatrice nods assent: he may speak to this soul

19–21 Dante: “Show me that you can read my thoughts”

22–24 this splendor, **Cunizza da Romano**, addresses Dante

25–30 Cunizza speaks first of her brother, **Ezzelino da Romano**

31–36 and then goes on to speak briefly of her present joy

37–38 next she turns to her “neighbor” here, **Folco di Marsiglia**

39–42 her prediction of the fame on earth that Folco will enjoy

43–45 Cunizza indicates the area of the **March of Treviso** by the the cities **Padua, Vicenza, Treviso**, and **Feltre**

46–48 her first prophecy: the battle at Vicenza (1314)

49–51 her second prophecy: **Riccardo da Camino** will die (1312)

52–60 her third prophecy: the bishop of Feltre, **Alessandro Novello**, will betray three **Ferrarese brothers** (1314)

61–63 Cunizza ends her speech by taking joy in God’s judgment

64–66 Cunizza turns back to dancing among the other Venusians

67–72 the living soul of Folco of Marseilles glows

73–81 Dante wants to know, since Folco reads his mind in God, why he insists on being asked to speak

82–93 Folco's circumlocutory indication of his city, Marseilles

94–96 his charity now stamps the heaven of Venus as that heaven had first "imprinted" him

97–102 Folco's aptness for love was none less than that of **Dido, Phyllis,** and **Hercules**

103–108 Folco: the awareness of their sins had ceased when these souls went through Lethe; now they discern God's plan

109–114 Folco: so that all the desires Dante has felt in this sphere be satisfied, he will tell Dante who is near him

115–126 **Rahab**, the harlot, is rewarded for helping the invading Jews take **Jericho**, in the Holy Land

127–132 Folco: the lamentable condition of **Florence** in 1300

133–138 further, that churchmen, from priest to pope, seek to enrich themselves by studying decretals instead of sacred texts, results in leaving the Holy Land to the infidel

139–142 But the **Vatican** (where **Peter** was put to death) and other Roman sites of martyrs' deaths will soon be free of stain.

PARADISO IX

Da poi che Carlo tuo, bella Clemenza,
m'ebbe chiarito, mi narrò li 'nganni
che ricever dovea la sua semenza;

ma disse: "Taci e lascia muover li anni";
sì ch'io non posso dir se non che pianto
giusto verrà di retro ai vostri danni.

E già la vita di quel lume santo
rivolta s'era al Sol che la rïempie
come quel ben ch'a ogne cosa è tanto.

Ahi anime ingannate e fatture empie,
che da sì fatto ben torcete i cuori,
drizzando in vanità le vostre tempie!

Ed ecco un altro di quelli splendori
ver' me si fece, e 'l suo voler piacermi
significava nel chiarir di fori.

Li occhi di Bëatrice, ch'eran fermi
sovra me, come pria, di caro assenso
al mio disio certificato fermi.

"Deh, metti al mio voler tosto compenso,
beato spirto," dissi, "e fammi prova
ch'i' possa in te refletter quel ch'io penso!"

Onde la luce che m'era ancor nova,
del suo profondo, ond' ella pria cantava,
seguette come a cui di ben far giova:

"In quella parte de la terra prava
italica che siede tra Rïalto
e le fontane di Brenta e di Piava,

After your Charles had enlightened me,
fair Clemence, he told of the deceptions
3 his seed was destined still to bear,

but said: 'Be silent, and let the years roll by.'
And so I can reveal no more than this: fitting grief
6 shall find the ones who do your family wrong.

By now the spirit in its holy light
had turned back to the Sun that fills its being,
9 as to the goodness that suffices in all things.

Ah, souls beguiled, creatures without reverence,
who wrench your hearts away from so much good
12 and set your minds on emptiness!

Now another of those splendors moved
in my direction, while its brightened glow
15 proclaimed its wish to bring me joy.

The eyes of Beatrice, fixed on me,
as they had been before, held loving reassurance
18 of her glad consent to my desire.

'Please let my wish receive its quick reward,
blessèd spirit,' I asked, 'and give me proof
21 that what I think reflects itself in you.'

At that the radiance, as yet unknown to me,
out of the very depth from which it sang before,
24 responded as does someone who delights in doing good:

'In that part of degenerate Italy
that extends from the Rialto
27 to the sources of the Brenta and the Piave

si leva un colle, e non surge molt' alto,
là onde scese già una facella
30 che fece a la contrada un grande assalto.

D'una radice nacqui e io ed ella:
Cunizza fui chiamata, e qui refulgo
33 perché mi vinse il lume d'esta stella;

ma lietamente a me medesma indulgo
la cagion di mia sorte, e non mi noia;
36 che parria forse forte al vostro vulgo.

Di questa luculenta e cara gioia
del nostro cielo che più m'è propinqua,
39 grande fama rimase; e pria che moia,

questo centesimo anno ancor s'incinqua:
vedi se far si dee l'omo eccellente,
42 sì ch'altra vita la prima relinqua.

E ciò non pensa la turba presente
che Tagliamento e Adice richiude,
45 né per esser battuta ancor si pente;

ma tosto fia che Padova al palude
cangerà l'acqua che Vincenza bagna,
48 per essere al dover le genti crude;

e dove Sile e Cagnan s'accompagna,
tal signoreggia e va con la testa alta,
51 che già per lui carpir si fa la ragna.

Piangerà Feltro ancora la difalta
de l'empio suo pastor, che sarà sconcia
54 sì, che per simil non s'entrò in malta.

Troppo sarebbe larga la bigoncia
che ricevesse il sangue ferrarese,
57 e stanco chi 'l pesasse a oncia a oncia,

'there rises a hill of no great height
from which a firebrand came hurtling down
to scourge the region with its fierce assault.

'This torch and I were born from a single root.
Cunizza was my name and, overcome
by this star's splendor, I shine here.

'I gladly pardon in myself the reason for my lot,
nor does it grieve me—a fact that may
seem strange, perhaps, to those unschooled among you.

'Of this scintillating, precious jewel beside me
in this heaven, great fame was left on earth.
And, before it dies away completely,

'this centennial year will come again five times.
Consider, then, should a man not strive to excel
so that his first life leave behind a better?

'Of this the present rabble there enclosed
by the Tagliamento and the Àdige have no thought,
nor, for all their scourgings, do they yet repent.

'But soon the time will come when Padua shall stain
the color of the water of Vicenza's marshes,
because the people there resist their duty.

'Where the rivers Sile and Cagnano converge,
one man lords it, with his head held high—
but even now the web is spun to catch him.

'Feltre must still bewail the perfidy
of her godless shepherd. This shall be so foul
that, for its like, none yet has gone to prison.

'Large indeed the vat would have to be
to hold so much of Ferrarese blood,
and weary he who had to weigh it ounce by ounce,

che donerà questo prete cortese
per mostrarsi di parte; e cotai doni
conformi fieno al viver del paese.

Sù sono specchi, voi dicete Troni,
onde refulge a noi Dio giudicante;
sì che questi parlar ne paion buoni."

Qui si tacette; e fecemi sembiante
che fosse ad altro volta, per la rota
in che si mise com' era davante.

L'altra letizia, che m'era già nota
per cara cosa, mi si fece in vista
qual fin balasso in che lo sol percuota.

Per letiziar là sù fulgor s'acquista,
sì come riso qui; ma giù s'abbuia
l'ombra di fuor, come la mente è trista.

"Dio vede tutto, e tuo veder s'inluia,"
diss' io, "beato spirto, sì che nulla
voglia di sé a te puot' esser fuia.

Dunque la voce tua, che 'l ciel trastulla
sempre col canto di quei fuochi pii
che di sei ali facen la coculla,

perché non satisface a' miei disii?
Già non attendere' io tua dimanda,
s'io m'intuassi, come tu t'inmii."

"La maggior valle in che l'acqua si spanda,"
incominciaro allor le sue parole,
"fuor di quel mar che la terra inghirlanda,

tra ' discordanti liti contra 'l sole
tanto sen va, che fa meridïano
là dove l'orizzonte pria far suole.

'the blood this generous priest will offer as a gift
to show his party just how staunch he is—
such gifts will suit that city's way of life.

'Above us are the mirrors you call Thrones.
From them the judging God shines down on us,
so that we think it good to say such things.'

Here she was silent and it seemed to me
her thoughts had turned to other cares
as she rejoined the ring where she had been before.

The other joy, already known to me
as precious, before my eyes became a splendid ruby,
sparkling in the bright rays of the sun.

There above, brightness is gained by joy,
as is laughter here, but down below
a shade shows dark when sadness clouds its mind.

'God sees all, and your sight is so in-Himmed,
blessèd spirit,' I said, 'that no wish of any kind
is able to conceal itself from you.

'Why then does your voice, which ever pleases Heaven,
together with the singing of those loving flames
that form their cowls from their six wings,

'not offer my desires their satisfaction?
I would not await your question
if I in-you'd me as you in-me'd you.'

'The widest expanse of water inside shores,'
were the initial words of his response,
'drawn from the sea encircling all the world,

'between its opposing shores extends so far
against the wheeling sun, it places the meridian
where at first lay only the horizon.

Di quella valle fu' io litorano
tra Ebro e Macra, che per cammin corto
parte lo Genovese dal Toscano.

Ad un occaso quasi e ad un orto
Buggea siede e la terra ond' io fui,
che fé del sangue suo già caldo il porto.

Folco mi disse quella gente a cui
fu noto il nome mio; e questo cielo
di me s'imprenta, com' io fe' di lui;

ché più non arse la figlia di Belo,
noiando e a Sicheo e a Creusa,
di me, infin che si convenne al pelo;

né quella Rodopëa che delusa
fu da Demofoonte, né Alcide
quando Iole nel core ebbe rinchiusa.

Non però qui si pente, ma si ride,
non de la colpa, ch'a mente non torna,
ma del valor ch'ordinò e provide.

Qui si rimira ne l'arte ch'addorna
cotanto affetto, e discernesi 'l bene
per che 'l mondo di sù quel di giù torna.

Ma perché tutte le tue voglie piene
ten porti che son nate in questa spera,
procedere ancor oltre mi convene.

Tu vuo' saper chi è in questa lumera
che qui appresso me così scintilla
come raggio di sole in acqua mera.

Or sappi che là entro si tranquilla
Raab; e a nostr' ordine congiunta,
di lei nel sommo grado si sigilla.

'I was a dweller on that water's shore
between the Ebro and the brief run of the Magra
that separates the Tuscan from the Genovese.

'So close they nearly share sunset and dawn
lie Bougie and the city that I came from.
Once it made its harbor warm with its own blood.

'Folco the people called me, if they knew
my name, and now this heaven
is marked by me, as I was marked by it,

'for the daughter of Belus was no more aflame,
bringing grief to Sychaeus and to Creusa,
than I, until the color of my hair began to fade,

'nor was she of Rhodope, who was deceived
by Demophoön, nor Alcides,
when he embraced Iole in his heart.

'Yet here we don't repent, but smile instead,
not at our fault, which comes not back to mind,
but for that Power which ordered and foresaw.

'Here we contemplate the craft that beautifies
such love, and here discern the good
with which the world above informs the one below.

'However, so that you may leave this sphere
with every wish that here has been engendered
satisfied, I must go on.

'You want to know who occupies this luminescence
that scintillates beside me here,
like a sunbeam gleaming in clear water.

'Know then that within it Rahab is at peace,
and, since she is of our number,
our highest rank receives its seal from her.

Da questo cielo, in cui l'ombra s'appunta
che 'l vostro mondo face, pria ch'altr' alma
120 del trïunfo di Cristo fu assunta.

Ben si convenne lei lasciar per palma
in alcun cielo de l'alta vittoria
123 che s'acquistò con l'una e l'altra palma,

perch' ella favorò la prima gloria
di Iosüè in su la Terra Santa,
126 che poco tocca al papa la memoria.

La tua città, che di colui è pianta
che pria volse le spalle al suo fattore
129 e di cui è la 'nvidia tanto pianta,

produce e spande il maladetto fiore
c'ha disvïate le pecore e li agni,
132 però che fatto ha lupo del pastore.

Per questo l'Evangelio e i dottor magni
son derelitti, e solo ai Decretali
135 si studia, sì che pare a' lor vivagni.

A questo intende il papa e ' cardinali;
non vanno i lor pensieri a Nazarette,
138 là dove Gabrïello aperse l'ali.

Ma Vaticano e l'altre parti elette
di Roma che son state cimitero
a la milizia che Pietro seguette,
142 tosto libere fien de l'avoltero."

'Into this heaven, where the shadow of your world
comes to a point, before any other,
first in Christ's triumph, she was taken up.

'Fitting it was indeed to leave her in one heaven,
a trophy of the lofty victory
He gained with both of His two palms,

'because she aided Joshua when he gained
his first triumph in the Holy Land—a place
that hardly touches the memory of the pope.

'Your city, which was planted by him,
the first to turn his back upon his Maker
and from whose envy comes such great distress,

'puts forth and spreads the accursèd flower
that has led astray both sheep and lambs,
for it has made a wolf out of its shepherd.

'For it the Gospels and the lofty doctors
are neglected and the Decretals alone are studied,
as is readily apparent from their margins.

'To it the pope and his cardinals devote themselves,
without a single thought for Nazareth,
where Gabriel spread out his wings.

'But Vatican hill and other chosen Roman places
that became the burial-ground
for the solidiery that followed Peter
will soon be free of this adultery.'

1–6. For a fair-minded consideration of this passage, about which it may at first seem difficult to formulate a definitive opinion, see Oelsner's gloss (comm. to vv. 1–6). He points out that a reader is faced with a choice between "two impossibilities," either the poet is addressing Clemenza, Charles's dead wife, or his daughter, of the same name, for whose presence here there are even more decisive problems. And it should be pointed out that the intimacy of that familiar "tuo" at least implies relationship (Dante had once seen Charles's Clemenza, according to Chimenz [comm. to verse 1], in 1281, when she was thirteen, on her way to Naples, but had no dealings of any kind with his daughter, married to the king of France). In addition, the plural "vostri" refers to Clemenza ("tu") and at least one other, most likely Charles's and her son, Caroberto. Chimenz (comm. to vv. 5–6) finds this last piece of evidence decisive, referring to those who actually lost something to the political chicanery of King Robert. However, perhaps the single most convincing piece of negative evidence deals with the detail that led to the objection that there is something odd or impossible in Dante's addressing Charles's dead wife. Against this frequently offered objection, Porena (comm. to vv. 1–3) indicates that Dante on several other occasions apostrophizes the dead, for example, Constantine (*Inf.* XIX.115), Saul (*Purg.* XII.40), Rehoboam (*Purg.* XII.46), and Buondelmonte (*Par.* XVI.140). It thus seems overwhelmingly likely that Dante presents himself as addressing the Clemenza who was Charles's wife.

7. This is the first appearance of the word *vita* when it has the meaning "living soul" in the poem. It is used 23 times in *Inferno* with its usual meaning ("life," in various senses), and then 24 times in *Purgatorio*. In *Paradiso* it is used 32 times in all, but, to indicate a soul in grace, only here (of Charles) and then of five other denizens of Heaven, as follows: *Paradiso* XII.127 (Bonaventure), XIV.6 (Thomas), XX.100 (Trajan), XXI.55 (Peter Damian), and XXV.29 (James). Gragnolati (Grag.2005.1), p. 242, n. 5, is simply incorrect when he states that the "same term 'vita' is used throughout the *Comedy* to define the human soul."

8–9. As we will learn in vv. 95–96, Folco is swathed in the light of his glory, as a saved soul. Here Charles turns to God (metaphorically, the Sun), the source of his own brightness; if you are filled with that light, there is no need of anything else.

10–12. This has not always been included among listings of addresses to the reader (see the note to *Inf.* VIII.94–96), but surely should be. (Previous addresses to the reader in *Paradiso* have occurred at II.1–18 and V.109–114.) Some may have realized that it is one, but the first to say as much is Daniello (comm. to this tercet), and he has been followed by only a few others, none in the current age of Dante studies. A probable reason for such reticence is the missing main verb. Nonetheless, it is clearly addressed to living mortals and, at least inferentially, to readers of the poem. To whom else?

12. The rhyme position is possibly the cause of Dante's choice of *tempie* (literally, "temples," but here, in metonymy, "head"). Indeed, half of the six uses of the word in the poem occur in rhymes.

13. To mark the change in personnel, or scene, Dante uses once again the formulaic *ed ecco*. See *Inferno* I.31; III.82; etc. In all, he does so a total of twenty-two times.

14–15. The increasing brightness of the living soul of Cunizza, as yet unidentified, signifies that she will gladly answer Dante's questions, in order to please him.

18. That is, his desire to speak with this living soul.

19. Literally, let my desire have its "counterweight" (*compenso*), that is, and thus be brought back into balance.

21. That is, show me that you can read my thoughts because you are saved.

23. In the last canto (*Par.* VIII.29) the souls were singing "Hosanna" from within their light. Here this one speaks from within as well.

25–36. This is the first part of the ample speech (vv. 25–63) given by Cunizza da Romano; it is devoted to her brother and to herself. (The second part, vv. 37–42, serves to introduce the second speaker of the canto, Folco of Marseilles, while the third and longest part, vv. 43–63, is devoted to the troubles that the March of Treviso soon shall experience.) Cunizza (ca. 1198–1279), after a long life of love affairs (Jacopo della Lana says that she was in love at every stage of her life [comm. to vv. 32–33]), came to

Florence in April 1265 and signed a notarial document freeing her family slaves in the house of Cavalcante de' Cavalcanti (seen in *Inf.* X), father of Dante's friend Guido. She was still alive in 1279 and probably died soon after that.

25–28. Tozer (comm. to these verses): "The place of which Dante speaks in line 28 as situated on a low hill is the castle of Romano, the patrimony of the Ezzelini. The exact position of this spot is not known, but the part of Italy which is here described as situated between Rialto and the 'fountains' of the Brenta and the Piave is the Marca Trivigiana, which lay between Venice (here represented by the island of Rialto) and the neighbouring part of the Alps, in which those two rivers rise." Ezzelino da Romano (1194–1259) was a Ghibelline leader, famed for his oppressive ways. "Ezzelino, whose lordship over the March of Treviso lasted for more than thirty years, was a ruthless and bloodthirsty tyrant, and was guilty of the most inhuman atrocities. . . . In 1255 Pope Alexander IV proclaimed a crusade against Ezzelino, styling him 'a son of perdition, a man of blood, the most inhuman of the children of men, who, by his infamous torture of the nobles and massacre of the people, has broken every bond of human society, and violated every law of Christian liberty.' After a war of three years' duration, in the course of which he committed the most terrible atrocities, Ezzelino was finally defeated (Sept. 16, 1259) by the marquis of Este at Cassano, where he was desperately wounded and taken prisoner. Eleven days after, having torn open his wounds, he died in his prison at Soncino, at the age of 64, after a reign of thirty-four years" (T).

29–30. We have seen Ezzelino briefly (with his menacing black hair) in *Inferno* XII.109–110. Pietro di Dante tells the following anecdote about him (Pietro1, comm. to vv. 31–33): "When his mother was close to parturition, she had a dream that she was giving birth to a flaming torch (*facem igneam*) that was setting afire the entire area of the March of Treviso."

In fact, it may be Ezzelino who is responsible for his sister's presence in *Paradiso*, if only because he was the subject of Albertino Mussato's *Ecerinis*, the first Senecan tragedy written in the postclassical age, which along with his historical account of Henry VII was the reason for his receiving the laurel in a tumultuous ceremony at Padua at Christmas 1315. Padua was in many respects the most advanced center for the birth of early forms of humanism in Italy. The exchange of Latin verse serving as letters between Giovanni del Virgilio and Dante (ca. 1320) included an invitation to Dante to write a Latin poem about major Italian political figures and then to come to Bologna for his laureation, an offer clearly counting on Dante's emulous feelings toward Mussato (1261–1329) and desire to be laureated himself, as Dante comes close to admitting in the opening lines of *Paradiso* XXV. For what had been a neglected aspect of Dante's relationship with other writers, see Manlio Pastore Stocchi (Past.1966.1) and Ezio Raimondi (Raim.1966.1). The first points to several passages in Dante, including the *Epistle to Cangrande*, which perhaps ought to be considered polemical against the never-mentioned Mussato. Raimondi, on the other hand, indicates several passages in Mussato, including a brief account of a dream of the afterworld that he had in Florence that was caused, it turns out, by stomach problems, a fairly obvious shot at the rival whom he, like that rival, never names. And see Arnaldi (Arna.1966.1) for more on the differing reactions to Cunizza and Ezzelino on the part of Mussato and of Dante. For the state of the question in 1970, see Guido Martellotti, "Mussato, Albertino," *ED* III (1970). While Martellotti admits that there is no hard evidence connecting these two writers (p. 1068a), he suggests that verses 25–33 are possibly a sly attack on Mussato (p. 1067b). It may seem that Dante and Mussato had no cause for mutual dislike. Both were champions of Henry VII (of whom Mussato was the historian of his Italian activities). But Mussato despised the Scaligeri, and especially Cangrande. In fact, in an event almost certainly referred to in vv. 46–48, the battle at Vicenza in September 1314, not only was Mussato present to fight against Cangrande, he was taken prisoner by that lord (see Benvenuto [comm. to vv. 46–48]: "multi capti sunt, . . . et Mussatus poeta" [many were captured, . . . including the poet Mussato]) and brought back to Verona, where he was treated less like a prisoner than an honored guest. One story that circulated had it that when Cangrande, impressed by Mussato's bravery in battle (he was wounded several times and yet, in his desire to avoid capture, leaped into the castle moat, out of which he was pulled by Cangrande's troops), came to see him in his comfortable quarters in the Scaliger castle, which served as his dungeon, and asked whether he could have a few words with his prisoner, Mussato replied that surely he might, but only if he were able to converse in Latin. We do not know how long Mussato was held prisoner in Verona, but not for very long, one supposes. But we do know that Dante was a resident of that castle at this period. It would seem inconceivable that Mussato was not much on Cangrande's mind and tongue. One can imagine Dante having to listen to his patron's lavish praise of this "other poet" who was "given the laurel," who was such a great Latinist, and who had put up such a brave fight in combat. It must have been galling.

As Bosco/Reggio remark (comm. to this canto, Intro.), this canto is more datable than most, referring to a number of events that occurred in 1314 and 1315. Thus it may have been written hot on the heels of the news of Mussato's laureation at the close of 1315. If the original plan for the canto called for the presence of Folco alone, perhaps including his presentation of Rahab, Dante may have decided to add another woman (it is a rare canto in the *Commedia* that has two women in starring or major supporting roles; only *Paradiso* III, with Piccarda and Constance, comes to mind) because Cunizza offered Dante a way to address the question of Mussato through her brother (who enjoys brief enough treatment here, but several lines more than he receives in *Inferno* XII).

31–33. Cunizza now identifies herself both as the sister of the "firebrand" and as, in the words of Benvenuto da Imola (comm. to vv. 13–15), "recte filia Veneris" (indeed a daughter of Venus). The words she uses to do so might suggest that she dwells permanently in this planet, as Pompeo Venturi (comm. to vv. 32–33) seems to believe. (For a later instance in the canto that seems indeed to indicate that Rahab was "assumed" by Venus, see the note to vv. 119–123.)

It has been difficult for commentators to accept Dante's salvation of Cunizza. Some show their hostile disbelief (she was, according to Benvenuto [comm. to vv. 31–36], "widely known to be a whore" [*famosa meretrix*], but he goes on to find her youthful conduct excusable [he does not mention her mature amorous adventures]). *Meretrix* was a label affixed to her on a half dozen other occasions (deriving from an unpublished early commentary), while others attempt to put forward the unbelievable claim that she only affected the manner of carnal lovers. For the amply documented list of Cunizza's various love affairs and marriages, including a famous fling with the poet Sordello during her first marriage, see Scartazzini (comm. to vv. 32–33) and Baranski (Bara.1993.2). (Sordello names himself at *Purg.* VI.74 but is present in the poem during four cantos, until the protagonist goes to sleep at the beginning of Canto IX.) To Daniele Mattalia (comm. to verse 32) she is a modern version of Rahab (but what service she performed for Church or state he does not say); however, Mattalia (comm. to verse 32) is apparently the only commentator before the seventh centenary observations in 1965 to face the question of the relation of the present situation of Cunizza in the afterworld to her eternal one, and he sees that they are different (what Dante would consider a correct view), but he then goes on to make a further distinction unwarranted by the text: She will be in the same rank in the Empyrean as Venus is in the heavens, that is, "in the third level of merit/happiness (*merito-felicità*)." Again, see the note to vv. 119–123.

31. Cunizza's formulation, once we consider that one sibling is seen by Dante in Hell while the other addresses him from this planet, is surely meant to remind us of the remark of Charles Martel about the differing natures of members of the same family (Esau and Jacob) in the last canto (VIII.130–131).

34–36. Cunizza is saying that she no longer begrudges herself her sins because she neither feels the impulse that led to them nor the remorse that followed them (both in the world and in Purgatory), which were washed away by Lethe. See the similar view of Francesco da Buti (comm. to vv. 25–36), dealing with the notion that Dante is contradicting himself when he presents Cunizza as remembering her sins. Folco will state the proposition a little more clearly than she does in vv. 103–104: "Here we don't repent, but smile instead, / not at our fault, which comes not back to mind" but at God's Providence, that foresaw the sin and its redemption. The "common herd" will not understand that she is not wracked by penitential thoughts of her sins.

37. Cunizza indicates Folco di Marsiglia, who will follow her in speaking to Dante at verse 82.

38–42. Dante would seem to hold to two positions, one "orthodox" in its condemnation of vainglory (see *Purg.* XI.100–102, where fame in the world is but a "gust of wind," variable and of short durance) and one less so, if still more or less acceptable in a Christian universe, renowned for the performance of good deeds. While the commentators are not of one opinion, it does not seem likely that Dante here is talking about the vain sort of fame, but of the second sort. See the even stronger positive evaluation of such renown in *Paradiso* XVIII.31–33, that enjoyed by the last souls whom Dante observes in the heaven of Mars, those who in the world made such a mark "that any poet's page would be enriched" by containing their names.

40. Most readers take this line as we do, that is, this century marker shall occur five more times before Folco's fame dies down. There was apparently a tradition, if it is referred to derisively by St. Augustine (*Enarr. Ps.* 6.1), that the history of humankind, from Adam until Judgment Day,

would last 7,000 years. That would, according to Dante's time line, make human history on this earth extend roughly to the year 1800, since 6,498 years have passed since God formed Adam (see *Par.* XXVI.118–123).

41. Aversano (Aver.2000.2), p. 39, contrasts this use of the word *eccellente* with the *eccellenza* of *Purgatorio* XI.87, where it has the clear sense of a need to excel based on pride. Here (if not all the commentators are in accord with this view), it clearly refers to extraordinary goodness, which lives on after one has died, forming a model for others to follow. St. Francis, for example, had exactly this effect on the world, galvanizing countless people to set their lives to doing good.

43–45. The current inhabitants of the Marca Trivigiana, its confines traced (to the west) by the Tagliamento and (to the east) by the Adige, although they have been "scourged" by the various tyrants of the region, Ezzelino, his brother Alberigo, and others, have not, according to Cunizza, learned their lesson.

46–48. But they shall learn that lesson, one of obedience to Cangrande, insisting on his role as imperial vicar even after the death of Henry VII. Cunizza first foretells the disastrous defeat of the Guelph Paduan army in the fall of 1314 in Vicenza, a Ghibelline city that it had retaken the day before, only to be completely routed in a surprise attack by a small imperial force led by Cangrande. For more on this battle, and the role of Albertino Mussato in it, see the note to vv. 29–30.

49–51. Next Cunizza prophesies the brutal death of Rizzardo da Camino, ruler of Treviso (1306–12), murdered in his own palace while playing chess by a peasant wielding a pruning hook. He was married to a daughter of Nino Visconti (see *Purg.* VIII.53) in 1308. Thus Dante would have probably looked with special disfavor on his notorious philandering, which may have been the motivating cause for his murder. As Bosco/Reggio (comm. to this tercet) point out, Dante nods here in the present tenses of the verbs in vv. 50–51: Rizzardo was not ruling the city in 1300, nor was the plot to kill him being hatched in that year.

The presence of Rizzardo here is perhaps intended to remind the reader of the high praise lavished upon his father, captain-general of Treviso (1283–1306), "il buon Gherardo" of *Purgatorio* XVI.124. See also *Convivio* IV.xiv.12, with its praise of Gherardo and mention of the rivers Sile and Cagnano. Thus we have here another of the examples, so dear to

Dante, of the unpredictability of nobility's being passed on through the seed of a noble father. "Good wombs have borne bad sons" is King Lear's version of this reflection.

52–60. Finally, Cunizza turns her prophetic attention to Feltro (Feltre; see *Inf.* I.105). Alessandro Novello, a Trevisan, was bishop of Feltre (1298–1320). In 1314 he gave three Ferrarese brothers, Ghibellines, refuge in the city, but then turned them over to the Guelphs of Ferrara, who cut their heads off.

54. The word *malta* has caused difficulty. Before Petrocchi, most texts capitalized it. (There were at least six prisons in Italy that bore the name Malta.) But it is also possible that Dante meant what Petrocchi thought he did (a generalized sense of "prison"). If, however, he was referring to a particular place, most recent discussants prefer the choice of the prison for ecclesiastics situated in Lake Bolsena.

61–63. Cunizza concludes her speech by reminding Dante of the actual location of the angelic order of Thrones, "above," that is, just below the Cherubim (and thus third from the highest rank, occupied by the Seraphim). For the implicit rebuke to Dante, both here and there, see the note to *Paradiso* VIII.34–39. Edward Peters (Pete.1991.1) points out that Thomas Aquinas associates the order of the Thrones with theologically correct human governance.

63. Cunizza is aware that to mortals her three prophecies (vv. 43–60), all of them detailing the just punishment of her "countrymen" from the Marca Trivigiana, may seem cruel, while to the saved they are a cause for further celebration of God's justice.

64–66. As soon as she breaks off her words to Dante (and she has been speaking quite a while, vv. 25–63), she joins her companions in dance and, like them, contemplates God.

67–68. Dante "knew" the next soul from Cunizza's words at vv. 37–42.

69. Bosco/Reggio (comm. to vv. 67–69) report that the *balasso* is a ruby found in Asia, in Balascam (today Badakhshan, a region including north-eastern Afghanistan and southeastern Tajikistan [see Eric Ormsby, "A mind emparadised," *The New Criterion* 26 {Nov. 2007}: 73f.]), according to the thirty-fifth chapter of Marco Polo's *Il milione*.

70–72. The meaning is fairly clear: Here in Paradise (*là sù*) a living soul, grown more joyful, becomes more refulgent; on earth (*qui*), a person, made happier, smiles; in Hell (*giù*), a damned soul, caused to feel greater sadness, darkens in its outer aspect. We never actually see such change in *Inferno*. This is another example (cf. *Inf.* XVI.106–108; *Inf.* XX.127–129) of Dante adding details to his descriptions of earlier scenes.

73–81. The protagonist's nine verses indulge in rhetorical flights and playful reproof. For "fancy" rhetoric, consider Dante's three coinages (vv. 73 and 81), which spectacularly turn pronouns into verbs ("to in-him," "to in-you," "to in-me") at either end of his address to Folco. And then there is his mock impatience with his interlocutor for holding his tongue when Folco can surely see, in God, Dante's eagerness to know his story. Is this the most "literary" pose we have as yet watched and heard the protagonist assume? Whatever its degree of novelty, it is a delight to observe.

When we look back from *Paradiso* XIV.96, we realize that these were the last words spoken by the protagonist until then. This is by far the longest stretch in the poem in which he remains silent, from here near the end of his stay in Venus, right through his time in the Sun, until just after his arrival in Mars.

77–78. It is probably no accident that Dante speaks here of the Seraphim, the highest order of angels and associated with the highest form of affection, spiritual love. Folco was, after all, a poet of carnal love, but one who transformed himself into a better kind of lover when he took orders and then when he became God's flail for heresy. Starting with Jacopo della Lana (comm. to vv. 73–79) and the Ottimo (comm. to vv. 73–78), the early commentators found biblical sources of the six wings of the Seraphim either in the Apocalypse or in Ezechiel. However, beginning with Lombardi (comm. to vv. 77–78), the consensus had moved to Isaiah 6:2, the only passage specifically naming them in the Bible: "And above [the Lord's throne] stood the seraphim; each one had six wings; with two he covered his face, and with two he covered his feet, and with two he did fly."

82–93. The poet, through the words of Folco, locates the Mediterranean, the second largest sea on the earth's surface after Oceanus (verse 84), which surrounds all the land on our globe, on the map of Europe. Moving from west to east, Folco makes the Mediterranean extend 90 degrees in latitude, more than twice its length in modern cartography. Folco places his birthplace, the as-yet-unnamed Marseilles, between the Ebro's mouth in Spain and that of the Magra, in Italy, which separates Liguria from Tuscany. Nearly sharing the time of both sunrise and sunset, Folco continues, his native city and Bougie (on the North African coast) thus nearly share the same meridian of longitude. This rebus leads a patient reader to his city's name. Carroll (comm. to vv. 82–92), at least in part to excuse the twelve-verse periphrasis for "I was born in Marseilles," insists that Folco is looking down, from the epicycle of Venus, with an astronaut's view of the Mediterranean, and describing what he sees.

85. For the context offered by the citation of *Aeneid* IV.622–629, see Balfour (Balf.1995.1), p. 137. He points out that IV.628, "litora litoribus contraria" (shore with opposing shore), recognized by some as the source of Dante's "tra ' discordanti liti" (between its opposing shores) is drawn from Dido's penultimate utterance, her curse on Aeneas and his offspring. "Dante's allusion to Dido's curse, therefore, underlines the far-reaching consequences of Aeneas's illicit love, for the conflict between Islamic East and Christian West is, for Dante, a continuation of the enmity between Carthage and Rome."

93. For the citation of Lucan here (*Phars.* III.453), see the notes to *Purgatorio* XVIII.101–102 and *Paradiso* VI.55–72.

94. Folchetto di Marsiglia was born circa 1160 and died in 1231. His poems, written in Provençal roughly between 1180 and 1195, were known to Dante, who praises them highly (if the only one referred to is his canzone "Tan m'abellis l'amoros pensamen" [So greatly does the thought of love please me]), naming him by his more familiar name as poet (*Folchetus* in Latin, which would yield *Folchetto* in Italian, as many indeed do refer to him) in *De vulgari eloquentia* II.vi.6. Dante "recycles" the opening of the first line of that canzone in the first line he gives to Arnaut Daniel (*Purg.* XXVI.140, "Tan m'abellis vostre cortes deman" [So greatly does your courteous question please me]). At least several years before 1200, Folchetto left the life of the world behind (including a wife and two sons), becoming first a friar, then abbot of Torronet in Toulon, and finally bishop of Toulouse in 1205. He was deeply involved in a leadership role in the bloody and infamous Albigensian Crusade (1208–29). As Longfellow has it (comm. to this verse), "The old nightingale became a bird of prey."

One wonders if Dante's use of Folco (rather than Folchetto) for him in this canto mirrors his sense of the "new man" that eventuated once he turned from love and amorous poetry to the religious life. For a perhaps similar appreciation, if it is not clearly stated, see Bertoldi (Bert.1913.1), p. 27, noting that St. Dominic was at Rome in 1216 "in compagnia del vescovo Folco, l'amoroso Folchetto di Marsiglia. . . ." On Dante's sense of Folco's two-part "career," see Barolini (Baro.1984.1), pp. 114–22.

95–96. Folco's meaning is that the heaven of Venus has its light increased by the presence of his soul, now wrapped in a sheath of light because he is saved, just as it once stamped his nature with an amorous disposition.

96. While Folchetto's status as poet seems not to be alluded to here at all, many deal with it as part of the context of his presence, understandably assuming that Dante is centrally interested in that. Among those involved in examining the possible Old French and Provençal sources of Dante's poems, Michelangelo Picone has been particularly active. Opposing the views advanced by Picone (Pico.1980.1 and Pico.1983.1) and Rossi (Ross.1989.1) and reaffirmed by Antonelli (Anto.1995.2), p. 347, Pietro Beltrami (Belt.2004.1), p. 33n., argues that Folco is *not* to be taken as the highest exponent of Troubadour lyrics found in the poem, but rather as a poet who has given over poetry for religion and is saved for that reason alone. That is, Folco's distinction in Paradise lies in his rejection of poetry, not in his continued embrace of it. Compare the similar opinion of Luca Curti (Curt.2002.1), p. 146: ". . . but now [we hear not the troubadour] but only the bishop Folco, in whose discourse poetry has not even a marginal presence. . . ."

97–102. Dido ("the daughter of Belus") was no more aflame with love (bringing grief to Sychaeus [Dido's dead husband; see *Aen.* IV.552 and *Inf.* V.62] and Creusa [Aeneas's dead wife; see *Aen.* II.736–794 and the note to *Purg.* II.79–81]) than Folco was. (However, since the next two classical lovers are both apparently drawn from Ovid's *Heroides*, Dante may be thinking of the portrait of Dido found there [Book VII].) Nor was Phyllis more in love with Demophoön, who betrayed her (see Ovid, *Heroides* II); nor was Hercules more in love with Iole (see Ovid, *Heroides* IX). Allegretti (Alle.2002.1), p. 142, suggests that Dante wants us to think of the *Heroides* in part because the work insists on the adulterous nature of most of the loves it recounts, using faithful Penelope as a counter *exemplum* to them.

103–105. The tercet clarifies the similar, but more occluded, statement of Cunizza (vv. 34–36). All the pain of sin is utterly erased from the memory of every saved soul. On this simile, see Jacoff (Jaco.1980.1).

106–108. A problematic passage. We have followed Bosco/Reggio's reading of it (see their comm. to this tercet), in which a Florentine form of the verb *torniare* (to turn, as on a lathe) is seen as bringing the meaning into focus, as follows: "Here, in Paradise, we contemplate the craft revealed in the creation that God's love makes beautiful; we also discern the goodness through which the heavens give form to the world below."

For a lengthy and unapologetic negative response to Dante's saving of Folco, see the judgment of John S. Carroll (comm. to vv. 82–102), which concludes as follows: "It certainly gives us a shock to find a noble spirit like Dante's so subdued to the colour and temper of its time that deeds which sink Ezzelino to perdition exalt Folco to Paradise, because done in the name of Christ and authority of His Vicar."

For the other appearance of the phrase "cotanto affetto," see *Inferno* V.125, where it applies to carnal affections. Folco's use of it now is very different, we may imagine, than it would have been in his flaming youth.

109–114. Having read Dante's mind, Folco changes the subject from himself to the particularly dazzling light ("like a sunbeam gleaming on clear water") about which he knows Dante is curious. Once we find out who it is, we understand why he has tried to create a sense of excited mystery around this being.

115–117. The enjambment in the second line of the tercet creates Dante's desired effect: surprise. Not only does Rahab's name cause us (at least temporary) consternation, what Folco goes on to say of her does also. Not only is a whore among the saved, she is among the loftiest souls whom we see here.

Among the first commentators, only the author of the Codice Cassinese (comm. to verse 117) said that by the "highest rank" Dante indicates the Empyrean, which is what he *should have* meant, since none of the Hebrew (and a very few other) souls saved in the Harrowing of Hell is anywhere recorded as going anywhere else, not even by Dante. That anonymous commentator would wait for nearly five and a half centuries for company (Torraca in 1905 [comm. to this tercet]). Torraca also believes the reference is to the Empyrean. The passage is, as many commentators protest, difficult to understand. Nonetheless, Benvenuto da Imola (comm. to vv. 115–117) seems quite certain that her highest "rank" pertains to the hierarchy of the souls gathered in Venus. Most of those after him who elect to identify her location also think the reference is to the planet. Only in the last one hundred years has the pendulum of scholarly opinion begun to swing, if only slightly, in the direction of the Empyrean. Allegretti (Alle.2002.1), pp. 143–44, makes a strong case for that resolution. The only problem is that in the entire passage, all other references are unquestionably to the sphere of Venus (vv. 113 [*qui*]; 115 [*là*]; 116 [*di nostr' ordine congiunta*]; 118–120 [*questo cielo . . . fu assunta*]; 122 [*in alcun cielo*]). And so it would seem that this is yet another instance of an authorial slip (see the note to vv. 119–123).

118–119. The point at which ends the shadow of the earth cast by the Sun, a cone stretching nearly 900,000 miles above the earth according to Alfraganus, reaches only as far as the sphere of Venus (and thus marks the planet only when it is on the lower half of its epicyclical rotation). Most early commentators, if they cite any astronomical authority, refer to Ptolemy (for the relevance of his chapter on eclipses, first by Jacopo della Lana). Beginning in the late nineteenth century, Alfraganus becomes more widely used as Dante scholars begin to understand the extent of the poet's debt to the Latin translation of the ninth-century Arabian astronomer's work, in fact the probable source for whatever Ptolemy he knew.

In the Old Testament, Rahab has a major role in the second chapter of Joshua (2:1–21), where she aids and abets two spies from Joshua's army; then she is rescued during the destruction of the city by a grateful Joshua (Joshua 6:22–25). Bosco/Reggio (comm. to vv. 118–126) point out that her salvation is not original with Dante, but is a matter of biblical record, with such witness as offered by St. Paul (Hebrews 11:31) and St. James (James 2:25), the first of whom insists on her faith in God, while the second extols her good works. And see Matthew 1:5, where Rahab is listed as the mother of Boaz, and thus a distant ancestress of Jesus. For a figural understanding of Rahab, see Auerbach (Auer.1946.1), pp. 482–84.

119–123. Dante slips back into the language of *Paradiso* III, where Piccarda and Constance seem to be located in the Moon on a permanent basis. See Bosco/Reggio (comm. on verse 120), who are of the opinion that Dante does not in fact mean what he seems to, since the souls of all those who were harrowed from Hell by Christ (see *Inf.* IV.52–63) were assumed at once into the Rose, as have been, indeed, all those who have been "graduated" from Purgatory (not to mention those few [we assume] in the Christian era who went straight to Heaven). However, we may once again be witnessing the trace of an earlier plan (see the note to *Paradiso* III.29–30). Bosco/Reggio's alternative explanation seems weak (repeating the explanation of Grabher [comm. to vv. 118–120]): Dante only means that in the Empyrean their rank corresponded to the rank of Venus among the planets. Dante, in fact (and deliberately?), never clarifies the relationship between the order of the eight heavens in which he sees the saved arranged for his edification (nor indeed between the hierarchy among the souls who appear in each heavenly sphere) and the seating plan in the Rose. One probable cause of his avoidance of this question is that there are obvious distinctions among the degrees of blessedness of the saved who appear in various spheres, as we have just seen (Rahab is the highest in rank among these visitors to Venus). To calibrate *both* scales of beatitude probably proved too much even for a Dante, who thus simply avoided a question that we sometimes choose to force on him.

123. Benvenuto (comm. to vv. 118–126) perhaps exhausted the possible interpretations of this line. The two "palms" refer to (1) the palms of Rahab's hands when she lowered her line to Joshua's two spies from the window of her room so that they could climb up; (2) the palms that Joshua and those who followed him raised in prayer. Benvenuto says these interpretations have been suggested by other readers and dismisses both of them in favor of (3): the palms of the hands of Jesus, nailed to the Cross. While there is still a certain amount of uncertainty, most current commentators support Benvenuto's reading.

124–126. In his *voce* dedicated to "Folchetto (Folco) di Marsiglia," *ED* II (1970), p. 955b, Antonio Viscardi makes the interesting suggestion that parallels exist between Folco's destruction of the fortified town of Lavaur in the Albigensian Crusade in 1211, accompanied by the voices of priests raised in song, and the fall of Jericho, accomplished by the sound of trumpets and shouts; he also suggests that both Folco and Rahab are humans stained by the sin of lust and ultimately redeemed by good works.

127–129. Satan is traditionally thought of as being prideful (in that he cannot accept being less important than God); but he is also thought of as envious, particularly in his dealings with Adam and Eve, whose happiness he cannot abide. Dante uses the rhetorical figure periphrasis here to rousing effect, for who does not know the "answer" to this riddle? We seem to be invited to shout the name of Lucifer. But note also the crushing result when we consider the adverb *pria* (first): Satan may have been the first to deny his Creator, but he was hardly the last, dear reader. . . .

The sins of Eve and Adam brought all of us "distress" in that we weep for our lost immortality.

For Satan's fall as a "foundation myth" of humankind, see the note to *Inferno* XXXIV.121–126. This text would seem to offer another version of that myth, with Satan's envy as the founding sin of Florence.

130–132. The gold florin, currency of Florence, has a lily stamped on its face, and, "accursèd flower" that it is, has corrupted the citizens of the town, whether old ("sheep") or young ("lambs"), because it had first corrupted the clergy, turned from caretaker ("shepherd") to greedy marauder of the flock ("wolf"). The avarice of the clergy caused major complaint in the Middle Ages, even more so than the runners-up, sexual license and gluttony.

133–135. The blackened margins of collections of decretals, or books of ecclesiastical law, tell what interests lure the clergy to study: the material advantage furthered, or so they believe, by mastering the ins and outs of canon law. For this they have given over not only consulting the Gospels, but studying the Fathers of the Church. And in one of his own letters (to the Italian cardinals gathered in France to choose a new pope after the death of Clement V), Dante makes the same charge, mentioning some specific names of those whom these cardinals do not read: "Gregory lies among the cobwebs; Ambrose lies forgotten in the cupboards of the clergy, and Augustine along with him; and Dionysius, Damascenus, and Bede" (*Epist.* XI.16 [tr. P. Toynbee]).

See Cassell (Cass.2004.1), pp. 12–13, adducing the fact that all the popes of Dante's time (except, of course, Celestine V) were canon lawyers, a fact that may help explain some of Dante's hostility to decretals.

In the early centuries of the Catholic Church, canon law was formed by the member churches themselves at synods of bishops or church councils. By the sixth century, papal letters settling points in canon law (a practice dating perhaps to the third or fourth century) began to be included in collections of the decisions of synods and councils. Sometime between the late eighth and late ninth century there was produced a collection, the so-called *False Decretals*. These spurious documents included "papal letters" that had in common the desire to strengthen papal authority. Gratian, a sort of Justinian of canon law, published his *Decretum* circa 1150. It codified the laws of the Church (although it included many documents collected in the *False Decretals*) and enjoyed a great deal of authority. To the surprise of some, given Dante's dislike of those churchmen who are interested in studying decretals as a path to maintaining or augmenting their financial privilege, we find Gratian in the heaven of the Sun (*Par.*

X.103–105). See J. Michael Gaynor, "Canon Law and Decretals" (http://jmgainor.home stead.com/files/PU/PF/cld.htm).

136. "To it" refers, again, to the florin, to which the highest ranks of the officialdom of the Church, the pope and his cardinals, pay much more serious attention than their vows of poverty should allow.

137–142. The two references are, first, to the Annunciation (when Gabriel "opened his wings" to Mary in Nazareth); second, to all those martyred in Rome for their belief in Christ, starting with Peter (buried on the Vatican hill) and filling many a catacomb. Thus the two exemplary groups bracket the birth and resurrection of Jesus, the one preparing the way for Him, the second following his path into a glorious death (and eventual resurrection).

Scartazzini (comm. to vv. 127–142) suggests that Dante's muffled prophecy is set in the context of crusading (see vv. 125–126), without going on to suggest that it calls for a new crusade. However, that does seem a real possibility. At any rate, most commentators have given up on finding a precise formulation for understanding Folco's prophecy. The "usual suspects" have been, more or less in this order of popularity, the death of Boniface VIII, the removal of the papacy to Avignon, the coming of a great leader (e.g., on the model of the *veltro* and/or the DXV). It would not seem like Dante to have a negative prophecy at this point (furthermore, the death of Boniface did *not* lead to a rejuvenation of the Church, nor did the "Avignonian captivity"); nor would it seem like him to repeat a prophecy that he would then repeat still again in *Paradiso* XXVII.145 (the *fortuna* [storm at sea]) and which is primarily imperial, not ecclesiastical, as this one is. And so it seems reasonable to suggest that Scartazzini may have been on the right track. Fallani (comm. to vv. 139–142) comes close to saying so (without referring to Scartazzini). And see Angelo Penna, "Raab," *ED* IV (1973), p. 817a, who says in passing that vv. 112–142 reflect crusading. Mark Balfour (Balf.1995.1), pp. 140–41, sees the desire for renewed crusading in the Holy Land as permeating the conclusion of the canto, but follows exegetical tradition in seeing its very last lines as referring to the *veltro* or DXV. The Church (and the entire context of this passage, vv. 133–142, which we hear in the voice of a [crusading] churchman, *is* ecclesiastical) will reorder itself only when it returns to its original purpose; for Dante, no matter how this may trouble modern readers, that meant recapturing Jerusalem.

PARADISO X

OUTLINE

THE SUN

1–27 *God's three Persons & Dante's addresses to his readers*

- 1–6 Trinitarian prologue to the heaven of the Sun
- 7–15 address to the reader, urging attention to the stars
- 16–21 the effects of the Zodiac's ecliptic path on the earth
- 22–27 second address to the reader, urged to be self-sufficient

28–39 *the ascent to the heaven of the Sun*

- 28–33 the Sun, in Aries, seen as fructifying and measuring
- 34–39 both Dante's ascent and Beatrice's guidance seem timeless

40–138 *the habitation of the Sun: first circle*

- 40–48 the brightness within the Sun defeats Dante's telling
- 49–51 God exhibits His threefold "art"
- 52–54 Beatrice advises Dante to give thanks to the "sun of the angels" for allowing him to rise to the Sun
- 55–63 no mortal was then more devoted to God than Dante; his love for God eclipsed his love for Beatrice; her smile
- 64–69 the souls make a circle with Beatrice and Dante as center that is compared in simile to the halo around the Moon
- 70–75 in the Empyrean, whence Dante has returned, there are "jewels" that these souls in the Sun now celebrate

76–81 the circling souls compared in simile to dancing ladies

82–96 Thomas Aquinas's first speech:

- 82–90 Since Dante's presence here reveals him to be one who lives in grace, Thomas must answer his question,
- 91–93 which concerns the souls who are circling Beatrice;
- 94–96 the speaker identifies himself as a Dominican friar
- 97–99 (1) **Albertus Magnus** (ca. 1193–1280)
- 99 (2) **Thomas Aquinas** (1225–74)
- 100–102 Thomas will now name the rest of the twelve:
- 103–105 (3) **Francesco Graziano** (ca. 1090–ca. 1160)
- 106–108 (4) **Peter Lombard** (ca. 1095–1160)
- 109–114 (5) **King Solomon** (author of four books of the Bible)
- 115–117 (6) **Dionysius the Areopagite** (converted by St. Paul)
- 118–120 (7) **Paulus Orosius** (flourished first half of fifth century)
- 121–123 the importance of the next soul is underlined
- 124–129 (8) **Severinus Boethius** (ca. 475–525)
- 130–132 (9) **Isidore of Seville** (ca. 560–636)
  (10) the **Venerable Bede** (674–735)
  (11) **Richard of St. Victor** (ca. 1123–73)
- 133–138 (12) **Siger of Brabant** (ca. 1225–ca. 1283)

139–148 coda: simile (mechanical clock calling monks to matins).

PARADISO X

Guardando nel suo Figlio con l'Amore
che l'uno e l'altro etternalmente spira,
lo primo e ineffabile Valore

quanto per mente e per loco si gira
con tant' ordine fé, ch'esser non puote
sanza gustar di lui chi ciò rimira.

Leva dunque, lettore, a l'alte rote
meco la vista, dritto a quella parte
dove l'un moto e l'altro si percuote;

e lì comincia a vagheggiar ne l'arte
di quel maestro che dentro a sé l'ama,
tanto che mai da lei l'occhio non parte.

Vedi come da indi si dirama
l'oblico cerchio che i pianeti porta,
per sodisfare al mondo che li chiama.

Che se la strada lor non fosse torta,
molta virtù nel ciel sarebbe in vano,
e quasi ogne potenza qua giù morta;

e se dal dritto più o men lontano
fosse 'l partire, assai sarebbe manco
e giù e sù de l'ordine mondano.

Or ti riman, lettor, sovra 'l tuo banco,
dietro pensando a ciò che si preliba,
s'esser vuoi lieto assai prima che stanco.

Messo t'ho innanzi; omai per te ti ciba;
ché a sé torce tutta la mia cura
quella materia ond' io son fatto scriba.

Gazing on His Son with the Love
the One and the Other eternally breathe forth,
the inexpressible and primal Power

made with such order all things that revolve
that he who studies it, in mind and in space,
cannot but taste of Him.

With me, then, reader, raise your eyes
up to the lofty wheels, directly to that part
where the one motion and the other intersect,

and from that point begin to gaze in rapture
at the Master's work. He so loves it in Himself
that never does His eye depart from it.

See how from there the oblique circle
that bears the planets on it branches off
to satisfy the world that calls for them.

And if their pathway were not thus deflected,
many powers in the heavens would be vain
and quite dead almost every potency on earth.

And, if it slanted farther or less far
in the upper or the lower hemisphere,
much would be lacking in the order of the world.

Stay on your bench now, reader,
thinking of the joy you have but tasted,
if, well before you tire, you would be happy.

I have set your table. From here on feed yourself,
for my attention now resides
in that matter of which I have become the scribe.

Lo ministro maggior de la natura,
che del valor del ciel lo mondo imprenta
e col suo lume il tempo ne misura,

con quella parte che sù si rammenta
congiunto, si girava per le spire
in che più tosto ognora s'appresenta;

e io era con lui; ma del salire
non m'accors' io, se non com' uom s'accorge,
anzi 'l primo pensier, del suo venire.

É Bëatrice quella che sì scorge
di bene in meglio, sì subitamente
che l'atto suo per tempo non si sporge.

Quant' esser convenia da sé lucente
quel ch'era dentro al sol dov' io entra'mi,
non per color, ma per lume parvente!

Perch' io lo 'ngegno e l'arte e l'uso chiami,
sì nol direi che mai s'imaginasse;
ma creder puossi e di veder si brami.

E se le fantasie nostre son basse
a tanta altezza, non è maraviglia;
ché sopra 'l sol non fu occhio ch'andasse.

Tal era quivi la quarta famiglia
de l'alto Padre, che sempre la sazia,
mostrando come spira e come figlia.

E Bëatrice cominciò: "Ringrazia,
ringrazia il Sol de li angeli, ch'a questo
sensibil t'ha levato per sua grazia."

Cor di mortal non fu mai sì digesto
a divozione e a rendersi a Dio
con tutto 'l suo gradir cotanto presto,

Nature's sublime and greatest minister,
who imprints Heaven's power on the world
and in his shining measures out our time,

in conjunction with the place I note above,
was wheeling through those spirals
in which he comes forth earlier each day.

And I was in it, aware of my ascent
no more than one becomes aware
of the beginnings of a thought before it comes.

It is Beatrice who leads from good
to better so suddenly that her action
has no measurement in time.

Whatever I saw within the sun, how shining
it must have been, for, when I entered,
it revealed itself, not by color, but by light.

Were I to call on genius, skill, and practice,
I could not ever tell how this might be imagined.
Enough if one believes and longs to see it.

And if the powers of our imagination
are too earthbound for such height, it is no wonder,
for eye has never seen light brighter than the sun.

So brilliant the fourth family of the highest Father,
who forever gives it satisfaction, shone,
revealing how He breathes and how begets.

And Beatrice began: 'Give thanks, give thanks
to the Sun who makes the angels shine and who,
by His grace, has raised you to this visible sun.'

Never was mortal heart so well prepared
for worship, nor so swift to yield itself
to God with absolute assent

come a quelle parole mi fec' io;
e sì tutto 'l mio amore in lui si mise,
che Bëatrice eclissò ne l'oblio.

Non le dispiacque, ma sì se ne rise,
che lo splendor de li occhi suoi ridenti
mia mente unita in più cose devise.

Io vidi più folgór vivi e vincenti
far di noi centro e di sé far corona,
più dolci in voce che in vista lucenti:

così cinger la figlia di Latona
vedem talvolta, quando l'aere è pregno,
sì che ritenga il fil che fa la zona.

Ne la corte del cielo, ond' io rivegno,
si trovan molte gioie care e belle
tanto che non si posson trar del regno;

e 'l canto di quei lumi era di quelle;
chi non s'impenna sì che là sù voli,
dal muto aspetti quindi le novelle.

Poi, sì cantando, quelli ardenti soli
si fuor girati intorno a noi tre volte,
come stelle vicine a' fermi poli,

donne mi parver, non da ballo sciolte,
ma che s'arrestin tacite, ascoltando
fin che le nove note hanno ricolte.

E dentro a l'un senti' cominciar: "Quando
lo raggio de la grazia, onde s'accende
verace amore e che poi cresce amando,

multiplicato in te tanto resplende,
che ti conduce su per quella scala
u' sanza risalir nessun discende;

as was mine when I heard those words,
and all my love was so set on Him
that it eclipsed Beatrice in forgetfulness.

This did not displease her. Instead, she smiled,
so that the splendor of her smiling eyes
divided my mind's focus among many things.

I saw many living lights of blinding brightness
make of us a center and of themselves a crown,
their voices sweeter than the radiance of their faces.

Thus ringed we sometimes see Latona's daughter
when the air has grown so heavy
that it retains the thread that forms her belt.

In the court of Heaven, from which I have returned,
there are many gems of such worth and beauty
that they may not be taken from the realm.

These lights were singing of those jewels.
He who fails to wing himself to fly there
might as well await the dumb to tell the news.

When, with just such songs, those blazing suns
had three times made their way around us,
like stars right near the still and steady poles,

they seemed to me like ladies, poised to dance,
pausing, silent, as they listen,
until they have made out the new refrain.

And from one of them I heard: 'Since the ray
of grace by which true love is kindled
and which, by loving, sees itself increase,

'multiplied in you, is so resplendent
that it conducts you up that stair
which none descends except to mount again,

qual ti negasse il vin de la sua fiala
per la tua sete, in libertà non fora
se non com' acqua ch'al mar non si cala.

Tu vuo' saper di quai piante s'infiora
questa ghirlanda che 'ntorno vagheggia
la bella donna ch'al ciel t'avvalora.

Io fui de li agni de la santa greggia
che Domenico mena per cammino
u' ben s'impingua se non si vaneggia.

Questi che m'è a destra più vicino,
frate e maestro fummi, ed esso Alberto
è di Cologna, e io Thomas d'Aquino.

Se sì di tutti li altri esser vuo' certo,
di retro al mio parlar ten vien col viso
girando su per lo beato serto.

Quell' altro fiammeggiare esce del riso
di Grazïan, che l'uno e l'altro foro
aiutò sì che piace in paradiso.

L'altro ch'appresso addorna il nostro coro,
quel Pietro fu che con la poverella
offerse a Santa Chiesa suo tesoro.

La quinta luce, ch'è tra noi più bella,
spira di tale amor, che tutto 'l mondo
là giù ne gola di saper novella:

entro v'è l'alta mente u' sì profondo
saver fu messo, che, se 'l vero è vero,
a veder tanto non surse il secondo.

Appresso vedi il lume di quel cero
che giù in carne più a dentro vide
l'angelica natura e 'l ministero.

'he who would deny your thirst the wine
out of his bottle would not be free to do so,
as water has no option but to flow into the sea.

'You want to know with what plants and blossoms
this garland is in flower, encircling with delight
the lovely lady who strengthens you for Heaven.

'I was a lamb among the holy flock
led by Dominic along the road
where sheep are fattened if they do not stray.

'He that is nearest to me on the right
was both my brother and my teacher—
he, Albert of Cologne, I, Thomas of Aquino.

'If you would like to find out who the others are,
follow, as I name them, with your eyes,
turning up your gaze along the blessèd wreath.

'The next flame issues from the smile of Gratian,
who served one and the other court so well
his service now gives joy in Paradise.

'The next one to adorn our choir
was the Peter who, like the poor widow,
offered up his treasure to Holy Church.

'The fifth light, the most beautiful among us,
breathes forth such love that all the world below
is greedy to discover how his soul has fared.

'Within his light there dwells a lofty mind,
its wisdom so profound, if truth is true,
there never rose another of such vision.

'Next to him behold the flaming of the candle
that in the flesh below saw farthest
into the nature and the ministry of angels.

Ne l'altra piccioletta luce ride
quello avvocato de' tempi cristiani
del cui latino Augustin si provide.

Or se tu l'occhio de la mente trani
di luce in luce dietro a le mie lode,
già de l'ottava con sete rimani.

Per vedere ogne ben dentro vi gode
l'anima santa che 'l mondo fallace
fa manifesto a chi di lei ben ode.

Lo corpo ond' ella fu cacciata giace
giuso in Cieldauro; ed essa da martiro
e da essilio venne a questa pace.

Vedi oltre fiammeggiar l'ardente spiro
d'Isidoro, di Beda e di Riccardo,
che a considerar fu più che viro.

Questi onde a me ritorna il tuo riguardo,
è 'l lume d'uno spirto che 'n pensieri
gravi a morir li parve venir tardo:

essa è la luce etterna di Sigieri,
che, leggendo nel Vico de li Strami,
silogizzò invidïosi veri."

Indi, come orologio che ne chiami
ne l'ora che la sposa di Dio surge
a mattinar lo sposo perché l'ami,

che l'una parte e l'altra tira e urge,
tin tin sonando con sì dolce nota,
che 'l ben disposto spirto d'amor turge;

così vid' ïo la gloriosa rota
muoversi e render voce a voce in tempra
e in dolcezza ch'esser non pò nota
se non colà dove gioir s'insempra.

'In the other little light there
smiles that defender of the Christian Church
of whose account Augustine made good use.

'If the eye of your mind is being drawn
from light to light, following my praises,
you are already thirsting for the eighth.

'Within it rejoices, in his vision of all goodness,
the holy soul who makes quite plain
the world's deceit to one who listens well.

'The body from which it was driven out
lies down there in Cieldauro, and he has risen
from martyrdom and exile to this peace.

'See, blazing just beyond him, the fiery breath
of Isidore, of Bede, and then of Richard,
the last in contemplation more than human.

'This one, from whom your look comes back to me,
is the light of a spirit to whom it seemed,
in his grave meditation, that death came on too slow.

'It is the eternal light of Siger,
who, instructing in the Street of Straw,
demonstrated enviable truths.'

Then, like a clock that calls us at the hour
when the bride of God gets up to sing
matins to her bridegroom, that he should love her still,

when a cog pulls one wheel and drives another,
chiming its ting-ting with notes so sweet
that the willing spirit swells with love,

thus I saw that glorious wheel in motion,
matching voice to voice in harmony
and with sweetness that cannot be known
except where joy becomes eternal.

1–6. Like the other tenth *canti*, this one marks the crossing of a borderline (in *Inferno*, it separated the sins of Incontinence from the walls of the City of Dis, enclosing the sins of the hardened will; in *Purgatorio*, Antepurgatory from Purgatory proper). The first of these is fairly indistinctly marked; the next more formally established. But this one is as though a double line had been drawn across the space separating Canto IX from Canto X, separating the planets attained by the earth's shadow from those, beginning with the Sun, that are free of such darkening. None of the souls we will meet from now on suffered from the human weakness that we found among those who lacked a vigorous faith, or those who placed too much hope in the things of this world, or those who failed to understand the nature of true love (for the program of the defective Theological Virtues in the first three heavens of *Paradiso*, see the note to *Par.* III.47–48; and see Andreoli [comm. to *Par.* III.16]: "The fact is that it is only in the fourth heaven that we shall begin to find souls who are completely beyond reproach").

On this opening, see Forti (Fort.1968.1), p. 352: After the several references in the last canto to human strife, Dante now turns to "celestial harmony instead of earthly disorder." Forti later says (p. 380) that the celestial Athens (see *Conv.* III.xiv.15) is the point at which we have now arrived.

These six verses might be paraphrased: "God the Father (the Power), gazing on His Son (Wisdom) with the Holy Spirit (Love) that breathes forth eternally from both Father and Son, created all things that revolve above, whether in angelic consciousness or in the sphere that they govern (e.g., that ruled by the Principalities, Venus), with the result that anyone who (as Dante now is doing) contemplates the Father's Power cannot fail to savor it."

1–3. Dante seizes the opportunity to underline his adherence to orthodox doctrine: The Holy Spirit breathes forth from both the Father and the Son. The so-called *filioque* controversy, caused by the addition of that phrase (meaning "and from the Son") in the Nicene Creed, which was one of the eventual causes of the split between the Eastern and Western Churches (which became final in 1054), was centered in the dispute over the emanation of the Holy Spirit. Against the decision of the Council of Nicea (325), the Eastern position was that the Spirit proceeded only from the Father. See Carroll (comm. to vv. 1–6): "Probably Dante had here a special interest in asserting the orthodox doctrine, because the two chief spokesmen of this Heaven were summoned to defend it against the Greek deputies at the Council of Lyons in 1274. Aquinas died on the way, and Bonaventura during the sitting of the Council."

4–5. These lines have caused difficulty. Where some have thought the references are to thoughts of things and things themselves in the created universe, most contemporary readers (perhaps following Forti [Fort. 1968.1], p. 353) think the references are to angelic intelligences (the nine orders of angels) and to the things impelled by them (the heavens with their planets).

6. This verse initiates the theme of ingestion in the canto, a part of the metaphor of eating first deployed as a governing trope by Dante in *Convivio*. It has a perhaps surprising presence in this canto that, in light of its higher interests, might seem an inappropriate place for such concerns. See also vv. 23 ("tasted"), 25 ("feed yourself"), 88 ("thirst" for "wine"), 96 ("where sheep are fattened").

7–15. This is the fourth address to the reader in *Paradiso* (see also *Par.* II.10–18; V.109–114; IX.10–12) and is in fact triple, with three imperatives, each in the first line of a tercet, marking its triune shape, which breaks a single action into three moments, matching the opening Trinitarian proem of the canto (vv. 1–6), with the reader being asked first to elevate his or her sight (verse 7), then to begin to gaze (verse 10), and finally to perceive (13).

9. "The heavenly bodies have two opposing movements: the one, daily (or equatorial), from east to west in the plane of the Equator, the other, annual (or zodiacal), from west to east in the plane of the ecliptic" (Bosco/Reggio, comm. to vv. 8–9).

10–12. God, apparently an aesthetician, loves contemplating His own work, just as the reader is encouraged to do as well. Barely out of sight in this tercet is Dante the maker, contemplating his own God-bearing poem with wonder and delight.

16–21. See Tozer (comm. to vv. 16–18) for the following paraphrase and explanation: " 'And if their path (the zodiac) were not inflected (i.e., oblique), much influence in Heaven would be fruitless, and almost every agency on earth below would fail.' It is the obliquity of the zodiac which causes the changes of the seasons; without it the sun could not produce the effect for which it was designed, and such agencies as those which originate life and growth in plants and animals, movement in winds and streams, changes of temperature, and the like, would no longer exist." See also Carroll (comm. to vv. 7–27): "Dante asks the reader to lift his eyes to 'the high wheels' at that point 'where the one motion on the other strikes'—that is the equinoctial point, where the ecliptic, 'the oblique circle which bears the planets,' crosses the circle of the Equator. The reference is to the annual revolution of the Sun. Its *daily* motion is from east to west, and parallel to the Equator; but its *annual* motion is from west to east, and along the Zodiac at a certain angle to the Equator."

22–27. There is some dispute as to whether this is a distinct address to the reader or a continuation of that found in vv. 7–15. Because they are rhetorically separate entities ("Leva dunque, lettore, . . ." and "Or ti riman, lettor, . . .") and enjoy temporal separation (the reader is asked three times to look along with Dante up at the circling heavens, and then to think upon what he or she has seen, unaided by the poet, who now must return to his narrative), one does not find an easy objection to consider them as being in fact more than one. The controlling element in this central metaphor of these two *terzine* moves from a scholar's bench (verse 22), on which we readers sit, listening to Dante's lecture, to (in verse 25) a seat at a banquet, at which chef Dante is preparing the meal, a "feast of knowledge" indeed. He does, however, beg off from serving us, leaving us to do that for ourselves, since he must attend to continuing his narrative.

23. For the interesting verb *prelibare*, appearing here for the first time in the poem, see the note to *Paradiso* XIV.4.

27. A *hapax*, the Latinism *scriba*, rhyming with two other Latinisms, *preliba* (tasted [and not yet swallowed]) and *ti ciba* (feed yourself), is one of the key words in Dante's self-presentation as veracious author, which occupies a privileged space here, the last line of one of the longest introductory passages to a canto in this poem at the point where it has reached the first stage of its destination, what we might refer to as "God's country." Poletto (comm. to vv. 25–27) points to the apt phrase in *Monarchia* II.x.6 where Luke is referred to as the scribe of Christ ("Cristus, ut scriba eius Lucas testatur"). And see Sarolli, "Dante *scriba Dei*" (in Saro.1971.1, pp. 189–336)

and the note to *Paradiso* V.85. For a meditation on this verse as encapsulating Dante's self-presentation as scribe throughout the poem, see Jacomuzzi (Jaco.1968.1). Dante's claim here, to be merely the "scribe" of God, is at once part of the topos of modesty and a shattering denial of it, since Dante's "mere scribal" activity lifts him to the level of the authors of Scripture, including the Solomon whom we will see in this very canto.

28–39. The ascent to the Sun, we are perhaps surprised to discover, has not until now been accomplished. We must surmise that the view of the heavens purveyed in vv. 1–27 derives from what Dante saw looking up from the planet Venus. His movement up from there, as is Beatrice's guidance while leading him up, seems instantaneous, seems not to occur in time. Compare the earlier insistence on the sense of the ascent to a higher sphere without awareness of time in *Paradiso* I.91–93; V.91–93; and VIII.13.

28–30. The Sun is seen as redirecting God's beneficial gifts (e.g., the warmth that causes vegetative growth) down to earth, as well as, while everlasting itself, giving us, who live here, our main means of telling time.

31. This "point," to which the poet has referred (in verse 9), is in the constellation Aries.

32–33. For this motion, see Dante's description of the diurnal movement of the Sun in *Convivio* III.v.14, "rising upward like the screw of a[n olive] press" (tr. R. Lansing). The spring ushers in the lengthening sunlight of early summer (March 21 to June 21), which begins to subside only after the summer solstice.

35–36. Grandgent (comm. to vv. 35–36) cites A. Fazzi (*GSLI*, vol. 73, p. 112), making the distinction between an uncaused, spontaneous thought, which is what Dante is describing here, and the sort of thought he had referred to earlier (*Inf.* XXIII.10: "Just as one thought issues from another, / so, from the first, another now was born").

37–39. Beatrice is described in terms that recall *Convivio* I.ii.14, describing the life of St. Augustine: "the progress of his life, which proceeded from bad to good, good to better, and better to best" (tr. R. Lansing).

40–42. Placella (Plac.1987.1), p. 222, follows Petrocchi in thinking that this effulgence is not that emanating from Beatrice (as most early commentators believed, perhaps encouraged by her presence in the preceding *terzina*), but of the souls in the Sun, who are so bright that they outshine even that brightest of all celestial bodies. For a fairly early instance (ca. 1791) of the current majority sense of this tercet, see Lombardi (comm. to vv. 40–45), citing the prophet Daniel, whose final vision (Daniel 12:3) portrays the wise as shining with the brightness of the sun.

43–48. The brightness that Dante saw in these souls, which made them stand out from the Sun, not by being a different color, but by being even brighter than the brightest thing known to our mortal vision, simply cannot be described by the poet, outdone by God's art, as it were. For discussion of this contrast in these lines between Dante's limited ability as artist in comparison to God's, see Barolini (Baro.1992.1), pp. 196–97.

49–51. Dante refers to those who show themselves in the Sun, the fourth of the planets, as the "fourth family"; God makes them happy by demonstrating his other two Trinitarian aspects, Wisdom (manifest in the Son) and Love (present in the Holy Spirit). See the opening of this canto, vv. 1–3.

If the preceding six verses described Dante's inability to portray the brightness of God's creatures, this tercet proclaims God's "art" in demonstrating His triune nature.

52–54. Beatrice plays with one of the most present medieval metaphors, the Sun as representing God (see *Conv.* III.xii.7), the "sun" of the angels, his "planets" in the Empyrean, who has raised Dante to the height of this heaven, home of the physical sun.

59–60. Discussing these lines, Curti (Curt.2002.1), pp. 150–52, paraphrases them as follows: ". . . my mind, so concentrated on God that Beatrice was eclipsed and forgotten, divided His splendor into many things, so that I saw many splendors sparkling" (p. 151). As opposed to his "forgetting" of Beatrice while he was still on earth, looked back upon with horror in *Purgatorio* XXX and XXXI, this forgetful behavior is laudable, as, in the next tercet, Beatrice's own reaction indicates.

61–63. Beatrice's delighted smile at being forgotten in favor of God brings Dante's attention back to her and, surely we are meant to understand, to the souls in the Sun.

64–69. The souls in the Sun make Beatrice and Dante the center of their circle ("crown") just as the halo around the Moon (dwelling of the former huntress, Diana) is formed by the vapor in our atmosphere that attaches "cloth" to the "belt" of Latona's daughter.

70–75. In the Empyrean (*la corte del cielo*), whence Dante has returned, there are jewels (the saints and/or the angels?) so precious that they may not be removed from the kingdom (resolved from metaphor, be described here on earth), and it was of them that these souls in the Sun sang. In this canto we are given less indication than in any we have read (in which the souls are making musical tribute) about what exactly the souls were singing; eventually we learn that the conjoined choruses of the two groups of twelve theologians are singing of the Incarnation (*Par.* XIII.27) and of the Trinity (*Par.* XIII.26; XIV.28–31), as Carroll has pointed out (comm. to vv. 70–93). One who does not put wings on himself (Icarus-like?), as Dante has, to fly up to see these "jewels" might as well await word about them from the dumb. One has to see for oneself, apparently (since not even Dante is telling), that is, take the trip through the heavens that, as far as we learn, only Paul and Dante were privileged to enjoy while still in this life.

A question remains unanswered in the commentaries. Are the singing souls, clearly presented as being situated in the Sun, distinguished from the "jewels," about whom they are singing and who are in the Empyrean, or are they counted among their companions here in the Sun? While many commentators cite *Inferno* II.125 for the phrase *corte del cielo*, no one seems to be bothered by the fact that it there clearly refers to the Empyrean, specifically referring to Mary, Lucy, Rachel, and Beatrice. It seems necessary to understand that the twelve theologians are singing of exalted "colleagues" whom they have temporarily left behind them in the Empyrean, for instance, the Virgin Mary, possibly St. Francis himself, and other "stars" of the afterlife, too precious to be sent below for Dante's instruction or to be identified by their descending colleagues in beatitude.

To explain the mercantile reference in this passage, Torraca (comm. to vv. 70–73) refers to Marco Polo's *Il milione* (XXV, LXXIX), where the traveler reports that the Great Khan would not allow rubies (see *Par.* IX.69 and note), in the first case, or pearls, in the second, to leave his kingdom in order to protect their value, not letting them become common by allowing their export. For Portirelli's views on Dante's knowledge of Marco Polo's voyage, see the note to *Purgatorio* I.22–24.

76–81. After the "suns" in the Sun had circled Dante and Beatrice three times, like the stars that circle the poles, they seemed to Dante to resemble ladies in the dance who pause, awaiting the resumption of singing in order to continue with their dance steps. See the description of the practice of ladies who danced to the singing of *ballate* in Dante's time in Casini/Barbi (comm. to verse 79).

For a meditation on this canto that takes its departure from these lines, see Freccero, "The Dance of the Stars" (1968), in *Dante: The Poetics of Conversion* (Frec.1986.1), pp. 221–44.

82–99. Thomas's first word, "Quando," is matched by only one other speaker's first word similarly occupying the last place in its line, that uttered by Ulysses (*Inf.* XXVI.90). Where Ulysses has epic pretensions in his self-narrative (see the note to *Inf.* XXVI.90–93), Thomas, another kind of "hero," one who indeed vigorously pursued virtue and knowledge (and not merely in what we might regard as an advertisement for himself) is a foil to prideful Ulysses. The Greek adventurer's pride is matched by Thomas's humility. (His name occurs only after he finishes the eighteen-line introductory portion of his speech, and then only after he has named his teacher. Can anyone imagine Ulysses referring to someone who had been his teacher?) His first self-description (vv. 94–96) intrinsically suggests that he is dramatically different from Ulysses, who in his pursuit of knowledge had companions whom he treated as the mere instruments of his own adventure and whom he destroyed along with himself; Thomas, on the other hand, "was a lamb among the holy flock / led by Dominic along the road / where sheep are fattened if they do not stray." That last word (*vaneggia*) surely has a kinship with Ulysses, whose wandering brings him under the spell of the Siren (at least according to Dante: See *Purg.* XIX.19–24). What Ulysses did, Thomas chose not to do.

86–96. It is interesting that this portion of the first utterance of St. Thomas, the great opponent of poetry for its seductive figurative quality, beautiful but simply untrue, contains several metaphors: the "stair" (the ascent of the heavens toward God) that Dante is on; the "wine" (knowledge) that Thomas will share with Dante; the "plants" (souls) that surround Beatrice and him; the "lambs" (friars) who were Thomas and his fellow Dominicans on earth; the "path" (the way to God) that led to his salvation; the "fattening" (knowledge of God's truth) found in the nourishment of the Word. One can only imagine Thomas's objection had he been able to read those words, put by Dante into his mouth. The last metaphor will have its second moment in the next canto (*Par.* XI.25), and then its last and triumphal appearance in the final verse of that canto (XI.139).

87. The "stair" that is climbed only twice is the pathway to Heaven negotiated by a living soul in grace, who is thus promised a return trip (we again think of St. Paul, Dante's only known precursor, though unreported miraculous journeys are not ruled out). Grandgent (comm. to this verse) notes that this is a clear prediction of Dante's ultimate salvation, and refers the reader to a similar earlier gesture in *Purgatorio* II.91–92 (and see, of course, *Purg.* XXXII.100–102).

97–99. Thomas begins his "catalogue of saints," twelve in number perhaps to remind us of the original apostles, with Albertus Magnus (1193–1280), often referred to as "Doctor Universalis" because of his extensive learning; he taught at Cologne, where Aquinas was one of his pupils. In some quarters it has become fashionable, after the exertions of Bruno Nardi, to argue for the actual preeminence in Dante's thought of Albert over Thomas. But see Cogan (Coga.1999.1), pp. xxiii–xxiv: "Despite Nardi's efforts to convince us that Albert the Great was Dante's preferred philosophical source, it is Aquinas whom Dante chooses as the principal spokesman for theology in the *Paradiso*, not Albert or any other theologian." For more detailed arguments that are in basic agreement with this position, see Dumol (Dumo.1998.1), especially pp. 139–66.

99. Thomas Aquinas (1225–74), often referred to as "Doctor Angelicus," was, in the minds of many, the greatest theologian of his time. It is perhaps fair to say that the position of those of Dante's readers most interested in the question has swung from the strict Thomistic construction of Dante sponsored by Giovanni Busnelli to the far more concessive views (which perhaps yield too much of Dante's allegiance to Thomism) of Casella (Case.1950.1) and of two of the leading non-Italian students of the poet's theology, Étienne Gilson and Kenelm Foster. For an extensive treatment of Dante's intellectual response to Aquinas, see Gilson's classic study (Gils.1939.1); and see Foster's entry "Tommaso d'Aquino," *ED* V (1976), pp. 626–49, as well as his much briefer English essay (Fost.1977.1), pp. 56–65. Dante criticism is currently a good deal more "ecumenical," a position that undergirds Amilcare Iannucci's fine, brief treatment of this subject ("Theology" in Lansing [Lans.2000.1], pp. 811–15). It would not be going too far to say that Dante is a precursor of at least one aspect of Renaissance humanism, its pleasure in syncretism, a delight in putting together things that would prefer to be kept separate, making new concepts out of the ideas of the unsuspecting (and defenseless) great figures of the past, about some of which they would, had they a voice, surely bellow

in complaint. For a cautionary note, indicating the complexity of the entire question of Dante's various philosophic allegiances, see Simon Gilson (Gils.2001.2), passim. Indeed, while Dante may honor Thomas more than any other theologian, that does not mean that he always agrees with him—far from it.

103–105. Gratian, the twelfth-century collector and organizer of canon law, who in his *Decretum*, according to some of Dante's commentators, tried to harmonize secular and ecclesiastical law, the two courts referred to in verse 104; others believe Dante is referring to two functions of the Church, the sacramental and the judgmental.

After the slam Dante has put in Folco's mouth against decretals (*Par.* IX.133–135), it seems strange to some that Gratian is so well rewarded. See Forti (Fort.1968.1), pp. 371–73, for the history of the dispute among the commentators caused by Dante's inclusion of Gratian here. And see Adversi (Adve.1995.1).

106–108. An almost exact contemporary of Gratian, Peter Lombard, the "Master of the Sentences" (his major work was the compendium *Sententiarum Libri*, presenting an elaborate overview of dogmatic theology). He says, in his preface to that work, that, like the poor widow in Luke's Gospel (21:1–4), he hopes to make his small contribution to God's treasury.

109–114. Solomon, son of David and king of Israel, the question of whose salvation was much discussed during the Middle Ages (see the reference to the world's hunger for news of him in vv. 110–111, along with its prime reasons for doubting that he was saved, his prodigious carnal affections in his old age, and his falling into idolatry as part of these *amours* [I Kings 11:1–9]; these missteps were compounded, for some, by his authorship of the Canticle of Canticles). However, if the Truth be true (i.e., if we are to believe what we read in the Bible), God specifically (I Kings 3:12) singles Solomon out for the highest praise: "I have given you a wise and understanding heart, so that there was none like you before you, neither after you shall any arise like you (*nec post te surrecturus sit*)," this last the source of Dante's "non surse il secondo" (verse 114). This passage is probably remembered in Matthew 11:11, "Among them that are born of women there has not risen a greater than John the Baptist," which was cited by Tommaseo (comm. to *Par.* X.112–114).

Michele Scherillo (Sche.1896.1) reviews Solomon's many "disqualifications" from being considered an author of Scripture and then his checkered career among the exegetes, the most authoritative of whom, from Dante's own point of view (e.g., St. Augustine, Brunetto Latini), deny him salvation (if St. Jerome granted it). (For three twelfth-century theologians who differ [Philip of Harvengt, Peter Comestor, and Joachim of Flora], saying that Solomon was indeed saved, see Sarolli [Saro.1971.1], pp. 210–15.) Scherillo suggests that it was primarily his kingship that inspired Dante to consider him among the blessed, but does not overlook the force of the fact that Solomon was indeed, in Dante's eyes (and, of course, not in his alone), the author of canonical texts: Proverbs (see, e.g., *Conv.* III.xi.12; *Mon.* III.1.3), Ecclesiastes (see, e.g., *Conv.* II.x.10), the Canticle of Canticles (see, e.g., *Conv.* II.v.5); though he never refers to Solomon's authorship of the Book of Wisdom, he cites its first line in *Paradiso* XVIII.91–93. In other words, for Dante, Solomon is *scriba Dei* (a scribe of God). No matter how anyone might call into question his credentials, he has them. We may reflect that Dante shares both a "monarchical" and a "theological" identity with Solomon, poet of empire and of God, his new "Book of Wisdom" (replacing the previous and abandoned attempt, the *Banquet*) railing against the enemies of the true and God-centered empire. The more one thinks of Dante's Solomon, the more he becomes a likely choice as precursor of this poet (perhaps even in the light of his sexual trespass, something that he, his father, David, and Dante Alighieri, by his own confession [*Purg.* XXX and XXXI], have in common).

On Solomon's *auctoritas* see Minnis (Minn.1984.1), pp. 94–96; 110–12. For the view of Solomon of early Christian exegetes, see Bose (Bose.1996.1). On the sense of the overwhelming importance, for Dante's view of Solomon, of his authorship of the Book of Wisdom, see Pelikan (Peli.1997.1), p. 3: Wisdom "was the book that brought together the *Timaeus* and Genesis on the beginning of the world" (cited by Herzmann [Herz.2003.1], p. 330). For a study of Dante's sense of identity with Solomon, see Seem (Seem.2006.1).

110. Aversano (Aver.2000.2), p. 43, points out that this is the third appearance in this canto of a form of the verb *spirare* (so closely and often associated with the "spiration" of the Holy Spirit), the only one to contain so many occurrences (see also vv. 2 and 51).

115–117. Dionysius the Areopagite, converted by St. Paul at Athens (as mentioned by Luke in Acts 17:34) and martyred there in A.D. 95. He was erroneously assumed to be the author of the *De caelesti hierarchia*, a work particularly prized for its description of the orders of the angels and of their nature. (Dante makes wide use of it in the *Paradiso*.) The *Celestial Hierarchy* and three others of the reputed works of Dionysius were actually produced some five centuries later by Greek neoplatonists and were translated into Latin only in the ninth century.

118–120. Orosius, whose historical compendium, entitled *Historiae adversus paganos*, was written at the suggestion of St. Augustine, as a defense of the Christian religion's beneficial role in human history. Augustine made use of it in writing his *De civitate Dei*, and it is frequently used by Dante. See Toynbee (Toyn.1902.1), "Dante's obligations to the *Ormista*," pp. 121–36, for the opinion that the reference is indeed to Orosius, which for a long time has been the view of the majority of the commentators. Alberto Pincherle, "Agostino," *ED* I (1970), p. 82b, mentions the usual suspects (Orosius, Ambrose, Tertullian, Paulinus of Nola, and Lactantius), and settles on Marius Victorinus. For continued insistence that the *avvocato de' tempi cristiani* is in fact Orosius, see Brugnoli (Brug.1998.1), pp. 491–92. The early commentators were divided, with the majority favoring St. Ambrose, but others backing Orosius. After them, the majority opinion has settled on Orosius by a wide margin, with many convinced by Venturi's argument (comm. to this tercet) that Dante would never have spoken of the great St. Ambrose as a "piccioletta luce" (little light). Moore should still be consulted (Moor. 1889.1), pp. 457–60, for three strong arguments for the reference's being to Orosius and not to Ambrose. But see Lieberknecht (Lieb.1996.1) for a thoughtful attempt to resuscitate Ambrose's candidacy, even if the author ends by admitting that Orosius remains the front-runner.

121–129. In the first of these three tercets, as a unique instance among this bevy of *illuminati*, Dante calls attention to the importance of a particular soul, a signal honor done Boethius, the author of the *De consolatione Philosophiae*. Dante mentions him, always with this particular text in mind, some dozen times in *Convivio* (first in I.ii.13). He was active in the first half of the sixth century, holding the consulship at Rome, but earned the displeasure of the emperor, Theodoric, who imprisoned him at Pavia and finally had him put to death by torture. See the note to verse 128.

See Trucchi (comm. to vv. 1–6) for the notion that, where Aquinas (*ST* Supp., q. 69, a. 2) says that only some will have to spend time in Purgatory before they pass on to Heaven, Dante has all go, with exceptions of those like Boethius, Francis, and Cacciaguida, the auspicious few, according to Isidoro del Lungo (in an unspecified text); that is, Dante's view is the exact negative counterpart to that of Thomas. See the note to *Paradiso* XI.109–117.

128. Curti (Curt.2002.1), p. 159, reminds us that Augustine's remains were circa 725 removed from Sardegna (where they had been taken from Hippo) and taken to Pavia by the Lombard king, Liutprand, who reinterred them in the basilica of Cieldoro. Where might Dante have learned this? In the opinion of Curti, from the *Chronicon* of the Venerable Bede (present in verse 131). (Casini/Barbi [comm. to this verse] had already pointed out that *both* Augustine and Boethius were reburied beneath imposing monuments in that church by Liutprand.)

130–131. Isidore (bishop) of Seville compiled one of the first great medieval encyclopedias in the seventh century, his twenty books of *Etymologies*. He was, either directly or indirectly (e.g., through the derivative work of Uguccione da Pisa), one of Dante's main authorities on any number of subjects.

131. The Venerable Bede, the ecclesiastical historian of Britain, lived well into the eighth century. See Pasquini (Pasq.2001.1), pp. 283–91, for claims on behalf of the writings of Bede (*Historia ecclesiastica gentis Anglorum, De natura rerum, De metrica arte*) as hitherto unexplored sources for a number of passages in the *Commedia*.

131–132. Richard of St. Victor wrote during the twelfth century. He and his master, Hugo of St. Victor (for whom see *Par.* XII.133), were mystical theologians in the monastery of St. Victor near Paris. "He was said to be a native of Scotland, celebrated Scholastic philosopher and theologian, chief of the mystics of the twelfth century. He was, with Peter Lombard, a pupil of the famous Hugh of St. Victor, and a friend of St. Bernard, to whom several of his works are dedicated; he died at St. Victor in 1173. His writings, which are freely quoted by Thomas Aquinas, consist of commentaries on parts of the Old Testament, St. Paul's Epistles, and the Apocalypse, as well as of works on moral and dogmatic subjects, and on mystical contemplation, the last of which earned him the title of 'Magnus Contemplator' " (T). Dante in his *Epistle to Cangrande* (*Epist.* XIII.28), when justifying his dealing with transcendental subjects in the *Paradiso*, appeals to Richard's work *De contemplatione*.

133–138. Siger of Brabant, thirteenth-century philosopher and theologian who taught at the Faculty of the Arts of the Sorbonne, located near "the Street of Straw," the Rue du Fouarre in Paris (one of the few pieces of "evidence" seized on by those who believe, as few today do, that Dante visited Paris; but the street's name was apparently widely known; and Dante might have heard details about the theological disputes in Paris, for instance from the Dominican Remigio Girolami, who had studied with St. Thomas in Paris and who lectured at S. Maria Novella between 1289 and 1303). In 1270, Thomas wrote his *De Unitate intellectus contra averroistas*, clearly attacking some of Siger's teaching (along with that of others). Between 1270 and 1277, Siger was prosecuted by the archbishop of Paris Étienne Tempier (and in 1276 by the inquisitor for France, Simon du Val) for heretical ideas and found guilty. He went to Orvieto to face the Roman Curia and apparently owned up to his wayward philosophizing, and perhaps was absolved for it. He then stayed in Orvieto, in a condition perhaps resembling house arrest, where he apparently met his death beneath the knife of a mad cleric, possibly a man assigned to him as a servant, circa 1283–84. The author of *Il Fiore* (XCII.9–11) mentions Siger's terrible end. For a compact bibliography of Siger's extensive body of work, those considered genuine, those possibly or probably by others, and those now lost, as well as a short list of studies of his impact on Dante, see Cesare Vasoli, "Sigieri (Sighieri) di Brabante," *ED* V (1976), pp. 241b–42a.

For an invaluable survey of the state of the question regarding the interrelationships among Aristotle, Averroës, Albertus Magnus, and Aquinas, as they affect Dante's own philosophical views, see the first half of the study by Simon Gilson (Gils.2004.1). For a brief but most helpful summary in English of the strands of Dante's Aristotelianism, see Scott, "Aristotle" (Lans.2000.1), pp. 61–65. For a discussion of the major "heresies" current in Dante's time, see Comollo (Como.1990.1). We in the twenty-first century may not have enough feel for the huge change in theology wrought by the rediscovery of Aristotle in the thirteenth century. Dante clearly felt himself drawn to the new philosophy, as is evident by his placing Aristotle higher than Plato as a figure of classical philosophical authority, as is first reflected in the *Commedia* in *Inferno* IV.131.

133–135. What the reader is supposed to understand about these thoughts that made death seem welcome to Siger is debated; perhaps it is his concern, mirrored in his retraction in (or perhaps after) 1276 that his earlier erring notions might condemn him to damnation in God's eyes, despite his finally having chosen the true faith. Vasoli ("Sigieri," *ED* V [1976], pp. 238a–42b) is not certain of Siger's sincerity in hewing to the line.

Nonetheless, Dante may have decided that his appearance before the Roman Curia in Orvieto "cured" him of his heretical bent, and that, when he was murdered, he was living in the bosom of Mother Church.

138. See Tulone (Tulo.2000.1) for a review of the problem caused by the phrase *invidiosi veri* (enviable truths). Tulone's hypothesis is that Dante's text refers to the envy of those who hypocritically oppose Siger's sound doctrinal teaching by claiming it is other than Christian. And see Mazzotta (Mazz.2003.1), p. 155, who is of the opinion that *invidiosi* means "not logically evident or demonstrable," on what grounds it is difficult to say. Benvenuto (comm. to vv. 133–138) distinguishes between the words *invidiosus* and *invidus* as follows: "invidiosus enim est ille cui invidetur propter suam felicitatem: et sic capitur in bona parte; invidus vero est ille qui invidet alteri; et sic capitur in mala parte" (for the man who is *invidiosus* is one who is envied because of his happiness, and the word is then understood positively; the man who is *invidus*, on the other hand, is one who is envious of another, and the word is then understood negatively). Curti (Curt.2002.1), p. 162, while not referring to Benvenuto, may have cited one of the fourteenth-century commentator's sources: Isidore of Seville (*Etym.* X.134): One who is *invidus* envies the happiness of another, while the man who is *invidiosus* suffers the envy of others. As for the word *sillogizzò* (which we have translated as "demonstrated"), from the beginning there has been dispute as to whether it is to be taken negatively or positively. Jacopo della Lana (comm. to vv. 133–138) argues that these syllogisms are untrue, while Benvenuto da Imola (commenting on the same passage) is of the opposite opinion, namely that the syllogisms of Siger's making are indeed truthful, and for that reason the subject of envy on the part of those who heard and admired them. Over the years a large majority of the commentators are of Benvenuto's opinion; and see Veglia (Vegl.2000.1), p. 103 and note, for a concordant reflection. That Siger is saved has undoubtedly contributed to the forming of this view; the words themselves might seem far less generous in a different context. See, for example, the second verse of the next canto.

139–148. According to Scott (Scot.2004.2), p. 297, this is the first reference in literature to a mechanical clock. He cites Dronke (Dron.1986.1), pp. 101–2, who suggests that Dante might have seen the one built in Milan in 1306 when he was there for the coronation of Henry VII (in 1310). And see Moevs (Moev.1999.2) for the nature and location of clocks in Dante's time.

144. For *turge* see Pertile (Pert.2005.2), pp. 173–76, pointing out, with numerous examples, that the word has never before been used, in Latin, with a sexual denotation, a meaning it acquired only later on. Dante, having conflated love and intellect, at least by the opening of this canto, can use the vocabularies interchangeably, or substitute the former for the latter, as he does here. Psychologists refer to another version of this process as sublimation, an attempt to skirt a painful awareness of sexual desire by replacing it with a more "acceptable" activity. In Jesus' teaching (e.g., the wise virgins preparing for the arrival of the bridegroom [Matthew 25:1–13]) we can see a more positive sense of sexuality, if it is also simultaneously seen as the basis for its own supersession, taking carnal pleasure past its physical expression and its physical limits. For example, "If you enjoy the thought of consummating a marriage, oh, will you enjoy the kingdom of Heaven!" It would seem likely that Dante's transposition of terms generally associated with sexual desire to descriptions of the longing for God, as innovative as it may seem to be, is in fact a continuation of a highly similar practice in Jesus' teaching, as is found with some frequency in the Gospels.

PARADISO XI

OUTLINE

THE SUN

1–9 apostrophe: eight false "cares" of mortals (law, medicine, priesthood, political power, robbery, civic affairs, sexuality, idleness)

10–12 removed from all that: Dante with Beatrice in the Sun

13–18 spirits of first solar circle finish their circling and become fixed in place; one of them (Thomas) speaks:

19–21 "I know your thoughts and the reasons for them:

22–27 you want to know what I meant at *Par.* X. 96 and X.114"

28–139 a self-commentary by Thomas on Paradiso X.96:

- 28–36 God chose two to serve as guides to Christ's Church
- 37–39 one seraphic **(Francis)** in his ardor, the other cherubic **(Dominic)** in his wisdom
- 40–42 I will speak of one, but that is to do so of both.

(43–117 inset: Thomas's "Life of Francis")

- 43–54 the situation of Francis's birthplace in Umbria, not to be called "Ascesi" but "Orïente"
- 55–57 Francis's early proofs of his powers:
- 58–63 his youthful love for and marriage to **Lady Poverty**
- 64–72 left a widow by **Jesus**, she had previously been in **Amyclas**'s company; but neither association helped her
- 73–75 Thomas spoke, he explains, of Francis and Poverty
- 76–78 their love caused holy, loving thoughts in others:

79–81 **Bernard of Quintavalle** decided to go forth barefoot;
82–84 **Egidius** and **Silvester** did so too;
85–87 and off they all went, cinctured with their cord
88–93 Francis appeared before **Pope Innocent III**, receiving the first seal for his order (1214)
94–99 once the number of followers had grown, **Pope Honorius III** gave Francis his "second crown" (1223)
100–108 after failing to convert the **Sultan** (1219), Francis received the third seal on **Mount Alvernia** (1224)
109–117 he preferred to die in Lady Poverty's bosom and told his followers to love her in faith.

(118–139 Thomas resumes his "commentary")

118–123 Dominic's worth in sharing such a role with Francis
124–132 but his sheep are so hungry for new food, the more scattered they become and the less milk they produce if they return; and they are few who keep to the fold
133–139 and that is why he said, "where sheep are fattened if they do not stray." QED.

PARADISO XI

O insensata cura de' mortali,
quanto son difettivi silogismi
quei che ti fanno in basso batter l'ali!

Chi dietro a *iura* e chi ad amforismi
sen giva, e chi seguendo sacerdozio,
e chi regnar per forza o per sofismi,

e chi rubare e chi civil negozio,
chi nel diletto de la carne involto
s'affaticava e chi si dava a l'ozio,

quando, da tutte queste cose sciolto,
con Bëatrice m'era suso in cielo
cotanto glorïosamente accolto.

Poi che ciascuno fu tornato ne lo
punto del cerchio in che avanti s'era,
fermossi, come a candellier candelo.

E io senti' dentro a quella lumera
che pria m'avea parlato, sorridendo
incominciar, faccendosi più mera:

"Così com' io del suo raggio resplendo,
sì, riguardando ne la luce etterna,
li tuoi pensieri onde cagioni apprendo.

Tu dubbi, e hai voler che si ricerna
in sì aperta e 'n sì distesa lingua
lo dicer mio, ch'al tuo sentir si sterna,

ove dinanzi dissi: 'U' ben s'impingua,'
e là u' dissi: 'Non nacque il secondo';
e qui è uopo che ben si distingua.

O foolish cares of mortals, how flawed
are all the arguments that make you flap
your wings in downward flight!

One pursued the law, one the Hippocratic
Aphorisms, while yet another sought
the priesthood, and another, rule by force or fraud,

one was set on plunder, one on the public weal,
one wearied himself in the toils of flesh
and its delights, another gave himself to idleness,

while I, set free from all these things,
was, high in heaven with Beatrice,
thus gloriously received.

When each flame had returned to the same point
on the circle where it had stood before,
it stopped, like a candle on its sconce,

and now the light that had already spoken
from deep within began again to speak,
smiling and shining still more bright:

'Even as I reflect its radiant beams, so,
gazing into the Eternal Light, I grasp
your thoughts and the source of their beginnings.

'You are in doubt and would have me restate
my words, to make them clear and plain,
matching the level of your understanding,

'as when I said, "Where sheep are fattened,"
as well as, "There never rose another."
And here one needs to make a clear distinction.

La provedenza, che governa il mondo
con quel consiglio nel quale ogne aspetto
creato è vinto pria che vada al fondo,

però che andasse ver' lo suo diletto
la sposa di colui ch'ad alte grida
disposò lei col sangue benedetto,

in sé sicura e anche a lui più fida,
due principi ordinò in suo favore,
che quinci e quindi le fosser per guida.

L'un fu tutto serafico in ardore;
l'altro per sapïenza in terra fue
di cherubica luce uno splendore.

De l'un dirò, però che d'amendue
si dice l'un pregiando, qual ch'om prende,
perch' ad un fine fur l'opere sue.

Intra Tupino e l'acqua che discende
del colle eletto dal beato Ubaldo,
fertile costa d'alto monte pende,

onde Perugia sente freddo e caldo
da Porta Sole; e di rietro le piange
per grave giogo Nocera con Gualdo.

Di questa costa, là dov' ella frange
più sua rattezza, nacque al mondo un sole,
come fa questo talvolta di Gange.

Però chi d'esso loco fa parole,
non dica Ascesi, ché direbbe corto,
ma Orïente, se proprio dir vuole.

Non era ancor molto lontan da l'orto,
ch'el cominciò a far sentir la terra
de la sua gran virtute alcun conforto;

'The providence that rules the world
with such deep wisdom that any God-created eye
must fail before it reaches to the very depth—

'so that the bride of Him who, crying out
in a loud voice, espoused her with His sacred blood,
should go in joy to her belovèd

'sure of herself and now to Him more faithful—
ordained in her behalf two princes,
one on this side, one on that, to serve as guides.

'One was all seraphic in his ardor,
the other, by his wisdom, was on earth
resplendent with cherubic light.

'I shall speak of one, since praising one,
whichever one we choose, is to speak of both,
for they labored to a single end.

'Between the Topino and the waters that descend
down from the hilltop chosen by the blessèd Ubaldo
there hangs a fertile slope from one high peak

'that makes Perugia feel both heat and cold
at Porta Sole, while behind its other flank
Nocera and Gualdo mourn their heavy yoke.

'From this slope, where it interrupts
its steep descent, a sun rose on the world,
as from the Ganges our sun sometimes does.

'Therefore, let anyone who would speak of this place
not say *Ascesi*, which would come up short,
but call it *Orient*, to sound its proper worth.

'Not much time as yet had passed
when he first lent his comfort to the earth
by the greatness of his virtuous power.

ché per tal donna, giovinetto, in guerra
del padre corse, a cui, come a la morte,
la porta del piacer nessun diserra;

e dinanzi a la sua spirital corte
et coram patre le si fece unito;
poscia di dì in dì l'amò più forte.

Questa, privata del primo marito,
millecent' anni e più dispetta e scura
fino a costui si stette sanza invito;

né valse udir che la trovò sicura
con Amiclate, al suon de la sua voce,
colui ch'a tutto 'l mondo fé paura;

né valse esser costante né feroce,
sì che, dove Maria rimase giuso,
ella con Cristo pianse in su la croce.

Ma perch' io non proceda troppo chiuso,
Francesco e Povertà per questi amanti
prendi oramai nel mio parlar diffuso.

La lor concordia e i lor lieti sembianti,
amore e maraviglia e dolce sguardo
facieno esser cagion di pensier santi;

tanto che 'l venerabile Bernardo
si scalzò prima, e dietro a tanta pace
corse e, correndo, li parve esser tardo.

Oh ignota ricchezza! oh ben ferace!
Scalzasi Egidio, scalzasi Silvestro
dietro a lo sposo, sì la sposa piace.

Indi sen va quel padre e quel maestro
con la sua donna e con quella famiglia
che già legava l'umile capestro.

'For, still a youth, he fought against his father's wish
for the favor of a lady to whom, as to death,
no one unlocks the door with gladness,

'and before his spiritual court *et coram patre*
he joined himself to her and, from then on,
each passing day, he loved her more.

'She, bereft of her first husband, scorned and unknown
one thousand and one hundred years and more,
remained without a suitor till he came.

'Nor did it profit her when men heard that she stood
unmoved, with Amyclas, despite the voice
of him who put the whole wide world in fear.

'Nor did it profit her when, being fiercely loyal
and undaunted, while Mary stayed below,
she wept with Christ upon the cross.

'But, lest I make my meaning dark,
let it be understood, in all that I have said,
that these two lovers are Francis and Poverty.

'Their happy countenances and their harmony,
their love and wonder and sweet contemplation
made them a cause for holy thoughts,

'so that the venerable Bernard was the first
to shed his shoes and run, pursuing such great peace,
and, running, thought himself too slow.

'O unknown riches and prolific good! Barefoot goes Giles,
barefoot goes Sylvester, following the groom,
so greatly pleasing is the bride.

'Then that father and teacher went his way
in company of his lady and that family,
each one girt with the same humble cord.

Né li gravò viltà di cuor le ciglia
per esser fi' di Pietro Bernardone,
né per parer dispetto a maraviglia;

ma regalmente sua dura intenzione
ad Innocenzio aperse, e da lui ebbe
primo sigillo a sua religïone.

Poi che la gente poverella crebbe
dietro a costui, la cui mirabil vita
meglio in gloria del ciel si canterebbe,

di seconda corona redimita
fu per Onorio da l'Etterno Spiro
la santa voglia d'esto archimandrita.

E poi che, per la sete del martiro,
ne la presenza del Soldan superba
predicò Cristo e li altri che 'l seguiro,

e per trovare a conversione acerba
troppo la gente e per non stare indarno,
redissi al frutto de l'italica erba,

nel crudo sasso intra Tevero e Arno
da Cristo prese l'ultimo sigillo,
che le sue membra due anni portarno.

Quando a colui ch'a tanto ben sortillo
piacque di trarlo suso a la mercede
ch'el meritò nel suo farsi pusillo,

a' frati suoi, sì com' a giuste rede,
raccomandò la donna sua più cara,
e comandò che l'amassero a fede;

e del suo grembo l'anima preclara
mover si volle, tornando al suo regno,
e al suo corpo non volle altra bara.

'Nor did an unworthy shame weigh on his brow
for being Pietro Bernardone's son,
90 nor for being an object of amazed contempt,

'but he regally laid bare his stern resolve
to Innocent and, from him, he received
93 the first seal of his order.

'When his followers, sworn to poverty,
increased their number, he, whose admirable life
96 were better sung in the glorious realm of Heaven,

'was affirmed with a second crown
by the eternal Breath, through Honorius,
99 in his holy purpose as shepherd of this flock.

'And when, in his thirst for martyrdom,
he preached Christ and the apostles who came after
102 in the proud presence of the Sultan,

'finding the people unripe for conversion
and unwilling to remain to no good purpose,
105 he returned to reap the harvest of Italian fields.

'On the harsh rock between the Tiber and the Arno
from Christ he had the final seal, then for two years
108 he bore His wounds upon his limbs.

'When He who had chosen him for so much good
was pleased to take him to the high reward
111 that he had won with his devoted meekness,

'he recommended his most cherished lady
to his brothers, as to his rightful heirs,
114 commanding them to love her faithfully.

'From his lady's bosom the illustrious soul
chose to set forth, returning to its kingdom,
117 and for its corpse would have no other bier.

Pensa oramai qual fu colui che degno
collega fu a mantener la barca
di Pietro in alto mar per dritto segno;

e questo fu il nostro patrïarca;
per che qual segue lui, com' el comanda,
discerner puoi che buone merce carca.

Ma 'l suo pecuglio di nova vivanda
è fatto ghiotto, sì ch'esser non puote
che per diversi salti non si spanda;

e quanto le sue pecore remote
e vagabunde più da esso vanno,
più tornano a l'ovil di latte vòte.

Ben son di quelle che temono 'l danno
e stringonsi al pastor; ma son sì poche,
che le cappe fornisce poco panno.

Or, se le mie parole non son fioche,
se la tua audïenza è stata attenta,
se ciò ch'è detto a la mente revoche,

in parte fia la tua voglia contenta,
perché vedrai la pianta onde si scheggia,
e vedra' il corrègger che argomenta
'U' ben s'impingua, se non si vaneggia.' "

'Now think what kind of man it took
to be a fit companion to maintain
120 the steadfast course of Peter's bark upon the sea,

'and just such was our patriarch. From this
you may perceive that he who follows him
123 as he commands is freighted with good cargo.

'But his flock has grown so greedy
for new sustenance that it is forced
126 to scatter through remote and distant pastures,

'and the farther his sheep go wandering off
from him, the emptier of milk
129 do they at last come back into the fold.

'There are some, indeed, who, fearing harm,
huddle near the shepherd, but these are so few
132 that a tiny piece of cloth can furnish all their cowls.

'And so, if my words are not too dark,
and if your ears have been intent,
135 and if you can recall exactly what was said,

'then shall your wish be in part fulfilled
and you shall see the reason why the plant is cleft
and what is meant by the rebuke
139 "where sheep are fattened if they do not stray." '

PARADISO XI

1–12. In sharp contrast to both the opening six and concluding nine verses of the preceding canto, with their visionary taste of a trinitarian and ordered love and then the sound made by the singing souls in the Sun (compared to the harmonious chiming of matins calling monks to prayer), the opening nine verses of this canto summon images of ceaseless and futile human activity, from which Dante is happy to have been, at least temporarily, liberated.

1. Dante's reflection of the opening verse of Persius's *Satires* ("*O curas hominum*, o quantum est in rebus inane" [O wearisome cares of men, o emptiness of the things we care for]) had an early-twentieth-century notice in Bertoldi (Bert. 1903.1), p. 7. However, it was first observed in the late fourteenth century by the author of the *Chiose ambrosiane.*

2. Depending on whether we have read verse 138 of the previous canto *in bono* or *in malo*, that is, whether we have thought Dante meant to praise or blame Siger's "syllogizing," we decide that the noun form of that word is here used oppositionally or with the same intonation. See the note to *Paradiso* X.138 for reasons to prefer the first alternative; where Siger is admirable for his powers of reasoning, the normal run of men is not, using reason merely to advance their cupidinous designs.

3. The metaphor of lowered wings suggests that we mortals, born worms but with the ability to be transformed into angelic butterflies (according to *Purg.* X.124–125), nevertheless choose to direct our cares to the things of this world, lowering the level of our desires.

4–9. Dante's list of vain human activities starts out with law (whether civil or canonical); medicine (identified by one of the earliest known doctors, Hippocrates, author of the medical text that bore the title *Aphorisms*); priesthood (as a position rather than as a calling); political power (whether achieved by force or guile).

5. Bosco/Reggio (comm. to this verse) point out that Dante's word *sacerdozio* for "priesthood" has the sense of an ecclesiastical office that yields a good living to its holder, and refer to Dante's previous attack on those religious (almost all of them, Dante has previously said) who study only in order to gain wealth or honors (see *Conv.* III.xi.10).

10–12. Punning on the first noun in *Paradiso*, the glory (*la gloria*) of God, Dante separates himself from the eight activities he has just catalogued by noting his freedom from such preoccupations as are caused by them and enjoying his presence here in the Sun, welcomed by these souls who live, still higher above, *in gloria* with God.

13–18. The spirits moving in this first solar circle, having surrounded Beatrice and Dante, become fixed, like candles on their holders, and one of them (Thomas) speaks.

19–21. Dante here gives Thomas one of the relatively few similes allowed to a speaker in the poem. One feels compelled to wonder what, had he been able to read these cantos of *Paradiso*, he would have thought of his inclusion in them. See the note to *Paradiso* X.86–96.

22–27. Perhaps we are meant to be amused that Thomas's eulogy of Francis begins as a gloss on two difficult passages on his own "poem" (see *Par.* X.96 and X.114), the veiled speech that made the historical Thomas distrust poetry.

28–36. This convoluted and difficult passage may be paraphrased as follows: "God's foresight, with such deep wisdom that none may fathom it, selected two guides for the Church so that she, married to Him at the moment when Christ cried out in pain on the Cross [Daniello, comm. to vv. 28–34: See Luke 23:46] and shed His blood to wed her [Lombardi, comm. to vv. 31–34: See Acts 20:28], might proceed joyously, and with greater confidence and faith, following Him." Thus Francis and Dominic, the first of whom was indeed often portrayed as a "second Christ" (see, among others, Auerbach [Auer.1944.2], p. 85), each takes on the role of Christ in husbanding the Church through her many tribulations both in his lifetime and thereafter, by instrument of the mendicant order that he, having founded, left behind him.

34–39. See Cosmo (Cosm.1936.1), pp. 123–25, for the view that Dante nourished his hopes for the Church's renewal with the writings of Ubertino da Casale, particularly his *Arbor vitae crucifixae Iesu*.

37–42. The complementarity of the founders of the two orders is insisted on here, not their distinguishing features. Thus before we hear a word about either Francis or Dominic, respectively associated with the Seraphim (the highest angelic order) and love and with the Cherubim (the next order down) and knowledge, we are informed in no uncertain terms that we should not rank one higher than the other. See the note to *Paradiso* XII.46–57. And see Carroll (comm. to vv. 37–39) for a similar attempt to bridge what he refers to as "mysticism" and "scholasticism."

It may have been Bernardino Daniello (comm. to vv. 40–42) who first brought historical fact into play in interpreting this part of the canto. It was a matter of record, he reports, that on Francis's feast day (4 October) one of the friars of his order would preach the virtues of Dominic, while on the feast of Dominic (8 August), a Dominican would do the same for Francis. Daniello suggests that this practice lies behind Dante's here. As many have ruefully noted, that spirit of fraternity between these two groups of friars did not present an accurate picture of the relations, in fact emulous, between these two mendicant orders in Dante's time.

37–39. For a likely source in the *Arbor vitae crucifixae Iesu* of Ubertino da Casale for Dante's making Francis seraphic and Dominic cherubic, see Mineo (Mine.1992.1), p. 273.

43–117. Here begins Dante's *Vita Francisci*. On Dante's sense of the life of Francis as a model for his once prideful and now exiled self, see Herzmann (Herz.2003.1), p. 323. For a brief essay on the canto as a whole, see Bruno Nardi (Nard.1964.1); for a much longer treatment, see Mineo (Mine. 1992.1). For bibliography, see Stanislao da Campagnola, "Francesco di Assisi, santo," *ED* III (1971). For the various lives of Francis known to Dante, see da Campagnola's article (Daca.1983.1). And for the relationship between the historical Francis and Dante's portrait of him, see Mellone (Mell.1987.1). For some more recent bibliography, see Barolini (Baro. 1992.1), p. 334, n. 6.

43–51. These three tercets of Thomas might be paraphrased as follows: "Between the Topino and the Chiascio, which flows down from Gubbio, perched on a fertile slope on mount Subasio, whence Perugia, some twelve miles to the west, feels both cold air from the mountains and the heat of the easterly sun, sits Assisi, while further to the east the towns Nocera and Gualdo suffer both from the cold and from being misgoverned by the Guelph Perugians. From here, where the mountain is least steep, arose a sun, just as the Sun we are in rises from Ganges in summer (when it is brightest)."

44. The "blessed Ubaldo," canonized in 1192, was born Ubaldo Baldassini in 1084 and served as bishop of Gubbio (1129–60). Before he

allowed himself an ecclesiastical life, he lived as a hermit on a hill near that town, along the stream named Chiascio.

47. Before it was destroyed, Porta Sole was one of the city gates of Perugia. Located on the southeast side of the city, it faced Assisi.

48. Nocera is a town in Umbria, some fifteen miles northeast of Assisi; Gualdo Tadino is also in Umbria and like it on the eastern slope of Mt. Subasio. The two towns "mourn beneath their heavy yoke" perhaps in two senses: Literally, they are beneath the peaks of the Apennine Range (and thus overshadowed by them); metaphorically, they suffer under Guelph rule.

51. The Ganges, about which we will hear again in *Paradiso* XIX.71, was for Dante the defining eastern limit of his world. (Seville [*Inf.* XX.126 and XXVI.110] was close to the western limit, as Ulysses discovered]). For earlier reference to the Ganges, see *Purgatorio* II.5 and XXVII.4.

53–54. *Ascesi*: For the phrase describing Francis as "quasi Sol oriens in mundo" (like the Sun rising on the world) by one of his chroniclers, Bernardo da Bessa, see Baldelli (Bald.1973.1), p. 105; this source was perhaps first cited by Daniello (comm. to verse 50). Perhaps the only commentator to be properly puzzled by what this verse means, whether in Dante's formulation itself or in more than six hundred years of commentary that have yet to produce a convincing resolution, is Chimenz (comm. to vv. 52–54). But no one apparently has thought of the most simple reason that might have made Dante prefer "Orïente" to "Ascesi": the tenses of the Latin verb and participle. "Ascesi" ("I have risen," certainly a Christlike enough word) yields to "Orïente" (rising) because the second word is present tense, that is, not confined to the past. Francis, like Christ, is *always* rising, leading us Heavenward.

The first commentator to turn to Bonaventure's life of Francis for a source, a practice of many contemporary glossators, was apparently Lombardi (comm. to vv. 53–54): "Vidi Alterum Angelum ascendentem ab ortu Solis, habentem signum Dei vivi" (I saw another angel ascending from the east, having the seal of the living God [Apocalypse 7:2]). We may note that St. Bonaventure's biblical formula also makes use of a present participle—two of them, in fact. Bosco (Bosc. 1966.1), p. 322, privileges the Apocalypse over Franciscan writings as compelling Dante's attention, but not convincingly, since Dante may have been reminded of the Apocalypse precisely by Bonaventure.

55. Dante puns on the Sun again, using a metaphoric valence for his birth (*orto* [rising]) more readily associated with the rising of a star or planet in the sky.

56–57. Again Francis, beginning his career of service to God and humankind, is seen as the Sun, now preparing the earth to be fruitful.

58–60. Francis's father raised his son to pursue the life of commerce, as he himself had done. Dante has boiled down into a single tercet the dramatic story of Francis's public rejection of his father's plans for him, taking the clothes off his back to return them to him in a public square of Assisi. This choice is represented here by his "marrying" Lady Poverty. (One of the popular Franciscan narratives of the thirteenth century was the *Sacrum commercium beati Francisci cum domina Paupertate*. For an attempt to establish Dante's acquaintance with this work as already revealed in passages in *Purgatorio*, see Havely [Have.1996.1].) That conceit gives the controlling image to the next fifty verses (58–117). And, while even indirect reference to the conflict between the Spiritual and Conventual Franciscans will not confront the reader until the next canto (XII.124), it is clear from the outset that Dante essentially sides with the Spirituals, whose central and urgent position was the radical insistence on the Church owning nothing, a view that happens to coincide with Dante's political views. This is not to say that his religious feelings about poverty were ungenuine, but merely to point out that a secondary reason for them does exist. Manselli, "francescanesimo," *ED* III (1971), pp. 14a–16b, points out that the fourteenth-century struggle within the order had its roots in the papacy of Celestino V, in the waning years of the thirteenth century, when a group of Franciscans received permission to split off and form their own "sub-order." They were fairly soon forced to flee Italy (most of them for Greece). This group included John of Peter Olivi and Ubertino of Casale, both of whom eventually resurfaced in Florence. For a recent discussion in English of Dante's views of the Spiritual Franciscans, see Havely (Have.2004.1).

60. In the past sixty years there has been dispute over the somewhat curious phrase "la porta del piacere" (lit., "the door of pleasure"), generally understood to understate the aversion to poverty, that is, none opens the door to her gladly, none welcomes poverty into his heart. This became "the doorway to pleasure" (*die Pforte der Lust* [*Neue Dantestudien*, Istanbul, 1944, p. 80]) in Auerbach's (Auer.1944.2, pp. 88–89) formulation (his translator does not help his case, making *porta* plural, while it is singular, and mistranslating *piacere* in her "gates of desire," if one must admit that

translating the phrase presents something of a problem). If most were scandalized by this reading, it has found support in some quarters, for example, Marguerite Mills Chiarenza (Chia.1993.1). The core of Auerbach's interpretation, possibly the most controversial point in a series of works dealing with Dante that were hardly intended to be without cause for controversy, may be represented in a single sentence: "It seems to me absolutely necessary to interpret the opening of the gates of desire in the proper sense as a sexual act, and thus *porta* as the gateway to the feminine body" (p. 88). For some of the many counterarguments, see Bonora (Bono.1987.1), pp. 242–43; Pasquini (Pasq.1996.1), pp. 422–23; see also Pasquini (Pasq.2001.1), pp. 193–94. What supporters of Auerbach's reading fail to take into account is that it is the male in the metaphor who opens *his* "porta del piacere" to the lady, thus rendering his entire argument inapplicable.

61–63. In 1207, before the court of the bishop of his hometown and *coram patre* (Latin: "in the presence of his father"), he renounced his family and the life that had been chosen for him to follow Christ. In no other figure in the history of the Church does the concept of the "imitation of Christ" have so obvious and central a relation as it has in the life of Francis of Assisi.

His "spouse," Poverty, once chosen, becomes increasingly more precious to him; as we will shortly find out (vv. 64–66), she had been married once before, and her previous husband had been no one less than Jesus.

64–66. While at first the reader is perhaps not sure as to the identity of Poverty's first husband, it will soon (at verse 72) become clear that she was Jesus' "wife," left a widow by the Crucifixion in A.D. 34, and remaining "unmarried" for 1,173 years, unwanted by any other suitor, until Francis's vow in 1207.

Dante has outdone himself. The writings about Francis (who was practically the cause of the explosion of the biography industry all by himself [there were at least eight "lives" produced within the century of his death]) have, except for the Gospels, no antecedents. Dante's addition to existing Franciscan material is spectacularly original in its reworking of the basic narrative found in Bonaventure and others. Dante expands the role of poverty not so much conceptually (the devotion to poverty is the keystone of all Franciscan writings) but stylistically, making his saintly life an allegorical tale of his relationship to her. He can, given the abundance of "official lives," count on his readers to fill in the by-then familiar historical details.

For the influence of Franciscan lyric poetry (and especially that of Iacopone da Todi) on Dante, see Vettori (Vett.2004.1), pp. 120–22. Luciano Rossi (Ross.2002.1), pp. 170–72, follows up a suggestion of Lucia Battaglia Ricci (Batt.1997.1), p. 42, and argues that Dante's eleventh canto reflects Francis's *Laudes Creaturarum* (see the note to *Inf.* I.117).

It seems possible that the author of the *Commedia* has, improbable as this may seem, gone beyond the prideful bearing that afflicted so much of his earlier work and attained a kind of humility (see Hollander [Holl.2003.2]). For the crucial role of Francis in the development of that humility, particularly as counterforce to the arid intellectual pride that leads to heresy, see Veglia (Vegl.2000.1), pp. 75–97.

67–69. Not content with making Poverty the "wife" of Jesus and then of Francis, Dante invents her presence in classical epic, adding her to the participants in that scene in Lucan (*Phars.* V.515–531) in which Caesar's bellowing, bullying manner cannot impress the poverty-stricken fisherman, Amyclas (see Dante's earlier treatment, without mention of Lady Poverty, in *Convivio* IV.xiii.12), not evincing fear because he has nothing of which to be robbed.

Occasionally, a reader (e.g., Carlo Grabher, comm. to vv. 64–75) complains that this bit of business seems overly cerebral (along with the next *exemplum*, the presence of Poverty on the Cross with Jesus). It surely reveals the high regard Dante held for Lucan's text, putting a moment from its narrative not only alongside one from the Bible (a familiar enough Dantean technique), but alongside one of the supreme moments in the Bible, Jesus' death on the Cross; yet Grabher's point is well taken.

70–72. If Lady Poverty's loyalty to Amyclas had won her no friends for more than a millennium, this result is all the more surprising in that she was the last one to solace Jesus in His final agony.

72. A much-debated line, from the earliest days to the present. Is the verb in this line *pianse* (wept), as Petrocchi has decided, or is it *salse* (climbed), as Benvenuto da Imola insisted (comm. to vv. 70–72)? Evidently, the shocking and otherwise unheard-of act that is portrayed if the reader accepts the second option has kept some commentators on the side of the version of this verse contained in the Codice Cassinese, in which we find *pianse*. As always, we are constrained (as we should be) by our decision to follow Petrocchi's text; on this occasion, we would have gladly been governed by Benvenuto's reading of the line.

73. Thomas is concerned lest he had allowed his speech to become *chiuso* (dark, unclear), and we consequently not understand of whom and of what he spoke, thus reflecting his characterization (vv. 22–24) of his figurative speech in the previous canto (most specifically *Par.* X.96, his metaphor of fattening sheep, on which he has been expanding here) as not being *aperta* (clear). Once again one may witness, behind the text, Dante's desire to deal with Thomas's attacks on the unreliable nature of poetic speech (see Hollander [Holl.1976.1]).

74. Finally we hear the name of this hero of the religious life. Ernesto Trucchi (comm. to vv. 55–57) revives the account of a certain preacher, named Chalippe, who, in town to address the faithful of Lucca during the Lenten observances of 1689, was shown names engraved in stone by a canon of Lucca named Moriconi. These were two Luccan brothers, one of whom, Bernardo Moriconi, left his native city and settled in Assisi. His son, Pietro (Bernardone, after his father) Moriconi, married a noblewoman by the name of Pica Bourlement. In 1181 they had a son, baptized (at the mother's instigation, since the father was away at the time) as Giovanni. Upon his return to Assisi, Pietro Bernardone was furious, since he had wanted his son to bear the name of Francesco (the adjective for "French" in Italian) to honor his own pleasure in association with France, the country where he had made his fortune as a merchant. Accordingly, the day of the boy's confirmation, Pietro had his name changed. And that, apparently, is how Francesco d'Assisi got his name.

76. See Porcelli (Porc.2000.1), pp. 1–5, for a discussion of the word *concordia* (harmony) as a key to understanding the cantos of the Sun.

77–78. Indeed, the growing love between Francis and his lady, Poverty, is a form of *concordia* developed out of apparent discord: the first description of poverty as something, like death, that no one willingly welcomes.

79–84. The first followers of Francis, those who were eventually gathered into the Order of Friars Minor (so called by Francis in his first Rule, indicating their humility, i.e, that they were "lesser brothers"), are now presented: Bernard of Quintavalle (a fellow townsman of Assisi, also from a wealthy family, who was so impressed by Francis's actions that he sold all his possessions in benefit of the poor and became his first follower; Francis considered Bernard his "first born"); Giles and Silvester, both also of Assisi—the first was also among the earliest of Francis's followers and lived until 1262;

Silvester was already a priest, who, when he had a dream in which Francis killed a dragon menacing the city, joined the group; he died circa 1240.

The sensuous delights of going barefoot are portrayed as the freedom of the soul in unstinting love of Christ. We note how the heat increases in these lines: Bernard is described with a past definite (*si scalzò*) as having taken his shoes off, but then the verb is repeated in the present tense (*scalzasi*) for Giles and Silvester. Those uses of the "historical present" intensify the feeling of liberation as, one by one, Francis's followers begin also to fall in love with this ugly woman.

82. The adjective *ferace* (literally, fertile, fecund), a hapax in the poem (as is, more surprisingly, the parallel adjective that precedes it, *ignota* [unknown]), contrasts with the notion of ordinary life, based as it is in acquiring wealth and possessions, not in living one's faith. Like its unique status among the words of the poem, its unusualness in ordinarily sterile human experience sets it apart.

84. On this verse, see Ulivi (Uliv.1982.1), p. 22, attacking Erich Auerbach (Auer.1944.2) for not understanding how changed she is in Francis's eyes. But see the line itself ("si la sposa piace"): One can almost hear the suppressed assonantal "spiace" (displeases), the normal reaction of almost everyone who is forced to contemplate the visage of Poverty.

85–86. These lines summarize the result of the family struggle between Pietro Bernardone and his son, once known as Giovanni (Sigmund Freud must have enjoyed this passage): Francis, having rejected his own father, has himself become a father and a teacher; having rejected his own family, he has created a group of apostolic brethren.

87. The word *capestro* refers to the rope used to control horses or oxen, that is, a halter, and was used as a belt by Francis and his first followers as an outward sign both of their inner control and of their humility before God. See its other two occurrences as identifying marks of Franciscan friars, *Inferno* XXVII.92 and *Paradiso* XI.132. And see the note to *Inferno* XVI.106–108 for the word *corda* (cord), also used to designate the cincture of a garment worn by a member of a religious order (of its fourteen appearances in the poem, however, only two others refer to such a use [*Inf.* XXVII.67; *Purg.* VII.114]).

88–93. In 1214, Francis went to Rome and had an audience with Pope Innocent III, who approved the founding of the order (he gave it its "first seal"). See Tozer's paraphrase (comm. to these vv.): "On that occasion he was not shamefaced on account of the meanness of his origin or his contemptible appearance, but 'like a prince declared to Innocent his stern intention' of founding his Order: It is a little difficult to reconcile the statement about the meanness of his origin with the fact that his father was a well-to-do merchant; but this appears to be the meaning, for St. Bonaventura in his Life of St. Francis says that, when the epithets 'boorish' and 'mercenary' were applied to him, the Saint was wont to reply, that such reproaches were suitably addressed to Pietro Bernardone's son ('Talia enim licet audire filium Petri de Bernardone' [*Legenda maior* VI.2])."

91. Pasquini (Pasq.2001.1), p. 241, points out that words in Dante's narrative at times are at radical odds with their counterparts in the various *vitae* of St. Francis, as here *regalmente* (regally) replaces the adverb *humiliter* (humbly); similarly, in verse 101, the Sultan's presence is described as being *superba* (prideful) while in the lives of Francis he is presented as offering a respectful welcome; or, in verse 106, Mt. Alvernia is portrayed as a *crudo sasso* (rugged rock) rather than as the *locus amoenus* (pleasant place) of his biographers' accounts. What these changes commonly reflect is Dante's desire to make Francis's story more heroic than did his own biographers, who dwelled on his humility. As opposed to those who would only contrast Francis and Dominic, Dante matches them as "militant heroes" of the Church. See the note to *Paradiso* XII.35.

92. Dante suppresses reference to the narrative that appears not only in all the early lives of Francis, but which has a role in Giotto's representation of his life in the upper church at Assisi. Pope Innocent III at first was not favorable to Francis's petition and was planning to deny it. He had a dream, however, in which he saw Francis holding the tottering Church of St. John Lateran on his shoulders, and that won him over.

94–99. In fewer than ten years the order had grown from a relatively tiny band (those who had joined by the time Francis first went to Rome) into some five thousand members in 1223, by the time he goes there to appear before Pope Onorius III and to receive the "second seal" of his mission from him.

94. The *gente poverella* (his followers, sworn to poverty) are to be distinguished from "ordinary" *povera gente* (poor people): Francis and his followers *chose* poverty, not necessarily having been born to it.

96. There are three basic constructions of the possible meaning of this contested line: Francis's life (1) is only to be praised for the greater glory of God, (2) were better sung in Heaven than by his (corrupt?) followers down there on earth, (3) were better sung in the Empyrean than (by me [Thomas]?) here in the Sun. Sapegno argues (comm. to this verse) briefly and cogently against the first two hypotheses and makes a convincing case for the third, giving it its first complete statement: "The life of Francis is more worthy of being sung in the Empyrean by choruses of angels and of souls in bliss than it is of being described in pedestrian ways by me alone." Thus, in this canto based on praise for Francis's humility, Thomas displays his own as well.

99. The word *archimandrita*, a word formed out of a Greek ecclesiastical term meaning "chief shepherd" (from *arch* + *mandra* ["sheepfold"]), and thus the head of more than one monastic community, a hapax in the poem (but which appears, denoting the apostle Peter, in *Mon.* III.ix.17; it also is present, referring to the pope, in *Epist.* XI.13). This word is not, as some might expect, a Dantean coinage, but may have been found by him in the *Magnae derivationes* of Uguccione da Pisa, as Grandgent (comm. to vv. 97–99) seems to have been the first commentator to suggest.

100–105. Drawn by his hope for martyrdom, in imitation of Christ, Francis, accompanied by twelve of his followers (a number obviously meant to recall Jesus' twelve disciples) went to Egypt during a crusade. He insisted, at great risk to all of their lives, on trying to convert the Sultan, Malik al-Kamil, and preached before him to no avail. The Mohammedan, showing great restraint (and perhaps some political astuteness), sent Francis and his fellows back to the Christian army. Francis, seeing his plans for martyrdom during crusade foiled by his gracious adversary, returned to Italy.

Dante presents this episode out of sequence, since the Egyptian journey occurred in 1219, four years before his second trip to Rome, presented in vv. 94–99.

106–108. A year after his receiving the second seal from the pope, Francis receives his third and final seal on Mt. Alvernia directly from Christ, the five stigmata that marked his body as they had marked His.

109–117. Francis's death receives more poetic space than any other element in Thomas's biography. His soul flies back to its Maker. (This is one of the few specific notices we have that some of the saved bypass purgation in order to proceed directly to Heaven. See the note to *Paradiso* X.121–129.)

The merchant in him, now totally redefined, does what all merchants are sure to do: make a will in favor of their surviving family or friends. Thus does Francis leave his "treasure" to his "family," commending them to love his "wife," Poverty, and commending his body to the dust, whence we all came. In good Franciscan fashion, he does not even want a plain coffin, only the earth itself.

Thomas's narrative has moved first along a vertical axis, beginning in the mountains above Assisi (vv. 43–45) and descending from there; then along a horizontal axis, as Francis moves around Italy and the Near East; and finally ending, once more on a mountain (Alvernia, verse 106), with his soul moving up still higher, to Heaven, while his body's latent movement is down, back into nothingness, without a containing bier (*bara*, the last word in Thomas's narrative), in the earth. He was canonized within two years of his death (1228).

111. Veglia (Vegl.2000.1), pp. 94–95, points out that there is a Franciscan sort of magnanimity that is seen by Dante precisely as *pusillo* (meek), as St. Thomas also believed (*ST* II–II, q. 129, a. 3).

118–123. Now our *archimandrita*, Francis (verse 99) is placed in relation to Thomas, a *patrïarca*. It is probably not accidental that Peter, referred to as *archimandrita* in *Monarchia* (see the note to verse 99), is mentioned here, as Dante obviously sees the first *archimandrita* and the second (Francis) as well as the new *patrïarca* (Dominic) as all playing a major role in the shaping of the Church, past and present, when the weakness and corruption in the papacy made the mendicant orders especially necessary in his eyes.

The whole metaphorical passage is developed in nautical terms, in which Peter is the first captain, followed by Francis and Dominic as cocaptains, of the Church. She is portrayed as a merchant ship (surprisingly, perhaps, until one thinks of the commercial metaphors that are present in some of Jesus' parables), with a precious cargo in its hold, the true believers who (we must assume) will be numbered among the saved.

124–132. And now a switch in metaphor: Dominic's "sheep" are so hungry for new food that they have become widely scattered; the farther afield they go, the less milk they produce (i.e., the less their lives give evidence of having taken in the lessons of life under the Franciscan Rule) when they finally return. And, if a few keep close to the shepherd, it does not take much cloth to have enough for their cowls. Thus does Thomas follow his praise of Francis with a denunciation of his own Order, as Bonaventure will do for his fellow Franciscans in the next canto (*Par.* XII.112–126).

For a consideration of the identical elements in these obviously paired cantos, see the note to *Paradiso* XII.142–145.

133–135. Heavily rhetorical (three "if" clauses in as many lines), the opening tercet of Thomas's conclusion draws Dante's attention back to his words in the previous canto (see the note to verse 139). Note that Thomas does not say, in the final clause, "what I said," but "what was said," in a painstakingly modest way of avoiding the use of the first person.

136–139. Thomas reminds Dante that he has been answering the first of his unvoiced "doubts" (see vv. 22–25), caused by Thomas's phrasing in the last canto (*Par.* X.96).

137. The word "plant" (*pianta*) introduces still another metaphor, that of Dominic's Order as despoiled plant, the reason for which defoliation Thomas has just made plain (vv. 124–132).

138. A dispute found in the commentaries involves the understanding of the word *correggier*, whether it is a noun (*correggér*), formed from the noun *correggia*, the Dominican equivalent of the Franciscan *capestro* (see the note to verse 87), and meaning "he who wears the Dominican cincture" and thus, here, Thomas (a formulation first proposed by Francesco da Buti [comm. to vv. 133–139], who, however, believed the noun referred to Dominic, not Thomas). Most today, following the self-styled "first modern commentator," Pompeo Venturi, who, in the eighteenth century, found an equivalent for the word *correggier* in "reprensione" (rebuke), think it is either a verb or an infinitive used as a verbal noun, meaning, in the first case, "correction" (we have translated it "rebuke") and, in the second, "guidance." And see Lombardi (comm. to vv. 138–139) for a return to Buti's interpretation. For his customary lengthy review (and also a return to Buti), see Scartazzini (comm. to vv. 138–139). However, see the nearly equally lengthy treatment offered by Campi (comm. to vv. 136–139), opting for Venturi's solution, which is much as our own. Since then, the basic disagreement lies between followers of Buti/Scartazzini and Venturi/Campi, with most who deal with the problem falling in behind Venturi/Campi.

139. Thomas, in good Thomistic fashion, rounds off his "gloss" on *Paradiso* X.96 by repeating the entire line here.

It is amusing to think that Dante's revenge on his major intellectual rival in the debate over the truth-telling capacity of poetry comes from making Thomas a commentator on Dante's poetry, a role that he himself, perhaps prodded by Thomas's attacks on his profession, felt called upon to play in his *Epistle to Cangrande.*

PARADISO XII

OUTLINE

THE SUN

1–2 retrospective opening phrase: Thomas had fallen silent

3–9 a second group surrounds his, matching movement to movement and song to song; the song outdid mortal music and song **(Muses, Sirens)** as a shining its reflection

10–21 the simile (comparing the two circles to twin rainbows **[Juno, Iris, Noah]**) contains a second simile (comparing the second rainbow to the voice of the nymph **Echo**)

22–27 the pause in all that dancing, singing, and shining is compared in its simultaneity in both circles to that evidenced in two eyes responding as one to beauty

28–30 a voice from the second circle is to Dante's attention as the Pole Star to the needle of a compass

31–36 that soul **[Bonaventure]** speaks: The love that makes him beautiful induces him to speak of **Dominic,** whose (and **Francis**'s common) warfare is matched by a common glory

37–45 the army of Christ, which it cost so much to rearm, was still in weakened condition when God's grace provided for it two champions to rally the wayward people.

46–111 *Bonaventure's Life of St. Dominic:*

- 46–54 Dominic's birthplace, Calaroga, in Spain:
- 55–57 a strong opponent of heresy
- 58–66 his mother's dream; baptism; his **godmother**'s dream
- 67–69 his naming
- 70–72 his role as keeper of Christ's garden, the Church
- 73–75 first signs of his love for Christ
- 76–78 his acceptance of his charge while still a baby

79–81 his rightly named parents, **Felice** and **Giovanna**

82–84 **Enrico di Susa** and **Taddeo d'Alderotto**: two wrong-spirited examples of the intellectual life

85–87 he readied himself to rid the Church of heresy,

88–102 not asking the pope for preferment, he fought

103–105 growing numbers of friars followed his example

106–111 this praise of Dominic matches Thomas's of Francis

112–126 Bonaventure on the degeneracy of the Franciscan Order:

112–114 Bonaventure now denounces Franciscan degeneracy:

115–126 where the first leader went forward, the flock now retreats; but soon there will come a reckoning for such as **Ubaldino di Casale** and **Matteo d'Acquasparta**

127–145 the habitation of the second circle in the Sun

127–129 Bonaventure

130–132 **Illuminato** and **Augustino**: early followers of Francis

133–135 **Hugh of St. Victor, Petrus Comestor, Petrus Hispanus** (Pope John XXI)

136–138 **Nathan, Chrysostom, Anselm, Donatus** the grammarian

139–141 **Rabanus Maurus** and the Abbot **Joachim of Flora**

142–145 Thomas's courtesy moved him to praise Dominic.

PARADISO XII

Sì tosto come l'ultima parola
la benedetta fiamma per dir tolse,
a rotar cominciò la santa mola;

e nel suo giro tutta non si volse
prima ch'un'altra di cerchio la chiuse,
e moto a moto e canto a canto colse;

canto che tanto vince nostre muse,
nostre sirene in quelle dolci tube,
quanto primo splendor quel ch'e' refuse.

Come si volgon per tenera nube
due archi paralelli e concolori,
quando Iunone a sua ancella iube,

nascendo di quel d'entro quel di fori,
a guisa del parlar di quella vaga
ch'amor consunse come sol vapori,

e fanno qui la gente esser presaga,
per lo patto che Dio con Noè puose,
del mondo che già mai più non s'allaga:

così di quelle sempiterne rose
volgiensi circa noi le due ghirlande,
e sì l'estrema a l'intima rispuose.

Poi che 'l tripudio e l'altra festa grande,
sì del cantare e sì del fiammeggiarsi
luce con luce gaudïose e blande,

insieme a punto e a voler quetarsi,
pur come li occhi ch'al piacer che i move
conviene insieme chiudere e levarsi;

As soon as the blessèd flame
had spoken its last word
the holy millstone once again began to wheel,

and had not yet come full around
before another circle closed it in,
matching it motion for motion, song for song,

song that, heard from such sweet instruments,
as far excels our muses and our sirens
as a first shining its reflected rays.

As twin rainbows, parallel in shape and color,
arc in their pathway through translucent clouds
when Juno gives the order to her handmaid—

the outer one born of the inner,
like the voice of that wandering nymph
whom love consumed as the sun does vapors—

and allow the people here on earth to know the future
because of the covenant God made with Noah,
that the world would not again be flooded,

so the two wreaths of those eternal roses
circled all around us and, thus reflected,
the outer circle shone in answer to the inner.

When the dance and all the other celebration—
the singing and the brilliant blaze of flames,
light with light blent in ardent joy—

came to a stop together and of one accord,
as eyes, when beauty moves them,
must open wide or close as one,

del cor de l'una de le luci nove
si mosse voce, che l'ago a la stella
parer mi fece in volgermi al suo dove;

e cominciò: "L'amor che mi fa bella
mi tragge a ragionar de l'altro duca
per cui del mio sì ben ci si favella.

Degno è che, dov' è l'un, l'altro s'induca:
sì che, com' elli ad una militaro,
così la gloria loro insieme luca.

L'essercito di Cristo, che sì caro
costò a rïarmar, dietro a la 'nsegna
si movea tardo, sospeccioso e raro,

quando lo 'mperador che sempre regna
provide a la milizia, ch'era in forse,
per sola grazia, non per esser degna;

e, come è detto, a sua sposa soccorse
con due campioni, al cui fare, al cui dire
lo popol disvïato si raccorse.

In quella parte ove surge ad aprire
Zefiro dolce le novelle fronde
di che si vede Europa rivestire,

non molto lungi al percuoter de l'onde
dietro a le quali, per la lunga foga,
lo sol talvolta ad ogne uom si nasconde,

siede la fortunata Calaroga
sotto la protezion del grande scudo
in che soggiace il leone e soggioga:

dentro vi nacque l'amoroso drudo
de la fede cristiana, il santo atleta
benigno a' suoi e a' nemici crudo;

from the core of one of these new lights,
as the North Star makes a compass needle veer,
rose a voice that made me turn to where it came from.

And it began: 'The love that makes me beautiful
bids me, in turn, to laud that other leader
because of whom my own has won such praise.

'It is fitting that, in naming one, we name the other
so that, just as they were joined as one in combat
with a single goal, their fame should shine as one.

'Rearmed at such high cost, the troops of Christ
moved with halting steps behind the standard,
full of doubt and few in number,

'when the Emperor who reigns forever
provided for His soldiers in their peril—
only of His grace, not for their merit—

'and, as was said, gave comfort to His bride
through these two champions, whose deeds and words
brought together the scattered people.

'In that place where gentle Zephyr's breath
rises to open the unfolding leaves
in which Europe sees herself reclad,

'not far from the pounding waves
beyond which the sun, having finished his long course,
sometimes hides himself from human sight,

'favored Calaroga lies
behind the shelter of the noble shield
that shows one lion in defeat and one in triumph.

'In that town was born the amorous lover
of the Christian faith, the holy athlete,
gentle to his own and savage to his foes.

e come fu creata, fu repleta
sì la sua mente di viva virtute
che, ne la madre, lei fece profeta.

Poi che le sponsalizie fuor compiute
al sacro fonte intra lui e la Fede,
u' si dotar di mutüa salute,

la donna che per lui l'assenso diede,
vide nel sonno il mirabile frutto
ch'uscir dovea di lui e de le rede;

e perché fosse qual era in costrutto,
quinci si mosse spirito a nomarlo
del possessivo di cui era tutto.

Domenico fu detto; e io ne parlo
sì come de l'agricola che Cristo
elesse a l'orto suo per aiutarlo.

Ben parve messo e famigliar di Cristo:
ché 'l primo amor che 'n lui fu manifesto,
fu al primo consiglio che diè Cristo.

Spesse fïate fu tacito e desto
trovato in terra da la sua nutrice,
come dicesse: 'Io son venuto a questo.'

Oh padre suo veramente Felice!
oh madre sua veramente Giovanna,
se, interpretata, val come si dice!

Non per lo mondo, per cui mo s'affanna
di retro ad Ostïense e a Taddeo,
ma per amor de la verace manna

in picciol tempo gran dottor si feo;
tal che si mise a circüir la vigna
che tosto imbianca, se 'l vignaio è reo.

'His mind, at the moment of its making,
was so full of living power that,
60 yet in his mother's womb, he made of her a prophet.

'After his nuptials with the Faith
were celebrated at the holy font
63 at which each dowered the other's safety,

'the lady who offered her assent for his
saw in a dream the admirable fruit
66 destined to spring from him and from his heirs.

'And, that he might be known as what he was indeed,
a spirit from Heaven came and named him
69 from the possessive form of Him whose he already was.

'He was called Dominic, and I shall speak of him
as that laborer chosen by Christ
72 to help Him dress and keep His garden.

'He seemed indeed a messenger and intimate of Christ,
since the first love made manifest in him
75 was for the initial precept taught by Christ.

'Many a time did his nurse find him
awake and silent on the ground,
78 as if he said, "It is for this I have come."

'O happy father, indeed Felix!
O blessèd mother, indeed Giovanna,
81 if, rightly construed, her name means what they say!

'Not for this world, for which men toil today,
following Taddeo and the Ostian,
84 but for love of the true manna,

'he soon became a teacher so renowned
that he began to travel through the vineyard,
87 which quickly withers if the keeper is corrupt.

E a la sedia che fu già benigna
più a' poveri giusti, non per lei,
ma per colui che siede, che traligna,

non dispensare o due o tre per sei,
non la fortuna di prima vacante,
non *decimas, quae sunt pauperum Dei,*

addimandò, ma contro al mondo errante
licenza di combatter per lo seme
del qual ti fascian ventiquattro piante.

Poi, con dottrina e con volere insieme,
con l'officio appostolico si mosse
quasi torrente ch'alta vena preme;

e ne li sterpi eretici percosse
l'impeto suo, più vivamente quivi
dove le resistenze eran più grosse.

Di lui si fecer poi diversi rivi
onde l'orto catolico si riga,
sì che i suoi arbuscelli stan più vivi.

Se tal fu l'una rota de la biga
in che la Santa Chiesa si difese
e vinse in campo la sua civil briga,

ben ti dovrebbe assai esser palese
l'eccellenza de l'altra, di cui Tomma
dinanzi al mio venir fu sì cortese.

Ma l'orbita che fé la parte somma
di sua circunferenza, è derelitta,
sì ch'è la muffa dov' era la gromma.

La sua famiglia, che si mosse dritta
coi piedi a le sue orme, è tanto volta,
che quel dinanzi a quel di retro gitta;

'And to the papal seat, not now as benevolent
to the upright poor as it was once—not flawed in itself,
but degenerate in its occupant—he made appeal,

'not to give away just two or three instead of six,
not for his chance at the first vacancy,
not for the *decimas, quae sunt pauperum Dei,*

'but for the privilege of fighting
against the errors of the world, thus to preserve the seed
of the twenty-four plants now wreathing you in light.

'Then, both with learning and with zeal,
secure in apostolic office, he went forth,
like a torrent gushing from its lofty source,

'and fell upon the tangled weeds of heresy,
attacking with his overwhelming force
wherever the resistance was most stubborn.

'From him there sprang still other streams
from which the Catholic garden draws its moisture,
so that its saplings grow with greater vigor.

'If such was one of the wheels of the chariot
used by Holy Church in self-defense
to overcome the rebels in the field,

'surely the excellence of that other'
about whom Thomas spoke so courteously
before I came, must be well known to you.

'But the track left by the outer rim
of its circumference is abandoned,
so that where once was crust, there now is mold.

'His family, which started out setting their feet
upon his footprints, is now turned backward,
setting their toes where once they placed their heels.

e tosto si vedrà de la ricolta
de la mala coltura, quando il loglio
si lagnerà che l'arca li sia tolta.

Ben dico, chi cercasse a foglio a foglio
nostro volume, ancor troveria carta
u' leggerebbe 'I' mi son quel ch'i' soglio';

ma non fia da Casal né d'Acquasparta,
là onde vegnon tali a la scrittura,
ch'uno la fugge e altro la coarta.

Io son la vita di Bonaventura
da Bagnoregio, che ne' grandi offici
sempre pospuosi la sinistra cura.

Illuminato e Augustin son quici,
che fuor de' primi scalzi poverelli
che nel capestro a Dio si fero amici.

Ugo da San Vittore è qui con elli,
e Pietro Mangiadore e Pietro Spano,
lo qual giù luce in dodici libelli;

Natàn profeta e 'l metropolitano
Crisostomo e Anselmo e quel Donato
ch'a la prim' arte degnò porre mano.

Rabano è qui, e lucemi dallato
il calavrese abate Giovacchino
di spirito profetico dotato.

Ad inveggiar cotanto paladino
mi mosse l'infiammata cortesia
di fra Tommaso e 'l discreto latino;
e mosse meco questa compagnia."

'Soon that harvest of bad tillage
shall occur, when the tares complain
that the barn is shut against them.

'I readily admit that, should one search our volume
leaf by leaf, one still could find some pages
where one might read, "What once I was, I am."

'But these will not come from Casale or Acquasparta,
for those from there come to the Rule
either to flee it or constrict it further.

'I am the living soul of Bonaventura
from Bagnoregio, who in great office
ever put last the left-hand care.

'Here are Illuminato and Augustine,
among the first brothers barefoot in poverty,
who, with the cord, became God's friends.

'Here with them is Hugh of St. Victor,
Peter the Bookworm, and Peter the Spaniard—
who casts light from his twelve books below,

'Nathan the prophet, Chrysostom
the Metropolitan, Anselm, and that Donatus
who, to the first art, deigned to set his hand.

'Rabanus is here and, shining at my side,
abbot Joachim of Calabria,
who was endowed with prophetic spirit.

'To sing the praises of so great a champion
the ardent courtesy and fitting discourse
of Brother Thomas has inspired me
and did the same to my companions.'

1. The action of this canto begins, if we take its first line literally, before the preceding one ends, that is, before Thomas utters the last syllables (or syllable) of *vaneggia*. That seems fitting, since these two cantos are, perhaps more than any other pair in the work, mirror images of one another. See Bertoldi (Bert.1903.1), referring to them, despite their differing subjects and feelings, as "twin cantos." See also the note to vv. 142–145.

3. Dante had earlier resorted to the image of the millstone (*mola*) to refer to the rotation of the Sun, seen from either pole, around the earth (*Conv.* III.v.14).

4–6. The matching circles of twelve saints, each moving in such a way as to match the other both in the eye and in the ear of the beholder, anticipates the final image of the poem (*Par.* XXXIII.143–145).

4. The first circle of saints was described (*Par.* XI.14) as having completed a first full rotation; now it is seen as being on the point of completing a second one.

6. The double repetition (*moto/moto*; *canto/canto*) underlines the matching quality of these two circles.

7–8. The previous tercet had divided the activity of the souls into circling movement and song; this one divides that song itself (repeating the word *canto*) into two components, words (*muse*) and melody (*sirene*). Dante had used the word *Muse* (capitalized by Petrocchi, if we have little idea of Dante's actual practice with regard to capitalization) in *Inferno* I.7, in *Purgatorio* II.8 and XXII.102, then in *Paradiso* II.9, to indicate the Muses of classical antiquity. Beginning here, however, and then in two later passages (*Par.* XV.26 and XVIII.33), Petrocchi obviously believes that Dante uses the lower-case word *musa* metaphorically, here to refer to poets (the next use will refer to Virgil [or his poetry] as "nostra maggior musa" [our greatest muse], and finally [*Par.* XVIII.33], to poetry itself—or so most readers believe).

Torraca (comm. to vv. 7–9) seems to have been the first to remark on the similar conjoining of Sirens and Muses in Boethius (*Cons. Phil.* I.1[pr]).

These two verses contain four words relating to music: *canto* (song), *musa* (muse), *sirena* (siren), *tuba* (brass musical instrument [more precisely, "horn"]). For the echoing effect that results from the repetition of the first two, Dante may have had in mind the similar effect found in Ovid's story of Echo and Narcissus, referred to in vv. 14–15. The next (and last) time we read the noun *tuba* (*Par.* XXX.35), it will be the metaphoric expression for Dante's poetic voice, while here it refers to the voices of the singing saints.

9. The word *splendore* is, in Dante, always the result of light (*luce*), proceeding along its ray (*raggio*), and then reflected by an object. (For these interrelated terms, describing the three major aspects of light, see Dante's earlier statement [*Conv.* III.xiv.5].) This verse makes clear Dante's belief that a second reflection (e.g., as in a mirror) is less vivid than that original splendor (but cf. *Par.* II.94–105, which seems to contradict this understanding). As we have learned in Canto X (vv. 64–69), these crowns of dancing saints are presented as circles of musical lights. And in that earlier passage, a simile, the comparison is to the rainbow, as will also be true in the simile that begins in the next verse.

10–21. This simile, explicitly formal in its construction (*Come . . . così*) and, balanced in its content, containing one classical and one biblical reference (Iris and the rainbow that God offered as a sign to Noah), gives a sense of the identity of the two circles of saints, despite their evident differences.

10. Dante apparently thought of thin (and thus "translucent") clouds as actually being constituted of a layer of water-soaked dust suspended in the atmosphere in which the rainbow appears.

11–18. There are a number of candidates for the classical source at work here, primarily texts in Virgil and Ovid. It seems likely that Dante would have had the reference (*Metam.* I.270–271) to Juno's sending Iris (her "handmaid," the rainbow) as a result of Jove's huge storm, sent below in his attempt to extirpate, in a flood, the human race (typified in the first murderer, Lycaon [the wolf-man], and hence abandoned by piety and justice [*Metam.* I.149–150]). That would nicely balance these gestures toward "famous rainbows," since the second of them is without doubt reflective of the rainbow that God sent as the sign of his covenant (Genesis 9:13) with Noah and the few other surviving members of humankind based on

His promise never to send such a destructive flood again. (The first book of the *Metamorphoses* is, as it were, the pagan equivalent of Genesis.) We are also probably meant to compare the unchecked vengeful desires of the king of the pagan gods with the moderated sternness of God the Father.

Dante adds a second rainbow, as his context demands, not as he found in his sources, but as may at least occasionally be observed in Tuscany even today.

13. The second circle is, like the second rainbow, wider than the first. Dante's science believed that the second rainbow was born from the first, not that it was part of a double refraction of light.

14–15. The reference is to the nymph Echo (*Metam.* III.356–510), who fell in love with Narcissus. She wasted away with unrequited passion until all that was left of her was a voice. This second simile, within the overarching simile that compares the two circles of saints to the double rainbow, replicates the form of such a rainbow.

18. As Tommaseo suggests (comm. to vv. 16–18), the present tense of the verb *allagare* (to flood) suggests the past, present, and future application of God's covenant with humankind: This global flood has not recurred and will never do so.

22–25. Dante seemingly intuits the extraordinary effect made by large symphony orchestras when called upon to modulate huge sound suddenly into silence. If the reader imagines Beethoven as the background music to this scene, perhaps he or she will better experience what is projected by these verses. Of course, the miraculous sound has not so much to do with extraordinary musical abilities as it does with the result of living in God's grace, in which all is harmonious, even sudden silence.

26–30. These similetic elements of this passage (vv. 22–30), two eyes opening or closing as one and Dante ineluctably being drawn to the voice of a new spirit (it will turn out to be Bonaventure), speak to the sense of the overpowering quality of the love and beauty that affects both the performers and their observer. Torraca (comm. to vv. 28–30) points out that the compass, invented only a short while before, had already become a familiar image in thirteenth-century Italian poetry, for example, in poems by Guido Guinizzelli and in Ristoro d'Arezzo.

31–33. St. Bonaventure is about to praise the leader of Thomas's order, St. Dominic, in response to Thomas's praise of Francis, the leader of his own. For information about the speaker, see the note to vv. 127–128.

34–36. In the previous canto (*Par.* XI.40–42) Thomas had gone out of his way to insist that praise of either Francis or Dominic is necessarily praise of the other; Bonaventure matches him.

35. While Dante has made every effort to "militarize" the sweetness of St. Francis, making both him and Dominic share the verb *militaro* (lit. "soldiered"), the following three tercets show that he is willing to associate himself with the traditional portrayal of Dominic as warlike, while the traditional depiction of Francis is decidedly not (see the note to *Par.* XI.91). On the other hand, it is again notable that he has included Francis within the construct of the Christian soldier.

37–45. These three tercets contain seven words that associate the two friars with militarism and imperial rule: *essercito* (army), *riarmar* (to rearm), *insegna* (battle standard), *imperador* (emperor), *regna* (reigns), *milizia* (soldiers), *campioni* ("champions," i.e., those who excel in single combat).

37–39. The "troops" obviously form the Church Militant, now led by the newly approved mendicant orders, expensive to rearm, since it took the blood of the apostles to accomplish that task (see Aversano [Aver.2000.2], p. 53, for reasons to prefer this gloss to that which insists the reference is to Christ's blood, an interpretation unopposed since the earliest days of the commentary tradition; Aversano refers the reader to *Par.* XXVII.40–45 for confirming evidence). Despite that, the soldiers, apparently, still lack resolve.

38. The "standard" of this army is obviously the Cross.

40–45. The meaning is that God succored His "troops," not because they were particularly worthy, but because He extended them His grace. For a clear summary of the two kinds of grace at work in Dante's world, operating grace (which Dante received from God, through the agency of Beatrice, in *Inferno* II) and cooperating grace, see Scott (Scot.2004.2), pp. 187–90. Once a sinner is justified by the receipt of operating grace, which is gratuitous (i.e., cannot be earned), he or she must "cooperate" in order to merit eventual reward (salvation). Scott reviews the American discussion of this issue, which was dominated by the views of Charles Singleton, until Antonio Mastrobuono (Mast.1990.1) clarified the nature of the problem.

40. That God is here referred to as "emperor" (as He is on only two other occasions: *Inf.* I.124 and *Par.* XXV.41) makes Dante's comfort with imperial trappings clear, especially to his Guelph enemies. This term for God is not in itself unwarranted in Christian tradition, far from it. But Dante uses it here in an ecclesiastical context where it might seem, at least to some, improper.

43. The reference ("as was said") is to *Paradiso* XI.31–36, where Thomas tells of God's appointment of these two stalwarts to succor the bride of Christ, Lady Poverty.

44. Francis (typified by love) is best represented by his *deeds*, Dominic (typified by knowledge), by his *words*.

46–57. Dominic was "born 1170, in the village of Calaroga, in Old Castile; he is supposed to have belonged to the noble family of Guzmàn, his father's name being Felix, his mother's Joanna. The latter is said to have dreamed before he was born that she gave birth to a dog with a torch in its mouth, which set the world on fire. At the age of fourteen he went to the university of Palencia, where he studied theology for ten or twelve years. He was early noted for his self-denial and charity. In 1195 he became canon of the cathedral of Osma. In 1215 he accompanied Folquet, bishop of Toulouse, to the Lateran Council; and in the same year, on his return to Toulouse, he founded his order of Preaching Friars, which was formally recognized by Honorius III in 121[7]. He died in Aug. 1221 at Bologna, where he was buried. He was canonized soon after his death (in 1234) by Gregory IX" (T). And see G. R. Sarolli, "Domenico, santo," *ED* II (1970), pp. 546–51. Sarolli points out that, when Dominic, with six companions, arrived in Toulouse in 1215, on the verge of forming a more structured group, he associated with Folco di Marsiglia (whom we encountered in *Par.* IX.88–102), the newly appointed bishop of that city.

46. Spain is located in the westernmost part of Europe.

47. Zephyr is the west wind. For the association of Dominic with the west and Francis with the east, see Bertoldi (Bert.1913.1), p. 47, n. 27, adding the details that for Dante, the Florentine, the main Dominican

church (S. Maria Novella) was situated in the western part of the city, while the main Franciscan church (S. Croce) was located in eastern Florence.

49–51. Torraca (comm. to vv. 56–57) thinks that the waves are found on the surface of the Ebro, the river running two miles from Dominic's native city, an argument contested vigorously by Bertoldi (Bert.1913.1), pp. 45–46, who supports the early commentators' belief that the reference is to the Atlantic Ocean. Others specify the Bay of Biscay. After Scartazzini (comm. to vv. 49–51), however, the ruling understanding is that the passage refers to the Gulf of Gascony, a more precise location off the Atlantic shoreline.

The sun hides itself from human sight when, at or near the summer solstice, it sets beyond the sight of those on land, because it has moved so far out over the Atlantic. For Dante, we must remember, to the west of the Gates of Hercules lies "the world where no one lives" (*Inf.* XXVI.117).

52. Calaruega ("Calaroga," in Dante's Italian), a small town in Castile, "fortunate" in having been the birthplace of Dominic.

53–54. "The royal arms of Castile bear a castle in the first and third quarters, and a lion in the second and fourth. Thus on one side of the shield the lion is subdued by the castle, and on the other subdues it" (Oelsner, comm. to these verses). The images represent the kingdoms of Castile and Leon, respectively.

55. The vocabulary of feudal times (*drudo*, "vassal") combines with that of erotic poetry (*amoroso*, "loving") to interrupt the military associations of Dominic, and eventually presents him, like Francis, as a "husband" (see verse 61, *sponsalizie*, "nuptials"). The word *drudo*, a triple hapax, that is, a word appearing once in each *cantica* (see Hollander [Holl.1988.3] for a listing of all examples of this phenomenon in the poem), occurs previously in *Inferno* XVIII.134 and *Purgatorio* XXXII.155, in both cases referring to a male partner in an illicit sexual liaison, in the first case, the man sleeping with the whore Thaïs; in the second, the giant beating his harlot, the Church in its Avignonian captivity. Thus its context in the poem works against those who would read Dante's treatment of Dominic as sugar-coated (see the note to verse 57).

The new interpretation of the second scene offered by Bognini (Bogn.2007.1) does not change the valence of the preceding remark, but does alter the identities of the "actors" in the pageant in *Purgatorio* XXXII. In a new (and entirely convincing) reading of the major characters in that scene, Bognini demonstrates that the whore is Ezechiel's Jerusalem and thus Dante's Florence, while the giant reflects Goliath as Robert of Anjou, the king of Naples and the Guelph leader in Italy, prime enemy of Henry VII.

56. If Francis is presented as a lover, Dominic is (here) presented as a fighter, but even here he is first described (verse 55) as *l'amoroso drudo*. See the note to verse 55.

57. Spiazzi (Spia.1989.1), pp. 339–41, thinks that the word *crudo* (cruel) is uncalled for, and he sets off on a lengthy defense: St. Dominic was in fact, and despite his crusading spirit, the most mild-mannered person imaginable. However, others take this verse at face value, and see its pertinence to Dominic's labors against the Cathars (e.g., Ghisalberti [Ghis.2002.1], pp. 184–86), during the period 1203 to 1210, when Dominic moved from preaching and debate to more violent means; but even Ghisalberti insists on the predominance of the "sweet" approach. Others have been less tolerant of Dominic's behavior. This is the last of thirteen appearances of the adjective *crudo* in the poem (leaving to one side the related words *crudele, crudeltà*, etc.); in none of the preceding dozen presences of the word does it have a mitigated meaning. As a result, the motives of those who argue for such mitigation here seem suspect. Dominic, as presented by Dante, is a tough warrior whom he goes out of his way also to present as a "lover."

58–60. The embryonic mind of Dominic was so powerful that it could send concepts (or at least images) to the mother who was bearing him. In this way he lent his mother the gift of prophecy. The early commentators are frequently misled, and think the reference of "lei" is not to the mother but to Dominic's *mente* in the preceding line, thus making a prophet of *him*. However, legend has it that, before his birth, his mother had a dream of a black-and-white dog who carried a torch in its mouth, which set fire to the whole world. That is what most of its interpreters today believe is referenced in the line, the mother's vision of her unborn son's wide effect on humanity. Since the colors of the habits of the Dominicans are black and white and since an easily available pun (*Domini canes* = the dogs of God) was in circulation at the time and was included in the first official "Life" of Dominic (by Teodorico d'Appoldia), the dream became a permanent piece of Dominican lore.

Frequent in discussions of this passage are citations of Isaiah 49:1, "Dominus ab utero vocavit me" (The Lord has called me from the womb); but see also Luke 1:15, "Spiritu Sancto replebitur adhuc ex utero matris suae" (and he shall be filled with the Holy Spirit, even from his mother's womb), describing John the Baptist, referred to by Di Biase (Dibi.1992.1), p. 40n. (first cited by Tommaseo [comm. to vv. 58–60]).

62. Where Francis married Poverty, Dominic took Faith as his wife.

63. A difficult line to translate convincingly, partly because the noun *salute* has different meanings in Dante. In Dominic's case, he will find *salvation* in his faith; he cannot "save" her, but he does keep her *safe* from heresy. Vellutello's gloss (comm. to vv. 61–66) has guided us as far as the sense is concerned: "because he saved the Faith, battling for it against heretics, and she in turn kept him safe."

64–66. A woman present at the baptismal ceremony, the child's godmother, answers (saying "I do") for the child when the priest asks whether he or she wishes to be baptized.

Dominic's godmother dreamed that he appeared with a bright star in his forehead that illumined the world; his "heirs" are, obviously, his fellow Dominicans.

67–69. The riddling diction yields its meaning after only a little effort. As Tozer (comm. to this tercet) unravels it: "An inspiration from Heaven (*Quinci*) was communicated to his parents to name him by the possessive adjective (viz. *Dominicus*) derived from the name of the Lord (*Dominus*), who possessed him entirely."

67. The word *costrutto* has caused a certain difficulty. In modern Italian it means "sense, meaning," but that meaning is not easily assigned to the word here. Tozer (comm. to vv. 67–69) sorts things out as follows: ". . . 'that he might be in name what he was in reality'; *costrutto*: 'the form of his name'; similarly in *Purg.* XXVIII.147 *costrutto* means 'a form of words' or 'sentence': and in *Par.* XXIII.24 *senza costrutto* is 'without putting it into words.' "

68. From the Empyrean (and not this heaven of the Sun), the text suggests, the Holy Spirit inspired the baby's parents to call him "Dominicus" (*Domini*-cus—the Latin form of his name, Domenico [its root is the genitive of *Dominus*, the Lord]).

71–75. This is the first set of the so-called Cristo rhymes. There will be three others, occurring in *Paradiso* XIV.104–108, XIX.104–108, and XXXII.83–87. For a valuable early study of this phenomenon, see

Francesco D'Ovidio (Dovi.1901.1). It is clear that, for Dante's purposes, no other word is good enough to rhyme with "Christ," who is the Word. For the tercet that contains the word *Cristo* four times, see the note to *Paradiso* XIV.103–108.

Porena (comm. to vv. 73–78) holds that D'Ovidio was correct to argue that the word *Cristo* is allowed to rhyme only with itself because, as a penitential gesture, Dante wants to undo the scabrous act he had perpetrated when, in one of his sonnets attacking Forese Donati's behaviors, he had rhymed the name of the Lord with *tristo* (distraught) and *malo acquisto* (ill-gotten gains).

71–72. The chore given Dominic to perform can hardly fail to remind a Christian reader of the task that Adam and Eve were given and failed to perform, to dress and keep the garden. See Genesis 2:15.

74–75. What exactly was Christ's "first counsel" to his followers? In the past one hundred years there has been continuing and uncertain discussion of this seemingly simple question. But it was not always thus. Almost every early commentator seizes on the same biblical passage, Matthew 19:21, Christ's advice to the rich young man to sell all that he possesses, give the proceeds to the poor, and then follow Him. For a summarizing sense of nearly six hundred years of near-total agreement, see Oelsner (comm. to verse 75): "The counsel of poverty (Matth. 19:21, whence the phrase 'counsels of perfection'). Thomas Aquinas, while distinguishing between the *precepts* and the *counsels* of Christ, says that the latter may all be reduced to three—Poverty, Continence, and Obedience. The first counsel, then, is Poverty."

The problem of the precise reference in verse 75 is complicated by the neighboring presences of two instances of the adjective *primo* (first). Are they used as synonyms, in both cases having a temporal relevance, or not? We think that they are, and thus have translated as we have ("since the first love manifest in him / was for the initial precept taught by Christ"). Some, however, believe that the first *primo* is temporal, that the second has to do with order of importance, that is, the most important of Christ's teachings, which would offer a bit more latitude as one searched through the Gospels. If we are correct, what then is "the initial precept" taught by Jesus? (Salsano, "consiglio," *ED* II [1970], p. 159b, understands *consiglio* to equate with "precetto divino.") That can in fact be the first Beatitude. Or, if Oelsner (see above) is correct, and Dante's sense of the word *consiglio* flows through St. Thomas's distinction between it and "precept," then the first "counsel" may indeed be thought of as accepting poverty, first among the three "counsels" of Christ, poverty, continence, obedience. Either way, poverty is the issue focal to this line. This seems more than acceptable, since Dominic is presented as parallel in his virtues to Francis (Grandgent [comm. to verse 75] points out that vv. 73–75 of both cantos thus deal with poverty), since Dominicans as well as Franciscans took vows of poverty, and since the next tercet, although also less clear than some might like, would seem to associate him both with Francis and with poverty as well.

76–78. "For this have I come": See Mark 1:38, "ad hoc enim veni," as Jesus announces his intention to preach. The baby Dominic's closeness to the earth reminds us of the similar association of Francis, indelibly associated with the dust at the end of his life (*Par.* XI.115–117). Poverty and humility, more usually associated with Francis, are both present in this vignette, as preconditions for Dominic's preacherly calling.

79. Dominic's father's name, Felice, means "happy" (*felix*) in Latin.

80–81. Bosco/Reggio (comm. to these verses) say that Dante, in the life of Dominic by Theodoric of Appoldia, could have read that his mother's name, Giovanna, meant "grace of God" or "full of grace." Theodoric's source (and Dante's) may have been, says Torraca (comm. to vv. 79–81), Uguccione da Pisa.

82–105. This passage presents the life and accomplishments of Dominic, after his engendering and childhood (vv. 58–81), the ensemble paralleling that portion of the preceding canto dedicated to the life and works of Francis (XI.55–117).

82–85. Dominic's honest religiosity is contrasted with the eye-on-the-prize sort of sham activities of two intellectuals, both of whom died within Dante's lifetime. The first, Enrico di Susa, from Ostia (died in 1271), was a famous canon lawyer (and thus Dante fires another salvo at the venal practitioners of this profession), while Taddeo d'Alderotto (the probable reference is to him) was a Florentine (died in 1295) who studied and then taught medicine at Bologna. Dante mocks his translation of Aristotle's *Ethics* in *Convivio* I.x.10. In these two men Dante pillories two kinds of false intellectual activity—religious law and Aristotelian science—both of which were of great importance to him.

87. The metaphorical vineyard (fairly obviously the Church) turns gray with rot if its keeper (obviously the pope) does not take good care of it. This reference to Boniface VIII is thinly veiled.

88–96. Carroll (comm. to vv. 46–105) paraphrases this elegant pastiche of a canon lawyer's style as follows: "[Dominic] asked from the Head of the Church none of the evil privileges so eagerly sought for by others: to distribute only a third or a half of moneys left for charitable purposes, retaining the rest; to receive the first vacant benefice; or to use for himself the tithes which belong to God's poor. His one request was for leave to fight against an erring world for the seed of the Faith."

88–90. Bonaventure, here most assuredly Dante's mouthpiece, distinguishes between the papacy, in its design supportive of the poor, and the pope (the hated Boniface VIII in 1300), ignoring that design.

91–93. These three corrupt practices all reveal the avarice of prelates, the first and third involving theft of monies destined for the poor, the second, advancement in ecclesiastical position. For this last, see Tozer (comm. to this tercet): "The reference is to the *expectationes*, or nominations to posts not yet vacant that popes of the day were pleased to make." Obviously, none of these self-aggrandizing activities had as their goal support for the benevolent tasks that customarily fell to the Church.

93. The Latin ("the tenth part that belongs to the poor," the tax collected by the clergy) refers to the tithe, the 10 percent of a parishioner's income that the Church collected in order to help feed and clothe the poor. Not even this was safe from predatory clergy, who took these funds for their own use.

95. See Bosco/Reggio (comm. to this verse): Dominic's request for approval of his order was made to Pope Innocent III in 1215, and approved only in late 1216 by Pope Honorius III, the newly elected pope (the Church had for a time prohibited the formation of new orders). However, in 1205, Dominic had gone to Rome, seeking permission to wage a campaign against heretics, which was granted. Between 1207 and 1214 he was part of the eventually bloody attempt to bring the Albigensian Cathars back into the fold, alongside of Folco di Marsiglia (see the notes to *Par.* IX.40 and to *Par.* IX.94). Bosco/Reggio try to keep Dominic's hands free of Albigensian blood, saying that on the day of the terrible battle of Muret (12 September 1213), Dominic was at prayer in a church. However, given the poet's praise of Folco, who was the leader of that crusade (if Simon de Montfort was in charge of the army at that particular battle), he may have imagined a Dominic as warlike as his Folco.

See vv. 97–102, where Dominic's forcefulness in combating heresy is applauded.

96. This indication reminds us of the precise balance in the two circles of saints that we have seen in these two cantos, each containing twelve souls.

97–102. While the militarism of Dominic's order may be metaphorical, referring to his preaching, that his "career" began with a literal war, the crusade against the Albigensians, certainly colors these lines, whatever Dante's intention.

98. Dominic fought against heresy with the support of Pope Honorius III, who had approved his request to found a new order. However, he had also had the approval of Pope Innocent III to subdue the Albigensians and bring them back to the fold (see the note to verse 95). In that effort, the crusaders' military force was more than metaphoric.

101–102. The "resistance was most stubborn" in Provence, with the Albigensian Cathars. This detail again tends to erode the distinction between Dominic the Christian debater and Dominic the Christian soldier. See the note to vv. 97–102.

103–105. Raoul Manselli (Mans.1973.1), p. 118, characterizes this tercet, moving from Dominic's day into Dante's, with the order burgeoning with new chapters, as setting a tranquil conclusion to a story that began with military roughness. One might add that it has hardly moderated its tone until now.

106–111. These verses offer a kind of summary of both saints' lives. The resulting image, the two wheels of a chariot of war, already deployed in the earthly paradise (introduced at *Purg.* XXIX.107 and on the scene until *Purg.* XXXII.147), is perhaps remembered in the final verses of the poem.

112–113. Here begins the denunciation of the current Franciscan Order (cf. the similar attack on the wayward Dominicans, *Par.* XI.118–123). Where in the last canto the image of Thomas's order was a merchant ship, here that founded by Francis is presented as a chariot of war. Bosco/Reggio (comm. to these verses) complain that, after the fresh and convincing images of the last canto, some of those encountered in this one, beginning with these chariot wheels, seem forced. Here Dominic is compared to the rim of a wheel that leaves a clear imprint in the earth, while his followers do no such thing.

114. Abruptly switching semantic fields, Bonaventure compares the good old days of Francis's leadership and the current condition of the order to wine casks: Good wine leaves crust in the barrel it was contained in, while bad wine leaves mold.

115–117. The faltering order is depicted as reversing its track; see the parallel moment in Thomas's denunciation of the Dominicans (*Par.* XI.124–132), portrayed as sheep wandering astray, away from the Rule, in search of new nourishment.

117. There is agreement among the commentators about the difficulty of making exact sense of this verse. We have not attempted to do more than give its obvious general meaning, though it happens that we are in fairly close agreement with the gloss of Daniele Mattalia to this tercet, who takes issue with some of the more strained attempts to make sense of this line, that is, the understanding, begun with Michele Barbi (Barb.1934.1, p. 287), that the Franciscan backsliders retrogress while facing forward, moving their front foot back toward (and then behind?) the other. Even if Dominic has been described as "the holy athlete" (verse 56), that way of retrogression seems to require muscular skills and patience well beyond those of most corrupt barefoot friars. Momigliano (comm. to vv. 115–117) justly complains that this line seems forced and lays some of the blame for that on the verb form *gitta* (lit. "throws"), forced by rhyme.

118–120. The obvious Scriptural allusion (to Matthew 13:24–30, the parable of the wheat and the tares) somehow seems to have escaped the earliest commentators. It appears first in Landino (comm. to these verses) and then is repeated in almost all subsequent comments. The reference of the tercet is a cause of some debate. See Manselli, "francescanesimo," *ED* III (1971), pp. 115–16; his view is that the word "loglio" (tares) does not refer to the Spiritual Franciscans, as some believe, but to all corrupt members of the order, whatever their leaning in the controversy between Spirituals and Conventuals.

122. The word *volume* (volume), occurring first in *Inferno* I.84 and last in *Paradiso* XXXIII. 86, literally runs from one end of the poem to the other. It

occurs nine times and always either refers to God's book (the Scriptures) or to his "other book," the created universe (except in its first use, where it refers to the *Aeneid* [see the note to *Inf.* I.84]). Thus, to refer to the slender booklet, the Rule of the Franciscan Order, as a *volume* is to employ a heavy word.

124–126. Cosmo (Cosm.1936.1), pp. 149–54, contrasts the inner tension among the Franciscan ranks with the struggles that afflicted Dominic's order, shaped by external enemies. For a study locating Francis, as Dante does here, in the middle, see Stanislao da Campagnola (Daca.1983.1); and for his indebtedness to Ubertino's very words for his characterizations of Francis (*seraphicus*) and Dominic (*cherubicus*), see p. 182n. See also Manselli (Mans.1982.1) for an overview of Dante's response to the Spiritual Franciscans, with many bibliographical indications in the notes. Mario Trovato (Trov.1995.1), p. 168, on the additional basis of his interpretation of *Paradiso* XI.109–114, lends his support to Manselli's position. And for what has been the standard view of the tension among the Conventual and Spiritual Franciscans themselves (at least after Manselli's work), see Manselli (Mans.1982.1), pp. 57–58: Matteo d'Acquasparta is criticized for loosening the strictures of the Rule of the order, while Ubertino da Casale is seen as being too rigid in his adherence to the founder's insistence on the importance of poverty in a true Christian life.

125. We have translated "la scrittura" in the narrowest sense ("the Rule"). In Dante's Italian the word has meant both writing in general and, on some occasions, the Bible. Here it is a third form of writing, something more than ordinary words and to be taken as postbiblical, but having a similar authority. (See the note to verse 122 for the similar status of the noun *volume*.) Aversano (Aver.1984.2), pp. 23–24, points out that Francis was so concerned that his Rule would be fraudulently emended that he encouraged his friars to memorize it.

127–141. For a helpful discussion of the participants of this second circle of souls found in the heaven of the Sun, see Di Biase (Dibi.1992.1), pp. 71–83. Comparing the two circles, Cosmo (Cosm.1936.1), pp. 106–7, argues that there is no sense of rigid separation between the two, rather, in fact, that there are many similarities between them.

127–128. "St. Bonaventura was born at Bagnoregio (now Bagnorea) near Orvieto in 1221, the year of St. Dominic's death. As a child he was attacked by a dangerous disease, which was miraculously cured by St. Francis of

Assisi. When the latter heard that the child had recovered he is said to have exclaimed 'buona ventura,' whereupon the boy's mother changed his name to Bonaventura. In 1238 or 1243 he entered the Franciscan order. After studying in Paris under Alexander of Hales, he became successively professor of philosophy and theology, and in 1257 was made doctor. Having risen to be general of the Franciscan order (in 1257), he was offered the archbishopric of Albano by Gregory X, whom he accompanied to the second Council of Lyons, where he died, July 15,1274, 'his magnificent funeral being attended by a pope, an emperor, and a king.' St. Bonaventura was canonized in 1482 by Sixtus IV, and placed among the doctors of the Church, with the title of *Doctor Seraphicus*, by Sixtus V" (T). The word *vita*, used here by Bonaventure to identify himself as a soul in grace, is used with this sense for the second time in the poem (see the note to *Par.* IX.7).

For Dante's debt to mysticism, as focused for him in the writings of Bonaventure, see Meekins (Meek.1997.1). For the possibility that Dante read the apparent contradictions between the positions of Aquinas and Bonaventure syncretistically, see Mazzotta (Mazz.2003.1) and Gragnolati (Grag.2005.1), pp. 58–77. Di Somma (Diso.1986.1), p. 50n., argues for the central importance of Bonaventure's *Itinerarium mentis in Deum* for all of Dante's poem, not only for this canto. A survey of Bonaventure's presence in the Dartmouth Dante Project reveals that the vast majority of references to "Bonaventura" before the end of the nineteenth century occur only in notes to this canto, in which he is a named (and thus inescapable) presence. Thus we realize, after a few minutes of searching, that a serious use of Bonaventure's texts as a guide to Dante is a fairly recent development. In fact, it is only in Scartazzini's commentary that one finds a total of more references to him in all the other cantos than one finds to him in this one. After Scartazzini, that situation begins to change. (English readers will find that in this particular, as well as in others, John Carroll outstrips his competitors.) See Hagman (Hagm.1988.1) for a study of Bonaventure's extensive and overall importance to Dante. But see Sofia Vanni Rovighi, "Bonaventura da Bagnoreggio, santo," *ED* I (1970), p. 673, arguing that attempts to show a direct textual dependence of Dante on Bonaventure have had only dubious results; all one can say is that his work (the *Itinerarium mentis in Deum* in particular) is a generic model for the outline of the *Comedy*, without being able to make more of a claim for it than that.

129. The "left-hand care" reflects the traditional link between left- and right-handedness as reflecting, respectively, "sinister" (the Latin word for "left") and positive purposes. The former here signifies "worldly concerns." Francesco da Buti (comm. to vv. 127–141) does not attempt to

banish cares of the world from the curate's interest, but does say that he does not (and must not) treat them as having the same importance as issues related to eternal life.

130. Illuminato and Augustino were among Francis's earliest followers. The first was a nobleman from Rieti, who accompanied him on his voyage to Egypt. Augustino was a townsman of Francis and eventually became head of a chapter of the order in Terra di Lavoro. Neither one of them is particularly associated with knowledge, which causes Benvenuto (comm. to vv. 130–132) to wonder why these two *homines ignorantes* were included here. He goes on to admire Dante's subtlety in doing so, for they, if not great intellects themselves, helped others to become, by their labor and example, more wise.

It was only in 1960 that a commentator on this verse (Mattalia), responding to a number of Dantists who raised the issue, suggested that a predictable reaction in one who is reading this line might very well be: "But that's not Saint Augustine of Hippo; where is he in all this?" (And we have to wait for *Paradiso* XXXII.35 to find that he is indeed among the blessed; see the note to that tercet.) For the last time he was named, see *Paradiso* X.120, but without mention of his eventual fate. Is it possible that Dante is playing a game with us? He mentions the actual St. Augustine in the last canto, where we might have expected to find him, among other theologians in the Sun; he now mentions a saved soul named "Augustine" who is not he but who *is* here. Both these gestures lead us to contemplate the possibility that Dante is teasing us. There will be some speculation as to his reasons for doing so in a note to *Paradiso* XXXII.34–36, a passage that situates Augustine among the inhabitants of the celestial Rose.

132. See the note to *Paradiso* XI.87 for the *capestro* as signal of adherence to the Franciscan Order.

133. "Hugh of St. Victor, celebrated mystic and theologian of the beginning of cent. xii; he was born near Ypres in Flanders c. 1097 or, as some believe, at Hartingham in Saxony, and was educated during his early years in the monastery of Hammersleben near Halberstadt in Saxony; in 1115 he removed to the abbey of St. Victor near Paris, which had recently been founded by William of Champeaux, the preceptor of Abelard, and which during cent. xii was a centre of mysticism; he became one of the canons-regular of the abbey, and was in 1130 appointed to the chair of theology, which he held until his death in 1141, his reputation being so great that he was known as 'alter Augustinus' [a second Augustine] and 'lingua Augustini'

[Augustine's tongue]. He was the intimate friend of Bernard of Clairvaux, and among his pupils were Richard of St. Victor and Peter Lombard. His writings, which are very numerous, and are characterized by great learning, are frequently quoted by Thomas Aquinas" (T).

134. Petrus Comestor (*comestor* is the Latin word for "eater" and was the nickname that Peter was given by his fellow priests because of his tremendous appetite for books), "priest, and afterwards dean, of the cathedral of Troyes in France, where he was born in the first half of cent. xii; he became canon of St. Victor in 1164, and chancellor of the University of Paris, and died at St. Victor in 1179, leaving all his possessions to the poor. His chief work was the *Historia scholastica*, which professed to be a history of the Church from the beginning of the world down to the times of the apostles" (T).

134–135. "Petrus Hispanus (Pedro Juliani), born at Lisbon, c. 1225, where he at first followed his father's profession of medicine; he studied at Paris, probably under Albertus Magnus; subsequently he was ordained and became (1273) archbishop of Braga; in 1274 he was created cardinal bishop of Tusculum (Frascati) by Gregory X; on Sept. 13, 1276, he was elected pope, under the title of John XXI, at Viterbo, in succession to Adrian V; he died May 20, 1277, after a reign of a little more than eight months, his death being caused by the fall of the ceiling of one of the rooms in his palace at Viterbo" (T). His manual of logic, the *Summulae logicales*, in twelve books, had a large audience.

That Dante calls no attention whatsoever to the fact that Peter was a pope (if very briefly) has caught the attention of many commentators. For the "scorecard" of the perhaps twelve popes who, in Dante's opinion, were saved (and the probably larger number who were damned), see the note to *Inferno* VII.46–48. John XXI is the last saved pope mentioned in the poem.

136. "Nathan, the prophet, who was sent by God to reprove David for his sin in causing the death of Uriah the Hittite in order that he might take Bathsheba to wife" (T).

For Nathan as *figura Dantis* and the question of why he, a relatively minor prophet, is given such high relief in this poem, see Sarolli (Saro.1971.1), pp. 189–246.

136–137. "St. John Chrysostom (i.e., in Greek his name means 'golden-mouthed'), celebrated Greek father of the Church, born at Antioch c.

345, died at Comana in Pontus, 407. He belonged to a noble family, and was first a lawyer; he afterward became a monk, in which capacity he so distinguished himself by his preaching that the Emperor Arcadius appointed him (in 398) patriarch of Constantinople. His severity toward the clergy in his desire for reform made him an object of hatred to them, and led to his deposition (403) at the instance of Theophilus, patriarch of Alexandria, and the Empress Eudoxia, whose excesses he had publicly rebuked. Sentence of exile was pronounced against him, but the people, to whom he had endeared himself by his preaching, rose in revolt, and he was reinstated in his office. Shortly afterward, he was again banished (404), and he finally died in exile on the shores of the Black Sea. He left nearly 1,000 sermons or homilies as evidence of his eloquence" (T).

137. "Anselm, archbishop of Canterbury, 1093–1109; he was born at Aosta in Piedmont in 1033, and in 1060, at the age of 27, he became a monk in the abbey of Bec in Normandy, whither he had been attracted by the fame of Lanfranc, at that time prior; in 1063, on the promotion of Lanfranc to the abbacy of Caen, he succeeded him as prior; fifteen years later, in 1078, on the death of Herluin, the founder of the monastery, he was made abbot, which office he held till 1093, in that year he was appointed archbishop of Canterbury by William Rufus, in succession to Lanfranc, after the see had been vacant for four years; in 1097, in consequence of disputes with William on matters of ecclesiastical jurisdiction, he left England for Rome to consult the pope, and remained on the Continent until William's death in 1100, when he was recalled by Henry I; he died at Canterbury, April 21, 1109; canonized, in 1494, by Alexander VI" (T).

137–138. "Aelius Donatus, Roman scholar and rhetorician of cent. iv, said to have been the tutor of Jerome; he was the author of a commentary on Virgil (now lost, but often alluded to by Servius), and of another on Terence, but his most famous work was an elementary Latin grammar, *Ars Grammatica* in three books; part of this work, the *Ars minor*, or *De octo partibus orationis*, served as a model for subsequent similar treatises. Owing to the popularity of this work in the Middle Ages it was one of the earliest books, being printed even before the invention of movable type—the name of its author became a synonym for grammar, just as Euclid for geometry" (T).

Donatus was the "people's grammarian" in that his *Ars*, unlike Priscian's (see *Inf.* XV.109), kept grammar as simple as possible. And grammar was itself the "first art" in the sense that it was the first subject taught to children, the first of the seven liberal arts. Thus his "intellectual humility" may have, in Dante's mind, paralleled that of Illuminato and Augustino. Both the Ottimo (comm. to these verses) and John of Serravalle (comm. to vv. 136–138) cite the *incipit* of the work: "Ianua sum rudibus" (I am the doorway through which the unlettered may pass [to learning]).

139. Rabanus Maurus was "born at Mainz of noble parents, c. 776; while quite a youth he entered the monastery at Fulda, where he received deacon's orders in 801; he shortly after proceeded to Tours to study under Alcuin, who in recognition of his piety and diligence gave him the surname of Maurus, after St. Maurus (d. 565), the favourite disciple of St. Benedict. He was ordained priest in 814, and after a pilgrimage to the Holy Land returned to Fulda in 817, where he became abbot in 822. He held this office for twenty years until 842, when he retired in order to devote himself more completely to religion and literature. Five years later, however, he was appointed to the archbishopric of Mainz, which he held until his death in 856. Rabanus, who was considered one of the most learned men of his time, wrote a voluminous commentary on the greater portion of the Bible, and was the author of numerous theological works . . ." (T). And see Nicolò Mineo, "Rabano Mauro," *ED* IV (1973), pp. 817–18. Most are content with the traditional identification of the ninth-century biblical commentator; however, for the view that this Rabanus is not Maurus but Anglicus, see Lerner (Lern.1988.1), pp. 631–32.

140–141. Joachim of Flora "appears to have enjoyed in his own day, and long afterwards, a reputation for prophetic power"; hence Bonaventure speaks of him as "di spirito profetico dotato," words which are said to be taken verbatim from the anthem still chanted on the Festival of St. Joachim in the churches of Calabria.

"Joachim was born c. 1145 at Celico, about 4 miles NE. of Cosenza in Calabria. He made a pilgrimage to the Holy Land, and on his return to Italy became a monk, entering (c. 1158) the Cistercian monastery of Sambucina. In 1177 he was made abbot of Corazzo in Calabria. In 1185, Pope Urban III appointed a deputy abbot in order that Joachim might have leisure to devote himself to his writings. In 1189 Joachim founded a monastery, San Giovanni in Fiore in the forest of the Sila among the mountains of Calabria, whence he was named 'de Floris.' From this institution, the rule of which was sanctioned by Celestine III in 1196, ultimately sprang the so-called Ordo Florensis (absorbed by the Cistercians, 1505). Joachim died c. 1202" (T).

On Dante's relationships with Joachim's work and various of its followers, see Calvet (Calv.2001.1). And see Nardi (Nard.1965.1).

Veglia (Vegl.2000.1), p. 71, points out that Averroës (*Inf.* IV.144), Siger (*Par.* X.136), and Joachim is each the last figure in a group (fortieth, twelfth, and twelfth, respectively); they have in common the surprise generated by their presence in these groups.

Rather than attempting, as some do, to "Franciscanize" this second circle in the Sun (while "Dominicanizing" the first in Canto X), Botterill (Bott.1995.1), p. 184, speaks of (and he is also referring to the first circle, seen in *Par.* X) the "images of celebration, reconciliation, and harmony" that typify this entire heaven.

142. There has been dispute over the reference of *paladino*, but most today seem content to believe that it refers to Dominic, rather than to Francis, Thomas, or Joachim. See Scotti (Scot.1987.1), p. 257n.

On the verb *inveggiar*, see Singleton (comm. to this verse): "The most plausible interpretation would seem to be that *inveggiar*, deriving from *invidiare*, to envy, would mean (as does its Provençal equivalent *envejar*) to envy in a good sense, hence to praise."

143–145. It has long been observed that Dante constructed these two cantos so as to make them reflect one another in a thoroughgoing way. See the chart offered by Bosco/Reggio (who at times seem to be forcing the details to fit) for the parallel elements in Cantos XI and XII (numbers in parentheses refer to the number of *terzine* dedicated to each subject; square brackets contain one element not included in their table):

	Canto XI	*Canto XII*
General introduction:	28–36 (3)	37–45 (3)
Actions performed by the two saints:	40–42 (1)	34–36 (1)
Place of birth:	43–51 (3)	46–54 (3)
Birth:	49–51 (1)	55–57 (1)
[Saint's Life:	55–117 (21)	58–105 (16)]
Transition from biography to condemnation:	118–123 (2)	106–111 (2)
Condemnation of his own Order:	124–129 (2)	112–117 (2)
Faithful friars:	130–132 (1)	121–123 (1)

143. See Fassò (Fass.1998.1) for the several elements that inform Dante's notion of courtesy.

144. Ettore Bonora (Bono.1987.1), pp. 281–83, discusses the phrase describing Aquinas's speech as "discreto latin" and says that it is obvious that Thomas is not speaking Latin, but using Latin stylistic devices (in the

lingua franca of the poem, Italian) that ennoble speech. (And it should be pointed out that Dante several times uses the word *latino* to indicate either the Italian language or "Italy" itself. See the note to *Inf.* XXII.64–66, the passage in which it first appears; and see the note to *Par.* XVII.34–35, its last appearance in the poem.)

PARADISO XIII

OUTLINE

THE SUN

1–24 the reader is asked to imagine the two circles of souls as belonging to a new constellation, comprised of fifteen stars of the first magnitude, seven from the **Great Bear**, and two from the **Little Bear**, that whirls around Dante in the shape of **Ariadne**'s crown

25–30 the souls all sing praises, not of **Bacchus** nor **Apollo,** but of the **Trinity**

31–36 **Thomas** resumes his role as narrator, turning to Dante's second question:

37–51 Thomas says that Dante thinks Thomas has said that Solomon is of superior mind to **Adam** (**Eve** was his rib) and to **Jesus**

52–87 Thomas clarifies: (1) Adam and Christ indeed have superior natures because they were made by God directly;

88–111 (2) among other mortals, he was discussing only kings, and of these Solomon is the wisest because he asked for wisdom

112–123 thus, be slow in coming to judgment, being sure to make necessary distinctions, avoiding erroneous opinions,

124–129 unlike **Parmenides, Melissus, Bryson; Sabellius, Arius,**

130–142 and withhold judgment until you really have good grounds, unlike most people, who are fools like **Bertha** and **Martin**.

PARADISO XIII

Imagini, chi bene intender cupe
quel ch'i' or vidi—e ritegna l'image,
mentre ch'io dico, come ferma rupe—,

quindici stelle che 'n diverse plage
lo cielo avvivan di tanto sereno
che soperchia de l'aere ogne compage;

imagini quel carro a cu' il seno
basta del nostro cielo e notte e giorno,
sì ch'al volger del temo non vien meno;

imagini la bocca di quel corno
che si comincia in punta de lo stelo
a cui la prima rota va dintorno,

aver fatto di sé due segni in cielo,
qual fece la figliuola di Minoi
allora che sentì di morte il gelo;

e l'un ne l'altro aver li raggi suoi,
e amendue girarsi per maniera
che l'uno andasse al primo e l'altro al poi;

e avrà quasi l'ombra de la vera
costellazione e de la doppia danza
che circulava il punto dov' io era:

poi ch'è tanto di là da nostra usanza,
quanto di là dal mover de la Chiana
si move il ciel che tutti li altri avanza.

Lì si cantò non Bacco, non Peana,
ma tre persone in divina natura,
e in una persona essa e l'umana.

Let him, who would fully understand
what I now saw, imagine—and let him, while I speak,
hold that image, steady as a rock—

fifteen stars that light up various regions
of the sky, and with such brightness
as to overcome the intervening haze.

Let him imagine the Wain, nestling
in the bosom of our sky both night and day
so that its wheeling shaft is never out of sight.

Let him imagine the mouth of that horn
descending from the axle's endpoint
around which the first wheel revolves,

and all these seen together to have formed, up in the sky,
a double constellation, like the ring once formed
of Minos' daughter when she felt the chill of death,

the rays of one reflected in the other,
with both revolving in such manner
that one went first and then the other followed.

Then he will have, as it were, the shadow
of the true constellation and the double dance
that wheeled around the point where I now was,

for it is as far beyond our understanding
as the speed of the heaven that exceeds all others
outstrips the muddy stirrings of the Chiana.

There they sang the praises not of Bacchus nor of Paean
but praised the divine nature in three Persons,
and in one Person sang that nature joined with man.

Compié 'l cantare e 'l volger sua misura;
e attesersi a noi quei santi lumi,
felicitando sé di cura in cura.

Ruppe il silenzio ne' concordi numi
poscia la luce in che mirabil vita
del poverel di Dio narrata fumi,

e disse: "Quando l'una paglia è trita,
quando la sua semenza è già riposta,
a batter l'altra dolce amor m'invita.

Tu credi che nel petto onde la costa
si trasse per formar la bella guancia
il cui palato a tutto 'l mondo costa,

e in quel che, forato da la lancia,
e prima e poscia tanto sodisfece,
che d'ogne colpa vince la bilancia,

quantunque a la natura umana lece
aver di lume, tutto fosse infuso
da quel valor che l'uno e l'altro fece;

e però miri a ciò ch'io dissi suso,
quando narrai che non ebbe 'l secondo
lo ben che ne la quinta luce è chiuso.

Or apri li occhi a quel ch'io ti rispondo,
e vedräi il tuo credere e 'l mio dire
nel vero farsi come centro in tondo.

Ciò che non more e ciò che può morire
non è se non splendor di quella idea
che partorisce, amando, il nostro Sire;

ché quella viva luce che sì mea
dal suo lucente, che non si disuna
da lui né da l'amor ch'a lor s'intrea,

Having done the measure of their song and circling dance,
these holy lights turned toward us,
rejoicing as they passed from task to task.

The silence among those holy souls in harmony
was broken by the light that had told me
the wondrous life of the poor man of God.

He said: 'Now that one sheaf is threshed
and its grain now gathered,
sweet charity bids me thresh the other.

'You believe that, into the side from which
the rib was drawn to form the lovely features
of her whose palate costs the world so dear,

'and into His, pierced by the spear, which gave
such satisfaction for sins, both done or yet to be,
as outweighs any fault found in the balance,

'all the light that is allowed to human nature
was infused by the very Power
which made the one and made the other.

'And thus you marvel at what I said before,
when I told you that the goodness
contained in the fifth light never had an equal.

'Open your eyes to the answer I shall give
and you shall find your thoughts and what I say
meet at the truth as in the center of a circle.

'That which does not die and that which must
are nothing but a bright reflection of that Idea
which our Lord, in loving, brings to birth.

'For that living Light, which so streams forth
from its shining Source that it neither parts from it
nor from the Love that is intrined with them,

per sua bontate il suo raggiare aduna,
quasi specchiato, in nove sussistenze,
etternalmente rimanendosi una.

Quindi discende a l'ultime potenze
giù d'atto in atto, tanto divenendo,
che più non fa che brevi contingenze;

e queste contingenze essere intendo
le cose generate, che produce
con seme e sanza seme il ciel movendo.

La cera di costoro e chi la duce
non sta d'un modo; e però sotto 'l segno
idëale poi più e men traluce.

Ond' elli avvien ch'un medesimo legno,
secondo specie, meglio e peggio frutta;
e voi nascete con diverso ingegno.

Se fosse a punto la cera dedutta
e fosse il cielo in sua virtù supprema,
la luce del suggel parrebbe tutta;

ma la natura la dà sempre scema,
similemente operando a l'artista
ch'a l'abito de l'arte ha man che trema.

Però se 'l caldo amor la chiara vista
de la prima virtù dispone e segna,
tutta la perfezion quivi s'acquista.

Così fu fatta già la terra degna
di tutta l'animal perfezïone;
così fu fatta la Vergine pregna;

sì ch'io commendo tua oppinïone,
che l'umana natura mai non fue
né fia qual fu in quelle due persone.

'of its own goodness gathers its own shining,
as though it were a mirror, in nine subsistences,
and yet eternally endures as one.

'From that height light descends to the lowest elements,
passing down from act to act, becoming such
that it produces nothing more than brief contingencies.

'By these contingent things I mean
things generated, with seed or without,
produced by the movements of the heavens.

'Their wax and that which molds it vary so
that, beneath the Idea's imprint,
light shines in varying degrees.

'And so it happens that trees of the very same kind
bear fruit, some of it better and some of it worse,
and that you are born with differing talents.

'If the wax were perfectly prepared
and the heaven at the height of its power,
in all its brightness would the seal be seen.

'But nature always fashions it defective,
working like the craftsman who, to the practice
of his craft, brings an unsteady hand.

'However, if the clear vision of the primal Power
is moved by burning Love and makes of that its seal,
then all perfection is attained in it.

'In that way was the dust made ready to receive—
once—perfection in a living creature,
in that way was the Virgin made to be with child.

'Thus do I agree with your opinion
that human nature never was—nor shall it be—
what it was in these two creatures.

Or s'i' non procedesse avanti piùe,
'Dunque, come costui fu sanza pare?'
comincerebber le parole tue.

Ma perché paia ben ciò che non pare,
pensa chi era, e la cagion che 'l mosse,
quando fu detto 'Chiedi,' a dimandare.

Non ho parlato sì, che tu non posse
ben veder ch'el fu re, che chiese senno
acciò che re sufficïente fosse;

non per sapere il numero in che enno
li motor di qua sù, o se *necesse*
con contingente mai *necesse* fenno;

non *si est dare primum motum esse,*
o se del mezzo cerchio far si puote
trïangol sì ch'un retto non avesse.

Onde, se ciò ch'io dissi e questo note,
regal prudenza è quel vedere impari
in che lo stral di mia intenzion percuote;

e se al 'surse' drizzi li occhi chiari,
vedrai aver solamente respetto
ai regi, che son molti, e ' buon son rari.

Con questa distinzion prendi 'l mio detto;
e così puote star con quel che credi
del primo padre e del nostro Diletto.

E questo ti sia sempre piombo a' piedi,
per farti mover lento com' uom lasso
e al sì e al no che tu non vedi:

ché quelli è tra li stolti bene a basso,
che sanza distinzione afferma e nega
ne l'un così come ne l'altro passo;

'Now, if I went no farther,
"How, then, was that other without equal?"
would be the first words from your mouth.

'But, to make quite clear what still remains obscure,
think who he was and what it was that moved him
to his request when he was bidden "Ask."

'I did not speak so darkly that you cannot see
he was a king and asked for wisdom
that he might become a worthy king.

'He did not ask to know the number of the angels
here above, nor if *necesse*
with a contingent ever made *necesse*,

'nor *si est dare primum motum esse,*
nor if in a semicircle a triangle can be formed
without its having one right angle.

'Therefore, if you reflect on this and what I said,
kingly prudence is that peerless vision
on which the arrow of my purpose strikes.

'And if you examine my use of "rose" with open eyes,
you will see that it referred alone to kings—
of whom there are so many, but the good ones rare.

'Take my words, along with this distinction,
and they can stand alongside your beliefs
concerning the first father and the One we love.

'And let this always be as lead upon your feet
to make you slow, just like a weary man, in moving,
whether to yes or no, unless you see both clearly.

'For he ranks low among the fools
who, without making clear distinctions,
affirms or denies in one case or another,

perch' elli 'ncontra che più volte piega
l'oppinïon corrente in falsa parte,
120 e poi l'affetto l'intelletto lega.

Vie più che 'ndarno da riva si parte,
perché non torna tal qual e' si move,
123 chi pesca per lo vero e non ha l'arte.

E di ciò sono al mondo aperte prove
Parmenide, Melisso e Brisso e molti,
126 li quali andaro e non sapëan dove;

sì fé Sabellio e Arrio e quelli stolti
che furon come spade a le Scritture
129 in render torti li diritti volti.

Non sien le genti, ancor, troppo sicure
a giudicar, sì come quei che stima
132 le biade in campo pria che sien mature;

ch'i' ho veduto tutto 'l verno prima
lo prun mostrarsi rigido e feroce,
135 poscia portar la rosa in su la cima;

e legno vidi già dritto e veloce
correr lo mar per tutto suo cammino,
138 perire al fine a l'intrar de la foce.

Non creda donna Berta e ser Martino,
per vedere un furare, altro offerere,
vederli dentro al consiglio divino;
142 ché quel può surgere, e quel può cadere."

'since it often happens that a hasty opinion
inclines one to the erring side, and then
fondness for it fetters the working of the mind.

'He who casts off from shore to fish for truth
without the necessary skill does not return the same
as he sets out, but worse, and all in vain.

'Clear proof of this was given to the world
by Parmenides, Melissus, Bryson, and others,
who went to sea without a port in mind.

'Such were Sabellius and Arius and the fools
who misread Scripture as a sword reflecting
the distorted image of a face upon its blade.

'Let the people, then, not be too certain
in their judgments, like those that harvest in their minds
corn still in the field before it ripens.

'For I have seen the briar first look dry and thorny
right through all the winter's cold,
then later wear the bloom of roses at its tip,

'and once I saw a ship, which had sailed straight
and swift upon the sea through all its voyage,
sinking at the end as it made its way to port.

'Let not Dame Bertha and Master Martin,
when they see one steal and another offer alms,
think that they behold them with God's wisdom,
for the first may still rise up, the other fall.'

1–24. If the punctuation here is as Dante left it, this is the longest single-sentence canto-opening in the poem. See the note to *Paradiso* VIII.1–12 for other cantos marked by lengthy openings. This is also the longest address to the reader in the entire poem, if it is an indirect one (marked by the thrice-uttered hortatory subjunctive "imagini" [let him imagine] in vv. 1, 7, and 10). And thus here we have another (cf. *Par.* XI.1–3) "pseudo-apostrophe" beginning a canto in the heaven of the Sun.

1–18. Dante's reconstruction of two perfect twelve-studded circles (each of which he has already seen and described in the immediately preceding cantos [*Par.* X.64–69; XII.1–21]) into apparently fanciful constituent groupings has, understandably, drawn some perplexed attention. (It is perhaps difficult not to think of the role that the poet assumes as being analogous to that of the geomancers, *Purg.* XIX.4–6, who similarly construct their "Fortuna Major" out of existing constellations.) What is the reason, we might wonder, for the numbering of the three subgroups as fifteen, seven, and two to equal twenty-four? For Bosco/Reggio (comm. to these verses), this is a rare case of Dante's taste for arid preciosity (*un preziosismo tutto intellettualistico*). In any case, the fifteen brightest stars found in the eighth heaven are to be imagined as being conjoined with all the seven that make up the Big Dipper and with two from the Little Dipper (see the note to vv. 13–15), thus representing the twenty-four "stars" to whom we have already been introduced. In order to formulate a reason for the fifteen in the first group, Francesco da Buti points out (comm. to vv. 1–21) that Alfraganus, in the nineteenth chapter of his *Elementa astronomica*, says that in the eighth sphere there are precisely fifteen stars of the first magnitude (i.e., in brightness and size). Niccolò Tommaseo (comm. to vv. 4–6) cites Ptolemy's *Almagest* for the same information (first referred to in this context by Jacopo della Lana [comm. to vv. 1–6]), adding the detail that these fifteen may be found situated variously in either hemisphere. However, that there should be nine in the last two groupings, both of which are associated with locating the position of the North Star, may reveal the design of a plan. As we have seen (*Par.* II.7–9), the Pole Star stands in for divine guidance; thus here the twin circles of Christian sapience are associated both with divine intellectual purpose and with the number that represents Beatrice, who is more clearly associated with the Wisdom of God, Christ, the Second Person of the Trinity, than with anything else.

2–3. This self-conscious literary gesture seeks to involve us as coconspirators in manufacturing a substitute solar system. We, as "secondary artists," are asked to collaborate, making ourselves responsible for literalizing the details of Dante's vision and keeping them in memory. It is really a quite extraordinary request, even in a poem that perhaps asks for more involvement on the part of its reader than any fictive work in Western literary history before *Don Quijote*.

7–8. The Wain is Ursa Major, the Big Dipper, close enough to the Pole Star never to leave the Northern Hemisphere.

10–12. See Bosco/Reggio (comm. to these verses) for the following explanation of what is surely the most convoluted element in an already convoluted passage: Dante asks us to imagine two stars of the Little Dipper farthest from its tip as the bell of a trumpet for which the Pole Star (at that tip) is the mouthpiece. This last point intersects, according to Dante (forcing the issue to his own purpose, according to Porena [comm. to vv. 10–12]), with the Primum Mobile. The universe is thus conceived of as a gigantic wheel, with a diameter running between our earth and the Crystalline sphere (even if, as Porena points out, the situation of the North Star in the eighth sphere precludes its having contact with the ninth).

13–15. The daughter of Minos here referred to is Ariadne. Her "crown" refers to the garland taken from her head by Bacchus after she died, having been abandoned by Theseus. Bacchus placed it in the heavens, where it is known as the Corona Borealis (see Ovid, *Metam.* VIII.174–182). Dante compares it, a single thing, to a double rainbow. (That Dante refers to Ariadne as herself being translated to the heavens, and not only her garland of flowers, has troubled some commentators. However, in a sort of reverse metonymy, Dante has given the whole for the part; he clearly wants us to think of Ariadne's garland as representing a circle of saints—twice. In the last canto (*Par.* XII.12) Juno's handmaid (the unnamed Iris) is doubled in the sky, just as here Minos's daughter (the unnamed Ariadne) is.

That the canto eventually finds its fullest expression of its central theme in Daedalus's trembling hand (see discussion in the note to vv. 67–78), an object that probably has its source in the next episode in Ovid (*Metam.* VIII.183–235), tends to strengthen the case for the aptness of the citation from that same *locus* here.

16–18. Still another troubled tercet. The first difficulty that it presents is fairly easy to resolve: Does the second circle extend beyond the first or does it stand within it? Most commentators sensibly take the first view, since the third circle clearly is wider than the second (*Par.* XIV.74–75), which at least implies that the second is wider than the first and, indeed, contains it. The really obdurate problem, on the other hand, is how to construe verse 18. If one says "one went first and then the other followed" (as we translate the line), the meaning is that one of the circles begins to move only after the other does (and probably the first is followed by the second). This hypothesis is seconded by the rhyme position of the word *poi*, used for the only time in the poem as a substantive, a usage that pretty clearly is forced by rhyme. What would Dante have said had he been writing *parole sciolte* (words not bound by meter—see *Inf.* XXVIII.1) and not been constrained by the need to rhyme? A good case can be made for "secondo" (i.e., next). And for this reason, we have translated the line as we have. See also Fasani (Fasa.2002.1), p. 194, buttressing this position with the early gloss of Francesco da Buti (comm. to vv. 1–21). After centuries of inconclusive debate, refusing to choose between the two established and conflicting views, Trucchi (comm. to this tercet) came up with a new hypothesis: Since the two concentric circles move so that the rays sent out by each reflect one another perfectly (he was thinking of facing pairs, Thomas and Bonaventure, Siger and Joachim, etc.), the circles, since they are of different extent, to maintain this unwavering relationship between themselves, must move at different speeds. Giacalone (comm. to this tercet) shares Trucchi's view, but credits Buti's less clear statement (comm. to vv. 1–21) for preparing the way.

19–21. What Dante asks the reader to be aware of seeing is *l'ombra de la vera / costellazione* (the "shadow of the real constellation"—cf. the similar phrases "l'ombra del beato regno" [the shadow of the blessèd kingdom]—*Par.* I.23, "di lor vero umbriferi prefazi" [shadowy prefaces of their truth]—*Par.* XXX.78). Here the reference to the *vera costellazione* has a similar typological rhythm: What Dante saw yields to its realer version, the two circles of moving, singing saints in their "double dance."

22–24. Now the purpose of our "imagining" along with Dante that starry construct becomes clear: The reality to which it corresponds is as far beyond our conceiving as the circling of the Primum Mobile exceeds in speed the movement of the Chiana, a sluggish stream in Tuscany that turned to marsh in some places, probably referred to, without being named, in *Inferno* XXIX.46–49.

25–27. In those two circles the souls were celebrating the triune God and, in the Person of Christ, His human nature as well (a song beyond our mortal understanding), not Bacchus or Apollo (songs all too understandable to us). The word *Peana* may refer either to cries of praise to Apollo or, as seems more likely here, to the god himself.

For the program of song in the last *cantica*, see the note to *Paradiso* XXI.58–60.

28–30. This part of the canto comes to a close with the souls turning their attention from their celebration of their trinitarian God, in dance and song, to dealing with Dante's doubts, a process that also brings them pleasure. They shift their attention from Dante's first question (rephrased at *Par.* XI.25), now answered, to his second (see *Par.* XIII.89).

31–36. Thomas, who is identified as the one who had narrated the life of Francis, as circumlocutory as ever, refers to his having answered Dante's first question (see *Par.* X.91–93) and now prepares (finally) to deal with the second.

31. The word *numi*, a hapax and a Latinism (from *numen*), here means "divinities" (translated as "holy souls"). It seems to owe its presence to the exigencies of rhyme.

34–36. Thomas's agricultural metaphor combines pedantic heaviness with one perhaps surprising touch: affection.

37–51. Thomas corrects Dante's misprision of what he had told him about Solomon in Canto X. Reduced to its core, this is what he conveys to the protagonist: "You believe that God, when he created Adam and (the human part of) Christ, gave each of them as much intellect as it was possible to create in a human being; if that is so, you wonder, how can I have said that Solomon's intelligence never was bettered by another's? I will now clear up your confusion."

37–42. Metonymic periphrasis abounds in these lines about Adam and Eve and Jesus, respectively identified by his rib cage, her pretty face and fatal appetite, and His rib cage. Dante treats the "wound" in Adam's side from which God formed Eve and that in Christ's side as corresponding, for the sin of the first parents was atoned for by the latter wound.

40–41. Exactly what is referred to by these words is much debated. See the summarizing treatment offered by Giacalone (comm. to vv. 37–45), which offers the following sense of the matter in dispute. Christ redeemed, with his death on the Cross, sins committed either (1) in the past or in the future; or (2) before His life on earth and after it; or (3) before His flesh was pierced on the Cross and after the Crucifixion. While it seems that the third of these alternatives is the most appealing (because it builds on the parallel structure of the entire passage, moving from Adam's rib to Christ's wounded side), it is also true that all three interpretations cause similar reflection: Christ died for our sins.

According to Schwarz (Schw.1966.1), pp. 147–48, these lines reflect the opinion of Peter Olivi (against the account found in John 19:30) that Jesus was pierced by the lance while he was still alive. Schwarz believes that *Paradiso* XXXII.128 reflects the same understanding. For the view that Dante was deeply aware of Olivi's work and essentially agreed with it, but never mentions his name because the Franciscan was being vigorously attacked by Church officials in Provence, who managed to have his *Lectura super Apocalypsim* condemned, see Manselli, "francescanesimo," *ED* III (1971), p. 16.

43–48. God the Father made the corporeal natures of Adam and Christ directly. All other human bodies are formed with the influence of intermediating agencies (i.e., the angels and the stars). And thus, in Dante's view, Thomas's statement of Solomon's singular intellectual gifts (*Par.* X.112–114) does indeed require further explanation, to which a goodly portion of the rest of the canto (vv. 49–111) will be devoted.

49–51. This tercet perhaps exemplifies the "unpoetic" quality of this canto (representing the sort of "philosophic discourse" that Benedetto Croce so often inveighed against [e.g., Croc.1921.1]), the cause of its being denigrated even by those to whose lot it fell to write *lecturae* dedicated to it. For documentation, see Cahill (Cahi.1996.1), p. 245 and note 1 (p. 266).

50–51. Thomas's figure of speech, insisting that Dante's view of Adam's and Christ's knowledge and his own championing of Solomon's not only do not contradict one another, but are equally close to the truth as are two points, along the circumference of a circle, to the center.

52–87. This portion of Thomas's speech is one of the most "philosophical" in the entire poem. It may serve as a pretext for answering the protagonist's concern about Solomon's relative perfection as knower; at the same time we sense that the poet simply wanted to posit his view of primary and secondary creation.

For a straightforward explanation, in simplified terms, of the passage, see Tozer (comm. to these verses): "What is created directly by God is perfect, whereas that which is created indirectly by Him through intermediate agencies and materials is imperfect; and therefore Dante is right in thinking that Adam, and Christ in His human nature, who belong to the former class, must have been superior in wisdom to all men, and therefore to Solomon."

52. "That which does not die" resolves into God, the angels, the heavens, prime matter, and the human soul; "that which must [die]" refers to all corruptible things (see *Par.* VII.133–141 and the note to vv. 124–138).

53–54. All that God makes, eternal and bound by time, is made radiant by reflecting the Word (Christ as Logos) made by the Father (Power) in his Love (the Holy Spirit).

55–60. The first step in this procession of God into His universe is for the Trinity to be reflected in the nine orders of angels (see the note to verse 59). See Moevs on these six verses: "The Trinity evoked in the [preceding] tercet is evoked again [in this one]: the Word-Son is a living light . . . which flows from the source of light (. . . the Father), but is not other than . . . its source: both are a power of love, . . . which 'en-threes' itself with them" (Moev.2005.1), p. 121.

57. Dante's coinage *intrearsi* (literally, "to inthree oneself") represents a form of linguistic boldness to which the reader has perhaps become accustomed. See, for example, the verb *s'incinquare* (literally, "to infive oneself") in *Paradiso* IX.40.

59. This is the first appearance (see *Par.* XXXIII.115; and see *Par.* XXIX.15 for the shining angelic substance announcing itself in the Latin verb *Subsisto*) of the Scholastic-flavored noun "subsistence," that is, existence as purely related to God's nature as is possible, here, in the nine orders of angels. Compare *Paradiso* XIV.73 and the note thereto. And see Alfonso Maierù, "sussistenza," *ED* V (1976), pp. 493a–494b, who cites Boethius, in *De duabus naturis*, referring to "a being, which, in order to be able itself to exist, has no need of any other being." See also Tozer (comm. to vv. 58–59): "These are called 'subsistences,' because this is the Scholastic term for that which exists by itself, and not in anything else; cp. Aquinas [*ST* I, q. 29, a. 2]." Among the earliest commentators there is a certain

hesitation in choosing between angels and heavens (e.g., Jacopo della Lana [comm. to vv. 55–60]). Benvenuto (comm. to vv. 55–60), however, is definitive in seeing the angels here ("idest in novem ordines angelorum"). The dispute meandered along until Scartazzini's magisterial review (comm. to this verse) of that errancy and his interpretation fixed the identification (Benvenuto's) for nearly all later discussants: the nine orders of angels. Scartazzini invokes passages in Dante's own texts: *Epistle* XIII, *Convivio* II.v and III.xiv, and most particularly *Paradiso* XXIX.142–145. Today one cannot find a discussant who has not benefited from Scartazzini's gloss, whether directly or indirectly; at the same time one can find no commentator (at least not among those included in the DDP) who even mentions him, although Singleton (comm. to this verse) does cite two of the Dantean passages that he cited.

60. The presence of Christ, Itself three-personed but unitary, is reflected by myriads of angels in nine groups.

61–66. The second stage of God's progression (for the first see the note to vv. 55–60) is into that part of the universe created out of the four elements and, not directly by God, but indirectly and by various agencies. Lombardi (comm. to vv. 55–63) refers the reader to *Paradiso* II.112–141 for an earlier exposition of this process. The light of the Word (verse 55) blends its creative power with the angelic presences in each heavenly sphere, moving downward "from act to act" and reaching the elements, until it finally interacts with the most short-lived perishable things, *brevi contingenze* (brief contingencies). According to Scholastic philosophy, contingent things have the potential either to be or not to be, depending on the presence or absence of a conjoined formal property. Those perishable things that are shaped by form are, if produced from seed, animal or vegetable; if not, mineral.

67–78. To explain the principle of difference, the results of which are so noticeable to any observer of any species, Thomas, wanting to avoid imputing to God a causal relation with mortality, ugliness, and/or failure, puts the blame for such things on Great Creating Nature. Thus the angel-derived powers of the planetary spheres are seen as waxing and waning, and the resultant creations (e.g., human beings, horses, zucchini, and garnets) variable.

Courtney Cahill (Cahi.1996.1), pp. 256–65, discusses this passage at some length (in a portion of her study subtitled "The Limitations of the *artista* in Thomas's Discourse on Creation"). Among other things, she puts forward the telling argument (p. 268, n. 25) that Thomas's initial presentation of Nature as perfect maker of God's creation is intentionally contradicted here, in order to account for the difference we find all around us in the world. She also finds that the image of the artist's trembling hand reflects that of Daedalus, as portrayed by Ovid (*Metam.* VIII.211), citing Hollander (Holl.1992.2), pp. 229–30, for an earlier and identical observation. See also Hollander (Holl.1983.1), p. 135n., for the suggestion that this passage may also reflect *Aeneid* VI.32–33, recounting Daedalus's double fatherly failure as artist to portray in gold his son's fall from the skies.

As opposed to her performance in God's direct creation, Nature, when she is working with the "wax" of secondary creation (i.e., not the first man, Adam, but his descendants; not the first apple, but the succeeding "generations" of the fruit, etc.), is *always* defective, coming up short of the archetype.

77. For the word *artista* and its four appearances in the poem (here and *Par.* XVI.51; XVIII.51; XXX.33), see Hollander (Holl.1992.2), p. 217; Cahill (Cahi.1996.1), p. 257.

79–87. Once again the Trinity is referred to—Spirit, Son, Father (in that order)—in order to distinguish between direct creation, under God's unshared auspices, as distinct from the natural secondary creation of which we have just heard. Thus twice in history human beings were made outside the natural process, with the creation of Adam (as well as Eve, now not referred to by Dante, perhaps, but we can hardly forget that she was indeed remembered in vv. 37–39) and of Jesus marking the limits of human perfection, well beyond the otherwise unmatchable king of Israel.

88–96. Without further explanation, Thomas says, Dante might still remain dubious; if he only considers who Solomon was and what moved him to ask for wisdom, he will understand. See III Kings 3:5–12, in which passage God appears to Solomon in a dream and promises to grant him whatever he asks for. Solomon responds by saying that God has made His servant into a king, but a king who has need of a knowing heart to judge his people. God, pleased by his answer, replies (in the passage quoted in *Par.* X.114 [and see the note to vv. 109–114]) "dedi tibi cor sapiens et intelligens, in tantum ut nullus ante te similis tui fuerit *nec post te surrecturus sit*" (I have given you a wise and an understanding heart; so that there was none like you before you, nor after you shall any arise who is like you [III Kings 3:12—italics added]).

According to Toffanin (Toff.1968.1), p. 453, Dante's veneration of Solomon the king is the high point of his Ghibellinism.

97–102. Thomas now contrasts practical kingly wisdom with typical Scholastic speculations, drawn from the following four fields: speculative theology (How many are the angels?), dialectic (Will a mixture of a necessary and a contingent premise ever yield a necessary conclusion?), natural science (Must we grant that motion had a beginning?), and geometry (Can a triangle be constructed in a semicircle in such a way that it not contain a right angle?). (All four answers are negative, beginning with the fact that, according to Dante, the angels are not numerable.) In Dante's view, Solomon's practical wisdom trumps all such formal intelligence. However, for a far different appraisal of Solomon's kingly wisdom, see Carroll (comm. to vv. 88–111): "The real difficulty is that, history being the witness, all Solomon's wisdom did not make him 'sufficient as a king.' The outward brilliance of his reign was but a veil which hid for the moment the slow sapping of his people's strength and character through his luxury and licentiousness, his tyrannies, exactions, and idolatries. He sowed the wind, and his son reaped the whirlwind when the downtrodden people rent the greater part of the kingdom out of his hand. Whatever Dante may say, Solomon as a king was perhaps the wisest fool who ever lived. In saying this, I am quite aware that I may be incurring the censure on hasty judgments with which Canto XIII closes."

On Solomon's song as leading to truthful (and not seductive, deceiving) love, see Chiarenza (Chia.2000.1).

97. For Dante's own thoughts on this question, see *Convivio* II.iv.3–15 and II.v.4–5, *Paradiso* XXVIII.92–93 and XXIX.130–135. The angels are "quasi innumerabili" (all but innumerable [*Conv.* II.v.5]).

98–99. For a helpful guide through the maze of medieval logical procedures, see Oelsner (comm. to vv. 97–102): "It is a general principle that no limitation that occurs in either of the premises can be escaped in the conclusion. Thus, if either of the premises is negative you cannot get a positive conclusion; if either of them is particular you cannot get a general conclusion; if either is contingent you cannot get a necessary conclusion. For instance, from 'The man on whom the lot falls *must* be sacrificed,' and 'The lot *may* fall on you,' you can infer: 'therefore you *may* be sacrificed,' but not 'therefore you *must* be sacrificed.' Ingenious attempts to get a necessary conclusion out of a necessary and a contingent premise are exposed by the logicians, *e.g.* 'Anyone who may run from the foe must be a coward; some of these troops may run from the foe, therefore some of them must be cowards.' The fallacy lies in the ambiguous use of 'may run from the foe.' In the first instance it means, 'is, *as a matter of fact*, capable of running away'; in the second, 'may, *for anything I know*, run away.' So that the two propositions do not hang together, and the conclusion is invalid."

100. That is, whether one can accept the notion that there existed a first motion, preceding all other motion. Benvenuto (comm. to vv. 97–102), after saying that, according to Aristotle's *Physics* [VIII.1] motion is eternal, insists that theologians find that it, like the world, has a beginning, and goes on to cite Genesis 1:1: "In the beginning God made the heavens and the earth." That was the First Mover's first motion; before that nothing moved.

101–102. See Euclid, *Geometria* III.31: All triangles inscribed in a circle, if the line bisecting that circle is used as their base, will have a right angle at their apex.

103–105. And so, rounding off his oratory, Thomas insists that kingly prudence is to be valued more highly than speculative philosophy (a position that coincides with that put forth in the *Epistle to Cangrande* [*Epist.* XIII.40–41], where Dante says that the branch of philosophy that the *Comedy* embraces is ethics, since the project of the poem is not speculation, but action).

106–108. For Dante (or Thomas) to insist that what was said of Solomon earlier (*Par.* X.114) corresponds to what is said now strains credulity, and not a little. If Dante had offered something to the effect that neither Adam nor Christ had to "rise," since they were made differently from all other mortals (except for Eve, conveniently lost from sight in all discussions of this passage), since they were directly produced by God, without intermediation (a tactic attempted by both the Ottimo [comm. to vv. 103–108] and Benvenuto [comm. to vv. 103–108]), then we might see the problem as resolved. However, the text rather pointedly fails to offer any such limitation.

If one examines the commentaries to *Paradiso* X.114, hardly anyone before the twentieth century thinks that the reference is to Solomon as king. For one who did, see Benvenuto (comm. to *Par.* X.109–114), who says that the phrase means that he has "no equal among kings." Benvenuto, perhaps the most competent reader of poetic text among all the earlier students of Dante, had likely remembered the addition found in this later passage, even if he does not refer to it. Scartazzini (comm. to *Par.* X.114) also makes this point, referring to the later passage and interpreting it in Thomas's way. But this may be said of few others before 1900 (twentieth-century readers of *Paradiso* X nearly all do look ahead to this passage). In fact, the biblical text that lies behind both passages (III Kings 3:12) does not qualify Solomon's excellence by reference to a "peer group," that is, that text represents him as the wisest among all humans, not only kings. Thus we once again have a sense that the text of *Paradiso*, in comparison with its predecessors, was left in a relatively unfinished condition at Dante's death; he could have handled the issue better when he introduced it.

109–111. With the distinction added in the preceding tercet (Dante's wording almost gives away the fact that no such distinction was intended in his first utterance on the subject), the protagonist can understand how Solomon was first among the wise kings without infringing upon the primacy of either Adam (the "first father") or of Jesus (the "One we love").

112–142. The final thirty-one lines of this canto, a text that has, on the authority of none other than Thomas Aquinas, just established Solomon's kingly wisdom as a defining part of Dante's theocratic view of the world's affairs, nonetheless offer a warning to all of us who tend to rush to judgment, whether in relation to matters philosophical or theological. As we shall see (vv. 133–138), there is an autobiographical component to this plea.

For Dante to have used so much poetic space on so apparently simple, even banal, a topic tells his readers how keenly he felt involved in the problem. Once again we sense how, as he looks back over his intellectual development from the vantage point of the making of this great work, he realizes how self-centered some of his earlier attitudes were (see Hollander [Holl.2003.2]).

112–114. We have seen how slowly the hypocrites made their way forward in *Inferno* XXIII, in their leaden capes. Just so should we approach affirming or denying the truth of matters we have not fully examined.

115–120. A rush to judgment is, unsurprisingly, condemned. In the last verse, Dante's genial understanding of the way we humans tend to fall in love with whatever opinion we contrive to form rescues the passage from banality. If there is one passage in the last four cantos in which the voice of Thomas, usually so fully "captured" by the poet and so distinct from his own, seems to be indistinguishable from Dante's, it is found in these six lines.

121–127. The metaphor for the search for truth moves to fishing. We hear first of three Greek philosophers of the fifth century B.C., then of two heretical thinkers of the early Christian era. Each of these groups is represented as standing for many another thinker who also lacks rigor.

121–123. Within the metaphor, the fisherman without the necessary skills of his craft not only returns home without a catch, but tired (or worse) from the voyage; outside of it, the thinker who lacks the proper intellectual tools not only fails to arrive at the truth, but enmeshes himself in failure.

125. The founder of the Eleatic school of philosophy and his pupil, Parmenides and Melissus, are both mentioned in *Monarchia* III.iv.4 as, according to Aristotle, using false premises and invalid syllogisms. Bryson, a less-known figure living in the same fifth century, was criticized by Aristotle for using invalid methods in his attempts to square the circle.

127. Sabellius and Arius, Christians of the third and fourth centuries, respectively. Longfellow characterizes them as follows: "Sabellius was by birth an African, and flourished as Presbyter of Ptolemais, in the third century. He denied the three persons in the Godhead, maintaining that the Son and Holy Ghost were only temporary manifestations of God in creation, redemption, and sanctification, and would finally return to the Father.

"Arius was a Presbyter of Alexandria in the fourth century. He believed the Son to be equal in power with the Father, but of a different essence or nature, a doctrine which gave rise to the famous Heterousian and Homoiousian controversy, that distracted the Church for three hundred years."

Aversano (Aver.2000.2), p. 59, points out that both of these thinkers were confused about the relationships among God's *substance* and his *persons*, and suggest that Dante may have been led to his thought by a sentence attributed to Athanasius by Alain de Lille (*PL* CCX.749): "Neque confundentes personas, ut Sabellius, neque substantiam separantes, ut

Arius" (Neither confounding the Persons, as did Sabellius, nor putting asunder His substance, as did Arius).

128–129. Sabellius, Arius, and their ilk are compared to swords in which human faces are reflected in distorted ways; just so were they to Scripture distorting mirrors of revealed truth. This comparison has disturbed many recent readers, to whom it seems either forced or unintelligible. The early commentators, however, were apparently more at ease with it, as though they thought of faces reflected on the irregular surfaces of shiny sword blades as a matter of course. Lombardi (comm. to these verses) at the close of the eighteenth century loses control of himself when confronting Venturi's continuance of that tradition. Swords, he shouts, were metaphorically the instruments of heretics who mutilated Scripture to make it accord with their nefarious purposes. For a while his intervention ruled in Italy (at Harvard, Longfellow just mentioned the two interpretations and took no side). Then Scartazzini (comm. to these verses) took Lombardi's argument apart (e.g., the language in the passage really does speak of mirroring rather than destruction), as did Poletto (comm. to vv. 127–129). Still, the debate continues into our own day, with the older position holding the edge, but not without challenge.

Strangely enough, hardly anyone has turned his attention to the Bible as a potential source, since the reference is to it. (It is not surprising that the single exception is Scartazzini [comm. to these vv.], if his two passages in the Psalms [56:5 and 63:4] are not exactly germane.) No one has apparently adduced the Scriptural passage containing one of the Bible's surprisingly few references to mirrors (as was pointed out by Carolyn Calvert Phipps in a graduate seminar on the *Paradiso* in 1980): the Epistle of James 1:23–24: "For if any be a hearer of the word, and not a doer, he is like a man beholding his natural face in a glass; for he beholds himself, and goes his way, and straightway forgets what manner of man he was." That is not a perfect fit, either, but it does at least share the basic context of these verses.

Carroll (comm. to vv. 121–128) reminds the reader that Thomas (who is, after all, the speaker here) had refuted both these heresies (Sabellius on the Trinity, Arius on the nonconsubstantiality of the Son with the Father). See *Summa contra Gentiles* IV.5–8.

130–132. We find a shift in the object of Thomas's measured scorn, from the schooled (philosophers and theologians) to the unschooled, ordinary folk (*Donna Berta e ser Martino*), as well as in the subject in which their misprision functions, from thoughts about the nature of things to the afterlife of one's neighbors.

133–138. The two examples, in reverse order, reminded John Carroll (comm. to vv. 129–142) of the father and son, Guido and Buonconte da Montefeltro. Guido, according to Dante in *Convivio* (IV.xxviii.8), was saved, but then was registered as one of the damned in *Inferno* XXVII, his story presented in both texts as a sea voyage; his son, Buonconte, although suffering a cruel death, in his agony spoke the name of Mary, the "rose," and was saved (*Purg.* V). Trucchi (comm. to vv. 139–142) makes the same point, but with less effect. And see Pézard (Peza.1965.1), ad loc., for an attempt to locate both the rose and the ship of this passage in *Convivio* IV.xxvii.7 and IV.xxviii.8.

For readers of *Convivio*, Dante has placed his former writing self among the Berthas and Martins (see verse 139) of the world. Perhaps recognizing ourselves described in vv. 118–120, we may share that sense.

135. For the phrase "la rosa in su la cima" (the bloom of roses at its tip), see *Purgatorio* XI.92.

136–138. For this tercet as referring to Ulysses and his ill-conceived final voyage, see Cahill (Cahi.1996.1), pp. 254–55. Trucchi (comm. to vv. 133–138) seems to have been her only precursor, if his mention of Ulysses (and Manfred) is only in passing.

139. The foolish "donna Berta e ser Martino" remind Carlo Grabher (comm. to vv. 34–142) of what Dante says in *Convivio* (IV.v.9) about those vile beasts who desire to know what is known only to God. A woman named Bertha had already enjoyed a role in Dante's displeasure with less-than-sophisticated writing; see *De vulgari eloquentia* II.vi.5: "Petrus amat multum dominam Bertam" (Peter loves Mistress Bertha a lot).

140–142. These verses have made many a reader uncomfortable with Dante's behavior in them. Is not *he* one who claims to have knowledge of divine wisdom? Furthermore, the concealed reference to his failed judgment of such things in *Convivio* (see the note to vv. 133–138) reads back at him in upsetting ways. Bosco/Reggio (comm. to vv. 112–142) point out that this entire passage needs to be read in the context of the medieval dispute over the damnation/salvation of Solomon (see the note to *Par.* X.109–114). We remember that such great figures as Jerome (who thought

Solomon was saved) and Augustine (who thought he was not) disagreed over this matter. It is clear that Dante is willing to risk considerable intellectual capital in the presentation of his case for Solomon. Sarolli has done a great deal to explain the choice of the other Old Testament figure, Nathan, for inclusion here (see the note to *Par.* XII.136). As a "type" of Dante the prophet, he joins Solomon, the overwhelmingly important figure among twenty-four "stars" of theological and religious importance, as agents of explanation of Dante's function in his own poem, as prophet, as poet, as supporter of the imperial monarchy.

142. As a coda to the Solomon theme, present on and off since *Paradiso* X.109 and that was almost immediately accompanied by its hallmark, the verb *surgere* (*Par.* X.114; X.140; XIII.106), the poet marks the conclusion of that thematic unit with its final presence.

PARADISO XIV

OUTLINE

THE SUN; MARS

1–9 the canto begins with an "implicit simile": water in a bowl that moves in waves from outer rim to center (or the obverse) and Thomas's voice at "perimeter" (and Beatrice's at "center") of the circle made by theologians

10–18 Beatrice intuits Dante's two questions: (1) Will the bodies of the saints shine eternally? (2) If so, how will onlookers' eyes endure so brilliant a light?

19–24 simile (2): as dancers in a circle become more excited in their singing and gestures as the dance continues, so did the holy circle react to Dante's question

25–27 and no one witnessing this could lament its price, death

28–33 this trinitarian sphere (of the Sun—see *Par.* X.1f.) is thrice marked again by the souls' trinitarian song.

34–36 The voice of the most divine member of the inner circle **[Solomon]** is compared to the voice of **[Gabriel]** to **Mary**:

37–42 [Solomon]: "our brightness corresponds to our ardor, our ardor to our power of sight, and that power to our grace

43–45 "once we are in flesh again, we will be more acceptable to God for being more complete

46–51 "when this is true, God's gift of grace will be increased as must our vision of Him, as must the ardor of our love, as must the brightness of our light

52–57 [simile (3)] "a glowing coal seen within the flame that it produces resembles the glowing body that will be added to the shining presences of these souls

58–60 "our bodily organs will be strong enough to sustain the sight of the glorified body."

61–66 The two circles of saints make Solomon's prayer their own

67–69 simile (4): the main "event," the third circle of lights

70–75 simile (5): evening stars compared to newly visible souls

76–78 the poet's apostrophe: true sparkling of the Holy Spirit!

79–81 Beatrice's smiling beauty too affecting to be remembered

82–87 the ascent to **Mars**, the smiling, reddening star

88–96 Dante's prayer of thanksgiving to God; the star's warm reaction; Dante's mixed-language response

97–102 simile (6): Milky Way seen as cross of crusading saints

103–108 the poet remembers the moment but cannot express it

109–117 simile (7): souls moving along the limbs of the cross and motes in rays of sunlight passing through slats of shades

118–123 simile (8): harmonies (not melody) of bowed instruments and harps compared to melody sung from cross (not words)

124–129 Dante heard "Risurgi" and "Vinci" but not the rest and is moved to love more than he has ever been before

130–132 perhaps that goes too far for seeming to slight Beatrice

133–139 the poet's complicated self-exculpation.

PARADISO XIV

Dal centro al cerchio, e sì dal cerchio al centro
movesi l'acqua in un ritondo vaso,
secondo ch'è percosso fuori o dentro:

ne la mia mente fé sùbito caso
questo ch'io dico, sì come si tacque
la glorïosa vita di Tommaso,

per la similitudine che nacque
del suo parlare e di quel di Beatrice,
a cui sì cominciar, dopo lui, piacque:

"A costui fa mestieri, e nol vi dice
né con la voce né pensando ancora,
d'un altro vero andare a la radice.

Diteli se la luce onde s'infiora
vostra sustanza, rimarrà con voi
etternalmente sì com' ell' è ora;

e se rimane, dite come, poi
che sarete visibili rifatti,
esser porà ch'al veder non vi nòi."

Come, da più letizia pinti e tratti,
a la fiata quei che vanno a rota
levan la voce e rallegrano li atti,

così, a l'orazion pronta e divota,
li santi cerchi mostrar nova gioia
nel torneare e ne la mira nota.

Qual si lamenta perché qui si moia
per viver colà sù, non vide quive
lo refrigerio de l'etterna ploia.

From center to rim, as from rim to center,
the water in a rounded vessel moves
as it is struck from outside or within.

This thought, just as I phrase it,
dropped into my mind the very instant
the glorious living soul of Thomas fell silent,

because of the like effects that sprang
from his speech and from the words of Beatrice,
who, responding, graciously began:

'This man has need, but does not tell of it
either by word or yet in thought,
because he seeks the root of still another truth.

'Tell him if the light that blooms
and makes your substance radiant shall remain
with you eternally the way it shines today,

'and, if it remains, tell him how,
when all of you are visible once more,
this would not prove distressing to your sight.'

As, impelled and drawn by heightened joy,
dancers in a round may raise their voices,
their pleasure showing in their movements,

so, at that eager and devout appeal,
the holy circles showed new joy in wheeling
as well as in their wondrous song.

Whoever here on earth laments that we must die
to find our life above knows not the fresh relief
found there in these eternal showers.

Quell' uno e due e tre che sempre vive
e regna sempre in tre e 'n due e 'n uno,
non circunscritto, e tutto circunscrive,

tre volte era cantato da ciascuno
di quelli spiriti con tal melodia,
ch'ad ogne merto saria giusto muno.

E io udi' ne la luce più dia
del minor cerchio una voce modesta,
forse qual fu da l'angelo a Maria,

risponder: "Quanto fia lunga la festa
di paradiso, tanto il nostro amore
si raggerà dintorno cotal vesta.

La sua chiarezza séguita l'ardore;
l'ardor la visïone, e quella è tanta,
quant' ha di grazia sovra suo valore.

Come la carne glorïosa e santa
fia rivestita, la nostra persona
più grata fia per esser tutta quanta;

per che s'accrescerà ciò che ne dona
di gratüito lume il sommo bene,
lume ch'a lui veder ne condiziona;

onde la visïon crescer convene,
crescer l'ardor che di quella s'accende,
crescer lo raggio che da esso vene.

Ma sì come carbon che fiamma rende,
e per vivo candor quella soverchia,
sì che la sua parvenza si difende;

così questo folgór che già ne cerchia
fia vinto in apparenza da la carne
che tutto dì la terra ricoperchia;

That ever-living One and Two and Three
who reigns forever in Three and Two and One,
uncircumscribed and circumscribing all,

was sung three times by each and every one
of these spirits, and with such melody
as would be fit reward for any merit.

And I heard in the most resplendent light
of the lesser circle a modest voice,
such perhaps as the angel's was to Mary,

reply: 'Just as long as the festival of Paradise
shall last, that is how long our love
shall dress us in this radiance.

'Its brightness answers to our ardor,
the ardor to our vision, and that is given
in greater measure of grace than we deserve.

'When we put on again our flesh,
glorified and holy, then our persons
will be more pleasing for being all complete,

'so that the light, granted to us freely
by the Highest Good, shall increase,
the light that makes us fit to see Him.

'From that light, vision must increase,
and love increase what vision kindles,
and radiance increase, which comes from love.

'But like a coal that shoots out flame
and in its glowing center still outshines it
so that it does not lose its own appearance,

'just so this splendor that enfolds us now
will be surpassed in brightness by the flesh
that earth as yet still covers.

né potrà tanta luce affaticarne:
ché li organi del corpo saran forti
a tutto ciò che potrà dilettarne."

Tanto mi parver sùbiti e accorti
e l'uno e l'altro coro a dicer "Amme!"
che ben mostrar disio d'i corpi morti:

forse non pur per lor, ma per le mamme,
per li padri e per li altri che fuor cari
anzi che fosser sempiterne fiamme.

Ed ecco intorno, di chiarezza pari,
nascere un lustro sopra quel che v'era,
per guisa d'orizzonte che rischiari.

E sì come al salir di prima sera
comincian per lo ciel nove parvenze,
sì che la vista pare e non par vera,

parvemi lì novelle sussistenze
cominciare a vedere, e fare un giro
di fuor da l'altre due circunferenze.

Oh vero sfavillar del Santo Spiro!
come si fece sùbito e candente
a li occhi miei che, vinti, nol soffriro!

Ma Bëatrice sì bella e ridente
mi si mostrò, che tra quelle vedute
si vuol lasciar che non seguir la mente.

Quindi ripreser li occhi miei virtute
a rilevarsi; e vidimi translato
sol con mia donna in più alta salute.

Ben m'accors' io ch'io era più levato,
per l'affocato riso de la stella,
che mi parea più roggio che l'usato.

'Nor will such shining have the power to harm us,
for our body's organs shall be strengthened
to deal with all that can delight us.'

So quick and eager seemed to me both choirs
to say their *Amen* that they clearly showed
their desire for their dead bodies,

not perhaps for themselves alone, but for their mothers,
for their fathers, and for others whom they loved
before they all became eternal flames.

And lo, all around and all of equal brightness,
rose a splendor, surpassing what had been,
as the horizon, at the rising sun, grows brighter.

And just as, at the approach of evening,
new lights begin to show throughout the sky,
so faint they seem both real and yet unreal,

it seemed to me that I began to see
new subsistences there that formed a ring
beyond the other two circumferences.

Ah, true incandescence of the Holy Breath!
How suddenly its glowing shone before me,
so bright my eyes could not endure it!

But Beatrice showed herself to me so fair
and smiling, this vision of her must remain
among those sights that have escaped my memory.

At this my eyes regained their sight and, raising them,
I saw myself translated, alone now with my lady,
to a more exalted state of bliss.

I was assured that I had risen higher
by the planet's fiery smile. It seemed to me
to glow more red than usual.

Con tutto 'l core e con quella favella
ch'è una in tutti, a Dio feci olocausto,
qual conveniesi a la grazia novella.

E non er' anco del mio petto essausto
l'ardor del sacrificio, ch'io conobbi
esso litare stato accetto e fausto;

ché con tanto lucore e tanto robbi
m'apparvero splendor dentro a due raggi,
ch'io dissi: "O Elïòs che sì li addobbi!"

Come distinta da minori e maggi
lumi biancheggia tra ' poli del mondo
Galassia sì, che fa dubbiar ben saggi;

sì costellati facean nel profondo
Marte quei raggi il venerabil segno
che fan giunture di quadranti in tondo.

Qui vince la memoria mia lo 'ngegno;
ché quella croce lampeggiava Cristo,
sì ch'io non so trovare essempro degno;

ma chi prende sua croce e segue Cristo,
ancor mi scuserà di quel ch'io lasso,
vedendo in quell' albor balenar Cristo.

Di corno in corno e tra la cima e 'l basso
si movien lumi, scintillando forte
nel congiugnersi insieme e nel trapasso:

così si veggion qui diritte e torte,
veloci e tarde, rinovando vista,
le minuzie d'i corpi, lunghe e corte,

moversi per lo raggio onde si lista
talvolta l'ombra che, per sua difesa,
la gente con ingegno e arte acquista.

With all my heart and in that tongue
which is the same for all, I made
burnt-offering to God befitting the new grace.

And the burning of the sacrifice
had not yet finished in my breast before I knew
my offering was propitious and accepted,

for splendors of such brightness, glowing red,
appeared to me within two beams that I cried out:
'O Helios, who so adorn them!'

As the Milky Way, arrayed with greater and lesser lights,
glows white between the universal poles,
making even sages wonder how and why,

these rays, thus constellated, made, deep within Mars,
the venerable sign that the crossing
of its quadrants fixes in a circle.

Here my memory outstrips my skill,
for that cross so flamed forth Christ
that I can find no fit comparison.

But he who takes his cross and follows Christ
shall yet forgive me what I leave untold,
for shining in that dawn I did see Christ.

From arm to arm, and between the head
and foot, moved brilliant lights
that scintillated as they met and passed.

Just so we see on earth, straight and slanting,
swift and slow, changing in appearance,
tiny motes of matter, long and short,

move through the beam of light that sometimes streaks
the shades that men devise for their protection
both with cunning and with skill.

E come giga e arpa, in tempra tesa
di molte corde, fa dolce tintinno
a tal da cui la nota non è intesa,

così da' lumi che lì m'apparinno
s'accogliea per la croce una melode
che mi rapiva, sanza intender l'inno.

Ben m'accors' io ch'elli era d'alte lode,
però ch'a me venìa "Resurgi" e "Vinci"
come a colui che non intende e ode.

Ïo m'innamorava tanto quinci,
che 'nfino a lì non fu alcuna cosa
che mi legasse con sì dolci vinci.

Forse la mia parola par troppo osa,
posponendo il piacer de li occhi belli,
ne' quai mirando mio disio ha posa;

ma chi s'avvede che i vivi suggelli
d'ogne bellezza più fanno più suso,
e ch'io non m'era lì rivolto a quelli,

escusar puommi di quel ch'io m'accuso
per escusarmi, e vedermi dir vero:
ché 'l piacer santo non è qui dischiuso,
perché si fa, montando, più sincero.

And as viol and harp strung with many strings
in their harmony will sound sweet
120 even to one who fails to catch their tune,

so from the lights that there appeared to me
a melody gathered and came from the cross,
123 enchanting me, though I could not make out the hymn.

I could tell that it contained high praise,
for the words 'Arise' and 'Conquer' came to me
126 as to one who hears but does not understand.

I was moved to such great love by this
that up until that moment I had not been bound
129 by chains so sweet and gentle.

My words, perhaps, may seem too bold,
slighting the beauty of those lovely eyes—
132 gazing into them my longing finds repose.

But one who understands that the living seals
of all that's beautiful gain potency with each ascent
135 and that I had not turned to her eyes there

may excuse me for that of which, accusing myself,
I make my excuse and see that I speak the truth:
for holy beauty may not be excluded here
139 because, as it ascends, it gains in purity.

1–9. A simile, with the formal markers of the trope suppressed (e.g., "just as," "so," "like") but with reference to its literary kind embedded in it (*similitudine* [a hapax, verse 7]), this comparison of the sounds of Thomas's voice, at the circumference of the smaller circle of saints, and of Beatrice's, issuing from near Dante at the center of that circle, draws attention to the mind of its maker, a witness of such celestial phenomena. The meaning is clear enough, if some have stumbled over the question of how water in the center of a bowl may be struck (answer: by something falling from above [like the thought that drops into Dante's mind—see the last part of the note to vv. 7–9]).

4. The Latinism *caso*, for "fall," is used uniquely here; ordinarily in the *Commedia* the word means either "chance" or "instance."

6. The use of the word "vita" to designate the soul of Thomas echoes *Paradiso* XII.127, describing the living soul (*vita*) of Bonaventure. See the note to *Paradiso* IX.7.

7–9. Just as the previous canto, in order to introduce a new group of saved souls, had begun with two instantaneously coupled links in a chain of events, the first of which is Thomas's speaking his concluding word (*Par.* XI.139 and XII.1–3), so now does this one. The utterance of Beatrice here comes hard upon Thomas's last word. It is probably not accidental that the Latinism *caso* in verse 4 reflects that particular word, *cadere*. Thomas says "fall" and it "falls" into Dante's mind that the discourses of Thomas and Beatrice are similar. That similarity is assumed to be obvious by most of the commentators, who, at any rate, do not trouble to discuss it. However, it is not finally clear what is meant. Thomas has just finished a longish discourse (*Par.* XIII.112–142) about the limited capacity of human knowledge. Beatrice's nine verses insist on the same thing: She knows what Dante wants to know even before he does. What these two saved souls share intellectually is the ability common to those who dwell in the Empyrean to know all that is knowable, and to know it in God (including, clearly, as the next tercet demonstrates, the future thoughts of mortals before they think them).

10–18. These are Beatrice's first words since *Paradiso* X.52–54 (her longest silence since she entered the poem in *Purgatorio* XXX; she will not speak again until *Par.* XVII.7, and then only briefly), just before Thomas began speaking at X.82. Thomas and Cacciaguida are two of the most voluble characters Dante meets in the afterlife. While they speak less than do the most present and loquacious of the guides, Virgil and Beatrice, not even the more mobile Statius or the presiding figure in the Empyrean, St. Bernard, speaks as much as either of these within their respective heavens. They are allowed to push Beatrice to the periphery of the discourse.

Dante, Beatrice says, will want to know two related things. She is addressing her request to all the saints in both the circles (all her pronouns are plural; we shall see that she is addressing all twenty-four of them by the plural *cerchi* [circles] of verse 23). One of them will step forward to deal with Dante's questions; if we expect Thomas—we would be excused if we did—we will be surprised.

The questions she attributes to Dante are: (1) Will the light that you give off be yours in eternity? (2) If it will, how will you not be blinded by one another once you get your bodies back (and become all the more resplendent)?

19–24. As opposed to the first simile in the canto (see the note to vv. 1–9), this one is fully expressed in the conventional mode, both tenor and vehicle keyed by the expected terms of comparison (*Come . . . così*). As circling dancers here on earth sometimes show greater pleasure by moving more animatedly and singing, so these twenty-four souls revealed (by moving more animatedly and singing) that they were pleased by Beatrice's request (they obviously take delight in being able to make others feel more joy).

25–27. Contemporary readers, who think of rain only as an inhibitor of outdoor relaxation or of light chores on a summer's day, will not see the point in this exaltation of a cooling shower in the sweltering Tuscan (un-air-conditioned) summertime. For the opposite sort of rain, see *Inferno* VI.7–12.

28–29. Lombardi (comm. to vv. 28–32) points out that none of the earlier commentators had revealed the plan in the first two lines, which is to set the "one" of the first verse against the "three" of the second, and the "three" of the first against the "one" of the second, thus making dramatic the relations of the Trinity, one-in-three as well as three-in-one. He also discusses the significance of the parallel relation between the two "two"s in the lines, representing the human and divine united in the Second Person of the Trinity. Porena (comm. to these verses) summarizes what is presented here succinctly: "Theological designation of God, who lives and reigns eternally as a single Substance, two Natures, and three Persons."

It took a bit longer until the palindromatic structure of these verses was understood as reflecting Joachim of Flora's structure of history, with its three great Ages: the first, of the Father; the second, of the Son; the third, of the Spirit. See the note to vv. 67–78. And see one of the "additional drawings" in the *Liber figurarum* (Reev.1972.1) for the three overlapping circles representing the three Ages. See also Dronke (Dron.1975.2), pp. 7–9.

30. Compare *Purgatorio* XI.1–2: "Our Father, who are in Heaven, / circumscribed only by the greater love. . . ."

31–32. This hymn to the Trinity, like that which it celebrates, blends multiplicity and unity, in this case twenty-four voices heard as one.

33. The Latinism *muno* (from the noun *munus*), a hapax in the poem clearly forced by rhyme, means "gift, reward." The reader may choose to honor (or not to) the Ottimo's apparent acceptance of the claim (comm. to *Inf.* X.85–87) that he says Dante once made to him: Not only did rhyme never force him into saying other than he intended to say, but he was able to make words in the rhyme position mean other than what they had meant in the work of previous poets.

See the note to *Paradiso* 1.13–15 for the use of *munus* in the *Epistle to Cangrande*.

34–36. From the earliest commentators on, for example, Jacopo della Lana (comm. to verse 34), writers have identified this unnamed figure as Solomon. In light of *Paradiso* X.109, which says that his light was the most beautiful in his circle, it is difficult not to. However, Francesco da Buti is the first commentator to hesitate to the point of not naming any one of the twelve in the first circle; perhaps his hesitation, shared by several, as we shall see, accounts for some of the continuing doubt about the identity of this singer. Landino (comm. to this tercet) advocates the candidacy of Peter Lombard; we find Vellutello (comm to vv. 34–39) denying that this is he, and joining those who believe it is Solomon. Both Gabriele (comm. to verse 34) and his pupil, Daniello (comm. to this tercet) abstain. In more modern times a similar profile describes the debate, with almost all thinking it is Solomon to whom reference is made. However, Porena's uneasiness is perhaps instructive (comm. to vv. 34–35). He suggests that Solomon may be here only because he was seen as the brightest star in his circle in *Paradiso* X (one would like to ask Porena why Dante has so described him if he did not mean anything by the remark). He goes on to wonder why Solomon is never mentioned by name—a worthy question. It is also clear that he is a bit concerned by the fleshly activities and celebrations of the king. Chiarenza (Chia.2000.1), p. 206, on the other hand, insists on Solomon's value, in Dante's eyes, for his heightened sense of the importance of the flesh. She also points out Dante's practice of not naming him, but always (*Purg.* XXX.10, *Par.* X.109, and here) presenting him as a privileged member of a group (pp. 206–7), thus looking at the same phenomenon that makes Porena feel that Dante is uncomfortable with his own treatment of Solomon, while Chiarenza sees, much more steadily, that he is playing off *our* discomfort. (For an example of that discomfort, see Carroll's remarks in the note to *Paradiso* XIII.97–102.)

It seems clear that this is indeed Solomon, and that Dante values him very highly, ranking him even higher than Thomas, both in the description of his brightness in Canto X and in choosing him to hold the last and privileged position in the heaven of the Sun. If we reflect how surely we expect Thomas to answer Beatrice's formulations of Dante's doubts (let the reader start reading again at Canto X and come to this canto innocent of both knowledge and inclination: Will not he or she expect Thomas to take command once more?), we can recapture some of our original surprise at finding not Thomas but Solomon here. And, as Scartazzini (comm. to verse 34) reminds us (Carroll [comm. to vv. 34–60] allows the same point), a passage in Ecclesiastes (3:18–22) reveals Solomon's skepticism about the destination of the soul after the death of the body. Carroll's treatment, unlike Scartazzini's, goes on to argue that an expert of no less authority than Aquinas asserts (*ST* I, q. 75, a. 6) that in this passage Solomon is speaking "in the character of the foolish" about an error of others that he states in order to refute. Whether Scartazzini or Carroll is right, it does seem that Dante knows that even in asserting that Solomon was saved, he was taking on some pretty estimable adversaries (e.g., Augustine); in making him an authority on the Trinity and the general resurrection, he has, once again, chosen to live dangerously.

34. The adjective *dia* can mean (and it has had both meanings in the poem) "divine" or "shining." We have followed Bosco/Reggio (comm. to vv. 34–35) and many others in believing that here it possesses the latter meaning.

35. The word *modesta* sent Tommaseo (comm. to vv. 34–36) in a direction Erich Auerbach would explore more amply in his essay *"Sermo humilis"* (Auer.1958.1). Tommaseo hears the voice of Beatrice beneath this verse. See *Inferno* II.56–57, where she is reported by Virgil to have spoken to him on her visit to Limbo "soave e piana, / con angelica voce, in sua favella" (gentle and clear . . . —/ an angel's voice was in her speech). And see the note to *Inferno* II.56–57. See also Nasti (Nast.2001.1), p. 120.

36. The reference to Gabriel and the Annunciation is a brief, iconographic way to connect this passage to the Song of Solomon, the wedding song of Christ and his Bride (the Church), as it was interpreted by generations of Christian exegetes.

37–60. Solomon's hymn, so different in technique from Thomas's "Scholastic" verses in these cantos, really does seem intended to imitate the warmth and poetic quality of the Canticle of Canticles. He answers Dante's two questions (vv. 37–57: In the rest of time the saved shall shine as brightly as we do here and now, until, after the general resurrection, the renewed presence of our bodies will make us shine more brightly still; vv. 58–60: Indeed, our restored senses, stronger than they are now, will be capable of looking on this even greater brightness). However, he does so by singing what can only be regarded as a hymn to the general resurrection, to borrow from Momigliano (comm. to vv. 28–33), a passage of critical prose that captures, as well perhaps as any has ever done, the thread uniting this entire canto, a celebration that combines praise of the Trinity and of the Resurrection. In an only human view, these two moments are registered as the birth and death of Jesus.

37–39. Solomon responds to Beatrice's question on Dante's behalf of all the spirits gathered in the Sun (see vv. 13–15), the answer to which is "we shall be resplendent eternally."

40–51. For a discussion of previous notice (that of Umberto Bosco and of Patrick Boyde) of the way in which this passage is complementary to *Inferno* VI.106–111, where Virgil tells Dante that after the Last Judgment and the recovery of their bodies, the sinners will feel more pain, see Gragnolati (Grag.2005.1), pp. 154–57. Solomon's words clearly state that the reclad soul will have greater powers of sight, and thus, it would follow, greater joy in seeing both the "soldiery of Paradise" and God Himself.

For interesting and pertinent remarks about the rhetorical figure *chi-*

asmus in this canto, beginning with its first verse and culminating in Solomon's speech, in these twelve verses, see Sowell (Sowe.1995.1), pp. 201–5. This trope derives its name from the Greek character transliterated as *chi* and expressed as "X"; thus, like the two major elements in the letter "x" (> <), a mirror image, for example, "apple baby castle . . . castle baby apple." Depending on its context, it may also put the reader in mind of the chiasmus-shaped Cross of Christ, as well as of the first letter of His name.

40–42. In the first of two "interlaced" tercets, Solomon, like Gabriel in verse 35, is modest, more modest than reading him might prepare us to find. The more grace he and his fellow saints experience, the better they see God; the better they see Him, the more they love Him; the more they love Him, the brighter they will shine. The verses run back down the chain of cause and effect. Compare the tercet at vv. 49–51 for a second example of this sort of interlacing. There the order is natural, that is, we move from seeing to loving to shining.

49–51. See the note to vv. 40–42.

52–57. In marked contrast to Thomas, who only rarely sounds "poetic" (but see the note to *Par.* XI.19–21), Solomon here is granted one of the few similes allowed a speaker in the poem (we have not encountered a simile since the one on Iris in *Par.* XII.10–21). This further identifies him with Dante and the world of poetry, eclipsing Thomas at least a little. This is not to say that Dante does not value Thomas; he values hardly anyone more. But it is also time for taking some good-natured revenge on the man who labored to belittle poetry and poets.

There are some 628 verses in the heaven of the Sun, nearly half of them (287) spoken by Thomas, poetry's confirmed enemy. Further, Dante is silent in all of this heaven, as though to match Thomas by opposition, switching roles with him. This is the only "zone" of the entire poem in which the protagonist does not say a single word.

58–60. Solomon concludes by responding to Beatrice's representation of Dante's second question (see vv. 16–18). The glorified body will not be too strongly bright for the eyes of the saved, perhaps because their own resurrected bodies will possess capacities their earthly ones did not, in this case superhuman eyesight. Dante's question was based solely on a normal human understanding of immortality, that is, on ignorance.

61–66. The twenty-four souls in the first two circles, moved by Solomon's words, show their desire to put on their resurrected flesh, and perhaps for the same result for all those other saved souls whom they love.

The reader who believes that Dante is not sympathetic to our physical selves will have to acknowledge that this passage establishes his credibility as a human being who, like Solomon, accepts the fact of our corporeal existence and finds it good. For Dante's view of the resurrected body, see Jacoff (Jaco.2000.1). See also Bynum (Bynu.1995.1), pp. 291–305. And see Picone (Pico.2002.4), pp. 212–13, n. 21, for a bibliography of some European contributions on this subject.

62. The Hebrew word "amen" is given here in its Tuscan form, *amme,* as part of Dante's program of expressing sacred truth in the low vernacular. See the note to verse 64.

64. The use of the word *mamme,* although forced by rhyme, is nonetheless striking. Such usage of the low-vernacular "mommies" is at one with the context, a soft-hued family portrait of saved humanity, as it were. Our translation deploys the less disturbing "mothers" because of its pairing with *padri* (rather than *babbi,* "daddies"). See the notes to *Inferno* XXXII.1–9 and *Purgatorio* XXI.97–99.

67–78. This supercharged passage has begun to be understood only in the past 101 years. An undergraduate student, Randy Mamiaro (Princeton '80), caused a stir in class when (in December 1979) he suggested that this third circle, tacitly parallel in number with the first two, contained the twelve apostles, who manifested themselves here as a sign of their approval of Solomon's words. Were not the apostles closely associated with the Holy Spirit, referred to in verse 76, represented as descending on them with the gift of tongues (Acts 2:3–4)? And would not they represent a fitting final group of twelve to accompany the first two that have come forward? Mamiaro's might still be a promising hypothesis, had not Peter Dronke in an article (Dron.1975.2, esp. pp. 10–16) shown convincingly that what Dante has built into his poem is a highly structured reference to Joachim of Flora's "Third Age," "the Age of the [Holy] Spirit," when the Church shall be taken up and each Christian living in the Spirit will be his or her own priest (and thus the numerically unspecified multitude of these many souls [a problem not well dealt with by Mamiaro's hypothesis]). Consequently, the first two circles in the Sun probably are related to Joachim's Age of the Father and Age of the Son, respectively. Dronke's thesis should have found more favor than it has. But see Picone (Pico.2002.4), p. 211, and Merlante and Prandi (Merl.2005.1), in notes to vv. 28 and 76–78, acknowledging his contribution. How often in Dante studies can one say that a new reading has completely altered our sense not only of the meaning of a text, but of its intellectual provenance as well? However, Dronke's discovery (he gives credit, for a first effort in this direction, to Leone Tondelli [Tond.1940.1, pp. 260–62]), had in fact been made by another, some three score and ten years earlier, John S. Carroll (comm. to these verses). (And Carroll, as far as one can see, has been omitted from the post-Dronke discussion.) In a long gloss, a portion of which follows, Carroll makes his case: "Now, it seems to me clear that Dante in this third circle wished to show how far his sympathy with these Joachimite views went. In general, he accepts the doctrine of a third era of the Holy Spirit. If we take the three circles to correspond to the Trinity, we may say that the first, the Dominican, represents the Father, the reign of law and fear; and the second, the Franciscan, the Son, the favour of the grace of Christ, whose image St. Francis bore. But Dante believes that these two types do not exhaust the possibilities of Theology. Joachim and his followers were not mistaken in their hope of a third era worthy to be called, in comparison with the others, the 'true sparkling of the Holy Spirit,' far wider in its range, far more brilliant in its shining. Dante cannot describe it definitely; it lies far off on the dim horizon of the future. It has the mystery of the evening when the stars are scarcely seen, for it is the passing away of one era. It has the mystery of the morning when the dawn whitens, for it is the beginning of a new day of the Spirit—perhaps the eternal day itself." John Saly (Saly.1989.1), pp. 14–15, also sees this third circle of souls as signifying Joachim's Third Age, but seems unaware of his precursors in this belief.

The only problem inherent in the Carroll/Dronke hypothesis is that, while the souls in the first two circles have all finished their lives on earth and assumed their seats in the Empyrean, those in Joachim's prophetic text have not. On the other hand, there is no reason to believe that Dante thought Joachim's Third Age had begun yet. Thus his text, like Joachim's, is prophetic, and Joachim is not the only presence in the poem "di spirito profetico dotato" (endowed with the spirit of prophecy—*Par.* XII.141). Further, the imprecise nature of their number and the fact that they are not recognizable to Dante accords with their status as the unnumbered and unnamed ranks of a Joachite New Age. Singleton (comm. to vv. 74–76) correctly notes that "the context and simile clearly suggest that they are a multitude and not merely twelve lights."

67. Bosco/Reggio point out (comm. to this verse) that, as usual, the phrasing "Ed ecco" (And lo) alerts the reader to a change in focus. We might expect, as a result, a change of venue, that is, the ascent to a higher sphere. But this is rather a totally new experience contained within the current heaven, one that is marked off as being exceptional in every way.

68. The word *lustro* (the noun "shining") occurs only one other time in the poem (*Purg.* XXIX.16). There it describes the brightness of the Church Triumphant in procession as Matelda and Dante first behold that pageant.

70–75. This simile, matching in its sweet tones and glowing, soft colors the tranquility of verses 61–66, misled Vellutello (comm. to vv. 70–78) into thinking the *novelle sussistenze* were angels (as they were in *Par.* XIII.59) rather than souls, and Lombardi (comm. to vv. 70–75) into believing this circle is the first thing seen in the sphere of Mars rather than the last in the Sun.

73. The word *sussistenza* (see the note to *Par.* XIII.59) is here used, by the consent of most discussants, to refer not to angelic substances but to saved souls. Tommaseo is quite sure, however, that even that last use of the word refers to angels. Benvenuto (comm. to vv. 70–75) was perhaps the first reader to identify the *sussistenze* as "the blessed souls in this third circle."

76–81. If Dante is unable to look upon the working of the Holy Spirit, evident in the movements of this circle, he can fix his eyes on Beatrice's smile—if he cannot bring that back to mind, for her increased beauty is beyond the capacity of his memory.

While one can understand the theological reasons that make it imperative to realize that Beatrice becomes more beautiful both as she gets closer to God and as Dante's capacity to perceive her true nature improves, had the poet stinted on the number of occasions he informs us of their reciprocal progress, the likelihood is that few of us would have complained.

82–87. The ascent to Mars is accomplished with relatively little fanfare and as little poetic space as all but one ascent to a higher sphere (Venus, at *Par.* VIII.13–15) before it. Compare *Paradiso* I.61–81; V.88–99; X.28–39.

83. This is Dante's only use in his poem of the Latinism *translato* (in this context, literally "carried up to"). See Sowell (Sowe.1995.1), p. 201, for

the recognition of a biblical precursor. Paul speaks of God's having snatched us from the power of darkness and *translated* us to His Son's kingdom, where we will dwell in light (Colossians 1:13). But see as well the only other presence of *transferre* in the New Testament, also Pauline (as far as Dante knew, Paul was the writer of the Epistle to the Hebrews): Hebrews 11:5.

86–87. That Mars is the "red planet" is an ancient tradition. That it becomes more red as a sign of welcome to Beatrice echoes the sign made in response to her arrival in the planet Mercury (*Par.* V.96).

88–96. If the ascent to Mars is not particularly noteworthy, the description of Dante's prayer of thanksgiving most certainly is. There are nine occurrences of hapax in these nine verses (*olocausto, essausto, litare, accetto, fausto, lucore, robbi, Eliòs, addobbi*), a sure sign of heightened emotion. And the passage concludes with Dante's first spoken words since Canto X (verse 81), as Barolini (Baro.1992.1), p. 334, n. 8, has observed. Language, as we shall see, is a continuing concern as we move through this entire sphere. Those who like to find Dante's identification of the seven liberal arts with the planets in the *Convivio* (II.xiii.8–30) at work in *Paradiso* must here justify the prior identification of Mars with music (*Conv.* II.xiii.20), a relationship in *Paradiso* perhaps more plausibly adduced from the sphere of the Sun.

88. Portirelli (comm. to vv. 88–96) interprets the phrase "that tongue which is the same for all" as meaning "the inner feelings of the mind, the same in all languages," a view that had been widely embraced as early as the fourteenth century. Dante is evidently referring to mental constructions, preverbal thoughts, which match one another perfectly until they are put into expression in various languages, when they may have small resemblance to one another. See John of Serravalle (comm. to vv. 88–90): "Conceptus mentis sunt idem in omnibus hominibus, loquela vero non sic" (Mental constructs are identical in all humans, but not the words [that are used to express them]). Dante is perhaps suggesting that there exists an ideal universal vernacular innate in all of us. See the note to *Paradiso* XV.39.

89. The word *olocausto* means, literally, "burnt offering," as verse 92 makes plain. For such sacrifice recorded in the Old Testament, most memorably in Abraham's eventually jettisoned intention to make a burnt offering of his son Isaac, see Genesis 22:2, 22:7, 22:8, 22:13. See the prior reference in *Paradiso* V.29.

Jacopo della Lana (comm. to vv. 88–90), the Ottimo (comm. to vv. 88–89), and Pietro Alighieri (comm. to vv. 85–90) all say that "olocausto" involves sacrifice of the whole object, while "sacrificio" involves only a part of it.

94. The redness of Mars is insisted on once again, this time increasing in its glow in response to Dante's offering of his gratitude.

95. The two beams, as we shall see, in fact constitute the cross of Mars.

96. For the meaning of *Eliòs*, Torraca (comm. to vv. 94–96) may have been the first to cite Toynbee (Toyn.1902.1), p. 112, for Dante's dependence on Uguccione da Pisa: "Ab *ely*, quod est deus, dictus est sol *elyos*, quod pro deo olim reputabatur" (From *ely*, which means "God," the sun, which once was considered God, is called *elyos*). The protagonist may here be presented as speaking in tongues, or at least a mixture of two biblical languages. His first word in particular, the name of God, reflects Hebrew (*Eli* [see *Purg.* XXIII.74]) and Greek (*Helios*).

The verb *addobbare* (a hapax in the poem, probably meaning "to adorn") is generally understood to refer to the wearing of ornamental clothing, since it usually refers to a person as being adorned, with the range of the verb's meaning here being extended to light. However, a persistent temptation in the commentaries is to see the verb as reflecting the French verb *adober* (English "dub"), as in striking a knight on the shoulder with a sword as part of the ceremony that reflects his worthiness. See Giacalone (comm. to verse 96).

97–102. The first simile in the heaven of Mars compares the small, nearly invisible stars that make up the Milky Way (*la Galassia*) to the souls who make up the cross of Mars (for Dante's learned discussion of the conflicting theories accounting for the existence of this celestial phenomenon, see *Convivio* II.xiv.5–8). Again, those who want to argue for a correspondence between *Convivio*'s alignment of the human arts and sciences with the heavens of *Paradiso* face a large (insurmountable?) problem. In *Convivio* (II.xiv.5), Dante associates *la Galassia* with metaphysics. Here it is associated neither with the Sun (which may have created it) nor with the Fixed Stars (where Dante locates it in *Convivio*) but with Mars, associated with music in *Convivio* (see the end of the note to vv. 88–96).

101. Mars seems previously to have had both negative and positive associations for Dante (see *Conv.* II.xiii.20–24), if not the same positive ones

that we find in the *Commedia*; in the earlier work Mars is associated with musical harmony as well as the destructiveness of war. In the *Commedia*, as the pagan god of war (e.g., *Inf.* XXIV.145; *Inf.* XXXI.51; *Purg.* XII.31), he is hardly praised. In his second aspect, he is sanitized (as he intrinsically is here) as the representative of the Christian warrior. C. S. Lewis (Lewi. 1964.1), p. 106, pegs Dante's positive sense of the pagan god to the term *martire* (martyr), as derivative of "Mars."

103–108. These tercets contain the second set (of four) triple identical rhymes on *Cristo* found in the poem (for the first, see *Par.* XII.71–75; also see the note to that passage).

Beginning with the notice of the fact that the *Cristo*-rhymes in Cantos XIV and XIX of the *Paradiso* appear in exactly the same lines (104, 106, and 108), Thomas Hart performs a series of calculations to demonstrate that Dante had employed ratios used to calculate the circumference of a circle to predetermine the precise locations in the poem of all four of these rhymes; these ratios in turn suggest the quadrants of a circumscribed Greek cross (formed by two diameters at right angles to one another). For more on the question of Dante's numerical composition, see Hart's various studies, as referred to in what may serve as a sort of compendium of them (Hart.1995.1).

103. The ineffability of what the narrator has seen will become increasingly a theme of the poem as it nears its (ineffable) vision of God. His poetic ability (and here *ingegno* clearly refers to Dante's art, not God's [see the note to *Inf.* II.7–9]) is simply not able to represent adequately the amazing things that he is indeed capable of holding in mind. By the end of the poem he will not be able to do that, either.

106. Dante's phrasing follows closely the words of Christ in Matthew 16:24: "Let him who wishes to follow me deny himself and take up his cross and follow me" (see Jacopo della Lana [comm. to vv. 106–108] and many others).

108. See Bosco/Reggio (comm. to this verse) for a summary of the debate over this line. We have followed them in thinking the gerund *vedendo* describes Dante, and not the Christian soldier he is addressing indirectly. One of the main justifications for their argument is the fact that no soul on its way to God should come by this route (we are allowed to assume that all go directly to the Empyrean). Further, and perhaps more tellingly, this cross of Christian soldiers will no longer be here, since all who appear

in all the spheres are there only temporarily, for the sake of Dante's education. On the other hand, the passage does read more readily the "wrong" way. And it was only fairly recently that anyone objected to that understanding (e.g., Torraca [comm. to vv. 106–108]), if that objection is both well founded and fairly common, especially after Porena's final note to this canto (found in the DDP at his comm. to vv. 106–108), entitled "una distrazione di Dante." Is this another instance of the unfinished quality of Dante's last *cantica*? See the notes to *Paradiso* III.29–30 and IX.119–123.

For the verb *balenare* (to flash [said of lightning]), Carroll (comm. to vv. 103–108) points to Matthew 24:27: "As the lightning comes out of the east, and shines even unto the west, so shall also be the coming of the Son of Man." Carroll goes on to say that this is the first of three visions of Christ in *Paradiso*, the second occurring in Canto XXIII.28–39, amidst the Church Triumphant. The final vision occurs, of course, in the concluding tercets of the poem.

109–117. The first of two consecutive similes, this one has armies of admirers for its small detail drawn from ordinary daily life, an experience that all have known but never expected to find in an "important" poem, the motes suspended in air irradiated in the streaks of sunlight making their way through shutters. We can almost observe Dante observing them (see the note to *Inf.* XXXII.70–72) and wondering how to use them in his poem. The range of this poet, his ability to move back and forth between the lofty and the simple, is perhaps unparalleled. One is content to be counted among his admirers.

109. Singleton (comm. to this verse) reminds us that in Italian (and, one might add, in Latin) the word *corno* can refer to the flank of an army. The observation is well taken, given, as Singleton says, the "military context" of the setting here (of which there will be more in the notes to the next canto).

110–111. The rapid movements of the souls along the two bands of the cross have certain logistical implications, as we learn from these verses, that is, there seems to be more than one file of saints along each band, since these souls catch up to and pass one another. We remember that in the preceding heaven, also, the souls, in their circles, were both dancing and singing as, we are about to learn, those in this new group are also.

114. Whether these *minuzie* (tiny motes) are, as we think, motes of dust or, as some of the early commentators believe, "atoms" is not a matter easily resolved.

117. This is the fourth (and final) appearance of the conjoined pair, *ingegno* and *arte*. See the note to *Inferno* II.7–9.

118–126. See the note to *Purg.* XXXII.61–62. This melody, like the "hymn" in that earlier passage, leaves Dante (at first) unable to make out its words. Here, however, he almost immediately does make out two of them, "Resurgi" and "Vinci" (Arise and Conquer). Landino (comm. to vv. 124–126) points out that these two "Scriptural" words are sung to Christ: "Arise and conquer," that is, "Arise from death and conquer the devil." Grandgent (comm. to verse 125) finds a source in the missal for Thursday of Easter Week (a most appropriate day, since it coincides with the beginning of the poem), the sequence "Resumpta carne *resurgit victor* die in tertia" (He rose again, having taken on once more His flesh, victorious on the third day).

For the program of song in the last *cantica*, see the note to *Paradiso* XXI.58–60.

118–123. The second simile in this set (eighth and last in the canto) captures the sonorous condition of the souls in Mars accompanying their rapid movement along the arms of the cross. This is a canto that is more characterized by simile than perhaps any other. (See Picone [Pico.2002.4], p. 205, who counts nine [including one that may not be considered formally a simile, if it does involve comparison, at vv. 34–36], differing from Blasucci [Blas.1991.1], enumerating ten, because he includes the simple comparison [see the note to *Inf.* I.22–27] at verse 126.) For bibliography on the Dantean simile, see Sowell (Sowe.1983.1) and, for more recent Italian work, see Picone, op. cit., p. 205n., including reference to Pagliaro, "similitudine," *ED* V (1976), esp. pp. 254a–257b, and Baldelli, "lingua e stile," *ED* VI (1978), esp. pp. 94a–97b.

Dante habitually uses similes in profusion at moments of heightened emotional or conceptual challenge, typically when the protagonist experiences stress (e.g., when he meets Beatrice and is castigated by her in *Purg.* XXX), or when the poet requires expanded intellectual powers (e.g., arriving in the Empyrean from the lower heavens in *Par.* XXX).

In *Paradiso* X.143 we have seen an earlier occurrence of the phrase *dolce tintinno* in the poem. There it refers to the sound issuing from a distant clock tower, here of two differing stringed instruments playing in harmony. The pleasure that a listener may take from music without recognizing the tune was like the pleasure Dante took from hearing the song these souls were singing without being able to make out most of its words.

127–129. The tercet concludes with a playful but meaningful identical rhyme: *vinci* (verb form derived from the Latin noun *vinculum* [shackles, bond]). Christ conquered death, we conquer by being bound to Him. This is the highest recognition that Dante has yet achieved, based on the experience of his selfless love of God.

130–139. Dante realizes that his reader may object to his apparent slight of Beatrice. These final ten verses of this extraordinary canto function as a commentary on the previous tercet (vv. 127–129), detailing Dante's increased love of God. Here is Tozer's explanation (comm. to vv. 133–139) of this convoluted, witty passage: "Dante here justifies himself for having said that the melody which he had just heard delighted him more than anything he had hitherto met with in Paradise, by doing which he had assigned the second place to the joy of seeing Beatrice's eyes. In order to justify himself (*Per escusarmi*), he accuses himself of not having looked at Beatrice's eyes since his arrival in the Heaven of Mars (l. 135); and his excuse for this (*Escusar puommi*) is that he was attracted by the delights of that Heaven, which surpassed those of the previous Heavens, according to the system of Paradise, in which the beauty and joy increase in ascending from sphere to sphere (ll. 133, 134). Consequently, what he had said about the delight of the melody of this Heaven surpassing all previous delights was true, inasmuch as it is reconcilable with the superior attractions of Beatrice's eyes, for their beauty had increased since the Heaven of Mars had been reached, but Dante was not aware of this because he had not seen them (ll. 138, 139)." Tozer and most other commentators take the verb *dischiudere*, which usually (in the *Commedia* as well as in Italian generally) means something like its English cognate, "to disclose," to signify, as they argue it also does once earlier (*Par.* VII.102), "to exclude." (But for disagreement with this generally accepted variant meaning in both cases, see Cardellino [Card.2006.1]). Our understanding of most of the literal sense of these verses coincides with that of Benvenuto da Imola (comm. to vv. 133–139). That the word "here" (*qui*) refers to the poem is nearly guaranteed by its distinction from the "there" (*lì*) of line 135. (See the similar situation addressed in the note to *Inf.* XXIX.54–57.)

PARADISO XV

OUTLINE

MARS

1–6 the goodwill of these singers reduced them to silence
7–12 how will such souls as these be deaf to our prayers? and how right is it that those who commit their lives to lower things shall spend eternity in Hell?
13–24 simile: the soul descending from the cross compared to a shooting star
25–27 simile: **Cacciaguida** compared to **Anchises**
28–30 his first words, the only Latin tercet in the poem
31–36 Dante's stupefaction and Beatrice's smile
37–42 Cacciaguida's second "tongue": ununderstandable speech
43–48 his third "tongue": thanks to God for His grace to Dante
49–69 Cacciaguida's first discourse:
- 49–54 Dante has pleased him by coming, winged by Beatrice
- 55–69 he understands that Dante is silent because he knows that his ancestor intuits both his questions, but urges him to speak that he may be moved by his words

70–72 Dante turns to Beatrice, who smiles her assent,
73–84 and addresses himself to Cacciaguida, expressing the reasons for his inability to offer adequate thanks
85–87 Dante concludes, after all that, by asking his name
88–148 Cacciaguida's second discourse:
- 88–96 family history: Dante's name **(Alighiero)** from Cacciaguida's son, Dante's great-grandfather; Dante should pray for him, since he's in Purgatory
- 97–129 the "good old days" in early-twelfth-century Florence:

97–99 peace within the ancient walls
100–102 pomp was a thing unknown
103–105 neither marriage age nor dowries were askew
106–108 no families were childless; no unbridled luxury
109–111 **Rome** was not yet bested in show by **Florence**:
112–114 **Bellincion Berti** and his family lived modestly
115–117 as did the **de' Nerli** and **del Vecchio** families
118–120 Florentine wives were neither exiled with their husbands nor left alone by husbands in France
121–126 portrait of family life: baby talk and woolwork
127–129 bad citizens then **(Cianghella** or **Lapo Salterello)** would have been as surprising as good ones **(Cincinnatus** or **Cornelia)** today

130–148 Cacciaguida's *vita*: his birth, baptism **(Baptistry)**, family (**Moronto, Eliseo** [brothers]), wife, warfare (under emperor, **Conrad**), martyr's death, salvation.

PARADISO XV

Benigna volontade in che si liqua
sempre l'amor che drittamente spira,
come cupidità fa ne la iniqua,

silenzio puose a quella dolce lira,
e fece quïetar le sante corde
che la destra del cielo allenta e tira.

Come saranno a' giusti preghi sorde
quelle sustanze che, per darmi voglia
ch'io le pregassi, a tacer fur concorde?

Bene è che sanza termine si doglia
chi, per amor di cosa che non duri
etternalmente, quello amor si spoglia.

Quale per li seren tranquilli e puri
discorre ad ora ad or sùbito foco,
movendo li occhi che stavan sicuri,

e pare stella che tramuti loco,
se non che da la parte ond' e' s'accende
nulla sen perde, ed esso dura poco:

tale dal corno che 'n destro si stende
a piè di quella croce corse un astro
de la costellazion che lì resplende;

né si partì la gemma dal suo nastro,
ma per la lista radïal trascorse,
che parve foco dietro ad alabastro.

Sì pïa l'ombra d'Anchise si porse,
se fede merta nostra maggior musa,
quando in Eliso del figlio s'accorse.

Benevolent will, in which a righteous love
whose breath is true must always show itself,
as does cupidity within an evil will,

had silenced the sweet-sounding lyre
and hushed the sacred strings that Heaven's right hand
loosens and draws taut.

How can they be deaf to righteous prayers,
the very spirits who, to prompt my prayers,
fell silent as with one accord?

It is well that endless be his grief
who, for love of things that do not last,
casts off a love that never dies.

As through the clear and tranquil evening sky
from time to time a sudden fire will shoot,
drawing the eyes that just before had calmly gazed,

and seems a star escaping from its place—
except from where it first was kindled
no star is missing and it lasts but a brief while—

so from the arm of that great cross
extending on the right a star raced to the foot
of the resplendent constellation there.

Nor did this jewel leave its ribbon,
but ran along the shining band so that
it seemed a flame that glows in alabaster.

With such affection did Anchises' shade reach out,
if our greatest muse is owed belief,
when in Elysium he knew his son.

"O sanguis meus, O superinfusa
gratïa Deï, sicut tibi cui
bis unquam celi ianüa reclusa?"

Così quel lume: ond' io m'attesi a lui;
poscia rivolsi a la mia donna il viso,
e quinci e quindi stupefatto fui;

ché dentro a li occhi suoi ardeva un riso
tal, ch'io pensai co' miei toccar lo fondo
de la mia gloria e del mio paradiso.

Indi, a udire e a veder giocondo,
giunse lo spirto al suo principio cose,
ch'io non lo 'ntesi, sì parlò profondo;

né per elezïon mi si nascose,
ma per necessità, ché 'l suo concetto
al segno d'i mortal si soprapuose.

E quando l'arco de l'ardente affetto
fu sì sfogato, che 'l parlar discese
inver' lo segno del nostro intelletto,

la prima cosa che per me s'intese,
"Benedetto sia tu," fu, "trino e uno,
che nel mio seme se' tanto cortese!"

E seguì: "Grato e lontano digiuno,
tratto leggendo del magno volume
du' non si muta mai bianco né bruno,

solvuto hai, figlio, dentro a questo lume
in ch'io ti parlo, mercé di colei
ch'a l'alto volo ti vestì le piume.

Tu credi che a me tuo pensier mei
da quel ch'è primo, così come raia
da l'un, se si conosce, il cinque e 'l sei;

'O sanguis meus, o superinfusa
gratïa Deï, sicut tibi cui
bis unquam celi ianüa reclusa?'

Thus spoke that light. And I gave heed,
then turned my eyes back to my lady—
whichever way I looked I was amazed,

for there glowed such a smile within her eyes
I thought that with my own I had attained
my ultimate bliss, my final paradise.

Then, a joy to hear and a joy to see,
the spirit added to what first he said
words so profound I could not understand them.

Nor did he hide his thoughts from me by choice
but by necessity, for his conceptions
were set beyond our mortal limit.

And when his bow of ardent love
relaxed enough to let his speech descend
down toward the limits of our intellect,

the first thing I could understand was:
'May you be blessed, Threefold and One,
who show such favor to my seed!'

And he went on: 'That long and welcome craving,
derived from reading in the massive book
where neither black nor white is ever altered,

'you have satisfied, my son, within this light
from which I speak to you by grace of her
who dressed you out in wings for this high flight.

'You think your thoughts flow into mine through Him
who is the First, as from the number one
will radiate the five and six, if one is known.

e però ch'io mi sia e perch' io paia
più gaudïoso a te, non mi domandi,
che alcun altro in questa turba gaia.

Tu credi 'l vero; ché i minori e ' grandi
di questa vita miran ne lo speglio
in che, prima che pensi, il pensier pandi;

ma perché 'l sacro amore in che io veglio
con perpetüa vista e che m'asseta
di dolce disïar, s'adempia meglio,

la voce tua sicura, balda e lieta
suoni la volontà, suoni 'l disio,
a che la mia risposta è già decreta!"

Io mi volsi a Beatrice, e quella udio
pria ch'io parlassi, e arrisemi un cenno
che fece crescer l'ali al voler mio.

Poi cominciai così: "L'affetto e 'l senno,
come la prima equalità v'apparse,
d'un peso per ciascun di voi si fenno,

però che 'l sol che v'allumò e arse,
col caldo e con la luce è sì iguali,
che tutte simiglianze sono scarse.

Ma voglia e argomento ne' mortali,
per la cagion ch'a voi è manifesta,
diversamente son pennuti in ali;

ond' io, che son mortal, mi sento in questa
disagguaglianza, e però non ringrazio
se non col core a la paterna festa.

Ben supplico io a te, vivo topazio
che questa gioia prezïosa ingemmi,
perché mi facci del tuo nome sazio."

'For that reason you do not ask me who I am
nor why I seem to you more filled with joy
60 than any other in this happy throng.

'And you are right, for the humble and the mighty
up here in this life gaze into the mirror
63 in which before you think them, thoughts shine clear.

'But, that the sacred love, which keeps me watching
with enduring vision and makes me thirst
66 with sweet desire, may be more happily fulfilled,

'let your voice resound sure, bold, and joyful,
to proclaim the will, proclaim the desire,
69 for which my answer is already set.'

I turned to Beatrice, who had heard
before I spoke and smiled a sign
72 that made my will put forth its wings.

And I began: 'Love and intelligence,
once the prime Equality appeared to you,
75 then became yours in equal measure,

'since that Sun that lit your way and made you warm
distributes both its heat and light so evenly
78 that all comparisons fall short.

'But for mortals, as you well know,
the will to act and the power to carry through
81 have wings that are not feathered equally,

'so that I, who am mortal, feel in myself
this inequality and thus can only offer thanks
84 for your paternal welcome with my heart.

'But I implore you, living topaz
set into this priceless ornament,
87 that you reward my longing with your name.'

"O fronda mia in che io compiacemmi
pur aspettando, io fui la tua radice":
cotal principio, rispondendo, femmi.

Poscia mi disse: "Quel da cui si dice
tua cognazione e che cent' anni e piùe
girato ha 'l monte in la prima cornice,

mio figlio fu e tuo bisavol fue:
ben si convien che la lunga fatica
tu li raccorci con l'opere tue.

Fiorenza dentro da la cerchia antica,
ond' ella toglie ancora e terza e nona,
si stava in pace, sobria e pudica.

Non avea catenella, non corona,
non gonne contigiate, non cintura
che fosse a veder più che la persona.

Non faceva, nascendo, ancor paura
la figlia al padre, ché 'l tempo e la dote
non fuggien quinci e quindi la misura.

Non avea case di famiglia vòte;
non v'era giunto ancor Sardanapalo
a mostrar ciò che 'n camera si puote.

Non era vinto ancora Montemalo
dal vostro Uccellatoio, che, com'è vinto
nel montar sù, così sarà nel calo.

Bellincion Berti vid' io andar cinto
di cuoio e d'osso, e venir da lo specchio
la donna sua sanza 'l viso dipinto;

e vidi quel d'i Nerli e quel del Vecchio
esser contenti a la pelle scoperta,
e le sue donne al fuso e al pennecchio.

'O bough of my tree, in whom I have rejoiced
even in expectation, I was your root.'
Such was the preface of his words to me.

Then: 'He from whom your house derives its name
and who for a hundred years and more
has circled the mountain on its lowest bank

'was your great-grandfather and my son.
It is most fitting that you shorten
his long and weary labor with your prayers.

'Florence, within the circle of her ancient walls
from which she still hears tierce and nones,
dwelled then in peace, temperate and chaste.

'No bracelet, no tiara did she wear,
no embroidered gown, no waistband
more striking to the eye than was its wearer.

'Nor did a newborn daughter make her father fear,
for marriage age and dowry were not yet extreme,
the one too low, the other one too high.

'No houses then stood uninhabited,
nor had Sardanapalus as yet arrived
to show what might be done behind closed doors.

'Not yet did your Uccellatoio surpass
in splendor Montemario but, exceeding
in its rise, it shall surpass it in its fall.

'I saw Bellincion Berti wear a belt of leather
and plain bone, and saw his lady step back
from the glass, her face untouched by paint.

'And I saw one of the Nerli and a del Vecchio
both content with wearing simple, unlined skins,
their ladies busy with their spindles and their flax.

Oh fortunate! ciascuna era certa
de la sua sepultura, e ancor nulla
120 era per Francia nel letto diserta.

L'una vegghiava a studio de la culla,
e, consolando, usava l'idïoma
123 che prima i padri e le madri trastulla;

l'altra, traendo a la rocca la chioma,
favoleggiava con la sua famiglia
126 d'i Troiani, di Fiesole e di Roma.

Saria tenuta allor tal maraviglia
una Cianghella, un Lapo Salterello,
129 qual or saria Cincinnato e Corniglia.

A così riposato, a così bello
viver di cittadini, a così fida
132 cittadinanza, a così dolce ostello,

Maria mi diè, chiamata in alte grida;
e ne l'antico vostro Batisteo
135 insieme fui cristiano e Cacciaguida.

Moronto fu mio frate ed Eliseo;
mia donna venne a me di val di Pado,
138 e quindi il sopranome tuo si feo.

Poi seguitai lo 'mperador Currado;
ed el mi cinse de la sua milizia,
141 tanto per bene ovrar li venni in grado.

Dietro li andai incontro a la nequizia
di quella legge il cui popolo usurpa,
144 per colpa d'i pastor, vostra giustizia.

Quivi fu' io da quella gente turpa
disviluppato dal mondo fallace,
lo cui amor molt'anime deturpa;
148 e venni dal martiro a questa pace."

'O fortunate women! Each knew for certain
where she would be buried, nor was any yet
forsaken in her bed at France's call.

'One kept eager watch upon the cradle,
using sounds and words that first delight
fathers and mothers when they soothe their child.

'Another, while drawing the wool from its spool,
would delight her household with the tales
of Troy, Fiesole, and Rome.

'A Cianghella or a Lapo Salterello,
in those days would have caused the same surprise
as now would Cincinnatus or Cornelia.

'It was to a municipal life so peaceful
and so fair, to a citizenry so loyal,
to so sweet a place to live,

'that Mary gave me when invoked with cries
of childbirth, and in your ancient Baptistry,
I was at once Cacciaguida and a Christian.

'Moronto was my brother, as was Eliseo.
My wife came from the valley of the Po,
and from her you took the surname that you bear.

'Later, I became a partisan of Emperor Conrad,
who girded me to be his knight
once, with my faithful service, I had won his favor.

'I followed him to oppose the iniquity
of that false creed whose people, by the failure
of your shepherds, usurp your right.

'There was I freed by that foul race
from all the snares of the deceitful world—
the love of which corrupts so many souls—
and came from being martyred to this peace.'

1–6. Perhaps it is the result of the only necessary relative absence of narrative in *Paradiso*, but the opening passages of many of its cantos show contorted construction and convoluted phrasing, an authorial self-consciousness that is more present than it had been in the first two *cantiche*. Narrative has its own excuse for being; theology at least seems to require justification, perhaps nowhere more so than in a poem. These two tercets are among those least afflicted, but still are not exactly easy. A possible paraphrase is: "The will that would perform good deeds and that always reveals itself in well-purposed love (as does evil will in a love of the things of this world) silenced the singing that God Himself makes harmonious." That is, the dancing choir of saints (see *Par.* XIV.109–123) grew quiet (and ceased moving) in order to welcome Dante to this heaven and to invite his questions. Their "harmony" is, in Dante's metaphor, the result of God's "hand" having tuned the "strings" of the "instrument" that their voices represent.

1–2. The themes of love and will may remind us of the discourse in the middle cantos of *Purgatorio*, Marco Lombardo's lofty praise of the (free) will.

1. A question here involves the verb, whether it is a form of *liquare* (to liquify) or *liquere* (to make manifest). Most choose the latter alternative, believing Dante treated the second-conjugation Latin verb as though it were among those of the first conjugation and also made it reflexive. Since it occupies the rhyme position, thus preparing the reader to grant the poet a perhaps larger amount of license, it is difficult to fault this view, and we have followed it in our translation.

4–6. For the recent deployment of a similar image (of a stringed instrument that has been tuned), see *Paradiso* XIV.118–120.

7–12. Resembling an indirect address to the reader, this passage begins with a rhetorical question (vv. 7–9) and ends in an apothegm. The courtesy of these saved souls in ceasing their joyful celebrative behavior in order to attend to a still-mortal being is adduced as evidence for the efficacy of prayer and as a rebuke to all on earth who think present pleasures exceed in value such exalted ones as these.

8. The word *sustanze* here, like *sussistenze* in the last canto (*Par.* XIV.73), does not refer to angels but to saved souls. See the note to *Paradiso* XIII.59.

12. This is the third time the word *amor* (love) appears in these verses: See also lines 2 and 11. After *Inferno* V, with 10 appearances in 68 lines (and two "triplets" at vv. 61–69 and 100–106, occurring in nine and seven lines, respectively), this is one of the densest groupings of the word in the poem, with three occurrences in 11 lines.

13–24. Only the first nine verses of this passage formally constitute a simile. From the first (e.g., Jacopo della Lana [comm. to vv. 13–18]), commentators have insisted that the celestial phenomena are not falling stars, but ignited vapors, referring to Aristotle's *Meteora* as their authority. Beginning with Daniello (comm. to vv. 13–15), later commentators have sought a classical poetic source for this "shooting star" in one of three places: in Ovid (*Metam.* II.319–322 [Phaeton]) or in Virgil (*Georg.* I.365–367 [stars falling from the skies]) and *Aen.* II.692–703 (the portentous shooting star or—more likely—comet that appears to Anchises' request for an omen of Jupiter's approval of his flight from Troy). Since the neighboring tercet's context (vv. 25–27) aligns Anchises with Cacciaguida, that has seemed to some the more likely source. However, it is only in Ovid that we find words that seem to be mirrored in Dante's description of the celestial phenomenon: The star has not in fact fallen, if it seemed to have fallen ("etsi non cecidit, potuit cecidisse videri").

22–24. That is, in its approach before its descent, this "star" follows the right angle made by the "arm" and the "stem" of the cross. For Dante's earlier treatment of the cross of Mars, see *Convivio* II.xiii.22: "This is also why in Florence, at the beginning of its ruin, there was seen in the sky in the shape of a cross a great quantity of these vapors which accompany the star of Mars" (tr. R. Lansing).

The apsidal chapel dedicated to the local martyr of Ravenna, St. Apollonaris, in the church dedicated to his memory, S. Apollinare in Classe, displays over the altar a mosaic cross that has jewels depicted as being embedded in it, with Christ's face as the central jewel, located at the transverse of its two elements. Is it possible that Dante was thinking of that particular cross? We do not know whether he visited Ravenna before he moved there, circa 1317–19, nor when he composed these cantos (but see the last paragraph of the note to *Par.* IX.29–30, reporting on the possibility that that canto reflected the pressure of the recent past, the years

1314–15). Petrocchi's dating of the composition of the last *cantica* would have it begun circa 1317. And so it is at least possible that the greater portion of *Paradiso* was composed in Ravenna. At any rate, Jeffrey Schnapp (Schn.1986.1), pp. 171–203, offers detailed arguments that locate various architectural features of Ravenna in the texts of the central cantos of *Paradiso*, including the mosaic found in this chapel, with its jeweled cross (pp. 180–85).

24. Alabaster is a creamy white stone, softly translucent, so that it could, when hollowed in such a way as to contain wax and a wick, be used as a light (particularly for votive purposes). Dante goes existing technology one better, imagining the cross of Mars as hollow and somehow having moving lights within that space.

25–27. All are in agreement about the Virgilian provenance of this simile. Itself representing paternal affection, it is perhaps the most obvious and filial affection shown by the poet to *his* poetic father, Virgil, since he left the poem in the earthly paradise (*Purg.* XXX). See *Aeneid* VI.684–686, a description of the shade of Anchises welcoming his living son to the Elysian Fields. (See the note to *Purgatorio* II.79–81.) What exactly we are to make of the reference is a matter of some dispute and more than a little complexity.

Surprisingly, this may be the first obvious citation of Virgil's text (*Aen.* VI.684–686) in quite some time and it is surely the most vibrant one so far in *Paradiso*. While there have been several at least generally Virgilian contaminations, this is the first pellucidly precise one since *Paradiso* VIII.9. Before that, the last great Virgilian flowering occurred in *Purgatorio* XXX (vv. 21, 48, 49–51, 52, 59–60—see Hollander [Holl.1993.1], pp. 317–18). From the beginning of the *Paradiso* it may have seemed that Virgil had been left behind as the main classical source in favor of Ovid (see the last paragraph of the note to *Par.* I.68). For discussion see Hollander (Holl.1983.1), pp. 134–35.

26. It is a commonplace in the commentaries to say that "musa" here means "poet." See, among others, Pietro di Dante (Pietro1, comm. to vv. 25–27): "qui major musa, idest poeta, latinorum est" (who was the greatest muse, that is, poet, among the Romans). And see *Convivio* IV.xxvi.8, where Dante refers to Virgil as "lo maggiore nostro poeta," and *Monarchia* II.iii.6, where the Latin master is "divinus poeta noster Virgilius." However, Bosco/Reggio (comm. to *Par.* XVIII.33) offer strong reasons for taking *musa* to mean the text of the *Aeneid* rather than its author.

The first commentator apparently even to sense the possible condescension toward Virgil in this verse was Steiner (comm. to vv. 26–27), who attempts to downplay its significance. That it took seven hundred years for a reader to say that this compliment might even seem to be backhanded is, one might say, remarkable. Dante could easily have avoided introducing this concern about how much faith we should give to Virgil's poem as a record of event. Merely to lodge the doubt is enough to identify Dante's motive, which is to call into question Virgil's final authority when faced with the certainties of the world of Revelation, in which the protagonist now finds himself. (Of course, we can turn the same question back onto Dante, whose poem also may not merit our belief, either; it is a dangerous game that he has chosen to play. And he knows that.) Mattalia (comm. to verse 26) is a good deal more firm than Steiner and sees the point of Dante's insistence on the fictitious nature of Virgil's account, but goes on to claim that Dante believed in the historicity of the events he narrates (a difficult position to accept as soon as one asks the inevitable question, "Do the events narrated as taking place in the Elysian Fields have any verifiable reality outside of Virgil's text?"). The firmest sense of the failing being lodged against Virgil found in contemporary commentaries is perhaps that of Singleton (comm. to verse 26), sending the reader to his comment on *Inferno* II.13. And see the note to *Inferno* II.28, above. Nonetheless, the first clear statement of the problematic aspects of these dubiety-creating references to the *Aeneid* is probably Grandgent's (comm. to *Inf.* II, intro. note): "It is worth noting that in introducing the example of Aeneas, Dante begins with 'tu dici che . . . ,' and a few lines further on he uses the phrase 'questa andata onde gli dai tu vanto'; so in *Par.* XV, 26, referring to the same episode, he adds 'se fede merta nostra maggior Musa,' meaning Virgil. These expressions seem to imply a mental reservation with regard to the literal veracity of Aeneas's adventure." And see Hollander (Holl.1983.1), pp. 135–36.

28–30. This is the only tercet in the poem entirely in Latin: "O blood of mine, O grace of God poured down from above, to whom, as to you, have the gates of heaven ever been opened twice." Indeed, only St. Paul is, alongside of Dante, in such glorious company, as far as we (or Dante) can know.

While it has pronouncedly Virgilian and biblical elements, the tercet is also Dante's brief answer to an unspoken challenge (until Giovanni del Virgilio, around 1320, had the dubious taste to offer him a chance at the laurel from Bologna in exchange for a truly worthy poem, a political one cast, more nobly than was this lowly *Comedy*, in Latin [see the note to *Par.*

IX.29–30]). He undoubtedly earlier had come into contact with others who thought that he should have eschewed the vernacular to write his poem in Latin, in the tradition of classical poetry. That, after all, is what Albertino Mussato had done.

For an overview of the situation of Latin writing in relation to the formation and development of the European vernaculars, see Marc Van Uytfanghe (Vanu.2003.1).

The Virgilian elements in the tercet include the words *sanguis meus*, widely recognized as a citation of *Aen.* VI.835. Anchises is addressing Julius Caesar and asking him to cast away his sword (rather than put it to use in bloody civil war): "proice tela manu, sanguis meus!" That speech ends with Anchises' fervid hope that Rome will spare the defeated and bring down the prideful (*Aen.* VI.853: "parcere subiectis et debellare superbos"). If that was her mission, Virgil knows how badly she failed in it. But there is a much less frequently cited possible second citation, in verse 30, a reference to the Sibyl's admonition; if Aeneas is so eager for his perilous journey, she will guide him. She expresses the danger awaiting him in two examples of passage into the land of the dead and back (*Aen.* VI.134–135), twice crossing the Styx, twice seeing black Tartarus (bis Stygios innare lacus, bis nigra videre / Tartara). It can certainly be argued that what Dante has done here is to take the fairly glum passage in Virgil and brighten the context considerably, the futile challenge to civil discord in Rome become the crusader's welcome to his "son," Aeneas's journey through Hell become this son's unique voyage to salvation.

That Cacciaguida's first words are in Latin, both biblical (at least generically) and Virgilian, accomplishes one of Dante's aims. It establishes his ancestor as speaker of the doubly significant "grammatical" tongue, that of God and man, Church and empire. As Dante's spiritual and fleshly father, he is perfectly fitted to meet his son's needs.

28. Aversano (Aver.2000.2), p. 66, points out that the protagonist has himself once used *sangue* in this precise sense (i.e., to denote bloodline), referring to Geri del Bello (*Inf.* XXIX.20). And now his ancestor uses the word, in Latin, to identify Dante as his seed.

29. Some readers have reflected that this verse would seem to put Dante in a class by himself, since Paul claims (II Corinthians 12:2) a celestial ascent only as far as the third heaven. But see the note to *Paradiso* I.73 for notice that traditional understanding of the passage identified Paul's "third heaven" with the Empyrean.

30. Benvenuto (comm. to vv. 28–30) says that this, Dante's first visit to the realms of Paradise, is made in the flesh, while the next one will not be (i.e., Dante's soul will fly up without his body after his death). Of course, he is destined to get that body back at the general resurrection.

31. While this "light" does not choose to identify himself until verse 135, it is perhaps good to have some sense of Dante's great-great-grandfather, who is speaking in this scene, "of whose life nothing is known beyond what Dante himself tells us; viz. that he was born in Florence (*Par.* XV.130–133) in the Sesto di Porta san Piero (*Par.* XVI.40–42) about the year 1090 (*Par.* XVI.34–39); that he belonged (possibly) to the Elisei, one of the old Florentine families which boasted Roman descent (*Par.* XV.136; *Par.* XVI.40); that he was baptized in the baptistery of San Giovanni in Florence (*Par.* XV.134–135); that he had two brothers, Moronto and Eliseo (*Par.* XV.136); that his wife came from the valley of the Po, and that from her, through his son, Dante got his surname of Alighieri (*Par.* XV.91–94, *Par.* XV.137–138); that he followed the Emperor Conrad III on the Second Crusade, and was knighted by him (*Par.* XV.139–144), and finally that he fell fighting against the infidel about the year 1147 (*Par.* XV.145–148)" (T).

32–33. The protagonist makes up for his previous "failure" to look at Beatrice in the last canto (XIV.127–132).

Aversano claims that stupefaction is experienced only twice in the Bible, both times in the responses of those who beheld Christ, citing Mark 9:14 (regarding the populace after the Transfiguration) and Acts 9:6–7 (regarding those who witness what is to them strange behavior on the part of Saul on the road to Damascus). But see also Acts 2:7–12, which perhaps contains a more relevant context than those two passages. After the apostles found they were able to "translate" words spoken in tongues into their own language, they were amazed. This is the first use of the word *stupefatto* in the poem. It will twice be used again (*Par.* XXVI.80 and *Par.* XXXI.35). On the last of these it will refer to the reaction of the pilgrim approaching Rome who sees the city for the first time.

34–36. Beatrice's smile recognizes that Dante has understood his identity better than ever before, biologically, but more important in terms of his family's heritage, and, still more important, as "Roman" and as Christian, assured of his salvation.

37–42. This is Cacciaguida's second kind of speech, one that the protagonist is unable to understand. For some reason André Pézard (Peza.1967.1) does not include this passage in his consideration of the "tongues" spoken by Cacciaguida (he deals with items 1, 3, and 4 in the listing below). This list is found in Hollander (Holl.1980.2), pp. 125–27 (for some further consideration, see Hollander [Holl.1992.1], pp. 38–39, n. 57). However, it seems clear that the reader must consider four languages as spoken by Cacciaguida: (1) vv. 28–30, Latin; (2) 37–42, speech that the protagonist could not recognize; (3) vv. 47–48, the Italian of Dante's time; (4) *Paradiso* XVI.34–36, the vernacular of Cacciaguida's day. For support for this view, see Honess (Hone.1997.1), p. 130.

39. Poletto (comm. to vv. 37–39) seems to have been the first commentator to notice the closeness of this line to the tenth verse of the last poem of the *Vita nuova* (XLI.12): "io non lo intendo, sì parla sottile" (I cannot understand the subtle words it [his pilgrim spirit, having visited Paradise and seen Beatrice] speaks [tr. M. Musa]). Benvenuto explains (comm. to vv. 37–42) that Cacciaguida was speaking of pure mental constructs (*conceptiones mentales*) that transcend mere humans' ability to understand. (See the note to *Par.* XIV.88.) On the other hand, Francesco da Buti (comm. to vv. 37–48) and Cristoforo Landino (comm. to vv. 37–39) both think the context of his first words in Latin, regarding Dante's status as one of the elect (vv. 28–30), point to the issue of predestination, a position that Sapegno (comm. to vv. 37–42) brings back into consideration, as several others do also. Hollander (Holl.1980.2) is of the opinion that this linguistic behavior on the part of Dante's ancestor may reflect either Adamic vernacular or the apostles' speaking in tongues. There is, in short, no consensus about how to read this verse. But see the note to vv. 43–48.

40–42. Benvenuto's hypothesis (see the note to verse 39) concerning "mental constructs" would seem to be certified by these lines, which tell us that Cacciaguida was not trying to hide his words from Dante but that the language he employed simply overshot its human target, that is, Cacciaguida had momentarily forgotten that Dante was not yet "immortal," that, in other words, his intelligence still was limited by his humanity.

The word *concetto* represents an important element in Dante's vocabulary of consciousness. Used as a singular noun for the first time in *Inferno* XXXII.4 (where it refers to the mental construct Dante has in his brain of the lowest landscape of Hell), it does not reappear until here (for the rest of its "career" in the poem, see the note to *Par.* XXXIII.127).

43–48. These six lines perhaps offer some clarification of the nature of Cacciaguida's unundersandable utterance (vv. 37–42). First, he seems to have been addressing God, and certainly not Dante; second, if the words he speaks now flow from the ones he uttered then, they, too, were words of thanksgiving for God's grace to his descendant.

48. This is the last appearance in the poem of the adjective *cortese* (literally "courtly" [i.e., of the court], and hence "courteous" [i.e., behaving as a courtier does—or should do]). It transforms the usual sense of the word, which often associates it with "courtly love," into heavenly affection, a rather pronounced Nietzschean "transvaluation of values." Dante had already availed himself of a similar strategic displacement at the end of the *Vita nuova*, when he refers to God as the "sire de la cortesia" (the Lord of graciousness [tr. M. Musa]).

50. For *volume*, see the note to *Paradiso* XII.122. To what "volume" does Cacciaguida refer? Where today commentators are unanimous in their opinion, it is amusing to read Jacopo della Lana on the problem. According to him (comm. to vv. 49–50) and to perhaps one other (the Anonimo Fiorentino [comm. to vv. 49–51]), it is the *Aeneid*. The Codice Cassinese (comm. to this verse) is perhaps the first to deliver the standard gloss: the mind of God. With few exceptions this is the common opinion during seven hundred years of commentatary. Tommaseo (comm. to vv. 49–51) suggests that the reference may also be to the Apocalypse (3:3), the Book of Life, in which the names of all the saved are recorded. Insofar as we are supposed to think of God's mind as containing this book (and, since it contains infinity, it must), we realize that Cacciaguida has read in it Dante's salvation.

50–54. Cacciaguida is using lofty diction to say that Dante's arrival has satisfied the long craving he has experienced (dating, we assume, from his arrival in the Empyrean circa 1147) to see his descendant's arrival in the heavens, about which he read in God's mind, credit for which he gives to Beatrice.

51. That is, the words in this "book" are unchanging, unlike those in human manuscripts, where scribes variously blot, erase, add to, and cross out previous texts. Compare *Paradiso* XVII.37–39. And see Torraca (comm. to vv. 49–51) for a reflection of this verse in the opening line of Dante's first *Eclogue* to Giovanni del Virgilio: "Vidimus in nigris albo patiente lituris . . ." (In letters black, upon receptive white, I saw . . .).

54. It is not difficult to believe that Dante is here revisiting a theme dear to him, the ill-fated flight of Icarus (see *Inf.* XVII.109–111 and XXIX.113–116; *Par.* VIII.125–126), but now starring Beatrice as a better-artificing Daedalus and Dante as nonfalling wonder boy. See the note to verse 72.

55–69. "Cacciaguida tells Dante that he understands the reason why he does not inquire his name and the cause of his interest in him, which is, that he (Dante) is aware that the denizens of Heaven see the thoughts of others through the medium of the mind of God which reflects them in every detail; and consequently that it is unnecessary for him to state in words what he wishes to be told him, because his wishes are already fully known to Cacciaguida. Still, he encourages Dante to speak, because his (Cacciaguida's) love will be increased by complying with his request" (Tozer, comm. to these verses).

56–57. See Grandgent (comm. to verse 56): "*Raia*, 'radiates.' Unity is the beginning of number, as God is the beginning of thought; from the conception of unity is derived the conception of all numbers, and in the divine mind all thought is contained."

68. Will and desire are the hallmarks of the soul's affective knowing and wise loving in Paradise. As Tommaseo pointed out long ago (comm. to vv. 67–69), the *cantica* will conclude with these two spiritual movements in Dante operating harmoniously (*Par.* XXXIII.143).

72. Dante apparently could not resist a second reference to Beatrice as Daedalus (see the note to verse 54). And see Hollander (Holl.1983.1), p. 135n., pointing out that there seems to be a "Daedalus program" in this part of the poem: *Paradiso* VIII.125, X.74–75, XIII.77–78, and here, representing, according to him (p. 136n.), something bordering on the obsessive.

73–84. This tortured preamble to a simple question ("What's your name?") is paraphrased by Tozer (comm. to these verses) as follows: "Dante here excuses himself for being unable to thank Cacciaguida as he would wish to do for his benevolence. The ground of his excuse is that, whereas in Heaven a feeling (*affetto*) is accompanied by an equivalent power of thought (*senno*), through which that feeling can find expression, this is not the case with mortal men, for in them the means (*argomento*) of expressing feeling fall short of the wish to do so (*voglia*)."

74. The term *equalità*, a hapax, has considerable theological weight. Aversano (Aver.2000.2), p. 68, cites Richard of St. Victor, *De Trinitate* VI.xxi: "Quid summa aequalitas sit in illa Trinitate, ubi oportet omnes aeque perfectos esse" (What very great equality there must be in that Trinity, in which it is necessary for all the elements to be equally perfect). Aversano continues by adducing the gloss of Alain de Lille (*PL* CCX.445) to his fourth *regula theologica*: "in Patre unitas, in Figlio [*sic*] aequalitas, in Spiritu sancto unitatis aequalitatisque connexio" (in the Father, uniqueness; in the Son, likeness; in the Holy Spirit, the link between uniqueness and likeness).

If one thinks about the "aesthetics" of the Christian religion (and of Dante's poem), one has a sense of the centrality of both uniqueness and of likeness. This is nowhere more readily apparent than in the Second Person of the Trinity, Jesus Christ, a uniquely human being (because He is also the immortal God) and yet a commonly human being (because He was also mortal). And, it is perhaps fair to suggest, this theme has nowhere before in the poem been quite so evident or so important as it has become in this canto.

81. The phrase "pennuti in ali" (feathered wings) picks up (from verse 54 ["vestì le piume"] and verse 72 ["crescer l'ali"]) to make this one of the densest insistences on Dante's heavenly flight in the poem. See Shankland's two studies (Shan.1975.1; Shan.1977.1) for discussion of the pun on the poet's surname (Alighieri) available in the Latin adjective for "winged," *aliger*.

85. The protagonist addresses his ancestor as "topaz." Alain de Lille, cited by Aversano (Aver.2000.2), p. 68, says that there are two colors of topaz, sky blue and golden.

87. We perhaps have already forgotten the elaborate preparation for this simple question. Cacciaguida says that he already knows what Dante wants to ask but wants him to ask it anyway, to bring him greater pleasure (vv. 55–69); and then Dante spends nearly as much poetic space (vv. 73–84) explaining why he cannot express his gratitude for Cacciaguida's welcome. That the inquiry about Cacciaguida's identity took so long to make it from Dante's lips is, perhaps, amusing, a sort of Scholastic joke, the sort of thing that would offer Rabelais, two centuries later, endless opportunity for spirited (and antagonistic) amusement at the expense of medieval modes of expression. However, Dante may have felt that the reader (even

the fourteenth-century reader) may have needed to be reminded of the gulf that separates souls that have come to God, enjoying an eternal and quasi-angelic spiritual existence, and even ultimately favored mortals, like Dante Alighieri. When we consider this aspect of the third *cantica*, we probably all agree that the poet manages to present himself as feeling proper humility at finding himself prematurely among the blessed, something that is not perhaps as often observed as it might be. For a useful presentation of what is known about Cacciaguida, see Fiorenzo Forti, "Cacciaguida," *ED* I (1970).

88–135. For the perhaps surprising presence of so many virtuous women representing "the good old days" in Florence, see Honess (Hone.1997.2), esp. pp. 108–14.

88–89. Cacciaguida's presentation of a genealogical "tree" (Bosco/Reggio point to the presence of the image of the family tree in *Purg.* VII.121, *Purg.* XX.43, and *Par.* IX.31) of Dante's family, of which he declares himself the root, begins his wider exploration of the history of Florence, the subject of some forty verses (88–129). Beginning with Benvenuto (comm. to vv. 88–90), there has been appreciation of the fact that Cacciaguida's words remember those attributed to God the Father (Matthew 3:17; Mark 1:11; Luke 3:22): "This is my beloved Son, in whom I am well pleased."

91–94. Cacciaguida refers to his son Alighiero (Dante's great-grandfather) as the source of the poet's surname (since Alighiero's own son, Dante's grandfather, was known as Bellincione degli Alighieri). Alighiero was perhaps given a Christian name reflecting his mother's maiden name, Alaghieri (see the note to vv. 137–138). We know from documentary evidence that he was alive in 1201, which means that Dante was misinformed as to the date of his death, since the poet has Cacciaguida represent him as having spent more than one hundred years in Purgatory purging his pridefulness (there results a certain family resemblance [see *Purg.* XIII.136–138]) and the calendar in the poem stands at 1300.

95–96. The news of Alighiero's presence on the terrace of Pride comes with an admonition of Dante's family duty, to pray for the deliverance of his soul from torment. There is a parallel moment in *Inferno* (XXIX.18–36), Dante's discovery of his ancestor, Geri del Bello, a cousin of his father, among the sowers of discord, an apparition that causes him to feel guilty for not having avenged a relative's violent death. For another similar distribution of a family, consider the case of the Donati (Corso in Hell, Forese in Purgatory, and Piccarda in Heaven [see the note to *Purg.* XXIII.42–48]; but there are several other examples as well).

See the note to *Paradiso* I.35–36 for the understanding that the purpose of the poem is to affect its readers' prayers. Here is an internal example of precisely that effect.

97–99. "The old line of walls dated from 1078 A.D. (Villani, iv. 8); it was now 'old,' because the wall of Dante's time was commenced in 1284. . . . The Badia [the church of S. Stefano in Badìa], the chimes of which are here referred to, stood just within the ancient walls; the Florentines took their time from these. . . . The factions and civil dissensions in Florence did not commence until 1177" (Tozer, comm. to this tercet).

100–102. Dante, in Cacciaguida's voice, has harnessed his wagon of complaint about a typical target of medieval moralizers, luxurious living, to a misogynistic diatribe against costly female overdecoration (for a cry against related but opposite behavior in Florentine women, see *Purg.* XXIII.98–105).

103–105. The tirade now turns toward marriage contracts, with their two related ills: the lowering age at which fathers feel forced to "sell" their daughters to a man, and the rising cost of doing so, represented by the dowry the girl's family had to put up. The two details manage to make the Florentine institution of marriage sound more like sexual bondage than matrimony.

106. The line has caused difficulty. The early commentators thought it referred to the thirteenth-century Florentine luxurious living in the early Renaissance equivalent of McMansions, showier houses than family life required; later ones believed that Dante was referring to marriages that were only for show, allowing the couple to lead dissolute lives. Scartazzini (comm. to this verse), reviewing the dispute, sides with the older view, because it better accords with the context, which is unnecessary luxury, as the following two lines demonstrate.

107–108. "Sardanapalus, last legendary king of the Assyrian empire of Ninus, noted for his luxury, licentiousness, and effeminacy. He spent his days in his palace, unseen by any of his subjects, dressed in female apparel, and surrounded by concubines. The satrap of Media, having determined to renounce allegiance to such a worthless monarch, rebelled against him, and for two years besieged him in Nineveh, until Sardanapalus, unable to hold out any longer, collected all his treasures, wives, and concubines, and placed them on an immense funeral pile, to which he set fire destroying himself at the same time" (T). The identity of Dante's source here is debated; those most commonly proposed are Juvenal (*Satires* X.362), Cicero (*Tuscul.* V), Justinus (*Hist.* 1.3), Orosius (*Hist. contra paganos* I.xix.1), and Aegidius Colonna (*De regimine principum* II.xvii), this last favored by Toynbee (in the entry from which the opening passage is cited) because it specifically refers to Sardanapalus's nefariously luxurious activity as being confined to a single room. For discussion of the likely sources of Dante's Sardanapalus, see Brugnoli (Brug.1999.1).

109–111. The thought here is that Florence after Cacciaguida's day rapidly eclipsed Rome in urban splendor, but its fall from supremacy will be even more swift. In synecdoche, Monte Mario and Uccellatoio represent Rome and Florence, respectively. Explaining these lines, Carroll has this to say (comm. to vv. 97–120): "Montemalo (now Monte Mario) is the hill on the way from Viterbo from which the splendour of the Eternal City is first seen; and Uccellatoio is the point on the road from Bologna from which the first flash of the greater splendour of Florence breaks on the traveller's view."

112–113. Bellincion Berti is exemplary of the citizenry of "the good old days" of Florence. Giovanni Villani (*Cronica* IV.1) speaks of him in similar terms. He was father of the "good Gualdrada" of *Inferno* XVI.37. While males, with the exception of the effeminate Sardanapalus and the corrupt Lapo (see verse 128), are not used to exemplify improper municipal behavior, they surely are present in the rest of the canto as representatives of Florentine virtue.

114. A good woman, as we would expect in this context, eschews facial cosmetics.

115–117. The heads of noble Florentine families (the Nerli and the Vecchietti) are, like Bellincion Berti, content with simple clothing, without adornment; their wives exhibit their virtue by what they take pleasure in doing: household chores.

118–120. Two different sort of ills befalling Florentine wives are referred to here: Some were taken along by their husbands when they were exiled and eventually died in foreign lands; others, married to men who took themselves off to a life of trade in France (cf. the first story in Boccaccio's *Decameron*), led lonely lives at home.

121–123. This vignette from "Scenes from Florentine Family Life, ca. 1125," by Dante Alighieri, features baby talk (see Hollander [Holl.1980.2], p. 127), a phenomenon that Dante is (perhaps surprisingly) most interested in. Florentine babies, goo-gooing in their cribs, are represented as teaching their mommies (and daddies, too) to speak in that "idiom." That word, which first appears here and then will be used only once more in the poem (*Par.* XXVI.114), where it is used to delineate Adam's first speech, is unmistakably "vernacular" Hebrew. And thus the word *idïoma*, here, may offer an insight into Dante's theory of the history of language: Each infant recapitulates the primal linguistic moment, speaking a version of Adamic vernacular, until, in the push and pull of maternal and paternal instruction and the infant's response, that vernacular takes on a local flavor, in this case Florentine. See Benvenuto (comm. to vv. 121–126): "scilicet, maternum linguagium, scilicet, *la ninna nanna*." It is perhaps useful to know that Vellutello regularly uses the word *idioma* to refer to various Italian vernaculars.

124. A second female presence is probably the husband's mother, also doing useful chores, working at her loom.

125–126. This grandmother narrates for the children in the family (but heard by all) the prehistory of Florence, with its roots in Troy, Rome, and Fiesole. Torraca (comm. to vv. 121–126) explains the details, common to many chronicles of the time, as follows: "The Florentines told of the origins of their city in the following way. After the linguistic division made as a result of the attempt to construct the tower of Babel, Atlas built the first city, which thus *fu sola* [stood alone] and was therefore called Fiesole. Another of Atlas's sons, Dardanus, traveling in the East, built Troy there. From Troy Aeneas came to Italy. One of his descendants founded Rome. The Romans destroyed Fiesole. Romans and Fiesolans founded Florence."

127–129. Dante alludes to two of his Florentine contemporaries, first Cianghella, daughter of Arrigo della Tosa. She married a man from Imola, after whose death she returned to her birthplace and behaved in such fashion as customarily gave widows a very bad name (cf. Boccaccio's *Corbaccio*), leading a life marked by lust and luxury. The profile of Lapo Salterello sounds a good bit like that of Dante (to what must have been the poet's dismay). He was a jurist and poet who, in 1294, represented his city to the papacy, and was then elected prior of Florence; further, in 1300 he denounced several of his cocitizens for collaborating with Pope Boniface VIII; in 1302 he, like Dante, was sent into exile (for fomenting discord and for barratry) by the victorious Black Guelphs. In chiastic order, Cianghella and Lapo are compared with two virtuous figures from the era of the Roman republic, Cincinnatus and Cornelia (see *Inf.* IV.128), the mother of the Gracchi. For Dante's overwhelming admiration of the Romans of those days, see Hollander and Rossi (Holl.1986.1). And for a revisionist (and convincing) analysis of the republican roots of Dante's imperialist views, see Armour (Armo.1997.2)

130–148. Cacciaguida's self-narrative, the longest in *Paradiso*, nonetheless seems brief when compared to some of the epic autobiographical performances of characters in *Inferno*, e.g., Ulysses (53 lines), Ugolino (72 lines). For discussion of the nature of speeches in *Paradiso*, see the fourth section of the introduction.

For a global study of these three *canti* dedicated to Dante's ancestor, see Figurelli (Figu.1965.1).

130–132. This *terzina* repeats a theme that we have encountered before (the "good old days"), but does so with such emphasis and fluidity (both lines are enjambed, so that the entire tercet has the feeling of a single line of thought, with four iterations of the adverb *così* upping the emotional effect), as to leave us in suspense, wondering about the subject and predicate that it introduces.

Dante's radical notion of the responsibility of the citizen, based on ethics more than on politics, may have been shaped by the "radical corporationalism" of Remigio de' Girolami; the characterization is that of Ernst Kantorowicz (Kant. 1957.1), p. 478, cited by Claire Honess (Hone.1997.2), p. 104. For an overview of the still underinvestigated question of Remigio's possible influence on Dante, with bibliography (including three important essays in English by Charles Till Davis), see Ovidio Capitani, "Girolami, Remigio dei," *ED* III (1971).

133–135. The first three words of the line offer subject, verb, and object: "Mary gave me." The tercet is based on the moments of birth and baptism, the crusader's mother calling out for the aid of Mary in the pain of parturition and the ceremonial pronouncing of the child's name at his baptism (in the Florentine Baptistery, where Dante himself would also receive his Christian identity and name); the last word of the tercet, reflecting its first word, also a name (Maria), is Cacciaguida. (He has delayed Dante's gratification for some time now; Dante asked to know who he was at verse 87.)

136. Cacciaguida now names his brothers, Moronto and Eliseo, of whom we know absolutely nothing. There has been some dispute over the years about the exact content of the line and some speculation that Dante means to associate himself with the great Florentine Ghibelline family, the Elisei, but with no convincing result to the process.

137–138. Cacciaguida's wife came, he says, from the valley of the Po (over the years, Ferrara remains perhaps the favorite location among the discussants, but, since there is a lot at stake [as, for some Americans, there is with regard to George Washington's dining and sleeping habits], the debate goes on). It was from her, he continues, that Dante got his surname, Alaghieri or Alighieri. Since one of her and Cacciaguida's sons was named Alighiero, it seems more than likely that he was named for his mother.

139–144. He follows the emperor, Conrad III, on the (disastrous) Second Crusade (in 1147) against Islam, against which the popes even now in Dante's day fail to take up arms (not even *preaching* crusade, much less fighting one). There still remains some debate over the question of which emperor Dante really means, Conrad II or III. But see Carroll (comm. to vv. 130–148): "Some doubt has been thrown on the commonly accepted view that the Emperor whom Cacciaguida followed to the Crusades was Conrad III of Suabia, but without reason. Founding on a passage in Villani (IV.9), Cassini suggests Conrad II, the Salic, who was Emperor from 1024 to 1039. According to Villani, this Emperor (whom he calls Conrad I and misdates) visited Florence frequently and knighted many of its citizens. The only crusade he undertook was against the Saracens in Calabria, so that on this view Cacciaguida never was in the Holy Land, and his birth must be pushed back at least a century before the generally received time. It is obviously impossible that he could in that case be the father of the Alighiero whom he calls his son, who died more than a hundred and sixty years later. There is no reason for giving up the ordinary view that the Emperor referred to is Conrad III, who in 1147, with Louis VII of France, undertook the disastrous Second Crusade, so enthusiastically preached by

St. Bernard of Clairvaux. (Bernard's defence for the failure of this Crusade which roused all Europe against him is that it was due to the sins of the Crusaders themselves. They fell as the Israelites fell in the wilderness, and from the same cause. His remedy is—faith and a third Crusade [*De Consideratione*, II.1].)"

145–148. He died in the Holy Land and came from martyrdom to this peace (cf. the words for Boethius's similar journey, *Par.* X.128–129). While some twentieth-century commentators seem to be open to the idea, no one before Chimenz (comm. to vv. 145–148) states clearly that the text surely accommodates the view of medieval clergy that those who died on crusade in the Holy Land went straight to Heaven, bypassing Purgatory.

Botterill's entry "Martyrdom" (Lans.2000.1, p. 596) offers reflections on Dante's daring in making Cacciaguida one among the otherwise canonical martyrs of the Church.

PARADISO XVI

OUTLINE

MARS

1–9 Dante's apostrophe of foolish pride in ancestry

10–12 his use of the honorific *voi*

13–15 Beatrice's smile like **[Lady of Malehault]**'s cough when she, unobserved, sees **Guinevere** wooing **[Lancelot]**

16–21 Dante to Cacciaguida: "You are my father"; his joy

22–27 Dante's four questions: (1) who were Your ancestors? (2) when were You a child? (3) how large was Florence then? (4) who were her most worthy citizens?

28–30 simile: Cacciaguida is like a coal quickened into flame

31–33 Cacciaguida's fourth "tongue": earlier vernacular

34–39 Cacciaguida answers (2): I was born in 1091

40–45 he answers (1): my people were from the heart of town, but let me not speak (with pride) of them

46–51 he answers (3): we were only one-fifth of you in number but purer (no taint of **Campi**, **Certaldo**, or **Figline**);

52–57 unfortunate that these have settled within city limits,

58–66 thus bringing misfortune to the city,

67–72 which became too large for its own good, as though it had eaten too much; two similes: blind bull (vs. blind lamb), five swords (vs. a single sword);

73–78 if you study the decline of four cities, you will wonder less that individual families suffer similar declines,

79–81 for, if death is evident in individuals, it may be perceived as present in cities that still seem alive

82–84 simile: as tides ebb and flow so does Florence's fate;

85–87 and so what follows should not be surprising: the decline of the once-great Florentine houses

88–139 Cacciaguida answers (4): the great families of Florence

140–144	Dante's apostrophe of **Buondelmonte**
145–147	Buondelmonte's body at the feet of the **statue of Mars**
148–154	Cacciaguida's ending: good old days before the wars.

PARADISO XVI

O poca nostra nobiltà di sangue,
se gloriar di te la gente fai
qua giù dove l'affetto nostro langue,

mirabil cosa non mi sarà mai:
ché là dove appetito non si torce,
dico nel cielo, io me ne gloriai.

Ben se' tu manto che tosto raccorce:
sì che, se non s'appon di dì in die,
lo tempo va dintorno con le force.

Dal "voi" che prima a Roma s'offerie,
in che la sua famiglia men persevra,
ricominciaron le parole mie;

onde Beatrice, ch'era un poco scevra,
ridendo, parve quella che tossio
al primo fallo scritto di Ginevra.

Io cominciai: "Voi siete il padre mio;
voi mi date a parlar tutta baldezza;
voi mi levate sì, ch'i' son più ch'io.

Per tanti rivi s'empie d'allegrezza
la mente mia, che di sé fa letizia
perché può sostener che non si spezza.

Ditemi dunque, cara mia primizia,
quai fuor li vostri antichi e quai fuor li anni
che si segnaro in vostra püerizia;

ditemi de l'ovil di San Giovanni
quanto era allora, e chi eran le genti
tra esso degne di più alti scanni."

O insignificant nobility of blood,
if you make us glory in you here below,
where our affections are ephemeral,

I will not ever think it strange,
for there, where appetite is never warped—
in, I mean, the heavens themselves—I gloried in you too.

You are indeed a cloak that quickly shrinks,
so that, if we do not add to it day by day,
time trims the edges with its shears.

With that *You* which had its origin in Rome
and which her offspring least preserve by use,
I once again began to speak,

and Beatrice, who stood somewhat apart,
smiled, like the lady who discreetly coughed
at the first fault inscribed of Guinevere.

I began: 'You are my father,
You prompt me to speak with bold assurance.
You raise me up, so I am more than I.

'My mind is flooded by such rivers of delight
that it exults it has not burst
with so much happiness and joy.

'Tell me then, belovèd stock from which I spring,
who were Your ancestors, and say what were the years
written in the record of Your childhood.

'Tell me of the sheepfold of Saint John,
how many people lived there and who among them
were worthy of its highest offices.'

Come s'avviva a lo spirar d'i venti
carbone in fiamma, così vid' io quella
luce risplendere a' miei blandimenti;

e come a li occhi miei si fé più bella,
così con voce più dolce e soave,
ma non con questa moderna favella,

dissemi: "Da quel dì che fu detto '*Ave*'
al parto in che mia madre, ch'è or santa,
s'allevïò di me ond' era grave,

al suo Leon cinquecento cinquanta
e trenta fiate venne questo foco
a rinfiammarsi sotto la sua pianta.

Li antichi miei e io nacqui nel loco
dove si truova pria l'ultimo sesto
da quei che corre il vostro annüal gioco.

Basti d'i miei maggiori udirne questo:
chi ei si fosser e onde venner quivi,
più è tacer che ragionare onesto.

Tutti color ch'a quel tempo eran ivi
da poter arme tra Marte e 'l Batista,
erano il quinto di quei ch'or son vivi.

Ma la cittadinanza, ch'è or mista
di Campi, di Certaldo e di Fegghine,
pura vediesi ne l'ultimo artista.

Oh quanto fora meglio esser vicine
quelle genti ch'io dico, e al Galluzzo
e a Trespiano aver vostro confine,

che averle dentro e sostener lo puzzo
del villan d'Aguglion, di quel da Signa,
che già per barattare ha l'occhio aguzzo!

As embers leap to flame on a puff of wind,
I watched that light become resplendent
at my respectful and persuasive words.

And as it became more pleasing to my sight,
so, with a voice more sweet and gentle,
but not in this our modern tongue,

he said: 'From the day *Ave* was first spoken
until the birthpangs by which my mother,
now blessed, was lightened of me, her burden,

'this fiery star came to its Lion
five hundred fifty times and thirty more
to be rekindled underneath its paw.

'My ancestors and I were born just where
the horsemen in your yearly race
first come upon the farthest district.

'Let that be enough for you about my forebears.
As to who they were and where they came from,
it is more modest to be silent than to speak.

'All who lived there then, fit to bear arms,
and who dwelt between Mars and the Baptist,
amounted to a fifth of those who live there now,

'but the city's bloodline, now mixed
with that of Campi, of Certaldo, and Figline,
was then found pure in the humblest artisan.

'Ah, how much better would it be
had those cities which I name remained but neighbors,
had you kept your borders at Galluzzo and Trespiano,

'than to have them in your midst and bear the stench
of the lout from Aguglion and of him from Signa
who already has so sharp an eye for graft!

Se la gente ch'al mondo più traligna
non fosse stata a Cesare noverca,
ma come madre a suo figlio benigna,

tal fatto è fiorentino e cambia e merca,
che si sarebbe vòlto a Simifonti,
là dove andava l'avolo a la cerca;

sariesi Montemurlo ancor de' Conti;
sarieno i Cerchi nel piovier d'Acone,
e forse in Valdigrieve i Buondelmonti.

Sempre la confusion de le persone
principio fu del mal de la cittade,
come del vostro il cibo che s'appone;

e cieco toro più avaccio cade
che cieco agnello; e molte volte taglia
più e meglio una che le cinque spade.

Se tu riguardi Luni e Orbisaglia
come sono ite, e come se ne vanno
di retro ad esse Chiusi e Sinigaglia,

udir come le schiatte si disfanno
non ti parrà nova cosa né forte,
poscia che le cittadi termine hanno.

Le vostre cose tutte hanno lor morte,
sì come voi; ma celasi in alcuna
che dura molto, e le vite son corte.

E come 'l volger del ciel de la luna
cuopre e discuopre i liti sanza posa,
così fa di Fiorenza la Fortuna:

per che non dee parer mirabil cosa
ciò ch'io dirò de li alti Fiorentini
onde è la fama nel tempo nascosa.

'If that tribe, which is the most degenerate
in all the world, had not been like a stepmother
to Caesar, but kind as a mother to her son,

'there is one, become a Florentine, who is in trade
and changes money, who would be sent straight back
to Semifonte, where his granddad scoured the country.

'Montemurlo would still owe fealty to the Conti,
the Cerchi would be in the parish of Acone,
and the Buondelmonti might remain in Valdigreve.

'Intermingling of peoples has ever been
the source of all the city's ills,
as eating in excess is to the body.

'A blind bull is more prone to fall
than a blind lamb, and frequently a single sword
cuts deeper and more sharp than five.

'If you consider Luni, Urbisaglia—
how they've ceased to be—and how Chiusi
and Senigallia soon will join them,

'then to hear how families come to nothing
will not seem strange or difficult to grasp,
since even cities cease to be.

'All your concerns are mortal, even as are you,
but in some things that are more lasting
this lies hidden, because all lives are brief.

'And, as the turning of the lunar sphere covers
and endlessly uncovers the edges of the shore,
thus does fortune deal with Florence.

'Then it should not seem strange or marvelous to you
to hear me talk of noble Florentines,
whose fame is buried in the depth of time.

Io vidi li Ughi e vidi i Catellini,
Filippi, Greci, Ormanni e Alberichi,
già nel calare, illustri cittadini;

e vidi così grandi come antichi,
con quel de la Sannella, quel de l'Arca,
e Soldanieri e Ardinghi e Bostichi.

Sovra la porta ch'al presente è carca
di nova fellonia di tanto peso
che tosto fia iattura de la barca,

erano i Ravignani, ond' è disceso
il conte Guido e qualunque del nome
de l'alto Bellincione ha poscia preso.

Quel de la Pressa sapeva già come
regger si vuole, e avea Galigaio
dorata in casa sua già l'elsa e 'l pome.

Grand' era già la colonna del Vaio,
Sacchetti, Giuochi, Fifanti e Barucci
e Galli e quei ch'arrossan per lo staio.

Lo ceppo di che nacquero i Calfucci
era già grande, e già eran tratti
a le curule Sizii e Arrigucci.

Oh quali io vidi quei che son disfatti
per lor superbia! e le palle de l'oro
fiorian Fiorenza in tutt' i suoi gran fatti.

Così facieno i padri di coloro
che, sempre che la vostra chiesa vaca,
si fanno grassi stando a consistoro.

L'oltracotata schiatta che s'indraca
dietro a chi fugge, e a chi mostra 'l dente
o ver la borsa, com' agnel si placa,

'I saw the Ughi, I saw the Catellini,
Filippi, Greci, Ormanni and Alberichi,
90 illustrious citizens already in decline,

'and I saw, as great as they were ancient,
dell'Arca alongside della Sannella,
93 and Soldanieri and Ardinghi and Bostichi.

'Over the gate, which today is weighed down
with such burden of new and unspeakable treachery
96 that some cargo soon shall be hurled from the ship,

'lived the Ravignani, from whom Count Guido
and all those who since have taken their name
99 from the noble Bellincione are descended.

'The Della Pressa already knew the way to rule,
and in their house the Galigaio already had
102 the gilded hilt and pommel.

'Great already was the stripe of fur,
great were the Sacchetti, Giuochi, Fifanti, Barucci,
105 Galli, and those who blush because of the bushel.

'The stock from which the Calfucci sprang
was already great, and already called
108 to the seats of power were Sizii and Arrigucci.

'Ah, in what glory I saw those,
now quite undone by pride! And the golden balls
111 made Florence flower with all their glorious deeds.

'Thus did the fathers of those who now,
whenever your church needs to fill the bishop's seat,
114 fatten themselves by sitting long in council.

'The proud and insolent race, playing the dragon
at the back of him who flees, but mild as a lamb
117 to him who shows his teeth—or else his purse,

già venìa sù, ma di picciola gente;
sì che non piacque ad Ubertin Donato
che poï il suocero il fé lor parente.

Già era 'l Caponsacco nel mercato
disceso giù da Fiesole, e già era
buon cittadino Giuda e Infangato.

Io dirò cosa incredibile e vera:
nel picciol cerchio s'entrava per porta
che si nomava da quei de la Pera.

Ciascun che de la bella insegna porta
del gran barone il cui nome e 'l cui pregio
la festa di Tommaso riconforta,

da esso ebbe milizia e privilegio;
avvegna che con popol si rauni
oggi colui che la fascia col fregio.

Già eran Gualterotti e Importuni;
e ancor saria Borgo più quïeto,
se di novi vicin fosser digiuni.

La casa di che nacque il vostro fleto,
per lo giusto disdegno che v'ha morti
e puose fine al vostro viver lieto,

era onorata, essa e suoi consorti:
o Buondelmonte, quanto mal fuggisti
le nozze süe per li altrui conforti!

Molti sarebber lieti, che son tristi,
se Dio t'avesse conceduto ad Ema
la prima volta ch'a città venisti.

Ma conveniesi, a quella pietra scema
che guarda 'l ponte, che Fiorenza fesse
vittima ne la sua pace postrema.

'was already on the rise, but of mean stock,
so that it gave no joy to Ubertin Donato
when his father-in-law made him their kinsman.

'The Caponsacchi had already made their way
from Fiesole to the marketplace, and both Giuda
and Infangato were already citizens of note.

'I will tell a thing incredible but true:
The old city walls were entered through a gate
that took its name from the della Pera.

'Everyone bearing the noble coat of arms
of the great baron whose name and praise
are celebrated at the feast of Thomas

'had from him their knighthood and their privilege,
although he that decks it with a golden fringe
today takes the side of the common folk.

'Gualterotti and Importuni were already there,
and the Borgo would even now be more at peace
had they been left hungry for new neighbors.

'The house that is the wellspring of your tears,
whose just disdain brought death among you
and put an end to your lighthearted life,

'was honored then, both it and its allies.
O Buondelmonte, how ill-fated that you fled
those nuptials at another's urging!

'Many would be happy who now grieve
if God had let the river Ema take you
the first time that you came into our town.

'But it was destined that, to the shattered stone
that guards the bridge, Florence should offer
a sacrificial victim in her final days of peace.

Con queste genti, e con altre con esse,
vid' io Fiorenza in sì fatto riposo,
che non avea cagione onde piangesse.

Con queste genti vid' io glorïoso
e giusto il popol suo, tanto che 'l giglio
non era ad asta mai posto a ritroso,
né per divisïon fatto vermiglio."

'With these noble families, and with others still,
I saw Florence in such tranquility
that there was nothing that might cause her grief.

'With these noble families I saw her people
so glorious and just, that the lily
had not yet been reversed upon the lance
nor by dissension changed to red.'

1–9. Dante, in the course of celebrating his noble birthright, uses the occasion to condemn any such self-aggrandizing sentiments. The appeal of noble bloodlines is so great, the poet explains, that he took pride in his ancestry even now in the heavens, where he assuredly should have known better. For a meditation on the problematical nature of Dante's ideas about nobility, see Borsellino (Bors.1995.1), pp. 39–41.

Boethius (*Cons.* III.6[pr]) proclaims the emptiness of a noble name in a passage also probably echoed by Dante in *Convivio* (IV.xx.5). See also *Monarchia* (II.iii.4), words that sound much like Francesco da Buti's gloss to these verses, citing Boethius in distinguishing nobility of soul from "corporeal" nobility (i.e., that established by bloodline).

Where at the close of Canto XIV Dante claims that he was not wrong in not praising Beatrice there, here he states that it was wrong indeed to feel himself glorified in his ancestry.

7–9. This apostrophe of nobility of blood employs a metaphor, in which the mantle (or cloak) of nobility of blood grows shorter each generation that fails to ornament its reputation by earning further genuine honors (as did Cacciaguida, dying a martyr's death on crusade).

10–12. Dante, finally knowing who it is whom he addresses, used the honorific *voi* to hail his ancestor, the "You" that was first given to Julius Caesar, according to Lucan (*Phars.* V.383–386), but is now little used by the contemporary Romans, descended into a state approaching barbarism in Dante's eyes (see *Dve* I.xi.2). (Perhaps the first to observe the Lucanian source was Pietro di Dante [comm. to this tercet].) Lucan, prompted by his hatred of Julius (and of Nero, for whom Julius occasionally stands in), has invented this particular in his True History of Authoritarian Language, a fabrication that eventually came to light. According to him, since Julius, assuming his role as dictator, also assumed the many roles of those Romans who had previously held positions of responsibility in republican Rome, he needed to be addressed in a way that represented the plurality of his roles. Gabriele (comm. to verse 10) was perhaps the first to express some doubt about Lucan's observation; Lombardi spiked it through the heart (comm. to vv. 10–15). The "honorific You" actually came into use, explains Scartazzini (comm. to verse 10), only in the third century.

13–15. This tercet returns to a scene that had been focal to the pivotal moment in the adulterous passion between Francesca and Paolo in *Inferno* V, the kiss exchanged by Lancelot and Guinevere in the twelfth-century Old French prose romance *Lancelot du lac*. "During [Gallehault's] residence at King Arthur's court a warm friendship sprang up between him and Lancelot, who confided to him his love for Queen Guenever. The latter, who secretly loved Lancelot, was easily persuaded by Gallehault to meet the knight privately. In the course of the interview Gallehault urged the queen to give Lancelot a kiss, which was the beginning of their guilty love. . . . [Dante here] alludes to the cough given by the Lady of Malehault, one of the queen's companions, on perceiving the familiarity between them (she herself being in love with Lancelot, who was aware of the fact, and was in great anxiety lest it should injure him with the queen)" (T). Umberto Carpi (Carp.2004.1), vol. I, pp. 24–25 and 256, refines the general appreciation of the reference, pointing out (and crediting Pietro Beltrami for the observation leading to his insight) that Guinevere's handmaid did not cough when the queen and Lancelot kissed, but before that, when she revealed to her admirer that she was aware of his name and of his lofty lineage. Her words cause the lady-in-waiting to cough as a way of informing Lancelot that *she* finally knows his identity and nobility of blood. Thus Beatrice, hearing Dante's response to his own genealogical distinction, the *voi* with which he addresses his ancestor, smiles in knowing response to that. That she does so as a warning against such pride seems clear, even if some commentators insist on a friendlier, less critical attitude at this height in the heavens.

16–18. The poet again contorts the order of events for his narrative purposes; the words that the protagonist speaks *precede*, naturally, Beatrice's reaction to them (vv. 13–15). Indeed, we may realize that the preceding *terzina* (vv. 10–12) also reflects what he has said just now.

These three parallel uses of the honorific *voi* for Cacciaguida, emotive anaphora (see Francesca's *Amor . . . Amor . . . Amor* in *Inf.* V.100–106), offer an outpouring of ancestral affection, but more than tinged with vainglory, the sin we saw punished on the terrace of Pride in Purgatory.

This program (of honorific address uttered by the protagonist) began in *Inferno* X, with Farinata and Cavalcante. It had one more appearance in the first *cantica*, with Brunetto Latini. In *Purgatorio*, Currado Malaspina, Pope Adrian V, Guinizzelli, and Beatrice all received the respectful *voi* in salutation. In this concluding canticle, Beatrice receives it three times (*Par.* IV.122–134), and Cacciaguida also three times, all in this tercet, in a final "explosion" that lays it to rest. (See the notes to *Inf.* X.49–51 and to *Purg.* XIX.131; also to *Par.* XXXI.79–90.)

16. The protagonist addresses seven beings as "father" in the poem: first of all Virgil, a total of seven times (between *Purg.* IV.44 and XXIII.13); then God (in the guise of Apollo) in *Paradiso* I.28; Cacciaguida (here and in *Par.* XVII.106); St. Benedict (*Par.* XXII.58); St. Peter (*Par.* XXIV.62 and XXIV.124); Adam (*Par.* XXVI.92); and finally St. Bernard (*Par.* XXXII.100). Dante the poet refers to five others as being his "fathers": Brunetto Latini (*Inf.* XV.83); Cato (*Purg.* I.33); Guido Guinizzelli (*Purg.* XXVI.97); St. Francis (*Par.* XI.85); and the Sun (*Par.* XXII.116).

17. For *baldezza* (here translated "bold assurance"), see Vallone (Vall.1967.1).

19. These "rivers" are, resolved from metaphor, the sources of the protagonist's pleasure in the knowledge of his lineage and in his election to join Cacciaguida among the saved souls here and, eventually, in the Empyrean.

22–27. The protagonist wants to know (1) the root of his roots, as it were; (2) about the times in Florence when Cacciaguida was a youth; (3) the number of inhabitants in the city in those days; and (4) the best people in the city then. His first question is reminiscent of Farinata's to him (*Inf.* X.42), "Chi fuor li maggior tui?" (Who were your ancestors?).

28–32. This simile, at least from the time of Scartazzini (comm. to vv. 28–33), has been recognized as Ovidian in provenance, reflecting the similar comparison (*Metam.* VII.79–81) describing Medea's renewed infatuation with Jason. It seems odd that, for a description of Cacciaguida's rekindled affection for his great-great-grandson, Dante should resort to Ovid's description of Medea's reignited passion for the handsome youth who will, as she almost fully realizes, betray her. (Dante had previously visited a part of this long passage dedicated to Medea and Jason [VII.1–403] in *Par.* II.16–18. For the "rewriting" of Ovid involved in that tercet, see the note to *Par.* II.17–18.)

33. What language does Cacciaguida speak? Breaking ranks with the vast majority of modern commentators who believe that it is twelfth-century

Florentine, Porena (in his second endnote to the canto, found in his comm. to verse 154 in the DDP) suggests that it is Latin. This solution had already been proposed by Daniello (comm. to this verse). It was held in favor until Poletto, some 330 years later, perhaps rightly sensing that Dante never would have used the terms "dolce" or "soave" to describe Latin as contrasted with the vernacular, cited Beatrice's use of Florentine vernacular, as referred to at *Inferno* II.57, as part of his understanding that the text refers to the Italian spoken in Cacciaguida's time. Grabher (comm. to vv. 28–33) is firm in denying Daniello's hypothesis; he favors a reference to Cacciaguida's use of the Florentine vernacular. (Grabher also denigrates a second theory, which had occasionally been pressed into service after Vellutello introduced it [comm. to vv. 28–33], that Cacciaguida spoke in "the tongues of angels.") He, like Poletto, is sure that it is best to understand that Dante is concerned here with the transitory nature of any stage in a vernacular tongue's development, as reflected in *Convivio* I.v.9, a concern that led to his promise, in the next sentence, to take up that matter in *De vulgari eloquentia* (which he did: see *Dve* I.ix.6). Pézard (Peza.1967.1), for all intents and purposes, resolved the issue in favor of the Florentine vernacular of the twelfth century.

34–36. The Annunciation, occurring on March 25 of the first year of Christian history, marked by the words "Ave Maria" in Gabriel's Latin, coincides with the date of the new year as measured by Florentines in Dante's age. It is probably not an accident that we are supposed to understand that the poem itself begins on that date in 1300. See the note to *Inferno* I.1.

37–39. " 'This fire (Mars) came 580 times to its Lion, to be rekindled under its paw.' Between the Conception—the beginning of the year 1—and the birth of Cacciaguida, Mars returned 580 times to the constellation of Leo, which, being of like disposition to Mars, reinforces the influence of that planet. As Mars completes its revolution in 687 days, we shall get the year of Cacciaguida's birth by multiplying 687 by 580 and dividing by 365: 1091. He was therefore 56 when he followed the crusade, having lived from 1091 to 1147. Cf. Moore [Moor.1903.1], III, 59–60. G. Federzoni, *In quale anno nacque Cacciaguida?* in *Fanfulla della Domenica*, 22 Nov. 1914 (XXXVI, no. 39), would adopt a reading *tre* for *trenta*, as Pietro Alighieri and some others did, giving *fiate* three syllables as usual, and thus would get a date 1106 instead of 1091" (Grandgent, comm. to vv. 37–39). The variant *tre* has now mainly been dismissed from the discussion, perhaps as a result of Lombardi's strong opposition (comm. to vv. 34–39), which even countered the opinion put forward by the Accademia della Crusca.

40–42. Here is John Carroll (comm. to vv. 40–45) clearing up this difficult passage: "The use of the word *sesto* by Cacciaguida is, strictly speaking, an anachronism. It is proper to a later time when the city was much larger, was enclosed in a second line of walls, and was divided into *six* wards or *sestieri*. The smaller city of Cacciaguida's day lay within the first wall, and was divided into *four* wards—*quartieri*, formed by a line of streets running from the ancient Porta del Duomo on the north to the Ponte Vecchio on the south, and crossed by another line from east to west, running through the Mercato Vecchio, now demolished to make way for the hideous Piazza Vittorio Emanuele. The *quartiere* in which the house of his ancestors stood was that named after the eastern gate, Porta San Piero. An annual game was run on June 24, the day of the patron saint of the city [John the Baptist], and, as its course was from west to east, this quarter was the last the competitors reached. And what Cacciaguida says is that the house in which he and his forefathers were born stood just at the point where the runners entered this last quarter of the city. This would localize it in the Via degli Speziali which runs off the Piazza Vittorio Emanuele towards the Corso, . . ."

42. Elements in this canto, including the reference to the annual *palio*, the race around the inner routes traversing the city, remind some readers of Brunetto Latini (*Inf.* XV.121–124). As the civic/political figure closest to the center of *Inferno*, he seems to have a certain similar placement and function both to Marco Lombardo (*Purg.* XVI) and to Cacciaguida (*Par.* XV–XVII).

43–45. A series of debates has followed this tercet. Nonetheless, the context offered by the opening of the canto, where the protagonist is portrayed as glorying in his ancestry and is cautioned by Beatrice's cough against so doing, perhaps offers us all we need to know to unravel this skein. Cacciaguida will not feed his great-great-grandson's pride by narrating his heroic noble past, which may be traced back to the Romans. This is the sense offered by Bosco/Reggio (comm. to verse 45), who sensibly go on to explain that in fact necessity lies behind the author's reticence: No one knows (or perhaps ever knew) the family history that is supposedly here suppressed in the service of modesty.

46–48. Answering the protagonist's third question, Cacciaguida leaves us in a quandary because his response is not clear. The males of "draft age" (as we would say today) in early-twelfth-century Florence were 20 percent of (a) the entire population in 1300 or (b) the males of draft age in 1300. The Italian would clearly (as our translation suggests) indicate that the first is what is meant.

47. The phrase "between Mars and the Baptist" is a way of describing the confines of the city in Cacciaguida's day by its nothernmost and southernmost monuments within the original walls (the Baptistry and the statue of Mars at the Ponte Vecchio).

50. These three small towns are today known as Campi Bizenzio (the nearest), Figline, and Certaldo (the farthest away from Florence; Boccaccio was born there in 1313). Readers have assumed that, in his choices, Dante expected local readers in the fourteenth century to recognize certain families that had recently arrived from these towns and associated themselves with nefarious activities.

51. Cacciaguida is referring to the "unmixed" (i.e., Roman and pure) blood of the original inhabitants, pure in even the least artisan and not yet diluted by the bad bloodlines of those descended from the Fiesolans—or from those even worse.

52–57. Cacciaguida is of the opinion that the quality of urban life would have been much improved had these new folk kept outside the boundaries north (Trespiano) and south (Galluzzo). However, they instead entered the city, bringing with them the "stench" of men like Baldo d'Aguglione and Fazio da Signa, both of whom, renegade White Guelphs, were involved in the "exile question" during Dante's attempts to return to Florence and both of whom were also opposed to the city's welcoming Henry VII. In short, each was a personal and political enemy of Dante.

58–66. See Tozer's paraphrase of this passage (comm. to verse 58): "If the clergy had not set themselves in opposition to the Imperial power, there would not have been those feuds between the small Italian towns, which ruined them, and caused their inhabitants to take refuge in Florence, where they became traders." For a more developed consideration, also in English, of the political situation referred to in these lines, see Carroll's commentary to them.

59. There soon results a linguistic "family resemblance" between the emperor and Dante (see *Par.* XVII.47), to both of whom the city behaves like a cruel stepmother (*noverca*).

61–63. Ever since Grandgent (comm. to verse 61, referring to two contemporary Italian sources), there has been a tradition among commentators to assign an identity to this exiled family from Semifonte (a town conquered and "colonized" by Florence in 1202), that of Lippo Velluti. One of the things that makes this hypothesis especially attractive is that Lippo was instrumental in sending Giano della Bella (see vv. 131–132), author of the *Ordinamenti di Giustizia* (1293), into exile. Dante, like Giano, was a prior of Florence and shared with him a noble bloodline (at least Dante may have sensed a similarity in this regard) as well as a deep distrust of the great noble houses, which abused their powers easily and often. Giano's *Ordinamenti* placed severe limits on their ability to do so. While neither Lippo nor Giano is mentioned by name, their antagonistic relationship may help unriddle the references in this passage as well as in the later one.

64–66. Continuing in the same vein, Cacciaguida argues that the Conti Guidi, the Cerchi, and the Buondelmonti (about whom we shall hear more at the end of this canto) all would have been better off had they not become Florentine citizens, staying in their original homes outside the city.

67–72. The mixing of peoples, like overeating, ruins a city, with the result that it becomes too large and too cumbersome. Its resulting unwieldiness is compared to that of a bull or of a superfluity of swords in the hand of a swordsman. This last is perhaps meant to mirror the 500 percent growth in Florence's population referred to in verse 48 (if it was to so great an increase that Dante was there referring [see the note to vv. 46–48]).

73–81. Two Roman cities, Luni (near Carrara) and Urbisaglia (near Macerata), had fallen into ruins well before Dante's time and remained in that condition. Two others, Chiusi (near Siena) and Senigallia (near Ancona), seemed to be suffering a similar fate. If cities show such mortal tendencies, reflects Cacciaguida, how much more subject to mortality are mere families? This unhappy thought leads toward the death-list of the great Florentine families that will occupy much of the rest of the canto.

82–87. Introduced by a simile (as the Moon causes tidal change that variously inundates and lays bare litoral planes, so the goddess Fortune does with Florence), Cacciaguida's task will be the recording of the great families who are dying out and whose remembrance is also growing faint. His purpose is to rescue their fame from "the dark backward and abyss of time."

88–139. The catalogue of once-great families of Florence includes the following, arranged here in groups of five [with those referred to by periphrasis in square brackets] and numbering forty: **Ughi, Catellini, Filippi, Greci, Ormanni; Alberichi, dell'Arca, della Sannella, Soldanieri, Ardinghi; Bostichi, Ravignani** (the noble and ancient family of Bellincion Berti [*Par.* XV.112], mentioned with the later-arriving Conti Guidi and with those who took their name from the first Bellincione), **della Pressa, Galigaio, [Pigli]** ("the stripe of fur"); **Sacchetti, Giuochi, Fifanti, Barucci, Galli; [Chiaramontesi]** ("those who blush because of the bushel"), **[Donati]** ("from which the Calfucci sprang"), **Sizii, Arrigucci, [Uberti]** ("those now undone by pride"); **[Lamberti]** ("balls of gold"), **[Visdomini]** ("the fathers"), **[Tosinghi]** ("the fathers"), **[Adimari]** ("the proud and insolent race"), **Caponsacchi; Giudi, Infangati, della Pera** (the Peruzzi?), the **Baron** (Hugh of Brandenburg), **Gualterotti; Importuni, [Buondelmonti]** ("new neighbors"), **[Amidei]** ("the house that is the wellspring of your tears"), **[Gherardini], [Uccellini]** (these last two are referred to as "allies" of the Amidei).

"Il XVI è quasi tutto una cronaca irta di puri nomi, ed è la più lunga e più arida pagina di cronaca di tutto il poema" (Canto XVI is nearly entirely a chronicle bristling with mere names; it is the longest and most arid page of chronicle in the entire poem [Momigliano, comm. to vv. 22–27]). Momigliano's judgment is, if more harsh than most, not atypical. Not only does it miss the aesthetic point of the catalogue of families (which might be compared to Homer's masterful catalogue of ships in *Iliad* II—if it cannot hope to rival that first and possibly best of literary catalogues), it severely overstates its length: not "quasi tutto una cronaca irta di puri nomi," but only a little over one-third of the canto, occupying verses 88–139.

For praise of the nostalgic poetic quality of *Paradiso* XVI, so roundly criticized by so many readers precisely for its unpoetic qualities, see Porena's first endnote in his commentary to this canto (appended to his comm. to verse 154 in the DDP).

94–99. Carroll: "[These lines] refer to the Cerchi (see note [in Carroll's comm. to vv. 58–66]). Their houses were above the Porta San Piero, and had been acquired by this wealthy family from the Conti Guidi, who sprang from the ancient house of the Ravignani, the head of which was the

Bellincion Berti of *Par.* XV. 112. The *fellonia* or treason charged against the Cerchi seems to be their failure as leaders of the Whites to defend the city against the Blacks in Nov. 1301. Dino Compagni says 'their hearts failed them through cowardice': the Priors gave them orders to prepare for defense and urged them 'to play the man.' But 'from avarice' they refused to pay the hired troops, made practically no preparations, and so handed over the city to six terrible days of outrage and pillage. The exile of the Whites which followed is the 'lightening of the barque' to which Dante refers in line 96. For a full account of this disastrous struggle between the Bianchi and the Neri, see Dino Compagni's *Chronicle*, Bk. II, and Villani's, VIII.38–49."

These six lines have been the cause of a certain confusion and of considerable debate; Carroll's view, however, seems sensible. For an English translation of Dino Compagni's chronicles of Florence in Dante's time, written by one of his contemporaries, see Compagni (Comp.1986.1).

101–102. As knights, members of the Galigaio family had, as their emblem, the gilded hilt and handle of a sword.

103. The Pigli had a stripe of squirrel-fur on a red field as their insignia.

105. For Dante's earlier reference to corrupt procedures in Florentine weights and measures, see *Purgatorio* XII.105 and the last paragraph in the note to XII.100–108.

109–111. Carroll: "Those 'undone by their pride' are the Uberti, the great Ghibelline family, banished in 1258, and never allowed to return. Farinata, who saved Florence after Montaperti (1260), belonged to it (*Inf.* X.22 ff.). The other family, referred to by its coat of arms, the 'balls of gold,' is the Lamberti. To it belonged Mosca, whose famous phrase, *Cosa fatta capo ha*, sealed Buondelmonte's fate—and his own (*Inf.* XXVIII.103 ff.)."

112–114. Carroll: "The reference is to the Tosinghi and the Visdomini, whom Villani (IV.10) calls 'patrons and defenders of the Bishopric.' During a vacancy, they enjoyed the use of the Bishop's palace until a successor was appointed, and apparently they did not spare the larder."

115–120. Carroll: "A bitter stroke at the Adimari,—dragons to the timid, but to men with teeth or purse, lambs. Dante's bitterness is not unnatural when we remember that, according to early commentators, one of this family, Boccaccino, gained possession of the poet's property, and therefore opposed strenuously his recall from exile. This might account also for his scorn of Filippo Argenti (*Inf.* VIII.31–64), who belonged to a branch of the Adimari."

The wife of Ubertino Donati, a member of the twenty-second family referred to in Cacciaguida's social registry of ancient Florence, was a daughter of Bellincion Berti; Ubertino was displeased when Bellincione, his father-in-law, arranged for the marriage of another of his daughters to a member of the Admiari clan, thus making Ubertino their kinsman.

124–126. Carroll: "That one of the gates of 'the small circuit'—the first city-wall—viz., the Porta Peruzza, was named after the Della Pera family might seem incredible for various reasons that have been suggested: (a) how small the circuit must have been when this was one of the city-gates; or (b) how free of jealousy ancient Florence must have been when one of its gates was named after a private family; or (c) how hard to believe that a family so forgotten now was so ancient that a gate in the earliest circuit of walls was named after it. The drift of the comments on the other families favours the last interpretation."

127–132. Carroll: " 'The great baron' was the Marquis Hugh of Brandenburg, viceroy in Tuscany of Otho III. Villani says he knighted five Florentine families, who for love of him bore his arms. One of these, the Della Bella, is here referred to as having surrounded the arms with a border of gold. It was a member of this family, the famous Giano della Bella, who in 1293 proposed the *Ordinances of Justice*, in order to curb the lawlessness of his own order, the nobles, and it is probably he who is referred to as having 'joined himself with the people.' How the Marquis Hugh was converted, built the Badia, died on S. Thomas' Day, and was buried in the monastery, will be found in Villani, IV.2."

133–135. While both families, the Gualterotti and the Importuni, were Guelph in the views of the local chroniclers (Villani, Compagni, Malispini), according to other documents, as reported by Bosco/Reggio (comm. to verse 133), the Gualterotti were in fact Ghibellines. Bosco/Reggio suggest the contradiction may be explained by the diverse political sympathies found in diverse branches of the family.

136–150. This is Cacciaguida's rueful contemplation of the wrack and ruin caused by a single event. Here is Carroll (comm. to *Par.* XIV. 79–87) on this pivotal moment in the history of Florence: "The reference is to the well-known story of the murder of Buondelmonte de' Buondelmonti in 1216. This young nobleman was betrothed to a lady of the Amidei family, but forsook her for a daughter of the house of the Donati. The kinsmen of the insulted lady waylaid and slew him at the foot of the statue of Mars, 'that mutilated stone,' as he rode into the city on Easter Day [Villani, *Chron.* V.38; Dino Compagni, 1.2]. Well for the city, says Cacciaguida, if the first time he came to it he had been drowned in the little stream of the Ema which flows through the Valdigreve, a little south of Florence, where his castle lay. The murder was generally regarded as the beginning of the feuds of Guelphs and Ghibellines of which Dante himself was a victim; although, as Villani admits, 'long before there were factions among the noble citizens, and the said parties existed by reason of the strifes and questions between the Church and the Empire' [*Chronicle* V.38]."

136–138. The Amidei are portrayed as justly angered by the snub to their name revealed in Buondelmonte's behavior; it is from their rage that originated the current sorrow of the city.

139. The allies of the Amidei were the Gherardini and Uccellini families.

145–147. It is difficult to imagine a more "operatic" or fitting symbol of the end of the era of peace in Florence than Buondelmonte's body, lying where it fell, at the feet of the statue of Mars, on Easter Sunday 1216. Mars as the pagan god of war is in this canto deployed against the Christian militancy that typifies the crusading spirit. See Borsellino (Bors.1995.1), p. 46, on the ambiguity of the sign of Mars in this canto, representing, in different contexts, both Heaven-approved crusading and damnable internecine broils.

148. For the question of the actual number of noble families in Florence in the eleventh and thirteenth centuries, see Scartazzini (comm. to vv. 59–154). Villani (*Cron.* V.39) accounts for seventy noble families in 1215. (He also reports on the numbers for 1015 [*Cron.* IV.10–13].) The discrepancies between Dante's figures and Villani's lead Scartazzini to think that Dante is not to be relied on for particulars of this kind. However, in this verse Dante has Cacciaguida say that there were more than these forty famous families that he has mentioned flowering at that time.

152. This verse will be remembered at *Paradiso* XXXI.39. See the note to that passage.

153–154. Cacciaguida takes pride in the fact that Florence, in his day, never lost a battle. The image of the flag reversed upon its staff is apparently a reference to the following practice: Members of the victorious army would drag the losers' battle-flags upside down over the field of combat.

In 1251 the Guelphs changed the design of the Florentine flag from a white lily on a red field to a red lily on a white field, while the ousted Ghibellines retained the traditional arrangement (according to Villani, *Cronica*, VI.43). As Stephany (Step.1973.1) points out, the original flag mirrors Cacciaguida's situation in the fifth heaven, red Mars quartered by a white Greek cross.

154. Fachard (Fach.2002.1), p. 231, points out that the first and last lines of this canto, so involved with the concepts of the nobility of bloodlines and the (at times consequent) spilling of human blood, both end with words for blood or bleeding.

PARADISO XVII

OUTLINE

MARS

1–6 simile: As **[Phaeton]** came to **Clymene** to have assurance that **[Apollo]** was his father, such did Dante seem;

7–12 Beatrice: "decide exactly what it is you want to know";

13–18 Dante: "Since you know what things will come to pass,

19–27 and since while I was with **Virgil** I heard harsh things about my future, I would like to be forewarned";

28–30 thus does Dante honor the will of Beatrice.

31–36 Cacciaguida responds, not in enigmas, but clearly;

37–99 his prophetic speech:

- 37–42 Contingent things are known to God without limiting the freedom of the will
- 43–45 simile: harmony from discordant sounds compared to the view of Dante's life possessed by Cacciaguida
- 46–48 simile: perfidy of **[Phaedra]** to **Hippolytus** and of Florence to Dante
- 49–51 (1) This last is the plan of **[Boniface]** who ponders the fate of Florence in the Roman Curia;
- 52–54 (2) the offended party will of course be blamed but God's judgment will be clear in His vengeance;
- 55–60 (3) in exile Dante will first leave behind what he loves most and then (4) know the pain of begging;
- 61–69 (5) worst will be the backbiting of his fellows: he will do well to make himself a party of one;

70–75 (6) Dante, leaving the exiled Whites, will be welcomed to Verona by a gracious host **[Bartolommeo]**

76–99 (7) **[Cangrande]**:

- 76–78 with Bartolommeo Dante will find Cangrande,
- 79–81 only nine years old and not much noticed,
- 82–84 but before **[Clement]** deceives **Henry VII** he will be marked as special;
- 85–87 his munificence will be so renowned that not even his enemies will be mute about it;
- 88–90 look to his generosity; he will change the condition of rich and poor alike;
- 91–93 Cacciaguida's suppressed prophecy (Cangrande)
- 94–96 his "gloss" on the negative things Dante has heard about his life in Hell and Purgatory;
- 97–99 yet he should not envy his false neighbors, who shall be punished in his lifetime.

100–111 Dante's worrisome doubts about the future and his poem:

112–120 dilemma: to tell the truth or not; lose "friends" or fame?

121–123 Cacciaguida, his smiling *tesoro*, resplendent, replies;

124–142 Cacciaguida's encouragement: "Tell the truth."

PARADISO XVII

Qual venne a Climenè, per accertarsi
di ciò ch'avëa incontro a sé udito,
quei ch'ancor fa li padri ai figli scarsi;

tal era io, e tal era sentito
e da Beatrice e da la santa lampa
che pria per me avea mutato sito.

Per che mia donna "Manda fuor la vampa
del tuo disio," mi disse, "sì ch'ella esca
segnata bene de la interna stampa:

non perché nostra conoscenza cresca
per tuo parlare, ma perché t'ausi
a dir la sete, sì che l'uom ti mesca."

"O cara piota mia che sì t'insusi,
che, come veggion le terrene menti
non capere in trïangol due ottusi,

così vedi le cose contingenti
anzi che sieno in sé, mirando il punto
a cui tutti li tempi son presenti;

mentre ch'io era a Virgilio congiunto
su per lo monte che l'anime cura
e discendendo nel mondo defunto,

dette mi fuor di mia vita futura
parole gravi, avvegna ch'io mi senta
ben tetragono ai colpi di ventura;

per che la voglia mia saria contenta
d'intender qual fortuna mi s'appressa:
ché saetta previsa vien più lenta."

Like him who came to Clymene to cast out doubt
upon the rumor he had heard against himself,
who still makes fathers cautious with their sons,

such was I and such was I perceived to be
both by Beatrice and by the holy light
that earlier for me had changed its place.

And so my lady said to me: 'Send forth
the flame of your desire, and let it issue
with the clear imprint of its inner stamp,

'not that our knowledge be increased by what you say
but that you rehearse the telling of your thirst
so that the drink be poured for you.'

'O my precious root, you are raised so high
that, even as earthly minds discern no triangle
can contain two angles, both of them obtuse,

'so you, gazing on the point that holds all time
are able to discern contingencies
before they are apparent in themselves.

'While I was still in Virgil's company,
both on the mountain that restores our souls
and during our descent into the region of the dead,

'grave words were said to me about my future life—
however much I feel myself prepared
foursquare against the blows of chance—

'so that my will would be content
if I could know what fate draws near,
for the arrow one expects comes slower.'

Così diss' io a quella luce stessa
che pria m'avea parlato; e come volle
Beatrice, fu la mia voglia confessa.

Né per ambage, in che la gente folle
già s'inviscava pria che fosse anciso
l'Agnel di Dio che le peccata tolle,

ma per chiare parole e con preciso
latin rispuose quello amor paterno,
chiuso e parvente del suo proprio riso:

"La contingenza, che fuor del quaderno
de la vostra matera non si stende,
tutta è dipinta nel cospetto etterno;

necessità però quindi non prende
se non come dal viso in che si specchia
nave che per torrente giù discende.

Da indi, sì come viene ad orecchia
dolce armonia da organo, mi viene
a vista il tempo che ti s'apparecchia.

Qual si partio Ipolito d'Atene
per la spietata e perfida noverca,
tal di Fiorenza partir ti convene.

Questo si vuole e questo già si cerca,
e tosto verrà fatto a chi ciò pensa
là dove Cristo tutto dì si merca.

La colpa seguirà la parte offensa
in grido, come suol; ma la vendetta
fia testimonio al ver che la dispensa.

Tu lascerai ogne cosa diletta
più caramente; e questo è quello strale
che l'arco de lo essilio pria saetta.

I said these words to the very light
that had just spoken and, as Beatrice wished,
my wish was now declared.

Not with cloudy sayings, by which the foolish folk
were once ensnared, before the Lamb of God,
who takes away our sins, was slain,

but in plain words and with clear speech
that paternal love replied,
hidden and yet revealed in his own smile:

'Contingent things, which do not extend
beyond the pages of your material world,
are all depicted in the Eternal Sight,

'yet are by that no more enjoined
than is a ship, moved downstream on a river's flow,
by the eyes that mirror it.

'And thus, as harmony's sweet sound may rise
from mingled voices to the ear, so rises to my sight
a vision of the time that lies in store for you.

'As Hippolytus was forced to flee from Athens,
because of his stepmother, treacherous and fierce,
so shall you be forced to flee from Florence.

'This is the plan, already set in motion,
that soon will bring success to him who plots it
where Christ is bought and sold all day.

'The populace shall blame the injured party,
as it always does, but vengeance
shall bear witness to the Truth that metes it out.

'You shall leave behind all you most dearly love,
and that shall be the arrow
first loosed from exile's bow.

Tu proverai sì come sa di sale
lo pane altrui, e come è duro calle
60 lo scendere e 'l salir per l'altrui scale.

E quel che più ti graverà le spalle,
sarà la compagnia malvagia e scempia
63 con la qual tu cadrai in questa valle;

che tutta ingrata, tutta matta ed empia
si farà contr' a te; ma, poco appresso,
66 ella, non tu, n'avrà rossa la tempia.

Di sua bestialitate il suo processo
farà la prova; sì ch'a te fia bello
69 averti fatta parte per te stesso.

Lo primo tuo refugio e 'l primo ostello
sarà la cortesia del gran Lombardo
72 che 'n su la scala porta il santo uccello;

ch'in te avrà si benigno riguardo,
che del fare e del chieder, tra voi due,
75 fia primo quel che tra li altri è più tardo.

Con lui vedrai colui che 'mpresso fue,
nascendo, sì da questa stella forte,
78 che notabili fier l'opere sue.

Non se ne son le genti ancora accorte
per la novella età, ché pur nove anni
81 son queste rote intorno di lui torte;

ma pria che 'l Guasco l'alto Arrigo inganni,
parran faville de la sua virtute
84 in non curar d'argento né d'affanni.

Le sue magnificenze conosciute
saranno ancora, sì che ' suoi nemici
87 non ne potran tener le lingue mute.

'You shall learn how salt is the taste
of another man's bread and how hard is the way,
going down and then up another man's stairs.

'But the heaviest burden your shoulders must bear
shall be the companions, wicked and witless,
among whom you shall fall in your descent.

'They, utterly ungrateful, mad, and faithless,
shall turn against you. But soon enough they, not you,
shall feel their faces blushing past their brows.

'Of their brutish state the results
shall offer proof. And it shall bring you honor
to have made a single party of yourself alone.

'You shall find welcome and a first refuge
in the courtesy of the noble Lombard,
the one who bears the sacred bird above the ladder.

'It is he who will hold you in such gracious favor
that, as for granting and asking, between you two,
that shall be first which, between all others, happens after.

'In his company you shall find one who, at birth,
so took the imprint of this mighty star
that his deeds will truly be renowned.

'As yet the people, because of his youth,
take small note of him, since these wheels
have revolved above him only for nine years.

'But, before the Gascon can deceive the noble Henry,
sparks of his virtue shall at first shine forth
in his indifference to wealth or toil,

'and his munificence shall one day be so widely known
even his enemies will not contrive
to keep their tongues from praising it.

A lui t'aspetta e a' suoi benefici;
per lui fia trasmutata molta gente,
cambiando condizion ricchi e mendici;

e portera'ne scritto ne la mente
di lui, e nol dirai"; e disse cose
incredibili a quei che fier presente.

Poi giunse: "Figlio, queste son le chiose
di quel che ti fu detto; ecco le 'nsidie
che dietro a pochi giri son nascose.

Non vo' però ch'a' tuoi vicini invidie,
poscia che s'infutura la tua vita
via più là che 'l punir di lor perfidie."

Poi che, tacendo, si mostrò spedita
l'anima santa di metter la trama
in quella tela ch'io le porsi ordita,

io cominciai, come colui che brama,
dubitando, consiglio da persona
che vede e vuol dirittamente e ama:

"Ben veggio, padre mio, sì come sprona
lo tempo verso me, per colpo darmi
tal, ch'è più grave a chi più s'abbandona;

per che di provedenza è buon ch'io m'armi,
sì che, se loco m'è tolto più caro,
io non perdessi li altri per miei carmi.

Giù per lo mondo sanza fine amaro,
e per lo monte del cui bel cacume
li occhi de la mia donna mi levaro,

e poscia per lo ciel, di lume in lume,
ho io appreso quel che s'io ridico,
a molti fia sapor di forte agrume;

'Look to him and trust his gracious deeds.
On his account many will find alteration,
rich men changing states with beggars.

'And you shall bear this written in your memory,
but shall not tell of it'—and he foretold events
that even those who witness them shall not believe.

Then he added: 'Son, these are the glosses
on what was told you, these are the snares
that lurk behind a few revolving years.

'Yet I would not have you feel envious disdain
for your fellow-townsmen, since your life shall far outlast
the punishment of their treachery.'

After the holy soul, by falling silent,
showed that he had done with putting the woof
into the web for which I had set the warp,

I began, like a man in doubt,
but one filled with great desire for advice
from someone of clear sight, right will, and love:

'I can see, father, that time is spurring toward me
to deal me such a blow as falls most heavily
on one proceeding heedless on his way.

'Thus it is good I arm myself with forethought
so that, if my belovèd town is torn from me,
I may not lose still others through my songs.

'Down through the world of endless bitterness,
and upward on the mountain from whose lovely peak
my lady raised me with her eyes,

'and after, rising through the heavens, light to light,
I have learned things that, should I retell them,
would discomfort many with their bitter taste.

e s'io al vero son timido amico,
temo di perder viver tra coloro
che questo tempo chiameranno antico."

La luce in che rideva il mio tesoro
ch'io trovai lì, si fé prima corusca,
quale a raggio di sole specchio d'oro;

indi rispuose: "Coscïenza fusca
o de la propria o de l'altrui vergogna
pur sentirà la tua parola brusca.

Ma nondimen, rimossa ogne menzogna,
tutta tua visïon fa manifesta;
e lascia pur grattar dov' è la rogna.

Ché se la voce tua sarà molesta
nel primo gusto, vital nodrimento
lascerà poi, quando sarà digesta.

Questo tuo grido farà come vento,
che le più alte cime più percuote;
e ciò non fa d'onor poco argomento.

Però ti son mostrate in queste rote,
nel monte e ne la valle dolorosa
pur l'anime che son di fama note,

che l'animo di quel ch'ode, non posa
né ferma fede per essempro ch'aia
la sua radice incognita e ascosa,
né per altro argomento che non paia."

'Yet, should I be a timid friend to truth,
I fear that I shall not live on for those
to whom our times will be the ancient days.'

The light, in which the treasure that I found there
had been smiling, now became resplendent
as a mirror, golden in the sun,

and then made this reply: 'A conscience dark,
whether with its own or with a kinsman's shame,
is sure to feel your words are harsh.

'Nonetheless, forswear all falsehood,
revealing all that you have seen,
and then let him who itches scratch.

'For, if your voice is bitter at first taste,
it will later furnish vital nourishment
once it has been swallowed and digested.

'This cry of yours shall do as does the wind
that strikes the highest peaks with greater force—
this loftiness itself no little sign of honor.

'That is why you have been shown, within these wheels,
upon the mountain, and in the woeful valley,
those souls alone that are well known to fame,

'since the mind of one who listens will not heed
nor fix its faith on an example
that has its roots in things unknown or hidden
or on some other proof not clearly shown.'

PARADISO XVII

1–12. We have come to the midpoint of *Paradiso*. See, for a reading of this central canto, Brugnoli (Brug.1995.1), pointing out, among other things, that the poet has underlined numerically this mathematical fact. Brugnoli demonstrates that the central cantos of the last canticle, XI–XXIII, are arranged, at least in terms of the number of verses that they contain, in a pattern, as follows (the two bordering cantos, excluded from the pattern, are listed, in the table below, in *italics*, only to indicate how noticeably they break it):

X	*148*	*= 13*	---
XI	139	= 13	★★★★★★
XII	145	= 10	★★★★★
XIII	142	= 7	★★★★
XIV	139	= 13	★★★
XV	148	= 13	★★
XVI	154	= 10	★
XVII	142	= 7	midpoint
XVIII	136	= 10	★
XIX	148	= 13	★★
XX	148	= 13	★★★
XXI	142	= 7	★★★★
XXII	154	= 10	★★★★★
XXIII	139	= 13	★★★★★★
XXIV	*154*	*= 10*	---

Apparently Brugnoli did not know the work of John Logan (Loga.1971.1), pp. 95–98, who had already made the identical observation, also pointing out that this pattern mirrored the pattern found in the line lengths of the central thirteen cantos of *Purgatorio* precisely. (For treatments of the numerical center of the whole poem, see the reference at the conclusion of the note to *Purg.* XVII.124–125.)

For another and more recent attempt to deal with the "centers" of the three canticles, see Ambrosini (Ambr.2002.1), pp. 253–54. His discussion begins and ends with Singleton (Sing.1965.2), but is without reference to the work of Logan and (still more surprisingly) of Brugnoli.

1–6. Phaeton sought reassurance from his mother, Clymene, against the denial (on the part of his "half-brother in divinity," as it were, Epaphus, a son of Io by Jove) of his origin from divine Apollo's seed (see *Metam.* I.747–789 [setting up the lengthy narrative of Phaeton's disastrous chariot-ride, *Metam.* II.1–400]). So now does Dante wish to be enlightened about the nature of the ills that will afflict him after 1300, ills that he has heard prophesied in Hell and in Purgatory (for all those prophetic passages [three of the last four are positive, not worrisome], see the note to vv. 43–99), even if he is assured of his eventual salvation. Beatrice and Cacciaguida share the role of a wiser Apollo, confirming his purpose without destroying him by allowing a runaway journey through the heavens. In Ovid's "tragic" narrative, Phaeton is, we remember, allowed to destroy himself through overenthusiastic evaluation of his own capacities as rookie sun-driver; in Dante's comically resolved tale of his journey through the heavens, we see the protagonist as a wiser (and better-aided) version of Phaeton.

See Moore (Moor.1896.1), p. 175, comparing Cacciaguida's assurance that Dante will survive his troubles to the Sibyl's similar gesture toward Aeneas (*Aen.* VI.95–96); Moore goes on to mention both heroes' calm acceptance of their fates (cf. *Aen.* VI.103–105). And see Schnapp (Schn.1991.2), pp. 217–19, and Picone (Pico.1994.1), pp. 181–82, for two particularly interesting responses to these verses. Also see Brownlee (Brow.1984.1) for the "Phaeton program" in the *Commedia.*

7–12. These are the first words uttered by Beatrice since *Paradiso* XIV.18. They repeat something we have been told several times now (first at *Par.* I.85–87), that the souls of the saved have the capacity to read minds; thus speech addressing them, while technically unnecessary, has the benefit to a mortal speaker of making his thoughts clear to himself so that his questioners, all of whom are necessarily saved souls, will have sufficient indication of what is "on his mind." This only seems a curious notion; upon reflection it makes perfectly good sense (i.e., if he has a confused thought in his mind, *that* is what his celestial interrogator will read in it). And what other writer can we imagine having such a complex thought about thinking's relationship to speech?

The metaphor of thirst as representing desire for knowledge has also been before us previously in this canticle (first at *Par.* II.19). It is here used by Beatrice as part of a severely mixed metaphor, since she has at verse 7 referred to the *vampa* (ardor, flame) of Dante's desire, now translated into water. Heavenly stylists are obviously not bound by the petty rules of mortal grammarians.

13–18. Dante's words to Cacciaguida make plain that he has understood a vital difference between mortal intelligence and that of the saints: The latter see, in the eternal present in God, even contingencies (i.e., those things that might either happen or not happen, in other words all possible occurrences, even those that in fact never did, or do, or will occur [see *Par.* XIII.63 and the note to *Par.* XIII.61–66]). The best we mortals can do, by contrast, is to grasp certain definitional truths, for example, that no triangle (containing a total of 180 degrees) can possess two angles each of which is greater than 90 degrees.

Where Phaeton wanted to know about his ancestry, Dante wants to know from his ancestor (as we will learn in vv. 22–27) the path of his future life. However, both "sons" have absolutely in common the need to be reassured.

13. The word *piota* refers to the sole of the foot (see *Inf.* XIX.120); here it may literally mean footprint while, in metaphor, it would rather seem to signify "root"; Scartazzini (comm. to this verse) discusses the Tuscan use of the noun to indicate the clump of earth around the root system of blades of grass, etc. And this seems the best way to take this passage: Cacciaguida is the patch of earth from which has sprung Dante's "plant." Cf. *Paradiso* XV. 88–89, where Cacciaguida refers to himself as the "root" (*radice*) that has produced Dante as its "bough" (*fronda*). See Petrocchi (Petr.1988.2), p. 338.

15. This is the second (and last) appearance of the word "triangle" in the poem (see *Par.* XIII.102 for the first).

19–27. Dante refers to the various predictions of the course of his future life that dot the first two canticles (see the note to vv. 46–99) and claims a serenity in the face of difficulty that some readers find belied by his very questions.

19. It comes as something of a surprise to hear Virgil's name on Dante's lips at this point, and for the first time in this canticle. It is as though the Virgilian resonances of Canto XV.25–30 had stirred the protagonist's loyalties (the last time we heard Virgil's name was in company of Dante's unique nominal presence [*Purg.* XXX.55]). This is the penultimate of 32 appearances of the Roman poet's name in the poem; the last will occur, in Adam's mouth, surprisingly enough, at *Paradiso* XXVI.118 (an occurrence somehow overlooked by Foster [Fost.1976.1], p. 72). Among denizens of the afterworld, only Beatrice is more often present in name (63 occurrences), if that of God occurs even more often than hers (more than 100 times).

24. For the word "tetragon," see Chiavacci Leonardi (Chia.1989.2), pp. 312–13, and Raffa (Raff.2000.1), pp. 164–78, both of whom consider the two sets of meanings of the geometrical figure that may have influenced Dante's choice of the word here, defensive (it was reckoned by several authorities, including Aristotle and St. Thomas, to be the strongest shape capable of withstanding assault) and more positive (in one medieval tradition it is associated with Christ).

Chiavacci Leonardi (pp. 314–16) also adduces Boethius here, as model in the widest possible sense. In her view, he, like Dante, persecuted and unjustly condemned, wrote a work of which he, again like Dante, was both author and protagonist.

For the Cacciaguida episode as also reflecting the sixth book of Cicero's *De re publica*, known as the *Somnium Scipionis* (and in this form commented on by Macrobius), see Schnapp (Schn.1986.1, e.g., p. 62, but passim) and Raffa (Raff.2000.1), pp. 147–64. And see Schnapp (Schn.1991.2), p. 216, discussing the similarities and differences between the prophecy offered by Brunetto in *Inferno* XV and that by Cacciaguida here.

27. Starting with Jacopo della Lana (comm. to this tercet), some early commentators attribute a version of this saying ("Jaculum praevisum minus laedit" [A javelin blow hurts the less if it is foreseen]) to "Solomon"; others, later along, beginning with Daniello (comm. to verse 27), say that it derives from a saying of Ovid's: "Nam praevisa minus laedere tela solent" (For the blows of weapons that one sees coming do not usually hurt as much) but without specifying where in Ovid it is to be found. (Daniello also refers to the "Solomonic" *dictum* first found in Jacopo della Lana.) It was Venturi (comm. to verse 27) who, while maintaining the attribution to Ovid, also kept the first citation alive, but (correctly) reassigned it to Gregory the Great and spiked the attribution to Solomon. However, the phantom attribution to Ovid lasted into the twentieth century, despite the fact (which should have raised more suspicion than it did) that it had never been assigned a specific source in any Ovidian text. Finally, Vandelli (in the Scartazzini/Vandelli comm. to verse 27), referring to an article in *BSDI* (25 [1918], p. 108), reassigns the popular tag to the Esopics of *Waltherius anglicus* (for Waltherius, see the note to *Inf.* XXIII.4–18). In this "school" are found also Brezzi (Brez.1989.1), p. 447, and Chiamenti (Chia.1995.1), p. 188. However, Aversano (Aver.2000.2) argues for the pivotal role of Gregory the Great's *Homilies* (to Luke 21:9–19): "Minus enim iacula feriunt quae praevidentur" (For javelins that

one sees coming wound the less), rather than that of Waltherius because, both in Gregory and in Dante, the context is of the greater pain one suffers at the betrayal of one's friends than at the hands of one's known enemies (Aversano points to Dante's sense of betrayal by his fellow exiles as registered in vv. 61–66).

31–36. Set off against pagan dark and wayward speech is Christian clarity of word and purpose. Perhaps Dante refers to Sibylline prophecy that resulted in human sacrifice (see the muffled but telling reference to the killing of Iphigenia in *Inferno* XX.110–111). Such is opposed by a better sacrifice, that of the Lamb, who took on all our sins (see, for the eventual biblical source of the phrase in the liturgy, which pluralizes our sins [*peccata*], John 1:29: "Ecce agnus Dei; ecce qui tollit peccatum mundi" [Behold the lamb of God; behold the one who takes away the sins of the world]).

31. The word *ambage* has an interesting history. Dante probably found its most troubling presence in *Aeneid* VI.99, where *ambages* was used to typify the animal-like sounds of the cave-dwelling Sibyl's prognostications. On the other hand, and as Pio Rajna (Rajn.1902.1) has pointed out, in Virgil, Ovid, and Statius it is also used to describe the twisting path found in the Cretan labyrinth; it also in Virgil indicates an enigmatic way of speaking. In *De vulgari eloquentia* (I.x.2), giving the palm for prose eloquence to the French (to the Provençals and Italians is reserved that for vernacular poetry [I.x.3–4]), Dante had referred to the term. The northerners are recorded as composing biblical narratives, tales of Troy and Rome, and the beautiful *ambage* (fictions) of King Arthur's court. Thus the word, a hapax in the poem, arrives in this context loaded with negative associations.

32. The verb *inviscarsi* has been used twice before (*Inf.* XIII.57 and XXII.144). In the first instance (where the verb's root is spelled *invesc-*), Pier delle Vigne speaks of the guileful properties of words (see Marchesi [Marc.1997.1]); the second passage describes winged demons caught in the pitch over which they are playing a cruel game with a sinner who temporarily outwits them. The verb describes the effects of birdlime, spread to entrap birds. It was a favorite word to Petrarch, who liked to describe Laura's beauty as imprisoning him.

34–35. The word "latino" has caused debate, with the primary warring interpretations being (1) it refers, as it has throughout *Inferno*, to things

Italian (whether the country or, as twice in *Paradiso*, its language) and (2) it here means "Latin," for the negative reason that, if it does not, then Dante has committed himself to a tautological expression, since "chiare parole" (plain words) and "preciso latin" (clear speech) signify the same thing.

For examples of arguments devoted to each of these views, see (for [1]) Honess (Hone.1994.1), pp. 51–52, and (for [2]) Vianello (Vian. 1968.1), pp. 593–94. The view put forward by Vianello does not admit that the two terms may predicate differing things of Cacciaguida's speech. However, the first term (*chiare parole*) may refer to his diction, the second (*preciso latin*) to his syntactical command of the language, his substance and his style, as it were. See, for an example (and it is only the very first example) of this poet's pleasure in "multi-predication," *Inferno* 1.5, "esta selva *selvaggia* e *aspra* e *forte*"; in short, Dante's usual habit would seem to support the first view. Furthermore, in the rest of the poem "latino" only once seems surely to refer to the Latin language (*Par.* X.120). On most other occasions it clearly means "Italian" (*Inf.* XXII.65; XXVII.27; XXVII.33; XXVIII.71; XXIX.88; XXIX.91; *Purg.* XI.58; XIII.92; and here, where it is employed for the last [thirteenth] time in the poem).

37–42. The old (and apparently never successfully disposed of [if what one hears in one's own classroom even now is any guide]) problem that many an early Christian theologian felt he had to grapple with, how God's foreknowledge does not limit freedom of the will, is here resolved in imagistic terms: God's knowing what you will do does not cause you to do it, just as when you watch a ship moving downstream, its motion is not propelled by your observing eyes.

37. Brezzi (Brez.1989.1), p. 448, underlines the importance of the concept of contingency in this canto, first at verse 16 ("contingenti") and then here ("contingenza"), as opposed to those things that are eternal. (See also the "cluster" of concern with contingent things in *Par.* XIII.63, XIII.64, and XIII.69.) The word (used as a verb) will reemerge for a final appearance in *Paradiso* XXV.1.

43–99. Cacciaguida's lengthy personal prophecy of the course of Dante's future life, the ninth and final one in the poem (stopping, strictly speaking, at verse 93, it is nonetheless exactly the same length as the preceding eight put together), eclipses all that we have learned from the four in *Inferno* (Ciacco, VI.64–75; Farinata, X.79–81; Brunetto, XV.55–57, 61–66, 70–75; Vanni Fucci, XXIV.143–150) and the four found in *Purgatorio* (Currado

Malaspina, VIII.133–139; Oderisi, XI.140–141; Bonagiunta, XXIV.37–38; Forese, XXIV.82–90). See Pasquini (Pasq.1996.1), p. 419. This is clearly meant to be taken as the most important prognostication of Dante's personal involvement in the political affairs of his world. If we consider that each of the first two canticles has four such passages and that this one, coming in the central canto of the third, is so detailed, it becomes clear that it is meant to overwhelm in importance all those that have preceded.

Chiarenza (Chia.1983.3), p. 145, juxtaposes the two Ovidian myths found in this canto, Phaeton and Hippolytus (see the note to vv. 46–48), arguing that the first is emblematic of damnation, the second of salvation.

43–45. The first commentator to be clear about the problems of this passage is Fallani (comm. to this tercet), referring to his gloss on *Purg.* IX.144, in which he cites Casimiri's lecture of 1924. Casimiri insisted that there were no instances of singing to organ accompaniment until the fifteenth century. Fallani is of the opinion that some of the early commentators (e.g., Jacopo della Lana, the Ottimo, Francesco da Buti, the Anonimo Fiorentino), when speaking of "il cantare degli organi," probably were referring only to the harmony established by two or more voices singing different notes, not to the musical instrument, the organ. For earlier discussion of this material, see the note to *Purgatorio* IX.139–145. And see Heilbronn-Gaines (Heil.1995.2), arguing that here the singular form *organo* clearly marks this reference as being to vocal polyphony, while the plural *organi* (as in *Purg.* IX.144) refers to the musical instrument.

No matter how discordant the sounds of his great-great-grandson's coming travails may seem, Cacciaguida would seem to be insisting, they will eventually be heard as harmony, at least once Dante's task is completed.

46–48. At least since the time of Scartazzini, commentators have recognized that the word indicating a cruel stepmother (*noverca*: Phaedra, Florence) and that indicating a man unjustly exiled (*immeritum*: Hippolytus, Dante) are found in a passage in Ovid's *Metamorphoses* (XV.497–505). Bosco/Reggio (comm. to this tercet) point out that the words *exul immeritus* found in four of Dante's thirteen epistles likely come from this passage in Ovid and that Hippolytus, as a result, should be considered a *figura Dantis*. And for Dante's sense of himself as sharing with Ovid the experience of exile, see the note to verses 55–57.

As Cacciaguida begins his lengthy series of predictions concerning Dante's life, we may perhaps remember that two passages in *Inferno* (X.130–132 and XV.88–90) surely seem to promise that Beatrice will be the one to reveal to Dante the course of his future life. Several readers have advanced hypotheses in order to account for Dante's obvious change in plan, most notably Marguerite Mills Chiarenza. For a summary of her argument, see the note to *Inferno* X.130–132.

46. Chiarenza (Chia.1966.1 [and see also Chia.1983.3]) was perhaps the first to examine the import to Dante of the rest of the tale of Hippolytus: his restoration from death and his ensuing life in exile from Athens under the name "Virbius." She argues that Dante could have known this part of Hippolytus's tale from Virgil (*Aen.* VII.777) and from Ovid (*Metam.* XV.497–546 [a connection first observed by Jacopo della Lana, comm. to vv. 46–48, if without naming Virbius]). (Dante might not have required the authority of Servius [alluded to by Chiarenza] who etymologizes Hippolytus's posthumous name as "bis vir" [twice a man], but simply seen these obvious Latin roots himself.) Chiarenza's conclusion is that the Virbius tradition gives Dante much more than a political self-justification, namely, a sense of his own spiritual second life. On the other hand, it does limn in precise parallel the Florentine's escape from the political dangers of the world of "Thebes" (in *Inferno* an insistent stand-in for the ailing and divided city of man on earth, the city of destruction that surely reminded the poet of the internecine woes of Florence [see *Inf.* XIV.69; XX.32; XXV.15; XXX.2; XXX.22; XXXII.11; XXXIII.89; there are three references to the Greek city in *Purgatorio*, but these are rather more neutral in tone]).

49–51. If the reader has been missing Virgil, this canto brings his name back into play (see the note to verse 19). And if the reader has missed the presence of one of Dante's favorite whipping boys, Pope Boniface VIII, here he is, officiating over a corrupt Roman clergy that makes its profit out of selling Christ. We might almost be back in *Inferno* XIX rather than at the midpoint of *Paradiso*.

51. How to translate *tutto dì*? We have decided, finding little help in the commentaries, that the phrase is more likely to refer to an imagined single long day in the "marketplace" of the Vatican rather than to an endless succession of days. Both solutions are found in the commentaries, the second more often. However, it seems to us that the sense of "all day long" is both more caustic and less obvious.

52–54. The poet looks back at his banishment, an "injured party" indeed, from Florence; then he turns to God's swift retributive justice, evident at least in the death of Boniface in 1303. Some dates that are pertinent here: Boniface was plotting against the Florentine White Guelphs as early as April 1300 (or so Dante probably believed); Dante was nearly certainly in Rome circa October 1301; on 27 January 1302 the Whites were banished from Florence. Possibly the most painful period in Dante's life is rehearsed in these lines.

Perhaps encouraged by the use of the same noun at verse 69, where it obviously does refer to a political party, some take the noun *parte* in verse 52 to refer to the White Guelphs. On the other hand, since Cacciaguida's entire prophecy is directed toward Dante's personal future, we probably should understand that Dante himself is the "offended party" whose innocence will be proclaimed in the vengeance he will enjoy once God intervenes to set things right. However, the first to take the passage in this way appear to have been the sixteenth-century commentators Alessandro Vellutello and Bernardino Daniello (comms. to this tercet); nearly all the earlier ones take the victims to be the exiled White Guelphs (including Dante, of course). Since we will shortly hear, in only thinly veiled ways, of the enmity Dante felt from his fellow Whites in exile (vv. 61–66), it would be extremely odd for him to think of them as sharing his status as victim here. It really seems necessary to believe that this *parte*, like that in verse 69, is a party of one.

Vellutello, perhaps following the lead of Francesco da Buti (comm. to vv. 46–57) in citing these particulars, is of the opinion that signs of Dante's "revenge" were evident in the various Florentine disasters of the spring of 1304; these are recounted more fully elsewhere (in his comm. to *Inf.* XXVI.7–9): the collapse of the Ponte alla Carraia because of the vast crowds of those who had assembled on the bridge to watch a spectacle enacted on the river below in which Hell was displayed (a "spectacle" that Dante himself would within several years begin to produce in writing, possibly with this one in mind); the civil war between the White and the Black Guelphs; and the terrible fire that destroyed seventeen hundred houses in the city (see Villani, *Cron.* VIII.70–71). Over the years there have been other candidates as well. The facts that these events were so cataclysmic (two major disasters and a civil war), involved such dramatic loss of life and destruction of property, seemed indeed like God's punishment upon the city, and occurred so soon after Dante was exiled (a mere two years) all combine to give continuing support to Vellutello's hypothesis. Of course, there were other notable events that the poet might have considered the result of God's hand smiting the enemies of Dante Alighieri, "a Florentine by birth but not in his behaviors" (as he describes himself in the salutation of the *Epistle to Cangrande*), for instance the death of Boniface VIII in 1303 (the choice of some commentators) or of Corso Donati in 1308 (the choice of others). However, everything in this lengthy passage is centered both on Dante and on his feckless fellow Florentines. For this reason Vellutello's interpretation seems more worthy of attention than others.

55–57. The protagonist has asked his ancestor to provision him against the "slings and arrows of outrageous Fortune" (verse 27); Cacciaguida now responds by referring to the sharpest wound of all: his exile. For Dante's sense of himself as the Italian Ovid, see Smarr (Smar.1991.1). From her observation that Ovid casts himself in the role of wandering Ulysses in both the *Tristia* and the *Ars amatoria*, she argues that Dante takes Ovid as a negative version of himself. For another treatment of Ovid as Dante's counterpart in exile, see Picone (Pico.1999.3). And see the note to vv. 46–48.

58–60. One of the most celebrated tercets in the poem, bringing home to the reader the poet's daily sense of abandonment in his exilic condition, a necessary guest even under the best of circumstances (and with the most benign of hosts). The poet's understatement catches perfectly the rhythm of the exile's daily round, going downstairs with perhaps some sense that this day may bring tidings betokening a possible return to Florence, and then mounting back up at night with the deadened senses of one who knows that life will probably merely continue as it is.

58. Strangely enough, the meaning of this verse is much debated. From the beginning, all have agreed that it refers to the bitter taste of bread (or anything else) eaten in bitter conditions. The "unofficial commentary tradition," that is, ordinary readers, however, senses a reference to the way bread is prepared in Florence (to this day): It is baked without salt. Pietrobono (comm. to vv. 58–60) is the first commentator even to refer to that fact and simply denies its relevance (thus revealing that some discussants had raised this issue), insisting on the larger and obvious meaning. (He cites the often-cited passage in *Convivio* [I.iii.4] in which Dante laments his exilic experience.) Fallani (comm. to vv. 58–60) explains that the salty taste is supplied by the exile's tears.

Longfellow (comm. to this verse) cites several pertinent passages, including Ecclesiasticus 29:24 [29:31–32 in the Vulgate] and 40:28–29 [29–30]: "It is a miserable thing to go from house to house; for where thou art a stranger, thou darest not open thy mouth. Thou shalt entertain and feast, and have no thanks: moreover, thou shalt hear bitter words. . . ." "My son, lead not a beggar's life, for better it is to die than to beg. The life of him that dependeth on another man's table is not to be counted for a life."

61–69. Dante became "a party of one" (verse 69) when he was disgusted with the efforts of his fellow exiles to make their way back into Florence, circa 1304. His correctness (we imagine a large meeting in which Dante was able to accomplish what the American comedian Mort Sahl, some five minutes into one of his scabrous and rollicking routines, used to ponder: "Is there anyone here I haven't offended yet?") about the folly of their preparations was, as far as he was concerned, reflected in their crushing defeat (an army of more than 10,000 men was routed, leaving 400 dead behind) by the Black Guelphs at the fortress Lastra a Signa, three kilometers from the walls of Florence, on 20 July 1304, during which battle Dante was in Arezzo. By a twist of circumstance, that put him there on the very day Francesco Petrarca was born in that city.

65–66. While some of the earlier commentators (e.g., Portirelli to vv. 61–69) see the red of bloody wounds to the head, the majority of them think only of the red of a guilty blush. Dante's point would seem to be that theirs would be no ordinary blushes (infusing only the cheeks with color), but would cover their entire countenances, even up to the hairline. In modern times, Scartazzini (comm. to verse 66) began the tradition of seeing both meanings in the line. That line of attack has, however, had little success, and twentieth-century commentators are fairly evenly divided in choosing one or the other. However, the phrase does seem a strange way to indicate those lying dead on the field of battle, since we assume that most of them were not killed by blows to the head (nor imagined as having blood from their other wounds or from the wounds of others staining their heads), while all of his former allies must (in Dante's view) now feel ashamed (i.e., are blushing) for having turned against him, reviling his opposition to their bankrupt and eventually anti-Florentine schemes. Bosco/Reggio (comm. to vv. 64–66) object that blushes cover one's cheeks, not the forehead. But that, perhaps, is exactly Dante's point: This is no ordinary blush, but burns on all the exposed parts of the face, "blushing to the roots of their hair," as the English expression has it.

67–69. The only other appearance of the noun *bestialitade* is in *Inferno* XI.83, where its meaning is much debated. See the note to *Inferno*

XI.76–90 and Fosca's commentary to that passage (vv. 79–84) for the minority opinion, followed here, that *bestialitade* refers to the lowest form of fraud, treachery, as surely Dante sees his supposed allies among the White Guelphs (and those fellow-traveling exiled Ghibellines who had joined forces with them), who deserted Dante's advocacy of the proper initiative against the Black Guelph rulers of the city. (Of course we know nothing of the matter[s] in dispute, just that there was a dispute and that it was pivotal and had a dramatic result, the defeat at La Lastra.) We remember that Antenora was the zone of Cocytus in which we found those who had betrayed country or party (*Inferno* XXXII.70–XXXIII.90), possibly the very sin Dante attributed to his fellow exiles, effectively dooming the cause and leaving him to form a "party of one."

The context of this entire passage, vv. 52–75, is unabashedly Dante-centered, so much so that even the most zealous lover of this poet may feel the stinging warmth of embarrassment stealing up and over his face, blushing to the roots of his hair.

70–71. Some commentators explain that, while Verona was not in fact the first place that Dante was received as he began his twenty years of exile (he did not arrive there for between one year and two [in 1303 or 1304] after he left Rome in 1302), it was nonetheless his first "real" shelter.

The succession of the Scaligeri, the ruling family of Verona in Dante's time, was as follows: Mastino della Scala had become the ruler in 1262; he was succeeded by his brother Alberto in 1277. Alberto died in 1301 and was succeeded, in turn, by each of his three sons: Bartolommeo (who died in March 1304), Alboino (who died late in 1311, having just been named by Henry VII his imperial vicar, a title passed along at his death to his younger brother, who had joined him in joint rulership in 1308), and Cangrande (the youngest, born in 1291 and who died in 1329, eight years after Dante's death). (Alberto also sired their illegitimate half brother Giuseppe, abbot of San Zeno [see *Purg.* XVIII.124].) According to what, after Petrocchi's work, has become a widespread understanding, Dante left Verona soon after the accession of Alboino in 1304 and returned in 1312 or 1313, that is, once Cangrande had assumed sole power. It has become an assumption in Dante studies that for some reason Dante and Alboino just did not get along, thus explaining the poet's eight years or more of absence from a city for which he obviously felt deep affection.

For a sketch of the historical situation after Cangrande's accession to unshared power, after Alboino died in 1311, see Manselli (Mans.1966.1). Manselli takes Dante's praise of Cangrande as genuine, since he was the only one active on the scene whom Dante considered capable, both in his personal qualities and by virtue of his political position, of carrying out the lofty imperial mission unsuccessfully initiated by Henry VII.

There is a large literature devoted to what was at one time a vexed question: Which Scaliger governed Verona when Dante first arrived? Now just about all agree that it was Bartolommeo. For a summary of the dispute, in English, see Carroll (comm. to vv. 70–75). For a fuller treatment, summarizing the entire debate and concluding, with nearly all the early commentators, that Bartolommeo was indeed Dante's first meaningful supporter in his exile, see Scartazzini (comm. to vv. 70–93).

72. See Tozer (comm. to vv. 71–72): "The arms of the Scaligers were a golden ladder in a red field, surmounted by a black eagle, which was the imperial ensign." Unfortunately for Dante's sake, this insignia was not chosen by the Scaligeri (at the earliest, by Bartolommeo) before 1301. By making it present now, in 1300, the poet hurries history along faster than it wants to go.

73–75. That is to say, Bartolommeo and Dante will grant one another's requests even before the other can make them, while in most cases the granting follows much later than the asking (i.e., it may not be forthcoming at all).

76–90. Commentators agree that this passage refers to Cangrande della Scala, one of the great figures of his time in northern Italy. He was indeed a "son of Mars," a fearless and fabled warrior, and a man of, in Dante's eyes, impeccable political convictions, an extreme supporter of Emperor Henry while he lived, and a man who refused to relinquish his title as imperial vicar even when the pope insisted that he do so (since there was no longer an emperor to be vicar to). For a portrait of the man and his court, see Carroll (comm. to vv. 76–93).

It has seemed reasonable to some to point out that Cangrande was too young in 1300 to be the subject of so dramatic a prophecy (not to mention the one in *Inf.* I, if that, also, applies to him), since he was only nine years old in 1300 and only around fourteen or fifteen when Dante began writing the poem. However, those who have made this argument have neglected to take three things into account: First, stories about Cangrande as a child prodigy were abundant (e.g., in one such the boy is depicted as being shown a chest, opened to reveal the coins and jewels it contains; he reaches out and covers that pelf back over with its cloth: See Cacciaguida's words in vv. 83–84 and Benvenuto's gloss to them [comm. to

vv. 82–84]; and see the similar sentiment expressed of the *veltro, Inf.* I.103); second, Cangrande had been named commander in chief of the Veronese armies before he was in his teens; third, and in general, expectations of the princes of royal houses and other such luminaries were simply out of all proportion to our own expectations of the young. See the note to *Inferno* I.100–105. Further, if this later passage was written when Cangrande was well into his twenties, as it undoubtedly was, it is not surprising that it looks to him to take over the role of the *veltro* and of the "five hundred ten and five." But see the note to *Paradiso* XXVII.142–148.

78. What does Dante imagine Cangrande will accomplish politically? Somehow, he apparently must think, Cangrande will finish the task that Henry started but failed to complete, the reëstablishment of conditions leading to the refounding of Aeneas's Rome. That is the only surmise possible that might justify the amazingly positive things said throughout this eventually unexpressed (or better, suppressed [see vv. 92–93]) prophecy. It is not, perhaps, "officially" one of the three "world prophecies" that appear, one in each *cantica* (*Inf.* I, *Purg.* XXXIII, *Par.* XXVII), but it reflects the first two of them and informs the third.

79–81. Dante takes the sticks out of the hands of those who would beat him about the head for prognosticating such things about a mere child. See the note to verses 76–90.

82–84. The "Gascon" (Pope Clement V) first led Henry on and then tried to undermine his imperial efforts. The date most commentators affix to the pope's open hostility to Henry is 1312, when the emperor hoped to be crowned (a second time in Italy) in St. Peter's, but was put off and finally relegated by decision of Clement to St. John Lateran, outside the walls of the city and in ruins. The "sparks" of virtue with which Cangrande is credited here may have been his demonstrations of support for the emperor; similarly, his "toil" is perhaps his effort, unrewarded, on Henry's behalf (for this view, see Carroll [comm. to vv. 76–93]). More likely, the first signs of virtue apparent in his not caring for worldly possessions was, apparently, a part of his "legend" (see the note to vv. 76–90); as for the *affanni* (toils) he does not complain about, most who remark on them take them as referring to his military exercises.

85. Poletto (comm. to vv. 85–87) makes the point that only Beatrice (*Par.* XXXI.88) and the Virgin (*Par.* XXXIII.20) are allowed to share this word with Cangrande. See also the first word of the dedication to him of *Epistle* XIII, "Magnifico."

89–90. Steiner was the first among the commentators to see the possible connection with a part of Mary's hymn of praise for her Son, Luke 1:52–53: "He has put down the mighty from their seats, and exalted them of low degree. He has filled the hungry with good things; and the rich he has sent away empty" (comm. to vv. 89–90). In light of this scriptural connection, Porena (comm. to these verses) thinks of Cangrande as a sort of Lombard Robin Hood.

91–93. It is difficult to see how this blank "prophecy" of the things that will be accomplished by Cangrande, imperial vicar that he was and insisted on being even after Henry's death, is anything but "imperial" in nature. (Henry, betrayed by Pope Clement V in 1312, is referred to a few lines ago [verses 82]). See Di Scipio's (Disc.1983.1) convincing attack on Passerin D'Entrèves (Pass.1955.1) for denying Dante's significant involvement with imperial ideas (in favor of religious orthodoxy), a position that simply fails to account for such clearly political (and imperial) passages as these.

It seems likely that Dante's optimism about Cangrande's future deeds is more the result of desperation than hope. Here was a man who had decided, upon precious little evidence, when he was writing the fourth book of *Convivio*, that the Roman Empire would be active once more. Within a decade an emperor comes down to Italy and behaves like the new Charlemagne, as far as Dante is concerned. One can only imagine (but the edgy tone of his second epistle to the emperor tells us a great deal about his growing disillusionment) the bitterness he felt once Henry had died in 1313. And now, some four or five years later, here he is, shouting at the top of his lungs, "The emperor is dead, long live the emperor!" He had, with little in the way of hard evidence, simply decided that Rome must rise again. And events made him correct. If Italy had not been ready for Henry (see *Par.* XXX.137–138), it would have to be ready for what Cangrande would do to clear the path for the *next* emperor. It may not be excessive to suggest that Dante felt as "keyed in" to the political events of his day, even before they occurred, as Fyodor Dostoyevski felt himself endowed with prescience about those of his time.

Carolyn Calvert Phipps (in a seminar in 1980) pointed out that there is a possible dependence here on the prophetic book referred to in the Apocalypse (10:4): "Signa quae locuta sunt septem tonitrua: et noli ea scribere" (Seal up those things which the seven thunders said and write them not). This is the instruction given John by the angel who brings him God's prophetic book for him to ingest. What makes Professor Phipps's observation particularly worthy of study is that there may be another possible visitation of the tenth chapter of the Apocalypse in this canto; see the note to vv. 130–132.

94–96. Concluding, Cacciaguida characterizes his utterances over the last seventeen tercets (vv. 43–93) as *chiose* (glosses); this long prophetic passage is unique in the poem, both for its length and for its personal import for the protagonist. It is divided into three sections, lines 43–69 (the pains of exile [Dante]); 70–75 (the first stay in Verona [Bartolommeo]); 76–93 (the second stay in Verona [Cangrande]).

What exactly do these "glosses" predict of Dante's difficult life as an exile? See the note to verses 52–54 for the range of possibilities according to the commentators. And to what specific prognostications do they respond, only Cacciaguida's here or to some of the earlier ones we heard in the first two *cantiche*, and if so, to which ones? We can say with some security that only the first section of his ancestor's prophecy, that concerning Dante's harsh political fate, is involved. It is worth remarking that the time frame that Cacciaguida seems to have in mind is short (*a pochi giri*), and that thus we should probably think that the events of 1304, just four revolutions of the heavens away from the date on which he speaks (1 April 1300), are likely what he has in mind.

97–99. Cacciaguida's repeated promise of Dante's vindication in the punishment of his enemies sounds very much as it did when it first was uttered in vv. 53–54. As for the notion contained in the neologism *s'infutura* (present tense of Dante's coinage, *infuturarsi* [lit. "to infuture oneself"]), ever since the early days of the commentary tradition at least some have argued that it would have been bad taste and out of keeping with Christian doctrine (not to mention the poet's own stated views) for Dante to have boasted at having survived his enemies in the flesh. Benvenuto da Imola (comm. to this tercet) does not even consider this possibility, referring only to Dante's honorable name as what will survive him, and survive longer than the dishonor of his enemies. Nonetheless, such a vaunt has been a long-standing trait in those who have survived the threatening behaviors of such powerful enemies as Boniface VIII (dead in 1303) or Corso Donati (dead in 1308). (Boniface is mentioned in this context by several commentators, although it is a bit of a stretch to believe that Dante thought of him as a "neighbor.") Porena points out (comm. to this tercet) that the "orthodox" interpretation, ridding Dante of a perhaps petty desire to outlive his enemies, makes little sense, since his immortal longings (see vv. 119–120) are considerably grander than the afterlives he foresees for his Florentine enemies, clearly meant to be in oblivion while Dante lives on. If that was his wish, he has been rewarded.

100–102. The metaphor, drawn from weaving, has it that Cacciaguida has finished answering Dante's question (the "warp") with his response (the "woof"), thus completing the pattern. See the earlier use of a similar metaphor, describing Piccarda's words (*Par.* III.95–96).

103–105. A "pseudo-simile" (see the note to *Inf.* XXX.136–141) in which the protagonist is compared to someone—very much like himself—asking a question of a person whom he trusts and loves—exactly such a one as Cacciaguida.

106–107. The metaphorical presentation of time as a (currently unseen) adversary in a duel on horseback captures the feelings of a person surprised by history and now realizing the enormity of his self-deluding former sense of security.

108. That is, time saves its heaviest blows for the one who is least aware of its relentless advance. See the similar thought expressed at vv. 23–24.

109–111. This tercet sounds a rare (and disingenuous) note of caution on the poet's part. If he will lose his native city within two years because of his obstinate adherence to telling the truth, should not he then consider mitigating his bitter words in complaint of the human iniquity found in other parts of Italy lest he be denied shelter and support in his exile? Since we have read the poem (which he only imagines writing at this point), we know that he did not succumb to the Siren song of "safety first." However, and as Carroll suggests (comm. to vv. 106–120), "In those days of the vendetta it is a marvel that a sudden knife in the heart did not send Dante to make actual acquaintance with that invisible world whose secrets he feigned to know."

111. For a source of this verse, Brugnoli (Brug.1995.1), pp. 56–57, cites Ovid, *Tristia* II.207: "Perdiderint cum me duo crimina, carmen et error. . . ." (Although two crimes, one a poem, one a mistake, shall have brought me to perdition . . .). This text, highly familiar and certainly most applicable to Dante, is somehow almost entirely lacking from the commentary tradition, appearing only once before, in Boccaccio's *Vita Ovidii*

(in his comm. to the literal sense of *Inf.* IV.90), and never, or so it seems, in the context of Dante's own exile.

112–120. Less an example of *captatio benevolentiae* than a sort of insistence on an inexcusable but necessary rudeness, this passage, recapitulating the journey until here and now, the midpoint of the third "kingdom," seeks our acceptance of the poet's revealing the harsh things that he has learned in Hell, Purgatory, and the first five of the heavens. While he might have won the goodwill of some of us by gilding the lily, as it were, he would have lost his claim on the rest of us (we do indeed call Dante's time "ancient," do we not?). For we want truth in our poetry, not blandishment.

118. Beginning with Scartazzini (comm. to this verse), the Aristotelian provenance of this gesture has been amply noted (the beginning of the *Ethics* [I.4]): "For friends and truth are both dear to us, but it is a sacred duty to prefer the truth." Dante himself has quoted or referred to this *dictum* on at least three occasions (*Conv.* IV.viii.13; *Mon.* III.i.3; *Epist.* XI.11). Cf. also the frequently cited Aristotelian tag, "Assuredly, I am Plato's friend, but I am still more a friend to truth."

119. Brunetto had taught him how to make himself immortal, "come l'uom s'etterna" (*Inf.* XV.85). It is not, we can assume, by flattering one's hosts. Brunetto seems to have been on Dante's mind in this context; see the note to verses 121–122.

121–122. Cacciaguida's shining presence is verbally reminiscent of the identical phrasing found in *Inferno* XV.119, where Brunetto refers to his own work (for the question of exactly which work, whether *Tresor* or *Tesoretto*, see the note to *Inf.* XV.119, and Hollander [Holl.1992.2], p. 228, n. 82) as *il mio Tesoro*, the same words that we find here, used of Cacciaguida. Are we perhaps to believe that, for Dante, Cacciaguida is a better, truer "father" than Brunetto? See Quinones (Quin.1979.1), pp. 174–76, and Ordiway (Ordi.1990.1) on Brunetto's replacement by Cacciaguida.

This is the sixth appearance (of seven) in the poem of the word *tesoro*. It first appeared in *Inferno* XV.119 (where Brunetto Latini alludes to his book of that title); then in *Inferno* XIX.90 (where Christ wants no "treasure" from Peter in compensation for the spiritual gifts He bestows upon him [as opposed to Simon Magus, who wants to acquire such gifts for a price]). In the first canto of the last canticle (*Par.* I.11), the poet refers to the "treasure" of God's kingdom that he has been able to store in his memory; the word is then found in *Paradiso* V.29 (where it refers to God's greatest gift to humankind, the freedom of our will); X.108 (representing the worldly goods that Peter Lombard renounced in order to follow Christ); and finally in XXIII.133 (designating the treasure in heaven of Matthew 6:20 [and/or 19:21], as Tommaseo [comm. to vv. 133–135] was apparently the first commentator to observe). That last reference eventually colors all that precedes it. In the final reckoning, worldly treasure is measured against this sole standard. And thus the word *tesoro*, which begins its course through the poem as the title for one of Brunetto Latini's works (by which he hopes to have achieved "immortality" in the world, a contradiction in terms), is examined and reexamined in such ways as to suggest either the desirability of renunciation of earthly "treasure" or the preferability of its heavenly counterpart, that "treasure in Heaven" that we may discover through the exercise of God's greatest gift to us, our true treasure here on earth, the free will, in our attempt to gain a better (and eternal) reward.

The poet's clear enthusiasm for his ancestor's noble sacrifice at least casts into doubt the central thesis of Brenda Deen Schildgen's article (Schi.1998.1) and book (Schi.2002.1), namely, that Dante did not promote crusading in the Holy Land, a position that may have the advantage of having a certain vogue among those who find crusading distasteful, but no other.

124–135. Cacciaguida admits that Dante's truth-telling will hurt all those who either themselves have given offense or who bear the sins of their relations on their consciences, but encourages him to tell the whole truth and nothing but the truth.

127–129. This tercet contains terms that have a possible relevance to Dante's sense of his own poeticizing. First, there is *menzogna* (a reference to the *bella menzogna* [beautiful lie] that represents a kind of poetry, as in *Conv*. II.i.3). Next we come upon the term *visione* (see *Par.* XXXIII.62), a kind of writing distinguished by being (or by claiming to be) literally true. This lofty word has barely ceased resonating when Dante descends the stylistic ladder to perhaps the lowest level of the vernacular that we encounter in this canticle, *grattar dov' è la rogna* (scratch where it itches). In three lines he puts forward what the poem is not (a tissue of lies, a "mere" fiction), what it is (an inspired vision), and what style its author insists that he employs (the comic, or low vernacular, style). See the notes to *Inferno*

XX.1–3, XX.106–114, and XX.130; *Purgatorio* IX.34–42 and XXX.21; and *Paradiso* I.20–21.

130–132. While few of the commentators suggest a source for this tercet, Pietro di Dante is a rare early exception (comm. to vv. 127–132 [only in his first redaction]). He cites, after various other potential sources, the text that alone has had a "career" among Dante's commentators to this passage, Boethius (*Cons. Phil.* III.1[pr]), a citation only recurring nearly five centuries later in Campi (comm. to this tercet). In the first half of the twentieth century it is found in Grandgent (comm. to this tercet) and in Scartazzini/Vandelli (comm. to verse 132). Porena (comm. to verse 132) also cites it, but sees a possible problem with its pertinence to Dante's context. However, it currently enjoys a certain stability, finding its way to most recent commentaries. Boethius's text reads: "Talia sunt quae restant, ut degustata quidem mordeant, interius autem recepta dulcescant" (You will find what I have yet to say bitter to the taste, but, once you have digested it, it will seem sweet [tr. R. Green]). However, there is no instance of a commentator referring to a biblical text (a close neighbor of one that may have been on Dante's mind only shortly before [see the note to vv. 91–93]), one found in John's Revelation (Apocalypse 10:9 [repeated nearly verbatim in 10:10]), where the angel is addressing the apostle: "Accipe librum, et devora illum: et faciet amaricari ventrem tuum, sed in ore tuo erit dulce tanquam mel" (Take the book and eat it; it will make your stomach bitter, but in your mouth it will be sweet as honey).

133–142. Cacciaguida's concluding ten lines (and he will speak only nine more as he leaves the poem in the next canto, vv. 28–36) establish, if not the *ars poetica* of this poem, then its mode of employing *exempla* for our moral instruction. This passage has caused no little confusion, especially three elements contained in it. (1) Some commentators seem to assume that it is only concerned with those in Hell; (2) others think that the poem ennobles its subjects (rather than the obverse); and (3) still others object that not all the populace of the afterworld seen by Dante may be considered famous. The first two problems are easily dealt with, for it is obvious that the poet means to indicate the famous dead in all three canticles and also that the honor accrues to the poem (one that eschews the commonplace for the extraordinary) rather than to its subjects. As for the third, one example of this complaint will suffice. Singleton (comm. to verse 138) argues that this claim cannot be taken as literally true, since there are many "unknown characters" found in the cast of the *Comedy*. "One has only to think," he says, "of the riff-raff, generally, of the eighth circle of *Inferno*." However, those crowds of "extras" do not count in Dante's scheme of things; those who are *named* are famous (or were, in Dante's time at least, better known than they are in ours).

There is one other problem of literal understanding that is as present today as it has always been, perhaps because it has never been treated, since readers do not see that it is problematic and simply assume that they understand what is meant. The word *cima* can mean various things (see the note to *Purg.* XI.91–93), but here it refers either to mountaintops (as we believe it does) or treetops (as it apparently does for most readers). The general sense is clear enough: Exemplary figures and clear arguments are both required to convince a reader.

133–134. The metaphors and similetic comparisons (the poem is a "cry," equated with the wind; its human subjects, metaphorically mountain peaks [or, according to not a few, treetops]) now make the poem lofty, that is, "tragic" in its stylistic reach. See the note to vv. 127–129. If there the author insisted on the comic essence of his work, he now insists equally vehemently on its tragic (or stylistically lofty) dimension.

139. The reader notes that Dante does not here imagine people reading his poem, but hearing it being read.

142. The poet surely forgets what he has *not* said at vv. 92–93. If ever there existed a "proof that remains obscure," that lacuna qualifies.

This canto, with its lavish praise of Cangrande, may be thought of as Dante's farewell to Verona, written between 1317 and 1318 according to Petrocchi (Petr.1988.2), pp. 335, 337. For the question, still somewhat vexed, of the exact date of Dante's arrival in Ravenna (we assume soon after he left Verona), see Eugenio Chiarini, "Ravenna," *ED* (IV [1973]), pp. 861–64.

PARADISO XVIII

OUTLINE

MARS; JUPITER

1–3 Cacciaguida and Dante with their different thoughts;
4–6 Beatrice: "There is no need to be pessimistic here."
7–12 Beatrice, Dante's "comfort," showed such love for him in her eyes that he can neither describe nor recall it;
13–18 he says he was loving God in the "mirror" of Beatrice;
19–21 her third and last speech in Mars is accompanied by her third and last smile in this heaven
22–27 simile: here on earth a face shows that all its soul is suffused by love as there Cacciaguida's flaming glow reveals his desire for further speaking
28–36 Cacciaguida's last (eighth) speech: metaphor of tree
37–48 Dante's **"Nine Worthies"**
49–51 Cacciaguida's singing makes him an "artista"
52–57 Dante seeks a sign from Beatrice as to what to do next and finds her aspect more joyous than ever before
58–69 the ascent to **Jupiter**
    58–63 simile: Dante, like a man improving day by day, finds himself making a greater arc
    64–69 simile: the change from the red of Mars to the white of Jupiter is like a blush leaving a face
70–72 Dante watches as souls in Jupiter spell out five words
73–78 simile: waterbirds, rising, like the souls, spelling;
79–81 at first they sang, then, forming a letter, fell silent
82–87 sixth invocation: **"divine Pegasean"**
88–93 Dante is shown thirty-five letters, one by one, and
94–96 (1) the souls linger on the "m";
97–99 (2) they are joined by new souls that form a lily

100–108 (3) simile: sparks flying up from burning logs when they are struck, from which fools make augury, compared to the souls atop the "M" rising higher: the **Eagle**

109–111 and He who depicts there needs no model as His guide, by the same principle by which birds make their nests

112–114 the new souls, who had first formed the lily, now finish their design

115–117 apostrophe: "O [Jupiter], I understood that earthly justice is the effect of the heaven that you engem!"

118–123 Dante's prayer to God that He look down with wrath upon the corruption of the **[papacy]**

124–126 apostrophe: "O heavenly militia, whom I look upon, pray for all those led astray by its example!"

127–129 the Church once made war with swords but now by decree

130–136 apostrophe: but you who write only to cancel, remember that Peter and Paul, who died for the vineyard that you lay waste, still live.

PARADISO XVIII

Già si godeva solo del suo verbo
quello specchio beato, e io gustava
lo mio, temprando col dolce l'acerbo;

e quella donna ch'a Dio mi menava
disse: "Muta pensier; pensa ch'i' sono
presso a colui ch'ogne torto disgrava."

Io mi rivolsi a l'amoroso suono
del mio conforto; e qual io allor vidi
ne li occhi santi amor, qui l'abbandono:

non perch' io pur del mio parlar diffidi,
ma per la mente che non può redire
sovra sé tanto, s'altri non la guidi.

Tanto poss' io di quel punto ridire,
che, rimirando lei, lo mio affetto
libero fu da ogne altro disire,

fin che 'l piacere etterno, che diretto
raggiava in Bëatrice, dal bel viso
mi contentava col secondo aspetto.

Vincendo me col lume d'un sorriso,
ella mi disse: "Volgiti e ascolta;
ché non pur ne' miei occhi è paradiso."

Come si vede qui alcuna volta
l'affetto ne la vista, s'elli è tanto,
che da lui sia tutta l'anima tolta,

così nel fiammeggiar del folgór santo,
a ch'io mi volsi, conobbi la voglia
in lui di ragionarmi ancora alquanto.

That blessèd mirror continued to rejoice
in his own thoughts and I was tasting mine,
tempering the bitter with the sweet,

when that lady, who was leading me to God,
said: 'Change your thoughts. Consider that I dwell
with Him who lifts the weight of every wrong.'

At the loving sound of my comfort's voice
I turned, and the great love I saw then,
in her holy eyes, I have to leave untold,

not just because I cannot trust my speech,
but because memory cannot retrace its path
that far unless Another guide it.

This much only of that moment can I tell again,
that, when I fixed my gaze on her,
my affections were released from any other longing

as long as the eternal Beauty,
shining its light on Beatrice, made me content
with its reflected glow in her fair eyes.

Conquering me with her radiant smile,
she said: 'Turn now and listen:
not in my eyes alone is Paradise.'

As, on occasion, here on earth, affection
may be read in someone's face
if it is strong enough to capture all the soul,

so, in the flaming of that holy radiance
to which I turned, I recognized his wish
to share some further thoughts with me.

El cominciò: "In questa quinta soglia
de l'albero che vive de la cima
e frutta sempre e mai non perde foglia,

spiriti son beati, che giù, prima
che venissero al ciel, fuor di gran voce,
sì ch'ogne musa ne sarebbe opima.

Però mira ne' corni de la croce:
quello ch'io nomerò, lì farà l'atto
che fa in nube il suo foco veloce."

Io vidi per la croce un lume tratto
dal nomar Iosuè, com' el si feo;
né mi fu noto il dir prima che 'l fatto.

E al nome de l'alto Macabeo
vidi moversi un altro roteando,
e letizia era ferza del paleo.

Così per Carlo Magno e per Orlando
due ne seguì lo mio attento sguardo,
com' occhio segue suo falcon volando.

Poscia trasse Guiglielmo e Rinoardo
e 'l duca Gottifredi la mia vista
per quella croce, e Ruberto Guiscardo.

Indi, tra l'altre luci mota e mista,
mostrommi l'alma che m'avea parlato
qual era tra i cantor del cielo artista.

Io mi rivolsi dal mio destro lato
per vedere in Beatrice il mio dovere,
o per parlare o per atto, segnato;

e vidi le sue luci tanto mere,
tanto gioconde, che la sua sembianza
vinceva li altri e l'ultimo solere.

And he began: 'On this fifth tier of the branches
of the tree that draws its sustenance from above
and always is in fruit and never sheds its leaves

'are blessèd spirits who below, on earth,
before they rose to Heaven, were of such renown
that any poet's page would be enriched by them.

'Look, therefore, at the two arms of the cross,
and each one whom I name will, flashing, dart
as does swift fire from within a cloud.'

I saw a streak of light drawn through the cross
at Joshua's name as soon as it was spoken,
nor could I tell the naming and the deed apart.

And, at the name of valorous Maccabaeus,
I saw shoot by another whirling light—
and it was joy that whipped that spinning top.

My watchful gaze was fastened
on Charlemagne and Roland there, as well,
just as the eye pursues the falcon in its flight.

William, Renouard, and then Duke Godfrey
next drew my eyes along that cross,
and Robert Guiscard also did so.

Then, leaving me to mingle with the other lights,
the soul who'd spoken last with me displayed
his artistry among the singers of that heaven.

I turned to my right to learn
from Beatrice what I ought to do,
whether signaled by some word or gesture,

and I saw her eyes so clear, so joyful,
that her aspect in its radiance outshone
her former glory, even that most recent.

E come, per sentir più dilettanza
bene operando, l'uom di giorno in giorno
s'accorge che la sua virtute avanza,

sì m'accors' io che 'l mio girare intorno
col cielo insieme avea cresciuto l'arco,
veggendo quel miracol più addorno.

E qual è 'l trasmutare in picciol varco
di tempo in bianca donna, quando 'l volto
suo si discarchi di vergogna il carco,

tal fu ne li occhi miei, quando fui vòlto,
per lo candor de la temprata stella
sesta, che dentro a sé m'avea ricolto.

Io vidi in quella giovïal facella
lo sfavillar de l'amor che lì era
segnare a li occhi miei nostra favella.

E come augelli surti di rivera,
quasi congratulando a lor pasture,
fanno di sé or tonda or altra schiera,

sì dentro ai lumi sante creature
volitando cantavano, e faciensi
or *D*, or *I*, or *L* in sue figure.

Prima, cantando, a sua nota moviensi;
poi, diventando l'un di questi segni,
un poco s'arrestavano e taciensi.

O diva Pegasëa che li 'ngegni
fai gloriosi e rendili longevi,
ed essi teco le cittadi e ' regni,

illustrami di te, sì ch'io rilevi
le lor figure com' io l'ho concette:
paia tua possa in questi versi brevi!

And as, from feeling more delight in doing good,
a man becomes aware from day to day
of his increasing virtue,

seeing that miracle adorned with greater brightness,
I became aware my wheeling circles
through the heavens had grown wider in their arc.

And such a change as passes in a moment
from the blushing face of a fair-skinned lady,
unburdened of the reason for her shame,

greeted my eyes once I had turned around,
because of the white radiance of the temperate
sixth star, which had gathered me into itself.

In that torch of Jupiter I watched
the sparkling of the love resplendent there
make signs, before my eyes, of our speech.

And as birds risen from the river's edge,
seeming to celebrate their pleasure in their food,
form now a rounded arc, and now another shape,

so, radiant within their lights, the holy creatures
sang as they flew and shaped themselves
in figures, now *D*, now *I*, now *L*.

At first, singing, they danced to their own tune.
And then, taking on one of these shapes,
they paused in their movement and were silent.

O divine Pegasean, who bestow glory
and long life on genius, as, with your help,
it gives life to towns and kingdoms,

inspire me with your light so that I may set down
their shapes as I conceived them in my mind.
May your power appear in these few lines.

Mostrarsi dunque in cinque volte sette
vocali e consonanti; e io notai
le parti sì, come mi parver dette.

"DILIGITE IUSTITIAM," primai
fur verbo e nome di tutto 'l dipinto;
"QUI IUDICATIS TERRAM," fur sezzai.

Poscia ne l'emme del vocabol quinto
rimasero ordinate; sì che Giove
pareva argento lì d'oro distinto.

E vidi scendere altre luci dove
era il colmo de l'emme, e lì quetarsi
cantando, credo, il ben ch'a sé le move.

Poi, come nel percuoter d'i ciocchi arsi
surgono innumerabili faville,
onde li stolti sogliono agurarsi,

resurger parver quindi più di mille
luci e salir, qual assai e qual poco,
sì come 'l sol che l'accende sortille;

e quïetata ciascuna in suo loco,
la testa e 'l collo d'un'aguglia vidi
rappresentare a quel distinto foco.

Quei che dipinge lì, non ha chi 'l guidi;
ma esso guida, e da lui si rammenta
quella virtù ch'è forma per li nidi.

L'altra bëatitudo, che contenta
pareva prima d'ingigliarsi a l'emme,
con poco moto seguitò la 'mprenta.

O dolce stella, quali e quante gemme
mi dimostraro che nostra giustizia
effetto sia del ciel che tu ingemme!

They then displayed themselves in five times seven
consonants and vowels, and I saw these letters
singly, and in the order they were traced.

DILIGITE IUSTITIAM—these letters,
placed together, verb and noun, came first,
QUI IUDICATIS TERRAM, last.

Then they came to rest in the fifth word's *M*
so that this place in Jupiter was shining
as does silver overlaid with gold.

And I saw other lights descend and settle
on the *M*'s high crest to sing, I think,
of that great Good which draws them to Itself.

Then, as when someone strikes a burning log,
causing innumerable sparks to fly,
sparks from which the foolish form their divinations,

just so a thousand lights and more appeared
to rise from there and mount, some more, some less,
as the Sun that kindles them ordained.

When each had settled in its place
I saw an eagle's head and neck
take shape out of that overlay of fire.

He who fashions there has need of none to guide Him
but Himself. Thus we recognize as His
the form that every bird takes for its nest.

The other blessèd spirits, who seemed at first content
to turn themselves into a lily on the *M*,
with gentle motion joined, completing the design.

O lovely star, how many and how bright the jewels
that showed me that our earthly justice
comes from that heaven, brilliant with your gems!

Per ch'io prego la mente in che s'inizia
tuo moto e tua virtute, che rimiri
120 ond' esce il fummo che 'l tuo raggio vizia;

sì ch'un'altra fiata omai s'adiri
del comperare e vender dentro al templo
123 che si murò di segni e di martìri.

O milizia del ciel cu' io contemplo,
adora per color che sono in terra
126 tutti svïati dietro al malo essemplo!

Già si solea con le spade far guerra;
ma or si fa togliendo or qui or quivi
129 lo pan che 'l pïo Padre a nessun serra.

Ma tu che sol per cancellare scrivi,
pensa che Pietro e Paulo, che moriro
132 per la vigna che guasti, ancor son vivi.

Ben puoi tu dire: "I' ho fermo 'l disiro
sì a colui che volle viver solo
e che per salti fu tratto al martiro,
136 ch'io non conosco il pescator né Polo."

Therefore, I entreat the Mind, in which your motion
and your power begin, to look down on the source
120 of smoke that dims your radiant beam,

so that your wrath come down once more
on those who buy and sell within the temple,
123 whose walls were built of miracle and martyrdom.

O soldiery of Heaven, whom I contemplate,
pray for those still on the earth,
126 those led astray by bad example!

It was the custom once to go to war with swords.
Now wars are fought withholding here and there
129 the bread our loving Father keeps from none.

But you who write only to cancel,
remember this: Peter and Paul, who died
132 to save the vineyard you lay waste, still live.

Well may you say: 'I have so set my heart
on him who chose to live in solitude
and who for a dance was dragged to martyrdom
136 that I know neither the Fisherman nor Paul.'

1–3. This is a more difficult tercet than it may seem. The standard view in the first commentators is that Cacciaguida was delighting in what he had said to his great-great-grandson, while the protagonist was sharing in that joy. Scartazzini (comm. to verse 1) disentangles the tortuous skein of debate over this line, pointing out that the text suggests that each of the two participants contemplates different "words." He offers what has become the standard modern view: The word *verbo* must here be understood as a translation of the Scholastic Latin term *verbum* (e.g., as defined by Thomas Aquinas, *ST* I, q. 34, a. 1), meaning "concept of the inner mind." Thus, we at least may conjecture, Cacciaguida was enjoying his understanding, beyond these contingent events, of a higher form of being, in the light of Eternity, while Dante was seeing, *sub specie humanitatis*, the harmonious relation of his exile to his eventual happiness. This would mark an improvement in his cognition (seeing eventual concord where he was expecting only grief), which, nonetheless, remained limited by his mortal aspirations. To mark the differences in their levels of experience, as Torraca (comm. to this tercet) observes, Dante uses very different verbs: Cacciaguida savors (*godeva*) completely his inner concept of deity, while the protagonist has but a first taste (*gustava*) of his own higher awareness.

3. Few commentators point out the obvious (but see at least Carroll [comm. to vv. 1–18]): The third verse reflects Cacciaguida's promise (*Par.* XVII.43–45) of an eventual harmonious resolution of the problems inherent in Dante's exile. The protagonist is now capable of a larger and wider view of the impending events in his life, knowing that they are a part of the divine plan, one that includes his writing this text and that corroborates the rightness of his political decisions in the greater scheme of things. Unlike Cacciaguida, however, he is not yet capable of seeing essences without their contingent trappings.

5–6. Beatrice, perhaps having tuned in on the inner thoughts of both Cacciaguida and Dante, reminds her charge that God takes away any sense of loss in earthly circumstances that the saved may feel, according to Dante's current understanding. Once saved, a soul is *in patria*, not in exile any longer.

Beatrice, who has been uncharacteristically silent in Mars (to make room for the poet's "Cacciaguida voice," which is expansive), now speaks for only the second time in this heaven. She has smiled twice (*Par.* XV.71

and XVI.14) and spoken once (*Par.* XVII.7–12); she will speak once more (vv. 20–21), as briefly as she does now.

7–15. The insistent presence of first-person pronouns and pronominal adjectives in this passage (*io* is heard four times, the rhyming *mio*, three) is striking. It reminds us that, from the beginning, we have had to consider the strategic difference between the writing agent and the behaving protagonist, the first seeing all things in the light of his final vision of God, the second experiencing them cumulatively.

8–12. This passage reflects the earlier one at *Paradiso* I.5–9, which similarly insists on the poet's incapacity to retell what he has experienced and forgotten, since his memory was not up to containing so momentous an experience.

8. The word *conforto*, used as a noun to describe another human being (e.g., "that person was my comfort"), has been employed three times before now (*Inf.* IV.18; *Purg.* III.22, IX.43), on each occasion assigned to Virgil; here, for the first (and last) time referring to anyone else, it obviously refers to Beatrice.

16–18. Beatrice's beauty is now understood to mirror the greatest beauty of all, that of God. See the note to *Purgatorio* XXXI.47–54 for a discussion of the verbal noun *piacere*, denoting the aesthetic aspect of divinity. For Aquinas on God's aesthetic dimension, see *ST* I, q. 39, a. 8, where he argues that "the highest form and paradigm of beauty is the splendor of God as manifested through Christ, to whom . . . the name 'Beauty' is most fittingly attributed" (Masciandaro [Masc.1995.1], p. 329).

19–21. Beatrice "conquers" Dante's will by compelling him to look away from her eyes in order to turn his attention a final time to the words of his great-great-grandfather. This is the last smile she will direct at Dante for quite some time. See the note to *Paradiso* XXIII.46–48.

22–27. This simile compares a particularly affection-bearing glance, perceived on earth, to the visibly increased flame of Cacciaguida's desire to speak again to his descendant.

28–36. Apparently having finished his performance, Cacciaguida, like Solomon (*Par.* XIV.37–60), returns for an encore. And, like Solomon's, his has ramifications for our understanding of the genre of his poem. Solomon's was a hymn to the Resurrection; his is a piece from a Christian martial epic. For this last as a Dantean genre, see Hollander (Holl.1989.1), arguing that, after an initial series of rebuffs to martial epic in *Inferno*, eventually in *Paradiso* the poet begins to associate himself, through Cacciaguida, with a Christian poetry of crusade, surely a martial subject.

29. The image of the tree that is nourished from its topmost tip, that is, the "tree" of the saved in the Empyrean by God Himself, may reflect, as Battaglia Ricci suggests (Batt.1995.1, p. 11), biblical language in general or perhaps Matthew 13:22 and/or Ezechiel 47:12.

31–33. See the note to *Paradiso* IX.38–42 for the sort of fame that is praiseworthy, even in a Christian context.

33. For the word *musa* as meaning "poet" (or, as seems more likely, "poem," according to Bosco/Reggio [comm. to this verse]), see the note to *Paradiso* XV.26. For the meaning "poem," Bosco/Reggio cite Virgil, *Eclogues* III.84 and VIII.5; Horace, *Epistles* I.xix.28; *Satires* II.vi.17.

34–36. Cacciaguida promises that, as he names each of these heroic figures, it will traverse the "arms" of the cross, looking like lightning flashing in a cloud (cf. the first description of these lights as flames glowing behind alabaster, *Par.* XV.22–24).

36. This verse is the last spoken by Cacciaguida. See the note to *Paradiso* XIV.52–57 for the similarly talkative Thomas Aquinas. Of the 628 verses in the heaven of the Sun, 287 are spoken by him (46 percent); of the 553 in Mars, 297 are spoken by Cacciaguida (54 percent).

37–51. For Dante's knowledge of the French tradition of the *Neuf preus* (Nine Worthies), see Hollander (Holl.1989.1), pp. 83–85, citing Joan Ferrante (Ferr.1984.1), p. 277n., and pointing to the first frontal study of Dante's eclectic treatment of this traditional subject, a then-forthcoming article by Lauren Scancarelli Seem. See also the discussion in Picone (Pico.2002.5), pp. 268–71. Picone rightly notes that Seem's article (accepted by *Forum Italicum* around 1989) never appeared. See also Battaglia Ricci (Batt.1995.1), pp. 13–14. Trucchi (comm. to vv. 34–36) observes only that the exemplary fighters are nine, "a symbolic and perfect number," but is unaware, as is the entire commentary tradition, of the likely presence of a reference to the Nine Worthies. Seem, in her unpublished article, argues that Dante knew the tradition of these nine heroes, three Jewish, three pagan, three Christian, from either *Les Voeux du paon*, by Jacques de Longuyon (ca. 1298–1309), or from the earlier Latin and French tradition, dating from the eleventh century (with somewhat differing lists of heroes), that Jacques himself relied on.

The traditional list of the *Nove prodi* includes five not included in Dante's revised list (the right-hand column in the two lists below):

Joshua	[1 in Dante also]
David	Roland [4]
Judas Maccabeus	[2 in Dante]
Hector	William of Orange [5]
Alexander the Great	Renouard [6]
Julius Caesar	Robert Guiscard [8]
King Arthur	Cacciaguida [9]
Charlemagne	[3 in Dante]
Godfrey of Bouillon	[7 in Dante]

It seems clear that Dante is taking a canonical list and recasting it to conform to his special purposes. He includes two of the first three and the last pair of names (Joshua, Judas Maccabeus; Charlemagne, Godfrey), dropping the middle four, and then adding five more recent "Christian heroes," three drawn from fictional treatments, sometimes of historical characters (Roland and William of Orange, if not Renouard) and two from history itself (Robert Guiscard, Cacciaguida), and "updating" the list, which had ended with Duke Godfrey, leader of the First Crusade (1096), by adding last his own ancestor, who had perished, a martyr, in the second (1147).

38. Joshua, successor of Moses as leader of the Israelites, was, in Dante's Christian eyes, the "first crusader" in that he conquered the Holy Land, restoring it to its rightful populace.

39. This line makes it clear that the protagonist hears the names of the heroes spoken by his ancestor, who thus becomes, for a moment, the "author" of this part of the poem, and thus of a crusading epic. See the note to verse 51. However, and as Iorio (Iori.1989.1), p. 474, reminds us, there is not a word about their battles; this text presents them as they are, now and forever, in the sight of God, literally *sub specie aeternitatis*, with all that violence behind them.

40. Judas Maccabeus fought successfully against two kings of Syria, both of whom wanted to extirpate the Jewish religion. He eventually was killed by a third in 160 B.C., but his mission had been accomplished by then.

42. "It was joy that whipped that spinning top": That is, joy "was the impulse which caused the rotation. The homely simile is borrowed from Virgil, *Aeneid* VII.378–384, where it is applied to Amata's wild excitement when under the influence of the Fury" (Tozer, comm. to vv. 40–42).

In the days before mechanized toys, children used to keep their top spinning (once they had imparted energy to it by rapidly pulling a cord wrapped around its top) by following it and "whipping" its sides with a long, thin stick, thus maintaining its rotating motion.

43. Charlemagne (742–814) fought against the Saracens in Spain. He is the only emperor in the group. Roland, while a historical figure (counted among the Christian dead at the battle of Roncesvalles), is better known from the *Chanson de Roland* and other medieval epic poems.

46. William, Duke of Orange (ca. 750–812), adviser of Charlemagne and leader in several military successes of the Christian forces, but still better known from the cycle of poems celebrating his valor. Renouard, while not a historical figure, was perhaps believed by Dante to be one. As Charlemagne and Roland were paired in one cycle of French *chansons de geste*, so were William and Renouard in another.

47. Godfrey of Bouillon (1058–1100) led the First Crusade, resulting in the conquest of Jerusalem.

48. Robert Guiscard ("Robert the Astute"), a historical figure (1015–85), was also celebrated in a Latin poem, *Gesti Roberti Wiscardi*. Exactly why Dante wanted to include him in this list is not clear, indeed is the subject of a certain scholarly puzzlement. Further, he violates the chronology established by the inclusion of Godfrey before him. Dante has previously mentioned him (*Inf.* XXVIII.13–14) as having defeated the Saracens in Puglia, and that may have been his single largest qualification in the poet's eyes.

49. Cacciaguida has rejoined the temporary residents of the cross and now he also streaks along its radial beam.

51. The word *artista*, as Hollander (Holl.1992.2), pp. 217–18, has argued, is perhaps used here for the first time in Italian with its modern sense, that is, not only as the practitioner of one of the liberal arts (in this case, music), but as a full-fledged "artist," both composer and performer of his own work, performing his "mini-epic" of nine crusading spirits, his personal version of the Nine Worthies. Its second such use will be in *Paradiso* XXX.33, where Dante will join his great-great-grandfather as one of the only two "artists" so designated in the *Commedia*.

The musical reference of this canto, its concerns so often expressed in musical terms, is studied by Heilbronn-Gaines (Heil.1995.2).

52–69. The ascent from Mars to Jupiter is accomplished during the course of a single action (Dante looks into Beatrice's eyes [vv. 52–57]), which is amplified by two similes (vv. 58–63, 64–69). The first combines awareness of the slowness of process with the suddenness of the realization that a change has finally occurred; the second presents a subtle change (the return of normal complexion) that follows a fairly dramatic event (a blush of modesty in response to some sort of embarrassment) that recedes perceptibly over a brief period. See the note to vv. 64–66. The first simile refers to the ascent from Mars and arrival in Jupiter in spatial terms, while the second reflects the colors of the two planets, respectively red and silvery white. Each refers to a subtle process, occurring over an indeterminate period of time, that is suddenly perceived as having involved fairly dramatic change.

56–57. As we may have suspected, Beatrice, in this her latest presence to Dante as they both ascend to a new realm, is even more beautiful than ever. See vv. 7–21, the last time he looked upon his lady in the heaven of Mars.

61–62. Dante has become aware that the segment of the ideal circle traversed by his body in each sphere is increasing in circumference the higher he rises, a natural result of his progress up through the heavens.

64–66. Beginning with Scartazzini (comm. to verse 64) and Poletto (comm. to vv. 64–69), some readers have turned to Ovid for a source for this blush in Arachne's face (*Metam.* VI.45–49). The scene is a troubling one: Athena appears (first disguised as an old woman) to accept Arachne's challenge to a contest in weaving. When the goddess reveals herself, the other mortals present show reverence, except for Arachne, whose involuntary blush is only momentary, and quickly fades, like the red sky at dawn. Picone (Pico.2002.5), p. 272, points out that the figuring element and the thing figured are reversed in Dante's use of the passage, reflecting an even more significant reversal, from a negative experience (Arachne's transformation into a spider) to a positive one (the letter M's transmutation into a lily and then an eagle).

For some resonances of this Ovidian moment, see, among others, Barolini (Baro.1987.1) and Macfie (Macf.1991.1).

70. As Poletto (comm. to vv. 70–72) points out, the word *facella* (from Latin *fax*, "torch") has been used once before to mean "star"; see *Purgatorio* VIII.89.

72. The phrase *nostra favella* has caused minor difficulty among those who (rightly) understand the noun usually to refer to vernacular speech and who therefore wonder why Dante uses this term for words that are Latin, and not Italian. The rhyme position obviously forced Dante's hand a little here. Most readers understand, along with Steiner (comm. to this verse) and, even more pointedly, Momigliano (comm. to vv. 70–72), that we should take the phrase more broadly and as referring to human speech in general.

73–78. Poletto (comm. to these verses) seems to have been the first to link them to *Purgatorio* XXIV.64–69. And Benvenuto (comm. to vv. 73–78) the first to see that this image is derived from Lucan (*Phars.* V.711–716).

Picone (Pico.2002.5), p. 274, points out that, while the avian "skywriting" observed by Lucan is aleatory and quickly obliterated, Dante's is lasting, by virtue of its inscription here in his pages.

73. Carroll (comm. to vv. 70–81) succinctly ties together the avian imagery that, beginning here, is so present in Jupiter: "It is to be noted that in this Heaven of the Eagle nearly all the similes are taken from bird-life (e.g., in addition to the Eagle and the present passage: XVIII.111, the mysterious reference to *nests*; XIX.34, the *falcon* issuing from its hood; XIX.91, the comparison of the Eagle to the *stork* hovering over its young; XX.73, the *lark* pausing, content with 'the last sweetness' of its song. See the chap. on 'The Birds of Dante' in Christopher Hare's *Dante the Wayfarer*)."

74. Cf. the doves, also at their *pastura* (feeding), in an earlier simile: *Purgatorio* II.124–125, as Torraca (comm. to vv. 73–75) suggests. These birds

seem of better purpose. While those earlier "doves," temporarily seduced by an ode from Dante's *Convivio*, failed to distinguish between wheat and tares (see the note to *Purg.* II.124–132), these "cranes" are singing God's song to Dante.

76. These "holy creatures" (*sante creature*) will later (*Par.* XIX.100–101) be identified as "lucenti incendi / de lo Spirito Santo" (the Holy Spirit's fiery lights).

82–87. This is the sixth invocation of the poem and second in *Paradiso*. What the Muse is asked to perform, the inspiration of Dante so that he may give long life to cities and kingdoms, might seem to require that Clio, the Muse of history, is called upon here. However, only one commentator even mentions her as a possibility (Momigliano [comm. to verse 82]), and he says only that the imperial context most fits Calliope or Clio.

The words *ingegno* (*Inf.* II.7; here; *Par.* XXII.114) and *concetto* (*Inf.* XXXII.4; here; *Par.* XXXIII.68) are both twice elsewhere present in passages containing invocations.

82. The winged horse Pegasus struck the ground on Mt. Helicon with his hoof. There sprang forth Hippocrene, the fountain sacred to the Muses. Which one of them does the poet invoke here? The most popular choices (given in historical order) are (1) Minerva, "Wisdom," as a sort of "super muse" (first suggested by Jacopo della Lana [comm. to vv. 82–87]); (2) a nonspecific, "generic" muse (first, Benvenuto [comm. to vv. 82–87]); (3) invoked for the second time in the poem (see *Purg.* I.9), Calliope, the Muse of epic (first, Vellutello [comm. to vv. 82–84], and the "majority candidate"); (4) also invoked for the second time (see *Purg.* XXIX.41), Urania, the heavenly Muse (first, Andreoli [comm. to this verse]). This is a vexed question, with four fairly popular solutions (and a few others, e.g., Euterpe [Torraca, comm. to vv. 82–84] and Clio [Momigliano, comm. to this verse]) and no clear consensus. All one can say is that the poet really seems to have a particular Muse in mind, since he addresses her with the singular "tu" in verse 87.

88–96. Perhaps the single most self-conscious, "artificial" passage in a poem that hardly lacks aesthetic exertion, the sort of thing Romantic readers, in the wake of De Sanctis and Croce, despise in the *Commedia*. However, for the view that this sort of calculated performance is a sign of the poet's "bello stile," see Parodi (Paro.1915.1).

88–89. For the poet to have counted his letters (there are 13 different ones in all), 35 instances of vowels (18, with "i" dominant [occurring 10 times]) and consonants (17, with "t" dominant [occurring 5 times]), tells us that he was making a point that he considered central to his purpose.

91–93. These seven words ("Love justice, you who judge the earth") constitute the opening sentence of the book of the Bible called "Sapientia" (Wisdom), attributed, by Dante at least, to Solomon. That attribution was a matter of some dispute for Christians, from the early Fathers on (e.g., in a fairly rare moment of concord, both Jerome and Augustine deny Solomon paternity [if both err in attributing it to Philo Judaeus]). For discussions of Dante's knowledge of this text, see G. R. Sarolli, "Salomone" (*ED* IV [1973]) and the unsigned article (apparently by Alessandro Niccoli), "Sapientia, Libro della" (*ED* V [1976]). Sarolli shows that Dante, in one of his many references to the biblical king (*Conv.* IV.xvi.1), refers, by citing Wisdom 6:23, to Solomon as the author of that now-apocryphal book. This passage in *Paradiso* is treated by most (including Sarolli) as the only reference to Wisdom in the *Commedia* (but see the note to verse 101), if there are two references in the *Epistle to Cangrande* (*Epist.* XIII.6 and XIII.62).

For the program of St. Paul's "five words with understanding" in the poem and its possible relevance here, see Hollander (Holl.1992.1), pp. 39–43.

It seems probable that this is the third passage in the poem to involve a phenomenon that might be described as "visible speech," formally similar expressions that also prominently involve the idea of justice. This one joins the "visible speech" found in the writing over the gate of Hell (*Inf.* III.1–9) and the words "seen" in the intaglio presenting Trajan and the widow (*Purg.* X.73–96). See Hollander (Holl.1969.1), pp. 297–300; Pertile (Pert.1991.3), p. 38; and Martinelli (Mart.2002.1), p. 283.

91. It is not surprising that justice, most blatantly evident as a guiding concern for this poet in this canto (where it is literally spelled out in capital letters), has caught the attention of nearly all who deal with it. Giglio's *lectura* (Gigl.1988.1) is little more than a meditation on Dante's conception of justice. And see Chimenz (Chim.1956.1), p. 1735, supporting a definition of the *Commedia* as a "poem of justice, both human and divine." In this vein, see also Scott (Scot. 1996.1), p. 55, citing Dante's epistle (*Epist.* XII.7), where he refers to himself as a "preacher of justice" (*vir predicans iustitiam*).

For a consideration of the centrality of justice to Cantos XVIII–XX and to the poem as a whole, see Took (Took.1997.1). Scartazzini (comm. to vv. 70–99) refers to two earlier passages that reveal Dante's overwhelming respect for this ideal: "Thus, although every virtue in man is deserving of love, that is most deserving of love in him which is most human, and that is justice" (*Conv.* I.xii.9, tr. R. Lansing); ". . . Justice, which disposes us to love and conduct ourselves with rectitude in all things" (*Conv.* IV.xvii.6, tr. R. Lansing).

94. Francesco da Buti (comm. to vv. 94–108) says that the "m," last letter of the word *terram*, stands for *mondo* (the world), a reading immediately supported by the meaning of the word itself in Wisdom 1:1. He continues by reading the souls making up the letter as being minor public officials and private citizens who have in common a love of justice; they will be the body politic for the emperor, figured in the eagle's head into which the central stem of the letter will eventually be transformed at its top. It has become far more common, but only in the twentieth century, for interpreters to claim that the letter stands for *monarchia*. On the other hand, the early interpretation has the virtue of separating the human desire for justice from its expression in actual imperial rule, which would certainly correspond with Dante's own experience, most of which was of a world that hoped for empire but was denied its presence. (See the note to vv. 100–108.)

95–96. The planet itself is seen as a silver globe inlaid with ornamentation worked in gold, the mobile souls carrying out God's artisanship for Dante's pleasure and instruction.

97–99. Other souls, descending (from where we are not told, but it is difficult to imagine from anywhere else but the Empyrean), not those who had paused in their "skywriting," appear to make a "cap" on the midpoint of the top of the "m," which then resembles (as we learn in verse 113) a lily, as well as a capital "M" in Gothic script.

99. For the program of song in the last *cantica*, see the note to *Paradiso* XXI.58–60.

100–108. The simile accounts for the rising of the souls (probably from the second group alone [i.e., that which had just formed the cap] and not from both groups, as some would understand) to represent the head and neck of an eagle. That physical detail remains a matter in question (i.e., whether the souls forming the eagle derived only from the new group or from both). Also a cause for debate is the more important question of what the three embodiments of the "m" represent. There are many solutions proposed. The more plausible explanations limit the possible choices to the following: (1) whether the "m" stands for *monarchia* or *mondo*, (2) whether the "M" (as lily) stands for France or Florence (its two most widely known identities), (3) whether the "M" (as eagle) stands for Christ or the empire. While arguments can and have been made for all these interpretations (and more), and in varying combinations, it does seem plausible to hold that the first image indicates the "world" of would-be imperial citizens, while the third indicates the empire once it is established (e.g., as Dante knew it briefly under Henry VII, 1310–13, and hoped to know it again). As for the second stage in the transformation (the most difficult to interpret—if no element of this puzzle is easily resolved), those who argue that it indicates the ideal primitive Florence (i.e., as Cacciaguida has described it in *Par.* XVI), a template for the civic virtues necessary to develop a populace capable of being led to empire, are most in accord with what we know of Dante's predilections in these matters.

100. For the connection of this image, "corrective" of divination, with Dante's harsh views of that practice put forward in *Inferno* XX, see Hollander (Holl.1980.1), pp. 197–99.

101. Pertile (Pert.1991.3), p. 41, cites Wisdom 3:7: "Fulgebunt iusti, / Et tamquam scintillae in harundineto discurrent" (The just will shine forth, / And they will show themselves like sparks in the stubble), crediting Pietrobono (comm. to this verse) as being the only other reader to note this clear citation (but also see Fallani [comm. to vv. 100–102]).

105. This Sun is God and these arriving souls sing, apparently, of their desire to return to Him. It is of some interest that, forming the head of the Eagle, they are in fact moving up, and thus back toward Him.

109–111. Just as birds need no exemplar to design their nests, but follow some inner imprinting, so God needs no "model" for his creating. This simple paraphrase of the tercet would have come as a great surprise to almost all who either avoided dealing with it or who labored over it in order to find something "more profound" in it. Indeed, its first clear statement had to await Brunone Bianchi (comm. to this tercet) in 1868. However, it is perhaps prudent to observe that the main opposing argument (there are several to choose from) has it that not the nests but the creatures within them, referred to by synecdoche, are portrayed as developing in accord with their archetypal form. And this just may be what Dante had in mind.

It was Grandgent (comm. to this tercet) who was perhaps the first to point to Thomas Aquinas for a potential source (*ST* I, q. 19, a. 4). Perhaps still closer is the reference put forward by Becker (Beck.1988.1) to Thomas's *Quaestiones disputatae de veritate*, XXIV, a. 1, resp. 3, which has it that "all swallows build their nests in the same way."

112–114. The rest of the spirits who had at first seemed to be content to make up the "enlilying" cap of the "M" now fill out the Eagle's shape (his wings?). This detail would argue against those who claim that some of the first group are drawn up into this further design. It would seem rather that they stay in the original "m." See the note to vv. 100–108.

113. For a consideration of a range of possible significances of this figure, see Sarolli (Saro.1971.1), pp. 337–56. Picone (Pico.2002.5), pp. 277–78, argues effectively for the fugitive vision that Dante has of the "M" as lily being the representation of the civic principles of Florence of the "buon tempo antico" as being consistent with the restoration of Roman imperial virtue in the city. Fumagalli (Fuma.2005.1) attempts to resuscitate the "French connection," arguing that the passage (vv. 88–114) presents St. Louis (King Louis IX of France) in a better light than is customarily perceived. He admits that Fenzi (Fenz.2004.1) has offered a strong argument against such a view, but presents it anyway.

115–117. The first of the apostrophes with which this canto concludes is addressed (as will be the second) to the positive forces in God's universal plan, first the tempering planet, just Jupiter. This tercet offers a clear example of Dante's belief in astral influence on earthly behaviors, with Jupiter conceived as the heavenly shaper of human embodiments of justice. See *Paradiso* VIII.97–99 and VIII.122–126 and the appended notes.

Lenkeith's chapter "Jupiter and Justice" (Lenk.1952.1, pp. 73–131) concludes with a citation of this tercet. She offers an evaluation of Dante's debt to Cicero's Stoic statecraft (with which the poet is in accord except for a total disavowal of its Godless theory of politics) and his total disagreement with Augustine's theologically determined rejection of the state's ability to have anything to do with "real justice" altogether.

118–136. The reader can hardly fail to notice the sudden and sustained shift in the tense of the verbs (from past definite in verse 116) to present, fifteen verbs in all, from *prego* (I pray [118]) to *conosco* (I know [136]). The most dramatic is perhaps the resurrective "are alive" (*son vivi*) for Saints Peter and Paul in verse 132. But the ostensible reason for the shift in tenses is clear: Dante looks up from composing his text to see again the souls he had previously seen in this sphere (we will meet them only in *Par.* XX), first among them David, those of just rulers, to pray for their intervention with God to alleviate the civic distress of all on earth who have been led astray by corrupt clergy, presided over by a corrupt pope. For reasons to believe that Dante here is thinking specifically of the papacy and particularly of Pope John XXII, see the note to verse 130.

118–123. Now the poet turns his attention from this planetary home of justice, where he was suspended, to God the Father, who is the source of the justice that Jupiter rays down to earth, and prays that He will observe the "smoke" that extinguishes those just rays before they reach our world and will feel wrath at the offenders.

122–124. Each of these three verses is constructed from a different verse of the Bible. For the commerce in the temple, see Matthew 21:12; for the bloody cost of building the Church out of sacrifice and martyrdom, see Acts 20:28; for the heavenly militia, see Luke 2:13.

124. The second of the three concluding apostrophes is addressed to the souls of the just rulers, whom he contemplates, as he writes these words, in the Empyrean. Nowhere in this passage does the poet rise to a higher pitch of blissful contemplation than here, where he even now "holds in mind" those whom he has previously seen in this heaven. See the note to vv. 118–136.

126. Surely Dante does not mean that all on earth are misled by corrupt prelates; his negative enthusiasm runs away with him. But he clearly does mean to indicate the population of Italy (and of France?) that is misgoverned by the Church.

127–129. The "bread" that God the Father bars to none is generally understood as the sacraments of the Church, and in this instance most particularly the sacrament of the Eucharist.

Since it is the Church that "makes war" by denying the sacrament of communion (an inevitable consequence of excommunication), in a better age the Church (and not, as some commentators believe, ancient Roman warriors) must have been brave on the field of battle. Exactly what Dante means by this is perhaps as puzzling as the commentaries have allowed it to become. However, in this very canto we have heard about those worthies who battled against the soldiery of Mohammed in order to regain the Holy Land, the Crusaders. Is this an approving recollection of the Crusades? No commentator apparently thinks so, but that fact in itself seems surprising. (Commentators who do attempt to identify the objects of these Christian weapons are content with a general sense, heretics and/or pagans.)

130–136. The third and final apostrophe is hurled at the sitting pope, and perhaps explains Dante's reasons for shifting out of the normal "time zone" of the poem to a "now" in which Pope John XXII is very much alive. See the note to verse 130.

The rhythmn of the three apostrophes is noteworthy, the first two addressed to the temporary inhabitants of Jupiter and the permanent residents of the Empyrean (*O dolce stella, . . . O milizia del ciel*), lofty in tone; the last, brutally personal and in the casual intonation not far removed from that of the gutter (*Ma tu . . .*). This conclusion of the canto is meant to be scabrous, because it is concerned with scabrous deeds, the repeated selling of Christ for personal gain. These verses offer what may be considered an appendix to *Inferno* XIX (where we first met simoniac popes) in which we hear the sitting pontiff, his words lent him by the acid-tongued Signor Alighieri, sounding like a mobster in *The Godfather* or *The Sopranos*, speak of his dead "buddies," one who was killed (John the Baptist, whose image, of course, adorns the florin) so that a political functionary could watch a striptease performed by his stepdaughter, and another two (whom we heard rightly named in the poet's voice just now, Peter and Paul) disparagingly referred to as a fisherman and "Paulie"—to whom he greatly prefers the florin.

130. A probable reference to Pope John XXII, who acceded to the Holy See in 1316 (he would survive in it for thirteen years past Dante's death, until 1334). John was not only French, but he decided to keep the Church in France, in its Avignonian "captivity," thus managing to draw Dante's ire. It has seemed to some that this diatribe against papal use of excommunication for political purpose is grounded in John's excommunication of the imperial vicar Cangrande in 1317.

The last pope who had a speaking part in the poem was Adrian V, on his way to Paradise, addressed by the protagonist with the honorific *voi* (*Purg.* XIX.131). Now, in the poem called *Paradiso*, we hear the protagonist speak to the sitting pope, using the familiar *tu*, in the most disparaging terms and tone of voice.

131–132. Dante's threat to Pope John is advanced in two lines hinged on the past tense of the verb "to die" (*moriro[no]*) and culminating in the triumphant assertion that the first keepers of the vineyard of the Church, who gave their lives for it as martyrs, are indeed alive (*vivi*). Peter and Paul (and John the Baptist, as we shall shortly hear), for the pope and his cofunctionaries, are dead indeed; but not for believers like Dante.

PARADISO XIX

OUTLINE

JUPITER

1–6 joyous in their enjoyment of God, these souls appeared to Dante as one, yet each seemed itself a glowing ruby;

7–12 the wonder of what Dante saw and heard the Eagle say;

13–18 the Eagle speaks: "For being just and dutiful I am here exalted; on earth my example of virtue is not followed"

19–21 simile: many embers make a single warmth as many loves combine to sing in unison from the beak of the Eagle

22–24 Dante now addresses the souls (metaphorically flowers):

25–33 he hopes that they will speak and clarify once and for all the reason for the damnation of virtuous pagans

34–39 simile: falcon, unhooded and preening, is like a banner woven of lauds, songs known to the saved, of divine grace

40–63 The Eagle: "God's wisdom exceeds that of his creations; if **[Lucifer]** failed to understand, how can you expect to?

64–66 "His light alone reveals all, your senses being faulty

67–69 "and now you understand why you cannot understand;

70–78 "where is," you want to know, "the justice that condemns a just **Indian**, living outside the Christian dispensation?

79–84 "and who are you, Dante, to question God's justice?

85–90 "O you gross minds, not understanding God's goodness!"

91–96 simile: mother stork hovering over the chick she has fed compared to the Eagle hovering over Dante

97–99 simile (Eagle speaks): "the notes I sing to you, Dante, escape your ken, just as God's judgment evades mortals."

100–102 Now the shining flames of the Holy Spirit grow quiet,

103–108 only to start up again: "No one ever came up here who did not believe in **Christ**;

109–114 "condemned pagans will themselves condemn erring Christians at the Judgment, seeing their many sins.

115–141 ACROSTIC: THE PESTILENCE OF TWELVE KINGS IN 1300

115–117 (1) **Emperor Albert** (1298–1308), Austria

118–120 (2) **[Philip the Fair]** (1285–1314), France

121–123 (3) **[Edward I]** (1272–1307), England

124–125 (4) **[Ferdinand IV of Castile]** (1295–1312), Spain

125–126 (5) **[Wenceslaus IV]** (1278–1305), Bohemia

127–129 (6) **[Charles II]** (1285–1309), Naples ("Jerusalem")

130–135 (7) **[Frederick II]** (1296–1337), Sicily

136–138 (8) **[James of Aragon]** (1276–1311), Majorca & Minorca

(9) **[James II of Aragon]** (1291–1327), Aragon

139–140 (10) **[Dionysius]** (1279–1325), Portugal

(11) **[Haakon V]** (1299–1319), Norway

140–141 (12) **[Stephen (Urosh) II]** (1275–1321), Serbia

142–148 CODA: THREE OTHER KINGDOMS

142–143 (13) **[Andrea III]** (1290–1301), Hungary

143–144 (14) **[Joanna]** (1284–1305), Navarre

145–148 (15) **[Henry II of Lusignan]** (1285–1324), Cyprus."

PARADISO XIX

Parea dinanzi a me con l'ali aperte
la bella image che nel dolce *frui*
liete facevan l'anime conserte;

parea ciascuna rubinetto in cui
raggio di sole ardesse sì acceso,
che ne' miei occhi rifrangesse lui.

E quel che mi convien ritrar testeso,
non portò voce mai, né scrisse incostro,
né fu per fantasia già mai compreso;

ch'io vidi e anche udi' parlar lo rostro,
e sonar ne la voce e "io" e "mio,"
quand' era nel concetto e "noi" e "nostro."

E cominciò: "Per esser giusto e pio
son io qui essaltato a quella gloria
che non si lascia vincere a disio;

e in terra lasciai la mia memoria
sì fatta, che le genti lì malvage
commendan lei, ma non seguon la storia."

Così un sol calor di molte brage
si fa sentir, come di molti amori
usciva solo un suon di quella image.

Ond' io appresso: "O perpetüi fiori
de l'etterna letizia, che pur uno
parer mi fate tutti vostri odori,

solvetemi, spirando, il gran digiuno
che lungamente m'ha tenuto in fame,
non trovandoli in terra cibo alcuno.

Before my eyes, its open wings outstretched,
appeared the lovely image of those interwoven souls,
reveling in sweet enjoyment.

Each one seemed to be a single ruby
in which the sun's ray burned with such a flame
it felt as though a sunbeam struck my eyes.

And what I now must tell
no voice has ever uttered, nor ink ever wrote,
nor was it ever seen in phantasy.

For I saw and heard it was the beak that spoke,
sounding with its voice the words for *I* and *my*
when, in conception, it meant *we* and *our*.

It said: 'For being just and merciful
I here am raised unto that glory
which by itself desire cannot attain.

'On earth I left behind such vestiges
as even wicked people there commend,
without, however, hewing to the form.'

Just as from many coals we feel a single heat,
so from that image there came forth
the undivided sound of many loves.

And I then answered: 'O everlasting blossoms
of eternal bliss, you make all odors
blend into what seems a single fragrance,

'breathe forth and free me from this endless fast
that ever keeps me famished,
since I can find no food for it on earth.

Ben so io che, se 'n cielo altro reame
la divina giustizia fa suo specchio,
che 'l vostro non l'apprende con velame.

Sapete come attento io m'apparecchio
ad ascoltar; sapete qual è quello
dubbio che m'è digiun cotanto vecchio."

Quasi falcone ch'esce del cappello,
move la testa e con l'ali si plaude,
voglia mostrando e faccendosi bello,

vid' io farsi quel segno, che di laude
de la divina grazia era contesto,
con canti quai si sa chi là sù gaude.

Poi cominciò: "Colui che volse il sesto
a lo stremo del mondo, e dentro ad esso
distinse tanto occulto e manifesto,

non poté suo valor sì fare impresso
in tutto l'universo, che 'l suo verbo
non rimanesse in infinito eccesso.

E ciò fa certo che 'l primo superbo,
che fu la somma d'ogne creatura,
per non aspettar lume, cadde acerbo;

e quinci appar ch'ogne minor natura
è corto recettacolo a quel bene
che non ha fine e sé con sé misura.

Dunque vostra veduta, che convene
essere alcun de' raggi de la mente
di che tutte le cose son ripiene,

non pò da sua natura esser possente
tanto, che suo principio non discerna
molto di là da quel che l'è parvente.

'It is clear to me that, even though God's Justice
has its mirror in another realm of heaven,
in yours it also shines without a veil.

'You know with what care I prepare myself
to listen, and you know the nature of the doubt
that now has kept me fasting for so long.'

As the falcon, freed from its encumbering hood,
raises its head, and flapping, as in winged applause,
displays its beauty and its eagerness,

just so I witnessed that emblem, made with strands
of praise for God's own grace, surge into songs
known but to those who live above in bliss.

Then it began: 'He who with His compass
drew the boundaries of the world and then, within them,
created distinctions, both hidden and quite clear,

'did not imprint His power so deep
throughout the universe that His Word
would not with infinite excess surpass His making.

'In proof of this, the first and prideful being,
who was created highest of all creatures,
by not waiting for the light, plummeted unripe.

'And thus it is clear that every lesser nature
is too small a vessel for that goodness
which has no limit, which is measured by itself alone.

'Thus your vision, which must be
but a single ray of many in the mind
of Him of whom all things are full,

'by its nature must not have such power
that it should not perceive its source
as lying far beyond all it can see.

Però ne la giustizia sempiterna
la vista che riceve il vostro mondo,
com' occhio per lo mare, entro s'interna;

che, ben che da la proda veggia il fondo,
in pelago nol vede; e nondimeno
èli, ma cela lui l'esser profondo.

Lume non è, se non vien dal sereno
che non si turba mai; anzi è tenèbra
od ombra de la carne o suo veleno.

Assai t'è mo aperta la latebra
che t'ascondeva la giustizia viva,
di che facei question cotanto crebra;

ché tu dicevi: 'Un uom nasce a la riva
de l'Indo, e quivi non è chi ragioni
di Cristo né chi legga né chi scriva;

e tutti suoi voleri e atti buoni
sono, quanto ragione umana vede,
sanza peccato in vita o in sermoni.

Muore non battezzato e sanza fede:
ov' è questa giustizia che 'l condanna?
ov' è la colpa sua, se ei non crede?'

Or tu chi se', che vuo' sedere a scranna,
per giudicar di lungi mille miglia
con la veduta corta d'una spanna?

Certo a colui che meco s'assottiglia,
se la Scrittura sovra voi non fosse,
da dubitar sarebbe a maraviglia.

Oh terreni animali! oh menti grosse!
La prima volontà, ch'è da sé buona,
da sé, ch'è sommo ben, mai non si mosse.

'Thus, the vision granted to your world
may make its way into eternal justice
as deep as eyes may penetrate the sea.

'From shore they well may glimpse the bottom,
but not once out upon the open sea,
and yet it is there, hidden in the depths.

'No light is never overcast unless it comes
from that clear sky which always shines. All others
darken in the shadow or the bane of flesh.

'Now the hiding-place has been laid bare
that concealed from you the living justice
about which you have posed so many questions.

'For you have often asked: "A man is born
upon the bank along the Indus, with no one there
to speak, or read, or write of Christ,

' "and all that he desires, everything he does, is good.
As far as human reason can discern,
he is sinless in his deeds and in his words.

' "He dies unbaptized, dies outside the faith.
Wherein lies the justice that condemns him?
Wherein lies his fault if he does not believe?"

'Now, who are you to sit upon the bench,
judging from a thousand miles away
with eyesight that is shorter than a span?

'To be sure, for one who wanted to debate this,
had the Scripture not been set above you,
there might be ample room for question.

'Oh, earthly creatures! oh, gross minds!
The primal Will, good in Itself,
has never from Itself, the highest good, declined.

Cotanto è giusto quanto a lei consuona:
nullo creato bene a sé la tira,
ma essa, radïando, lui cagiona."

Quale sovresso il nido si rigira
poi c'ha pasciuti la cicogna i figli,
e come quel ch'è pasto la rimira;

cotal si fece, e sì levài i cigli,
la benedetta imagine, che l'ali
movea sospinte da tanti consigli.

Roteando cantava, e dicea: "Quali
son le mie note a te, che non le 'ntendi,
tal è il giudicio etterno a voi mortali."

Poi si quetaro quei lucenti incendi
de lo Spirito Santo ancor nel segno
che fé i Romani al mondo reverendi,

esso ricominciò: "A questo regno
non salì mai chi non credette 'n Cristo,
né pria né poi ch'el si chiavasse al legno.

Ma vedi: molti gridan 'Cristo, Cristo!'
che saranno in giudicio assai men *prope*
a lui, che tal che non conosce Cristo;

e tai Cristian dannerà l'Etïòpe,
quando si partiranno i due collegi,
l'uno in etterno ricco e l'altro inòpe.

Che poran dir li Perse a' vostri regi,
come vedranno quel volume aperto
nel qual si scrivon tutti suoi dispregi?

Lì si vedrà, tra l'opere d'Alberto,
quella che tosto moverà la penna,
per che 'l regno di Praga fia diserto.

'Only what accords with It is just: It is not drawn
to a created good but, sending forth Its rays,
It is the source of every good.'

As a stork will circle above her nest
after she has fed her young,
and as the one just fed looks up at her,

so, lifting up my brow, I watched
as over me the blessèd image flew on wings
that took their thrust from such shared counsel.

Wheeling, it sang, then spoke:
'As my notes exceed your understanding,
such is eternal judgment to all mortals.'

When these, the Holy Spirit's fiery lights,
grew quiet, still shaped into the sign
that made the world revere the Romans,

the eagle once again began: 'To this kingdom
no one ever rose without belief in Christ,
whether before or after He was nailed up on the tree.

'But observe that many shout out "Christ, O Christ!"
who shall be farther off from Him,
on Judgment Day, than such as know not Christ.

'The Ethiopian shall condemn such Christians
when the two assemblies go their separate ways,
the one forever rich, the other poor.

'What shall the Persians say then to your kings
when they see that volume lying open
in which their many infamies are all inscribed?

'There they shall see, among the deeds of Albert,
the deed—now soon to move the pen—
through which the realm of Prague shall suffer desolation.

Lì si vedrà il duol che sovra Senna
induce, falseggiando la moneta,
quel che morrà di colpo di cotenna.

Lì si vedrà la superbia ch'asseta,
che fa lo Scotto e l'Inghilese folle,
sì che non può soffrir dentro a sua meta.

Vedrassi la lussuria e 'l viver molle
di quel di Spagna e di quel di Boemme,
che mai valor non conobbe né volle.

Vedrassi al Ciotto di Ierusalemme
segnata con un i la sua bontate,
quando 'l contrario segnerà un emme.

Vedrassi l'avarizia e la viltate
di quei che guarda l'isola del foco,
ove Anchise finì la lunga etate;

e a dare ad intender quanto è poco,
la sua scrittura fian lettere mozze,
che noteranno molto in parvo loco.

E parranno a ciascun l'opere sozze
del barba e del fratel, che tanto egregia
nazione e due corone han fatte bozze.

E quel di Portogallo e di Norvegia
lì si conosceranno, e quel di Rascia
che male ha visto il conio di Vinegia.

O beata Ungheria, se non si lascia
più malmenare! e beata Navarra,
se s'armasse del monte che la fascia!

E creder de' ciascun che già, per arra
di questo, Niccosïa e Famagosta
per la lor bestia si lamenti e garra,
che dal fianco de l'altre non si scosta."

'There they shall see the sorrow brought upon the Seine
by one who falsifies his country's coin
and who will die assaulted by a boar.

'There they shall see the pride that makes men thirst
and so drives both the Englishman and Scot to fury
that neither will remain within his borders.

'Of him from Spain, and of Bohemia's king,
the text will show their wanton luxury and lazy ways
and that they never knew nor searched for valor.

'Of the Cripple of Jerusalem the text will show
an *I* to mark his only generous act,
while an *M* will mark the other traits in him.

'Of him who rules the isle of fire,
where the long life of Anchises had its end,
the text will show the greed and cowardice.

'Displayed will be his utter worthlessness,
requiring the use of shorthand
that will note much in little space.

'Displayed for all to see will be the wicked deeds
by which his uncle and his brother brought disgrace
to so renowned a line and both their kingdoms.

'Displayed will be the kings of Portugal and Norway,
and he of Rascia, who, to his own hurt,
laid his eyes upon Venetian coinage.

'O happy Hungary, if only she no longer lets
herself be poorly led! Happy Navarre, if she but takes
protection from the mountains that surround her!

'And, in proof of this, all men should know
that Nicosia and Famagosta
lament and complain of their own beast,
who takes his place among the others.'

1–6. The Eagle is first seen as a discrete entity (*la bella image*) and then as its components, the individual just rulers who constitute this beautiful image of justice, each appearing as a much-prized precious stone, the ruby. The text goes on to suggest that all of them were glowing as though the sun were equally reflected in all of them at once (something that would not happen in earthbound optics, where uneven surfaces reflect a distant light variously). In fact, these "rubies," red with the glow of *caritas*, are shining with their own light of affection, if that is eventually a reflection of God's love for them.

Dante's radical (and revolutionary, at least from an Augustinian point of view) notion is that earthly justice is the direct product of a divine principle. And, as we learned in the last canto (see the note to *Par.* XVIII.115–117), the souls of the shapers of those human institutions that serve justice are themselves shaped by the agency of this heaven.

1. The image of the Eagle, with its open wings, suggests, to Baranski (Bara.1995.4), p. 277, a passage from Deuteronomy 32:11, "expandit alas suas" (spreading out its wings), in the song about himself that Moses intones near the end of his life, in which he is presented as an eagle taking his chicks upon his back for an exodal ride. (Scartazzini cited that passage, but at *Purgatorio* IX.30.)

2. The term *frui* (to enjoy), first identified as deriving from St. Augustine by Benvenuto (comm. to vv. 1–3), probably arrives in Dante via Aquinas (*ST* I–II, q. 11, a. 3), as Scartazzini may have been the first to suggest.

7–12. What Dante must now report was never reported by voice, nor written in ink, nor present in the image-receiving faculty of the mind, for he had seen the beak speak and had heard it, too, when it uttered with its voice "I" and "mine," while in its conception it meant "we" and "our." We have had a similar experience once before, hearing Dante introduce himself as "we" and then speak as "I" in the first two lines of the poem (*Inf.* I.1–2): "Nel mezzo del cammin di *nostra* vita / *mi* ritrovai per una selva oscura. . . ."

St. Paul describes similar marvelous truths (I Corinthians 2:9) that "the eye has not seen, nor ear heard, nor the heart of man imagined," an observation dating back to Jacopo della Lana (proem to this canto). For discussion of this example of Dante's exploitation of the familiar topos of novelty, see Ledda (Ledd.2002.1), pp. 81–82.

9. For "phantasy" as a technical term in medieval versions of Aristotelian "physiology of mind," see Carroll (comm. to *Par.* IV.28–48) and Singleton (comm. to *Purg.* XVII.13–18); see also the note to *Purgatorio* XVII.13–18. This faculty is the image-receiving element in the mind. Carroll, Singleton, and Hollander consequently use this spelling in order to distinguish this term from the modern one, "fantasy," a daydream or another form of fictive flight.

10. The first commentator to report the resonance here of Apocalypse 8:13, "Then I looked, and I heard an eagle crying with a loud voice as it flew directly overhead," was Tommaseo (comm. to vv. 10–12). The context is the fourth angelic trumpet blast, and the eagle is announcing woe to those who dwell on earth. Dante's Eagle, on the other hand, has a more eupeptic message.

It seems clear that Geoffrey Chaucer was amused when he read this verse; his loquacious eagle in that delightful send-up of Dante's poem, *The House of Fame*, surely was one poet's laughing salute to another.

13. Bosco/Reggio (comm. to this verse) point out the resonance of the description of Trajan (shortly himself to appear in the poem at *Par.* XX.44–45) in *Purgatorio* X.93, where he is portrayed as moved by *giustizia* and *pietà*.

14–15. These verses were initially and widely interpreted to refer to that glory (salvation) that is greater than any desire for it. Scartazzini (comm. to verse 15), however, cites Bartolomeo Perazzini (*Note alla "Divina Commedia"* [Venice, 1844], p. 155), who says that the heavenly glory won by these souls, even more than did their desire, reflected (and rewarded) their deeds. Given the context of their virtuous acts as rulers, this interpretation has won support ever since it was presented by Scartazzini and Campi (comm. to vv. 13–15). Nonetheless, there is still no consensus, with various commentators advancing the one or the other explanation. Here is Carroll (comm. to vv. 1–18), summarizing the debate before attempting to find a way out: "Two interpretations are suggested: (1) that this glory of Jupiter is superior to all human desire; (2) that it does not allow itself to be won by mere desire—it must be worked for (Matth. 7:21). I venture to suggest a third: the common way in which kings aim at glory is at their own 'desire' or ambition, and earthly glory may be so won. But not so the glory of this Heaven: it can be 'conquered' only 'by being just and merciful.' "

16–18. We may need to remind ourselves that the Eagle is speaking as a corporate entity, his "I" really meaning "we," that is, the virtuous rulers composing his shape have all left exemplary lives behind them that draw lip service but no imitative good actions.

18. The commentators, from Benvenuto (comm. to vv. 16–18) onward, generally take *storia* here in the sense of *exemplum*, that is, according to the fourteenth-century Dantist, the wicked on the earth do not follow the positive examples of these virtuous rulers, present here in the Eagle, of whom we shall see some in the next canto.

19–21. The simile pounds home the poet's insistence that the plurality of souls making up the Eagle's unity sing as a single voice.

22–24. The protagonist himself, as it were, picks up the theme of the simile only to express it in metaphor: He hopes that these souls will become a garden of flowers giving off a single perfume, that is, speaking as one.

25–33. We probably are reminded of the presence in Limbo of the virtuous pagans (unauthorized by previous authority, e.g., St. Thomas, who denies them a place alongside the only inhabitants of the "orthodox" Limbus, the innocent but unbaptized infants [see the note to *Inf.* IV.30]). It was clear from that earlier passage that our poet had a problem with traditional Christian views of the "guilt" of otherwise morally good (or even excellent) human beings. The last words of his request to the souls in the Eagle make it plain that in his life he had been bothered by the Church's teaching on the postmortal situation of the virtuous heathen.

25. The gerund (perhaps used here as a present participle) *spirando* (breathing forth) is a form of the verb (*spirare*) that Dante uses to indicate the "spiration" of the Holy Spirit. For confirmation of this association, see verse 101.

28–30. The poet here refers, as Tommaseo (comm. to this tercet) was apparently the first commentator to point out, to Cunizza's words in *Paradiso* IX.61–62, from which he has learned that the angelic order of

Thrones, presiding over the heaven of Saturn, is designated as reflecting divine justice. But this does not mean that these just souls here in Jupiter are innocent of such knowledge, since they know about earthly justice and, further, like all the saved, see the higher form reflected in God Himself.

34–39. This is the first of two similes based on avian behavior in this canto. This one shows a tamed falcon being prepared to go off on a hunt for prey, while the next, at vv. 91–96, completes the implicitly joined image with a stork that has fed its young.

For six other references to falconry in the poem, see Bosco/Reggio (comm. to vv. 34–36).

35. For the double sense here of the Latin verb *plaudere* (both "to beat one's wings" and "to express approval" [as found in both Ovid and Virgil]), see Scartazzini (comm. to this verse).

40–63. The following is Tozer's paraphrase of these lines: "God, who created all things, infinitely surpasses in Himself the wisdom which appears in His creation (ll. 40–45). Lucifer, the highest of created beings, fell, because he lacked as yet the light which would have enabled him to see God perfectly (ll. 46–48). How much more feeble must be the vision of beings inferior to him! (ll. 49–51). Hence our minds cannot have any true conception of God's attributes (ll. 52–57), and, in particular, of His justice (ll. 58–63)."

40. For the image of the compass in God's designing of the universe, see Proverbs 8:27, as was perhaps first noted by Tommaseo (comm. to vv. 40–42). Torraca added the information that Dante himself cited this passage in *Convivio* III (xv.16).

46–48. Lucifer's fall (and that of the other rebellious angels) will have an entire passage to itself for Beatrice's elucidation in *Paradiso* XXIX.49–66. For Adam's contrasting "ripeness," see *Paradiso* XXVI.91. Lucifer did not await God's finishing His creation of him, which would have made him "perfect" with the light of grace.

58–60. Some commentators follow Scartazzini (comm. to verse 58) in ascribing this thought to Psalm 35:7 [36:6], "Your judgments are like the great deep," first cited, if without ascription, by John of Serravalle (comm. to vv. 70–78).

64–66. The answer to Dante's question will be found in God alone (in the metaphor, such shining as is never clouded over), as opposed to human sight, obfuscated by clouds of unknowing (products of our fallible or, worse, corrupt senses).

67–69. Marked by two Latinisms used as rhymes (*latebra*, "hiding-place"; *crebra*, "frequent"), this tercet marks the Eagle's finally coming to grips with Dante's insistent question about the justice of the condemnation of pagans who had apparently committed no positive sin.

69. The poet, allowing the Eagle to do so for him, insists once again that his life has been marked by a sort of prehumanist zeal to defend the pagans from unfair Christian treatment. But see the note to vv. 88–90.

70–78. This passage gives the fullest and most affecting version of this question, one that was directed at, as we have seen, perhaps the single most troubling aspect of Christian orthodoxy for Dante. The language, if indirectly, revisits a scene from *Purgatorio* (XXI.7–13), the appearance of Statius, himself led to salvation by Virgil, represented so as to be reminiscent of Jesus, resurrected, appearing to Cleopas and his wife. See Luke 24:19, a description of Jesus given by Cleopas (to Jesus Himself, whom he did not at first recognize), "vir propheta potens in opere et sermone" (a prophet mighty in deed and word), perhaps first cited by Tommaseo (comm. to vv. 73–75). In *Purgatorio* XXI.17–18, Virgil, hoping Statius will soon enjoy the fruits of salvation, refers to his own situation, condemned by "the unerring court / that confines me in eternal exile," with full acceptance of his guilt in God's eyes. It is difficult to read the passage at hand and not think of Virgil. Once we encounter some of the virtuous pagans who were saved in the next canto, it will once more be difficult not to think of him.

70–72. For a meditation on the challenge to Dante's claim to universality presented by those dwelling beyond the Indus (i.e., in India or even farther to the east), see Schildgen (Schi.1993.1).

77. As Foster explains (Fost.1976.1), p. 83, this hypothetical Indian must be condemned to Limbo, for he is (verse 73) without sin.

79–90. Up until now we have probably been sympathizing with the protagonist's unwillingness to embrace the justice that would condemn such an essentially admirable human being who, through no fault of his own, has not heard the Word. Suddenly the Eagle pounces on Dante (his "tu" is most personal, where in most of the rest of his long speech [vv. 40–90], with the exception of five other second-person singular pronouns or verbs within four lines, 67–70, he seems to be thinking of all mortals, three times addressing us as "voi"). "Who are you, Dante, to judge God's judgment?" Further (and now the Eagle resorts to third-person attack, Dante being offhandedly treated as a caviling subtilizer), is he not aware of what the Bible says? See the discussion of Romans 9:20 in the note to vv. 79–81.

79–81. As a biblical source for this tercet, Venturi (comm. to verse 79) adduces the Pauline formula (Romans 9:20) that will have most currency among later commentators: "o homo tu quis es qui respondeas Deo?" (But who are you, O man, that you answer back to God? [Is this the source of the Eagle's "tu"?]) Tommaseo adds a reference to Dante himself speaking in this vein (*Conv.* IV.v.9).

For the notion that this is the most important tercet of the canto, see Scrivano (Scri.1995.1), p. 29.

81. A "span" is as much as can be covered by a human palm, that is, not very much, at least not in comparison with one thousand miles.

83. See the extensive treament of this verse by Battistini (Batt.1988.1).

85. Compare Boethius (*Cons. Phil.* III.3[pr]) on *terrena animalia* (earthly beasts), first cited by Poletto (comm. to vv. 85–87), who also points out that Dante had previously cited this phrase in *Convivio* IV.v.9.

87. See Scartazzini's citation (comm. to this verse) of Malachi 3:6: "ego enim Dominus et non mutor" (for I am the Lord and I change not).

88–90. All that is just in the world accords with God's will; on the other hand, no created good draws God's will to itself; its goodness is the manifestation of that will, not its cause. Scartazzini/Vandelli (comm. to this tercet) point to Dante's similar phrasing in *Monarchia* II.ii.5, a passage that, in turn, may reflect the concept of God's inability to be unjust in Romans 9:14–15.

Having set himself up as a "liberal" on the question of the eternal punishment of virtuous pagans, Dante now embraces the "conservative" position, which has it that pagans are justly damned for not having intuited the truth of Christ. He will play this hand out again in the next canto, where he will see saved pagans (their presence in Heaven surely reflects a "liberal" mind-set), but will contrive to convince us (and himself?) that they had somehow found Christ. As we will see, moral perfection alone will not procure the most just among pagans a place in Heaven, this poet's Christian pantheon.

91–96. For the earlier and related avian simile, see the note to vv. 34–39.

96. The meaning of this expression is that the Eagle is propelled by the shared wills of its constituent souls.

97–99. Just as the second avian simile completed the first one (see the notes to vv. 34–39 and 91–96), so this second simile, pronounced by the Eagle itself, completes the pattern established by the first simile. There (vv. 19–21), many were resolved as one (many embers sensed as a single heat, many affectionate voices heard as a single song); here celestial harmony is not audible to human ears, which can hear only the individual voices and cannot make sense of them. See *Inferno* XX.29–30 for a similar insistence on the necessary failure of humans to understand God's justice.

101–102. This formulation might help clarify an issue that confuses some readers. The Eagle is not so much a symbol of Roman *imperium* as it is of God's justice made apparent in this world in whatever embodiment it should happen to take.

103–105. The Eagle's words are pellucidly clear; nevertheless, some readers contrive not to understand them. Salvation without belief in Christ is simply not possible. We should tuck this notice away in order to reexamine it in the light of the salvation of both Trajan and Ripheus in the next canto; in the light of this absolute qualification, their salvations seem dubious, at the very least.

For an excursus (in English) on the concept of implicit faith, which alone can make a bit more understandable Dante's unshakable embrace of the Church's firm ruling in this matter, see Carroll (comm. to vv. 79–84).

104–108. This is the third set (there will eventually be four [see *Par.* XXXII.83–87] of identical rhymes on the word *Cristo*. See the notes to *Paradiso* XII.71–75 and XIV.103–108.

106–108. Mowbray Allan (Alla.1993.1) restates and widens some of his earlier conclusions about the poem's openness to the possibility of Virgil's salvation. He reads this tercet as promising more than Dante probably intends. The text states only that, after the Judgment, some of these failed Christians will be still farther from God than certain pagans. That statement probably should not be interpreted as arguing for the possible eventual salvation of Virgil (or other pagans). They are *already* nearer God, in the Limbus (see Baranski [Bara.1995.4], p. 292, making this point), than most of the damned, who are predominantly (at least nominally) Christians. There is nothing here that requires us to think that Dante thinks that God will change his mind about Virgil—although of course He has the ability to do exactly that should He choose. The evidence of the text, however, does not in any way suggest that Dante thought that He would. For example, Virgil is allowed to describe his place in Limbo as eternal (*Purg.* XXI.18), not something the poet would have put in his mouth were he to have disagreed, as is (or ought to be) abundantly clear.

109–114. In response to this passage, perhaps Venturi (comm. to this verse) was the first commentator to cite the following pertinent text in Matthew (12:41–42): "The men of Nineveh will rise up at the judgment with this generation and condemn it, for they repented at the preaching of Jonah, and behold, a greater than Jonah is here. The queen of the South will rise up at the judgment with this generation and condemn it, for she came from the ends of the earth to hear the wisdom of Solomon, and behold, a greater than Solomon is here."

110. This verse has been a stumbling block for some readers. The clause "when the two assemblies go their separate ways" almost certainly does not mean, as some have taken it to do, that the Ethiopians shall depart from the wicked Christians and go to Heaven. Rather, it signifies that when the sheep (the saved "soldiery of Heaven") are separated from the goats (both decent Ethiopian nonbelievers *and* sinful Christians), these virtuous heathen will (justly) castigate their Christian counterparts, who were given the key to Heaven and chose not even to try to unlock its gates.

112. The word "kings" sets up the acrostic with its list of those rotten rulers that fills the rest of the canto.

113. The noun *volume* was first used, we may remember, to indicate Virgil's *Aeneid* (see *Inf.* 1.84 and note). Of its nine occurrences in the poem

(see Hollander [Holl.1969.1], pp. 78–79, unaccountably mentioning only seven of these, omitting the two occurrences found at *Par.* XXIII.112 and XXVI.119), only this one refers more or less directly to the Bible, more precisely, to the Apocalypse (20:12), as was first pointed out in specific terms by Pietro Alighieri ([Pietro1] comm. to vv. 112–114). These two uses do not make Virgil's book a Christian book by association; rather, they underline the tragic distance separating Virgil from salvation. The biblical text refers to the Book of Life, in which are recorded the names of the saved, and other unnamed "Books of the Dead" (see discussion of *Inf.* XXIX.57 in Hollander [Holl.1982.1]): "And I saw the dead, great and small, standing before the throne, and the books were opened. Then another book was opened, which is the book of life. And the dead were judged by what was written in the books, according to what they had done." It is more than sufficiently clear that Dante is here referring not to the "good" book in Revelation 20:12, but to the "bad" one(s).

114. That the word *dispregio* (here translated "infamy") has already been seen at *Inferno* VIII.51 has been noted in the commentaries at least since the appearance of Poletto's (1894, to vv. 112–114). This is its seventh and last appearance in the poem, in one form or another.

115–139. Dante's second (and last) full-scale acrostic in the poem (for the first, see the note to *Purgatorio* XII.25–63). There can be little doubt but that this one, too, is a deliberate contrivance, whatever the strength of the feelings one happens to harbor against such literary behavior. Three sets of three consecutive tercets begin with the same letter, L, V, and E, respectively, thus spelling the word *lue*, or "plague." However, even such astute readers as Bosco and Reggio (comm. to verse 115) seem to want to join Savi-Lopez (*BSDI* 10 [1903], p. 328) in thinking Dante's LVE the result of mere chance. While that seems extreme, at the other end of extremity we find Taylor (Tayl.1987.1), who wants to extend the acrostic by adding the "i" and "emme" of its central tercet (vv. 128–129) so as to get the scrambled word "lueim," an anagram for *umile* (humble). For her more than questionable procedure in so doing, see Barolini's complaint (Baro.1992.1), pp. 309–10. Barolini (pp. 308–9) also dismisses three other "discoverers" of "acrostics" elsewhere in the poem. However, see Allegretti (Alle.2004.2) for a study of yet another (and hitherto unobserved) acrostic in Dante's poetic response to Giovanni del Virgilio's invitation to compose a pastoral eclogue.

115–117. *Lì*, here and in the next two tercets, means "in that volume," that is, in the "Book of the Dead." Albert (emperor from 1298–1308, i.e., in precedence of Henry VII), was previously denounced by Dante for his neglect of Italy (*Purg.* VI.97–126). In 1304 he invaded and devastated Bohemia. In the assemblage of fifteen crowned heads appearing here, Albert is the only one to be named, thus giving us a sense of how much knowledge of "current events" Dante believed he could count on in his readers.

118–120. "On the banks of the Seine," that is, at Paris, where Philip the Fair caused his subjects great distress when he adulterated the coinage. See the note to verse 119.

119. For Philip's monetarist failings, see Oelsner (comm. to vv. 119–120): "[the king] debased the coinage to one-third of its value, in order to meet the expenses of his Flemish campaigns in 1302. This is one of several passages in which we see the horror of tampering with the coinage entertained by Dante, the citizen of the greatest commercial city of Europe. As the symbol of greed the *Florin* was the 'accursed flower' of *Par.* IX.130, but as the foundation of all commercial relations it was worthy of such reverence that he who tampered with it was to be ranked with him who falsified the very personality of human beings, the ultimate basis of human intercourse." Toynbee ("Filippo[2]") points out that Philip is always named by periphrasis in the poem, never by his name, and lists his other main periphrastic appearances: *Inferno* XIX.87; *Purgatorio* VII.109, XX.91.

120. This mention of the death of the French king dates the canto as having been composed (or, at least, modified) after November 1314, according to Campi (comm. to vv. 118–120); see also Foster (Fost.1976.1), p. 85. The Ottimo (comm. to vv. 118–120), writing in 1333, knew about the death of Philip the Fair, caused by a boar. (The word *cotenna*, in Tuscany, meant the hide of a wild pig and perhaps, in Dante's day [as nineteenth-century commentators report, even then on the tongues of peasants in the Romagna], referred to the whole dangerous animal.) Lombardi (comm. to this verse) explains what happened (citing Villani [*Cron.* IX.66]): A boar ran among the legs of Philip's horse and the frightened animal threw his royal rider, killing him.

121–123. "The pride that makes men thirst" is evidently the craving to dominate. Dante is probably referring to the border wars between Scotland and England in the reign of Edward I (1272–1307). However, just which monarch Dante has in mind is debated. Since the poet had previously praised Edward I (*Purg.* VII.130–132), some readers have suggested that Dante was thinking of Edward II, even if he ruled at a period that places him outside the limits established for everyone else mentioned in this list (i.e., to have been governing in 1300). Thus it probably seems necessary to believe one of two things: Either Dante had received information that made him change his mind about Edward I, or else he had incorrect dates for Edward II. The Scottish leader referred to is perhaps Robert the Bruce (1306–29). That would put him also outside the allotted time zone. However, as Tozer points out (comm. to this tercet), since Villani (*Cron.* VIII.90) represents him as the Scottish leader during Edward I's reign, Dante may have fallen into the same error.

124–126. Ferdinand IV of Castile and Wenceslaus IV of Bohemia. For the latter see *Purgatorio* VII.101–102, where he is described in much the same way.

127–129. "The Cripple of Jerusalem" was the derogatory name for the lame Charles II, king of Apulia and Naples (1285–1309), who claimed the title "King of Jerusalem" enjoyed by his father, even though it never was granted to him as the son. Tozer (comm. to vv. 127–129) paraphrases and comments: "His virtues will be seen marked by a unit (I), his vices by an M (for Lat. *mille*, 'a thousand'). The one virtue here intended was liberality, which Dante attributes to him in *Paradiso* VIII.82." Steiner (comm. to vv. 128–130) says that others have suggested that "I" and "M" refer to the first and last letters of his desired and fraudulent title, "King of *I*erusale*m*."

130–132. The reference is to Frederick II, son of Pedro of Aragon (see *Purg.* VII.119), and first regent (1291) and then king of Sicily (1296–1337). Sicily is referred to as "the isle of fire" because of the volcanic activity of Mt. Etna. For the death of Anchises on its western shore, see Virgil (*Aen.* III.707–710). This Frederick II is not to be confused with the emperor Frederick II (see *Inf.* X.119 and note), who died in 1250.

133–138. See Russo (Russ.1983.1), p. 105, for discussion of the rhymes based in the sound of *-zz* as typical of the low style, citing *De vulgari eloquentia* II.vii.5–6 on "hirsute" words that are not fitting for the tragic style.

133–135. Frederick is the only one of the pestilential dozen to receive more than a single tercet for his dispraises. With a wry sense of humor, Dante claims that Frederick is unworthy of attention, yet he gives Frederick's unworthiness more space than any of his competitors in malfeasance.

Tozer paraphrases the tercet as follows and then comments: " 'In order to let men know how paltry he is, that which is written against him will take the form of abbreviations, which will enumerate many vices within a small space.' Abbreviations were commonly used in MSS. to save space; so they would be used in God's record of Frederic, because he was too insignificant for a large space to be allotted to him."

137–138. The uncle, *barba*, of Frederick II of Sicily was James, king of Majorca (and of Minorca). He lost his crown for ten years as a result of joining Philip the Bold of France in a disastrous invasion of Catalonia. His brother, James of Aragon (see *Purg.* VII.119), in 1291 succeeded to the throne of Aragon, surrendering his kingship of Sicily, which his father had acquired, and appointed his younger brother, Frederick, to it in 1296. By these acts the James boys dishonored both family and their kingship.

137. Seven times in the first two canticles the word *barba* meant, what it still means, "beard." Here it means "uncle," as Francesco da Buti (comm. to vv. 136–148) informs us it does in Lombard.

139–141. The concluding royal triad share a single tercet: Dionysius, king of Portugal; Haakon V, king of Norway; and Stephen Ouros, king of Rascia, the modern Illyria and Dalmatia. Tozer (comm. to this tercet): "[Stephen] struck coins of debased metal in imitation of the Venetian ducat; the resemblance of the two is seen in the figures given by Philalethes, p. 259."

142–148. The acrostic comes to a close, but Dante is not yet finished cataloguing the ills of Europe's suffering kingdoms. This ungainly departure from the acrostic mode suggested to Bosco/Reggio that the acrostic itself may have occurred without design (see the note to vv. 115–139). The reader notes that these three examples offer mixed messages: the first of a good monarch leading to continued good governance, the second of a good monarch whose work will be undone at her death, and the third of a disastrous monarch.

142–144. Tozer (comm. to this tercet): "Hungary had been governed by corrupt princes until the time of Andrea III (1290–1301), who was a good sovereign. 'Happy Navarre, if she should defend herself with the mountain that girds her,' the Pyrenees. Joan of Navarre had married Philip the Fair in 1284, but governed her kingdom independently. On her death in

1305 it passed to her son Louis Hutin, and when he succeeded to the throne of France as Louis X in 1314, it was annexed to the French crown."

145–147. Tozer (comm. to this tercet): "Cyprus, of which Nicosia and Famagosta were the chief cities, was badly governed in 1300 by Henry II of Lusignan, who was a man of corrupt life."

148. As a coda to the whole parade of princes, we are told that Henry (as opposed to Andrea III and Joanna of Navarre?), a bad ruler, keeps the (metaphoric) company of the dirty dozen referred to in the acrostic.

PARADISO XX

OUTLINE

JUPITER

1–12 implicit simile: voices of the saved in Jupiter resemble the stars shining once the sun has set

13–15 Dante apostrophizes the love issuing from the spirits

16–78 the souls that form the eye of the Eagle

16–21 the silence of the souls, having ceased their song

22–27 simile: sounds issuing from lutes or bagpipes and from the Eagle's neck

28–30 the voice of the Eagle began again, uttering words that Dante inscribed upon his heart

31–36 the Eagle: "Gaze on my eye to study my greatest souls:

37–42 "**[David]** (as singer of the Holy Spirit)

43–48 "**[Trajan]** (as humble servant of a widow)

49–54 "**[Hezekiah]** (as penitent king)

55–60 "**[Constantine]** (his way to Heaven paved with good intention)

61–66 "**William the Good** of Sicily (mourned as a just ruler)

67–72 "**Ripheus** the Trojan (now he truly knows divine grace)";

73–78 simile: the Eagle is silent with satisfaction like a lark that has sung its song and silently enjoys satiety in it.

79–138 Dante: pagans in Paradise? the Eagle's answer:

79–84 Dante, while he knows that his question is obvious to the Eagle, cannot restrain himself from giving it voice;

85–87 the Eagle acknowledges Dante's confusion and responds:

88–93 "You see the what but not the why,

94–99 "that is, God wills to be conquered and thus conquers;

100–105 "[Trajan] and [Ripheus] both died believers in Christ:

106–117 "tale of Trajan: the prayer of **Gregory** and his rebirth,

118–129 "tale of Ripheus: vision of salvation in Christ to come;

130–138 "even we, elect, know not the identities of all the elect."

139–141 Thus were the poet's weak eyes made strong by Justice;

142–148 final simile: as a lutenist accompanies a singer, so did the flames of Trajan and of Ripheus move in accord with the Eagle's words.

PARADISO XX

Quando colui che tutto 'l mondo alluma
de l'emisperio nostro sì discende,
che 'l giorno d'ogne parte si consuma,

lo ciel, che sol di lui prima s'accende,
subitamente si rifà parvente
per molte luci, in che una risplende;

e questo atto del ciel mi venne a mente,
come 'l segno del mondo e de' suoi duci
nel benedetto rostro fu tacente;

però che tutte quelle vive luci,
vie più lucendo, cominciaron canti
da mia memoria labili e caduci.

O dolce amor che di riso t'ammanti,
quanto parevi ardente in que' flailli,
ch'avieno spirto sol di pensier santi!

Poscia che i cari e lucidi lapilli
ond' io vidi ingemmato il sesto lume
puoser silenzio a li angelici squilli,

udir mi parve un mormorar di fiume
che scende chiaro giù di pietra in pietra,
mostrando l'ubertà del suo cacume.

E come suono al collo de la cetra
prende sua forma, e sì com' al pertugio
de la sampogna vento che penètra,

così, rimosso d'aspettare indugio,
quel mormorar de l'aguglia salissi
su per lo collo, come fosse bugio.

When he who floods the whole world with his light
sinks steadily from sight within our hemisphere
until the day is spent on every side,

the sky, lit up before by him alone,
suddenly sparkles with a multitude of lights
which all reflect a single one.

I was reminded of this alteration in the sky
when the emblem of the world and of its lords
ceased speaking from within its blessèd beak,

and all those living lights, shining
still more bright, began their songs
that slip, and fade, and fall from memory.

O sweet love, mantled in a smile,
how ardent did you sound within those pipes,
filled with the breath of holy thoughts alone!

Once the bright and precious stones of the sixth light,
which scintillated in their setting there,
had silenced their angelic tones,

it seemed to me I heard the murmur of a stream,
its waters falling crystal clear from rock to rock,
revealing the abundance of its source above.

And as a sound is given shape
at the neck of the lute or by the wind
forced through the vent-holes of a bagpipe,

so, holding me no longer in suspense,
the murmur of the eagle issued through its neck
as though it had been hollowed out.

Fecesi voce quivi, e quindi uscissi
per lo suo becco in forma di parole,
quali aspettava il core ov' io le scrissi.

"La parte in me che vede e pate il sole
ne l'aguglie mortali," incominciommi,
"or fisamente riguardar si vole,

perché d'i fuochi ond' io figura fommi,
quelli onde l'occhio in testa mi scintilla,
e' di tutti lor gradi son li sommi.

Colui che luce in mezzo per pupilla,
fu il cantor de lo Spirito Santo,
che l'arca traslatò di villa in villa:

ora conosce il merto del suo canto,
in quanto effetto fu del suo consiglio,
per lo remunerar ch'è altrettanto.

Dei cinque che mi fan cerchio per ciglio,
colui che più al becco mi s'accosta,
la vedovella consolò del figlio:

ora conosce quanto caro costa
non seguir Cristo, per l'esperïenza
di questa dolce vita e de l'opposta.

E quel che segue in la circunferenza
di che ragiono, per l'arco superno,
morte indugiò per vera penitenza:

ora conosce che 'l giudicio etterno
non si trasmuta, quando degno preco
fa crastino là giù de l'odïerno.

L'altro che segue, con le leggi e meco,
sotto buona intenzion che fé mal frutto,
per cedere al pastor si fece greco:

There it became a voice and, coming from the beak,
it formed the words my heart was waiting for,
and on my heart I wrote them down.

'The part of me that, in mortal eagles,
sees and endures the sun, you now must watch
with fixed attention,' were its words to me,

'for, from the flames from which I take my form,
those that make my eye shine so brightly in my head,
those are the very highest spirits in their ranks.

'He that blazes as the pupil with a central spark
was the one who sang the praises of the Holy Ghost
and brought the ark from town to town.

'Now he knows the merit of his song,
insofar as it derived from his own thought,
by the fit reward he now enjoys.

'Of the five who arc to form my eyebrow,
the one who is closest to my beak
consoled the widow when she lost her son.

'Now he knows how dear the cost, should one fail
to follow Christ, since he has lived
both this sweet life and, long ago, that other.

'And he that follows on the arc of which I speak,
there on its upward curve, delayed his death
by offering up his true repentance.

'Now he knows God's irrevocable decree
remains unaltered even when a worthy prayer postpones
what might occur on earth today until tomorrow.

'The next one there, with good intent that bore bad fruit,
turned Greek, along with both the laws and me,
thus yielding his position to the shepherd.

ora conosce come il mal dedutto
dal suo bene operar non li è nocivo,
avvegna che sia 'l mondo indi distrutto.

E quel che vedi ne l'arco declivo,
Guiglielmo fu, cui quella terra plora
che piagne Carlo e Federigo vivo:

ora conosce come s'innamora
lo ciel del giusto rege, e al sembiante
del suo fulgore il fa vedere ancora.

Chi crederebbe giù nel mondo errante
che Rifëo Troiano in questo tondo
fosse la quinta de le luci sante?

Ora conosce assai di quel che 'l mondo
veder non può de la divina grazia,
ben che sua vista non discerna il fondo."

Quale allodetta che 'n aere si spazia
prima cantando, e poi tace contenta
de l'ultima dolcezza che la sazia,

tal mi sembiò l'imago de la 'mprenta
de l'etterno piacere, al cui disio
ciascuna cosa qual ell' è diventa.

E avvegna ch'io fossi al dubbiar mio
lì quasi vetro a lo color ch'el veste,
tempo aspettar tacendo non patio,

ma de la bocca, "Che cose son queste?"
mi pinse con la forza del suo peso:
per ch'io di coruscar vidi gran feste.

Poi appresso, con l'occhio più acceso,
lo benedetto segno mi rispuose
per non tenermi in ammirar sospeso:

'Now he knows that the evil which derived
from his good act does him no harm,
even if it brought the world to ruin.

'And the one you see on the downward arc was William,
for whom those lands lament which weep in woe
because of living Charles and living Frederick.

'Now he knows how Heaven is moved by love
for a righteous king, as the effulgence
of his aspect still makes plain.

'Who in the erring world below would think
that Trojan Ripheus should be the fifth
among the holy lights along this arc?

'Now he knows much the world cannot discern
of heavenly grace, although his sight
cannot make out the bottom of this sea.'

Like the lark that soars in air,
first singing, then silent, content and rejoicing
in the final joyous sweetness of its song,

such did that image seem to me, the very imprint
of the eternal Beauty, by whose will
all things become that which they truly are.

And even though I was as clear in my perplexity
as color shows through glass that covers it,
my question could not bear to wait its turn in silence,

but, by the pressure of its weight,
forced from my lips: 'What are these things I see?'
For there I saw a glittering revelry of lights.

And then, its eye lit up with greater brilliance,
the blessèd emblem, to set me free
from suspense and wonder, gave its answer:

"Io veggio che tu credi queste cose
perch' io le dico, ma non vedi come;
sì che, se son credute, sono ascose.

Fai come quei che la cosa per nome
apprende ben, ma la sua quiditate
veder non può se altri non la prome.

Regnum celorum vïolenza pate
da caldo amore e da viva speranza,
che vince la divina volontate:

non a guisa che l'omo a l'om sobranza,
ma vince lei perché vuole esser vinta,
e, vinta, vince con sua beninanza.

La prima vita del ciglio e la quinta
ti fa maravigliar, perché ne vedi
la regïon de li angeli dipinta.

D'i corpi suoi non uscir, come credi,
Gentili, ma Cristiani, in ferma fede
quel d'i passuri e quel d'i passi piedi.

Ché l'una de lo 'nferno, u' non si riede
già mai a buon voler, tornò a l'ossa;
e ciò di viva spene fu mercede:

di viva spene, che mise la possa
ne' prieghi fatti a Dio per suscitarla,
sì che potesse sua voglia esser mossa.

L'anima glorïosa onde si parla,
tornata ne la carne, in che fu poco,
credette in lui che potëa aiutarla;

e credendo s'accese in tanto foco
di vero amor, ch'a la morte seconda
fu degna di venire a questo gioco.

'I see that you believe these things because I say them
but fail to see, how, though you believe them,
90 they came to pass, because their cause is hidden.

'You are like the man who knows a thing by name
but does not understand its quiddity
93 unless another makes that plain to him.

'*Regnum celorum* suffers violence
from fervent love and living hope.
96 These conquer the very will of God,

'not as man may master man, but conquer it
because it would be conquered, and,
99 once conquered, itself conquers by its goodness.

'The first living soul in the eyebrow and the fifth
make you wonder to find them adorning
102 the dwelling-place of angels.

'They left their bodies not as gentiles
but as Christians, firm in their beliefs, the one
105 before, the other after, the piercing of His feet.

'For from Hell, where no one may return
to righteous will, the one came back into his bones—
108 this his reward for living hope,

'the living hope that furnished power to the prayers
addressed to God to raise him from the dead
111 so that his will might find its moving force.

'The blessèd soul of whom I speak,
back in his flesh for but a while,
114 believed in Him who had the power to help,

'and, believing, was kindled to such fire
of the one true love that, on his second death,
117 he was deemed worthy to enjoy our happiness.

L'altra, per grazia che da sì profonda
fontana stilla, che mai creatura
120 non pinse l'occhio infino a la prima onda,

tutto suo amor là giù pose a drittura:
per che, di grazia in grazia, Dio li aperse
123 l'occhio a la nostra redenzion futura;

ond' ei credette in quella, e non sofferse
da indi il puzzo più del paganesmo;
126 e riprendiene le genti perverse.

Quelle tre donne li fur per battesmo
che tu vedesti da la destra rota,
129 dinanzi al battezzar più d'un millesmo.

O predestinazion, quanto remota
è la radice tua da quelli aspetti
132 che la prima cagion non veggion *tota*!

E voi, mortali, tenetevi stretti
a giudicar: ché noi, che Dio vedemo,
135 non conosciamo ancor tutti li eletti;

ed ènne dolce così fatto scemo,
perché il ben nostro in questo ben s'affina,
138 che quel che vole Iddio, e noi volemo."

Così da quella imagine divina,
per farmi chiara la mia corta vista,
141 data mi fu soave medicina.

E come a buon cantor buon citarista
fa seguitar lo guizzo de la corda,
144 in che più di piacer lo canto acquista,

sì, mentre ch'e' parlò, sì mi ricorda
ch'io vidi le due luci benedette,
pur come batter d'occhi si concorda,
148 con le parole mover le fiammette.

'The other soul, through grace, which wells up
from a source so deep there never was a creature
who could thrust his vision to its primal spring,

'set all his love below on righteousness.
And for that reason, from grace to grace,
God opened his eyes to our redemption yet to come,

'so that he believed and, from that time on,
endured no longer paganism's stench
but rebuked the wayward peoples for it.

'The three ladies you saw near the right-hand wheel
served to baptize him one thousand years and more
before the sacrament existed.

'O predestination, how distant is your root
from the gaze of those who cannot grasp
the Primal Cause in its entirety!

'And you mortals, find some restraint
in making judgments, for we, who gaze on God,
have yet to know all those who are elect.

'And to us this very lack is sweet,
because in this good is our good perfected,
for that which God wills we will too.'

Thus did that holy image,
to cure the shortness of my vision,
apply sweet medication to my eyes.

And, as a practiced lute player will follow
a practiced singer with his quivering chords,
giving the song a sweeter sound,

so, all the while the eagle spoke, as I recall,
I kept my eyes on those two blessèd lights and saw,
just as blinking eyes keep time as one,
they timed their flames' pulsations to the words.

1–12. Any aesthetic performance is likely, at moments, to leave its observer wondering as to the motives of the performer. For example, here one might inquire why Dante did not decide to make this already highly wrought passage a perfectly turned simile. It has all the requisite elements, lacking only the initial *Come* (Just as) and the pivotal *così* (so) at the beginning of the seventh verse. With regard to the classical simile, it almost seems as though he had decided to ring the changes on an established form as frequently as he could. See the notes to *Purgatorio* XXVII.76–87; *Paradiso* XIV.19–24 and XIV.118–123.

The Eagle has stopped speaking as a corporate entity. That allows the individual voices of this particular collective of the saved to speak as themselves. Had their actual words been recorded here, it probably would have been clear, as it is when they speak as themselves at the end of the canto, that their descriptor for themselves is "we" (verse 134) and not "I" (verse 31). In simile, they are like the shining of the stars after the sun has left the sky (in Dante's further comparison, once the Eagle's beak has gone silent).

6. According to Dante's astronomy, stars did not glow with their own energy, but derived their light from the Sun (see *Conv*. III.xii.7): ". . . il sole. Lo quale di sensibile luce sé prima e poi tutte le corpora celestiali e [le] elementali allumina" (the Sun, which illuminates with perceptible light first itself and then all the celestial and elemental bodies [tr. R. Lansing]). And see the discussion in the introduction to *Paradiso*, section 2.

8. The "emblem of the world" is the Eagle, symbol of universal empire, the ideal that Dante embraced so warmly in his *Monarchia*.

13–15. The poet apostrophizes the love emanating from these spirits, wreathed in "smiles": How ardent did this love appear in those "pipes" (or in those "flames" [there is much debate in the commentaries over this choice]) that were so full of holy thoughts! As Bosco/Reggio (comm. to verse 14) point out, the word *flaillo* is an absolute hapax, meaning that this is its unique appearance, not only in the *Commedia*, not only in all the works of Dante, but in the history of the Italian language. In their opinion, there is no way to decide between the two possible meanings, "flute" (see French *flavel*) or "flame" (from O Fr. *flael*), since both find resonance in the surrounding context. However, Benvenuto states unambiguously that the reference is to sound. And his opinion is given further weight by the musical reference of the simile in vv. 22–27.

16–18. The silence of the souls, having left off their singing (which Dante could not hold in mind [verse 12]), begun when the Eagle had ceased its speech, gives way to what seems to be the rumbling sound of a river, giving evidence of the profusion of its lofty source (it will be the voice of the Eagle, rumbling like an organ pipe filling with new air). This tercet marks the beginning of the first of the two central elements of the canto, a presentation of the souls that make up the eye of the Eagle (vv. 16–78); the second, the Eagle's explanation of the presence in Paradise of those who certainly appear to be pagans, runs through vv. 79–129.

18. The phrase *li angelici squilli* is probably not to be understood as the "song of the angels" (Bosco/Reggio [comm. to this verse]), but as the "angelic songs" of the blessed.

19–21. If Tommaseo (comm. to this tercet) is correct, these lines reflect both a passage in the *Georgics* (I.108–110) and one in the *Aeneid* (XI.296–299). The passage in Virgil's epic describes the rumor of the many voices of the native Italians being quieted by King Latinus's voiced decision to make peace with the invading future Romans. Chiarenza (Chia.1995.3), p. 302, makes the point that this decision is thus in accord "with the unchangeable will of Providence."

22–29. This double simile, reflecting the fingering of two kinds of musical instruments in order to produce varying sounds (along the neck of a lute or at the vents of a bagpipe), describes the sound produced from within the Eagle's neck, eventually issuing from his beak as a series of notes (or words).

Landino (comm. to vv. 25–29) expresses his admiration for Dante's ability, plainly visible here, to "make the impossible seem believable" and compares him to Ovid in this respect.

30. The Eagle uttered words that Dante, once more reverting to the image of his scribal role, wrote down upon his heart. See the notes to *Purgatorio* XXIV.55–63; *Paradiso* V.85, X.27, and X.109–114.

31–33. The Eagle's invitation to Dante to gaze upon its eye revisits a bit of lore already placed in evidence. We learned that mortal eagles are able to look into the sun without harm from *Paradiso* I.46–48; see the accompanying note, referring to possible sources in Aristotle and in Brunetto Latini.

31. Returning to speech from song, the Eagle now again speaks as a single voice. We will hear it switch back again to the first-person plural in its final words (see verse 134).

34–36. The Eagle now reports that the souls that form its eye (we only see one of the two, if it in fact happens to possess more in the way of orbs of sight than its profiled appearance as the emblem of empire requires—a dubious eventuality) are the greatest among the many that give its form an aquiline shape.

37–72. The Eagle's thirty-six verses in six segments, each of six lines, and each involving use of anaphora (the phrase *ora conosce*), identify the six "chiefs" of justice: David, Trajan, Hezekiah, Constantine, William the Good, and Ripheus (their fame is at first insisted on when the first four of them are named only by circumlocution; the last two understandably require more assistance). It seems possible that the poet wanted us to reflect that the thirty-six lines in praise of these half dozen dead rulers mirror, if adversely, the twenty-seven verses, also marked by anaphora, describing the dozen defective living rulers in the preceding canto, *Paradiso* XIX.115–141.

The number of these just rulers (six) may also be meant to put us in mind of the six "world-historical" emperors presented in *Paradiso* VI: Julius Caesar, Augustus, Tiberius, Titus, Justinian, and Charlemagne. Those seemed to have been significant primarily for the events over which they presided; these, for their personal justness. That distinction may or may not explain their appearing here (only temporarily, we at times may struggle to remember) in a higher heaven. Dante never gives us the grounds on which to establish the relative advancement of the blessed in the Empyrean, except for the eighteen souls whom we are allowed to see in *Paradiso* XXXII; and none of these saved rulers is seen among them.

37–39. The first of these most just among just rulers is David, in the *Commedia* most honored as the singer of the Holy Spirit (as are also all his companions in the Eagle: see *Par.* XIX.101). (David is prominently mentioned in *Purg.* X.65 [and see the appended note]; *Par.* XXV.71–72 and XXXII.11–12). He is, in fact, the figure from the Old Testament most present in Dante's work, referred to perhaps fifty times in all.

For his service to the Lord in transporting the Ark of the Covenant, see *Purgatorio* X.55–69.

40–42. Some think the words *suo consiglio* (his own thought) refer to the "thought" of the Holy Spirit; most, to that of David (as is reflected in our translation).

The question of the "merit" of David's song disturbs some readers. See, for instance, Tozer (comm. to vv. 40–42), pointing out that David could benefit only insofar as his song proceeded from his own free will (and thus was not the effect of inspiration, in which case it would not, as the text suggests, in itself make him worthy of salvation). However, is David's worthiness not similar to the unexpressed claim for his own "merit" that Dante might have considered most convincing? He presents himself as the "new David" from the outset (see *Inf.* I.65), that is, as a man directly inspired by God to lift his eyes from worldly distraction. In Dante's mind, there does not seem to be any limitation on the freedom of his will imposed thereby.

43–48. Trajan, the Roman emperor (A.D. 98–117), is closest to the Eagle's beak in the semicircle that describes the "eyebrow," as it were, above David, located as the pupil of the eye. For his humble service to the widow and the tradition of his salvation, see *Purgatorio* X.73–93 and the appended note. For some of the twists and turns in the history of the accounts of the salvation of Trajan, see Picone (Pico.2002.6), pp. 313–19.

Now Trajan appreciates, both by now being here with God and by having been in Limbo, the cost of not following Christ.

48. For the phrase *dolce vita* (sweet life), see the note to *Paradiso* IV.35.

49–51. Hezekiah, a king of Judah in the seventh century B.C., was a just monarch, according to the Bible, at least in his own accountancy (see II Kings 20:3).

His tears (but were they shed in penitence?) are found in Isaiah 38:3, as was first noted by Jacopo della Lana (comm. to verse 51). Here is the pertinent passage (38:1–5): "In those days Hezekiah became sick and was at the point of death. And Isaiah the prophet the son of Amoz came to him, and said to him, 'Thus says the Lord: Set your house in order, for you shall die, you shall not recover.' Then Hezekiah turned his face to the wall and prayed to the Lord, and said, 'Please, O Lord, remember how I have walked before you in faithfulness and with a whole heart, and have done what is good in your sight.' And Hezekiah *wept* bitterly. Then the word of the Lord came to Isaiah: 'Go and say to Hezekiah, Thus says the Lord, the God of David your father: I have heard your prayer; I have seen your *tears*. Behold, I will add fifteen years to your life' " (italics added). Hezekiah in fact here does not weep out of penitence, as Dante says he did, but the detail that God saw his tears and then remitted his sentence of death was perhaps enough to suggest to the poet that the king was contrite for his sins, and not merely brokenhearted and afraid.

Now Hezekiah knows that answered prayers are part of God's plan, rather than representing a change in it (cf. *Purg.* VI.28–42, where the same question is raised about Virgil's views on this matter). Carroll (comm. to vv. 49–54) puts this well: "In short, what Hezekiah now knows in Heaven is the mystery of how prayer harmonizes with and fulfils 'the eternal judgment,' instead of being, as it seems, an alteration of it."

For Hezekiah as "type" of Dante, see Charity (Char.1966.1), p. 230, and the note to *Inferno* I.1.

52–54. Tozer (comm. to this tercet) paraphrases and interprets this passage as follows: " 'when a worthy prayer causes that which was ordained for the present time to be postponed to a future time'; this was what happened in Hezekiah's case through the postponement of his death. The meaning of the entire passage here is, that what God has ordained is not changed in answer to prayer, because God has already provided for it."

55–60. Since the spatial arrangement of the inhabitants of the Eagle's semicircular eyebrow is not chronological, the fact that Constantine (274–337) is the middle figure in it, and thus the highest, takes us by surprise, given the number and vehemence of Dante's outbursts against the Donation (e.g., *Inf.* XIX.115–117, *Purg.* XXXII.124–129; and see *Monarchia*, which fairly seethes with them). In this passage Dante settles for Constantine's good intent in his governance of the Eastern empire. However, now this emperor knows that if the evil he unwittingly committed has not harmed him, it has nonetheless destroyed the world. Dante may allow him salvation, but makes him pay for it eternally and dearly with this permanent wound in his self-awareness. This does not efface the glory his good intention won him, but it does mar its beauty.

61–66. William the Good, king of (Naples and) Sicily (ruled 1166–89), is presented as mourned by his subjects (he died young, at thirty-five), who now must suffer the misdeeds of his two successors, Charles of Anjou (who ruled Apulia) and Frederick II of Aragon (who ruled Sicily itself—see *Par.* XIX.127–135, where these two are the sixth and seventh unworthy rulers in that pestilential anagram). Now William, who was widely celebrated in his lifetime for his lawful reign and his generosity, knows that God loves a just king.

67–72. Ripheus is unlike the first five identified rulers in not ever having been mentioned within a Christian context by anyone at all; he is also the only one of them not to have been a king or an emperor. Indeed, he is a sort of "extra," a bit player (if a heroic and probably highborn one) in the *Aeneid*, barely mentioned but for his death fighting along with Aeneas (*Aen.* II.426–428; see also II.339, II.394). Dante does not refer to a particular good deed that he performed, insisting instead on the general fact of his justness. The not inconsiderable poetic space (vv. 118–129) devoted to "explaining" his Christian belief has never diminished readers' amazement at finding him here. That is not surprising, as even he is portrayed (in verse 72) as not knowing the reason for his being among the elect.

For a recently discovered (it had been hiding in plain view for centuries) and probable source, or at least confirmation, of Dante's view of Ripheus, see Scott (Scot.1994.1), pp. 190–92, pointing out that a passage in Boethius (*Cons. Phil.* IV.6[pr].127–131) offers several reasons to think it was in Dante's mind as he wrote this passage: (1) that Boethius is referring to the same passage that scholars habitually point to as Dante's source in *Aeneid* II seems highly likely; (2) the Boethian context is utterly appropriate, since it involves the surprising nature, in human eyes, of providence; (3) the passage includes a specific reference to Lucan's Cato of Utica (*Phars.* I.128), approving Cato's worth (even though he lost his war) against that of Caesar, though Julius (and not Cato) was victorious (see Dante's presentation of Cato in the first two cantos of *Purgatorio*). The text in question reads in part as follows (tr. W. V. Cooper, italics added): "For, to glance at *the depth of God's works* with so few words as human reason is capable of comprehending, I say that what you think to be most fair and most conducive to *justice*'s preservation, that appears *different to an all-seeing Providence.* Has not our fellow-philosopher *Lucan* told us how 'the conquering cause did please the gods, but the conquered, *Cato*?'" One can only imagine how Dante felt, seeing that his own radical and dangerous ideas had some justification in no less an authority than Boethius. For an earlier, similar, but not quite as pointed recognition of the influence of the *Consolatio* (and particularly its fourth book) on Dante's thought here, see Chiarenza (Chia.1983.2).

On the other hand, one may be excused a certain dubiety concerning the genuineness of Dante's belief in the salvation of this pagan. Virgil has handed Dante the stick with which to beat him: After he calls Ripheus the most just of the Trojans ("iustissimus"), he concludes with the phrase "dis aliter visum" (to the gods it seemed otherwise [*Aen.* II.428]); the muffled meaning seems to be that the gods do not care about just humans, and "kill us for their sport" (as King Lear phrased it). Dante lands hard upon Virgil for this judgment: His Christian God reverses pagan justice. (For this view, see Hollander [Holl.1983.1], p. 138; for a more conciliatory one, Bosco/Reggio, comm. to verse 68.)

Chiarenza (Chia.1995.3), pp. 304–5, puts into intelligent focus the way so much of *Paradiso* XX reopens the "question of Virgil" in our minds: "Virgil's drama is based on the contingency that he died just nineteen years before the birth of Christ. If God could extend Hezekiah's life by fifteen years, why did He not extend Virgil's by little more? It was said that St. Paul, moved by the beauty and wisdom of Virgil's poetry, prayed at the poet's tomb for his salvation. (For this topic, she adverts to the work of Comparetti [Comp.1872.1], p. 98; Davis [Davi.1957.1], pp. 103–4; and Vickers [Vick.1983.1], p. 72.) If God could answer Gregory's prayers for Trajan, why did He reject the similar prayer of the great St. Paul? How could a minor figure in Virgil's poem have caught the attention of God, while Virgil himself failed to?" Whether we like it or not, we have heard the answer to our question in the last canto, when the Eagle came down hard upon Dante for his similar question (*Par.* XIX.79–90): We cannot weigh God's intent, only recognize it.

On the question of God's disposition of the virtuous pagans, see G. Fallani, "salvezza dei pagani," *ED* IV (1973) and Picone (Pico.2002.6), pp. 311–13, and, with specific reference to Ripheus, pp. 317–20. For the interesting observation that Dante might have found an equally "salvable" pagan in the person of Galaesus, also referred to by Virgil as "iustissimus" (in *Aeneid* VII.536), see Camerino (Came.1995.1), pp. 55–56, who sees Dante as observing this rather striking phenomenon and considering that the two "most just" pagans point only, again, to the inscrutable nature of God's justice—as well, we might want to add, as of Dante's.

Apparently first among the few to hear the echo here of the salvation of the Roman (and thus pagan) centurion Cornelius (see Acts 10:22–23; 34–35) was Scartazzini (comm. to vv. 68–69); most recently see Aversano (Aver.2000.2), p. 91, building the evidence for his point better than his (unacknowledged) predecessors: Cornelius the centurion, "vir *iustus* et timens Deum" (a just and God-fearing man [Acts 10:22; Aversano's italics]). He concludes, "In patristic exegesis this centurion is the type of the gentiles saved by the grace of God"; Cornelius "because of his great faith and his justness, received the gift of the Holy Spirit before he was baptized" (Aversano is citing Rabanus Maurus for this judgment).

Perhaps our poet was tempted to push his reading of Virgil past the point of no return. At any rate, that is what he has accomplished, making the condemned author of the *Aeneid*, alongside the similarly Limbo-bound hero of his epic, spend their eternities in the lower world of an afterlife they neither believed in nor deserved, while this "bit player" enjoys the fruits of Heaven. For him to be here, Ripheus necessarily had to welcome Christ into his life; again, one has a difficult time believing that Dante really thought so. But that is what he decided he thought.

69. Dante is aware that his treatment of Ripheus will astound at least some of his readers. That he wants them to couple it with his similarly contentious insistence on Solomon's salvation (despite the warmly contrary opinions of some "big guns" of Christian theology, none bigger or more negative about the possibility of Solomon's salvation than Augustine) is the opinion of Lauren Seem (Seem.2006.1), p. 77. She points out that both Solomon (*Par.* X.109) and Ripheus are the fifth lights in the shapes that they and their colleagues have temporarily assumed in order to display themselves to Dante, a circle and the eyebrow of an eagle, and that both were spectacularly provocative selections for salvation.

73–78. The Eagle, delighted by its own report of the salvation of Ripheus (and by the fact that not even he understands why he was saved), is like a lark satisfied by its own song, silent in its flight, savoring that melody in memory. The ensuing description of the silent emblem is not easy to decode, but it seems to refer to the Eagle (*l'imago*) as stamped (*de la 'mprenta*) by the eternal Beauty that is God (*l'etterno piacere*), by whose will each thing becomes that which it is. In this case that last and rather puzzling general statement probably refers most directly to Ripheus's saved soul, as the context suggests.

This passage has understandably caused a certain amount of debate (for a summary, see Scartazzini [comm. to vv. 76–78]). Its key phrase ("la 'mprenta / de l'etterno piacere") either means that the Eagle bears the imprint of God's will or is the imprint of His beauty. Most of the commentators, including Scartazzini, are of the first persuasion. However, when speaking of the *etterno piacere* of God, Dante elsewhere seems to refer to His everlasting beauty (see Took [Took. 1984.1], pp. 10–11, 17–22). The phrase also occurs in *Purgatorio* XXIX.32 and *Paradiso* XVIII.16. In addition, in *Paradiso* the word *piacere*, standing alone and referring to God, frequently seems to indicate His beauty (see *Par.* XXVII.95, XXXII.65, and XXXIII.33). And so we have translated the phrase, if gingerly, as we have. This is a possible reading, but not a certain one.

73. John of Serravalle (comm. to vv. 73–78) is alert to the charming pun available in the name of the bird (*allodetta*, lark). He puts Latin words into its beak: "Surge, Deum *lauda*, iam lux est, cantat *alauda*" ('Arise, *praise* God, for it is light,' sings the *lark* [italics added, even though John's play on words is lost in English]).

79–84. This simple comparison, less developed than a "classical" simile, makes the heavy question within Dante evident to the souls configuring the Eagle. Despite knowing that, he nonetheless bursts out in amazement and perplexity. We may need to remind ourselves that for eighty-five cantos the protagonist has resisted the notion that virtuous pagans should be condemned to Hell. Then the Eagle insisted on that harsh truth in Canto XIX. And now that same Eagle tells Dante that two of the greatest souls that produce his shape are saved pagans. It is small wonder the protagonist is both amazed and perplexed.

79–81. Tozer (comm. to this tercet) explains the passage as follows: "The metaphor is from coloured glass, the reference being to 'coated' glass, i.e. white glass coated with a coloured film on one side only. As this colour could be clearly seen through the glass, so the spirits could look through Dante's mind, and see the doubt within it."

85–90. The Eagle, its eye more ardent, acknowledges the protagonist's confusion and prepares to explain its causes.

91–93. Commentators, beginning with Scartazzini (comm. to vv. 91–92), suggest the trace here of Aquinas's distinction between *cognitio sensitiva* and *cognitio intellectiva* (*ST* II–II, q. 8, a. 1), that is, between knowledge based on sense perception and that based on reason, penetrating to the true meaning of phenomena.

92. The word *quiditate* is a Scholastic term for "essence."

93. Scartazzini (comm. to vv. 91–92) deals with the Latinism *prome* as meaning "extract," "draw out," that is, as one grasps the essence of a concept.

94–96. See Matthew 11:12: "*Regnum caelorum* vim patitur, et violenti rapiunt illud" (the kingdom of heaven suffers violence, and the violent bear it away [italics added])—in these cases at the behest of the hopeful prayers of Pope Gregory and the ardent affection of Ripheus. As we will see (vv. 108, 121), the virtues of Hope and Love will be specifically aligned with the salvations of Trajan and of Ripheus, respectively.

97. Rhyme may have forced Dante to use a Provençalism, *sobranza* (overcomes, conquers), but he seems to welcome the excuse, as his project for the language of the *Commedia* is inclusive rather than exclusive.

98–99. The chiasmus (*vince, vinta; vinta, vince*) underlines the power of the paradox: God wills to be conquered and thus conquers.

103–105. This tercet is built on still another chiasmus: Trajan, Ripheus; Christ to come, Christ come.

As opposed to a more comfortable understanding, in other words, that Trajan and (more pointedly) Ripheus had been won to the God of the Christians through implicit faith (see Aquinas, *ST* II–II, q. 2, a. 7), Dante insists that he believes that we believe that they believed explicitly in Christ, in Trajan's case (less difficult to accept, but involving a major miracle [see vv. 106–117], after the fact; in Ripheus's, before [see vv. 118–129]). And so they died, not as unbelievers, but as full-fledged Christians. The trick here is to add a disclaimer for Trajan (he died a Christian only when he died a *second time*) and to swallow hard at the claim made on behalf of Ripheus.

The feet of Jesus, transfixed to the Cross by a single spike, offered one of the most piteous physical images drawn from the Passion. See, for example, Bonvesin de la Riva's *De scriptura rubra* in his *Libro de le tre scritture*, vv. 153–170 (cited by Gragnolati [Grag.2005.1], pp. 95–96; and see p. 231, n. 57), where, in eighteen verses, the word *pei* (Milanese dialect for "feet") occurs six times in Bonvesin's bloody account of the Crucifixion.

106–117. The somewhat grudging authority of St. Thomas (*ST*, Suppl., q. 71, a. 5) sustains the widely disseminated tale that Trajan was resuscitated by agency of Gregory's accepted prayers, believed in Christ, was baptized, died a second time, and was received in Heaven (see the note to *Purg.* X.73–93). Thomas, however, seems in fact to have been drawn to the story of Gregory's intervention on Trajan's behalf, referring to it in some six *loci* in his other works. See the indispensable online *Corpus Thomisticum* (www.corpusthomisticum.org), the project in which Father Roberto Busa convinced IBM to become his partner in 1946.

108. What is perhaps most surprising about Trajan's reward is that it was won not by *his* hope, but by that of Pope Gregory. We are reminded of the fate of those in Limbo (where, we assume, Trajan was first lodged), who exist (according to *Inf.* IV.42) longing for a better lot, if without hope for it (*sanza speme*). Gregory's hope "conquered" God on Trajan's behalf; the emperor himself, the evidence that we gather from Limbo would seem to assert, was hopeless.

118–129. Some early commentators (e.g., Pietro di Dante [Pietro1, comm. to these verses], John of Serravalle [comm. to vv. 31–36 and 127–129]) speak of the "baptism of fire" in those inspired by the Holy Spirit to love God perfectly. For Dante, Virgil's single word, *iustissimus*, seems to have been the key for this incredible invention. (For the centrality of justice to Dante's design, see the note to *Inferno* III.4.)

To Ripheus Virgil has dedicated a total of only five lines in the *Aeneid*; Dante doubles that (and then some) in this passage alone.

121. The word *drittura* is a hapax in the poem, but has a Dantean history before it puts in its appearance here, first in *Convivio* (IV.xvii.6), where, as rectitude, it is an attribute of the eleventh and final of Aristotle's moral virtues, Justice. *Drittura* also appears in the exilic *canzone*, "Tre donne intorno al cor mi son venute" (*Rime* CIV.35), where she seems as much a despised exile from Florence as does the poet.

126. As provocation, this detail is over the top. Nonetheless, the commentators are amazingly willing to accept what Dante says without protest. The whole story of Ripheus is nothing less than outrageous, and now the poet tops it off by turning him, as Poletto (comm. to vv. 124–126) had the strength of mind to observe, into a sort of Trojan St. Paul. Why not? Dante seems to have thought; if he became a Christian, he must have hated those shoddy pagan gods and the religious practices of his fellow pagans, doesn't that makes sense? And so he preached against those practices. Is Dante having fun with us? And at Virgil's expense? Perhaps.

127–129. The three ladies are obviously the three theological virtues, whom we saw at the right wheel of the chariot of the Church Triumphant in *Purgatorio* XXIX.121–129. In what sense did they "serve to baptize" Ripheus? Since that ritual was not available to him, and since he was born with original sin upon him, he required something in its place. Somehow he acquired the three theological virtues and these brought him to Christ. Dante's text here may reflect a passage in St. Augustine's *De doctrina christiana* (I.xxxix.43): "Thus a man supported by faith, hope, and charity, with an unshaken hold upon them, does not need the Scriptures except for the instruction of others" (tr. D. W. Robertson, Jr.).

130–148. The fourth and final section of this canto addresses itself to a question that has always troubled Christians (as is focally shown in many of the writings of Augustine): predestination. Reiterating Thomas's criticism of our all-too-human desire to speculate upon the likely salvation or damnation of our neighbors (*Par.* XIII.139–142), the Eagle now portrays as cosmic the unknowing that surrounds God's purpose. Not even the immortal just souls in the Empyrean know all the elect (see verse 72 for the less dramatic notice of the shortness of mortal vision in this regard). This comes as something of a surprise, as Torquato Tasso noted (comm. to vv. 133–135), since everything we have previously learned about this topic would clearly seem to indicate that the saved know, in God, all things that exist (see, inter alia, *Par.* V.4–6, VIII.85–90, IX.73–75, XV.49–51, XVII.13–18, and XIX.28–30, as well as the notes to *Par.* IV.16–18 and XIV.7–9); however, Dante's enthusiasm for the subject seems to have led him into at least a possible self-contradiction, since what is said here denies that even the blessed can have complete knowledge of what God has in His mind. Gragnolati (Grag.2005.1, passim) argues that after the general resurrection God's thought will be knowable by all the saved. Dante's apparent assertion that the blessed do not know the identities of those not yet saved certainly seems to violate the principle that whatever God knows the saved are able to read in His mind, as Tasso noted. From *Paradiso* XV.49–51 we have learned that Cacciaguida *knew* that Dante was inscribed in the Book of Life. And so we must wonder how thoroughly the poet held to this apparent revision of his earlier view, as much as we must honor it.

Venturi (comm. to verse 135) was apparently the first commentator to refer to part of the *collecta* ("collect"—originally a short prayer recited to Christians gathered ["collected"] for a service) known as "the Collect for the living and the dead": "Deus, cui soli cognitus est numerus electorum in superna felicitate locandus" (God, to whom alone is known the number of the elect that is to be set in supernal bliss). This prayer, once it was cited by Venturi, had a certain afterlife in the commentators right through the nineteenth century, but for some reason has been allowed to vanish in our time. Nonetheless, while it does give us an official teaching of the Church regarding the limits of the knowledge of those in the Empyrean, it certainly is at odds with what the poem has led us to expect, as Tasso observed.

134. The Eagle once again, concluding its presence in the poem, speaks as a plural entity, in the collective voice of the individual souls of the just.

139–141. Thus were Dante's weak eyes strengthened by Justice (cf. the Eagle's very first words at XIX.13, speaking in the first-person singular: "Per esser *giusto* e pio" [For being just and merciful]).

141. The phrase "soave medicina" (sweet medication) recalls the *medicina* of *Inferno* XXXI.3. It also probably refers to the "pestilence" the protagonist's eyes had encountered in the counterpoised object of vision to this briefer catalogue of the justly saved, the group of twelve damned rulers found in Canto XIX. As Marino Barchiesi (Barc.1973.1), pp. 73–74, realized, it also recalls the "disease" of sympathy for classical divination demonstrated by the protagonist in *Inferno* XX. And, in this vein, see Hollander (Holl.1980.2), p. 199: "The disease which has been cured in *Paradiso* XX revealed its etiology in *Inferno* XX."

142–148. This is the final simile of the canto and of this simile-filled heaven (there are twelve in Cantos XVIII–XX, four in each): As a lutenist accompanies a singer, Trajan and Ripheus move their flames, as though in accompaniment, to the Eagle's words.

PARADISO XXI

OUTLINE

SATURN

1–24 *The ascent to the sphere of Saturn*

- 1–3 Dante gazes on Beatrice as they rise;
- 4–6 were she to smile, Dante, like **Semele**, would burn to ash
- 7–12 because, as she rises, she has become more beautiful
- 13–15 Saturn in Leo in March–April 1300
- 16–18 Beatrice: "Pay attention to the shape [the ladder] that will be visible to you in the mirror of this planet";
- 19–24 one who knew his joy in beholding her would understand his greater joy in obeying her, even if it meant denying his eyes their pleasure in her;

25–42 *the golden ladder in the sky*

- 25–30 **Jacob's Ladder**
- 31–33 the numerous saints shining in their descent on it
- 34–42 simile: different movements of three groups of jackdaws

43–102 *Dante's two questions of* ***[Peter Damian]*** *and his answers:*

- 43–51 the protagonist does not ask his question aloud until Beatrice reads his mind and tells him to do so:
- 52–60 (1) "Why do you approach me?"; (2) "why the quiet here?"
- 61–63 (2) "No singing here for the same reason she did not smile;
- 64–72 (1) "I've come to do God's bidding by greeting

you, not from personal affection, but in accord with God's will";

73–78 (1) [Dante again]: "But why were *you* destined to do this?"

79–81 The soul spins like a millstone around itself in joy

82–96 and tells Dante that, although he knows all that he can know of God's plan, not the most enlightened soul in Heaven, not even one of the Seraphim, has that answer;

97–102 when Dante returns to earth, he should try to dissuade people from wanting answers to such questions.

103–126 Peter Damian answers Dante's third question:

103–105 Dante asks this spirit who he is

106–120 and he identifies himself in a familiar geographical way:

121–126 he was called both Peter Damian and "Peter the sinner" and was made cardinal and Bishop of Ostia.

127–142 Peter denounces the excesses of prelates:

127–129 Peter and Paul, though thin, ate only what they could;

130–135 now it takes four men to prop up, guide, and carry the train of one of these double beasts;

136–142 the rest of the souls thunder their approval as they surround Peter in their brightening flames.

PARADISO XXI

Già eran li occhi miei rifissi al volto
de la mia donna, e l'animo con essi,
e da ogne altro intento s'era tolto.

E quella non ridea; ma "S'io ridessi,"
mi cominciò, "tu ti faresti quale
fu Semelè quando di cener fessi:

ché la bellezza mia, che per le scale
de l'etterno palazzo più s'accende,
com' hai veduto, quanto più si sale,

se non si temperasse, tanto splende,
che 'l tuo mortal podere, al suo fulgore,
sarebbe fronda che trono scoscende.

Noi sem levati al settimo splendore,
che sotto 'l petto del Leone ardente
raggia mo misto giù del suo valore.

Ficca di retro a li occhi tuoi la mente,
e fa di quelli specchi a la figura
che 'n questo specchio ti sarà parvente."

Qual savesse qual era la pastura
del viso mio ne l'aspetto beato
quand' io mi trasmutai ad altra cura,

conoscerebbe quanto m'era a grato
ubidire a la mia celeste scorta,
contrapesando l'un con l'altro lato.

Dentro al cristallo che 'l vocabol porta,
cerchiando il mondo, del suo caro duce
sotto cui giacque ogne malizia morta,

Now my eyes were fixed again
upon my lady's face. And with my eyes,
my mind drew back from any other thought.

She was not smiling. 'If I smiled,'
she said, 'you would become what Semele became
when she was turned to ashes,

'for my beauty, which you have seen
flame up more brilliantly the higher we ascend
the stairs of this eternal palace,

'is so resplendent that, were it not tempered
in its blazing, your mortal powers would be
like tree limbs rent and scorched by lightning.

'We have risen to the seventh splendor,
which, beneath the burning Lion's breast,
sends down its rays, now mingled with his power.

'Set your mind behind your eyes
so that they may become the mirrors for the shape
that in this heaven's mirror will appear to you.'

When I was told to set my mind on other things,
only one who knew how much my eyes could feast
upon that blessèd countenance

would understand what joy it was to me
but to obey my heavenly guide,
weighing one side of the scale against the other.

Within the crystal, circling our earth,
that bears the name of the world's belovèd king,
under whose rule all wickedness lay dead,

di color d'oro in che raggio traluce
vid' io uno scaleo eretto in suso
tanto, che nol seguiva la mia luce.

Vidi anche per li gradi scender giuso
tanti splendor, ch'io pensai ch'ogne lume
che par nel ciel, quindi fosse diffuso.

E come, per lo natural costume,
le pole insieme, al cominciar del giorno,
si movono a scaldar le fredde piume;

poi altre vanno via sanza ritorno,
altre rivolgon sé onde son mosse,
e altre roteando fan soggiorno;

tal modo parve me che quivi fosse
in quello sfavillar che 'nsieme venne,
sì come in certo grado si percosse.

E quel che presso più ci si ritenne,
si fé sì chiaro, ch'io dicea pensando:
"Io veggio ben l'amor che tu m'accenne.

Ma quella ond' io aspetto il come e 'l quando
del dire e del tacer, si sta; ond' io,
contra 'l disio, fo ben ch'io non dimando."

Per ch'ella, che vedëa il tacer mio
nel veder di colui che tutto vede,
mi disse: "Solvi il tuo caldo disio."

E io incominciai: "La mia mercede
non mi fa degno de la tua risposta;
ma per colei che 'l chieder mi concede,

vita beata che ti stai nascosta
dentro a la tua letizia, fammi nota
la cagion che sì presso mi t'ha posta;

The color of gold in a ray of sunlight,
I saw a ladder, rising to so great a height
my eyesight could not rise along with it.

I also saw, descending on its rungs,
so many splendors that I thought that every light
shining in the heavens was pouring down.

And as, following their normal instinct,
rooks rise up together at the break of day,
warming their feathers, stiffened by the cold,

and some of them fly off, not to return,
while some turn back to where they had set out,
and some keep wheeling overhead,

just such varied motions did I observe
within that sparkling throng, which came as one
as soon as it had reached a certain rung.

And the one that stayed the closest there to us
grew so shining bright I said, but not aloud,
'This sign makes clear your love for me.

'But she, upon whose word I wait to know
when and how to speak or to be silent, she keeps still
and I do well, against my will, to ask no question.'

She, therefore, who could see my silence plain
in the sight of Him whose sight beholds all things,
then said: 'Satisfy the ardent wish that burns within you.'

And I: 'My merit does not make me worthy
of your answer, but for the sake of her
who gives me leave to ask,

'blessèd living soul, still hidden
in the radiance of your joy, make known to me
the cause that made you draw so near

e dì perché si tace in questa rota
la dolce sinfonia di paradiso,
che giù per l'altre suona sì divota."

"Tu hai l'udir mortal sì come il viso,"
rispuose a me; "onde qui non si canta
per quel che Bëatrice non ha riso.

Giù per li gradi de la scala santa
discesi tanto sol per farti festa
col dire e con la luce che mi ammanta;

né più amor mi fece esser più presta,
ché più e tanto amor quinci sù ferve,
sì come il fiammeggiar ti manifesta.

Ma l'alta carità, che ci fa serve
pronte al consiglio che 'l mondo governa,
sorteggia qui sì come tu osserve."

"Io veggio ben," diss' io, "sacra lucerna,
come libero amore in questa corte
basta a seguir la provedenza etterna;

ma questo è quel ch'a cerner mi par forte,
perché predestinata fosti sola
a questo officio tra le tue consorte."

Né venni prima a l'ultima parola,
che del suo mezzo fece il lume centro,
girando sé come veloce mola;

poi rispuose l'amor che v'era dentro:
"Luce divina sopra me s'appunta,
penetrando per questa in ch'io m'inventro,

la cui virtù, col mio veder congiunta,
mi leva sopra me tanto, ch'i' veggio
la somma essenza de la quale è munta.

'and tell me why, within this wheel,
the sweet symphony of Paradise falls silent,
which lower down resounds with such devotion.'

'Your hearing is as mortal as your sight,'
he answered. 'Thus here there is no song
for the very reason Beatrice has not smiled.

'I have come down the sacred ladder's rungs this far
only to bid you welcome with my words
and with the light that wraps me in its glow.

'It was not greater love that made me come more swiftly,
for as much and more love burns above,
as that flaming luminescence shows,

'but the profound affection prompting us
to serve the Wisdom governing the world
has brought about the outcome you perceive.'

'I see indeed, O sacred light,' I said,
'how acts of love, unbidden, serve this court
in concord with that knowledge which foresees,

'but it is hard for me to understand
why you alone among your peers
were foreordained to act upon this charge.'

I had not yet quite finished with my words
when the light began to spin around its core,
whirling like a quickly turning millstone.

Then the love that was within it spoke:
'Divine light focuses on me, piercing
the radiance that holds me in its womb.

'Its power, conjoined with my own sight,
raises me so far above myself that I can see
the Highest Essence, the source from which it flows.

Quinci vien l'allegrezza ond' io fiammeggio;
per ch'a la vista mia, quant' ella è chiara,
la chiarità de la fiamma pareggio.

Ma quell' alma nel ciel che più si schiara,
quel serafin che 'n Dio più l'occhio ha fisso,
a la dimanda tua non satisfara,

però che sì s'innoltra ne lo abisso
de l'etterno statuto quel che chiedi,
che da ogne creata vista è scisso.

E al mondo mortal, quando tu riedi,
questo rapporta, sì che non presumma
a tanto segno più mover li piedi.

La mente, che qui luce, in terra fumma;
onde riguarda come può là giùe
quel che non pote perché 'l ciel l'assumma."

Sì mi prescrisser le parole sue,
ch'io lasciai la quistione e mi ritrassi
a dimandarla umilmente chi fue.

"Tra 'due liti d'Italia surgon sassi,
e non molto distanti a la tua patria,
tanto che' troni assai suonan più bassi,

e fanno un gibbo che si chiama Catria,
di sotto al quale è consecrato un ermo,
che suole esser disposto a sola latria."

Così ricominciommi il terzo sermo;
e poi, continüando, disse: "Quivi
al servigio di Dio mi fe' sì fermo,

che pur con cibi di liquor d'ulivi
lievemente passava caldi e geli,
contento ne' pensier contemplativi.

'And this inflames the joy with which I burn:
for, in the clarity of my sight,
I match the clearness of my flame.

'Nonetheless, the most enlightened soul in Heaven,
that seraph who fixes most his eye on God,
could not produce an answer to your question,

'for what you ask is hidden in the depths
of the abyss of God's eternal law, so that the sight
of any being He created is cut off from it.

'And to the mortal world, when you return,
bear this report, so that it shall no more presume
to set its steps toward such a goal.

'The mind, here bright, is dimmed by smoke on earth.
Ask yourself, then, how could it do down there
what it cannot, though Heaven raise it to itself?'

His words so reined me in
that I withdrew the question, limiting myself
to asking humbly who he was.

'Between Italy's two shores
and not far distant from your homeland,
crags rise so high that thunder rolls below them.

'They form a ridge called Càtria.
A consecrated monastery stands below,
once dedicated wholly to God's worship.'

Thus a third time he began,
addressing me, and then went on:
'There I became so constant serving God,

'my simple fare seasoned with olive oil alone,
that I readily endured the heat and frost,
content in contemplation.

Render solea quel chiostro a questi cieli
fertilemente; e ora è fatto vano,
sì che tosto convien che si riveli.

In quel loco fu' io Pietro Damiano,
e Pietro Peccator fu' ne la casa
di Nostra Donna in sul lito adriano.

Poca vita mortal m'era rimasa,
quando fui chiesto e tratto a quel cappello,
che pur di male in peggio si travasa.

Venne Cefàs e venne il gran vasello
de lo Spirito Santo, magri e scalzi,
prendendo il cibo da qualunque ostello.

Or voglion quinci e quindi chi rincalzi
li moderni pastori e chi li meni,
tanto son gravi, e chi di rietro li alzi.

Cuopron d'i manti loro i palafreni,
sì che due bestie van sott' una pelle:
oh pazïenza che tanto sostieni!"

A questa voce vid' io più fiammelle
di grado in grado scendere e girarsi,
e ogne giro le facea più belle.

Dintorno a questa vennero e fermarsi,
e fero un grido di sì alto suono,
che non potrebbe qui assomigliarsi;
né io lo 'ntesi, sì mi vinse il tuono.

'That cloister which used to yield abundant harvest
to these heavens now is barren,
120 but soon its barrenness must be revealed.

'In that place I was known as Peter Damian,
but Peter the Sinner in the House
123 of Our Lady on the Adriatic shore.

'Little of mortal life on earth was left to me
when I was singled out and dragged to that red hat
126 which now is passed from bad to worse.

'Cephas came, and the exalted vessel
of the Holy Spirit came, lean and barefoot,
129 receiving their food at any doorway.

'Now our modern shepherds call for one on this side,
one on that, to support them, they are so bloated,
132 and one to go before, one to boost them from behind.

'Their fur-lined mantles hang upon their horses' flanks
so that two beasts go underneath one skin.
135 O patience, what a heavy load you bear!'

As he spoke, I saw more flickering flames
descend, spinning from rung to rung,
138 at every turn more lovely.

They thronged around him and then stopped and raised
a cry so loud that nothing here
could be compared to it—nor could I make it out,
142 so did its thunder overwhelm me.

1–4. As has always been the case (*Par.* I.64–66 [Moon]; V.88–96 [Mercury]; VIII.14–15 [Venus]; X.37–39 [Sun]; XIV.79–84 [Mars]; XVIII.52–57 [Jupiter]; and in these verses), as he ascends to a new heaven, Dante fixes his eyes on Beatrice's face so that nothing else can attract his attention. And it will be much the same in the three ascents still before him (*Par.* XXII.97–105 [Starry Sphere]; XXVII.88–96 [Crystalline Sphere]; XXX.14–27 [Empyrean]). In most of these moments, Beatrice is either explicitly or indirectly portrayed as smiling. This time, however, there is something quite different about the heavenly guide's disposition, as we discover in the following tercet: For the first time in this situation, an ascent to the next celestial heaven, Beatrice is rather pointedly *not* smiling. The little mystery that this fact engenders is left for Peter Damian to resolve (see vv. 61–63).

5–12. The reference to Ovid's Semele (*Metam.* III.256–315) may at first seem out of place in this context (as it did not when it occurred in *Inf.* XXX.1–2, where the vengeance of God upon the counterfeiters is compared to the vengeance taken by Juno upon Semele). "Semele, daughter of Cadmus, king of Thebes; she was beloved by Jupiter, by whom she became the mother of Bacchus. Juno, in order to avenge herself upon Jupiter, appeared to Semele in the disguise of her aged nurse Beroe, and induced her to ask Jupiter to show himself to her in the same splendour and majesty in which he appeared to Juno. Jupiter, after warning Semele of the danger, complied with her request, and appeared before her as the god of thunder, whereupon she was struck by lightning and consumed to ashes" (T). Here, Beatrice, as Jove, withholds her sovereign and celestial beauty from her mortal "lover" until such time as he will be able to bear her divine beauty. Thus Ovid's "tragic" tale, embellished with a Christian and "comic" conclusion, is rewritten; unlike Semele, Dante will become capable of beholding the immortals face-to-face. See Brownlee (Brow.1991.2) for a discussion in this vein, also demonstrating that this myth functions as the "spine" of the narrative of Dante's spiritual growth in this heaven.

8. The phrase *l'etterno palazzo* (eternal palace) recalls, according to Aversano (Aver.2000.2), p. 94, the *domus Dei* (house of God) mentioned by Jacob in Genesis 28:17, a passage not distant from the one describing his

dream of the ladder, so prominently visited in this canto. See the note to vv. 28–30.

13–15. Beatrice announces that they have arrived in the seventh heaven, that of Saturn, characterized, as we shall find, by monastic silence. As the tenth canto of this *cantica* marked a transition to a higher realm (from the sub-solar heavens of Moon, Mercury, and Venus), so does this canto lift the pilgrim into a still higher realm, beyond that dedicated to the praise of those associated with knowledge, just warfare, and just rulership, for Dante the highest forms of human activity in the world. Contemplation, as a form of direct contact with divinity, is thus marked off as a still higher form of human activity, one that itself borders on the divine. The major exemplary figures in this realm, Peter Damian and Benedict, are presented as, even during their lives on earth, having been nearly angelic in their comprehension, if, however, maintaining contact with the ordinary in their daily rituals of monastic labor (a monastery was, among other things, a sort of single-sex farming community). The eighth sphere will present us with still holier humans, writers of the Christian Bible (Saints Peter, James, and John), while in the ninth we find the reflection of the angelic intelligences. Thus we are here entering the final triad in the poet's tripartite division of the created universe.

That the constellation Leo should be described as warm ("ardente"—v. 14) seems to allow the understanding that Dante is speaking only metaphorically (the Sun being in Leo, and thus "warming" it). But, as Torraca (comm. to vv. 13–15) and others, after him, point out, an antecedent text (*Par.* XVI.39) also seems to make the constellation itself heat-producing.

16–18. Beatrice's monitory metaphor is precise: Dante should put his mind/memory behind his eyes in order to make them mirrors, by agency of such "backing," in order to understand and remember what he is about to see in Saturn.

19–24. As Tozer (comm. to these verses) paraphrases: "The man who could conceive the greatness of my joy in feasting my eyes on Beatrice's face, would also be able to understand that I felt still greater delight in obeying her injunctions, when I looked away from her to the object which she indicated."

19. It is not unusual for Dante to present his intellectual quest in terms of metaphors of ingestion. See the note to *Paradiso* X.22–27.

24. The line "balancing the one side of the scale against the other" reflects the strength of the protagonist's desire to look at Beatrice as measured against his even greater desire to obey her.

25–27. For a previous (and similarly circumlocutory) reference to Saturn, see *Inferno* XIV.95–96; and, for Dante's overall assessment of this best of the pagan gods, who presided over a golden age, see Iannucci (Iann.1992.2).

The planet is mentioned by name only once in the poem (*Purg.* XIX.3). It is a larger presence in *Convivio*, where it is mentioned several times, including in the following description: "The heaven of Saturn has two properties by which it may be compared to Astrology: one is the slowness of its movement through the 12 signs, for according to the writings of the astrologers, a time of more than 29 years is required for its revolution; the other is that it is high above all the other planets" (*Conv.* II.xiii.28—tr. R. Lansing). This makes it symbolically the most lofty philosophical pursuit of all, since astrology is the highest and most difficult science for its students to master. Theology alone is more lofty—and more difficult.

28–30. This ladder, as has been recognized at least since the fourteenth century (see the Codice Cassinese, comm. to *Par.* XXII.67), derives from the Bible, the ladder to Heaven seen by Jacob in his dream (Genesis 28:12), as Dante's reference in the next canto will underline (*Par.* XXII.70–72). Further, and as Bosco/Reggio (comm. to vv. 29–30) point out, both these saints, Peter Damian and Benedict, had written of Jacob's Ladder as emblematizing the purpose of (monastic) life. However, we probably ought also to consider Boethius, who presents the Lady Philosophy as having the image of a ladder on her gown (*Cons. Phil.* I.1[pr]), connecting the Greek letters *pi* (at the bottom, for practical knowledge) and *theta* (at the top, for theoretical or, we might say, contemplative knowledge [Dante knew enough Greek to realize that *theta* is also the first letter of the word for God, *theos*]). Singleton (comm. to vv. 29–30) credits Grandgent for the reference to Boethius. See the note to Paradiso XXII.1.

That the ladder is golden reminds us that Saturn reigned in the golden age.

29. See Pecoraro (Peco.1968.1), pp. 745–49, for a discussion of this *scaleo*, which eventually settles on the traditional interpretation; the ladder, built of rungs of humility, leads to the contemplation of God. Pecoraro takes an

interesting detour through the writings of Paolo Amaducci, a neglected figure in Dante studies, who effectively was the first modern critic (Filippo Villani was arguably the first ancient one) to apply the fourfold method of Scriptural exegesis to interpreting Dante (for Amaducci, without reference to Pecoraro's earlier notice, see Hollander [Holl.1976.1, pp. 128–29, n. 49, and Holl.2001.1, p. 187, n. 45]). (Pecoraro discusses only one of his five studies of Dante's supposed reliance on Peter Damian [Amad.1921.1].)

31–33. It is eventually clear (e.g., vv. 64–66) that all these spirits (compared to all the stars in the nighttime sky), descending, are coming from the Empyrean for the sole purpose of welcoming Dante to his higher degree of contemplative awareness; that they, like all the spirits we see in the heavens, are only temporary visitors to these realms; that all the saved souls and the angels populate the Empyrean (as far as we can tell, they have never manifested themselves to anyone in a lower heaven before Dante's most extraordinary visit to the heavens that concludes his journey through the afterworld).

Jacob saw angels on the ladder in his dream, ascending *and* descending. Dante sees the souls of the blessed only descending, at least for now.

34–42. This is the sole "classical" simile in these two cantos devoted to the monastic sphere of Saturn (but see *Par.* XXII.1–6) and perhaps represents the only joyous moment in them. It describes those souls who descend from the Empyrean, where such behavior is not only appropriate but natural, for it is the realm of everlasting joy.

This fairly extended simile is complex enough to have caused considerable difficulty. For an interesting and original interpretation, see Carroll (comm. to these verses). He argues that Dante has carefully followed Thomas Aquinas (*ST* II–II, q. 180, a. 3–6) for every detail of this passage (Torraca [comm. to these verses] will later cite the same passage without treating it as fully). Here is an abbreviated version of Carroll's argument: Thomas is responding to Richard of St. Victor's six steps of contemplation, reduced by Richard himself to three: *Cogitatio*, *Meditatio*, *Contemplatio*. When the descending spirits, the jackdaws in the simile, reach a certain step, groups of them begin moving in one of three ways (about which there will be more shortly). That step, Carroll says, represents Richard's second step, Meditation, or speculation, an intellectual activity that draws, in Aquinas's treatment here, on the image of mirroring (as Carroll points out Dante has done in vv. 17–18). The descending spirits, we must remember, are used to seeing in the third way, Contemplation. Now, reentering the protagonist's realm of experience, which necessarily falls short of seeing face-to-face (as even he will be able to do shortly, once he enters the Empyrean), these saved souls behave in three different ways. Carroll associates each of these behaviors in turn with Thomas's discussion of Richard of St. Victor's three modes of intellectual activity: "Some of the souls 'go away without return,' that is, without doubling back: they represent the *straight* motion which goes direct from things of sense to things of intellect. Some 'turn back to where they started from'—to the certain step from which their flight began: they represent the *oblique* motion, which is composed, says Aquinas, of a mixture of straight and circular, of reason and divine illumination. And some, 'wheeling, make a sojourn': they represent the *circular* motion,—that perfect movement by which the intellect turns uniformly round one centre of Divine truth, the 'sojourn' signifying the immobility of this motion, as of a revolving wheel that sleeps upon the axle."

As for the birds themselves, Carroll cites Benvenuto (comm. to these verses) to the effect that they love solitude and choose the desert for their habitation. *Pole*, according to some commentators, are *cornacchie grige* (gray crows, or jackdaws), having black wings, silver eyes, and large red beaks encircled by yellow.

34. For *costume* as "natural instinct" or "inner law," see the note at its first appearance in the poem, where it also seems to have this sense (*Inf.* III.73).

37–39. It is perhaps needless to say that there have been several ingenious attempts to explain these three movements of the birds. It is perhaps fair to say that none has seemed ultimately convincing. Carroll's, based in the texts of Richard of St. Victor and of Aquinas (see the note to vv. 34–42), remains the most interesting.

42. It may be fair to suggest that the significance of this "rung" of Jacob's Ladder has also escaped even the few who choose to discuss it. It seems unlikely to represent a mere "realistic" detail, for example, the "rung" of the "ladder" that is at a level with the heaven of Saturn. Again, see Carroll's interesting hypothesis (see the note to vv. 34–42), that this is the "grade" of meditation, the earthly form of divine contemplation, as it were.

43. This soul will eventually identify himself as Peter Damian at verse 121. See the note to vv. 106–126.

46–48. Dante underlines his obedience to Beatrice as the reason he does not respond more fully to Peter Damian's affection for this special visitor to the sphere of Saturn. This tercet casts her in the role of leader of a monastic community, setting the rules for conversation and all other aspects of the social life of the "monk" under her care, Dante Alighieri.

49–50. Once again we are given to understand that the souls in bliss are able to know all that may be known in their contemplation of the mind of God, the mirror of all creation. The identical nature of such knowledge with its source is suggested by the three uses of the verb *vedere* in these two lines.

51. Beatrice only now releases Dante to open his mind and heart to Peter.

52–60. From Peter, Dante wants to know two things: why he seemed, by his proximity, so affectionate toward him and why, for the first time in the heavens, song has yielded to silence.

58–60. Saturn is marked by an atmosphere of monastic self-denial. It is the home of the cardinal virtue temperance and of religious meditation. The absence of melody in Saturn is singular thus far in *Paradiso*, for we and the protagonist have become accustomed to hearing sacred songs as we ascend the spheres: "Ave Maria" in the Moon (*Par.* III.121–122); an "Osanna" in both Mercury (VII.1) and Venus (VIII.29); the singing of the souls in the Sun is referred to a good half dozen times, but it is only in XIII.25–27 that we are informed that they sing, not of Bacchus nor of Apollo, but of the Trinity; next we learn that the unidentified song in Mars contains the words *Risurgi* and *Vinci* (XIV.125) and that the souls in Jupiter sing of God (XVIII.99). Underscoring the uniqueness of the silence of this sphere, the final three heavens are also marked by song: the Starry Sphere by Gabriel's song for Mary (XXIII.103–108) and by the other members of the Church Triumphant crying out, to the ascending mother of God, "Regina celi" (XXIII.128). In the succeeding sphere, various moments in Dante's progress among his saintly interlocutors are punctuated by voices raised in song: "Dio laudamo" (XXIV.113), "Sperino in te" (XXV.73), "Sperent in te" (XXV.98), "Santo, santo, santo" (XXVI.69), "Al Padre, al Figlio, a lo Spirito Santo, *gloria*" (XXVII.1–2); in the Crystalline Sphere the angelic choirs resonate with "Hosannah" (XXVIII.94); in the Empyrean we hear once more the "Ave Maria" (XXXII.95). See the note to *Paradiso* XXVII.1–3.

59. The adjective *dolce* (sweet) occurs with some regularity from one end of the poem (*Inf.* I.43) to the other (*Par.* XXXIII.63), 106 times in all.

61–63. Peter Damian gives his answer to the second of Dante's questions first. It is brutally frank: Dante still thinks as the world thinks and is not yet ready to experience the higher degree of divinity that songs at this level represent. And now we also learn that this was precisely the reason for Beatrice's withholding of her customary smile as well (see verse 4).

64–72. Peter's answer to Dante's first question is more circuitous, but reflects the same problem: Dante's inability to think beyond the limits of a human comprehension of love. Peter's affection for Dante is not greater than that felt by any others among the saved in Paradise, that is to say, it is not "personal." We may remember Casella in *Purgatorio* II, whose greeting was very personal indeed, as a kind of control for our measurement of this affection.

73–78. Still a slow learner, Dante gets part of the message: In the Court of Heaven, freedom in loving is to follow God's will, a similar paradox to that developed in Beatrice's lengthy discussion of free will in *Paradiso* V.19–33. On the other hand, his follow-up question reveals that he is still eager to understand the *reason* for the choice of Peter Damian as the deliverer of heavenly greeting.

77. For Aquinas's distinction (*ST* I, q. 23, a. 1) between providence and predestination, see Torraca (comm. to these verses). Carroll, in another context (comm. to *Par.* XX.130–132), cites this same passage in the *Summa* and paraphrases it as follows: "Hence Predestination is defined as 'Divine Providence leading rational creatures to their supernatural end, the Beatific Vision,' the entire process, from beginning to end, having its reason in the Divine will alone. It is not dependent on the foreseen merits of the elect; and the prayers of saints (such as Gregory's for Trajan) are only part of the second causes by means of which the decree of Predestination is worked out." Bosco/Reggio (comm. to verse 78) also cite Thomas (*ST* I, q. 22, a. 3): "Two things belong to providence—namely, the type of the order of things foreordained towards an end; and the execution of this order, which is called government." They go on to suggest that Dante was in accord with this view in *Paradiso* XI.28–30. Their point is that the subject here is not predestination, but divine foreknowledge of the actions of particular individuals.

For more on predestination, see the note to *Paradiso* XX.130–148.

83–90. Peter's preamble tells Dante how he was filled with divine love for his mission, but *not* why, as his final point will insist.

Bosco/Reggio (comm. to these verses) paraphrase the passage as follows: "The light of grace descends on me, penetrating the light that wraps me round, in whose womb I am enclosed, and its power, conjoined with my intellect, lifts me so far above myself that I can see the supreme essence, God, from whom this light bursts forth. From this sight comes the joy with which I shine, since the splendor of my flame is as great as the clarity of my vision of God."

84. Muresu (Mure.1996.2), p. 30, reports discomfort at the Dantean coinage *inventrarsi* on the part of several commentators. Among those he mentions are Tommaseo (comm. to this verse): *"non bello"* (not beautiful) is his laconic reaction. Andreoli (comm. to this verse) has this to say: The term is "unfit to describe a heavenly spirit speaking of his divine light." But see Mattalia (comm. to this verse) for an understanding of Dante's sense of the Scriptural relevance of the word, reflecting the Gospels' references to Mary's womb (e.g., Luke 11:27, cited by Virgil, as character, at *Inf.* VIII.45). As usual, Scartazzini (comm. to this verse) has a lengthy discussion of the variant readings. See also the two appearances of the noun *ventre* (womb, belly) in this *cantica* (*Par.* XXIII.104 and *Par.* XXXIII.7 and the notes thereto).

90. For the word *pareggio*, see the note to *Paradiso* XXIII.67.

91–102. Neither the most exalted soul in Heaven, Peter explains, possibly referring to Mary (see *Par.* XXXI.116–117), nor one of the most enlightened of the highest order of angels, a seraph, can ever know the reasons for God's decisions. This is the only limit, then, on even angelic intelligence. All those in the Empyrean can know, in God, all relations among all things, in heaven and on earth, but not the eventual reasons that might explain their causes. The urgency of Peter's explanation to Dante is clearly aimed past him, to us on earth, who so enjoy imagining that we understand the root causes of events even though our normal sinful disability should probably deprive us of such baseless optimism in this regard. But we are little more mature than babies, forever asking "Why?" See, on this passage, Hawkins (Hawk.1995.1), p. 313.

94–95. The description of providence (God's foreknowledge, which alone can account for the causes that lie behind the interrelations of things) as an "abyss" suggests a "plurality of worlds," this universe (known by the angels and the blessed) and the vast inner mind of God that extends (if it may be said to extend) to regions of which we cannot possess even the slightest knowledge nor indeed verify the existence. At least as early as *Purgatorio* III.37, Dante should have understood that such things were beyond knowing. Virgil then advised him that humans were not behaving rationally when they hoped to know the "why" behind things. Dante is, as we are frequently forced to acknowledge, a slow learner.

103–105. Discouraged from pursuing his quest for knowledge beyond both human and, indeed, angelic potential, Dante contents himself with asking Peter, in the form of his third question, to identify himself.

106–126. The seven tercets dedicated to the life of Peter Damian (1007–72) are reminiscent of the earlier saints' lives that we have heard in *Paradiso*. Once again we begin with a geographical indicator (the mountain called Catria, in the Apennines, that rises some five thousand feet above sea level, near the town of Gubbio). Peter's narrative is brief and self-abnegating (those of Francis [*Par.* XI] and of Dominic [*Par.* XII] are considerably more full, but then they are narrated by praiseful others, not by their abstemious selves). Peter's is modesty itself, concluding with the ironic and bitter reflection on his having been made to give over the life of prayer that truly pleased him for that of "administration."

"St. Peter Damian, proclaimed doctor of the Church by Leo XII in 1828; born of an obscure family at Ravenna *c.* 1007. In his childhood he was much neglected, and after the death of his parents was set by his eldest brother to tend swine. Later on, another brother, named Damian, who was archdeacon of Ravenna, took compassion on him and had him educated. Peter in gratitude assumed his brother's name and was thenceforth known as Peter Damian (Petrus Damiani). After studying at Ravenna, Faenza, and Parma, he himself became a teacher, and soon acquired celebrity. At the age of about 28, however, he entered the Benedictine monastery of Fonte Avellana on the slopes of Monte Catria, of which in 1043 he became abbot. In this capacity he rendered important services to Popes Gregory VI, Clement II, Leo IX, Victor II, and Stephen IX, by the last of whom he was in 1057, much against his will, created cardinal bishop of Ostia. He appears to have been a zealous supporter of these popes, and of Hildebrand (afterwards Gregory VII), in their efforts to reform Church discipline, and made journeys into France and Germany with that object. After fulfilling several important missions under Nicholas II and Alexander II, he died at an advanced age at Faenza, Feb. 22, 1072.

"Dante represents Peter Damian as inveighing against the luxury of the prelates in his day; the commentators quote in illustration a passage from a letter of his to his brother cardinals, in which he reminds them that the dignity of a prelate does not consist in wearing rare and costly furs and fine robes, nor in being escorted by troops of armed adherents, nor in riding on neighing and mettlesome steeds, but in the practice of morality and the exercise of the saintly virtues" (T). While he was never formally canonized, he was venerated as a saint from the time following his death in several places in Italy and at Cluny.

111. John of Serravalle (comm. to vv. 106–111) distinguishes among *latrìa* (the accent in the poem may be due to the requirements of rhyme or, as Scartazzini suggests [comm. to this verse], to Dante's small Greek), *dulia*, and *yperdulia*. The first is defined as honoring God alone; the second, those who are virtuous (e.g., the saints); the third, "things excellent" (examples are Mary and the cross). Tommaseo (comm. to vv. 109–111) mentions the appearance of the term in both Augustine (*DcD* X.1) and Aquinas (*ST* II–II, q. 81, a. 1). Pietro di Dante (Pietro1, comm. to vv. 106–111) was the first to cite Isidore of Seville for the term (*Etym.* VIII.xi.11).

115–117. This tercet contains one (of two) references to "contemplative" intellectual behavior or to those who perform it (see the reference to *contemplanti* in *Par.* XXII.46) in the heaven of Saturn. In neither case does it seem to refer to *contemplatio Dei*, but would rather seem to indicate monastic rumination, or meditation, thoughts that lead to God, but not a direct vision of Him. In fact, of the seven uses of the words derived from *contemplare* in the poem, beginning in *Purgatorio* XXIV.132, where Virgil, Dante, and Statius meditate upon Gluttony, only one would clearly seem to indicate contemplation of the highest kind, St. Bernard in *Paradiso* XXXI.111; but even that may have been contemplation of the Virgin (as his contemplation referred to in *Par.* XXXII.1 clearly is).

121–123. There has been controversy over the reference of the second Peter in this tercet. Petrocchi's text has "fu'" (*fui* [I was]). And the logic of the phrasing also indicates a single reference: In place 1, I was called "x," in place 2, "y." Later historical certainty, which would make Dante responsible for knowing that there was another Peter, a monk in the monastery to which he has Pietro allude and who died there in 1119, may not apply. Scholars have pointed out that Dante's knowledge of Peter Damian was itself suspect; he could easily have conflated these two religious of Ravenna in this passage written, one assumes, after his settling in Ravenna circa 1317. However, since Peter Damian died in 1072, nearly fifty years before the death of Pietro Peccatore, Dante's phrasing would seem quite odd: "In that place (his monastery at Fonte Avellana) I was known as Peter Damian, and Peter the Sinner was (*fu*, not *fu'*, abbreviation of *fui*) in the House of Our Lady . . ." The syntax and logic seem beyond rescue. The first version may be historically inaccurate, but it does make grammatical sense: "In that place I was (*fu'*, not *fu*) known as Peter Damian, and as Peter the Sinner in the House of Our Lady." This view is in accord with the generally authoritative Michele Barbi (Barb.1941.2), pp. 257–96, and with the later discussion in Chiavacci Leonardi (Chia.1997.1), pp. 596–97 (with updated bibliography).

For a review of the history of the issue (and eventual agreement with Barbi's analysis), see Pecoraro (Peco.1968.1), pp. 771–77. For strong support of Barbi's views on the single identity of the two Peters, see Muresu (Mure.1996.2), p. 35n. That Benvenuto da Imola (comm. to vv. 121–123), who knew that part of Italy well, spoke so forcefully about the "deception" of those who believe that Dante is talking about two Peters probably should have concluded the debate long ago.

125. Like Shakespeare's "hats and clocks" in *Julius Caesar* (II.i), Peter's "cappello," the red hat worn by cardinals, is a gratuitous anachronism on Dante's part. As Torraca was the first commentator to point out (comm. to vv. 124–126, citing an article in *BSDI* 6 [1899]), it was only during the papacy (1243–54) of Innocent IV that this clerical accoutrement began to be worn by the princes of the Church.

127–135. Peter concludes his words to Dante with a denunciation of corrupt clergy, culminating in one of the more memorable anticlerical images in the poem, the pastor on horseback as beast with attendants, his poor horse sagging under the weight of his flesh.

Dante may have known Peter's own imprecations against the corruptions of the clergy in his *Liber Gomorrhianus* (as was often suggested in the last century, first by Torraca [comm. to vv. 121–123]). As a number of commentators suggest, Peter was a man after Dante's heart, not only for his surprising openness to "imperial" politics, but especially for his scurrilous tongue for the malfeasance of the clergy, for which he apologizes but apparently delights in allowing free rein. That Dante was recognized as anticlerical by the clergy is not a matter to doubt. There is the obvious case of the *Monarchia* (which spent some three centuries and one-third [from the first index of prohibited books until 1881] as unfit for Catholic eyes). However, and as Comollo (Como.1990.1), pp. 49–50, points out, there were any number of rough spots, for a cleric respectful of his pope, in the poem (particularly *Inf.* XI.6–9; XIX.106–117; *Purg.* XIX.106–116; and *Par.* IX.136–142).

127–128. Cephas (stone [*pietra*]) is the [Aramaic] name that Christ gave to Simon (see John 1:42), thereafter known as Simon Peter (Pietro, in Italian, keeps the pun alive better than does the English "Peter"). The "exalted vessel of the Holy Ghost" is Paul (see *Inf.* II.28).

129. Scartazzini (comm. to this verse) points to biblical sources for this fraternal abnegation: I Corinthians 10:27 ("eat whatever is set before you") and Luke 10:7 (Christ advising his disciples not to go from house to house in search of food, but to stay wherever they chance to be).

136–142. Peter's collegial souls, as they descend the ladder to greet him, glow with righteous indignation at these words. Surrounding him, having ceased their circular movement, they let loose a cry so loud and angry that Dante cannot make out the words of what they shout. Where earlier in the canto he had been denied both Beatrice's smile and the singing of the blessed, now he is allowed to hear a superfluity of sound with a similar net result. (The canto moves from monastic silence to monkish outrage, both leaving the protagonist stunned, uncomprehending.) It is a final reminder of his human incapacity even now, when he has attained the height of Saturn in the heavens.

For this "thunder" as resonating with that found in Ovid's description of Jupiter, preparing to descend to seduce Semele by taking his thunder and his lightning bolts along (*Metam.* III.300), see Brownlee (Brow.1991.2), pp. 226–27.

PARADISO XXII

OUTLINE

SATURN

1–21 *Beatrice explains the reason for the shouting*

1–6 Dante as frightened child, Beatrice as reassuring mother:

7–9 in Heaven, she explains, only righteous zeal can account for such apparently dissonant sounds;

10–12 now he should see that her smile or their song would have been too much for him, since their shout has so moved him;

13–15 had he understood their words, he would understand the vengeance of God that awaits such prelates;

16–18 such vengeance comes slow for mortals who, in longing or in fear, await it anxiously;

19–21 now he should pay attention to the other souls here.

22–51 *first part of the discussion with St. Benedict*

22–24 Dante sees a crowd of joyous souls;

25–30 he represses the question ("who are you?") that the largest and brightest of these pearls advances to answer:

31–36 "You should have understood the charity that governs us here and spoken; I will answer without making you do so":

37–51 Benedict's autobiography.

52–72 *Dante's premature request*

52–60 "Show yourself to me uncovered," without his light

61–72 Benedict: Dante will see him thus in the Empyrean.

73–99 *Benedict denounces the corruption of his order*

- 73–75 No mortals now try to reach meditative heights;
- 76–78 the monasteries and their monks are now derelict;
- 79–84 his attack on monastic abdication of duty;
- 85–87 humans start out well but quickly reveal their faults;
- 88–93 **Peter, Francis,** and he built on very little, but now one sees the institutions they founded totally corrupted;
- 94–96 God's revenge will show His power: e.g., **Jordan, Red Sea;**
- 97–99 Benedict and his companions all disappear above

100–111 *Ascent to the heaven of the fixed stars*

- 100–105 Dante and Beatrice move upward with supernatural speed;
- 106–111 address to the reader: how quickly he went up and entered the Starry Sphere [in Gemini]

112–123 *seventh invocation in the poem (to the stars of Gemini)*

124–154 *Dante looks back down*

- 124–126 Beatrice: "You are so near the final happiness that your sight is clear and keen;
- 127–132 "therefore, look back at what you have already traversed."
- 133–138 Dante sees the seven spheres and the earth,
- 139–150 and then the seven planets,
- 151–154 with a final glance at our globe before turning back to the eyes of Beatrice.

PARADISO XXII

Oppresso di stupore, a la mia guida
mi volsi, come parvol che ricorre
sempre colà dove più si confida;

e quella, come madre che soccorre
sùbito al figlio palido e anelo
con la sua voce, che 'l suol ben disporre,

mi disse: "Non sai tu che tu se' in cielo?
e non sai tu che 'l cielo è tutto santo,
e ciò che ci si fa vien da buon zelo?

Come t'avrebbe trasmutato il canto,
e io ridendo, mo pensar lo puoi,
poscia che 'l grido t'ha mosso cotanto;

nel qual, se 'nteso avessi i prieghi suoi,
già ti sarebbe nota la vendetta
che tu vedrai innanzi che tu muoi.

La spada di qua sù non taglia in fretta
né tardo, ma' ch'al parer di colui
che disïando o temendo l'aspetta.

Ma rivolgiti omai inverso altrui;
ch'assai illustri spiriti vedrai,
se com' io dico l'aspetto redui."

Come a lei piacque, li occhi ritornai,
e vidi cento sperule che 'nsieme
più s'abbellivan con mutüi rai.

Io stava come quei che 'n sé repreme
la punta del disio, e non s'attenta
di domandar, sì del troppo si teme;

Overcome by wonder, I turned to my guide,
as does a child who always scurries back
to the one who has his utmost trust.

And she, like a mother, quick in comforting
her son when he is pale and out of breath
with a voice that often calmed him in the past,

said: 'Don't you understand you are in Heaven?
Don't you understand that all of Heaven is holy,
that all things done here spring from righteous zeal?

'It should be clear to you just how their song,
and then my smile, would have confused you,
since you were so startled by their cry.

'In it, had you understood their prayers,
you would already recognize
the vengeance you shall see before you die.

'The sword of Heaven never cuts in haste
nor in delay, but to the one who waits
in longing or in fear, it well may seem so.

'Now turn around and see the others,
for you shall look on many illustrious spirits
if you but set your gaze to where I say.'

I turned my eyes as she had urged and saw
one hundred little globes that made each other brighter
in the glittering reflections of one another's rays.

I was as one who in himself restrains
the spur of his desire and, fearing to presume,
dares not pose his question.

e la maggiore e la più luculenta
di quelle margherite innanzi fessi,
per far di sé la mia voglia contenta.

Poi dentro a lei udi': "Se tu vedessi
com' io la carità che tra noi arde,
li tuoi concetti sarebbero espressi.

Ma perché tu, aspettando, non tarde
a l'alto fine, io ti farò risposta
pur al pensier, da che si ti riguarde.

Quel monte a cui Cassino è ne la costa
fu frequentato già in su la cima
da la gente ingannata e mal disposta;

e quel son io che sù vi portai prima
lo nome di colui che 'n terra addusse
la verità che tanto ci soblima;

e tanta grazia sopra me relusse,
ch'io ritrassi le ville circunstanti
da l'empio cólto che 'l mondo sedusse.

Questi altri fuochi tutti contemplanti
uomini fuoro, accesi di quel caldo
che fa nascere i fiori e ' frutti santi.

Qui è Maccario, qui è Romoaldo,
qui son li frati miei che dentro ai chiostri
fermar li piedi e tennero il cor saldo."

E io a lui: "L'affetto che dimostri
meco parlando, e la buona sembianza
ch'io veggio e noto in tutti li ardor vostri,

così m'ha dilatata mia fidanza,
come 'l sol fa la rosa quando aperta
tanto divien quant' ell' ha di possanza.

The largest and most lustrous of those pearls
advanced to satisfy my longing
to find out more about him.

Then, from deep within, I heard him say: 'Could you see,
as I do, the charity burning in our midst,
you would have shared your thoughts with us.

'And that your arrival at the lofty goal
be not delayed by waiting, I shall answer
your guarded thoughts, which you dare not express.

'The summit of the mountain on whose slope
Cassino lies was once much frequented
by people both deluded and perverse.

'I am he who first brought up the slope
the name of Him who carried down to earth
the truth that so exalts us to the heights.

'And such abundant grace shone down on me
I led the neighboring towns away
from impious worship that misled the world.

'All these other flames spent their lives in contemplation,
kindled by that warmth which brings
both holy flowers and holy fruits to birth.

'Here is Macarius, here is Romualdus,
here are my brothers whose feet never strayed
beyond their cloisters and whose hearts were firm.'

And I to him: 'The affection you display
when you speak with me and the signs of kindness
that I see and mark in all your fires

'have enhanced my confidence,
as the sun expands the rose
when it opens to its fullest bloom.

Però ti priego, e tu, padre, m'accerta
s'io posso prender tanta grazia, ch'io
ti veggia con imagine scoverta."

Ond' elli: "Frate, il tuo alto disio
s'adempierà in su l'ultima spera,
ove s'adempion tutti li altri e 'l mio.

Ivi è perfetta, matura e intera
ciascuna disïanza; in quella sola
è ogne parte là ove sempr' era,

perchè non è in loco e non s'impola;
e nostra scala infino ad essa varca,
onde così dal viso ti s'invola.

Infin là sù la vide il patriarca
Iacobbe porger la superna parte,
quando li apparve d'angeli sì carca.

Ma, per salirla, mo nessun diparte
da terra i piedi, e la regola mia
rimasa è per danno de le carte.

Le mura che solieno esser badia
fatte sono spelonche, e le cocolle
sacca son piene di farina ria.

Ma grave usura tanto non si tolle
contra 'l piacer di Dio, quanto quel frutto
che fa il cor de' monaci sì folle;

chè quantunque la Chiesa guarda, tutto
è de la gente che per Dio dimanda;
non di parenti nè d'altro più brutto.

La carne d'i mortali è tanto blanda,
che giù non basta buon cominciamento
dal nascer de la quercia al far la ghianda.

'Therefore, I pray you, father, reassure me—
if I may hope to gain so great a favor—
that I may see you with your face unveiled.'

And he: 'Brother, your lofty wish
shall find fulfillment in the highest sphere,
where all desires are fulfilled, and mine as well.

'There only all we long for is perfected,
ripe, and entire. It is there alone
each element remains forever in its place,

'for it is not in space and does not turn
on poles. Our ladder mounts right up to it
and thus its top is hidden from your sight.

'Jacob the patriarch saw the ladder's highest rungs
attain that height when, teeming with
a throng of angels, it appeared to him.

'But no one bothers now to raise his foot
up from the earth to climb those rungs,
and my Rule is but a waste of paper.

'The walls that were constructed for an abbey
have been converted into dens for thieves, and sacks,
now filled with rotten flour, once served as cowls.

'But the highest rates of usury are not exacted
against God's will so much as is the harvest
that turns the hearts of monks to madness.

'For whatever the Church has in its keeping
is reserved for those who ask it in God's name,
and not for kindred or more vile relations.

'The flesh of mortals is so weak and dissolute
that good beginnings go astray down there, undone
before the newly planted oak can bring forth acorns.

Pier cominciò sanz' oro e sanz' argento,
e io con orazione e con digiuno,
e Francesco umilmente il suo convento;

e se guardi 'l principio di ciascuno,
poscia riguardi là dov' è trascorso,
tu vederai del bianco fatto bruno.

Veramente Iordan vòlto retrorso
più fu, e 'l mar fuggir, quando Dio volse,
mirabile a veder che qui 'l soccorso."

Così mi disse, e indi si raccolse
al suo collegio, e 'l collegio si strinse;
poi, come turbo, in sù tutto s'avvolse.

La dolce donna dietro a lor mi pinse
con un sol cenno su per quella scala,
sì sua virtù la mia natura vinse;

né mai qua giù dove si monta e cala
naturalmente, fu sì ratto moto
ch'agguagliar si potesse a la mia ala.

S'io torni mai, lettore, a quel divoto
trïunfo per lo quale io piango spesso
le mie peccata e 'l petto mi percuoto,

tu non avresti in tanto tratto e messo
nel foco il dito, in quant' io vidi 'l segno
che segue il Tauro e fui dentro da esso.

O glorïose stelle, o lume pregno
di gran virtù, dal quale io riconosco
tutto, qual che si sia, il mio ingegno,

con voi nasceva e s'ascondeva vosco
quelli ch'è padre d'ogne mortal vita,
quand' io senti' di prima l'aere tosco;

'Peter started his community with neither gold
nor silver, and I mine with fasting and with prayer,
90 while Francis with humility established his.

'If you consider where each started out,
and then consider how far it now has strayed,
93 you shall see how dark its white has turned.

'Still, the sight of Jordan driven back and of the sea
that opened at the will of God were greater wonders
96 to behold than would be His intervention here.'

This he said to me, and then withdrew
to his companions, who, drawing close together,
99 now swirled up as in a whirlwind.

My sweet lady, with but a single gesture, urged me on
to follow right behind them up that stairway,
102 so did her power overcome my nature.

And never once down here below,
where we mount and descend by natural law,
105 was there motion swift enough to match my flight.

So may I, reader, once again return
there to that holy triumph for whose sake
108 I frequently bewail my sins and beat my breast,

you could not have withdrawn and thrust your finger
into the fire faster than I saw the sign
111 that follows on the Bull and was within.

O glorious stars, O light made pregnant
with a mighty power, all my talent,
114 whatever it may be, has you as source.

From you was risen and within you hidden
he who is the father of all mortal life
117 when first I breathed the Tuscan air.

e poi, quando mi fu grazia largita
d'entrar ne l'alta rota che vi gira,
la vostra regïon mi fu sortita.

A voi divotamente ora sospira
l'anima mia, per acquistar virtute
al passo forte che a sé la tira.

"Tu se' sì presso a l'ultima salute,"
cominciò Bëatrice, "che tu dei
aver le luci tue chiare e acute;

e però, prima che tu più t'inlei,
rimira in giù, e vedi quanto mondo
sotto li piedi già esser ti fei;

sì che 'l tuo cor, quantunque può, giocondo
s'appresenti a la turba trïunfante
che lieta vien per questo etera tondo."

Col viso ritornai per tutte quante
le sette spere, e vidi questo globo
tal, ch'io sorrisi del suo vil sembiante;

e quel consiglio per migliore approbo
che l'ha per meno; e chi ad altro pensa
chiamar si puote veramente probo.

Vidi la figlia di Latona incensa
sanza quell' ombra che mi fu cagione
per che già la credetti rara e densa.

L'aspetto del tuo nato, Iperïone,
quivi sostenni, e vidi com' si move
circa e vicino a lui Maia e Dïone.

Quindi m'apparve il temperar di Giove
tra 'l padre e 'l figlio; e quindi mi fu chiaro
il varïar che fanno di lor dove;

And afterward, when I was granted grace
to enter the high wheel that keeps you turning,
it was your zone to which I was assigned.

To you now, with devotion, my soul sighs
that it gain strength for the next daunting task
that with such power draws it to itself.

'You are so near the final blessedness,'
Beatrice then began,
'your eyes from now on shall be clear and keen.

'Thus, before you become more one with it,
look down once more and see how many heavens
I have already set beneath your feet,

'so that your heart, filled with joy,
may greet the triumphant throng that comes
in gladness to this aethereal sphere.'

With my eyes I returned through every one
of the seven spheres below, and saw this globe of ours
to be such that I smiled, so mean did it appear.

That opinion which judges it as least
I now approve as best, and he whose thoughts
are fixed on other things may truly be called just.

I saw Latona's daughter shining bright,
without that shadow for which I once believed
she was both dense and rare.

The visage of your son, Hyperion, I endured
and saw how Maia and Dïone move
around him in their circling near.

Then I saw the tempering of Jove between his father
and his son, and the changes that they make
in their positions were now clear.

e tutti e sette mi si dimostraro
quanto son grandi e quanto son veloci
e come sono in distante riparo.

L'aiuola che ci fa tanto feroci,
volgendom' io con li etterni Gemelli,
tutta m'apparve da' colli a le foci;
poscia rivolsi li occhi a li occhi belli.

All seven planets there revealed
their sizes, their velocities,
and how distant from each other their abodes.

The little patch of earth that makes us here so fierce,
from hills to rivermouths, I saw it all
while I was being wheeled with the eternal Twins.
Then I turned my eyes once more to those fair eyes.

1–6. This simile is perhaps better described as two simple comparisons combined into a single trope. (Francesco da Buti [comm. to vv. 1–21] did, however, describe it as a "similitudine.") It first compares Dante to a distressed child running to its mother and then portrays Beatrice as a mother calming her child. Poletto (comm. to vv. 1–3) was apparently the first to indicate the nearly certain reference to *Purgatorio* XXX.43–45 (Dante as child [*fantolin*] running to his mommy [*mamma*]), but the Anonimo Fiorentino (comm. to vv. 1–3) pretty clearly had been thinking of that same text.

These verses continue the action of the preceding canto, which ended with Dante being unable to make out the meaning of a thunder-like utterance (one of the loudest noises we hear from the pages of the poem, perhaps bringing to mind the similarly stunning noise of the infernal waterfall at *Inferno* XVI.94–105). This shout emanated from Peter Damian's outraged colleagues, departing from the silent meditation that marked their presence once they descended to this sphere (see *Par.* XXI.58). Naturally enough, the protagonist, unable to make out their words, fears lest their rebuke, so loud as to be incomprehensible, be aimed at him. His apparent logic is clear enough: In this realm, if Beatrice does not smile and if the souls do not sing, he must be being rebuked for something he has (or has not) done.

1. Tommaseo (comm. to vv. 1–3) was perhaps the first to identify the citation here of Boethius (*Cons. Phil.* 1.2[pr]): Philosophy appearing to the befuddled "hero" at the beginning of that work (the two passages share versions of the phrase *stupor oppressit*). Thus the text of the *Consolatio* stands behind Dantean expressions at either end of the canto. See the note to verse 151 (but also see the note to *Par.* XXI.28–30). Baranski (Bara.2002.1), p. 357, makes the telling point that Boethius presents the Lady Philosophy's gown as bearing a ladder that moves from lower practical matters to higher and theological concerns, an emblem resembling the ladder we see here in Saturn, which configures both ascent and descent, the life of meditation and of work in the world, the monastic practices of meditation and labor. (Benedict's "motto," as is reported by Fallani [comm. to verse 40], was "ora et labora" [pray and work].)

4–6. Beatrice's increasing feminization (for her "male" attributes, see *Purg.* XXX.19, 43–48, 58, and the notes thereto) is, clearly, not the sign of her sexualization, as some contrive to believe. Never in the poem does she appear as other than chaste, here, in simile, as Dante's mother.

7–9. Beatrice corrects his misapprehension, explaining that anger in the heavens cannot be produced by anything but righteous indignation (*buon zelo*). Thus the shout he heard could not have been directed against him, but rather against those on earth who offend in their desecration of the religious life, "li moderni pastori" (modern shepherds [*Par.* XXI.131]). Once again we are made to see how poorly prepared this mortal is for this higher realm.

10–15. Beatrice explains that Dante's inability to comprehend the "prayers" of the visitors to Saturn, prophesying God's vengeance on His enemies, is in itself proof that he was not ready to bear either Beatrice's beatific smile or the contemplatives' singing, both of which were, for that reason, withheld from him.

10–12. Carroll (comm. to vv. 1–18) restates a passage in St. Bernard's *De Consideratione* (V.xiv) that may throw considerable light on this tercet: There are four kinds of divine judgments, each one defined by its breadth, or length, or depth, or height. Consideration of God's judgments coincides with "depth." Carroll continues: "This kind of contemplation 'may violently shock the beholder with the fearful vision, but it puts vice to flight, firmly bases virtue, initiates in wisdom, preserves humility.' It is plainly the shock of this contemplation of the 'depth' which here stuns the Pilgrim. The cry is an echo from the Thrones of the Divine judgments who preside over this Heaven, and the very echo shakes Dante to the soul; and Beatrice asks how, if the 'depth' so shook him, he could have borne the 'height'—the lofty ecstatic joy of contemplation represented by her smile."

13–15. This sort of righteous indignation is itself a sort of joy, since it involves, as Beatrice says, the celebration of just punishment, visible in the vengeance of God, that Dante will be able to observe on earth before he dies. This "minor prophecy" (for another see *Purg.* XXIII.97–102) about the punishment of the corrupt clergy resembles the similar promise (*Par.* XVII.98–99), made by Cacciaguida, that Dante will witness the just punishment of his Florentine enemies. The death of any of Dante's major adversaries, occurring while he was still alive, would indeed seem to make elements of these "prophecies" correct. On the religious side of the roster, major deaths that succored Dante's hopes included those of the popes Boniface VIII (1303) and Clement V (1314); in the secular ledger, that of Corso Donati (1308 [see *Purg.* XXIV.82–90]).

16–18. For Dante's enemies, obviously, this sword will make itself felt all too soon, while for him it will be slow indeed in coming.

This feeling had already raced through Dante's veins. Mattalia (comm. to verse 16) indicates the second of Dante's "political epistles" (*Ep.* VI.4, written in March of 1311), addressed to Henry VII, for the sword of God and vendetta. The text speaks of the "gladius Eius qui dicit: 'Mea est ultio' " (the sword of Him who says, "Vengeance is mine").

19–21. Beatrice's urging would lead us to believe that we shall learn of the presence of at least a number of great contemplatives in this sphere. We shall, however, meet only one more, St. Benedict (named only by periphrasis at verses 40–42), although he is accompanied by two other named monastics, Macarius and Romuald (verse 49), who are merely said to be here and must share a single line of verse. The others, of whom we are about to see many dozens, do not receive even that much notice, a perhaps fitting anonymity in this environment of self-abnegation. For whatever reason, Dante has limited his panoply of great contemplatives to Peter Damian and Benedict of Norcia, with an assisting cast of only two named supporting players.

The phrasing of her command to Dante reflects similar urgings on Virgil's part (*Inf.* IX.55, X.31; *Purg.* XXVII.31–32) and one earlier one by Beatrice herself (*Par.* XVIII.20). The ability to turn and face that which he fears or has not yet understood is what his two guides both encourage in him.

20. For the phrase *illustri spiriti* (glorious spirits), Tommaseo (comm. to vv. 19–21) adduces a Virgilian text (*Aen.* VI.758): "inlustris animas."

23. These "one hundred little globes" are neither precisely one hundred in number nor little globes, but a large number of descended saints who, in their joy (we remember that they are spending eternity in the most joyful place there is) make one another more joyous, as can be perceived by their increasing brightness.

25–30. The protagonist, getting with the spirit of this place, overrules "la punta del disio" (the spur of his desire) and suppresses his desire to know who these spirits are—but of course he has communicated with them in

God, despite his reticence. One light, the best and the brightest "pearl" among them, advances to reveal his identity.

For a study of Dante's adaptation of sexually charged terms to express the desire for God, see Pertile (Pert.1990.1), using verse 26 as his point of departure. And now see his book (Pert.2005.2), which includes this essay and builds upon it.

28–29. We know, as did those who painted and those who "read" medieval paintings, that size is a measure of importance; this is, accordingly, the most important personage of the group (as is also underlined by his greater brightness among the *margherite* [pearls] who make up his company). Thus it is that Mary will be the greatest among the flames (at least once Christ goes back to the Empyrean) seen in the descended Church Triumphant (*Par.* XXIII.90).

Benedict will make his identity knowable (he will not actually name himself then or ever) at vv. 40–42. See the note to vv. 37–45.

31–36. Once again a personage of Paradise alludes to the fact that speech is here an unnecessary form of communication (to any understanding but that of mortal Dante). The speaker assures him that, had he only known the inner dispositions of these "globes," he would have spoken up (even as we remind ourselves that there obviously was no need to, since they know his thoughts even as he suppresses his desire to give voice to them).

31. For the extraordinary number of verbs of seeing in this canto (twenty-one), all but two of them referring to Dante's sight, see Baranski (Bara.2002.1), p. 344n.

37–45. Benedict (480–543), born in the Umbrian city of Norcia, became the founder of what is considered the oldest monastic order in the West, which bears his name. Son of wealthy parents, he went to Rome to study, and there witnessed the debauchery of the clergy. His response was to take up a solitary eremitic life in a cave. His fame brought him the attention of those who had chosen to live a cloistered life. He agreed to become the head of the convent of Vicovaro, thus moving from the existence of a hermit to that of a cenobite. This was not in all respects a propitious decision on his part, since his fellow monks, resentful of his extremely strict Rule, tried to poison him. He managed to survive the attempt on his life and once again retreated to his cave. Monks loyal to him and to his vision of the cenobitic life eventually followed him to Montecassino, where he destroyed a temple of Apollo and a grove sacred to Venus (according to Oelsner [comm. to vv. 37–39]), converted the locals (until his advent, still pagans), and founded his order. As commentators point out, beginning with Jacopo della Lana (*Nota* to this canto), Dante's brief version of Benedict's *vita* is indebted to that found in his biographer, St. Gregory the Great, *Dialogues*, II.2. It may seem surprising that Benedict was canonized only in 1220, nearly seven centuries after his death, while Francis had to wait only two years for his sainthood (1228).

39. The adjectives assigned to the indigenous pagan locals pretty clearly seem to distinguish between, in Tommaseo's view (comm. to vv. 37–39), their confused mental state and their misdirected affections (in Oelsner's formulation [see the note to vv. 37–45], worship of Apollo and devotions to Venus).

45. As opposed to verse 39, which seems to point to two unacceptable forms of behavior among the locals, this one would rather indicate the worship of Apollo alone.

46–48. Once again (see the note to verse 1) the text indicates the special nature of the monastic vocation, a combination of prayerful meditation and labor, in Benedict's own prescription for cenobitic activity, "ora et labora."

48. Francesco da Buti (comm. to vv. 37–51) resolves the metaphoric *fiori* (flowers) and *frutti* (fruits) into "words" and "deeds." It seems at least possible, given Benedict's own division of monkish occupation into prayer and work, that this is how we should interpret the "flowers" that Dante has in mind: the words that give shape to prayer.

49. Saints Macarius and Romuald were surely also monks, but, especially with regard to the first, there is little certainty as to his absolute identity. For Macarius, the two main candidates were both dead before Benedict was born. "It is uncertain which of the several saints of the name of Macarius is the one intended by Dante. The two best known, between whom perhaps Dante did not very clearly distinguish, are St. Macarius the Elder, called the Egyptian, and St. Macarius the Younger of Alexandria—both disciples of St. Anthony. St. Macarius the Elder (born in 301) retired at the age of 30 into the Libyan desert, where he remained for sixty years, passing his time between prayer and manual labour, until his death, at the

age of 90, in 391. St. Macarius the Younger had nearly 5,000 monks under his charge (d. 404); he is credited with having established the monastic rule of the East, as St. Benedict did that of the West" (T).

As for St. Romuald (956–1027), he began (in 1012) the Camaldolese Order, a reformed group of Benedictines. It was named for the donor of its holding, *campus Maldoli* (the field of Maldolus), or "Camaldoli." (Its monastery, in Tuscany, is referred to in *Purgatorio* V.96.) Thus Benedict is bracketed, chronologically, by a precursor and a follower. Dante may have learned about Romuald, born in Ravenna, from the *vita Romualdi* composed by his townsman, Peter Damian.

50–51. It sounds as though Benedict is readying himself to give a denunciation of the corruption of his order, in the style of Peter Damian (*Par.* XXI.130–135); however, Dante interrupts him with a surprising question, one that detains him for some time; he will deliver his broadside only at vv. 73–96.

52–54. The protagonist allows that he has interpreted (correctly) his temporary companions' increased brightness as an expression of their affection for him.

58–60. Benedict is awarded the role of Dante's penultimate "father" in this poem, with only St. Bernard to come (for the others, see the note to *Par.* XVI.16).

He also has the honor of preceding St. James (see *Par.* XXV.122–129) in causing Dante to ask questions about the fleshly aspect of the condition of the blessed. There also circulated a medieval legend that St. John, for his particular closeness to Jesus, was unique among the rest of the blessed (Jesus and Mary being the sole other exceptions) in having his resurrected body in Heaven before the general resurrection (see Jacoff [Jaco.1999.1]). Dante's curiosity about Benedict's fleshly nature, however, has no ascertainable "source," at least none supported by Dante's commentators. In the case of Benedict, the protagonist's question (and his desire) is somewhat different. He would like to see Benedict *now* as he shall be when he is found again, seated in Heaven (*Par.* XXXII.35), that is, with his sheathing flame removed so that his face's features will be utterly plain to a beholder. Once in the Empyrean, Dante will see *all* the blessed as though they had already been given back their fleshly selves (*Par.* XXX.43–45), that is, even before the general resurrection. Thus he will there experience the reality of Benedict and of James (and of all the other saints) in identical ways.

Why, the commentators are left to ask, does Dante introduce this concern here, one that seems to have no historical footing? The least that one can hazard is that, given his "fatherhood" and this exceptional request, Benedict played a more vital role in Dante's intellectual and spiritual development than has been ascertained, if in what precise ways remains unknown.

Brownlee points out (Brow.1991.2), pp. 227–28, that Dante's desire to see Benedict in his flesh uncomfortably parallels Semele's request to Jove, but that he will see Benedict as though resurrected in the flesh in *Paradiso* XXXII.35. His story, unlike hers, has a happy ending.

61–72. At some length Benedict corrects the supposition that lay behind Dante's desire to see him in his true human resemblance. His conclusion, with its reference to Jacob's Ladder and its function as the connecting point between the rest of the timebound universe and the unchanging Empyrean, brings his attention back to his monks, last heard of at verse 51.

61. This represents the last use of the word "brother" (*frate*) as a term of address in the poem. See the note to *Purgatorio* IV.127.

See Carroll (comm. to vv. 61–63) for the notion that Benedict is gently reproving Dante for having called him "father" (verse 58) by insisting that they are better considered brothers in Christ. Compare the desire of Pope Adrian V *not* to have Dante kneel before him in obeisance, since they enjoy a similar brotherhood (*Purg.* XIX.133–135).

64. Aversano (Aver.2000.2), p. 101, points out that, rather than redundant through some failing on the poet's part, as some commentators hold, these three adjectives reproduce a phrase in an apostolic epistle (James 1:4): "And let steadfastness have its full effect, that you may be perfect and complete, lacking in nothing" (*perfecti et integri, in nullo deficientes*).

67. The Empyrean *non s'impola* (does not turn on poles), as does the terrestrial globe and as do the planets, but is the place that T. S. Eliot might have described as "the still point of the turning world" (the phrase occurs once in the second section of "Burnt Norton," the first of the *Four Quartets*, and once again in the fourth).

68–69. This ladder "mounts right up to it," that is, to the Empyrean, which is why Dante cannot yet see its terminus.

70–72. The tercet puts into play, in case we have missed it, the reference to Genesis 28:12: "And he dreamed, and behold, there was a ladder set up on the earth, and the top of it reached to heaven. And behold, the angels of God were ascending and descending on it."

73–87. Beginning with the foot of Jacob's Ladder, as it were, Benedict now rounds on the current members of his order. Their degeneracy is reflected in the crumbling physical plant of the monastery; in the attempt to find *some* use for the cowls of the monks (since apparently those who wear them are few) as bags for flour; in the flagrant usury employed by them; and, still worse, in their charging exorbitant prices for the foodstuffs that they grow. On this last charge, see Tozer (comm. to vv. 79–84), describing it as "covetousness in misappropriating the revenues of the Church, which rightfully belong to God's poor, to the purposes of nepotism and licentiousness. This in the sight of God is a worse sin than usury."

Benedict's remarks come to momentary cessation in the image of human sinfulness quickly undoing even the fresh beginnings of the lives of the young.

77. Christ, driving the moneychangers from the temple (Matthew 21:12–13), portrays them as turning His "house of prayer" into a "den of thieves" (*speluncam latronum*), as was noted by John of Serravalle (comm. to vv. 76–78). Dante's *spelonche* nearly certainly reflects that passage.

85–87. Oaks take a while to grow mature enough to produce acorns—twenty years, according to Jacopo della Lana (comm. to this tercet) and Francesco da Buti (comm. to vv. 73–87). However, Dante seems to be underlining the relative brevity of their acornless state. Sapegno (comm. to this tercet) looks forward to a similar sense of the brief durance, there of innocence among us humans, at *Paradiso* XXVII.121–138.

88–96. In the first of these three tercets, Benedict reviews high points in the establishments of communities within the Church: the apostle Peter's first "papacy" (first century); the founding of his own order (sixth century); the founding of Francis's (twelfth century). The reader has a clear sense that Benedict does not expect any major renewal in the Church. And yet his speech ends with a curiously optimistic (and typically Dantean) reversal, in the promise of better days, with which his harangue comes to its close. If bodies of water could have been halted in their flow to let the Hebrews cross to safety, as Psalm 113:3 (114:5) attests, that would still seem a greater miracle than if God were to intervene in the world now. In short, as unlikely as that possibility seems, its odds are shorter than they were for the miracles of Jordan and of the Red Sea. In Dante's scheme of things, there is always room for hope, a view that we will find again in *Paradiso* XXVII.142–148, in a passage that similarly surmounts a decidedly pessimistic view of human sinfulness with hopes for a better world in the near future.

88. See the relevant passage in Acts 3:6: "Petrus autem dicit: Argentum et aurum non est mihi" (But Peter said, "Silver and gold have I none"), its relevance first suggested in the *Chiose ambrosiane* (comm. to this verse).

89. A possible *arrière pensée* of Ugolino (*Inf.* XXXIII.75), who knew *digiuno* (fasting) all too well, but prayer too little. See the note to *Inferno* XXXIII.49.

93. See *Paradiso* XXVII.136 for a similar description of a thing changed into its opposite, in that case, innocence into sinfulness.

94–96. God's miracles (Joshua 3:14–17), Jordan turned back and (Exodus 14:21–29) the crossing of the Red Sea (both remembered in Psalm 113:3 [114:5]), will have accustomed the eventual witnesses of His vengeance against these prelates to see that such relatively minor miracles are also signs of His power.

97–99. The departure of Benedict and his fellow monastics, headed back "home," to the Empyrean at the upper end of Jacob's Ladder, where, we may assume, they will no longer think of the world's many corruptions, is accompanied by a whirlwind, sign of God's power and of His love for these saints.

100–111. In their wake, Beatrice leads Dante up the "ladder," but not yet to Benedict's companions' goal, the Empyrean, but to the eighth of the nine heavenly spheres, that of the Fixed Stars. The ascent is brief and briefly described, but the point of arrival will be treated at greater length.

102. Andreoli (comm. to this verse) paraphrases as follows: "the natural gravity of my body." Is this an admission that Dante indeed visited the heavens in the body? However, it could suggest that the protagonist thinks of himself in corporeal terms out of habit. But see the note to *Paradiso* I.73.

106–111. Dante apostrophizes us (for the distribution of the addresses to the reader throughout the poem, see the note to *Inf.* VIII.94–96) for the final time in the poem (as Tommaseo noted). Are we to think it a coincidence that this last occurrence falls just before the first of the final triad of invocations, now to higher powers directly (God's creative powers in the stars and then the Deity Itself in *Par.* XXX and XXXIII)? It is as though the poet is underlining the distance between human and divine experience by leaving us behind. After Dante looks down through the planets, the next sight he will see is the Church Triumphant, which we will see again in the penultimate canto of the poem. For all of the next canto, for the last third of the thirtieth, and for all the final three we are seeing "face-to-face."

As the space travelers near their eventual goal, the time taken for the ascent from sphere to sphere decreases, since the "gravitational pull" of the Empyrean naturally increases as one nears it.

109–111. The poet allows us to learn, inferentially, where his visit to the Starry Sphere has been situated by Providence, in "the sign following the Bull" (Taurus), and thus in Gemini, the sign under which, in 1265, he was born and which shaped whatever genius he possesses. With Gemini the Sun rose and set the day Dante was born in Tuscany; and now he comes to this heaven in this constellation. (Singleton [comm. to vv. 127–154] cites an interesting observation of Grandgent's: "Thus, in a spiritual sense, [Dante] returns, like Plato's departed, to his native star: cf. *Par.* IV.52–57.") From the stars of Gemini the poet invokes aid in acquiring the necessary capacity to tell of the final things of Heaven, beginning in the next canto with the appearance of the "hosts of Christ's triumph" (*Par.* XXIII.20–21).

109–110. The by-now fairly familiar trope *hysteron proteron* is used to describe the speed of their upward movement and attainment of the next sphere. See the note to *Paradiso* I.23–26.

112–123. Adding to the reader's sense of the poet's self-consciousness at this moment in his creation, this seventh invocation also underlines the importance of the visit to the stars that shaped his human abilities. In *Inferno* II.7, when Dante invoked *alto ingegno* for aid, it is at least possible that he was invoking God's power to help him make his poem (see the notes to *Inf.* II.7–9 and *Par.* XXV.2). Here, especially in light of the equation between God's powers and the heavenly spheres suggested by *Paradiso*

II.9, Dante would seem to be aligning his own powers as a poet with those specifically allotted him by God through the agency of the alignment of the stars at his birth, when the Sun ("he who is father to all mortal life") was under the sign of Gemini.

121–123. The actual invocation occurs only now, as the first three tercets of the passage define the power of these stars and give the nature and history of Dante's relationship with them. What is the specific "daunting task" for which the poet seeks heavenly aid? Most commentators are content to see this as a general appeal, called for by the heightening of the poem's subject, rising above the realms in which Dante and we are allowed to see the temporarily present souls of saved mortals and looking forward to the final vision in the poem's final canto. This seems a sensible view. (For a review of the varied [and rather vague or general] interpretations offered through the nineteenth century, see Scartazzini [comm. to vv. 122–123].) Del Lungo (comm. to this tercet) offers a stronger reading, arguing that the specific appeal is made for a specific reason: Dante in the next canto must describe the triumph presided over by Christ and Mary. Indeed, in Canto XXIII the protagonist will be seeing "face-to-face." And what he will see is the ultimate destination of the justified portion of our race, the Church Triumphant, which will descend from the Empyrean in order to make itself visible to a mortal (for the first [and only!] time in human history, we may embarrassedly consider). And thus this invocation is "special" for that reason. Having made it, the poet reports first on his downward glance, as he readies himself to see better things; the passage describing that vision will complete this canto. In the next, the intricate opening simile leads directly into the vision of the Church Triumphant, the first thing above him that Dante will describe after the invocation (see *Par.* XXIII. 19–21, Beatrice's words, "Now look upon the hosts / of Christ in triumph, all the fruit / gathered from the wheeling of these spheres!"). It is with this immediate destination in mind that one might want to understand the "clue" to such an understanding found in Beatrice's earlier statement, a few lines farther on in this canto, at verse 124 ("You are so near the final blessedness"), as a reference *not* to his eventual destination in the Empyrean, as most imagine it to be, but in fact to this immediately proximate vision of the citizenry of that place in the next canto. In fact, the vast majority of commentators believe the passage looks forward only to the last canto, drawn by the phrase *ultima salute,* for God, in *Paradiso* XXXIII.27. Only Trucchi (comm. to vv. 124–126) resists this "easy" solution, seeing that the presence of Christ in the next one is what is at stake.

Of similar effect is Beatrice's ensuing remark (vv. 131–132), encouraging Dante to look back to see how much heavenly territory he has already traversed, a journey that makes him ready to appear before "the triumphant throng / that comes rejoicing to this celestial sphere." In light of such indications, it seems more than likely that the invocation is meant to be read as a preparation for that near-at-hand experience, not one some ten cantos distant.

123. The phrase "passo forte" (daunting task) caught Benvenuto's attention (comm. to vv. 121–123). Why is it so? "Because," Benvenuto says, "here is that which all things strive toward. In what follows [Dante] describes God's Church in its triumph, with all the celestial court, including God."

124–129. See Boyle (Boyl.2000.1), pp. 3–5, on Dante's awareness of Thomas's failure to complete his three-part *Summa* and consequent diminution in comparison with Dante's tripartite poem. She continues by claiming that the *Comedy* uses both agricultural and navigational metaphors to demonstrate that poetry is more fitting than philosophy or theology to articulate "the ascent to divine contemplation." While her sense of Dante's hostility to Thomas is surely overblown, she is among those who realize that all is not peaches and cream in Dante's presentation of his relations with Thomas.

124–126. Beatrice is not so much admonishing Dante to prepare his eyes for such exalted vision as insisting that, trained as they have been, they are now necessarily ready for that vision, and will be so for the duration of his visit to the rest of the heavens and to the Empyrean. This is to agree with Bosco/Reggio (comm. to this tercet). For the sense in which Dante is at this moment near his "final blessedness," see the note to vv. 121–123.

127. Dante's neologism here is close to untranslatable. The coinage is possibly to be taken as a verb of the first conjugation, "inleiarsi," to "in-it oneself," that is, to make oneself one with something external to one's being.

129. Beatrice's reference to the great extent of the universe that Dante can now make out "beneath his feet" reminds us again that we are still not sure whether we are meant to understand that Dante is in *Paradiso* in the flesh. While something like certainty awaits us, as will be made clear in a few cantos, here we sense a certain coyness. Beatrice may be speaking figuratively,

meaning "Look down beneath you, where your feet would be if you were here in the flesh." Or she may simply be saying, "Look beneath your feet," feet that are really there, dangling beneath him in the heaven of the Fixed Stars.

131–132. Once again Beatrice clearly alludes to what Dante will see next, in the verses early in the next canto (19ff.), the Church Triumphant, having left Heaven to appear to Dante in this heaven.

132. The word *etera*, literally translated, means "(a)ether," in Aristotle's sense of the "fifth element," as understood by Jacopo della Lana (comm. to vv. 130–132), that which composes the "stuff" of which a celestial sphere consists and in which other bodies (e.g., the stars) are contained. It is thus differentiated from both stars (and what we refer to as planets) and nothingness (what we used to refer to as "space").

133–153. This remarkable passage is almost as interesting in its antecedence as in its immediate progeny. There are similar scenes in Boccaccio's *Filostrato* and *Teseida*; Chaucer visits both of these, in the moment that is perhaps central to the understanding of his intentions for the ending of the *Troilus*; and both writers evidently pay close attention to Dante as well as to his and their classical precursors. While there continues to be debate about Dante's firsthand knowledge of the portion of Cicero's lost *De re publica* known as the "Dream of Scipio," it really does seem to most that Dante knew this text (VI.xvi.16). On the other hand, there is and can be no debate about his knowledge of the similar passage in Boethius's *De consolatione* (II.m7.1–6), if that seems less directly resemblant. (Singleton [comm. to vv. 127–154] presents both texts, with English translations.) In Cicero, Dante's great Roman hero Scipio, appearing in a dream to his grandson after his death, speaks of this paltry world, seen from the heavens, in much the same tone as we find here; in Boethius, there is a vision of this narrow earth.

134. Some readers may benefit from a reminder: For Dante the seven "planets" circling over our earth are Moon, Mercury, Venus, Sun, Mars, Jupiter, and Saturn. All the stars are contained in the next sphere, the heaven of the Fixed Stars, to which point the protagonist has just now risen (see vv. 100–111).

139–150. Dante examines the planets beneath his feet; these are seen in a somewhat unusual order and are mainly named by their "parents":

(1) Moon (daughter of Latona), (4) Sun (son of Hyperion), (2) Mercury (daughter of Maia), (3) Venus (daughter of Dïone), (6) Jupiter, (7) Saturn (father of Jupiter), (5) Mars (son of Jupiter).

Carroll (comm. to these verses) makes a helpful distinction between St. Bernard's terms *consideratio* and *contemplatio*: "St. Bernard (***De Consideratione*** [II.ii]) thus distinguishes: '*Contemplation* may be defined as the soul's true unerring intuition, or as the unhesitating apprehension of truth. But *consideration* is thought (*cogitatio*) earnestly directed to research, or the application of the mind to the search for truth; though in practice the two terms are indifferently used for one another' (Lewis' transl.). Both words are believed to come from augurial rites: Contemplation, from *com* and *templum*, the marking out of a *templum*, or sacred space open to the sky; and consideration, from *com* and *sidus* (*sideris*) a star, or constellation, observation of the stars." In Bernard's language then, Dante is "considering" the stars; contemplation of God remains ahead of him.

139–141. The reference is, obviously, to the Moon (Latona's daughter, Diana) and to Dante's earlier misprisions of the reasons for its differing degrees of brightness (see *Par.* II.49–51). Now that he is seeing her from "behind," from the side turned away from earth, her surface is uniform in appearance.

142–143. Dante's improved eyesight (see vv. 124–126) quickly bestows a new benefit: He can look directly at the Sun, the son of Hyperion in some classical myths, including Ovid's (*Metam.* IV.192).

144. Referring to them by the names of their mothers, Dante sees Mercury (Maia) and Venus (Dïone). The literal sense of this tercet has caused problems; Bosco/Reggio (comm. to vv. 143–144) propose a reading that is mirrored in our translation.

145–146. Perhaps the best gloss available for these verses was written by Dante himself (*Conv.* II.xiii.25): "The heaven of Jupiter may be compared to Geometry because of two properties: one is that it moves between two heavens that are antithetical to its fine temperance, namely that of Mars and that of Saturn; consequently Ptolemy says, in the book referred to [Dante mentions his *Quadripartitus* in section 21], that *Jupiter is a star of temperate constitution between the cold of Saturn and the heat of Mars*; the other is that among all the stars it appears white, almost silvery" ([italics added] tr. R. Lansing).

146. Saturn, the father of Jupiter, thus lent his name to the only planet that cannot be named by a parent.

148–150. From his vantage point in the eighth celestial sphere, Dante is now able to observe the relationships among the seven planets (see the note to verse 134) with regard to their varying sizes, the differing speeds of their rotations around the earth, and the distances between their *ripari*, that is, what medieval astronomers refer to as their "houses," or their stations in the heavens.

151. The word "aiuola," frequently translated as "threshing floor," is almost without a doubt, as Scott (Scot.2003.1) has argued, without the biblical resonance of Matthew 3:12 and Luke 3:17 that is heard by some from the nineteenth century into our own time. He also believes that the word reflects its presence in a phrase found in Boethius's *De consolatione*, II.7[pr], *angustissima . . . area*. Scott cites Kay (Kay.1998.1), p. 317, n. 22, glossing *Monarchia* III.xvi.11, where Dante uses the Latin equivalent of "aiuola": "Latin *areola* is a diminutive form of *area*, and hence is 'a little space' " (see also Pasquini [Pasq.1988.1], p. 439). (For the long-standing but frequently overlooked knowledge of the reference to Boethius, see first Pietro di Dante [Pietro1, comm. to vv. 145–150] and then Francesco da Buti [comm. to vv. 149–154], who are joined by several later practitioners, including Landino, Daniello, and Tommaseo. Longfellow [comm. to this verse] gets the Boethius right but is responsible [according to Scott] for the invention of "threshing floor" in his translation.) This rendering of the word has had a long run, but may in fact still need winnowing. Scott continues: "Dante uses it here in this general, etymological sense, although often both *areola* and its Italian calc *aiuola* are used for specific small spaces, e.g. a flowerbed, seedbed, open courtyard, threshing floor, or even a blank space on a page [. . .]. Dante probably had in mind Boethius's description of the inhabitable world as an 'angustissimum [*sic*] . . . area' (*Cons. Phil.* II.7[pr].3), which Dante echoed in *Epist.* [VII.15]: 'in angustissima mundi area' [such a narrow corner of the world]."

See Dante's second use of *aiuola* at *Paradiso* XXVII.86.

152–154. Because of the high-speed revolution of the celestial sphere in which he is currently lodged, Dante is able to see all of the physical contour of our earth. He does so without particular enthusiasm, and is quick to turn his eyes back to the eyes of Beatrice, which are undoubtedly to be understood as gazing up toward God and not down toward Dante's (and our) paltry patch of earth.

This passage inevitably leads a reader to wonder exactly how much time Dante spent in the heavens (and in the Empyrean). He left our terrestrial globe at noon on Wednesday (either 30 March or 13 April in the year 1300, as the reader will recall [see the note to *Inf.* I.1]). How long was he in Paradise? When did he come "home"? For discussion, see the note to *Paradiso* XXVII.79–81.

PARADISO XXIII

OUTLINE

STARRY SPHERE

1–12 simile (1): mother bird, anxiously awaiting dawn, and Beatrice awaiting "sunrise" in order to "nourish" Dante

13–15 comparison (1): Dante is like a man who longs for what he has not and who is satisfied by the hope itself

16–18 but the moments of hoping and seeing are near resolution: the sky is brightening

19–21 Beatrice: "See those first and then later saved by **Christ**"

22–24 Beatrice's indescribable joy: her "home" has come to her;

25–30 simile (2): a full moon **(Trivïa)** and all the stars likened to this "sun" lighting up all the descended souls

31–33 and Dante's sight cannot bear its brightness;

34 his apostrophe of Beatrice;

35–39 she: "You are conquered by Christ, desired since **[Adam]**"

40–45 simile (3): lightning swelling in cloud and crashing to earth likened to Dante's feasting mind leaving itself;

46–48 her command: "See me as I truly am; now you can bear my smile, because of what you have witnessed";

49–51 comparison (2): Dante is as one awakening from a dream

52–54 when he heard Beatrice's invitation, worthy of gratitude;

55–60 "non-invocation": should all the poets best nourished by the Muses now aid him, the result would not be worth much;

61–62 describing Paradise, the sacred poem must make a leap

63 simile (4): poem like a man at an obstruction on his path

64–66 "indirect" address to reader: whoever reflected on the mortal shoulder bearing such a weighty theme would not blame the shoulder for trembling;

67–69 this voyage not for a little bark but for a bold prow and unsparing helmsman.

70–72 Beatrice: "Why look at me and not the 'garden'?"

73–75 the rose (representing **Mary**); the lilies (the **Apostles**)

76–78 Dante tries again to look into the effulgence of Christ

79–84 simile (5): sunbeam shining through rift in cloud upon flowers is like risen Christ's ray on his companions in beatitude

85–87 apostrophe of Christ, expressing gratitude for His ascent

88–139 fifty-two verses for Mary, her first "moment" in the poem:

- 88–90 Mary as greatest "flame" of that host; Dante prays to her twice each day
- 91–96 a "torch" descends and circles Mary, "crowning" her
- 97–102 "simile" (6): Gabriel's melody makes the sweetest human music seem grating by comparison
- 103–108 Gabriel to Mary: "I will circle you until you rejoin Jesus in the Empyrean"
- 109–111 at end of Gabriel's song, host call out Mary's name
- 112–117 Primum Mobile too distant yet to be visible to Dante
- 118–120 Dante's eyes cannot follow Mary's ascent
- 121–125 simile (7): infant, after suckling, reaches up to mamma; so the host extend themselves up toward Mary
- 126–129 the remaining host sing "Regina celi"
- 130–132 the poet's exclamation of joy: those good sowers!
- 133–135 here they enjoy the treasure gained in exile
- 136–139 here, with the keys to such glory, Peter triumphs.

PARADISO XXIII

Come l'augello, intra l'amate fronde,
posato al nido de' suoi dolci nati
la notte che le cose ci nasconde,

che, per veder li aspetti disïati
e per trovar lo cibo onde li pasca,
in che gravi labor li sono aggrati,

previene il tempo in su aperta frasca,
e con ardente affetto il sole aspetta,
fiso guardando pur che l'alba nasca;

così la donna mïa stava eretta
e attenta, rivolta inver' la plaga
sotto la quale il sol mostra men fretta:

sì che, veggendola io sospesa e vaga,
fecimi qual è quei che disïando
altro vorria, e sperando s'appaga.

Ma poco fu tra uno e altro quando,
del mio attender, dico, e del vedere
lo ciel venir più e più rischiarando;

e Bëatrice disse: "Ecco le schiere
del trïunfo di Cristo e tutto 'l frutto
ricolto del girar di queste spere!"

Pariemi che 'l suo viso ardesse tutto,
e li occhi avea di letizia sì pieni,
che passarmen convien sanza costrutto.

Quale ne' plenilunïi sereni
Trivïa ride tra le ninfe etterne
che dipingon lo ciel per tutti i seni,

As the bird among the leafy branches that she loves,
perched on the nest with her sweet brood
all through the night, which keeps things veiled from us,

who in her longing to look upon their eyes and beaks
and to find the food to nourish them—
a task, though difficult, that gives her joy—

now, on an open bough, anticipates that time
and, in her ardent expectation of the sun,
watches intently for the dawn to break,

so was my lady, erect and vigilant,
seeking out the region of the sky
in which the sun reveals less haste.

I, therefore, seeing her suspended, wistful,
became as one who, filled with longing,
finds satisfaction in his hope.

But time was short between one moment and the next,
I mean between my expectation and the sight
of the sky turned more and more resplendent.

And Beatrice said: 'Behold the hosts
of Christ in triumph and all the fruit
gathered from the wheeling of these spheres!'

It seemed to me her face was all aflame,
her eyes so full of gladness
that I must leave that moment undescribed.

As, on clear nights when the moon is full,
Trivia smiles among the eternal nymphs
that deck the sky through all its depths,

vid' i' sopra migliaia di lucerne
un sol che tutte quante l'accendea,
come fa 'l nostro le viste superne;

e per la viva luce trasparea
la lucente sustanza tanto chiara
nel viso mio, che non la sostenea.

Oh Bëatrice, dolce guida e cara!
Ella mi disse: "Quel che ti sobranza
è virtù da cui nulla si ripara.

Quivi è la sapïenza e la possanza
ch'aprì le strade tra 'l cielo e la terra,
onde fu già sì lunga disïanza."

Come foco di nube si diserra
per dilatarsi sì che non vi cape,
e fuor di sua natura in giù s'atterra,

la mente mia così, tra quelle dape
fatta più grande, di sé stessa uscìo,
e che si fesse rimembrar non sape.

"Apri li occhi e riguarda qual son io;
tu hai vedute cose, che possente
se' fatto a sostener lo riso mio."

Io era come quei che si risente
di visïone oblita e che s'ingegna
indarno di ridurlasi a la mente,

quand' io udi' questa proferta, degna
di tanto grato, che mai non si stingue
del libro che 'l preterito rassegna.

Se mo sonasser tutte quelle lingue
che Polimnïa con le suore fero
del latte lor dolcissimo più pingue,

I saw, above the many thousand lamps,
a Sun that kindled each and every one
as ours lights up the sights we see above us,

and through that living light poured down
a shining substance. It blazed so bright
into my eyes that I could not sustain it.

O Beatrice, my sweet belovèd guide!
To me she said: 'What overwhelms you
is a force against which there is no defense.

'Here is the Wisdom and the Power that repaired
the roads connecting Heaven and the earth
that had so long been yearned for and desired.'

As fire breaks from a cloud,
swelling till it finds no room there,
and, against its nature, falls to earth,

just so my mind, grown greater at that feast,
burst forth, transported from itself,
and now cannot recall what it became.

'Open your eyes and see me as I am.
The things that you have witnessed
have given you the strength to bear my smile.'

I was like a man who finds himself awakened
from a dream that has faded and who strives
in vain to bring it back to mind

when I heard this invitation, deserving
of such gratitude as can never be erased
from the book that registers the past.

If at this moment all the tongues
that Polyhymnia and her sisters nurtured
with their sweetest, richest milk

per aiutarmi, al millesmo del vero
non si verria, cantando il santo riso
e quanto il santo aspetto facea mero;

e così, figurando il paradiso,
convien saltar lo sacrato poema,
come chi trova suo cammin riciso.

Ma chi pensasse il ponderoso tema
e l'omero mortal che se ne carca,
nol biasmerebbe se sott' esso trema:

non è pareggio da picciola barca
quel che fendendo va l'ardita prora,
né da nocchier ch'a sé medesmo parca.

"Perché la faccia mia sì t'innamora,
che tu non ti rivolgi al bel giardino
che sotto i raggi di Cristo s'infiora?

Quivi è la rosa in che 'l verbo divino
carne si fece; quivi son li gigli
al cui odor si prese il buon cammino."

Così Beatrice; e io, che a' suoi consigli
tutto era pronto, ancora mi rendei
a la battaglia de' debili cigli.

Come a raggio di sol, che puro mei
per fratta nube, già prato di fiori
vider, coverti d'ombra, li occhi miei;

vid' io così più turbe di splendori,
folgorate di sù da raggi ardenti,
sanza veder principio di folgóri.

O benigna vertù che sì li 'mprenti,
sù t'essaltasti per largirmi loco
a li occhi lì che non t'eran possenti.

should sound to aid me now, their song could not attain
one-thousandth of the truth in singing of that holy smile
and how it made her holy visage radiant.

And so, in representing Paradise,
the sacred poem must make its leap across,
as does a man who finds his path cut off.

But considering the heavy theme
and the mortal shoulder it weighs down,
no one would cast blame if it trembled with its load.

This is no easy voyage for a little bark,
this stretch of sea the daring prow now cleaves,
nor for a pilot who would spare himself.

'Why does my face arouse you so to love
you do not turn to see the lovely garden
now blossoming beneath the rays of Christ?

'There is the rose in which the Word of God
was turned to flesh. There are the lilies
for whose fragrance the right way was chosen.'

Beatrice said these words. And I, all eager
to follow her instruction, again resumed
the struggle, despite my feeble power of sight.

As, lit by the sun's rays streaming through broken clouds,
my eyes, sheltered by the shade,
once saw a field of flowers,

so now I saw a many-splendored throng
illuminated from above by blazing rays,
but could not see the source of all that brightness.

O gracious Power, who did thus imprint them!
You rose to more exalted heights to grant
their sight to eyes not ready to behold you.

Il nome del bel fior ch'io sempre invoco
e mane e sera, tutto mi ristrinse
90 l'animo ad avvisar lo maggior foco;

e come ambo le luci mi dipinse
il quale e il quanto de la viva stella
93 che là sù vince come qua giù vinse,

per entro il cielo scese una facella,
formata in cerchio a guisa di corona,
96 e cinsela e girossi intorno ad ella.

Qualunque melodia più dolce suona
qua giù e più a sé l'anima tira,
99 parrebbe nube che squarciata tona,

comparata al sonar di quella lira
onde si coronava il bel zaffiro
102 del quale il ciel più chiaro s'inzaffira.

"Io sono amore angelico, che giro
l'alta letizia che spira del ventre
105 che fu albergo del nostro disiro;

e girerommi, donna del ciel, mentre
che seguirai tuo figlio, e farai dia
108 più la spera suprema perché lì entre."

Così la circulata melodia
si sigillava, e tutti li altri lumi
111 facean sonare il nome di Maria.

Lo real manto di tutti i volumi
del mondo, che più ferve e più s'avviva
114 ne l'alito di Dio e nei costumi,

avea sopra di noi l'interna riva
tanto distante, che la sua parvenza,
117 là dov' io era, ancor non appariva:

The name of the fair flower I invoke
each morning and at evening time, enthralled my mind
as I gazed at the brightest of the flames.

When the quality and magnitude of the living star,
who surpasses up above as she surpassed below,
were painted on my eyes,

there descended through the sky a torch that,
circling, took on the likeness of a crown.
It encircled her and wheeled around her.

The sweetest melody, heard here below,
that most attracts our souls
would seem a burst of cloud-torn thunder

compared with the reverberation of that lyre
with which the lovely sapphire that so ensapphires
the brightest heaven was encrowned.

'I am angelic love and I encircle
the exalted joy breathed from the womb
that was the dwelling place of our desire,

'and I shall circle you, Lady of Heaven,
until you follow your Son to the highest sphere,
making it the more divine because you enter.'

Thus that circling music, sealing itself,
came to its conclusion, while all the other lights
made Mary's name resound.

The royal mantle of the universal turning spheres,
which most burns and is most quickened
in the breath of God and in His works,

was, at its inner boundary,
so very far above us that as yet,
from where I was, it was well beyond my seeing,

però non ebber li occhi miei potenza
di seguitar la coronata fiamma
che si levò appresso sua semenza.

E come fantolin che 'nver' la mamma
tende le braccia, poi che 'l latte prese,
per l'animo che 'nfin di fuor s'infiamma;

ciascun di quei candori in sù si stese
con la sua cima, sì che l'alto affetto
ch'elli avieno a Maria mi fu palese.

Indi rimaser lì nel mio cospetto,
"Regina celi" cantando sì dolce,
che mai da me non si partì 'l diletto.

Oh quanta è l'ubertà che si soffolce
in quelle arche ricchissime che fuoro
a seminar qua giù buone bobolce!

Quivi si vive e gode del tesoro
che s'acquistò piangendo ne lo essilio
di Babillòn, ove si lasciò l'oro.

Quivi trïunfa, sotto l'alto Filio
di Dio e di Maria, di sua vittoria,
e con l'antico e col novo concilio,
colui che tien le chiavi di tal gloria.

so that my eyes had not the power
to fasten on the crown-tipped flame
that rose along the path left by her sowing.

And, like a baby reaching out its arms
to *mamma* after it has drunk her milk,
its inner impulse kindled into outward flame,

all these white splendors were reaching upward
with their fiery tips, so that their deep affection
for Mary was made clear to me.

Then they remained there in my sight,
singing *Regina celi* with such sweetness
that my feeling of delight has never left me.

Oh, how great is the abundance
that is stored in granaries so rich above,
that down on earth were fields ripe for the sowing!

There they live, rejoicing in the treasure
they gained with tears of exile,
in Babylon, where they spurned the gold.

Beneath the exalted Son of God and Mary,
up there he triumphs in his victory,
with souls of the covenants old and new,
the one who holds the keys to such great glory.

PARADISO XXIII

1–12. This warm-hued and extended simile opens a canto that has long been admired as one of the most lyrical of the entire *Commedia.* It contains more similes than any canto since *Purgatorio* XXX (which has seven) and *Paradiso* XIV (eight), by merit of offering seven in all (and two simple comparisons). In contrast, the preceding two cantos together offered only a single striking example (XXI.34–42). When one considers them, their burden unabashedly religious and explanatory, one senses at once the differing register introduced by the presence here of affective poetry.

The first nine verses of the simile portray a mother bird awaiting the dawn so that she can find the food with which to feed her nestlings; the final tercet makes the terms of the comparison clear: Beatrice hopes soon to be able to nourish Dante with a vision of the final and best thing knowable by humankind, eternal beatitude in the presence of God. Nonetheless, for all the resemblances (and few of Dante's similes are as "neat" as this one) between mother bird and Beatrice, between soon-to-be-awake, soon-to-be-satisfied nestlings and Dante, we also can see that there is at least one crucial difference here as well. In the imagined earthly scene, the physical sun rises in the east; in the reported scene in the eighth sphere, the metaphoric "sun" descends from the zenith, a supernatural sun having risen at noon, as it were. Dante's theologized "transvaluation of value," so crucial a part of his strategy, especially in *Paradiso,* following examples found in the teaching of Jesus, is observable here. What will the joys of Heaven be like? Like the pleasure of being fed, but having nothing to do with eating; like the pleasure of the bride when her bridegroom comes to her, but having nothing to do with sexuality; like the pleasure of possessing great wealth, but having nothing to do with money.

See Goffis (Goff.1968.1), p. 838, for notice of Dante's reliance here on Lactantius's *De ave Phoenice,* vv. 39–42, in the portrait of his mother bird, as was first claimed by Enrico Proto (*BSDI 22* [1915], pp. 72–73). This attribution is now supported by a number of commentators. The passage presents the bird at the top of a tree, turned to where the sun will rise and waiting for its rays. Some have objected that the phoenix, as near-immortal bird, does not seem appropriate to this context and deny its presence behind Dante's lines. Lactantius, who lived into the early fourth century, was imbued with the Christian faith, so much so that he was hired by the emperor Constantine to instruct his children. It is not certain he was in fact the author of the poem; what is certain is that, as a Christian symbol (precisely of the reborn Christ), the bird, whoever was its author, is appropriate to the atmosphere of Dante's moment, preparing for a vision of Christ in His flesh.

1. It seems entirely fitting that a canto centrally devoted to the mother of Jesus begin with this image of the selfless and loving mother bird. Such is the retrograde nature of some commentators that they debate whether this bird is meant to be taken as male or female. While it is true that the gender of the bird is not specified, and while male birds do indeed care for nestlings, the context of the simile and of the canto as a whole makes a father bird an otiose thought.

2. The phrase *dolci nati* (sweet brood) may have its origin in Virgil, *Georgics* II.523, "dulces . . . nati," in that glowing tableau of the bucolic life in the "good old days" of pre-Roman Italy. Indeed, as Bosco points out in his introductory note to this canto, there are many classical references peeking out at us from these lines, including that one. Apparently the first to cite this passage in the *Georgics* was Scartazzini (comm. to this verse); see also Marigo (Mari.1909.1).

3. For the blackness of the night that hides things from view, Tommaseo was the first to point to Virgil (*Aen.* VI.271–272): "ubi caelum condidit umbra / Iuppiter, et rebus nox abstulit atra colorem" (when Jupiter has buried the sky in shade, and black Night has stolen from the world her hues [tr. H.R. Fairclough]).

4. There seems no reason to honor the views of those who see in the *aspetti disïati* anything other than the "faces" of the nestlings. Yet some believe that the phrase refers to the locations of nourishment for the young birds or even the "aspects" of the soon-to-rise Sun.

As Tommaseo (comm. to vv. 4–6) points out, words for "desire" and "desiring" occur four times in this canto (see also vv. 14, 39, 105).

7. The bird now ventures from the nest farther along the branch, where the leaves are less thick, in order to have a better view of sunrise.

9. For the medieval *alba* (a love-song, lamenting the coming of dawn, sung to one's beloved after a night of lovemaking), see Saville (Savi.1972.1). And see Picone (Pico.1994.2), pp. 211–13, for the relevance also of the religious *alba*. Picone points out that in Dante's scene the dawn

is a welcome presence, betiding the renewal of affection rather than the sad time of necessary separation for lovers.

10–11. This language for Beatrice's attitude recalls that found in *Purgatorio* XIX.26, where Beatrice (if that is she in Dante's dream) is *santa e presta* (holy and alert); in that dream it is Dante who makes "straight" the deformed witch he wants to love.

11–12. Unriddled, these lines indicate the heavenly equivalent of noon on earth, the zenith of the universe. We remember that the physical sun lies *below* the place where Dante finds himself. Beatrice is expecting "sunrise" there, at the zenith, not at the "horizon." The descent of the blessed spirits of the Empyrean, naturally, is from "true north," the very top of the universe. Lombardi points out (comm. to these verses) that the heavenly Jerusalem is directly over the earthly one; this "supernatural sunrise" calls our attention to the fact that the "sun" that is about to "dawn" is indeed extraordinary.

12. The Sun at its zenith seems to "move" more slowly because it covers the smaller part of its arc, as seen by us; see Tozer (comm. to *Purg.* XXXIII.103–105): "At noon the sun is brightest, and the imagination naturally conceives that it pauses or slackens its speed when it reaches the highest point of its course."

13–18. Dante, as nestling, must await his "food." Like the subject it describes, delayed satisfaction both for giver and recipient, the passage continues to draw out that moment of satisfaction, until the "sun" is finally described as having risen.

19–21. While a great deal of preparation has led up to this moment (and it should now be clear that it is this moment that necessitated the invocation in the last canto), it is nonetheless a vast surprise, once we realize that what has just occurred is a "visit" by the entire Church Triumphant to the second of the heavenly spheres beneath the placeless, timeless Empyrean. There the object of their "visit" is no other and no more than Dante Alighieri, "a Florentine by birth but not in his behaviors." There are few moments in the poem, not even the final vision of the triune God, that come close to reaching the level of daring found here. The saved who dwell with Christ are thought of as the souls that have been harvested by Him (some in the Harrowing [see *Inf.* IV.52–63], slightly fewer than half of them later), in part because of the positive qualities bred in them by the stars at their birth. Aversano (Aver.2000.2), p. 104, suggests that the descent of these souls from the Empyrean may mimic that described in the Apocalypse (Apoc. 21:2), "And I saw the holy city, new Jerusalem, coming down out of heaven from God, . . ." (*descendentem de coelo a Deo*).

There has been and remains dispute as to who exactly comes down to be seen by Dante. Some embarrassment is felt on the poet's behalf had he wanted the reader to believe that all the saints in Heaven came down to greet him. Embarrassing or not, that seems the only possible reading: *tutto il frutto* (all the fruit) does not allow for a more modest, gentlemanly selectivity.

We are forced also to reflect that Dante has seen some of these souls before. If all of them now descend, their number includes all the souls since Piccarda whom he has already seen in the various seven previous heavens.

20. For a meditation on the "triumph of Christ" announced by Beatrice, see Lo Cascio (Loca.1974.1), pp. 76–92.

22–24. The by-now customary (and, within the poet's strategy, necessary) upward gradation in Beatrice's joy as she gets nearer her God may seem more justified here than at other times. She is now once more in the presence of those with whom she shares Eternity; and now for the first time she is accompanied by her Dante. She is "home," and escorting Dante to his home as well.

24. The phrase *sanza costrutto* ("without putting it in words") is a bit unusual. For more on *costrutto*, see the note to *Paradiso* XII.67. Mattalia (comm. to this verse) explains that it means "the parts and elements of 'discourse' " and goes on to suggest that, in *De vulgari eloquentia*, Dante refers to it as *constructio*, that is, the building blocks of language.

25–30. The second simile in the canto compares the Moon, when it is largest and brightest, surrounded by the other astral presences, to this "sun," irradiating the host of the blessed. There can be no doubt as to what this "sun" is. For here Dante is looking at (if unable to see) the living light that is Jesus Christ, like His mother, present here in the resurrected flesh worn, at least now, before the general resurrection, by them alone. Some commentators, perhaps puzzled by the strange and lone occurrence in which the assembled citizenry of the Empyrean descends as a unit to the nether heavens, believe that this "sun" is a "symbol" of Christ; however, we are meant to understand that it *is* Christ (see the note to vv. 31–33). Here is Jacopo della Lana (comm. to these verses) on this passage: "Or qui dà esemplo come la substanzia della umanità di Cristo, ch'era sopra tutti li predetti beati, luceva più di tutti, e tutti li illuminava, simile a questo sensibile sole, che illumina tutti li corpi celesti" (Now [Dante] here gives an example of how the substance of the humanity of Christ, which was above all the aforementioned blessed souls, shone more brightly than all of them, and illumined them all, just as does this material Sun, which illumines all the heavenly bodies).

25–27. For Trivia, the Moon, see Picone (Pico.1994.2), pp. 213–17. He insists on a source, not in Horace or Virgil, as is proposed by some, but in Ovid (*Metam*. III.138–252). Picone's treatment of Dante's interpretation of Actaeon resembles Brownlee's reading of his Semele (see the note to *Par.* XXI.5–12); it is a subversive reading of the "tragic" original, in which Actaeon is torn apart by Diana's hounds. Now Dante/Actaeon finds a better resolution.

31–33. The resurrected body of Christ shines down upon Dante's blinded eyes. Singleton, who on seven separate occasions in his comments to this canto insists that what we witness of Christ's presence is not to be taken literally but "symbolically," here (comm. to vv. 31–32) believes that "*Sustanza* is used in the scholastic sense (*substantia*), denoting that which has separate existence, as contrasted with 'accident,' which is a quality existing in a substance. See Dante's use of these terms in *Vita nuova* XXV.1–2. With this term the stress is rather on the human Christ. The whole vision is symbolic, however—a point not to be forgotten." In fact "the whole vision" is to be taken as the most "real" experience Dante has yet had, as any such seeing of Christ in His flesh would have to be.

34. In a single verse Dante culminates his long and varying experience of Beatrice in this recognition of what her guidance has meant and where it has finally led him. When she came to him as *mediatrix*, one whose being was imprinted by Christ in order to lead him back to his Savior, he was often uncertain. Now the identity between them is finally sensed on his pulses, and he is properly grateful. This is a line that many readers find themselves greatly moved by, without perhaps being able to verbalize the reasons for their emotion. It was amazing, he must reflect, that she had faith in such as him.

For an essay on the relationship between Beatrice and Virgil as Dante's guides, see Punzi (Punz.1999.1). For the sense that Dante, here and elsewhere, has totally revised his earlier and earthly sense of Beatrice, see Paolo Cherchi (Cher.2004.1): "This is the true praise. Beatrice loses nothing of her physical beauty; indeed, she remains the most fair among the fair. However, the 'diseroticization,' so to speak, comes . . . from Dante, who comes to understand, at a certain point in his narrative, that the lady whom he desires is truly 'venuta da cielo in terra a miracol mostrare' " (come from Heaven to earth to reveal a miracle—*VN* XXVI.6).

Masciandaro's *lectura* of this canto (Masc.1995.1) demonstrates the importance of aesthetic concerns throughout this particularly beautiful canto.

35. For the only other use of the Provençalism *sobranza* (overwhelms), see the note to *Paradiso* XX.97.

37–39. Beatrice's discourse leaves little doubt but that she and Dante are gazing on Jesus Himself. See I Corinthians 1:24, Paul's description of Christ as "the Wisdom of God."

39. It was 4,302 years that Adam waited for Christ to harrow him from Limbo. See the note to *Paradiso* XXVI.118–120.

40–45. The third simile of the canto compares the swelling lightning bolt, escaping from the cloud that can no longer contain it, and falling, against its nature, downward, to Dante's mind, swelling with its rapt vision of Christ, escaping from its "container," and becoming other than it had been.

Dante's meteorology (for this phenomenon Steiner [comm. to vv. 40–42] cites Albertus Magnus, *Meteor.* I.iv.7) held that lightning resulted when contention between fiery and aquatic elements within a cloud resulted in the fiery part becoming too large and bursting the edges of the aqueous envelope, as it were. Theorists of the phenomenon were hard pressed to explain *why* this excess of fire should, only in this instance, fall downward rather than follow its natural inclination up.

43. The noun *dape* (Latin *dapes*, viands), a hapax in the poem, shows Dante's hand once again being forced by rhyme. Lombardi (comm. to this verse) refers to the hymn composed by St. Ambrose, describing a saintly man who thus "dapes supernas obtinet" (obtains supernal food).

45. It seems clear that the author wishes us to understand that the protagonist, blinded by Christ, has had a Pauline (or Johannine) *raptus*.

46–48. Dante's vision has now readied him, if not to see Christ in His splendor, then at least to be able to have a version of that experience with respect to Beatrice. Heretofore, she has made herself his mirror (e.g., *Par.* XVIII.13–18); now she invites him to see her as herself; in the previous sphere (*Par.* XXI.4–12, XXI.63, XXII.10–11) he was denied her smile (which he last saw in Mars [*Par.* XVIII.19]). Now he possesses the capacity to behold her true being, since his experience of the Church Triumphant under Christ has raised his ability to deal with such lofty things.

As Brownlee points out (Brow.1991.2), pp. 230–31, this marks the completion of the "Semele program" *in bono*, Dante's being able to look upon his "goddess" in her true nature.

49–51. The tercet, while offering a simple comparison rather than, strictly speaking, a simile (see, e.g., *Par.* XXII.2–3, 4–6 for like phenomena), continues the similetic tonality of the canto. Here we find another comparison involving a state of mind (see the note to *Inf.* XXX.136–141). We may be reminded both of Dante's final vision of Beatrice in Christ in *Vita nuova* XLII and (if we have already read this poem at least once) of the final vision in *Paradiso* XXXIII. In both those cases, as here, there is at stake a *visione* that cannot be brought back to consciousness. In all three cases we are speaking of what is clearly presented as a true vision, not a dream, even if here this is *compared* to an ordinary dreamer's attempt to revive in himself the experience of the dream from which he has awakened. Our task as interpreters of text is not made easier by the fact that in Dante's Italian both ordinary dreaming and privileged sight of the highest kind may be signified by the same word, *visione*. For an attempt to demonstrate how carefully Dante developed and deployed necessary distinctions in his vocabulary of seeing as early as in his *Vita nuova*, see Hollander (Holl.1974.1).

In the last tercet the poet has used the verb *vedere* to register Dante's vision of Jesus, the "sun" that is too bright for him as yet to take in; Beatrice invites him to look upon *her* as she truly is (if he cannot yet sustain a vision of Christ). He had never before enjoyed, in the narrative of her presence in the *Commedia*, from *Purgatorio* XXX until right now, such beholding of Beatrice "face-to-face." However, it seems probable that we are meant to consider that she was present to his vision in an at least approximately similar manifestation in the last chapter of the *Vita nuova*.

And thus this moment is meant to draw that one back to mind. There, too, Beatrice was a living soul in the presence of God.

50. Poletto (comm. to vv. 49–54) notes that this hapax, the Latinism *oblita* (forgotten, faded from memory) is deployed in the *Epistola a Cangrande* (XIII.80). The context of that passage is perhaps remembered here: "This again is conveyed to us in Matthew, where we read that the three disciples fell on their faces, and record nothing thereafter, as though memory had failed them (*quasi obliti*). And in Ezekiel it is written: 'And when I saw it, I fell upon my face.' And should these not satisfy the cavillers, let them read Richard of St. Victor in his book *On Contemplation*; let them read Bernard in his book *On Consideration*; let them read Augustine in his book *On the Capacity of the Soul*; and they will cease from their cavilling" (tr. P. Toynbee). Perhaps unsurprisingly, some of these texts (particularly those of Richard of St. Victor and of Bernard) have been before our eyes in notes to the last contemplative heaven. This portion of the *Epistola* (XIII.77–84) is a fairly lengthy commentary on *Paradiso* I.7–9. The context is supplied by the extramundane experiences of Paul and Dante, those uniquely favored humans who had seen God in their ascent to the Empyrean.

52–53. Beatrice's "offer" to let Dante see her face-to-face, as she truly is, that is, blessed in the company of the elect, is the greatest gift she has ever bestowed on Dante. Among other things, it promises his own blessedness to come, for how would God sanction such a vision to a mortal bound to perdition?

54. The language here, too, puts us in mind of the *Vita nuova*, now of the opening reference (*VN* I.1) to Dante's *libro della mia memoria* (book of my memory), in which Beatrice's significant presences are recorded. Strangely enough, because the self-citation does seem obvious, surprisingly few (ten) commentators to *Paradiso* XXIII refer to the *Vita nuova* as being focally present behind the phrasing of verse 54. Once again the first is Scartazzini (comm. to vv. 52–54).

55–59. Not even if all the most inspired (pagan) poets, inspired by all the Muses (led, in this consideration, by the one associated with sacred song, Polyhymnia), should come to Dante's aid, would that serve to reveal more than a tiny bit of the Christian truth he now saw in Beatrice.

There happen to be in the poem nine invocations (no more than five of them addressed to traditional Muses) and nine references to the Muses; see Hollander (Holl.1976.2), n. 3, who also offers an account of the inaccuracies of Muse-counting from 1896 to 1973, from Scartazzini to Singleton. Since we have known for a long time of the importance of the number nine to Dante, such failed accounting is surprising. But see Hollander's belated discussion (in his later version of this article [Holl.1980.1], p. 32, n. 1a) of Fabio Fabbri (Fabb.1910.1), p. 186, who lists the nine invocations correctly.

For this trope (nursing Muses) as it is developed in the (only slightly?) later *Eclogues*, see Heil (Heil.2003.1). And see Cestaro (Cest.2003.1), pp. 139, 162, 166, for the Muses as nourishing in *Purgatorio* and *Paradiso*.

55–57. It has become fairly usual (beginning with Tommaseo [comm. to this tercet]) for commentators to cite *Aeneid* VI.625–627, for example, Poletto (comm. to vv. 55–60): "No, had I a hundred tongues, a hundred mouths, and voice of iron, I could not sum up all the forms of crime, or rehearse all the tale of torments" [tr. H. R. Fairclough]. The Sibyl is here reacting to what she and Aeneas might have seen had they entered Tartarus instead of proceeding to the Elysian Fields. Since we are seeing the inhabitants of the Christian version of those "fields," the passage in the *Aeneid* seems doubly apt.

56. Polyhymnia is mentioned as one of the nine Muses by all the early commentators; most of them go on to identify her with memory rather than a specific artistic form, as she is in handbooks today (with the sacred hymn). The first commentator to associate her with hymns was Andreoli (comm. to vv. 55–57), etymologizing her Greek name; with him she becomes, for the modern commentary tradition, the Muse "of many hymns."

61–63. Read as literally as it probably should be, Dante's remark indicates that his poem *right now* is "representing Paradise," and doing so for the very first time. That is why he required a preparatory invocation (*Par.* XXII.121–123) for this portion of the poem (now combined with an at least equally attention-summoning "non-invocation," vv. 55–63). True Paradise is found only, one may respond, after *Paradiso* XXX.90, once Dante begins to see the courts of Heaven as they are. However, singularly and strikingly, it is here, in the Fixed Stars, that he is allowed to see those who dwell there, whom he will see again once he himself has reached the Empyrean. In this vein, among many, see Goffis (Goff.1968.1), p. 826, referring to this canto as beginning the "second part" of *Paradiso*. However, see Benvenuto da Imola, for the kind of misapprehension that dogs him whenever Dante represents himself as having looked upon reality. Here is Benvenuto's response to this tercet: "*figurando il paradiso*, that is, representing poetically, figuratively; for this passage does not represent real things. . . ."

Scartazzini (comm. to verse 61) documents the confusion caused by these lines: If "figurando il paradiso" means "representing [true] paradise," that is, the Church Triumphant, citizenry of the Empyrean (and that is not everyone's understanding, if it seems to be a just one), then why does the "sacred poem" indeed "have to make a leap"? There is a fairly straightforward interpretation: The poem "overleaps" an intervening heaven, the Primum Mobile, in finding its subject matter in those who inhabit the Empyrean. It is in that sense that he is like a man "who finds his path obstructed" and has to leap over the impediment.

Tommaseo (comm. to this tercet) puts it into relationship with *Inferno* XXXII.9, where Dante is concerned with the difficulty of describing the bottom of the universe (here, with the top of it). There we find, immediately following this expression of concern, an invocation; here, immediately preceding an expression of similar difficulty, a non-invocation.

61. In the *Commedia* the word *paradiso* has only a single presence outside the *cantica* that bears its name (*Purg.* I.99). Its first clear reference to the Empyrean (rather than to the celestial regions in general) perhaps occurs only in its sixth appearance, in *Paradiso* (XV.36).

64–66. This is an "indirect address to the reader," as it were; for the extent of the real kind in the poem, see the notes to *Inferno* VIII.94–96 and *Paradiso* X.22–27.

Daniello, Lombardi, Tommaseo, Scartazzini, Torraca (all in their comments on this tercet) cite Horace's much-quoted passage ("sumite materiam") from his *Ars poetica* (vv. 38–41): "Take a subject, you writers, equal to your strength, and ponder long what your shoulders refuse, and what they are able to bear. Whoever shall choose a theme within his range, neither speech will fail him, nor clearness of order" (tr. H. R. Fairclough). Torraca reminds the reader that Dante had earlier cited this passage in *De vulgari eloquentia* (II.iv.4).

The altogether possible pun on Homer's name, unrecorded in the commentaries, in Dante's rephrasing of Horatian *humerus* (shoulder) as *òmero mortal* (mortal shoulder), since *Omèro* is Homer's name in Italian (see

Inf. IV.88), was noted in the 1970s by Professor Janet Smarr, while she was a graduate student at Princeton. That Dante may have for a moment thought of himself as the "Italian Homer" would not come as a surprise. If he did, the profoundly famous Homer (see Horace, *Ars poetica* 401: *insignis Homerus*), by any stretch of the imagination "immortal," has an Italian counterpart in the very mortal Dante. For Dante's earlier reference to a Homeric being seeming like a god (and thus immortal), see *Vita nuova* II.8.

67–69. This tercet, recapping the nautical imagery that shapes the beginnings of each of the last two canticles of the poem, allows us to realize that, in some real sense, Dante put forward this canto as a liminal space, at the border of the infinite, as it were. In that perspective, the text that follows directly after this one is the final third of *Paradiso* XXX, where we are again in the direct presence of Eternity.

These verses pick up various thematic elements from earlier in the poem. For the "little bark" with its unworthy readers, see *Paradiso* II.1; for the *Commedia* as a *legno*, see *Paradiso* II.3; for the angelic steersman as *celestial nocchiero*, see *Purgatorio* II.43. We have progressed to that point at which the poet has himself become the pilot who will not spare himself in guiding us to our heavenly destination.

Is this tercet a boundary stone for a "fourth part" of the *Commedia*, consisting in Dante's experience of the Empyrean, begun here, only to be interrupted by six more cantos that take place in the last two spheres?

67. The word *pareggio* has caused difficulty. Its other use in the poem (*Par.* XXI.90) has not seemed problematic to the commentators (it is a verb form meaning "I match" or "I equal"). Here, on the other hand, where it is a predicate nominative, it has caused traffic jams. The value of the word in its two most favored forms (there have been as many as seven candidates at one time or another) is close enough that one may say that the difference is not worth a large investment of effort: Some sense of a voyage over an extensive piece of sea is what most think is meant, however they arrive at their conclusion.

70–75. That the protagonist is looking upon the Church Triumphant is beyond question, despite occasional shilly-shallying about how many of the saved are represented as having come down to be seen by Dante (since Beatrice's words at verse 20 make it plain that all are here). The question that remains is *why* the poet engineered this extraordinary scene. The commentators have not ventured an opinion, perhaps because they do not fully take in what an extraordinary moment this is. It is simply amazing to find that all the blessed have appeared in space and time, that is, in the Starry Sphere and before we enter the Empyrean. One might counter that this is similar to their appearances through the spheres. But there they came as "emissaries" of themselves; now they *are* themselves (without, of course, their flesh), and are arranged as they shall be for eternity. For a precise understanding of the difference, see Borzi (Borz.1989.1), p. 644: "Il Canto XXIII del *Paradiso* segna il passaggio dalla rappresentazione dei beati distribuiti, per ragioni didattiche, nei sette cieli, alla visione di un Paradiso còlto nella realtà teologica della sua unità" (Canto XXIII marks the passage from the representation of the blessed souls distributed, for didactic reasons, through the seven heavens, to the vision of a Paradise caught in the theological reality of its oneness).

71. The word *giardino* (garden), absent from the poem since *Purgatorio* VI.105, where it was used in the phrase "the garden of the empire," now, referring to the members of the Church Triumphant, reappears. It will do so again at *Paradiso* XXVI.110, where it refers to the garden of Eden, and then in XXXI.97 and XXXII.39, where it will signify the Empyrean, Eden regained.

73–75. We hear that there are at least two kinds of flowers in this "garden" (verse 71). The single rose, by common consent, is Mary; the lilies, if with slightly less unanimous support, represent the apostles, leading humankind toward salvation in Christ (along "the right way"). See Jacopo della Lana (comm. to verse 74) on three reasons for identifying the lilies with the apostles: (1) because lilies are white (signifying faith), vermilion in their inner petals (signifying incorruptibility and charity), and fragrant (signifying preaching and hope).

78. For a second time (see vv. 31–33), the brightness of Jesus overwhelms Dante's ability to look at Him. (The line literally means "the battle of the weak brows.")

79–84. The precondition for this simile, as we finally will realize in verse 86, is that Jesus has withdrawn, going back up to the Empyrean. And so now He, as the Sun, shines through a rift in clouds and illuminates a spot of earth, representing, resolved from the simile, the host of Christ's first triumph (the Harrowing) and the souls of all those saved after that.

82–84. On a beam of light passing through a cloud as an expression of Dante's light physics, see Gilson (Gils.2000.1), pp. 150–69. Boyde (Boyd.1993.1), pp. 67–68, deals with its three prime elements: *luce* (the source of light), *lumen* (in Dante's Italian, *raggio*, the beam along which the *luce* travels), *splendor[e]* (the surface that the light irradiates). Perhaps nowhere else in the poem is this arrangement articulated so neatly, each element receiving one line in the tercet, but that is not to say it is not often present. See the note to *Paradiso* XII.9.

85–87. Christ, addressed as His paternal attribute, Power, is now thanked by the poet for having made, by withdrawing, his experience of the scene possible. His overwhelming light, which is compared to the sun being present only through a chink in the clouds (His "ray" that illuminates the resplendent flowers in a field without blinding the onlooker by shining full on him as well), is thus only resplendent on the souls that constitute the "garden" of the Church Triumphant.

88–89. This passage brings out emotional responses in even hardened commentators, as demonstrated by a quick sampling of their responses to it in the DDP. And surely they are correct in thinking that Dante is revealing a personal trait, what a stern Protestant would describe, with perhaps an Anglo-Saxon *harrumph*, as "Mariolatry." This is, nonetheless, one of the few touches in the poem that allow us to feel the presence of an ordinary human being beneath the writer's words (we often are allowed to share Dante's thoughts, only rarely his doings), one who is occupied with the details of daily living, praying to the Intercessor before he descends the stairs in a stranger's house and then again after he climbs them in the evening (see *Par.* XVII.60).

90. For the significance of Mary's appearing to be greater in size than the other saints, see the note to *Paradiso* XXII.28–29.

91–102. This little scene reflects a genre familiar from paintings of the time, an Annunciation, with its two familiar figures, the archangel Gabriel and the mother of Jesus. It ends with the canonical color for Mary, her earmark glowing blue. Porena (comm. to vv. 106–108), however, denies that the angelic presence here is that of Gabriel, urging rather the candidacy of an unnamed Seraph.

93. Mary is as elevated over all the other saints in Heaven as she exceeded in virtue all other living beings while she was on earth.

95. For the Virgin's crown, created by Gabriel's circling, see Carroll (comm. to vv. 91–108): "Aquinas distinguishes between the *essential bliss* of heaven and the *accidental reward*. The essential bliss he calls the *corona aurea*, or simply *aurea*; and the accidental reward, *aureola*, a diminutive of *aurea*. All saints in the Fatherland receive the *aurea*, the essential bliss of perfect union of the soul with God; but the *aureola*, or accidental reward, is given only to those who, in the earthly warfare, have won an excellent victory over some special foe: virgins, martyrs, and doctors and preachers [*Summa*, Supp., q. xcvi, a. 1]."

97–102. Similetic in its feeling, this passage does without the trope's traditional markers but surely has telling effect: "Ave Maria," for instance, would sound like a cloud crackling with thunder if compared with the "song" created by the angelic affection for Mary.

100. While the poet never explicitly says that Gabriel is singing, he makes it clear that the angel is indeed doing so by referring to him as a "lyre."

103–108. The Starry Sphere is the one most characterized by singing. (For the program of song in the last *cantica*, see the note to *Par.* XXI.58–60.)

104. The word *ventre* (womb, belly), about as explicitly a low-vernacular word as a Christian poet could employ in this exalted context, brought forth a wonderfully numb-brained remark in complaint by Raffaele Andreoli (comm. to vv. 103–105): "più nobilmente il Petrarca: 'Virginal chiostro' " (Petrarch says this more nobly: "virginal cloister"). His insistence on the desirability of a "higher," more "civilized" stylistic level strikes a reader sympathetic to Dante's strategy as inept.

107–108. If we needed clarification, here it is: Jesus has returned, and Mary is about to return, to the Empyrean. As far as we can tell, all the other members of the Church Triumphant are meant to be understood as still being present down here in the eighth heaven.

110. The "other lights" are clearly the members of the Church Triumphant, not including Jesus and Mary.

112–120. Trucchi (comm. to these verses) considers this scene, surmounting those that previously reflected the Annunciation and the Coronation of the Virgin, a revisitation of her Assumption; as Carroll already had suggested (comm. to vv. 91–108), this scene represents "the heavenly counterpart of the Assumption of the body of Mary, which, according to the belief of the Church, God did not suffer to see corruption. Like her Son, she rose from the dead on the third day, and was received by Him and the angels into the joy of Paradise."

It would be like Dante to have worked those three major episodes in her life into his scene, the first representing her being chosen, the second her victory over death, and the third her bodily Assumption into Heaven, a reward she shares with her Son alone. The other commentators, with the exception of Carroll (comm. to vv. 109–129), do not mention it.

112–114. The poet refers to the *primo mobile*, the ninth sphere, also known as the Crystalline Sphere (because, even though it is material, it contains no other heavenly bodies in addition to itself). It is "royal" because it is the closest of the nine "volumes" (revolving heavens, or spheres) to God.

115–120. Since his eyes could not yet see the Crystalline Sphere, they of course could not follow Mary's rising still farther, that is, beyond that sphere and back "home" into the Empyrean.

120. Mary sowed her seed, Jesus, in the world.

121–126. This final simile of the canto portrays the denizens of the Empyrean, currently visiting Dante in the eighth heaven, as infants reaching up with gratitude to their mommies who have just nursed them. We remember that, in the non-invocation (vv. 55–60), Dante referred to the Muses' milk that had nourished classical poets (verse 57), whose songs would not be much help at all in singing Beatrice's smile. That milk is evidently in contrast with the one referred to here. This milk, we understand, is a nourishing vernacular, one quite different from the Latin *latte* that is of little nutritional value for a Christian poet. (See Hollander [Holl.1980.2].)

The word "mamma" has an interesting presence in this poem (see the notes to *Inf.* XXXII.1–9 and to *Purg.* XXI.97–99). It is used a total of five times, once in *Inferno*, twice in *Purgatorio* (last in *Purg.* XXX.44), and twice in this final canticle (first in *Par.* XIV.64). Here it picks up on its last use in *Purgatorio*. It is always a part of Dante's rather boisterous championing of the "low vernacular," and never more naturally than in this warmly affectionate scene that represents the members of the Church Triumphant stretching upward in expression of their love for Mary.

128. In the wake of Mary's ascent, following Jesus back up to the Empyrean, the rest of the members of the Church Triumphant sing her praise. From the beginning of the commentary tradition, with Jacopo della Lana (comm. to this verse), the hymn "Queen of Heaven" has been identified as an antiphon sung at Easter, celebrating the resurrection of Jesus. (An antiphon is a responsive song, based on a psalm, sung by the congregation, after the reading of that psalm, which forms the text of the lesson at Matins or Vespers. This particular antiphon was used in the eight-day period defining the Easter season, Palm Sunday to Easter itself.) Scartazzini (comm. to this verse) gives the complete Latin text, six verses, each ending with the cry of praise "hallelujah." (For the English text, see Singleton [comm. to this verse].) Both the third and sixth verses of the antiphon refer to the resurrection of Jesus; since He has recently (verse 86) Himself gone back up, we probably (and are meant to) think of His first ascent, in the flesh then as now.

130–135. In our translation, we have mainly followed Carroll (comm. to vv. 130–139), who has Dante turning from his admiration of Mary to "the heavenly treasures stored up in the Apostles. The metaphors, it must be confessed, are somewhat mixed. The Apostles are at once the sowers or the soil (depending on how we understand *bobolce*) and the chests in which the abundant harvest is stored. The harvest is not simply their own personal bliss, but the life and joy they have in the treasure of redeemed souls all round them in this Heaven, won in weeping in the Babylonian exile of earth, where for this wealth, they abandoned gold."

130–132. Lino Pertile (Pert.2006.1) demonstrates that many elements found in this canto are reprocessed in Dante's first *Eclogue*, and goes on to hypothesize that this, the first modern European classical eclogue, was written soon after Dante had finished working on this canto, and that his reference, in the eclogue, to the ten "pails of milk" that he hopes soon to send to Giovanni del Virgilio, his poetic correspondent, are precisely the final ten cantos of the *Paradiso*, a bold and interesting idea first proposed by Carroll (comm. to *Par.* XXV.1–12).

132. The word *bobolce*, a hapax, one, more than most, the deployment of which is obviously forced by rhyme. See Enrico Malato, "bobolca," *ED* I

(1970), for the various interpretations. We believe that it probably refers, as most of the early commentators believed, to the apostles as "sowers" of the "seeds" of the new faith.

133–135. The first tercet of the concluding seven-line flourish celebrates the victory of the triumphant Church, seen for the last time in this realm. There is no valediction for them, only celebration.

Pietro Alighieri (Pietro1, comm. to vv. 130–136) was apparently the first (and remains one of the surprisingly few) to note the presence here of an allusion to Psalm 136 [137]:1: "By the waters of Babylon, there we sat down and wept when we remembered Zion," a text Dante himself had previously remembered in *Epistola* VII.30 (as was noted by Poletto [comm. to vv. 130–135]).

It is worth noting here (it will be unmistakably clear in *Paradiso* XXXII) that Dante specifically refers to the Hebrews who were saved ("the treasure / they gained with tears of exile, / in Babylon"). It will come as a shock to some readers to learn that fully half of those in Paradise are, in fact, ancient Hebrews who believed in Christ as their savior. (See *Par.* XXXII.22–24.)

133. For the importance (and changing significance) of the word *tesoro* (treasure), see the note to *Par.* XVII.121.

Tommaseo (comm. to vv. 133–135) here puts into play both Matthew 6:20 (about laying up *true* treasure in Heaven) and 19:29 ("And everyone who has left houses or brothers or sisters or father or mother or children or lands, for my name's sake, will receive a hundredfold and will inherit eternal life").

136–139. Now the poet sets all his attention on St. Peter, who will examine the protagonist on faith, the first of the three theological virtues, in Canto XXIV, serving as guide in the first and the last of the following four cantos. In this heaven, he will share speaking parts with two other of the original disciples, James and John, as well as with the first father, Adam. Peter will speak in both *Paradiso* XXIV (eight times for a total of 54 verses) and XXVII (an utterance in 36 verses and in two parts, both devoted to a ringing denunciation of the corrupt papacy).

PARADISO XXIV

OUTLINE

STARRY SPHERE

1–9 Beatrice's apostrophe of the host (minus Mary and Christ)
10–12 in response the souls whirl in delight while Dante looks;
13–18 simile (1): clock-mechanisms and the various "dancers";
19–21 a "flame," as bright as any other there, approached them;
22–27 three times it circled Beatrice with a song so divine that Dante's phantasy could not preserve it;
28–33 **Peter** (not yet named) addresses Beatrice, whose prayer drew him from his colleagues to minister to Dante;
34–45 Beatrice to Peter: "question this man on Faith";
46–51 simile (2): bachelor preparing for his examination and Dante readying himself for questioning;
52–57 Peter's first question: "What is Faith?"
58–66 Dante's first response, addressed to Peter, citing Paul.
67–69 Peter's follow-up: "Why did Paul refer to 'substances' and then 'evidences'?"
70–78 Dante's second response: "Because Faith gives the most substantial help we mortals have for finding evidence."
79–85 Peter is pleased, and continues with his third question: "The alloy and the weight of this coin are well examined, but have you got it in your purse?"
86–87 Dante's third response: "Yes, I do."
88–90 Peter's fourth question: "Where did you get this gem?"
91–96 Dante's fourth response: "From the two Testaments."
97–99 Peter: "What makes them divinely inspired?"
100–102 Dante's fifth response: "The proof is found in miracles."
103–105 Peter: "But who assures you that these ever happened? Is your argument not a circular one?"
106–111 Dante's sixth response: "The greatest miracle is that the world turned to Christ without miracles."

112–114 The host sang "Te Deum laudamus" in Italian;
115–123 Peter examines Dante on his faith's substance and source.
124–138 Dante's seventh response: Peter at Christ's tomb;
139–147 Dante's belief in the Trinity; the evidence for it;
148–154 simile (3): master embraces servant bearing good news as Peter, singing, circles Dante three times.

PARADISO XXIV

"O sodalizio eletto a la gran cena
del benedetto Agnello, il qual vi ciba
sì, che la vostra voglia è sempre piena,

se per grazia di Dio questi preliba
di quel che cade de la vostra mensa,
prima che morte tempo li prescriba,

ponete mente a l'affezione immensa
e roratelo alquanto: voi bevete
sempre del fonte onde vien quel ch'ei pensa."

Così Beatrice; e quelle anime liete
si fero spere sopra fissi poli,
fiammando, volte, a guisa di comete.

E come cerchi in tempra d'orïuoli
si giran sì, che 'l primo a chi pon mente
quïeto pare, e l'ultimo che voli;

così quelle carole, differente-
mente danzando, de la sua ricchezza
mi facieno stimar, veloci e lente.

Di quella ch'io notai di più carezza
vid' ïo uscire un foco sì felice,
che nullo vi lasciò di più chiarezza;

e tre fïate intorno di Beatrice
si volse con un canto tanto divo,
che la mia fantasia nol mi ridice.

Però salta la penna e non lo scrivo:
ché l'imagine nostra a cotai pieghe,
non che 'l parlare, è troppo color vivo.

'O company of the elect chosen to feast
at the great supper of the blessèd Lamb,
who feeds you so that your desire is ever satisfied,

'since by God's grace this man enjoys a foretaste
of whatsoever falls beneath your table,
before death sets a limit to his time,

'heed his immeasurable craving and with dewdrops
from that fountain where you drink forever,
refresh him at the very source of all his thoughts.'

Thus Beatrice. And those joyful spirits
transformed themselves to rings around fixed poles,
circling, like blazing comets, in their brightness.

And as wheels in the movements of a clock
turn in such a way that, to an observer,
the innermost seems standing still, the outermost to fly,

just so those dancers in their circling,
moving to a different measure, fast or slow,
let me gauge their wealth of gladness.

From the dancer I made out to be most precious
I saw come forth a flame so full of joy
that not one there produced a greater brightness.

Three times it circled Beatrice,
its song so filled with heavenly delight
my phantasy cannot repeat it.

And so my pen skips and I do not write it,
for our imagination is too crude, as is our speech,
to paint the subtler colors of the folds of bliss.

"O santa suora mia che sì ne prieghe
divota, per lo tuo ardente affetto
da quella bella spera mi disleghe."

Poscia fermato, il foco benedetto
a la mia donna dirizzò lo spiro,
che favellò così com' i' ho detto.

Ed ella: "O luce etterna del gran viro
a cui Nostro Segnor lasciò le chiavi,
ch'ei portò giù, di questo gaudio miro,

tenta costui di punti lievi e gravi,
come ti place, intorno de la fede,
per la qual tu su per lo mare andavi.

S'elli ama bene e bene spera e crede,
non t'è occulto, perché 'l viso hai quivi
dov' ogne cosa dipinta si vede;

ma perché questo regno ha fatto civi
per la verace fede, a gloriarla,
di lei parlare è ben ch'a lui arrivi."

Sì come il baccialier s'arma e non parla
fin che 'l maestro la question propone,
per approvarla, non per terminarla,

così m'armava io d'ogne ragione
mentre ch'ella dicea, per esser presto
a tal querente e a tal professione.

"Dì, buon Cristiano, fatti manifesto:
fede che è?" Ond' io levai la fronte
in quella luce onde spirava questo;

poi mi volsi a Beatrice, ed essa pronte
sembianze femmi perch'ïo spandessi
l'acqua di fuor del mio interno fonte.

'O my holy sister, who pray to us
with such devotion, by the ardor of your love
you draw me forth from that fair circle.'

Once the blessèd fire had come to rest,
for my lady it breathed forth these words,
just as here I've set them down.

And she: 'O everlasting light of that great man
with whom our Lord did leave the keys,
which He brought down from this astounding joy,

'test this man as you see fit on points,
both minor and essential, about the faith
by which you walked upon the sea.

'Whether his love is just, and just his hope and faith,
is not concealed from you because your sight
can reach the place where all things are revealed.

'But since this realm elects its citizens
by measure of true faith, it surely is his lot
to speak of it, that he may praise its glory.'

Just as the bachelor arms himself and does not speak
while the master is setting forth the question—
for discussion, not for final disposition—

so I armed myself with all my arguments
while she was speaking, readying myself
for such an examiner and such professing.

'Speak up, good Christian, and make your declaration.
What is faith?' At that I lifted up my brow
to the light from which this breathed,

and then I faced Beatrice, who quickly signaled,
with a glance, that I should now pour forth
the waters welling from the source within me.

"La Grazia che mi dà ch'io mi confessi,"
comincia' io, "da l'alto primipilo,
faccia li miei concetti bene espressi."

E seguitai: "Come 'l verace stilo
ne scrisse, padre, del tuo caro frate
che mise teco Roma nel buon filo,

fede è sustanza di cose sperate
e argomento de le non parventi;
e questa pare a me sua quiditate."

Allora udi': "Dirittamente senti,
se bene intendi perché la ripuose
tra le sustanze, e poi tra li argomenti."

E io appresso: "Le profonde cose
che mi largiscon qui la lor parvenza,
a li occhi di là giù son sì ascose,

che l'esser loro v'è in sola credenza,
sopra la qual si fonda l'alta spene;
e però di sustanza prende intenza.

E da questa credenza ci convene
silogizzar, sanz' avere altra vista:
però intenza d'argomento tene."

Allora udi': "Se quantunque s'acquista
giù per dottrina, fosse così 'nteso,
non lì avria loco ingegno di sofista."

Così spirò di quello amore acceso;
indi soggiunse: "Assai bene è trascorsa
d'esta moneta già la lega e 'l peso;

ma dimmi se tu l'hai ne la tua borsa."
Ond' io: "Sì ho, sì lucida e sì tonda,
che nel suo conio nulla mi s'inforsa."

'May the grace that allows me to make confession
to the great centurion,' I began,
'grant clear expression to my thoughts.'

And I continued: 'As the truthful pen,
father, of your dear brother wrote it,
he who, with you, set Rome upon the path to truth,

'faith is the substance of things hoped for,
the evidence of things that are not seen.
And this I take to be its quiddity.'

Then I heard: 'You reason rightly if you understand
why he placed it, first, among the substances,
only then to set it down as evidence.'

And I: 'The profound mysteries
that here so richly manifest themselves to me,
to our eyes below are so concealed

'that they exist there through belief alone,
on which is based our hope to rise above.
And therefore it assumes the name of substance.

'It is from this belief that we must argue,
when there is nothing else we can examine.
And it therefore has the name of evidence.'

Then I heard: 'If all that is acquired below
from doctrine taught were this well learned,
there would be left no room for sophistry.'

This breathed forth from that kindled love.
And it continued: 'Now this coin's alloy
and weight are well examined,

'but tell me if you have it in your purse.'
And I: 'I do indeed, so bright and round
that of its coinage I am not in doubt.'

Appresso uscì de la luce profonda
che lì splendeva: “Questa cara gioia
sopra la quale ogne virtù si fonda,

onde ti venne?” E io: “La larga ploia
de lo Spirito Santo, ch’è diffusa
in su le vecchie e ’n su le nuove cuoia,

è silogismo che la m’ha conchiusa
acutamente sì, che ’nverso d’ella
ogne dimostrazion mi pare ottusa.”

Io udi’ poi: “L’antica e la novella
proposizion che così ti conchiude,
perché l’hai tu per divina favella?”

E io: “La prova che ’l ver mi dischiude,
son l’opere seguite, a che natura
non scalda ferro mai né batte incude.”

Risposto fummi: “Dì, chi t’assicura
che quell’ opere fosser? Quel medesmo
che vuol provarsi, non altri, il ti giura.”

“Se ’l mondo si rivolse al cristianesmo,”
diss’ io, “sanza miracoli, quest’ uno
è tal, che li altri non sono il centesmo:

ché tu intrasti povero e digiuno
in campo, a seminar la buona pianta
che fu già vite e ora è fatta pruno.”

Finito questo, l’alta corte santa
risonò per le spere un “Dio laudamo”
ne la melode che là sù si canta.

E quel baron che sì di ramo in ramo,
essaminando, già tratto m’avea,
che a l’ultime fronde appressavamo,

Then came forth from the depth of the light
refulgent there: 'This precious gem
90 upon which all the virtues rest,

'what was its origin and how did you obtain it?'
And I: 'The abundant rain of the Holy Ghost,
93 poured out onto the parchments old and new,

'is the syllogism that has proven it to me
with such great force that any other demonstration,
96 compared with it, would seem completely pointless.'

Then I heard: 'The premises, both old and new,
that you find so convincing in their truth,
99 why do you take them for the word of God?'

And I: 'The proof that revealed the truth to me
are the works that followed, for which nature
102 neither makes iron red with heat nor smites an anvil.'

'Say,' came the answer, 'who assures you that these works
all really happened? The very thing requiring proof,
105 and nothing else, is your sole warrant of them.'

'For the world to have turned to Christ,'
I said, 'without miracles, that indeed was one
108 to outdo all others more than hundredfold.

'For poor and fasting did you come into the field
to sow the good plant that was once a vine
111 and now has turned into a thornbush.'

My words ended, the high and holy court resounded
through all its starry spheres with 'Lord, we praise you'
114 with such melody as is only sung above.

And that nobleman who now had led me thus
from branch to branch in his examination
117 so that we neared the highest boughs,

ricominciò: "La Grazia, che donnea
con la tua mente, la bocca t'aperse
infino a qui come aprir si dovea,

sì ch'io approvo ciò che fuori emerse;
ma or convien espremer quel che credi,
e onde a la credenza tua s'offerse."

"O santo padre, e spirito che vedi
ciò che credesti sì, che tu vincesti
ver' lo sepulcro più giovani piedi,"

comincia' io, "tu vuo' ch'io manifesti
la forma qui del pronto creder mio,
e anche la cagion di lui chiedesti.

E io rispondo: Io credo in uno Dio
solo ed etterno, che tutto 'l ciel move,
non moto, con amore e con disio;

e a tal creder non ho io pur prove
fisice e metafisice, ma dalmi
anche la verità che quinci piove

per Moïsè, per profeti e per salmi,
per l'Evangelio e per voi che scriveste
poi che l'ardente Spirto vi fé almi;

e credo in tre persone etterne, e queste
credo una essenza sì una e sì trina,
che soffera congiunto 'sono' ed 'este.'

De la profonda condizion divina
ch'io tocco mo, la mente mi sigilla
più volte l'evangelica dottrina.

Quest' è 'l principio, quest' è la favilla
che si dilata in fiamma poi vivace,
e come stella in cielo in me scintilla."

began again: 'The grace that woos your mind
has until this moment opened your lips
and made your mouth say what it should,

'so that I approve what has come forth from it.
But now you must declare what you believe
and through what means you came to such belief.'

'O holy father, spirit who now can see
that which you once believed with such conviction
you outstripped younger feet to reach the sepulcher,'

I began, 'you would have me here declare
the substance of my ready faith, and also tell
the source of it, the reason why I hold it dear.

'And I reply: I believe in one God,
one and eternal, who, Himself unmoved, moves
all the heavens with His love and their desire.

'In defense of this belief I do have proof, not only
physical and metaphysical, but offered
also by the truth that pours like rain from here

'through Moses and the Prophets and the Psalms,
through what the Gospel says and what you wrote
once the burning Spirit made you holy.

'I believe in three eternal Persons. I believe
these are a single Essence, at once threefold and one
so as to allow agreement both with "are" and "is."

'The profound truth of God's own state of which I speak
is many times imprinted in my mind
by the true instructions of the Gospel.

'This is the beginning, this the living spark
that swells into a living flame
and shines within me like a star in heaven.'

Come 'l segnor ch'ascolta quel che i piace,
da indi abbraccia il servo, gratulando
per la novella, tosto ch'el si tace;

così, benedicendomi cantando,
tre volte cinse me, sì com' io tacqui,
l'appostolico lume al cui comando
io avea detto: sì nel dir li piacqui!

As the master to whom a servant brings good news
rejoices when he hears it, and puts his arms around
the speaker just as soon as he has finished,

thus, blessing me as he sang,
the apostolic light, at whose command I spoke,
encircled me three times once I was silent,
because my words had brought him such delight.

1–9. Beatrice apostrophizes the heavenly host (minus Christ and Mary, who have now both ascended to the Empyrean) on behalf of Dante. She hopes that they will share their "meal," as it were, with her pupil.

This is one of the three cantos (of the thirty-three in which she might have done so, *Purg.* XXXI through *Par.* XXX) in which she speaks the opening lines. See also *Purgatorio* XXXI and *Paradiso* V.

1. This verse/tercet is made up of "loaded" terms, the first of which is *sodalizio*: Jacopo della Lana says there are four kinds of fellowship: in battle, "cumpagni"; on voyages, "comiti"; in business, "cumlega"; at table, "sodali." For a likely "source" for Dante's choice of the word *eletto*, see Matthew 22:14: "Multi enim sunt vocati, pauci vero *electi*" (For many are called, but few are chosen). For the phrase *la gran cena*, see Apocalypse 19:9: "Beati qui ad *coenam* nuptiarum agni vocati sunt" (Blessed are they who are called to the marriage supper of the Lamb) and Luke 14:16: "*coenam magnam*" (great banquet).

4. The verb *prelibare* (to have a foretaste) is a striking one. We have seen it once before (at *Par.* X.23). It has also been used in *De vulgari* (I.iv.5) and in *Epistle* VI.24. All these occurrences are recorded in the entry "prelibare" by Antonio Lanci in the *Enciclopedia dantesca* (*ED* IV [1971]), which, however, omits the two occurrences in the *Epistle to Cangrande* (XIII.42 and XIII.46). Its use here may remind us of its presence there, where it indicates the opening passage of the *cantica*, the foretaste of (or prologue to) what is coming.

5. For the crumbs of bread that fall from the banquet of philosophy, see *Convivio* I.i.10; is this a correction of that passage, substituting a better "meal," communion in Christ, for the one portrayed there? For the last canticle as the "completed *Convivio*," see the note to *Paradiso* III.91–96.

8. For this image, see *Aeneid* VI.230, *rore levi* (light dew), as was first suggested by Tommaseo (comm. to vv. 7–9).

10–12. These souls whirl, upon a central point, in circles. They look like comets because they have tails of light; however, they apparently maintain their circular orbits, that is, are not errant in their motions, as actual comets are.

13–18. The simile clarifies the motion of these "comets." Like the flywheels of a mechanical clock, some move more quickly than others; however, here greater speed is the mark of greater worthiness, as we learn from vv. 19–21.

Among the earlier commentators, only John of Serravalle (comm. to these verses) perceives and expresses the precise resemblance between the simile's tenor and vehicle. For him the circling groups of dancers and the flywheels are precisely related in their varying grades of joy, their greater and lesser speeds revealing their relative degrees of blessedness. He does not go on to observe, and nearly five centuries would pass until Poletto would do so (comm. to these verses), that, since we are seeing the Church Militant, the circles that we are observing here might well be the circles we observe there (in Canto XXXII), that is, the "rows" in the round "amphitheater" of the Rose. In that case, all those who seem to believe that this circle contains only apostles need to revise their opinion. The highest tier of the Rose contains Mary (*Par.* XXXII.1); John the Baptist (XXXII.31); Adam, Peter, John (as scribe of the Apocalypse), Moses, Anna, and Lucy (all referred to in XXXII.118–137). All of these, we must assume, are in that circling dance from which issues Peter now, and James and John in the next canto. It is difficult to understand why Poletto's understanding of these verses has not entered the discussion of them, which remains, as a result, maddeningly vague. See Hollander (Holl.2006.2).

For a much earlier listing, which also refers to the population of the top tier of the Rose, see the note to *Paradiso* IV.29–30. In those lines we learn that Moses, both Johns, Mary, and Samuel are probably there; the first four are indeed confirmed as being in the highest row by the text of *Paradiso* XXXII.

16. The word *carola* (lit. "carol") here refers to a style of dancing. See Greco (Grec.1974.1), pp. 112–13, for the distinction between a *danza* (dance) and a *carola* (reel), in which dancers in circles or in straight lines hand each other off to a next (temporary) partner. But see Landino (comm. to vv. 16–18) for the most economical explanation: "Chosì quelle carole, *idest* anime che si giravono; proprio carola che significa ballo tondo, *differentemente danzando*, et per questa differentia dimostra più et meno beatitudine, et però dice *mi si faceano stimare veloci et lente* della sua richeza" (Thus were these "carols," i.e., souls, turning. "Carol" signifies "round dance." "Moving to a different measure" in such a way as to reveal more and less beatitude; and therefore [the poet] says "made me gauge their gladness" by its wealth).

19–21. From among the "dancers" and from the group of them that was most joyful, evidently the one that includes the apostles, came a "flame" that was as bright as any other there. We perhaps need to be reminded that Dante is beholding the Church Triumphant, minus Jesus and Mary. When we examine the inhabitants of the Rose (*Par.* XXXII.118), we will see that the only two apostles mentioned there (Peter and John) are in the highest rank in that great stadium. Their situation here lends support to those who believe that the group set apart here is also apostolic. But see the note to vv. 13–18.

19. The dancer who is most precious ("of greater value") is St. Peter; he will not be named until Canto XXV.12. For the second appearance of the noun *carezza*, see *Paradiso* XXV.33.

20–21. Peter's higher worth among even such exalted company as this is indicated by his greater brightness.

22. Peter circles Beatrice three times, as he will do again at the end of the canto (verse 152), on that occasion circling Dante. This number, that of the Trinity, is obviously auspicious. (Some later commentators see it as the number of the three theological virtues; since Peter appears here as the representative of only one, Faith, that would seem a less likely reference here.) However, and as other passages will remind us, it is also the number of times Peter betrays Jesus (see Matthew 26:34, 26:75; Mark 14:30, 14:72; Luke 22:34, 22:61). This might not be a case convincingly made on the basis of this verse alone; but see the note to vv. 124–126.

24. The *fantasia*, the image-receiving capacity of the brain, receives sounds as well, as this passage makes clear.

25. The familiar image of Dante as scribe is before us again, but now in nonforthcoming mode. His *dictator* (his phantasy) cannot bring Peter's song of affection for Beatrice back to mind, and so his pen must omit it.

26. Daniello (comm. to vv. 22–27) is apparently the only reader of this canto to think of the context offered this scene by the weaving contest between Athena and Arachne. He does so in order to place the painterly technique (the representation of folds in a garment) referred to here in an Ovidian context (*Metam.* VI.61–66). Jacopo della Lana (comm. to vv. 26–27) was the first to make the now common observation that this verse

describes the way a painter would depict the folds in a garment, by using darker colors for them.

27–30. Dante laments the coarseness of the art of his time (his own included), which is simply not up to the challenge of representing such delicate shadings, whether visually or verbally. What he does reproduce is what Peter says to Beatrice, i.e., the words that he speaks after he has stopped singing. She, he reports, has loosed him from the sphere he was circling in (see verse 11) and he, as a result, may serve as Dante's interlocutor.

31–33. And now Dante does reassume his role as scribe, setting down the words that Peter uttered after he had finished his (unrecorded) song. No other section of the poem has more uses of the noun for "breath," *spiro,* and the verb for "inspire" or "breathe into," *spirare* (*Par.* XXIII.104, XXIV.82, XXV.82, XXV.132, XXVI.3, XXVI.103). The self-consciousness of these lines is telling: Peter, inspired (the word the poet uses for his breath, *spiro,* is nearly surely intended to remind us of the spiration of the Holy Spirit), utters words that Dante, his scribe, can tell us (and just has). See the notes to *Purgatorio* XXIV.55–63 and *Paradiso* VI.88.

34–36. From this tercet we realize that the "everlasting light" (we remember that this light was the most brilliant among its companions in the Church Triumphant at verse 21) addressed by Beatrice is St. Peter. For Jesus left the "keys of the kingdom" (Matthew 16:19) to Peter. In the tradition of Roman Catholicism, this signified that Jesus picked him to be the first pope, presiding over, among other things, the departure of the saved and damned souls for the afterlife.

37–38. Beatrice invites Peter to examine Dante on the theological virtue Faith, both its major tenets and its lesser aspects. For the word *tenta*, see the note to verse 48.

39. Peter's walking on water displayed his faith in Jesus, but also revealed the tenuous nature of that faith when he doubts and begins to sink, causing Jesus to castigate him: "O you of little faith" (Matthew 14:28–33). And so here Beatrice is remembering Peter's noble beginning and suppressing reference to the far less impressive conclusion of the biblical narrative. See the note to vv. 124–126.

40–45. Beatrice concludes her intervention on Dante's behalf by acknowledging that Peter already knows that her pupil passes muster on the three theological virtues. On the other hand, it is Dante's responsibility to glorify these, most of all Faith.

40. The three verbs of this verse obviously reflect the three theological virtues, Love, Hope, and Faith, in that order, as was apparent from the very beginning of the commentary tradition (see Jacopo della Lana on this verse).

46–51. The medieval bachelor's examination in theology, some elements of which still persist in oral doctoral examinations in a few fields at a few institutions in our day, is rehearsed here. A bachelor was a candidate for the first degree in the field, just as today. The examination was administered by a *magister* (master); he certified the bachelor as being worthy of entering the pursuit of the doctorate in theology, probably his own goal as well.

48. The *magister* intervenes, not to settle the question (*quaestio*, a formal exercise in debate in which the answer is known or assumed), but to formulate it—as Peter is about to do.

See Scartazzini (comm. to vv. 47–48) for a full discussion of the dispute that has followed this verse through the centuries. And see Tozer's explanation (comm. to vv. 46–48): "The allusion here is to what took place in the mediaeval Universities. The 'Master' is a duly licensed teacher, and the Bachelor a student who is preparing for the office of teacher. The Bachelor at one stage of his preparatory course was required to pass through a form of examination, which was called 'Disputatio tentativa,' before a Master, who propounded the subject of this (*la question*). Usually in such cases a number of opponents were appointed to combat the candidate's arguments (see Rashdall, *The Universities of Europe in the Middle Ages*, vol. I., p. 466). In the present instance, however, this is not supposed to happen, and the proofs advanced lead up to a conclusion which is recognized as well established, so that the candidate has no need [to] *terminar la questione*. Similarly, St. Peter propounds the question, and Dante adduces what he considers to be the fitting arguments, but the conclusion is determined beforehand. The title 'disputatio tentativa' is probably referred to in the word *tenta* in 1. 37."

52–111. Tozer (comm. to these verses) divides the ensuing "examination" into five parts, as follows: "The subjects of the questions and answers in what follows are: (1) what faith is (ll. 52–66); (2) how Dante understands St. Paul's definition of faith (ll. 67–82); (3) whether Dante possesses faith (ll. 83–87); (4) whence he derived his faith (ll. 88–96); (5) what is the evidence of the inspiration of Scripture, on which he bases his faith (ll. 97–111)."

52–57. Dante turns to Peter and then to Beatrice, who signals that he should, in metaphor, "pour forth the waters" of his answer. As Grandgent was apparently the first to notice, the passage is possibly a calque on Christ's words (John 7:38: "He who believes in me, as the Scripture says, 'From within him there shall flow rivers of living water' "). It is interesting that here, as later (vv. 64–65, when he will turn to Paul for the definition of Faith), Dante never uses the words of his examiner to define this theological virtue. It is all very well to explain (as does Carroll [comm. to vv. 52–66]) that Peter never offered a definition of it, with the result that Dante had, therefore, to resort to St. Paul. The question then remains (in addition to the nagging question of Paul's absence from the cast of characters who perform a part in the poem), why did Dante choose to give Peter so prominent a role with regard to Faith? And, for the question of Paul's importance to Dante, see the last items in the note to *Inferno* XXXI.67.

56–57. Cf. *Inferno* I.79–80: "Or se' tu quel Virgilio e quella *fonte* / che *spandi* di parlar sì largo fiume?" (Are you then Virgil, the fountainhead / that pours so full a stream of speech?). Consultation of the DDP reveals that apparently no one has seen what seems a fairly obvious self-citation, perhaps because it would seem to have Beatrice promote Dante to Virgil's status, making him, and not the Latin poet, a "source" or "fountainhead"; nonetheless, that is approximately what has transpired within the narrative.

58–60. While this tercet would qualify, formally, as a true invocation, it is uttered by the protagonist rather than by the poet, and thus falls outside the set of nine authorial invocations (see the note to *Inf.* II.7–9); cf. Ledda (Ledd.2002.1), p. 32n.

59. "Centurion," our translation, is the generic term; Dante, however, uses a word that needs some explanation. Peter is presented as the *primipilus* among "Christian soldiers." The term refers to the standard-bearer in the Roman army who throws the first javelin (*primum pilum*) in battle.

Benvenuto da Imola (comm. to vv. 58–60) was the first to say that the word was found in Isidore of Seville; he has been followed by several later commentators. However, none offers a specific textual location for the description; furthermore, consultation of the *Etymologies* does not reveal any even promising leads. (Daniello [comm. to vv. 58–60] indicates a possible source in the Roman military historian Vegetius [cited by Dante in *Mon.* II.ix.3], in particular *De re militari* II.viii.)

61. Dante's claim for the trustworthiness of even the writing instruments of sacred texts, clear from the phrase "the truthful pen," reflects his concern for that basic distinction between two kinds of writing, truthful and fabulous (i.e., historical and fictive), that runs from one end of the *Commedia* to the other.

62–63. Dante's locution necessarily calls attention to the fact that Peter did not in fact write about faith, a task that he left for Paul. See the notes to vv. 52–57 and to vv. 124–126.

64–66. As Paul said (Hebrews 11:1): "Faith is the substance of things hoped for and the evidence of things not seen—that is its quiddity." Greco (Grec.1974.1), p. 120, reports that Aquinas, in his *De fide*, says that it is in fact the best definition of this theological virtue.

We should remember that Hebrews 11:4–40 recounts the salvations, by their faith in Christ to come, of major Hebrew figures, from Abel to Samuel.

67–69. Peter challenges Dante to explicate Paul's words, and especially the related concepts of faith as the "substance" of hope and the "evidence" for things not seeable.

70–78. Tozer (comm. to these verses) translates the protagonist's thoughts as follows: "Heavenly mysteries cannot be known on earth by sight, but are discerned by faith only; and as hope is founded on this, faith is the substance, or foundation, of things hoped for. It is also the proof of things unseen, because we are justified in arguing from faith in matters where sight is unavailing."

75. Dante's *intenza* translates the Scholastic term *intentio* (notion, concept). And so the thought is (Grandgent [comm. to this verse]) "assumes the concept," that is, "falls into the category."

79–85. Peter approves Dante's intellectual grasp of the doctrinal aspect of faith; now he wants to know if his pupil really has it, or is only talking a good game, like the sophist Dante seems to have convinced him he is not.

89–96. To Peter's question about the source of his faith, Dante responds, "The rain of the Holy Spirit poured over the two testaments is the syllogism of syllogisms."

97–102. Peter's follow-up question, in which he asks why the protagonist considers Scripture inspired, elicits Dante's avowal that nature cannot have been responsible for the miracles recounted in both testaments.

103–105. Peter persists in his testing of Dante's faith, asking whether it might be true that the argument from miracles is not verifiable, that is, that such argument is based on the truth of the proposition that is being tested. (We may reflect that the obvious subtext here, for a Christian discussant, is the resurrection of Jesus.)

106–110. Tozer (comm. to these verses) paraphrases Dante's rejoinder as follows: "The reply to such an objection is that the conversion of the world to Christianity without miracles by men of no position like the Apostles would be incomparably the greatest of all miracles, and would be in itself a sufficient proof of the divine origin of Christianity." See Augustine, the final words of the fifth chapter *De civitate Dei* XXII: "[O]ne grand miracle suffices for us, that the whole world has believed without any miracles" (tr. M. Dods).

108. For the word *centesmo*, see Matthew 19:29 (another passage in which the authority of Peter may seem challenged; see the note to vv. 124–126): "And everyone who has left houses or brothers or sisters or father or mother or children or lands, for my name's sake, will receive *a hundredfold* and will inherit eternal life" (italics added). It was Peter's troubling question (what shall he and the other disciples have for giving up the things of this world to follow Jesus) that elicited that remark.

111. Gratuitous in terms of the argument being made (but thoroughly in keeping with what we expect from Dante) is this biting thrust at the Church, corrupted under (and, in some cases, by) Peter's successors. For a survey of saved and damned popes, see the note to *Inferno* VII.46–48.

113–114. "Dio laudamo" is of course the Italian version of the Latin hymn "Te Deum laudamus," which we heard intoned in *Purgatorio* IX.140, when the gate of Purgatory swung open (see the note to *Purg.* IX.139–145). And see Casagrande (Casa.1976.1), pp. 260–64, for the relationship between all the Italian hymns of praise in the eighth heaven and the Hebrew word of praise "alleluia." Also see Brownlee (Brow.1984.2) for reflections on "Why the Angels Speak Italian."

There is a profusion of hymns in this heaven: *Paradiso* XXIII.128 ("Regina celi"); XXV.73 ("Sperino in te"); XXV.98 ("Sperent in te"); XXVI.69 ("Santo, santo, santo"); XXVII.1 ("Al Padre, al Figlio, a lo Spirito Santo, *gloria*"), including this one, six musical outbursts in all.

It is curious that the commentary tradition is silent on the fact that the "Te Deum" is represented as being sung in the vernacular, surely connected to the Italian identity of the poet/bachelor of theology who has just concluded the crucial part of his "examination" here. Further, the commentators, without dispute among themselves, either think that the outburst of the Church Triumphant celebrates Dante's profession of faith *or* the triumph of the Christian faithful. Scartazzini/Vandelli (comm. to these verses) were the first to suggest that possibly both are intended, as Momigliano (comm. to these verses) concurs.

115–123. Although verse 121 makes it plain that Peter has accepted Dante's profession of faith, it is also clear that he wants the new professor to expatiate on two points (they correspond to his first and fourth questions and Dante's responses [vv. 52–53 and 61–66; and then vv. 89–96]). Peter wants Dante to spell out precisely *what* he believes and exactly *where* he learned it.

115. Peter's baronial title will be given to James as well (see *Par.* XXV.17). It probably reflects its use as the term of address for a feudal lord, as Mestica observes (comm. to vv. 115–117). Lombardi (comm. to vv. 115–117) reports that it was not uncommon in the late medieval period to give saints the titles of those who were indeed powerful in this world. One example (of the two) he adduces is Giovanni Boccaccio's (repeated) reference to "baron messer santo Antonio" (*Decameron* VI.x.9, VI.x.11, VI.x.44).

118. See Tozer (comm. to this verse): "*Donneare* is from Provençal *domnear*, and that from Lat. *domina*; it expresses the chivalrous treatment of a lady by her cavalier. Here it is used of the grace of God gently operating on the mind of man."

124–138. Dante's seventh response involves the experience of Peter and John at Christ's tomb (see John 20:3–8); Dante's *credo* in God the Creator; his proofs: philosophical, theological, and Scriptural (from Genesis to Peter's Epistles).

124–126. Here is a part of Carroll's comment to vv. 115–138: "That is, Peter *sees* now the risen body of Christ, concerning which he had only *faith* as he ran to the sepulchre; but even faith made him conquer the younger feet of John, who at the time had no faith in the Resurrection. The difficulty is that it was John who outran Peter and came first to the sepulchre. It is not in the least likely that Dante forgot this. His meaning undoubtedly is that while the younger feet, through lack of faith, lingered at the entrance, Peter's faith carried him past his doubting companion to the inside. (In *De Mon.* III.ix, however, the incident is given as an instance of Peter's impulsiveness rather than his faith: 'John says that he went in immediately when he came to the tomb, seeing the other disciple lingering at the entrance.' Perhaps Dante wished to retract his former judgment.) This does no injustice to John, since he himself says it was only after he entered and saw how the grave-clothes were folded up, that he believed (John 20:5–8). It is somewhat strange, however, that Dante should choose this incident as an example of Peter's faith."

Is this more than a slight dig in the ribs for Peter? See the notes to vv. 22, 39, 52–57, 62–63, and 108. The reader would do well to turn immediately to *Monarchia* III.ix.1–19, a diatribe against Peter *as a stand-in for the papacy*. Discussing the context of the passage in Luke 22:38, which was among the biblical texts that the hierocrats used to assert papal authority over the emperor, Dante has this to say about Peter's intellectual capacity: "Peter, as was his habit, answered unreflectingly, only considering the surface of things" (*Mon.* III.ix.2); later (III.ix.8) he adds that, had Peter actually said what the hierocrats claimed he did, Christ would have reproached him for that remark about the two swords "as He did reproach him many times, when he replied not knowing what he was saying." Dante continues in a similar vein (III.ix.9): "And that Peter was in the habit of speaking without reflecting is proved by his hasty and unthinking impulsiveness, which came not just from the sincerity of his faith, but, I think, from his simple and ingenuous nature." Finally, having listed a whole series of Peter's inadequacies, both as thinker and as loyal follower of Jesus, Dante moves toward his conclusion: "It is helpful to have listed these episodes involving our Archimandrite in praise of his ingenuousness, for they show quite clearly that when he spoke of the two swords he was answering

Christ with no deeper meaning in mind" (all these translations are from P. Shaw's edition). According to Carroll, this passage may serve as a partial retraction of those views. The reader has, nonetheless, to wonder why Dante should, if more circumspectly than in the anti-Petrine diatribe in *Monarchia*, be chipping away at the veneer of authority lodged in the man whom he considered the first pope. Is it possible that his widely represented distrust of particular popes prompts him to protest any emerging sense that a pontiff, because of his tenure in the highest ecclesiastical office, is necessarily without doctrinal error? See Bennassuti's unintentionally amusing insistence (comm. to *Inf.* XI.8) that Dante could not have condemned Pope Anastasius II as a heretic because the poet believed in papal infallibility (Bennassuti, as a priest, should have known better, since this did not become a doctrine of the Church until his own nineteenth century); as a result the reader is to understand that demons put that inscription on the tomb for Dante to read. This is perhaps one of the most extravagant misreadings of the text of the poem and of Dante's intentions in a commentary tradition that is not deprived of amusingly wrongheaded insistences on what Dante supposedly would never do.

130–132. Bosco/Reggio (comm. to this tercet) interpret what has proven to be a surprisingly controversial line as having two focal points, the love on God's part for His creation, the love on its part for Him. We have followed them in our translation.

134. For Dante's distinction between physics and metaphysics here (and the relation of this passage to discussions found in *Convivio* II), see Alfonso Maierù (Maie.2004.1), especially his concluding remarks.

136. This verse repeats, nearly verbatim, Luke 24:44, as was pointed out by Tommaseo (comm. to vv. 136–138). Jesus speaks: "These are my words that I spoke to you while I was still with you, that everything written about me in the Law of Moses and the Prophets and the Psalms must be fulfilled."

137–138. See Tozer's paraphrase of these lines: "*voi*, &c.: St. Peter and the other apostles, who derived the inspiration of their writings from the descent of the Holy Ghost at Pentecost."

139–147. Dante recites his *credo* in the Trinity. He goes on to say that his proofs for God's trinitarian nature are Scriptural, without specifying where these appear. Somehow it does not come as a surprise that Scartazzini (comm. to vv. 143–144) was the first to offer such a list: Matthew 28:19; John 14:16–17; II Corinthians 13:14 (this passage, however, seems not to appear in the Vulgate); I Peter 1:2; and I John 5:7.

148–150. A source for this vehicle of the concluding simile, which seems to be based on a particular scene as described in some previous work, has escaped the commentators. However, see Aversano (Aver.2000.2), pp. 113–14, suggesting that two passages in St. Luke may be conflated in Dante's text, Luke 19:17 and (somewhat more convincingly) 15:20–32, the parable of the Prodigal Son. As Aversano admits, the connections may seem a bit tenuous; however, as he points out, Dante's gerund *gratulando* may pick up Luke's two uses of *congratularsi* in this chapter (15:6 and 15:9), according to him the only two uses of that verb in the Gospels. (He has overlooked one other, also in Luke [1:58].)

151–154. St. Peter now "laureates" Dante in Faith. While the phrase *tre volte* (three times) occurs on seven other occasions in the poem, its first and last appearances are the only ones that occur in the final four verses of a canto, here and in *Inferno* XXVI.139. It would seem possible that this use remembers *in bono* that first occurrence, in which the ship of Ulysses spins around three times before it sinks. Here Dante is not being punished for his presumption, but rewarded for his faith.

PARADISO XXV

OUTLINE

STARRY SPHERE

1–12 should the sacred poem overcome the cruelty of the Florentines, Dante will return to his city a poet, taking the laurel in the Baptistry, where he became a Christian (and now Peter has encircled his brow);

13–18 Peter is joined by a second "baron" **[James]**;

19–24 simile (1): dove joining mate and James joining Peter;

25–27 they are so aflame that Dante is blinded by them;

28–33 Beatrice: "Make hope resound up here, since you 'figured it' on earth";

34–36 James to Dante: "Raise your head and make yourself certain; for mortal sight, up here, must be ripened";

37–39 Dante now is able to gaze on these "hills" (apostles).

40–45 James: "Since the Emperor, in His grace, wants you to see His Counts in His most secret hall so that you may make yourself stronger in Hope—and others too—

46–48 "(1) say what Hope is, (2) say how it blossoms in your mind, and (3) say whence it came to you."

49–51 Beatrice, [as **Daedalus**], intervenes on his behalf on (2):

52–57 "The Church Militant has no son of greater hope;

58–63 "he may answer your other two questions for himself."

64–66 simile (2): eager pupil to his master as Dante to James;

67–69 Dante's answer to question (1): "Hope is the sure and certain hope of the resurrection, produced by Divine Grace and preceding merit";

70–78 Dante's answer to question (3): "David was the first who instilled hope in my heart, and then James."

79–81 James's flame seems to be convulsed by internal lightning;

82–86 James: "I, hopeful even in my martyrdom, rebreathe my love of this virtue to you in your gladness in it."

87–88 James's fourth question: the promise Hope holds for him?

89–96 Dante: "Scripture offers the emblem for those God loves";

97–99 angels herald his finished examination with "Sperent in te"

100–102 **John** appears (unnamed and as yet unidentified)

103–108 simile (3): happy virgin, rising to dance to honor the bride, compared to John approaching Peter and James;

109–111 the three sing and dance while Beatrice watches them.

112–114 Beatrice: "This is the apostle loved by Christ."

115–117 Beatrice remains fixed upon Peter, James, and John;

118–121 simile (4): a man trying to see the beginning of an eclipse compared to Dante trying to make out John's body;

122–129 John, who has clearly divined Dante's desire, scolds him;

130–135 simile (5): as a whistle's sound arrests oars in air, so John's first words stilled the other two apostles;

136–139 Dante's mind was shaken when he could not see Beatrice.

PARADISO XXV

Se mai continga che 'l poema sacro
al quale ha posto mano e cielo e terra,
sì che m'ha fatto per molti anni macro,

vinca la crudeltà che fuor mi serra
del bello ovile ov' io dormi' agnello,
nimico ai lupi che li danno guerra;

con altra voce omai, con altro vello
ritornerò poeta, e in sul fonte
del mio battesmo prenderò 'l cappello;

però che ne la fede, che fa conte
l'anime a Dio, quivi intra' io, e poi
Pietro per lei sì mi girò la fronte.

Indi si mosse un lume verso noi
di quella spera ond' uscì la primizia
che lasciò Cristo d'i vicari suoi;

e la mia donna, piena di letizia,
mi disse: "Mira, mira: ecco il barone
per cui là giù si vicita Galizia."

Sì come quando il colombo si pone
presso al compagno, l'uno a l'altro pande,
girando e mormorando, l'affezione;

così vid' ïo l'un da l'altro grande
principe glorïoso essere accolto,
laudando il cibo che là sù li prande.

Ma poi che 'l gratular si fu assolto,
tacito *coram me* ciascun s'affisse,
ignito sì che vincëa 'l mio volto.

Should it ever come to pass that this sacred poem,
to which both Heaven and earth have set their hand
so that it has made me lean for many years,

should overcome the cruelty that locks me out
of the fair sheepfold where I slept as a lamb,
foe of the wolves at war with it,

with another voice then, with another fleece,
shall I return a poet and, at the font
where I was baptized, take the laurel crown.

For there I came into the faith
that recommends the soul to God, and now,
because of it, Peter encircled thus my brow.

At that a light moved toward us from the circle
out of which had come the first-fruit of the stock
of vicars Christ did leave for us on earth,

and my lady, brimming with joy, said to me:
'Look, look, here is the nobleman
who down below draws pilgrims to Galicia.'

As, when the dove alights beside its mate
and each displays, circling and cooing,
its fondness for the other,

so I saw one great and glorious prince
welcomed by the other, both giving praise
for the feast that there above they share.

But after they had shown their pleasure in each other,
they both stopped, silent, *coram me*,
so brightly flaming that they overcame my sight.

Ridendo allora Bëatrice disse:
"Inclita vita per cui la larghezza
de la nostra basilica si scrisse,

fa risonar la spene in questa altezza:
tu sai, che tante fiate la figuri,
quante Iesù ai tre fé più carezza."

"Leva la testa e fa che t'assicuri:
ché ciò che vien qua sù del mortal mondo,
convien ch'ai nostri raggi si maturi."

Questo conforto del foco secondo
mi venne; ond' io levăi li occhi a' monti
che li 'ncurvaron pria col troppo pondo.

"Poi che per grazia vuol che tu t'affronti
lo nostro Imperadore, anzi la morte,
ne l'aula più secreta co' suoi conti,

sì che, veduto il ver di questa corte,
la spene, che là giù bene innamora,
in te e in altrui di ciò conforte,

dì quel ch'ell' è, dì come se ne 'nfiora
la mente tua, e dì onde a te venne."
Così seguì 'l secondo lume ancora.

E quella pïa che guidò le penne
de le mie ali a così alto volo,
a la risposta così mi prevenne:

"La Chiesa militante alcun figliuolo
non ha con più speranza, com' è scritto
nel Sol che raggia tutto nostro stuolo:

però li è conceduto che d'Egitto
vegna in Ierusalemme per vedere,
anzi che 'l militar li sia prescritto.

Then, smiling, Beatrice said:
'Illustrious living soul, you who wrote
of the abundant gifts of our heavenly court,

'make Hope resound here at this height,
since you know how, you who were the very figure of it
when Jesus showed most favor to the three.'

'Lift up your head and then take heart,
for all that comes here from the mortal world
will here be ripened in our radiance.'

The second fire offered this assurance.
Therefore I raised my eyes up to the hills
whose blazing light had weighed them down before.

'Since our Emperor, of His grace,
wills that you come, before your death,
to meet His nobles in His secret chamber,

'so that, having known the reality of this court,
you may then strengthen in yourself and others
the hope that brings true love to those on earth,

'tell what it is and how it blossoms in your mind,
and tell from where it came to you.'
Thus spoke the second light.

And the compassionate soul who guided
the feathers on my wings to that great height
answered for me before I could reply:

'The Church Militant has no other son
so filled with hope, as it is written
in the Sun that shines its rays on all our host.

'Therefore is it granted him to come from Egypt
to Jerusalem that he may see the city
before his time of warfare has its end.

Li altri due punti, che non per sapere
son dimandati, ma perch' ei rapporti
quanto questa virtù t'è in piacere,

a lui lasc' io, ché non li saran forti
né di iattanza; ed elli a ciò risponda,
e la grazia di Dio ciò li comporti."

Come discente ch'a dottor seconda
pronto e libente in quel ch'elli è esperto,
perché la sua bontà si disasconda,

"Spene," diss' io, "è uno attender certo
de la gloria futura, il qual produce
grazia divina e precedente merto.

Da molte stelle mi vien questa luce;
ma quei la distillò nel mio cor pria
che fu sommo cantor del sommo duce.

'Sperino in te,' ne la sua tëodia
dice, 'color che sanno il nome tuo':
e chi nol sa, s'elli ha la fede mia?

Tu mi stillasti, con lo stillar suo,
ne la pistola poi; sì ch'io son pieno,
e in altrui vostra pioggia repluo."

Mentr' io diceva, dentro al vivo seno
di quello incendio tremolava un lampo
sùbito e spesso a guisa di baleno.

Indi spirò: "L'amore ond'ïo avvampo
ancor ver' la virtù che mi seguette
infin la palma e a l'uscir del campo,

vuol ch'io respiri a te che ti dilette
di lei; ed emmi a grato che tu diche
quello che la speranza ti 'mpromette."

'Two other points regarding which you asked—
not for your enlightenment, but for him to tell
how much this virtue means to you—

'I leave to him. For they will not be difficult,
nor offer grounds for boasting of himself.
Now let him answer, and may God's grace be his aid!'

Like the student answering his teacher,
ready and eager in the subject he prepared,
intending to display his worth,

'Hope,' I said, 'is the certain expectation
of future glory, springing
from heavenly grace and merit we have won.

'This light comes down to me from many stars,
but he who first instilled it in my heart
was that exalted singer of our exalted Lord.

' "Let them have hope in you," he declares
in his god-song, "those who know your name."
Among those who share my faith, who does not know it?

'After he had imbued me with his song,
you poured your epistle down on me so that I,
overflowing, now rain your rain on others.'

While I spoke, within the living core
of fire appeared a flare, quivering
like lightning in sudden and repeated flashes.

Then it breathed forth: 'The love with which I burn,
for the Virtue that was my companion,
even to the palm and my departing from the field,

'bids me breathe words again to you who take delight
in Hope. And I would like to hear you say
what promise Hope holds out to you.'

E io: "Le nove e le scritture antiche
pongon lo segno, ed esso lo mi addita,
de l'anime che Dio s'ha fatte amiche.

Dice Isaia che ciascuna vestita
ne la sua terra fia di doppia vesta:
e la sua terra è questa dolce vita;

e 'l tuo fratello assai vie più digesta,
là dove tratta de le bianche stole,
questa revelazion ci manifesta."

E prima, appresso al fin d'este parole,
"*Sperent in te*" di sopr' a noi s'udì;
a che rispuoser tutte le carole.

Poscia tra esse un lume si schiarì
sì che, se 'l Cancro avesse un tal cristallo,
l'inverno avrebbe un mese d'un sol dì.

E come surge e va ed entra in ballo
vergine lieta, sol per fare onore
a la novizia, non per alcun fallo,

così vid' io lo schiarato splendore
venire a' due che si volgieno a nota
qual conveniesi al loro ardente amore.

Misesi lì nel canto e ne la rota;
e la mia donna in lor tenea l'aspetto,
pur come sposa tacita e immota.

"Questi è colui che giacque sopra 'l petto
del nostro pellicano, e questi fue
di su la croce al grande officio eletto."

La donna mia così; né però piùe
mosser la vista sua di stare attenta
poscia che prima le parole sue.

And I: 'The new and the ancient Scriptures
set forth the goal for souls that God has made his friends
and this directs me to that promise.

'Isaiah says that each in his own land
shall be vested in a double garment,
and their own land is this sweet life.

'And then your brother, turning his attention
to the shining robes, explains to us
this revelation with still greater clarity.'

At once, as soon as these words ended,
Sperent in te was heard above us,
to which all circles of the blessed responded.

Then one light, among them all, shone out so bright
that, if the Crab held such a gem,
to winter would belong a month of endless day.

As a happy maiden rises and comes forward,
joining the dancers only to show honor
to the bride, not prompted by desire for display,

so I saw that now brighter splendor gliding
toward the two already whirling to the notes
most fitted to the ardent burning of their love.

He joined them there in singing and in dance,
and my lady, her gaze fixed on them, stood
as a bride stands, silent and motionless.

'This is he who lay upon the breast
of our Pelican, who from the cross
elected him to bear the heavy charge.'

These were my lady's words, nor did her gaze
waver after she had spoken, but stayed intent
and fixed as it had been before.

Qual è colui ch'adocchia e s'argomenta
di vedere eclissar lo sole un poco,
che, per veder, non vedente diventa;

tal mi fec'ïo a quell' ultimo foco
mentre che detto fu: "Perché t'abbagli
per veder cosa che qui non ha loco?

In terra è terra il mio corpo, e saragli
tanto con li altri, che 'l numero nostro
con l'etterno proposito s'agguagli.

Con le due stole nel beato chiostro
son le due luci sole che saliro;
e questo apporterai nel mondo vostro."

A questa voce l'infiammato giro
si quïetò con esso il dolce mischio
che si facea nel suon del trino spiro,

sì come, per cessar fatica o rischio,
li remi, pria ne l'acqua ripercossi,
tutti si posano al sonar d'un fischio.

Ahi quanto ne la mente mi commossi,
quando mi volsi per veder Beatrice,
per non poter veder, benché io fossi
presso di lei, e nel mondo felice!

As one who strains his eyes in his attempt to see
the sun when it is partly in eclipse,
and, his seeing overwhelmed, has lost his sight,

such did I become before that final flaming
until I heard these words: 'Why do you blind your eyes
trying to behold what is not here to see?

'In earth, earth is my body and there shall it lie
among the others until our number
shall be equal to the eternal purpose.

'With the two robes in the blessèd cloister
are the two lights alone who have ascended,
and let this be the news you bring back to your world.'

At these words, the fiery dance was ended,
together with the sweetly mingled notes
that issued from the blended threefold breath,

just as, to avoid fatigue or danger,
oars until that moment driven through the water
stop all at once when the whistle sounds.

Ah, how troubled was my mind
when I looked back for Beatrice
and could not see her, even though I was
so near to her and in that happy world!

1–9. This passage is surely one of the most personal statements Dante makes in the entire poem. However, it tends to cause disagreement, the central issue of which is whether Dante presents himself as vigorous in his hope for laureation or as sardonic about its likelihood. As representative of the first school of thought, which has its roots in Jacopo della Lana (comm. to verse 1) and, more vociferously, in the Ottimo (comm. to vv. 1–12), one might choose the recent treatment of Scott (Scot.2004.2). His "optimistic" reading (and it is a reading at least apparently in keeping with Dante's "hopefulness," the subject on which he is being examined by St. James) is found both in Scott's translation and paraphrase of these lines. In the first, he supplies the following (the square brackets are in his text): "If it comes [and may it come] to pass that the sacred poem to which both heaven and earth have lent a hand . . ." (p. 98); in the second, he offers his eventual sense of the passage (p. 295), intrinsically denying to Dante a proper Christian sense of the contingency of all earthly things. Scott considers the two subjunctives in vv. 1 and 4 optative, expressing "what the exiled poet longs for with all his being, a burning desire that opens the canto dedicated to the theological value of hope."

On the other hand, see, among others, Sarolli (Saro.1971.1), pp. 384–89, Chiarenza (Chia.1983.3), pp. 147–48, and Chiavacci Leonardi (Chia.1988.2), p. 268, for appreciations of the *contingent* nature of Dante's hope for laureation in Florence, which they find in the passage. Such an attitude is typified by a resigned tone rather than the hopeful one that most readers, like Scott, assign to him. A playful paraphrase in tune with this second view of the passage might run as follows: "Should it ever fall out [even if it seems most unlikely to do so] that I return to Florence [but those bastards will *never* allow me to come back home] and then [perhaps equally implausibly] that those fools decide to give me the laurel [which Giovanni del Virgilio has already offered me if I write a Latin poem for those sharing his dreadful Bolognese taste in poetry]. . . ." In such a view, where the first two verbs are circumspectly (and correctly) dubious, and thus in the subjunctive mood, the last two are triumphantly (and illogically) indicative ("I shall return," "I shall take"). (The subjunctive in a dependent clause almost necessarily causes a reader or a listener to expect the conditional ["I would return," "I would take"].) Indeed, in one sense Dante already has crowned himself (he allows St. Peter to be the agent of his heavenly "laureation" at the conclusion of Canto XXIV, an "event" he refers to in verse 12). In this reading, the desired but improbable hometown laureation is represented as being both totally unlikely and as inescapable, were the world (and particularly Florence) only honest; thus the truculently aggressive tone of the indicatives. To summarize, to those of this persuasion, Dante seems to be saying, "Well, I do not think it is really likely to occur but, if I do make it back home, I'm going to take the laurel (since I deserve it)." It is notable that Dante, on both occasions on which he considers the prospect of his own laureation (see *Par.* I.26, *coronarmi* [crown myself]), imagines the wreath, not as being bestowed upon him by some benevolent figure, but as being taken by himself. (For this appreciation, see Mattalia [comm. to verse 9].)

Scott (p. 296) observes that the *vello* (fleece) in verse 7 aligns Dante, as well as with Jason, with the biblical prophet John the Baptist, that patron of Florence and figure celebrated by its Baptistry, who wore camel skins as his garment in the wilderness, his fleece. For the only slightly more widely recognized reference here, to Jason's search for the Golden Fleece, see Sarolli (Saro.1971.1), p. 401, and Pohndorf (Pohn.1965.1), p. 189, the latter in particular supported by Hollander (Holl.1969.1), pp. 223–24. (It is a perhaps surprising fact that no commentator in the current version of the DDP seems to have associated this *vello* with Jason, although their connection here seems obvious.)

1. We may do well to remember the offer made to Dante by Giovanni del Virgilio, that he should follow his vernacular *Commedia* with a more worthy instrument of procuring the laurel (see the note to *Par.* XV.28–30), a Latin poem with a political subject. If the hypothesis shared by John Carroll and Lino Pertile is correct (see the note to *Par.* XXIII.130–132), Dante composed his answering eclogue soon after he was writing that canto. It is inviting to think that this insistence on his poem's being, on the contrary, dedicated to sacred things, is a defiant answer to that invitation, even if that may stretch chronological possibilities a bit much. However, for Dante's sense of a recent (1315) Italian laureation and its impact on him, see the note to *Paradiso* IX.29–30. And see Hollander (Holl.2003.2), pp. 54–55, for the poet's handling of the temptations of fame.

Villa (Vill.2001.1) considers both the term *poema sacro* and the related phrase "sacrato poema" at *Paradiso* XXIII.62.

This is the only presence in the poem of the verb *contingere*. For the occurrences of the noun *contingenza* (*Par.* XIII.63; XIII.64; XVII.37) and the participial adjective *contingente* (*Par.* XIII.99; XVII.16), see the entries for those terms, both prepared by Alfonso Maierù, *ED* (II [1970]).

2. In response to this challenging verse, Pasquini (Pasq.2001.1, pp. 145, 147) moves away from the traditional exegesis, which has it that the words *cielo* and *terra* both refer to what God has created, the twin subject of the poem, as it were, heaven and earth. That is, he realizes that the verse is not about the subject of the poem but about its heavenly agency. However, while an improvement in one respect, his reading seems deficient in the main one. For what may seem a radical (but perhaps only a necessary) view of the matter, see Hollander (Holl.1997.1) and, for a similar view, Baranski (Bara.2001.2), pp. 393–94. Such a reading of this line has it that Dante insists, however covertly, that the poem has two makers, God (the divine "dictator") and himself (the human "scribe"). The notion that he thus portrays his own hand writing the poem finds support in *Rime* CXIV.8, Dante's answer to a sonnet from Cino da Pistoia, in which he portrays his tired fingers grasping the pen with which he writes his own responsive sonnet.

3. For the sense of this verse, Benvenuto (comm. to vv. 1–9) looks back to the *fami, freddi o vigilie* that Dante claims to have suffered on behalf of his poem. See *Purgatorio* XXIX.37–38: "O sacred Virgins, if fasting, cold, or sleepless nights / I've ever suffered for your sake. . . ."

4. For *fuor mi serra* (locks me out), see the envoy of *Rime* 116, the so-called Montanina: "My mountain song, go your way. Perhaps you will see Florence, my city, that shuts me out from her [*che fuor di sé mi serra*], void of love and stripped of compassion" (tr. Foster and Boyde). The self-citation was first noted by Tommaseo (comm. to vv. 4–6).

5–6. The figurative speech is oversimplified and dramatic: Florence as "sheepfold," youthful Dante as "lamb," his enemies (Black Guelphs, others) as "wolves."

7. *altra voce . . . altro vello:* lit., deeper voice and facial hair or gray hair (see Dante, *Eclogue* I.42–44) of the mature man; metaphorically, with prophetic speech and this book, written on *vellum* (?); in addition, new "golden fleece" (see Ovid, *Metam.* VI.720: "vellera," and Dante, in his first *Eclogue* [II.1]: "Velleribus Colchis" [Colchian fleece])—Dante as Jason (cf. *Par.* II.16–18; XXXIII.94–96).

7–9. Tommaseo (comm. to this tercet) was perhaps the first to point to a passage in Dante's first *Eclogue*, which is addressed to Giovanni del Virgilio, who had made a conditional invitation that he come to Bologna to receive the poet's crown there. In that poem Dante says (vv. 42–44): "Nonne triumphales melius pexare capillos, / et, patrio redeam si quando, abscondere canos / fronde sub inserta solitum flavescere, Sarno?" (Were it not better my triumphant locks should hide beneath the green their hoariness, erst auburn-glowing, by the ancestral stream, should ever I return to deck them there, of Arno? [tr. Wicksteed and Gardner]). It seems evident that either this passage is reflected in that one—unless, as seems less likely, this one was written after that one. In any case, it seems clear that Dante was much involved with thoughts reflecting both Mussato's laureation in 1315 and his own desire for that reward, whether before Giovanni's goading offer or after it. See the note to verse 1.

8. In this use of the word *poeta*, we have the closest Dante ever comes to calling himself "poet" outright, though he has been issuing statements that all but said as much as early as *Vita nuova* XXV. No vernacular writer of lyric had ever used this term for himself before; it is traditionally reserved for the classical (Latin and Greek) poets.

9. Exactly what Dante means by this word has been a matter of some dispute. See Rigo (Rigo.1994.1), pp. 135–63, for a complex meditation on possible meanings of the poet's putting on the *cappello* ("crown," according to her, in the sense of "reward for accomplishment in poetry"), in which she advances the theory that it refers most significantly to Dante's desire to be given back his Florentine citizenship.

10–12. Whatever we make of the first nine verses (e.g., do they present Dante's hunger for a not truly Christian poetic immortality or his shrugging it off?), this tercet says the "right" things about the "right" kind of immortality. He wants to be "crowned" in the Baptistry because it was there he entered the Catholic faith. His belief in Jesus Christ has just now (*Par.* XXIV.152) been celebrated when his temples were thrice circled by St. Peter, named for the first time since his appearance in the last lines of Canto XXIII.

13–15. While James is never named, he is clearly identified (the same will be true of John at the end of this canto and in XXVI).

The *spera* (circle) referred to is surely that most precious one among those making up the Church Triumphant (see *Par.* XXIV.13–18 and note), the one containing at least some of the apostles. For *primizie* (first-fruits), see James 1:18: "Of his own will he brought us forth by the word of truth, that we should be a kind of first-fruits of his creatures." James is speaking of all the apostles; here Dante uses his word in the singular to refer to Peter alone.

17. For the term *barone*, see the note to *Paradiso* XXIV.115.

18. "St. James, to whose tomb at Compostella, in Galicia [Spain], pilgrimages were and are still made. The legend says that the body of St. James was put on board a ship and abandoned to the sea; but the ship, being guided by an angel, landed safely in Galicia. There the body was buried; but in the course of time the place of its burial was forgotten, and not discovered again till the year 800, when it was miraculously revealed to a friar" (Longfellow, comm. to verse 17). Compostella, after Rome, was the most popular goal of pilgrims inside Europe's borders. See Dante's divisions of pilgrims into three groups in *Vita nuova* XL.7: "palmers" (to the Holy Land), "pilgrims" (to Galicia), "romers" (to Rome).

What was Dante's knowledge of the distinctions between the two saints named James? Historians distinguish between James the Major (son of Zebedee) and James the Minor (son of Alpheus). For the undeveloped claim (and death has deprived us of such development) that Dante here deliberately conflates the two James, see Karl Uitti (Uitt.2005.1), p. 650n.

19–24. See Shoaf (Shoa.1975.1), who argues for the presence of a "dove program" in the poem, moving from the damned sinners Francesca and Paolo in *Inferno* V.82, through the muddled saved souls on the shore, unable to distinguish between wheat and tares in *Purgatorio* II.125, to these brotherly apostles, redeeming earthly affection by turning it toward heavenly nourishment (see *Par.* XXIV.1–2, "the elect invited to / the glorious supper of the blessèd Lamb"), thus tacitly rebuking the careless eating habits of the freshly saved souls on the shore of Purgatory. There are only these three presences of doves in the poem, each in a carefully turned simile, one to a canticle; it is difficult to believe Dante was *not* paying close attention to their distribution and significance.

26. The reader has once before encountered the first word of the Latin phrase *coram me* (in front of me): See *Paradiso* XI.63: *coram patre*, when, "in the presence of his father," Francis "married" Lady Poverty.

28–33. Tozer (comm. to vv. 29–30) says that the passages in St. James's Epistle that are referred to are 1:5, "If any of you lacks wisdom, let him ask

God, who gives generously to all without reproach, and it will be given him"; 1:17, "Every good gift and every perfect gift is from above, coming down from the Father of lights"; other commentators add 2:5, "Has not God chosen those who are poor in the world to be rich in faith and heirs of the kingdom?" Tozer continues, "It is to be remarked that Dante has here and in vv. 76–77, by a strange error, attributed this epistle, which was written by St. James the Less, to St. James the Greater; the same mistake is found in Brunetto Latini (*Tesoro*, Bk. II, Ch. 8)." For the favor of Jesus, Grandgent (comm. to vv. 32–33) offers the following: "Three of the disciples (Peter, James, John) were chosen by Jesus to be present, and to receive the clearest revelation of his character, on three different occasions: at the Transfiguration (Matth. 17:1–8), in the Garden of Gethsemane (Matth. 26:36–38), and at the raising of the daughter of Jairus (Luke 8:50–56). On these three occasions Peter, James, and John stand respectively for Faith, Hope, and Love."

30. The Greek word "basilica" is defined by Jacopo della Lana (comm. to vv. 29–30) as *Domus regia* (royal palace). Benvenuto (comm. to vv. 28–30) says that Beatrice is referring to the Church Triumphant (in the Empyrean, if it is now present here).

32. For James as the "figure" of Hope in the technical sense (i.e., he is said to "figure" it), see Hollander (Holl.1969.1), pp. 64–66. For his more general association with hope, see Tartaro (Tart.1989.1), p. 680, referring to the earlier arguments of Conrieri (Conr.1971.1) and Battaglia Ricci (Batt.1972.1).

37. James, lending his presence to that of Peter, is the one who speaks.

38–39. The plain meaning of this circumlocution is that, at the invitation of James, Dante looked up at both apostles, since he had at first lowered his gaze in respect. See Psalm 120:1: "Levavi oculos meos in montes, unde veniet auxilium mihi" (I have lifted up my eyes to the hills, whence shall come my help).

40–45. One might paraphrase the apostle's words as follows: "Since the Emperor, in his grace, wants you to see his counts in his most secret hall while you still live so that, experiencing the truth of this court, you may make yourself stronger in Hope—and others, too." For the language of worldly titles, used of the members of the "court" of Heaven, see the note to *Paradiso* XXIV.115.

46–48. James asks the protagonist three questions: (1) "What is Hope?" (2) "How does your mind blossom with it?" (3) "From where did it make its way to you?"

49–51. In the poet's barely suppressed reference to Daedalus, Beatrice is portrayed as having done well in guiding Dante's pens/wings to such lofty flight. She now intervenes for him, answering James's second question—perhaps because it would have been awkward for Dante to have responded, since his answer might have seemed self-praising.

52–57. Mazzotta (Mazz.1988.2), p. 98, sees this passage as confirming the pattern of Exodus as a model for the poem, as has already been made explicit in *Purgatorio* II.46. It also contains two (of only three) uses of the verb *militare* in the poem. We are dealing here with an armed exodus, a Christian militancy. Beatrice presents Dante's claims to the theological virtue of Hope. Inscribed in Christ, he has been chosen to come from "Egypt" to "Jerusalem" and to this vision before he finishes his militancy (Daniello [comm. to vv. 55–57] was apparently the first commentator to cite Job 7:1 in this connection: "Militia est vita hominis super terram" [Man's life on this earth is a warfare]; it has since become fairly commonplace to do so).

58–63. Beatrice continues: As for the first and third questions, which you put to him not to know the answer but so that he may please you in his responses (cf. *Par.* XXIV, 40–45), and which will not be difficult for him, let him reply.

67–69. See Singleton (comm. on this tercet): "The definition of hope given by Dante here is that of Peter Lombard in *Sentences* III.xxvi.1: 'Est enim spes certa expectatio futurae beatitudinis, veniens ex Dei gratia et meritis praecedentibus' (Now hope is a certain expectation of future beatitude proceeding from God's grace and antecedent merits). He adds: 'Sine meritis aliquid sperare non spes sed praesumptio dici potest' (Without merits, to hope for something is not hope but presumption)."

70–78. See Psalm 9:11 (9:10 in our Bible): "And those who know your name shall put their trust in you [*sperent in te*])." The protagonist credits David with being the first who had instilled hope in his heart, and then James (James 1:12) instilled it there, too, so that Dante is filled with it and "rerains" both of these "rains" on others.

73–78. William Stephany (Step.1995.1), pp. 377–78, invites a closer examination of these two tercets, which reveal, first, hidden in the words describing David's *tëodia*, Augustine's association of the name of God and hope; second, in the very words of the Epistle of James (see the note to *Inf.* XXVI.32 for the presence of James 3:4–6 behind that tercet), the imperative to be a maker of words producing a love for God, an imperative fulfilled by Dante's *tëodia* as well.

73. See David (Davi.1993.1), pp. 441–44, on *tëodia* as a "chant provenant de Dieu" (song deriving from God) and as being, *sub rosa*, a generic denominator of the poem. But see Barolini's earlier (and fuller) exposition of this theme (Baro.1984.1), pp. 276–77.

79–81. James responds to Dante's formulation with an accepting lightning flash.

82–87. See Tozer (comm. to vv. 83–84) for a paraphrase and explanation: "St. James is still kindled with love for the virtue of Hope, though the Blessed can no longer feel hope themselves, because they have fruition; *la palma*: the palm of martyrdom, *l'uscir del campo*: his quitting the field of battle was his death. St. James was put to death by Herod Agrippa the Elder, Acts 12:1–2."

89–96. Tozer (comm. to vv. 91–93): "Isaiah 61:7: 'Therefore in their land they shall possess the double; everlasting joy shall be unto them.' Dante interprets 'the double' as meaning the blessedness of soul and body; cf. *doppia vesta* here with *due stole* in 1. 127." And see John (in Apocalypse 3:5; 7:9–17), speaking more directly of the general resurrection.

Stephany (Step.1995.1), p. 381, suggests that, although not cited directly in this canto, Isaiah 61 offers an indirect gloss on it. In Luke 4, Jesus reads from this chapter of Isaiah in the temple; when he sees that his words are offensive he insists that "no prophet is honored in his native land" (Luke 4:24), words that certainly must have seemed to the exiled poet to fit his own condition as well.

89. Chiavacci Leonardi (Chia.1988.2), p. 266n., writes that *segno* here means, not *termine a cui si tende* or *meta* ("goal"), as is supposedly the "general understanding among exegetes" of this verse, but "sign," citing Torraca (comm. to vv. 88–90) as her precursor. However, consultation of the full and sensible review of the problem by Scartazzini (comm. to vv.

88–90) would have revealed an earlier, better, and more convincing understanding of the line, taken in precisely this sense.

91–93. For a meditation upon resurrection, so clearly referred to here, as being the central concern of the entire poem, see Chiavacci Leonardi (Chia.1988.2).

93. For the two previous appearances of the phrase *dolce vita,* see the note to *Paradiso* IV.35.

94–96. For the "shining robes," see Apocalypse 3:5 and 7:9–17. And for the concept of the glorified body, see Gragnolati (Grag.2005.1), p. 198; also pp. 165–66, discussing St. James.

97–99. Among the commentators, only Carroll (comm. to these verses) looks up from this Latin "translation" of the vernacular version of a line from Psalm 9, which we have heard in verse 73, to think of Psalm 30, also involving hope in the Lord. This is what he has to say: "It is probably meant to be the reversal of the incident in the Earthly Paradise. . . . There, when the Angels, pitying Dante's distress, sang '*In te, Domine, speravi,*' they were promptly silenced by Beatrice—he had then no title to hope. Now everything is changed. Beatrice herself proclaims him a child of hope."

98. The identity of the singer(s) of the words of the psalm is not given. The commentators are universally puzzled (if only Chimenz [comm. to vv. 97–99] has the good sense to complain that Dante had left the issue unresolved and problematic). It is thus perhaps necessary to assume that angels, whether in the ninth sphere or, as seems more likely, in the Empyrean, are their source. The only human souls above them now are Jesus and Mary. And while one cannot rule out the possibility that it is one of them that we hear (or even both of them), that does not seem likely, nor has anyone, perhaps, ever argued for that solution. And so an angelic voice or group of voices is probably an acceptable solution, but not one that there is consensus about. However, the inhabitants of the "spheres" (circles) of the Church Triumphant are probably ruled out, since they are now here in the eighth heaven and not up above. It is as though whoever, singular or plural, is doing that singing were answering Dante's Italian version of the psalm in Latin, as though to underline his acceptance as a hopeful member of the Church.

100–102. For the dazzling brightness of John's transfigured body, Toynbee (Toyn. 1905.1) refers to the legendary accounts found, for instance, in Vincent of Beauvais (whom he cites), Petrus Comestor, and Jacopo da Varagine.

He is so bright that were the constellation Cancer (which shines all night from mid-December to mid-January) to have in it a single star as bright, it would turn one month into unbroken "day."

103–108. See Grandgent (comm. to vv. 103–111): "The three representatives of the Christian virtues dance before Beatrice, as the Virtues themselves did (in allegorical form) in *Purg.* XXIX.121–129."

109–111. John joins his fellow apostles (Peter and James) in song as Beatrice, as bride, looks on.

112–114. The references are to the disciple who leaned on Jesus (John 13:23) and who was chosen by Christ on the cross to care for Mary (John 19:27). The pelican seemed a fitting image of Christ because the bird was supposed to feed its young by piercing its own breast with its beak to feed them with its blood. The bird is mentioned (if not with these characteristics) in Psalm 101:7 (102:6). For a fairly extensive note devoted to Christ as pelican, see Carroll (comm. to vv. 100–114).

118–121. Dante's blindness, as Carroll observes (comm. to these verses), is a form of punishment for his vain curiosity about the bodily condition of the apostle's soul; he goes on to note that it is curious that Thomas (*ST* suppl., q. 77, a. 1, ad 2) supports the truth of the legend.

122–129. John says that his body has returned to earth as clay, and will so remain until the general resurrection; only Christ and Mary are in Heaven in the flesh, as Dante is instructed to tell those "back home" whom he shall meet when he returns.

124–126. Jacoff (Jaco.1999.1), p. 52, believes that Dante cancels the version of the tale that has John being in Heaven in his flesh in order to privilege Mary.

127–129. John, who is the very model of the biblical scribe (see, e.g., Apocalypse 22:18–19) here has become the dictator, with Dante acting as *his* scribe. He specifically licenses Dante to write the words he has just written.

130–135. Poletto (comm. to these verses), citing Casini, is the first commentator to find the original of this simile in Statius, mentioning *Thebaid* IV.804–807 and VI.799–801. But see Porena (comm. to these verses [actually his second "nota finale" to this canto in the printed version of his commentary]), who attacks such attributions as "scholarship" run amok. (Torraca [comm. to these verses] had previously suggested as much, if a bit more gently.) Bosco/Reggio (comm. to vv. 133–135) are in accord with Porena. However, it should be pointed out that Porena does not discuss the Statian simile that is closest to Dante's text (that in the sixth book), but deals with that in *Thebaid* IV and another not adduced by Poletto (*Theb.* X.774–777).

131–132. Our translation reflects Gaffney's suggestion (Gaff.1973.1, p. 111) that the verb, *si quietò*, preserves the ambiguity between sound and movement.

136–139. See Acts 9:7, when Saul's companions, "hearing a voice but seeing no man," try to see Jesus. We may want to remember that John, as visionary, was frequently portrayed as "blind" (see, e.g., *Purg.* XXIX. 143–144), a familiar iconographical representation of inner sight.

PARADISO XXVI

OUTLINE

STARRY SPHERE

1–6 Dante, blinded, hears the voice of John as a breath, posing his first question: "What is your soul's goal?"

7–12 and then offering his reassurance: Beatrice his **Ananias**;

13–18 Dante answers (1): "the good that makes you happy";

19–24 John's second question: "Who made you aim at that target?"

25–27 Dante answers (2): "rational examination and authority";

28–36 reason: the greater good draws the greater love:

37–39 **[Aristotle]**: love as the cause of all celestial movement;

40–45 authority: John himself revealed God in the Bible;

46–48 John summarizes and accepts Dante's answer

49–51 John's third question: "But what are the cords that draw you? the teeth that bite you?"

52–54 John's intention is clear (he wants Dante to tell of the role of love in leading him to understanding):

55–66 Dante answers (3): the "bites" are Creation, Redemption, and promise of eternal Glory—these have "drawn" him from the sea of perverse love to the shore of good love;

67–69 the blessed (the host, not only the apostles) and Beatrice sing the "Sanctus"—in Italian;

70–78 simile: a man, awakened from sleep by a light, who does not know what he is looking at until he can decipher it: just so were Dante's eyes cleared by Beatrice's;

79–81 Dante's stupefaction at the presence of a fourth light;

82–84 Beatrice: "This is Adam";

85–90 simile: as the tip of a tree bent down by wind snaps back on its own, so Dante, silenced by her words, now wants to speak:

91–96 Dante addresses Adam as God's direct creation and as the father of humankind;

97–102 simile: cloth covering an animal reveals its feelings, as Adam's inner gladness was visible within his glowing form

103–108 Adam: I read your thoughts in God, the mirror that reflects all things, while nothing can mirror it

109–142 Adam states and then answers Dante's four questions:

109–114 (1) how long has it been since God put him in Eden? (2) how long did he stay there? (3) what was the reason for God's anger? (4) what were the languages (a) that he used and (b) that he made?

the answers:

115–117 (3) not the eating itself, but the transgression;

118–123 (1) 930 years on earth, 4,302 years in Limbo;

124–138 (4) the language he spoke was extinct before Nimrod's attempt to build Babel; language is mortal;

139–142 (2) he lived in Eden, sinless, then guilty, into the seventh hour after he was created.

PARADISO XXVI

Mentr'io dubbiava per lo viso spento,
de la fulgida fiamma che lo spense
uscì un spiro che mi fece attento,

dicendo: "Intanto che tu ti risense
de la vista che haï in me consunta
ben è che ragionando la compense.

Comincia dunque; e dì ove s'appunta
l'anima tua, e fa ragion che sia
la vista in te smarrita e non defunta:

perché la donna che per questa dia
regïon ti conduce, ha ne lo sguardo
la virtù ch'ebbe la man d'Anania."

Io dissi: "Al suo piacere e tosto e tardo
vegna remedio a li occhi, che fuor porte
quand' ella entrò col foco ond' io sempr' ardo.

Lo ben che fa contenta questa corte,
Alfa e O è di quanta scrittura
mi legge Amore o lievemente o forte."

Quella medesma voce che paura
tolta m'avea del sùbito abbarbaglio,
di ragionare ancor mi mise in cura;

e disse: "Certo a più angusto vaglio
ti conviene schiarar: dicer convienti
chi drizzò l'arco tuo a tal berzaglio."

E io: "Per filosofici argomenti
e per autorità che quinci scende
cotale amor convien che in me si 'mprenti:

While I was still bewildered at my loss of sight,
from the resplendent flame that blinded me
there breathed a voice that caught my ear:

'Until you have regained the sight
you have consumed on me, you will do well
to make good for its loss with speech.

'Begin, and tell what goal your soul has set.
And be assured your power of sight
is but confounded, not forever lost,

'for the lady who guides you through
this holy place possesses in her glance
the power the hand of Ananias had.'

And I said: 'As soon or as late as she wishes,
may the cure come to eyes that were the portals
she entered with the fire in which I always burn.

'The good that satisfies this court
is alpha and omega of whatever scripture
Love teaches me in loud or gentle tones.'

The same voice that had set me free
from fear at my sudden blindness
made me hesitate before I spoke again,

when it said: 'It is clear you need to sift
with a finer sieve, for you must reveal
who made you aim your bow at such a target.'

And I: 'Both philosophic reasoning
and the authority that descends from here
made me receive the imprint of such love,

ché 'l bene, in quanto ben, come s'intende,
così accende amore, e tanto maggio
quanto più di bontate in sé comprende.

Dunque a l'essenza ov' è tanto avvantaggio,
che ciascun ben che fuor di lei si trova
altro non è ch'un lume di suo raggio,

più che in altra convien che si mova
la mente, amando, di ciascun che cerne
il vero in che si fonda questa prova.

Tal vero a l'intelletto mïo sterne
colui che mi dimostra il primo amore
di tutte le sustanze sempiterne.

Sternel la voce del verace autore,
che dice a Moïsè, di sé parlando:
'Io ti farò vedere ogne valore.'

Sternilmi tu ancora, incominciando
l'alto preconio che grida l'arcano
di qui là giù sovra ogne altro bando."

E io udi': "Per intelletto umano
e per autoritadi a lui concorde
d'i tuoi amori a Dio guarda il sovrano.

Ma dì ancor se tu senti altre corde
tirarti verso lui, sì che tu suone
con quanti denti questo amor ti morde."

Non fu latente la santa intenzione
de l'aguglia di Cristo, anzi m'accorsi
dove volea menar mia professione.

Però ricominciai: "Tutti quei morsi
che posson far lo cor volgere a Dio,
a la mia caritate son concorsi:

'for the good, by measure of its goodness, kindles
love as soon as it is known, and so much more
the more of goodness it contains.

'To that essence, then, which holds such store of goodness
that every good outside of it is nothing
but a light reflected of its rays,

'the mind of everyone who sees the truth
on which this argument is based
must, more than anything, be moved by love.

'This truth is set forth to my understanding
by him who demonstrates to me the primal love
of all eternal substances.

'And the voice of the truthful Author sets it forth
when, speaking of Himself, He says to Moses:
"I will make all My goodness pass before you."

'You also set it forth to me in the beginning
of your great message, which, more than any other herald,
proclaims the mystery of this high place on earth.'

And I heard: 'In accord with human reason
and with the authorities concordant with it,
the highest of your loves is turned to God.

'Say further if you feel still other cords
that draw you to Him, so that you may declare
the many teeth with which this love does bite.'

The holy purpose of Christ's Eagle was not hidden.
Indeed, I readily perceived the road
on which he set my declaration on its way.

Thus I began again: 'All those things
the bite of which can make hearts turn to God
converge with one another in my love.

ché l'essere del mondo e l'esser mio,
la morte ch'el sostenne perch' io viva,
e quel che spera ogne fedel com' io,

con la predetta conoscenza viva,
tratto m'hanno del mar de l'amor torto,
e del diritto m'han posto a la riva.

Le fronde onde s'infronda tutto l'orto
de l'ortolano etterno, am' io cotanto
quanto da lui a lor di bene è porto."

Sì com' io tacqui, un dolcissimo canto
risonò per lo cielo, e la mia donna
dicea con li altri: "Santo, santo, santo!"

E come a lume acuto si disonna
per lo spirto visivo che ricorre
a lo splendor che va di gonna in gonna,

e lo svegliato ciò che vede aborre,
sì nescïa è la sùbita vigilia
fin che la stimativa non soccorre;

così de li occhi miei ogne quisquilia
fugò Beatrice col raggio d'i suoi,
che rifulgea da più di mille milia:

onde mei che dinanzi vidi poi;
e quasi stupefatto domandai
d'un quarto lume ch'io vidi tra noi.

E la mia donna: "Dentro da quei rai
vagheggia il suo fattor l'anima prima
che la prima virtù creasse mai."

Come la fronda che flette la cima
nel transito del vento, e poi si leva
per la propria virtù che la soblima,

'The world's existence and my own,
the death He bore that I might live,
and that which all believers hope for as do I,

'all these—and the certain knowledge of which I spoke—
have drawn me from the sea of twisted love
and brought me to the shore where love is just.

'I love the leaves with which the garden
of the eternal Gardener is in leaf
in measure of the good He has bestowed on them.'

As soon as I was silent, the sweetest song
resounded through that heaven, and my lady
chanted with the others: 'Holy, holy, holy!'

As sleep is broken by a piercing light
when the spirit of sight runs to meet the brightness
that passes through its filmy membranes,

and the awakened man recoils from what he sees,
his senses stunned in that abrupt awakening
until his judgment rushes to his aid—

exactly thus did Beatrice drive away each mote
from my eyes with the radiance of her own,
which could be seen a thousand miles away,

so that I then saw better than I had before.
And almost dazed with wonder I inquired
about a fourth light shining there among us.

My lady answered: 'Within these rays
the first soul ever made by the First Power
looks with love upon his Maker.'

As the tree that bends its highest branches
in a gust of wind and then springs back,
raised up by natural inclination,

fec'io in tanto in quant' ella diceva,
stupendo, e poi mi rifece sicuro
un disio di parlare ond' ïo ardeva.

E cominciai: "O pomo che maturo
solo prodotto fosti, o padre antico
a cui ciascuna sposa è figlia e nuro,

divoto quanto posso a te supplìco
perché mi parli: tu vedi mia voglia,
e per udirti tosto non la dico."

Talvolta un animal coverto broglia,
sì che l'affetto convien che si paia
per lo seguir che face a lui la 'nvoglia;

e similmente l'anima primaia
mi facea trasparer per la coverta
quant' ella a compiacermi venìa gaia.

Indi spirò: "Sanz' essermi proferta
da te, la voglia tua discerno meglio
che tu qualunque cosa t'è più certa;

perch' io la veggio nel verace speglio
che fa di sé pareglio a l'altre cose,
e nulla face lui di sé pareglio.

Tu vuogli udir quant' è che Dio mi puose
ne l'eccelso giardino, ove costei
a così lunga scala ti dispuose,

e quanto fu diletto a li occhi miei,
e la propria cagion del gran disdegno,
e l'idïoma ch'usai e che fei.

Or, figliuol mio, non il gustar del legno
fu per sé la cagion di tanto essilio,
ma solamente il trapassar del segno.

so was I overcome while she was speaking—
awestruck—and then restored to confidence
90 by the words that burned in me to be expressed.

I began: 'O fruit who alone were brought forth ripe,
O ancient father, of whom each bride
93 is at once daughter and daughter-in-law,

'as humbly as I am able, I make supplication
for you to speak with me. You know what I long for.
96 To have your answer sooner I leave that unsaid.'

Sometimes, beneath its covering, an animal
stirs, thus making its desire clear
99 by how its wrappings follow and reveal its movement.

In just this manner the very first soul
revealed to me, through its covering,
102 how joyously it came to do me pleasure.

Then it breathed forth: 'Without your telling me,
I can discern your wishes even better
105 than you can picture anything you know as certain.

'For I can see them in that truthful mirror
which makes itself reflective of all else
108 but which can be reflected nowhere else.

'You wish to know how long it is since God
placed me in the lofty garden where this lady
111 prepared you for so long a stairway,

'and how long it was a pleasure to my eyes,
and the true cause of the great wrath,
114 and the language that I used and that I shaped.

'Know then, my son, that in itself the tasting of the tree
was not the cause of such long exile—
117 it lay in trespassing the boundary line.

Quindi onde mosse tua donna Virgilio,
quattromilia trecento e due volumi
120 di sol desiderai questo concilio;

e vidi lui tornare a tutt' i lumi
de la sua strada novecento trenta
123 fïate, mentre ch'ïo in terra fu'mi.

La lingua ch'io parlai fu tutta spenta
innanzi che a l'ovra inconsummabile
126 fosse la gente di Nembròt attenta:

ché nullo effetto mai razïonabile,
per lo piacere uman che rinovella
129 seguendo il cielo, sempre fu durabile.

Opera naturale è ch'uom favella;
ma così o così, natura lascia
132 poi fare a voi secondo che v'abbella.

Pria ch'i' scendessi a l'infernale ambascia,
I s'appellava in terra il sommo bene
135 onde vien la letizia che mi fascia;

e *El* si chiamò poi: e ciò convene,
ché l'uso d'i mortali è come fronda
138 in ramo, che sen va e altra vene.

Nel monte che si leva più da l'onda,
fu'io, con vita pura e disonesta,
da la prim' ora a quella che seconda,
142 come 'l sol muta quadra, l'ora sesta."

'In the place from which your lady sent down Virgil
I longed for this assembly more than four thousand
three hundred and two revolutions of the sun,

'and I saw it return to all the lights
along its track nine hundred thirty times
while I was living on the earth.

'The tongue I spoke was utterly extinct
before the followers of Nimrod turned their minds
to their unattainable ambition.

'For nothing ever produced by reason—
since human tastes reflect the motion
of the moving stars—can last forever.

'It is the work of nature man should speak
but, if in this way or in that, nature leaves to you,
allowing you to choose at your own pleasure.

'Before I descended to anguish of Hell,
I was the name on earth of the Sovereign Good,
whose joyous rays envelop and surround me.

'Later *El* became His name, and that is as it should be,
for mortal custom is like a leaf upon a branch,
which goes and then another comes.

'On the mountain that rises highest
from the sea, I lived, pure, then guilty,
from the first hour until the sun changed quadrant,
in the hour that follows on the sixth.'

1. As a continuation of its predecessor, this canto begins with Dante's concerns about his blindness. The verb *dubbiava* underlines the combination of fear and uncertainty that he is experiencing, as Sapegno (comm. to vv. 1–2) points out (citing Francesco da Buti [comm. to vv. 1–12]); he reflects on some of the previous and varying meanings of the verb *dubbiare* (*Inf.* IV.18 and *Purg.* XX.135: being fearful; *Purg.* III.72: being dubious).

3. For the noun *spiro*, see *Paradiso* XXIV.32, where it refers to Peter's "breath" (and see the related verb [*spirò*] at XXIV.82; and XXV.82, with similar significance for James as well). Thus each apostle is identified with the word connected to the spiration of the Holy Spirit; it is probably not accidental that all three of them are associated with this spiration in *Paradiso* XXV.132.

5–6. These lines bring back to mind a similar tactic on the part of Virgil (*Inferno* XI.10–15), where Dante's olfactory sense must be rested from the infernal stench before the downward journey into the pit may be continued; therefore, Virgil, in order to pass the time profitably, offers his "lecture" on the order of the sins. Here, in response to Dante's temporary blindness, John will use the time to give Dante his examination on Love, which begins with the next tercet.

6. Aversano (Aver.2000.2), p. 121, points out that here the verb *ragionare*, so intimately connected with the phrase *d'amore* (and thus "to speak of love") in Dante's own and other amorous lyrics, here is put to the service of discussing a higher form of love, the third (and highest) of the three theological virtues (see Paul's statement to that effect [that among faith, hope, and love, "the greatest of these is love"] in I Corinthians 13:13). (The verb is repeated in verse 21.)

At the same time, it is necessary to keep in mind, as Scartazzini (comm. to vv. 1–18) reminds us, citing Thomas (*ST* I–II, q. 65, a. 5), the necessary relations among Charity, Faith, and Hope. We may be tempted to conclude that, like the Persons of the Trinity, the presence of one of them implies the presence of the other two.

9–12. The protagonist's blindness, John assures him, is but temporary. For the reference, see Acts 9:10–18, where Ananias, a disciple of Christ, is sent to cure Saul of his blindness. Once he does so, Paul begins to preach Jesus Christ. This is thus the pivotal moment in the life of Saul/Paul. While Beatrice, bringing back Dante's sight, is thus Ananias-like, there is much less at stake here, and the comparison may seem at least a bit overblown.

9. The past participle, *smarrita*, of the verb *smarrire* (to confuse, discourage, bewilder) is used to suggest Dante's inner state in *Inferno* I.3, II.64, V.72, X.125, and XIII.24 (see the note to *Inf.* X.125). In most of those situations, the protagonist felt sympathy for the damned. Here, in the penultimate occurrence of the word to indicate his inner state, his loss of the faculty of vision is not the result of his sinfulness, but represents only a temporary failing (a result of his remaining tendency to see with carnal eyes?) in his increasing capacity to understand things divine. A final occurrence of the verb to indicate that condition awaits (*Par.* XXXIII.77); there it will refer to a rather different (and loftier) "confusion" on the protagonist's part.

13–15. Getto (Gett.1968.1), p. 933, has observed that this canto enters into an intimate relationship with the *Vita nuova* (see also Brownlee [Brow.1990.1], p. 390). And these verses, more pointedly than most in this *cantica* dedicated to Dante's love for Beatrice, recall the physical basis of Dante's first desires for her (and one also refers to the even clearer sexual reference of that Virgilian reminiscence found in a similar moment, *Purg.* XXX.46–48, equating Beatrice and Dido). The language here is unmistakably reminiscent of the language of sexual desire found in Dante's lyrics (and in those of other poets). Reassembling arguments made in her three previous essays in this vein, Regina Psaki (Psak.2003.1) argues that Dante's heavenly love for Beatrice conflates that early form of love in his present one. Opponents of this view are accused of "cultural nervousness about the notion that sexual love may be sacred" (p. 119). Nonetheless, it is difficult to believe that Dante wants his reader to think that the old flame still burns beneath angelic clothing; and it is still more difficult to believe that, at least within the confines of the *Comedy*, he would consider any form of extramarital sexual love "sacred."

16–18. Dante's answer is simple (at least it seems so at first). Love "reads" instruction to him, as might a professor at the Sorbonne. The poet's word *leggere* refers to the practice of instruction in theology from which the word "lecture" derives (for a previous use, see *Par.* X.137); see Poletto (comm. to *Par.* X.136–138). Dante's heart is instructed by the Holy Spirit to love God.

The problem for the reader results from the phrasing of the thought "whatever scripture Love teaches me in loud or gentle tones." Since the precise meaning of this tercet is much contested, there are many instances of commentators who outdo themselves in improbable readings (for a review, see Scartazzini [comm. to vv. 17–18]; his own attempt, however, leaves much to be desired with respect to the last four words [*o lievemente o forte*]). To characterize them with the words of Origen, hurling invective at those copyists of the Gospels who twisted the sense of the text in order to arrive at a meaning of which they approved, such commentators are guilty of "perverse audacity" (see Ehrman [Ehrm.2005.1], p. 52). However, see Carroll (comm. to vv. 1–18): "Much difficulty is made of these words, but the meaning is quite simple: 'God is the beginning and the end of all my love.' The figurative form is taken from the Alpha and Omega of Revelation 1:8: God is the entire alphabet of the sacred writings which love reads to his soul—the scripture of the universe. Many meanings are suggested for '*o lievemente o forte*,' 'with light voice or strong': such as reason and revelation, or human and Divine love, or God loved for Himself and for His benefits. Dante's own words which follow seem to me to give the answer. The *loud* voice corresponds to the arguments of Philosophy and the assurance of Revelation in ll. 25–45; and the *low* voice to the secondary causes of love in ll. 55–66. But whether low or loud, God is the one and only object of love." For a different view, see Benvenuto (comm. to this tercet), who interprets "lievemente o forte" as "easy or difficult," a view accepted by Simone Marchesi (Marc.2002.2).

For "Alfa ed O" Dante is of course citing John's own words (Apocalypse 1:8, 21:6, 22:13), as he has already done in the *Epistle to Cangrande* (XIII.90): "And since, when the Beginning or First, which is God, has been reached, there is nought to be sought for beyond, inasmuch as He is Alpha and Omega [*Alfa et O*], that is, the Beginning and the End, as the Vision of John tells us, the work ends in God Himself, who is blessed for evermore, world without end" (tr. P. Toynbee).

16. For "lo ben" (the good), see *Inferno* III.18, "il ben dell'intelletto" (the good of the intellect), or, as most commentators agree, God.

17. For some bibliography dealing with this verse, see Valerio (Vale.2003.1), p. 98, n. 65, citing not only Nardi's discussion (Nard.1964.2), pp. 317–20, but three studies by Del Popolo from the 1990s. Nardi demon-

strated that the reading he had grown up with ("Alfa ed Omega") is metrically impossible.

21. The words *mi mise in cura* (made me hesitate) are not understood by everyone in the same way, with some believing that they mean "gave me a reason," an opinion that we do not share.

22–24. John asks the protagonist to go down to a second level in his disquisition on this theological virtue, to put his answer through a "finer sieve." However, and as Singleton (comm. to vv. 1–79) points out, "no definition of love is given in the examination, as it is with faith and hope. This serves to stress the fact that love is primarily a matter of the will, not of the intellect. Dante is simply asked *what* he loves, and why."

25–27. Dante replies briefly but thoroughly, refining his first response (vv. 13–18). Love is imprinted in him by two agents, philosophical arguments and "authority," or, in a shorthand of sorts, Aristotle and the Bible.

28–36. For the gist of these tercets, see Tozer's paraphrase: "The argument derived from Reason is this:—That which is good awakens love in the soul of him who understands its nature, and the love increases in proportion as the goodness is greater. Consequently, the Being who is perfect goodness must attract more love than any other object."

37–39. To whom does Dante refer here? Aristotle is the nearly unanimous opinion of the commentators, who are divided only about the precise passage, whether in the *Metaphysics*, the *Ethics*, or *On Causes* (attributed to Aristotle during the Middle Ages), explaining how the spheres' love for the Godhead set the universe into motion.

40–45. Dante now adduces two texts in evidence, the first plainly identifiable. It reports that God says to Moses (Exodus 33:19), "Ego ostendam omne bonum tibi" (I will make all My goodness pass before you). Perhaps the first commentator to deal with the context of this passage was Vellutello (comm. to vv. 40–42), noting that it continues by having God reveal to Moses only His "back parts," not His face. Apparently he was the only commentator to do so before Carroll, whose discussion is informative (comm. to vv. 19–45): "It seems to me difficult to believe that Dante, when quoting this, did not remember that God proceeds to say: 'Thou canst not see my face: for there shall no man see me and live. . . . Thou shalt see my back parts: but my face shall not be seen.' And, as I understand it, the passage which he takes from the New Testament is chosen just because it is the fulfillment of the imperfect revelation given to Moses." Then Carroll turns to the less clearly identified source: "It is taken from St. John's writings, the particular reference being much disputed. . . . Dante is thinking of all [of John's writings] as *one* proclamation of the secret of heaven to earth; and if so, 'the *beginning* of the high heralding' is the Prologue to the Fourth Gospel. Now it happens that the closing words of the Prologue allude to this very fulfillment of the imperfect revelation through Moses of which I have spoken: 'The law was given by Moses; grace and truth came by Jesus Christ. No man hath seen God at any time; the only begotten Son, which is in the bosom of the Father, he hath declared him.' The evident connection of this with the passage quoted from Moses seems to me conclusive. Moses saw the back of God; Christ reveals the 'secret' of heaven—the bosom of the Father" [*Par.* XXVI.40–45].

42. For Guido Cavalcanti's version of this statement, see *Vita nuova* III.14: "Vedeste, al mio parere, onne valore" (I think that you beheld all worth—tr. M. Musa), as cited by Valerio (Vale.2003.1), pp. 90–91. And see the discussion of Exodus 33:19 in the note to vv. 40–45.

44. The word *preconio* (proclamation, message) and the word *arcano* (mystery) is each a hapax. Benvenuto begins the understanding that this *preconio* is the opening verse of John's Gospel, "In the beginning was the Word." However, and as Scartazzini (comm. to this verse) argues, most of the ancient commentators are of the opinion that the Apocalypse is on Dante's mind here; he follows them. It would have been hard to oppose the combined authority of Benvenuto and Scartazzini; the former's judgment (supported, as it was in this particular, by that of Francesco da Buti) should perhaps have weighed more heavily with the latter.

46–48. John accepts Dante's answer. Depending on whether the verb *guarda* is to be taken as a present indicative (as we translate it) or as an imperative strongly influences one's understanding of the tercet. See, inter alia, discussions in Scartazzini, brusquely dismissive (if perhaps rightly so) of those who decide for the imperative, and Bosco/Reggio, more balanced in keeping the options open (both in their comms. to this tercet).

49–51. John now sets his third question for the protagonist, involving the subjects of what draws him (by pulling him with *corde* [cords]) and what goads him (by bites of its *denti* [teeth]) toward God. The reader may be reminded of the stimuli on the seven terraces of the purgatorial mountain, which featured (see, e.g., *Purg.* XIV.147) *freno* or *richiamo* ("curb" or "lure"). In *Paradiso* XXVIII.12, Beatrice's eyes will be presented as the "cord" (in the sense of "noose") that captured him.

In response to Venturi's complaint against the bitterness of Dante's metaphor for such a sweet feeling (love), Lombardi (comm. to verse 51) points out that Dante has always used harsh metaphors for love (presented as burning, wounding, etc.).

53. The authors of the Gospels were portrayed as four different creatures, the "four living creatures" of Apocalypse 4:7: Matthew as man, Mark as lion, Luke as ox, John as eagle.

55–66. Carroll (comm. to vv. 46–63) continues his global explanation of this passage: "But [John's] examination is not finished. 'The Eagle of Christ' pursues the subject into its secondary causes. We come at this point to the scripture which Love reads with a *low* voice (l.18)—the collateral and subsidiary sources of charity, or as John puts it, the cords that draw, and the teeth that bite into the heart." And then, interpreting the verses 58–60, Carroll concludes: "In other words, the creation of the world and man, the cross of Christ, and the hope of glory: these are 'the teeth' with which the love of God bites into his heart, for all are operations of that love. Yet it is to be noted that they are not 'the interior act of charity,' the clinging of the soul to God, but only cords to draw men to the act."

62–63. Once more Dante turns to the large motif of the exodus to express his personal journey from sin to redemption. See the previous uses of *pelago* (*Inf.* I.23 and *Par.* II.5).

64–66. Scartazzini (comm. to verse 65) was apparently the first (and still among the few) to see that Dante was again resorting to the text of John's Gospel (John 15:1): "Ego sum vitis vera et Pater meus agricola est" (I am the true vine, and my Father is the vinedresser). See also Singleton (comm. to this tercet), Bosco/Reggio (comm. to this tercet), and Getto (Gett.1968.1), p. 941.

67–69. See Getto (Gett.1968.1), pp. 942–43, discussing Dante's formula for concluding the apostles' examinations of him on the three theological virtues. These occur at *Paradiso* XXIV.112–114, XXV.97–99, and in these verses. Getto finds the three texts sharing the following earmarks: Each passage (1) is contained in no more or no less than a single *terzina*; (2) contains reference to Dante's completion of his utterance; (3) cites the opening words of the celebrative song raised at its conclusion; (4) includes some description of the quality of that song; (5) refers to those who sang it.

Once again we find a Latin hymn (the "Sanctus"), which had become a part of the liturgy, performed in Italian ("Holy, holy, holy"). See the note to *Paradiso* XXIV.113–114. The original "Sanctus" is found in both Isaiah 6:3 and Apocalypse 4:8 (where it follows the description of the "four living creatures" [see the note to verse 53]).

70–79. This simile portrays Dante/Saul becoming Dante/Paul as a result of the ministrations of Beatrice, who restores his temporarily vanquished sight. See the note to vv. 9–12.

70–75. Dante seems to have been fascinated by the processes both of falling to sleep and of awakening from it. Is there another work from this period that has more frequent or more detailed references to both? See, for example, *Inferno* I.111, III.136, XXV.90, XXX.136–141, XXXIII.38; *Purgatorio* IX.11, IX.33–42, IX.63, XV.119–123, XVII.40–42, XVIII.87–88, XVIII.143–145, XXVII.92, XXVII.113, XXXII.64–69, XXXII.76–78; *Paradiso* XXXII.139.

See Boyde (Boyd.1993.1), pp. 74–75, for an analysis of the "mechanics" of seeing in these six lines.

73. The verb *ab[b]or[r]ire* (or, as we believe, *ab[b]or[r]are*)—and both forms (along with others, as well) are found with orthographical variants in the interpretive tradition—has caused a great deal of puzzlement. See Casagrande (Casa.1997.2) for a thorough study of the history of the problem, concluding that (1) the verb is nearly certainly the first conjugation one, used by Dante twice in *Inferno* (XXV.144; XXXI.24); (2) it probably, on the basis of observations found in Uguccione da Pisa, derives from a Latin synonym for *balbus* (not speaking clearly [see *Purg.* XIX.7 and *Par.* XXVII.130 and 133]) and here means "loses the power of speech." Casagrande, following Porena (comm. to vv. 73–75), treats the form of the verb here as metaplasmic, that is, believing that Dante, his hand forced by the exigencies of rhyme, has switched conjugational endings (*-ire*) for (*-are*). Our translation accepts the basic interpretation of Porena (as restated by Bosco/Reggio [comm. to vv. 73–75])—but does not accept the new

reading proposed by Casagrande, for the reason that the action resulting from Beatrice's intervention is not that the protagonist can speak clearly so much as it is that he can *see better* (see verse 79). Since what is revealed as the object of his eventually clear vision is still another soul, it would seem reasonable to argue that what at first appears unclear to the protagonist is that "fourth light," what turns out to be the radiance of Adam.

76. For the word *quisquilia*, a hapax in Dante, see Amos 8:6, where it is a hapax in the Bible, indicating the chaff from grain.

80–81. The totally unexpected "fourth light," we habitual readers realize, without surprise, is Adam. If we remember our first reading, we probably recall our amazement at what Dante (who reports himself "stupefatto" [dazed]) has done, putting the first father before us for an interview about Edenic existence.

80. For the word *stupefatto*, see Aversano (Aver.2000.2), p. 125, citing Acts 9:7, all the more plausible as a reference, given the Pauline context of the canto (introduced at vv. 10–12). "The men who were traveling with him [Saul] stood speechless [*stupefacti*], hearing the voice but seeing no one." Jesus, invisible, has called Saul to Him. Saul rises from the ground blind and is led by the hand by his fellow travelers into Damascus, where he will be cured of his blindness as the new man, Paul, by Ananias.

82–84. The theological dimensions of this tercet are large indeed: God the Father created all things and then Adam, who gazes up at his maker with the love sponsored by the Holy Spirit. That love is made manifest in turn by the redemptive act of Christ, who has saved fallen Adam and some of those who were born in his sinfulness.

85–90. This is an at least somewhat puzzling simile, equating Beatrice with a gust of wind, forcing the top of a tree down from its normal inclination upward. It then goes on to equate Dante with that treetop, regaining its natural upward direction once the gust has blown itself out. The meaning is plain, but the negative associations that surround Beatrice seem strange, and the positive ones that accumulate around Dante's desires to do something that Beatrice seems to want to inhibit seem so, too.

91–92. Adam was, by tradition, thought to have been created by God as though he were thirty or (more usually) thirty-three years old (thus matching the years of Christ on earth). Tommaseo (comm. to vv. 91–93) remarks that the protagonist's phrasing is not very kind, since it brings to Adam's mind the appetite (for the apple) that caused his fall.

On this passage see Moevs (Moev.2005.1), pp. 101–2, distinguishing between Adam as indeed ripe in himself, as he was made by God (and now again is), and the creature he had mistakenly thought he could improve by opposing God's will and stealing His forbidden fruit.

93. Every bride is both Adam's daughter and his daughter-in-law. Of course, the same holds true for grooms, if with genders exchanged. See Carroll (comm. to vv. 88–96), explaining that this verse is "an echo of St. Augustine's *City of God*, XV.16: '*Father* and *father-in-law* are the names of two relationships. . . . But Adam in his single person was obliged to hold both relations to his sons and daughters, for brothers and sisters were united in marriage. So too Eve his wife was both mother and mother-in-law to her children of both sexes.' "

95–96. The poet (and protagonist) play with the convention established and embellished as we proceed through the last canticle: Souls in Heaven read the thoughts of others in the mind of God. That being true, the protagonist acknowledges, an unvoiced question begets its answer more rapidly, avoiding the time otherwise lost in verbal duplication. Adam himself will underline this point at some length (vv. 103–108).

97. This line has caused confusion, even anger, and (perhaps consequently) flights of fancy. It was only with Lombardi (comm. to vv. 97–102) that a commentator disagreed with the earlier commentators' assumption that the covering was the creature's own fur. Now almost all agree that the imagined animal is covered (if for a reason not readily discerned) with a cloth of some kind. (Porena [comm. to vv. 97–99] would eventually draw on a childhood experience, when he once carried a cat in a sack, to suggest that Dante was referring to a similarly ensacked feline.) Torraca (comm. to vv. 97–102) suggests the possible reference to a caparisoned horse (if Pézard mainly receives the credit for Torraca's in fact earlier observation), but then wisely backs away from making any definite identification; he continues by reminding us of the highly similar similetic moment in *Paradiso* VIII.52–54, in which Dante compares the glad soul of Charles Martel to a silkworm clothed in its own glowing light. (And see the earlier and altogether similar appreciation of Poletto [comm. to vv. 97–102].) This, one thinks, is assuredly the model for any attempt at an interpretation; however, it is rare that the verse has been considered in this light.

If one wants to crown a particular exercise for its fervid imagination, one might well favor Daniello's opinion (comm. to vv. 97–102) of male horses sniffing on the wind the maddening odor of female horses in heat and shuddering thereat. In short, a number of animals have been called (including, in addition to those already mentioned, piglets, dogs, even birds [in particular, the hooded falcon]), but none has been chosen.

103–108. See the note to vv. 95–96.

104. See Moore (Moor.1889.1), pp. 483–86, supporting the traditional reading ("da te") against that strange but, for some people, overpoweringly attractive variant, "Dante": "There are few passages where we can pronounce with greater confidence as to the true reading than we can here. . . ." (p. 483). A goodly number of Dantists are firmly committed to the notion that the appearance of the poet's name in the poem, his signature, as it were, occurs only once, as the first word spoken by Beatrice, in *Purgatorio* XXX.55. Such as they are most grateful to Moore's exertions, since there had been, before his intervention, more than a few who were most eager to find "Dante" uttered by Adam, the first namer (see Genesis 2:19–20).

107–108. Tozer (comm. to vv. 106–108) paraphrases Adam's remark as follows: "I see those wishes depicted in the mind of God, in which, as in a faithful mirror, the thoughts of His creatures are reflected; whereas their minds (and therefore your [i.e., Dante's] mind) cannot know what is passing in the mind of God, so that you cannot reach the same certainty." He continues as follows: "According to this interpretation, *pareglio* is a substantive, meaning a 'parhelion' or mock-sun; from which sense—as a parhelion is a reflected or refracted image of the sun—it is taken to signify simply a 'reflexion.' The literal translation, then, of vv. 107–108 will be—'who makes [H]imself the reflexion of (i.e., in [H]im are reflected) the other things (and, in particular, men's minds), while none of them makes itself a reflexion of [H]im ([H]is thoughts are not reflected in their minds).' " For an exhaustive (it contains more than fifteen hundred words) review of the word *pareglio*, which, if its general sense is understood, has caused considerable difficulty, see Scartazzini (comm. to vv. 106–108).

109–114. Adam "repeats" Dante's four questions: (1) How much time has passed since God put Adam in Eden? (2) How long did he reside there? (3) What caused God's anger against him? (4) What were the languages that he was given and that he developed? (This fourth question has been variously understood.)

110–111. Dante's "thought question," intuited by Adam from the mind of God, included his reverent feelings toward Beatrice (unsurprisingly enough), who came to him in Eden, the very place that Adam lost, prepared to lead him on this great spiritual and intellectual journey.

114. The early commentators did not realize how problematic (and how important) this verse is. It presents Adam as having two separate linguistic "pools," each deriving from a different source, from which he first gathered and then formed the first human speech. It was Lombardi (comm. to this verse), at the early dawn of the "modern age" in Dante studies, in the last decade of the eighteenth century, who first made the (fairly obvious) point that the first speaking task performed by Adam was to name the animals God had just created as sharers of his world (Genesis 2:19–20). What was the *source* of that language? That is, did Adam learn it or was it innate in him, put there by God when He formed him from earth? Tommaseo (comm. to vv. 112–114) is (and correctly so) of the second opinion. Andreoli (comm. to this verse) appropriates Tommaseo's words to this effect, but then adds an important piece of evidence from Dante himself (*De vulgari eloquentia* [I.vi.4]): "I say that a certain form of language was created by God *along with the first soul*; I say 'form' with reference both to the words used for things, and to the construction of words, and to the arrangement of the construction; and this form of language would have continued to be used by all speakers, had it not been shattered through the fault of human presumption, as will be shown below" (tr. S. Botterill [italics added]). Thus did Dante at that time account for the origins of human vocabulary, of grammar, and of syntax; these all came directly from God and were inherent in Adam (and Eve, we imagine, though Dante never pays any positive attention to Eve as speaker; that is not something for which he considers her interesting). It is Adam who will name Eve *virago* ("woman"—Genesis 2:23). What Dante believed to have been Adam's creative process in developing his God-given language by adding words to it may be apparent here: From the pre-Hebrew equivalent of Latin *vir*, implanted in him by God, he derived "*vir*ago" (for "wo*man*").

While it is clear that Dante had changed his thinking, by the time he was writing the *Commedia*, about the second part of this history of the language (the length of time that the original Adamic speech survived—see the note to verse 134), there is no reason to believe he had altered that first opinion very much, if at all: The first Adamic speech was given by God, but (and we will be surprised by this, as some today still are, even to the point of simply getting it wrong) it was given as perishable. It was, as we shall shortly see, the core, or seedbed, of the first vernacular and, like all vernacular speech, doomed to die out to be replaced by other always changeful "idioms." God gave his *Ursprache* to Adam as a form, containing models for his development of vocabulary, of grammar, and of rhetoric. Simultaneously, He granted him the privilege of naming the animals himself. As a result, "dog," "owl," "lion" were terms invented by Adam, not by God. The language that he got from God was thus immediately, even if it first served as a model, in flux, a part of the mortal world of becoming, as was, we shall shortly learn, the one word that we can safely assume he got directly from his Creator, His name. This was "I," but became "El" (again, see the note to verse 134). (For God's changing His own name, see Exodus 6:2–3: "I [*Dominus*] appeared to Abraham, to Isaac, and to Jacob, as God Almighty [*in Deo omnipotente*], but by my name the Lord [*Adonai*] I did not make myself known to them").

For the word *idïoma*, which we have here translated "language," but which seems to be identified by Dante with vernacular speech, see the note to *Paradiso* XV.121–123, the passage in which it has its only other occurrence in the poem. On the language of Adam, see Mengaldo, "La lingua di Adamo," *ED* (IV [1970]), pp. 47b–48b; Imbach (Imba.1996.1), pp. 197–214. For the treatment of Adam in *De vulgari eloquentia*, see Corti (Cort.1978.1), pp. 243–56.

115–142. Tozer summarizes the rest of the canto (comm. to these verses): "Of Dante's four questions, which have just been stated, Adam answers first No. 3—'What was the real cause of the Fall of Man?' (vv. 115–117); next No. 1—'How long a time had elapsed from the Creation to the present moment?' (vv. 118–123); then No. 4—'What language did Adam speak?' (vv. 124–138); and finally No. 2—'How long a time did he spend in the Earthly Paradise?' (vv. 139–142)."

115–117. Adam answers first the third question that Dante has put to him, a question that, as many commentators point out, reflects the gravest issue that Adam knows: his own disobedience, which cost him and all our race Eden. This is "paradisal" behavior that we witness here; what sinner in *Inferno* would voluntarily recite his worst sin first (or at all)? There are a few exceptions, beginning with Ciacco (see *Inf.* VI.53), but most, as we saw, try to avoid this subject.

Hardly anyone dealing with this tercet recently (and this is particularly true with respect to American Dantists, who are perhaps more drawn to Ulysses than may seem reasonable) fails to discuss the obvious "quotation" in the phrase "il trapassar del segno" (the trespass of the boundary line) of *Inferno* XXVI.107–109: ". . . we reached the narrow strait / where Hercules marked off [*segnò*] the limits, / warning all men to go no farther." Surprisingly, the only apparent mention in the commentaries collected in the DDP (but see, e.g., Chiavacci Leonardi [Chia.1997.1], p. 728) is in Bosco/Reggio (comm. to vv. 109–117), referring to this passage's relationship with the theme of transgression, as embodied in the canto of Ulysses. However, cf. (among others) Iannucci (Iann.1976.1), p. 426; Hawkins (Hawk.1979.1); Brownlee (Brow.1990.1), p. 394; and Barolini (Baro.1992.1), pp. 49, 52, 58, 106, 108, 112, and 238, whose treatment begins with reference to Nardi's consideration (Nard.1942.1) of both Ulysses and Adam as having trespassed boundaries. See also Rati (Rati.1988.1), pp. 513–14.

116. The last occurrence of the noun *cagione* (reason, cause), of its forty-six instances in the poem, is found here (and for the penultimate, see verse 113). As the poem concludes, discursive reasoning yields to more intuitive forms of understanding and expression.

The use of the noun *essilio* (exile) binds two other figures to Adam in having shared this bitter experience, Dante and Virgil (who sees his after-life as exilic—see *Purg.* XXI.18). It is not surprising to find "Virgilio" as its rhyme in verse 118.

118–120. For the first notice of Adam's long life of exile from God's kingdom, first on earth and then in Limbo, see *Purgatorio* XXXIII.58–63 and the note thereto. See also the note to *Paradiso* IX.40 and to vv. 121–123, below.

Eusebius (whose dates were the basis for Jerome's authoritative *Chronicon* [which served most medieval encyclopedists, such as Isidore of Seville and Uguccione da Pisa]) is credited by the more recent commentators (beginning with Lombardi [comm. to vv. 119–120]) as being Dante's source for the 4,302 years between Adam's death and the Harrowing.

118. This represents the thirty-first and final appearance of Virgil's name in the poem. It thus occurs slightly less than half as often as that of Beatrice, which appears sixty-three times. (See the notes to *Purg.* XV.77 and *Par.* XVII.19.)

121–123. Adam says that he had lived on earth for 930 solar years (see Genesis 5:5). This means that he was harrowed (in A.D. 34) after 5,232 years (930 + 4,302) of sinful life, first on earth, then in Limbo, where his punishment was, apparently, to live without hope yet in desire. At least that is Virgil's description of the suffering of him and his cosufferers in Limbo (*Inf.* IV.42: "without hope we live in longing"), and it certainly fits him and all other damned pagans. But what of the Hebrew saints, like Adam? During their time in Hell were they equally without hope? Or, because they believed in Christ to come, were they in fact hopeful? Adam, however, does refer to his time in Hell as being typified by "anguish" (verse 133). In short, this is not an issue that Dante has chosen to confront, and we cannot say whether Dante thought that Adam and his eventually to-be-harrowed companions knew that Christ was coming for them or not, or whether they even hoped that He would.

Adam has now enjoyed 1,266 years of grace in Heaven. Adam's years coincide, of course, with the course of human life in general, 6,498 years along its road in 1300. See the note to *Paradiso* IX.40 for one traditional estimate of the future duration of human time. And see, for a fuller discussion of three views of that future, involving the Platonic Great Year (36,000 years), a medieval variant of that tradition (13,000 years), and St. Augustine's (possible) view that the world will last seven millennia, the last paragraph of the note to *Inferno* I.1 and the note to *Paradiso* IX.40 in the PDP.

124–126. Pietro di Dante explicitly identifies (comm. to vv. 124–132) Adam's first *lingua* as being vernacular speech. It was extinct, this tercet insists, before construction of the Tower of Babel began. Many have realized that this is a direct contradiction of what Dante had said in *De vulgari* (I.vi.4–7), where he specifically says that the first language was Hebrew and that it was spoken until after the construction of the Tower. (For a study of the literary history of this topos, see Borst [Bors.1957.1].)

From Genesis, Dante might have learned several things about the history of the language that squared with his spectacularly idiosyncratic theory of that history. The tenth chapter teaches that Noah's three sons (Japheth, Ham, and Shem) each had children, and all these groups of progeny spoke different languages (*linguae*); that is, the "confusion" was apparently in progress *before* the launch of Nimrod's "unachievable" linguistic project. Nonetheless, Genesis 11 begins with the earth still being of a single tongue (*terra labii unius*), and this passage is what Dante "revises," whatever justification he might have thought he had found, in the previous chapter, for doing so. God puts humankind into confusion for trying to build the tower (and that is the version found both in Genesis and in *De vulgari*); in the *Commedia*, however, the result of Babel is pre-Babelic. This is not the only time that we find Dante revising the text of the Bible to suit his own purpose. To seize on only one other blatant example, found in a neighboring passage in *De vulgari* (I.iv.2–3), Dante denies the authority of Genesis in making Eve the first speaker (God, he says, would not have wanted a woman to utter the first spoken word). And see his similarly high-handed treatment of classical text, e.g., of the *Aeneid* in *Purgatorio* XXII.40–41. Fortunately, there is a good deal of playfulness that lies behind these otherwise numbingly troglodytic gestures; nonetheless, there they are, and they are certainly challenging.

130. See P. V. Mengaldo, "lingua," *ED* (III [1971]), p. 661b, discussing the source of this verse in Egidio Romano, *De regimine principum* (III.ii.24): "It is a natural thing that man should speak, and nature teaches him to do so; but whether the speech should be German or French or Tuscan nature does not instruct him. On the contrary, a man must himself learn it, either by himself or with the aid of others."

132. Daniello (comm. to vv. 130–132) makes the astute observation that Dante is here citing the first line of the poem in Provençal he composes and attributes to Arnaut Daniel (it actually derives from a poem by Folchetto—see the note to *Purg.* XXVI.140–147—"Tan m'abellis l'amoros pensamen"). See *Purgatorio* XXVI.140.

133. Adam dates the change in the pre-Hebrew vernacular as having occurred before his death at the age of 930. His words do not allow any greater precision than that.

It is striking that we do not hear his name in this scene (we have heard it five times in *Inferno* and *Purgatorio*). See Andrea Ciotti, "Adamo," *ED* (I [1970]), pointing out that medieval Scriptural exegesis related Greek *'âdhâm* to *âdâhmah* ("man" to "earth"), thus *homo* to *humus*. This would surely have been of interest to Dante, since it would tend to locate Adamic vernacular within the low style, Dante's own (or so at least he chose to present it as being).

134. This verse has been the cause of a great deal of confusion, as some of its interpreters are honest enough to admit. Scartazzini, after an exhaustive survey of the history of its interpretation, concludes with the notice that, while it is most embarrassing for a commentator to admit such a thing, he has not resolved its problems. (For another noteworthy attempt to clarify [if not to solve] the problem, see Porena [comm. to this verse].)

The most enduring, among the several desperate stabs it has caused, has been the following: Vellutello (comm. to vv. 130–138) was apparently the first to claim that "I" was to be read numerically, as "one." Another notion has periodically reappeared (after having been introduced by Scartazzini [comm. to this verse]): "I" (or "J") is the first letter of "Jah" or "Jehovah." A much rarer but still interesting proposed solution is only found as late as Trucchi's commentary (comm. to vv. 133–138): Dante wanted "I" and not "El" because "I" (or "J," the same character in his Italian) was the first letter of "Jesus." Nonetheless, the formulation that "I" equals "un" ("one") found favor, over the years, with many interpreters (including several editors, who replace what is "I" in our text with "un"), beginning with Francesco da Buti (comm. to vv. 133–142). Lombardi (comm. to this verse) was apparently the first commentator to refer to Dante's earlier treatment of the nature of Adam's first word in *De vulgari;* he also pointed out that Dante was (whether deliberately or not he does not say) in disagreement with Isidore, who had been plain that "El" was the name that God was first called. That this is a possible meaning of this verse is reinforced by the presence of the same alpha-numerical pun on the Roman "i" as "one" at *Paradiso* XIX.128.

See Casagrande (Casa.1976.1) for a careful consideration of the problems of this verse. He ends up linking it, through the commentary of the Ottimo *ad loc.*, to Isidore's eighth (of ten appellations) name of God (*Etym.* VII.i), *ia*, itself connected to the Hebrew word *alleluia*, as praise of God's name. Hollander (Holl.1969.1), p. 144n., had previously argued for Isidore's *ninth* name of God, the *tetragrammaton*, transliterated as *ia ia*, as being the text that Dante had in mind, as evidenced by the parodic reference to it and the sixth name of God ("Ego *sum*, qui *sum*" [I am that I am]) found first in the Siren's self-naming (*Purg.* XIX.19), "*Io son, io son* dolce serena" and then corrected in Beatrice's self-naming (*Purg.* XXX.73), "*Ben son, ben son* Beatrice." (All of these phrases have repetition as a common feature.)

Hollander (Holl.1980.2), p. 128, returning to this subject, offers a hypothetical reason for Dante's change of mind: The poet wanted to associate his own vernacular Italian, in which the name of God coincides with Adamic pre-Hebrew vernacular, with that first of all vernaculars. And he might have cited (but in fact did not) the following passage in *De vulgari* (I.vi.2): "For whoever is so misguided as to think that the place of his birth is the most delightful spot under the sun may also believe that his own language—his mother tongue, that is—is pre-eminent among all others; and, as a result, he may believe that his language was also Adam's" (tr. S. Botterill). This mocking of boosters of their own inconsequential towns perhaps also conveys Dante's own hidden claim in the *Commedia*: Dante's version of Tuscan is to be seen as in some way resurrecting Adamic vernacular, coinciding in the vowel "I," which is the name of God in each. For a similar opinion, see Moevs (Moev.2005.1), p. 183. And see *Paradiso* XXIX.17 for the dative pronoun "i" referring to God.

One might also speculate that Dante considered *El* as the name of God associated with Hebrew "grammaticality," the written language of the scribes of the Bible; for this reason he must retract his earlier opinion (*El*) in favor of a truly "vernacular" solution (*I*). Further, we may reflect that when he considered the context of his remark in *De vulgari* (I.iv.4), he surely would have noted that there he had characterized Adam's first word as an emotive exclamation, indeed a cry of joy. The word *I*, which we have just heard Adam use in the preceding verse ("pria ch'*i*' scendessi"), may sound and feel "vernacular," while *El* may sound and feel "grammatical," that is, like a language learned in school.

135. God the Father had been stern with sinful Adam for more than five thousand years; then his Son drew him forth from the Limbus up to the Empyrean. We hear nothing of the possibility of purgation for pre-Christian Christians and so must assume that in His triumph (*Par.* XXIII.20), when he harrowed Hell, He brought them straight "home." Anything less charitable (i.e., a visit to Purgatory) would seem picky, wouldn't it? And so here is a paradox: Some saved Christians, even most (and it seems likely that this restriction applies to all but the saintliest of saints), bound for Heaven must pass through purgation, while the virtuous Hebrews who were harrowed by Christ (if not all the saved pagans—we do see Cato and Statius on the Mount of Purgatory) apparently do not have to repay any of their sins on earth. Merely a moment's reflection puts David and Solomon in the dock of our understandable sense of retributive justice. . . .

136. For *El* as a name of God, see the note to verse 134. And see Moore (Moor.1889.1), pp. 487–92, for the history of this tormented verse in the manuscripts.

137–138. The recognition of the Horatian source (*Ars poetica* 60–63) of these verses begins with Benvenuto da Imola (comm. to vv. 124–129). Here is Horace, as cited, with a translation by Singleton (comm. to these verses):

ut silvae foliis pronos mutantur in annos,
prima cadunt; ita verborum vetus interit aetas,
et iuvenum ritu florent modo nata vigentque.
debemur morti nos nostraque. . . .

[As forests change their leaves with each year's decline,
and the earliest drop off: so with words, the old race dies,
and, like the young of human kind, the new-born bloom and thrive.
We are doomed to death—we and all things ours.]

139–142. The question of the length of time spent by Adam in Eden before the Fall is not uniformly dealt with. On the other hand, and as Thomas Hill (Hill.1982.1), p. 94, has demonstrated, Dante is not alone in stating that the first man's innocence lasted only between six and seven hours, citing Petrus Comestor and Gulielmus Durandus as preceding him in this opinion.

Dante obviously felt that the detail was of great enough interest to make it the climactic, canto-ending detail.

Brownlee (Brow.1990.1), p. 396, points out that this period corresponds more or less exactly to the amount of time Dante himself has recently spent in the garden of Eden (see *Purg.* XXVII.133 and XXXIII.103–105). He might have added that Dante also spends six hours with Adam and his companions here in the Starry Sphere (starting at *Par.* XXII.129). See the note to *Paradiso* XXVII.79–81. And see the similar observation offered by P. Sabbatino, *L'Eden della nuova poesia: Saggi sulla "Divina Commedia"* (Florence: Olschki, 1991), p. 99, pointing out that Dante enters the earthly paradise on the sixth day of his otherwordly journey at the sixth hour of the day, while Adam, on the sixth day of Creation, fell at the sixth hour and while Christ was crucified to redeem fallen mankind at the sixth hour as well. Sabbatino's observation of these numerical similarities is cited by Bognini (Bogn.2007.1), p. 82 (n. 32).

PARADISO XXVII

OUTLINE

STARRY SPHERE; CRYSTALLINE SPHERE

1–3 the "Gloria" sung by all the saints makes Dante drunk;

4–6 they seemed to be smiling, so that his "drunkenness" was brought about by both his hearing and his sight;

7–9 the poet apostrophizes joy, gladness, a life of love and peace, and wealth.

10–18 Peter, Luke, John, and Adam flame before Dante, Peter more than the other three; God has quieted the rest.

19–21 Peter: "If you think *I* changed color, wait until you see the rest of these souls!"

22–27 Peter's denunciation of **Boniface VIII,** Christ's vicar

28–30 the redness promised by Peter overspreads the host;

31–36 double simile: chaste lady blushing at another's fault, Beatrice's shame (the eclipse at the **Crucifixion**);

37–39 Peter's voice now as changed as his color:

40–45 (1) amassing wealth not the aim of Peter or of his martyred successors,

46–48 (2) nor that the pope should divide his flock into two,

49–51 (3) nor that the Guelphs should bear the papal keys as their military insignia;

52–54 (4) nor that the popes should sell indulgences under the seal bearing Peter's likeness;

55–57 the corrupt clergy: why does God delay His vengeance?

58–60 foreign [popes] drink Peter's and his followers' blood

61–63 but Providence, which sided with **Scipio,** will act soon;

64–66 Peter to Dante: "When you return, tell them the truth!"

67–72 Simile: as in winter, under Capricorn, snowflakes fall downward, so the souls of the blessed "fall" upward

73–78 Dante follows their upward flight as long as he can, at which point Beatrice invites him to look down:

79–87 Dante's second look down into the revolving universe;
88–96 ascent to the ninth sphere: Beatrice's smiling face;
97–99 as Dante gazes, he is transported out of Gemini in the sphere of the fixed stars and into the Primum Mobile;
100–102 this sphere has no recognizable "landmarks," all its "parts" being uniform;
103–105 smiling, Beatrice explains to Dante where they are:
106–120 Beatrice on the Primum Mobile as imparting motion to the rest of the universe and thus as the source of time
121–141 Beatrice's apostrophe of greed;
142–148 Beatrice's prophecy: the coming "storm at sea."

PARADISO XXVII

"Al Padre, al Figlio, a lo Spirito Santo,"
cominciò, "gloria!" tutto 'l paradiso,
sì che m'inebrïava il dolce canto.

Ciò ch'io vedeva mi sembiava un riso
de l'universo; per che mia ebbrezza
intrava per l'udire e per lo viso.

Oh gioia! oh ineffabile allegrezza!
oh vita intègra d'amore e di pace!
oh sanza brama sicura ricchezza!

Dinanzi a li occhi miei le quattro face
stavano accese, e quella che pria venne
incominciò a farsi più vivace,

e tal ne la sembianza sua divenne,
qual diverrebbe Iove, s'elli e Marte
fossero augelli e cambiassersi penne.

La provedenza, che quivi comparte
vice e officio, nel beato coro
silenzio posto avea da ogne parte,

quand'ïo udi': "Se io mi trascoloro,
non ti maravigliar, chè, dicend' io
vedrai trascolorar tutti costoro.

Quelli ch'usurpa in terra il luogo mio,
il luogo mio, il luogo mio che vaca
ne la presenza del Figliuol di Dio,

fatt' ha del cimitero mio cloaca
del sangue e de la puzza; onde 'l perverso
che cadde di qua sù, là giù si placa."

'To the Father, to the Son, and to the Holy Ghost,
glory,' cried all the souls of Paradise,
and I became drunk on the sweetness of their song.

It seemed to me I saw the universe
smile, so that my drunkenness
came now through hearing and through sight.

O happiness! O joy beyond description!
O life fulfilled in love and peace!
O riches held in store, exempt from craving!

Before my eyes four torches were aflame.
The one who, luminous, had come forth first
began to glow more brilliantly,

his aspect changing, as would Jupiter's
if he and Mars were birds
and had exchanged their plumage.

The providence that there assigns
both time and duty had imposed silence
on every member of the holy choir,

when I heard: 'If my color changes, do not be amazed,
for while I am speaking you shall see
the color of each soul here change as well.

'He who on earth usurps my place,
my place, my place, which in the eyes
of God's own Son is vacant,

'has made my tomb a sewer of blood and filth,
so that the Evil One, who fell from here above,
takes satisfaction there below.'

Di quel color che per lo sole avverso
nube dipigne da sera e da mane,
vid'ïo allora tutto 'l ciel cosperso.

E come donna onesta che permane
di sé sicura, e per l'altrui fallanza,
pur ascoltando, timida si fane,

così Beatrice trasmutò sembianza;
e tale eclissi credo che 'n ciel fue
quando patì la supprema possanza.

Poi procedetter le parole sue
con voce tanto da sé trasmutata,
che la sembianza nons i mutò piùe:

"Non fu la sposa di Cristo allevata
del sangue mio, di Lin, di quel di Cleto,
per essere ad acquisto d'oro usata;

ma per acquisto d'esto viver lieto
e Sisto e Pïo e Calisto e Urbano
sparser lo sangue dopo molto fleto.

Non fu nostra intenzion ch'a destra mano
d'i nostri successor parte sedesse,
parte da l'altra del popol cristiano;

né che le chiavi che mi fuor concesse,
divenisser signaculo in vessillo
che contra battezzati combattesse;

né ch'io fossi figura di sigillo
a privilegi venduti e mendaci,
ond' io sovente arrosso e disfavillo.

In vesta di pastor lupi rapaci
si veggion di qua sù per tutti i paschi:
o difesa di Dio, perché pur giaci?

Then I saw that all this heaven was suffused
with the very color painted on those clouds
that face the sun at dawn or dusk.

As a chaste woman, certain of her virtue,
merely on hearing of another's fault,
makes evident the shame she feels for it,

just so did Beatrice change in her appearance,
and just such an eclipse, I think, there was above
when the Omnipotent felt pain.

Then he added these words to his first
with voice so altered from its former state
that even his looks were not more changed:

'The Bride of Christ was not nurtured with my blood—
nor that of Linus and of Cletus—
to serve the cause of gaining gold.

'Rather, to gain this joyous way of life
Sixtus, Pius, Calixtus, and Urban
shed their blood after many tears.

'It was never our intention that the one part
of Christ's fold should be seated on the right
of our successors, and the other on the left,

'nor that the keys entrusted to my keeping
should become devices on the standards
borne in battles waged against the baptized,

'nor that I become the imprint in a seal
on sale for fraudulence and bribes
so that I blush, in turn, with rage and shame.

'Ravenous wolves in shepherds' clothing
can be seen, from here above, in every pasture.
O God our defender, why do you not act?

Del sangue nostro Caorsini e Guaschi
s'apparecchian di bere: o buon principio,
a che vil fine convien che tu caschi!

Ma l'alta provedenza, che con Scipio
difese a Roma la gloria del mondo,
soccorrà tosto, sì com' io concipio;

e tu, figliuol, che per lo mortal pondo
ancor giù tornerai, apri la bocca,
e non asconder quel ch'io non ascondo."

Sì come di vapor gelati fiocca
in giuso l'aere nostro, quando 'l corno
de la capra del ciel col sol si tocca,

in sù vid' io così l'etera addorno
farsi e fioccar di vapor trïunfanti
che fatto avien con noi quivi soggiorno.

Lo viso mio seguiva i suoi sembianti,
e seguì fin che 'l mezzo, per lo molto,
li tolse il trapassar del più avanti.

Onde la donna, che mi vide assolto
de l'attendere in sù, mi disse: "Adima
il viso e guarda come tu se' vòlto."

Da l'ora ch'ïo avea guardato prima
i' vidi mosso me per tutto l'arco
che fa dal mezzo al fine il primo clima;

sì ch'io vedea di là da Gade il varco
folle d'Ulisse, e di qua presso il lito
nel qual si fece Europa dolce carco.

E più mi fora discoverto il sito
di questa aiuola; ma 'l sol procedea
sotto i mie' piedi un segno e più partito.

'Cahorsines and Gascons prepare to drink our blood.
O lofty promise,
to what base end are you condemned to fall?

'But Providence on high, which by the deeds of Scipio
preserved in Rome the glory of the world,
shall, as I can clearly see, soon bring assistance.

'And you, my son, who, for your mortal burden,
must return below, make sure they hear this
from your mouth, not hiding what I do not hide.'

As when the sun touches the horn
of the heavenly Goat and the air
lets its frozen vapors fall in flakes,

so I saw the celestial sphere adorned
with triumphant flakes of vapor soaring upward,
souls who had now been with us for some time.

My eyes were following their forms
and followed them until the wider intervening space
made me unable to pursue them higher.

My lady, therefore, who saw that I was freed
from staring upward, said: 'Cast your sight below
and see how wide a circle you have traveled.'

Since the last time I looked down
I saw I had traversed all of the arc
from the midpoint of the first clime to its end,

so that on the one side I could see, beyond Gades,
the mad track of Ulysses, on the other, nearly
to the shore where Europa made sweet burden of herself.

More space of this small patch of earth
could I have seen, had not the sun, beneath my feet,
now moved a sign and more away.

La mente innamorata, che donnea
con la mia donna sempre, di ridure
ad essa li occhi più che mai ardea;

e se natura o arte fé pasture
da pigliare occhi, per aver la mente,
in carne umana o ne le sue pitture,

tutte adunate, parrebber nïente
ver' lo piacer divin che mi refulse,
quando mi volsi al suo viso ridente.

E la virtù che lo sguardo m'indulse,
del bel nido di Leda mi divelse
e nel ciel velocissimo m'impulse.

Le parti sue vivissime ed eccelse
sì uniforme son, ch'i' non so dire
qual Bëatrice per loco mi scelse.

Ma ella, che vedëa 'l mio disire,
incominciò, ridendo tanto lieta,
che Dio parea nel suo volto gioire:

"La natura del mondo, che quïeta
il mezzo e tutto l'altro intorno move,
quinci comincia come da sua meta;

e questo cielo non ha altro dove
che la mente divina, in che s'accende
l'amor che 'l volge e la virtù ch'ei piove.

Luce e amor d'un cerchio lui comprende,
sì come questo li altri; e quel precinto
colui che 'l cinge solamente intende.

Non è suo moto per altro distinto,
ma li altri son mensurati da questo,
sì come diece da mezzo e da quinto;

My loving mind, which always lingers lovingly
on my lady, ardently longed, still more than ever,
to let my eyes once more be fixed on her.

And if nature or art have fashioned lures
of human flesh, or of paintings done of it,
to catch the eyes and thus possess the mind,

all these combined would seem as nothing
compared to that divine beauty that shone on me
when I turned back and saw her smiling face.

And the power that her look bestowed on me
drew me from the fair nest of Leda
and thrust me into heaven's swiftest sphere.

Its most rapid and its most exalted parts
are so alike I cannot tell
which of them Beatrice chose to set me in.

But she, who knew my wish, began to speak,
smiling with such gladness that her face
seemed to express the very joy of God.

'The nature of the universe, which holds
the center still and moves all else around it,
starts here as from its boundary line.

'This heaven has no other where
but in the mind of God, in which is kindled
the love that turns it and the power it pours down.

'Light and love enclose it in a circle,
as it contains the others. Of that girding
He that girds it is the sole Intelligence.

'Its motion is not measured by another's,
but from it all the rest receive their measures,
even as does ten from its half and from its fifth.

e come il tempo tegna in cotal testo
le sue radici e ne li altri le fronde,
omai a te può esser manifesto.

Oh cupidigia, che i mortali affonde
sì sotto te, che nessuno ha podere
di trarre li occhi fuor de le tue onde!

Ben fiorisce ne li uomini il volere;
ma la pioggia continüa converte
in bozzacchioni le sosine vere.

Fede e innocenza son reperte
solo ne' parvoletti; poi ciascuna
pria fugge che le guance sian coperte.

Tale, balbuzïendo ancor, digiuna,
che poi divora, con la lingua sciolta,
qualunque cibo per qualunque luna;

e tal, balbuzïendo, ama e ascolta
la madre sua, che, con loquela intera,
disïa poi di vederla sepolta.

Così si fa la pelle bianca nera
nel primo aspetto de la bella figlia
di quel ch'apporta mane e lascia sera.

Tu, perché non ti facci maraviglia,
pensa che 'n terra non è chi governi;
onde sì svïa l'umana famiglia.

Ma prima che gennaio tutto si sverni
per la centesma ch'è là giù negletta,
raggeran sì questi cerchi superni,

che la fortuna che tanto s'aspetta,
le poppe volgerà u' son le prore,
sì che la classe correrà diretta;
e vero frutto verrà dopo 'l fiore."

'How time should have its roots in a single flowerpot
and its foliage in all the others
may now become quite clear to you.

'O greed, it is you who plunge all mortals
so deep into your depths that not one has the power
to lift his eyes above your waves!

'The will of man bursts into blossom
but the never-ceasing rain reduces
the ripening plums to blighted rot.

'Loyalty and innocence are found
in little children only. Then, before
their cheeks are bearded, both are fled.

'One, still babbling, observes the fastdays,
who later, once his tongue is free,
devours any kind of food no matter what the month.

'Another, babbling, loves and heeds his mother,
who later, once his speech has been developed,
longs to see her buried in her grave.

'Thus does the white skin turn to black
in the first aspect of the lovely daughter
of him who brings the day and leaves behind the night.

'Lest you wonder at this, consider
that, on earth, there is no one to govern
and, in consequence, the human family strays.

'But, before all January leaves the winter
for the hundredth part neglected there below,
rays from these lofty circles shall shine forth

'so that the long-awaited tempest turn the ships,
setting their poops where now they have their prows.
Then shall the fleet run its true course
and the blossom shall be followed by good fruit.'

1–3. In celebration of the completion of Adam's "education" of Dante in the eighth sphere—where Dante spends six hours (see *Par.* XXII.152, XXVII.79–81, and cf. Adam's six hours in Eden) and six cantos, the longest time spent in any sphere—the entire consistory of heaven, first seen in *Paradiso* XXIII.19–33 and 82–139, now sings the "Gloria" to the Trinity. Bosco/Reggio point out that the poem contains the "great prayers" of the Church: "Paternoster" (*Purg.* XI.1–24), "Credo" (*Par.* XXIV.130–41), "Ave Maria" (*Par.* XXXIII.1–21), "Te Deum" (*Purg.* IX.139–41; *Par.* XXIV.112–14), and "Sanctus" (*Par.* XXVI.69). Here once again the souls sing in Italian. It seems possible that the blessed and the angels use Latin when they sing to one another and that, when they sing of Dante, their language is Italian. For the songs heard in this canticle, see the note to *Paradiso* XXI.58–60.

For Dante's "drunkenness" see Jeremiah 23:9, "quasi vir ebrius" (like a man who is drunk); but see also, as Bosco/Reggio cite Consoli as noting, *Vita nuova* III.2, where Dante, upon first hearing Beatrice's voice, was taken by "tanta dolcezza, che come inebriato mi partio da le genti" (became so ecstatic that, like a drunken man, I turned away from everyone [tr. M. Musa]). He has come full circle.

4–6. Insisting on his "drunkenness," the poet now says that to the first cause (the singing) was added a second inebriant, what seemed to him no less than a smile of universal proportions.

7–9. The five conditions apostrophized by the poet (happiness, joy, love, peace, riches) are all usually associated with life in this world. Here they are all rather imagined in their transmuted spiritual forms.

9. The word *brama* occurs six times in the poem and is always associated with a low longing, especially for wealth; in fact, it is twice associated with wolves (*Inf.* I.49; *Par.* IV.4). Bosco/Reggio (comm. to verse 9) cite *Convivio* III.xv.3: "[il desiderio] essere non può con la beatitudine, acciò che la beatitudine sia perfetta cosa e lo desiderio sia cosa defettiva" (desire is something that cannot coexist with blessedness, since blessedness is something perfect and desire something defective—tr. R. Lansing).

10–15. Peter, about to reenter the action as the *primus inter pares* yet again, has his flame turn from white to red. The pseudo-simile has it that Peter went from white to red as would Jupiter were he to exchange plumage with Mars; against those who find the figure of speech "strange" or "forced," Chiavacci Leonardi (Chia.1997.1), p. 743, points out that an ancient tradition of representation presented the planets as birds, with rays as their feathers. Scott, in his essay "Su alcune immagini tematiche di *Paradiso* XXVII" (Scot.1977.1, pp. 195–237), demonstrates the precision of Dante's apparently forced figure: The just God (Jove) will demonstrate His justness by righteous indignation (i.e., Mars-like—pp. 196–202).

16–18. Tozer (comm. to vv. 16–17) explains the reference as being to that aspect of Providence " 'which in Heaven assigns to each his fitting time and part'; *vice* is the occasion when this or that person is to act, *offizio* the function which he is to perform. For the general principle which is here expressed, cp. *Par.* XXI.67–72" (i.e., Peter Damian expressing his subservience to God in accepting his mission to Dante).

19–21. Peter looks ahead to the transmogrification of every member of the Church Triumphant, reddening with righteous anger, when he unleashes his harsh words. Significantly enough, this is treated as occurring only after his reference to Satan in verse 27.

22–24. Despite Peter's vehemence about Rome's centrality to the papacy, it is good to keep in mind the observation of V. H. H. Green (cited by Scott [Scot.2004.1], p. 253n.), that between 1100 and 1304 (and we should be aware of Dante's insistence on the rightness of their being there), the popes were more absent from Rome than present, 122 years vs. 82 years. Further, for Dante, Boniface was both a bad pope and an improperly elected one. On either (or both) of those grounds, he may have considered the Papal See "vacant" in 1300, and thus felt he could represent Satan's particular pleasure in Boniface's improper stewardship. However, it seems likely that the passage is also meant to reflect the scandalously long period between the death of Bertrand de Got, Pope Clement V (20 April 1314), and the election of yet another Frenchman, Jacques d'Euse, as Pope John XXII (5 September 1316). On the other hand, it also seems probable that, to Dante's eyes, if Boniface had left the papacy "vacant" because of his various shortcomings, both of his successors, one having moved the papacy to France and the other having kept it there, had left its true seat, in Rome, vacant. (Scartazzini [comm. to vv. 10–27] is of a somewhat different opinion, believing that Dante considered the Papal See "vacant" when John XXII, a simoniac pope if ever there was one, ruled the Church; half a dozen more recent commentators are also of this opinion.)

Tommaseo (comm. to vv. 22–24) was apparently the first to point out that the repeated phrase "il luogo mio" recapitulates Jeremiah 7:4, the thrice-repeated "templum Domini" (the Lord's temple). He is seconded by a number of other commentators between Poletto and Fallani, but then the commentaries go silent on this ascription.

Peter's triple repetition, not quite unique in the poem (see the *santo, santo, santo* of *Par.* XXVI.69), is nonetheless notable, perhaps reminding the reader of the Trinity as well as of the triple-tiered tiara worn by the pope.

25–27. For a discussion of this penultimate, if intrinsic, assault on Boniface, see Massimo Seriacopi (Seri.2003.1), pp. 220–25. The author goes on to describe Dante's general attitude toward this great figure in the history of the papacy as follows: "[Boniface is to Dante] at once the pope and a simoniac; magnificent and yet obtuse; full of energy but arrogant" (p. 226). His book concludes with a helpful review of the varying views of Boniface, found in Dante's margins, put forward by the fourteenth-century commentators (pp. 239–57). For a papal attempt (that of Benedict XV in 1921) to square Dante's poem with the Church's teaching, see Maria Lorena Burlot (Burl.2003.1), p. 551.

28–30. This detail is drawn from Ovid (*Metam.* III.183–185): Diana's blush as seen by Actaeon. (See Grandgent [comm. to verse 28].) That blush fits the context of the blush of shame attributed to Beatrice in verse 34.

31–36. D'Ancona (Danc.1913.1), p. 460, was among the first to insist (see Steiner [comm. to vv. 31–34], in disagreement) that Beatrice went pale, that is, did not grow red with indignation. (But see Poletto's [comm. to vv. 31–34] earlier report of Giuliani's still earlier and similar interpretation, which he, similarly, does not accept.) This view has, nonetheless, been followed by a number of twentieth-century Dantists. But see Scott (Scot.1977.1), p. 209, for a rebuke of those who so argue. And see Bosco/Reggio (comm. to vv. 28–36) for a view similar to his; however, they go on to argue that the reference to the eclipse at Christ's Passion (see Matthew 27:45) reflects not only her darkening, but that of all the saints of the Church Triumphant temporarily gathered here.

33. What probably makes the passage more difficult than it really should be is the adjective *timido*, understood by the early commentators as

"ashamed" (a word readily associated with blushing), while modern ones think it means "timid" (an adjective more likely associated with facial pallor). The last seems a less likely significance, given the context.

37–39. Peter's voice (vv. 19–27) was, we may be surprised to learn, not as angry in that utterance as it is soon to be. When we read back over the passage (vv. 19–39), we realize that the poet has carefully staged the development of this scene: (1) preparation for the change in color (vv. 19–21); (2) the occurrence of that change (vv. 28–36); (3) the further change in the quality of Peter's voice (vv. 37–39). Cf. Dante's own two-stage "drunkenness" in vv. 1–6, first at a sound, then at a sight. Here Peter modulates his appearance first, and then his voice.

40–45. Peter begins a list of some martyred popes with himself; he refers to or names six others in all. These may be broken down into three pairs, one from each of the first three centuries of the Church's life (Linus and Cletus, Sixtus and Pius, Calixtus and Urban).

46–48. Christ will come in judgment and divide his flock into sheep (those who are saved) and goats (those eternally damned). The sitting pope (in 1300, Boniface VIII) is charged with dividing his people into two political factions, the Guelphs loyal to him (his sheep) and his Ghibelline enemies (the goats). This does not mean that Dante limited his list of papal offenders in this respect to one.

49–51. The first four of Peter's complaints (vv. 40–54) about papal misconduct seem both generalizable and yet specific to Boniface's reign (1294–1303). The papacy was often portrayed by Dante as using its temporal power incorrectly; this passage may particularly remember Boniface's "crusade" against the Colonna family, already alluded to in *Inferno* XXVII.85–90, as Benvenuto (comm. to vv. 49–54) was the first to suggest.

52–54. This tercet reflects the sale of ecclesiastical privileges that bore the papal seal, the image of St. Peter.

55–57. Now we descend to the lesser ranks of the clergy. See Matthew 7:15 for the warning against wolves in sheep's clothing, applied to those priests who betray their calling (and their parishioners).

See Marietti (Mari.2003.1), pp. 435–40, for the way in which Dante considers himself a descendant of the prophet Jeremiah here and throughout the *Comedy*. And see Sapegno (comm. to these verses) for a citation of the prophet's outcry against those shepherds who harm their flocks (Jeremiah 23:1).

58–60. Two French popes, the Gascon Clement V (1305–14—see the note to *Inf.* XIX.79–87) and John XXII (1316–34) of Cahors (for that city's association with usury, see the note to *Inf.* XI.46–51), will attempt to gather wealth from the Church founded by the blood of the first martyred popes, representing the good beginning that will have so foul an end.

61–63. A first prophetic utterance, leading into the fuller prophecy at the end of the canto (vv. 142–148): Providence, which sided with Scipio (in 202 B.C. at the battle of Zama) to maintain Rome's glory in the world (and it is clear that the text refers to imperial, and not ecclesiastical, Rome), will soon act to set things straight, as Peter *conceives* (for the force of this verb, see the notes to *Inf.* II.7–9, *Inf.* XXXII.1–9, and *Purg.* XXIX.37–42).

For Dante's lofty sense of Scipio, see Hollander and Rossi (Holl.1986.1), pp. 65–69. For his persistent presence in *Convivio* (IV.v), *Monarchia* (II.ix), and *Commedia* (*Inf.* XXXI, *Purg.* XXIX, *Par.* VI, and here), see the table (Holl.1986.1), p. 75, also listing the various appearances of the dozen and a half republican heroes referred to in Dante's works.

It is surely striking that, at the climax of his antipapal outburst, he turns to a great political figure and not to a religious one. For an earlier and more developed presentation of this view, see Scott (Scot.1977.1), pp. 216–20. A similar political frame of reference may inform Beatrice's prophecy of the *fortuna* (verse 145) at the end of the canto.

64–66. These are the last words spoken by any character in the poem, except for Dante, Beatrice, and Bernard. Peter joins those who charge mortal Dante with his prophetic task, Beatrice (*Purg.* XXXII.103–105; XXXIII.52–57) and Cacciaguida (*Par.* XVII.124–142), thus making threefold the source of the poet's authority to reveal his vision. This represents his final investiture in his role as God's prophet.

Peter's flat-out acknowledgment that Dante is here in his flesh finally sets that question to rest. See previous discussions in the notes to *Paradiso* I.73, II.37–45, and XXII.129.

67–72. The Sun is in Capricorn (the Goat) in late December and the first two-thirds of January, when we earthlings may well witness snowflakes falling downward through the air. Just so did Dante see the souls in whom the celestial Rose consists making their way back up (and thus through the Primum Mobile) to the Empyrean. This is not, as we may first think, a reversal of gravity. The celestial pull is the obverse of the terrestrial one, upward toward God. They are snowing themselves back home. They have been away since *Paradiso* XXIII.19, more than five hundred verses in five cantos, and for roughly the same six hours that Dante has spent here.

Scartazzini (comm. to vv. 67–68) was apparently the first to cite as "source" the upside-down "rain of manna" of angels returning to Heaven in *Vita nuova* XXIII.25, in the *canzone* "Donna pietosa e di novella etate." The context of that central poem (sixteenth of thirty-one poems in all, second of three *canzoni*) is, however, the opposite of this passage, for in it Dante imagines the death of Beatrice, and does so in human, tragic terms. Here, Beatrice is very much alive, watching as her companions in beatitude joyfully return to their immortal stations.

It seems extraordinary that *leggere Dante per Dante* ("reading Dante through the lens of Dante," in a free translation), as Scartazzini is doing here, took so long to establish itself as a critical method. There is very little reference to other *loci* in the *Commedia* (and hardly any to Dante's other works) in the first five hundred years of the poem's life among its commentators. And, in a related phenomenon, there is hardly any citation of the poet's "competitors" in vernacular lyric; the major sources of literary reference are the Bible and the Latin classics. Today, readers take all of these as necessary and useful avenues for exploring the poem. See, for example, Pasquini, "Fra Dante e Guido: la neve e i suoi segreti" (in Pasq.2001.1, pp. 66–67), discussing the Cavalcantian elements of this simile.

70. Standing at either end of this heaven is a reference to it as "aether" (*etera*), the denser-than-air substance of the planetary spheres (see the note to *Par.* XXII.132).

71. The adjective attached to these souls (*trïunfanti*) is both descriptive and designative, the latter insofar as they are members of the Church Triumphant—in case we had forgot.

73–75. The space is that between the Starry Sphere and the Empyrean (i.e., situated above the Crystalline Sphere), and thus defeats Dante's ability to see them return.

76–78. Beatrice, seeing that Dante can no longer make out the members of the Church Triumphant as they return home, invites him, once again, to look beneath his feet, down through the universe, toward the earth (see *Par.* XXII.127–129).

79–87. The formally similar beginnings and conclusions of the two passages (this one and *Par.* XXII.133–153) devoted to the protagonist's earthward gazing back down through the heavens underline the formulaic aspect of both scenes. See Moore (Moor.1903.1), pp. 62–71, for a full discussion.

Dante's reference points are noteworthy: He is over the trackless ocean to the west of the two islands referred to as Gades (*Insulae Gades* [see the note to verse 82]) where Ulysses began his *folle volo* (*Inf.* XXVI.125) and can almost see the shore of Asia Minor, where Europa was raped by Jupiter. Some suggest that these two myths reflect the two most insistent temptations of man, prideful or transgressive intellectual behavior and lust. It may also be tempting to see them in autobiographical terms for Dante, his besetting sins of wayward philosophizing and sexual misconduct, these two sins finding an echo (and a model?) in St. Augustine's *Confessions* (see Hollander [Holl.1969.1], p. 165n.).

As Jacoff points out (Jaco.1991.2), p. 237, Ovid tells the story of Europa in three different places (*Metamorphoses* II and VI; *Fasti* II) with quite diverse treatments; she meditates upon the possibility that Dante has at once paired Europa with Ulysses *in malo*, as transgressive voyager (even if she is a victim of Jove's lustful forcing), and also *in bono*, as a sort of classical prefiguration of Dante, in that she was conjoined with the divine. On this passage, see Moevs (Moev.2005.1), pp. 132–33, arguing that Ulysses and Europa have opposed valuations, he being identified with selfish seeking, while she represents "loving surrender to the divine." For expression of the more usual view, see Scott (Scot.1977.1), p. 223, finding in Ulysses a man who fell victim to the temptations of the intellect and the will, while seeing in Europa a victim of her own sensual desires. However, it might be objected that Europa is not the character who is paired with Ulysses, but that Jove is. That is, Ulysses and Jupiter are both portrayed as embarking on voyages, spurred by curiosity in the first case and by lust in the second, that are harmful to their "mates."

79–81. How long was Dante away from our terrestrial globe? In Carroll's words (comm. to *Par.* XXII. 151–154), this is "one of the most difficult problems in the poem." But then Carroll himself neglects the question of how long Dante actually remained in the heavens. Most Dantists today seem likely to agree that he was there some thirty hours.

If we limit our inquiry to how long he was in *this* heaven, we can establish that period from the celestial details we are given here (see, e.g., Moore [Moor.1903.1], p. 68): Six hours have passed since the protagonist last looked down (at the conclusion of *Par.* XXII). And see the note to *Paradiso* XXVI.139–142, pointing out that Dante spends six hours in the Starry Sphere, as did Adam in Eden and as he does here. (This is not to mention that [all but two] members of the Church Triumphant were also present here for that amount of time [see the note to vv. 67–72]).

See Tozer's clarifying paraphrase of this passage (comm. to this tercet): "Hence Dante, in describing himself as passing, while he was in Gemini, from the meridian of Jerusalem to that of Gades, says that he moved along the arc formed by the *primo clima*. The interval between those two points is represented as reaching from the middle to the end of the first *clima*, because to Alfraganus the *climata* were divisions not of the entire globe, but of the habitable globe (thus he says 'Loca quadrantis *habitabilis* dividuntur in septem climata'), and he regarded their extension from E. to W. as corresponding to twelve hours in time ('longitudo omnium climatum ab oriente in occasum spatio 12 horarum a revolutione caelesti conficitur'), which represent 180° in space. Consequently, the half of this extension (*dal mezzo al fine*) would be six hours in time, or 90° in space, thus corresponding to the difference between Jerusalem and Gades. *Fine* is appropriately used of the western extremity of the *clima*, because the movement of the sun, and that of Dante himself in the zodiac, which are here regarded, are from E. to W. It is hardly necessary to add that, when it is said that Dante was on the meridian of Jerusalem or of Gades, it does not follow that he was over those places, but only that he was in the same longitude with them."

82. See Kirkham (Kirk.1995.1), p. 347n., on "Gade": "Dante's 'Gades' refers not to Cadiz, but to the *Gades Insulae* described by Paulus Orosius, the foundations upon which Hercules built his pillars, marking the outermost limit of the western world. See for this clarification M. A. Orr, *Dante and the Early Astronomers* (London: Wingate, 1913), p. 222."

83. Ulysses reappears once more. Again he figures a voyage quite different from Dante's, a voyage to destruction. Those who attempt to read the central character of *Inferno* XXVI as positive here must deal with Dante's firm rejection of the hero, which surely makes it even more difficult to heroicize him than did the ironic treatment offered in the earlier episode. See, in a similar vein, Picone (Pico.2002.7), p. 430.

86. It is nearly certainly hazardous to translate *aiuola* (little patch of earth) as "threshing-floor"; see the note to *Paradiso* XXII.151. Boyle (Boyl.2000.1) is among the many who simply assume that it is what is meant by the word.

For the twin problems, exactly how far Dante had moved with the heavens and, consequently, how much of our globe he was able to observe, see Carroll (comm. to *Par.* XXII.151–154). His hypothesis is that the reader is supposed to identify each of the three apostles with whom Dante has conversed as having been particularly identified with efforts located in specific parts of the Mediterranean world, John with Asia Minor, Peter with Rome, and James with Spain. And thus, with regard to the second question, the protagonist's vision of earth coincides with those regions.

85–87. This tercet repeats two distinctive elements we found at the arrival in the Starry Sphere: The poet again (see *Par.* XXII.151) refers to the little globe below as the "small patch of earth" that it seems (*aiuola*) and the protagonist again (*Par.* XXII.129) sees it beneath his feet (*sotto li piedi*)—see the appended note concerning the possibility that we are supposed to conclude that those feet make the protagonist present in his body. When we read the phrase now, however, it is difficult to come to any other conclusion, since Peter has already (see verse 64) referred to Dante's "mortal burden"—with him now, his flesh.

88–99. Only the last of these four tercets allotted to the ascent to the next heaven, the Crystalline Sphere, is devoted to the ascent itself. Once again, Beatrice has become unspeakably more beautiful, outdoing either natural beauty or artistic rendering. With his eyes fixed on hers, Dante moves up to the next realm. The passage includes, perhaps surprisingly, a reference to Beatrice's *physical* beauty (vv. 91–93). We are close enough to the Empyrean for that to come as a surprise, even as a shock. However, when we examine the text, we find that the poet tells us that such carnally delightful images would be nothing compared to her beauty as a reflection of God's divinity.

98. Her eyes draw him aloft out of Gemini, the "nest of Leda," a reference that may have been chosen to remind us of Jupiter, seducer of Europa (verse 84) and Leda, among others.

100–102. The Crystalline Sphere is uniform and transparent. Those of us who have been hoping to have confirmation that somehow the specifications made in *Convivio* about the intellectual activities sponsored by the various heavens, as these are described there, might seem reflected in these same heavens, as they are described here, must once again suffer disappointment, as the Primum Mobile, according to *Convivio* (II.xiv.14–18), is supposed to resemble moral philosophy—not angelology. It certainly seems plain that Dante abandoned this schematic design of the earlier work in the *Comedy*, for whatever reason. But see Armour (Armo.1995.1), p. 410, claiming that Beatrice's turning to invective is indeed the sign of this heaven's alignment with moral philosophy.

100. There is considerable contention about the possible reading *vicissime* (nearest), defended vigorously and even nastily by Scartazzini (comm. to vv. 100–102). Petrocchi (Petr.1966.1), pp. 245–47, defends his choice of *vivissime*. As always, whatever our opinion, we have followed Petrocchi, who argues that it here means "moving most quickly." There are a number of other candidates, as sketched by Bosco/Reggio (comm. to vv. 100–102).

103. Beatrice, reading Dante's mind, knows that he wants to find out exactly where he is.

106–114. These verses make clear the relationship of this sphere to the Empyrean, which, without having any recognizable shape at all, is like a tenth celestial circle, if only in that it "surrounds" the Primum Mobile.

107. The word *mezzo*, which also can have a quite different technical meaning (e.g., at *Purg.* I.15), here apparently means "midpoint" or "center," indicating the earth as the center of the universe.

109. For the notion that Dante's universe is four-dimensional, a hypersphere, see Peterson (Pete.1979.1), who believes that Dante's vision of the cosmos looks forward to Einstein's; Osserman (Osse.1995.1), pp. 89–91, suggesting that Peterson overlooks the earlier model proposed by Riemann; Freccero (Frec.1998.1); and Egginton (Eggi.1999.1). However, the reader probably should temper an enthusiasm for such "premodern physics" on Dante's part with an awareness of his possible dependence, for his "ontological, neoplatonic, and theocentric" vision of the rest of the universe, on such models as he found in his precursors. For instance, see Chiarenza (Chia.1988.1), pp. 232–34, reacting to *Paradiso* XXVIII.14–15 with the suggestion that Dante's "picture" derives from Bonaventure (*Itinerarium mentis*, V).

For a quick introduction to the properties of the hypersphere, one may visit the following site: http://www.hypersphere.com/hs/abouths.html.

115–120. The Crystalline Sphere rules the temporal relationships among the parts of the rest of the universe. Dante employs the word *testo* ("flowerpot"; in modern Italian "baking dish"), a hapax when having this sense (but see *Inf.* XV.89 and *Purg.* VI.29 for its use with the meaning "text") to portray the ninth (and invisible) sphere as the container of all time, with its invisible roots here, displaying its leaves, pushed downward, in the visible portions of the rest of the spheres (the stars and planets). (The Crystalline Sphere's "likeness" to a flowerpot would seem to be based on the fact that we cannot see the "roots of time," just as we cannot see the root system of a plant when it is in a pot.)

The author of the Codice Cassinese was perhaps the first to point to Dante's source here, Aristotle's *Physics* (IV.x–xiii); Francesco Torraca (comm. to vv. 118–120) appears to have been the first commentator to cite Dante's citation of that passage in *Convivio* (IV.ii.6).

121–126. Ever since the protagonist encountered the wolf of cupidity in the first canto, *cupidigia* has been a constant presence in the poem. It now becomes, in metaphor, the very sea in which we must attempt to steer our lives toward the harbor of good deeds. Since we naturally long for the good, it is the blight of cupidity that turns our first flowering into rotten fruit.

126. Casini/Barbi (comm. to this verse, citing *BSDI* 9 [1902]:161) refer to the Tuscan saying (given here in a rough English version) that offers the following meteorological pearl: "If it rains on Ascension Day / the plums will suffer quick decay."

127. We follow Chimenz (comm. to vv. 127–129) and most recent commentators in reading the word *fede* in the moral (rather than the theological) sense, and thus "loyalty" or "honesty."

130–135. In these two examples of failing human conduct, does Dante rehearse the first two sins of mankind, eating and killing? An air of puzzlement about the poet's reasons for choosing these particular examples pervades the early commentaries. John of Serravalle (comm. to vv. 133–135) is among the few to offer a motive, in the second instance, for such nasty thoughts on the part of the grown child, putting in his mouth the following maledictive question: "When will she be dead, this damned widow?" Baldassare Lombardi (comm. to vv. 134–135) suggests two motives: to be done with her pious corrections and to dissipate her property. This two-part motive is repeated by any number of later commentators; Luigi Pietrobono (comm. to verse 135) is the first of them to think of Cecco Angiolieri's sonnet "S'io fossi fuoco" (If I were fire) in which he says, "S'i' fosse morte, andarei a mi' padre;—s'i' fosse vita, non starei con lui:—similemente faria da mi' madre" (If I were Death, I'd go to my father; if I were life, I would not abide with him: and [I'd have] the same dealings with my mother).

130. The gerund *balbuzïendo*, used as participle (repeated in verse 133), picks up the adjective *balba* (stammering) from *Purgatorio* XIX.7, the description of the foul seductress in Dante's second Purgatorial dream. There it contrasted with the false beauty and eloquence that the dreaming protagonist lent her; here it is the sign of innocence and immaturity that is preferable to mature and calculated evildoing.

136–138. A widely debated tercet, one of the most vexed passages in the entire poem. And yet, at least at first glance and if we listen only to its first interpreters, it seems easier to resolve than it has in fact turned out to be. The Ottimo, Benvenuto, and Landino, obviously reflecting on the context of the preceding six verses, argue that the *bella figlia* is human nature itself, "created" by the Sun (the Ottimo refers us to *Par.* XXII.116 for Dante's presentation of the Sun as "father" of every mortal life). Starting with John of Serravalle (comm. to this tercet), who also believes that the reference is to human nature, commentators refer to Aristotle's tag, "Homo et sol generant hominem" (Man and the Sun generate men), found near the end of the second section of the *Physics* (and quoted by Dante [*Mon.* I.ix.1].) This is then repeated by numerous later glossators.

What tends to be obscured in the conflicting studies of the tercet is the difficulty in making out the literal sense of the phrase "nel primo aspetto." This phrase may be understood in at least three mutually exclusive ways: the *aspetto* (1) belongs to the daughter (it is probably located in the skin of her face, her "aspect," what she looks like) and is darkened by the Sun; (2) belongs to the daughter and is *her* gaze; (3) is what is seen by the Sun, that is, is in *his* sight (whatever the Sun represents, whether itself or God). Since there is no sure way of determining which of these possibilities governs, one has to proceed "backward," arguing from the context to the meaning of this phrase. (Indeed, that is how we arrived at the first option.)

What may seem surprising today, in light of the wildly differing responses that begin with Carmine Galanti (as reported by Poletto [comm. to this tercet in 1894], he introduced Circe into the list of "candidates") and continue into our own time, is the near unanimity of the ancients. Major exceptions are Jacopo della Lana (comm. to this tercet), who interprets her as representing the Church; the Anonimo Fiorentino (comm. to this tercet), who, in a variation, thinks that she represents the priesthood. (For passages in Bonaventure's *Collationes in Hexaemeron* [XII and XXV] that portray the Church as *filia solis*, see Pierotti [Pier.1981.1].) On the other hand, and for something completely different, see Francesco da Buti (comm. to vv. 121–138), who uniquely is of the opinion that, reflecting her presence in *Aeneid* VI.142 (the next two verses detail the plucking of the golden bough), she is Proserpina, or the Moon. The most complete summary of interpretations until 1921 is found in Casini/Barbi (comm. to verse 136) and is still useful, to a point, today.

Strangely enough, it was only eighty years ago that what has come to be considered an essential reference in verse 136 was brought to light by H. D. Austin (Aust.1936.1): Song of Solomon (1:5), "I am black but comely." Once Auerbach (Auer.1946.1), pp. 485–88, also treated this as an evident borrowing, it began to be more widely noticed. (For discussion of this tercet [and these two contributions], see Hollander [Holl.1969.1], pp. 174–80, and Pertile [Pert.1991.2], pp. 5–6.)

Scartazzini (comm. to this tercet) resurrects Jacopo della Lana's solution: the Church. In the twentieth century Circe became the favored choice, supported by the Virgilian (*Aen.* VII.11) and Ovidian (*Metam.* XIV.346) phrase, *filia solis*, describing her (see Barbi [Barb.1934.1], pp. 292–93; Scott [Scot.1977.1], p. 229). More recently, Guthmüller (Guth. 1999.1), pp. 248–50, takes issue with Pertile's anti-Circean view. Pertile (Pert.1991.2), who mines commentary to the Canticle of Canticles by Guillaume de Saint-Thierry (pp. 7–18), had argued that for Dante, in this passage, at least, the *sposa* (bride) of the Canticle represents the human soul.

The Third Vatican Mythographer (XI.6) offers the following list of those to whom the name *filia solis* was given: Pasiphae, Medea, Circe, Phaedra, Dirce. For the first of these, Pasiphae, see Sarteschi (Sart.2000.2), referring to Servius as source; but see the previous article of Cassata (Cass.1971.3), who had arrived at this interpretation before her. Lanza (Lanz.1996.1), ad loc., accepts Cassata's argument.

However, for still another candidate, see Hollander (Holl.1969.1), p. 191n.: If Dante knew either the *Dittochaeon* (Prudentius's poeticized version of Scriptural narrative) or some digest or listing in which at least its first line is found (cf. the online catalogue of the holdings of the monastery at Melk, where it does in fact appear), he would have seen some version of the following: "Eva columba fuit tunc candida; nigra deinde / facta per anguinum malesuada fraude venenum" (Eve was at first white as a dove; she then became black because of the venomous serpent and its persuasive fraudulence). Hollander begins by citing Ovid (*Metam.* V.568–571) for the *facies* (face, aspect) of Proserpina turning, in the obverse of what is described here, from sadness to sunlit gladness; he then presses his case for Dante's figural melding of Proserpina and Eve (a familiar enough equation, e.g., both women as sinful "eaters" [Hollander, p. 179]).

There are problems with all the solutions heretofore proposed except, perhaps, for the most generic one: human nature, or human beings in general (or, in Pertile's formulation, the human soul). This last hypothesis is accompanied by only one slight problem: Dante has, in the two preceding tercets, exemplified human conduct in a male child; why should he, if his subject remains the same, suddenly switch to a generic female child? This would make a reader believe that the reference changes to feminine for a reason, a hidden identity that we are meant to puzzle out. And we have certainly puzzled. However, and to take only the two most popular modern readings, Circe and the Church, both of these seem flawed. Circe does not have the virginal aspect that these lines at least seem to confer upon the *bella figlia.* And she really doesn't fit the context; she does not change from good to bad, from lovely to ugly, etc.; she changes *others* into something that they were not before. In order to support this reading, one must interpret Circe as changing the complexion of her captives, hardly what Dante seems to be interested in here. And what about the Church? As a possible interpretation, it gains support from its longevity (it first was broached by Jacopo della Lana), from a modern authority (Scartazzini), and from a skillful argument (Chiavacci Leonardi's [Chia.1997.1], p. 763). However, if one reads the entire context as political and civil, as it surely seems to be, one finds that solution awkward. Indeed, it could be argued that Dante's thoughts about the Church's reform and revitalization *outside a political context* at the time he was writing the last parts of *Paradiso* (with the Church, by electing John XXII pope, having thereby confirmed its election of the Avignonian captivity) are never anything but grim. All we hear about the Church in upper paradise is given in thundering invectives against her failings. It does not appear that Dante spent much thought on ways in which it might be amended.

As for the proposal of Eve, it faces (as do all the others but that putting forward human nature) a formidable challenge: the present tense of the verb *fa*. If the verse read, in the original, *fé*, as Lanza suggests it might have (Lanz.1996.1, ad loc.), then the reference to Eve would be a lot more plausible. But such proposals must be advanced only with a sense of restraint.

139–141. Perhaps because we are so near the Empyrean, many Dantists do not observe the clearly political interests of the following prophecy (vv. 142–148), which concludes the canto. Any sort of open-minded reading of this tercet makes it plain that the governance Dante has in mind is not that of a pope, is not ecclesiastical in any way. It is instructive to compare the similar moment in *Purgatorio* XVI.94–96 (and see the appended note). It is also instructive to study the lengthy and concerted gloss to this passage of Francesco da Buti (comm. to vv. 139–148), which interprets the entire prophecy as having to do with the corruption and necessary reform of the Church. That so gifted a commentator can go astray is a warning to us lesser readers.

142–148. Tozer interprets: "The reckoning of the Julian calendar involved a yearly error in excess of somewhat less than a hundredth part of a day (*la centesma*), and this in Dante's time amounted to an error of about nine days, so that January was advanced by so much towards the end of winter and beginning of spring. It was this which was corrected by the Gregorian calendar two centuries and a half later. The general meaning, then, of *prima che*, &c., is 'before a very long time has passed'; but it is intended to be understood ironically as meaning 'before long,' 'soon,' somewhat in the same way as when we say 'not a hundred miles off' for 'near.' " Whatever the time involved, it is clear that this is a major prophecy in the poem, in line with those found in *Inf.* I ("veltro") and *Purg.* XXXIII ("DXV"), as Hollander (Holl.1969.1), pp. 180–91, has argued. One of the medieval meanings of "fortuna" was "storm at sea"—cf. *Purg.* XXXII, 116—and that clearly seems to be the image Dante uses here. The word for "fleet" (*classe*) is here used for the first time in Italian (according to the *Grande Dizionario* [Batt.1961.1]); it comes from Latin *classis*, the name for Ravenna as home of the Roman fleet and (for a time) capital of the empire. Within the context of the canto, Peter's slam of the papacy also ends with a Roman thought (Scipio defeating Hannibal); it is not really surprising that

Beatrice here should prophesy the coming of an emperor who will set things right. (See, among others, Scott [Scot.1977.1], pp. 232–33; Hollander [Holl.2001.1], pp. 142–44.) Only then will the human race steer a good course—and the papacy, too, get straightened out.

142–143. See Moore (Moor.1903.1), pp. 95–101, for an extended presentation of what still coincides with the "standard" interpretation of this problematic expression. He shows that the Julian calendar, itself developed to adjust "seasonal slippage" of considerable extent, mismeasured the solar year by the one-hundredth part of a day. Richard Kay (Kay.2003.2) argues that, on the contrary, Dante refers to the hundredth part of a degree of sidereal movement.

144. For medieval views that the stars were involved in shaping these major human events, see Woody (Wood.1977.1).

145–148. The word *fortuna*, as only several earlier commentators have pointed out (e.g., the Anonimo Fiorentino and Tommaseo, both to vv. 145–148 [although both eventually hedge their bets]), here nearly certainly has the meaning "storm at sea." In the nineteenth century, beginning with Andreoli (comm. to vv. 145–147), that became the dominant reading (and see Hollander [Holl.1969.1], pp. 181n., 190). Tommaseo (comm. to these verses) had previously cited an analogous passage (*Purg.* XXXII.116), "come nave in fortuna" (like a ship tossed in a tempest), which might have offered a clue to others. Perhaps the vastly different context of that passage (the nascent Church is being attacked by Roman emperors) is responsible for the failure of attention. However, for a recent and differing opinion, see Prandi (Pran.1994.1), p. 120, who does not consider pertinent the meteorological meaning of *fortuna* in this occurrence of the word; the same may be said of Antonelli (Anto.2002.1), pp. 422–23.

For notice of a similar and entirely relevant passage, see Scott (Scot.1996.1), p. 100, in his discussion of *Purgatorio* VI.76–78, pointing to *Epist.* VI.3: ". . . When the throne of Augustus is vacant, the whole world goes out of course, the helmsman and rowers slumber in the ship of Peter, and unhappy Italy, forsaken and abandoned to private control, and bereft of all public guidance, is tossed with such buffeting of winds and waves as no words can describe, . . ." (tr. P. Toynbee). See Tommaseo (comm. to these verses [and see the note to verse 148]), citing an earlier form of the image in a discussion of empire in *Convivio* IV.v.8. Kleinhenz (Klei.1986.2), pp. 229–30, thinks that the prophecy is of "a powerful temporal ruler." Vazzana (Vazz.1989.1), p. 726, sees the storm at sea as representing the next and very angry emperor, "un nuovo Scipione, salvatore armato" (a new Scipio, a savior in arms).

146. For some of the earlier presences (there are six of them in all) of the word *poppa*, signifying "poop deck," see the note to *Purgatorio* XXX.58. And here *prora*, of which this is the fifth and final appearance (see *Inf.* VIII.29 and XXVI.141; *Purg.* XXX.58; *Par.* XXIV.68), joins its naval counterpart for a shared final appearance.

148. The canto ends with a corrective return to the image of failed fruition (found in verse 126). We are promised that the eventual imperial reemergence, latent in history (one perhaps thinks of the model represented by *kairos*, the "fullness of time" in the coming of Christ during the *Pax romana*), will be, amazing even to Dante, fulfilled before our very eyes. This underlying reference had already been precisely expressed in *Convivio* IV.v.8: "Nor was the world ever, nor will it be, so perfectly disposed as at the time when it was guided by the voice of the one sole prince and commander of the Roman people [Augustus], as Luke the Evangelist testifies. Since universal peace reigned everywhere, which it never did before nor ever shall again, the ship of human society was speeding on an even course directly toward its proper port" (tr. R. Lansing). This is, "reading Dante through the lens of Dante" (see the last paragraph of the note to vv. 67–72), perhaps the single best gloss to this difficult passage, even if it appears to have been cited only by Tommaseo (see the note to vv. 145–148). Much has recently been written about Dante's rejection of the values he espoused in his earlier works, particularly *Convivio* (see the notes to *Par.* VIII.34–39 and XVIII.91–93). While it seems nothing less than obvious, to any sort of objective examination that this is true, it surely needs also to be observed that such retrospective change of heart is not total. These notes refer to the minor works frequently, and to the *Convivio* most frequently (roughly one hundred times). In some respects it was the pre-study for *Paradiso* (see the note to *Par.* III.91–96), embodying several of its major themes and images (centrally, the intellectual banquet [the "bread of angels"]). Thus, while some of its matter may have been "heretical" from the standpoint of the author of the later poem, many of its judgments, particularly in the fourth treatise, in which the *Convivio* changed its course dramatically, now embracing Roman history as one of its new themes, are exactly as we find them in *Paradiso* (see Hollander [Holl.2001.1], pp. 86–90).

PARADISO XXVIII

OUTLINE

CRYSTALLINE SPHERE

1–3 retrospective attention to Beatrice's prophecy;
4–12 simile: as a man, seeing a torch in a mirror, looks back to see if it is actually behind him, so Dante turned back to see the reflection in Beatrice's eyes;
13–21 he sees [reflected?] in the sphere itself a tiny **point**
22–42 and then **nine concentric circles** of light [nine orders of angels] revolving around that point, which is God
43–45 Beatrice on the **Seraphim,** the order closest to God
46–57 Dante's question about the inverse relations between speed and distance in these two "universes"
58–63 Beatrice's first response: "If you cannot undo this knot, it is no wonder, since no one else has tried to"
64–78 and her second: the "astronomy" of the Empyrean
79–87 similes: **Boreas** clears out the night sky just as Beatrice explains these things; her truthful words resemble a star in the heavens
88–90 the angels' response to her explanation:
91–96 myriads of them emit Hosannahs to God
97–139 Beatrice explains the hierarchy of the angels:
- 97–114 the first triad: Seraphim, **Cherubim,** and **Thrones;**
- 115–126 the next two triads: **Dominions, Virtues, Powers; Principalities, Archangels, Angels;**
- 127–129 all angelic orders look up but interact below
- 130–135 **Dionysius** had the order right, but not **Gregory**
- 136–139 and Dionysius was informed directly by **St. Paul.**

PARADISO XXVIII

Poscia che 'ncontro a la vita presente
d'i miseri mortali aperse 'l vero
quella che 'mparadisa la mia mente,

come in lo specchio fiamma di doppiero
vede colui che se n'alluma retro,
prima che l'abbia in vista o in pensiero,

e sé rivolge per veder se 'l vetro
li dice il vero, e vede ch'el s'accorda
con esso come nota con suo metro;

così la mia memoria si ricorda
ch'io feci riguardando ne' belli occhi
onde a pigliarmi fece Amor la corda.

E com' io mi rivolsi e furon tocchi
li miei da ciò che pare in quel volume,
quandunque nel suo giro ben s'adocchi,

un punto vidi che raggiava lume
acuto sì, che 'l viso ch'elli affoca
chiuder conviensi per lo forte acume;

e quale stella par quinci più poca,
parrebbe luna, locata con esso
come stella con stella si collòca.

Forse cotanto quanto pare appresso
alo cigner la luce che 'l dipigne
quando 'l vapor che 'l porta più è spesso,

distante intorno al punto un cerchio d'igne
si girava sì ratto, ch'avria vinto
quel moto che più tosto il mondo cigne;

When she who does imparadise my mind
had revealed the truth against
the present life of wretched mortals,

then, as one whose way is lit by a double-candled lamp
held at his back, who suddenly in a mirror sees
the flame before he has seen or even thought of it

and turns to see if the glass is telling him the truth,
and then sees that it reflects things as they are—
as notes reflect the score when they are sung—

just so do I remember having done,
gazing into the beautiful eyes
which Love had made into the snare that caught me.

When I turned back and my eyes were struck
by what appears on that revolving sphere—
if one but contemplates its circling—

I saw a point that flashed a beam of light
so sharp the eye on which it burns
must close against its piercing brightness.

The star that, seen from here below, seems smallest
would seem a moon if put beside it,
as when one star is set beside another.

As near, perhaps, as a halo seems to be
when it encircles the light that colors it,
where the vapor that forms it is most dense,

there whirled about that point a ring of fire
so quick it would have easily outsped
the swiftest sphere circling the universe.

e questo era d'un altro circumcinto,
e quel dal terzo, e 'l terzo poi dal quarto,
dal quinto il quarto, e poi dal sesto il quinto.

Sopra seguiva il settimo sì sparto
già di larghezza, che 'l messo di Iuno
intero a contenerlo sarebbe arto.

Così l'ottavo e 'l nono; e ciascheduno
più tardo si movea, secondo ch'era
in numero distante più da l'uno;

e quello avea la fiamma più sincera
cui men distava la favilla pura,
credo, però che più di lei s'invera.

La donna mia, che mi vedëa in cura
forte sospeso, disse: "Da quel punto
depende il cielo e tutta la natura.

Mira quel cerchio che più li è congiunto;
e sappi che 'l suo muovere è sì tosto
per l'affocato amore ond' elli è punto."

E io a lei: "Se 'l mondo fosse posto
con l'ordine ch'io veggio in quelle rote,
sazio m'avrebbe ciò che m'è proposto;

ma nel mondo sensibile si puote
veder le volte tanto più divine,
quant' elle son dal centro più remote.

Onde, se 'l mio disir dee aver fine
in questo miro e angelico templo
che solo amore e luce ha per confine,

udir convienmi ancor come l'essemplo
e l'essemplare non vanno d'un modo,
ché io per me indarno a ciò contemplo."

This ring was encircled by another ring,
and that by the third, the third by the fourth,
the fourth by the fifth, and the fifth by the sixth.

Higher there followed the seventh, now spread so wide
that the messenger of Juno, in full circle,
would be unable to contain its size.

And so, too, the eighth and ninth,
each one revolving with diminished speed
the farther it was wheeling from the first.

And that one least removed from the blazing point of light
possessed the clearest flame, because, I think,
it was the one that is the most intruthed by it.

My lady, who saw me in grave doubt
yet eager to know and comprehend, said:
'From that point depend the heavens and all nature.

'Observe that circle nearest it,
and understand its motion is so swift
because it is spurred on by flaming love.'

And I to her: 'If the universe were arranged
in the order I see here among these wheels
I would be content with what you've set before me.

'However, in the world of sense we see
the farther from the center they revolve
the more divinity is in their orbits.

'And so, if my desire to know shall gain its end
in this rare temple of the angels,
which has but light and love for boundaries,

'then I still need to learn exactly why
the model and its copy fail to follow the same plan,
for, using my own powers, I reflect on this in vain.'

"Se li tuoi diti non sono a tal nodo
sufficïenti, non è maraviglia:
tanto, per non tentare, è fatto sodo!"

Così la donna mia; poi disse: "Piglia
quel ch'io ti dicerò, se vuo' saziarti;
e intorno da esso t'assottiglia.

Li cerchi corporai sono ampi e arti
secondo il più e 'l men de la virtute
che si distende per tutte lor parti.

Maggior bontà vuol far maggior salute;
maggior salute maggior corpo cape,
s'elli ha le parti igualmente compiute.

Dunque costui che tutto quanto rape
l'altro universo seco, corrisponde
al cerchio che più ama e che più sape:

per che, se tu a la virtù circonde
la tua misura, non a la parvenza
de le sustanze che t'appaion tonde,

tu vederai mirabil consequenza
di maggio a più e di minore a meno,
in ciascun cielo, a süa intelligenza."

Come rimane splendido e sereno
l'emisperio de l'aere, quando soffia
Borea da quella guancia ond' è più leno,

per che si purga e risolve la roffia
che pria turbava, sì che 'l ciel ne ride
con le bellezze d'ogne sua paroffia;

così fec'ïo, poi che mi provide
la donna mia del suo risponder chiaro,
e come stella in cielo il ver si vide.

'That your fingers are not fit to undo this knot
is not surprising, so entangled
has it become from never being tried.'

My lady said this, then went on: 'Take
what I shall tell you if you would be fed,
and see you sharpen your wits on it.

'The material heavens are wide or narrow
according as power, greater or less,
is diffused through all their parts.

'Greater goodness makes for greater blessedness,
and greater blessedness takes on a greater body
when all its parts are equal in perfection.

'This sphere, therefore, which sweeps into its motion
the rest of the universe, must correspond
to the ring that loves and knows the most,

'so that, if you apply your measure,
not to their appearances but to the powers themselves
of the angels that appear to you as circles,

'you will see a marvelous congruence,
larger with more, smaller with less, in each sphere
according to its celestial Intelligence.'

As the vault of our air is left
serene and shining when Boreas
blows from his gentler cheek

and the dark refuse of the sky is cleared
and purged away so that the heavens smile
as all their quarters fill with loveliness,

just so did I feel when my lady
bestowed on me her lucid answer,
and, like a star in heaven, the truth shone clear.

E poi che le parole sue restaro,
non altrimenti ferro disfavilla
che bolle, come i cerchi sfavillaro.

L'incendio suo seguiva ogne scintilla;
ed eran tante, che 'l numero loro
più che 'l doppiar de li scacchi s'inmilla.

Io sentiva osannar di coro in coro
al punto fisso che li tiene a li *ubi*,
e terrà sempre, ne' quai sempre fuoro.

E quella che vedëa i pensier dubi
ne la mia mente, disse: "I cerchi primi
t'hanno mostrato Serafi e Cherubi.

Così veloci seguono i suoi vimi,
per somigliarsi al punto quanto ponno;
e posson quanto a veder son soblimi.

Quelli altri amori che 'ntorno li vonno,
si chiaman Troni del divino aspetto,
per che 'l primo ternaro terminonno;

e dei saper che tutti hanno diletto
quanto la sua veduta si profonda
nel vero in che si queta ogne intelletto.

Quinci si può veder come si fonda
l'esser beato ne l'atto che vede,
non in quel ch'ama, che poscia seconda;

e del vedere è misura mercede,
che grazia partorisce e buona voglia:
così di grado in grado si procede.

L'altro ternaro, che così germoglia
in questa primavera sempiterna
che notturno Arïete non dispoglia,

And, when she paused in her speech,
as boiling iron shoots out sparks
so did these circles sparkle,

each spark keeping to its flaming ring. They were
so many that their number ran to thousands more
than the successive doubling of a chessboard's squares.

From choir to choir I heard *Hosanna* sung
to the fixed point, which holds them—and forever shall—
in those *ubi* that have always been theirs.

And she, who understood the puzzled thoughts
now present in my mind, said: 'The closer rings
reveal to you both Seraphim and Cherubim.

'They seek their bonds so swiftly, hoping they may gain
as much as they can hold of likeness to the point,
and this they can attain, the loftier their vision.

'These other loving spirits circling them
are called the Thrones of God,
and with them the first triad was complete.

'And you should know that all of them delight
in measure of the depth to which their sight
can penetrate the truth, where every intellect finds rest.

'From this, it may be seen, beatitude itself
is based upon the act of seeing,
not on that of love, which follows after,

'and the measure of their sight reveals their worth,
which grace and proper will beget in them.
Such, then, is the process, step by step.

'The second triad thus blossoming
in this eternity of spring
which no nocturnal Ram lays waste

perpetüalemente *'Osanna'* sberna
con tre melode, che suonano in tree
ordini di letizia onde s'interna.

In essa gerarcia son l'altre dee:
prima Dominazioni, e poi Virtudi;
l'ordine terzo di Podestadi èe.

Poscia ne' due penultimi tripudi
Principati e Arcangeli si girano;
l'ultimo è d'Angelici ludi.

Questi ordini di sù tutti s'ammirano,
e di giù vincon sì, che verso Dio
tutti tirati sono e tutti tirano.

E Dïonisio con tanto disio
a contemplar questi ordini si mise,
che li nomò e distinse com' io.

Ma Gregorio da lui poi si divise;
onde, sì tosto come li occhi aperse
in questo ciel, di sé medesmo rise.

E se tanto secreto ver proferse
mortale in terra, non voglio ch'ammiri:
ché chi 'l vide qua sù gliel discoperse
con altro assai del ver di questi giri."

'ever sings hosannas, the threefold strain
resounding in the threefold ranks
of bliss by which they are intrined.

'In this hierarchy are found the next divinities—
Dominions first, then Virtues,
and the third are Powers.

'The penultimate two of these festive throngs
are whirling Principalities and then Archangels,
while the last one is all Angels at their play.

'All these orders gaze in ecstasy above.
The highest there are linked with those below,
so that the rest are drawn, and also draw, to God.

'Dionysius with such passion set his mind
to contemplate these orders
that he named them and arranged them as do I.

'But later Gregory took a different view,
so that, opening his eyes here in this heaven,
he saw his errors, laughing at himself.

'And if a mortal man on earth set forth
such hidden truth, you need not wonder,
for he who saw it here above revealed it then to him,
along with many other truths about these circlings.'

1–3. This retrospective opening tercet reminds us that, if humanity is in parlous condition (cf. *Par.* XXVII.127–141, Beatrice's lament for our lost innocence), the protagonist's guide has prophesied better times to come (*Par.* XXVII.142–148). Dante's gaze, in this canto, will also reflect a double focus, first fixing on Beatrice's mirroring eyes, and then behind him on what they reflect, God and the angels, themselves as seen, we are perhaps to understand, on the convex outer surface of the Crystalline Sphere (see the note to vv. 13–15).

2. Contini (Cont.1968.1), p. 1002, insists on the importance of the word "vero" (true) and the concept of truthfulness to this canto; it is, in his opinion, its "parola chiave"; indeed a major portion of his *lectura* (pp. 1002–12) is a meditation in this vein.

3. See Bosco/Reggio (comm. to this verse), who claim that we may read Beatrice here either allegorically (as "Theology") or literally (as herself). They, doubtless wisely, prefer the second understanding; nonetheless, some readers may find it a bit disquieting to discover intelligent critics even raising the possibility, so near the final vision, of "poets' allegory" being used as an interpretive tool for what the poet presents as being both actual and experienced.

4–9. This return to the conditions of the experiment alluded to in the second canto (see the note to *Par.* II.94–105) shows how captious some readers are in their insistence that Dante deliberately presents that experiment as being literally impossible. Such a reader will once again object that, if the flame is behind the subject's back, it cannot be reflected in a mirror set directly in front of him. And once again a less positivistic reader will realize that, if the flame is, for instance, only a few centimeters above the observer's head (as it is in the reproduction of a fifteenth-century illustration of the experiment [see Boyd.1995.1, p. 15)]), the result will be as Dante says. In any case, this is a poem and not a physics lab. And yet we should realize that Dante only says "behind" (*dopo, retro*) the observer, without in any way suggesting that the flame might not be visible from a point directly in front of him.

4. A *doplerus* was a torch formed by twisting two candles together. Picone (Pico.2002.7), p. 433, adduces Guinizzelli's previous use (in the

third stanza of his *canzone* "Al cor gentil," well known to Dante) of a slightly different Italian form, *doplero.*

8–9. See Bosco/Reggio (comm. to these verses). In our translation we have followed their suggestion that the only exact "fit" would be between a note that is sounded and its scoring in musical notation. Aside from Gabriele (comm. to verse 9), who shrugs the verse away with the description "a very ugly comparison," most commentators struggle with these lines, until Porena (comm. to these verses) sees that all previous attempts at suggesting resemblance (e.g., singing with its accompaniment, song with its meter, words with their music, etc.) are not as precise as the image to which this musical analogue is likened, the reflection of a thing in a mirror.

10–12. Psaki (Psak.1995.1), p. 426, is eloquent defending Dante's right to present Beatrice's sexual being as somehow *still* being a part of her attraction for him. The problem with her argument is that this text is clearly past-oriented, the verb *fece* (past definite) in evident contrast with the present tense of Dante's coinage *imparadisa* (imparadises). The girl toward whom he had been drawn sexually had turned out to be valuable for other and (in this poem) better reasons.

12. For this use of the word *corda* (cord, here translated "snare") as having only metaphorical valence as a "simbolo di virtù" (symbol of virtue), see Padoan (Pado.1974.1), p. 177n. He says that this usage is found also at *Inferno* XVI.106 (the famous, or infamous, "cord" that holds Dante's garments together and is used by Virgil as an invitation and challenge to Geryon) and *Purgatorio* VII.114 (where Pedro III of Aragon is "girt with the cord of every virtue," perhaps the only occurrence in which Padoan's formulation really works). However, it is not clear that the word in any of these appearances has only a metaphorical sense.

In the thirteen presences of the word *corda* in the poem, five times it refers to a bowstring; three times, to the strings of musical instruments; once, to the cords on a whip. That leaves one other form of *corda* that seems identical with (or at least highly similar to) Padoan's three: *Paradiso* XXVI.49, the cords (*corde*) of love that draw us after it. And that seems to be the same (or a closely related) meaning as is found in these three.

13–15. Exactly what Dante sees reflected in Beatrice's eyes is a matter of considerable dispute, although some commentators have possibly begun to sever the Gordian knot. Torraca (comm. to this tercet) was perhaps the first to realize that God and his angels have not descended to this sphere from the Empyrean, if without specifying how it is exactly that they are seen here. Sapegno (comm. to vv. 13–16) improves that formulation, insisting that the protagonist sees God and the angels in the Empyrean *through* the perfectly transparent sphere of the Primum Mobile. This view has the benefit of keeping God and his angels where they belong (in the "tenth heaven"), but does not do very well by the poet's insistence that he saw them "in quel volume" (in [or "on"] that revolving sphere). The fullest and best discussion of the problem, one that is aware of the pitfalls into which all his precursors have slipped, is that of Siro Chimenz (comm. to this tercet). He gets all the details right, but in the end confesses that he simply cannot come up with a solution. See the note to the opening tercet of this canto for an attempt at a resolution: Dante portrays the surface of the Primum Mobile as where the highest realities of all, God and His angelic partners in creation, are visible. In support of this hypothesis, we might consider the fact that the introductory simile itself speaks of a reflection (in Beatrice's mirroring eyes). That, in turn, may be considered (if this hypothesis is correct) a reflection of a reflection. Possible confirmation is found in *Paradiso* XXX.106–108, where the Rose is presented as a self-reflection off the convex surface of the Primum Mobile.

Bosco/Reggio (comm. to this tercet) point out that the commentators are confused by this apparently simple utterance. How can God and the angels be present *in the Crystalline Sphere* anytime one looks intently into it? It is not easy to see how or why they, Bosco/Reggio continue, would now or ever descend to this sphere (despite, they might have added, the descent of the Church Triumphant in Canto XXIII), nor how any other hypothesis might account for the apparition (e.g., a vision, an allegory, some sort of unusual perception). Our hypothesis is as follows: Dante looks from a mirror (Beatrice's eyes) into a second "mirror" (the convex surface of the Crystalline Sphere) where first the Point and then the angelic circlings are what he sees, painted, as it were, upon the surface of this Primum Mobile, the circling of which moves all the universe by its influence. Cf. *Paradiso* I.1–3: "La Gloria di colui che tutto move / per l'universo penetra, e risplende / in una parte più e meno altrove" (The glory of Him who moves all things / pervades the universe and shines / in one part more and in another less). God's glory is to be considered as completely penetrating and at the same time visible here, in the first and purest sphere (and reflected least clearly of all by earth, spiritually even "denser" than the Moon, itself a less than perfect mirror, as we learned in *Paradiso* II). Seeing this highest and purest "universe," God and his angels, on the surface of the Crystalline Sphere, the protagonist experiences the "copy" as though it were actually present. For possible confirmation of this view, see the note to *Paradiso* XXX.103–108.

Mellone (Mell.1989.1), pp. 733–34, demonstrates the congruence between the language of Alfragano (whose view is accepted and cited by Giovanni di Sacrobosco) and that of Dante here. Alfragano presents the earth as a tiny point in relation to even the smallest star that can be seen from earth. In Mellone's judgment, Dante has deliberately misapplied the astronomer's picture of our physical universe to God's spiritual one.

14. For the word *volume*, see the note to *Paradiso* XII.122. Here it evidently refers to the revolving sphere of the Primum Mobile itself, although that interpretation is not widely shared.

15. Mellone (Mell.1989.1), pp. 734–35, politely but firmly (and correctly) dismisses those Dantists (most significantly Bruno Nardi) who believe that this *giro* is in fact found in (or simply is) the Empyrean, rather than referring to the Crystalline Sphere itself. In fact, we should probably understand that it *is* the Crystalline Sphere. It is true that Dante once refers to the Empyrean as a *giro*, but he probably should not have (see the note to *Par.* IV.34).

16–21. The point is so terribly bright that whoever looks at it must close his eyes, so terribly small that the tiniest star in our sky would seem large as the Moon if placed beside it.

On the relation between what Dante sees here and the earth-centered Aristotelian universe, see Cornish (Corn.2000.2), pp. 108–18.

22–39. See the note to *Paradiso* III.51 for the apparent contradiction here, in that "the nine ranks of angels, each associated with one of the planetary spheres, rotat[e] around the point that represents the Godhead faster the *nearer* they are to that point," while in the lower universe the spheres rotate more slowly the closer they are to their center. Beatrice determinedly resolves this issue at vv. 58–78.

22–24. Cf. *Paradiso* X.67–69, Dante's description of the Moon's halo.

25–27. In earth-centered astronomy, we learn that the Primum Mobile, the outermost sphere, rotates the fastest (see *Par.* XXVII.99). Now we learn that the first ring of angels, the Seraphim, rotates even more quickly.

If we reflect only a moment, what seems an inverse relation between these two universes is in fact one of parallelism when considered from the perspective of the Empyrean's God-centered astronomy. In such a view, the closer a sphere is to God, the faster it rotates on its axis, no matter where that axis is.

Between vv. 99 and 126 we shall hear the names of the angelic bands in descending order, exactly as they are presented anonymously here. Looking back from there, we can add to the highest rank, the Seraphim, the names of Cherubim, Thrones; Dominions, Virtues, Powers; Principalities, Archangels, and Angels.

27. For *mondo* as meaning not "world" but "universe," see (as Poletto [comm. to vv. 22–27] advises) *Convivio* III.v.3, where Dante rehearses the difference between these two meanings of the word.

28–30. Surely a highly competitive candidate in any annual "Worst Tercet in the *Divine Comedy*" contest, this *terzina* does possess the merit of a matter-of-fact tone that encourages the reader to take Dante's celestial reportage at face value by suggesting that a certain value lies in prosaic verse.

31–33. The seventh circle out from the Godhead is that of the Principalities, one of the orders that Dante had misplaced in the *Convivio*. See the note to *Paradiso* VIII.34–39. Were we able to see a rainbow as an entire circle, it still would not be large enough to contain the arc made by this angelic order. For the varying "size" of these angelic bands, see vv. 64–66. And for Dante's previous reference to Iris, see *Paradiso* XII.12 (and the note to *Par.* XII.11–18).

34–36. The eighth and ninth circles, containing respectively the Archangels and the Angels, round out the assemblage, each rotating still more slowly around the Point.

37–39. The Seraphim, associated with love, are here presented as associated with knowledge (they are "entruthed"). At verse 45, however, they will again be associated with love. And see the note to verse 72.

41–42. As was first pointed out by Daniello (comm. to vv. 40–45), this statement reflects a passage in Aristotle's *Metaphysics*. And see Singleton (comm. to these verses): "This clearly reflects Aristotle's statement in the

Metaphysics summarizing his speculations on the unmoved mover as final cause and supreme good. In the Latin translation of Aristotle known to Thomas Aquinas this reads (*Metaphys.* XII, 7, 1072b): 'Ex tali igitur principio dependet caelum et natura.' (It is on such a principle, then, that the heavens and the natural world depend.) Aquinas, in his commentary on this point in the *Metaphysics*, states (*Exp. Metaphys.* XII, lect. 7, n. 2534): 'Hence it is on this principle, i.e., the first mover viewed as an end, that the heavens depend both for the eternality of their substance and the eternality of their motion. Consequently the whole of nature depends on such a principle, because all natural things depend on the heavens and on such motion as they possess.' "

See Vasoli (Vaso.1972.1), pp. 44–50, for a discussion of the neoplatonizing elements in Dante's emanationist view of God's stellar creations and their effect on the lower world. This is, according to Vasoli, not really Aristotelian at all, but essentially and clearly neoplatonic, "closer to Avicenna's metaphysical imagination than to the texts of [Aristotle's] *De caelo*, . . ." (p. 47).

41. The point about this *punto* is that in the Empyrean it is both a mathematically unlocatable and tiny point, a speck, containing everything, and/or an unimaginably large space in which everything that exists in the lower spheres—as a reflection of this point—truly exists. See *Paradiso* XXXIII.85–87.

43–45. Love may or may not "make the world go round," but it certainly is the motive force of the universe. The Seraphim's love of God, Aristotle's unmoved mover, imparts motion to everything beneath Him.

46–57. These four tercets are the protagonist's only words in this sphere, and once again indicate that his intelligence is still earthbound. See Tozer's recapitulation (comm. to vv. 46–57): "Dante here states the difficulty which he feels, viz. that, whereas in the world of sense the spheres move more swiftly in proportion to their distance from the centre, i.e., the earth, the celestial circles which he is now contemplating move more swiftly in proportion to their nearness to the centre, i.e., God. As the latter of these systems is the pattern of the former, it would be natural that they should correspond." That is to say, the physics of the highest heavens is counter to expectation; the smallest circle runs fastest, the most distant, slowest, the exact opposite of what the protagonist experienced as he moved upward and outward from the earth. As Beatrice will explain, that inverse ratio is puzzling only to an earthling; the spiritual physics that she explains is only (super)natural. See the note to vv. 25–27.

52–54. The protagonist refers to the Primum Mobile as a "temple" and to its "boundary," the Empyrean, in terms of love and light, its two most notable characteristics, as we shall see.

55–57. See the note to *Paradiso* XXVII.109 for discussions of Dante's possible "anticipation" of modern cosmic theory, in particular, the hypersphere. He wants to know the relationship between the actual universe and the spiritual one.

Pietro di Dante (Pietro1, comm. to vv. 70–78) was the first among many to cite Boethius, *Cons. Phil.* (III.m9), already cited by Dante at *Convivio* III.ii. 17; the last lines of this poem, a favorite during the Middle Ages, contain the phrase *te cernere finis* cited in the *Epistle to Cangrande* (*Epist.* XIII.89).

58–60. Dante, through Beatrice's characterization of his question, is revealed as not yet being capable of confronting the counterintuitive relations between the physical universe and its spiritual substrate.

64–78. See Tozer's paraphrase (comm. to vv. 64–78): "The argument is as follows:—In the material universe the size of the spheres [i.e., their circumference] corresponds to the amount of divinely infused power (*virtute*) which they possess, and which is diffused by them throughout their whole range (*per tutte lor parti*), i.e., from sphere to sphere and to the earth (ll. 64–66). A larger amount of the benefits thus communicated and received below (*maggior bontà*) is the result of a larger amount of salutary influence (*maggior salute*), and the larger amount of salutary influence is contained in a larger body—supposing always that that body has complete receptive power throughout (ll. 67–69). Consequently, the ninth sphere, or *Primum Mobile*, which is the largest, is also the highest in its nature of all the spheres; and thus it corresponds to the first and highest circle of the angels, that of the Seraphim (ll. 70–72). Hence, if you estimate the angelic circles, not by their size, as you see them, but by the rank and relative power of the spirits which compose them, you will perceive that each material Heaven corresponds exactly to the Order of Intelligences that guides it, the wider sphere to the superior, the narrower to the inferior power."

72. Those who believe that Dante is either "Franciscan," privileging love over knowledge, or "Thomist," placing knowledge higher than love, find

here only one of several clear indications that he wants to combine intellect and will in a common activity, "loving-knowledge" or "knowing-love," that bridges this divide. This has been apparent since we encountered a similar formulation lying behind the harmonious presentation of these two fraternal communities in the heaven of the Sun. And see the note to vv. 37–39.

79–87. The four main winds were, in Dante's day and for centuries after, portrayed as faces. Boreas, the north wind, blows straight ahead or from his left (from the northeast) or from his right (from the northwest). This last was considered the mildest of these three winds, swelling up his right cheek and clearing out the night sky. However, there is some disagreement on this point. Those who find Dante's source in the *Tresor* of Brunetto Latini (I.cvi.14) maintain that the passage refers to the northeast wind.

Tommaseo (comm. to vv. 79–81) locates a source in Boethius (*Cons. Phil.* I.m3.1–10).

87. Not so much a developed simile as a simple comparison, this verse equates Beatrice's fairly lengthy and complex explanation (vv. 61–78) and the clear light from a star (in a sky that has been rid of its obscuring clouds by the wind, if we remember the first simile, vv. 79–84). All that complexity—two dozen verses of it—yields to the simplest illustration of the protagonist's new comprehension.

88–90. Pleased with Beatrice's explanation, the angelic circles (in the Empyrean, we remember) throw out sparks (i.e., the angels themselves, each order keeping to its circle) like molten iron.

For Dante's previous use of this image, see *Paradiso* I.60.

91–93. See Longfellow (comm. to verse 93) for the reference: "The inventor of the game of chess brought it to a Persian king, who was so delighted with it, that he offered him in return whatever reward he might ask. The inventor said he wished only a grain of wheat, doubled as many times as there were squares on the chess-board; that is, one grain for the first square, two for the second, four for the third, and so on to sixty-four. This the king readily granted; but when the amount was reckoned up, he had not wheat enough in his whole kingdom to pay it."

One commentator (Oelsner [comm. to verse 93]) reports that this number is greater than 18,000,000,000,000,000,000. The reader will want to remember that such an astoundingly high figure is the result of simple doubling; the result of squaring (unless one begins with one [what the king should at least have offered as his counterproposal]) would be beyond astronomical.

This anecdote, deriving from the East, has several potential European intermediaries, as has been duly noted (e.g., among others, Peire Vidal, as reported by Torraca [comm. to these verses]; but see Ledda [Ledd..2002.1], p. 297n., for fuller documentation). The question of Dante's direct knowledge of Arabic material has focused, in the last century, on the *Libro della scala*, the account of the Prophet's night journey to another world. Theodore Silverstein (Silv.1952.1) for a while seemed to have silenced those who argued, encouraged by two books by Asín Palacios (Asin.1919.1 and Asin.1927.1), that there was a direct relationship between the Arabic *Libro della scala* and the *Commedia*. His book is still most valuable, although it has often been forgotten in the rekindled debate. Silverstein examined critically Asín's evidentiary procedures and found them deeply flawed, pointing out that more likely sources are to be found in familiar Jewish and Christian texts. However, a new stage in the debate was initiated by Cerulli (Ceru.1949.1), who produced a palliative argument in support of a basic relationship between Dante's poem and Arabic sources (see the discussion of his book by Nardi [Nard.1960.4].) More recently, as respected a critic as Maria Corti (Cort.1995.1) attempted to resuscitate Asín Palacios's thesis; but see Chiamenti (Chia.1999.3) for an effective debunking of her effort. For more recent support of at least the thrust of Asín Palacios's views, see Schildgen (Schi.2002.1). And for an enthusiastic return to most of the original positions of Asín, see Carlo Saccone (Sacc.2002.1).

94–96. The angelic choruses, responding to one another, sing glory to God while remaining fixed eternally in their circles.

For the program of song in the last *cantica*, see the note to *Paradiso* XXI.58–60.

95. Poletto (comm. to vv. 94–96) points out that Dante here uses the Scholastic Latin term *ubi* ("where," with the sense of "place"), which he had three times previously "translated" into Italian (*dove*); see, among the forty appearances of that word in *Paradiso*, only those occurring at III.88, XII.30, XXII.147, and XXVII.109 (this fourth added by Bosco/Reggio [comm. to vv. 95–96]).

97–129. Beatrice here details the order of the angelic hierarchy, an order at variance from the one Dante had presented in *Convivio* (II.v.7–11). For the source of that celestial plan, see the note to vv. 130–135 (and see the discussion in Pasquazi [Pasq.1972.1], pp. 375–78).

While he substantially alters his ordering of the angelic hierarchy from his presentation in *Convivio*, Dante remains firmly in disagreement with St. Thomas about a crucial detail, as Scott (Scot.2004.2), p. 109, takes care to point out. In the *Summa contra Gentiles* (III.1xxx.11), Thomas said that the angelic order of the Virtues was alone responsible for the movement of *all* the heavenly spheres, while Dante, first in *Convivio* (II.v.6) and then here, carefully associates a particular order of angels with a particular sphere, and goes on to say that the various angelic orders are the causes of the movements of the corresponding heavenly spheres (*Conv.* II.v.13; vv. 127–129).

98–102. The Seraphim and Cherubim, associated primarily with love and with knowledge, respectively, are seen as hurrying in their circling in order to resemble God more closely.

103–114. Four tercets are devoted to completing the discussion of the highest group of angels, adding one other to the Seraphim and Cherubim, the Thrones.

103–105. These other "loving spirits" (we note that both Seraphim *and* Cherubim are here associated, along with the Thrones, with loving [see the note to vv. 109–111]).

This tercet is problematic. But see Torraca's solution (comm. to this tercet): The causal clause does not clarify the reason for the name "Thrones" (as most assume), but relates to God's having completed the first triad of angels when He created the Thrones. Bosco/Reggio (comm. to verse 105) uneasily accept this saving understanding of what they consider an "infelice terzina" (infelicitous tercet).

104. The Thrones convey the judgments of God below, as Dante has explained in *Paradiso* IX.62. It seems possible that Dante thought of these first three orders as being particularly related to the Trinity, Love, Knowledge, and Divine Judgment, related to, in order, the Spirit, the Wisdom, and the Power of God. On the other hand, like the Trinity itself, each of the Persons (and each order of angels) has a triune identity along with its individual primary characteristic. There were in fact quite elaborate systems available relating each of the three main groups of angels to each of the three Persons of the Trinity.

Carroll (comm. to vv. 97–105) has a different understanding of the first three orders: "The Thrones are, as they are called elsewhere, 'mirrors' (*Par.* IX.61–63) by which the Divine judgments are flashed throughout the universe. These judgments, however, descend to the Thrones through the Seraphim and Cherubim, that is, through love and knowledge. The Thrones, therefore, are the *terminus*, so to speak, of the love and knowledge of God issuing in judgment. 'The Seraphim,' says Bonaventure, 'contemplate the goodness of God, the Cherubim the truth, the Thrones the equity' (*Compend. Theol. Veritatis*, II.12; St. Bernard, *De Consideratione*, V.4–5); and this equity contains the goodness and truth, the love and light, which flow down through the two higher Orders."

105. The past definite tense of the verb *terminare* here is used in a dialectal form (as is *vonno*, with which it rhymes, in verse 103). In *De vulgari eloquentia* (I.xiii.2), Dante had disparaged this (Pisan) dialectal form of the past definite ending (*-onno*), as commentators (beginning with Andreoli [comm. to vv. 104–105]) have taken pleasure in pointing out. While both these words are forced by rhyme with (the apocopated form of *possono*) *ponno*, it seems evident that Dante enjoyed being forced into this "ungrammatical" posture (i.e., presenting himself as employing a surprisingly low vernacular). See the note to *Paradiso* XVII.127–129.

106–108. Now all three comprising the highest angelic triad are identified, not with love for, but with knowledge of, God.

109–111. This tercet offers apparent aid and comfort to those who propose a "Dominican" Dante, one who values knowledge over love. However, here the poet is saying that knowledge precedes love temporally, not that it is better than it. Clearly, we are meant to understand that, in a Christian soul, they work together. If not, the poet would have found a way to present the Cherubim as the highest order of angels.

112–114. See Grandgent (comm. to verse 114): "These are the 'steps': Grace begets good will, Grace and good will constitute desert, desert determines the degree of sight, and sight is the source of love." He goes on by referring the reader to *Paradiso* XXIX.61–66 and Thomas, *ST*, I, q. 62, a. 4.

115–126. Where six tercets were lavished upon the first triad, the second two (Dominions, Virtues, Powers; Principalities, Archangels, Angels) receive only four altogether.

115–120. For a celebration of Dante's wildly innovative use of metaphor in this passage, see "Un esempio di poesia dantesca (il canto XXVIII del *Paradiso*)," in Contini (Cont.1976.1), p. 213.

116–117. Unlike earthly springtimes, condemned to experience the mortal cycle when Aries becomes a constellation of the night sky in autumn, signaling the end of fruitfulness for the agricultural year, this "spring" is everlasting.

118–120. Scott (Scot.2004.2), p. 384, cites Bemrose (Bemr.1983.1), p. 85, n. 20, for the observation that, as far as he has found, no one before Dante had apparently ever joined the nine ranks of angels to nine particular spheres.

118. The word *sberna* we have translated as "sings" because to do it justice would have taken several words. It has been used in the last canto (*Par.* XXVII.141) with a slightly different spelling and where it means "unwinters," as it also does here, but with the further latent sense of "to sing like birds welcoming the springtime."

121–123. The second triad, composed of orders that have feminine nouns representing them in Latin and in Italian (Dominions, Virtues, Powers) are referred to as *dee* (goddesses).

124–126. The third triad (Principalities, Archangels, Angels) terminates this catalogue.

127–129. All these angelic orders look up; nonetheless, they have their effects below, all created things being affected by them.

128. The first commentator to object to the standard understanding of the verb form *vincon* as being not from *vincere* (conquer) but from *vincire* (bind) was apparently Torraca (comm. to vv. 127–129). Most contemporary commentators, if not all, accept his reading, as do we.

130–135. Dante had perhaps followed Gregory (*Moralia* XXXII.48) indirectly by following the version (Seraphim, Cherubim, *Powers, Principalities*, Virtues, *Dominions, Thrones*, Archangels, Angels) found in Brunetto Latini, *Tresor* (I.xii.5). (Oelsner [comm. to verse 133] was apparently the first commentator to discuss Dante's reliance here on Brunetto.) Gregory, in the *Homiliae* (XXXIV), had only two orders at variance from Dionysius's, the order Dante employs here. See Tozer (comm. to verse 130): "Dionysius the Areopagite, the convert of St. Paul at Athens (Acts 17:34), was the reputed author of the *De Caelesti Hierarchia*, . . . In reality that work seems to have been written in the fifth or sixth century. It was translated from the original Greek into Latin by John Scotus Eriugena (Cent. IX), and became the textbook of angelic lore in the middle ages. The names of the Orders were derived from Scripture, for five of them, viz. Thrones, Dominions, Virtues, Powers, and Principalities, occur in St. Paul's Epistles (cp. Romans 8:38 [Vulg.]; Ephesians 1:21; Colossians 1:16), and the remaining four, viz. Seraphim, Cherubim, Archangels, and Angels, in other parts of the Bible; but the system which Dante here gives was due to the work just mentioned." For Dante's own earlier version, which is probably much more on the poet's mind than Gregory's, see *Convivio* II.v.7–11. This is a large "oops!" that has Dante laughing at himself even more than Gregory might be imagined as doing.

For an essay in English on the importance of Dionysius for Dante, see Gardner (Gard.1913.1), pp. 77–110. For the commentary to this canto that is fullest in terms of reference to the actual texts of Dionysius, see Aversano (Aver.2000.2), pp. 135–41.

131. Aversano (Aver.2000.2), p. 138, points out that Dante's use of this term, *contemplar*, which surely has no need of any particular "source," nonetheless reflects Dionsysius's frequent use of it as a "technical term" for the highest form of contemplation.

133–135. Seem (Seem.2006.1), p. 79, points out that Isidore, who appears conjointly with Solomon in the heaven of the Sun, must similarly be laughing at himself, for he had expressed the opinion that Solomon was damned (*PL* XLII, p. 459).

135. Has Dante forgotten himself again? (See the note to *Par.* IX.119–123.) Porena (comm. to vv. 130–135) thinks Dante has nodded here. Bosco/Reggio (comm. to vv. 134–135) deal with the problem by claiming, less than convincingly, that the poet really meant Heaven in general, and not the Primum Mobile. The only way around the obstacle is to insist that Gregory, passing through this heaven on his way to his seat in the Rose, saw the image of the nine angelic orders present on this sphere as Dante did (see the note to vv. 13–15); however, this seems a forced argu-

ment. Are we faced with another inconsistency that the poet would have cleared up had he lived long enough?

136–139. Beatrice concludes her lengthy speech, begun at verse 61. If, she advises Dante, it was a mortal, Dionysius, who informed humankind of these things, we earthlings should remember that he got his information from St. Paul (see Acts 17:34), who had himself been here. For the significance of Dante's preference for Dionysius over Gregory (the authority of Pauline direct experience as told to a truthful *scriptor* as opposed to later gatherings of an encyclopedic kind), see Picone (Pico.2002.7), pp. 437–38, and Moevs (Moev.2005.1), p. 162.

PARADISO XXIX

OUTLINE

CRYSTALLINE SPHERE

1–9 simile: the moment of the vernal equinox (sun and moon in "balance") and Beatrice's silent smile

10–12 Beatrice will tell Dante what he wants to know: she has seen his question in God.

Beatrice explains God's creation of the angels:

13–21 motive: (WHY?) not for "gain" to Himself (impossible), but that His splendor might "subsist" (WHEN? & WHERE?) in time and space, after creation out of time and space

22–24 (HOW?) form (angels), unformed matter (earth), form and matter joined (heavens) all were created simultaneously

25–30 simile: instantaneous flash of light in clear objects and God's three-stringed bow's three creations

31–36 the three orders of the substances God made (repeated)

37–45 against Jerome [and with Thomas], angels not created before the material universe

46–48 now Dante knows where, when, and how angels were made

49–66 the fallen angels and the good: nearly immediate fall of first, while rest circle God in joy; Lucifer's pride vs. humility of the good angels. Dante should not doubt their worth: it lies in their affection for God

67–69 Beatrice: this suffices for him to understand angels;

70–126 however, because Dante may have been incorrectly taught she digresses on how the angels, if they have intellection and will, do not need memory, since they always live in God's present;

82–96 attack on vain philosophizing on earth (which is, nonetheless, not as troublesome as distortion of the Bible), and of foolish preachers; examples:

- 97–102 eclipse at Crucifixion: miracle, not natural
- 103–126 indulgences: lying clergy and foolish flocks

127–145 Beatrice adds further intelligence about the angels:

- 130–135 their number is beyond calculation;
- 136–141 the varying degrees in which they partake of God;
- 142–145 God's glory is reflected in them.

PARADISO XXIX

Quando ambedue li figli di Latona,
coperti del Montone e de la Libra,
fanno de l'orizzonte insieme zona,

quant' è dal punto che 'l cenìt inlibra
infin che l'uno e l'altro da quel cinto,
cambiando l'emisperio, si dilibra,

tanto, col volto di riso dipinto,
si tacque Bëatrice, riguardando
fiso nel punto che m'avëa vinto.

Poi cominciò: "Io dico, e non dimando,
quel che tu vuoli udir, perch' io l'ho visto
là 've s'appunta ogne *ubi* e ogne *quando*.

Non per aver a sé di bene acquisto,
ch'esser non può, ma perché suo splendore
potesse, risplendendo, dir *'Subsisto,'*

in sua etternità di tempo fore,
fuor d'ogne altro comprender, come i piacque,
s'aperse in nuovi amor l'etterno amore.

Né prima quasi torpente si giacque;
ché né prima né poscia procedette
lo discorrer di Dio sovra quest' acque.

Forma e materia, congiunte e purette,
usciro ad esser che non avia fallo,
come d'arco tricordo tre saette.

E come in vetro, in ambra o in cristallo
raggio resplende sì, che dal venire
a l'esser tutto non è intervallo,

When the two offspring of Latona,
one covered by the Ram, one by the Scales,
together make a belt of the horizon

for the moment that the zenith
holds them balanced, until each of them,
in changing hemispheres, now leaves that belt,

for just that long, her face lit by a smile,
Beatrice was silent, staring intently
at the point that overcame me.

Then she began: 'I tell, I do not ask,
what you would like to hear. For I have seen it there
where every *ubi* and every *quando* has its center.

'Not to increase His store of goodness,
a thing impossible, but that His splendor,
shining back, might say *Subsisto*,

'in His eternity, beyond time, beyond
any other limit, as it pleased Him,
in these new loves, Eternal Love unfolded.

'Nor, before then, did He rest in torpor,
for until God moved upon these waters
there existed no "before," there was no "after."

'Form and matter, conjoined and separate,
came into being without defect,
shot like three arrows from a three-stringed bow.

'And, as a ray shines right through glass, amber,
or crystal, so that between its presence
and its shining there is no lapse of time,

così 'l triforme effetto del suo sire
ne l'esser suo raggiò insieme tutto
sanza distinzïone in essordire.

Concreato fu ordine e costrutto
a le sustanze; e quelle furon cima
nel mondo in che puro atto fu produtto;

pura potenza tenne la parte ima;
nel mezzo strinse potenza con atto
tal vime, che già mai non si divima.

Ieronimo vi scrisse lungo tratto
di secoli de li angeli creati
anzi che l'altro mondo fosse fatto;

ma questo vero è scritto in molti lati
da li scrittor de lo Spirito Santo,
e tu te n'avvedrai se bene agguati;

e anche la ragione il vede alquanto,
che non concederebbe che ' motori
sanza sua perfezion fosser cotanto.

Or sai tu dove e quando questi amori
furon creati e come: sì che spenti
nel tuo disïo già son tre ardori.

Né giugneriesi, numerando, al venti
sì tosto, come de li angeli parte
turbò il suggetto d'i vostri alimenti.

L'altra rimase, e cominciò quest' arte
che tu discerni, con tanto diletto,
che mai da circüir non si diparte.

Principio del cader fu il maladetto
superbir di colui che tu vedesti
da tutti i pesi del mondo costretto.

'just so did the threefold creation flash—
with no intervals in its beginning—
from its Lord into being, all at once.

'With it, order was created and ordained
for the angels, and these were the summit
of the universe, for in them God produced pure act.

'Pure potential held the lowest place.
Between them, potential and act were held together
by such a bond as may not be unbound.

'Jerome's writing tells you all the angels
were created many centuries before
the rest of the universe came into being.

'Yet the scribes of the Holy Ghost declare
the truth on many pages,
as you shall find on searching with some care.

'And even reason sees it, in some measure,
for it would not grant that the movers of the heavens
should remain so long without becoming perfect.

'Now you know both where and when these loving spirits
were created, and you know how, as well.
And thus three flames of your desire have been quenched.

'Then, sooner than one might count to twenty,
one band of angels had disturbed
the lowest of your elements.

'The other band remained and gave itself
with such abandon to this task, which you behold,
that never does it cease its circling motion.

'The cause accounting for the fall
was the accursèd pride of him you saw
crushed beneath the weight of all the world.

Quelli che vedi qui furon modesti
a riconoscer sé da la bontate
che li avea fatti a tanto intender presti:

per che le viste lor furo essaltate
con grazia illuminante e con lor merto,
sì c'hanno ferma e piena volontate;

e non voglio che dubbi, ma sia certo,
che ricever la grazia è meritorio
secondo che l'affetto l'è aperto.

Omai dintorno a questo consistorio
puoi contemplare assai, se le parole
mie son ricolte, sanz' altro aiutorio.

Ma perché 'n terra per le vostre scole
si legge che l'angelica natura
è tal, che 'ntende e si ricorda e vole,

ancor dirò perché tu veggi pura
la verità che là giù si confonde,
equivocando in sì fatta lettura.

Queste sustanze, poi che fur gioconde
de la faccia di Dio, non volser viso
da essa, da cui nulla si nasconde:

però non hanno vedere interciso
da novo obietto, e però non bisogna
rememorar per concetto diviso;

sì che là giù, non dormendo, si sogna,
credendo e non credendo dicer vero;
ma ne l'uno è più colpa e più vergogna.

Voi non andate giù per un sentiero
filosofando: tanto vi trasporta
l'amor de l'apparenza e 'l suo pensiero!

'These whom you observe here all were humble,
acknowledging the Goodness that had made them fit
to be endowed with an intelligence so vast.

'Thus their vision was exalted
by illuminating grace, along with their own merit,
so that theirs is a will both whole and steadfast.

'And I would not have you doubt, but rather be assured,
that there is merit in receiving grace
in measure as the heart inclines to it.

'Henceforth, if you have understood my words,
you may examine anything you like
in this assembly without need of aid.

'But since in schools on earth you still are taught
that the angelic nature is possessed
of understanding, memory, and will,

'I will continue, so that you clearly see
how truth is made unclear down there
by such equivocation in its teaching.

'These angelic beings, since they first rejoiced
in the face of God, from which nothing may be hidden,
have never turned their eyes away from it,

'so that their sight is never interrupted
by some new object. And thus they have no need
to search the past for some forgotten construct.

'Thus down there men are dreaming while they wake,
believing that they speak the truth. And those
who don't believe so share the greater guilt and shame.

'Down there, when you philosophize, you fail
to follow one true path, so does the love of show
preoccupy your mind and carry you away,

E ancor questo qua sù si comporta
con men disdegno che quando è posposta
la divina Scrittura o quando è torta.

Non vi si pensa quanto sangue costa
seminarla nel mondo e quanto piace
chi umilmente con essa s'accosta.

Per apparer ciascun s'ingegna e face
sue invenzioni; e quelle son trascorse
da' predicanti e 'l Vangelio si tace.

Un dice che la luna si ritorse
ne la passion di Cristo e s'interpuose,
per che 'l lume del sol giù non si porse;

e mente, ché la luce si nascose
da sé: però a li Spani e a l'Indi
come a' Giudei tale eclissi rispuose.

Non ha Fiorenza tanti Lapi e Bindi
quante sì fatte favole per anno
in pergamo si gridan quinci e quindi:

sì che le pecorelle, che non sanno,
tornan del pasco pasciute di vento,
e non le scusa non veder lo danno.

Non disse Cristo al suo primo convento:
'Andate, e predicate al mondo ciance';
ma diede lor verace fondamento;

e quel tanto sonò ne le sue guance,
sì ch'a pugnar per accender la fede
de l'Evangelio fero scudo e lance.

Ora si va con motti e con iscede
a predicare, e pur che ben si rida,
gonfia il cappuccio e più non si richiede.

'and even this is tolerated here
with less wrath than when holy Scripture
90 is neglected or its doctrines are mistaught.

'There is no thought among you of the blood it costs
to sow the world with it, or how acceptable he is
93 who humbly makes his way to it.

'Each strives to gain attention by inventing new ideas,
expounded by the preachers at some length—
96 but the Gospel remains silent.

'One says that at Christ's passion the moon turned back
and interposed itself in such a way
99 the sun's light did not reach below.

'He lies, for the light chose to hide itself.
And therefore Spaniards and Indians,
102 as well as Jews, could all see that eclipse take place.

'Florence has not as many named Lapo and Bindo
as it has tales like these that are proclaimed
105 from the pulpit, here and there, throughout the year,

'so that the ignorant flocks return from feeding
fed on wind. And that they fail
108 to see their loss does not excuse them.

'Christ did not say to His first congregation:
"Go preach idle nonsense to the world,"
111 but gave to them a sound foundation.

'And that alone resounded from their lips,
so that, in their warfare to ignite the faith,
114 they used the Gospel as their shield and lance.

'Now preachers ply their trade with buffoonery and jokes,
their cowls inflating if they get a laugh,
117 and the people ask for nothing more.

Ma tale uccel nel becchetto s'annida,
che se 'l vulgo il vedesse, vederebbe
120 la perdonanza di ch'el si confida:

per cui tanta stoltezza in terra crebbe,
che, sanza prova d'alcun testimonio,
123 ad ogne promession si correrebbe.

Di questo ingrassa il porco sant' Antonio,
e altri assai che sono ancor più porci,
126 pagando di moneta sanza conio.

Ma perché siam digressi assai, ritorci
li occhi oramai verso la dritta strada,
129 sì che la via col tempo si raccorci.

Questa natura sì oltre s'ingrada
in numero, che mai non fu loquela
132 né concetto mortal che tanto vada;

e se tu guardi quel che si revela
per Danïel, vedrai che 'n sue migliaia
135 determinato numero si cela.

La prima luce, che tutta la raia,
per tanti modi in essa si recepe,
138 quanti son li splendori a chi s'appaia.

Onde, però che a l'atto che concepe
segue l'affetto, d'amar la dolcezza
141 diversamente in essa ferve e tepe.

Vedi l'eccelso omai e la larghezza
de l'etterno valor, poscia che tanti
speculi fatti s'ha in che si spezza,
145 uno manendo in sé come davanti."

'But such a bird nests in their hoods
that, if the people saw it, they would see
120 the kind of pardoning to which they give their trust.

'Because of these such foolishness has grown on earth
that, with no warrant vouching for its truth,
123 they still would flock to any promise.

'On this Saint Anthony fattens his swine,
along with many others who are still more swinish,
126 repaying them with unstamped coin.

'But, since we have digressed enough,
now turn your eyes to the true road again,
129 that the way may be made shorter—and the time.

'The angelic host mounts by degrees
to such high numbers, no mortal speech or thought
132 could ever count so far,

'and, if you consider what Daniel reveals,
you shall see that in his many thousands
135 a finite number stays concealed.

'The Primal Light that irradiates them all
is received by them in just as many ways
138 as there are splendors joined with It.

'Therefore, since affection follows
the act of conceiving, love's sweetness glows
141 with differing radiance, more brightly or subdued.

'See now the height and breadth of the Eternal Worth,
one light, which shines dispersed among
so many mirrors yet remains
145 in Itself one, just as It was before.'

PARADISO XXIX

1–6. Alison Cornish (Corn.1990.1 [repr. Corn.2000.2, pp. 119–41]) has furnished a bravura performance on this opening simile, connecting its consideration of a single moment separating two very different states (balance/imbalance) to the moment separating God's creation of the angels from that of their first choices. See also Moevs (Moev.2005.1), pp. 151–60.

1–3. Cornish begins her treatment of this moment with the following observation: "We have no way of knowing whether the planetary configuration that opens [this canto] describes dawn or dusk" (Corn.1990.1), p. 1. In the first three centuries it was a rare commentator (but, for exceptions, see Francesco da Buti [comm. to vv. 1–12] and Vellutello [comm. to vv. 1–9]) who did not assume that Dante presented the Sun as being in Aries, the Moon in Libra. After Vellutello there is a period in which everyone gets this "right"; in fact, among the Italians it is only in the twentieth century with Steiner (comm. to verse 2) that the old error returns (until Bosco/Reggio [comm. to vv. 1–9] restore the better reading; but see Chiavacci Leonardi [Chia.1997.1], p. 797, who reverts to the discredited interpretation). Among Dante's English-writing commentators, however, only Oelsner (comm. to these verses) understood that Dante leaves it absolutely opaque as to whether it is the Sun or Moon that is in Aries (the Ram) or in Libra (the Scales). The reference to the Sun's being in Aries at the Creation in the first canto of the poem (*Inf.* I.39–40) has, understandably perhaps, been the controlling factor for such readers.

1. For discussion of Latona's role in the poem (she is also named at *Purg.* XX.131, *Par.* X.67, and XXII.139), see Aversano (Aver.2000.2), pp. 141–42, suggesting that her maternal role may have seemed to Dante reminiscent of Mary (in particular in her having given birth to Apollo, treated several times as Christ [see the notes to *Par.* I.13–15, 13, 19, 25–27]). He continues by suggesting that Dante also was drawn to the figure of Latona by her exilic condition, particularly as this was presented by Ovid (*Metam.* VI.186–191), and by her eventual stability, shared by the former wandering isle, Delos, in a sort of pagan version of eternal peace and light.

4–6. The Sun and the Moon are described as being momentarily balanced (an instant immeasurably brief because both are always in their orbital motion); their being "out of balance" is recognized after a certain duration, when both are perceived as having changed position, moving away from (the one above, the other below) the horizon. Strangely, Cornish (Corn.1990.1), p. 7, believes that Porena was of the opinion that this instant also corresponds to that of a total lunar eclipse. Porena, in fact, first in his earlier article (Pore.1930.1) and then in his commentary (to vv. 4–6), "dismisses the eclipse as an accident" (the words are Kleiner's [Klei.1994.1], p. 166, n. 14). Porena is in polemic against those of Dante's commentators who take his scientific lore too seriously.

7–8. Some (incorrectly) believe that what is described as being of immeasurably short duration is Beatrice's smile (see Payton [Payt.1995.1], p. 439): "The longer it is thought about, the smaller the exact instant is. . . . How long did Beatrice smile? How brief a moment can you conceive?" Payton has not digested Cornish's explanation (Corn.1990.1, pp. 6–7), not of Beatrice's smile, but of her *silence*, which is the issue here: "For Aristotle an instant (or the 'now,' as he called it) is the temporal equivalent of a point on a line; yet time is no more made up of these 'nows' than a line is composed of geometrical points" (p. 7). She points out that Porena before her had correctly characterized the temporal nature of Beatrice's silence (see his comm. to vv. 4–6) as indeed having measurable duration. Porena suggests that the amount of time for half the rising or setting Sun or Moon to rise completely above or to sink completely below the horizon is a little more than a minute, certainly a measurable time. Cornish might have observed that Bosco/Reggio (comm. to vv. 1–9) had supported Porena's thesis.

9. For the poet's contrastive inner reference to Francesca's words (*Inf.* V.132, "ma solo un punto fu quel che ci vinse" [still, it was a single instant overcame us]), here and in *Paradiso* XXX.11, see Hollander (Holl.1993.5), pp. 7–8, nn. 18–19, citing Contini (Cont.1976.1), p. 206, as having preceded him in pointing out this parallel. But see also Chiampi (Chia.1981.1), p. 66. And now see Moevs (Moev.2005.1), p. 157.

10–12. By now a most familiar claim of Beatrice's: She reads Dante's thoughts in the point (God) where all space (Latin for "where": *ubi*) and time (Latin for "when": *quando*) most purely and truly exist.

13–18. We are in the highest part of God's creation in time, a mixture of form and matter, the heavens. This sphere, we remember, is governed by the Seraphim, the highest order of angels, dedicated to loving God. Dante has asked a most difficult theological question: If God is self-sufficient, if He has no "needs," why did He bother to create anything at all? The answer that Beatrice offers is simplicity itself: He created because He loves and wanted the angels to enjoy His love in their being, loving Him in return.

For consideration of Dante's reflections on the Creation, see Boyde (Boyd.1981.1), pp. 235–47. On the canto as a whole, see Nardi's *lectura* (Nard.1956.1). For Dante's recasting in it of the relatively anthropomorphic view of creation found in Genesis for a more abstract and philosophical one, see Boitani (Boit.2002.1). Boitani further maintains (p. 95) that Dante's rescripting of Genesis goes far beyond what is authorized by the Bible in portraying the creation of the angels, a subject about which Scripture is silent.

15. The Latin verb form *subsistere* is used here, as Bosco/Reggio point out, voluntarily (Dante had used the Italian form of the noun *substantia* [*sussistenza*] at *Paradiso* XIII.59 and easily could have used *sussisto* here, which rhymes perfectly with *visto* and *acquisto*). And so we may conclude that he wanted the Scholastic flavor that the Latin term affords. See verse 12, where the parallelism with the Latin word *ubi* causes the reader to realize that a perfectly usual Italian word *quando* is there a Latin word.

17. The Italian dative pronoun "i" (*gli* in modern Italian) is used some eight times in the poem, but this is the only time it refers to God after Adam informs us that "I" was the first name that human speakers used to address Him, and that Adam was the first to use it. See the note to *Paradiso* XXVI.134.

19–21. Two major issues are touched on here. If our sense of the history of the world begins with Creation (i.e., Genesis 1:1), what was God doing *before* then? (Attributed to St. Augustine is the retort, "preparing a Hell for the inquisitive" [see Carroll, comm. to vv. 19–30].) Dante's point is that whatever He was doing, He was not lazing about, even if there was, strictly speaking, no time before the Creation.

The second problem is of a different order. What exactly does "God moved upon these waters" mean? Precisely what "waters" are referred to? The obvious reference is to Genesis 1:2. The first commentator (but hardly the last) to point to the work of Bruno Nardi was Porena (comm. to this tercet). Nardi had shown (see Nard.1944.1), pp. 307–13, that one traditional medieval interpretation of this biblical text was that these waters are above the rest of the heavens (the Primum Mobile was also referred to as the "acqueous sphere"). As Bosco/Reggio (comm. to this tercet) point out, Dante's use of the demonstrative adjective "queste" (these) makes that solution even more attractive, since Dante and Beatrice are currently in the Primum Mobile.

22–36. Boitani (Boit.2002.2), p. 446, adduces *Paradiso* VII.64–66, with its sense of God's creation being motivated by love, as lying behind this passage. For the distinctions between *forma* and *atto* and between *materia* and *potenza*, see Bemrose (Bemr.1983.1) and Baranski's rejoinder (Bara. 1984.1), pp. 298–99.

22–24. From the fourteenth century onward, commentators (e.g., the author of the notes to the *Commedia* found in the Codice Cassinese [comm. to verse 22]) have entered into the question of what exactly Dante envisioned when he thought of "pure matter." The author of that early commentary resorts to Plato's term *ylem* ["hyle"], for primordial matter without form, the "stuff" of the four elements that God would give shape in creating the physical world. See O'Keeffe (Okee.1924.1), pp. 56–57, for why this is *not* the same as the "prime matter" of Averroës. And, for a recent discussion in English, taking issue with Nardi's various pronouncements that would make Dante less orthodox than even he probably wanted to be perceived, see Moevs (Moev.2005.1), pp. 40–45. For instance, Moevs believes that Dante's ideas about *materia puretta* accord with Thomas's views.

For the three entities "shot" by this "three-stringed bow," see the note to vv. 31–36.

25–30. Dante insists on the simultaneity of all parts of God's instantaneous creation, heavenly and sublunar. The three elements of that creation (pure form, mixed form and matter, and pure matter) obviously are in hierarchical relation to one another; but their creation occurred in the same instant.

26–27. According to Mellone (Mell.1974.1), p. 196, n. 1, this is the only time in all his works that Dante refers to the notion in medieval physics that light traveled at infinite velocity.

31–36. The standard gloss is found in Bosco/Reggio (comm. to these verses), who say that the angels, "pure act" (i.e., pure form or substance, unmodified by accidents), were created in the Empyrean; that "pure matter" (unformed matter before God created the universe) was the condition of the earth before the event recorded in Genesis 1:1–2; that the nine heavens, between the Empyrean and earth, were created out of a mixture of form and matter ("act" [*atto*] and "potential" [*potenza*]). However, for a nuanced and more complex discussion of Dante's unique integration of elements from many sources in this passage, orthodox (e.g., Thomas Aquinas) and unorthodox (e.g., Averroës), see Mellone (Mell.1974.1), pp. 198–200.

There is a persistent counterview, one that understands the second aspect of the Creation differently, as humankind. But see Poletto's stern remonstrance (comm. to vv. 22–24).

31–32. On these lines, see Kay (Kay.2003.1), p. 45: "Order and structure were created together in the substances [= angels]."

Singleton (comm. to vv. 8–9) makes the following observation: "For a reader unfamiliar with the standard procedure of a *summa* of theology, it should perhaps be pointed out that the poem is proceeding thematically in the opposite direction to that of a *summa*: the journey moves ever upwards, toward God, and here comes to a treatise on angels, in these two cantos so near the end, whereas a *summa* begins with God, in its first section of questions, and then passes to the creation or procession of creatures from God (cf. *Summa theol.* I of Thomas Aquinas as it passes from question 43 to question 44), beginning with the highest creatures, which are the angels."

37–45. As Scripture (e.g., Genesis 1:1, Ecclesiasticus 18:1, Psalm 101:26 [102:25]) and reason (for Dante's own contribution under this heading, see vv. 43–45) attest, God created the angels, not as St. Jerome asseverated (in his commentary on Paul's Epistle to Titus 1:2), many, many centuries before He created the heavens and the earth, but simultaneously with them. Dante's disagreement with Jerome is confrontational and dismissive, all the more so since it issues from the mouth of Beatrice, and we cannot lay the blame on a somewhat intemperate protagonist. (For the text of Thomas's far more conciliatory packaging of his own dissent [*ST* I, q. 61, a. 3], see Singleton [comm. to vv. 37–39]).

43–45. Beatrice's point is that, were Jerome to have been correct, the angels would have had nothing to do for all those centuries, since their only task is governing the heavens.

46–63. Mellone (Mell.1974.1), p. 194, locates this part of Beatrice's discourse in Peter Lombard's discussion of the angels (*Sententiae* I.ii.2), where he sets out the problems to be resolved exactly as they are represented here: "Concerning the angelic nature the following must first be considered: when it was created, and where, and how; then what the result was of the defection of certain of them and of the adhesion of certain others." Cf. Boitani (Boit.2002.2), p. 452, for the same citation.

46–48. In good Scholastic style, Beatrice summarizes the first three elements in her exposition. See the note to vv. 46–63.

49–51. No one seems to have found a reason or a source for this segment of time that Dante decides it took the angels to fall from the Empyrean into Hell. In fact, normal gravitational force, applied to normal objects, would have left them falling a far longer time. Their sin, self-loving rebellion against God, occurred the moment of/after their creation, for all intents and purposes instantaneously. Their fall, traversing the entire universe to its core, took less than half a minute.

50. See *Convivio* II.v.12 for Dante's previous handling of the question of the fallen angels: It was about one-tenth of the whole group who sinned and fell; God was moved to create humankind as a kind of replacement for these ("alla quale restaurare fue l'umana natura poi creata").

For Augustine's absolute unwillingness to consider that God created the eventually fallen angels anything less than completely good, see Cornish (Corn.1990.1), pp. 10–14. On the other hand, he clearly thought that angelic nature would have come into being making choices. And so Augustine, caught between two very strong theological imperatives (God never created evil; Satan never enjoyed the bliss of loving God), invented an amorphous *mora* (delay) between his creation and his fall. According to Cornish, for Augustine "the devil was not created sinful, yet his sin was not deferred even for a split-second. He makes the distinction that by nature the devil was good, by choice he became evil, so that the beginning of Lucifer's being and the beginning of his sin occurred at two separate moments. Whether these are logical or chronological moments is not clear" (p. 11). Dante's view, while never clearly stated, is probably not very different.

51. For *suggetto*, see Bemrose (Bemr.1983.1), pp. 197–201, siding with the majority; the word refers to "terra" (earth). See, for instance, Lombardi's gloss (comm. to vv. 49–51), saying that earth is *subject to* (i.e., lies beneath) the other three elements, water, air, and fire. But see Mazzoni (Mazz.1979.2 [Intro. to *Questio*], pp. 712–32) and Baranski (Bara.1984.1),

p. 300, both of whom suggest that we are meant to realize that what is under discussion is "prime matter" (*la materia prima*). And see Cestaro (Cest.2003.1), p. 248, n. 87: "Dante alludes here to the common Scholastic notion of a *subiectum elementorum*, the primal elemental material prior to the definition of four distinct elements, akin to Plato's *silva* ['hyle']. . . ." A hedged bet is found in Oelsner's notes (comm. to vv. 49–51): "*Il suggetto dei vostri elementi* is usually (and perhaps rightly) taken to mean 'that one of your elements that underlies the rest,' *i.e.*, earth. Compare *Inf.* XXXIV.121–126. But if we take this passage on its own merits, it seems better to understand the *substrate* of the elements to mean the *prima materia* (compare [*Par.*] II.106–108; VII.133–136, and lines 22–24 of this canto); the elaboration of the elements being the subsequent work of the Angels and the heavens." The strongest case against this second interpretation was made by Porena (comm. to vv. 49–51), pointing out that *Inferno* XXXIV.122–126 reveals that Dante thought that, by the time Satan had penetrated our globe, water and earth had already been separated. However, Chimenz (comm. to vv. 49–51) countered that argument as follows: The words inscribed over the gate of Hell (*Inf.* III.7–8) would seem to suggest that before the creation of Hell (and, Chimenz insists, the contemporary creation of the angels), nothing existed except eternal things, and thus Satan fell into unformed matter. Nonetheless, it is certainly possible that we are meant to understand that earth was formed while Satan was falling and (at least in part) in order to receive him and his partners in rebellion.

52–57. The verb *circuir* does not suggest that the remaining (loyal) angels are flying around the heavens freestyle, but that they form nine angelic circlings around God, as opposed to the fallen angels, who, along with their leader, Lucifer, are imprisoned in Hell. The text (vv. 56–57) specifically reminds readers of their vision of Satan at the center of the universe (*Inferno* XXXIV.110–111).

58–60. The good angels, unlike the prideful members of their cohort, are portrayed as "modesti" (humble), possessing the virtue opposite to their brethren's vice of pride.

61–63. See Singleton's gloss (comm. to this tercet): "The angels who waited for the bestowal of the higher light, the light of glory, received that light (here termed 'grazia illuminante'). Their merit (*merto*) was precisely that humility and their waiting upon the Lord to bestow that higher light.

With that bestowal they were forever confirmed in this highest grace, and accordingly they are now bound thereby to the good and to *do* the good. They have fullness of vision and of will, and they cannot sin. See Thomas Aquinas, *Summa theol.* I, q. 62, a. 8, resp.: 'The beatified angels cannot sin. The reason for this is, because their beatitude consists in seeing God through His essence. Now, God's essence is the very essence of goodness. Consequently the angel beholding God is disposed towards God in the same way as anyone else not seeing God is to the common form of goodness. Now it is impossible for any man either to will or to do anything except aiming at what is good; or for him to wish to turn away from good precisely as such. Therefore the beatified angel can neither will nor act, except as aiming towards God. Now, whoever wills or acts in this manner cannot sin. Consequently the beatified angel cannot sin.' "

64. Dante, Beatrice divines, may be wondering what the angels actually *did* in order to merit illuminating grace.

65–66. See Singleton (comm. to these verses), citing Aquinas (*ST* I, q. 62, a. 5): "As the angel is of his nature inclined to natural perfection, so is he by merit inclined to glory. Hence instantly after merit the angel secured beatitude. Now the merit of beatitude in angel and man alike can be from merely one act; because man merits beatitude by every act informed by charity. Hence it remains that an angel was beatified straightway after one act of charity."

70–126. Dante's corrosive attack on bad preaching reveals heartfelt annoyance, probably reflecting extensive personal experience. Tasked with the representation of the Word, preachers should control their desires for recognition of their powers of speaking.

70–81. Discussing the questions pertaining to the natures of angelic language (see *De vulgari eloquentia* I.ii.3) and memory, see Barbara Faes de Mottoni (Faes.2001.1). Her discussion of this passage, found on pp. 243–53, concludes (p. 253) with the assertion, difficult to fault, that the angels, knowing everything in God, have, at least in Dante's possibly heterodox opinions (potentially opposed to those of Peter Lombard, Bonaventure, Albert the Great, and Thomas Aquinas), need of neither language nor memory. However, see the further distinction offered by Attilio Mellone (Mell.1974.1), pp. 205–8, who suggests that, while a passage in *Monarchia* (I.iii.7) clearly seems to require that we conceive that Dante there denies that the angels have memories, here the poet only seems to assert that they do not need to make use of them.

70. See the observation of Hawkins (Hawk.1999.1), p. 192: With the exception of *Purgatorio* XXXII.79, "where 'scuola' describes the Old Testament precursors of Christ, . . . [the word] always denotes what is pagan or in some sense defective. . . ."

75. Bosco/Reggio (comm. to this verse) allow that possibly Dante believes that, projecting human experience onto the terms "intellect," "will," and "memory" (see verse 72), some earthly judges distort the nature of the angelic versions of these capacities. That would "save" Dante from opposing some pretty potent authorities (see the note to vv. 70–81).

79–80. See Imbach (Imba.1996.1), p. 147, averring that Dante embraces at least one heretical position of Siger de Brabant when, in these lines, he argues, against the authorities mentioned in the note to verses 70–81, that the angels have no memory. For discussion, see Curti (Curt.2002.1), pp. 161–62. It seems likely that Dante wants, as is often the case, to formulate his own position on an issue, one that accords with elements found in several other authorities.

82–84. The explanation seems clear enough (and is found in many early commentaries): There are those on earth who are totally confused (i.e., they "dream" even while they are not sleeping) in believing that the angels have need of memory, while others, those who maintain such a view while knowing it to be false, are guilty not of ignorance but of fraud. These Christian sophists care more about making a splash than seeking the truth.

Boitani (Boit.2002.2), p. 451, is effective in joining two responses that are rarely seen together in the commentary tradition when he understands (1) that the focus of Beatrice's anger is completely on the question of angelic memory (and does not spill over into the sins of bad preachers, which dominate the following verses [91–126], as so many allow their discussion to do) and (2) that the zeal behind her (Dante's) insistence is passionate and fully conscious of the famous feathers that will be ruffled thereby, those of Saints Jerome, Augustine, and Thomas, for starters. However, he perhaps goes too far in asserting that Dante *denies* that angels have memory; the text only asserts (vv. 80–81) that they have no *need* of memory, which may imply either that they have or do not have this capacity. Dante is obviously outraged at the notion of angels requiring (and actually using) memory, since they live in the eternal present. However, whether he goes as far as Averroës (and Siger) in denying that they have this capacity, that question he leaves us to wonder about. He could not have left the issue more ambiguous, as he obviously desired to—which may imply that he did in fact buy into Siger's argument.

85–90. These two tercets form the pivot on which Beatrice's argument turns from heavenly theology (involving the nature of angelic mind) to religious concerns of a lower intellectual order, from the disputes of theologians to the fables told by preachers—and Dante almost certainly has in mind itinerant friars.

91–93. The "cost" of the benefits of Scripture in blood (of Jesus, the martyred apostles, and the other martyrs [see Pasquini/Quaglio, comm. to this tercet, for these three references]) is not taken into account.

Poletto (comm. to this tercet) at least reacts to the curious present tense of the verb *costa* (costs), and "translates" it as *costò* (cost). Grabher (comm. to this tercet) does take the present tense as meaningful, believing that Dante is not speaking literally of the blood of martyrs, but metaphorically—of the inner sacrifice made by all Christians. This does not seem a convincing gloss. And thus, while the constraints of rhyme may be all the explanation one requires for the presence of the form, the reader is forced to wonder. Did Dante think of the past sacrifices of the heroes of the Church as occurring in the vivid present tense, or is his point that such sacrifices are being made even now, in his day? His opinions on the current condition of the City of Man, expressed volubly throughout the poem (most recently at *Par.* XXVII.121–141), would seem to gainsay this second possible explanation.

94–126. Pasquazi (Pasq.1968.1), p. 1031, begins his *lectura* with this invective against preachers, which is a frequent cause of complaint among less stern readers of the last canticle. His view is that it should be dealt with not as aberrant, but as of a piece with the texture and purpose of the canto. Mellone (Mell.1974.1), p. 209, is of a similar opinion. For discussion of a similar discomfort among the commentators with Beatrice's last words in the poem in the following canto, see Hollander (Holl.1993.5), pp. 31–33.

94–96. Preaching as preening now becomes Beatrice's subject. Her insistence on the fictitious nature of this sort of public utterance is underlined by the word *invenzioni* (inventing new ideas) here and *favole* (tales) at verse 104, *ciance* (idle nonsense) at verse 110, *motti* and *iscede* (buffoonery and jokes) at verse 115. Cf. Giovanni Boccaccio's portrait of a fiction-dealing friar, Fra Cipolla (*Decameron* VI.x), which probably owes more than a certain debt to this passage. (See Longfellow [comm. to verse 115] and Hollander [Holl.1997.2], pp. 41–45).

97–102. For the "darkness at noon" that overspread the world during the Crucifixion of Jesus, see Luke 23:44: "It was now about the sixth hour, and there was darkness over the whole land until the ninth hour." (See also Matthew 27:45 and Mark 15:33.) And see Grandgent (comm. to these verses): "To explain this darkness at the Crucifixion, some said that the moon left its course to make an eclipse, others that the sun hid its own rays. Dionysius (*Par.* XXVIII.130) favored the first explanation, St. Jerome the second. Both are recorded by St. Thomas in *Summa Theologiae* III, q. 44, a. 2. The second theory has the advantage of accounting for an obscuration 'over all the land,' whereas an ordinary eclipse would darken only a part of it."

100. This line has caused scandal. Does Dante really want to say that those who say that the Moon retroceded six constellations in the Zodiac in order to blot out the Sun (and, according to Scartazzini [comm. to this verse] and Bosco/Reggio [comm. to vv. 97–102], some fairly illustrious authorities, including Dionysius the Areopagite, Albert the Great, and Thomas Aquinas, took this explanation seriously) are *liars*? Those are strong words. Scartazzini was the first to point out that Dante had a precursor in such a harsh view, Petrus Comestor (*PL* CXCVIII.1631), who says that those who uphold such tales "have lied" (*mentiti sunt*). Eventually Nardi (Nard.1944.1), pp. 375–76, would also turn to this source and argue that, despite the commentators' discomfort, both the manuscript tradition and Petrus's harsh words underline the fact that Dante meant exactly what he said. We should remember the poet's harsh treatment of Jerome, specifically mentioned as totally incorrect (Dante could have been less direct!) in this very canto (verses 37–45); on that occasion, concerning the dating of the creation of the angels, St. Thomas was right (if Dante doesn't say so specifically). And now it is *his* turn to be told off, if indirectly. Bosco/Reggio try to diminish the force of the verb *mentire* in Dante's day (i.e., rather than lying, it meant something more like "does not tell the truth"). Nonetheless, it is plain enough that Dante is belittling an opinion that is to be thought of as having the same merit as the idle tales told by

not-very-well-educated friars. And if Dionysius, Albert, or Thomas chooses to align himself with such drivel, he gets only what he deserves—that seems to be the poet's attitude.

Dante disposes of this "scientific" account of the miracle recorded in three Gospels on truly experimental grounds. If it were true, then the resulting eclipse would have been only partial. And so we are forced to follow Jerome, whose miraculous "self-eclipse" of the Sun indeed was visible in all the world, and not merely in the area around Jerusalem.

103–108. This picture of religious ceremony in the Florence of Dante's day has its kinship with that found in the series of (often hilarious) representations of preaching found in the *Decameron*. All over the city, in parish after parish, all through the year, the leaders of the flock trade in "wind," notions that are clearly estranged from truth. Such intellectual vagrancy, however, does not excuse the individual sheep, who should realize that what they listen to so avidly has nothing to do with the Bible or with the fundamental truths of their religion. In other words, they are not innocent because they are stupid.

103. Daniello (comm. to this verse) was the first glossator to identify the source of the nickname *Lapo* as Jacopo. That *Bindo* derived from Ildebrando was first noted by Fanfani (in his *Vocabulary of Tuscan Usage*), according to Andreoli (comm. to this verse).

105. Dante's verb *gridare* tells all one needs to know about the quality of mind that lies behind these "shouted" sermons.

106–114. For a sermon of St. Bernard that may be reflected in this passage, see Payton (Payt.1995.1), pp. 448–49.

109. Christ's first "congregation" was comprised of the apostles.

111. The "sound foundation" was based on the Bible.

112–114. Some think that the phrase "le sue guance" (lit. "cheeks" [a choice forced by rhyme?] understood as metonymic for "lips") refers to the lips of Jesus rather than to those of the apostles. In choosing the latter, we follow Bosco/Reggio (comm. to this tercet) and the large majority of the commentators. However, the estimable Francesco da Buti (comm. to vv. 109–117) begins the tradition of treating the utterances as coming from

Christ's mouth, and has had a narrow but fairly distinguished band of adherents (Landino, Costa, Tommaseo, Andreoli, etc.).

117. The *cappuccio* (cowl) worn by friars balloons figuratively with their pride. Literally, a large and well-tailored cowl was the sign of wealth of the Order and/or importance of an individual. Bosco/Reggio (comm. to vv. 115–117) point out that the only other *cappuccio* found in this poem is worn by the hypocrites in Malebolge, *Inferno* XXIII.61. They are attired in leaden costume that mimics the garb of Cluniac monks.

118. Bosco/Reggio (comm. to this verse) point out that Satan was often, in medieval iconography, represented as a black crow (in contrast to the white dove that represented the Holy Spirit) and that Dante has spoken (*Inf.* XXXIV.47) of Lucifer as an *uccello* (bird).

121–123. Believing in the truthfulness of pardons (and pardoners) is the height of credulity. It is hard to blame the trickster when his victims almost insist on being gulled.

124–126. See Tozer's gloss on this tercet: " '[O]n this (credulity) St. Antony fattens his pig.' The hog which appears in pictures at the feet of St. Antony, the Egyptian hermit [ca. 250–355], represents the demon of sensuality which he conquered. In the middle ages the swine of the monks of St. Antony were allowed to feed in the streets of cities, and were fed by devout persons (Jameson, *Sacred and Legendary Art*, pp. 750, 751); this is what Dante refers to." The obvious reversal in the values of the Antonines, who became the representatives of the vice that their founder had conquered, is apparent.

126. The friars of Antony's order are "repaying" the contributions of their foolish flocks with counterfeit coin: meaningless pieces of paper on which is written their forgiven sins.

127–129. Beatrice concludes her tirade with an ironic verbal gesture, making it a mere digression. Now let us return, she says, to the true way, the path chosen by the loyal angels, a subject turned aside from in verse 94 for her savage attack upon friars, difficult to accept as a mere digression.

130–132. The numbers of the angels increases the higher they are found. Dante's coinage, the verb *ingradarsi*, is found in slightly altered form (*digradarsi*) in *Paradiso* XXX.125. In both cases it seems to have the meaning "to increase step-by-step." Thus, the higher the eyes of an observer mount, the more angels they are able to take in. And that number is beyond both human vocabulary and mortal conception.

133–135. Discussing this passage, Ledda (Ledd.2002.1), pp. 297–98, points out that Daniel's numeration of the angels (Daniel 7:10, "a thousand thousands served him, and ten thousand times one hundred thousand stood before him" [according to the Vulgate]), while incalculable for most human beings, was probably a finite number in Dante's opinion. Similarly, the wording of verse 135, "a particular number lies concealed" (*determinato numero si cela*), would clearly seem to indicate a very large but determinable number. Most commentators think the poet is saying something quite different, namely that the number of angels cannot be represented by *any* finite number. However, Dante's sense for mathematics may be more sophisticated than that of his commentators; apparently he knows the distinction between "numberless" (i.e., beyond counting because of limited human capacity) and "infinite," a concept of which he knew at least from the extended discussion in Aristotle's *Physics* (III.iv–viii).

Behind this passage, according to Mellone (Mell.1974.1), pp. 210–11, there lies a dispute between "Aristotelians" (who propose a limited number of angels) and the Bible (e.g., Daniel 7:10, Apocalypse 5:11). However, see Thomas Aquinas (*ST* I, q. 112, a. 4), as cited by Bosco/Reggio (comm. to verse 135): "The multitude of the angels transcends any material multitude." It is clear what position Dante does not share, that of the "Aristotelians," who argue for a strictly limited number (as few as sixty). However, whether he believes that the angels are infinite or numbered is not entirely clear, although verse 135 may be more specific than it is generally understood as being. Aversano (Aver.2000.2), p. 148, supports the second opinion, citing Gregory's gloss on Job 25:3 from the *Moralia*: "And if the number of angels is finite to the eye of God [Dante's 'particular number'?], in the human view it is infinite [Dante's 'lies concealed'?]" (*PL* LXXV.542).

136–141. God's brilliance irradiates the angelic nature in such ways that it is received by these creatures (*splendori* because they reflect the divine light [for Dante's "light physics" see the note to *Par.* XXIII.82–84]) variously, each in accord with its capacity to absorb and return God's love.

142–145. Seemingly infinite in its application, God's love for the highest creatures that He made nonetheless still issues from the single entity that made them.

PARADISO XXX

OUTLINE

PRIMUM MOBILE; EMPYREAN

1–13 simile: advancing dawn hiding stars, God hiding angels
14–15 blinded by the light and constrained by love: Beatrice
16–21 her beauty greater than ever; only God can truly enjoy it
22–24 the poet defeated by his subject
25–27 comparison: sun on eyes, as her smile blots out his memory
28–33 elaboration: his continual praise has reached its limit
34–36 and so he leaves her to a greater trumpeting
37–45 Beatrice, her task over, tells Dante where he is and that here he will see angels and saints, the latter in flesh
46–51 simile: lightning and perceived objects; the point of light and Dante's blindness
52–54 a voice within Dante: so this Light welcomes here
55–60 Dante, enraptured, gradually can see the Light
61–69 his first vision: light as river, two banks, sparks
70–75 Beatrice commends his desire to know; first he must drink
76–81 she indicates the relation between what he sees and what he will see once he can *really* see
82–87 simile: babe awaking moves to suckle, Dante bends to river
88–90 even as he drinks the river becomes round, not linear
91–96 simile: unmasked revelers, flowers and sparks
97–99 eighth invocation: splendor of God
100–102 the new place: God as Light that his creatures can see
103–105 its circumference wider than the sun's
106–108 it is formed by a ray reflected from the Primum Mobile, which in turn takes its movement and influence from it

109–114 simile: hill reflected in river, one thousand tiers above the Light

115–117 if the lowest ring encloses the Light, imagine the upper circumference of the Rose!

118–123 Dante sees it all as one, since where God rules without mediation far and near do not matter

124–148 Beatrice's last speaking role in the poem:

- 124–132 she draws Dante into the Rose: "see the blessed"
- 133–138 Henry VII, the first soul, seen as coming to Paradise
- 139–141 Italy's failure to welcome Henry
- 142–144 the devious behavior of Clement V
- 145–148 Clement will soon go to Hell and displace Boniface.

PARADISO XXX

Forse semilia miglia di lontano
ci ferve l'ora sesta, e questo mondo
china già l'ombra quasi al letto piano,

quando 'l mezzo del cielo, a noi profondo,
comincia a farsi tal, ch'alcuna stella
perde il parere infino a questo fondo;

e come vien la chiarissima ancella
del sol più oltre, così 'l ciel si chiude
di vista in vista infino a la più bella.

Non altrimenti il trïunfo che lude
sempre dintorno al punto che mi vinse,
parendo inchiuso da quel ch'elli 'nchiude,

a poco a poco al mio veder si stinse:
per che tornar con li occhi a Bëatrice
nulla vedere e amor mi costrinse.

Se quanto infino a qui di lei si dice
fosse conchiuso tutto in una loda,
poca sarebbe a fornir questa vice.

La bellezza ch'io vidi si trasmoda
non pur di là da noi, ma certo io credo
che solo il suo fattor tutta la goda.

Da questo passo vinto mi concedo
più che già mai da punto di suo tema
soprato fosse comico o tragedo:

ché, come sole in viso che più trema,
così lo rimembrar del dolce riso
la mente mia da me medesmo scema.

About six thousand miles away from here
the sixth hour burns and even now this world
3 inclines its shadow almost to a level bed,

when, deep in intervening air, above us,
begins such change that here and there,
6 at our depth, a star is lost to sight.

And, as that brightest handmaid of the sun advances,
the sky extinguishes its lights,
9 even the most beautiful, one by one.

Not otherwise the victory that revels
in eternal joy around the point that overcame me
12 and seems enclosed by that which it encloses

little by little faded from my sight,
so that, compelled by seeing nothing and by love,
15 I turned my eyes to gaze on Beatrice.

If all things said of her up to this point
were gathered in a single hymn of praise,
18 it would be paltry, matched to what is due.

The beauty that I saw transcends
all thought of beauty, and I must believe
21 that only its maker may savor it all.

I declare myself defeated at this point
more than any poet, whether comic or tragic,
24 was ever thwarted by a topic in his theme,

for, like sunlight striking on the weakest eyes,
the memory of the sweetness of that smile
27 deprives me of my mental powers.

Dal primo giorno ch'i' vidi il suo viso
in questa vita, infino a questa vista,
non m'è il seguire al mio cantar preciso;

ma or convien che mio seguir desista
più dietro a sua bellezza, poetando,
come a l'ultimo suo ciascuno artista.

Cotal qual io la lascio a maggior bando
che quel de la mia tuba, che deduce
l'ardüa sua matera terminando,

con atto e voce di spedito duce
ricominciò: "Noi siamo usciti fore
del maggior corpo al ciel ch'è pura luce:

luce intellettüal, piena d'amore;
amor di vero ben, pien di letizia;
letizia che trascende ogne dolzore.

Qui vederai l'una e l'altra milizia
di paradiso, e l'una in quelli aspetti
che tu vedrai a l'ultima giustizia."

Come sùbito lampo che discetti
li spiriti visivi, sì che priva
da l'atto l'occhio di più forti obietti,

così mi circunfulse luce viva,
e lasciommi fasciato di tal velo
del suo fulgor, che nulla m'appariva.

"Sempre l'amor che queta questo cielo
accoglie in sé con sì fatta salute,
per far disposto a sua fiamma il candelo."

Non fur più tosto dentro a me venute
queste parole brievi, ch'io compresi
me sormontar di sopr' a mia virtute;

From the first day, when in this life I saw her face
until my vision of her now, pursuit
of her in song has never been cut off.

But now I must desist in my pursuit,
no longer following her beauty in my verse,
as every artist, having reached his limit, must.

Thus I leave her to more glorious trumpeting
than that of my own music, as, laboring on,
I bring my difficult subject toward its close.

With the voice and bearing of a guide
who has discharged his duty, she began: 'We have issued
from the largest body to the Heaven of pure light,

'light intellectual, full of love,
love of true good, full of joy,
joy that surpasses every sweetness.

'Here you shall see both soldieries of Paradise,
one of them in just such form
as you shall see it at the final judgment.'

Like sudden lightning that confounds
the faculty of sight, depriving eyes
of taking in the clearest objects,

thus did a living light shine all around me,
leaving me so swathed in the veil of its effulgence
that I saw nothing else.

'The love that calms this heaven
always offers welcome with such greetings,
to make the candle ready for its flame.'

No sooner had these few words reached my mind
than I became aware of having risen
above and well beyond my powers,

e di novella vista mi raccesi
tale, che nulla luce è tanto mera,
che li occhi miei non si fosser difesi;

e vidi lume in forma di rivera
fulvido di fulgore, intra due rive
dipinte di mirabil primavera.

Di tal fiumana uscian faville vive,
e d'ogne parte si mettien ne' fiori,
quasi rubin che oro circunscrive;

poi, come inebrïate da li odori,
riprofondavan sé nel miro gurge,
e s'una intrava, un'altra n'uscia fori.

"L'alto disio che mo t'infiamma e urge,
d'aver notizia di ciò che tu vei,
tanto mi piace più quanto più turge;

ma di quest' acqua convien che tu bei
prima che tanta sete in te si sazi":
così mi disse il sol de li occhi miei.

Anche soggiunse: "Il fiume e li topazi
ch'entrano ed escono e 'l rider de l'erbe
son di lor vero umbriferi prefazi.

Non che da sé sian queste cose acerbe;
ma è difetto da la parte tua,
che non hai viste ancor tanto superbe."

Non è fantin che sì sùbito rua
col volto verso il latte, se si svegli
molto tardato da l'usanza sua

come fec' io, per far migliori spegli
ancor de li occhi, chinandomi a l'onda
che si deriva perché vi s'immegli;

and such was the new vision kindled within me
that there exists no light so vivid that my eyes
could not have borne its brightness.

And I saw light that flowed as flows a river,
pouring its golden splendor between two banks
painted with the wondrous colors of spring.

From that torrent issued living sparks
and, on either bank, they settled on the flowers,
like rubies ringed in gold.

Then, as though intoxicated by the odors,
they plunged once more into the marvelous flood,
and, as one submerged, another would come forth.

'The deep desire that now inflames and prods you
to understand at last all that you see
pleases me the more the more it surges.

'But you must drink first of these waters
before your great thirst may be satisfied.'
Thus the sun of my eyes spoke to me.

Then she continued: 'The river, the topazes
that enter and leave it, and the laughter of the meadows
are all shadowy prefaces of their truth,

'not that these things are in themselves unripe,
but because the failure lies with you,
your vision is not yet strong enough to soar.'

No infant, waking up too late
for his accustomed feeding, will thrust his face
up to his milk with greater urgency,

than I, to make still better mirrors of my eyes,
inclined my head down toward the water
that flows there for our betterment,

e sì come di lei bevve la gronda
de le palpebre mie, così mi parve
90 di sua lunghezza divenuta tonda.

Poi, come gente stata sotto larve,
che pare altro che prima, se si sveste
93 la sembianza non süa in che disparve,

così mi si cambiaro in maggior feste
li fiori e le faville, sì ch'io vidi
96 ambo le corti del ciel manifeste.

O isplendor di Dio, per cu' io vidi
l'alto trïunfo del regno verace,
99 dammi virtù a dir com'ïo il vidi!

Lume è là sù che visibile face
lo creatore a quella creatura
102 che solo in lui vedere ha la sua pace.

E' si distende in circular figura,
in tanto che la sua circunferenza
105 sarebbe al sol troppo larga cintura.

Fassi di raggio tutta sua parvenza
reflesso al sommo del mobile primo,
108 che prende quindi vivere e potenza.

E come clivo in acqua di suo imo
si specchia, quasi per vedersi addorno,
111 quando è nel verde e ne' fioretti opimo,

sì, soprastando al lume intorno intorno,
vidi specchiarsi in più di mille soglie
114 quanto di noi là sù fatto ha ritorno.

E se l'infimo grado in sé raccoglie
sì grande lume, quanta è la larghezza
117 di questa rosa ne l'estreme foglie!

and no sooner had the eaves of my eyelids
drunk deep of that water than to me it seemed
it had made its length into a circle.

Then, like people wearing masks,
once they put off the likeness not their own
in which they hid, seem other than before,

the flowers and the sparks were changed before my eyes
into a greater celebration, so that I saw,
before my very eyes, both courts of Heaven.

O splendor of God, by which I saw
the lofty triumph of the one true kingdom,
grant me the power to tell of what I saw!

There is a light above that makes the Creator
visible to every creature
that finds its only peace in seeing Him.

It spreads itself into so vast a circle
that its circumference would be larger
than the sphere that is the sun.

All that is seen of it comes as a ray reflected
from the summit of the Primum Mobile,
which draws from this its motion and its powers.

And as a hillside is mirrored by the water
at its foot, as if it saw itself adorned
when it is lush with grass and flowers,

so I saw, rising above the light and all around it
mirrored in more than a thousand tiers,
all those of us who have returned on high.

And, if the lowest of its ranks encloses
a light so large, how vast is the expanse containing
the farthest petals of this rose?

La vista mia ne l'ampio e ne l'altezza
non si smarriva, ma tutto prendeva
il quanto e 'l quale di quella allegrezza.

Presso e lontano, lì, né pon né leva:
ché dove Dio sanza mezzo governa,
la legge natural nulla rileva.

Nel giallo de la rosa sempiterna,
che si digrada e dilata e redole
odor di lode al sol che sempre verna,

qual è colui che tace e dicer vole,
mi trasse Bëatrice, e disse: "Mira
quanto è 'l convento de le bianche stole!

Vedi nostra città quant' ella gira;
vedi li nostri scanni sì ripieni,
che poca gente più ci si disira.

E 'n quel gran seggio a che tu li occhi tieni
per la corona che già v'è sù posta,
prima che tu a queste nozze ceni,

sederà l'alma, che fia giù agosta,
de l'alto Arrigo, ch'a drizzare Italia
verrà in prima ch'ella sia disposta.

La cieca cupidigia che v'ammalia
simili fatti v'ha al fantolino
che muor per fame e caccia via la balia.

E fia prefetto nel foro divino
allora tal, che palese e coverto
non anderà con lui per un cammino.

Ma poco poi sarà da Dio sofferto
nel santo officio: ch'el sarà detruso
là dove Simon mago è per suo merto,
e farà quel d'Alagna intrar più giuso."

Within that breadth and height,
my sight was not confused but shared
120 the full extent and quality of that rejoicing.

There, near and far do neither add nor take away,
for where God, unmediated, rules
123 natural law has no effect.

Into the yellow of the sempiternal rose,
which rises in its ranks, expands, and exhales
126 fragrances that praise the Sun's perpetual spring,

I, like a man who is silent but would speak,
was led by Beatrice, and she said: 'Behold
129 how vast the white-robed gathering!

'See our city, with its vast expanse!
See how many are the seats already filled—
132 few are the souls still absent there!

'And in that great seat which draws your eyes
for the crown already set above it,
135 before you shall dine at this wedding feast,

'shall sit the soul of noble Henry,
who on earth, as emperor, shall attempt
138 to set things straight for Italy before she is prepared.

'Blind cupidity, bewitching you,
has made you like the infant, dying of hunger,
141 who shoves his nurse's breast away.

'At that time the prefect of the sacred court
will be a man who will not make his way
144 on the same road by daylight as he will by night.

'But short shall be the time God suffers him
in holy office, for he shall be thrust
down there where Simon Magus gets what he deserves,
148 and push that fellow from Anagni deeper down.'

1–3. Tozer's paraphrase (comm. to verse 1) of this complex tercet runs as follows: "The dawn, instead of being mentioned by name, is here described, by an elaborate periphrasis, as the time when it is about midday 6,000 miles off from us on the earth's surface. This calculation is arrived at in the following manner. Seven hours are approximately the period of time which the sun takes to pass over 6,000 miles of the earth's surface; for, according to the computation of Alfraganus (cap. VIII), which Dante accepted (*Conv.* III.v.11—see Toynbee, *Dict.*, p. 522, s.v. "Terra"), the entire circumference of the earth was 20,400 miles, and consequently the amount of that circumference corresponding to seven hours out of the complete revolution of twenty-four hours was 5,950 miles (20,400 x 7/24 = 5,950), or in round numbers 6,000 miles. Hence, when Dante says that the sixth hour is 6,000 miles distant from us, he means that with us it is seven hours before noon, or an hour before sunrise, the sun being regarded as rising at 6 a.m. The word *Forse* intimates that the calculation is made in round numbers." For an analysis of the entire opening passage (vv. 1–15), see Salsano (Sals.1974.1), pp. 215–24.

1. Aversano (Aver.2000.2), p. 149, points out that this is the only time the much-used adverb (sixty-seven occurrences) *forse* ("perhaps," but here "about," as Aversano advises) is employed to begin either a verse or a canto.

2. Strictly speaking, the "sixth hour" is 11 to noon (see *Par.* XXVI.141–142), but here it represents noon itself, six hours after dawn (ideally considered 6 A.M., whenever it actually occurs).

3. The phrase *letto piano* (level bed) refers to the moment when the sun's midpoint is in the plane of the horizon. Grandgent (comm. to vv. 1–3): "The sun is below our horizon on one side, and the earth's conical shadow, projected into space, is correspondingly above our horizon on the other. As the sun rises, the shadow sinks; and when the middle of the sun shall be on the horizon line, the apex of the shadow will be on the same plane in the opposite quarter."

4–6. For *mezzo* as "center of the sky," in the sense of zenith, see Salsano (Sals.1974.1), pp. 222–24, and Chiavacci Leonardi (Chia.1997.1), pp.

825–26. For centuries this was the standard gloss. That is, commentators believed that Dante was referring to the midpoint of the Starry Sphere, directly overhead. Porena (comm. to vv. 1–6 [= "Nota finale" to this canto]) sharply objected. How can the sky directly above an observer be the first part of the heavens seen growing lighter at the approach of dawn, when obviously the eastern horizon is? He goes on to cite a text that, he says, explains this verse perfectly, *Convivio* III.ix.11–12, where Dante discusses the obscuring qualities of the earth's atmosphere itself. Most of the commentators who follow Porena accept his explanation (a few even crediting him). See, for example, Bellomo (Bell.1996.1), pp. 52–53. At least three aspects of Porena's argument are, however, problematic: (1) Dante does not say that the predawn sky grows lighter *first* at its zenith, only that it does so, and does so very gradually; (2) his description seems to imply invariable phenomena (i.e., celestial events that happen in the same manner every night at its juncture with dawn), while atmospheric hindrances are variable; (3) the relationship between this and the following *terzina* is such that the process initiated in this one is completed in that, which would at least imply a continuous movement in these celestial "candles" becoming dimmer and finally being snuffed out. In short, it seems unwise to jettison the old reading for Porena's.

4. For Dante's *cielo . . . profondo* it has been traditional (at least since the time of Lombardi [comm. to vv. 1–6]) to cite Virgil, *Georgics* IV.222, *caelumque profundum*.

7–8. The traditional understanding, of uninterrupted currency until the last decade of the nineteenth century, is that the "brightest handmaid of the Sun" is Aurora, who announces the arrival of her lord at sunrise. Scartazzini (comm. to verse 7), however (if without changing that interpretation), reminds us that Dante refers to the hours of the day as *ancelle* [*del giorno*] (*Purg.* XII.81, XXII.118). That bit of lore about the personified hours (which hardly dispatches the traditional literary association of Aurora as the handmaid of the Sun indirectly referred to at *Purg.* IX.2, with its presentation of the brightening predawn sky) remained offstage until Poletto (comm. to vv. 1–15 [of course not mentioning Scartazzini]) casually refers to it as his only comment on this verse. He was joined by Mattalia (comm. to verse 7 [of course not mentioning either Scartazzini or Poletto]), who was the first commentator to insist that the first hour of the day is the particular brightness referred to. However, several considerations cast serious doubt on this solution: (1) It would be strange for Dante to have referred to the first hour of the day as its brightest, since most would doubtless consider noon to be that; (2) the passage refers to a gradual process (like that of the aurora of the Sun), while the passing of even a single minute when the Sun is rising is marked by a dramatic change indeed; (3) it is difficult once the Sun rises to see any stars at all, much less to watch a gradual extinguishing process across the eastern half of the heavens. Perhaps it was such considerations that governed the continuing response among the commentators, all of whom represented in the DDP remain wedded to the traditional gloss, Aurora. However, inexplicably (if tentatively), Chiavacci Leonardi (Chia.1997.1), p. 826, cites and accepts Mattalia's interpretation. For the proposal of a totally new understanding, see Leuker (Leuk.2004.1), who claims that the "handmaid" is Venus as morning star. He does not find it problematic that Venus will be referred to in verse 9, believing, rather, that both these periphrases refer to her.

9. The traditional understanding, which has no need of revaluation, is that the brightest and most beautiful light in the predawn sky is Venus as morning star.

10–15. The lengthy and elaborate simile now presents its second term: As the light of the stars in the dawn sky yields to the increasing brilliance of the Sun, so the nine angelic orders, whirling around God, extinguish their glow. The result is that their self-effacement encourages him to yield to his desire, which is to look at Beatrice.

11. See Contini (Cont.1968.1), p. 1018, for recognition of the self-citation here. The line contains a fairly obvious revisitation, in the phrase "al punto che mi vinse" (around the point that overcame me), of Francesca's description of the *punto* in the Lancelot romance that aroused her and Paolo (*Inf.* V.132): "ma solo un *punto* fu quel che ci *vinse*" (still, it was a single instant overcame us [italics added]). It is perhaps only the oppositional nature of this *punto*, not a "point" in a text describing sexual arousal, but God, the Point of the universe, that had kept the close resemblance in phrasing apparently unobserved for so many centuries. For other notice, see Hollander (Holl.1983.1), pp. 139–40, Dronke (Dron.1989.1), p. 32 (both without reference to any precursor), and De Robertis (Dero.1990.1), p. 141 (citing Contini). And see Hollander (Holl.1993.5), pp. 7–8, acknowledging Contini, if belatedly. See also Stierle (Stie.2002.2), pp. 407–8, who mentions no precursor. And see the note to *Paradiso* XXIX.9.

12. The circles of angels seem to surround God; in fact He "contains" them (and all else).

16–18. The poet, seeing Beatrice at the edge of eternity, as it were, begins his valedictory remarks by insisting that all his preceding praise together would not do to fulfill the need he feels to express her beauty.

17. The word *loda* (praise) has a "technical" overtone. As recorded in *Vita nuova*, Dante began to grow toward comprehending the meaning of Beatrice when he turned from poems about the pain his loving her had caused him to those in praise of her (see *VN* XVIII.9).

18. For the Latinism *vice* (here translated "that which is due"), the commentators are torn among several possibilities. Perhaps the most popular is the usage found in the Latin phrase *explere vicem*, meaning "to fulfill one's duties," probably the most likely sense of the word here. But see Scartazzini (comm. to this verse) for the majority opinion (which he does not share) that it means *volta* with the sense of "time" or "occasion." Several add "place" to the possibilities, and there are still other options. Singleton (comm. to this verse) cites the other use of *vice* (at *Par.* XXVII.17), where it is paired with *officio* (duty), to argue that it therefore cannot mean that here; but see Scartazzini (comm. to *Par.* XXVII.17–18), who deals with *vice* as there being the "duty" of silence incumbent on the rest of the spirits while St. Peter fulfills *his* duty, which is to hold forth against papal turpitude, the two words sharing a sense approaching that of synonyms.

Scott (Scot.1977.2), p. 163, comments on the extraordinary incidence of Latinisms in this canto, which he puts at fifty.

19–21. Dante will see Beatrice once more, after she resumes her seat in the Rose (from which she arose once, on 24 March 1300 [also Maundy Thursday according to Dante's Idealized Earth Time], in order to draw Virgil forth from Limbo; and then again, around noon the following Wednesday, in order to descend to the earthly paradise for her reunion with Dante). This, however, is his last attempt to describe her beauty, which has been increasing from his second description of it (in the heaven of the Moon, *Par.* IV.139–142) every time he sees her anew until now. That this "program" has come to its end is clear from the seven tercets (vv. 16–36) devoted to a final description of her increased beauty, which offer a kind of history (esp. vv. 28–33) of that beauty's effect on Dante.

On the point of returning to her undivided attention to God, she is already being retransformed into a more-than-human being, pure soul, as it were, without the hindrance of human concerns that she has taken on for Dante's sake. Thus only God can fully enjoy her beauty.

22–27. And thus the human poet who is speaking to us, confined by the two modes (and only two generic possibilities are referred to in the entire text, unlike *De vulgari eloquentia*, which mentions several others), tragic or comic, that are available to him, must acknowledge his necessary failure. The poem of the triumph of Beatrice needs a new genre, one that Dante has defined at *Paradiso* XXV.73, and that shares with David's psalms, expressing his love for God, the generic tag of *tëodia* (god song).

For this last, see Barolini (Baro.1984.1), p. 277. Only a new form might seem capable of describing such things.

See Shaw (Shaw.1981.1), p. 196: "There is a chain of inadequacy in Dante because of the visionary nature of the experience he is describing. The mind cannot fully grasp what it experiences, because this transcends the human capacity for understanding; the memory cannot now recall even that which the mind did grasp at the time; and finally, the poet's words cannot do justice even to what he *can* recall to mind. The poet's words are three stages removed from what he is attempting to represent."

For discussion of reference here to Virgil and Dante as, respectively, writers of tragedy and of comedy, see Scartazzini (comm. to verse 24) and Hollander (Holl.1993.5), p. 10, n. 23.

25–27. Like a mortal with weak eyes, unable even more than most to look directly at the Sun, the poet finds his inner sight blinded by the memory of this last and transformed beauty evident in Beatrice. Scartazzini (comm. to vv. 25–27) was apparently the first commentator (but not the last, though none of the others cites him) to call attention to three passages in the minor works that offer similar images, *Vita nuova* (XLI.6) and *Convivio* (III.0.59–60; III.viii.14 [this last the commentary on those verses]). It is amusing to discover that in the first case, it is Beatrice's soul, ascended to Heaven, that is too bright for Dante to behold, while in the two passages in *Convivio* the blinding is accomplished by the glow of Lady Philosophy. The first is entirely germane to the present context, which has Beatrice about to ascend to exactly where Dante first saw her seated in Heaven in the *libello*. Dante would have preferred, however, that we forget the second, in praise of the lady who replaced Beatrice in his affections.

27. Porena (comm. to vv. 26–27) is perhaps the first to discuss the two possible meanings of *mente*, "mind" (here with the sense of "intellect")

and "memory," making a good case for the former, as we have translated the word. See also Maierù, "mente," *ED* (III [1971]), pp. 899a–905a, who agrees (p. 902b). However, if it is his mind that Dante is separated from, in what specific ways ought we consider the possible meaning(s) of the verse? This is a difficult line to translate.

28–29. If we accept the "history" put forward in *Vita nuova*, the first time that he saw Beatrice was shortly before Dante's ninth birthday (*VN* II.1–2), thus no later than June of 1274, and probably a little before then. The current date in the poem is perhaps 31 March 1300 (see the note to *Inf.* I.1).

28. The word *viso* may here be rendered with either "eyes" or "face." We have chosen the latter, even though most of the commentators who actually choose one alternative over the other, beginning with Benvenuto (comm. to vv. 28–30), prefer "eyes."

30. "This verse is more problematic than it generally seems to be to most commentators: [H]ow can Dante say this when he has displayed such a marked deviation from singing of Beatrice in *Convivio*? Are we to understand that that work, even if it records her being eclipsed in Dante's affection by the *donna gentile*, nonetheless is about her? Or are we to imagine that, since Dante has been through the rivers Lethe and Eunoe, he forgets his past wrongdoing and remembers only the good in the history of his affections?" (Hollander [Holl.1993.5], p. 11, n. 26).

31–36. "The poet is able to represent aspects of divinity but cannot know it directly. Beatrice, at one with God, resists any human poet's capacity, even Dante's. And thus Dante must leave her to a *maggior bando*, the angelic trumpets' heralding at the [G]eneral Resurrection. . . . [Beatrice] is better than all mortals because she is immortal, a condition [that] she shares utterly with her fellow saints. In a sense, Dante's inability to sing of her results not from her being unique, but from her being absolutely the same as all the blessed in her love of God" (Hollander [Holl.1993.5], pp. 11–12). Naturally, that is true of any other saved soul as well.

33. See Binni (Binn.1968.1), p. 1070, for a paraphrase of this verse: "il limite estremo delle sue forze espressive" ([at] the outer limit of his powers of expression).

34. Rossi (Ross.1981.1 and Ross.1985.1), p. 65 and p. 89, respectively, points out that the word *bando* here looks back at *Purgatorio* XXX.13 in

such a way as to make its meaning clear. All the early commentators who make an effort to identify the source of that trumpeting say that it will be a later poet (Benvenuto [comm. to vv. 34–39] specifies "a poet-theologian," in which judgment he is followed by John of Serravalle [comm. to vv. 34–42]); some, their discomfort more or less apparent, go along, perhaps because they do not understand to what else the sonorous reference might refer. That was the muddled condition of appreciation of this passage until Scartazzini (comm. to this verse) cut through centuries of weak responses and magisterially solved (or should have) the riddle once and for all (the text refers to the trump of Judgment Day), even if his reward for doing so was to be ridiculed by Poletto (comm. to vv. 34–37) and to be ignored even by those relative few who agree with him. Mestica (comm. to vv. 34–38), without reference to Scartazzini (do we hear the strains of a familiar tune? [see the note to *Purg.* XXX.115–117]), also settles on this daring but sensible explanation, as does Del Lungo (comm. to vv. 34–38). Still more blameworthy than Poletto, Vandelli, revising his master's work, simply substitutes his own version of the ancient view for Scartazzini's radical new interpretation (comm. to vv. 34–36), attributing the trumpet blast to a "voce poetica più possente della mia" (poetic voice more powerful than mine). In more recent times, Scartazzini's position has found support in Rossi (Ross.1981.1), pp. 65, 72; Hollander (Holl.1993.5), pp. 10–13 [with a review of the status of the debate]; Chiavacci Leonardi (Chia.1997.1), p. 830; and Ledda (Ledd.2002.1), p. 301. However, see Shaw (Shaw.1981.1), p. 197, for a return to the old solution, the *bando* will issue from "a greater poetic talent than his own."

For a similar problem, what Dante refers to by the phrase "con miglior voci" (with better words) at *Paradiso* I.35, and the utter unlikelihood that he might be thinking of future poets better than he, see the note to I.35–36.

38–42. On these verses see Bortolo Martinelli (Mart.1985.1), pp. 113–14, arguing that the Empyrean is to be considered as having corporeal being. Dante (in *Conv.* II.iii.8) has been interpreted as saying that this was indeed the case. (Although there are those who do not hold to this opinion, finding that Dante attributes this opinion to "Catholics" without necessarily embracing it himself, this would not mark the first time that Dante changed his mind about an opinion expressed in the *Convivio*). Here, however, it seems totally clear that Dante is reiterating his thoughts about the triform Creation (see *Par.* XXIX.22–24), which included pure form unalloyed with matter (i.e., the Empyrean and the angels). As Aversano

(Aver.2000.2), p. 151, points out, if the Primum Mobile is the largest material sphere in the heavens, that requires that the Empyrean not be material, for it contains (i.e., is larger than) all else.

It is quite striking, as Aversano points out, that after *Inferno* II.21 Dante never uses the word *empireo* again. It had, in fact, appeared more often in the *Convivio* (twice: II.iii.8 and II.xiv.19).

39–42. These four verses, weaving their three line-beginning/ending nouns *luce*, *amore*, *letizia* into a knot expressing the nature of God's kingdom (intellectual light and love, the latter yielding joy) in a pattern of linkage new to the poem, are perhaps calculated to offer a first sense of the higher spiritual reality of the Empyrean.

43. The two "militias" found here are, of course, the angels and the saved souls. Scartazzini (comm. to vv. 43–45) says the first fought against the rebel angels, the second, against the vices.

44–45. The poet, in his enthusiasm for incarnation, restrains himself only enough not to insist that the angels are seen as though they, too, are embodied. There is no preexisting tradition that allows this daring invention (seeing the blessed as though they were already incarnate) on Dante's part. And yet, once we read his instruction, we accept their phantom flesh as a necessary element of his vision.

This is all the more striking as we have just been assured that we left "corporality" behind when we left the Primum Mobile (vv. 38–39). See discussion in Scott (Scot.1977.2), pp. 164 and 179, and Hollander (Holl.1993.5), p. 14: "[T]his resubstantiation occurs exactly at the moment at which we have apparently left corporality behind us. . . . 'From nature and history to spirituality and eternity' is one way to translate [Beatrice's] phrase."

46–51. Again Dante is blinded by the light, one last time before he begins seeing the higher reality of God's Heaven as it really is. The simile makes use of a fitting biblical precursor, St. Paul (see the note to verse 49).

For the blending of scientific and biblical elements in this simile, see Gilson (Gils.2001.2), p. 56.

49. Tommaseo (comm. to vv. 49–51) was apparently the first commentator to hear the echo of the passage in the Book of Acts (22:6) that features the fairly rare verb *circumfulgere*. Scartazzini (comm. to this verse) also did

so. Their view was shared by Poletto (comm. to vv. 46–51) and at least nine commentators in the following century, from Torraca to Bosco/Reggio. Disagreeing with such as these, who think that Dante's Latinizing verb form *circunfulse* (shone all around) reflects the *circumfulgere* of Acts 22:6 (or either of two other passages in that book), Dronke (Dron.1989.1), p. 37–38, insists on the greater relevance of Luke 2:9, the only other biblical passage that contains this verb, describing the shepherds keeping watch on the night of the Nativity: "And the glory of the Lord shone around them" (*et claritas Dei circumfulsit eos*). Dronke objects to claims for a linkage here between Dante and Saul, "the fanatical persecutor whom the circumfulgent light blinds for three days, stunning him into a change of heart." However, what works against Dronke's hypothesis is the very context that he tries to turn against those who take the reference as being to Saul/Paul, since he fails to take into account the noticeable fact that Dante, like Paul (and unlike the shepherds), is blinded by the light. For Dante's Pauline identity here, see Foster (Fost.1977.1), pp. 70–73; Di Scipio (Disc.1980.1); and Shaw (Shaw.1981.1), p. 201: "There can be no doubt that Dante expects us at this point to think of Saul on the road to Damascus." And see Hollander (Holl.1993.5), pp. 14–15 (n. 34). Kleinhenz (Klei.1995.1), pp. 458–59, is also of this opinion; on p. 468, n. 5, he refers to Dronke's hypothesis with dubiety, as does Bellomo (Bell.1996.1), p. 45, n. 19.

52–54. Beatrice explains that the blinding brightness of the Empyrean welcomes all newcomers just as Dante is welcomed now (and will be again, we realize), prepared to see God face-to-face and to flame with love for Him.

53. The word *salute* (greetings), ever since its teasing presence in the *Vita nuova* as meaning either "greeting" or "salvation" or an enigmatic union of the two, appears here, also, with ambivalent meaning.

55–60. The protagonist is now ready for the final stage of his journey, as is betokened by the fact that he has internalized Beatrice's words. Not all commentators agree that such is the case, claiming that Dante is uncertain as to the source of the words, even that he may have spoken them himself. But see Benvenuto (comm. to these verses) who, with whatever justification, has no doubt—the words are indeed spoken by Beatrice. It certainly seems a part of the protagonist's preparation for being rapt in his vision of God that distinctions between objective and subjective reality should begin to break down. In *Paradiso* XXXIII.131 he will see himself in the image of Christ.

61–69. The last accommodative metaphor in the part of the poem that precedes seeing face-to-face presents what Dante observes with imperfect vision in such a way as to reveal the substance hidden in these "shadowy prefaces" (verse 78).

For the river of light, and its possible dependence on a passage in the *Anticlaudianus* of Alanus ab Insulis (Alain de Lille), see Witke (Witk.1959.1). Hollander (Holl.1969.1), pp. 196–202, discusses the complex way in which Dante's use of metaphor morphs into absolute reality, which had first been available to his still-strengthening mind as only an approximation of itself.

61. Notice of the dependence of Dante on Apocalypse 22:1 ("Then the angel showed me the river of the water of life, bright as crystal, flowing from the throne of God and of the Lamb") apparently begins with the author of the commentary in the Codice Cassinese (comm. to this verse). Sapegno (comm. to this verse) cites, as do many others, this biblical text, but adds St. Bonventure's commentary to it: "Flumen aeternae gloriae est flumen Dei, plenum congregatione sanctorum. . . . Aeterna gloria dicitur fluvius, propter abundantiam; aquae vivae, propter indeficientiam; splendidus, propter munditiam; tamquam cristallum, propter transparentiam" (The river of eternal glory is the river of God, filled by the congregation of the saints. . . . Eternal glory is said to be flowing water because of its abundance; the water of life because it has no impurities; shining because of its clarity; like crystal because of its transparency). (The second most cited potential biblical source is Daniel 7:10.)

Chiavacci Leonardi (Chia.1975.2), p. 16, reminds us that this is not a river of light, but light in the form of a river. (See Jacopo della Lana [comm. to vv. 61–69] for a similar understanding.)

62–66. Seeing metaphorically, as it were (thus reversing our usual practice, which is to understand the truth of things and then express that in metaphor), the protagonist sees light in the form of a river, its two banks covered with flowers, with sparks flying up and then settling back down on the blossoms. All these elements will be metamorphosed into their realer selves, a round stadium-rose nearly filled with saved souls, with angels ("bees") moving quickly back and forth between the souls ("flowers") and God (the "hive"). There is, as well there should be, general agreement about the identities of these three elements, resolved from metaphor. The identity of the light in the form of a river is frequently passed over in silence. However, Benvenuto (comm. to vv. 61–63) was apparently the first to associate it with grace.

62. Exactly what adjective Dante set down (and what it means) has been a matter of some dispute, with four possible choices (*fulvido, fulgido, fluvido, fluido*) doing battle over the centuries. See Scartazzini, who rejects the last two, and supports most of the first commentators in choosing the first (or the second, which has, according to him, the same meaning). It means, he says, "resplendent." Others, for instance Torraca (comm. to vv. 61–63), say that Dante's word derives from Latin *fulvus* (reddish yellow).

64–66. For Virgil's Elysian Fields as the model for this passage, see Gmelin (Gmel.1957.1), p. 52 (his note to *Paradiso* XXXI.7). For the view that this passage may, in its own right, be a veiled first presentation of that text, see Hollander (Holl.1976.2), p. 240 (repr. Holl.1980.1, p. 38). In the *Aeneid* (VI.703–709), the protagonist is looking at the souls of the blessed, those happy inhabitants of the Elysian Fields. (At least they probably seem happy to us when first we see them; but see the note to *Par.* XXXI.7–12 for Aeneas's eventual view.) In simile, they are compared to bees nestling in flowers. To Dante, not one to leave a fine poetic moment only as fine as he found it, the "bees" are the angels, while the blessed are the "flowers." This becomes clearer in the next canto (see the note to *Par.* XXXI.7–12), as several commentators testify. Yet it is nonetheless true, once we see the allusion, that we can carry it back with us to this passage. And then we may begin to understand that, for all the apparent discarding of Virgil that sets the last *cantica* apart from the first two, the Latin poet is rewarded by his greatest medieval admirer with a new life in the conclusion of his poem. See Hollander (Holl.1983.1), p. 140; Rossi (Ross.1981.1), pp. 55–58; Rossi (Ross.1989.2), pp. 306–7; and Hollander (Holl.1993.5), pp. 17–19, making the additional point (p. 18) that the reference thus makes this reference, along with that in verse 49 to Saul, reverse the negative version of the protagonist's typology (*Inf.* II.32). Where before, at least in the protagonist's own view, he failed to match up to his two precursors, now he is indeed the new Paul and the new Aeneas:

> Interea videt Aeneas in valle reducta
> seclusum nemus et virgulta sonantia silvae,
> Lethaeumque domos placidas qui praenatat amnem.
> hunc circum innumerae gentes populique volabant:

ac veluti in pratis ubi apes aestate serena
floribus insidunt variis et candida circum
lilia funduntur, strepit omnis murmure campus.

. . .

And now Aeneas sees in the valley's depths
a sheltered grove and rustling wooded brakes
and the Lethe flowing past the homes of peace.
Around it hovered numberless races, nations of souls
like bees in meadowlands on a cloudless summer day
that settle on flowers, riots of color, swarming round
the lilies' lustrous sheen, and the whole field comes alive
with a humming murmur. (Tr. R. Fagles [Viking 2006])

This is a powerful moment in which Virgil's and Dante's mimetic proclivities are shown in their warmest tones; at least in Dante's case we witness the imitation of nature engineered by another kind of imitation altogether. See McLaughlin (Mcla.1995.1), p. 5, for the distinction between mimesis of external reality and imitation of previous literature. And for an earlier brief discussion of the distinction and of how the two techniques may be found joined, see Hollander (Holl.1975.2), p. 122.

66. For the ruby set in gold, it has become commonplace, after Scartazzini (comm. to this verse), to cite *Aeneid* X.134: "qualis gemma micat, fulvum quae dividit aurum" (glittered like a jewel set in yellow gold [tr. H. R. Fairclough]).

67. For the inebriation of the angels, Scartazzini (comm. to vv. 46–81) cites the Psalms (35:9–10 [36:8–9]): "They feast on the abundance of your house, / and you give them drink from the river of your delights. / For with you is the fountain of life; / in your light do we see light."

68. A discussion of another Virgilian text that may stand behind Dante's Latinate phrase *miro gurge* (marvelous flood) is found in Rossi (Ross.1985.1), pp. 83–91, examining the parallels between Dante's river and that found in *Georgics* IV.348–356, the Peneüs, into whose depths Aristaeus will penetrate and see (p. 84) "the place where all the earth's streams converge" (IV.365–366).

70–75. Beatrice intervenes again, preparing Dante for his baptismal ingestion of the waters of Life. Hollander (Holl.1969.1), p. 196, and

(Holl.1993.5), p. 19, points out that he has experienced "baptism" in two previous scenes: *Purgatorio* I.121–129 and XXXIII.127–129.

76–81. His guide now explains what we may have already understood, that what Dante was seeing was not really what he thought it was, that it was only a "shadowy forecast" of its true nature.

For the notion that all of *Paradiso* up to verse 90 is best conceived as a series of accommodative metaphors, see discussion in Hollander (Holl.1969.1), pp. 192–202; (Holl.1993.5.1), pp. 19–21.

77. Resolved from metaphor, the "laughter" of the "meadows" is represented in the "flowers" that cover it, that is, the saints.

78. For the figural sense of history that stands behind this expression (*umbriferi prefazi*), see Pasquini (Pasq.1999.2). See also Ledda (Ledd. 2002.1), pp. 302–3. For more on the figural dimensions of the word *umbra*, see the note to *Paradiso* I.22–24.

82–90. In nine lines Dante "drinks in" his "baptismal" "milk" and, as a result, has his vision transformed; he will shortly be able to see the realities of Heaven as they truly are. This simile is the opening gesture in staging his identity as newborn "babe," culminating in *Paradiso* XXXIII.106–108.

85–89. The conclusion of this simile is effortful indeed: Dante "drinks" his "baptism" with his eyelids and thus moves his eyesight to the next level of seeing.

90. In a single verse the meaning of Dante's changed "eyesight" is manifest: For him time has become eternity; history has become its own fulfillment in revelation. His previous linear sense of things has moved to a new dimension, the circularity of perfection. This new vision, unlike that of some, maintains its relation to the things of the world, which now for the first time may be really understood. See *Paradiso* XXXIII.88–90.

91–96. The first moment of face-to-face seeing is presented with this simile. The protagonist now perceives the "flowers" as the saints they are, the "sparks" as angels. While no one said so for centuries, the only apparent "source" for this image of unmasking was a festive occasion, a masked ball of some kind. Poletto (comm. to vv. 91–96) somewhat uneasily defends the poet's choice of material; however, the noun *feste* (lit., "festivals," or "celebrations") in verse 94 at least seems to help establish a frame of reference. Nonetheless, Fallani (comm. to vv. 91–93) suggested that the reference is to masked actors. A potential literary source for this image has apparently never been suggested. It is probably fair to say that most readers feel puzzled as to the poet's motivation at such an important moment.

For another sort of unmasking, in which the protagonist again has his initial vision yield to a greater reality, see the note to *Paradiso* XXXIII.28–33.

95–99. On identical rhymes, see Wlassics (Wlas.1975.1), p. 121. He points out that this repetition of *vidi* (I saw) underlines the claim for a poetics based in seeing and making seen. As several commentators have observed (apparently the first was Scartazzini [comm. to vv. 97–99]), aside from the four occurrences of the identical rhymes of "Cristo" (see the note to *Par.* XII.71–75), there are only two other cases of triple identical rhymes in the poem, the bitterly ironic repetition of "per ammenda" in *Purgatorio* XX.65–69 and the occurrences of "vidi" here.

Responding to the word's presence in verse 61, Aversano (Aver.2000.2), p. 152, points to the repetitive pattern of the same form, *vidi*, in John's Apocalypse (Apoc. 5:1, 5:2, 5:6, and 5:11). Dante uses that form seven times in all in this canto, the most of any canto in the *cantica* (*Par.* XVIII is the nearest challenger, with six uses; however, *Inferno* IV, with its list of forty virtuous pagans whom the protagonist saw in the Limbus, has fully eleven appearances of *vidi*; and in *Purgatorio* XXXII, there are eight. There are 166 occurrences of this form of the verb *vedere* in the poem, all but thirteen of them spoken by the poet; exceptions include Virgil [at *Inf.* IV.53 and XXIX.25], the protagonist [at *Inf.* XXIV.129], and several souls to whom Dante listens [*Inf.* XXVI.103, XXVII.79, XXVIII.71, XXXII.116; *Par.* XIII.136; XV.115; XVI.88, 91, 109]). *Vidi* is one of Dante's favorite locutions, reflecting his strategic insistence on the reality of his experience.

95. The *fiori* (flowers) are the saved souls, the *faville* (sparks) are the angels, as is commonly agreed (see the note to vv. 62–66). We see them again in the next canto, verses 7–9, the sparks now transformed, in simile, into bees. Once we see that, we can understand that these first "real substances," noncontingent and sempiternal, that we see "face-to-face" in the entire poem have models in a scene in the *Aeneid* (VI.703–708 [see the note to vv. 64–66]).

97–99. This is the eighth and penultimate invocation in the poem (see the note to *Inf.* II.7–9), addressing God's reflected light, possibly his grace (the ninth and final invocation will be addressed to God as *luce*, the source of light, in *Par.* XXXIII.67).

100–102. The first line of this tercet marks a borderline as sharply etched as that, involving similar stylistic traits, separating lower from upper Hell (*Inf.* XVIII.1): "Luogo è in inferno detto Malebolge" (There is a place in Hell called Malebolge). Here the light of grace that makes God visible to once-mortal souls introduces the final (and visionary) part of the poem.

100. There is a certain amount of indecision in the commentaries as to whether this *lume* is reflected light rather than its source (which would be *luce*). Some argue that it is the Holy Spirit, others Jesus as Logos, still others some form of grace. For this last, see Carroll (comm. to vv. 100–123): "It will be noticed that I speak of this central circular sea as *lumen gratiae*, for it is still the light of grace which once flowed in form of a river; but that light of grace has now reached its perfect form of eternity, the *lumen gloriae*. The change of the river into the circular sea is Dante's symbolic way of stating that the grace by which a soul is saved and strengthened to persevere to the end of the earthly life, is not something different in kind from the glory to which it leads. According to Aquinas, 'grace is nothing else than a certain beginning of glory in us' [*ST* II–II, q. 24, a. 3: 'Gratia et gloria ad idem genus referuntur; quia gratia nihil est aliud quam quaedam inchoatio gloriae in nobis'], and the light of glory is simply the perfected form of the grace of earth [*ST* I–II, q. 111, a. 3]. Aquinas is here laying down the distinction between prevenient and subsequent grace." Hollander (Holl.1993.5), p. 25, n. 63, claims that, among the first commentators, only Benvenuto (comm. to *Par.* VII.1–6) discusses the *lumen gloriae* (even if elsewhere); but see his remarks on this passage (vv. 100–102) and those of his student, John of Serravalle (comm. to vv. 100–105). He does go on (correctly) to credit Scartazzini (comm. to vv. 115–117) as being the first of the moderns to do so.

103–108. The enormous size of the Rose may come as something of a surprise. Dante never tells us the number of places that are found there, whether it is the precise number (144,000) offered in the Apocalypse (see the note to *Par.* XXXI.115–117), or the approximate number on the basis of the "replacement value" of the fallen angels (see the note to *Par.* XXIX.50), or still another figure. There are some questions that we are simply not encouraged to pose.

The disc of the Sun, even populated by souls on thrones with first-class legroom, would hold more saints than are imaginable, millions of millions. See Poletto (comm. to vv. 100–105) for discussion of what Dante knew about such measurements, including that of the diameter of the Sun, 37,750 miles according to *Convivio* IV.viii.7.

The Rose is made up of a beam of light (the Godhead) reflected upward from the convex surface of the Primum Mobile, which rotates because of its love for that beam and spreads its influence through the celestial spheres beneath it.

This passage may help in understanding the difficult text at *Paradiso* XXVIII.13–15 (see the note thereto). There the poet, in the Primum Mobile, has his first vision of the Godhead and the surrounding spheres of angels. Exactly where he sees them is a matter in dispute. This passage might help establish that they are here (in the Empyrean) but are seen down there, on the surface of the Crystalline Sphere, whence they, along with the Rose, are also reflected back up here.

For the shape of the Rose as being neither a cylinder nor a cone, but hemispheric, see Kay (Kay.2003.1), pp. 46–48.

109–114. In the vehicle of this simile, the stadium in which the saints are seated is "personified" as a hillside that can look down to its foot and see itself, alive with spring (see the *primavera* of verse 63), reflected back up to its gaze. The tenor presents the seeing hill's counterpart, the protagonist, as looking up (not down), and seeing, not himself, but all the blessed as reflections of the beam, reaching upward a thousandfold. (We are aware that Dante frequently uses this number as a synonym for an uncountable multitude; see at least the next [and last] time he does so, *Par.* XXXI.131.)

115–117. Daniello (comm. to this tercet) wonders, if the circumference of the lowest row in the Rose is greater than the circumference of the sphere that holds the Sun (see the note to vv. 103–108), how great must be the circumference of the highest row, at least one thousand rows higher (and wider by a factor of at least one thousand times a probably constant yet indeterminate measurement).

117. Francesco da Buti (comm. to vv. 109–117) says that the rows of the Rose "are like those in the *arena di Verona*." He is followed by two modern commentators, Trucchi (comm. to vv. 118–123) and Sapegno (comm. to vv. 112–113). Trucchi, however, prefers the notion of Gioachino Brognoligo that the structure Dante has in mind is the Colosseum at Rome. Both

Dante's more recent and more certain visit to the Arena and its greater intimacy as a built space give the edge to Verona.

118–123. For a concise statement of the "resemblant difference" of the Empyrean, its way of not relating and yet totally relating to the literally underlying realms of the created universe, see Moevs (Moev.2005.1), p. 82: "The Empyrean is out of space-time, untouched by physical law; it is a dimensionless point, in which all is immediately present, a 'space' of consciousness, in which the 'sight' of awareness 'takes' (*prendeva*) as itself all it sees, all that exists."

As we will discover, Dante is allowed to see with a new sense of dimension, which abrogates spatial perspective and makes all things equidistant one from another (see *Par.* XXXI.73–78). This passage prepares for that one, and both offer further evidence of the poet's extraordinarily vivid and inventive scientific imagination.

124–129. Ever since Jacopo della Lana, the yellow has been understood as the center of the Rose (the reader should remember that Dante is not talking about cultivated roses but wild ones, with their flatter profile). Beatrice and Dante are standing at the midpoint of the Rose when she directs him to look up and see the citizenry of the City of God.

As has been suggested (see the note to verse 117), Dante may have found a model for the Rose in the Arena di Verona. The reader is in fact urged to visit that place, to find a way to walk, without looking up, into the very center of its floor, and then to experience the sight of the inner tiers of the amphitheater. And it is just possible that he or she then will share the experience that Dante had there some seven hundred years ago. It really looks like the model for the Rose, vast yet intimate.

124. For the notion that Dante's Rose is a kind of counterimage to the flower plucked at the end of the *Roman de la Rose*, with its evident reference to the female *pudenda*, see Shaw (Shaw.1981.1), pp. 209–10. Shaw, who accepts Contini's argument for attributing the *Fiore*, the sonnet sequence based on the *Roman*, to Dante, consequently argues that this passage is a "case of the mature poet making amends for the aberrations of his youthful self" (p. 210). (For discussion of the status of these questions, Dante's knowledge of the *Roman* and his authorship of the *Fiore*, see the note to *Par.* II.59–60.) Among the surprisingly few commentators to express an opinion on this matter (one that no one considers unimportant), Mestica (comm. to vv. 115–123) raises the possibility that Dante had read it

(and that he had written the *Fiore*). Giacalone (comm. to vv. 124–129) cites Savj Lopez (Savj.1964.1), who thinks that Dante would have made allowances for the profane love championed by the *Roman* and thus seen it as a worthy precursor.

125. The Latinism *redole* (exhales fragrance) is traced to *Aeneid* I.436 first by Tommaseo (comm. to vv. 124–126).

126. For this "springtime" sense of the verb *vernare*, see the note to *Paradiso* XXVIII.118. The verb usually means "to spend the winter" (see *Inf.* XXXIII.135 and *Purg.* XXIV.64).

129. For the phrase *bianche stole* (white robes), see its previous use at *Paradiso* XXV.95, where it clearly signifies the bodies to be returned at the general resurrection. Beatrice has promised Dante that this is the way the saved will seem to him, even though they are not yet resurrected, and so the phrase here allows us to understand that this is indeed how they appear, in the flesh.

For an overview of the history and significance of the concept of resurrection of the flesh in the Western Church (with some consideration of Dante), see Bynum (Bynu.1995.1). For a close look at the importance of the resurrected body, in several writers preceding Dante and (primarily) in the *Commedia*, see Gragnolati (Grag.2005.1). For Dante's sense of this subject, see also Jacoff (Jaco.1999.1 and Jaco.2000.1).

At least since reading *Paradiso* XIV.61–66 (the passage shows the first two groups, the twenty-four contemplatives, who have shown themselves to Dante and Beatrice in the heaven of the Sun, all longing for their own resurrected flesh as well as for their saved relatives to regain their own), we have been aware that there is something missing in the beatific life. Against more usual views, Dante presents the afterlife of those currently in Paradise as being less than perfect (and less than perfected) because, against the orthodox notion that blessedness itself is the ultimate and eternal reward, there is, according to Dante, one thing that is felt as currently lacking: the resurrection of the flesh. Taught by Jesus (e.g., Luke 14:14) and insisted on by St. Paul, that future event is promised to all the saved. However, the early medieval view (e.g., that of Augustine) was, unsurprisingly, that once with God, the condition of the soul in a blessed and blissful member of the Church Triumphant was already perfected, both in what it knew and what it desired. The general resurrection, promised by St. Paul (most extensively in I Corinthians 15:35–55), of course awaited that soul, but the admixture of corporality was only "decorative," at least in a sense. Certainly Paul does not tackle that issue in his curiously defensive insistence, against pagan (and Christian?) mockers (see Acts 17:18 and 17:32), that the saved will indeed regain their own flesh in the long passage in I Corinthians.

Only months more than ten years after Dante's death in 1321, his old nemesis, Pope John XXII, preached a series of sermons of which a central point was that, until the soul was reclad in its flesh, it would not see God, setting off a horrified reaction within the Church, the eventual result of which was that the next pope, Benedict XII, restored the earlier disposition of the matter, namely, that the saved soul immediately experiences both the highest bliss in and the fullest knowledge of God of which it is capable.

Dante might have been amused to find that John XXII, whom he despised (see the note to *Par.* XXVII.136–138), was in disagreement with him on this important and divisive issue as well as on more pressing "political" concerns.

130–148. For a global discussion of this final passage, see Hainsworth (Hain.1997.1), arguing that it not only fails to destroy the harmony or unity of this canto (a position shared by many—see p. 154n. for a concise bibliography of the question), but that it is part of its integrity. See the similar opinion of Salsano (Sals.1974.1), pp. 232–34, and of Hollander (Holl.1993.5), pp. 31–33.

For an attempt to "save" this passage despite itself, see Bosco/Reggio (comm. to these verses), who concede that Dante probably should not have turned aside from contemplating things eternal and divine for such a feverish concern with mere contingency, compounding that "fault" by putting this earth-centered speech in the mouth of holy Beatrice, and as her last utterance at that. One can hear awareness of centuries of complaint behind their words. To be just, one must admit that this concern with earthly things seems inconsistent with the usual sort of piety. No one ever said (or should have) that Dante is "usual" in any respect at all.

130–132. There are only two possible considerations of the significance of the few places left in the Rose: Either there are very few good people alive (or who will be born before the end of time), or the end is coming faster than we think. That we should combine these two responses seems prudent. However, for Dante's possible sense that there are some fifteen hundred years left to run in history, see the note to *Paradiso* IX.40.

133–138. Silverstein (Silv.1939.1) deals with the surprise that most readers exhibit at the empty throne of the emperor being the first object that the protagonist sees in the Empyrean by reminding us of the far more ample medieval tradition that displayed vacant seats in heaven awaiting "humble friars and simple monks" (pp. 116–17) rather than emperors. He thus sees the salvation of Henry VII not in terms of his imperial mission (failed as it was), but as an "accolade of kingly righteousness" (p. 129), showing that, in passages in the Gospels and one in the *Vision of Tundale* (see p. 124 and n. 19), Dante had available testimony to the personal justness of those kings who, rather than merely ruling them, truly served their people. (He might have referred to Dante's praise of William the Good; see the note on *Par.* XX.61–66.) However, it is probably a mistake to accept, as Silverstein does (p. 128), the notion that, with Henry's failure to establish lasting imperial rule in Italy "died all of Dante's hope on earth." For a view, apparently shaped in part by Silverstein's, that Dante had essentially given up his hopes for an imperial resurgence because of the derelictions of the fourteenth-century papacy, see Peters (Pete.1972.1), who goes further than Silverstein in seeing Dante as having modified his imperial hopes. But see Goudet (Goud.1974.1) and Rossi (Ross.1981.1), pp. 43–50 (with a rejoinder to Peters on p. 49) for a more convincing sense of Dante's continuing imperial hopes.

For Dante's fifth *Epistula* (addressed to the princes and peoples of Italy) as rechanneling biblical and liturgical reflections of Christ's majesty onto Henry VII, see Rigo (Rigo.1980.1).

For Henry VII as the seventh divinely selected emperor, see the last paragraph of the note to *Paradiso* VI.82–91.

134. Bosco/Reggio (comm. to this verse) point out that it is difficult to be certain just what Dante means. Is the crown (a) leaning against the throne? (b) a part of the design on its back? (c) suspended over it? This reader confesses that he has always assumed the third option was the right one.

135. The word *nozze* (wedding feast) drew Mattalia's attention (comm. to this verse) to Dante's *Epistle to the Italian Princes* (*Epist.* V.5): "Rejoice, therefore, O Italy, thou that art now an object of pity even to the Saracens, for soon shalt thou be the envy of the whole world, seeing that thy bridegroom, the comfort of the nations, and the glory of thy people, even the most clement Henry, Elect of God and Augustus and Caesar, is hastening to the wedding (*ad nuptias properat*)" (tr. P. Toynbee). This attribution is also found in Rossi (Ross.1981.1), p. 50.

136. The adjective *agosta* (imperial) still honors Henry's "Augustan" mission, which was to unite the Italians into a nation, as Aeneas had set out to

do. Augustus had presided over its flowering, bringing the world to peace under Rome's authority.

137. For Henry's first naming, see *Paradiso* XVII.82, where his betrayal by Pope Clement is clearly referred to. This second (and final) reference to him by name places his coming as "Augustus" in the future, thus reflecting Dante's willed optimism that the future harbors a "new Henry" even after this one has failed.

138. See Hainsworth (Hain.1997.1), p. 160, on the two main and opposing senses of the notion of "disposition" in Dante (the verb *disporre* in various forms). The word often refers to human choices (sometimes mistaken ones), but also to divine election. Here, Hainsworth argues, that Italy was not "disposed" when she should have been does not mean that she will not welcome her next opportunity to embrace a rightful ruler.

139–141. Florence as an ill-willed baby boy, who turns from his nurse's breast even as he feels the pangs of hunger, is reminiscent of the two good young boys who will turn bad quickly enough in *Paradiso* XXVII.130–135. The political context and the word *cupidigia* are other common elements in the two passages.

139. See, for a different tonality but similar formulations, Dante's earlier utterance, issued from exile, addressed to his fellow citizens when they were resisting the efforts of Henry VII to take control of Florence (*Epistula* VI.22): "Nec advertitis dominantem *cupidinem*, quia *ceci* estis, venenoso susurrio blandientem, minis frustatoriis cohibentem, nec non captivantem vos in lege peccati, ac sacratissimis legibus que iustitie naturalis imitantur ymaginem, parere vetantem; observantia quarum, si leta, si libera, non tantum non servitus esse probatur, quin ymo perspicaciter intuenti liquet ut est ipsa summa libertas" (Nor are ye ware in your *blindness* of the overmastering *greed* which beguiles you with venomous whispers, and with cheating threats constrains you, yea, and has brought you into captivity to the law of sin, and forbidden you to obey the most sacred laws; those laws made in the likeness of natural justice, the observance whereof, if it be joyous, if it be free, is not only no servitude, but to him who observes with understanding is manifestly in itself the most perfect liberty—tr. P. Toynbee [italics added]).

142–148. This concluding passage, with its rancor against the ecclesiastical enemies of the imperial idea, has disturbed many, who find it entirely inappropriate as Beatrice's last utterance in a theologically determined poem. One must admit that it may seem out of place in a Christian poem, with its necessary message of the unimportance of the things of the world coupled with Jesus' insistence that we forgive our enemies. Such a sensible view, however, disregards the thoroughgoing political concern of the poem and does not deal with Dante's stubborn insistence on the rectitude of his vision of the world order (see Hollander [Holl.1993.5], pp. 32–33).

The thirtieth cantos of the final *cantiche* are united, as Claudio Varese noted (Vare.1953.1), p. 25, in at least two major respects: They are cantos of departure for both beloved guides; they also are both "cantos of Beatrice," the first of arrival, the second of return (to the point of her departure, her seat in Heaven, as described in *Inferno* II.71, 101–102).

If we can remember our first reading of the poem, we will perhaps recall our eventual and retrospective surprise upon discovering that these were the last words spoken by Beatrice in the *Divine Comedy*. We, like the protagonist, have gotten used to her guidance. Unlike Virgil's departure, which is prepared for even as he enters the poem (*Inf.* I.121–126), Beatrice's departure is a total surprise (see the note to *Par.* XXXI.102).

142–144. This tercet undoubtedly is a last nasty glance at Pope Clement V, who made a show of welcoming Henry VII to Italy but then worked assiduously behind the scenes to defeat the emperor's efforts to unite her cities under his rule (see the note to *Par.* XVII.82–84).

145–146. Henry died 24 August 1313; Clement, 20 April 1314, soon enough after Henry for Dante to consider his death God's punishment for his treacherous opposition to the emperor and to his cause—even if Clement had been seriously ill a very long time. See the note to *Inferno* XIX.79–87.

147. Simon Magus gave the "naming opportunity" to Dante for the third of the *Malebolge* (see *Inf.* XXIX.1), where the simoniac popes and other clerics who traded in the goods and services of the Church are found, and where Dante so memorably is mistaken by Pope Nicholas III for Pope Boniface VIII (*Inf.* XIX.53).

148. The phrase "that fellow from Anagni" is Dante's own version of the false and slangy familiarity of the corrupt clergy (see the note to *Par.* XVIII.130–136). The reference, of course, is to Pope Boniface VIII, seen as forced deeper into his hole (that of the simoniac popes) by the advent of Clement, who now will be the topmost, and thus able to wave his burning

soles about in Hell. Dante didn't know it, but Clement's time would exceed that of Boniface, who waved his feet from 1303 to 1314. In the unwritten continuation of this poem, Clement would have twenty years in the relatively open air of the *bolgia*, since John XXII did not die until 1334 (surely Dante felt he was destined for eternal damnation, and would have continued to do so, especially had he learned of John's unenlightened views on the resurrection of the flesh [see the note to verse 129]).

PARADISO XXXI

OUTLINE

THE EMPYREAN

1–3 the blessed, in triumph, in the form of a white rose;

4–6 the angels, flying, see and sing God's glory

7–12 simile: like bees they descend into the Rose only to reascend with their pollen and make honey in "the hive";

13–15 angels: red faces, golden wings, whitest possible "bodies"

16–18 angels: take "honey" from the "hive" back to the "flowers"

19–24 angels: translucent, they do not cut off the sight of God;

25–27 the final "kingdom" of the poem: all gaze on God

28–29 triune God, how you do satisfy both these "militias"!

30 look down on our tempest here on this earth!

31–40 if northern barbarians, seeing Rome, were amazed, how much more so was Dante, coming from Florence and time to these good citizens in the true and eternal city!

41–42 joyful and amazed, Dante hears nothing, says nothing;

43–48 simile: pilgrim looking around the distant church he vowed to visit compared to Dante, looking around the Rose

49–51 the blessed, splendid and smiling, gesture with dignity

52–57 having seen the overall design of Paradise, Dante wants to ask Beatrice about specific aspects of the Empyrean;

58–63 in her place he finds a fatherly elder **(St. Bernard)**;

64 Dante's first spoken words in some time: "Where is she?"

65–69 Bernard: "she sent me to bring your desire to fulfillment and is up there above in the third row from the top";

70–72 Dante sees Beatrice in the Rose "crowned" by God's rays;

73–78 the bottom of the sea is no farther from the upper regions than Dante from her, but here distance is no bar to sight

79–90 Dante prays to Beatrice, giving thanks and hoping for help

91–93 Beatrice smiles and then turns back to the source of all;

94–99 Bernard: "to finish your quest, first study this garden";

100–102 Bernard burns with love for the Virgin, who will help them

103–111 simile: Croatian pilgrim coming to Rome and seeing the Veronica, just as Dante is gazing at Bernard

112–117 Bernard: "look up from here to Mary at the Rose's rim"

118–123 simile: Sun brightest spot on horizon like Mary on rim

124–129 simile: rising Sun like Mary, darker space to either side

130–135 band of angels, each distinct, surround Mary who, smiling, with her beauty brings joy to all the other saints;

136–138 even had Dante the words, he would not dare describe her;

139–142 Bernard, observing Dante's fervor for Mary, looks back at her so lovingly that he makes Dante's eyes more ardent.

PARADISO XXXI

In forma dunque di candida rosa
mi si mostrava la milizia santa
che nel suo sangue Cristo fece sposa;

ma l'altra, che volando vede e canta
la gloria di colui che la 'nnamora
e la bontà che la fece cotanta,

sì come schiera d'ape che s'infiora
una fïata e una si ritorna
là dove suo laboro s'insapora,

nel gran fior discendeva che s'addorna
di tante foglie, e quindi risaliva
là dove 'l süo amor sempre soggiorna.

Le facce tutte avean di fiamma viva
e l'ali d'oro, e l'altro tanto bianco,
che nulla neve a quel termine arriva.

Quando scendean nel fior, di banco in banco
porgevan de la pace e de l'ardore
ch'elli acquistavan ventilando il fianco.

Né l'interporsi tra 'l disopra e 'l fiore
di tanta moltitudine volante
impediva la vista e lo splendore:

ché la luce divina è penetrante
per l'universo secondo ch'è degno,
sì che nulla le puote essere ostante.

Questo sicuro e gaudïoso regno,
frequente in gente antica e in novella,
viso e amore avea tutto ad un segno.

In form, then, of a luminous white rose
I saw the saintly soldiery that Christ,
with His own blood, took as His bride.

But the others—who, even as they fly, behold
and sing the glory of Him who stirs their love,
and sing His goodness that raised them up so high,

as a swarm of bees that in one instant plunge
deep into blossoms and, the very next, go back
to where their toil is turned to sweetness—

these descended to the splendid flower,
adorned with many petals, and then flew up
to where their love forever dwells.

Their faces were of living flame,
their wings were gold, the rest
was of a whiteness never matched by snow.

When they descended to the flower, they bestowed
the peace and love acquired with their beating wings
upon the petals, row on row.

Nor did so vast a flying throng,
coming between the flower and the light above,
obstruct the looking up or shining down,

for the light of God so penetrates the universe,
according to the fitness of its parts to take it in,
that there is nothing can withstand its beam.

This sure and joyful kingdom,
thronged with souls from both the old times and the new,
aimed sight and love upon a single goal.

Oh trina luce che 'n unica stella
scintillando a lor vista, sì li appaga!
guarda qua giuso a la nostra procella!

Se i barbari, venendo da tal plaga
che ciascun giorno d'Elice si cuopra,
rotante col suo figlio ond' ella è vaga,

veggendo Roma e l'ardüa sua opra,
stupefaciensi, quando Laterano
a le cose mortali andò di sopra;

ïo, che al divino da l'umano,
a l'etterno dal tempo era venuto,
e di Fiorenza in popol giusto e sano,

di che stupor dovea esser compiuto!
Certo tra esso e 'l gaudio mi facea
libito non udire e starmi muto.

E quasi peregrin che si ricrea
nel tempio del suo voto riguardando,
e spera già ridir com' ello stea,

su per la viva luce passeggiando,
menava ïo li occhi per li gradi,
mo sù, mo giù e mo recirculando.

Vedëa visi a carità süadi,
d'altrui lume fregiati e di suo riso,
e atti ornati di tutte onestadi.

La forma general di paradiso
già tutta mïo sguardo avea compresa,
in nulla parte ancor fermato fiso;

e volgeami con voglia rïaccesa
per domandar la mia donna di cose
di che la mente mia era sospesa.

O threefold Light, which, in a single star
sparkling in their sight, contents them so!
Look down upon our tempest here below.

If the barbarians, coming from that region
which Helice covers every day,
wheeling with her son, in whom she takes delight,

were dumbstruck at the sight of Rome
and her majestic monuments,
when the Lateran surpassed all other works of man,

I, who had come to things divine from man's estate,
to eternity from time,
from Florence to a people just and sane,

with what amazement must I have been filled!
Indeed, between the wonder and my joy, I was content
neither to hear nor speak a word.

And, as a pilgrim, in the temple of his vow,
content within himself, looks lovingly about
and expects to tell his tale when he gets home,

so, through the living light I let my eyes
range freely through the ranks, now up, now down,
now circling freely all around again.

I saw visages informed by heavenly love, resplendent
with Another's light and their own smiles,
their every movement graced with dignity.

My gaze by now had taken in
the general form of Paradise
but not yet fixed on any single part of it,

and I turned, with newly kindled eagerness
to ask my lady many things
that kept my mind yet in suspense.

Uno intendëa, e altro mi rispuose:
credea veder Beatrice e vidi un sene
vestito con le genti glorïose.

Diffuso era per li occhi e per le gene
di benigna letizia, in atto pio
quale a tenero padre si convene.

E "Ov' è ella?" sùbito diss' io.
Ond' elli: "A terminar lo tuo disiro
mosse Beatrice me del loco mio;

e se riguardi sù nel terzo giro
dal sommo grado, tu la rivedrai
nel trono che suoi merti le sortiro."

Sanza risponder, li occhi sù levai,
e vidi lei che si facea corona
reflettendo da sé li etterni rai.

Da quella regïon che più sù tona
occhio mortale alcun tanto non dista,
qualunque in mare più giù s'abbandona,

quanto lì da Beatrice la mia vista;
ma nulla mi facea, ché süa effige
non discendëa a me per mezzo mista.

"O donna in cui la mia speranza vige,
e che soffristi per la mia salute
in inferno lasciar le tue vestige,

di tante cose quant' i' ho vedute,
dal tuo podere e da la tua bontate
riconosco la grazia e la virtute.

Tu m'hai di servo tratto a libertate
per tutte quelle vie, per tutt' i modi
che di ciò fare avei la potestate.

I expected one thing but found another:
instead of Beatrice, an old man, adorned
60 as were the rest of those in glory, met my eyes.

His eyes and cheeks were quite suffused
with kindly joy, and from his whole appearance shone
63 a loving father's tenderness.

Then 'Where is she?' I asked at once
and he replied: 'To lead your longing to its goal
66 Beatrice called me from my place.

'If you raise your eyes to the third circle
below the highest tier, you shall see her again,
69 now on the throne her merits have assigned.'

Without a word, I lifted up my eyes
and saw that she, reflecting the eternal rays,
72 appeared to be encircled by a crown.

From the highest region where the thunder breaks
down to the bottom of the deepest sea,
75 no mortal eye is ever quite so far

as was my sight removed from Beatrice.
Yet to me that mattered not, because her image
78 came down undimmed by anything between.

'O lady who give strength to all my hope
and who allowed yourself, for my salvation,
81 to leave your footprints there in Hell,

'of all the many things that I have seen,
I know the grace and virtue I've been shown
84 come from your goodness and your power.

'It is you who, on no matter what the path,
have drawn me forth from servitude to freedom
87 by every means that you had in your power.

La tua magnificenza in me custodi,
sì che l'anima mia, che fatt' hai sana,
piacente a te dal corpo si disnodi."

Così orai; e quella, sì lontana
come parea, sorrise e riguardommi;
poi si tornò a l'etterna fontana.

E 'l santo sene: "Acciò che tu assommi
perfettamente," disse, "il tuo cammino,
a che priego e amor santo mandommi,

vola con li occhi per questo giardino;
ché veder lui t'acconcerà lo sguardo
più al montar per lo raggio divino.

E la regina del cielo, ond'ïo ardo
tutto d'amor, ne farà ogne grazia,
però ch'i' sono il suo fedel Bernardo."

Qual è colui che forse di Croazia
viene a veder la Veronica nostra,
che per l'antica fame non sen sazia,

ma dice nel pensier, fin che si mostra:
"Segnor mio Iesù Cristo, Dio verace,
or fu sì fatta la sembianza vostra?";

tal era io mirando la vivace
carità di colui che 'n questo mondo,
contemplando, gustò di quella pace.

"Figliuol di grazia, quest' esser giocondo,"
cominciò elli, "non ti sarà noto,
tenendo li occhi pur qua giù al fondo;

ma guarda i cerchi infino al più remoto,
tanto che veggi seder la regina
cui questo regno è suddito e devoto."

'Keep your munificence alive in me, so that
my soul, which you have healed,
may please you when it leaves its mortal frame.'

This was my prayer. And she, however far away
she seemed, smiled and looked down at me,
then turned again to the eternal fountain.

And the holy ancient spoke: 'So that you may achieve
your journey's consummation now,
both sacred love and prayer have sent me here:

'Let your sight fly through this garden,
for seeing it will help prepare your eyes
to rise, along the beam of holy light.

'And Heaven's queen, for whom I burn
with love, will grant us every grace,
since I am her own, her faithful Bernard.'

As the man who, perhaps from Croatia, has come
to set his gaze on our Veronica,
his ancient craving still not satisfied,

and who thinks to himself while it is shown:
'My Lord Jesus Christ, God Himself,
was this then how you really looked?',

just so was I, gazing on the living love
of him who, still within the confines of this world,
in contemplation tasted of that peace.

'Child of grace,' he said, 'you will not know
this joyful state if you maintain your gaze,
instead of upward, fixed down here.

'Rather to the highest circles raise your eyes
so that you may behold the queen enthroned,
her to whom this realm is subject and devout.'

Io levai li occhi; e come da mattina
la parte orïental de l'orizzonte
soverchia quella dove 'l sol declina,

così, quasi di valle andando a monte
con li occhi, vidi parte ne lo stremo
vincer di lume tutta l'altra fronte.

E come quivi ove s'aspetta il temo
che mal guidò Fetonte, più s'infiamma,
e quinci e quindi il lume si fa scemo,

così quella pacifica oriafiamma
nel mezzo s'avvivava, e d'ogne parte
per igual modo allentava la fiamma;

e a quel mezzo, con le penne sparte,
vid' io più di mille angeli festanti,
ciascun distinto di fulgore e d'arte.

Vidi a lor giochi quivi e a lor canti
ridere una bellezza, che letizia
era ne li occhi a tutti li altri santi;

e s'io avessi in dir tanta divizia
quanta ad imaginar, non ardirei
lo minimo tentar di sua delizia.

Bernardo, come vide li occhi miei
nel caldo suo caler fissi e attenti,
li suoi con tanto affetto volse a lei,
che ' miei di rimirar fé più ardenti.

I raised my eyes. As, at break of day,
the eastern part of the horizon shines
with a brighter glow than where the sun goes down,

so, as though my eyes were moving from a valley
up a mountain, I saw that one far crest
surpassed in brightness all the others.

Where we await the shaft of Phaeton's
poorly guided car, there, where it is most aflame,
while on this side and on that the light shades off,

just so that peaceful oriflamme showed brightest
in the middle, while on either side
the flame was dimmed in equal measure.

Around that point I saw more than a thousand angels,
their wings outspread, in joyful festival,
each distinct in brightness and in motion.

I saw there, smiling at their games and songs,
beauty that brought pleasure to the gaze
of all the other gathered saints.

Were I as rich with words as in my store of images,
I still would never dare attempt to tell
the least of these delights that came from her.

Bernard, who saw my eyes were fixed, intent
upon the very fire that made him warm,
turned his own on her with such affection
that he made mine more ardent in their gaze.

1–3. For the resemblance of Dante's *candida rosa* to the rose-wheel windows of medieval cathedrals, see Leyerle (Leye.1977.1). He argues for the double significance of this design: the wheel of Fortune, symbol of the fleetingness of earthly success, and the rose, symbol of a higher and more ordered affection (one particularly related to the Blessed Virgin). He then goes on to suggest that Dante has this design in mind both in his depiction of Fortune's wheel (*Inf.* VII) and of the Rose found here in the Empyrean. Leyerle also believes that a particular rose-wheel window was in Dante's mind, the one that was completed in the façade of the basilica of S. Zeno in Verona at least by 1300. On the exterior of S. Zeno, carvings of human figures, all four of whom are either falling or rising, strengthen his first case; the lovely tracing of the light on the inner spaces of the cathedral are at least not unlike the design found in Dante's Rose. However, see Scott (Scot.2002.1), p. 477, citing Barnes (Barn.1986.1, pp. 25 and 31, n. 30) for the argument that the term for "rose window" only begins to appear in the European vernaculars, first in France, in the very late seventeenth century. This is hardly conclusive evidence that Dante did not think of one of these round, large, beautiful, and many-hued glass structures, piercing stone and splashing the interior space with colored light, as the model for his Rose. (In fact, Migliorini-Fissi's *lectura* of the canto [Migl.1989.1], pp. 609–11, certainly lends credence to Leyerle's argument; while she does not mention his article, but does note two later treatments found in Di Scipio's fifth chapter [Disc.1984.1] and in Demaray [Dema.1987.1], she points out that the idea was first broached in 1870 by Ozanam.) The term may be anachronistic, but nothing in Leyerle's case depends upon the availability of the term. And if one were to select a particular window, Leyerle has chosen well. Verona was, at least for two lengthy periods in both decades of the fourteenth century in which Dante lived, the focal point of his life as an exile, at least until his removal to Ravenna probably in the final third of the second decade. San Zeno was (and is) an astoundingly beautiful church.

1. Benvenuto (comm. to vv. 1–3) sees that the adverb *dunque* (then) is pointing to a previous discussion (Beatrice's first description of the Rose, in *Par.* XXX.124–132, "interrupted" by the "digression" [XXX.133–145] of her bitter words about Henry's death and the corrupt recent popes Boniface and Clement). With "dunque" the poet announces his return to her prior subject. The word's casual, "vernacular-sounding" nature caught the atten-

tion of Scaglione (Scag.1967.2), as is reported by Scott (Scot.2002.1), p. 476. Both of them refer to the term brought to bear in Dante studies by Auerbach (Auer.1958.1), *sermo humilis*, for the low style, in their classification of this linguistic gesture. Scott admires the juxtaposition of *dunque* with *candida rosa* (luminous white rose) as the expression of Dante's union of the low with the sublime.

Vellutello (comm. to vv. 1–3) was apparently the first commentator, in a long tradition, to link the "bianche stole" (white robes) last heard of in *Paradiso* XXX.129 with the adjective *candida* (luminous white) modifying *rosa*. Grandgent (comm. to this verse) is one of only two in the DDP to suggest a source in Albertus Magnus (*De laudibus beatae Mariae Virginis* [XII.iv.33]): "Et nota, quod Christus rosa, Maria rosa, Ecclesia rosa, fidelis anima rosa," equating Jesus, Mary, the Church, and the faithful soul of a believer with the rose.

For the fullest bibliography for this canto available in print, see Costa (Cost.1996.1), pp. 78–85.

2–3. The protagonist gazes at the *milizia* (soldiery) that fought on for the Church that Christ "adquisivit sanguine suo" (obtained with His own blood—Acts 20:28, first cited by Tommaseo [comm. to vv. 1–3]). And see the note to verse 127. Dante never stops seeing the Church as an army, even in its peaceful triumph.

4–6. The other host, the angels, now take the poet's attention, flying up to the "hive" while contemplating and singing Its glory.

5. The first five words of *Paradiso* I.1 are present here, verbatim.

7–12. The angelic host is given similetic expression. At first, by Pietro di Dante (Pietro1, comm. to vv. 7–9) and Benvenuto (comm. to vv. 4–12), these bees were seen as deriving from *Aeneid* I.430–431. However, from Vellutello (comm. to vv. 4–12) onward, commentators have heard the more relevant echo of the simile at *Aeneid* VI.703–709 (for that text, see the note to *Paradiso* XXX.64–66).

The conclusion of Rossi's study (Ross.1989.2), pp. 313–24, accounts for the disparities in the two similes by showing that the situation in the *Aeneid*, from a Christian perspective, is less propitious than it first may seem. As a central case in point, Aeneas discovers that all these happy shades are about to be (from Dante's perspective) "reincarnated." We can hardly imagine the joy felt by the hero of this "epic" when he sees the souls in the Rose as they will look when they are resurrected. Surely we are meant to remember Aeneas's quite different reaction, when he learns from Anchises about the flesh that these souls in the Elysian Fields will bear with them as they return to the world and its toils. Indeed, Aeneas laments their return to the world of flesh (*Aen.* VI.719–721). In the post-Platonic *Aeneid*, the world of flesh has nothing to do with spiritual perfection; in Dante's poem the beatified spirit has only a single unfulfilled desire: to be granted the return of its flesh. Thus, if Dante allows Virgilian text a renewed presence in his poem, he is not without the ironic distance that we have found present in even the first moments of the poem (for example, see the notes to *Inf.* II.28 and II.56–57).

For other possible sources for this passage, e.g., in St. Anselm and St. Bernard, see Scott (Scot.2002.1), p. 478. For several different passages in Bernard, see the following: Carroll (comm. to vv. 1–12), Torraca (comm. to these verses), Casini/Barbi (comm. to verse 7), and Trucchi (comm. to vv. 4–12), who also cites Anselm. A few later commentators also make gestures in both these directions, if without furnishing texts.

A discussion of the elaborate structural play in this simile is found in Lansing (Lans.1977.1), p. 37. The vehicle and tenor of the simile each mirrors both moments in the movement of the bees/angels, first down to the flowers/souls, then back up to the hive/God.

7. As we have seen (note to *Par.* XXX.64–66), Virgil's verb (*insidere*) for what the bees do at least suggests that, more than settling on the blossoms, they enter them. Thus Dante here follows Virgil faithfully, if others seem to believe he does not (see Bosco/Reggio [comm. to this verse]).

9. The word *laboro* is obviously a deliberate Latinism, since *lavoro*, Italian for "labor," is metrically the same, and Dante's hand was not forced by rhyme. Why does he choose this linguistic tactic here? Perhaps to underline his borrowing from Virgil.

12. We are given a clue as to the separate "dwelling" of God. Fallani (comm. to vv. 40–42) discusses the fact that among the Scholastics there was a tradition of a second "heaven" in the Empyrean, the *coelum Trinitatis* (the heaven of the Trinity), a "place" distinct from the Empyrean, where dwelt the triune God, separated from the blessed souls. In Fallani's opinion, Dante accepts that tradition. It is, however, not clear that he does. Perhaps he both honors and abrogates it, for his God is not in an "eleventh zone" of the heavens, but in the one He shares with the saints—if in a

higher and thus different *locus* from them (the distance between the "floor" and the top tier of the Rose is greater than that between the lowest place in the sea and the highest place beneath the Moon [see the note to vv. 73–78]; the distance between that point in the Rose and God would seem to be infinite). And thus Dante can have things both ways: Is God separate from the saints? Yes and no. He is infinitely farther aloft than they, but that does not require that He "inhabits" another "place," especially since His "habitation" is everywhere and nowhere. It seems clear that Dante intends to avoid this issue, of which he must have been aware. For the presence of the phrase *coelum Trinitatis*, in a context that is related, see Thomas Aquinas, *Super Evangelium S. Matthaei lectura* (51.2, referring to Psalm 36:11 [37:11] and Matthew 5:5, "The meek shall inherit the earth"; Aquinas explains that the *terra* [earth] promised them is the Empyrean). It is not entirely clear, but he seems to think of the Empyrean and the *coelum Trinitatis* as though they might be considered one and the same.

13–15. Dante's description of the angels, flaming red faces, golden wings, and white "bodies," is possibly based in biblical texts as well as popular iconography (as found, for instance, painted on church walls). Quite a few biblical sources have been a part of the indeterminate discussion down through the centuries. Perhaps the only sure citation (for the angels' red faces) is Scartazzini's (comm. to verse 13): Ezechiel 1:13: "their appearance was like burning coals of fire," which has quantitatively the most support. A second at least likely attribution is Tommaseo's (comm. to this tercet), who, for the white, cites Matthew 28:3: the angel who appears at the tomb of Jesus, his vestments "white as snow" (some later commentators join [or substitute] Matthew's supposed "source," Daniel 7:9). The gold has several suggestions based in Daniel 10:5, but this is not convincingly chosen, since the gold there described is that found on a belt, not on wings.

As for the "allegorical" meaning of the three colors, nearly all can agree that the red faces bespeak angelic love. However, the other two are the cause of disagreement. Some, unconvincingly, propose the Trinity (Love, Wisdom [?], and Power [??]); others select various abstractions, not much more convincingly. There is a general understanding that the angels and their colors are perfect in three respects: They love perfectly, fly on immortal pinions, and have "bodies" that are utterly pure. And that is probably enough.

17–18. In Dante's lovely transposition, these bees, now having gathered the "pollen" (God's love) from the hive, bring "honey" *back* from the hive to the souls: a celestial variant on nature's apiary artistry. These flowers have a second chance to enjoy their own (now enhanced) sweetness. Dante's "honey," like God's love and their love for Him, is bidirectional.

As Augustine knew and taught, mortal love can never satisfy or be satisfied: "inquietum est cor nostrum donec requiescat in te" (restless is our heart until it finds rest in you—*Confessiones* I.1). These two words, *pace* and *ardore* ("peace" and "love"), can be found together only here in the Empyrean, never in Dante's world below.

19–27. The numberless host of the angels, circling God in nine ranks (see the note to *Par.* XXVIII.25–27), do not hinder in any way either His ray from reaching the saints in the Rose or their ability to make out His splendor (which Aversano [Aver.2000.2], p. 159, particularizes as the Second Person, Christ, irradiated by the Father). Torraca (comm. to vv. 22–24) reminds us that, in *Convivio* (III.vii.5), Dante had in fact said that the angels were as though translucent (*diafani*). Indeed, all of them, those who believed in Christ to come and those who believed after the fact, are gazing lovingly on the triune God.

22–23. See *Paradiso* I.2 and the note to verse 5, above. Thus Dante, nearing his ending, reflects his beginning, a way of also signaling that the poem is approaching its conclusion.

25–27. We now see all the saints doing what, as we will learn in the next canto, they always do, looking up, fixing their gaze on God. There is no variety in Heaven, nor is it desired by the blessed.

We also learn, in that canto, what is intrinsic only to what we see here. There are more Jews in Heaven than Christians. This puzzled some commentators and infuriated others, the first group claiming that Dante could not possibly have meant this, the others believing him only too well. Pretty clearly Dante's neat division of the Rose into two equal parts, with a few empty seats in the Christian half and none in the Jewish one, is meant to force that conclusion upon a reader. As far as we know, there are only a very few gentiles among the Hebrew group. In fact, we know only that there are two, Cato (there thus *should* be at least one empty place in the full half, as Cato is still minding Purgatory) and Ripheus (Statius and Trajan were both alive in Christian times). Dante's point is clear: More Jews believed in Christ without the authority of His presence, as certified by the witness provided by the New Testament, than did Christians, even though they were given the answers before they took the exam.

28–29. In verse 27 the saints are said to aim their gaze at a single target. Now the poet speaks of that single essence as a "star," but also as the Trinity, a "threefold Light," bringing joy to all the blessed who behold it (and they all do). Some of the early commentators are less clear than they might be that this is not an "invocation" or part of the prayer that Dante will address to God in verse 30. This is an example of apostrophe, one of praise, and not part of a request.

30. The poet then addresses God, praying that He look down at the "storm" afflicting mortal lives on earth. Is there an implicit further request to be understood here? Most of the commentators think so. And all of them who are of this opinion believe that Dante is asking God to intervene on behalf of storm-tossed mortals. However, it seems at least as likely that he means no such thing. Rather, as the reference to Florence (verse 39) might also suggest, God ought to look down at the spectacle of human sin with grim recognition of the lostness of those living now on earth, almost all of them beyond redemption. Apparently the first to offer so point-blank a negative reading was Roffarè (Roff.1968.1), p. 1107. What stands in the way of accepting this pessimistic interpretation is the highly possible presence of a citation of a passage, first cited by Tommaseo (comm. to vv. 28–30), in Boethius's *Consolatio* (I.m5.42–48): "O God, whoever you are, who joins [*sic*] all things in perfect harmony, look down upon this miserable earth! We men are no small part of Your great work, yet we wallow here in the stormy sea of fortune. Ruler of all things, calm the roiling waves and, as You rule the immense heavens, rule also the earth in stable concord" (tr. R. Green). Also germane is *Monarchia* I.xvi.4, first cited by Torraca (comm. to vv. 28–30): "O human race, how many storms and misfortunes and shipwrecks must toss you about while, transformed into a many-headed beast, you strive after conflicting things" (tr. P. Shaw). This last is part of the bitter conclusion of the first book of that treatise, and would not encourage one to believe that, if Dante were thinking of it here, he foresaw any sort of divine aid coming to the human race. On the other hand, see the prophecy concluding *Paradiso* XXVII, which does predict God's positive intervention in the affairs of men (similarly presented as a storm at sea [*fortuna*]—see the note to *Par.* XXVII.142–148). It is thus difficult to decide what the author intended us to gather about the nature of his request for God's attention.

31–40. In this lengthy simile the poet compares barbarians, probably coming, in times of peace, from northern Europe to Rome, seeing the imperial buildings of the city before Constantine gave those buildings to the papacy just after his conversion in 312, to himself, moving in the opposite direction, "south" to "north," from Florence to the New Jerusalem above the heavens.

The magnificent church of St. John Lateran was destroyed by fire in 1308. Making things worse, Henry VII, denied a coronation in St. Peter's by Pope Clement, was crowned in the ruins of that church in 1312, nearly exactly one thousand years later, and died the next year (see note to *Paradiso*.XVII.82–84).

For a discussion of the various notions of what exactly Dante meant by the reference, see Costa (Cost.1996.1), pp. 65–66.

32–33. Callisto was exiled by Diana from the "nunnery" of chaste forest maidens for her affair with Jove, which resulted in her giving birth to Arcas. "The 'zone' that is always 'covered by Helice' is the North. The nymph Helice or Callisto was transformed into the constellation of the Great Bear, and her son Arcas or Boötes into the Little Bear: *Metam.* II.496–530, especially 515–517; cf. *Purg.* XXV.131. The Bears, or Dippers, are close to the North Star" (Grandgent, comm. to vv. 31–34).

37–39. The phrase "a people just and sane" is the third and last in a series of parallel pairs, with the parallelism inverted in the third term: good/bad, good/bad, bad/good. See *Paradiso* XVI.152, where Florentines in "the good old days" were portrayed in much more positive terms. Now things have changed, and Florentines are those left behind in order for Dante to associate with such people as they once were, now found only in Heaven.

39. This is the fifteenth and last time we hear the word *Fiorenza* in the poem; we first heard it in Farinata's voice (*Inf.* X.92). While in fact Florence had replaced Rome as the greatest city of Italy, Dante here reverses that equation, making old Rome the type of the celestial city, while new Florence is portrayed as the city of the lost.

43–48. The second simile in a series of three dedicated to the theme of pilgrimage (see the note to vv. 103–111), this one presents Dante as a traveler to a shrine, a journey he has vowed to make. For the pilgrimage motif in the entire poem, see Holloway (Holl.1992.3).

While Dante leaves the particular shrine he may have had in mind shrouded in silence, the early commentators variously suggested the Church of the Holy Sepulchre in Jerusalem, St. Peter's in Rome, and St.

James of Compostella in Galicia (Spain), the three most important destinations for pilgrims in his day.

48. The Tuscan word for "now" (*mo*) was first heard at *Inferno* X.21 and leaves the poem after a dazzling three uses in a single line (and the twenty-third through twenty-fifth in all), perhaps underlining Dante's desire to be considered a vernacularizing poet even at the sublime height of the Empyrean. The effect of the triple presence of the word accents the eager nature of his glance, unable to move quickly enough in taking in every aspect of the place he has so long desired to see, the goal of his pilgrimage. Verse 54 describes Dante's similar hurried and eager glances cast around the Rose in the attempt to take it all in.

49–51. What the protagonist sees, faces, reminds us that it was only the first few souls whom he saw in the heavens whose human features he could make out (see the note to *Par.* III.58–63). Now he is seeing, as Beatrice promised he would (*Par.* XXX.44–45), the souls as they will look when they are reincarnate.

51. The word *onestade* has only two occurrences in the poem. The last time we heard it was in the poet's description of Virgil when he was running up the slope of Mount Purgatory (*Purg.* III.11) after Cato chastised the souls who listened, charmed, to Casella's song. There Virgil is seen as having lost his dignity; here the souls in the Rose are seen by the protagonist as having theirs.

52–54. The mood is quiet, preparing us for a transition, moving from the general to the specific.

55–58. Compare the similar scene in *Purgatorio* XXX.43–54, when the protagonist turns back to speak to Virgil, only to find him gone. This scene, clearly reflective of that one, is much briefer and in an altogether different key. That one is three times as long, and in the tragic mode. Here, the disappearance of Beatrice has a quite different tonality. Among the differences is that she disappears from the "floor of the arena" only to reappear in her place in the Rose (see verse 71).

56–57. What were the questions Dante still wanted Beatrice to answer? Are we supposed to wonder? Or is this mere "realistic detail" (i.e., are we merely supposed to reflect, "Of course, anyone would have a lot of questions during a first visit to Paradise")? Some commentators, however, try to ascertain what questions Dante wanted to ask. For example, Jacopo della Lana (comm. to vv. 55–57): Dante wants to know the identities of those seated in the Rose; or Benvenuto (comm. to vv. 52–57): Dante wants to know where Mary and Beatrice are seated. Poletto (comm. to vv. 52–57) loses patience with such attempts, urging us not to seek what the poet has chosen not to reveal. Francesco da Buti (comm. to vv. 43–57) had solved the riddle acceptably, if obviously and unprofitably: Dante had questions about Paradise. . . . Steiner (comm. to these verses) has the wisest response: These lines refer to the questions that St. Bernard will eventually respond to, reading them in God. In fact, this is a rare occasion on which almost everyone is essentially correct. Bernard does answer Dante's voiced question (Where is Beatrice? [verse 64]) and one unvoiced one (Where is Mary? [verse 100]). He also in the next canto names a good number of souls seated in the Rose, as Jacopo suggested he might and as Bernard says he will (vv. 97–99).

58–60. In place of Beatrice, he finds, near him on the "floor" of the Rose, an "old man" (it will turn out to be Bernard, but we do not know that yet), looking like the other blessed souls.

59. See Bosco/Reggio (comm. to *Par.* XXXII.40–75), who point out that by portraying Bernard as an old man (*sene*), Dante is violating a commonly understood ground rule of *Paradiso*, that all souls are, in their perfected beings, of the age of Christ in His last year on earth, when he was thirty-three. (This is sometimes given as thirty, thirty-three, thirty-four, or even thirty-five.) Why Dante chose to violate this "rule" is not clear. Bosco/Reggio opt for an artist's rebellion against a view that would inhibit his artistic virtuosity, an old Bernard being more believable than one in his renewed youth. And see Carroll (comm. to *Par.* XXXII.1–48), discussing the babes seated in the lower half of the Rose: "Further, as we saw in the case of Bernard himself, Dante appears to ignore the doctrine of Aquinas that in the Resurrection the saints will rise at the age of thirty. Bernard, himself an old man, draws his attention to the child faces and voices of the lower ranks (*Par.* XXXII.46–48). Each soul, apparently, wears the form proper to the age it had attained on earth, freed of course from weakness and defect of the flesh. Dante evidently felt that there would have been something incongruous in making babies, who had never exercised true choice, appear full-grown in the flower of life. (Augustine thought otherwise: infants would receive 'by the marvellous and rapid

operation of God that body which time by a slower process would have given them' [*De civ. Dei*, XXII.xiv].)"

63. Bernard is Dante's last "father" in the poem. For a listing, see the note to *Paradiso* XVI.16.

64. See Scartazzini (comm. to this verse), reminding the reader of the Magdalen's remark to the resurrected Jesus, whom she mistakes for a "gardener," upon not seeing Jesus where she expects to see Him, in His sepulcher (John 20:15): "Si tu sustulisti *eum*, dicito mihi ubi. . . ." (If you have carried Him away, tell me where. . . ." [italics added]).

These are Dante's first spoken words since *Paradiso* XXVIII.57. See the note to *Paradiso* XIV.88–96 for a considerably longer silence on his part.

65–69. Bernard's first words answer Dante's most pressing concern, the whereabouts of Beatrice, who, he points out, is in the third row from the top. For a similar scene, see *Inferno* II.109–112, where Beatrice tells how Lucy came to her exactly where we see her now and got her to leave this seat in order to go into Limbo to enlist Virgil's aid. Just so has she now enlisted Bernard's help on Dante's behalf and then reassumed her place.

70–72. Dante sees Beatrice literally in glory, resplendent with the light of God.

71. For Beatrice's crown and Aquinas's discussion of the additional *aureola* accorded especially favored saints, see the note to *Paradiso* XXIII.95 and Scartazzini (comm. to vv. 71–72).

73–78. From the highest point in the earth's sublunar atmosphere to the deepest seabed was not so far as Dante found himself now from Beatrice; and yet he could see her as though there were no appreciable distance between them. The poet has already explained (*Par.* XXX.121–123) that in the Empyrean, the usual physical laws that we know on earth are suspended.

In a sense, Dante here "disinvents" the as-yet-to-be-discovered technique of perspectival representation that would distinguish Italian painting of the next century.

77. See Scott (Scot.2002.1), p. 485, for this striking word (*effige*), which is used only here and in *Paradiso* XXXIII.131, thus further associating Beatrice and Christ.

79–90. Apparently, the first commentator to pay any conscious attention to the protagonist's switch from the honorific *voi*, in addressing Beatrice, to the affectionate *tu*, was Grabher (comm. to vv. 70–93), if he does not make much out of it. Porena (comm. to vv. 79–90) also notices the change, but has quite a strong sense of what it signifies, only appearing to be a closing of the distance between them, but being in fact a distancing, because it is the *tu* addressed to a saint, or that is proffered both to God and to Mary. Indeed, both God and Mary, in Christian theology, have the unique gift of being divine and human simultaneously—as does Beatrice. Nonetheless, Chimenz (comm. to vv. 79–84) admires Porena's formulation. Giacalone (comm. to vv. 79–84) is also in their camp. A different view is advanced by Singleton (comm. to verse 80), one that proposes that the guide has become the individual soul of Beatrice (Singleton retains his sense that the guide is "allegorical," while the individual is not, a judgment that some would dispute in its first instance, others in the second). Bosco/Reggio (comm. to vv. 82–84) also support Porena's thesis.

For a different view, see Hollander (Holl.2001.1), pp. 126–27, pointing out that, as in the *Vita nuova*, Beatrice in Heaven may indeed be addressed with *tu*, "only when she is at one with God, where and when there are no human hierarchies." The fact would seem to be that these eleven second-person-singular pronouns and verb endings (in only twelve verses) do indicate a more personal sense of affection, in a sort of uncontrolled outburst of personal enthusiasm, allowable now that they are on an equal footing as lovers of one another in God. We cannot imagine Jesus addressing Mary as *Voi*.

79–81. For the figural equation, Beatrice as Dante's "Christ," see Hollander (Holl. 1969.1), p. 261. After calling attention to the poet's last words to Virgil in the poem (*Purg.* XXX.51), "Virgilio a cui per mia salute die'mi" (Virgil, to whom I gave myself for my salvation), he then continues as follows, discussing this tercet: "At Dante's beginnings we do well to have in mind his endings, and vice versa. It is Beatrice, the figure of Christ, who brings Dante to salvation; it is Virgil who brings Dante to Beatrice. Dante does not (and did not in the *Vita nuova*) use the word *salute* lightly. His last words to Virgil give him the highest function anyone less than Christ can perform, and that is to bring another to Christ." In this vein, see Scott (Scot.1973.1), p. 570. See also Iannucci (Iann.1995.2), p. 483 (citing his earlier article [Iann.1979.1]), who also notes Beatrice's Christlike attributes in this passage (as, once again, does Scott [Scot.2002.1], p. 486). This has become more or less the standard interpretation of those considered by some in Italy to be part of a so-called *scuola americana*, "the American school (of Dante studies)." And see Pasquini (Pasq.2001.1), p. 254, remarking on the "near-heterodoxy" of these verses.

To be honest, this reading seems so obvious that one feels apologetic for harping on it. However, to understand what blinders Dantists accustomed themselves to wearing whenever they came near the border of so "blasphemous" a theologized poetic for the poem, see the allegorizing glosses of such as Benvenuto da Imola (comm. to this tercet). In his reading (and he is far from being alone in it), Beatrice becomes "theology" who comes down to this "hell on earth" (our world, not Limbo) in order to bring her message to all mortals (including, we assume, Dante Alighieri). This is so flagrantly wrongheaded that one has to admire Benvenuto at least for his stubbornness in not yielding to a Christological interpretation of Beatrice nor to a personal one of Dante, who, in his treatment, is only a stand-in for all humankind. This, one of the most personal moments of the *Commedia*, is thus turned into a kind of simpleminded version of an uplifting moral tale, one only implausibly attributed to the genius of Dante. Reviewing responses to this passage in the DDP, one finds the word "Christ" only in Singleton's commentary (to verse 91) of 1975. How did (or does) anyone read this passage and *not* think of Christ's descent into Hell and His subsequent Harrowing of the Hebrew saints?

85. The typological equations (Beatrice = Moses; Dante = the Hebrews) once again align Beatrice with Christ. See the note to verses 79–81. Here, as there, the commentators seem to want to avoid such "blasphemous" associations. For the Exodus as the poem's controlling trope, see Singleton (Sing.1960.1).

88–90. As one who had sinned against Beatrice once before, Dante knows whereof he speaks. He thus prays that she will help him remain pure of soul for the rest of his time on earth when he is again without her. When he wrote these lines, he probably did not realize how brief that time would be.

91–93. This is the final tercet devoted to the interaction of the two lovers in the poem. Her final smile yields to her returning her attention to the source of all being.

94–99. Bernard summarizes the tasks that lie ahead for Dante: He must contemplate this resplendent gathering (*splendore*) to prepare himself to see, up through the ray (*raggio*), the source of the irradiating light (*luce*). See the note on Dante's light physics, *Paradiso* XXIII.82–84.

94. Dante uses the Latinism *sene* (from *senex*) again. See the note to verse 59.

96. A disputed verse. Some believe the prayer is Beatrice's, the love Bernard's; others think that both are Beatrice's. See Scartazzini (comm. to this verse) for a summary of the two positions and a strong vote for the first solution, but eventual openness to the second.

97–99. Bernard's suggestion might indicate that one of Dante's unasked questions (see the note to vv. 56–57) had to do with the population of the Rose.

102. Bernard names himself, having sounded like a lyric poet of Dante's youthful acquaintance talking about his lady, associating himself, however, not with a Giovanna, a Lagia, or a Selvaggia, but with the Blessed Virgin Mary. Everything about this moment comes as a surprise. We did not anticipate a new guide in the poem, if Dante surely decided that he wanted to have a chance to bid farewell to Beatrice, as well as to present her as being back in bliss. In addition, perhaps for reasons reflecting his personal devotion (for a possible confirmation, see *Par.* XXIII.88–89), he wanted a guide more associated with Mary for this highest part of the poem (not that Beatrice would have been in any way unqualified); perhaps he also felt a numerological tug in deciding to have a trinitarian third instructor. Still, one sympathizes with those who feel that there is something ungainly about the substitution of Bernard for Beatrice. (See the discussion in Botterill [Bott.1994.1], pp. 64–115.) And no one who defends the advent of a new guide can argue that it has been at all prepared for, as was Beatrice's (as early as *Inf.* I.121–126). Pertile (Pert.2001.1), pp. 67–69, goes so far as to argue, if not particularly convincingly, that Dante had planned (and the first sign of such a plan revealed itself, according to him, in *Inf.* II.24–25, with the indication of Mary, Lucy, and Beatrice) to have Beatrice replaced by Lucy. Whatever one thinks of that solution, one must admit that there is a problem here, one that a few strokes of the quill could have avoided. However, see Mazzoni (Mazz.1997.1), who insists on the influence of Bernard's work (or that which Dante considered Bernardine) behind the text of the poem from its outset. And see Iannucci (Iann.1995.2), pp. 481–82, for the notion that the

surprise of Bernard's presence is only a tactic to alert us to his importance for Dante. A series of essays discussing the reflection of several of Bernard's writings in the *Commedia* is found in Aversano (Aver.1990.1). For a summary of Bernard's importance for Dante and of the presence of his writing behind the cantos in which he appears, see Carroll (comm. to vv. 118–142). For the possible influence of Bernard's *De diligendo Deo* on the structure of the entire poem, see Hollander (Holl.1976.2, repr. Holl.1980.1, pp. 33–38). And see the notes to *Purgatorio* XXVII.139–141 and *Paradiso* XXXIII.127–132. For a compact treatment of Bernard's life, see Raoul Manselli, "Bernardo di Chiaravalle, santo," *ED* (I [1970]), pp. 601a–5b, which, however, skirts the question of the actual literary influence of Bernard on Dante. For an introductory treatment in English, one may, in addition to Botterill, consult Gardner (Gard.1913.1), pp. 111–43.

Dante does not refer to Bernard's urgent and frequent support of the Second Crusade (1145–1147) in his preaching. For a study of this crusade, inevitably linked to the adjective "disastrous," see Constable (Cons. 1953.1). Dante's silence is perhaps not surprising, given its failure.

Bernard names himself only at the end of his speech (vv. 94–102). The impression of humility is perhaps less pronounced than when similar behavior was exhibited by both Thomas Aquinas (*Par.* X.82–99) and Cacciaguida (*Par.* XV.88–135), who indeed speak longer before naming themselves. Nonetheless, his comportment is clearly intended to portray his modesty.

103–111. This long but essentially simple simile links Dante once again with a pilgrim arriving at his destination, in this case Rome, where the Veronica, a most holy relic, was preserved. Veronica was supposedly a woman of Jerusalem who offered Jesus a cloth (*sudarium*) to wipe the blood and sweat from His face on the way to Calvary. His features remained on the cloth, which was eventually taken to St. Peter's in Rome, where it was displayed to the faithful on certain occasions. That her name was actually Veronica is doubtful, since her name itself means "true likeness" (*vera icona*). The whole history of this image (and of other relics like it, particularly the Shroud of Turin) is controversial. But for Dante, there was not even a question of its authenticity. See his earlier reference, at the climactic moment of the *Vita nuova* (XL.1), to pilgrims on their way to Rome to see the Veronica, a moment fulfilled here in this poem by Dante's pilgrimage to "that Rome where Christ Himself is Roman" (*Purg.* XXXII.102).

See Lansing (Lans.1977.1), pp. 137–40, for consideration of three consecutive similes in this canto (see also vv. 31–40 and 43–48) dedicated to the theme of completion of a pilgrimage.

103. Croatia, for Dante's audience, represented a very distant and "foreign" place, as in the more recent expression "from here to Timbuktu."

109–111. See Singleton (comm. on these verses): "Bernard's two principal qualifications to serve as final guide in the journey stem from his special devotion to the Virgin Mary and from his fame as one dedicated to mystical contemplation with special emphasis on the affective movement of the mind as it rises to God, an emphasis which later Franciscan thought and devotion adopted and stressed. It was believed that Bernard, in such meditation, had a foretaste of the peace of Heaven. In the *Meditationes piissimae* (XIV, 36–37), ascribed to Bernard, there is a rhapsody on the joys of contemplation. See also Bernard, *Sermones in Cantica Canticorum*, XXIII, 15–16. As noted above, Dante in his *Letter to Can Grande* (*Epist.* XIII, 80) refers the reader of his *Paradiso* to Bernard's work *De contemplatione*."

112–117. Dante, in fixing his gaze on Bernard, who has descended from his seat in the Rose upon Beatrice's urging (see verse 66), has fixated on a lesser version of the good and true than that which Bernard will eventually bring him to see. At least for now the Virgin is the best sight available to him, and she is at the very highest point, in the top row of the stadium-rose.

115–117. How many souls are seated in the Rose? Dante keeps his counsel on that question. The Apocalypse numbers the saved as 144,000 (Apoc. 7:1, 7:4; 14:1, 14:3). Landino (comm. to *Par.* XXX.133–138) reports that some say that the number of blessed is equivalent to the number of fallen angels, while others are of the opinion that it is the same as that of the remaining good angels. (For Dante's previous opinion on a related matter, see the note to *Paradiso* XXIX.50.) Landino concludes that only God knows the number of angels, as Aquinas says.

118–142. This passage is seamless, a single action, Dante's raising his eyes (verse 118) at Bernard's command and seeing Mary, surrounded by angels and admired by the rest of the blessed. It is like a painting of the Virgin seated in glory. However, since it is only *like* a painting, the poet introduces his central scene with a double simile, each element of which begins "e come."

Until now, we have been shown the Empyrean with a long-range perspective, seeing all the Rose as a unit divided into many parts. Now we focus on a single part of it and are presented with a new sense of graduated selectivity, in which the things that are nearest Mary are brightest, while those farthest from her gradually fade from view.

118–123. The first simile pairs Mary with the brightness of the Sun at its rising, as compared with the entire rim of the sky. We are asked to imagine a 360° view: The east and the parts of the horizon nearest it are brightest, the west, where the Sun lit up the horizon the evening before, the darkest. As we will see, this arrangement is perfectly mirrored in the varying brightness of parts of the Rose.

124–129. In the second simile, the brightness at the *locus* of the rising Sun is contrasted with the diminished light on either side of it, and is compared either to all the Rose or to Mary (see the note to verse 127).

Once again, as in the first of these conjoined similes (vv. 118–123), the varied lightness in parts of the Rose is insisted on.

124. Rhyme forces Dante into synecdoche, the part *temo* (yoke-beam, or chariot-pole [i.e., that to which the horses are attached]) for the whole (chariot). For other occurrences of this word (*timone* in modern Italian), see *Purgatorio* XXII.119; XXXII.49, 140, 144; *Paradiso* XIII.9.

125. We last heard of Phaeton, a frequent presence in the poem, in *Paradiso* XVII.3 (see the note to XVII.1–6). Why Dante wants to recall that tragic adventure here is not immediately evident.

127. This arresting oxymoron, "peaceful oriflamme" (or "battle flag of peace"), has a varied history in the commentaries. Most trace its origin to the French royal battle standard. Scott (Scot.2002.1), p. 488, points out that, whereas many contemporary commentators say that this banner of the French kings, maintained at St. Denis, was red, it was actually red and gold, as its Latin derivation makes plain (*auri fiamma* [golden flame]). See Oelsner's brief exposition (comm. to this verse), which, however, reverses the more usual relations between the red and the gold: "The Oriflamme (*aurea flamma*) was the standard given by the Angel Gabriel to the ancient kings of France, representing a [red] flame on a golden ground. No one who fought under it could be conquered. The golden glow of heaven is the invincible ensign not of war but peace."

Most who write about this verse play up the opposed values of the two elements in this image, Mary's peaceful conquest as opposed to the French (or any) king's military exploits. However, we should remember that this gathering, too, is an army, if now a triumphant one, with all but a final battle (that of the returning Christ against Antichrist at the end of days) behind it. (For a view in absolute disagreement with this one, see Porena [comm. to this verse].) While there is some dispute about whether the *oriafiamma* is Mary alone, all the Rose (including her), or some portion of the blessed souls distinct from her, see Trucchi (comm. to vv. 124–129) for an interesting solution. The *oriafiamma* is the entire Rose, Mary is the golden flame, the rest of the blessed (the petals of the "rose") the red background. While this is not in accord with the minority explanation of what is figure, what background, it surely is worth serious consideration for its complete explanation of all the elements in the image. However, it is clear that Mary is the light referred to as the Sun in both similes. She is at the center (*nel mezzo*) of things as the protagonist now sees them.

130–132. Around Mary, the central object in this picture, the protagonist sees an assemblage of angels, apparently of all nine orders, since they seem differentiated from one another in how bright they shine and in what they do.

136–138. The *topos* of the inexpressibility of great beauty, now that it is no longer needed for Beatrice (see the note to *Par.* XXX.22–27), is made to accompany Mary.

137. Dante's verb *imaginar* (referring to the mind's ability to receive and store images received from outside it) is quite different from the more modern instance of the word, with its clear reference to invention of things not previously seen by the imaginer. See the note to *Purgatorio* XVII.13–18.

139–142. The canto concludes with Bernard, famous as the "lover-poet" of Mary, gazing, alongside her newest "lover-poet," Dante Alighieri. His awareness of Bernard's affection for her makes his own all the more ardent.

For a recent discussion of whether or not Dante is to be considered "a mystic," see Botterill (Bott.2003.1), who is mainly in the affirmative. It is difficult to believe that the final cantos of the poem, so obviously reflective of a great mystic, St. Bernard, and so triumphantly presenting a final vision, can be thought of as separate from the tradition of Western mysticism. At the same time, it is difficult to think of the earlier ninety-seven cantos of the poem as being essentially mystical in character. Thus the best answer seems to be "no" and "yes"—in that order. But see Scott (Scot.2004.2), pp. 407–8, for a cautious denial of even this much mysticism in Dante's poetry. One supposes that some (who find Dante's poetry more like Blake's than not) think of him as a mystic, while others (who do not so find) deny that he is one.

140. The phrase *fissi e attenti* (fixed and intent) is repeated here for the third time. We heard it first in *Purgatorio* II.118, used *in malo*, for Dante and the newly arrived souls who are seduced by Casella's song and require Cato's reprimand in order to get back on their path toward God. It then appears in *Purgatorio* XXXII.1, where it describes Dante's gaze, fixed on Beatrice, trying to slake his ten-year "thirst" for her presence. That repetition was perhaps intended to counter the first instance, the context of which was the song that Dante had composed in favor of Beatrice's rival, the Lady Philosophy (her identity at least according to the *Convivio* [first at II.xii.9]). Now it is used a second time *in bono*, here referring to Dante's new "lady," the Virgin. Unlike the last one, this ocular gesture does not reflect the rejection of one lady in favor of another. In Heaven there may be no marrying, but there is no limit to the number of objects of one's affection.

PARADISO XXXII

OUTLINE

THE EMPYREAN

1–3 Bernard, still fixed on (1) **Mary**, assumes the role of teacher and names some inhabitants of Paradise:
4–6 (2) [**Eve**] (her original sin sealed and healed by Mary)
7–9 (3) **Rachel** and (4) **Beatrice**
10–12 (5) **Sarah,** (6) **Rebecca,** (7) **Judith**, and [**David**]'s great-grandmother, (8) [**Ruth**]
13–15 moving downward in the "petals" of the rose
16–24 from Ruth on down more Hebrew women marking off the OT side of the rose, those who believed in Christ to come;
25–27 the NT side, where there are vacancies, in Christ come
28–33 and where we see (9) **John the Baptist** in the first tier;
34–36 (10) **Francis,** (11) **Benedict,** (12) **Augustine**, and others;
37–39 God's providence seen in so equal a division of the Rose;
40–48 all the lower half is children, saved by merit of others
49–51 Bernard sees that Dante is confused about this merit
52–66 Bernard: "Differences here reflect not merit but grace;
67–75 "think of [**Jacob** and **Esau**]; all these children are sorted not by their works but by their capacity to see God:
76–78 "from [**Adam to Abraham**]: faith of parents saved them
79–81 "from Abraham to Christ: circumcision
82–84 "from Christ to now: baptism
85–87 "look on the face [Mary's] that most resembles Christ's";
88–93 this greatest similarity to God yet experienced by Dante
94–99 an angel [**Gabriel**] opens his wings and sings; the court of Heaven, replying, sings in rapture
100–106 Dante replies: gratitude and a question (about the angel)
107–108 simile: morning star to sun as Bernard to Mary

109–114 Bernard identifies Gabriel (still by periphrasis)
115–117 Bernard continues to identify the blessed:
118–126 **(13) [Adam], (14) [Peter]**
127–132 **(15) [John], (16) [Moses]**
133–135 **(17) Anne**
136–138 **(18) Lucy**
139 Bernard: "Since the time before your rapture grows short
140–141 (simile) "we must stop, as a tailor prepares his cloth;
142–144 "it is now time to penetrate God's effulgence;
145–150 "for that, prayer to Mary is necessary; you should rehearse my words within you."
151 Bernard's prayer:

PARADISO XXXII

Affetto al suo piacer, quel contemplante
libero officio di dottore assunse,
e cominciò queste parole sante:

"La piaga che Maria richiuse e unse,
quella ch'è tanto bella da' suoi piedi
è colei che l'aperse e che la punse.

Ne l'ordine che fanno i terzi sedi,
siede Rachel di sotto da costei
con Bëatrice, sì come tu vedi.

Sarra e Rebecca, Iudìt e colei
che fu bisava al cantor che per doglia
del fallo disse *'Miserere mei,'*

puoi tu veder così di soglia in soglia
giù digradar, com' io ch'a proprio nome
vo per la rosa giù di foglia in foglia.

E dal settimo grado in giù, sì come
infino ad esso, succedono Ebree,
dirimendo del fior tutte le chiome;

perché, secondo lo sguardo che fée
la fede in Cristo, queste sono il muro
a che si parton le sacre scalee.

Da questa parte onde 'l fiore è maturo
di tutte le sue foglie, sono assisi
quei che credettero in Cristo venturo;

da l'altra parte onde sono intercisi
di vòti i semicirculi, si stanno
quei ch'a Cristo venuto ebber li visi.

Absorbed in his delight, that man of contemplation
took upon himself the teacher's role
and spoke these holy words:

'The wound that Mary closed up and anointed
was opened and inflicted
by the lovely woman now at Mary's feet.

'Below her, in the order
formed by the third tier of the seats,
as you can see, Rachel sits with Beatrice.

'Sarah and Rebecca, Judith and she—
great-grandmother of that singer who,
grieving for his sin, cried: *"Miserere mei"*—

'may be seen there, one beneath the other,
in their ordered ranks, while I, pausing for each name,
move petal by petal down through the rose.

'And downward from the seventh tier, or up,
parting all the petals of this flower,
are the appointed seats of Hebrew women.

'For, according to whether in their faith
they looked forward to Christ or back,
this is the wall that separates the sacred tiers.

'On this side, where the flower is in fullest bloom
with all its petals, those are seated
who believed in Christ as yet to come.

'On the other side, where the semicircles
are interspersed with vacant spaces, are seated
those who kept their eyes on Christ already come.

E come quinci il glorïoso scanno
de la donna del cielo e li altri scanni
di sotto lui cotanta cerna fanno,

così di contra quel del gran Giovanni,
che sempre santo 'l diserto e 'l martiro
sofferse, e poi l'inferno da due anni;

e sotto lui così cerner sortiro
Francesco, Benedetto e Augustino
e altri fin qua giù di giro in giro.

Or mira l'alto proveder divino:
ché l'uno e l'altro aspetto de la fede
igualmente empierà questo giardino.

E sappi che dal grado in giù che fiede
a mezzo il tratto le due discrezioni,
per nullo proprio merito si siede,

ma per l'altrui, con certe condizioni:
ché tutti questi son spiriti asciolti
prima ch'avesser vere elezïoni.

Ben te ne puoi accorger per li volti
e anche per le voci püerili,
se tu li guardi bene e se li ascolti.

Or dubbi tu e dubitando sili;
ma io disciogilerò 'l forte legame
in che ti stringon li pensier sottili.

Dentro a l'ampiezza di questo reame
casüal punto non puote aver sito,
se non come tristizia o sete o fame:

ché per etterna legge è stabilito
quantunque vedi, sì che giustamente
ci si risponde da l'anello al dito;

'And just as here the glorious seat
of heaven's lady and the other seats beneath it
30 form that long dividing line,

'so, opposite, does that of the exalted soul of John,
who, holy since his birth, endured the wilderness
33 and martyrdom, and then two years of Hell.

'Below him, and continuing that line,
sit Francis, Benedict, Augustine, and others,
36 assigned as far as this, down from tier to tier.

'Now behold the depth of God's foreseeing,
for both the ways of showing faith
39 shall fill this garden equally.

'And know that downward from the row
that midway cuts the two dividing lines
42 the seats are held by those who had no merit of their own,

'but through deserving others, under fixed conditions,
were freed from sin, for all of these are spirits
45 released before they exercised free choice.

'This, indeed, you may discover for yourself
from their faces and their childish voices,
48 if you look at them with care and if you listen.

'Now you are perplexed and silent in perplexity.
Let me untie the complicated knot
51 in which your oversubtle thoughts have bound you.

'In all the ample range of this domain
no trace of chance can find a place—
54 no more than sorrow, thirst, or hunger,

'for all you see here is ordained by law eternal,
so that the circling ring here fits
57 the finger that was meant for it.

e però questa festinata gente
a vera vita non è *sine causa*
intra sé qui più e meno eccellente.

Lo rege per cui questo regno pausa
in tanto amore e in tanto diletto,
che nulla volontà è di più ausa,

le menti tutte nel suo lieto aspetto
creando, a suo piacer di grazia dota
diversamente; e qui basti l'effetto.

E ciò espresso e chiaro vi si nota
ne la Scrittura santa in quei gemelli
che ne la madre ebber l'ira commota.

Però, secondo il color d'i capelli,
di cotal grazia l'altissimo lume
degnamente convien che s'incappelli.

Dunque, sanza mercé di lor costume,
locati son per gradi differenti,
sol differendo nel primiero acume.

Bastavasi ne' secoli recenti
con l'innocenza, per aver salute,
solamente la fede d'i parenti;

poi che le prime etadi fuor compiute,
convenne ai maschi a l'innocenti penne
per circuncidere acquistar virtute;

ma poi che 'l tempo de la grazia venne,
sanza battesmo perfetto di Cristo
tale innocenza là giù si ritenne.

Riguarda omai ne la faccia che a Cristo
più si somiglia, ché la sua chiarezza
sola ti può disporre a veder Cristo."

'Thus, the company of those who prematurely
came to this true life are not *sine causa*
placed more and less exalted here among themselves.

'The King, through whom this kingdom rests
in love so great and in so great delight
their will would never dare to ask for more,

'creating every mind in His own bliss,
variously bestows His grace and as He pleases—
and, in this case, let the fact suffice.

'This is clearly and expressly noted for you
by Holy Scripture in the account of twins
who, still in their mother's womb, were moved to wrath.

'Therefore, according to the color of the hair
bestowed with so much grace, the Sovereign Light
will crown them with their fitting aureoles.

'Not for what they've done or have not done
they thus are placed in separate ranks, separated
only by the keenness of the vision they were born to.

'In early times their parents' faith alone,
coupled with the innocence that they possessed,
gave sufficient proof of their salvation.

'Once the first age had run its course,
male children had to find the strength
for innocent wings in circumcision.

'But once the time of grace had come,
then, without perfect baptism in Christ,
such innocents were cast below.

'Look now on the face that most resembles Christ,
for nothing but its brightness
can make you fit to look on Christ.'

Ïo vidi sopra lei tanta allegrezza
piover, portata ne le menti sante
create a trasvolar per quella altezza,

che quantunque io avea visto davante,
di tanta ammirazion non mi sospese,
né mi mostrò di Dio tanto sembiante;

e quello amor che primo lì discese,
cantando *"Ave, Maria, gratïa plena,"*
dinanzi a lei le sue ali distese.

Rispuose a la divina cantilena
da tutte parti la beata corte,
si ch'ogne vista sen fé più serena.

"O santo padre, che per me comporte
l'esser qua giù, lasciando il dolce loco
nel qual tu siedi per etterna sorte,

qual è quell' angel che con tanto gioco
guarda ne li occhi la nostra regina,
innamorato sì che par di foco?"

Così ricorsi ancora a la dottrina
di colui ch'abbelliva di Maria,
come del sole stella mattutina.

Ed elli a me: "Baldezza e leggiadria
quant' esser puote in angelo e in alma,
tutta è in lui; e sì volem che sia,

perch' elli è quelli che portò la palma
giuso a Maria, quando 'l Figliuol di Dio
carcar si volse de la nostra salma.

Ma vieni omai con li occhi sì com' io
andrò parlando, e nota i gran patrici
di questo imperio giustissimo e pio.

I saw such joy rain down on her,
conveyed within the minds and borne
by holy spirits framed to soar those heights,

that, however much I had seen before,
nothing had held me in such wonder and suspense,
nor shown me so close a likeness to God,

and the loving spirit that had first descended,
singing *'Ave Maria, gratia plena'*
hovered before her with his wings outspread.

From every side the blessèd court all sang,
responding to the solemn sacred chant,
so that each face became more luminous with joy.

'O holy father, who on my behalf
deign to be here below, leaving the sweet place
where by eternal lot you have your seat,

'who is the angel gazing with such joy
upon the eyes of her our Queen,
so much in love he seems to be a flame?'

Thus I tried once more to gain instruction
from him who glowed in Mary's beauty
as the morning star reflects the sun.

And he: 'All confidence and grace of movement
that can be found in angel or in any blessèd soul
are found in him—and we would have it so,

'for it is he who brought the palm to Mary
when the Son of God elected to take on
the burden of our flesh.

'But let your eyes follow my words, as I continue,
noting the eminent patricians
of this most just and pious empire.

Quei due che seggon là sù più felici
per esser propinquissimi ad Agusta,
son d'esta rosa quasi due radici:

colui che da sinistra le s'aggiusta
è 'l padre per lo cui ardito gusto
l'umana specie tanto amaro gusta;

dal destro vedi quel padre vetusto
di Santa Chiesa a cui Cristo le chiavi
raccomandò di questo fior venusto.

E quei che vide tutti i tempi gravi,
pria che morisse, de la bella sposa
che s'acquistò con la lancia e coi clavi,

siede lungh' esso, e lungo l'altro posa
quel duca sotto cui visse di manna
la gente ingrata, mobile e retrosa.

Di contr' a Pietro vedi sedere Anna,
tanto contenta di mirar sua figlia,
che non move occhio per cantare osanna;

e contro al maggior padre di famiglia
siede Lucia, che mosse la tua donna
quando chinavi, a rovinar, le ciglia.

Ma perché 'l tempo fugge che t'assonna,
qui farem punto, come buon sartore
che com' elli ha del panno fa la gonna;

e drizzeremo li occhi al primo amore,
sì che, guardando verso lui, penètri
quant' è possibil per lo suo fulgore.

Veramente, *ne* forse tu t'arretri
movendo l'ali tue, credendo oltrarti,
orando grazia conven che s'impetri

'These two who are seated there above us,
most happy for being so near the Empress,
are, as it were, the two roots of this rose:

'He who sits beside her to her left
is that father for whose reckless tasting
mankind still tastes such bitterness.

'To her right behold that ancient father
of Holy Church to whose care Christ entrusted
the keys to this, the fairest flower.

'And he who was doomed to see before he died
the years of grief of the beautiful bride,
she who was won with the lance and the nails,

'sits next to him and, next to the other, rests
that leader under whose rule that stiff-necked people,
fickle and ungrateful, lived on manna.

'Look at Anna, where she sits across from Peter,
so content merely to gaze upon her daughter
she does not move her eyes as she sings hosanna.

'And opposite the greatest father of a family
sits Lucy, who urged on your lady, when
with eyes cast down, you headed on your path to ruin.

'But since the time runs short that readies you for sleep,
let us stop here, as a good tailor would,
who cuts the cloak as he is stocked with cloth.

'And let us fix our eyes on Primal Love,
so that, looking up toward Him, you penetrate,
as far as may be done, His brilliance.

'But, lest by any chance, beating your wings
and thinking to advance, you should fall back,
you must gain your grace through prayer,

grazia da quella che puote aiutarti;
e tu mi seguirai con l'affezione,
sì che dal dicer mio lo cor non parti."
E cominciò questa santa orazione:

'grace from her who has the power to help you.
You shall follow me with your devotion
so your heart does not stray from my words.'
151 He then began this holy supplication:

1. The opening verse of this canto has caused considerable difficulty. Without reviewing the various responses (for which see Scartazzini [comm. to this verse]), we should say that we have followed fairly freely Scartazzini's basic understanding, which takes "affetto" as being, here, a Latinism, formed out of the past participle (*adfectus*) of the deponent verb *adficior* (influence), and thus, loosely here, "intent upon" or "absorbed in." As for the noun *piacer*, we take it here not as "beauty" but as Bernard's "delight" in Mary. See also Tozer (comm. to vv. 1–2).

Perhaps the most compelling gloss to this opening word of the canto is found in Aversano's commentary (Aver.2000.2), p. 165. He, as did several modern commentators before him (e.g., Mestica and Mattalia [comms. to this verse]), traces the source of *affetto* to the past participle of the verb *afficere*, with the resulting sense of being affixed, or conjoined. Aversano attributes this sense of the word to St. Bernard on two occasions (*PL* CLXXXIII.1297, CLXXXIII.1384).

2–3. Porena (comm. to vv. 1–2) suggests that Bernard does not interrupt his personal adoration of Mary in order to carry out his new responsibility, as *doctor* (teacher), but names the inhabitants of the Rose from memory. This task, along with allied concerns, will occupy vv. 4–87 of the canto.

As Aversano points out, the adjective *santo* (holy) occurs more often in this canto than in any other. In fact, it occurs here seven times.

4–18. For discussion of Dante's choice of the Hebrew women he included in the Rose, see Di Scipio (Disc.1983.2). See also the remarks of Carroll (comm. to vv. 8–10).

4–6. Dante's use of the trope *hysteron proteron* is widely noticed. It offers an "instant replay" run backward, undoing the universal effect of the wound of Original Sin, incurred by Eve's eating of the forbidden fruit, when Mary gave birth to Jesus. Mary's position in the Rose, seated with Eve at her feet, reinforces that understanding.

8. Jacob's first and second wives, Leah and Rachel, as we saw in *Purgatorio* XXVII.100–108, represent (as they were traditionally understood as doing) the active and the contemplative life, respectively. Aversano

(Aver.2000.2), p. 166, points out that, according to Richard of St. Victor, in his *Benjamin major* (*PL* CXCVI.62), Rachel, as the first stage of contemplation, *dilatatio* (expansion), an identity she shares with Beatrice, yields to the second stage, represented by the son she died giving birth to, Benjamin, or *sublevatio* (i.e., being raised up), who has a counterpart in the poem, of course, in Bernard, Dante's Benjamin. That state in turn yields to *alienatio* (ecstasy), the passing beyond human limits to experience things as they are in themselves, absolute reality. Aversano also cites *PL* CXCVI.52 and CXCVI.170.

9. Beatrice is "out of pattern" with the crossing vertical and horizontal elements. This perhaps indicates that such an idiosyncratic pattern is meant to reflect the individual identity of the beholder. It thus results that Dante is like everyone else in being uniquely unlike everyone else, an only apparently paradoxical insight later developed centrally by Michel de Montaigne.

It does not seem to have caught the attention of any commentator that Beatrice's name appears in the ninth verse of the canto, that is, accompanied by her identifying (and trinitarian) number. Beatrice is named here for the sixty-second time. (For the last, see *Par.* XXXIII.38. Her name thus occurs over a span of ninety-nine cantos [her first nominal appearance is in *Inf.* II.70].) See the note to *Purgatorio* XV.77.

Costa (Cost.1996.1), p. 70, makes a telling point: Beatrice's presence in the Rose scotches any attempt to conclude that her status in the poem is merely "allegorical."

10. Sarah, Rebecca, and Judith were among the Old Testament heroines harrowed by Christ. Sarah was the wife of Abraham and mother of Isaac; Rebecca, the wife of Isaac and mother of Jacob; Judith, the savior of the Jews from Assyrian captivity when she murdered Holofernes (see *Purg.* XII.58–60).

11–12. Ruth is identified only by periphrasis and in her role as the great-grandmother of David, also indicated by periphrasis. He is represented by his sins of adultery and murder (Bathsheba and Uriah), the setting for Psalm 50 (51), *Miserere mei* (Have mercy on me), which served as the text of Dante's first spoken words as character in the poem (*Inf.* I.65). For the meaning of David for Dante, see the notes to *Purgatorio* X.65 and *Paradiso* XX.37–39. And see Carroll's discussion of a common theme behind at least most of Dante's choices (comm. to vv. 1–48), which offers another reason for the reference to David: "[T]hey were all regarded as types of the Church, and they are for the most part ancestresses of Christ according to the flesh (Rachel and Judith alone are not in the direct line of our Lord's ancestry. Judah, through whom the descent flows, was a son of Leah; and Judith had no children [Judith 16:22]): Ruth, for example, is described as the *bisava*, the great grandmother, of David, for the purpose, apparently, of indicating the descent of the Virgin, and therefore of her Son, from that king. The manner in which David is referred to—'the singer who for sorrow of his sin said *Miserere Mei*' (Ps. 51 [50]:1)—while apparently irrelevant to the question of descent, is in reality closely connected with it. Matthew 1:6 states plainly that 'David the king begat Solomon of her that had been the wife of Urias.' The reference therefore to David's repentance for his great sin, so far from being irrelevant, suggests in the most delicate way the continuation of the descent through Solomon."

13–15. Bernard indicates many more saints than we actually hear him name; therefore, we probably assume, the poet's selection of the eighteen who are named is not casually arrived at.

16–21. These Hebrew women, the seven whom we have just heard referred to by name or by periphrasis, are only the beginning of a long line down the Rose (until we would come to the first Hebrew female child, we assume) that separates pre-Christian and Christian saints. As Aversano (Aver.2000.2), p. 166, points out, neither Eve (obviously not a descendant of Abraham) nor Ruth (who was from Moab) can properly be considered Hebrews, despite Dante's insistence.

Singleton (comm. to vv. 40–42) believes that Dante intends us to believe that the dividing "walls" of Hebrew women and Christian men reach all the way to the "floor" of the Rose, and that thus the lower half of them are surrounded by babies. That seems a dubious notion, although Dante does not clearly portray the situation. If "neatness counts," he may have expected us to imagine a line of smiling Hebrew female babies looking across the Rose at equally happy Christian male babies, while spreading out to either side of those two lines are babies of the other gender, the first half of them of their own religion, the second group of the other. (See the third item in the note to vv. 37–39.)

25–33. Dante once again insists on the absence of some saints-to-be in the Christian half of the Rose (the only place for which he specifies the eventual tenant is the throne destined for Henry VII [see the conclusion of *Par.*

XXX]). He also refers to semicircles in order to alert us to the fact that there will be a matching descending line, one composed entirely of males, beneath John the Baptist. To Mary's left and John's right sit the Hebrew saints; to her right and to his left, the Christian ones. It is not stated, but seems clear, that we are to picture two *different* semicircles, with the midpoint of their arcs located at Mary and John, containing male saints (beneath Mary) and female saints (beneath John), except for the bisecting line, which is gendered as is each of them. See the chart in the note to vv. 37–39.

31. John's epithet *gran* (exalted) reflects, in the opinion of a great number of commentators, beginning with Scartazzini (comm. to this verse), Matthew 11:11: "[A]mong those born of women there has arisen no one greater than John the Baptist."

32–33. For John's holiness, see Luke 1:15: "and he will be filled with the Holy Spirit, even from his mother's womb"; for his martyrdom, see Matthew 14:3–12, Herod's beheading of John; for his period in Limbo before he was harrowed, see Tommaseo (comm. to vv. 31–33), being more precise: "between twenty and twenty-one months."

34–36. If Dante's treatment of Augustine remains one of the most puzzling aspects of his poem, he himself is to blame; he seems deliberately to conceal his debt to Augustine (see the note to *Par.* XII.130). Once Dante studies became more "scientific," in the nineteenth century, we might have expected that a great "detective" of Dante's reading habits, Edward Moore, would have started to set things right in this respect. However, when he takes up this subject in *Scripture* and *Classical Authors in Dante* (Moor.1896.1), pp. 291–94, he is both tentative and hesitant, lest he overstate the importance of Augustine to Dante. Here are his concluding words (p. 294): "I must confess, in conclusion, that I have not been able as yet to investigate the question of Dante's probable acquaintance with the works of St. Augustine nearly as fully as the subject seems to deserve. I am continually coming on fresh points of resemblance. There is, however, always this element of uncertainty, that many of his theories or arguments are reproduced by Aquinas, . . ." One does not want to blame Moore for the general underappreciation of Augustine's importance for Dante. Nonetheless, the great scholar's hesitance undoubtedly affected others, who felt excused thereby from studying the problem as carefully as it "seems to deserve." For better appreciations, if not the central study that is still badly needed, see Mazzoni (Mazz.1967.1), passim; Newman

(Newm.1967.1); Fallani (Fall.1976.1); Freccero (Frec.1986.1), especially pp. 1–15; Mazzotta (Mazz.1979.1), esp. pp. 147–91; Wingell (Wing. 1981.1); Took (Took.1990.1); Hawkins (Hawk.1991.2). Like Hawkins, Sarteschi (Sart.1999.1) believes that there is a widespread and often unacknowledged interaction between the texts of Augustine and those of Dante.

Augustine knew that imperial Virgil had to be resisted publicly and spiritedly, and yet he makes his *Confessions* a sort of epic Mediterranean countervoyage (see Hollander [Holl.1969.1], p. 12 and n.), in which the pivotal municipal moment occurs not in an imperial monument in Rome but in a church in Milan. And if the text is seemingly a-Virgilian, even anti-Virgilian, it is nonetheless studded with Virgilian references. If that sounds suggestive of Dante's later treatment of Virgil in his Christian epic, the differences are perhaps not so very great.

See the note to *Paradiso* XII.130 for discussion of the appearance of Augustine's name (but not the saint) in *Paradiso* X and XII. And see Seem (Seem.2006.1), p. 82, pointing out that these two nominal presences arouse our expectations, but when Augustine finally does appear (*Par.* XXXII.35), he is only a word from hitting the cutting-room floor, as it were, to be included, unbeknownst to us, among the unnamed others (*e altri*) seated in the Rose. This close call (and Dante's playful game with the reader over Augustine's fate in the Dantean afterworld) may possibly be explained by the fact of Augustine's strenuous opposition to the imperial (and republican) Roman ideal. Thus the Augustinian tale of two cities, which extols the City of God and its embattled earthly precursor, the Church Militant, but has no room for the empire in its worldview, is the work of an enemy. There is no question but that Dante knew Augustine's work and admired it deeply—as theology, but even as theology only up to a point, for that theology permeates his historical vision, and vice versa. And the point that divides these two thinkers is Rome.

35. See Bosco/Reggio (comm. to this verse): Dominic is not here only because his Order used the Augustinian Rule and the three others mentioned here, Augustine, Benedict, and Francis (to name them in chronological order), each composed the Rule for his Order. Others have tried to wrestle with the apparently slighting omission of reference to Dominic here, made all the more troublesome by the fact that in *Convivio* (IV.xxviii.9), Dante refers to Benedict, Augustine, Francis, and Dominic (in that order). There they are exemplars of the religious life. Among the early commentators, only Francesco da Buti apparently felt that the omis-

sion required comment. He revisits Thomas's insistence (*Par.* XI.40–42) that what is said in praise of one (Francis) is to be understood equally of the other (Dominic). The few others who tackle the problem do not suggest more convincing hypotheses than that offered by Bosco/Reggio.

36. From Bernard's remark at vv. 14–15, where he says that he will name many other saints in the line descending from Mary, we surely assume that this line beneath the Baptist, probably composed of other religious leaders, was also identified, but not reported. See the note to vv. 13–15.

37–39. John Carroll (comm. to vv. 1–48) was perhaps the first to claim that the arrangement of the named souls might have an iconographical effect: "It is not likely to be accidental that the Rose is thus blessed with the sign of the Cross on each side." The design formed in the Rose by those who are named is possibly reminiscent of the T or *tau*, the emblem of the cross so important in the iconography of St. Francis, as Fleming, among others, has demonstrated (Flem.1982.1), pp. 99–128. Francis knew that Ezechiel (9:4) had said that the faithful would all be marked with the *tau* on their foreheads and took it as his particular version of the sign of the cross.

When we consider the saints in the order they are named (the numeration is provided in the diagram below), our sense of that is reinforced, since the poet first fills up the I-stem of the figure (plus the idiosyncratic adjunct of Beatrice, for which see the note to verse 9), then arranges the bar of the T in a chiasmus (15-14-13-16), and then finally adds its foot, chronologically ordered (Anne, then Lucy).

John Evang. (15)	Peter (14)	Mary (1)	Adam (13)	Moses (16)
		Eve (2)		
	Beatrice (4)	Rachel (3)		
		Sarah (5)		
		Rebecca (6)		
		Judith (7)		
		Ruth (8)		
		Augustine (12)		
		Benedict (11)		
		Francis (10)		
	Lucy (18)	John Bapt. (9)	Anne (17)	

Montanari (Mont.1974.1), p. 256, points out the symmetries in the arrangement of this seating plan of Heaven; the stadium is divided into corresponding zones by the following six groups, further sorted into three pairs: Old Testament, New Testament; Men, Women (both of these groups on horizontal axes); Adults, Infants (on a vertical axis).

Since our subject is Dante, it will come as no surprise to the reader to learn that even this diagram (above) is controversial. While there is consensus among some, perhaps expressed in the clearest and briefest terms by Pernicone (Pern. 1965.1), p. 109, there is a surprising amount of disagreement over what seems close to self-evident. Among the issues found variously among the discussants are the following: (1) Do the indications "left" and "right" (vv. 121–124) indicate directions from the protagonist's perspective or from (respectively) the Virgin's and John's? (2) Does Dante consider Lucy and Anne as figures who should be present in the "Christian" or "Jewish" section of the Rose, and has he botched his placement of them as a result? (3) How many rows are there in this celestial stadium?

(1) There are intensely held views on either side of this issue. For a discussion of these, see Russi (Russ.1968.1), pp. 1176–87, who devotes a major portion of his *lectura* to a labored attempt at resolving the directional indications in the canto. Picone (Pico.2002.8), p. 494, is matter-of-fact in declaring that we are seeing them from the perspective of *Dante's* left and right. Such a view would require that the reader imagine the post-Advent saints as seated to Mary's left, and those pre-Advent to her right. It is true that the poet does not make their disposition clear, leaving us to deal with the question. On the other hand, placing the New Testament figures to Mary's left would seem an implausible choice. God would not be so rude a host to these heroes of Christianity in forming His Eternal Seating Plan.

(2) The question of the arrangement of the two souls on either side of John the Baptist (see vv. 133–138) has also been strangely controversial. Several commentators contrive to put Lucy to John's right, believing her a pre-Christian figure. Russi (Russ.1968.1), p. 1187, accepting this arrangement, goes on to argue that she is not the historical Lucy, but a symbol of illuminating grace. (It is surprising how long it was until a commentator treated Lucy as historical, the third-century martyr from Syracuse; the first appears to have been Portirelli [comm. to vv. 136–141] in the early nineteenth century. Did his precursors really believe that Dante had granted an allegory a seat in Heaven, in which it would eventually wear its own flesh?) The situation barely improves in more recent times, when, even after Lucy of Syracuse has entered the commentary tradition, some moderns revert to the age-old error.

(3) Picone (Pico.2002.8), p. 495, discussing verses 16–18, which enumerate the seven levels of the stadium down from Mary through Ruth, goes on to extrapolate from that passage an erroneous supposition,

namely, that there are only that many rows in the upper half of the Rose. From that assumption he (only logically) calculates that the lower half (the kindergarten, as it were) must be comprised of the same number of rows (seven). However, what we know does not accord easily with his hypothesis. See, for the vast upward expanse of the Rose, *Paradiso* XXX.115–118 and XXXI.73–75 (where we learn that Beatrice, not even in the highest rank of the Rose, is at a distance even greater than that between the lowest point on earth and the farthest reach of its atmosphere). If we were to accept Picone's calculations, we would have to understand that a mere twelve rows of the Rose rose upward in that vast a space. (Not to be preferred are other attempts at numerical precision, even if they seem properly more grandiose. See, for instance, Russi, p. 1169, citing G. Barone in 1906 as having calculated the rows as numbering 1,290.) Indeed, the text itself makes it quite clear that there are more Hebrew women beneath Ruth, forming the dividing line. (What it doesn't tell us is whether the line stops at the halfway mark [see the note to vv. 40–48] to be continued by female Hebrew babies, or whether, as at least Singleton believes, it goes all the way to the Rose's "floor" [see the note to vv. 16–21]). Further, if Dante accepted, at least as an approximate guide, the canonical 144,000 who make up the citizenry of the Empyrean (see the notes to *Par.* XXX.103–108 and *Par.* XXXI.115–117), Picone's fourteen rows would each need to seat more than ten thousand souls. To be fair, he was led to this view by his arguably possible interpretation of the word *soglie* (either "seats" or "tiers"; he chooses the former). That, however, is to neglect the clear significance of the word *soglia* at *Paradiso* XVIII.28, which clearly illuminates the next use of the word at verse 13 of this canto; in both these uses Dante is fairly obviously referring to "rows" and not individual "seats." Perhaps the rhyme position helps explain the use he made of an expanded meaning of the word.

Other, if less noticed, problems about the population of the Rose are caused by the location of Beatrice's presence in it. This is obviously idiosyncratic to this particular viewer, since it is the only element not part of a balanced design. And, compounding that problem, her placement itself seems to be problematic, out of order. From what we are nearly forced to extrapolate from the arrangement seen in the top row, the center lines divide male from female on both sides of the Rose. Thus Beatrice should be next to a male (e.g., Benedict). Iconography apparently trumped the boy-girl ordering principle in Dante's mind. Further, he had boxed himself into this arrangement in *Inferno* II.102, where Beatrice says that Lucy came to her in Heaven where she was seated next to Rachel. In any case, there does not seem to be a way around the fact that in placing Beatrice next to

Rachel, Dante has violated his own unstated but clearly formulated rules. The following arrangement is based on the left-right axis as provided for in item (1), above.

TOP RIGHT QUADRANT		TOP LEFT QUADRANT
Christian males	Hebrew females	Hebrew males
Christian male infants?	Hebrew female infants?	Hebrew male infants?
	"FLOOR"	
Christian female infants?	Christian male infants?	Hebrew female infants?
Christian females	Christian males	Hebrew females
BOTTOM RIGHT QUADRANT		BOTTOM LEFT QUADRANT

38–39. All those commentators who believe that Dante "doesn't mean" what he indicates, that in Heaven for the Last Judgment and general resurrection there will be an equal number of Christians and Hebrews (the latter including only a few gentiles in their number, at least two [see the note to *Par.* XXXI.25–27] and only possibly more), should have to recite these lines aloud before saying anything about the issue.

40–48. Dante now draws another boundary line, this one dividing the "north-south" axis of the Rose into two portions of equal height (though of unequal volume). There are three classes of saved babies, all of whom, because they had not attained the age of reason, died only in their inherited sinfulness (i.e., without positive sin): (1) Jewish infants who somehow shared their parents' faith in Christ to come; (2) Jewish infants whose parents, once circumcision was instituted as a ritual by the Jews, had them circumcised (see the note to vv. 76–81); (3) Christian infants who had the better form of "circumcision," baptism. In real terms, then, the rules for Christian infants were more stringent.

43. The "conditions" referred to indicate, of course, ritual circumcision.

46–48. Dante obviously enjoyed rewarding himself for his strict interpretation of the law of baptism in *Inferno* IV.30, when he agreed with St. Thomas that all unbaptized children will be found in Limbo. Now he sees a multitude of saved infants, and he dwells much longer on them.

See the note to *Paradiso* XXXI.59 for discussion of the presence of these babes not as the adults they should become (according to the standard view), but as the babies they were, back in their sweet flesh. See Nardi (Nard.1944.1), pp. 317–34, for the "age" of the babes in Heaven and other problems associated with their presence here.

49–84. Dante now chooses to deal, at some length, with a knotty problem: Do these sinless and saved innocents appear in the Rose in any meaningful pattern, as do the adults? This matter is set forth and resolved in three parts (vv. 49–60, 61–66, and 67–84).

49–60. *Part I:* Bernard has divined that Dante, observing that these infants seem to be ranked in some sort of preferential order, immediately counters that (true) perception with the perfectly sensible notion that they only *seem* to be ordered by their varying merit, but are in fact merely casually arranged (for how can one distinguish one infant's moral perfection from another's?). In response, he treats his pupil as though he were a balky schoolboy (the reader may understandably feel surprise; we are, after all, very near the final vision).

49. The Latin verb *silere* (to be silent) is the source of Dante's Latinism.

57. The metaphor refers to the hypothesis that lies behind Dante's question. No, Bernard says, there is no possibility, in this realm, of what exists existing without a reason. Thus, if you see gradation, there *is* gradation, and there is a reason for it.

61–66. *Part II:* The second stage of Bernard's response to Dante's unvoiced question is a clear answer: Nothing happens casually here. The reason for His ordering the infants' places as He does is in the mind of God and it is futile to try to fathom His reasons; just accept them. (And it may be particularly difficult to accept the idea that God creates human souls with unequal degrees of ability to know Him.)

67–84. *Part III:* The third and final stage of his response is to give examples of God's other and similar behavior, which might have made it clear even to Dante that His preference for preference has always been manifest in the varying degrees of his grace.

67–75. Dante might have learned, for instance, from the Bible that God loves variously. See Malachi 1:2–3: "Yet I have loved Jacob but Esau I have hated." And this while they were still in the womb. Distinguishing them was not what they have done (they have not *done* anything), but, as it may seem, the color of their hair (Esau; see Genesis 25:25). That is the uncomprehending human view. God sees what we do not, and knows what we do not: the inner sight of our fellow beings. Esau's red and Jacob's black hair were only the outward manifestations of their inner differences, their abilities to know and love God.

76–84. Making clear what was latent in lines 40–48, Bernard now details the "history of grace" for babies, at first their parents' love for Christ to come, then circumcision, and finally (in the age of Christ) baptism.

For the first two of these, see St. Thomas (*ST* III, q. 70, a. 4), cited by Bosco/Reggio (comm. to vv. 76–78): "Ante institutionem circumcisionis fides Christi futuri iustificabat tam pueros quam adultos" (Before the institution of circumcision, faith in Christ to come justified both little children and adults). Bosco/Reggio go on to point out that Thomas (*ST* III, q. 70, a. 2) also holds that Original Sin is passed along through males alone (though it affects all, since our race cannot rely on matrilineal parthenogenesis), which accounts for the emphasis on male circumcision in the second tercet of this passage. However, the rules became more stringent once Christ came, with baptism now mandatory for the salvation of the innocent.

79. Jacopo della Lana (comm. to vv. 79–81) understands that the "age of circumcision" began with Abraham. The author of the Codice Cassinese (comm. to this verse) was the first to understand the reference here as being to the first two ages, from Adam to the Flood, from the Flood to Abraham, some 3,184 years according to him.

83–87. Bernard's lecture ends with the fourth and concluding set of identical rhymes on *Cristo*. See the notes to *Paradiso* XII.71–75 and XIV.103–108.

85–87. This transitional tercet presents the face of Mary as preparation for the final vision of Christ's features in the next canto (verse 131), a stunning detail, suggesting a resemblance both physical for the human side of the

Godhead and spiritual (Mary's perfect purity of soul as the only human worthy of bearing the Christ).

88–93. And now, as a sort of coda to the foregoing "lecture," the angels radiate their pleasure in her down from above to Mary. Gabriel, who had before (see *Par.* XXIII.94–96) descended to reenact the Annunciation, does so once again, spreading his wings as the painters of this scene always show him doing, and singing her song.

95. Gabriel's praise of Mary is the last singing we hear in the poem. (For the program of song in the last *cantica*, see the note to *Par.* XXI.58–60.) If we recall the first parodic references to "hymns" (*Inf.* VII.125) or "songs" (*Inf.* XIX.118) or "psalms" (*Inf.* XXXI.69) to describe antimelodic utterance in Hell, we realize the care with which Dante organized his plan for the "musical score" of the *Commedia*, beginning *in bono* with the first singing heard in *Purgatorio* (II.46–48), the "theme song" of the entire work, Psalm 50, *In Isräel de Aegypto*.

97–99. The assembled choirs of Heaven, angelic and human, share a moment of joy in Mary, both singing and beaming with love.

97. The word *cantilena*, a hapax, would seem to refer specifically to Gabriel's song (although some think it is more general in its reference). The singers would seem to include (although there is some uncertainty about this also) everyone on the scene, all the angels and all the saints, and their response, according to Benvenuto (comm. to vv. 94–99), is both spoken and sung: "cantantes et dicentes Dominus tecum etc." (singing and saying "The Lord be with you," etc.). Francesco da Buti (comm. to vv. 85–99) fills in the "etc." by reciting the full response: "Blessed are you among women, and blessed is the fruit of your womb, Jesus."

Cantilena (at least in Italian) seems to be a coinage of Dante's. It happens that the word is also a hapax in the Vulgate (as Aversano has noted [Aver.2000.2], p. 169), occurring in the following passage of Ecclesiasticus (47:13–18): "Solomon reigned in days of peace, and God gave him rest on every side, that he might build a house for his name and prepare a sanctuary to stand for ever. / How wise you became in your youth! You overflowed like a river with understanding. / Your soul covered the earth, and you filled it with parables and riddles. / Your name reached to far-off islands, and you were loved for your peace. / For your songs [*cantilenis*] and proverbs and parables, and for your interpretations, the countries marveled at you. / In the name of the Lord God, who is called the God of Israel, you gathered gold like tin and amassed silver like lead." Aversano reasonably enough believes that the word *cantilenae* here reflects the songs of Solomon gathered in the *Cantica canticorum*. Thus *cantilena* may have a certain affinity with the last coinage for a God-derived song, *tëodia*, that we heard in *Paradiso* XXV.73, as Mattalia (comm. to verse 97) suggests.

100–102. Dante's last address to Bernard sounds like a conflation of his farewells to Beatrice (*Par.* XXXI.79–81) and to Virgil (*Purg.* XXX.46–51), his first "padre" in the poem. (See the note to *Par.* XVI.16.)

103–105. The protagonist does all of us who need assistance a favor by asking Bernard who that angelic presence was.

107–108. Mary is now presented as the morning star, Venus, a moment that certainly Nietzsche would have to agree is a pronounced "transvaluation of value," even if he might not approve of the result.

109–114. Bernard identifies Gabriel as the angel who carried the palm of victory down to Mary at the Annunciation when Jesus decided to give His life for our salvation. Whose victory? Ours, over death.

115. The three words at the beginning of this verse echo Virgil's similar urgings of Dante to come along in *Inferno* XX.124 and *Purgatorio* IV.137.

116–117. The language is that of imperial Rome ("patricians," "empire") "transvaluated" into Christian terms, or at least terms that are positive in either context: justice and piety, perhaps the values most readily translatable between, in many respects, two very different cultures.

118–120. The two "roots" of the Rose are Adam, "father" of all those who believed in Christ to come, and St. Peter, the first leader of His Church.

For a study in which the Rose is seen as the culmination of the vegetation motif in the poem, see Frankel (Fran.1982.1). Her article studies this motif, from the tree losing its leaves in the simile of *Inferno* III.112–116 through its culmination in the form of a repetaled rose, moving from Virgilian tragedy to Dantean comedy. See also Prandi (Pran.1994.1) for a similar appreciation, if from a different perspective.

119. Calling the Queen of Heaven "Agosta" is a daring "imperializing" touch. The last time we heard the adjective it was in Beatrice's mouth (*Par.*

XXX.136) and described a true emperor, Henry VII. This is perhaps as far as Dante can go in the vein initiated in *Purgatorio* XXXII.102, "that Rome where Christ Himself is Roman."

121–126. Adam and St. Peter each receive a *terzina*, the former the author of our woe, the latter the agent of our redemption as the founder of the Mystical Body of Christ, the Church, which holds the keys to the Kingdom.

121. Benvenuto (comm. to vv. 121–126) says that this verb, *aggiustarsi*, translates the Latin *appropinquare* (to near, approach). It is yet another hapax occurring in rhyme position.

127–129. St. John the Evangelist, who, as author/scribe of the Apocalypse, saw the final tribulations of the Church in his visions on the Isle of Patmos. See Dante's "portrait" of him (*Purg.* XXIX.144), *dormendo, con la faccia arguta* (as though he slept, despite his keen expression). Is this a prefiguration of Dante's visionary experience that is being prepared for in these concluding verses of this canto? See the note to verse 139.

130–132. Three spaces past Peter and next to Adam sits Moses, who led the stiff-necked Israelites (first in Exodus 32:9) through the desert, feeding them on manna (Exodus 16:14–15).

133–135. Diametrically opposite St. Peter sits Anne, the mother of Mary. She is apparently the only occupant of the Rose allowed the special privilege of *not* looking up at God, but across the rim of the stadium at her daughter.

136–138. This is St. Lucy's third appearance in the poem (see *Inf.* II.97 and *Purg.* IX.52–63). Bernard here reminds Dante of the first one, when he was "ruining" downward back toward death (*Inf.* I.61) when Virgil appeared to him, the result of the collaboration of the Virgin, Lucy, and Beatrice (seated at first where she is right now, next to Rachel [*Inf.* II.102]). The "greatest father" is, of course, Adam.

139. This verse has caused innumerable problems. Giacalone (comm. to vv. 139–144) compiles six differing attempts at interpretation; there are probably more, but one must admit it is hard to distinguish shadings of meaning from substantial differences. Most can agree that the verse refers to time and to sleep, but what exactly is time doing to the protagonist and

what sort of sleep is involved? Further, and pivotal, is a distinction about when the dreaming referred to occurred or is occurring or will occur. The basic disagreements have, it is probably fair to say, their roots in the temporal relation of Dante's dreaming. Either Dante (1) has been "dreaming" from the beginning of this special experience, as might be indicated by *Inferno* I.11, where Dante admits he was full of sleep when he lost the true way, and/or (2) is "dreaming" now (in the sense that he is having a more than normal experience of the afterworld), or (3) will be "out of time" (in both senses of the phrase) when he has the final vision of the Trinity, for which Bernard will seek Mary's aid, in a few minutes. Barolini (Baro.1992.1), pp. 144–51, carries on a long conversation with Barbi (Barb.1934.1), in which she unsuccessfully tries to undermine his objections to her position. Barolini wants to make the entire poem "visionary." Barbi, on the other hand, wants to distinguish between the "experiential" feel of most of the narrated journey and "vision" properly speaking. And the fact that there are "real" dreams presented in the poem (e.g., in *Purg.* IX, XIX, and XXVII) certainly implies that the rest of the time Dante is having "normal" experience of the decidedly postnormal things he witnesses in the afterworld. The crux of the issue found in this verse is to what precise (or for that matter general) dreaming the text refers. More than one hundred years ago, Torraca (comm. to vv. 139–141) read the verse as follows: "[P]erchè già cessa il tuo essere nel tempo, finisco, per non ritardare la tua partecipazione all'eternità, le tua visione suprema" (Because your presence in time already is ceasing, I finish speaking, so as not to delay your participation in eternity, your supreme vision). For a recent paper, not very distant from Torraca's finding, see Cuzzilla (Cuzz.2003.1), whose views influenced our reading of the verse. What he suggests is that the "sleep" is the mystic vision, already referred to in the picture of John "dreaming" in *Purgatorio* XXIX (see the note to vv. 127–129).

For some other discussions, see Passerini (Pass.1918.1), ad loc.; Gilson (Gils.1924.1), pp. 62–63; Pernicone (Pern.1965.1), pp. 120–21. Gilson cites Canticle of Canticles 5:2, "Ego dormio et cor meum vigilat" (I sleep and my heart wakes), a passage that Bonaventure uses to indicate the state of ecstatic vision. And see Boyde (Boyd.1993.1), pp. 130–39, for a discussion of *somnia* (dreams). See also the note to *Paradiso* XXVII.79–81.

140–141. Alessio (Ales.1989.1), p. 12, finds a source for Dante's much-admired image in the conclusion of a treatise on epistolary rhetoric, *Palma*, by Boncampagno da Signa. Advising his reader that he should measure out his epistolary space with care, so that his thoughts will all fit onto the amount of paper reserved for them, Boncompagno continues his thought with a simile: "sicut providus sartor pannum, de quo camisiam disposuit facere vel gunnellam" (just as a tailor, having thought ahead, has prepared the cloth from which to make a shirt or else a skirt).

142–144. Bernard calls our attention to the fact that Dante's sight, improving, is moving up within the *raggio* (ray) that irradiates the Rose, eventually to penetrate its source. See the note to *Paradiso* XXXI.94–99.

145–148. Unlike Icarus (see the note to *Par.* XV.54), Dante will not trust his own wings, but will listen to Bernard, a more successful "father" than Daedalus, perhaps because he recognizes the necessity of the grace that Mary can help obtain.

145. The word *ne* is not a Latinism (*ne* in Italian is a pronominal particle meaning "of it" or "of them"), but a Latin conjunction meaning "lest."

146. The neologism and hapax *oltrare* (move forward, advance), nearly certainly forced by the requirement of rhyme, will be echoed in the noun *oltraggio* in the next canto (verse 57).

149–150. Bernard uses the future tense as an imperative: "You shall follow me. . . ." The implication is that Dante would not want to do anything else but internalize his words.

151. The poet puts what clearly might have served as the opening line of the next canto here, apparently to give Bernard an uninterrupted presence at center stage for his prayer. Momigliano (comm. to vv. 149–151) describes this canto-ending as one of the most remarkable in the poem, "a long pause that sets apart, like a hush falling over the congregation, the prayer that will be raised in the holy atmosphere of the next canto."

PARADISO XXXIII

OUTLINE

THE EMPYREAN

- 1–39 Bernard's prayer:
  - 1–12 *salutatio*
    - 1–6 "[**Mary** defined in terms of four paradoxes];
    - 7–9 in your womb was rekindled love that made the Rose
    - 10–12 here you are torch of love; below, torch of hope
  - 13–21 *exordium*
    - 13–15 grace comes only through your intercession,
    - 16–18 love for those who ask it (even before the asking)
    - 19–21 your mercy, pity, and munificence account for whatever goodness exists in us
  - 22–27 *narratio*
    - 22–27 this man begs, by your grace, to see God
  - 28–33 *repetitio*
    - 28–33 and I pray for this, too
  - 34–39 *peroratio*
    - 34–37 finally, preserve his affections after such vision
    - 38–39 see how **Beatrice**, other saved souls pray for this"
- 40–45 Mary accepts his prayer, then turns her eyes to God.
- 46–51 Dante's ardor anticipates Bernard's signal to look up
- 52–54 Dante's sight entering the ray of light
- 55–57 what he saw exceeds his speech and his memory
- 58–63 simile: feelings of dreamer after dream and the sweet remnant of Dante's vision
- 64 simile: what he saw as pattern in snow melted by sun,
- 65–66 simile: as leaves of **Sibyl's** prophecies in the wind;

67–75 ninth invocation: to God as Light to grant humans power to conceive, if only a little, the nature of His being

76–81 danger of losing vision and thus his clasping of it

82–84 apostrophe: grace that allowed his sight into the Light

85–93 his vision of all things as unity

94–96 his momentary vision is more forgotten than **Neptune**'s vision of the *Argo* 2,500 years ago

97–99 simile: Dante as Neptune

100–105 perfection of Dante's intellect and will

106–108 his words will fall shorter, even of what he remembers, than those of a nursing infant

109–120 his view of the changing Godhead in its three circles

121–123 Dante's speech falls short of his conception

124–126 apostrophe: Light that loves and knows Itself

127–132 the second circling bears our likeness

133–139 simile: Dante as geometer trying to square the circle

140–141 the flash that makes all plain at last;

142–145 his vision failed, but his intellect and will rotate, both spun by the love that moves the heavens.

PARADISO XXXIII

"Vergine Madre, figlia del tuo figlio,
umile e alta più che creatura,
termine fisso d'etterno consiglio,

tu se' colei che l'umana natura
nobilitasti sì, che 'l suo fattore
non disdegnò di farsi sua fattura.

Nel ventre tuo si raccese l'amore,
per lo cui caldo ne l'etterna pace
così è germinato questo fiore.

Qui se' a noi meridïana face
di caritate, e giuso, intra ' mortali,
se' di speranza fontana vivace.

Donna, se' tanto grande e tanto vali,
che qual vuol grazia e a te non ricorre,
sua disïanza vuol volar sanz' ali.

La tua benignità non pur soccorre
a chi domanda, ma molte fïate
liberamente al dimandar precorre.

In te misericordia, in te pietate,
in te magnificenza, in te s'aduna
quantunque in creatura è di bontate.

Or questi, che da l'infima lacuna
de l'universo infin qui ha vedute
le vite spiritali ad una ad una,

supplica a te, per grazia, di virtute
tanto, che possa con li occhi levarsi
più alto verso l'ultima salute.

'Virgin Mother, daughter of your Son,
more humble and exalted than any other creature,
fixed goal of the eternal plan,

'you are the one who so ennobled human nature
that He, who made it first, did not disdain
to make Himself of its own making.

'Your womb relit the flame of love—
its heat has made this blossom seed
and flower in eternal peace.

'To us you are a noonday torch of charity,
while down below, among those still in flesh,
you are the living fountainhead of hope.

'Lady, you are so great and so prevail above,
should he who longs for grace not turn to you,
his longing would be doomed to wingless flight.

'Your loving kindness does not only aid
whoever seeks it, but many times
gives freely what has yet to be implored.

'In you clemency, in you compassion,
in you munificence, in you are joined
all virtues found in any creature.

'This man who, from within the deepest pit
the universe contains up to these heights
has seen the disembodied spirits, one by one,

'now begs you, by your grace, to grant such power
that, by lifting up his eyes,
he may rise higher toward his ultimate salvation.

E io, che mai per mio veder non arsi
più ch'i' fo per lo suo, tutti miei prieghi
ti porgo, e priego che non sieno scarsi,

perché tu ogne nube li disleghi
di sua mortalità co' prieghi tuoi,
sì che 'l sommo piacer li si dispieghi.

Ancor ti priego, regina, che puoi
ciò che tu vuoli, che conservi sani,
dopo tanto veder, li affetti suoi.

Vinca tua guardia i movimenti umani:
vedi Beatrice con quanti beati
per li miei prieghi ti chiudon le mani!"

Li occhi da Dio diletti e venerati,
fissi ne l'orator, ne dimostraro
quanto i devoti prieghi le son grati;

indi a l'etterno lume s'addrizzaro,
nel qual non si dee creder che s'invii
per creatura l'occhio tanto chiaro.

E io ch'al fine di tutt' i disii
appropinquava, sì com' io dovea,
l'ardor del desiderio in me finii.

Bernardo m'accennava, e sorridea,
perch' io guardassi suso; ma io era
già per me stesso tal qual ei volea:

ché la mia vista, venendo sincera,
e più e più intrava per lo raggio
de l'alta luce che da sé è vera.

Da quinci innanzi il mio veder fu maggio
che 'l parlar mostra, ch'a tal vista cede,
e cede la memoria a tanto oltraggio.

'And I, who never burned for my own seeing
more than now I burn for his, offer all my prayers,
and pray that they may not fall short,

'so that your prayers disperse on his behalf
all clouds of his mortality and let
the highest beauty be displayed to him.

'This too, my Queen, I ask of you, who can achieve
whatever you desire, that you help him preserve,
after such vision, the purity of his affections.

'Let your protection rule his mortal passions.
See Beatrice, with so many of the blessed,
palms pressed together, joining me in prayer.'

Those eyes belovèd and revered by God,
fixed on him who prayed, made clear to us
how dear to her all true devotion is.

Then she turned her gaze to the eternal Light.
It is incorrect to think that any living being
can penetrate that brightness with such unblinking eyes.

And, as I neared the end of all desire,
I extended to its limit, as was right,
the ardor of the longing in my soul.

With his smile, Bernard signaled
that I look upward, but of my own accord
I was already doing what he wished,

for my sight, becoming pure,
rose higher and higher through the ray
of the exalted light that in itself is true.

From that time on my power of sight exceeded
that of speech, which fails at such a vision,
as memory fails at such abundance.

Qual è colüi che sognando vede,
che dopo 'l sogno la passione impressa
rimane, e l'altro a la mente non riede,

cotal son io, ché quasi tutta cessa
mia visïone, e ancor mi distilla
nel core il dolce che nacque da essa.

Così la neve al sol si disigilla;
così al vento ne le foglie levi
si perdea la sentenza di Sibilla.

O somma luce che tanto ti levi
da' concetti mortali, a la mia mente
ripresta un poco di quel che parevi,

e fa la lingua mia tanto possente,
ch'una favilla sol de la tua gloria
possa lasciare a la futura gente;

ché, per tornare alquanto a mia memoria
e per sonare un poco in questi versi,
più si conceperà di tua vittoria.

Io credo, per l'acume ch'io soffersi
del vivo raggio, ch'i' sarei smarrito,
se li occhi miei da lui fossero aversi.

E' mi ricorda ch'io fui più ardito
per questo a sostener, tanto ch'i' giunsi
l'aspetto mio col valore infinito.

Oh abbondante grazia ond' io presunsi
ficcar lo viso per la luce etterna,
tanto che la veduta vi consunsi!

Nel suo profondo vidi che s'interna,
legato con amore in un volume,
ciò che per l'universo si squaderna:

Just as the dreamer, after he awakens,
still stirred by feelings that the dream evoked,
cannot bring the rest of it to mind,

such am I, my vision almost faded from my mind,
while in my heart there still endures
the sweetness that was born of it.

Thus the sun unseals an imprint in the snow.
Thus the Sibyl's oracles, on weightless leaves,
lifted by the wind, were swept away.

O Light exalted beyond mortal thought,
grant that in memory I see again
but one small part of how you then appeared

and grant my tongue sufficient power
that it may leave behind a single spark
of glory for the people yet to come,

since, if you return but briefly to my mind
and then resound but softly in these lines,
the better will your victory be conceived.

I believe, from the keenness of the living ray
that I endured, I would have been undone
had I withdrawn my eyes from it.

And I remember that, on this account,
I grew more bold and thus sustained my gaze
until I reached the Goodness that is infinite.

O plenitude of grace, by which I could presume
to fix my eyes upon eternal Light
until my sight was spent on it!

In its depth I saw contained,
by love into a single volume bound,
the pages scattered through the universe:

sustanze e accidenti e lor costume
quasi conflati insieme, per tal modo
che ciò ch'i' dico è un semplice lume.

La forma universal di questo nodo
credo ch'i' vidi, perché più di largo,
dicendo questo, mi sento ch'i' godo.

Un punto solo m'è maggior letargo
che venticinque secoli a la 'mpresa
che fé Nettuno ammirar l'ombra d'Argo.

Così la mente mia, tutta sospesa,
mirava fissa, immobile e attenta,
e sempre di mirar faceasi accesa.

A quella luce cotal si diventa,
che volgersi da lei per altro aspetto
è impossibil che mai si consenta;

però che 'l ben, ch'è del volere obietto,
tutto s'accoglie in lei, e fuor di quella
è defettivo ciò ch'è lì perfetto.

Omai sarà più corta mia favella,
pur a quel ch'io ricordo, che d'un fante
che bagni ancor la lingua a la mammella.

Non perché più ch'un semplice sembiante
fosse nel vivo lume ch'io mirava,
che tal è sempre qual s'era davante;

ma per la vista che s'avvalorava
in me guardando, una sola parvenza,
mutandom' io, a me si travagliava.

Ne la profonda e chiara sussistenza
de l'alto lume parvermi tre giri
di tre colori e d'una contenenza;

substances, accidents, and the interplay between them,
as though they were conflated in such ways
that what I tell is but a simple light.

I believe I understood the universal form
of this dense knot because I feel my joy expand,
rejoicing as I speak of it.

My memory of that moment is more lost
than five and twenty centuries make dim that enterprise
when, in wonder, Neptune at the *Argo*'s shadow stared.

Thus all my mind, absorbed,
was gazing, fixed, unmoving and intent,
becoming more enraptured in its gazing.

He who beholds that Light is so enthralled
that he would never willingly consent
to turn away from it for any other sight,

because the good that is the object of the will
is held and gathered in perfection there
that elsewhere would imperfect show.

Now my words will come far short
of what I still remember, like a babe's
who at his mother's breast still wets his tongue.

Not that the living Light at which I gazed
took on other than a single aspect—
for It is always what It was before—

but that my sight was gaining strength, even as I gazed
at that sole semblance and, as I changed,
it too was being, in my eyes, transformed.

In the deep, transparent essence of the lofty Light
there appeared to me three circles
having three colors but the same extent,

e l'un da l'altro come iri da iri
parea reflesso, e 'l terzo parea foco
che quinci e quindi igualmente si spiri.

Oh quanto è corto il dire e come fioco
al mio concetto! e questo, a quel ch'i' vidi,
è tanto, che non basta a dicer "poco."

O luce ettema che sola in te sidi,
sola t'intendi, e da te intelletta
e intendente te ami e arridi!

Quella circulazion che sì concetta
pareva in te come lume reflesso,
da li occhi miei alquanto circunspetta,

dentro da sé, del suo colore stesso,
mi parve pinta de la nostra effige:
per che 'l mio viso in lei tutto era messo.

Qual è 'l geomètra che tutto s'affige
per misurar lo cerchio, e non ritrova,
pensando, quel principio ond' elli indige,

tal era io a quella vista nova:
veder voleva come si convenne
l'imago al cerchio e come vi s'indova;

ma non eran da ciò le proprie penne:
se non che la mia mente fu percossa
da un fulgore in che sua voglia venne.

A l'alta fantasia qui mancò possa;
ma già volgeva il mio disio e 'l *velle*,
sì come rota ch'igualmente è mossa,
l'amor che move il sole e l'altre stelle.

and each one seemed reflected by the other
as rainbow is by rainbow, while the third seemed fire,
equally breathed forth by one and by the other.

O how scant is speech, too weak to frame my thoughts.
Compared to what I still recall my words are faint—
to call them "little" is to praise them much.

O eternal Light, abiding in yourself alone,
knowing yourself alone, and, known to yourself
and knowing, loving and smiling on yourself!

That circling which, thus conceived,
appeared in you as light's reflection,
once my eyes had gazed on it a while, seemed,

within itself and in its very color,
to be painted with our likeness,
so that my sight was all absorbed in it.

Like the geometer who fully applies himself
to square the circle and, for all his thought,
cannot discover the principle he lacks,

such was I at that strange new sight.
I tried to see how the image fit the circle
and how it found its where in it.

But my wings had not sufficed for that
had not my mind been struck by a bolt
of lightning that granted what I asked.

Here my exalted vision lost its power.
But now my will and my desire, like wheels revolving
with an even motion, were turning with
the Love that moves the sun and all the other stars.

1–39. This much (and justly) celebrated passage, Bernard's prayer to the Virgin, has the authority and unity of a separate poem. This is not to suggest that it is in any way incongruous in its context (quite the opposite is true), only that it could be published (as surely it has been) in an anthology of devotional lyrics and be one of the most moving and commanding of the collection.

For a study of this passage, see Auerbach (Auer.1949.1), who aligns it with examples of classical and Christian praise. And for the large extent to which Dante has borrowed from Bernard's own writings for the words of this prayer, see Aversano (Aver.2000.2), pp. 173–76.

Gian Carlo Alessio, in a lecture he presented at Princeton University during the autumn semester of 1981, broke down the rhetorical divisions of Bernard's prayer as follows:

1–12: *salutatio*
13–21: *exordium*
22–27: *narratio*
28–33: *repetitio*
34–39: *peroratio*

The tone of intimacy found in this prayer is emphasized by its extraordinary number of second-person-singular pronouns (*tu, te, ti*) and adjectives (*tuo, tua*), 17 of them in 39 verses (and that figure does not include second-person-singular endings of verbs). See the note to *Paradiso* XXXI.79–90.

1. This verse establishes the basic modality of the entire canto, making two references to what will be a common theme of so many verses in it: harmonious resolution of impossibly related contraries. "Virgin" and "mother" cannot logically be the shared properties of any woman; nor can any woman be the daughter of her son. This overriding of the logic of impossibility will culminate in the final simile of the poem, the geometer attempting to square the circle. The only answer to impossibility is miracle. Reacting to the entire canto, Güntert has said (Gunt.2002.2), p. 505, "No Christian poet had ever been so daring."

For the beginnings of the last cantos of the first two *cantiche*, see the note to *Purgatorio* XXXIII.1–3, which points out that each of the previous opening lines was in another poetic voice, first that of Venantius Fortunatus and second that of David, both of them speaking Latin. Here we have another poetic voice, that of St. Bernard, but he does not use his customary Latin tongue (apparently no writing of Bernard in French survives), but the vernacular. This opening line thus presents us first with a completed pattern and then, on further consideration, with a broken pattern: We expect Latin here, but do not find it.

For both elements of this verse as dependent on formulations found in the fifth book of Alain de Lille's *Anticlaudianus*, see Ledda (Ledd.2002.1), p. 308n., citing the previous notice by Jacomuzzi (Jaco.1965.1), p. 12n. Ledda also reports other medieval *formulae* that are similar to Dante's paradoxical expressions.

This marks the thirteenth time that a canto has begun with a speaker's words (see the note to *Par.* V.1).

2. If one had to choose a single line of the fourteen thousand two hundred and thirty-three verses of the *Commedia* to stand for its stylistic program, countering classical high style with Christian *sermo humilis*, this one might serve that purpose. It begins and ends with the humanity of Mary, humble and a mere human creature, who is, at the same time, lofty (*alta*), as is the poem itself.

3. See Carroll's explanation of this line (comm. to vv. 1–39): "The woman worthy to be the 'Mother of God' must have been elect from the beginning."

4–6. This tercet, remarkable for its triple play on the "making" of flesh (*fattore, farsi, fattura*), rises to the heights with the hapax (and coinage?) *nobilitasti* (ennobled). What is the noblest act ever done? God's making himself mortal for our sake.

7. Dante's use of the word *ventre* (here and once earlier for Mary's womb at *Par.* XXIII.104) was perhaps not intended to be controversial. See Bosco/Reggio (comm. to vv. 1–21), pointing out that Dante may have deliberately been echoing "et benedictus fructus ventris tui, Jesus" (blessed is the fruit of your womb, Jesus [originally found in Luke 1:42]). This is the end of the first part of the prayer: "Hail, Mary, full of grace, / blessed are you among women." Nonetheless, and as we have observed (see the notes to *Par.* XXI.84 and XXIII.104), some of Dante's readers find this a lowering of diction unbefitting such a lofty subject.

In a related and similar vein, see McLaughlin (Mcla.1995.1), pp. 20–21, remarking that "After Petrarch reasserts the absolute superiority of Latin over the *volgare*, Dante's vernacular echoes of classical *auctores* are regarded as a diminution of their status."

On the word *amore*, see Sacchetto (Sacc.1974.1), for whom love is the key to the poem, occurring 19 times in *Inferno*, 50 in *Purgatorio*, and 85 in *Paradiso*.

8–9. Christ's sacrifice was the evidence of the rekindling of God's love for humankind, resulting in the saved souls that populate the Rose.

10–12. For the elevation of Mary found here (and in all this passage), see Carroll (comm. to vv. 1–39): "[Dante] must have been familiar with the distinction of Aquinas between *latria*, the worship due to God; *dulia*, the veneration given to saints and Angels; and *hyperdulia*, the higher veneration given to Mary, as the most exalted of creatures (*ST* II–II, q. 103, a. 3, 4)."

11–12. For the saved, there is no more need for hope—their hope (as well as their faith) has been rewarded, and now they only love eternally. Meanwhile, while to those (few, we need to recall, lest we get carried away by the warmth of these verses) left on earth who will be saved, Mary offers the surest path of hope for their salvation.

14–15. Campi (comm. to vv. 13–15) cites Monsignor Cavedoni for the attribution of this image to St. Bernard, *Sermones in Vigilia Nativitatis Domini* III.10: "Nihil nos Deus habere voluit, quod per Mariae manus non transiret" (God does not wish us to have anything that has not first passed through the hands of Mary).

15. Geoffrey Chaucer, who knew and understood this poem better than any English writer for many centuries, appropriated this line in his *Troilus* with hilarious result. Stanza 182 of Book III (one stanza from the numerical midpoint of the work, 588 of 1178 stanzas) has Troilus in the midst of his three-stanza prayer to Venus (his "Mary"). Whoever wants to accomplish his love (he is thinking about carnal pleasure), he says, without Venus's help, "his desire will fly without wings," that is, will not be successful. It is *Paradiso* XXXIII done as *Some Like It Hot*, one of Billy Wilder's greatest films. (That Chaucer could do Dante "straight" is witnessed in many of his texts; in the context of this canto, see particularly

his rewriting of the first half of Bernard's prayer in "The Second Nun's Prologue" of *The Canterbury Tales*, vv. 29–77.)

As Simone Marchesi, in conversation, has pointed out, Chaucer's Billy Wilder was Giovanni Boccaccio, whose lascivious Venetian friar Albert (*Decam.* IV.ii), in illicit pleasure with a Venetian matron, "flew many times without his wings." Albert appears to the credulous woman as the angel Gabriel, decked out in a costume including wings that he takes off only in the darkness of her bedroom. Boccaccio is clearly pulling Dante's leg; now Chaucer does so also.

17–18. For liberality extending itself unrequested, see *Purgatorio* XVII.59–60 and *Paradiso* XVII.75.

19–20. Here we have a case of a Virgilian borrowing that has apparently remained hidden for centuries (in both texts, CAPITALS mark structural parallels and *italics* indicate secondary repeated sounds of *te*):

> In TE misericordia, in TE pieta*te*,
> in TE magnificenza, in TE s'aduna . . .

See *Georgics* IV.465–466 (Orpheus lamenting his dead Eurydice, a scene Dante has revisited in *Purg.* XXX.49–51 [see the note to that passage] as parallel to his plaint for lost Virgil, as is fairly widely agreed these days):

> TE, dulcis coniunx, TE solo in litore secum,
> TE venien*te* die, TE deceden*te* canebat.

> [thee, sweet wife, thee, alone on the lone shore,
> thee while day dawned, thee while it died, he sang.]

This seems an obvious revisitation. Perhaps we have not seen it because the situations are so opposed. But that is the point: Bernard is a better Orpheus singing a better Eurydice, Maria. It is a small but telling emblem of how Dante rewrites Virgilian tragedy as Christian comedy. And the Virgilian context is striking: We last heard the notes of *Georgics* IV in tragic mode for his disappearance as a character from the poem; now that poem becomes the subtext for a better moment, his own reentry to this Christian comedy at its highest point.

Notice of this echo is fairly recent. See Hollander (Holl.1993.1), p. 339, citing a communication from Professor Rachel Jacoff in 1987, suggesting the existence of this borrowing, which also possibly reflects *Paradiso* XXIII.88–89, where Dante presents himself as praying to Mary each morning and evening, while Orpheus presents himself as "singing" Eurydice morning and evening. The stark contrast between Virgilian "Orphic" love that leads to death and Marian affection that leads to eternal life could not be more striking.

We may remember that the first (and only) time we heard Dante's name in this poem (*Purg.* XXX.55), it was echoing a passage just a little farther along in this *Georgic* (see the note to *Purg.* XXX.63).

22–23. Bosco/Reggio (comm. to these verses) rightly express surprise that there is any debate at all over exactly which of the souls in which parts of the afterworld Bernard refers to, since he obviously refers to all of them.

28–33. The meaning of these verses is clear enough, but the discussion of them is uncertain with regard to a possible source. While several commentators hear a plausible echo of *Aeneid* II.604–606 (first Gabriele [comm. to vv. 31–32]) in these verses, and a few others hear one of Boethius (*Cons.* III.m9.25–28) and not of Virgil (first Vellutello [comm. to vv. 28–33]), neither text is really close enough to be a convincingly heard citation, if the Virgilian one has the largest following and the more likely context. If we believe that the Virgilian passage is being alluded to, the parallels are fairly inviting. Where Venus removes the shield of invisibility from the gods so that Aeneas may see his true enemies for what they are, Mary takes the cloud of his mortality away from Dante so that he may see his "friend," God, as He is.

29–39. These verses contain six words for praying, the densest occurrence of noun and verb forms of *priego* in the poem.

33. Once again the precise understanding one should have of the verbal noun *piacer* is an issue. See the note to *Purgatorio* XXXI.47–54. Grabher (comm. to vv. 28–33) believes that here it means *somma bellezza* (highest beauty), as do we.

34–39. See Bosco/Reggio (comm. to vv. 1–21), who observe that this final prayer offered by Bernard may reflect the second and final part of the *Ave Maria*: "Sancta Maria, Mater Dei, / ora pro nobis peccatoribus, nunc, / et in hora mortis nostrae. Amen" (Holy Mary, Mother of God, / pray for us sinners now / and at the hour of our death. Amen).

The traditional interpretation of these lines, as it is advanced by Sapegno (comm. to these verses); Chiavacci Leonardi (Chia.1997.1), p. 911; and Dronke (Dron.1994.1), p. 28, fits well with the Marian text. It sees the final moments of the prayer as turning to Dante's *Nachleben* back on earth, and hoping that Mary will intervene to help him remain pure, so that he will indeed be able to return here. This understanding is opposed by Pertile (Pert.1981.1); Bàrberi Squarotti (Barb.1995.1), pp. 367–71; and Ledda (Ledd.2002.1), pp. 309–10, all of whom find it inappropriate for Bernard's prayer to leave the subject of Dante's vision being pure for that of his post-Paradiso life back on earth being morally sound. Why is this an unseemly concern, either aesthetically or intellectually? It had already been before the reader in *Paradiso* XXXI.88–90, where Dante himself beseeches Beatrice for this kind of heavenly assistance. Pertile (p. 2) argues that, for the very reason that Dante's prayer has been accepted, as signified by Beatrice's smile, there is no longer any need to linger on this issue. Perhaps so. On the other hand, the language of these six verses (particularly at vv. 36 and 37) really does seem to be related to earthly concerns. In other words, even if it seems ungainly to some (but not to most), the standard interpretation seems more plausible.

40–45. The Virgin, evidently made of more august stuff than Beatrice, does not smile when Bernard finishes his prayer as Beatrice did when Dante finished his (*Par.* XXXI.92), but indicates by the expression in her eyes how much she is gratified by the prayers of the devout. Then she turns her gaze (as did Beatrice) back up to God.

46. As Güntert observes (Gunt.2002.2), p. 511, after the formal conclusion to Bernard's prayer (vv. 40–45), this verse begins the final "macrosequence" of the one-hundredth canto; it is precisely one hundred verses in length.

48. This verse has caused a central disagreement over its two main potential meanings. We follow Singleton's interpretation (comm. to this verse): "The meaning of the verb in this verse is much debated, but one aspect of that meaning seems beyond discussion: *finii* cannot here be in a normal signification of 'bring to an end.' Indeed, the context requires that the meaning be the exact opposite, i.e., 'I brought the ardor of my desire to its highest intensity.' " And see the similar position of Bosco/Reggio (comm. to this verse). Another difficult passage may be considered a "preview" of

this one (*Purg.* XVIII.31–33) and may help unscramble the sense of this line. See the note to that passage (*Purg.* XVIII.28–33).

49. As Aversano (Aver.2000.2), p. 177, points out, this is the third and last appearance of Bernard's name in the poem (see also *Par.* XXXI.102 and 139), as a sort of Trinitarian gesture of farewell.

50–51. Bernard was signaling, in his capacity as guide, what Dante should be doing, but Dante was already doing exactly that. He has not outrun his need for guidance so much as he has internalized his guide.

52–54. The poet could not be more precise. Up to now his powers of sight have improved so that he can finally see God's reflection in the universe perfectly, an ability that was far from his grasp when the poem began. Now he will see Him as Himself. Thus the protagonist's vision is about to move from reflections of His glory up into the beam of light emanating from Him. It is balanced for seconds between the two aspects of deity, reflection and source (see the note to *Par.* XXIII.82–84). In the next tercet we realize that he has recorded his breakthrough. No Christian except for St. Paul has seen so much—or such is the unspoken claim the poet makes us share.

55–57. The experience of seeing God face-to-face (1) is ineffable, not describable, and (2) the vision cannot be remembered in any of its details anyway (these twin disclaimers were made at the outset [see *Par.* I.7–9]). All that remains is the awareness of having had the experience.

57. For the word *oltraggio* as expressing Dante's version of the *excessus mentis* of the Christian mystical tradition, see Pertile (Pert.1981.1 [repr. Pert.2005.2]).

58–66. Given our previous experience reading in the *Paradiso*, we expect here exactly what we get. Moving into an area of heightened experience, which challenges his expressive powers (as it had challenged his perceptive powers), Dante has inevitably moved to simile. After, in the last tercet, understating the fact that he saw God, he now turns not to one simile, but to three of them, in order to express the nature of his loss. This is perhaps the only time in the poem that he deploys three similes back-to-back; in any case, the Trinitarian nature of what he has looked upon (which will be made clear to us before long) is perhaps reflected in their number.

These are the penultimate similes in a poem that turns to them more often than we might have expected, and surely his use of the technique reflects his sense of the classical Latin epic simile, so familiar to him, particularly from the pages of Virgil. And the last of these three will be unmistakably Virgilian.

58–63. The first and fullest of the three similes is one of a class defined by Tozer (see the note to *Inf.* XXX.136–141) as "drawn from mental experiences."

58. The present tense of the verb in the simile seems natural to us, since Dante usually bases his similes in the world of our present experience. We do not, however, expect to hear the narrative voice speaking in the present tense—but if we look ahead to verse 61, we find the poet speaking to us now, from his writing table back on earth. He won't stay there (see vv. 133–138, a parallel structure, in which the poet compares himself to the geometer and then says "such *was* I"), as we will see, but that is where he presents himself as being now, at least for the moment.

61. Switching from the experience itself to writing about his recording of the experience, the poet speaks in the present tense, which comes as a surprise, since we have not heard him use that tense in the Empyrean, and not since *Paradiso* XXX.34.

62–63. Benvenuto (comm. to vv. 58–63) says that Dante is claiming that even now he still tastes just a drop of this immense joy (*adhuc sentio aliquam stillam, idest, guttam illius immensae dulcedinis*).

62. This is the sixth and final appearance of the word *visione*, used here for the first time for the poem itself. It was apparently from here that the many writers who referred to the work as the *Visione* (perhaps wanting to avoid the embarrassing [to some] title, *Commedia*) took their cue. And see the note to *Paradiso* XVII.127–129.

64. Benvenuto (comm. to vv. 64–66) says that this is a fitting simile, because "the human mind, weak and infirm, loses the form of its phantasy's vision beneath the heat of the Eternal Sun." This second comparison is apparently not "literary" in its inspiration. There is in fact no citation of any text of any kind for this verse among the commentators gathered in the DDP.

65–66. When we read her name, we may wonder why we have not heard it before now; it is as though Dante were holding her in reserve for his hundredth canto (as we will see, that number is three times associated with her in the main passage involving her in the *Aeneid*). The Sibyl, we may sometimes fail to remember, was merely the conduit for Apollo's messages. Thus, and as Benvenuto (comm. to vv. 64–66) says, both the Sibyl and Dante lost track of a communication from a divinity. If we recall the first two cantos of this canticle, with their insistence on Apollo as God's "stand-in" (*Par.* I.13; II.8), we can see why Benvenuto makes them companions in losing track of the truth revealed by "Apollo."

The history of the commentators' response to this Virgilian reference is strange, beginning with the mistake of Francesco da Buti (or his scribe), who identifies (comm. to vv. 55–66) the source as being in *Aeneid* V, when he clearly means *Aeneid* III. All the other earlier commentators, beginning with Pietro (Pietro1, comm. to vv. 58–66), and including Benvenuto, John of Serravalle, Daniello, and Venturi, refer only to the appropriate passage in *Aeneid* VI. However, beginning with Lombardi (comm. to vv. 64–66), every commentator but two refers only to the passage in *Aeneid* III (443–451), which is the one in which the usual scattering of her leaves is described; the second passage, while also referring to that usual result, has Aeneas convincing the oracle to speak, and not write, her expression of Apollo's response. However, it is probably helpful to have both scenes in mind; the only two commentators in the DDP to refer to *both* passages are Oelsner and Singleton (comms. to these verses).

The passage in the *Aeneid* (VI.42–155) describing the Sibyl's cave is both long and full of arresting "Dantean" detail. The cave possesses one hundred mouths and one hundred gates (VI.43); Aeneas requests that the Sibyl *not* write her "poems" (*carmina*) on leaves to be scattered by the wind, but recite them aloud (VI.74–75); the hundred gates open and their breezes carry her reply (VI.81–82); Virgil (VI.99) typifies her utterance as "horrible enigmas" (*horrendas ambages*), a phrase that Dante has picked up in *Paradiso* XVII.31; Aeneas asks (VI.108) the Sibyl to bring him into his father's sight (*ad conspectum cari genitoris*), while Dante hopes to see his Father. (While there are other resonances in Dante's poem of the last four dozen verses, they are not relevant to this passage.)

If the obvious references to Virgil have been recognized, but not all that well exploited, there is also possibly a reference to Augustine, which has only rarely been noticed and not exploited at all. It is found in chapter xxiii of Book XVIII of *De civitate Dei*, a text vengefully hostile to Virgil for his prideful view of Rome's continuing and sempiternal hegemony (especially now that the city has been sacked in the year 410). Augustine says that the Sibyl (not the Cumaean [Virgil's] but the Erythraean—if he later hedges by saying it *may* have been the Cumaean) had, in a poem, prophesied the coming of Christ and ought to be considered as inhabiting the City of God. What led Augustine to make such claims may have been a desire to roast Virgil, either for not heeding his own Sibyl (who, after all, presides over the fourth *Eclogue*) or for choosing to sponsor the wrong one. Here is a portion of what he sets down in his lengthy analysis of this poem: The first letters of each successive line in the Greek Sibylline pronouncement spell out, Augustine reports: " 'Jesus Christ the Son of God, the Saviour.' And the verses are twenty-seven, which is the cube of three. For three times three are nine; and nine itself, if tripled, so as to rise from the superficial square to the cube, comes to twenty-seven. But if you join the initial letters of these five Greek words, . . . they will make the word *ikduj*, that is, 'fish,' in which word Christ is mystically understood, because He was able to live, that is, to exist, without sin in the abyss of this mortality as in the depth of waters" (tr. M. Dods). Notice of this passage in St. Augustine is not a frequent feature of the commentaries. However, see Benvenuto (comm. to these verses), who points to it at some length. He is followed apparently only by Campi (comm. to these verses). Hollander (Holl.1983.1), pp. 146–50, while suggesting this connection, neglected his two precursors (when he could have used all the help he could find).

For an article by Philippe Verdier on the Sibyl's appearance to Augustine at *Ara coeli* in Rome, see *Mélanges de l'École française à Rome* 94 (1982): 85–119. And for a collection of studies of the Sibyl's antique and medieval presence, see Allevi (Alle.1965.1) as well as Bouquet and Morzadec (Bouq.2004.1). Allevi discusses this passage on pp. 443–48.

66. On the Sibyl's leaves, see Boitani (Boit.1978.1), taking them as a starting point for his *lectura* of the canto.

67–75. The word *concetto* (conception, conceiving) is the linchpin of this passage, occurring in verses 68 and 75 (on the latter occasion as a verb). Dante, in this last of his nine invocations (see the note to *Inf.* II.7–9), asks God to make His reality "conceivable" by mortals. If He requites Dante's request, the poet promises, that will be the result. A scaled-back request, the poet insists, is all that he makes, underlined by the repetition of the phrase "un poco" (one small part).

This is the fourth time in the poem that the word *concetto* is connected with an invocation (see the notes to *Inf.* XXXII.1–9 and 10–12;

Par. XVIII.82–87; and, for a survey of all the presences of *concetto* in the poem, see the note to *Par.* XXXIII.127). It surely seems to be involved in Dante's sense of what the human agent needs from a higher source, not the mere substance of his vision, but its shaping conceptual formulation. And that is precisely what, the poet will tell us, he was granted in the lightning bolt that resolves all his questions in verses 140–141.

67. The poet here addresses God as source (*O somma luce*), not as what He irradiates, but as the *fonte* (spring, font) of everything.

76–84. The protagonist had entered the *raggio* (ray) in verse 53. Now he has issued from it and approached the source. Having uttered his ninth invocation a few lines earlier (vv. 67–75), he does not invoke the Deity. He does not *need* help to see Him any longer; he has accomplished that goal. And so he gives thanks for His grace in allowing this final vision, which he is about to unfold before us. See discussion in Ledda (Ledd.2002.1), pp. 313–14 and n.

77. For the past presence of the adjective *smarrito* in the poem, see the note to *Paradiso* XXVI.9.

85–93. For a most suggestive and yet concise reading of this passage, the universe explained and put into relationship with its Creator in three tercets, see Moevs (Moev.2005.1), pp. 78–79. God creates all things as unity. He is the ground of all being. And Dante, seeing the universal diversity as unity, experiences it as God saw it in creating it, as a simple yet "limitless and dimensionless reality" (Moevs, p. 78).

85–90. On the various dimensions of this passage, from medieval book production, in which a writer took his individual quartos (*quaderni*) to have them conflated and sewn into a "book," Ahern argues that Dante's poem reflects the "book" of God's created universe, even to its Trinitarian structure. For bibliography on the concept (God's "two books," the Bible and His creation), see Güntert (Gunt.2002.2), p. 511n.

85–87. Chiarenza (Chia.1972.1), p. 80, says that this tercet is "inspired by the doctrine of the double existence of creation, separate in the universe and unified in its Creator's conception."

91–93. Güntert (Gunt.2002.2), p. 508, hopes to convince us to see "three Dantes" in this tercet: the narrator (*credo*), the narrator speaking of the protagonist in the past tense (*i' vidi*), and the "post-vision protagonist" (*mi sento . . . i' godo*), a being somehow differentiated from the narrator in Güntert's view (see the similar argument advanced by Picone [Pico.2000.3], pp. 18–21). However, it is difficult to understand how his separation of the first and third voices can be supported, since they both use the present tense and surely seem to be the standard voice of the *io narrante* rather than two different voices, speaking from different times. Since it is not logically possible for one of those times to be post-writing, it must then fall between the vision and the writing, and thus in the past. To put this another way, had Dante had such a plan in mind, he needed to deploy a better-conceived tactic in order to make it effective. As it is, we have two moments in the poem. One is stable, the protagonist's voyage during a week in the spring of 1300, in which he *does* change over that time; that is *then*. The other is always in fact shifting between circa 1307 and circa 1321, but is treated without temporal distinction as the authorial *now*, if it has in fact finally reached its farthest point. The author who looks up at us from the pages of *Inferno* XXXII.71–72 to tell us his discomfort in winter's cold occupies the same moment as this one, as far as we can see from his text, which offers no temporal divisions of the writerly present except for the ones we may happen to supply. Proust would later choose to dramatize the subject of the author's mortal change through time; all times in which Dante, on the other hand, looks up at us from his writing table are equally "now." All that has changed is that he is finishing his book; in Hollander's formulation (Holl.1969.1, p. 227), "The Pilgrim he was has become the history of the Poet he is."

For the similarities between Dante's "deification" here and that of Glaucus in *Paradiso* I.67–79, see Hollander (Holl.1969.1), pp. 228–29. See also Longen (Long.1975.1) and Migliorini-Fissi (Migl.1982.1).

For the suggestion that this image of a ship, filled with armed men and headed for battle, underlines the poet's desire to associate his Christian poem with classical martial epic in this final reference to the world of men, see Hollander (Holl.1989.1), p. 85.

94–96. This tercet has called forth equal amounts of admiration and distress, admiration for the beauty and scope of its conception, distress at the indubious difficulty of its highly compacted literal sense. First things first. What does the tercet *mean*? Perhaps because of the difficulty of understanding why Dante might have wanted to present himself as *forgetting* the greatest insight he (or practically anyone) has ever had, there has been some attempt to understand *letargo* not as "forgetting," but as a form of visionary experience. However, most now think that the former meaning is far more likely here, as, obviously, do we. If all can agree (and that is to assume a good deal) that the term, in Dante's Italian, refers to oblivion, forgetting, that still leaves a deal of difficulty.

A good place to begin one's study of this tercet is with the extensive gloss of Scartazzini, not because he solves its mysteries (he almost certainly does not), but because he so thoroughly indicates what these are. Francesco da Buti's discussion of this tercet (a part of his comm. to vv. 82–99) makes a point based in mythographic history that stands as a helpful understanding even today. He (uniquely) offers a striking version of the classical background: Neptune had longed to see his "kingdom," the sea, "inhabited" as was the land. Therefore, he took great joy in seeing the first ship ever to bring men to his "territory," the sea, and has been painfully "forgetting" it (in the sense that he longs to see it without satisfaction every day) for twenty-five hundred years ever since. And thus Dante can say that his one moment of awareness of the final mystery of the Trinity, how humanity and divinity share the same being, now being lost, is more painful than Neptune's far longer period of experiencing oblivion. See Tozer's similar paraphrase (comm. to this tercet): " '[O]ne single moment is greater oblivion to me (*letargo*, lit. lethargy, dullness), than twenty-five centuries have been to the enterprise which caused Neptune to marvel at the shadow of *Argo*.' In other words: 'I forgot in a single moment more of what I saw . . . than men have forgotten, in twenty-five centuries, of the Argonautic expedition.' " Needless to say, there are other views. For instance, Chimenz (comm. to this tercet) believes that the twenty-five centuries are marked by remembrance, not by forgetting. However, others have noted that the structure of the passage simply forces the reader to accept the negative understanding (i.e., the view advanced by Tozer). And if the poet goes on to describe the vision in great detail (the main point put forward by those who read the text "positively"), he also will insist on its fleetingness, as Carroll (comm. to this tercet), objecting to Scartazzini's "positive" interpretation, rightly argues. Lombardi had offered, in addition to the classical modern statement later found in Tozer, two important additions to the sum of commentary knowledge: The word *letargo* derives from Greek *lethe* (forgetfulness), and the years between the voyage of the *Argo* and 1300 are, according to Dante's authorities, either 2,523 or 2,570. Tommaseo (comm. to this tercet) supports the first of these dates, which has now become "canonical" among the commentators. Either one is a promising date, since both sector the "history of sea voyages" in an arc of twenty-six centuries, 1223 (or 1270) B.C. to 1300, with its approximate midpoint in the Incarnation (as Hollander

[Holl.1969.1], pp. 231–32, has argued). The voyage of the Argonauts, preceding the Trojan War, was the first important event in the Greek portion of universal history. (See Gmelin [Gmel.1957.1], p. 572, for an examination of Dante's Argonautical chronology.)

94. See Jacomuzzi (Jaco.1965.1), p. 10, discussing the tension in this canto between *letargo* (forgetting) and the frequent presence of verbs for seeing. And see Picone (Pico.1994.1), pp. 200–202.

95. The word *impresa* (undertaking, enterprise) has an interesting history in the poem. See Hollander (Holl.1969.1), pp. 230–31, pointing out that, in *Inferno* II.41 and 47, the word refers to Dante's journey and that, in *Inferno* XXXII.7, it represents Dante's poem about that journey; here, on the other hand, it would seem to refer both to the journey and to the record of that journey, for the first is in process of becoming the second.

96. According to Ovid, Jason was the builder of the first ship ("primaeque ratis molitor" [*Metam.* VIII.302]). For the history of the *Argo*-motif, see Curtius (Curt.1950.1), favoring Ovid (*Metam.* VII.120), which assuredly lies behind Dante's earlier reference to Jason's voyage (see the note to *Par.* II.17–18), but does not seem quite so good a fit here.

The image of Neptune looking up from beneath the sea is reminiscent of what the poet tells us in Canto XXXI.73–78, where he looked up at Beatrice as though he were immersed in the deepest point in the sea and she were at the highest point in the earth's atmosphere. Both sightings involve the word *effige* (features), the first time as Beatrice's likeness, the second (*Par.* XXXIII.131), that of Jesus. The fact that Neptune saw the shadow (*ombra*) of the *Argo* makes it at least probable that the poet hoped we would consider that voyage as the prefiguration of his own (see Hollander [Holl.1969.1], p. 232).

And as for Ovidian inspiration for what is sometimes considered a Dantean invention, Hollander (Holl.1969.1), p. 222, has argued for the impact of the last line (721) of Ovid's Book VI, describing the *Argo* setting sail from Iolcos: "Per mare non notum prima petiere carina" (The first keel to cleave an unknown sea). That would leave Neptune alone unaccounted for. To be sure, we find him looking up from the seabed (wherever Dante found the source of the image) earlier in this very poem, *Inferno* XXVIII.83–84, where, in his only other appearance, he witnesses Malatestino's treachery as he has witnessed similar crimes on the part of Greeks (*gente argolica*), the "bad Argonauts" succeeding Jason, as it were.

97. For Dante's "sospesa," Gilson (Gils.1924.1), p. 59, cites the prologue of Bonaventure's *Itinerarium mentis ad Deum* for a similar use of the word *suspensio* to denote the mind's ecstatic rapture in its contemplation of God.

98. When Dante looked at Beatrice in Eden, the angels cried out (*Purg.* XXXII.9) that he was "troppo fiso!" (too fixed), in the sense that he was confounding the physical and the spiritual in his appreciation of Beatrice. Now there can be no question of that, since "fixation" on God is the condition of blessedness for eternity, as the following two tercets make absolutely plain.

100–105. Not only is the intellect satisfied by gazing on God, but the will is, too; for what other good, as object of the will, can supervene?

106–108. For a final time, the poet, having nearly completed a poem that has just reported having seen and understood the underlying principle ordering the entire universe, insists that, compared to the truth of that vision, his work is mere baby talk. (See the note to *Par.* XV.121–123 and Hollander [Holl.1980.2].)

111–114. Preparing us to see the Trinity through his eyes, the poet reassures us that he harbors no heretical notions about God's nature(s); if He is three, that does not mean that He is other than one; if He is one, that does not mean that He is other than three. Even the protagonist's vastly improved powers still have one more stage of visionary capacity to reach, one in which he will be able to experience the unchanging Trinity with his changed sight.

115–117. The Trinity is first experienced as three circles inhering in a single space, distinguished only by their colors, not their sizes, which are identical.

116–120. Bonanno (Bona.2001.1), p. 224, suggests that the rhymes here deliberately echo those found in *Donna me prega*, vv. 51–55 (*miri, tiri, giri*), with subversive intent, and indeed sees the entire final canto as entering into a corrective debate with the understanding of the nature of love proposed in Cavalcanti's *canzone*.

118–120. The tercet, as characterized by Carroll (comm. to vv. 115–123) as presenting "what Aquinas calls the Relations of Divinity according to the Procession of Persons out of identity of substance—the Relations of Paternity, Generation and Spiration (*Summa*, I, q. 28). From the circle of the Father appeared reflected the circle of the Son, as Iris [rainbow] from Iris [rainbow]; and from both was breathed forth equally the fire of Love which is the Holy Spirit (on the Procession of the Spirit from both Father and Son, and the *filioque* controversy, see above [Carroll's comm.], on *Par.* X.1–6). We must not think of these in the form of three rainbows one within another, or even as the three colours of a rainbow, for these are also one within another. The 'one dimension' shows that Dante conceived of them as co-existing in the one space, though he does not explain how he was able to see the three colours distinct within each other." One supposes that they manifested themselves as changing colors. Dante does not assign a particular color either to Father or Son; the Holy Spirit, as Love, is understandably red.

121. For this last use of *fioco* (weak, indistinct) in the poem, see Hollander (Holl.1983.1), tying together *Vita nuova* XXIII (see pp. 76–77), *Inferno* I.63, and this verse (pp. 150–51). For a similar view, see Bologna (Bolo.2002.1), p. 461. Torraca seems to have been the first commentator (and, among those gathered in the DDP, he seems to have been followed only by Mestica [comm. to this tercet]) even to note that we have seen this term before in *Inferno* I.63, but has no further comment. Hollander suggests that "this use of the word is intended to make us consider Virgil's initial *fiochezza*, with all its metaphoric insistence on the fact that he had failed to speak the Word. In this respect, the two poets find themselves once again together at the end, reunited in their failures, and yet so very far from one another, separated by the ground of their failures" (p. 151).

Bellomo (Bell.1996.1), p. 55n., believes that the question of Dante's Virgil needs to be reopened, beginning with a rereading of Bruno Nardi (Nard.1960.1), especially pp. 96–150.

124–126. Ledda (Ledd.2002.1), p. 317n., says he is following Jacomuzzi in seeing that the protagonist's final vision is of the Incarnation, and not the Trinity. Does one really have to make that choice? It would seem to be preferable to see it as Trinitarian, which includes the vision of Jesus as spirit in flesh, as He is.

127–132. Finally, Dante sees the Humanity of the Trinity, the Son, Jesus Christ, incarnate within the circle that abstractly represents the Second Person. Once again the differing colors of the Persons are insisted on, and once again (see the note to vv. 118–120) Dante does not report the color of the Son (nor of the Father).

It took centuries until a commentator (Scartazzini [comm. to verse 131]) realized that this image contained a reference to St. Paul (Philippians 2:7), "but made himself nothing, taking the form of a servant, being born in the likeness of men." This is currently a fairly widespread perception, but the only other writer in the DDP to observe it is Grandgent (comm. to verse 131).

The enormous presence of the Bible in the poem has at times simply overwhelmed its observers. This is a case in point. Moore (Moor.1896.1), pp. 321–34, lists over six hundred possible citations in all Dante's works, the bulk of them in the *Commedia*. Thus one needs to deal cautiously with Steiner's accountancy (Stei.2001.1), p. 89, which counts the actual citations (rather than more general forms of reference) as two in *Inferno*, eight in *Purgatorio*, and a dozen in *Paradiso*.

127. This is the final use of this word, whether as an abstract noun meaning "concept" or "conceiving" or a transitive verb (to conceive [an idea—see *Inf.* XII.13 for the first and only use of the verb to mean "to conceive offspring," although there is more than an overtone of that sense here]). There have been twelve previous uses of the noun or of the verb (*Inf.* XXVI.73, XXXII.4; *Par.* III.60, XV.41, XVIII.86, XIX.12, XXII.33, XXIV.60, XXIX.81 and 132, XXXIII.68 and 122), which has more uses in this canto than in any other (three). See the note to *Paradiso* XV.40–42. See also Ledda (Ledd.2002.1), pp. 316–19.

130–132. See Dronke (Dron.1965.1), pp. 389–90, and Baranski (Bara.2000.1), pp. 173–74, 217, both cited by Gilson (Gils.2004.1), p. 174n., as synthesizing Platonism and Aristotelianism.

131. For notice of a possible reflection here of the fourth and final stage of loving God in St. Bernard's *De diligendo Deo*, see Hollander (Holl.1976.2), p. 35 (repr. Holl.1980.2): "Commentators have for a long time annotated this passage with a reference to Philippians 2:7" (as we have seen [note to vv. 127–132], that is barely true; only two of them in the last 150 years). Hollander goes on to show that Bernard, in *De diligendo Deo* (*Sancti Bernardi Opera*, ed. J. Leclercq and H. M. Rochais, Vol. III [Rome: Editiones Cistercienses, 1963], p. 142), resorts to the same Pauline passage in a highly similar context, describing the height of the mystical love of God, when one loves oneself in God. For Bernard's four stages in

the love of God and their possible relation to the stages in the *Comedy* (first suggested by a student at Princeton, Donald J. Mathison, in 1968), see the note to *Purgatorio* XXVII.139–141. For later discussions that are in agreement, see Mazzoni (Mazz.1997.1), p. 176, as well as Moevs (Moev.2005.1), p. 81. And see E. G. Gardner (Gard.1913.1), p. 118, for the relation of *De diligendo Deo* X.27–28 to Dante's spiritual preparedness for the final vision.

133. For a study of this penultimate simile, a meditation on how Dante may be said to have "squared the circle," see Herzman and Towsley (Herz.1994.1). See also Ledda (Ledd.2002.1), p. 317n.

137–138. See Kay (Kay.2002.1), pp. 30–31, for the notion, advanced as a follow-up to his examination of the Vitruvian nature of Dante's calculations of the dimensions of both the giants (*Inf.* XXX) and of Satan (*Inf.* XXXIV), that what Dante sees is Vitruvius's image of man inscribed in a circle, his *umbelicus* at the center of the circle, his fingers and toes at the circumference, in what is the eventual model for Leonardo da Vinci's far more famous design. As charming as this notion is, the word *effige* in Dante (*Par.* XXXI.77, XXXIII.131) seems rather to indicate, as is generally the case in Italian, the visage, not the whole human body.

138. Jacomuzzi (Jaco.1965.1) offers a reading of these verses and of the poem as a whole in the mode of a theologically determined fourfold allegoresis. For discussion, with some bibliography, of Italian and American treatments of theological allegory in the poem, see Hollander (Holl. 2001.1), pp. 37–39 and p. 188, nn. 55–57.

139–141. For insistence on the role played, in this final vision, of both the *Benjamin major* of Richard of St. Victor and the *Itinterarium mentis in Deum* of Bonaventure, see Gilson (Gils.1924.1), pp. 56–57. Gilson (pp. 62–63) concludes that, given these two sources, Dante's vision is not a Pauline *raptus* (a function of the intellect), but a Franciscan *exstasis* (a function of the affective capacity). This, however, and despite Gilson's authority, is not the general current opinion, which rather insists that Dante did have a Pauline *raptus* (as the entire *cantica* has been preparing us to grant). For instance, Güntert (Gunt.2002.2), p. 507, cites Aquinas (*ST* II–II, q. 175, a. 3), distinguishing among three kinds of vision (but for an earlier and similar treatment see Pertile [Pert.1981.1], pp. 6–7). After discussions that are in strong agreement with positions taken on the issues by Augustine, Thomas explains, in his Reply to Objection 1: "Man's mind is rapt by God to the contemplation of divine truth in three ways. First, so that he contemplates it through certain imaginary pictures (*per similitudines quasdam imaginarias*), and such was the ecstasy that came upon Peter [Acts 10:10–16]. Secondly, so that he contemplates the divine truth through its intelligible effects (*per intelligibiles effectus*); such was the ecstasy of David, who said (Psalm 115 [116]:11): 'I said in my excess: Every man is a liar.' Thirdly, so that he contemplates it in its essence (*in sua essentia*). Such was the rapture of Paul, as also of Moses; and not without reason, since as Moses was the first Teacher of the Jews, so was Paul the first 'Teacher of the gentiles' " (tr. from the website of the *Catholic Encyclopedia*). It is typical of Gilson, a Dominican himself, to downplay the importance of Dominicans in favor of Franciscans. His graciousness is a model to us all. However, it may be that he is simply incorrect here. The reader will note that here, even at the conclusion of the great poem, commentators are divided among Franciscan and Dominican positions on the issues. For the difficult history of the intertwined strands of knowledge and love in St. Thomas, in whom, at least apparently, such distinctions would be clearer than they are in Dante, see Sherwin (Sher.2005.1). In Dante, we find at moments, like this one, knowledge eclipsing the claims of love; at others, that dynamic would seem to be reversed. One comes away with the feeling that Dante responds fully to the main competing voices in this continuing dialectic, "Franciscans" (Francis himself, Bonaventure, Bernard, and perhaps Joachim as well), who privilege love (but not *against* knowledge), and "Dominicans" (Thomas *primissimus inter impares*, but Albertus Magnus and Remigius Girolamus as well), who privilege knowledge (but not *against* love). For an article that strongly supports the notion that Dante was closely aware of the text of Ezechiel, see Bognini (Bogn.2007.1).

142–145. The final four lines are divided into two parts, the first referring to an apparent failure ("Here my exalted vision lost its power"), in which the protagonist/poet, so recently rewarded with the comprehension of Everything (verse 141), loses that vision, which is blotted out by his reemergent humanity. And then the poem's final sentence, begun with an adversative, *ma* (but), tells a quite different story: The protagonist's interior motions, that of his affective power (the will) and that of his intellective power (his transmuted desire), both move in harmony with God's cosmos.

142. See the *Grande Dizionario* for a definition of *facoltà*: "the property of every being endowed with sense to perceive, revive, and represent in the

soul sensations, perceptions, impressions, and images." On *fantasia* and *imaginazione*, see Lepschy (Leps.1987.1). And see the notes to *Purgatorio* XVII.13–18 and 25.

143. For discussion of Dante's use of Latin in the poem, including this final instance, see the note to *Paradiso* IV.25.

144. Pertile (Pert.2005.2), pp. 265–81 (a reprinting of an article published in 1995) and pp. 133–35, reopens the question of the meaning of this final image. The vast majority of readers have believed that Dante has a single wheel in mind (none more exigently and at greater length than Nardi [Nard.1944.1], pp. 337–50), all places on which move with uniform regularity. Pertile revives the view of those few twentieth-century readers who saw the tautological vacuity of this as a final image and, revisiting Ezechiel (1:19–21 and 10:16) and Boethius (*Cons.* II.m8.28–30), revives a better idea: Dante has *two* wheels in mind. Aversano (Aver.1984.2), pp. 203–6, also finds the source in Ezechiel (1:15–21), but in order to make a different point. But see Freccero (Frec.1986.1, pp. 246–50 of an essay entitled "The Final Image," first published in 1964) for whom there is but one wheel, despite the fact that he thinks it reflects Ezechiel's wheel within a wheel, which would seem to indicate two wheels.

For a new wrinkle, see Rizzardi (Rizz.2000.1), who makes a case for Dante's having an image in mind that would become a staple in later ages: the universe as the movements in a mechanical clock. She bolsters her argument by pointing back to previous clock imagery (at *Purg.* VIII.85–87; *Par.* X.139–146 and *Par.* XXIV.13–18).

Whatever the metaphor controlling this passage, whether biblical or astronomical or mechanical, the simplest solution of the literal sense of the line is to understand that line 144, "as a wheel that is moved in just the same way," is attached to the preceding (Latin) noun, *velle*. What the text then says is clear: "But already my desire was moving in a circle (around God), as was my will, revolving in just the same way." This was precisely the understanding put forward by Torraca (comm. to vv. 143–145) over one hundred years ago that Bruno Nardi belittled (Nard.1944.1), p. 349n. The protagonist/poet's soul has left our solar system behind and is moving in a circle, not around our earth, but, like the angelic orders, around God. See Pertile's concluding remarks on the last paradox in the poem: The pilgrim has found his peace in continual movement. It is not an accident that Goethe admired this final scene and used it in developing the conclusion of the second part of *Faust*.

145. While the fact that the word *stelle* is the last word of each canticle would seem to have been an early and lasting perception, John of Serravalle (comm. to vv. 133–145) appears to have been the first ever to have had it.

For the possibility that Dante's *stella* reflects Ovid's *astra* (*Metam.* XV.876) and *his* starry vision of his own personal immortality that concludes his great poem (vv. 871–879), reformulated by Dante to accord with quite a different (and less self-absorbed) view, see Levenstein (Leve.2003.1), p. 418.

For an essay on this "last word," see Ahern (Aher.1984.1), who, while not referring to Ovid, argues that this canto couches its central concerns, conflating two metaphors, in the images of the heavens as book and of the stars as alphabet.

Scartazzini (comm. to this verse) points out that the presence of the same form of the verb *muovere* in the first and last lines of the *cantica* creates a sort of ring composition. He also points out that Dante's practice in this regard resembles that found in *canzoni* of other poets in his time; he also suggests the pertinence of the ending (which happens to constitute its thirty-third paragraph) of the *Epistle to Cangrande* (XIII.90): "And since, when the Beginning or First, which is God, has been reached, there is nought to be sought for beyond, inasmuch as He is Alpha and Omega, that is, the Beginning and the End, as the *Vision* of John tells us, the work ends in God Himself, who is blessed for evermore, world without end" (tr. P. Toynbee).

AMDG 9.ix.MMVI

INDEX OF NAMES AND PLACES

Index of these items (in their English forms, where these exist) in the Italian text of *Paradiso*. NB: (1) if a character or a place is mentioned more than once in a canto, only the first reference is indicated; (2) no distinction has been made between direct and indirect references; that is, one will find "Lavinia" and not "Amata, daughter of."

INDEX OF SUBJECTS TREATED IN THE NOTES

This index is meant to help the reader find subjects, treated in the notes, that may not be readily remembered as being related to a particular passage.

Adve.1995.1
Adversi, Aldo, "Dante e il canonista Graziano (*Par.* X, 103–105)," *Il Diritto ecclesiastico* 106 (1995): 499–513.
Agne.1891.1
Agnelli, Giovanni, *Topo-cronografia del viaggio dantesco* (Milan: Hoepli, 1891).
Aher.1982.3
Ahern, John, "Singing the Book: Orality in the Reception of Dante's *Comedy*," in *Dante: Contemporary Perspectives*, ed. Amilcare A. Iannucci (Toronto: University of Toronto Press, 1997 [1982]), pp. 214–39.
Aher.1982.4
Ahern, John, "Binding the Book: Hermeneutics and Manuscript Production in *Paradiso* 33," *PMLA* 97 (1982): 800–809.
Aher.1984.1
Ahern, John, "Dante's Last Word: The *Comedy* as a *liber coelestis*," *Dante Studies* 102 (1984): 1–14.
Ales.1989.1
Alessio, Gian Carlo, "Un appunto su *Paradiso* XXXII.139–141," *Nozze Cociglio-Magnino* (Verona: Valdonega, 1989).
Alla.1993.1
Allan, Mowbray, "*Paradiso* XIX, 106, and St. Thomas's *Sed contra*," *Dante Studies* 111 (1993): 195–211.
Alle.1965.1
Allevi, Febo, *Con Dante e la Sibilla ed altri (dagli antichi al volgare)* (Milan: Edizioni Scientifico-Letterarie, 1965).
Alle.2002.1
Allegretti, Paola, "Canto IX," in *Lectura Dantis Turicensis: Paradiso*, ed. Georges Güntert and Michelangelo Picone (Florence: Cesati, 2002), pp. 133–44.
Alle.2004.1
Allegretti, Paola, "Argo: 'Dietro al mio legno che cantando varca' (*Par.* II 3)," *Studi Danteschi* 69 (2004): 185–209.
Alle.2004.2
Allegretti, Paola, "Un acrostico per Giovanni del Virgilio," *Studi Danteschi* 69 (2004): 289–93.
Amad.1921.1
Amaducci, Paolo, *Nel cielo de' contemplanti: S. Pier Damiano Ravennate; saggio di una interpretazione nuova della* Divina commedia (Rome: Alfieri e Lacroix, [1921]).
Ambr.2002.1
Ambrosini, Riccardo, "Canto XVII," in *Lectura Dantis Turicensis: Paradiso*, ed. Georges Güntert and Michelangelo Picone (Florence: Cesati, 2002), pp. 243–64.

Angi.1986.1
Angiolillo, Giuliana, "Canto IV," in *Lectura Dantis Neapolitana: "Paradiso,"* ed. P. Giannantonio (Naples: Loffredo, 2000 [1986]), pp. 59–72.
Anto.1995.2
Antonelli, Roberto, "La corte 'italiana' di Federico II e la letteratura europea," in *Federico II e le nuove culture (Atti del XXXI Convegno storico internazionale, Todi, 9–12 ottobre 1994)*, Spoleto, Centro Italiano di Studi sull'Alto Medioevo, 1995, pp. 319–45.
Anto.2002.1
Antonelli, Roberto, "Canto XXVII," in *Lectura Dantis Turicensis: Paradiso*, ed. Georges Güntert and Michelangelo Picone (Florence: Cesati, 2002), pp. 419–27.
Armo.1995.1
Armour, Peter, "*Paradiso* XXVII," in *Dante's "Divine Comedy," Introductory Readings III: "Paradiso,"* ed. Tibor Wlassics (*Lectura Dantis [virginiana]*, 16–17, supplement, Charlottesville: University of Virginia, 1995), pp. 402–23.
Armo.1997.2
Armour, Peter, "Dante and Popular Sovereignty," in *Dante and Governance*, ed. John Woodhouse (Oxford: Clarendon, 1997), pp. 27–45.
Arna.1996.1
Arnaldi, Girolamo, "La Marca Trevigiana 'prima che Federigo avesse briga', e dopo," in *Dante e la cultura veneta*, ed. V. Branca and G. Padoan (Florence: Olschki, 1966), pp. 29–37.
Arna.1992.1
Arnaldi, Girolamo, "La maledizione del sangue e la virtù delle stelle: Angioini e Capetingi nella *Commedia* di Dante," *La Cultura* 30 (1992): 47–74.
Asin.1919.1
Asín Palacios, Miguel, *La escatologia musulmana en la "Divina Comedia": historia y crítica de una polémica* (Madrid: Hiperión, 1984 [1919]).
Asin.1927.1
Asín Palacios, Miguel, *Dante y el Islam* (Madrid: Edit. Voluntad, 1927).
Auer.1944.2
Auerbach, Erich, "St. Francis of Assisi in Dante's *Commedia*," in *Scenes from the Drama of European Literature*, tr. C. Garvin (New York: Meridian Books, 1959 [1944]), pp. 77–98.
Auer.1946.1
Auerbach, Erich, "Figurative Texts Illustrating Certain Passages of Dante's *Commedia*," *Speculum* 21 (1946): 474–89.
Auer.1949.1
Auerbach, Erich, "Dante's Prayer to the Virgin (*Par.* XXXIII) and Earlier Eulogies," *Romance Philology* 3 (1949): 1–26.
Auer.1958.1
Auerbach, Erich, "*Sermo humilis*," in *Literary Language and Its Public in Late Latin Antiquity and in the Middle Ages*, tr. R. Manheim (Princeton: Princeton University Press, 1965 [1958]), pp. 25–66.
Aust.1936.1
Austin, H. D., " 'Black But Comely' (*Par.* XXVII, 136–138)," *Philological Quarterly* 15 (1936): 253–57.
Aver.1984.2
Aversano, Mario, *Dante e gli "scritti" di San Francesco* (Salerno: Palladio, 1984 [31 pp.]).
Aver.1988.2
Aversano, Mario, "La conclusione della *Commedia*," in *La quinta rota: Studi sulla "Commedia"* (Turin: Tirrenia, 1988), pp. 189–227.
Aver.1990.1
Aversano, Mario, *San Bernardo e Dante: Teologia e poesia della conversione* (Salerno: Edisud, 1990).

Aver.2000.2
Aversano, Mario, *Dante daccapo* ([glosses to the *Paradiso*], *copia d'eccezione*, sent by the author on 11 September 2001).
Azze.2003.1
Azzetta, Luca, "Le chiose alla *Commedia* di Andrea Lancia, l'*Epistola a Cangrande* e altre questioni dantesche," *L'Alighieri* 21 (2003): 5–76.
Bald.1973.1
Baldelli, Ignazio, "Il canto XI del *Paradiso*," *Nuove letture dantesche*, vol. VI (Florence: Le Monnier, 1973), pp. 93–105.
Bald.1993.2
Baldelli, Ignazio, "Il canto I del *Paradiso*," *L'Alighieri* 1/2 (1993): 59–74.
Balf.1995.1
Balfour, Mark, "*Paradiso* IX," in *Dante's "Divine Comedy," Introductory Readings III: "Paradiso,"* ed. Tibor Wlassics (*Lectura Dantis [virginiana]*, 16–17, supplement, Charlottesville: University of Virginia, 1995), pp. 131–45.
Bara.1984.1
Baranski, Zygmunt G., "Dante tra dei pagani e angeli cristiani," *Filologia e critica* 9 (1984): 293–302.
Bara.1993.2
Baranski, Zygmunt G., " 'Sordellus . . . qui . . . patrium vulgare deseruit': A Note on *De vulgari eloquentia*, I, 15, sections 2–6," in *The Cultural Heritage of the Italian Renaissance: Essays in Honour of T. G. Griffith*, ed. C. E. J. Griffiths and R. Hastings (Lewiston, N.Y.: Edwin Mellen Press, 1993), pp. 19–45.
Bara.1995.3
Baranski, Zygmunt G., "The Poetics of Meter: *Terza rima*, 'canto,' 'canzon,' 'cantica,' " in *Dante Now: Current Trends in Dante Studies*, ed. Theodore J. Cachey, Jr. (Notre Dame: University of Notre Dame Press, 1995), pp. 3–41.
Bara.1995.4
Baranski, Zygmunt G., "*Paradiso* XIX," in *Dante's "Divine Comedy," Introductory Readings III: "Paradiso,"* ed. Tibor Wlassics (*Lectura Dantis [virginiana]*, 16–17, supplement, Charlottesville: University of Virginia, 1995), pp. 277–99.
Bara.1997.3
Baranski, Zygmunt G., and Patrick Boyde, eds., *The "Fiore" in Context: Dante, France, Tuscany* (Notre Dame: University of Notre Dame Press, 1997).
Bara.2000.1
Baranski, Zygmunt G., *Dante e i segni* (Rome: Liguori, 2000).
Bara.2001.1
Baranski, Zygmunt G., "L'esegesi medievale della *Commedia* e il problema delle fonti," in his *"Chiosar con altro testo": Leggere Dante nel Trecento* (Fiesole: Cadmo, 2001), pp. 13–39.
Bara.2002.1
Baranski, Zygmunt G., "Canto XXII," in *Lectura Dantis Turicensis: Paradiso*, ed. Georges Güntert and Michelangelo Picone (Florence: Cesati, 2002), pp. 339–62.
Barb.1934.1
Barbi, Michele, *Problemi di critica dantesca* (Florence: Sansoni, 1934).
Barb.1941.2
Barbi, Michele, *Con Dante e coi suoi interpreti* (Florence: Le Monnier, 1941).
Barb.1995.1
Bàrberi Squarotti, Giorgio, "La preghiera alla Vergine: Dante e Petrarca," *Filologia e critica* 20 (1995): 365–74.
Barc.1973.1
Barchiesi, Marino, "Catarsi classica e 'medicina' dantesca, Dal canto XX dell'*Inferno*," *Letture classensi* 4 (1973): 9–124.
Barn.1986.1

Barnes, John C., "*Ut architectura poesis?* The Case of Dante's *candida rosa,*" *The Italianist* 6 (1986): 19–33.

Baro.1981.1
Barolini, Teodolinda, review of R. Kirkpatrick *(Dante's "Paradiso" and the Limits of Modern Criticism), Romance Philology* 35 (1981): 409–13.

Baro.1984.1
Barolini, Teodolinda, *Dante's Poets* (Princeton: Princeton University Press, 1984).

Baro.1987.1
Barolini, Teodolinda, "Arachne, Argus, and St. John: Transgressive Art in Dante and Ovid," *Mediaevalia* 13 (1987): 207–26.

Baro.1992.1
Barolini, Teodolinda, *The Undivine "Comedy": Detheologizing Dante* (Princeton: Princeton University Press, 1992).

Batt.1961.1
Battaglia, Salvatore, and Giorgio Bárberi Squarotti, eds., *Il Grande Dizionario della lingua italiana* (Turin: UTET, 1961–96 [up to "Sik"]).

Batt.1972.1
Battaglia Ricci, Lucia, "*Paradiso* XXV, 86–96," *Giornale storico della letteratura italiana* 149 (1972): 333–38.

Batt.1988.1
Battistini, Andrea, " 'Se la Scrittura sovra voi non fosse [. . .]': Allusioni bibliche nel canto XIX del *Paradiso,*" *Critica letteraria* 16 (1988): 211–35.

Batt.1989.1
Battaglia Ricci, Lucia, "Piccarda, o della carità: lettura del terzo canto del *Paradiso,*" *Critica e filologia* 14 (1989): 27–70.

Batt.1995.1
Battaglia Ricci, Lucia, "Con parole e segni: Lettura del XVIII del *Paradiso,*" *L'Alighieri* 6 (1995): 7–28.

Batt.1997.1
Battaglia Ricci, Lucia, "Figure di contraddizione: Lettura dell'XI canto del *Paradiso,*" in *Studi in onore di Emilio Bigi* (Milan: Principato, 1997), pp. 34–50.

Beck.1988.1
Becker, Christopher B., "Dante's Heretics," unpublished typescript read in 1988.

Bell.1996.1
Bellomo, Saverio, "Il canto XXX del *Paradiso,*" *L'Alighieri* 8 (1996): 41–56.

Belt.2004.1
Beltrami, Pietro G., "Arnaut Daniel e la 'bella scola' dei trovatori di Dante," in *Le culture di Dante: Atti del quarto Seminario dantesco internazionale,* ed. Michelangelo Picone et al. (Florence: Cesati, 2004), pp. 29–59.

Bemr.1983.1
Bemrose, Stephen, *Dante's Angelic Intelligences: Their Importance in the Cosmos and in Pre-Christian Religion* (Rome: Edizioni di Storia e Letteratura, 1983).

Bert.1903.1
Bertoldi, Alfonso, *Il canto XI del "Paradiso"* (["Lectura Dantis Orsanmichele"] Florence: Sansoni, [1903]).

Bert.1913.1
Bertoldi, Alfonso, *Il canto XII del "Paradiso"* (["Lectura Dantis Orsanmichele"] Florence: Sansoni, [1913]).

Binn.1968.1
Binni, Walter, "Canto XXX," in *Lectura Dantis Scaligera: "Paradiso,"* dir. M. Marcazzan (Florence: Le Monnier, 1968), pp. 1061–96.

Blas.1991.1
Blasucci, Luigi, "Discorso teologico e visione sensibile nel canto XIV del *Paradiso,*" *La Rassegna della letteratura italiana* 95 (1991): 5–19.

Blas.2000.1
Blasucci, Luigi, "Per una tipologia degli esordi nei canti danteschi," *La parola del testo* 4 (2000): 17–46.
Bogn.2007.1
Bognini, Filippo, "Gli occhi di Ooliba: Una proposta per *Purg.* XXXII 148-60 e XXXIII 44-45," *Rivista di Studi Danteschi* 7 (2007): 73–103.
Boit.1978.1
Boitani, Piero, "The Sibyl's Leaves: A Study of *Paradiso* XXXIII," *Dante Studies* 96 (1978): 83–126.
Boit.2002.1
Boitani, Piero, "Creazione e cadute di *Paradiso* XXIX," *L'Alighieri* 19 (2002): 87–103.
Boit.2002.2
Boitani, Piero, "Canto XXIX," in *Lectura Dantis Turicensis: Paradiso*, ed. Georges Güntert and Michelangelo Picone (Florence: Cesati, 2002), pp. 441–55.
Bolo.2002.1
Bologna, Corrado, "Canto XXX," in *Lectura Dantis Turicensis: Paradiso*, ed. Georges Güntert and Michelangelo Picone (Florence: Cesati, 2002), pp. 457–72.
Bona.2001.1
Bonanno, Danilo, "Guido in Paradiso: *Donna me prega* e l'ultimo canto della *Commedia*," *Critica del testo* 4 (2001): 223–43.
Bono.1987.1
Bonora, Ettore, "Canto XI," in *Lectura Dantis Neapolitana: "Paradiso,"* ed. P. Giannantonio (Naples: Loffredo, 2000 [1987]), pp. 237–53.
Bors.1957.1
Borst, Arno, *Der Turmbau von Babel,* 3 vols. (Stuttgart: A. Hiersemann, 1957–60).
Bors.1995.1
Borsellino, Nino, "Sotto il segno di Marte: la cronaca del padre antico (*Par.* XVI)," *L'Alighieri* 5 (1995): 37–46.
Borz.1989.1
Borzi, Italo, "Il Canto XXIV," in *"Paradiso": Letture degli anni 1979–'81*, ed. S. Zennaro (Rome: Bonacci, 1989), pp. 643–66.
Bosc.1966.1
Bosco, Umberto, *Dante vicino* (Caltanissetta: Sciascia, 1966).
Bose.1996.1
Bose, Mishtooni, "From Exegesis to Appropriation: The Medieval Solomon," *Medium Aevum* 65 (1996): 187–210.
Bott.1994.1
Botterill, Steven, *Dante and the Mystical Tradition: Bernard of Clairvaux in the "Commedia"* (Cambridge: Cambridge University Press, 1994).
Bott.1995.1
Botterill, Steven, "*Paradiso* XII," in *Dante's "Divine Comedy," Introductory Readings III: "Paradiso,"* ed. Tibor Wlassics (*Lectura Dantis [virginiana]*, 16–17, supplement, Charlottesville: University of Virginia, 1995), pp. 172–85.
Bott.2003.1
Botterill, Steven, "Mysticism and Meaning in Dante's *Paradiso*," in *Dante for the New Millennium*, ed. Teodolinda Barolini and H. Wayne Storey (New York: Fordham University Press, 2003), pp. 143–51.
Bouq.2004.1
Bouquet, Monique, and Françoise Morzadec, eds., *La Sibylle: Parole et représentation* (Rennes: Presses Universitaires de Rennes, 2004).
Boyd.1981.1
Boyde, Patrick, *Dante Philomythes and Philosopher: Man in the Cosmos* (Cambridge: Cambridge University Press, 1981).
Boyd.1993.1

Boyde, Patrick, *Perception and Passion in Dante's "Comedy"* (Cambridge: Cambridge University Press, 1993).

Boyd.1995.1

Boyde, Patrick, "L'esegesi di Dante e la scienza," in *Dante e la scienza*, ed. P. Boyde and V. Russo (Ravenna: Longo, 1995), pp. 9–23.

Boyl.2000.1

Boyle, Marjorie O'Rourke, "Closure in Paradise: Dante Outsings Aquinas," *Modern Language Notes* 115 (2000): 1–12.

Brez.1968.1

Brezzi, Paolo, "Canto VI," in *Lectura Dantis Scaligera: "Paradiso,"* dir. M. Marcazzan (Florence: Le Monnier, 1968), pp. 173–216.

Brez.1989.1

Brezzi, Paolo, "II Canto XVII," in *"Paradiso": Letture degli anni 1979–'81*, ed. S. Zennaro (Rome: Bonacci, 1989), pp. 443–67.

Brow.1978.1

Brownlee, Kevin, "Dante and Narcissus (*Purg.* XXX, 76–99)," *Dante Studies* 96 (1978): 201–6.

Brow.1984.1

Brownlee, Kevin, "Phaeton's Fall and Dante's Ascent," *Dante Studies* 102 (1984): 135–44.

Brow.1984.2

Brownlee, Kevin, "Why the Angels Speak Italian: Dante as Vernacular *Poeta* in *Paradiso* XXV," *Poetics Today* 5 (1984): 597–610.

Brow.1990.1

Brownlee, Kevin, "*Paradiso* XXVI," in *Dante's "Divine Comedy," Introductory Readings III: "Paradiso,"* ed. Tibor Wlassics (*Lectura Dantis [virginiana]*, 16–17, supplement, Charlottesville: University of Virginia, 1995 [1990]), pp. 388–401.

Brow.1991.2

Brownlee, Kevin, "Ovid's Semele and Dante's Metamorphosis: *Paradiso* 21–22," in *The Poetry of Allusion: Virgil and Ovid in Dante's "Commedia,"* ed. Rachel Jacoff and Jeffrey T. Schnapp (Stanford: Stanford University Press, 1991), pp. 224–32, 293–94.

Brug.1995.1

Brugnoli, Giorgio, "*Paradiso* XVII," *L'Alighieri* 5 (1995): 47–58.

Brug.1998.1

Brugnoli, Giorgio, "I tempi cristiani di Dante," *Critica del testo* 1 (1998): 469–92.

Brug.1999.1

Brugnoli, Giorgio, "Sardanapalo in camera," *Rivista internazionale di onomastica letteraria* 1 (1999): 55–76.

Burl.2003.1

Burlot, Maria Lorena, "Dante Alighieri y la Iglesia católica: La *Divina Comedia* y la Enciclica 'In praeclara' de Benedicto XV," in *Mito y religión en la lengua y la literatura italianas: Atti del convegno di italianistica*, ed. Gloria Galli de Ortega y María Troiano de Echegaray, vol. II (Mendoze: Editorial de la Facultad de Filosofía y Letras–Univ. Nac. de Cuyo, 2003), pp. 549–60.

Bynu.1995.1

Bynum, Caroline Walker, *The Resurrection of the Body in Western Christianity, 200–1336* (New York: Columbia University Press, 1995).

Cahi.1996.1

Cahill, Courtney, "The Limitations of Difference in *Paradiso* XIII's Two Arts: Reason and Poetry," *Dante Studies* 114 (1996): 245–69.

Calv.2001.1

Calvet, Antoine, "Dante et les joachimismes," in *Pour Dante: Dante et l'Apocalypse; Lectures humanistes de Dante*, ed. Bruno Pinchard and Christian Trottmann (Paris: Champion, 2001), pp. 77–98.

Came.1995.1

Camerino, Giuseppe Antonio, "*Paradiso* XX," *L'Alighieri* 6 (1995): 47–60.

Card.2006.1

Cardellino, Lodovico, " 'Dischiuso' in *Paradiso* 7.102 e 14.138: ha il senso usuale di 'aperto' o 'espresso,' non di 'escluso,' " *Electronic Bulletin of the Dante Society of America* (January 2006).

Carp.2004.1

Carpi, Umberto, *La nobiltà di Dante* (Florence: Polistampa, 2004).

Carr.2002.1

Carrai, Stefano, "Canto VI," in *Lectura Dantis Turicensis: Paradiso*, ed. Georges Güntert and Michelangelo Picone (Florence: Cesati, 2002), pp. 95–106.

Caru.1994.1

Carugati, Giuliana, "Retorica amorosa e verità in Dante: Il *De causis* e l'idea della donna nel *Convivio*," *Dante Studies* 112 (1994): 161–75.

Casa.1976.1

Casagrande, Gino, " 'I s'appellava in terra il sommo bene' (*Paradiso*, XXVI, 134)," *Aevum* 50 (1976): 249–73.

Casa.1997.2

Casagrande, Gino, "Parole di Dante: 'abborrare,' " *Studi Danteschi* 63 (1991 [1997]): 177–90.

Case.1950.1

Casella, Mario, "Nel cielo del Sole: l'anima e la mente di san Tommaso," *Studi Danteschi* 29 (1950): 5–40; 30 (1951): 5–22; 31 (1952): 5–30.

Cass.1971.3

Cassata, Letterio, "Tre *cruces* dantesche: III; La pelle di Pasifae," *Studi Danteschi* 48 (1971): 29–43.

Cass.2004.1

Cassell, Anthony K., *The "Monarchia" Controversy: An Historical Study with Accompanying Translations of Dante Alighieri's "Monarchia," Guido Vernani's "Refutation of the 'Monarchia' Composed by Dante," and Pope John XXII's Bull "Si fratrum"* (Washington, D.C.: Catholic University of America Press, 2004).

Ceru.1949.1

Cerulli, Enrico, *Il "Libro della scala" e la questione delle fonti arabo-spagnole della "Divina Commedia"* (Città del Vaticano: Biblioteca apostolica vaticana, 1949).

Cest.2003.1

Cestaro, Gary P., *Dante and the Grammar of the Nursing Body* (Notre Dame: University of Notre Dame Press, 2003).

Char.1966.1

Charity, A. C., *Events and Their Afterlife: The Dialectics of Christian Typology in the Bible and Dante* (Cambridge: Cambridge University Press, 1966).

Cher.2004.1

Cherchi, Paolo, "Dante e i trovatori," in *Le culture di Dante: Atti del quarto Seminario dantesco internazionale*, ed. Michelangelo Picone et al. (Florence: Cesati, 2004), pp. 93–103.

Chia.1966.1

Chiarenza, Marguerite Mills, "Hippolytus' Exile: *Paradiso* XVII, vv. 46–48," *Dante Studies* 84 (1966): 65–68.

Chia.1967.3

Chiappelli, Fredi, "Abstraction et réalité dans la structure figurative du *Paradiso*," in *Le Réel dans la littérature et dans la langue, actes du Xe congrès de la Féderation internationale des langues et littératures modernes (F.I.L.L.M.), Strasbourg, 29 août–3 septembre 1966*, ed. Paul Vernois (Paris: C. Klincksieck, 1967), pp. 7–22.

Chia.1972.1

Chiarenza, Marguerite Mills, "The Imageless Vision and Dante's *Paradiso*," *Dante Studies* 90 (1972): 77–91.

Chia.1975.2

Chiavacci Leonardi, Anna Maria, "Il canto XXX del *Paradiso*," *Paragone* 308 (1975): 3–34.

Chia.1981.1
Chiampi, James T., *Shadowy Prefaces* (Ravenna: Longo, 1981).
Chia.1983.2
Chiarenza, Marguerite, "Boethian Themes in Dante's Reading of Virgil," *Stanford Italian Review* 3 (1983): 25–35.
Chia.1983.3
Chiarenza, Marguerite Mills, "Time and Eternity in the Myths of *Paradiso* XVII," in *Dante, Petrarch, Boccaccio: Studies in the Italian Trecento in Honor of Charles S. Singleton*, ed. A. S. Bernardo and A. L. Pellegrini (Binghamton, N.Y.: Medieval & Renaissance Texts and Studies, 1983), pp. 133–50.
Chia.1988.1
Chiarenza, Marguerite Mills, " 'Legato con amore in un volume,' " in *Dante e la Bibbia*, ed. G. Barblan (Florence: Olschki, 1988), pp. 227–34.
Chia.1988.2
Chiavacci Leonardi, Anna, " 'Le bianche stole': il tema della resurrezione nel *Paradiso*," in *Dante e la Bibbia*, ed. G. Barblan (Florence: Olschki, 1988), pp. 249–71.
Chia.1989.2
Chiavacci Leonardi, Anna Maria, "*Paradiso* XVII," in *Filologia e critica dantesca: Studi offerti a Aldo Vallone* (Florence: Olschki, 1989), pp. 309–27.
Chia.1993.1
Chiarenza, Marguerite, "Dante's Lady Poverty," *Dante Studies* 111 (1993): 153–75.
Chia.1995.1
Chiamenti, Massimiliano, *Dante Alighieri traduttore* (Florence: Le Lettere, 1995).
Chia.1995.3
Chiarenza, Marguerite, "*Paradiso* XX," *Lectura Dantis [virginiana]* 16–17 (1995): 300–307.
Chia.1997.1
Chiavacci Leonardi, Anna Maria, *Paradiso, con il commento di A. M. C. L.* (Milan: Mondadori, 1997).
Chia.1999.3
Chiamenti, Massimiliano, "Intertestualità *Liber Scale Machometi-Commedia?*" *Semestrale di Studi (e Testi) italiani* 4 (1999): 45–51. [see also http://www.disp.let. uniroma1.it/contents/?idPagina=95]
Chia.2000.1
Chiarenza, Marguerite, "Solomon's Song in the *Divine Comedy*," in *Sparks and Seeds: Medieval Literature and Its Afterlife (Essays in Honor of John Freccero)*, ed. Dana E. Stewart and Alison Cornish (Turnhout: Brepols, 2000), pp. 199–208.
Chim.1956.1
Chimenz, Siro A., "Il canto XIX del *Paradiso*," in *Letture dantesche, III: "Paradiso,"* ed. G. Getto (Florence: Sansoni, 1965 [1956]), pp. 1733–59.
Clay.1985.1
Clay, Diskin, "The Art of Glaukos (Plato *Phaedo* 108D4–9)," *American Journal of Philology* 106 (1985): 230–36.
Coga.1999.1
Cogan, Marc, *The Design in the Wax: The Structure of the "Divine Comedy" and Its Meaning* (Notre Dame: University of Notre Dame Press, 1999).
Cogl.1990.1
Coglievina, Leonella, "Strutture narrative e 'vera sentenza' nel *Paradiso* dantesco: l'esempio del V canto," *Studi Danteschi* 58 (1986 [1990]): 49–80.
Como.1990.1
Comollo, Adriano, *Il dissenso religioso in Dante* (Florence: Olschki, 1990).
Comp.1872.1
Comparetti, Domenico, *Vergil in the Middle Ages*, tr. E. F. M. Benecke (Hamden, Conn.: Archon Books, 1966 [1872]).
Comp.1986.1

Boorstein, Daniel E., tr., *Dino Compagni's Chronicle of Florence* (Philadelphia: University of Pennsylvania Press, 1986).

Conr.1971.1

Conrieri, Davide, "San Giacomo e la speranza: osservazioni su *Paradiso* XXV, vv. 13–99," *Giornale storico della letteratura italiana* 148 (1971): 309–15.

Cons.1953.1

Constable, Giles, "The Second Crusade as Seen by Contemporaries," *Traditio* 9 (1953): 213–79.

Cont.1968.1

Contini, Gianfranco, "Canto XXVIII," in *Lectura Dantis Scaligera: "Paradiso,"* dir. M. Marcazzan (Florence: Le Monnier, 1968), pp. 999–1030.

Cont.1976.1

Contini, Gianfranco, *Un' idea di Dante* (Turin: Einaudi, 1976).

Cont.2001.1

Conte, Silvia, "Le finalità del comico: una nuova proposta per l'interpretazione della *intitulatio* della *Commedia*," *Critica del testo* 4 (2001): 559–74.

Cont.2006.1

Conte, Silvia, "Giustiniano e l'ispirazione divina dei *Digesta*," *L'Alighieri* 27 (2006): 25–40.

Corn.1990.1

Cornish, Alison, "Planets and Angels in *Paradiso* XXIX: The First Moment," *Dante Studies* 108 (1990): 1–28.

Corn.2000.1

Cornish, Alison, "Angels," in *The Dante Encyclopedia*, ed. Richard Lansing (New York: Garland, 2000), pp. 37–45.

Corn.2000.2

Cornish, Alison, *Reading Dante's Stars* (New Haven: Yale University Press, 2000).

Cort.1978.1

Corti, Maria, *Il viaggio testuale* (Turin: Einaudi, 1993 [1978]).

Cort.1983.1

Corti, Maria, *La felicità mentale: nuove prospettive per Cavalcanti e Dante* (Turin: Einaudi, 1983).

Cort.1995.1

Corti, Maria, "La *Commedia* di Dante e l'oltretomba islamico," *L'Alighieri* 5 (1995): 7–19.

Cosm.1936.1

Cosmo, Umberto, *L'ultima ascesa: Introduzione alla lettura del "Paradiso,"* ed. B. Maier (Florence: La Nuova Italia, 1965 [1936]).

Cost.1996.1

Costa, Gustavo, "Il canto XXXI del *Paradiso*," *L'Alighieri* 8 (1996): 57–85.

Croc.1921.1

Croce, Benedetto, *La poesia di Dante*, 2d ed. (Bari: Laterza, 1921).

Curt.1948.1

Curtius, Ernst Robert, *European Literature and the Latin Middle Ages*, tr. W. R. Trask (New York: Harper & Row, 1963 [1948]).

Curt.1950.1

Curtius, Ernst Robert, "The Ship of the Argonauts," in *Essays on European Literature*, tr. M. Kowal (Princeton: Princeton University Press, 1973 [1950]), pp. 465–96.

Curt.2002.1

Curti, Luca, "Canto VI," in *Lectura Dantis Turicensis: Paradiso*, ed. Georges Güntert and Michelangelo Picone (Florence: Cesati, 2002), pp. 145–65.

Cuzz.2003.1

Cuzzilla, Tony, "*Par.* 32.139: 'Ma perché 'l tempo fugge che t'assonna,' " *Electronic Bulletin of the Dante Society of America* (March 2003).

Daca.1983.1

da Campagnola, Stanislao, "Francesco d'Assisi in Dante," *Laurentianum* 24 (1983): 175–92.
Danc.1913.1
D'Ancona, Alessandro, *Scritti danteschi* (Florence: Sansoni, 1913).
Davi.1957.1
Davis, Charles Till, *Dante and the Idea of Rome* (Oxford: Oxford University Press, 1957).
Davi.1968.1
Davis, Charles T., "Il buon tempo antico," in *Florentine Studies: Politics and Society in Renaissance Florence*, ed. N. Rubenstein (Evanston, Ill.: Northwestern University Press, 1968), pp. 45–69.
Davi.1984.1
Davis, Charles T., *Dante's Italy and Other Essays* (Philadelphia: University of Pennsylvania Press, 1984).
Davi.1993.1
David, Michel, "Dante et sa théodie," in *Omaggio a Gianfranco Folena*, ed. Pier Vincenzo Mengaldo (Padua: Editoriale Programma, 1993), pp. 429–46.
Debo.1987.1
De Bonfils Templer, Margherita, "Genesi di un'allegoria," *Dante Studies* 105 (1987): 79–94.
Debo.1987.2
De Bonfils Templer, Margherita, "Il dantesco *amoroso uso di Sapienza*: sue radici platoniche," *Stanford Italian Review* 7 (1987): 5–27.
Defa.1995.1
De Fazio, Marina, "*Paradiso* V," in *Dante's "Divine Comedy," Introductory Readings III: "Paradiso,"* ed. Tibor Wlassics (*Lectura Dantis [virginiana]*, 16–17, supplement, Charlottesville: University of Virginia, 1995), pp. 68–90.
Dema.1987.1
Demaray, John G., *Dante and the Book of the Cosmos* (Philadelphia: American Philosophical Society, 1987).
Dero.1990.1
De Robertis, Domenico, "Dante e Beatrice in Paradiso," *Critica letteraria* 18 (1990): 137–54.
Desi.2001.1
Desideri, Giovannella, "Riscontri iconografici nell'*Epistola a Cangrande*," *Critica del testo* 4 (2001): 575–78.
Dibi.1992.1
Di Biase, Carmine, *II Canto XII del "Paradiso"* (Naples: Ermanno Cassitto, 1992).
Disc.1980.1
Di Scipio, Giuseppe, "Dante and St. Paul: The Blinding Light and Water," *Dante Studies* 98 (1980): 151–57.
Disc.1983.1
Di Scipio, Giuseppe, "Dante and Politics," in *The "Divine Comedy" and the Encyclopedia of Arts and Sciences: Acta of the International Dante Symposium, 13–16 November 1983, Hunter College, New York*, ed. G. Di Scipio and A. Scaglione (Amsterdam: John Benjamins, 1988), pp. 267–84.
Disc.1983.2
Di Scipio, Giuseppe, "The Hebrew Women in Dante's Symbolic Rose," *Dante Studies* 101 (1983): 111–21.
Disc.1984.1
Di Scipio, Giuseppe C., *The Symbolic Rose in Dante's "Paradiso"* (Ravenna: Longo, 1984).
Disc.1995.1
Di Scipio, Giuseppe, *The Presence of Pauline Thought in the Works of Dante* (Lewiston, N.Y.: Edwin Mellen Press, 1995).
Diso.1986.1
Di Somma, Paolo, "Canto III," in *Lectura Dantis Neapolitana: "Paradiso,"* ed. P. Giannantonio (Naples: Loffredo, 2000 [1986]), pp. 49–57.

Dovi.1901.1
D'Ovidio, Francesco, "*Cristo* in rima," in his *Studii sulla "Divina Commedia"* (Milan: Sandron, 1901), pp. 215–24.
Dron.1965.1
Dronke, Peter, " 'L'amore che move il sole e l'altre stelle,' " *Studi medievali* 6 (1965): 389–422.
Dron.1975.2
Dronke, Peter, " 'Orizzonte che rischiari,' " in his *Dante and Medieval Latin Traditions* (Cambridge: Cambridge University Press, 1986 [1975]), pp. 82–102.
Dron.1989.1
Dronke, Peter, "Symbolism and Structure in *Paradiso* 30," *Romance Philology* 43 (1989): 29–48.
Dron.1994.1
Dronke, Peter, "The Conclusion of Dante's *Commedia*," *Italian Studies* 49 (1994): 21–39.
Dron.1997.1
Dronke, Peter, *Dante's Second Love: The Originality and the Contexts of the "Convivio"* (Exeter: Society for Italian Studies, 1997).
Dumo.1998.1
Dumol, Paul Arvisu, *The Metaphysics of Reading Underlying Dante's "Commedia": The "Ingegno"* (New York: Peter Lang, 1998).
Eggi.1999.1
Egginton, William, "On Dante, Hyperspheres, and the Curvature of the Medieval Cosmos," *Journal of the History of Ideas* 60.2 (1999): 195–216.
Ehrm.2005.1
Ehrman, Bart D., *Misquoting Jesus* (San Francisco: Harper, 2005).
Fabb.1910.1
Fabbri, Fabio, "Le invocazioni nella *Divina Commedia*," *Giornale dantesco* 18 (1910): 186–92.
Fach.2002.1
Fachard, Denis, "Canto XVI," in *Lectura Dantis Turicensis: Paradiso*, ed. Georges Güntert and Michelangelo Picone (Florence: Cesati, 2002), pp. 231–42.
Faes.2001.1
Faes de Mottoni, Barbara, "Il linguaggio e la memoria dell'angelo in Dante," in *Pour Dante: Dante et l'Apocalypse; Lectures humanistes de Dante*, ed. Bruno Pinchard and Christian Trottmann (Paris: Champion, 2001), pp. 237–53.
Fall.1976.1
Fallani, Giovanni, "Dante e S. Agostino," in his *L'esperienza teologica di Dante* (Lecce: Milella, 1976), pp. 185–203.
Fall.1989.1
Fallani, Giovanni, "Il Canto VII" in *"Paradiso": Letture degli anni 1979–81*, ed. S. Zennaro (Rome: Bonacci, 1989), pp. 223–39.
Fasa.2002.1
Fasani, Remo, "Canto XIII," in *Lectura Dantis Turicensis: Paradiso*, ed. Georges Güntert and Michelangelo Picone (Florence: Cesati, 2002), pp. 193–202.
Fass.1998.1
Fassò, Andrea, "La cortesia di Dante," in *Filologia Romanza e cultura medievale: studi in onore di Elio Melli*, ed. A. Fassò, L. Formisano, and M. Mancini (Alessandria: Edizioni dell'Orso, 1998), vol. I, pp. 279–301.
Fede.1920.1
Federzoni, Giovanni, *"La Divina Commedia" di Dante Alighieri commentata per le scuole e per gli studiosi* (Bologna: L. Cappelli, 1920).
Fenz.2004.1
Fenzi, Enrico, "Tra religione e politica: Dante, il mal di Francia e le 'sacrate ossa' dell'esecrato san Luigi (con un excursus su alcuni passi del *Monarchia*)," *Studi Danteschi* 69 (2004): 23–117.

Fenz.2005.1
Fenzi, Enrico, "Ancora a proposito dell'argomento barberiniano (una possibile eco del *Purgatorio* nei *Documenti d'Amore* di Francesco da Barberino," *Tenzone* 6 (2005): 97–119.
Ferr.1983.1
Ferrante, Joan M., "Words and Images in the *Paradiso*: Reflections of the Divine," in *Dante, Petrarch, Boccaccio: Studies in the Italian Trecento in Honor of Charles S. Singleton*, ed. A. S. Bernardo and A. L. Pellegrini (Binghamton, N.Y.: Medieval & Renaissance Texts and Studies, 1983), pp. 115–32.
Ferr.1984.1
Ferrante, Joan, *The Political Vision of the "Divine Comedy"* (Princeton: Princeton University Press, 1984).
Figu.1965.1
Figurelli, Fernando, "I canti di Cacciaguida," *Cultura e scuola* 4 (1965): 634–61.
Flem.1982.1
Fleming, John V., *From Bonaventure to Bellini: An Essay in Franciscan Exegesis* (Princeton: Princeton University Press, 1982).
Fort.1968.1
Forti, Fiorenzo, "Canto X," in *Lectura Dantis Scaligera: "Paradiso,"* dir. M. Marcazzan (Florence: Le Monnier, 1968), pp. 349–82.
Fost.1976.1
Foster, Kenelm, "*Paradiso* XIX," *Dante Studies* 94 (1976): 71–90.
Fost.1977.1
Foster, Kenelm, *The Two Dantes and Other Studies* (Berkeley: University of California Press, 1977).
Frac.1906.1
Fraccaroli, Giuseppe, "Dante e il *Timeo*," in *Il Timeo*, tr. Giuseppe Fraccaroli (Turin: Fratelli Bocca, 1906), pp. 391–424.
Fran.1982.1
Frankel, Margherita, "Biblical Figurations in Dante's Reading of the *Aeneid*," *Dante Studies* 100 (1982): 13–23.
Frec.1986.1
Freccero, John, *Dante: The Poetics of Conversion*, ed. Rachel Jacoff (Cambridge, Mass.: Harvard University Press, 1986).
Frec.1998.1
Freccero, John, "Dante's Cosmos" (Bernardo Lecture Series, No. 6; Binghamton, N.Y.: CEMERS, 1998), pp. 1–16.
Fuma.2005.1
Fumagalli, Edoardo, "*Par.* XVIII, 88–114, l'enigma del giglio e la sapienza di re Salomone," *L'Alighieri* 26 (2005): 111–25.
Gaff.1973.1
Gaffney, James, "Dante's Blindness in *Paradiso* XXV–XXVI: An Allegorical Interpretation," *Dante Studies* 91 (1973): 101–12.
Gali.1968.1
Galimberti, Cesare, "Canto VII," in *Lectura Dantis Scaligera: "Paradiso,"* dir. M. Marcazzan (Florence: Le Monnier), pp. 217–52.
Garb.1971.1
Garboli, Cesare, "II canto V del *Paradiso*," *Paragone* 22 (1971): 3–19.
Gard.1913.1
Gardner, Edmund G., *Dante and the Mystics* (London: Dent), 1913.
Gett.1968.1
Getto, Giovanni, "Canto XXVI," in *Lectura Dantis Scaligera: "Paradiso,"* dir. M. Marcazzan (Florence: Le Monnier, 1968), pp. 929–60.
Ghis.2002.1

Ghisalberti, Alessandro, "Canto XII," in *Lectura Dantis Turicensis: Paradiso*, ed. Georges Güntert and Michelangelo Picone (Florence: Cesati, 2002), pp. 181–91.

Gigl.1988.1

Giglio, Raffaele, "Canto XVIII," in *Lectura Dantis Neapolitana: "Paradiso,"* ed. P. Giannantonio (Naples: Loffredo, 2000 [1988]), pp. 345–62.

Gils.1924.1

Gilson, Étienne, "La conclusion de la *Divine Comédie* et la mystique franciscaine," *Révue d'histoire franciscaine* 1 (1924): 55–63.

Gils.1939.1

Gilson, Étienne, *Dante and Philosophy*, tr. D. Moore (New York: Harper and Row, 1963 [1939]).

Gils.1997.1

Gilson, Simon A., "Dante and the Science of 'Perspective': A Reappraisal," *Dante Studies* 115 (1997): 185–219.

Gils.2000.1

Gilson, Simon A., *Medieval Optics and Theories of Light in the Works of Dante* (Lewiston, N.Y.: Edwin Mellen Press, 2000).

Gils.2001.2

Gilson, Simon A., "Medieval Science in Dante's *Commedia*: Past Approaches and Future Directions," *Reading Medieval Studies* 27 (2001): 39–77.

Gils.2004.1

Gilson, Simon A., "Rimaneggiamenti danteschi di Aristotele: *gravitas e levitas* nella *Commedia*," in *Le culture di Dante: Atti del quarto Seminario dantesco internazionale*, ed. Michelangelo Picone et al. (Florence: Cesati, 2004), pp. 151–77.

Gmel.1957.1

Gmelin, Hermann, *Kommentar: das Paradies* (Stuttgart: Klett, 1957).

Goff.1964.1

Goffis, Cesare Federico, "Canto I," in *Lectura Dantis Scaligera: "Paradiso"* (Florence: Le Monnier, 1968 [1964]), pp. 1–36.

Goff.1968.1

Goffis, Cesare Federico, "Canto XXIII," in *Lectura Dantis Scaligera: "Paradiso,"* dir. M. Marcazzan (Florence: Le Monnier, 1968), pp. 821–58.

Goud.1974.1

Goudet, Jacques, "La 'parte per se stesso' e l'impegno politico di Dante," *Nuove letture dantesche*, vol. VII (Florence: Le Monnier, 1974), pp. 289–316.

Grag.2005.1

Gragnolati, Manuele, *Experiencing the Afterlife* (Notre Dame: Notre Dame University Press, 2005).

Grec.1974.1

Greco, Aulo, "Il canto XXIV del *Paradiso*," *Nuove letture dantesche*, vol. VII (Florence: Le Monnier, 1974), pp. 107–25.

Gree.1962.1

Green, Richard, tr., Boethius, *The Consolation of Philosophy*, ed. O. Piest (New York: Bobbs-Merrill, 1962).

Gunt.2002.2

Güntert, Georges, "Canto XXXIII," in *Lectura Dantis Turicensis: Paradiso*, ed. Georges Güntert and Michelangelo Picone (Florence: Cesati, 2002), pp. 505–18.

Guth.1999.1

Guthmüller, Bodo, " 'Che par che Circe li avesse in pastura' (*Purg.* XIV, 42): Mito di Circe e metamorfosi nella *Commedia*," in *Dante: mito e poesia; Atti del secondo Seminario dantesco internazionale*, ed. M. Picone and T. Crivelli (Florence: Cesati, 1999), pp. 235–56.

Hagm.1988.1

Hagman, Edward, "Dante's Vision of God: The End of the *Itinerarium Mentis*," *Dante Studies* 106 (1988): 1–20.

Hain.1997.1

Hainsworth, Peter, "Dante's Farewell to Politics," in *Dante and Governance*, ed. John Woodhouse (Oxford: Clarendon, 1997), pp. 152–69.

Hart.1995.1

Hart, Thomas, " 'Per misurar lo cerchio' (*Par.* XXXIII 134) and Archimedes' *De mensura circuli*: Some Thoughts on Approximations to the Value of Pi," in *Dante e la scienza*, ed. P. Boyde and V. Russo (Ravenna: Longo, 1995), pp. 265–335.

Hatc.1971.1

Hatcher, Elizabeth R., "The Moon and Parchment: *Paradiso* II, 73–78," *Dante Studies* 89 (1971): 55–60.

Have.1996.1

Havely, Nicholas R., "Poverty in Purgatory: From *Commercium* to *Commedia*," *Dante Studies* 114 (1996): 229–43.

Have.2004.1

Havely, Nick, *Dante and the Franciscans: Poverty and the Papacy in the "Commedia"* (Cambridge: Cambridge University Press, 2004).

Hawk.1979.1

Hawkins, Peter S., "Trespassing on the Word: God's Book and Ours," *Journal of the American Academy of Religion* 47 (1979): 47–53.

Hawk.1991.1

Hawkins, Peter, "Watching Matelda," in *The Poetry of Allusion: Virgil and Ovid in Dante's "Commedia,"* ed. Rachel Jacoff and Jeffrey T. Schnapp (Stanford: Stanford University Press, 1991), pp. 181–201.

Hawk.1991.2

Hawkins, Peter, "Divide and Conquer: Augustine in the *Divine Comedy*," *PMLA* 106 (1991): 471–82.

Hawk.1995.1

Hawkins, Peter, "*Paradiso* XXI," in *Dante's "Divine Comedy," Introductory Readings III: "Paradiso,"* ed. Tibor Wlassics (*Lectura Dantis [virginiana]*, 16–17, supplement, Charlottesville: University of Virginia, 1995), pp. 308–17.

Heil.1984.1

Heilbronn, Denise, "*Concentus musicus*: The Creaking Hinges of Dante's Gate of Purgatory," *Rivista di studi italiani* 2 (1984): 1–15.

Heil.1984.2

Heilbronn, Denise, "Contrapuntal Imagery in *Paradiso* VIII," *Italian Culture* 5 (1984): 39–54.

Heil.1995.2

Heilbronn-Gaines, Denise, "*Paradiso* XVIII," in *Dante's "Divine Comedy," Introductory Readings III: "Paradiso,"* ed. Tibor Wlassics (*Lectura Dantis [virginiana]*, 16–17, supplement, Charlottesville: University of Virginia, 1995), pp. 266–76.

Heil.2003.1

Heil, Andreas, "Die Milch der Musen," *Antike und Abenland* 49 (2003): 113–29.

Herz.1994.1

Herzmann, Ronald B., and Gary W. Towsley, "Squaring the Circle: *Paradiso* 33 and the Poetics of Geometry," *Traditio* 49 (1994): 95–125.

Herz.2003.1

Herzmann, Ronald, "From Francis to Solomon: Eschatology in the Sun," in *Dante for the New Millennium*, ed. Teodolinda Barolini and H. Wayne Storey (New York: Fordham University Press, 2003), pp. 320–33.

Hill.1982.1

Hill, Thomas D. "Adam's Noon: *Paradiso* XXVI, 139–142," *Dante Studies* 100 (1982): 93–97.

Holl.1969.1

Hollander, Robert, *Allegory in Dante's "Commedia"* (Princeton: Princeton University Press, 1969).
Holl.1974.1
Hollander, Robert, "*Vita Nuova*: Dante's Perceptions of Beatrice," *Dante Studies* 92 (1974): 1–18.
Holl.1975.1
Hollander, Robert, "*Purgatorio* II: Cato's Rebuke and Dante's *scoglio*," *Italica* 52 (1975): 348–63.
Holl.1975.2
Hollander, Robert, "Literary Consciousness and the Consciousness of Literature," *Sewanee Review* 83 (1975): 115–27.
Holl.1976.1
Hollander, Robert, "Dante *Theologus-Poeta*," *Dante Studies* 94 (1976): 91–136.
Holl.1976.2
Hollander, Robert, "The Invocations of the *Commedia*," *Yearbook of Italian Studies* 3 (1976): 235–40.
Holl.1980.1
Hollander, Robert, "The Tragedy of Divination in *Inferno* XX," in *Studies in Dante* (Ravenna: Longo, 1980), pp. 131–218.
Holl.1980.2
Hollander, Robert, "Babytalk in Dante's *Commedia*," in *Studies in Dante* (Ravenna: Longo, 1980), pp. 115–29.
Holl.1982.1
Hollander, Robert, "Dante's 'Book of the Dead': A Note on *Inferno* XXIX, 57," *Studi Danteschi* 54 (1982): 31–51.
Holl.1983.1
Hollander, Robert, *Il Virgilio dantesco: tragedia nella "Commedia"* (Florence: Olschki, 1983).
Holl.1986.1
Hollander, Robert, and Albert Rossi, "Dante's Republican Treasury," *Dante Studies* 104 (1986): 59–82.
Holl.1988.3
Hollander, Robert, "An Index of Hapax Legomena in Dante's *Commedia*," *Dante Studies* 106 (1988): 81–110.
Holl.1989.1
Hollander, Robert, "Dante and the Martial Epic," *Mediaevalia* 12 (1989): 62–91.
Holl.1990.1
Hollander, Robert, "*Purgatorio* II: The New Song and the Old," *Lectura Dantis [virginiana]* 6 (1990): 28–45.
Holl.1992.1
Hollander, Robert, *Dante and Paul's "five words with understanding,"* Occasional Papers, No. 1, Center for Medieval and Early Renaissance Texts and Studies (Binghamton, N.Y.: Medieval and Renaissance Texts and Studies, 1992).
Holl.1992.2
Hollander, Robert, "Dante and Cino da Pistoia," *Dante Studies* 110 (1992): 201–31.
Holl.1992.3
Holloway, Julia Bolton, *The Pilgrim and the Book* (New York: Peter Lang, 1992).
Holl.1993.1
Hollander, Robert, "Le opere di Virgilio nella *Commedia* di Dante," in *Dante e la "bella scola" della poesia: Autorità e sfida poetica*, ed. A. A. Iannucci (Ravenna: Longo, 1993), pp. 247–343.
Holl.1993.2
Hollander, Robert, *Dante's Epistle to Cangrande* (Ann Arbor: University of Michigan Press, 1993).
Holl.1993.3

Hollander, Robert, "Dante and His Commentators," in *The Cambridge Companion to Dante*, ed. R. Jacoff (Cambridge: Cambridge University Press, 1993), pp. 226–36.

Holl.1993.5

Hollander, Robert, "*Paradiso* XXX," *Studi Danteschi* 60 (1988 [=1993]): 1–33.

Holl.1993.7

Hollander, Robert, "Why Did Dante Write the *Comedy*?" *Dante Studies* 111 (1993): 19–25.

Holl.1996.2

Hollander, Robert, "Dante's Deployment of *Convivio* in the *Comedy*," *Electronic Bulletin of the Dante Society of America* (October 1996).

Holl.1997.1

Hollander, Robert, " 'Al quale ha posto mano e cielo e terra' (*Paradiso* 25.2)," *Electronic Bulletin of the Dante Society of America* (January 1997).

Holl.1997.2

Hollander, Robert, *Boccaccio's Dante and the Shaping Force of Satire* (Ann Arbor: University of Michigan Press, 1997).

Holl.1999.1

Hollander, Robert, "Dante's 'dolce stil novo' and the *Comedy*," in *Dante: mito e poesia; Atti del secondo Seminario dantesco internazionale*, ed. M. Picone and T. Crivelli (Florence: Cesati, 1999), pp. 263–81.

Holl.2001.1

Hollander, Robert, *Dante: A Life in Works* (New Haven: Yale University Press, 2001).

Holl.2003.1

Hollander, Robert, and Heather Russo, "*Purgatorio* 33.43: Dante's 515 and Virgil's 333," *Electronic Bulletin of the Dante Society of America* (March 2003).

Holl.2003.2

Hollander, Robert, "Dante's Pride," in *Studi sul canone letterario del Trecento: Per Michelangelo Picone*, ed. J. Bartuschat and L. Rossi (Ravenna: Longo, 2003), pp. 43–55.

Holl.2005.1

Hollander, Robert, "*Paradiso* 4.14: Dante as Nebuchadnezzar?" *Electronic Bulletin of the Dante Society of America* (May 2005).

Holl.2005.2

Hollander, Robert, "The 'miglior voci' of *Paradiso* 1.35," *Electronic Bulletin of the Dante Society of America* (November 2005).

Holl.2006.1

Hollander, Robert, "*Paradiso* I.35–36: 'con miglior voci / si pregherà perché Cirra risponda,' " *Letteratura italiana antica* 7 (2006): 241–47.

Holl.2006.2

Hollander, Robert, "*Paradiso* 24.13–21: St. Peter's Companions," *Electronic Bulletin of the Dante Society of America* (May 2006).

Hone.1994.1

Honess, Claire, "Expressing the Inexpressible: The Theme of Communication in the Heaven of Mars," *Lectura Dantis [virginiana]* 14–15 (spring-fall 1994): 42–60.

Hone.1997.1

Honess, Claire, "Communication and Participation in Dante's *Commedia*," in *In amicizia: Essays in Honour of Giulio Lepschy*, ed. Z.G. Baranski and L. Pertile (*The Italianist* 17 [1997, special supplement]), pp. 127–45.

Hone.1997.2

Honess, Claire, "Feminine Virtues and Florentine Vices: Citizenship and Morality in *Paradiso* XV–XVII," in *Dante and Governance*, ed. John Woodhouse (Oxford: Clarendon, 1997), pp. 102–20.

Iann.1976.1

Iannucci, A. A., "Ulysses' *folle volo*: the Burden of History," *Medioevo romanzo* 3 (1976): 410–45.

Iann.1979.1
Iannucci, Amilcare, "Beatrice in Limbo: A Metaphoric Harrowing of Hell," *Dante Studies* 97 (1979): 23–45.
Iann.1992.2
Iannucci, Amilcare, "Saturn in Dante," in *Saturn: From Antiquity to the Renaissance*, ed. M. Ciavolella and A. A. Iannucci (Toronto: Dovehouse, 1992), pp. 51–67.
Iann.1995.2
Iannucci, Amilcare A., "*Paradiso* XXXI," in *Dante's "Divine Comedy," Introductory Readings III: "Paradiso,"* ed. Tibor Wlassics (*Lectura Dantis [virginiana]*, 16–17, supplement, Charlottesville: University of Virginia, 1995), pp. 470–85.
Imba.1996.1
Imbach, Ruedi, *Dante, la philosophie et les laïcs* (Fribourg: Editions Universitaires, 1996).
Iori.1989.1
Iorio, Giovanni, "Il Canto XVIII," in *"Paradiso": Letture degli anni 1979–81*, ed. S. Zennaro (Rome: Bonacci, 1989), pp. 469–96.
Jaco.1965.1
Jacomuzzi, Angelo, " 'L'imago al cerchio': Nota sul canto XXXIII del *Paradiso*," in his *L'imago al cerchio: Invenzione e visione nella "Divina Commedia"* (Milan: Silva, 1968 [1965]), pp. 5–27.
Jaco.1968.1
Jacomuzzi, Angelo, " 'Ond'io son fatto scriba,' " in his *L'imago al cerchio: Invenzione e visione nella "Divina Commedia"* (Milan: Silva, 1968), pp. 29–100.
Jaco.1980.1
Jacoff, Rachel, "The Post-Palinodic Smile: *Paradiso* VIII and IX," *Dante Studies* 98 (1980): 111–22.
Jaco.1985.1
Jacoff, Rachel, "Sacrifice and Empire: Thematic Analogies in San Vitale and the *Paradiso*," in *Renaissance Studies in Honor of Craig Hugh Smyth*, ed. Andrew Morrogh et al. (Florence: Giunti Barbèra, 1985), pp. 317–32.
Jaco.1991.2
Jacoff, Rachel, "The Rape/Rapture of Europa: *Paradiso* 27," in *The Poetry of Allusion: Virgil and Ovid in Dante's "Commedia,"* ed. Rachel Jacoff and Jeffrey T. Schnapp (Stanford: Stanford University Press, 1991), pp. 233–46, 294–95.
Jaco.1999.1
Jacoff, Rachel, "Dante and the Legend(s) of St. John," *Dante Studies* 117 (1999): 45–57.
Jaco.2000.1
Jacoff, Rachel, " 'Our Bodies, Our Selves': The Body in the *Commedia*," in *Sparks and Seeds: Medieval Literature and Its Afterlife (Essays in Honor of John Freccero)*, ed. Dana E. Stewart and Alison Cornish (Turnhout: Brepols, 2000), pp. 119–37.
Kant.1951.1
Kantorowicz, Ernst, "Dante's 'Two Suns,' " in *Semitic and Oriental Studies, a Volume Presented to William Potter on the Occasion of His Seventy-fifth Birthday, October 29, 1949*, ed. Walter J. Fischel (Berkeley: University of California Press, 1951), pp. 217–31.
Kant.1957.1
Kantorowicz, Ernst, *The King's Two Bodies* (Princeton: Princeton University Press, 1957).
Kay.1983.1
Kay, Richard, "Astrology and Astronomy," in *The "Divine Comedy" and the Encyclopedia of Arts and Sciences: Acta of the International Dante Symposium, 13–16 November 1983, Hunter College, New York*, ed. G. Di Scipio and A. Scaglione (Amsterdam: John Benjamins, 1988), pp. 147–62.
Kay.1994.2
Kay, Richard, *Dante's Christian Astrology* (Philadelphia: University of Pennsylvania Press, 1994).

Kay.1998.1
Kay, Richard, *Dante's "Monarchia,"* translated, with a commentary, by Richard Kay (Toronto: Pontifical Institute of Mediaeval Studies, 1998).
Kay.2002.1
Kay, Richard, "Vitruvius and Dante's Giants," *Dante Studies* 120 (2002): 17–34.
Kay.2003.1
Kay, Richard, "Dante's Empyrean and the Eye of God," *Speculum* 78 (2003): 37–65.
Kay.2003.2
Kay, Richard, "Unwintering January (Dante, *Paradiso* 27.142–143)," *Modern Language Notes* 118 (2003): 237–44.
Kirk.1978.1
Kirkpatrick, Robin, *Dante's "Paradiso" and the Limits of Modern Criticism* (Cambridge: Cambridge University Press, 1978).
Kirk.1995.1
Kirkham, Victoria, "Dante's Polysynchrony: A Perfectly Timed Entry into Eden," *Filologia e critica* 20 (1995): 329–52.
Klei.1986.2
Kleinhenz, Christopher, "Dante and the Bible: Intertextual Approaches to the *Divine Comedy*," *Italica* 63 (1986): 225–36.
Klei.1994.1
Kleiner, John, *Mismapping the Underworld: Daring and Error in Dante's "Comedy"* (Stanford: Stanford University Press, 1994).
Klei.1995.1
Kleinhenz, Christopher, "*Paradiso* XXIII," in *Dante's "Divine Comedy," Introductory Readings III: "Paradiso,"* ed. Tibor Wlassics (*Lectura Dantis [virginiana]*, 16–17, supplement, Charlottesville: University of Virginia, 1995), pp. 456–69.
Lans.1977.1
Lansing, Richard, *From Image to Idea: A Study of the Simile in Dante's "Commedia"* (Ravenna: Longo, 1977).
Lans.2000.1
Lansing, Richard, ed., *Dante Encyclopedia* (New York: Garland, 2000).
Lanz.1996.1
Lanza, Antonio, ed., Dante Alighieri, *La Commedia: Testo critico secondo i più antichi manoscritti fiorentini*, Nuova edizione (Anzio: De Rubeis, 1996).
Ledd.1997.1
Ledda, Giuseppe, "*Tópoi* dell'indicibilità e metaforismi nella *Commedia*," *Strumenti critici* 12 (1997): 117–40.
Ledd.2001.1
Ledda, Giuseppe, "Poesia, scienza e critica dantesca," *L'Alighieri* 18 (2001): 99–113.
Ledd.2002.1
Ledda, Giuseppe, *La guerra della lingua* (Ravenna: Longo, 2002).
Ledd.2006.1
Ledda, Giuseppe, "Osservazioni sul panegirico di San Domenico," *L'Alighieri* 27 (2006): 105–25.
Lego.1957.1
Le Goff, Jacques, *Intellectuals in the Middle Ages*, tr. Teresa Lavender Fagan (Oxford: Blackwell, 1993).
Lenk.1952.1
Lenkeith, Nancy, *Dante and the Legend of Rome* (London: Warburg Institute, 1952).
Leon.1996.1
Leonardi, Lino, "'Langue' poetica e stile dantesco nel *Fiore*: per una verifica degli 'argomenti interni'," in *Studi di filologia medievale in onore di d'Arco Silvio Avalle* (Milan: Ricciardi, 1996), pp. 237–91.
Leps.1987.1

Lepschy, Giulio, "Fantasia e immaginazione," *Lettere Italiane* 38 (1987): 20–34.

Lern.1988.1

Lerner, Robert E., "On the Origins of the Earliest Latin Pope Prophecies: A Reconsideration," *Monumenta Germaniae Historica* 33, Teil V (1988): 611–35.

Leuk.2004.1

Leuker, Tobias, " 'La chiarissima ancella / del sol,' *Par.* XXX, 7–8: Dante tra Marziano Capella e Boiardo," *L'Alighieri* 24 (2004): 93–96.

Leve.2003.1

Levenstein, Jessica, "The Re-Formation of Marsyas in *Paradiso* I," in *Dante for the New Millennium*, ed. Teodolinda Barolini and H. Wayne Storey (New York: Fordham University Press, 2003), pp. 408–21.

Lewi.1964.1

Lewis, C. S., *The Discarded Image* (Cambridge: Cambridge University Press, 1964).

Leye.1977.1

Leyerle, John, "The Rose-Wheel Design and Dante's *Paradiso*," *University of Toronto Quarterly* 46 (1977): 280–308.

Lieb.1996.1

Lieberknecht, Otfried, " 'L'avvocato de' tempi cristiani,' *Par.* 10.118–120: Ambrose of Milan Reconsidered," *Electronic Bulletin of the Dante Society of America* (September 1996).

Loca.1974.1

Lo Cascio, Renzo, "Il canto XXIII del *Paradiso*," *Nuove letture dantesche*, vol. VII (Florence: Le Monnier, 1974), pp. 67–105.

Loga.1971.1

Logan, John L., "The Poet's Central Numbers," *Modern Language Notes* 86 (1971): 95–98.

Long.1975.1

Longen, Eugene M., "The Grammar of Apotheosis: *Paradiso* XXX, 94–99," *Dante Studies* 93 (1975): 209–14.

Macf.1991.1

Macfie, Pamela Royston, "Ovid, Arachne and the Poetics of *Paradiso*," in *The Poetry of Allusion: Virgil and Ovid in Dante's "Commedia,"* ed. Rachel Jacoff and Jeffrey T. Schnapp (Stanford: Stanford University Press, 1991), pp. 159–72.

Maie.2004.1

Maierù, Alfonso, "Dante di fronte alla Fisica e alla Metafisica," in *Le culture di Dante: Atti del quarto Seminario dantesco internazionale*, ed. Michelangelo Picone et al. (Florence: Cesati, 2004), pp. 127–49.

Mala.1999.1

Malato, Enrico, *Dante* (Rome: Salerno, 1999).

Mans.1966.1

Manselli, Raoul, "Cangrande e il mondo ghibellino nell'Italia settentrionale alla venuta di Arrigo VII," in *Dante e la cultura veneta*, ed. V. Branca and G. Padoan (Florence: Olschki, 1966), pp. 39–49.

Mans.1973.1

Manselli, Raoul, "Il Canto XII del *Paradiso*," in *Nuove letture dantesche*, vol. VI (Florence: Le Monnier, 1973), pp. 107–28.

Mans.1982.1

Manselli, Raoul, "Dante e gli Spirituali francescani," *Letture classensi* 11 (1982): 47–61.

Marc.1997.1

Marchesi, Simone, "The Knot of Language: 'Sermocinatio' and 'Contrapasso' for the Rhetoricians in Dante's *Inferno*," *Romance Languages Annual* 11 (1997): 254–59.

Marc.2002.2

Marchesi, Simone, "A Rhetoric of Faith: Dante's Poetics in the Transition from *De vulgari eloquentia* to the *Commedia*" (doctoral dissertation, Princeton University, 2002).

Mari.1909.1

Marigo, Aristide, "Le *Georgiche* di Virgilio fonte di Dante," *Giornale dantesco* 17 (1909): 31–44.
Mari.2003.1
Marietti, Marina, "L'agnello al centro," *Letteratura italiana antica* 4 (2003): 435–44.
Mart.1964.1
Marti, Mario, "Il canto III del *Paradiso*," in *Letture dantesche, III: "Paradiso,"* ed. G. Getto (Florence: Sansoni, 1964 [1961]), pp. 1383–96.
Mart.1985.1
Martinelli, Bortolo, "La dottrina dell'Empireo nell'*Epistola a Cangrande* (capp. 24–27)," *Studi Danteschi* 57 (1985): 49–143.
Mart.2002.1
Martinelli, Bortolo, "Canto XIX," in *Lectura Dantis Turicensis: Paradiso*, ed. Georges Güntert and Michelangelo Picone (Florence: Cesati, 2002), pp. 281–305.
Mart.2003.1
Martinez, Ronald L., "Dante's Jeremiads: The Fall of Jerusalem and the Burden of the New Pharisees, the Capetians, and Florence," in *Dante for the New Millennium*, ed. Teodolinda Barolini and H. Wayne Storey (New York: Fordham University Press, 2003), pp. 301–19.
Masc.1995.1
Masciandaro, Franco, "*Paradiso* XXIII," in *Dante's "Divine Comedy," Introductory Readings III: "Paradiso,"* ed. Tibor Wlassics (*Lectura Dantis [virginiana]*, 16–17, supplement, Charlottesville: University of Virginia, 1995), pp. 329–51.
Mast.1990.1
Mastrobuono, Antonio C., *Dante's Journey of Sanctification* (Washington, D.C.: Regnery Gateway, 1990).
Mazz.1958.1
Mazzeo, Joseph A., *Structure and Thought in the "Paradiso"* (Ithaca: Cornell University Press, 1958).
Mazz.1960.1
Mazzeo, Joseph A., *Medieval Cultural Tradition in Dante's "Comedy"* (Ithaca: Cornell University Press, 1960).
Mazz.1967.1
Mazzoni, Francesco, *Saggio di un nuovo commento alla "Divina Commedia": "Inferno"—Canti I–III* (Florence: Sansoni, 1967).
Mazz.1979.1
Mazzotta, Giuseppe, *Dante, Poet of the Desert* (Princeton: Princeton University Press, 1979).
Mazz.1979.2
Mazzoni, Francesco, ed., Dante Alighieri, *Opere minori*, vol. II (Milan-Naples: Ricciardi, 1979), pp. 691–880.
Mazz.1982.1
Mazzoni, Francesco, "Il canto VI del *Paradiso*," *Letture classensi* 9–10 (1982): 119–59.
Mazz.1988.2
Mazzotta, Giuseppe, "Teologia ed esegesi biblica (*Par.* III–V)," in *Dante e la Bibbia*, ed. G. Barblan (Florence: Olschki, 1988), pp. 95–112.
Mazz.1993.1
Mazzotta, Giuseppe, *Dante's Vision and the Circle of Knowledge* (Princeton: Princeton University Press, 1993).
Mazz.1997.1
Mazzoni, Francesco, "San Bernardo e la visione poetica della *Divina Commedia*," in *Seminario Dantesco Internazionale: Atti del primo convegno tenutosi al Chauncey Conference Center, Princeton, 21–23 ottobre 1994*, ed. Z. G. Baranski (Florence: Le Lettere, 1997), pp. 171–241.
Mazz.2003.1
Mazzotta, Giuseppe, "The Heaven of the Sun: Dante between Aquinas and Bonaventure," in *Dante for the New Millennium*, ed. Teodolinda Barolini and H. Wayne Storey (New York: Fordham University Press, 2003), pp. 152–68.

Mcla.1995.1
McLaughlin, Martin, *Literary Imitation in the Italian Renaissance: The Theory and Practice of Literary Imitation in Italy from Dante to Bembo* (Oxford: Clarendon Press, 1995).
Meek.1997.1
Meekins, A. G., "The Study of Dante, Bonaventure, and Mysticism: Notes on Some Problems of Method," in *In amicizia: Essays in Honour of Giulio Lepschy*, ed. Z. G. Baranski and L. Pertile (*The Italianist* 17 [1997, special supplement]), pp. 83–99.
Mell.1974.1
Mellone, Attilio, "Il canto XXIX del *Paradiso* (una lezione di angelologia)," *Nuove letture dantesche*, vol. VII (Florence: Le Monnier, 1974), pp. 193–213.
Mell.1987.1
Mellone, Attilio, "Il san Francesco di Dante e il san Francesco della storia," in *Dante e il francescanesimo* (Cava de' Terreni: Avagliano, 1987), pp. 11–73.
Mell.1989.1
Mellone, Attilio, "Il Canto XXVIII," in *"Paradiso": Letture degli anni 1979–81*, ed. S. Zennaro (Rome: Bonacci, 1989), pp. 731–54.
Merl.2005.1
Merlante, Riccardo, and Stefano Prandi, eds., *La Divina Commedia* (Brescia: La Scuola, 2005).
Migl.1982.1
Migliorini-Fissi, Rosetta, "La nozione di *deificatio* nel *Paradiso*," *Letture classensi* 9–10 (1982): 39–72.
Migl.1989.1
Migliorini-Fissi, Rosetta, "Canto XXXI," in *"Paradiso": Lectura Dantis Neapolitana*, dir. P. Giannantonio (Naples: Loffredo, 2000 [1989]), pp. 605–61.
Mill.1977.1
Miller, James L., "Three Mirrors of Dante's *Paradiso*," *University of Toronto Quarterly* 46 (1977): 263–79.
Mine.1987.1
Mineo, Nicolò, "Canto VI," in *"Paradiso": Lectura Dantis Neapolitana*, dir. P. Giannantonio (Naples: Loffredo, 2000 [1987]), pp. 89–145.
Mine.1992.1
Mineo, Nicolò, "La 'vita' di San Francesco nella 'festa di paradiso,' " in *I primi undici canti del "Paradiso" (Lectura Dantis Metelliana)*, ed. Attilio Mellone (Rome: Bulzoni, 1992), pp. 223–320.
Minn.1984.1
Minnis, A. J., *Medieval Theory of Authorship: Scholastic Literary Attitudes in the Later Middle Ages* (London: Scolar, 1984).
Moev.1999.1
Moevs, Christian, "God's Feet and Hands (*Paradiso* 4.40–48): Non-duality and Non-false Errors," *Modern Language Notes* 114 (1999): 1–13.
Moev.1999.2
Moevs, Christian, "Miraculous Syllogisms: Clocks, Faith and Reason in *Paradiso* 10 and 24," *Dante Studies* 117 (1999): 59–84.
Moev.2005.1
Moevs, Christian, *The Metaphysics of Dante's "Comedy"* (Oxford: Oxford University Press, 2005).
Mont.1963.1
Montano, Rocco, *Storia della poesia di Dante*, vol. II (Naples: Quaderni di Delta, 1963).
Mont.1974.1
Montanari, Fausto, "Il canto XXXII del *Paradiso*," *Nuove letture dantesche*, vol. VII (Florence: Le Monnier, 1974), pp. 255–63.
Moor.1889.1
Moore, Edward, *Contributions to the Textual Criticism of the "Divina Commedia"* (Cambridge: Cambridge University Press, 1889).

Moor.1896.1
Moore, Edward, *Studies in Dante*, First Series: *Scripture and Classical Authors in Dante* (Oxford: Clarendon, 1969 [1896]).
Moor.1903.1
Moore, Edward, *Studies in Dante*, Third Series: *Miscellaneous Essays* (Oxford: Clarendon, 1968 [1903]).
Moor.1917.1
Moore, Edward, *Studies in Dante*, Fourth Series: *Textual Criticism of the "Convivio" and Miscellaneous Essays* (Oxford: Clarendon, 1968 [1917]).
Mure.1996.2
Muresu, Gabriele, "Lo specchio e la contemplazione (*Paradiso* XXI)," *L'Alighieri* 8 (1996): 7–39.
Musc.1968.1
Muscetta, Carlo, "Canto VIII," in *Lectura Dantis Scaligera: "Paradiso,"* dir. M. Marcazzan (Florence: Le Monnier, 1968), pp. 253–96.
Nard.1942.1
Nardi, Bruno, "La tragedia di Ulisse," in his *Dante e la cultura medievale* (Bari: Laterza, 1942), pp. 89–99.
Nard.1944.1
Nardi, Bruno, *Nel mondo di Dante* (Rome: Edizioni di "Storia e Letteratura"), 1944.
Nard.1956.1
Nardi, Bruno, "Il canto XXIX del *Paradiso*," in his *"Lecturae" e altri studi danteschi*, ed. Rudy Abardo (Florence: Le Lettere, 1990 [1960]), pp. 193–201.
Nard.1960.1
Nardi, Bruno, *Dal "Convivio" alla "Commedia,"* con premessa alla ristampa di O. Capitani (Rome: Istituto Storico Italiano per il Medio Evo, 1992 [1960]).
Nard.1960.2
Nardi, Bruno, *Studi di filosofia medievale* (Rome: Edizioni di Storia e letteratura, 1960).
Nard.1960.3
Nardi, Bruno, "Perché dietro la memoria non può ire' (*Paradiso*, I, 9)," in his *"Lecturae" e altri studi danteschi*, ed. Rudy Abardo (Florence: Le Lettere, 1990 [1960]), pp. 267–76.
Nard.1960.4
Nardi, Bruno, discussion of Cerulli (Ceru.1949.1) in *Dal "Convivio" alla "Commedia,"* con premessa alla ristampa di O. Capitani (Rome: Istituto Storico Italiano per il Medio Evo, 1992 [1960]), pp. 351–70.
Nard.1964.1
Nardi, Bruno, "Il canto di S. Francesco," in his *"Lecturae" e altri studi danteschi*, ed. Rudy Abardo (Florence: Le Lettere, 1990 [1964]), pp. 173–84.
Nard.1964.2
Nardi, Bruno, "Perché 'Alfa ed O' e non 'Alfa ed Omega' (Nota a *Par.* XXVI, 17)," in his *Saggi e note di critica dantesca* (Milan-Naples: Ricciardi, 1966 [1964]), pp. 317–20.
Nard.1965.1
Nardi, Bruno, "Dante e Gioacchino da Fiore," in his *"Lecturae" e altri studi danteschi*, ed. Rudy Abardo (Florence: Le Lettere, 1990 [1965]), pp. 277–331.
Nard.1985.1
Nardi, Bruno, "Il canto delle macchie lunari (II *Par.*)," *L'Alighieri* 26 (1985): 21–32.
Nast.2001.1
Nasti, Paola, "The Wise Poet: Solomon in Dante's Heaven of the Sun," *Reading Medieval Studies* 27 (2001): 103–38.
Newm.1967.1
Newman, Francis X., "St. Augustine's Three Visions and the Structure of the *Commedia*," *Modern Language Notes* 82 (1967): 56–78.
Obri.1979.1

O'Brien, William J., " 'The Bread of Angels' in *Paradiso* II: A Liturgical Note," *Dante Studies* 97 (1979): 97–106.

Okee.1924.1

O'Keeffe, David, "Dante's Theory of Creation," *Revue néoscolastique de philosophie* 26 (1924): 45–67.

Ordi.1982.1

Ordiway, Frank, "In the Earth's Shadow: The Theological Virtues Marred," *Dante Studies* 100 (1982): 77–92.

Ordi.1990.1

Ordiway, Frank Bryan, *Dante, Chaucer, and the Poetics of the Past* (unpublished doctoral dissertation, Princeton University, 1990).

Orr.1914.1

Orr, M.A., *Dante and the Early Astronomers* (London: Gail and Inglis, [1914]).

Osse.1995.1

Osserman, Robert, *Poetry of the Universe* (New York: Anchor, 1995).

Pado.1965.2

Padoan, Giorgio, "II Canto VII del *Paradiso*," *Lectura Dantis Romana* (Turin: S.E.I., 1965).

Pado.1974.1

Padoan, Giorgio, "Il canto XXVIII del *Paradiso*," *Nuove letture dantesche,* vol. VII (Florence: Le Monnier, 1974), pp. 175–91.

Pado.1993.1

Padoan, Giorgio, *Il lungo cammino del "Poema sacro": studi danteschi* (Florence: Olschki, 1993).

Palm.2003.1

Palma di Cesnola, Maurizio, *Questioni dantesche: "Fiore," "Monarchia," "Commedia"* (Ravenna: Longo, 2003).

Para.1989.1

Paratore, Ettore, "Il Canto VIII," in *"Paradiso": Letture degli anni 1979–81*, ed. S. Zennaro (Rome: Bonacci, 1989), pp. 241–67.

Paro.1915.1

Parodi, E. G., "Gli esempi di superbia punita e il 'bello stile' di Dante," in his *Poesia e storia della "Divina Commedia,"* ed. G. Folena and P. V. Mengaldo (Venice: Neri Pozza, 1965 [1915]), 149–61.

Pasq.1968.1

Pasquazi, Silvio, "Canto XXIX," in *Lectura Dantis Scaligera: "Paradiso,"* dir. M. Marcazzan (Florence: Le Monnier, 1968), pp. 1031–60.

Pasq.1972.1

Pasquazi, Silvio, *All'eterno dal tempo: Studi danteschi* (Florence: Le Monnier, 1972 [2d ed.]).

Pasq.1988.1

Pasquini, Emilio, "Canto XXII," in *Lectura Dantis Neapolitana: "Paradiso,"* ed. P. Giannantonio (Naples: Loffredo, 2000 [1988]), pp. 431–40.

Pasq.1996.1

Pasquini, Emilio, "Il *Paradiso* e una nuova idea di figuralismo," *Intersezioni* 16 (1996): 417–27.

Pasq.1996.2

Pasquini, Emilio, "Le icone parentali nella *Commedia*," *Letture classensi* 25 (1996): 39–50.

Pasq.1999.2

Pasquini, Emilio, "Dante and the 'Prefaces of Truth': From 'Figure' to 'Completion,' " *Italian Studies* 54 (1999): 18–25.

Pasq.2001.1

Pasquini, Emilio, *Dante e le figure del vero: La fabbrica della "Commedia"* (Milan: Bruno Mondadori, 2001).

Pass.1918.1

Passerini, G. L., *La "Divina Commedia" di Dante Alighieri commentata da G. L. Passerini* (Florence: Sansoni, 1918).

Pass.1955.1
Passerin D'Entrèves, Alessandro, *Dante as a Political Thinker* (Oxford: Oxford University Press, 1955).
Past.1966.1
Pastore Stocchi, Manlio, "Dante, Mussato, e la tragedia," in *Dante e la cultura veneta*, ed. V. Branca and G. Padoan (Florence: Olschki, 1966), pp. 251–62.
Past.1972.1
Pastore Stocchi, Manlio, "Il canto V del *Paradiso*," *Nuove letture dantesche*, vol. V (Florence: Le Monnier, 1972), pp. 341–74.
Past.1981.1
Pastore Stocchi, Manlio, "Dante e la luna," *Lettere Italiane* 33 (1981): 153–74.
Payt.1995.1
Payton, Rodney, "*Paradiso* XXIX," in *Dante's "Divine Comedy," Introductory Readings III: "Paradiso,"* ed. Tibor Wlassics (*Lectura Dantis [virginiana]*, 16–17, supplement, Charlottesville: University of Virginia, 1995), pp. 435–55.
Peco.1968.1
Pecoraro, Marco, "Canto XXI," in *Lectura Dantis Scaligera: "Paradiso,"* dir. M. Marcazzan (Florence: Le Monnier, 1968), pp. 733–86.
Peir.2006.1
Peirone, Luigi, "Parole di Dante: *fuia,*" *L'Alighieri* 27 (2006): 151–60.
Peli.1997.1
Pelikan, Jaroslav, *What Has Athens to Do with Jerusalem? Timaeus and Genesis in Counterpoint* (Ann Arbor: University of Michigan Press, 1997).
Pern.1965.1
Pernicone, Vincenzo, "II canto XXXII del *Paradiso*," in his *Studi danteschi e altri saggi*, ed. M. D. Wanke (Genoa: Università degli Studi, 1984 [1965]), pp. 105–21.
Pert.1981.1
Pertile, Lino, "*Paradiso* XXXIII: l'estremo oltraggio," *Filologia e critica* 6 (1981): 1–21.
Pert.1990.1
Pertile, Lino, " 'La punta del disio': storia di una metafora dantesca," *Lectura Dantis [virginiana]* 7 (1990): 3–28.
Pert.1991.2
Pertile, Lino, " 'Così si fa la pelle bianca nera': l'enigma di *Paradiso* XXVII, 136–138," *Lettere Italiane* 43 (1991): 3–26.
Pert.1991.3
Pertile, Lino, "*Paradiso* XVIII tra autobiografia e scrittura sacra," *Dante Studies* 109 (1991): 25–49.
Pert.1993.2
Pertile, Lino, "*Paradiso*: A Drama of Desire," in *Word and Drama in Dante: Essays on the "Divina Commedia,"* ed. J. C. Barnes and J. Petrie (Dublin: Irish Academic Press, 1993), pp. 143–80.
Pert.1998.2
Pertile, Lino, *La puttana e il gigante: Dal Cantico dei Cantici al Paradiso Terrestre di Dante* (Ravenna: Longo, 1998).
Pert.2001.1
Pertile, Lino, "Quale amore va in Paradiso?" in *"Le donne, i cavalieri, l'arme, gli amori": Poema e romanzo; la narrativa lunga in Italia*, ed. Francesco Bruni (Venice: Marsilio, 2001), pp. 59–70.
Pert.2005.2
Pertile, Lino, *La punta del disio: Semantica del desiderio nella "Commedia"* (Fiesole: Cadmo, 2005).
Pert.2006.1
Pertile, Lino, "Le *Egloghe*, Polifemo e il *Paradiso*," *Studi Danteschi* 71 (2006): 285–302.
Pete.1972.1

Peters, Edward M., "The Failure of Church and Empire: *Paradiso* 30," *Mediaeval Studies* 34 (1972): 326–35.

Pete.1979.1

Peterson, Mark A., "Dante and the 3-sphere," *American Journal of Physics* 47.12 (1979): 1031–35.

Pete.1991.1

Peters, Edward, "Human Diversity and Civil Society in *Paradiso* VIII," *Dante Studies* 109 (1991): 51–70.

Petr.1957.1

Petrocchi, Giorgio, "Intorno alla pubblicazione dell'*Inferno* e del *Purgatorio*," *Convivium* 25 (1957): 652–69.

Petr.1966.1

Petrocchi, Giorgio, *Dante Alighieri: La Commedia secondo l'antica vulgata*, ed. G. Petrocchi (Florence: Le Lettere, 1994 [1966]), vol. I, Introduzione.

Petr.1969.1

Petrocchi, Giorgio, *Itinerari danteschi*, Premessa a cura di C. Ossola (Milan: Franco Angeli, 1994 [Bari: Laterza, 1969]).

Petr.1988.2

Petrocchi, Giorgio, "Canto XVII," in *Lectura Dantis Neapolitana: "Paradiso,"* ed. P. Giannantonio (Naples: Loffredo, 2000 [1988]), pp. 335–43.

Peza.1965.1

Pézard, André, ed., Dante Alighieri, *Oeuvres complètes* (Paris: Gallimard, 1965).

Peza.1967.1

Pézard, André, "Les trois langues de Cacciaguida," *Revue des études italiennes* 16 (1967): 217–38.

Pico.1974.1

Picone, Michelangelo, "Il *Fiore*: struttura profonda e problemi attributivi," *Vox romanica* 33 (1974): 145–56.

Pico.1980.1

Picone, Michelangelo, "Giraut de Bornelh nella prospettiva di Dante," *Vox romanica* 39 (1980): 22–43.

Pico.1983.1

Picone, Michelangelo, "*Paradiso* IX: Dante, Folchetto e la diaspora trobadorica," *Medioevo romanzo* 8 (1981–1983): 47–89.

Pico.1994.1

Picone, Michelangelo, "Dante argonauta: la ricezione dei miti ovidiani nella *Commedia*," in M. Picone and B. Zimmermann, eds., *Ovidius redivivus: von Ovid zu Dante* (Stuttgart: M&P Verlag, 1994), pp. 173–202.

Pico.1994.2

Picone, Michelangelo, "Miti, metafore e similitudini del *Paradiso*: un esempio di lettura," *Studi Danteschi* 63 (1989 [1994]): 193–217.

Pico.1999.3

Picone, Michelangelo, "Dante, Ovidio e la poesia dell'esilio," *Rassegna europea di letteratura italiana* 14 (1999): 7–23.

Pico.2000.1

Picone, Michelangelo, "Il corpo della/nella luna: sul canto Il del *Paradiso*," *L'Alighieri* 15 (2000): 7–25.

Pico.2000.3

Picone, Michelangelo, "Leggere la *Commedia* di Dante," in *Lectura Dantis Turicensis: Inferno*, ed. Georges Güntert and Michelangelo Picone (Florence: Cesati, 2000), pp. 13–25.

Pico.2002.2

Picone, Michelangelo, "Canto II," in *Lectura Dantis Turicensis: Paradiso*, ed. Georges Güntert and Michelangelo Picone (Florence: Cesati, 2002), pp. 35–52.

Pico.2002.3

Picone, Michelangelo, "Canto VIII," in *Lectura Dantis Turicensis: Paradiso*, ed. Georges Güntert and Michelangelo Picone (Florence: Cesati, 2002), pp. 119–32.
Pico.2002.4
Picone, Michelangelo, "Canto XIV," in *Lectura Dantis Turicensis: Paradiso*, ed. Georges Güntert and Michelangelo Picone (Florence: Cesati, 2002), pp. 203–18.
Pico.2002.5
Picone, Michelangelo, "Canto XVIII," in *Lectura Dantis Turicensis: Paradiso*, ed. Georges Güntert and Michelangelo Picone (Florence: Cesati, 2002), pp. 265–79.
Pico.2002.6
Picone, Michelangelo, "Canto XX," in *Lectura Dantis Turicensis: Paradiso*, ed. Georges Güntert and Michelangelo Picone (Florence: Cesati, 2002), pp. 307–24.
Pico.2002.7
Picone, Michelangelo, "Canto XXVIII," in *Lectura Dantis Turicensis: Paradiso*, ed. Georges Güntert and Michelangelo Picone (Florence: Cesati, 2002), pp. 429–39.
Pico.2002.8
Picone, Michelangelo, "Canto XXXII," in *Lectura Dantis Turicensis: Paradiso*, ed. Georges Güntert and Michelangelo Picone (Florence: Cesati, 2002), pp. 491–503.
Pico.2005.1
Picone, Michelangelo, "Il tema dell'incoronazione poetica in Dante, Petrarca e Boccaccio," *L'Alighieri* 25 (2005): 5–26.
Pier.1981.1
Pierotti, Gian Luca, "La *filia solis* di Bonaventura e i cambiamenti di colore in *Par.* XXVII," *Lettere Italiane* 33 (1981): 216–21.
Plac.1987.1
Placella, Vincenzo, "Canto X," in *Lectura Dantis Neapolitana: "Paradiso,"* ed. P. Giannantonio (Naples: Loffredo, 2000 [1987]), pp. 207–36.
Plac.1995.1
Placella, Vincenzo, "Il pubblico del *Convivio* e quello del *Paradiso*," in *Miscellanea di studi in onore di Raffaele Sirri*, a cura di M. Palumbo and V. Placella (Naples: Federico e Ardia, 1995), pp. 365–73.
Pohn.1965.1
Pohndorf, Marie Catherine, "Conceptual Imagery Related to the Journey Theme in Dante's *Commedia*" (doctoral dissertation, University of Denver, 1965).
Porc.2000.1
Porcelli, Bruno, "Numeri e nomi nei canti danteschi del sole," *Giornale storico della letteratura italiana* 117 (2000): 1–13.
Pore.1930.1
Porena, Manfredi, "Noterelle dantesche," *Studi romanzi* 20 (1930): 201–6.
Pran.1994.1
Prandi, Stefano, *Il "Diletto legno": Aridità e fioritura mistica nella "Commedia"* (Florence: Olschki, 1994).
Psak.2003.1
Psaki, F. Regina, "Love for Beatrice: Transcending Contradiction in the *Paradiso*," in *Dante for the New Millennium*, ed. Teodolinda Barolini and H. Wayne Storey (New York: Fordham University Press, 2003), pp. 115–30.
Psak.1995.1
Psaki, Regina, *"Paradiso* XXVIII," in *Dante's "Divine Comedy," Introductory Readings III: "Paradiso,"* ed. Tibor Wlassics (*Lectura Dantis [virginiana]*, 16–17, supplement, Charlottesville: University of Virginia, 1995), pp. 424–34.
Punz.1999.1
Punzi, Arianna, "Oh Beatrice, dolce guida e cara! (*Paradiso* XXIII, v. 34)," *Critica del testo* 2 (1999): 771–99.
Quag.2001.1
Quaglio, Enzo, "Per l'antica fortuna del *Fiore*," *Rivista di Studi Danteschi* 1 (2001): 120–27.

Quin.1979.1
Quinones, Ricardo J., *Dante Alighieri* (Boston: Twayne, 1979).
Raff.2000.1
Raffa, Guy P., *Divine Dialectic: Dante's Incarnational Poetry* (Toronto: Toronto University Press, 2000).
Ragn.1989.2
Ragni, Eugenio, "*Folor, recta dilectio e recta politia* nel cielo di Venere," *Studi latini e italiani* 3 (1989): 135–52.
Raim.1966.1
Raimondi, Ezio, "Dante e il mondo ezzeliniano," in *Dante e la cultura veneta*, ed. V. Branca and G. Padoan (Florence: Olschki, 1966), pp. 51–69.
Raim.1986.1
Raimondi, Ezio, "Ontologia della metafora dantesca," *Letture classensi* 15 (1986): 99–109.
Rajn.1902.1
Rajna, Pio, "*Arturi regis ambages pulcerrimae*," *Studi Danteschi* 1 (1902): 91–99.
Rati.1988.1
Rati, Giancarlo, "Canto XXVI," in *Lectura Dantis Neapolitana: "Paradiso,"* ed. P. Giannantonio (Naples: Loffredo, 2000 [1988]), pp. 501–19.
Reev.1972.1
Reeves, Marjorie, and Beatrice Hirsch-Reich, *The "Figurae" of Joachim of Fiore* (Oxford: Clarendon Press, 1972).
Rigo.1980.1
Rigo, Paola, "Tempo liturgico nell'epistola ai Principi e ai Popoli d'Italia," in her *Memoria classica e memoria biblica in Dante* (Florence: Olschki, 1994), pp. 33–44.
Rigo.1994.1
Rigo, Paola, *Memoria classica e memoria biblica in Dante* (Florence: Olschki, 1994).
Rizz.2000.1
Rizzardi, Sandra, "Dante e l'orologio," *Studi e problemi di critica testuale* 60 (2000): 51–70.
Roff.1968.1
Roffarè, Francesco T., "Canto XXXI," in *Lectura Dantis Scaligera: "Paradiso,"* dir. M. Marcazzan (Florence: Le Monnier, 1968), pp. 1097–1134.
Ross.1981.1
Rossi, Albert, "*A l'ultimo suo: Paradiso* XXX and Its Virgilian Context," *Studies in Medieval and Renaissance History* [University of British Columbia] 4 (1981): 39–88.
Ross.1985.1
Rossi, Albert L, "*Miro gurge* (*Par.* XXX, 68): Virgilian Language and Textual Pattern in the River of Light," *Dante Studies* 103 (1985): 79–101.
Ross.1989.1
Rossi, Albert L., " 'E pos d'amor plus nom cal': Ovidian Exemplarity and Folco's Rhetoric of Love in *Paradiso* IX," *Tenso: Bulletin of the Société Guilhem IX* 5 (1989): 49–102.
Ross.1989.2
Rossi, Albert L., "The Poetics of Resurrection: Virgil's Bees (*Paradiso* XXXI, 1–12)," *Romanic Review* 80 (1989): 305–24.
Ross.2000.1
Rossini, Antonio, "Dante and Ovid: A Comparative Study of Narrative Technique" (unpublished doctoral dissertation, University of Toronto, 2000).
Ross.2002.1
Rossi, Luciano, "Canto XI," in *Lectura Dantis Turicensis: Paradiso*, ed. Georges Güntert and Michelangelo Picone (Florence: Cesati, 2002), pp. 167–79.
Ross.2003.1
Rossi, Luciano, "Dante, la *Rose* e il *Fiore*," in *Studi sul canone letterario del Trecento: Per Michelangelo Picone*, a cura di J. Bartuschat and L. Rossi (Ravenna: Longo, 2003), pp. 9–32.

Russ.1968.1
Russi, A., "Canto XXXII," in *Lectura Dantis Scaligera: "Paradiso,"* dir. M. Marcazzan (Florence: Le Monnier, 1968), pp. 1135–90.
Russ.1971.1
Russo, Vittorio, *Esperienze e/di letture dantesche (tra il 1966 e il 1970)* (Naples: Liguori, 1971).
Russ.1983.1
Russo, Vittorio, *"Paradiso* XIX: *similis fictio numquam facta fuit per aliquem poetam," Dante Studies* 101 (1983): 87–110.
Sacc.1974.1
Sacchetto, Aleardo, "Il canto XXXIII del *Paradiso," Nuove letture dantesche,* vol. VII (Florence: Le Monnier, 1974), pp. 265–87.
Sacc.2002.1
Saccone, Carlo, "Muhammad's Mi'raj: A Legend between East and West [Postface to *Il Libro della Scala*]," tr. E. Emery, paper presented at the conference on *Arabic and Judaic Influences in and around Dante Alighieri* (Venice, 11–12 September 2002). [Paper consultable at: http://www.geocities.com/DanteStudies/miraj.html]
Sals.1974.1
Salsano, Fernando, "Il canto XXX del *Paradiso," Nuove letture dantesche,* vol. VII (Florence: Le Monnier, 1974), pp. 215–34.
Saly.1989.1
Saly, John, *Dante's Paradiso: The Flowering of the Self; An Interpretation of the Anagogical Meaning* (New York: Pace University Press, 1989).
Sang.1999.2
Sanguineti, Federico, "Per *Paradiso* 4:55," *Dante Studies* 117 (1999): 195–97.
Saro.1971.1
Sarolli, Gian Roberto, *Prolegomena alla "Divina Commedia"* (Florence: Olschki, 1971).
Sart.1999.1
Sarteschi, Selene, "Sant'Agostino in Dante e nell'età di Dante," in her *Per la "Commedia" e non per essa soltanto* (Rome: Bulzoni, 2002 [1999]), pp. 171–94.
Sart.2000.2
Sarteschi, Selene, "Ancora sui versi 136–38 di *Paradiso* XXVII," *Giornale storico della letteratura italiana* 118 (2000): 401–21.
Savi.1972.1
Saville, Jonathan, *The Medieval Erotic "Alba"* (New York: Columbia University Press, 1972).
Savj.1964.1
Savj Lopez, Paolo, "Il canto XXX del *Paradiso,"* in *Letture dantesche, III: "Paradiso,"* ed. G. Getto (Florence: Sansoni, 1964), pp. 625–38.
Scag.1967.2
Scaglione, Aldo, "Periodic Syntax and Flexible Meter in the *Divina Commedia," Romance Philology* 21 (1967): 1–22.
Sche.1896.1
Scherillo, Michele, "Perché Dante salva Salomone," in his *Alcuni capitoli della biografia di Dante* (Turin: Loescher, 1896), pp. 299–311.
Schi.1993.1
Schildgen, Brenda Deen, "Dante and the Indus," *Dante Studies* 111 (1993): 177–93.
Schi.1998.1
Schildgen, Brenda Deen, "Dante and the Crusades," *Dante Studies* 116 (1998): 95–125.
Schi.2002.1
Schildgen, Brenda Deen, *Dante and the Orient* (Urbana: University of Illinois Press, 2002).
Schn.1986.1
Schnapp, Jeffrey T., *The Transfiguration of History at the Center of Dante's "Paradise"* (Princeton: Princeton University Press, 1986).
Schn.1991.2

Schnapp, Jeffrey T., "Dante's Ovidian Self-Correction in *Paradiso* 17," in *The Poetry of Allusion: Virgil and Ovid in Dante's "Commedia,"* ed. Rachel Jacoff and Jeffrey T. Schnapp (Stanford: Stanford University Press, 1991), pp. 214–23, 289–93.

Schw.1966.1

Schwarz, Willy, "Si trovano in Dante echi delle opinioni teologiche di Pietro Olivi?—Dante e i Templari," in *Atti del Congresso internazionale di studi danteschi*, vol. II (Florence: Sansoni, 1966), pp. 147–49.

Scot.1973.1

Scott, John A., "Dante's Allegory," *Romance Philology* 26 (1973): 558–91.

Scot.1977.1

Scott, John A., *Dante magnanimo; studi sulla "Commedia"* (Florence: Olschki, 1977).

Scot.1977.2

Scott, John A., "*Paradiso* XXX," in *Dante Commentaries*, ed. D. Nolan (Dublin: Irish Academic Press, 1977), pp. 159–80.

Scot.1987.1

Scotti, Mario, "Canto XII," in *Lectura Dantis Neapolitana: "Paradiso,"* ed. P. Giannantonio (Naples: Loffredo, 2000 [1987]), pp. 255–78.

Scot.1994.1

Scott, John A., "Dante, Boezio e l'enigma di Rifeo (*Par.* 20)," *Studi Danteschi* 61 (1989 [1994]): 187–92.

Scot.1995.1

Scott, John A., "The Unfinished *Convivio* as Pathway to the *Comedy*," *Dante Studies* 113 (1995): 31–56.

Scot.1996.1

Scott, John A., *Dante's Political Purgatory* (Philadelphia: University of Pennsylvania Press, 1996).

Scot.2002.1

Scott, John, "Canto XXXI," in *Lectura Dantis Turicensis: Paradiso*, ed. Georges Güntert and Michelangelo Picone (Florence: Cesati, 2002), pp. 473–89.

Scot.2003.1

Scott, John A., "*Paradiso* 22.151: 'L'aiuola che ci fa tanto feroci'; Philology and Hermeneutics," *Electronic Bulletin of the Dante Society of America* (April 2003).

Scot.2004.1

Scott, John A., "Genesi e sviluppo del pensiero politico di Dante," in *Le culture di Dante: Atti del quarto Seminario dantesco internazionale*, ed. Michelangelo Picone et al. (Florence: Cesati, 2004), pp. 243–70.

Scot.2004.2

Scott, John A., *Understanding Dante* (Notre Dame: Notre Dame University Press, 2004).

Scri.1995.1

Scrivano, Riccardo, "*Paradiso* XIX," *L'Alighieri* 6 (1995): 29–46.

Seem.2006.1

Seem, Lauren Scancarelli, "*Nolite iudicare*: Dante and the Dilemma of Judgment," in *Writers Reading Writers: A Festschrift in Honor of Robert Hollander*, ed. Janet Levarie Smarr (Newark: University of Delaware Press, 2007), pp. 73–88.

Seri.2003.1

Seriacopi, Massimo, *Bonifacio VIII nella storia e nell'opera di Dante* (Florence: Chiari, 2003).

Shan.1975.1

Shankland, Hugh, "Dante 'Aliger,' " *Modern Language Review* 70 (1975): 764–85.

Shan.1977.1

Shankland, Hugh, "Dante 'Aliger' and Ulysses," *Italian Studies* 32 (1977): 21–40.

Shaw.1981.1

Shaw, Prudence, "*Paradiso* XXX," in *Cambridge Readings in Dante's "Comedy,"* ed. K. Foster and P. Boyde (Cambridge: Cambridge University Press, 1981), pp. 191–213.

Sher.2005.1

Sherwin, Michael, *By Knowledge and By Love: Charity and Knowledge in the Moral Theology of St. Thomas Aquinas* (Washington, D.C.: Catholic University of America Press, 2005).

Shoa.1975.1

Shoaf, R. A., "Dante's *colombi* and the Figuralism of Hope in the *Divine Comedy*," *Dante Studies* 93 (1975): 27–59.

Shoa.1983.1

Shoaf, R. A., *Dante, Chaucer, and the Currency of the Word* (Norman, Okla.: Pilgrim Books, 1983).

Silv.1939.1

Silverstein, Theodore, "The Throne of the Emperor Henry in Dante's *Paradise* and the Mediaeval Conception of Christian Kingship," *Harvard Theological Review* 32 (1939): 115–29.

Silv.1952.1

Silverstein, Theodore, "Dante and the Legend of the Mirāj: The Problem of Islamic Influence in the Christian Literature of the Otherworld," *Journal of Near Eastern Studies* 11 (1952): 89–110, 187–97.

Sinc.1946.1

Sinclair, John D., *Dante's "Paradiso"* (New York: Oxford, 1961 [1946]).

Sing.1960.1

Singleton, Charles S., " 'In exitu Israel de Aegypto,' " *Annual Report of the Dante Society* 78 (1960): 1–24.

Sing.1965.2

Singleton, Charles S., "The Poet's Number at the Center," *Modern Language Notes* 80 (1965): 1–10.

Smar.1991.1

Smarr, Janet Levarie, "Poets of Love and Exile," in *Dante and Ovid: Essays in Intertextuality*, ed. Madison U. Sowell (Binghamton, N.Y.: Medieval & Renaissance Texts & Studies, 1991), pp. 139–51.

Sowe.1983.1

Sowell, Madison U., "A Bibliography of the Dantean Simile to 1981," *Dante Studies* 101 (1983): 167–80.

Sowe.1995.1

Sowell, Madison U., "*Paradiso* XIV," in *Dante's "Divine Comedy," Introductory Readings III: "Paradiso,"* ed. Tibor Wlassics (*Lectura Dantis [virginiana]*, 16–17, supplement, Charlottesville: University of Virginia, 1995), pp. 198–212.

Spia.1989.1

Spiazzi, Raimondo, "Il Canto XII," in *"Paradiso": Letture degli anni, 1979–81*, ed. S. Zennaro (Rome: Bonacci, 1989), pp. 331–52.

Stab.1989.1

Stabile, Giorgio, "Il Canto II del *Paradiso*," in *"Paradiso": Letture degli anni 1979–81*, ed. S. Zennaro (Rome: Bonacci, 1989), pp. 35–100.

Stee.1977.1

Steenberghen, Fernand Van, *Maître Siger de Brabant* (Louvain: Publications universitaires, 1977).

Stef.1992.1

Stefanini, Ruggero, "Piccarda e la luna," *Lectura Dantis [virginiana]* 11 (fall 1992): 25–41.

Stei.2001.1

Steiner, George, *Grammars of Creation* (New Haven: Yale University Press, 2001).

Step.1973.1

Stephany, William A., "A Note on *Paradiso* XVI, 154," *Dante Studies* 91 (1973): 151.

Step.1995.1

Stephany, William A., "*Paradiso* XXV," in *Dante's "Divine Comedy," Introductory Readings III: "Paradiso,"* ed. Tibor Wlassics (*Lectura Dantis [virginiana]*, 16–17, supplement, Charlottesville: University of Virginia, 1995), pp. 371–87.

Stie.2002.2
Stierle, Karlheinz, "Canto XXVI," in *Lectura Dantis Turicensis: Paradiso*, ed. Georges Güntert and Michelangelo Picone (Florence: Cesati, 2002), pp. 405–18.
Stul.1991.1
Stull, William, and Robert Hollander, "The Lucanian Source of Dante's Ulysses," *Studi Danteschi* 63 (1991 [1997]): 1–52.
Tart.1989.1
Tartaro, Achille, "Il Canto XXV," in *"Paradiso": Letture degli anni 1979–81*, ed. S. Zennaro (Rome: Bonacci, 1989), pp. 667–83.
Tate.1961.1
Tate, Allen, "The Symbolic Imagination: A Meditation on Dante's Three Mirrors," in *Discussions of the "Divine Comedy,"* ed. Irma Brandeis (Boston: Heath, 1961), pp. 102–11.
Tayl.1987.1
Taylor, Karla, "From *superbo Iliòn to umile Italia*": The Acrostic of *Paradiso* 19," *Stanford Italian Review* 7 (1987): 47–65.
Toff.1947.1
Toffanin, Giuseppe, *Sette interpretazioni dantesche* (Naples: Libreria scientifica editrice, 1947).
Toff.1968.1
Toffanin, Giuseppe, "Canto XIII," in *Lectura Dantis Scaligera: "Paradiso,"* dir. M. Marcazzan (Florence: Le Monnier, 1968), pp. 447–78.
Tond.1940.1
Tondelli, Leone, *Il libro delle figure dell'abate Gioachino da Fiore* (Turin: SEI, 1940).
Took.1984.1
Took, John, *"L'etterno piacer": Aesthetic Ideas in Dante* (Oxford: Clarendon, 1984).
Took.1990.1
Took, John, "Dante and the *Confessions* of St. Augustine," *Annali d'Italianistica* 8 (1990): 360–82.
Took.1997.1
Took, John, " 'Diligite iustitiam qui iudicatis terram': Justice and the Just Ruler in Dante," in *Dante and Governance*, ed. John Woodhouse (Oxford: Clarendon, 1997), pp. 137–51.
Toyn.1902.1
Toynbee, Paget, *Dante Studies and Researches* (Port Washington, N.Y.: Kennikat Press, 1971 [1902]).
Toyn.1905.1
Toynbee, Paget, "Of the Legend of St. John the Evangelist (*Par.* XXV.100–2; 112–24)," in his *Dante Studies* (Oxford: Clarendon, 1921 [1905]), pp. 92–95.
Trov.1995.1
Trovato, Mario, "*Paradiso* XI," in *Dante's "Divine Comedy," Introductory Readings III: "Paradiso,"* ed. Tibor Wlassics (*Lectura Dantis [virginiana]*, 16–17, supplement, Charlottesville: University of Virginia, 1995), pp. 156–71.
Tulo.2000.1
Tulone, Giampiero, "Gli 'invidiosi veri' nella *Commedia* e nelle fonti dantesche," *Lettere Italiane* 52 (2000): 345–78.
Ture.2004.1
Turelli, Federico, " 'Dopo il dosso / ti stea un lume' (*Par.* II 97–105): Beatrice, un progetto fisico sperimentale," *Letteratura italiana antica* 5 (2004): 321–24.
Uitt.2005.1
Uitti, Karl D., "The *Codex Calixtinus* and the European St. James the Major: Some Contextual Issues," in *"De sens rassis": Essays in Honor of Rupert T. Pickens*, ed. Keith Busby et al. (Amsterdam: Rodopi, 2005), pp. 645–66.
Uliv.1982.1
Ulivi, Ferruccio, "San Francesco e Dante," *Letture classensi* 11 (1982): 9–24.

Vale.2003.1
Valerio, Sebastiano, "Lingua, retorica e poetica nel canto XXVI del *Paradiso*," *L'Alighieri* 22 (2003): 83–104.
Vall.1967.1
Vallone, Aldo, " 'Baldanza'-'baldezza' dai Siciliani a Dante," in *Atti del Convegno di studi su Dante e la Magna Curia* (Palermo: Luxograph, 1967), pp. 315–32.
Vall.1989.1
Vallone, Aldo, "Il Canto XXX," in *"Paradiso": Letture degli anni 1979–'81*, ed. S. Zennaro (Rome: Bonacci, 1989), pp. 785–804.
Vanu.2003.1
Van Uytfanghe, Marc, "Le latin et les langues vernaculaires au Moyen Age: un aperçu panoramique," in *The Dawn of the Written Vernacular in Western Europe*, ed. M. Goyens and W. Verbeke, in *Mediaevalia Lovaniensia*, Series 1, Studia 33 (2003), pp. 1–38.
Vare.1953.1
Varese, Claudio, "Il canto trentesimo del *Paradiso*," in his *Pascoli politico, Tasso e altri saggi* (Milan: Feltrinelli, 1961 [1953]), pp. 23–31.
Vare.2002.1
Varela-Portas de Orduña, Juan, *Introducción a la semántica de la "Divina Commedia": teoría y análisis del simil* (Madrid: Ediciones de la Discreta, 2002).
Vaso.1972.1
Vasoli, Cesare, "Il canto II del *Paradiso*," in *Lectura Dantis Metelliana: I primi undici canti del "Paradiso"* (Rome: Bulzoni, 1992 [1972]), pp. 27–51.
Vazz.1989.1
Vazzana, Steno, "Il Canto XXVII," in *"Paradiso": Letture degli anni 1979–81*, ed. S. Zennaro (Rome: Bonacci, 1989), pp. 701–30.
Vegl.2000.1
Veglia, Marco, "Per un'ardita umiltà: L'averroismo di Dante tra Guido Cavalcanti, Sigieri di Brabante e San Francesco d'Assisi," *Schede Umanistiche* 1 (2000): 67–106.
Vett.2004.1
Vettori, Alessandro, *Poets of Divine Love: Franciscan Mystical Poetry of the Thirteenth Century* (New York: Fordham University Press, 2004).
Vian.1968.1
Vianello, Nereo, "Canto XVII," in *Lectura Dantis Scaligera: "Paradiso,"* dir. M. Marcazzan (Florence: Le Monnier, 1968), pp. 579–622.
Vick.1983.1
Vickers, Nancy, "Seeing Is Believing: Gregory, Trajan, and Dante's Art," *Dante Studies* 101 (1983): 67–85.
Vill.2001.1
Villa, Claudia, "*Comoedia: laus in canticis dicta?* Schede per Dante: *Paradiso*, XXV.1 e *Inferno*, XVIII," *Rivista di Studi Danteschi* 1 (2001): 325–31.
Weat.1975.1
Weatherby, Harold L., *The Keen Delight: The Christian Poet in the Modern World* (Athens: University of Georgia Press), especially pp. 6–26.
Wilk.1961.1
Wilkins, Ernest Hatch, "Voices of the *Divine Comedy*," *Annual Report of the Dante Society* 79 (1961): 1–9.
Wing.1981.1
Wingell, Albert E., "The Forested Mountaintop in Augustine and Dante," *Dante Studies* 99 (1981): 9–48.
Witk.1959.1
Witke, Edward C., "The River of Light in the *Anticlaudianus* and the *Divina Commedia*," *Classical Review* 11 (1959): 144–56.
Wlas.1975.1

Wlassics, Tibor, *Dante narratore* (Florence: Olschki, 1975).
Wood.1977.1
Woody, Kennerly M., "Dante and the Doctrine of the Great Conjunctions," *Dante Studies* 95 (1977): 119–34.
Wood.1997.1
Woodhouse, John, "Dante and Governance: Contexts and Contents," in *Dante and Governance*, ed. John Woodhouse (Oxford: Clarendon, 1997), pp. 1–11.

ALSO TRANSLATED BY

ROBERT AND JEAN HOLLANDER

INFERNO

The epic grandeur of Dante's masterpiece has inspired readers for seven hundred years, but the further we move from the late medieval world of Dante, the more a rich understanding and enjoyment of the poem depends on knowledgeable guidance. Robert Hollander, a renowned scholar and master teacher of Dante, and Jean Hollander, an accomplished poet, have written a beautifully accurate and clear verse translation of the first volume of Dante's epic poem, the *Divine Comedy*. Featuring the original Italian text opposite the translation, this edition also offers an extensive and accessible introduction and generous commentaries that draw on centuries of scholarship as well as Robert Hollander's own decades of teaching and research. The Hollander translation is the new standard in English of this essential work of world literature.

Poetry/Classics/978-0-385-49698-8

PURGATORIO

In the second book of the *Divine Comedy*, Dante has left hell and begins the ascent of the mount of purgatory. Just as hell had its circles, purgatory, situated at the threshold of heaven, has its terraces, each representing one of the seven mortal sins. With Virgil again as his guide, Dante climbs the mountain; the poet shows him, on its slopes, those whose lives were variously governed by pride, envy, wrath, sloth, avarice, gluttony, and lust. As he witnesses the penance required on each successive terrace, Dante often feels the smart of his own sins. His reward will be a walk through the garden of Eden, perhaps the most remarkable invention in the history of literature.

Poetry/Classics/978-0-385-49700-8

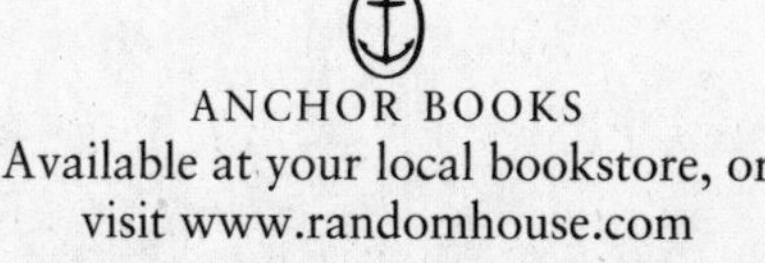

ANCHOR BOOKS
Available at your local bookstore, or
visit www.randomhouse.com